Pro C# 10 with .NET 6

Foundational Principles and Practices in Programming

Eleventh Edition

Andrew Troelsen
Phil Japikse

Apress®

Pro C# 10 with .NET 6: Foundational Principles and Practices in Programming

Andrew Troelsen
Chambersburg, PA, USA

Phil Japikse
West Chester, OH, USA

ISBN-13 (pbk): 978-1-4842-7868-0
ISBN-13 (electronic): 978-1-4842-7869-7
https://doi.org/10.1007/978-1-4842-7869-7

Managing Director, Apress Media LLC: Welmoed Spahr
Acquisitions Editor: Joan Murray
Development Editor: Laura Berendson
Coordinating Editor: Mark Powers
Copyeditor: Kim Wimpsett

Cover designed by eStudioCalamar

Cover image by Shutterstock (www.shutterstock.com)

Distributed to the book trade worldwide by Apress Media, LLC, 1 New York Plaza, New York, NY 10004, U.S.A. Phone 1-800-SPRINGER, fax (201) 348-4505, e-mail orders-ny@springer-sbm.com, or visit www.springeronline.com. Apress Media, LLC is a California LLC and the sole member (owner) is Springer Science + Business Media Finance Inc (SSBM Finance Inc). SSBM Finance Inc is a **Delaware** corporation.

For information on translations, please e-mail booktranslations@springernature.com; for reprint, paperback, or audio rights, please e-mail bookpermissions@springernature.com.

Apress titles may be purchased in bulk for academic, corporate, or promotional use. eBook versions and licenses are also available for most titles. For more information, reference our Print and eBook Bulk Sales web page at www.apress.com/bulk-sales.

Any source code or other supplementary material referenced by the author in this book is available to readers on GitHub. For more detailed information, please visit www.apress.com/source-code.

Printed on acid-free paper

To my family, Amy, Conner, Logan, and Skylar,
thank you for all of the support and patience you have given me.
Also, to my father (Cor);
father, husband, inventor, and my center of excellence.

—Phil

Table of Contents

About the Authors

Andrew Troelsen has more than 20 years of experience in the software industry. Over this time, he has worked as a developer, educator, author, public speaker, and now team lead and lead engineer at Thomson Reuters. He is the author of numerous books in the Microsoft universe covering C++-based COM development with ATL, COM, and .NET interoperability; Visual Basic; and the award-winning C# and the .NET platform. He has a master of science degree in software engineering (MSSE) from the University of St. Thomas and is working on a second master of science degree in computational linguistics (CLMS) from the University of Washington.

Phil Japikse is an international speaker, Microsoft MVP, ASPInsider, Professional Scrum Trainer, and passionate member of the developer community. Phil has been working with .NET since the first betas, developing software for more than 35 years, and heavily involved in the agile community since 2005. He is the lead director of the Cincinnati .NET User Group and the Cincinnati Software Architect Roundtable, founded the CincyDeliver (`cincydeliver.org`) conference, and volunteers for the National Ski Patrol. During the day, Phil works as the CTO/Chief Architect for Pintas & Mullins. He enjoys learning new tech and is always striving to improve his craft. You can follow Phil on his blog (`skimedic.com`) or on Twitter (`@skimedic`).

About the Technical Reviewers

Eric Smith is a consultant with Strategic Data Systems in Sharonville, Ohio, working on the .NET project team. He is a 2017 graduate of MAX Technical Training's .NET Bootcamp and previously received a master's degree in German Studies from the University of Cincinnati in 2014. He has been tinkering with writing software since the mid-1990s and still enjoys writing directly against hardware whenever the opportunity arises. Outside of computing, he spends most of his time reading, working in his machine shop, and endurance cycling.

William Pintas is a professional software engineer and project manager at Pintas & Mullins Law Firm. He graduated from New York University in 2018 with a degree in Computer Science. He has spent the past few years diving deep into the Microsoft tech stack. Currently, William is developing a business-to-business API platform using ASP.NET Core, C#, and Azure to seamlessly share legal information between law firms. In his free time, William loves kite boarding and composing classical piano music.

Acknowledgments

I want to thank Apress and the entire team involved in writing this book. As I've come to expect with all of my books for Apress, I am very impressed with the dedication and level of support we received during the writing process. I want to thank you, the reader, for reading this book and hope that you will find it as helpful in your career as it has been in mine. Lastly, I couldn't have done this without my family and the support I've had from them. Between reading my work and proofing it and your understanding of the time involved, I couldn't have done it without you! Love you all!

—Phil Japikse

Introduction

Choose Your Own Adventures

From the very first editions that Andrew wrote, and the ensuing editions since I have taken over the book, the goal has been (and always will be) to help you be productive and informed software engineers. This book, like C# and the .NET platform, continues to grow with every release. This provides an opportunity for you, the reader, to choose your own adventures. Whether you are new to software development or a seasoned veteran, this book has content to take you to the next level.

For the veteran C# developer, this book keeps you up to date with the latest that C# and .NET has to offer. Starting with C# 7, the section headers indicate when a feature was introduced or updated. Quickly scanning the table of contents highlights the new features so you can quickly read up on them and take them for a spin. This book can also serve as a reference manual, with code samples ready to help you complete that task that isn't quite muscle memory.

For the beginner, this book uses an organized approach to teaching C# and object oriented programming. Once you are comfortable with those topics, you can exercise them by skipping ahead and building application ASP.NET Core or Windows Presentation Foundation. Not ready to dive into data access? All of the code for each chapter is provide in the GitHub repo, so you can skip ahead in the book and use the provided code samples to explore in the order you choose.

As an author, I don't know what your individual needs are at any single point in time. As a CTO and Chief Architect, I know what our organization and software engineers need for the long haul. Not only for the software they build, but for their careers as the move towards tech lead and architect positions. My goal is to provide you with the same information that I provide my team and my organization. Chances are you don't need everything in this book – right now. Chances are also good that you will at some point in your development cycles. So, choose your own adventure, grab what you need to finish your task at hand, and know that we'll be ready for you when you come back to tackle another section.

The Source Code

The source code for this book is hosted on GitHub in the `https://www.Github.com/apress/pro-c-sharp-10` repository.

An Overview of This Book

Pro C# 10 with .NET 6 is logically divided into nine distinct parts, each of which contains a number of related chapters. Here is a part-by-part and chapter-by-chapter breakdown of the text.

Part I: Introducing C# and .NET 6

The purpose of Part I is to acclimate you to the nature of the .NET platform and various development tools used during the construction of .NET applications.

Chapter 1: Introducing C# and .NET 6

This first chapter functions as the backbone for the remainder of the text. The primary goal of this chapter is to acquaint you with a number of .NET-centric building blocks, such as the Common Language Runtime (CLR), Common Type System (CTS), Common Language Specification (CLS), and Base Class Libraries (BCL). Here, you will take an initial look at the C# programming language, namespaces, and the .NET assembly format.

Chapter 2: Building C# Applications

The goal of this chapter is to introduce you to the process of compiling C# source code files. After installing the .NET SDK and runtimes, you will learn about the completely free (and fully functional) Visual Studio Community edition as well as the extremely popular (and also free) Visual Studio Code. You learn how to create, run, and debug .NET C# applications using both Visual Studio and Visual Studio Code.

Part II: Core C# Programming

The topics presented in this part of the book are quite important because you will use them regardless of which type of .NET software you intend to develop (e.g., web applications, desktop GUI applications, code libraries, services, etc.). Here, you will learn about the fundamental data types of .NET, work with text manipulation, and learn the role of various C# parameter modifiers (including optional and named arguments).

Chapter 3: Core C# Programming Constructs, Part 1

This chapter begins your formal investigation of the C# programming language. Here, you will learn about the role of the `Main()` method, top-level statements, and numerous details regarding the intrinsic data types of the .NET platform and variable declaration. You will work with and manipulate textual data using `System.String` and `System.Text.StringBuilder`. You will also examine iteration and decision constructs, pattern matching, narrowing and widening operations, and the `unchecked` keyword.

Chapter 4: Core C# Programming Constructs, Part 2

This chapter completes your examination of the core aspects of C#, beginning with creating and manipulating arrays of data. Next, you examine how to construct overloaded type methods and define parameters using the `out`, `ref`, and `params` keywords. You will also learn about the enum type, structures, and nullable data types, and you will understand the distinction between value types and reference types. Finally, you will learn about tuples.

Part III: Object-Oriented Programming with C#

In this part, you will come to understand the core constructs of the C# language, including the details of object-oriented programming. This part will also examine how to process runtime exceptions and will dive into the details of working with strongly typed interfaces. Finally, you will learn about object lifetime and garbage collection.

Chapter 5: Understanding Encapsulation

This chapter begins your examination of object-oriented programming (OOP) using the C# programming language. After you are introduced to the pillars of OOP (encapsulation, inheritance, and polymorphism), the remainder of this chapter will show you how to build robust class types using constructors, properties, static members, constants, and read-only fields. You will also learn about partial type definitions, object initialization syntax, and automatic properties, and the chapter will wrap up with an examination of record types and record structs.

Chapter 6: Understanding Inheritance and Polymorphism

Here, you will examine the remaining pillars of OOP (inheritance and polymorphism), which allow you to build families of related class types. As you do this, you will examine the role of virtual methods, abstract methods (and abstract base classes), and the nature of the polymorphic interface. Then you will explore pattern matching with the `is` keyword, and finally, this chapter will explain the role of the ultimate base class of the .NET platform, `System.Object`.

Chapter 7: Understanding Structured Exception Handling

The point of this chapter is to discuss how to handle runtime anomalies in your code base through the use of structured exception handling. Not only will you learn about the C# keywords that allow you to handle such problems (`try`, `catch`, `throw`, `when`, and `finally`), but you will also come to understand the distinction between application-level and system-level exceptions. In addition, this chapter will show you how to set Visual Studio on break on all exceptions to debug the exceptions that escape your notice.

Chapter 8: Working with Interfaces

The material in this chapter builds upon your understanding of object-based development by covering the topic of interface-based programming. Here, you will learn how to define classes and structures that support multiple behaviors, how to discover these behaviors at runtime, and how to selectively hide particular behaviors using explicit interface implementation. In addition to creating a number of custom interfaces, you will also learn how to implement standard interfaces found within the .NET platform. You will use these to build objects that can be sorted, copied, enumerated, and compared.

Chapter 9: Understanding Object Lifetime

The final chapter of this part examines how the CLR manages memory using the .NET garbage collector. Here, you will come to understand the role of application roots, object generations, and the `System.GC` type. Once you understand the basics, you will examine the topics of disposable objects (using the `IDisposable` interface) and the finalization process (using the `System.Object.Finalize()` method). This chapter will also investigate the `Lazy<T>` class, which allows you to define data that will not be allocated until requested by a caller. As you will see, this feature can be helpful when you want to ensure you do not clutter the heap with objects that are not actually required by your programs.

Part IV: Advanced C# Programming

This part of the book will deepen your understanding of the C# language by walking you through a number of more advanced (but important) concepts. Here, you will complete your examination of the .NET type system by investigating collections and generics. You will also examine a number of more advanced features of C# (e.g., extension methods, operator overloading, anonymous types, and pointer manipulation). You will then examine delegates and lambda expressions, take a first look at Language Integrated Query, and finish the section with two chapters that focus on processes and multithreaded/async programming.

Chapter 10: Collections and Generics

This chapter explores the topic of *generics*. As you will see, generic programming gives you a way to create types and type members, which contain various *placeholders* that can be specified by the caller. In a nutshell, generics greatly enhance application performance and type safety. Not only will you explore various generic types within the `System.Collections.Generic` namespace, but you will also learn how to build your own generic methods and types (with and without constraints).

Chapter 11: Advanced C# Language Features

This chapter deepens your understanding of the C# programming language by introducing you to a number of advanced programming techniques. Here, you will learn how to overload operators and create custom conversion routines (both implicit and explicit) for your types. You will also learn how to build and interact with type indexers, as well as work with extension methods, anonymous types, partial methods, and C# pointers using an unsafe code context.

Chapter 12: Delegates, Events, and Lambda Expressions

The purpose of this chapter is to demystify the delegate type. Simply put, a .NET delegate is an object that points to other methods in your application. Using this type, you can build systems that allow multiple objects to engage in a two-way conversation. After you have examined the use of .NET delegates, you will then be introduced to the C# `event` keyword, which you can use to simplify the manipulation of raw delegate programming. You will wrap up this chapter by investigating the role of the C# lambda operator (`=>`) and exploring the connection between delegates, anonymous methods, and lambda expressions.

Chapter 13: LINQ to Objects

This chapter begins your examination of Language Integrated Query (LINQ). LINQ allows you to build strongly typed query expressions that can be applied to a number of LINQ targets to manipulate data in the broadest sense of the word. Here, you will learn about LINQ to Objects, which allows you to apply LINQ expressions to containers of data (e.g., arrays, collections, and custom types). This information will serve you well as you encounter a number of additional LINQ APIs throughout the remainder of this book.

Chapter 14: Processes, AppDomains, and Load Contexts

Now that you have a solid understanding of assemblies, this chapter dives deeper into the composition of a loaded .NET Core executable. The goal of this chapter is to illustrate the relationship between processes, application domains, and contextual boundaries. These topics provide the proper foundation for Chapter 15, where you will examine the construction of multithreaded applications.

Chapter 15: Multithreaded, Parallel, and Async Programming

This chapter examines how to build multithreaded applications and illustrates a number of techniques you can use to author thread-safe code. The chapter opens by revisiting the .NET delegate type to ensure explaining a delegate's intrinsic support for asynchronous method invocations. Next, you will investigate the types within the `System.Threading` namespace. The next section covers the Task Parallel Library (TPL). Using the TPL, .NET developers can build applications that distribute their workload across all available CPUs in a wickedly simple manner. At this point, you will also learn about the role of Parallel LINQ, which provides a way to create LINQ queries that scale across multiple machine cores. The remainder of the chapter covers creating nonblocking calls using the `async`/`await` keywords, local functions and generalized `async` return types, and asynchronous streams, and the `ForEachAsync()` method.

Part V: Programming with .NET Core Assemblies

Part V dives into the details of the .NET assembly format. Not only will you learn how to deploy and configure .NET code libraries, but you will also come to understand the internal composition of a .NET binary image. This section explains the role of .NET attributes and the role of resolving type information at runtime and the role of the Dynamic Language Runtime (DLR) and the C# `dynamic` keyword. The final chapter covers the syntax of Common Intermediate Language (CIL) and the role of dynamic assemblies.

Chapter 16: Building and Configuring Class Libraries

At a high level, *assembly* is the term used to describe a binary file created with a .NET compiler. However, the true story of .NET assemblies is far richer than that. Here, you will learn how to build and deploy assemblies and learn the difference between class libraries and console applications. The final section covers the new options available in .NET, such as single file executables and ready-to-run publishing.

Chapter 17: Type Reflection, Late Binding, Attribute, and Dynamic Types

This chapter continues your examination of .NET assemblies by checking out the process of runtime type discovery using the `System.Reflection` namespace. Using the types of this namespace, you can build applications that can read an assembly's metadata on the fly. You will also learn how to load and create types at runtime dynamically using late binding. The next topic of this chapter will explore the role of .NET attributes (both standard and custom). To illustrate the usefulness of each of these topics, the chapter shows you how to construct an extendable application complete with snap-ins. .NET 4.0 introduced a new aspect of the .NET runtime environment called the *Dynamic Language Runtime*. Using the DLR and the C# `dynamic` keyword, you can define data that is not truly resolved until runtime. Using these features simplifies some complex .NET programming tasks dramatically. In this final topic of the chapter, you will learn some practical uses of dynamic data, including how to leverage the .NET reflection APIs in a streamlined manner.

Chapter 18: Understanding CIL and the Role of Dynamic Assemblies

The goal of the final chapter in this section is twofold. The first part examines the syntax and semantics of CIL in much greater detail than in previous chapters. The remainder of this chapter will cover the role of the `System.Reflection.Emit` namespace. You can use these types to build software that can generate .NET Core assemblies in memory at runtime. Formally speaking, assemblies defined and executed in memory are termed *dynamic assemblies*.

Part VI: File Handling, Object Serialization, and Data Access

By this point in the text, you have a solid handle on the C# language and the details of the .NET assembly format. Part VI leverages your newfound knowledge by exploring a number of commonly used services found within the base class libraries, including file I/O, object serialization, and database access using ADO.NET.

Chapter 19: File I/O and Object Serialization

The `System.IO` namespace allows you to interact with a machine's file and directory structure. Over the course of this chapter, you will learn how to create (and destroy) a directory system programmatically. You will also learn how to move data into and out of various streams (e.g., file based, string based, and memory based). The latter part of this chapter will examine the XML and JSON object serialization services of the .NET platform. Simply put, serialization allows you to persist the public state of an object (or a set of related objects) into a stream for later use. Deserialization (as you might expect) is the process of plucking an object from the stream into memory for consumption by your application.

Chapter 20: Data Access with ADO.NET

This chapter covers database access using ADO.NET, the database API for .NET applications. Specifically, this chapter will introduce you to the role of .NET data providers and how to communicate with a relational database using ADO.NET, which is represented by connection objects, command objects, transaction objects, and data reader objects. This chapter also begins the creation of the AutoLot database, which will be enhanced in Part VII.

Part VII: Entity Framework Core

By this point in the text, you have a solid handle on the C# language and the details of the .NET assembly format. Part VI leverages your newfound knowledge by exploring a number of commonly used services found within the base class libraries, including file I/O, database access using ADO.NET, and database access using Entity Framework Core.

Chapter 21: Introducing Entity Framework Core

This chapter introduces Entity Framework (EF) Core. EF Core is an object-relational mapping (ORM) framework built on top of ADO.NET. EF Core provides a way to author data access code using strongly typed classes that directly map to your business model. Here, you will come to understand the building blocks of EF Core, including `DbContext`, entities, the specialized collection class `DbSet<T>`, and the `DbChangeTracker`. Next, you will learn about building your data model understanding EF Core conventions, data annotations, and the Fluent API. The next sections cover query execution and tracking versus non-tracking queries. The final piece of this chapter is the EF Core global tool for the .NET Core command-line interface (CLI).

Chapter 22: Exploring Entity Framework Core

This chapter continues exploring EF Core. The chapter begins by diving deep into create, read, update, and delete (CRUD) operations. The rest of the chapter covers some of the more notable features of EF Core, including global query filters, raw SQL queries with LINQ, projections, database generated values, concurrency checking, connection resiliency, database function mapping, batching of statements, value converters, and shadow properties. The final section covers SQL Server temporal table support, the newest feature in EF Core 6.

Chapter 23: Build a Data Access Layer with Entity Framework Core

This chapter builds the AutoLot data access layer. It begins with scaffolding the AutoLot database from Chapter 20 into a derived `DbContext` and entity classes. Then the project and database are updated to change to a code first approach. The entities are updated to their final version, and migration are used to update the database tables and add SQL Server objects. The final database change is to create a migration for the stored procedure from Chapter 21 and a new database view. The next section builds a rich set of repositories for code encapsulation, and the final update is to add data initialization code.

Chapter 24: Test Driving the AutoLot

Chapter 24 uses the xUnit testing framework to build automated integration tests for the AutoLot data access layer. In this chapter over 60 tests are used to explore querying, creating, updating, and deleting records.

Part VIII: Windows Presentation Foundation

The initial desktop GUI API supported by the .NET platform was termed Windows Forms. While this API is still fully supported, .NET 3.0 introduced programmers to an API called Windows Presentation Foundation (WPF). Unlike Windows Forms, this framework integrates a number of key services, including data binding, 2D and 3D graphics, animations, and rich documents, into a single, unified object model. This is all accomplished using a declarative markup grammar called Extensible Application Markup Language (XAML). Furthermore, the WPF control architecture provides a trivial way to restyle the look and feel of a typical control radically using little more than some well-formed XAML.

Chapter 25: Introducing Windows Presentation Foundation and XAML

In this chapter, you will begin by examining the motivation behind the creation of WPF (when there was already a desktop development framework in .NET). Then, you will learn about the syntax of XAML and, finally, take a look at the Visual Studio support for building WPF applications.

Chapter 26: WPF Controls, Layouts, Events, and Data Binding

This chapter will expose you to the process of using intrinsic WPF controls and layout managers. For example, you will learn to build menu systems, splitter windows, toolbars, and status bars. This chapter will also introduce you to a number of WPF APIs (and their related controls), including the Ink API, commands, routed events, the data-binding model, and dependency properties.

Chapter 27: WPF Graphics Rendering Services

WPF is a graphically intensive API; given this fact, WPF provides three ways to render graphics: shapes, drawings and geometrics, and visuals. In this chapter, you will evaluate each option and learn about a number of important graphics primitives (e.g., brushes, pens, and transformations) along the way. This chapter will also examine ways to incorporate vector images into your WPF graphics, as well as how to perform hit-testing operations against graphical data.

Chapter 28: WPF Resources, Animations, Styles, and Templates

This chapter will introduce you to three important (and interrelated) topics that will deepen your understanding of the Windows Presentation Foundation API. The first order of business is to learn the role of logical resources. As you will see, the logical resource (also termed an *object resource*) system provides a way for you to name and refer to commonly used objects within a WPF application. Next, you will learn how to define, execute, and control an animation sequence. Despite what you might be thinking, however, WPF animations are not limited to the confines of video games or multimedia applications. You will wrap up the chapter by learning about the role of WPF styles. Similar to a web page that uses CSS or the ASP.NET theme engine, a WPF application can define a common look and feel for a set of controls.

Chapter 29: WPF Notifications, Validations, Commands, and MVVM

This chapter begins by examining three core WPF framework capabilities: notifications, validations, and commands. In the notifications section, you will learn about observable models and collections and how they keep your application data and UI in sync. Next, you will dig deeper into commands, building custom commands to encapsulate your code. In the validations section, you will learn how to use the several validation mechanisms available in WPF applications. The chapter closes with an examination of the Model-View-ViewModel (MVVM) pattern and ends by creating an application that demonstrates the MVVM pattern in action.

Part IX: ASP.NET Core

Part VIII is devoted to an examination of constructing web applications using ASP.NET Core. The chapters in this section cover ASP.NET Core fundamentals as well as build a RESTful service, a web application using the MVC pattern, and a Razor page based web application.

Chapter 30: Introducing ASP.NET Core

This chapter introduces ASP.NET Core. After describing the Model-View-Controller (MVC) pattern, the solution and the three ASP.NET Core projects are created and the multiple ways to run and debug application is explored. Next, the chapter covers many of the features from ASP.NET MVC/ASP.NET WebAPI that were brought forward into ASP.NET Core. These include convention over configuration, controllers and actions, routing, model binding and validation, and filters.

Chapter 31: Diving into ASP.NET Core

The chapter covers the many new features introduced in ASP.NET Core, including Razor pages, the environmentally aware configuration system, built-in dependency injection and the options pattern, the HTTP client factory, deployment patterns, the HTTP request pipeline, and logging.

Chapter 32: RESTful Services with ASP.NET Core

This chapter finishes the ASP.NET Core RESTful service application. The chapter begins with a look at returning JSON from action methods and JSON configuration options. The functionality for API controllers that the `ApiAttribute` adds is explored. API Versioning is covered next, and the Swagger/OpenAPI configuration is updated to support versioned APIs. A base controller to provide standard CRUD operations is created and the entity specific controllers are added. An exception filter is added and basic authentication is added to the service.

Chapter 33: Web Applications with MVC

This chapter finishes the MVC-based web application. The chapter starts with a deep look into views and the Razor View Engine, including layouts and partials. Next, managing client-side libraries and the bundling/minification of those libraries is covered. The base controller is built along with the derived entity specific controller. An Area is added to the application for managing Make records. Next tag helpers (another new feature in ASP.NET Core) are explored, followed by creating custom tag helpers. The application's view component is added for the dynamic menu. Two custom validation attributes and their related server and client-side code are used to provide validation to a view model. The final section covers the General Data Protection Regulation (GDPR) support in ASP.NET Core.

Chapter 34: Web Applications Using Razor Pages

The chapter starts with a deep look into Razor pages and Razor page views and then completes the AutoLot. Web application. Many of the MVC application capabilities, like layouts, partial views, tag helpers, view components, GDPR support, and areas are supported in Razor page applications. All of the features of the AutoLot.Mvc application is replicated in the AutoLot.Web application, leveraging the similarities and highlighting the differences between MVC and Razor pages.

PART I

Introducing C# and .NET 6

CHAPTER 1

Introducing C# and .NET 6

Microsoft's .NET platform and the C# programming language were formally introduced circa 2002 and have quickly become a mainstay of modern-day software development. The .NET platform enables a large number of programming languages (including C#, VB.NET, and F#) to interact with each other. A program written in C# can be referenced by another program written in VB.NET. More on this interoperability later in this chapter.

In 2016, Microsoft officially launched .NET Core. Like .NET, .NET Core allows languages to interop with each other (although a limited number of languages are supported). More importantly, this new framework is no longer limited to running on the Windows operating system but can also run on iOS, and Linux and be developed on MacOS and Linux. This platform independence opened up .NET and C# to a much larger pool of developers. While cross-platform use of C# was supported prior to .NET Core, that was through various other frameworks such as the Mono project.

Note With the release of .NET 5, the "Core" part of the name was dropped. Throughout this book, the term .NET refers to .NET Core (up to 3.1) and .NET 5/6

Microsoft launched C# 10 and .NET 6 on November 8, 2021. C# 10 is tied to a specific version of the framework and will run only on .NET 6 and above. This relationship between language and .NET versions gives the C# team the freedom to introduce features into C# that couldn't otherwise be added into the language due to framework limitations.

As mentioned in the book's introduction, the goal of this text is twofold. The first order of business is to provide you with a deep and detailed examination of the syntax and semantics of C#. The second (equally important) order of business is to illustrate the use of numerous .NET development frameworks. These include database access with ADO.NET and Entity Framework (EF) Core, user interfaces with Windows Presentation Foundation (WPF), and finally RESTful services and web applications with ASP.NET Core. As it is said, the journey of a thousand miles begins with a single step; and with this, I welcome you to Chapter 1.

This first chapter lays the conceptual groundwork for the remainder of the book. Here, you will find a high-level discussion of a number of .NET-related topics such as assemblies, the Common Intermediate Language (CIL), and just-in-time (JIT) compilation. In addition to previewing some keywords of the C# programming language, you will also come to understand the relationship between the .NET Runtime, the Common Type System (CTS) and the Common Language Specification (CLS).

This chapter also provides you with a survey of the functionality supplied by the .NET base class libraries, sometimes abbreviated as BCLs. Here, you will get an overview of the language-agnostic and platform-independent nature of the .NET platform. As you would expect, these topics are explored in further detail throughout the remainder of this text.

A. Troelsen and P. Japikse, *Pro C# 10 with .NET 6*, https://doi.org/10.1007/978-1-4842-7869-7_1

■ **Note** Many of the features highlighted in this chapter (and throughout the book) also apply to the original .NET Framework.

Exploring Some Key Benefits of the .NET Platform

The .NET framework is a software platform for building web applications and services for the Windows, iOS, and Linux operating systems, as well as WinForms and WPF applications on Windows operating systems. To set the stage, here is a quick rundown of some core features provided, courtesy of .NET:

- *Support for numerous programming languages*: .NET applications can be created using C#, F#, and VB.NET programming languages (with C# and F# being the primary languages for ASP.NET Core).
- *A common runtime engine shared by all .NET languages*: One aspect of this engine is a well-defined set of types that each .NET language understands.
- *Language integration*: .NET supports cross-language inheritance, cross-language exception handling, and cross-language debugging of code. For example, you can define a base class in C# and extend this type in Visual Basic.
- *A comprehensive base class library*: This library provides thousands of predefined types that allow you to build code libraries, simple terminal applications, graphical desktop applications, and enterprise-level websites.
- *A simplified deployment model*: .NET libraries are not registered into the system registry. Furthermore, the .NET platform allows multiple versions of the framework as well as applications to exist in harmony on a single machine.
- *Extensive command-line support*: The .NET command-line interface (CLI) is a cross-platform tool chain for developing and packaging .NET applications. Additional tools can be installed (globally or locally) beyond the standard tools that ship with the .NET SDK.

You will see each of these topics (and many more) examined in the chapters to come. But first, I need to explain the new support lifecycle for .NET.

Understanding the .NET Support Lifecycle

.NET versions are released much more frequently than prior .NET Framework. With all of these releases available, it can be difficult to keep up, especially in an enterprise development environment. To better define the support lifecycle for the releases, Microsoft has adopted a variation of the Long-Term Support Model,[1] commonly used by modern open source frameworks.

Long-Term Support (LTS) releases are major releases that will be supported for an extended period of time. They will only receive critical and/or nonbreaking fixes throughout their life span. Prior to end-of-life, LTS versions will be changed to the designation of maintenance. LTS releases with .NET will be supported for the following time frames, whichever is longer:

- Three years after initial release
- One year of maintenance support after subsequent LTS release

[1] https://en.wikipedia.org/wiki/Long-term_support

Microsoft has decided to name Short-Term Support releases as Current, which are interval releases between the major LTS releases. They are supported for six months after a subsequent Current or LTS release.

As mentioned earlier, .NET 6 was released in November 2021. It was released as a Long Term Support version and will be supported at least until November 2024. .NET 5 will go out of support on May 8, 2022, six months after the .NET 6 release. The only other supported version at the time of this writing is .NET Core 3.1 which is supported until December 3, 2022.

It's important to check the support policy for each new version of .NET that is released. Just having a higher number doesn't necessarily mean it's going to be supported long term. The full policy is located here:

```
https://dotnet.microsoft.com/platform/support-policy/dotnet-core
```

Previewing the Building Blocks of the .NET Platform

Now that you know some of the major benefits provided by .NET, let's preview key (and interrelated) topics that make it all possible: the .NET Runtime, CTS, and the CLS. From a programmer's point of view, .NET can be understood as a runtime environment and a comprehensive base class library. The runtime layer contains the set of minimal implementations that are tied specifically to a platform (Windows, iOS, Linux) and architecture (x86, x64, ARM), as well as all of the base types for .NET.

Another building block of the .NET platform is the *Common Type System*, or *CTS*. The CTS specification fully describes all possible data types and all programming constructs supported by the runtime, specifies how these entities can interact with each other, and details how they are represented in the .NET metadata format (more information on metadata later in this chapter; see Chapter 17 for complete details).

Understand that a given .NET language might not support every feature defined by the CTS. The *Common Language Specification*, or *CLS*, is a related specification that defines a subset of common types and programming constructs that all .NET programming languages can agree on. Thus, if you build .NET types that expose only CLS-compliant features, you can rest assured that all .NET languages can consume them. Conversely, if you make use of a data type or programming construct that is outside of the bounds of the CLS, you cannot guarantee that every .NET programming language can interact with your .NET code library. Thankfully, as you will see later in this chapter, it is simple to tell your C# compiler to check all of your code for CLS compliance.

The Role of the Base Class Libraries

The .NET platform also provides a set of base class libraries (BCLs) that are available to all .NET programming languages. Not only does this base class library encapsulate various primitives such as threads, file input/output (I/O), graphical rendering systems, and interaction with various external hardware devices, but it also provides support for a number of services required by most real-world applications.

The base class libraries define types that can be used to build any type of software application and for components of the application to interact with each other.

The Role of .NET Standard

The number of base class libraries in the .NET Framework far exceeds those in .NET. This is understandable, as the .NET Framework had a 14-year head start on .NET. This disparity created issues when attempting to use .NET Framework code with .NET code. The solution (and requirement) for .NET Framework/.NET Core 3.1 interop is .NET Standard.

.NET Standard is a specification that defines the availability of .NET APIs and base class libraries that must be available in each implementation. The standard enables the following scenarios:

- Defines a uniform set of BCL APIs for all .NET implementations to implement, independent of workload
- Enables developers to produce portable libraries that are usable across .NET implementations, using this same set of APIs
- Reduces or even eliminates conditional compilation of shared source due to .NET APIs, only for OS APIs

The chart located in the Microsoft documentation (`https://docs.microsoft.com/en-us/dotnet/standard/net-standard`) shows the various compatibility between .NET Framework and .NET. This is useful for prior versions of C#. However, C# 9+ will only run on .NET 5+ or .NET Standard 2.1, and .NET Standard 2.1 is not available to the .NET Framework.

What C# Brings to the Table

C# is a programming language whose core syntax looks *very* similar to the syntax of Java. However, calling C# a Java clone is inaccurate. In reality, both C# and Java are members of the C family of programming languages (e.g., C, Objective-C, C++) and, therefore, share a similar syntax.

The truth of the matter is that many of C#'s syntactic constructs are modeled after various aspects of Visual Basic (VB) and C++. For example, like VB, C# supports the notion of class properties (as opposed to traditional getter and setter methods) and optional parameters. Like C++, C# allows you to overload operators, as well as create structures, enumerations, and callback functions (via delegates).

Moreover, as you work through this text, you will quickly see that C# supports a number of features, such as lambda expressions and anonymous types, traditionally found in various functional languages (e.g., LISP or Haskell). Furthermore, with the advent of *Language Integrated Query* (LINQ), C# supports a number of constructs that make it quite unique in the programming landscape. Nevertheless, the bulk of C# is indeed influenced by C-based languages.

Because C# is a hybrid of numerous languages, the result is a product that is as syntactically clean as (if not cleaner than) Java provides just about as much power and flexibility as C++. Here is a partial list of core C# features that are found in all versions of the language:

- No pointers required! C# programs typically have no need for direct pointer manipulation (although you are free to drop down to that level if absolutely necessary, as shown in Chapter 11).
- Automatic memory management through garbage collection. Given this, C# does not support a `delete` keyword.
- Formal syntactic constructs for classes, interfaces, structures, enumerations, and delegates.
- The C++-like ability to overload operators for a custom type, without the complexity.
- Support for attribute-based programming. This brand of development allows you to annotate types and their members to further qualify their behavior. For example, if you mark a method with the `[Obsolete]` attribute, programmers will see your custom warning message print out if they attempt to make use of the decorated member.

C# 10 is an already powerful language and, combined with .NET, enables building a wide range of application types.

Major Features in Prior Releases

Starting with C# 7, I started adding into the section headers the version when features were added (e.g. "(New 7.x)") or updated (e.g. "(Updated 7.x)").

New Features in C# 10

C# 10, released on November 8, 2021, with .NET 6, adds the following features:

- Record structs
- Improvements to structure types
- Global using directives and global implicit using directives
- File scoped namespaces
- Property pattern matching enhancements
- Constant Interpolated strings
- Improvements to lambda expressions
- Record type enhancements
- Assignment and declaration in deconstruction
- Removal of false warnings on definite assignment

In addition to this, there are also updates to the .NET framework that impact development. I have updated the section headers that are new (or updated) in C#10 /NET 6 with "(New 10)" or "(Updated 10")."

Managed vs. Unmanaged Code

It is important to note that the C# language can be used only to build software that is hosted under the .NET runtime (you could never use C# to build a native COM server or an unmanaged C/C++-style application). Officially speaking, the term used to describe the code targeting the .NET runtime is *managed code*. The binary unit that contains the managed code is termed an *assembly* (more details on assemblies in just a bit). Conversely, code that cannot be directly hosted by the .NET runtime is termed *unmanaged code*.

As mentioned previously, the .NET platform can run on a variety of operating systems. Thus, it is quite possible to build a C# application on a Windows machine and run the program on an iOS machine using the .NET runtime. As well, you can build a C# application on Linux using Visual Studio Code and run the program on Windows. With Visual Studio for Mac, you can also build .NET applications on a Mac to be run on Windows, macOS, or Linux.

Unmanaged code can still be accessed from a C# program, but it then locks you into a specific development and deployment target.

Using Additional .NET–Aware Programming Languages

Understand that C# is not the only language that can be used to build .NET applications. .NET applications can generally be built with C#, Visual Basic, and F#, which are the three languages supported directly by Microsoft.

Getting an Overview of .NET Assemblies

Regardless of which .NET language you choose to program with, understand that despite .NET binaries taking the same file extension as unmanaged Windows binaries (`*.dll`), they have absolutely no internal similarities. Specifically, .NET binaries do not contain platform-specific instructions but rather platform-agnostic *Intermediate Language* (*IL*) and type metadata.

■ **Note** IL is also known as Microsoft Intermediate Language (MSIL) or alternatively as the Common Intermediate Language (CIL). Thus, as you read the .NET literature, understand that IL, MSIL, and CIL are all describing essentially the same concept. In this book, I will use the abbreviation CIL to refer to this low-level instruction set.

When a `*.dll` has been created using a .NET compiler, the binary blob is termed an *assembly*. You will examine numerous details of .NET assemblies in Chapter 16. However, to facilitate the current discussion, you do need to understand four basic properties of this new file format.

First, unlike .NET Framework assemblies that can be either a `*.dll` or `*.exe`, .NET projects are *always* compiled to a file with a `.dll` extension, even if the project is an executable. Executable .NET assemblies are executed with the command `dotnet <assembly name>.dll`. New in .NET Core 3.0 (and later), the `dotnet.exe` command is copied to the build directory and renamed to `<assembly name>.exe`. Running this command automatically calls the `dotnet <assembly name>.dll` file, executing the equivalent of `dotnet <assembly name>.dll`. The `*.exe` with your project name isn't actually your project's code; it is a convenient shortcut to running your application.

Updated in .NET 6, your application can be reduced to a single file that is executed directly. Even though this single file looks and acts like a C++-style native executable, the single file is a packaging convenience. It contains all the files needed to run your application, potentially even the .NET runtime itself! But know that your code is still running in a managed container just as if it were published as multiple files.

Second, an assembly contains CIL code, which is conceptually similar to Java bytecode, in that it is not compiled to platform-specific instructions until absolutely necessary. Typically, "absolutely necessary" is the point at which a block of CIL instructions (such as a method implementation) is referenced for use by the .NET runtime.

Third, assemblies also contain *metadata* that describes in vivid detail the characteristics of every "type" within the binary. For example, if you have a class named `SportsCar`, the type metadata describes details such as `SportsCar`'s base class, specifies which interfaces are implemented by `SportsCar` (if any), and gives full descriptions of each member supported by the `SportsCar` type. .NET metadata is always present within an assembly and is automatically generated by the language compiler.

Finally, in addition to CIL and type metadata, assemblies themselves are also described using metadata, which is officially termed a *manifest*. The manifest contains information about the current version of the assembly, culture information (used for localizing string and image resources), and a list of all externally referenced assemblies that are required for proper execution. You'll examine various tools that can be used to examine an assembly's types, metadata, and manifest information over the course of the next few chapters.

The Role of the Common Intermediate Language

Let's examine CIL code, type metadata, and the assembly manifest in a bit more detail. CIL is a language that sits above any particular platform-specific instruction set. For example, the following C# code models a trivial calculator. Don't concern yourself with the exact syntax for now, but do notice the format of the `Add()` method in the `Calc` class.

```
//Calc.cs
Calc c = new Calc();
int ans = c.Add(10, 84);
Console.WriteLine("10 + 84 is {0}.", ans);
//Wait for user to press the Enter key
Console.ReadLine();

// The C# calculator.
class Calc
{
  public int Add(int addend1, int addend2)
  {
    return addend1 + addend2;
  }
}
```

Compiling this code produces a file `*.dll` assembly that contains a manifest, CIL instructions, and metadata describing each aspect of the `Calc` and `Program` classes.

■ **Note** Chapter 2 examines how to use graphical integrated development environments (IDEs), such as Visual Studio Community, to compile your code files.

For example, if you were to output the IL from this assembly using `ildasm.exe` (examined later in this chapter), you would find that the `Add()` method is represented using CIL such as the following:

```
.method public hidebysig instance int32 Add(int32 addend1,
            int32 addend2) cil managed
{
  // Method begins at RVA 0x2090
  // Code size       9 (0x9)
  .maxstack  2
  .locals /*11000002*/ init (int32 V_0)
  IL_0000:  /* 00   |                  */ nop
  IL_0001:  /* 03   |                  */ ldarg.1
  IL_0002:  /* 04   |                  */ ldarg.2
  IL_0003:  /* 58   |                  */ add
  IL_0004:  /* 0A   |                  */ stloc.0
  IL_0005:  /* 2B   | 00               */ br.s       IL_0007
  IL_0007:  /* 06   |                  */ ldloc.0
  IL_0008:  /* 2A   |                  */ ret
} // end of method Calc::Add
```

Don't worry if you are unable to make heads or tails of the resulting CIL for this method because Chapter 18 will describe the basics of the CIL programming language. The point to concentrate on is that the C# compiler emits CIL, not platform-specific instructions.

Now, recall that this is true of all .NET compilers. To illustrate, assume you created this same application using Visual Basic, rather than C#.

```
' Calc.vb
Module Program
  ' This class contains the app's entry point.
  Sub Main(args As String())
    Dim c As New Calc
    Dim ans As Integer = c.Add(10, 84)
    Console.WriteLine("10 + 84 is {0}", ans)
    'Wait for user to press the Enter key before shutting down
    Console.ReadLine()
  End Sub
End Module
' The VB.NET calculator.
Class Calc
  Public Function Add(ByVal addend1 As Integer, ByVal addend2 As Integer) As Integer
    Return addend1 + addend2
  End Function
End Class
```

If you examine the CIL for the Add() method, you find similar instructions (slightly tweaked by the Visual Basic compiler).

```
  .method public instance int32  Add(int32 addend1,
                                     int32 addend2) cil managed
  {
    // Code size       9 (0x9)
    .maxstack  2
    .locals init (int32 V_0)
    IL_0000:  nop
    IL_0001:  ldarg.1
    IL_0002:  ldarg.2
    IL_0003:  add.ovf
    IL_0004:  stloc.0
    IL_0005:  br.s       IL_0007
    IL_0007:  ldloc.0
    IL_0008:  ret
  } // end of method Calc::Add
```

As a final example, the same simple Calc program developed in F# (another .NET language) is shown here:

```
// Learn more about F# at http://fsharp.org

// Calc.fs
open System

module Calc =
    let add addend1 addend2 =
        addend1 + addend2

[<EntryPoint>]
let main argv =
```

```
let ans = Calc.add 10 84
printfn "10 + 84 is %d" ans
Console.ReadLine()
0
```

If you examine the CIL for the Add() method, once again you find similar instructions (slightly tweaked by the F# compiler).

```
.method public instance int32  Add(int32 addend1,
                                    int32 addend2) cil managed
{
  // Code size       9 (0x9)
  .maxstack  2
  .locals init (int32 V_0)
  IL_0000:  nop
  IL_0001:  ldarg.1
  IL_0002:  ldarg.2
  IL_0003:  add.ovf
  IL_0004:  stloc.0
  IL_0005:  br.s       IL_0007

  IL_0007:  ldloc.0
  IL_0008:  ret
} // end of method Calc::Add

} // end of class Calc.Vb.Calc
```

Benefits of CIL

At this point, you might be wondering exactly what is gained by compiling source code into CIL rather than directly to a specific instruction set. One benefit is language integration. As you have already seen, each .NET compiler produces nearly identical CIL instructions. Therefore, all languages are able to interact within a well-defined binary arena.

Furthermore, given that CIL is platform-agnostic, the .NET Framework itself is platform-agnostic, providing the same benefits Java developers have grown accustomed to (e.g., a single code base running on numerous operating systems). In fact, there is an international standard for the C# language. Prior to .NET Core, there were numerous implementations of the .NET framework for non-Windows platforms, such as Mono. These still exist, although the release of .NET 6 greatly reduced the need for those other platforms.

Compiling CIL to Platform-Specific Instructions

Because assemblies contain CIL instructions rather than platform-specific instructions, CIL code must be compiled on the fly before use. The entity that compiles CIL code into meaningful CPU instructions is a JIT compiler, which sometimes goes by the friendly name of *jitter*. The .NET runtime environment leverages a JIT compiler for each CPU targeting the runtime, each optimized for the underlying platform.

For example, if you are building a .NET application to be deployed to a handheld device (such as an iOS or Android phone), the corresponding jitter is well equipped to run within a low-memory environment. On the other hand, if you are deploying your assembly to a back-end company server (where memory is seldom an issue), the jitter will be optimized to function in a high-memory environment. In this way, developers can write a single body of code that can be efficiently JIT compiled and executed on machines with different architectures.

Furthermore, as a given jitter compiles CIL instructions into corresponding machine code, it will cache the results in memory in a manner suited to the target operating system. In this way, if a call is made to a method named PrintDocument(), the CIL instructions are compiled into platform-specific instructions on the first invocation and retained in memory for later use. Therefore, the next time PrintDocument() is called, there is no need to recompile the CIL.

Precompiling CIL to Platform-Specific Instructions

There is a utility in .NET called crossgen.exe, which can be used to pre-JIT your code. Fortunately, in .NET Core 6, the ability to produce "ready-to-run" assemblies is built into the framework. More on this later in this book.

The Role of .NET Type Metadata

In addition to CIL instructions, a .NET assembly contains full, complete, and accurate metadata, which describes every type (e.g., class, structure, enumeration) defined in the binary, as well as the members of each type (e.g., properties, methods, events). Thankfully, it is always the job of the compiler (not the programmer) to emit the latest and greatest type metadata. Because .NET metadata is so wickedly meticulous, assemblies are completely self-describing entities.

To illustrate the format of .NET type metadata, let's take a look at the metadata that has been generated for the Add() method of the C# Calc class you examined previously (the metadata generated for the Visual Basic version of the Add() method is similar, so we will examine the C# version only).

```
// TypeDef #2 (02000003)
// -------------------------------------------------------
//   TypDefName: Calc  (02000003)
//   Flags     : [NotPublic] [AutoLayout] [Class] [AnsiClass] [BeforeFieldInit]  (00100000)
//   Extends   : 0100000D [TypeRef] System.Object
//   Method #1 (06000003)
//   -------------------------------------------------------
//     MethodName: Add (06000003)
//     Flags     : [Public] [HideBySig] [ReuseSlot]  (00000086)
//     RVA       : 0x00002090
//     ImplFlags : [IL] [Managed]  (00000000)
//     CallCnvntn: [DEFAULT]
//     hasThis
//     ReturnType: I4
//     2 Arguments
//       Argument #1:  I4
//       Argument #2:  I4
//     2 Parameters
//       (1) ParamToken : (08000002) Name : addend1 flags: [none] (00000000)
//       (2) ParamToken : (08000003) Name : addend2 flags: [none] (00000000)
```

Metadata is used by numerous aspects of the .NET runtime environment, as well as by various development tools. For example, the IntelliSense feature provided by tools such as Visual Studio is made possible by reading an assembly's metadata at design time. Metadata is also used by various object-browsing utilities, debugging tools, and the C# compiler itself. To be sure, metadata is the backbone of numerous .NET technologies including reflection, late binding, and object serialization. Chapter 17 will formalize the role of .NET metadata.

The Role of the Assembly Manifest

Last but not least, remember that a .NET assembly also contains metadata that describes the assembly itself (technically termed a *manifest*). Among other details, the manifest documents all external assemblies required by the current assembly to function correctly, the assembly's version number, copyright information, and so forth. Like type metadata, it is always the job of the compiler to generate the assembly's manifest. Here are some relevant details of the manifest generated when compiling the `Calc.cs` code file shown earlier in this chapter (some lines omitted for brevity):

```
.assembly extern /*23000001*/ System.Runtime
{
  .publickeytoken = (B0 3F 5F 7F 11 D5 0A 3A )                         // .?_....:
  .ver 6:0:0:0
}
.assembly extern /*23000002*/ System.Console
{
  .publickeytoken = (B0 3F 5F 7F 11 D5 0A 3A )                         // .?_....:
  .ver 6:0:0:0
}
.assembly /*20000001*/ Calc.Cs
{
  .hash algorithm 0x00008004
  .ver 1:0:0:0
}
.module Calc.Cs.dll
.imagebase 0x00400000
.file alignment 0x00000200
.stackreserve 0x00100000
.subsystem 0x0003       // WINDOWS_CUI
.corflags 0x00000001    //  ILONLY
```

In a nutshell, the manifest documents the set of external assemblies required by `Calc.dll` (via the `.assembly extern` directive) as well as various characteristics of the assembly itself (e.g., version number, module name). Chapter 16 will examine the usefulness of manifest data in much more detail.

Understanding the Common Type System

A given assembly may contain any number of distinct types. In the world of .NET, *type* is simply a general term used to refer to a member from the set {class, interface, structure, enumeration, delegate}. When you build solutions using a .NET language, you will most likely interact with many of these types. For example, your assembly might define a single class that implements some number of interfaces. Perhaps one of the interface methods takes an enumeration type as an input parameter and returns a structure to the caller.

Recall that the CTS is a formal specification that documents how types must be defined in order to be hosted by the .NET Runtime. Typically, the only individuals who are deeply concerned with the inner workings of the CTS are those building tools and/or compilers that target the .NET platform. It is important, however, for all .NET programmers to learn about how to work with the five types defined by the CTS in their language of choice. The following is a brief overview.

CTS Class Types

Every .NET language supports, at the least, the notion of a *class type*, which is the cornerstone of object-oriented programming (OOP). A class may be composed of any number of members (such as constructors, properties, methods, and events) and data points (fields). In C#, classes are declared using the `class` keyword, like so:

```
// A C# class type with 1 method.
class Calc
{
  public int Add(int addend1, int addend2)
  {
    return addend1 + addend2;
  }
}
```

Chapter 5 will begin your formal examination of building class types with C#; however, Table 1-1 documents a number of characteristics pertaining to class types.

Table 1-1. *CTS Class Characteristics*

Class Characteristic	Meaning in Life
Is the class sealed?	Sealed classes cannot function as a base class to other classes.
Does the class implement any interfaces?	An interface is a collection of abstract members that provides a contract between the object and object user. The CTS allows a class to implement any number of interfaces.
Is the class abstract or concrete?	Abstract classes cannot be directly instantiated but are intended to define common behaviors for derived types. Concrete classes can be instantiated directly.
What is the visibility of this class?	Each class must be configured with a visibility keyword such as `public` or `internal`. Basically, this controls whether the class may be used by external assemblies or only from within the defining assembly.

CTS Interface Types

Interfaces are nothing more than a named collection of abstract member definitions and/or (introduced in C# 8) default implementations, which are implemented (optionally in the case of default implementations) by a given class or structure. In C#, interface types are defined using the `interface` keyword. By convention, all .NET interfaces begin with a capital letter *I*, as in the following example:

```
// A C# interface type is usually
// declared as public, to allow types in other
// assemblies to implement their behavior.
public interface IDraw
{
  void Draw();
}
```

On their own, interfaces are of little use. However, when a class or structure implements a given interface in its unique way, you are able to request access to the supplied functionality using an interface reference in a polymorphic manner. Interface-based programming will be fully explored in Chapter 8.

CTS Structure Types

The concept of a structure is also formalized under the CTS. If you have a C background, you should be pleased to know that these user-defined types (UDTs) have survived in the world of .NET (although they behave a bit differently under the hood). Simply put, a *structure* can be thought of as a lightweight class type having value-based semantics. For more details on the subtleties of structures, see Chapter 4. Typically, structures are best suited for modeling geometric and mathematical data and are created in C# using the `struct` keyword, as follows:

```
// A C# structure type.
struct Point
{
  // Structures can contain fields.
  public int xPos, yPos;

  // Structures can contain parameterized constructors.
  public Point(int x, int y)
  { xPos = x; yPos = y;}

  // Structures may define methods.
  public void PrintPosition()
  {
    Console.WriteLine("({0}, {1})", xPos, yPos);
  }
}
```

CTS Enumeration Types

Enumerations are a handy programming construct that allow you to group name-value pairs. For example, assume you are creating a video game application that allows the player to select from three character categories (Wizard, Fighter, or Thief). Rather than keeping track of simple numerical values to represent each possibility, you could build a strongly typed enumeration using the `enum` keyword.

```
// A C# enumeration type.
enum CharacterTypeEnum
{
  Wizard = 100,
  Fighter = 200,
  Thief = 300
}
```

By default, the storage used to hold each item is a 32-bit integer; however, it is possible to alter this storage slot if need be (e.g., when programming for a low-memory device such as a mobile device). Also, the CTS demands that enumerated types derive from a common base class, `System.Enum`. As you will see in Chapter 4, this base class defines a number of interesting members that allow you to extract, manipulate, and transform the underlying name-value pairs programmatically.

CTS Delegate Types

Delegates are the .NET equivalent of a type-safe, C-style function pointer. The key difference is that a .NET delegate is a *class* that derives from `System.MulticastDelegate`, rather than a simple pointer to a raw memory address. In C#, delegates are declared using the `delegate` keyword.

```
// This C# delegate type can "point to" any method
// returning an int and taking two ints as input.
delegate int BinaryOp(int x, int y);
```

Delegates are critical when you want to provide a way for one object to forward a call to another object and provide the foundation for the .NET event architecture. As you will see in Chapters 12 and 14, delegates have intrinsic support for multicasting (i.e., forwarding a request to multiple recipients) and asynchronous method invocations (i.e., invoking the method on a secondary thread).

CTS Type Members

Now that you have previewed each of the types formalized by the CTS, realize that most types take any number of *members*. Formally speaking, a type member is constrained by the set {constructor, finalizer, static constructor, nested type, operator, method, property, indexer, field, read-only field, constant, event}.

The CTS defines various *adornments* that may be associated with a given member. For example, each member has a given visibility trait (e.g., public, private, protected). Some members may be declared as abstract (to enforce a polymorphic behavior on derived types) as well as virtual (to define a canned, but overridable, implementation). Also, most members may be configured as static (bound at the class level) or instance (bound at the object level). The creation of type members is examined over the course of the next several chapters.

■ **Note** As described in Chapter 10, the C# language also supports the creation of generic types and generic members.

Intrinsic CTS Data Types

The final aspect of the CTS to be aware of for the time being is that it establishes a well-defined set of fundamental data types. Although a given language typically has a unique keyword used to declare a fundamental data type, all .NET language keywords ultimately resolve to the same CTS type defined in an assembly named `mscorlib.dll`. Consider Table 1-2, which documents how key CTS data types are expressed in VB.NET and C#.

Table 1-2. *The Intrinsic CTS Data Types*

CTS Data Type	VB Keyword	C# Keyword
System.Byte	Byte	byte
System.SByte	SByte	sbyte
System.Int16	Short	short
System.Int32	Integer	int
System.Int64	Long	long
System.UInt16	UShort	ushort
System.UInt32	UInteger	uint
System.UInt64	ULong	ulong
System.Single	Single	float
System.Double	Double	double
System.Object	Object	object
System.Char	Char	char
System.String	String	string
System.Decimal	Decimal	decimal
System.Boolean	Boolean	bool

Given that the unique keywords of a managed language are simply shorthand notations for a real type in the System namespace, you no longer have to worry about overflow/underflow conditions for numerical data or how strings and Booleans are internally represented across different languages. Consider the following code snippets, which define 32-bit numerical variables in C# and Visual Basic, using language keywords as well as the formal CTS data type:

```
// Define some "ints" in C#.
int i = 0;
System.Int32 j = 0;

' Define some  "ints" in VB.
Dim i As Integer = 0
Dim j As System.Int32 = 0
```

Understanding the Common Language Specification

As you are aware, different languages express the same programming constructs in unique, language-specific terms. For example, in C# you denote string concatenation using the plus operator (+), while in VB you typically make use of the ampersand (&). Even when two distinct languages express the same programmatic idiom (e.g., a function with no return value), the chances are good that the syntax will appear quite different on the surface.

```
// C# method returning nothing.
public void MyMethod()
{
  // Some interesting code...
}

' VB method returning nothing.
Public Sub MyMethod()
  ' Some interesting code...
End Sub
```

As you have already seen, these minor syntactic variations are inconsequential in the eyes of the .NET runtime, given that the respective compilers (`csc.exe` or `vbc.exe`, in this case) emit a similar set of CIL instructions. However, languages can also differ with regard to their overall level of functionality. For example, a .NET language might or might not have a keyword to represent unsigned data and might or might not support pointer types. Given these possible variations, it would be ideal to have a baseline to which all .NET languages are expected to conform.

The CLS is a set of rules that describe in vivid detail the minimal and complete set of features a given .NET compiler must support to produce code that can be hosted by the .NET Runtime, while at the same time be accessed in a uniform manner by all languages that target the .NET platform. In many ways, the CLS can be viewed as a *subset* of the full functionality defined by the CTS.

The CLS is ultimately a set of rules that compiler builders must conform to if they intend their products to function seamlessly within the .NET universe. Each rule is assigned a simple name (e.g., CLS Rule 6) and describes how this rule affects those who build the compilers as well as those who (in some way) interact with them. The crème de la crème of the CLS is Rule 1.

> *Rule 1*: CLS rules apply only to those parts of a type that are exposed outside the defining assembly.

Given this rule, you can (correctly) infer that the remaining rules of the CLS do not apply to the logic used to build the inner workings of a .NET type. The only aspects of a type that must conform to the CLS are the member definitions themselves (i.e., naming conventions, parameters, and return types). The implementation logic for a member may use any number of non-CLS techniques, as the outside world won't know the difference.

To illustrate, the following C# `Add()` method is not CLS compliant, as the parameters and return values make use of unsigned data (which is not a requirement of the CLS):

```
class Calc
{
  // Exposed unsigned data is not CLS compliant!
  public ulong Add(ulong addend1, ulong addend2)
  {
    return addend1 + addend2;
  }
}
```

However, consider the following code that makes use of unsigned data internally in a method:

```
class Calc
{
  public int Add(int addend1, int addend2)
  {
    // As this ulong variable is only used internally,
```

```
    // we are still CLS compliant.
    ulong temp = 0;
    ...
    return addend1 + addend2;
  }
}
```

The class still conforms to the rules of the CLS and can rest assured that all .NET languages are able to invoke the `Add()` method.

Of course, in addition to Rule 1, the CLS defines numerous other rules. For example, the CLS describes how a given language must represent text strings, how enumerations should be represented internally (the base type used for storage), how to define static members, and so forth. Luckily, you don't have to commit these rules to memory to be a proficient .NET developer. Again, by and large, an intimate understanding of the CTS and CLS specifications is typically of interest only to tool/compiler builders.

Ensuring CLS Compliance

As you will see over the course of this book, C# does define a number of programming constructs that are not CLS compliant. The good news, however, is that you can instruct the C# compiler to check your code for CLS compliance using a single .NET attribute.

```
// Tell the C# compiler to check for CLS compliance.
[assembly: CLSCompliant(true)]
```

Chapter 17 dives into the details of attribute-based programming. Until then, simply understand that the `[CLSCompliant]` attribute will instruct the C# compiler to check every line of code against the rules of the CLS. If any CLS violations are discovered, you receive a compiler warning and a description of the offending code.

Understanding the .NET Runtime

In addition to the CTS and CLS specifications, the final piece of the puzzle to contend with is the .NET Runtime. Programmatically speaking, the term *runtime* can be understood as a collection of services that are required to execute a given compiled unit of code. For example, when Java developers deploy software to a new computer, they need to ensure the Java virtual machine (JVM) has been installed on the machine in order to run their software.

The .NET platform offers yet another runtime system. The key difference between the .NET runtime and the various other runtimes I just mentioned is that the .NET runtime provides a single, well-defined runtime layer that is shared by *all* languages and platforms that are .NET.

Distinguishing Between Assembly, Namespace, and Type

Each of us understands the importance of code libraries. The point of framework libraries is to give developers a well-defined set of existing code to leverage in their applications. However, the C# language does not come with a language-specific code library. Rather, C# developers leverage the language-neutral .NET libraries. To keep all the types within the base class libraries well organized, the .NET platform makes extensive use of the *namespace* concept.

A namespace is a grouping of semantically related types contained in an assembly or possibly spread across multiple related assemblies. For example, the System.IO namespace contains file I/O-related types, the System.Data namespace defines basic database types, and so on. It is important to point out that a single assembly can contain any number of namespaces, each of which can contain any number of types.

The key difference between this approach and a language-specific library is that any language targeting the .NET runtime uses the *same* namespaces and *same* types. For example, the following two programs all illustrate the ubiquitous Hello World application, written in C# and VB:

■ **Note** The following code uses the C# 9 version of the Program class with a void Main() method to help illustrate the example. The new templates in C# 10 use top level statements (covered in Chapter 3) and global implicit using statements (covered later in this chapter).

```
// Hello World in C#.
using System;

public class MyApp
{
  static void Main()
  {
    Console.WriteLine("Hi from C#");
  }
}

' Hello World in VB.
Imports System
Public Module MyApp
  Sub Main()
    Console.WriteLine("Hi from VB")
  End Sub
End Module
```

Notice that each language is using the Console class defined in the System namespace. Beyond some obvious syntactic variations, these applications look and feel very much alike, both physically and logically.

Clearly, once you are comfortable with your .NET programming language of choice, your next goal as a .NET developer is to get to know the wealth of types defined in the (numerous) .NET namespaces. The most fundamental namespace to get your head around initially is named System. This namespace provides a core body of types that you will need to leverage time and again as a .NET developer. In fact, you cannot build any sort of functional C# application without at least making a reference to the System namespace, as the core data types (e.g., System.Int32, System.String) are defined here. Table 1-3 offers a rundown of some (but certainly not all) of the .NET namespaces grouped by related functionality.

Table 1-3. *A Sampling of .NET Namespaces*

.NET Namespace	Meaning in Life
`System`	Within `System`, you find numerous useful types dealing with intrinsic data, mathematical computations, random number generation, environment variables, and garbage collection, as well as a number of commonly used exceptions and attributes.
`System.Collections` `System.Collections.Generic`	These namespaces define a number of stock container types, as well as base types and interfaces that allow you to build customized collections.

`System.Data`
`System.Data.Common`
`System.Data.SqlClient`
	These namespaces are used for interacting with relational databases using ADO.NET.

`System.IO`
`System.IO.Compression`
`System.IO.Ports`
	These namespaces define numerous types used to work with file I/O, compression of data, and port manipulation.

`System.Reflection` `System.Reflection.Emit`	These namespaces define types that support runtime type discovery as well as dynamic creation of types.
`System.Runtime.` `InteropServices`	This namespace provides facilities to allow .NET types to interact with unmanaged code (e.g., C-based DLLs and COM servers) and vice versa.
`System.Drawing` `System.Windows.Forms`	These namespaces define types used to build desktop applications using .NET's original UI toolkit (Windows Forms).

`System.Windows`
`System.Windows.Controls`
`System.Windows.Shapes`
	The `System.Windows` namespace is the root for several namespaces that are used in Windows Presentation Foundation applications.

`System.Windows.Forms` `System.Drawing`	The `System.Windows.Forms` namespace is the root for several namespaces used in Windows Forms applications.
`System.Linq` `System.Linq.Expressions`	These namespaces define types used when programming against the LINQ API.
`System.AspNetCore`	This is one of many namespaces that allows you to build ASP.NET Core web applications and RESTful services.
`System.Threading` `System.Threading.Tasks`	These namespaces define numerous types to build multithreaded applications that can distribute workloads across multiple CPUs.
`System.Security`	Security is an integrated aspect of the .NET universe. In the security-centric namespaces, you find numerous types dealing with permissions, cryptography, etc.
`System.Xml`	The XML-centric namespaces contain numerous types used to interact with XML data.

Accessing a Namespace Programmatically

It is worth reiterating that a namespace is nothing more than a convenient way for us mere humans to logically understand and organize related types. Consider again the System namespace. From your perspective, you can assume that System.Console represents a class named Console that is contained within a namespace called System. However, in the eyes of the .NET runtime, this is not so. The runtime engine sees only a single class named System.Console.

In C#, the using keyword simplifies the process of referencing types defined in a particular namespace. Here is how it works. Returning to the Calc example program earlier in this chapter, there is a single using statement at the top of the file.

```
using System;
```

That statement is a shortcut to enable this line of code:

```
Console.WriteLine("10 + 84 is {0}.", ans);
```

Without the using statement, the code would need to be written like this:

```
System.Console.WriteLine("10 + 84 is {0}.", ans);
```

While defining a type using the fully qualified name provides greater readability, I think you'd agree that the C# using keyword reduces keystrokes. In this text, we will avoid the use of fully qualified names (unless there is a definite ambiguity to be resolved) and opt for the simplified approach of the C# using keyword.

However, always remember that the using keyword is simply a shorthand notation for specifying a type's fully qualified name, and either approach results in the same underlying CIL (given that CIL code always uses fully qualified names) and has no effect on performance or the size of the assembly.

Global Using Statements (New 10.0)

As you build more complex C# applications, you will most likely have namespaces repeated in multiple files. Introduced in C# 10, namespaces can be referenced globally, and then be available in every file in the project automatically. Simply add the global keyword in front of your using statements, like this:

```
global using System;
```

■ **Note** All global using statements must come before any non-global using statements.

A recommendation is that you place the global using statements along with your top level statements (covered in Chapter 3) or a completely separate file (such as GlobalUsings.cs) for better visibility. You will see many examples of this throughout this text.

In addition to placing the global using statements in Program.cs (or a separate file), they can be placed in the project file for the application using the following format:

```
<ItemGroup>
  <Using Include=”System.Text” />
  <Using Include=”System.Text.Encodings.Web” />
  <Using Include=”System.Text.Json” />
  <Using Include=”System.Text.Json.Serialization” />
</ItemGroup>
```

Implicit Global Using Statements (New 10.0)

Another new feature included with .NET 6/C# 10 are implicit global using statements. The implicit global using statements supplied by .NET 6 varies based on the type of application you are building. Table 1-4 lists the types of applications and the included namespaces.

Table 1-4. *A Sampling of .NET Namespaces*

.NET Application Type	Namespaces covered by implicit global using statements
Client (Microsoft.NET.Sdk)	System System.Collections.Generic System.IO System.Linq System.Net.Http System.Threading System.Threading.Tasks
Web (Microsoft.NET.Sdk.Web)	All from Microsoft.NET.Sdk plus: System.Net.Http.Json Microsoft.AspNetCore.Builder Microsoft.AspNetCore.Hosting Microsoft.AspNetCore.Http Microsoft.AspNetCore.Routing Microsoft.Extensions.Configuration Microsoft.Extensions.DependencyInjection Microsoft.Extensions.Hosting Microsoft.Extensions.Logging
Worker Service (Microsoft.NET.Sdk.Worker)	All from Microsoft.NET.Sdk plus: Microsoft.Extensions.Configuration Microsoft.Extensions.DependencyInjection Microsoft.Extensions.Hosting Microsoft.Extensions.Logging

The vast majority of the C# 10 project templates enable global implicit using statements by default with the ImplicitUsings element in the project's main Property group. To disable the setting, update the project file to the following:

```
<PropertyGroup>
  <TargetFramework>net6.0</TargetFramework>
  <Nullable>enable</Nullable>
  <ImplicitUsings>disable</ImplicitUsings>
</PropertyGroup>
```

To see the global using statements in your project, look for the <ProjectName>.GlobalUsings.g.cs file in the \obj\Debug\net6.0 folder. For the Calc.cs project, the following is the generated code:

```
// <auto-generated/>
global using global::System;
global using global::System.Collections.Generic;
global using global::System.IO;
global using global::System.Linq;
```

```
global using global::System.Net.Http;
global using global::System.Threading;
global using global::System.Threading.Tasks;
```

File Scoped Namespaces (New 10.0)

Also new in C# 10, file-scoped namespaces remove the need to wrap your code in braces when placing it in a custom namespace. Take the following example of the `Calculator` class, contained in the `CalculatorExamples` namespace. Prior to C# 10, to place a class in a namespace required the namespace declaration, an opening curly brace, the code (`Calculator`), and then a closing curly brace. In the example, the extra code is in bold:

```
namespace CalculatorExamples
{
  class Calculator()
  {
  ...
  }
}
```

As your code becomes more complex, this can add a lot of extra code and indentation. With file scoped namespaces, the following code achieves the same effect:

```
namespace CalculatorExamples
class Calculator()
{
...
}
```

■ **Note** Custom namespaces are covered in depth in Chapter 16

Referencing External Assemblies

Prior versions of the .NET Framework used a common installation location for framework libraries known as the *Global Assembly Cache* (GAC). Instead of having a single installation location, .NET does not use the GAC. Instead, each version (including minor releases) is installed in its own location (by version) on the computer. When using Windows, each version of the runtime and SDK gets installed into `c:\Program Files\dotnet`.

Adding assemblies into *most* .NET projects is done by adding NuGet packages (covered later in this text). However, .NET applications targeting (and being developed on) Windows still have access to COM libraries.

For an assembly to have access to another assembly that you are building (or someone built for you), you need to add a reference from your assembly to the other assembly and have physical access to the other assembly. Depending on the development tool you are using to build your .NET applications, you will have various ways to inform the compiler which assemblies you want to include during the compilation cycle.

Exploring an Assembly Using ildasm.exe

If you are beginning to feel a tad overwhelmed at the thought of gaining mastery over every namespace in the .NET platform, just remember that what makes a namespace unique is that it contains types that are somehow *semantically related*. Therefore, if you have no need for a user interface beyond a simple console application, you can forget all about the desktop and web namespaces (among others). If you are building a painting application, the database namespaces are most likely of little concern. You will learn over time the namespaces that are most relevant to your programming needs.

The Intermediate Language Disassembler utility (`ildasm.exe`) allows you to create a text document representing a .NET assembly and investigate its contents, including the associated manifest, CIL code, and type metadata. This tool allows you to dive deeply into how the C# code maps to CIL and ultimately helps you understand the inner workings of the .NET platform. While you never *need* to use `ildasm.exe` to become a proficient .NET programmer, I highly recommend you fire up this tool from time to time to better understand how your C# code maps to runtime concepts.

■ **Note** The `ildasm.exe` program no longer ships with the .NET 6 runtime. There are two options for getting this tool into your workspace. The first is to compile from the .NET 6 Runtime source located at `https://github.com/dotnet/runtime`. The second, and easier method, is to pull down the desired version from `www.nuget.org`. ILDasm on NuGet is at `https://www.nuget.org/packages/Microsoft.NETCore.ILDAsm/`. Make sure to select the correct version (for this book you will want version 6.0.0 or higher). Add the ILDasm NuGet package to your project with the following command: `dotnet add package Microsoft.NETCore.ILDAsm --version 6.0.0`.

This doesn't actually load `ILDasm.exe` into your project but places it in your package folder (on Windows): `%userprofile%\.nuget\packages\microsoft.netcore.ildasm\6.0.0\runtimes\native\`.

I have also included the 6.0.0 version of `ILDasm.exe` in this book's GitHub repo in the root folder for the code samples.

After you get `ildasm.exe` loaded onto your machine, you can run the program from the command line without any arguments to see the help comments. At a minimum, you have to specify the assembly to extract the CIL.

An example command line is as follows:

```
ildasm /all /METADATA /out=csharp.il calc.cs.dll
```

This will create a file named `csharp.il` exporting all available data into the file. This is the file where the previous IL examples came from.

Summary

The point of this chapter was to lay out the conceptual framework necessary for the remainder of this book. I began by examining a number of limitations and complexities found within the technologies prior to .NET and followed up with an overview of how .NET and C# attempt to simplify the current state of affairs.

.NET basically boils down to a runtime execution engine (the `.NET Runtime`) and base class libraries. The runtime is able to host any .NET binary (aka assembly) that abides by the rules of managed code. As you saw, assemblies contain CIL instructions (in addition to type metadata and the assembly manifest) that are compiled to platform-specific instructions using a just-in-time compiler. In addition, you explored the role of the Common Language Specification and Common Type System.

In the next chapter, you will take a tour of the common integrated development environments you can use when you build your C# programming projects. You will be happy to know that in this book you will use completely free (and feature-rich) IDEs, so you can start exploring the .NET universe with no money down.

CHAPTER 2

Building C# Applications

As a C# programmer, you can choose from among numerous tools to build .NET Core applications. The tool (or tools) you select will be based primarily on three factors: any associated costs, the OS you are using to develop the software, and the computing platforms you are targeting. The point of this chapter is to provide the information you need to install the .NET 6 SDK and runtime and to present a first look at Microsoft's flagship IDEs, Visual Studio Code and Visual Studio.

The first part of this chapter will cover setting up your computer with the .NET 6 SDK and runtime. The next section will examine building your first C# application with Visual Studio Code and Visual Studio Community Edition.

Note The screenshots in this and subsequent chapters are from Visual Studio Code v 1.61.2 or Visual Studio 2022 Community Edition v17.0.0 on Windows. If you want to build your applications on a different OS or IDE, this chapter will guide you in the right direction; however, the look and feel of your IDE might differ from the various screenshots in this text.

Installing .NET 6

To get started developing applications with C# 10 and .NET 6 (on Windows, macOS, or Linux), the .NET 6 SDK needs to be installed (which also installs the .NET 6 runtime). All of the installs for .NET and .NET Core are located at the convenient `www.dot.net`. On the home page, click Download and then click "All .NET downloads" under .NET. After clicking "All .NET downloads," you will see the LTS versions of .NET (6.0) and a link for .NET 6.0. Click ".NET 6.0 (recommended)." Once on that page, select the correct .NET 6 SDK for your operating system. For this book, you will need to install the SDK for .NET Core version 6.0.100 or higher, which also installs the .NET and ASP.NET Core runtimes. If you are using a Windows machine, it will also install the .NET Desktop runtime.

Understanding the .NET Version Numbering Scheme

At the time of this writing, the .NET 6 SDK is at version 6.0.100. The first two numbers (6.0) indicate the highest version of the runtime you can target. In this case, that's 6.0. This means the SDK also supports developing for a lower version of the runtime, such as .NET 5 or .NET Core 3.1. The next number (1) is the quarterly feature band. Since we are currently in the first quarter of the year since the release, it is a 1. The final two numbers (00) indicate the patch version. This is a little bit clearer if you add a separator into the version in your mind and think of the current version as 6.0.1.00.

A. Troelsen and P. Japikse, *Pro C# 10 with .NET 6*, https://doi.org/10.1007/978-1-4842-7869-7_2

Confirming the .NET 6 Install

To confirm the installation of the SDK and the runtimes, open a command window and use the .NET command-line interface (CLI), `dotnet.exe`. The CLI has SDK options and commands available. The commands include creating, building, running, and publishing projects and solutions, and you will see examples of those commands later in this text. In this section, we will examine the SDK options, of which there are four, as shown in Table 2-1.

Table 2-1. *.NET 5 CLI SDK Options*

Option	Meaning in Life
`--version`	Display the .NET SDK version in use
`--info`	Display .NET information
`--list-runtimes`	Display the installed runtimes
`--list-sdks`	Display the installed SDKs

The `--version` option displays the highest version of the SDK installed on your machine, or the version specified in a `global.json` located at or above your current directory. Check the current version of the .NET SDK installed on your machine, enter the following:

```
dotnet --version
```

For this book, the result needs to be 6.0.100 (or higher).

To show all of the .NET Core Runtimes installed on your machine, enter the following:

```
dotnet --list-runtimes
```

There are three different runtimes:

- `Microsoft.AspNetCore.App` (for building ASP.NET Core applications)
- `Microsoft.NETCore.App` (the foundational runtime for .NET)
- `Microsoft.WindowsDesktop.App` (for building WinForms and WPF applications)

If you are running a Windows OS, each of these must be version 6.0.0 (or higher). If you are not on Windows, you will just need the first two, `Microsoft.NETCore.App` and `Microsoft.AspNetCore.App`, and also be showing version 6.0.0 (or higher).

Finally, to show all of the SDKs installed, enter the following:

```
dotnet --list-sdks
```

Again, the version must be 6.0.100 (or higher).

Checking For Updates

New with .NET 6, the CLI has a new command that checks your installed versions of the .NET/.NET Core SDKs and runtimes for updates. This command is backwards compatible, so it also checks for updates for .NET Core 3.1. It will also inform you if any of the installed SDK or runtimes are out of support (like the 2.x versions). To check the versions, enter the following command:

```
dotnet sdk check
```

The command will not update any of the versions for you, it just reports the status. To update, follow the same procedure outlined above to download and install the new version(s).

Use an Earlier Version of the .NET (Core) SDK

Sometimes you might want to ensure you are using an older version of the .NET SDK. As an example, you are building your production applications using .NET 6. An early release candidate for .NET 7 is available, and you want to start experimenting with it while not putting your production work at risk. While Microsoft states that you can build previous versions of .NET applications with a later SDK, many developers and organizations aren't comfortable with release candidates, much less early beta/preview releases.

If you need to pin your project to an earlier version of the .NET SDK, you can do that with a `global.json` file. To create this file, you can use this command, which pins the current folder and all subfolders to SDK version 5.0.400:

```
dotnet new globaljson -sdk-version 5.0.400
```

This creates a `global.json` file that looks like this:

```
{
  "sdk": {
    "version": "5.0.400"
  }
}
```

Running `dotnet.exe --version` in this directory (or any subdirectory) will return 5.0.400.

Building .NET Core Applications with Visual Studio

If you have experience building applications using prior versions of Microsoft technologies, you are probably familiar with Visual Studio. The edition names and features sets have changed throughout the life of the product but have settled down since the release of .NET Core. Visual Studio is available in the following editions (for both Window and Mac):

- Visual Studio 2022 Community (free)
- Visual Studio 2022 Professional (paid)
- Visual Studio 2022 Enterprise (paid)

The Community and Professional editions are *essentially* the same. The most significant difference is in the licensing model. Community is licensed for open source, academic, and small-business uses. Professional and Enterprise are commercial products that are licensed for any development, including enterprise development. As one would expect, the Enterprise edition has many additional features compared to the Professional edition.

■ **Note** For specific licensing details, please go to `www.visualstudio.com`. Licensing Microsoft products can be complex, and this book does not cover the details. For the purposes of writing (and following along with) this book, Community is legal to use.

All Visual Studio editions ship with sophisticated code editors, integrated debuggers, GUI designers for desktop applications, and much more. Since they all share a common core set of features, the good news is that it is easy to move between them and feel quite comfortable with their basic operation.

Installing Visual Studio 2022 (Windows)

Before using Visual Studio 2022 to develop, execute, and debug C# applications, you need to get it installed. The installation experience changed dramatically with the 2017 version and is worth discussing in more detail. If you have been using 2019, you will find the experience very similar.

■ **Note** You can download Visual Studio 2022 Community from `www.visualstudio.com/downloads`.

The Visual Studio 2022 installation process is now broken down into application-type workloads. This allows you to install just the components you need for the type of applications you plan on building. For example, if you are going to build web applications, you would install the "ASP.NET and web development" workload.

Another (extremely) significant change is that Visual Studio 2022 supports true side-by-side installation. Note that I am not referring to just previous versions of Visual Studio but to Visual Studio 2022 itself! For example, on my main work computer, I have Visual Studio 2022 Enterprise installed for my professional work and Visual Studio 2022 Community for use in my books, courses, and conference lectures. If you have Professional or Enterprise supplied by your employer, you can still install the Community edition to work on open source projects (or the code in this book).

When you launch the installer for Visual Studio 2022 Community, you are presented with the screen shown in Figure 2-1. This screen has all of the workloads available, the option to select individual components, and a summary on the right side showing what has been selected.

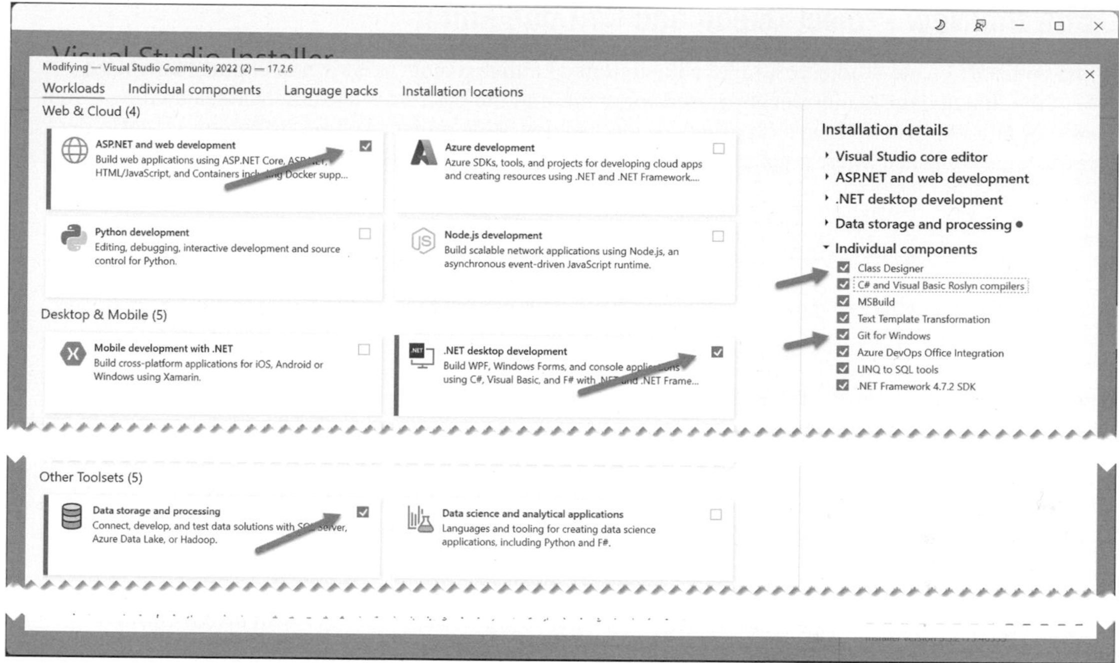

Figure 2-1. *The new Visual Studio installer*

For this book, you will want to install the following workloads:

- .NET desktop development
- ASP.NET and web development
- Data storage and processing

On the "Individual components" tab, also select Class Designer and Git for Windows (all under "Code tools"). Once you have all of them selected, click Install. This will provide you with everything you need to work through the examples in this book.

Taking Visual Studio 2022 for a Test-Drive

Visual Studio 2022 is a complete IDE for software development using .NET and C#. Let's take a quick look at Visual Studio by building a simple .NET 6 Console application.

Using the New Project Dialog and C# Code Editor

When you start Visual Studio, you will see the updated Launch dialog, as shown in Figure 2-2. The left side of the dialog has the most recently used solutions, and the right side has options for launching Visual Studio by launching code from a repository, opening an existing project/solution, opening a local folder, or creating a new project. There is also an option to continue without any code, which just launches the Visual Studio IDE.

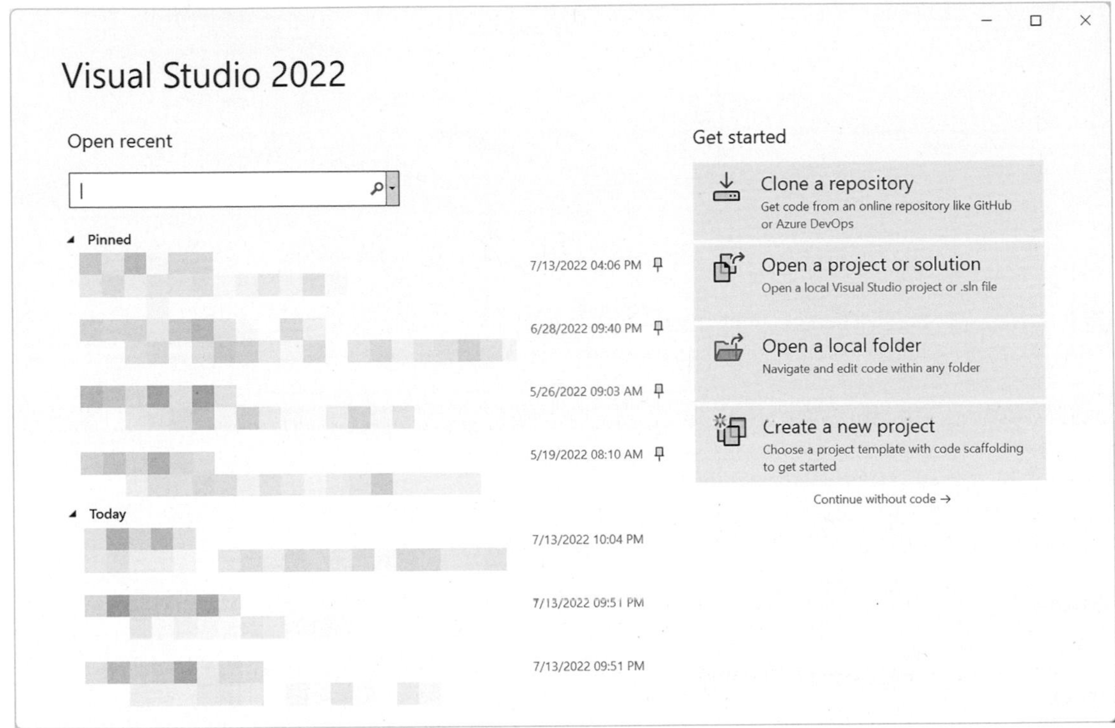

Figure 2-2. *The new Visual Studio launch dialog*

Select the "Create a new project" option, and you will be prompted with the "Create a new project" dialog. As shown in Figure 2-3, recently used templates (if any) are on the left, and all available templates are on the right, including a set of filters and a search box.

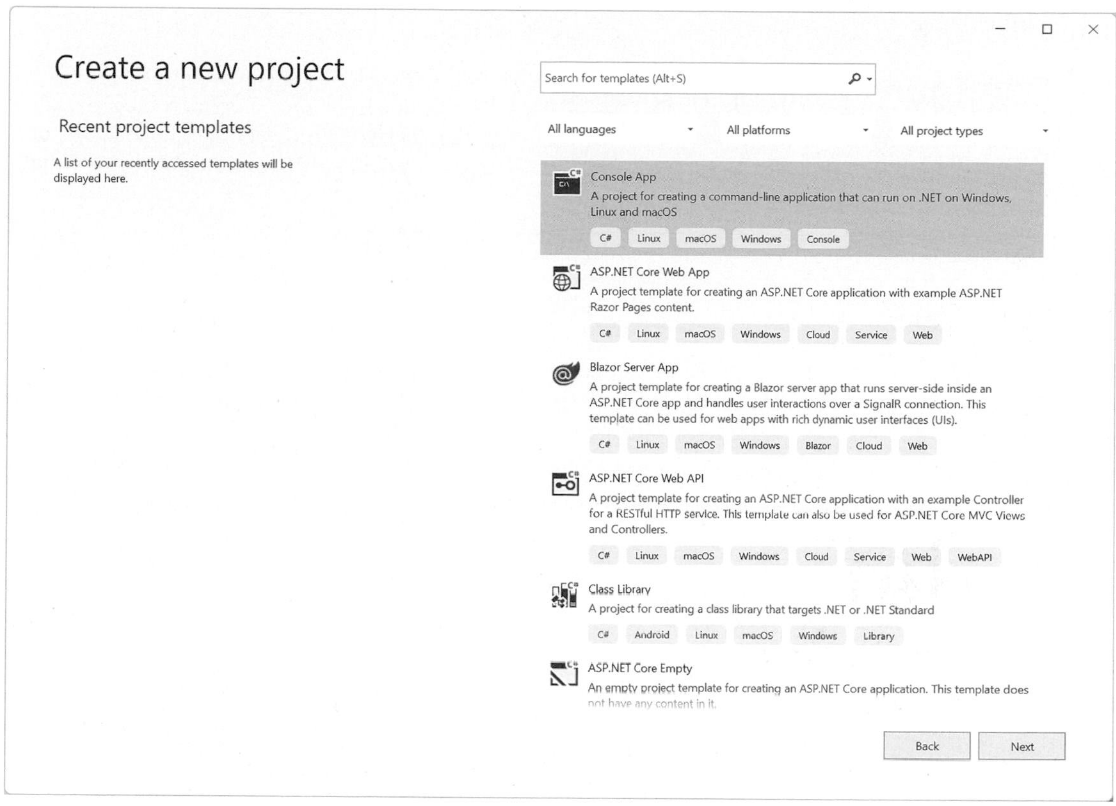

Figure 2-3. *The "Create a new project" dialog*

To start, create a new Console App, making sure to select the C# version and not the Visual Basic version.

The next screen is the "Configure your new project" dialog, as shown in Figure 2-4. Enter **SimpleCSharpConsoleApp** for the project name and select a location for the project. The wizard will also create a Visual Studio solution, by default named after the project name.

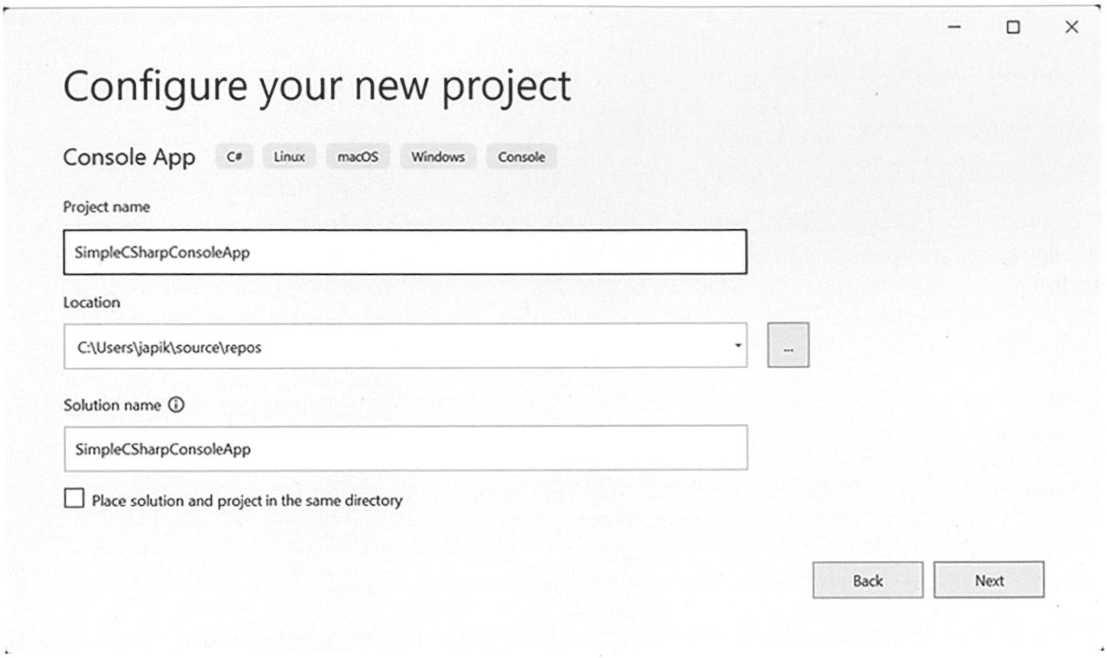

Figure 2-4. *The "Configure your new project" dialog*

■ **Note** Creating solutions and projects can also be accomplished using the .NET Core Command Line Interface (CLI). This will be covered with Visual Studio Code.

The next screen prompts for the version of .NET to use. Make sure ".NET 6.0 (Long-term support)" is selected, as shown in Figure 2-5.

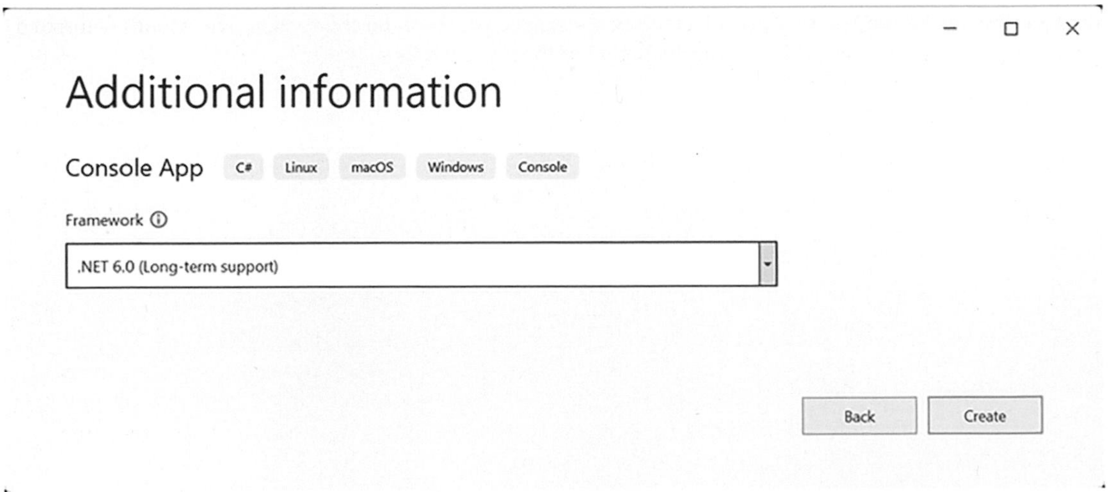

Figure 2-5. *Chosing the .NET Version*

Once the project has been created, you will see that the initial C# code file (named `Program.cs`) has been opened in the code editor. The initial template just has a comment (the line starting with `//`) and a single line of code that writes "Hello, World!" to the console:

```
// See https://aka.ms/new-console-template for more information
Console.WriteLine("Hello, World!");
```

Those two lines of code are referred to as top level statements and serve as the entry point into the application. The next chapter covers top level statements and application entry points in detail. For now, realize that this is where the execution starts for your app, and ends when all of the lines have executed.

Replace the comment and the single line of code with the following:

```
// Set up Console UI (CUI)
Console.Title = "My Rocking App";
Console.ForegroundColor = ConsoleColor.Yellow;
Console.BackgroundColor = ConsoleColor.Blue;
Console.WriteLine("*************************************");
Console.WriteLine("***** Welcome to My Rocking App *****");
Console.WriteLine("*************************************");
Console.BackgroundColor = ConsoleColor.Black;

// Wait for Enter key to be pressed.
Console.ReadLine();
```

■ **Note** You will notice as you type, Visual Studio attempts to complete the words for you. This is called IntelliSense (code completion help) and is integrated into Visual Studio and Visual Studio Code.

Here, you are using the `Console` class defined in the `System` namespace. The `System` namespace is included as part of the global implicit using statements, so it isn't explicitly needed. This program does not do anything too interesting; however, note the final call to `Console.ReadLine()`. This is in place simply to ensure the user must press a key to terminate the application. With Visual Studio 2022, this is unnecessary as the VS debugger will pause the program and prevent it from exiting. If you were to navigate to the compiled version and run it, the program would disappear almost instantly when debugging the program!

■ **Note** If you want to change the VS debugging experience to automatically end the program, select Tools ➤ Options ➤ Debugging ➤ Automatically close the console when debugging stops.

Changing the Target .NET Core Framework

When creating this project, you selected the version of .NET that you wanted to use. If you chose the wrong one (or want to change it for some other reason), double-click the project name in Solution Explorer. This opens the project file in the editor (this feature was introduced with Visual Studio 2019 and .NET Core). You can also edit the project file by right-clicking the project name in Solution Explorer and selecting "Edit Project file." You will see the following:

```
<Project Sdk="Microsoft.NET.Sdk">
  <PropertyGroup>
    <OutputType>Exe</OutputType>
    <TargetFramework>net6.0</TargetFramework>
    <ImplicitUsings>enable</ImplicitUsings>
    <Nullable>enable</Nullable>
  </PropertyGroup>
</Project>
```

To change the .NET version to version 5, for example, simply change the TargetFramework value to net5.0, as shown here:

```
<Project Sdk="Microsoft.NET.Sdk">
  <PropertyGroup>
    <OutputType>Exe</OutputType>
    <TargetFramework>net5.0</TargetFramework>
    <ImplicitUsings>enable</ImplicitUsings>
    <Nullable>enable</Nullable>
  </PropertyGroup>
</Project>
```

You can also change the target framework by right-clicking the project name in Solution Explorer and selecting Properties, opening the Application tab, and updating the Target Framework value, as shown in Figure 2-6.

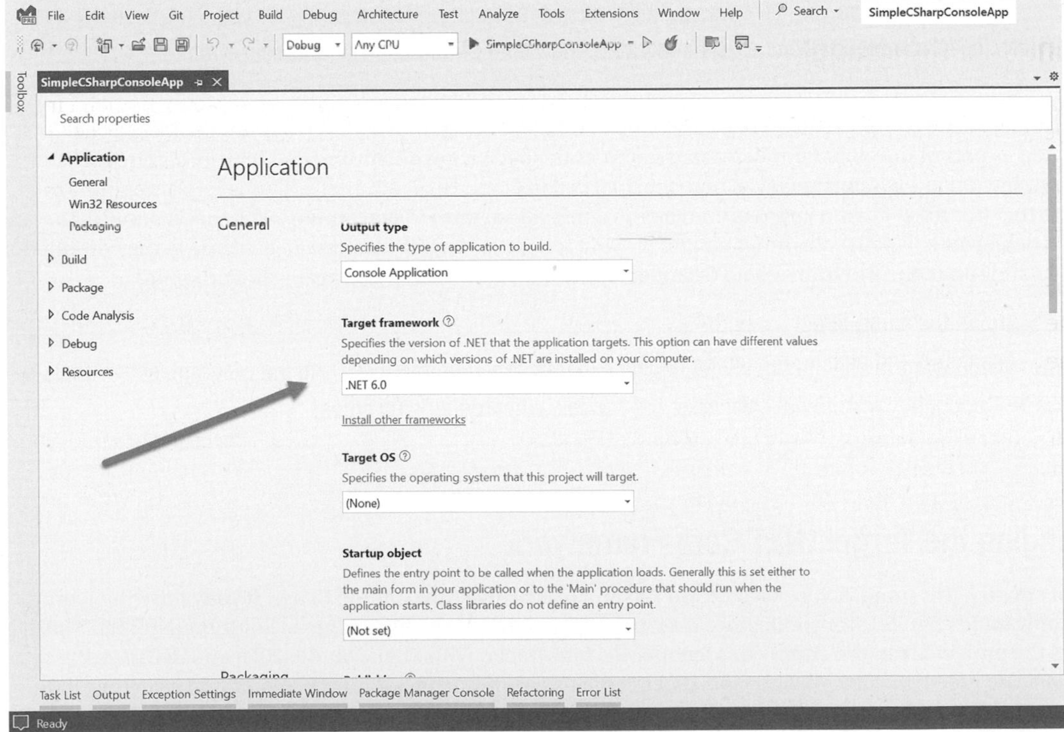

***Figure 2-6.** Changing the target framework for your application*

Using C# 10 Features

In versions of .NET and the .NET Framework, the version of C# supported by a project could be changed. Since the release of .NET Core 3.0 (and each subsequent.NET version), the version of C# used is tied into the .NET Core/.NET version. For .NET 6.0 projects, the language version is locked into C# 10. Table 2-2 lists the target frameworks (.NET, .NET Core, .NET Standard, and .NET Framework) and the default C# version utilized.

Table 2-2. *C# 8 Version and Target Framework*

Target Framework	Version	C# Language Version Default
.NET	6.x	C# 10.0
.NET	5.x	C# 9.0
.NET Core	3.x	C# 8.0
.NET Core	2.x	C# 7.3
.NET Standard	2.1	C# 8.0
.NET Standard	2.0	C# 7.3
.NET Standard	1.x	C# 7.3
.NET Framework	all	C# 7.3

Running and Debugging Your Project

To run your program and see the output, press the Ctrl+F5 keyboard command (which is also accessed from the Debug ➤ Start Without Debugging menu option). Once you do, you will see a Windows console window pop on the screen with your custom (and colorful) message. Be aware that when you "run" your program with Ctrl+F5, you bypass the integrated debugger.

■ **Note** .NET applications can also be compiled and executed using the CLI. To run your project, enter `dotnet run` in the same directory as the project file (`SimpleCSharpApp.csproj` in this example). The `dotnet run` command also automatically builds the project.

If you need to debug your code (which will certainly be important when building larger programs), your first step is to set breakpoints at the code statement you want to examine. Although there is not much code in this example, set a breakpoint by clicking the leftmost gray bar of the code editor (note that breakpoints are marked with a red dot icon; see Figure 2-7).

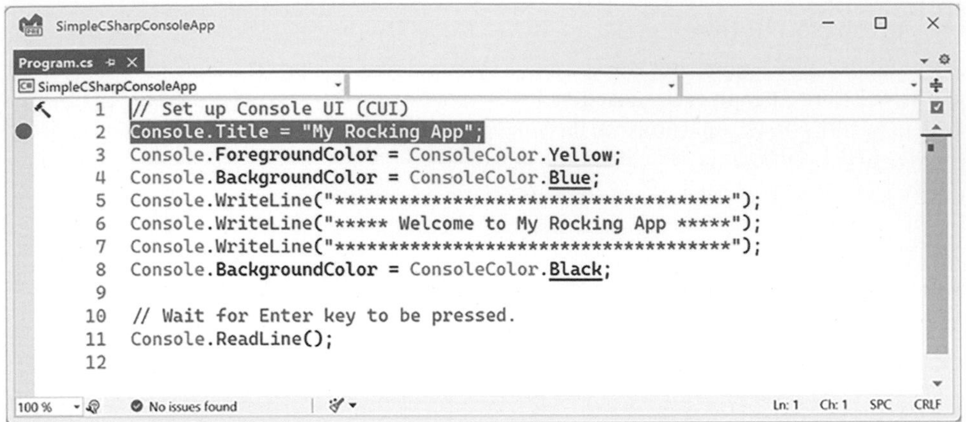

Figure 2-7. *Setting breakpoints*

If you now press the F5 key (or use the Debug ➤ Start Debugging menu option or click the green arrow with Start next to it in the toolbar), your program will halt at each breakpoint. As you would expect, you can interact with the debugger using the various toolbar buttons and menu options of the IDE. Once you have evaluated all breakpoints, the application will eventually terminate once the statements have completed.

■ **Note** Microsoft IDEs have sophisticated debuggers, and you will learn about various techniques over the chapters to come. For now, be aware that when you are in a debugging session, a large number of useful options will appear under the Debug menu. Take a moment to verify this for yourself.

Using Solution Explorer

If you look to the right of the text editor, you will see the Solution Explorer window, which shows you a few important things. First, notice that the new project wizard has created a solution along with the single project. This can be confusing at first, as they both have been given the same name (SimpleCSharpConsoleApp). The idea here is that a "solution" can contain multiple projects that all work together. For example, your solution might include three class libraries, one WPF application, and one ASP.NET Core web service. The earlier chapters of this book will almost always have a single for the example code; however, when you build some more complex examples, you will see how to add new projects to your initial solution.

■ **Note** Be aware that when you select the solution in the Solution Explorer window, the IDE's menu system will show you a different set of choices than when you select a project. If you ever find yourself wondering where a certain menu item has disappeared to, double-check you did not accidentally select the wrong node.

Using the Visual Class Diagram Tool

Visual Studio also gives you the ability to design classes and other types (such as interfaces or delegates) in a visual manner. The Class Diagram provides tools that allow you to create, view, and modify the objects in your project and their relationships with other objects. Using this tool, you are able to visually add (or remove) members to (or from) a type and have your modifications reflected in the corresponding C# file. Also, as you modify a given C# file, changes are reflected in the class diagram.

■ **Note** This book only uses the Class Diagram tool occasionally to accentuate certain concepts. It is shown here for completeness, and the choice to use it or the text editor is entirely up to you. The overwhelming majority of the examples use the text editor of Visual Studio/Visual Studio Code.

To access the visual class designer tools, the first step is to insert a new class diagram file. To do so, select project in the Solution Explorer, then activate the Project ➤ Add New Item menu option and locate the Class Diagram type (Figure 2-8).

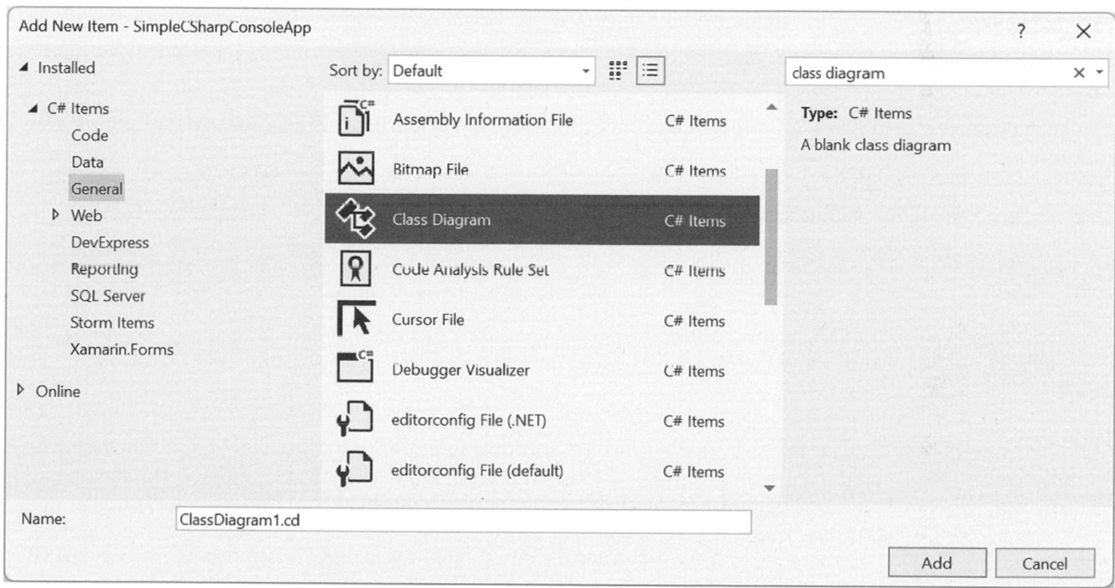

Figure 2-8. *Inserting a class diagram file into the current project*

Initially, the designer will be empty; however, you can drag and drop files from your Solution Explorer window on the surface or right click on the design surface to create new classes. To get started, create a new class in your project by right clicking on the project and selecting Add ➤ Class. In the Add New Item – SimpleCSharpConsoleApp dialog, select Class, and name it Car.cs, as shown in Figure 2-9.

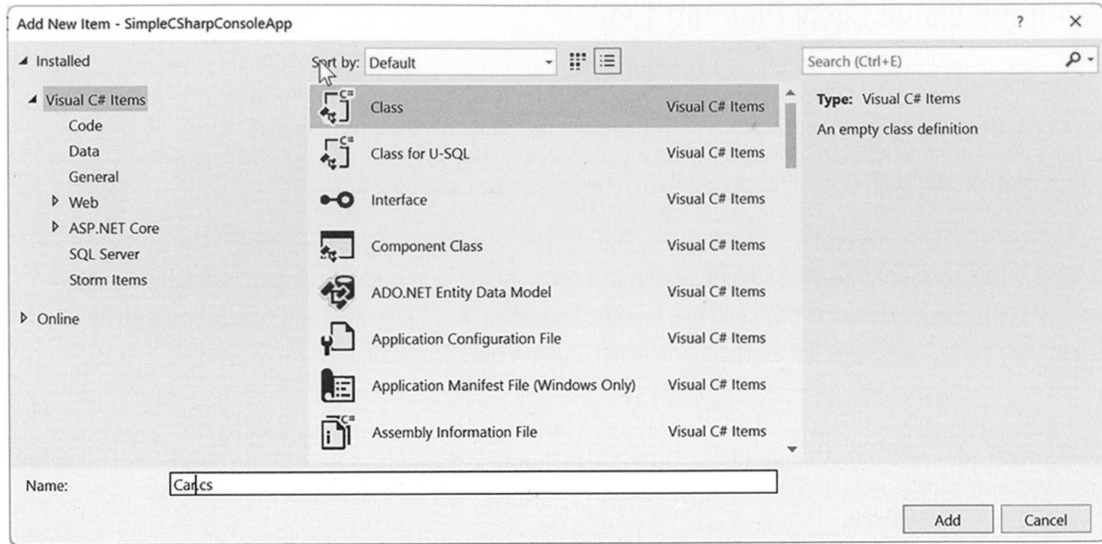

Figure 2-9. *The Add New Item Dialog*

Update the code to the following to create a `Car` class (you will learn all about classes over the next few chapters):

```
namespace SimpleCSharpConsoleApp;

public class Car
{
    public string PetName { get; set; }
    public string Make { get; set; }
}
```

After saving the file, drag the `Car.cs` file from the Solution Explorer onto the Class Diagram. Once you do this, you will find a visual representation of the class. If you click the arrow icon for a given type, you can show or hide the type's members. Underneath the Class Diagram is the Class Details window, which shows the specifics of the selected class diagram (see Figure 2-10).

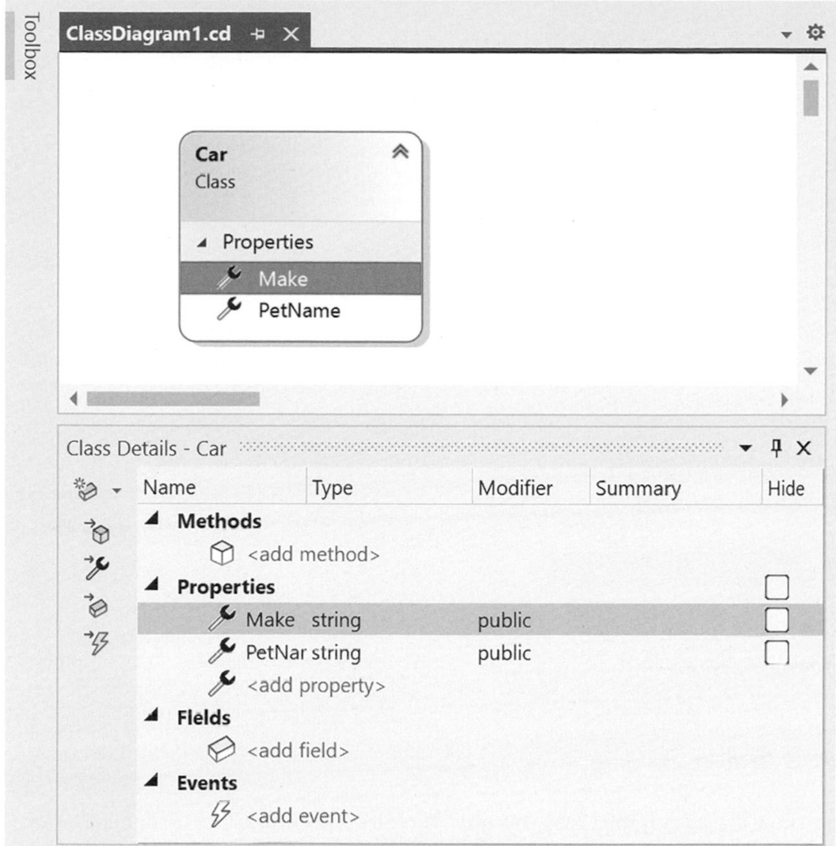

Figure 2-10. *The Class Diagram viewer*

■ **Note** Using the Class Designer toolbar, you can fine-tune the display options of the designer surface.

The Class Details window not only shows you the details of the currently selected item in the diagram but also allows you to modify existing members and insert new members on the fly.

The Class Designer Toolbox allows you to insert new types (and create relationships between these types) into your project visually (see Figure 2-11). (Be aware you must have a class diagram as the active window to view this toolbox.) As you do so, the IDE automatically creates new C# type definitions in the background.

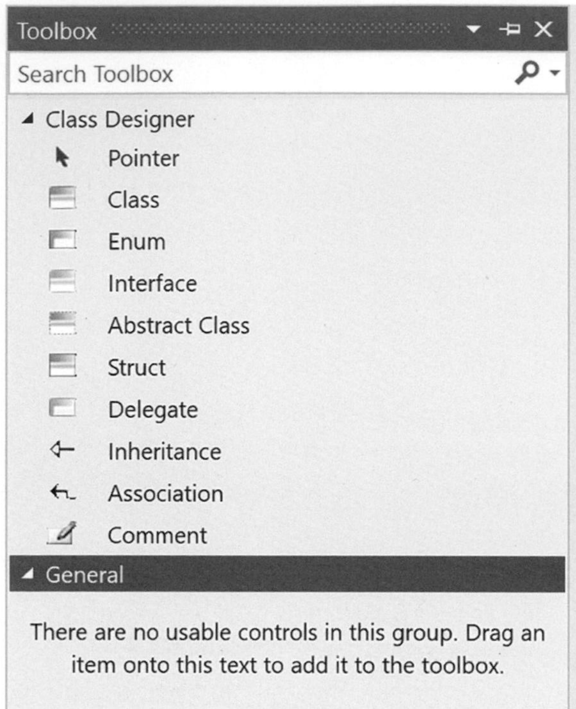

Figure 2-11. *The Class Designer Toolbox*

By way of example, drag a new class from the Class Designer Toolbox onto your Class Designer. Name this class `Make` with public access and select Create new file. This will result in the creation of a new C# file named `Make.cs` that is automatically added to your project. Now, using the Class Details window, add a `public string` property named `Name` (see Figure 2-12).

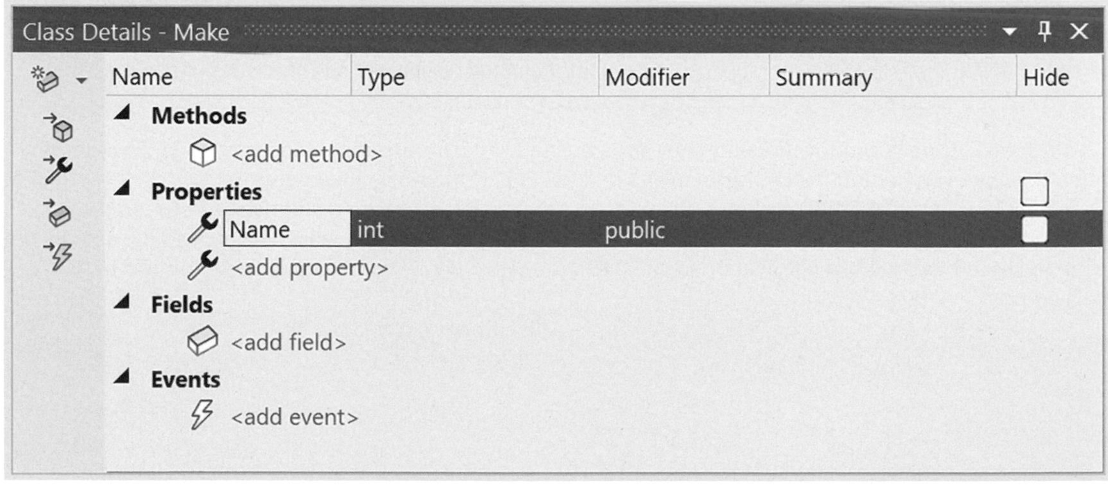

Figure 2-12. *Adding a property with the Class Details window*

If you now look at the C# definition of the Make class, you will see it has been updated accordingly:

```
using System;
using System.Collections.Generic;
using System.Linq;
using System.Text;

namespace SimpleCSharpConsoleApp
{
  public class Make
  {
    public int Name
    {
      get => default;
      set { }
    }
  }
}
```

■ **Note** Don't worry about the extra using statements or the syntax of property. This will all be covered in subsequent chapters.

Now, activate the designer file once again and drag another new class onto the designer and name it SportsCar. Click the Inheritance icon in the Class Designer Toolbox and click the top of the SportsCar icon. Next, click the mouse on top of the Car class icon. If you performed these steps correctly, you have just derived the SportsCar class from Car (see Figure 2-13).

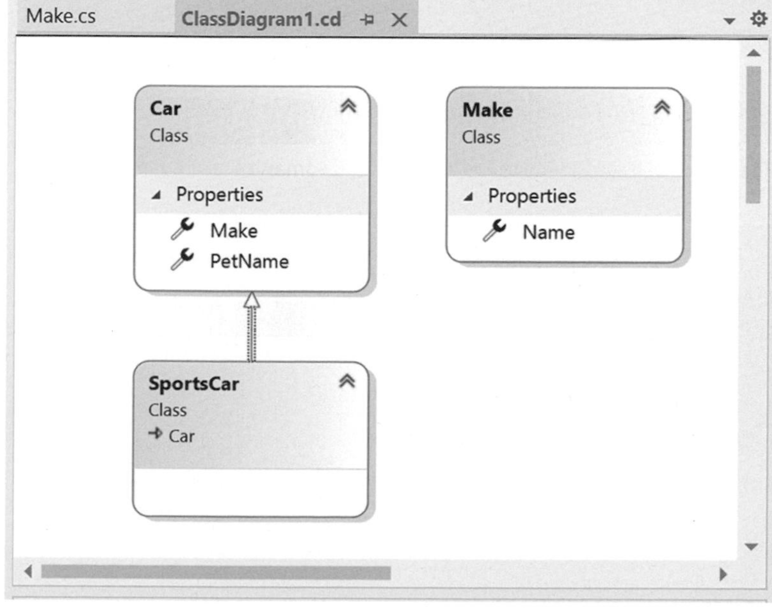

***Figure 2-13.** Visually deriving from an existing class*

■ **Note** The concept of inheritance will be fully examined in Chapter 6.

To complete this example, update the generated SportsCar class with a public method named GetPetName(), authored as follows:

```
public class SportsCar : Car
{
   public string GetPetName()
   {
     PetNam" = ""red";
     return PetName;
   }
}
```

As you would expect, the designer shows the added method to the SportsCar class.

This concludes your first look at Visual Studio. Now let's look at the most recent addition to the Visual Studio family, Visual Studio Code.

Building .NET Core Applications with Visual Studio Code

Another popular IDE from Microsoft is Visual Studio Code (VS Code). Visual Studio Code is a relatively new edition to the Microsoft family; is free, open source, and cross-platform; and has gained significant adoption among developers in and out of the .NET ecosystem. The focus of Visual Studio Code is (as the name suggests) the code of your application. While it does not have many of the built-in features that are included in Visual Studio, it is extremely fast, and additional functionality (like different language support) can be added through extensions. This allows you to have a fast IDE customized for your workflow. Many samples in this book are built and tested with Visual Studio Code. You can download it here:

```
https://code.visualstudio.com/download
```

After installing VS Code, you will want to add the C# extension found here:

```
https://marketplace.visualstudio.com/items?itemName=ms-dotnettools.csharp
```

■ **Note** Visual Studio Code is used to develop many different types of applications based on a multitude of languages. There are extensions for Angular, View, PHP, Java, and many, many, more.

Taking Visual Studio Code for a Test-Drive

Let's take a quick look at Visual Studio Code by building the same .NET 6 Console application from the Visual Studio example.

Creating Solutions and Projects

When you start Visual Studio Code, you are presented with a blank slate. Creating solutions and projects must be done through the .NET 6 command-line interface, also known as the CLI. To start, open a folder with Visual Studio Code by selecting File ➤ Open Folder, and navigate through the explorer window to where you want your solution and project to live. Next, open a terminal window by selecting Terminal ➤ New Terminal or by pressing Ctl+`.

In the terminal window, enter the following command to create an empty .NET 5 solution file:

```
dotnet new sln -n SimpleCSharpConsoleApp -o .\VisualStudioCode
```

This creates a new solution file with the name (-n) SimpleCSharpConsoleApp in a subdirectory (of the current directory) named VisualStudioCode. When using Visual Studio Code with a single project app, there is no need to create a solution file. Visual Studio is solution centric; Visual Studio Code is code centric. We created a solution file here to duplicate the process in the Visual Studio example.

■ **Note** These examples use the Windows directory separators. Adjust the separators based on your operating system.

Next, create a new C# 9/.NET 5 (-f net6.0) console application named (-n) SimpleCSharpConsoleApp in a subdirectory (-o) of the same name (note that this command must be all on one line):

```
dotnet new console -lang c# -n SimpleCSharpConsoleApp -o .\VisualStudioCode\
SimpleCSharpConsoleApp -f net6.0
```

Finally, add the newly created project to the solution with the following command:

```
dotnet sln .\VisualStudioCode\SimpleCSharpConsoleApp.sln add .\VisualStudioCode\
SimpleCSharpConsoleApp
```

■ **Note** This is just a small sample of what the CLI is capable of. To discover everything the CLI can do, enter `dotnet -h`.

Exploring the Visual Studio Code Workspace

As you can see in Figure 2-14, the Visual Studio Code workspace is focused on the code, but also provides a lot of additional features to aid your productivity. The explorer (1) is an integrated file explorer and is selected in the figure. The Source Control (2) integrates with Git. The Debug icon (3) launches the appropriate debugger (once the correct extension is installed). The next one down is the extension manager (4). The extension manager is context sensitive and will make recommendations based on the type of code in the open directory and subdirectories.

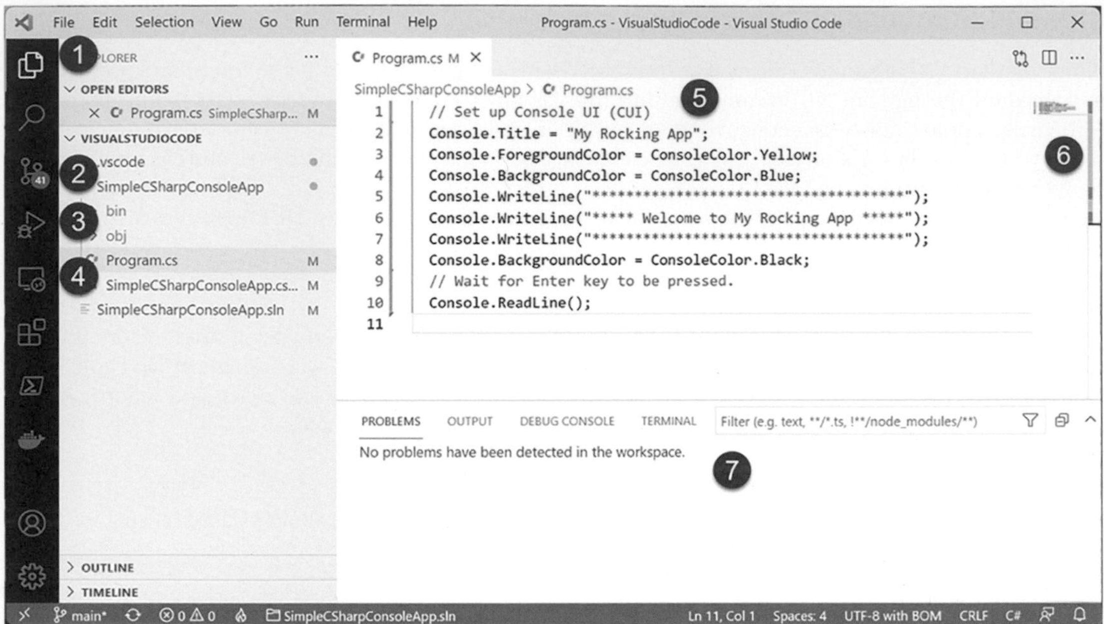

Figure 2-14. *The Visual Studio Code workspace*

The code editor (5) is complete with color coding and IntelliSense support. The code map (6) shows the map of your entire code file, and the Problems/Output/Debug Console/Terminal window (7) receives the output from debug sessions and accepts input from the user.

Restoring Packages, Building and Running Programs

The .NET 6 CLI has all of the power needed to create and build solutions and projects, add and restore NuGet packages, and run applications. To restore all of the NuGet packages required for your solution and project, enter the following command in the terminal window (or a command window outside of VS Code), making sure to run the command from the same directory as the solution file:

```
dotnet restore
```

■ **Note** Using `dotnet build` also restores all of the Nuget packages.

To restore and build all of the projects in your solution, execute the following in the terminal/command window (again, making sure the command is executed in the same directory as the solution file):

```
dotnet build
```

■ **Note** When `dotnet restore` and `dotnet build` are executed in a directory that contains a solution file, all of the projects in the solution are acted on. The commands can also be run on a single project by running the command in the directory of the C# project file (`*.csproj`).

To run your project without debugging, execute the following .NET CLI command in the same directory as the project file (`SimpleCSharpConsoleApp.csproj`):

```
dotnet run
```

Debugging Your Project

To debug your program after setting a break point, click the Debug icon (2 in Figure 2-14), then click Run and Debug (Figure 2-15).

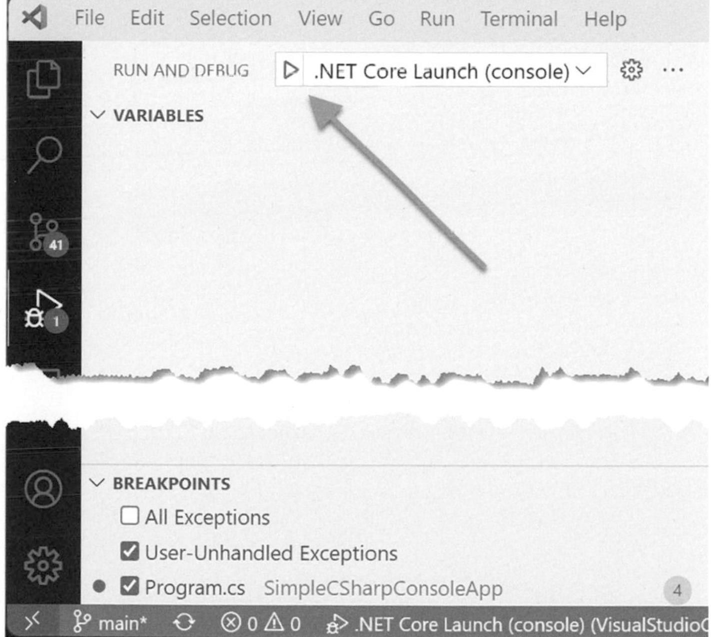

Figure 2-15. *Run and Debug in Visual Studio Code*

Finding the .NET Core and C# Documentation

The C# and .NET Core documentation are both extremely good, very readable, and full of useful information. Given the huge number of predefined .NET types (which number well into the thousands), you must be willing to roll up your sleeves and dig into the provided documentation. You can view all of the Microsoft documentation here:

```
https://docs.microsoft.com/en-us/dotnet/csharp/
```

The areas that you will use the most in the first half of this book are the C# documentation and the .NET Core documentation, found at the following locations:

```
https://docs.microsoft.com/en-us/dotnet/csharp/
https://docs.microsoft.com/en-us/dotnet/core/
```

Summary

The point of this chapter was to provide you the information to set up your development environment with the .NET 6 SDK and runtimes as well as provide a tour of Visual Studio 2022 Community Edition and Visual Studio Code. If you are interested in building cross-platform .NET Core applications, you have a host of choices. Visual Studio (Windows only), Visual Studio for the Mac (Mac only), and Visual Studio Code (cross platform) are all supplied by Microsoft. Building WPF or WinForms applications still requires Visual Studio on a Windows machine.

PART II

Core C# Programming

CHAPTER 3

Core C# Programming Constructs, Part 1

This chapter begins your formal investigation of the C# programming language by presenting a number of bite-sized, stand-alone topics you must be comfortable with as you explore the .NET Core Framework. The first order of business is to understand how to build your program's *application object* and to examine the composition of an executable program's entry point: the `Main()` method as well as a new C# 9.0 feature, top-level statements. Next, you will investigate the fundamental C# data types (and their equivalent types in the `System` namespace) including an examination of the `System.String` and `System.Text.StringBuilder` classes.

After you know the details of the fundamental .NET Core data types, you will then examine a number of data type conversion techniques, including narrowing operations, widening operations, and the use of the `checked` and `unchecked` keywords.

This chapter will also examine the role of the C# `var` keyword, which allows you to *implicitly* define a local variable. As you will see later in this book, implicit typing is extremely helpful, if not occasionally mandatory, when working with the LINQ technology set. You will wrap up this chapter by quickly examining the C# keywords and operators that allow you to control the flow of an application using various looping and decision constructs.

Breaking Down a Simple C# Program (Updated C# 10)

C# demands that all program logic be contained within a type definition (recall from Chapter 1 that *type* is a general term referring to a member of the set {class, interface, structure, enumeration, delegate}). Unlike many other languages, in C# it is not possible to create global functions or global points of data. Rather, all data members and all methods must be contained within a type definition. To get the ball rolling, create a new empty solution named `Chapter3_AllProject.sln` that contains a C# console application named SimpleCSharpApp.

From Visual Studio, select the Blank Solution template on the "Create a new project" screen. When the solution opens, right-click the solution in Solution Explorer and select Add ➤ New Project. Select "C# console app" from the templates, name it **SimpleCSharpApp**, and click Next. Select .NET 6.0 for the framework and then click Create.

To create a solution and console application and add that console application to the solution, from the command line (or the Visual Studio Code terminal window), execute the following:

```
dotnet new sln -n Chapter3_AllProjects
dotnet new console -lang c# -n SimpleCSharpApp -o .\SimpleCSharpApp -f net6.0
dotnet sln .\Chapter3_AllProjects.sln add .\SimpleCSharpApp
```


A. Troelsen and P. Japikse, *Pro C# 10 with .NET 6*, https://doi.org/10.1007/978-1-4842-7869-7_3

In the created project, you will see one file (named `Program.cs`) with one line of code.

```
Console.WriteLine("Hello, World!");
```

If you are new to C#, this line seems pretty straightforward. It writes the message "Hello, World!" to the standard console output window. Prior to C# 10, there was a lot more code required to achieve the same effect. When creating the same program in versions of C# prior to C# 10, you were required to write the following:

```
using System;

namespace SimpleCSharpApp
{
  class Program
  {
    static void Main(string[] args)
    {
      Console.WriteLine("Hello World!");
    }
  }
}
```

The `Console` class is contained in the `System` namespace, and with the implicit global namespaces provided by .NET 6/C# 10, the `using System;` statement is no longer needed. The next line creates a custom namespace (covered in Chapter 16) to wrap the `Program` class. Both the namespace and the `Program` class can be removed due to the top-level statement functionality introduced in C# 9 (covered shortly). That brings us back to the single line of code to write the message to the `Console`.

For now, to cover some important variations of the entry point into C# applications, we will use the older (more verbose) style of code instead of the streamlined C# 10 version. Given this, update the `Main()` method of your `Program` class with the following code statements:

```
class Program
{
  static void Main(string[] args)
  {
    // Display a simple message to the user.
    Console.WriteLine("***** My First C# App *****");
    Console.WriteLine("Hello World!");
    Console.WriteLine();

    // Wait for Enter key to be pressed before shutting down.
    Console.ReadLine();
  }
}
```

■ **Note** C# is a case-sensitive programming language. Therefore, *Main* is not the same as *main*, and *Readline* is not the same as *ReadLine*. Be aware that all C# keywords are lowercase (e.g., public, lock, class, dynamic), while namespaces, types, and member names begin (by convention) with an initial capital letter and the first letter of any embedded words is capitalized (e.g., Console.WriteLine, System.Windows.MessageBox, System.Data.SqlClient). As a rule of thumb, whenever you receive a compiler error regarding "undefined symbols," be sure to check your spelling and casing first!

The previous code contains a definition for a class type that supports a single method named Main(). By default, the C# project templates that don't use top-level statements name the class containing the Main() method Program; however, you are free to change this if you so choose. Prior to C# 9.0, every executable C# application (console program, Windows desktop program, or Windows service) must contain a class defining a Main() method, which is used to signify the entry point of the application.

Formally speaking, the class that defines the Main() method is termed the *application object*. It is possible for a single executable application to have more than one application object (which can be useful when performing unit tests), but then the compiler must know which Main() method should be used as the entry point. This can be done via the <StartupObject> element in the project file or via the Startup Object drop-down list box, located on the Application tab of the Visual Studio project properties window.

Note that the signature of Main() is adorned with the static keyword, which will be examined in detail in Chapter 5. For the time being, simply understand that static members are scoped to the class level (rather than the object level) and can thus be invoked without the need to first create a new class instance.

In addition to the static keyword, this Main() method has a single parameter, which happens to be an array of strings (string[] args). Although you are not currently bothering to process this array, this parameter may contain any number of incoming command-line arguments (you will see how to access them momentarily). Finally, this Main() method has been set up with a void return value, meaning you do not explicitly define a return value using the return keyword before exiting the method scope.

The logic of the Program class is within Main(). Here, you make use of the Console class, which is defined within the System namespace. Among its set of members is the static WriteLine(), which, as you might assume, sends a text string and carriage return to the standard output. You also make a call to Console.ReadLine() to ensure the command prompt launched by the Visual Studio IDE remains visible. When running .NET Core Console apps with Visual Studio (in either Debug or Release mode), the console window remains visible by default. This behavior can be changed by enabling the setting "Automatically close the console when debugging stops" found under Tools ➤ Options ➤ Debugging. The Console.ReadLine() method is there to keep the window open if the program is executed from Windows Explorer by double-clicking the product *.exe file. You will learn more about the System.Console class shortly.

Using Variations of the Main() Method (Updated 7.1)

By default, the .NET console project template will generate a Main() method that has a void return value and an array of string types as the single input parameter. This is not the only possible form of Main(), however. It is permissible to construct your application's entry point using any of the following signatures (assuming it is contained within a C# class or structure definition):

```
// int return type, array of strings as the parameter.
static int Main(string[] args)
{
  // Must return a value before exiting!
  return 0;
}
```

```
// No return type, no parameters.
static void Main()
{
}

// int return type, no parameters.
static int Main()
{
  // Must return a value before exiting!
  return 0;
}
```

With the release of C# 7.1, the `Main()` method can be asynchronous. Async programming is covered in Chapter 15, but for now realize there are four additional signatures.

```
static Task Main()
static Task<int> Main()
static Task Main(string[])
static Task<int> Main(string[])
```

■ **Note** The `Main()` method may also be defined as public as opposed to private. Note that private is assumed if you do not supply a specific access modifier. Access modifiers are covered in detail in Chapter 5.

Obviously, your choice of how to construct `Main()` will be based on three questions. First, do you want to return a value to the system when `Main()` has completed and your program terminates? If so, you need to return an `int` data type rather than `void`. Second, do you need to process any user-supplied, command-line parameters? If so, they will be stored in the array of `strings`. Lastly, do you need to call asynchronous code from the `Main()` method? We'll examine the first two options in more detail after introducing top-level statements. The async options will be covered in Chapter 15.

Using Top-Level Statements (New 9.0)

While it is true that prior to C# 9.0, all C# .NET Core applications must have a `Main()` method, C# 9.0 introduced top-level statements, which eliminate the need for much of the ceremony around the C# application's entry point. Both the class (`Program`) and `Main()` methods can be removed. To see this in action, update the `Program.cs` class to match the following:

```
// Display a simple message to the user.
Console.WriteLine("***** My First C# App *****");
Console.WriteLine("Hello World!");
Console.WriteLine();

// Wait for Enter key to be pressed before shutting down.
Console.ReadLine();
```

You will see that when you run the program, you get the same result! There are some rules around using top-level statements:

- Only one file in the application can use top-level statements.
- When using top-level statements, the program cannot have a declared entry point.
- The top-level statements cannot be enclosed in a namespace.
- Top-level statements still access a `string` array of args.
- Top-level statements return an application code (see the next section) by using a return.
- Functions that would have been declared in the `Program` class become local functions for the top-level statements. (Local functions are covered in Chapter 4.)
- The top-level statements compile to a class named `Program`, allowing for the addition of a `partial Program` class to hold regular methods. Partial classes are covered in Chapter 5.
- Additional types can be declared after all top-level statements. Any types declared before the end of the top-level statements will result in a compilation error.

Behind the scenes, the compiler fills in the blanks. Examining the generated IL for the updated code, you will see the following `TypeDef` for the entry point into the application:

```
// TypeDef #1 (02000002)
// -------------------------------------------------------
//     TypDefName: <Program>$  (02000002)
//     Flags     : [NotPublic] [AutoLayout] [Class] [Abstract] [Sealed] [AnsiClass]
       [BeforeFieldInit]  (00100180)
//     Extends   : 0100000D [TypeRef] System.Object
//     Method #1 (06000001) [ENTRYPOINT]
//     -------------------------------------------------------
//         MethodName: <Main>$ (06000001)
```

Compare that to the `TypeDef` for the entry point from Chapter 1:

```
// TypeDef #1 (02000002)
// -------------------------------------------------------
//     TypDefName: CalculatorExamples.Program  (02000002)
//     Flags     : [NotPublic] [AutoLayout] [Class] [AnsiClass]
       [BeforeFieldInit]  (00100000)
//     Extends   : 0100000C [TypeRef] System.Object
//     Method #1 (06000001) [ENTRYPOINT]
//     -------------------------------------------------------
//         MethodName: Main (06000001)
```

Notice for the example from Chapter 1, the `TypDefName` value is shown as the namespace (`CalculatorExamples`) plus the class name (`Program`), and the `MethodName` value is `Main`. In the updated example using top-level statements, the compiler has filled in the values of `<Program>$` for the `TypDefName` and `<Main>$` for the method name.

Specifying an Application Error Code (Updated 9.0)

While a vast majority of your Main() methods (or top-level statements) will return void as the return value, the ability to return an int (or Task<int>) keeps C# consistent with other C-based languages. By convention, returning the value 0 indicates the program has terminated successfully, while another value (such as -1) represents an error condition (be aware that the value 0 is automatically returned, even if you construct a Main() method prototyped to return void).

When using top-level statements (and therefore no Main() method), if the executing code returns an integer, that is the return code. If nothing is explicitly returned, it still returns 0, as with explicitly using a Main() method.

On the Windows operating system, an application's return value is stored within a system environment variable named %ERRORLEVEL%. If you were to create an application that programmatically launches another executable (a topic examined in Chapter 18), you can obtain the value of %ERRORLEVEL% using the ExitCode property of the launched process.

Given that an application's return value is passed to the system at the time the application terminates, it is obviously not possible for an application to obtain and display its final error code while running. However, to illustrate how to view this error level upon program termination, begin by updating the top-level statements, as follows:

```
// Note we are explicitly returning an int, rather than void.
// Display a message and wait for Enter key to be pressed.
Console.WriteLine("***** My First C# App *****");
Console.WriteLine("Hello World!");
Console.WriteLine();
Console.ReadLine();

// Return an arbitrary error code.
return -1;
```

If the program is still using a Main() method as the entry point, change the method signature to return int instead of void, as follows:

```
static int Main()
{
...
}
```

Now let's capture the return value of the program with the help of a batch file. Using Windows Explorer, navigate to the folder containing your project file (e.g., C:\SimpleCSharpApp) and add a new text file (named SimpleCSharpApp.cmd) to that folder. Update the contents of the folder to the following (if you have not authored *.cmd files before, do not concern yourself with the details):

```
@echo off
rem A batch file for SimpleCSharpApp.exe
rem which captures the app's return value.

dotnet run
@if "%ERRORLEVEL%" == "0" goto success

:fail
  echo This application has failed!
```

```
  echo return value = %ERRORLEVEL%
  goto end
:success
  echo This application has succeeded!
  echo return value = %ERRORLEVEL%
  goto end
:end
echo All Done.
```

At this point, open a command prompt (or use the Visual Studio Code terminal) and navigate to the folder containing your new *.cmd file. Execute the file by typing its name and pressing the Enter key. You should find the output shown next, given that your top-level statements (or Main() method) return -1. Had the top-level statements (or Main() method) returned 0, you would see the message "This application has succeeded!" print to the console.

```
***** My First C# App *****

Hello World!

This application has failed!
Return value = -1
All Done.
```

The PowerShell equivalent of the preceding *.cmd file is as follows:

```
dotnet run
if ($LastExitCode -eq 0) {
    Write-Host "This application has succeeded!"
} else
{
    Write-Host "This application has failed!"
}
Write-Host "All Done."
```

To run this, type PowerShell into the Visual Studio Code terminal and then execute the script by typing this:

```
.\SimpleCSharpApp.ps1
```

You will see the following in the terminal window:

```
***** My First C# App *****

Hello World!

This application has failed!
All Done.
```

■ **Note** If you receive a security policy error when running the PowerShell script, you can set the policy to allow unsigned local scripts by executing the following command in PowerShell:

```
set-executionpolicy -executionpolicy remotesigned -scope currentuser
```

A vast majority (if not all) of your C# applications will use void as the return value from Main(), which, as you recall, implicitly returns the error code of zero. To this end, the Main() methods used in this text (beyond the current example) will return void.

Processing Command-Line Arguments (Updated 9.0)

Now that you better understand the return value of the Main() method or top-level statements, let's examine the incoming array of string data. Assume that you now want to update your application to process any possible command-line parameters. One way to do this is using a C# for loop. (Note that C#'s iteration constructs will be examined in some detail near the end of this chapter.)

```
// Display a message and wait for Enter key to be pressed.
Console.WriteLine("***** My First C# App *****");
Console.WriteLine("Hello World!");
Console.WriteLine();
// Process any incoming args.
for (int i = 0; i < args.Length; i++)
{
  Console.WriteLine("Arg: {0}", args[i]);
}
Console.ReadLine();
// Return an arbitrary error code.
return 0;
```

■ **Note** This example is using top-level statements, which doesn't utilize a Main() method. Updating the Main() method to accept the args parameter is covered shortly.

Once again, examining the generated IL for the program using top-level statements, notice that the <Main>$ method accepts a string array named args, as shown here (abbreviated for space):

```
.class private abstract auto ansi sealed beforefieldinit '<Program>$'
       extends [System.Runtime]System.Object
{
  .custom instance void [System.Runtime]System.Runtime.CompilerServices.
  CompilerGeneratedAttribute::.ctor()=
    ( 01 00 00 00 )
  .method private hidebysig static
          int32  '<Main>$'(string[] args) cil managed
  {
    .entrypoint
...
```

```
  } // end of method '<Program>$'::'<Main>$'
} // end of class '<Program>$'
```

If the program is still using a `Main()` method as the entry point, make sure the method signature accepts a `string` array named args, as follows:

```
static int Main(string[] args)
{
...
}
```

Here, you are checking to see whether the array of `strings` contains some number of items using the `Length` property of `System.Array`. As you will see in Chapter 4, all C# arrays actually alias the `System.Array` class and, therefore, share a common set of members. As you loop over each item in the array, its value is printed to the console window. Supplying the arguments at the command line is equally simple, as shown here:

```
C:\SimpleCSharpApp>dotnet run /arg1 -arg2

***** My First C# App *****
Hello World!
Arg: /arg1
Arg: -arg2
```

As an alternative to the standard `for` loop, you may iterate over an incoming `string` array using the C# `foreach` keyword. Here is some sample usage (but again, you will see specifics of looping constructs later in this chapter):

```
// Notice you have no need to check the size of the array when using "foreach".
// Process any incoming args using foreach.
foreach(string arg in args)
{
  Console.WriteLine("Arg: {0}", arg);
}
Console.ReadLine();
return 0;
```

Finally, you are also able to access command-line arguments using the static `GetCommandLineArgs()` method of the `System.Environment` type. The return value of this method is an array of `strings`. The first entry holds the name of the application itself, while the remaining elements in the array contain the individual command-line arguments.

```
// Get arguments using System.Environment.
string[] theArgs = Environment.GetCommandLineArgs();
foreach(string arg in theArgs)
{
  Console.WriteLine("Arg: {0}", arg);
}
Console.ReadLine();
return 0;
```

■ **Note** The `GetCommandLineArgs` method does not receive the arguments for the application through the `Main()` method and does not depend on the `string[] args` parameter.

Of course, it is up to you to determine which command-line arguments your program will respond to (if any) and how they must be formatted (such as with a - or / prefix). Here, I simply passed in a series of options that were printed directly to the command prompt. Assume, however, you were creating a new video game and programmed your application to process an option named `-godmode`. If the user starts your application with the flag, you know he is, in fact, *a cheater*, and you can take an appropriate course of action.

Specifying Command-Line Arguments with Visual Studio 2022

In the real world, an end user has the option of supplying command-line arguments when starting a program. However, during the development cycle, you might want to specify possible command-line flags for testing purposes. To do so with Visual Studio, right-click the project name in Solution Explorer, select Properties, and then navigate to the Debug tab on the left side. From there, open the new Launch Profile UI, specify the values using the Command Line Arguments text box (see Figure 3-1), and save your changes.

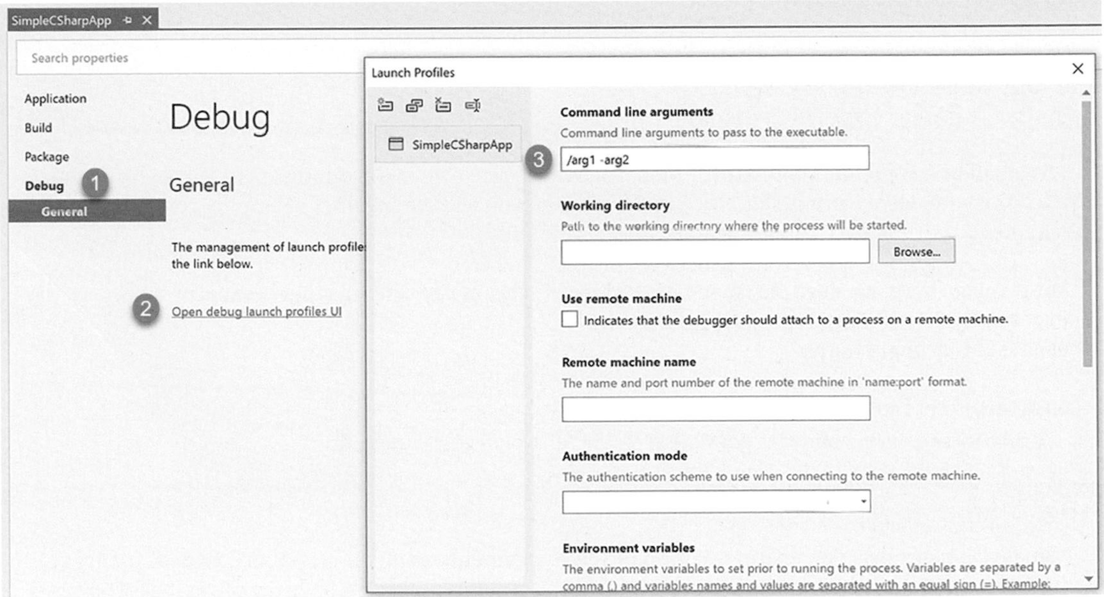

Figure 3-1. *Setting application arguments in Visual Studio*

After you have established such command-line arguments, they will automatically be passed to the `Main()` method when debugging or running your application within the Visual Studio IDE.

Additional Members of the System.Environment Class (Updated 10.0)

The `Environment` class exposes a number of extremely helpful methods beyond `GetCommandLineArgs()`. Specifically, this class allows you to obtain a number of details regarding the operating system currently hosting your .NET 6 application using various static members. To illustrate the usefulness of `System.Environment`, update your code to call a local method named `ShowEnvironmentDetails()`.

```
// Local method within the Top-level statements.
ShowEnvironmentDetails();

Console.ReadLine();
return -1;
}
```

Implement this method after your top-level statements to call various members of the `Environment` type:

```
static void ShowEnvironmentDetails()
{
  // Print out the drives on this machine,
  // and other interesting details.
  foreach (string drive in Environment.GetLogicalDrives())
  {
    Console.WriteLine("Drive: {0}", drive);
  }
  Console.WriteLine("OS: {0}", Environment.OSVersion);
  Console.WriteLine("Number of processors: {0}",
    Environment.ProcessorCount);
  Console.WriteLine(".NET Core Version: {0}",
    Environment.Version);
}
```

The following output shows a possible test run of invoking this method:

```
***** My First C# App *****

Hello World!

Drive: C:\
OS: Microsoft Windows NT 10.0.19042.0
Number of processors: 16
.NET Core Version: 6.0.0
```

The `Environment` type defines members other than those shown in the previous example. Table 3-1 documents some additional properties of interest; however, be sure to check out the online documentation for full details.

Table 3-1. *Select Properties of System.Environment*

Property	Meaning in Life
ExitCode	Gets or sets the exit code for the application
Is64BitOperatingSystem	Returns a bool to represent whether the host machine is running a 64-bit OS
MachineName	Gets the name of the current machine
NewLine	Gets the newline symbol for the current environment
ProcessId (new in 10.0)	Gets the unique identifier of the current process
ProcessPath (new in 10.0)	Returns the path of the executable that started the currently executing process; returns null when the path is not available
SystemDirectory	Returns the full path to the system directory
UserName	Returns the name of the user that started this application
Version	Returns a Version object that represents the version of the .NET Core platform

Using the System.Console Class

Almost all the example applications created over the course of the initial chapters of this book make extensive use of the System.Console class. While it is true that a console user interface (CUI) may not be as enticing as a graphical user interface (GUI) or web application, restricting the early examples to console programs will allow you to keep focused on the syntax of C# and the core aspects of the .NET 6 platform, rather than dealing with the complexities of building desktop GUIs or websites.

■ **Note** Access to the Console class is now implicitly provided by the global using statements provided by .NET 6, negating the need to add in the using System; statement that was required in previous versions of C#/.NET.

As its name implies, the Console class encapsulates input, output, and error-stream manipulations for console-based applications. Table 3-2 lists some (but definitely not all) members of interest. As you can see, the Console class does provide some members that can spice up a simple command-line application, such as the ability to change background and foreground colors and issue beep noises (in a variety of frequencies!).

Table 3-2. *Select Members of System.Console*

Member	Meaning in Life
Beep()	This method forces the console to emit a beep of a specified frequency and duration.
BackgroundColor ForegroundColor	These properties set the background/foreground colors for the current output. They may be assigned any member of the ConsoleColor enumeration.
BufferHeight BufferWidth	These properties control the height/width of the console's buffer area.
Title	This property gets or sets the title of the current console.
WindowHeight WindowWidth WindowTop WindowLeft	These properties control the dimensions of the console in relation to the established buffer.
Clear()	This method clears the established buffer and console display area.

Performing Basic Input and Output (I/O) with the Console Class

In addition to the members in Table 3-2, the Console type defines a set of methods to capture input and output, all of which are static and are, therefore, called by prefixing the name of the class (Console) to the method name. As you have seen, WriteLine() pumps a text string (including a carriage return) to the output stream. The Write() method pumps text to the output stream without a carriage return. ReadLine() allows you to receive information from the input stream up until the Enter key is pressed, while Read() is used to capture a single character from the input stream.

To illustrate simple I/O using the Console class, create a new Console Application project named BasicConsoleIO and add it to your solution with these CLI commands:

```
dotnet new console -lang c# -n BasicConsoleIO -o .\BasicConsoleIO -f net6.0
dotnet sln .\Chapter3_AllProjects.sln add .\BasicConsoleIO
```

Replace the Program.cs code with the following:

```
Console.WriteLine("***** Basic Console I/O *****");
GetUserData();
Console.ReadLine();
static void GetUserData()
{
}
```

■ **Note** Visual Studio and Visual Studio Code both support a number of "code snippets" that will insert code once activated. The cw code snippet is quite useful during the early chapters of this text, in that it will automatically expand to Console.WriteLine()! To test this for yourself, type in cw somewhere within your code and hit the Tab key. Note: In Visual Studio Code, you hit the Tab key once; in Visual Studio, you must hit the Tab key twice.

Implement this method after the top-level statements with logic that prompts the user for some bits of information and echoes each item to the standard output stream. For example, you could ask the user for a name and age (which will be treated as a text value for simplicity, rather than the expected numerical value), as follows:

```
static void GetUserData()
{
  // Get name and age.
  Console.Write("Please enter your name: ");
  string userName = Console.ReadLine();
  Console.Write("Please enter your age: ");
  string userAge = Console.ReadLine();

  // Change echo color, just for fun.
  ConsoleColor prevColor = Console.ForegroundColor;
  Console.ForegroundColor = ConsoleColor.Yellow;

  // Echo to the console.
  Console.WriteLine("Hello {0}! You are {1} years old.",
  userName, userAge);

  // Restore previous color.
  Console.ForegroundColor = prevColor;
}
```

Not surprisingly, when you run this application, the input data is printed to the console (using a custom color to boot!).

Formatting Console Output

During these first few chapters, you might have noticed numerous occurrences of tokens such as {0} and {1} embedded within various string literals. The .NET 6 platform supports a style of string formatting slightly akin to the printf() statement of C. Simply put, when you are defining a string literal that contains segments of data whose value is not known until runtime, you are able to specify a placeholder within the string literal using this curly-bracket syntax. At runtime, the values passed into Console.WriteLine() are substituted for each placeholder.

The first parameter to WriteLine() represents a string literal that contains optional placeholders designated by {0}, {1}, {2}, and so forth. Be aware that the first ordinal number of a curly-bracket placeholder always begins with 0. The remaining parameters to WriteLine() are simply the values to be inserted into the respective placeholders.

■ **Note** If you have more uniquely numbered curly-bracket placeholders than fill arguments, you will receive a format exception at runtime. However, if you have more fill arguments than placeholders, the unused fill arguments are ignored.

It is permissible for a given placeholder to repeat within a given string. For example, if you are a Beatles fan and want to build the string "9, Number 9, Number 9", you would write this:

```
// John says...
Console.WriteLine("{0}, Number {0}, Number {0}", 9);
```

Also, know that it is possible to position each placeholder in any location within a string literal, and it need not follow an increasing sequence. For example, consider the following code snippet:

```
// Prints: 20, 10, 30
Console.WriteLine("{1}, {0}, {2}", 10, 20, 30);
```

Strings can also be formatted using string interpolation, which is covered later in this chapter.

Formatting Numerical Data

If you require more elaborate formatting for numerical data, each placeholder can optionally contain various format characters. Table 3-3 shows the most common formatting options.

Table 3-3. *.NET Core Numerical Format Characters*

String Format Character	Meaning in Life
C or c	Used to format currency. By default, the flag will prefix the local cultural symbol (a dollar sign [$] for US English).
D or d	Used to format decimal numbers. This flag may also specify the minimum number of digits used to pad the value.
E or e	Used for exponential notation. Casing controls whether the exponential constant is uppercase (E) or lowercase (e).
F or f	Used for fixed-point formatting. This flag may also specify the minimum number of digits used to pad the value.
G or g	Stands for *general*. This character can be used to format a number to fixed or exponential format.
N or n	Used for basic numerical formatting (with commas).
X or x	Used for hexadecimal formatting. If you use an uppercase X, your hex format will also contain uppercase characters.

These format characters are suffixed to a given placeholder value using the colon token (e.g., {0:C}, {1:d}, {2:X}). To illustrate, update the top-level statements to call a new helper function named FormatNumericalData(). Implement this method in your Program.cs file to format a fixed numerical value in a variety of ways.

```
// Now make use of some format tags.
static void FormatNumericalData()
{
  Console.WriteLine("The value 99999 in various formats:");
  Console.WriteLine("c format: {0:c}", 99999);
  Console.WriteLine("d9 format: {0:d9}", 99999);
  Console.WriteLine("f3 format: {0:f3}", 99999);
  Console.WriteLine("n format: {0:n}", 99999);

  // Notice that upper- or lowercasing for hex
  // determines if letters are upper- or lowercase.
  Console.WriteLine("E format: {0:E}", 99999);
  Console.WriteLine("e format: {0:e}", 99999);
  Console.WriteLine("X format: {0:X}", 99999);
  Console.WriteLine("x format: {0:x}", 99999);
}
```

The following output shows the result of calling the FormatNumericalData() method:

```
The value 99999 in various formats:

c format: $99,999.00
d9 format: 000099999
f3 format: 99999.000
n format: 99,999.00
E format: 9.999900E+004
e format: 9.999900e+004
X format: 1869F
x format: 1869f
```

You will see additional formatting examples where required throughout this text; however, if you are interested in digging into string formatting further, look up the topic “Formatting Types” within the .NET Core documentation.

Formatting Numerical Data Beyond Console Applications

On a final note, be aware that the use of the string formatting characters is not limited to console programs. This same formatting syntax can be used when calling the static string.Format() method. This can be helpful when you need to compose textual data at runtime for use in any application type (e.g., desktop GUI app, ASP.NET web app, etc.).

The string.Format() method returns a new string object, which is formatted according to the provided flags. The following code formats a string in hex:

```
// Using string.Format() to format a string literal.
string userMessage = string.Format("100000 in hex is {0:x}", 100000);
```

Working with System Data Types and Corresponding C# Keywords

Like any programming language, C# defines keywords for fundamental data types, which are used to represent local variables, class data member variables, method return values, and parameters. Unlike other programming languages, however, these keywords are much more than simple compiler-recognized tokens. Rather, the C# data type keywords are actually shorthand notations for full-blown types in the `System` namespace. Table 3-4 lists each system data type, its range, the corresponding C# keyword, and the type's compliance with the Common Language Specification (CLS). All of the system types are in the System namespace, left off the chart for readability.

Table 3-4. *The Intrinsic Data Types of C#*

C# Shorthand	CLS Compliant?	System Type	Range	Meaning in Life
`bool`	Yes	`Boolean`	true or false	Represents truth or falsity
`sbyte`	No	`SByte`	-128 to 127	Signed 8-bit number
`byte`	Yes	`Byte`	0 to 255	Unsigned 8-bit number
`short`	Yes	`Int16`	-32,768 to 32,767	Signed 16-bit number
`ushort`	No	`UInt16`	0 to 65,535	Unsigned 16-bit number
`int`	Yes	`Int32`	-2,147,483,648 to 2,147,483,647	Signed 32-bit number
`uint`	No	`UInt32`	0 to 4,294,967,295	Unsigned 32-bit number
`long`	Yes	`Int64`	-9,223,372,036,854,775,808 to 9,223,372,036,854,775,807	Signed 64-bit to number
`ulong`	No	`UInt64`	0 to 18,446,744,073,709,551,615	Unsigned 64-bit number
`char`	Yes	`Char`	U+0000 to U+ffff	Single 16-bit Unicode character
`float`	Yes	`Single`	$-3.4\ 10^{38}$ to $+3.4\ 10^{38}$	32-bit floating-point number
`double`	Yes	`Double`	$\pm5.0\ 10^{-324}$ to $\pm1.7\ 10^{308}$	64-bit floating-point number
`decimal`	Yes	`Decimal`	$(-7.9 \times 10^{28}$ to $7.9 \times 10^{28})/(10^{0 \text{ to } 28})$	128-bit signed number
`string`	Yes	`String`	Limited by system memory	Represents a set of Unicode characters
`object`	Yes	`Object`	Can store any data type in an object variable	The base class of all types in the .NET universe

■ **Note** Recall from Chapter 1 that CLS-compliant .NET Core code can be used by any other .NET programming language. If you expose non-CLS-compliant data from your programs, other .NET languages might not be able to make use of it.

Understanding Variable Declaration and Initialization

When you are declaring a local variable (e.g., a variable within a member scope), you do so by specifying the data type, followed by the variable's name. To begin, create a new Console Application project named BasicDataTypes and add it into the solution using these commands:

```
dotnet new console -lang c# -n BasicDataTypes -o .\BasicDataTypes -f net6.0
dotnet sln .\Chapter3_AllProjects.sln add .\BasicDataTypes
```

Update the code to the following:

```
using System.Numerics;

Console.WriteLine("***** Fun with Basic Data Types *****");
```

Now, add the following static local function and call it from the top-level statements:

```
static void LocalVarDeclarations()
{
  Console.WriteLine("=> Data Declarations:");
  // Local variables are declared as so:
  // dataType varName;
  int myInt;
  string myString;
  Console.WriteLine();
}
```

Be aware that it is a *compiler error* to make use of a local variable before assigning an initial value. Given this, it is good practice to assign an initial value to your local data points at the time of declaration. You may do so on a single line or by separating the declaration and assignment into two code statements.

```
static void LocalVarDeclarations()
{
  Console.WriteLine("=> Data Declarations:");
  // Local variables are declared and initialized as follows:
  // dataType varName = initialValue;
  int myInt = 0;

  // You can also declare and assign on two lines.
  string myString;
  myString = "This is my character data";

  Console.WriteLine();
}
```

It is also permissible to declare multiple variables of the same underlying type on a single line of code, as in the following three bool variables:

```
static void LocalVarDeclarations()
{
  Console.WriteLine("=> Data Declarations:");
  int myInt = 0;
  string myString;
  myString = "This is my character data";

  // Declare 3 bools on a single line.
  bool b1 = true, b2 = false, b3 = b1;
  Console.WriteLine();
}
```

Since the C# bool keyword is simply a shorthand notation for the System.Boolean structure, it is also possible to allocate any data type using its full name (of course, the same point holds true for any C# data type keyword). Here is the final implementation of LocalVarDeclarations(), which illustrates various ways to declare a local variable:

```
static void LocalVarDeclarations()
{
  Console.WriteLine("=> Data Declarations:");
  // Local variables are declared and initialized as follows:
  // dataType varName = initialValue;
  int myInt = 0;

  string myString;
  myString = "This is my character data";

  // Declare 3 bools on a single line.
  bool b1 = true, b2 = false, b3 = b1;

  // Use System.Boolean data type to declare a bool.
  System.Boolean b4 = false;

  Console.WriteLine("Your data: {0}, {1}, {2}, {3}, {4}, {5}",
      myInt, myString, b1, b2, b3, b4);
  Console.WriteLine();
}
```

The default Literal (New 7.1)

The default literal assigns a variable the default value for its data type. This works for standard data types as well as custom classes (Chapter 5) and generic types (Chapter 10). Create a new method named DefaultDeclarations() and add the following code:

```
static void DefaultDeclarations()
{
  Console.WriteLine("=> Default Declarations:");
  int myInt = default;
  Console.WriteLine(myInt);
}
```

Using Intrinsic Data Types and the new Operator (Updated 9.0)

All intrinsic data types support what is known as a *default constructor* (see Chapter 5). This feature allows you to create a variable using the new keyword, which automatically sets the variable to its default value:

- bool variables are set to false.
- Numeric data is set to 0 (or 0.0 in the case of floating-point data types).
- char variables are set to a single empty character.
- BigInteger variables are set to 0.
- DateTime variables are set to 1/1/0001 12:00:00 AM.
- Object references (including strings) are set to null.

■ **Note** The BigInteger data type mentioned in the previous list will be explained in just a bit.

Although it is more cumbersome to use the new keyword when creating a basic data type variable, the following is syntactically well-formed C# code:

```
static void NewingDataTypes()
{
  Console.WriteLine("=> Using new to create variables:");
  bool b = new bool();              // Set to false.
  int i = new int();                // Set to 0.
  double d = new double();          // Set to 0.
  DateTime dt = new DateTime();     // Set to 1/1/0001 12:00:00 AM
  Console.WriteLine("{0}, {1}, {2}, {3}", b, i, d, dt);
  Console.WriteLine();
}
```

C# 9.0 added a shortcut for creating variable instances. This shortcut is simply using the keyword new() without the data type. The updated version of NewingDataTypes is shown here:

```
static void NewingDataTypesWith9()
{
  Console.WriteLine("=> Using new to create variables:");
  bool b = new();              // Set to false.
  int i = new();               // Set to 0.
  double d = new();            // Set to 0.
  DateTime dt = new();         // Set to 1/1/0001 12:00:00 AM
```

```
    Console.WriteLine("{0}, {1}, {2}, {3}", b, i, d, dt);
    Console.WriteLine();
}
```

Understanding the Data Type Class Hierarchy

It is interesting to note that even the primitive .NET data types are arranged in a *class hierarchy*. If you are new to the world of inheritance, you will discover the full details in Chapter 6. Until then, just understand that types at the top of a class hierarchy provide some default behaviors that are granted to the derived types. The relationship between these core system types can be understood as shown in Figure 3-2.

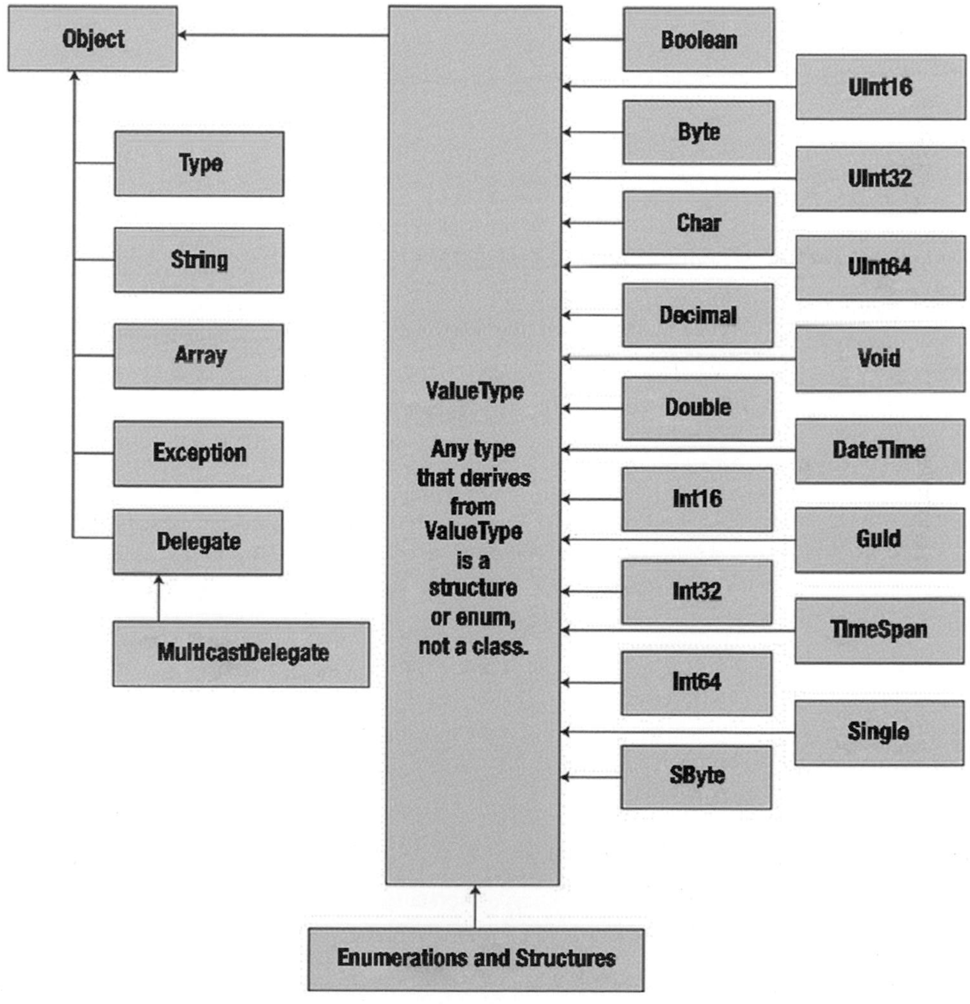

Figure 3-2. *The class hierarchy of system types*

Notice that each type ultimately derives from System.Object, which defines a set of methods (e.g., ToString(), Equals(), GetHashCode()) common to all types in the .NET Core base class libraries (these methods are fully detailed in Chapter 6).

Also note that many numerical data types derive from a class named System.ValueType. Descendants of ValueType are automatically allocated on the stack and, therefore, have a predictable lifetime and are quite efficient. On the other hand, types that do not have System.ValueType in their inheritance chain (such as System.Type, System.String, System.Array, System.Exception, and System.Delegate) are not allocated on the stack but on the garbage-collected heap. (You can find more information on this distinction in Chapter 4.)

Without getting too hung up on the details of System.Object and System.ValueType, just understand that because a C# keyword (such as int) is simply shorthand notation for the corresponding system type (in this case, System.Int32), the following is perfectly legal syntax, given that System.Int32 (the C# int) eventually derives from System.Object and, therefore, can invoke any of its public members, as illustrated by this additional helper function:

```
static void ObjectFunctionality()
{
  Console.WriteLine("=> System.Object Functionality:");

  // A C# int is really a shorthand for System.Int32,
  // which inherits the following members from System.Object.
  Console.WriteLine("12.GetHashCode() = {0}", 12.GetHashCode());
  Console.WriteLine("12.Equals(23) = {0}", 12.Equals(23));
  Console.WriteLine("12.ToString() = {0}", 12.ToString());
  Console.WriteLine("12.GetType() = {0}", 12.GetType());
  Console.WriteLine();
}
```

If you were to call this method from within the top-level statements, you would find the output shown here:

```
=> System.Object Functionality:

12.GetHashCode() = 12
12.Equals(23) = False
12.ToString() = 12
12.GetType() = System.Int32
```

Understanding the Members of Numerical Data Types

To continue experimenting with the intrinsic C# data types, understand that the numerical types of .NET Core support MaxValue and MinValue properties that provide information regarding the range a given type can store. In addition to the MinValue/MaxValue properties, a given numerical system type may define further useful members. For example, the System.Double type allows you to obtain the values for epsilon and infinity (which might be of interest to those of you with a flair for mathematics). To illustrate, consider the following helper function:

```
static void DataTypeFunctionality()
{
  Console.WriteLine("=> Data type Functionality:");

  Console.WriteLine("Max of int: {0}", int.MaxValue);
  Console.WriteLine("Min of int: {0}", int.MinValue);
  Console.WriteLine("Max of double: {0}", double.MaxValue);
  Console.WriteLine("Min of double: {0}", double.MinValue);
  Console.WriteLine("double.Epsilon: {0}", double.Epsilon);
  Console.WriteLine("double.PositiveInfinity: {0}",
    double.PositiveInfinity);
  Console.WriteLine("double.NegativeInfinity: {0}",
    double.NegativeInfinity);
  Console.WriteLine();
}
```

When you define a literal whole number (such as 500), the runtime will default the data type to an int. Likewise, literal floating-point data (such as 55.333) will default to a double. To set the underlying data type to a long, use suffix l or L (4L). To declare a float variable, use the suffix f or F to the raw numerical value (5.3F), and use the suffix m or M to a floating-point number to declare a decimal (300.5M). This becomes more important when declaring variables implicitly, which is covered later in this chapter.

Understanding the Members of System.Boolean

Next, consider the System.Boolean data type. The only valid assignment a C# bool can take is from the set {true || false}. Given this point, it should be clear that System.Boolean does not support a MinValue/MaxValue property set but rather TrueString/FalseString (which yields the string "True" or "False", respectively). Here is an example:

```
Console.WriteLine("bool.FalseString: {0}", bool.FalseString);
Console.WriteLine("bool.TrueString: {0}", bool.TrueString);
```

Understanding the Members of System.Char

C# textual data is represented by the string and char keywords, which are simple shorthand notations for System.String and System.Char, both of which are Unicode under the hood. As you might already know, a string represents a contiguous set of characters (e.g., "Hello"), while the char can represent a single slot in a string (e.g., 'H').

The System.Char type provides you with a great deal of functionality beyond the ability to hold a single point of character data. Using the static methods of System.Char, you are able to determine whether a given character is numerical, alphabetical, a point of punctuation, or whatnot. Consider the following method:

```
static void CharFunctionality()
{
  Console.WriteLine("=> char type Functionality:");
  char myChar = 'a';
  Console.WriteLine("char.IsDigit('a'): {0}", char.IsDigit(myChar));
  Console.WriteLine("char.IsLetter('a'): {0}", char.IsLetter(myChar));
  Console.WriteLine("char.IsWhiteSpace('Hello There', 5): {0}",
    char.IsWhiteSpace("Hello There", 5));
```

```
  Console.WriteLine("char.IsWhiteSpace('Hello There', 6): {0}",
    char.IsWhiteSpace("Hello There", 6));
  Console.WriteLine("char.IsPunctuation('?'): {0}",
    char.IsPunctuation('?'));
  Console.WriteLine();
}
```

As illustrated in the previous method, many members of `System.Char` have two calling conventions: a single character or a string with a numerical index that specifies the position of the character to test.

Parsing Values from String Data

The .NET data types provide the ability to generate a variable of their underlying type given a textual equivalent (e.g., parsing). This technique can be extremely helpful when you want to convert some user input data (such as a selection from a GUI-based, drop-down list box) into a numerical value. Consider the following parsing logic within a method named `ParseFromStrings()`:

```
static void ParseFromStrings()
{
  Console.WriteLine("=> Data type parsing:");
  bool b = bool.Parse("True");
  Console.WriteLine("Value of b: {0}", b);
  double d = double.Parse("99.884");
  Console.WriteLine("Value of d: {0}", d);
  int i = int.Parse("8");
  Console.WriteLine("Value of i: {0}", i);
  char c = Char.Parse("w");
  Console.WriteLine("Value of c: {0}", c);
  Console.WriteLine();
}
```

Using TryParse to Parse Values from String Data

One issue with the preceding code is that an exception will be thrown if the string cannot be cleanly converted to the correct data type. For example, the following will fail at runtime:

```
bool b = bool.Parse("Hello");
```

One solution is to wrap each call to `Parse()` in a `try-catch` block (exception handling is covered in detail in Chapter 7), which can add a lot of code, or use a `TryParse()` statement. The `TryParse()` statement takes an `out` parameter (the `out` modifier is covered in detail in Chapter 4) and returns a `bool` if the parsing was successful. Create a new method named `ParseFromStringWithTryParse()` and add the following code:

```
static void ParseFromStringsWithTryParse()
{
  Console.WriteLine("=> Data type parsing with TryParse:");
  if (bool.TryParse("True", out bool b))
  {
    Console.WriteLine("Value of b: {0}", b);
  }
```

```
  else
  {
    Console.WriteLine("Default value of b: {0}", b);
  }
  string value = "Hello";
  if (double.TryParse(value, out double d))
  {
    Console.WriteLine("Value of d: {0}", d);
  }
  else
  {
    Console.WriteLine("Failed to convert the input ({0}) to a double and the variable was
    assigned the default {1}", value,d);
  }
  Console.WriteLine();
}
```

If you are new to programming and do not know how if/else statements work, they are covered later in this chapter in detail. The important item to note from the preceding example is that if a string can be converted to the requested data type, the TryParse() method returns true and assigns the parsed value to the variable passed into the method. If the value cannot be parsed, the variable is assigned its default value, and the TryParse() method returns false.

Using System.DateTime and System.TimeSpan (Updated 10.0)

The System namespace defines a few useful data types for which there are no C# keywords, such as the DateTime and TimeSpan structures.

The DateTime type contains data that represents a specific date (month, day, year) and time value, both of which may be formatted in a variety of ways using the supplied members. The TimeSpan structure allows you to easily define and transform units of time using various members.

```
static void UseDatesAndTimes()
{
  Console.WriteLine("=> Dates and Times:");

  // This constructor takes (year, month, day).
  DateTime dt = new DateTime(2015, 10, 17);

  // What day of the month is this?
  Console.WriteLine("The day of {0} is {1}", dt.Date, dt.DayOfWeek);

  // Month is now December.
  dt = dt.AddMonths(2);
  Console.WriteLine("Daylight savings: {0}", dt.IsDaylightSavingTime());

  // This constructor takes (hours, minutes, seconds).
  TimeSpan ts = new TimeSpan(4, 30, 0);
  Console.WriteLine(ts);
```

```
  // Subtract 15 minutes from the current TimeSpan and
  // print the result.
  Console.WriteLine(ts.Subtract(new TimeSpan(0, 15, 0)));
}
```

The DateOnly and TimeOnly structs were added in .NET 6/C# 10, and each represents half of the DateTime type. The DateOnly struct aligns with the SQL Server Date type, and the TimeOnly struct aligns with the SQL Server Time type. The following code shows the new types in action:

```
static void UseDatesAndTimes()
{
  Console.WriteLine("=> Dates and Times:");
...
  DateOnly d = new DateOnly(2021,07,21);
  Console.WriteLine(d);

  TimeOnly t = new TimeOnly(13,30,0,0);
  Console.WriteLine(t);
}
```

Working with the System.Numerics Namespace

The System.Numerics namespace defines a structure named BigInteger. As its name implies, the BigInteger data type can be used when you need to represent *humongous* numerical values, which are not constrained by a fixed upper or lower limit.

■ **Note** The System.Numerics namespace defines a second structure named Complex, which allows you to model mathematically complex numerical data (e.g., imaginary units, real data, hyperbolic tangents). Consult the .NET Core documentation if you are interested.

While many of your .NET Core applications might never need to make use of the BigInteger structure, if you do find the need to define a massive numerical value, your first step is to add the following using directive to the file:

```
// BigInteger lives here!
using System.Numerics;
```

At this point, you can create a BigInteger variable using the new operator. Within the constructor, you can specify a numerical value, including floating-point data. However, C# implicitly types non-floating-point numbers as an int and floating-point numbers as a double. How, then, can you set BigInteger to a massive value while not overflowing the default data types used for raw numerical values?

The simplest approach is to establish the massive numerical value as a text literal, which can be converted into a BigInteger variable via the static Parse() method. If required, you can also pass in a byte array directly to the constructor of the BigInteger class.

■ **Note** After you assign a value to a BigInteger variable, you cannot change it, as the data is immutable. However, the BigInteger class defines a number of members that will return new BigInteger objects based on your data modifications (such as the static Multiply() method used in the following code sample).

In any case, after you have defined a BigInteger variable, you will find this class defines similar members as other intrinsic C# data types (e.g., float, int). In addition, the BigInteger class defines several static members that allow you to apply basic mathematical expressions (such as adding and multiplying) to BigInteger variables. Here is an example of working with the BigInteger class:

```
static void UseBigInteger()
{
  Console.WriteLine("=> Use BigInteger:");
  BigInteger biggy =
    BigInteger.Parse("9999999999999999999999999999999999999999999999");
  Console.WriteLine("Value of biggy is {0}", biggy);
  Console.WriteLine("Is biggy an even value?: {0}", biggy.IsEven);
  Console.WriteLine("Is biggy a power of two?: {0}", biggy.IsPowerOfTwo);
  BigInteger reallyBig = BigInteger.Multiply(biggy,
    BigInteger.Parse("8888888888888888888888888888888888888888888"));
  Console.WriteLine("Value of reallyBig is {0}", reallyBig);
}
```

It is also important to note that the BigInteger data type responds to C#'s intrinsic mathematical operators, such as +, -, and *. Therefore, rather than calling BigInteger.Multiply() to multiply two huge numbers, you could author the following code:

```
BigInteger reallyBig2 = biggy * reallyBig;
```

At this point, I hope you understand that the C# keywords representing basic data types have a corresponding type in the .NET Core base class libraries, each of which exposes a fixed functionality. While I have not detailed each member of these data types, you are in a great position to dig into the details as you see fit. Be sure to consult the .NET Core documentation for full details regarding the various .NET data types—you will likely be surprised at the amount of built-in functionality.

Using Digit Separators (New 7.0)

Sometimes when assigning large numbers to a numeric variable, there are more digits than the eye can keep track of. C# 7.0 introduced the underscore (_) as a digit separator (for integer, long, decimal, double data, or hex types). C# 7.2 allows for hex values (and the new binary literal, covered next, to start with an underscore, after the opening declaration). Here is an example of using the new digit separator:

```
static void DigitSeparators()
{
  Console.WriteLine("=> Use Digit Separators:");
  Console.Write("Integer:");
  Console.WriteLine(123_456);
  Console.Write("Long:");
  Console.WriteLine(123_456_789L);
```

```
  Console.Write("Float:");
  Console.WriteLine(123_456.1234F);
  Console.Write("Double:");
  Console.WriteLine(123_456.12);
  Console.Write("Decimal:");
  Console.WriteLine(123_456.12M);
  //Updated in 7.2, Hex can begin with _
  Console.Write("Hex:");
  Console.WriteLine(0x_00_00_FF);
}
```

Using Binary Literals (New 7.0/7.2)

C# 7.0 introduces a new literal for binary values, for example, for creating bit masks. The new digit separator works with binary literals, and C# 7.2 allows for binary and hex numbers to start with an underscore. Now, binary numbers can be written as you would expect. Here is an example:

```
0b_0001_0000
```

Here is a method that shows using the new literals with the digit separator:

```
static void BinaryLiterals()
{
  //Updated in 7.2, Binary can begin with _
  Console.WriteLine("=> Use Binary Literals:");
  Console.WriteLine("Sixteen: {0}",0b_0001_0000);
  Console.WriteLine("Thirty Two: {0}",0b_0010_0000);
  Console.WriteLine("Sixty Four: {0}",0b_0100_0000);
}
```

Working with String Data

`System.String` provides a number of methods you would expect from such a utility class, including methods that return the length of the character data, find substrings within the current string, and convert to and from uppercase/lowercase. Table 3-5 lists some (but by no means all) of the interesting members.

Table 3-5. *Select Members of System.String*

String Member	Meaning in Life
`Length`	This property returns the length of the current string.
`Compare()`	This static method compares two strings.
`Contains()`	This method determines whether a string contains a specific substring.
`Equals()`	This method tests whether two string objects contain identical character data.
`Format()`	This static method formats a string using other primitives (e.g., numerical data, other strings) and the `{0}` notation examined earlier in this chapter.
`Insert()`	This method inserts a string within a given string.
`PadLeft() \ PadRight()`	These methods are used to pad a string with some characters.
`Remove() \ Replace()`	These methods are used to receive a copy of a string with modifications (characters removed or replaced).
`Split()`	This method returns a `String` array containing the substrings in this instance that are delimited by elements of a specified `char` array or `string` array.
`Trim()`	This method removes all occurrences of a set of specified characters from the beginning and end of the current string.
`ToUpper() \ ToLower()`	These methods create a copy of the current string in uppercase or lowercase format, respectively.

Performing Basic String Manipulation

Working with the members of `System.String` is as you would expect. Simply declare a `string` variable and make use of the provided functionality via the dot operator. Be aware that a few of the members of `System.String` are static members and are, therefore, called at the class (rather than the object) level.

Assume you have created a new Console Application project named FunWithStrings and added it to your solution. Clear out the existing code and add the following:

```
using System.Runtime.CompilerServices;
using System.Text;
BasicStringFunctionality();

static void BasicStringFunctionality()
{
  Console.WriteLine("=> Basic String functionality:");
  string firstName = "Freddy";
  Console.WriteLine("Value of firstName: {0}", firstName);
  Console.WriteLine("firstName has {0} characters.", firstName.Length);
  Console.WriteLine("firstName in uppercase: {0}", firstName.ToUpper());
  Console.WriteLine("firstName in lowercase: {0}", firstName.ToLower());
  Console.WriteLine("firstName contains the letter y?: {0}",
    firstName.Contains("y"));
  Console.WriteLine("New first name: {0}", firstName.Replace("dy", ""));
  Console.WriteLine();
}
```

There is not too much to say here, as this method simply invokes various members, such as ToUpper() and Contains(), on a local string variable to yield various formats and transformations. Here is the initial output:

```
***** Fun with Strings *****

=> Basic String functionality:
Value of firstName: Freddy
firstName has 6 characters.
firstName in uppercase: FREDDY
firstName in lowercase: freddy
firstName contains the letter y?: True
firstName after replace: Fred
```

While this output might not seem too surprising, the output seen via calling the Replace() method is a bit misleading. In reality, the firstName variable has not changed at all; rather, you receive a new string in a modified format. You will revisit the immutable nature of strings in just a few moments.

Performing String Concatenation

String variables can be connected to build larger strings via the C# + (as well as +=) operator. As you might know, this technique is formally termed *string concatenation*. Consider the following new helper function:

```
static void StringConcatenation()
{
  Console.WriteLine("=> String concatenation:");
  string s1 = "Programming the ";
  string s2 = "PsychoDrill (PTP)";
  string s3 = s1 + s2;
  Console.WriteLine(s3);
  Console.WriteLine();
}
```

You might be interested to know that the C# + symbol is processed by the compiler to emit a call to the static String.Concat() method. Given this, it is possible to perform string concatenation by calling String.Concat() directly as shown in the following modified version of the method (although you really have not gained anything by doing so—in fact, you have incurred additional keystrokes!):

```
static void StringConcatenation()
{
  Console.WriteLine("=> String concatenation:");
  string s1 = "Programming the ";
  string s2 = "PsychoDrill (PTP)";
  string s3 = String.Concat(s1, s2);
  Console.WriteLine(s3);
  Console.WriteLine();
}
```

Using Escape Characters

As in other C-based languages, C# string literals may contain various *escape characters*, which qualify how the character data should be printed to the output stream. Each escape character begins with a backslash, followed by a specific token. In case you are a bit rusty on the meanings behind these escape characters, Table 3-6 lists the more common options.

Table 3-6. *String Literal Escape Characters*

Character	Meaning in Life
`\'`	Inserts a single quote into a string literal.
`\"`	Inserts a double quote into a string literal.
`\\`	Inserts a backslash into a string literal. This can be quite helpful when defining file or network paths.
`\a`	Triggers a system alert (beep). For console programs, this can be an audio clue to the user.
`\n`	Inserts a line feed (Unix-based systems).
`\r\n`	Inserts a line feed (non-Unix-based platforms).
`\r`	Inserts a carriage return.
`\t`	Inserts a horizontal tab into the string literal.

For example, to print a string that contains a tab between each word, you can make use of the `\t` escape character. Or assume you want to create a string literal that contains quotation marks, another that defines a directory path, and a final string literal that inserts three blank lines after printing the character data. To do so without compiler errors, you would need to make use of the `\"`, `\\`, and `\n` escape characters. The following method demonstrates this:

```
static void EscapeChars()
{
  Console.WriteLine("=> Escape characters:");
  string strWithTabs = "Model\tColor\tSpeed\tPet Name ";
  Console.WriteLine(strWithTabs);

  Console.WriteLine("Everyone loves \"Hello World\" ");
  Console.WriteLine("C:\\MyApp\\bin\\Debug ");

  // Adds a total of 4 blank lines (3 escaped, 1 from WriteLine).
  Console.WriteLine("All finished.\n\n\n ");
  Console.WriteLine();
}
```

Notice from Table 3-6 that there is a difference when creating a new line based on the operating system the code is executing on. The `NewLine` property of the static `Environment` type adds in the proper escape code(s) for adding blank lines into your text. Consider the following addition to the `EscapeChars()` method:

```
static void EscapeChars()
{
  //omitted for brevity
  // Adds a 4 more blank lines.
  Console.WriteLine("All finished for real this time.{0}{0}{0}",Environment.NewLine);
}
```

Performing String Interpolation

The curly-bracket syntax illustrated within this chapter ({0}, {1}, etc.) has existed within the .NET platform since version 1.0. Starting with the release of C# 6, C# programmers can use an alternative syntax to build string literals that contain placeholders for variables. Formally, this is called *string interpolation*. While the output of the operation is identical to traditional string formatting syntax, this new approach allows you to directly embed the variables themselves, rather than tacking them on as a comma-delimited list.

Consider the following additional method of your Program class (StringInterpolation()), which builds a string variable using each approach:

```
static void StringInterpolation()
{
    Console.WriteLine("=> String interpolation:\a");

    // Some local variables we will plug into our larger string
    int age = 4;
    string name = "Soren";

    // Using curly-bracket syntax.
    string greeting = string.Format("Hello {0} you are {1} years old.", name, age);
    Console.WriteLine(greeting);

    // Using string interpolation
    string greeting2 = $"Hello {name} you are {age} years old.";
    Console.WriteLine(greeting2);
}
```

In the greeting2 variable, notice how the string you are constructing begins with a dollar sign ($) prefix. Next, notice that the curly brackets still are used to mark a variable placeholder; however, rather than using a numerical tag, you are able to place the variable directly into the scope. The assumed advantage is that this new formatting syntax is a bit easier to read in a linear (left-to-right) fashion, given that you are not required to "jump to the end" to see the list of values to plug in at runtime.

There is another interesting aspect of this new syntax: the curly brackets used in string interpolation are a valid scope. Therefore, you can use the dot operation on the variables to change their state. Consider updates to each assembled string variable.

```
string greeting = string.Format("Hello {0} you are {1} years old.", name.ToUpper(), age);
string greeting2 = $"Hello {name.ToUpper()} you are {age} years old.";
```

Here, I have uppercased the name via a call to ToUpper(). Do note that in the string interpolation approach, you do *not* add a semicolon terminator when calling this method. Given this, you cannot use the curly-bracket scope as a fully blown method scope that contains numerous lines of executable code. Rather, you can invoke a single member on the object using the dot operator as well as define a simple general expression such as {age += 1}.

It is also worth noting that you can still use escape characters in the string literal within this new syntax. Thus, if you wanted to insert a tab, you can prefix a \t token as so:

```
string greeting = string.Format("\tHello {0} you are {1} years old.", name.ToUpper(), age);
string greeting2 = $"\tHello {name.ToUpper()} you are {age} years old.";
```

Performance Improvements (Updated 10.0)

When using string interpolation in versions prior to C# 10, under the hood the compiler is converting the interpolated string statement into a Format() call. For example, take a shortened version of the previous example and plug it into the Main() method of a .NET 5 (C# 9) console application (named CSharp9Strings).

```
using System;
namespace CSharp9Strings
{
  class Program
  {
    static void Main(string[] args)
    {
      int age = 4;
      string name = "Soren";
      string greeting = string.Format("\tHello {0} you are {1} years old.", name.
ToUpper(), age);
      string greetings = $"\tHello {name.ToUpper()} you are {age} years old.";
    }
  }
}
```

When the Main() method is examined with ILDasm, you can see that both the call to Format() and the string interpolation calls are implemented as the same Format() calls in the IL (lines in bold):

```
.method private hidebysig static void  Main(string[] args) cil managed
{
  .maxstack  3
  .entrypoint
  .locals init (int32 V_0, string V_1, string V_2)
  IL_0000:  nop
  IL_0001:  ldc.i4.4
  IL_0002:  stloc.0
  IL_0003:  ldstr  "Soren"
  IL_0008:  stloc.1
  IL_0009:  ldstr  "\tHello {0} you are {1} years old."
  IL_000e:  ldloc.1
  IL_000f:  callvirt   instance string [System.Runtime]System.String::ToUpper()
  IL_0014:  ldloc.0
  IL_0015:  box  [System.Runtime]System.Int32
  IL_001a:  call  string [System.Runtime]System.String::Format(string, object, object)
  IL_001f:  stloc.2
  IL_0020:  ldstr  "\tHello {0} you are {1} years old."
  IL_0025:  ldloc.1
  IL_0026:  callvirt  instance string [System.Runtime]System.String::ToUpper()
```

```
  IL_002b:  ldloc.0
  IL_002c:  box  [System.Runtime]System.Int32
  IL_0031:  call  string [System.Runtime]System.String::Format(string, object, object)
  IL_0036:  stloc.3
  IL_0037:  ret
} // end of method Program::Main
```

The problem with this is performance. When Format() is called at runtime, the method parses the format string to find the literals, format items, specifiers, and alignments, which the compiler already did at compile time. All items are passed in as System.Object, which means value types are boxed. If there are more than three parameters, an array is allocated. In addition to performance issues, Format() works only with reference types.

A major change in C# 10 is that all the work that can be done at compile time is retained in the IL using the DefaultInterpolatedStringHandler and its methods. This is the equivalent C# 10 code that interpolated strings are converted to:

```
static void StringInterpolationWithDefaultInterpolatedStringHandler()
{
  Console.WriteLine("=> String interpolation under the covers:\a");
  int age = 4;
  string name = "Soren";

  var builder = new DefaultInterpolatedStringHandler(3,2);
  builder.AppendLiteral("\tHello ");
  builder.AppendFormatted(name);
  builder.AppendLiteral(" you are ");
  builder.AppendFormatted(age);
  builder.AppendLiteral(" years old.");
  var greeting = builder.ToStringAndClear();
  Console.WriteLine(greeting);
}
```

The version of the DefaultInterpolatedStringHandler's constructor used in this example takes two integers. The first is the number of literals, and the second is the number variables. This enables the instance to make an educated guess as to how much memory to allocate. Literals are added in with the AppendLiteral() method, and variables are added in with the AppendFormatted() method.

Bench testing has shown a significant performance improvement in string handling in C# 10 when your code contains string interpolation, which is good news. The really good news is that you don't have to write all this extra code. The compiler takes care of it all when compiling string interpolation.

Defining Verbatim Strings (Updated 8.0)

When you prefix a string literal with the @ symbol, you have created what is termed a *verbatim string*. Using verbatim strings, you disable the processing of a literal's escape characters and print out a string as is. This can be most useful when working with strings representing directory and network paths. Therefore, rather than making use of \\ escape characters, you can simply write the following:

```
// The following string is printed verbatim,
// thus all escape characters are displayed.
Console.WriteLine(@"C:\MyApp\bin\Debug");
```

Also note that verbatim strings can be used to preserve whitespace for strings that flow over multiple lines.

```
// Whitespace is preserved with verbatim strings.
string myLongString = @"This is a very
     very
          very
               long string";
Console.WriteLine(myLongString);
```

Using verbatim strings, you can also directly insert a double quote into a literal string by doubling the " token.

```
Console.WriteLine(@"Cerebus said ""Darrr! Pret-ty sun-sets""");
```

Verbatim strings can also be interpolated strings, by specifying both the interpolation operator ($) and the verbatim operator (@).

```
string interp = "interpolation";
string myLongString2 = $@"This is a very
   very
         long string with {interp}";
```

New in C# 8, the order does not matter. Using either $@ or @$ will work.

Working with Strings and Equality

As will be fully explained in Chapter 4, a *reference type* is an object allocated on the garbage-collected managed heap. By default, when you perform a test for equality on reference types (via the C# == and != operators), you will be returned true if the references are pointing to the same object in memory. However, even though the string data type is indeed a reference type, the equality operators have been redefined to compare the *values* of string objects, not the object in memory to which they refer.

```
static void StringEquality()
{
  Console.WriteLine("=> String equality:");
  string s1 = "Hello!";
  string s2 = "Yo!";
  Console.WriteLine("s1 = {0}", s1);
  Console.WriteLine("s2 = {0}", s2);
  Console.WriteLine();

  // Test these strings for equality.
  Console.WriteLine("s1 == s2: {0}", s1 == s2);
  Console.WriteLine("s1 == Hello!: {0}", s1 == "Hello!");
  Console.WriteLine("s1 == HELLO!: {0}", s1 == "HELLO!");
  Console.WriteLine("s1 == hello!: {0}", s1 == "hello!");
  Console.WriteLine("s1.Equals(s2): {0}", s1.Equals(s2));
  Console.WriteLine("Yo!.Equals(s2): {0}", "Yo!".Equals(s2));
  Console.WriteLine();
}
```

The C# equality operators by default perform a case-sensitive, culture-insensitive, character-by-character equality test on string objects. Therefore, "Hello!" is not equal to "HELLO!", which is also different from "hello!". Also, keeping the connection between string and System.String in mind, notice that you are able to test for equality using the Equals() method of String as well as the baked-in equality operators. Finally, given that every string literal (such as "Yo!") is a valid System.String instance, you are able to access string-centric functionality from a fixed sequence of characters.

Modifying String Comparison Behavior

As mentioned, the string equality operators (Compare(), Equals(), and ==) as well as the IndexOf() function are by default case sensitive and culture insensitive. This can cause a problem if your program does not care about case. One way to overcome this is to convert everything to uppercase or lowercase and then compare, like this:

```
if (firstString.ToUpper() == secondString.ToUpper())
{
  //Do something
}
```

This makes a copy of each string with all lowercase letters. It is probably not an issue in most cases but could be a performance hit with a significantly large string or even fail based on culture. A much better practice is to use the overloads of the methods listed earlier that take a value of the StringComparison enumeration to control exactly how the comparisons are done. Table 3-7 describes the StringComparison values.

Table 3-7. *Values of the StringComparison Enumeration*

C# Equality/Relational Operator	Meaning in Life
CurrentCulture	Compares strings using culture-sensitive sort rules and the current culture
CurrentCultureIgnoreCase	Compares strings using culture-sensitive sort rules and the current culture and ignores the case of the strings being compared
InvariantCulture	Compares strings using culture-sensitive sort rules and the invariant culture
InvariantCultureIgnoreCase	Compares strings using culture-sensitive sort rules and the invariant culture and ignores the case of the strings being compared
Ordinal	Compares strings using ordinal (binary) sort rules
OrdinalIgnoreCare	Compares strings using ordinal (binary) sort rules and ignores the case of the strings being compared

To see the effect of using the StringComparison option, create a new method named StringEqualitySpecifyingCompareRules() and add the following code:

```
static void StringEqualitySpecifyingCompareRules()
{
  Console.WriteLine("=> String equality (Case Insensitive:");
  string s1 = "Hello!";
```

```
    string s2 = "HELLO!";
    Console.WriteLine("s1 = {0}", s1);
    Console.WriteLine("s2 = {0}", s2);
    Console.WriteLine();

    // Check the results of changing the default compare rules.
    Console.WriteLine("Default rules: s1={0},s2={1}s1.Equals(s2): {2}", s1, s2,
    s1.Equals(s2));
    Console.WriteLine("Ignore case: s1.Equals(s2, StringComparison.OrdinalIgnoreCase): {0}",
      s1.Equals(s2, StringComparison.OrdinalIgnoreCase));
    Console.WriteLine("Ignore case, Invariant Culture: s1.Equals(s2, StringComparison.
    InvariantCultureIgnoreCase): {0}", s1.Equals(s2, StringComparison.InvariantCulture
    IgnoreCase));
    Console.WriteLine();
    Console.WriteLine("Default rules: s1={0},s2={1} s1.IndexOf(\"E\"): {2}", s1, s2,
    s1.IndexOf("E"));
    Console.WriteLine("Ignore case: s1.IndexOf(\"E\", StringComparison.OrdinalIgnoreCase):
    {0}", s1.IndexOf("E", StringComparison.OrdinalIgnoreCase));
    Console.WriteLine("Ignore case, Invariant Culture: s1.IndexOf(\"E\", StringComparison.
    InvariantCultureIgnoreCase): {0}", s1.IndexOf("E", StringComparison.InvariantCulture
    IgnoreCase));
    Console.WriteLine();
}
```

While the examples here are simple ones and use the same letters across most cultures, if your application needed to consider different culture sets, using the StringComparison options is a must.

Strings Are Immutable

One of the interesting aspects of System.String is that after you assign a string object with its initial value, the character data *cannot be changed.* At first glance, this might seem like a flat-out lie, given that you are always reassigning strings to new values and because the System.String type defines a number of methods that appear to modify the character data in one way or another (such as uppercasing and lowercasing). However, if you look more closely at what is happening behind the scenes, you will notice the methods of the string type are, in fact, returning you a new string object in a modified format.

```
static void StringsAreImmutable()
{
    Console.WriteLine("=> Immutable Strings:\a");
  // Set initial string value.
  string s1 = "This is my string.";
  Console.WriteLine("s1 = {0}", s1);

  // Uppercase s1?
  string upperString = s1.ToUpper();
  Console.WriteLine("upperString = {0}", upperString);

  // Nope! s1 is in the same format!
  Console.WriteLine("s1 = {0}", s1);
}
```

If you examine the relevant output that follows, you can verify that the original `string` object (`s1`) is not uppercased when calling `ToUpper()`. Rather, you are returned a *copy* of the `string` in a modified format.

```
s1 = This is my string.

upperString = THIS IS MY STRING.
s1 = This is my string.
```

The same law of immutability holds true when you use the C# assignment operator. To illustrate, implement the following `StringsAreImmutable2()` method:

```
static void StringsAreImmutable2()
{
  Console.WriteLine("=> Immutable Strings 2:\a");
  string s2 = "My other string";
  s2 = "New string value";
  Console.WriteLine(s2);
}
```

Now, compile your application and run `ildasm.exe` (see Chapter 1). The following output shows what you would find if you were to generate CIL code for the `StringsAreImmutable2()` method:

```
.method assembly hidebysig static void  '<<Main>$>g__StringsAreImmutable2()|0,8'()
cil managed

{
  // Code size       32 (0x20)
  .maxstack  1
  .locals init (string V_0)
  IL_0000:  nop
...
  IL_000c:  ldstr      "My other string"
  IL_0011:  stloc.0
  IL_0012:  ldstr      "New string value"
  IL_0017:  stloc.0
  IL_0018:  ldloc.0
  IL_0013:  nop
...
  IL_0014:  ret
} // end of method Program::StringsAreImmutable2
```

Although you have yet to examine the low-level details of the CIL, note the two calls to the `ldstr` (load string) opcode. Simply put, the `ldstr` opcode of the CIL loads a new `string` object on the managed heap. The previous `string` object that contained the value `"My other string"` will eventually be garbage collected.

So, what exactly are you to gather from this insight? In a nutshell, the `string` class can be inefficient and result in bloated code if misused, especially when performing string concatenation or working with huge amounts of text data. If you need to represent basic character data such as a US Social Security number, first or last names, or simple bits of text used within your application, the `string` class is the perfect choice.

However, if you are building an application that makes heavy use of frequently changing textual data (such as a word processing program), it would be a bad idea to represent the word processing data using `string` objects, as you will most certainly (and often indirectly) end up making unnecessary copies of string data. So, what is a programmer to do? Glad you asked.

Using the System.Text.StringBuilder Type

Given that the `string` type can be inefficient when used with reckless abandon, the .NET Core base class libraries provide the `System.Text` namespace. Within this (relatively small) namespace lives a class named `StringBuilder`. Like the `System.String` class, the `StringBuilder` defines methods that allow you to replace or format segments, for example. When you want to use this type in your C# code files, your first step is to make sure the following namespace is imported into your code file (this should already be the case for a new Visual Studio project):

```
// StringBuilder lives here!
using System.Text;
```

What is unique about the `StringBuilder` is that when you call members of this type, you are directly modifying the object's internal character data (making it more efficient), not obtaining a copy of the data in a modified format. When you create an instance of the `StringBuilder`, you can supply the object's initial startup values via one of many *constructors*. If you are new to the topic of constructors, simply understand that constructors allow you to create an object with an initial state when you apply the new keyword. Consider the following usage of `StringBuilder`:

```
static void FunWithStringBuilder()
{
  Console.WriteLine("=> Using the StringBuilder:");
  StringBuilder sb = new StringBuilder("**** Fantastic Games ****");
  sb.Append("\n");
  sb.AppendLine("Half Life");
  sb.AppendLine("Morrowind");
  sb.AppendLine("Deus Ex" + "2");
  sb.AppendLine("System Shock");
  Console.WriteLine(sb.ToString());
  sb.Replace("2", " Invisible War");
  Console.WriteLine(sb.ToString());
  Console.WriteLine("sb has {0} chars.", sb.Length);
  Console.WriteLine();
}
```

Here, I have constructed a `StringBuilder` set to the initial value `"**** Fantastic Games ****"`. As you can see, I am appending to the internal buffer and am able to replace or remove characters at will. By default, a `StringBuilder` is only able to initially hold a string of 16 characters or fewer (but will expand automatically if necessary); however, this default starting value can be changed via an additional constructor argument.

```
// Make a StringBuilder with an initial size of 256.
StringBuilder sb = new StringBuilder("**** Fantastic Games ****", 256);
```

If you append more characters than the specified limit, the `StringBuilder` object will copy its data into a new instance and grow the buffer by the specified limit.

Narrowing and Widening Data Type Conversions

Now that you understand how to work with intrinsic C# data types, let's examine the related topic of *data type conversion*. Assume you have a new Console Application project named TypeConversions and added it to your solution. Update the code to match the following:

```
Console.WriteLine("***** Fun with type conversions *****");

// Add two shorts and print the result.
short numb1 = 9, numb2 = 10;
Console.WriteLine("{0} + {1} = {2}",
  numb1, numb2, Add(numb1, numb2));
Console.ReadLine();

static int Add(int x, int y)
{
  return x + y;
}
```

Notice that the `Add()` method expects to be sent two `int` parameters. However, the calling code is, in fact, sending in two `short` variables. While this might seem like a complete and total mismatch of data types, the program compiles and executes without error, returning the expected result of 19.

The reason the compiler treats this code as syntactically sound is because there is no possibility for loss of data. Given that the maximum value of a `short` (32,767) is well within the maximum range of an `int` (2,147,483,647), the compiler implicitly *widens* each `short` to an `int`. Formally speaking, *widening* is the term used to define an implicit *upward cast* that does not result in a loss of data.

■ **Note** Look up "Type Conversion Tables" in the .NET Core documentation if you want to see permissible widening (and narrowing, discussed next) conversions for each C# data type.

Although this implicit widening worked in your favor for the previous example, other times this "feature" can be the source of compile-time errors. For example, assume you have set values to `numb1` and `numb2` that (when added together) overflow the maximum value of a `short`. Also, assume you are storing the return value of the `Add()` method within a new local `short` variable, rather than directly printing the result to the console.

```
Console.WriteLine("***** Fun with type conversions *****");

// Compiler error below!
short numb1 = 30000, numb2 = 30000;
short answer = Add(numb1, numb2);

Console.WriteLine("{0} + {1} = {2}",
  numb1, numb2, answer);
Console.ReadLine();
```

In this case, the compiler reports the following error:

```
Cannot implicitly convert type 'int' to 'short'. An explicit conversion exists (are you
missing a cast?)
```

The problem is that although the `Add()` method is capable of returning an `int` with the value 60,000 (which fits within the range of a `System.Int32`), the value cannot be stored in a `short`, as it overflows the bounds of this data type. Formally speaking, the CoreCLR was unable to apply a *narrowing operation*. As you can guess, narrowing is the logical opposite of widening, in that a larger value is stored within a smaller data type variable.

It is important to point out that all narrowing conversions result in a compiler error, even when you can reason that the narrowing conversion should indeed succeed. For example, the following code also results in a compiler error:

```
// Another compiler error!
static void NarrowingAttempt()
{
  byte myByte = 0;
  int myInt = 200;
  myByte = myInt;

  Console.WriteLine("Value of myByte: {0}", myByte);
}
```

Here, the value contained within the `int` variable (`myInt`) is safely within the range of a `byte`; therefore, you would expect the narrowing operation to not result in a runtime error. However, given that C# is a language built with type safety in mind, you do indeed receive a compiler error.

When you want to inform the compiler that you are willing to deal with a possible loss of data because of a narrowing operation, you must apply an *explicit cast* using the C# casting operator, `()`. Consider the following update to the `Program.cs` file:

```
Console.WriteLine("***** Fun with type conversions *****");
short numb1 = 30000, numb2 = 30000;

// Explicitly cast the int into a short (and allow loss of data).
short answer = (short)Add(numb1, numb2);

Console.WriteLine("{0} + {1} = {2}",
  numb1, numb2, answer);
NarrowingAttempt();
Console.ReadLine();

static int Add(int x, int y)
{
  return x + y;
}

static void NarrowingAttempt()
{
  byte myByte = 0;
  int myInt = 200;
```

```
  // Explicitly cast the int into a byte (no loss of data).
  myByte = (byte)myInt;
  Console.WriteLine("Value of myByte: {0}", myByte);
}
```

At this point, the code compiles; however, the result of the addition is completely incorrect.

```
***** Fun with type conversions *****

30000 + 30000 = -5536
Value of myByte: 200
```

As you have just witnessed, an explicit cast allows you to force the compiler to apply a narrowing conversion, even when doing so may result in a loss of data. In the case of the NarrowingAttempt() method, this was not a problem because the value 200 can fit snugly within the range of a byte. However, in the case of adding the two shorts within the code, the end result is completely unacceptable (30,000 + 30,000 = -5536?).

If you are building an application where loss of data is always unacceptable, C# provides the checked and unchecked keywords to ensure data loss does not escape undetected.

Using the checked Keyword

Let's begin by learning the role of the checked keyword. Assume you have a new method within Program that attempts to add two bytes, each of which has been assigned a value that is safely below the maximum (255). If you were to add the values of these types (casting the returned int to a byte), you would assume that the result would be the exact sum of each member.

```
static void ProcessBytes()
{
  byte b1 = 100;
  byte b2 = 250;
  byte sum = (byte)Add(b1, b2);

  // sum should hold the value 350. However, we find the value 94!
  Console.WriteLine("sum = {0}", sum);
}
```

If you were to view the output of this application, you might be surprised to find that sum contains the value 94 (rather than the expected 350). The reason is simple. Given that a System.Byte can hold a value only between 0 and 255 (inclusive, for a grand total of 256 slots), sum now contains the overflow value (350 - 256 = 94). By default, if you take no corrective course of action, overflow/underflow conditions occur without error.

To handle overflow or underflow conditions in your application, you have two options. Your first choice is to leverage your wits and programming skills to handle all overflow/underflow conditions manually. Of course, the problem with this technique is the simple fact that you are human, and even your best attempts might result in errors that have escaped your eyes.

Thankfully, C# provides the checked keyword. When you wrap a statement (or a block of statements) within the scope of the checked keyword, the C# compiler emits additional CIL instructions that test for overflow conditions that may result when adding, multiplying, subtracting, or dividing two numerical data types.

If an overflow has occurred, you will receive a runtime exception: `System.OverflowException`. Chapter 7 will examine all the details of structured exception handling and the use of the `try` and `catch` keywords. Without getting too hung up on the specifics at this point, observe the following update:

```
static void ProcessBytes()
{
  byte b1 = 100;
  byte b2 = 250;

  // This time, tell the compiler to add CIL code
  // to throw an exception if overflow/underflow
  // takes place.
  try
  {
    byte sum = checked((byte)Add(b1, b2));
    Console.WriteLine("sum = {0}", sum);
  }
  catch (OverflowException ex)
  {
    Console.WriteLine(ex.Message);
  }
}
```

Notice that the return value of `Add()` has been wrapped within the scope of the checked keyword. Because the sum is greater than a `byte`, this triggers a runtime exception. Notice the error message printed out via the `Message` property.

```
Arithmetic operation resulted in an overflow.
```

If you want to force overflow checking to occur over a block of code statements, you can do so by defining a "checked scope" as follows:

```
try
{
  checked
  {
    byte sum = (byte)Add(b1, b2);
    Console.WriteLine("sum = {0}", sum);
  }
}
catch (OverflowException ex)
{
  Console.WriteLine(ex.Message);
}
```

In either case, the code in question will be evaluated for possible overflow conditions automatically, which will trigger an overflow exception if encountered.

Setting Project-wide Overflow Checking (Project File)

If you are creating an application that should never allow silent overflow to occur, you might find yourself in the annoying position of wrapping numerous lines of code within the scope of the checked keyword. As an alternative, the C# compiler supports the /checked flag. When it's enabled, all your arithmetic will be evaluated for overflow without the need to make use of the C# checked keyword. If overflow has been discovered, you will still receive a runtime exception. To set this for the entire project, enter the following into the project file:

```
<PropertyGroup>
    <CheckForOverflowUnderflow>true</CheckForOverflowUnderflow>
</PropertyGroup>
```

Setting Project-wide Overflow Checking (Visual Studio)

To enable the "Check for arithmetic overflow" flag, open the project's property page. Note that Visual Studio 2022 has updated the project settings dialog pretty significantly from Visual Studio 2019. Most of the options in the dialog now have a descriptor along with the setting. Select General from the Build menu (on the left side of the dialog) and then select the "Check for arithmetic overflow/underflow" check box (see Figure 3-3). Enabling this setting can be helpful when you are creating a debug build. After all the overflow exceptions have been squashed out of the code base, you are free to disable the /checked flag for subsequent builds (which can increase the runtime performance of your application).

■ **Note** The configuration selection is updated in Visual Studio 2022. The gear icon shows up only when you hover your mouse pointer by the check box or to the left of the title. Selecting the configuration is covered next.

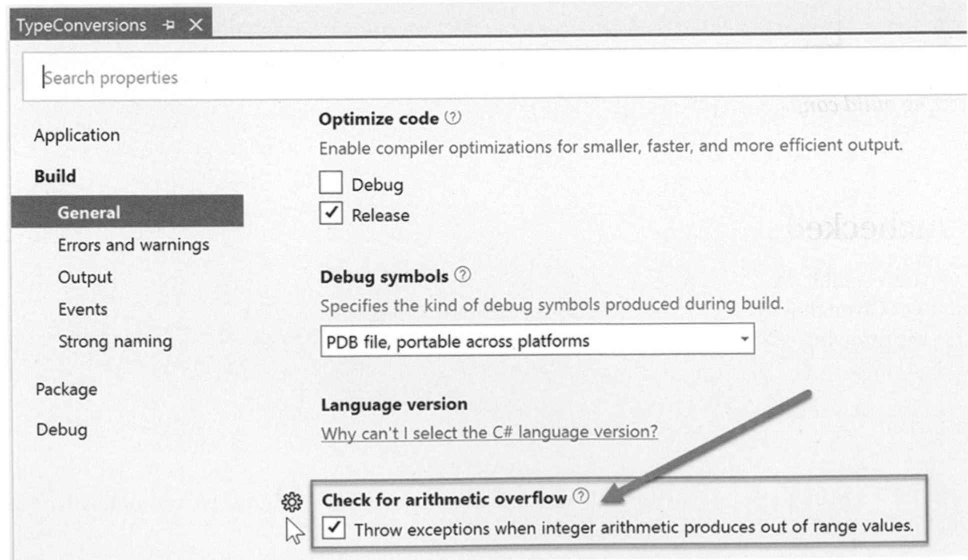

Figure 3-3. *Enabling project-wide overflow/underflow data checking*

Selecting the Build Configuration

To select all configurations or a specific configuration for a build option, hover with your mouse over the check box or to the left of the title. Click the gear that appears, and you will see the build configuration selector shown in Figure 3-4.

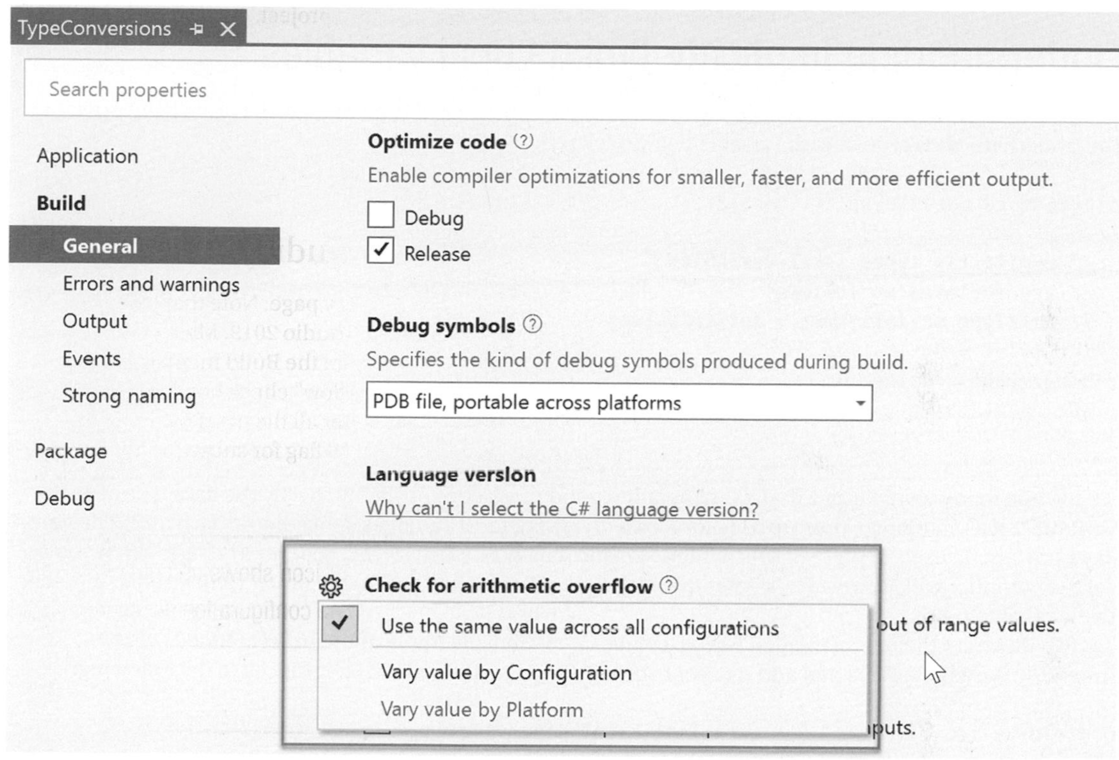

Figure 3-4. *Selecting build configuration(s) for build options*

Using the unchecked Keyword

Now, assuming you have enabled this project-wide setting, what are you to do if you have a block of code where data loss *is* acceptable? Given that the /checked flag will evaluate all arithmetic logic, C# provides the unchecked keyword to disable the throwing of an overflow exception on a case-by-case basis. This keyword's use is identical to that of the checked keyword, in that you can specify a single statement or a block of statements.

```
// Assuming /checked is enabled,
// this block will not trigger
// a runtime exception.
unchecked
{
  byte sum = (byte)(b1 + b2);
  Console.WriteLine("sum = {0} ", sum);
}
```

So, to summarize the C# checked and unchecked keywords, remember that the default behavior of the .NET Core runtime is to ignore arithmetic overflow/underflow. When you want to selectively handle discrete statements, use the checked keyword. If you want to trap overflow errors throughout your application, enable the /checked flag. Finally, the unchecked keyword can be used if you have a block of code where overflow is acceptable (and thus should not trigger a runtime exception).

Understanding Implicitly Typed Local Variables

Up until this point in the chapter, when you have been defining local variables, you have *explicitly* specified the underlying data type of each variable being declared.

```
static void DeclareExplicitVars()
{
  // Explicitly typed local variables
  // are declared as follows:
  // dataType variableName = initialValue;
  int myInt = 0;
  bool myBool = true;
  string myString = "Time, marches on...";
}
```

While many would argue that it is generally a good practice to explicitly specify the data type of each variable, the C# language does provide for *implicitly typing* local variables using the var keyword. The var keyword can be used in place of specifying a specific data type (such as int, bool, or string). When you do so, the compiler will automatically infer the underlying data type based on the initial value used to initialize the local data point.

To illustrate the role of implicit typing, create a new Console Application project named ImplicitlyTypedLocalVars and add it to your solution. Update the code in Program.cs to the following:

```
Console.WriteLine("***** Fun with Implicit Typing *****");
```

Add the following function to demonstrate implicit declarations:

```
static void DeclareImplicitVars()
{
  // Implicitly typed local variables
  // are declared as follows:
  // var variableName = initialValue;
  var myInt = 0;
  var myBool = true;
  var myString = "Time, marches on...";
}
```

■ **Note** Strictly speaking, var is not a C# keyword. It is permissible to declare variables, parameters, and fields named var without compile-time errors. However, when the var token is used as a data type, it is contextually treated as a keyword by the compiler.

In this case, the compiler is able to infer, given the initially assigned value, that `myInt` is, in fact, a `System.Int32`, `myBool` is a `System.Boolean`, and `myString` is indeed of type `System.String`. You can verify this by printing the type name via *reflection*. As you will see in much more detail in Chapter 17, *reflection* is the act of determining the composition of a type at runtime. For example, using reflection, you can determine the data type of an implicitly typed local variable. Update your method with the following code statements:

```
static void DeclareImplicitVars()
{
  // Implicitly typed local variables.
  var myInt = 0;
  var myBool = true;
  var myString = "Time, marches on...";

  // Print out the underlying type.
  Console.WriteLine("myInt is a: {0}", myInt.GetType().Name);
  Console.WriteLine("myBool is a: {0}", myBool.GetType().Name);
  Console.WriteLine("myString is a: {0}", myString.GetType().Name);
}
```

■ **Note** Be aware that you can use this implicit typing for any type including arrays, generic types (see Chapter 10), and your own custom types. You will see other examples of implicit typing over the course of this book.

If you were to call the `DeclareImplicitVars()` method from the top-level statements, you would find the output shown here:

```
***** Fun with Implicit Typing *****

myInt is a: Int32
myBool is a: Boolean
myString is a: String
```

Declaring Numerics Implicitly

As stated earlier, whole numbers default to integers, and floating-point numbers default to doubles. Create a new method named `DeclareImplicitNumerics`, and add the following code to demonstrate implicit declaration of numerics:

```
static void DeclareImplicitNumerics()
{
  // Implicitly typed numeric variables.
  var myUInt = 0u;
  var myInt = 0;
  var myLong = 0L;
  var myDouble = 0.5;
```

```
  var myFloat = 0.5F;
  var myDecimal = 0.5M;

  // Print out the underlying type.
  Console.WriteLine("myUInt is a: {0}", myUInt.GetType().Name);
  Console.WriteLine("myInt is a: {0}", myInt.GetType().Name);
  Console.WriteLine("myLong is a: {0}", myLong.GetType().Name);
  Console.WriteLine("myDouble is a: {0}", myDouble.GetType().Name);
  Console.WriteLine("myFloat is a: {0}", myFloat.GetType().Name);
  Console.WriteLine("myDecimal is a: {0}", myDecimal.GetType().Name);
}
```

Understanding Restrictions on Implicitly Typed Variables

There are various restrictions regarding the use of the var keyword. First, implicit typing applies *only* to local variables in a method or property scope. It is illegal to use the var keyword to define return values, parameters, or field data of a custom type. For example, the following class definition will result in various compile-time errors:

```
class ThisWillNeverCompile
{
  // Error! var cannot be used as field data!
  private var myInt = 10;

  // Error! var cannot be used as a return value
  // or parameter type!
  public var MyMethod(var x, var y){}
}
```

Also, local variables declared with the var keyword *must* be assigned an initial value at the exact time of declaration and *cannot* be assigned the initial value of null. This last restriction should make sense, given that the compiler cannot infer what sort of type in memory the variable would be pointing to based only on null.

```
// Error! Must assign a value!
var myData;

// Error! Must assign value at exact time of declaration!
var myInt;
myInt = 0;

// Error! Can't assign null as initial value!
var myObj = null;
```

It is permissible, however, to assign an inferred local variable to null after its initial assignment (provided it is a reference type).

```
// OK, if SportsCar is a reference type!
var myCar = new SportsCar();
myCar = null;
```

Furthermore, it is permissible to assign the value of an implicitly typed local variable to the value of other variables, implicitly typed or not.

```
// Also OK!
var myInt = 0;
var anotherInt = myInt;

string myString = "Wake up!";
var myData = myString;
```

Also, it is permissible to return an implicitly typed local variable to the caller, provided the method return type is the same underlying type as the `var`-defined data point.

```
static int GetAnInt()
{
  var retVal = 9;
  return retVal;
}
```

Implicit Typed Data Is Strongly Typed Data

Be aware that implicit typing of local variables results in *strongly typed data*. Therefore, use of the `var` keyword is *not* the same technique used with scripting languages (such as JavaScript or Perl) or the COM `Variant` data type, where a variable can hold values of different types over its lifetime in a program (often termed *dynamic typing*).

■ **Note** C# does allow for dynamic typing in C# using a keyword called—surprise, surprise—`dynamic`. You will learn about this aspect of the language in Chapter 17.

Rather, type inference keeps the strongly typed aspect of the C# language and affects only the declaration of variables at compile time. After that, the data point is treated as if it were declared with that type; assigning a value of a different type into that variable will result in a compile-time error.

```
static void ImplicitTypingIsStrongTyping()
{
  // The compiler knows "s" is a System.String.
  var s = "This variable can only hold string data!";
  s = "This is fine...";

  // Can invoke any member of the underlying type.
  string upper = s.ToUpper();

  // Error! Can't assign numerical data to a string!
  s = 44;
}
```

Understanding the Usefulness of Implicitly Typed Local Variables

Now that you have seen the syntax used to declare implicitly typed local variables, I am sure you are wondering when to make use of this construct. First, using var to declare local variables simply for the sake of doing so brings little to the table. Doing so can be confusing to others reading your code because it becomes harder to quickly determine the underlying data type and, therefore, more difficult to understand the overall functionality of the variable. So, if you know you need an int, declare an int!

However, as you will see beginning in Chapter 13, the LINQ technology set makes use of *query expressions* that can yield dynamically created result sets based on the format of the query itself. In these cases, implicit typing is extremely helpful because you do not need to explicitly define the type that a query may return, which in some cases would be literally impossible to do. Without getting hung up on the following LINQ example code, see whether you can figure out the underlying data type of subset:

```
static void LinqQueryOverInts()
{
  int[] numbers = { 10, 20, 30, 40, 1, 2, 3, 8 };

  // LINQ query!
  var subset = from i in numbers where i < 10 select i;

  Console.Write("Values in subset: ");
  foreach (var i in subset)
  {
    Console.Write("{0} ", i);
  }
  Console.WriteLine();

  // Hmm...what type is subset?
  Console.WriteLine("subset is a: {0}", subset.GetType().Name);
  Console.WriteLine("subset is defined in: {0}", subset.GetType().Namespace);
}
```

You might be assuming that the subset data type is an array of integers. That seems to be the case, but, in fact, it is a low-level LINQ data type that you would never know about unless you have been doing LINQ for a long time or you open the compiled image in ildasm.exe. The good news is that when you are using LINQ, you seldom (if ever) care about the underlying type of the query's return value; you will simply assign the value to an implicitly typed local variable.

In fact, it could be argued that the *only time* you would make use of the var keyword is when defining data returned from a LINQ query. Remember, if you know you need an int, just declare an int! Overuse of implicit typing (via the var keyword) is considered by most developers to be poor style in production code.

Working with C# Iteration Constructs

All programming languages provide ways to repeat blocks of code until a terminating condition has been met. Regardless of which language you have used in the past, I would guess the C# iteration statements should not raise too many eyebrows and should require little explanation. C# provides the following four iteration constructs:

- for loop
- foreach/in loop

- while loop
- do/while loop

Let's quickly examine each looping construct in turn, using a new Console Application project named IterationsAndDecisions.

■ **Note** I will keep this section of the chapter short and to the point, as I am assuming you have experience using similar keywords (if, for, switch, etc.) in your current programming language. If you require more information, look up the topics "Iteration Statements (C# Reference)," "Jump Statements (C# Reference)," and "Selection Statements (C# Reference)" within the C# documentation.

Using the for Loop

When you need to iterate over a block of code a fixed number of times, the for statement provides a good deal of flexibility. In essence, you are able to specify how many times a block of code repeats itself, as well as the terminating condition. Without belaboring the point, here is a sample of the syntax:

```
// A basic for loop.
static void ForLoopExample()
{
  // Note! "i" is only visible within the scope of the for loop.
  for(int i = 0; i < 4; i++)
  {
    Console.WriteLine("Number is: {0} ", i);
  }
  // "i" is not visible here.
}
```

All your old C, C++, and Java tricks still hold when building a C# for statement. You can create complex terminating conditions, build endless loops, loop in reverse (via the -- operator), and use the goto, continue, and break jump keywords.

Using the foreach Loop

The C# foreach keyword allows you to iterate over all items in a container without the need to test for an upper limit. Unlike a for loop, however, the foreach loop will walk the container only in a linear (n+1) fashion (thus, you cannot go backward through the container, skip every third element, or whatnot).

However, when you simply need to walk a collection item by item, the foreach loop is the perfect choice. Here are two examples using foreach—one to traverse an array of strings and the other to traverse an array of integers. Notice that the data type before the in keyword represents the type of data in the container.

```
// Iterate array items using foreach.
static void ForEachLoopExample()
{
  string[] carTypes = {"Ford", "BMW", "Yugo", "Honda" };
  foreach (string c in carTypes)
```

```
  {
    Console.WriteLine(c);
  }

  int[] myInts = { 10, 20, 30, 40 };
  foreach (int i in myInts)
  {
    Console.WriteLine(i);
  }
}
```

The item after the in keyword can be a simple array (seen here) or, more specifically, any class implementing the IEnumerable interface. As you will see in Chapter 10, the .NET Core base class libraries ship with a number of collections that contain implementations of common abstract data types (ADTs). Any of these items (such as the generic List<T>) can be used within a foreach loop.

Using Implicit Typing Within foreach Constructs

It is also possible to use implicit typing within a foreach looping construct. As you would expect, the compiler will correctly infer the correct "type of type." Recall the LINQ example method shown earlier in this chapter. Given that you do not know the exact underlying data type of the subset variable, you can iterate over the result set using implicit typing.

```
static void LinqQueryOverInts()
{
  int[] numbers = { 10, 20, 30, 40, 1, 2, 3, 8 };

  // LINQ query!
  var subset = from i in numbers where i < 10 select i;
  Console.Write("Values in subset: ");

  foreach (var i in subset)
  {
    Console.Write("{0} ", i);
  }
}
```

Using the while and do/while Looping Constructs

The while looping construct is useful should you want to execute a block of statements until some terminating condition has been reached. Within the scope of a while loop, you will need to ensure this terminating event is indeed established; otherwise, you will be stuck in an endless loop. In the following example, the message "In while loop" will be continuously printed until the user terminates the loop by entering yes at the command prompt:

```
static void WhileLoopExample()
{
  string userIsDone = "";

  // Test on a lower-class copy of the string.
```

```
  while(userIsDone.ToLower() != "yes")
  {
    Console.WriteLine("In while loop");
    Console.Write("Are you done? [yes] [no]: ");
    userIsDone = Console.ReadLine();
  }
}
```

Closely related to the while loop is the do/while statement. Like a simple while loop, do/while is used when you need to perform some action an undetermined number of times. The difference is that do/while loops are guaranteed to execute the corresponding block of code at least once. In contrast, it is possible that a simple while loop may never execute if the terminating condition is false from the onset.

```
static void DoWhileLoopExample()
{
  string userIsDone = "";

  do
  {
    Console.WriteLine("In do/while loop");
    Console.Write("Are you done? [yes] [no]: ");
    userIsDone = Console.ReadLine();
  }while(userIsDone.ToLower() != "yes"); // Note the semicolon!
}
```

A Quick Discussion About Scope

Like all languages based on C (C#, Java, etc.), a *scope* is created using curly braces. You have already seen this in many of the examples so far, including namespaces, classes, and methods. The iteration and decision constructs also operate in a scope, as in the following example:

```
for(int i = 0; i < 4; i++)
{
  Console.WriteLine("Number is: {0} ", i);
}
```

For these constructs (both in the previous section and the next section), it is permissible to not use curly braces. In other words, the following code is *exactly* the same as the previous example:

```
for(int i = 0; i < 4; i++)
  Console.WriteLine("Number is: {0} ", i);
```

While this is permissible, it is typically not a good idea. The problem is not the one-line statement, but the statement that goes from one line to more than one line. Without the braces, mistakes could be made when expanding the code within the iteration/decision constructs. For example, the following two examples are ***not*** the same:

```
for(int i = 0; i < 4; i++)
{
  Console.WriteLine("Number is: {0} ", i);
  Console.WriteLine("Number plus 1 is: {0} ", i+1)
}
for(int i = 0; i < 4; i++)
  Console.WriteLine("Number is: {0} ", i);
  Console.WriteLine("Number plus 1 is: {0} ", i+1)
```

If you are lucky (like in this example), the additional line of code generates a compilation error, since the variable *i* is defined only in the scope of the `for` loop. If you are unlucky, you are executing code that does not get flagged as a compiler error, but is a logic error, which is harder to find and debug.

Working with Decision Constructs and the Relational/Equality Operators

Now that you can iterate over a block of statements, the next related concept is how to control the flow of program execution. C# defines two simple constructs to alter the flow of your program, based on various contingencies:

- The `if/else` statement
- The `switch` statement

■ **Note** C# 7 extends the `is` expression and `switch` statements with a technique called *pattern matching*. The basics of how these extensions affect `if/else` and `switch` statements are shown here for completeness. These extensions will make more sense after reading Chapter 6, which covers base class/derived class rules, casting, and the standard `is` operator.

Using the if/else Statement

First up is the `if/else` statement. Unlike in C and C++, the `if/else` statement in C# operates only on Boolean expressions, not ad hoc values such as `-1` or `0`.

Using Equality and Relational Operators

C# `if/else` statements typically involve the use of the C# operators shown in Table 3-8 to obtain a literal Boolean value.

Table 3-8. C# Relational and Equality Operators

C# Equality/Relational Operator	Example Usage	Meaning in Life
`==`	`if(age == 30)`	Returns `true` only if each expression is the same
`!=`	`if("Foo" != myStr)`	Returns `true` only if each expression is different
`<`	`if(bonus < 2000)`	Returns `true` if expression A (`bonus`) is less than expression B (2000)
`>`	`if(bonus > 2000)`	Returns `true` if expression A (`bonus`) is greater than expression B (2000)
`<=`	`if(bonus <= 2000)`	Returns `true` if expression A (`bonus`) is less than or equal to expression B (2000)
`>=`	`if(bonus >= 2000)`	Returns `true` if expression A (`bonus`) is greater than or equal to expression B (2000)

Again, C and C++ programmers need to be aware that the old tricks of testing a condition for a value not equal to zero will not work in C#. Let's say you want to see whether the `string` you are working with is longer than zero characters. You might be tempted to write this:

```
static void IfElseExample()
{
  // This is illegal, given that Length returns an int, not a bool.
  string stringData = "My textual data";
  if(stringData.Length)
  {
    Console.WriteLine("string is greater than 0 characters");
  }
  else
  {
    Console.WriteLine("string is not greater than 0 characters");
  }
  Console.WriteLine();
}
```

If you want to use the `String.Length` property to determine truth or falsity, you need to modify your conditional expression to resolve to a Boolean.

```
// Legal, as this resolves to either true or false.
If (stringData.Length > 0)
{
  Console.WriteLine("string is greater than 0 characters");
}
```

Using if/else with Pattern Matching (New 7.0)

New in C# 7.0, *pattern matching* is allowed in `if/else` statements. Pattern matching allows code to inspect an object for certain traits and properties and make decisions based on the (non)existence of those properties and traits. Do not worry if you are new to object-oriented programming; the previous sentence will be explained in great detail in later chapters. Just know (for now) that you can check the type of an object using the `is` keyword, assign that object to a variable if the pattern matches, and then use that variable.

The `IfElsePatternMatching` method examines two object variables and determines if they are a string or an int and then prints the results to the console:

```
static void IfElsePatternMatching()
{
  Console.WriteLine("===If Else Pattern Matching ===");
  object testItem1 = 123;
  object testItem2 = "Hello";
  if (testItem1 is string myStringValue1)
  {
    Console.WriteLine($"{myStringValue1} is a string");
  }
  if (testItem1 is int myValue1)
  {
    Console.WriteLine($"{myValue1} is an int");
  }
  if (testItem2 is string myStringValue2)
  {
    Console.WriteLine($"{myStringValue2} is a string");
  }
  if (testItem2 is int myValue2)
  {
    Console.WriteLine($"{myValue2} is an int");
  }
  Console.WriteLine();
}
```

Making Pattern Matching Improvements (New 9.0)

C# 9.0 has introduced a host of improvements to pattern matching, as shown in Table 3-9.

Table 3-9. Pattern Matching Improvements

Pattern	Meaning in Life
`Type patterns`	Checks if a variable is a type
`Parenthesized patterns`	Enforces or emphasizes the precedence of pattern combinations
`Conjuctive (and) patterns`	Requires both patterns to match
`Disjunctive (or) patterns`	Requires either pattern to match
`Negated (not) patterns`	Requires a pattern does not match
`Relational patterns`	Requires input to be less than, less than or equal, greater than, or greater than or equal
`Pattern combinator`	Allows multiple patterns to be used together.

The updated `IfElsePatternMatchingUpdatedInCSharp9()` shows these new patterns in action:

```
static void IfElsePatternMatchingUpdatedInCSharp9()
{
    Console.WriteLine("======= C# 9 If Else Pattern Matching Improvements =======");
    object testItem1 = 123;
    Type t = typeof(string);
    char c = 'f';

    //Type patterns
    if (t is Type)
    {
        Console.WriteLine($"{t} is a Type");
    }

    //Relational, Conjuctive, and Disjunctive patterns
    if (c is >= 'a' and <= 'z' or >= 'A' and <= 'Z')
    {
        Console.WriteLine($"{c} is a character");
    };

    //Parenthesized patterns
    if (c is (>= 'a' and <= 'z') or (>= 'A' and <= 'Z') or '.' or ',')
    {
        Console.WriteLine($"{c} is a character or separator");
    };

    //Negative patterns
    if (testItem1 is not string)
    {
        Console.WriteLine($"{testItem1} is not a string");
    }
```

```
    if (testItem1 is not null)
    {
        Console.WriteLine($"{testItem1} is not null");
    }
    Console.WriteLine();
}
```

Using the Conditional Operator (Updated 7.2, 9.0)

The conditional operator (?:), also known as the *ternary conditional operator*, is a shorthand method of writing a simple if/else statement. The syntax works like this:

```
condition ? first_expression : second_expression;
```

The condition is the conditional test (the if part of the if/else statement). If the test passes, then the code immediately after the question mark (?) is executed. If the test does not evaluate to true, the code after the colon (the else part of the if/else statement) is executed. The previous code example can be written using the conditional operator like this:

```
static void ExecuteIfElseUsingConditionalOperator()
{
  string stringData = "My textual data";
  Console.WriteLine(stringData.Length > 0
    ? "string is greater than 0 characters"
    : "string is not greater than 0 characters");
  Console.WriteLine();
}
```

There are some restrictions to the conditional operator. First, both types of first_expression and second_expression must have implicit conversions to from one to another, or, new in C# 9.0, each must have an implicit conversion to a target type. Second, the conditional operator can be used only in assignment statements. The following code will result in the compiler error "Only assignment, call, increment, decrement, and new object expressions can be used as a statement":

```
  stringData.Length > 0
    ? Console.WriteLine("string is greater than 0 characters")
    : Console.WriteLine("string is not greater than 0 characters");
```

New in C# 7.2, the conditional operator can be used to return a reference to the result of the condition. Take the following example, which uses two forms of the conditional operator by ref:

```
static void ConditionalRefExample()
{
  var smallArray = new int[] { 1, 2, 3, 4, 5 };
  var largeArray = new int[] { 10, 20, 30, 40, 50 };

  int index = 7;
  ref int refValue = ref ((index < 5)
    ? ref smallArray[index]
    : ref largeArray[index - 5]);
  refValue = 0;
```

```
    index = 2;
    ((index < 5)
      ? ref smallArray[index]
      : ref largeArray[index - 5]) = 100;

    Console.WriteLine(string.Join(" ", smallArray));
    Console.WriteLine(string.Join(" ", largeArray));
}
```

If you are not familiar with the ref keyword, do not worry too much at this point, as it will be covered in depth in the next chapter. To sum up, the first example returns a *reference* to the array location checked with the condition and assigns the refValue variable to that reference. Think of the reference conceptually as a point to the location in the array and not the actual value of the position of the array. This allows for changing of the array's value in that position directly by changing the value assigned to the variable. The result of setting the value of the refValue variable to zero changes the second array's values to 10,20,**0**,40,50. The second example updates the first array's second value to 100, resulting in 1,2,**100**,4,5.

Using Logical Operators

An if statement may be composed of complex expressions as well and can contain else statements to perform more complex testing. The syntax is identical to C (and C++) and Java. To build complex expressions, C# offers an expected set of logical operators, as shown in Table 3-10.

Table 3-10. *C# Logical Operators*

Operator	Example	Meaning in Life
&&	`if(age == 30 && name == "Fred")`	AND operator. Returns true if all expressions are true.
||	`if(age == 30 || name == "Fred")`	OR operator. Returns true if at least one expression is true.
!	`if(!myBool)`	NOT operator. Returns true if false, or false if true.

■ **Note** The && and || operators both "short-circuit" when necessary. This means that after a complex expression has been determined to be false, the remaining subexpressions will not be checked. If you require all expressions to be tested regardless, you can use the related & and | operators.

Using the switch Statement

The other simple selection construct offered by C# is the switch statement. As in other C-based languages, the switch statement allows you to handle program flow based on a predefined set of choices. For example, the following logic prints a specific string message based on one of two possible selections (the default case handles an invalid selection):

```
// Switch on a numerical value.
static void SwitchExample()
{
  Console.WriteLine("1 [C#], 2 [VB]");
  Console.Write("Please pick your language preference: ");

  string langChoice = Console.ReadLine();
  int n = int.Parse(langChoice);

  switch (n)
  {
    case 1:
      Console.WriteLine("Good choice, C# is a fine language.");
      break;
    case 2:
      Console.WriteLine("VB: OOP, multithreading, and more!");
      break;
    default:
      Console.WriteLine("Well...good luck with that!");
      break;
  }
}
```

■ **Note** C# demands that each case (including `default`) that contains executable statements have a terminating `return`, `break`, or `goto` to avoid falling through to the next statement.

One nice feature of the C# `switch` statement is that you can evaluate `string` data in addition to numeric data. In fact, all versions of C# can evaluate `char`, `string`, `bool`, `int`, `long`, and `enum` data types. As you will see in the next section, C# 7 adds additional capabilities. Here is an updated `switch` statement that evaluates a string variable:

```
static void SwitchOnStringExample()
{
  Console.WriteLine("C# or VB");
  Console.Write("Please pick your language preference: ");

  string langChoice = Console.ReadLine();
  switch (langChoice.ToUpper())
  {
    case "C#":
      Console.WriteLine("Good choice, C# is a fine language.");
      break;
    case "VB":
      Console.WriteLine("VB: OOP, multithreading and more!");
      break;
    default:
      Console.WriteLine("Well...good luck with that!");
      break;
  }
}
```

It is also possible to switch on an enumeration data type. As you will see in Chapter 4, the C# `enum` keyword allows you to define a custom set of name-value pairs. To whet your appetite, consider the following final helper function, which performs a `switch` test on the `System.DayOfWeek` enum. You will notice some syntax I have not yet examined, but focus on the issue of switching over the `enum` itself; the missing pieces will be filled in over the chapters to come.

```
static void SwitchOnEnumExample()
{
  Console.Write("Enter your favorite day of the week: ");
  DayOfWeek favDay;
  try
  {
    favDay = (DayOfWeek) Enum.Parse(typeof(DayOfWeek), Console.ReadLine());
  }
  catch (Exception)
  {
    Console.WriteLine("Bad input!");
    return;
  }
  switch (favDay)
  {
    case DayOfWeek.Sunday:
      Console.WriteLine("Football!!");
      break;
    case DayOfWeek.Monday:
      Console.WriteLine("Another day, another dollar");
      break;
    case DayOfWeek.Tuesday:
      Console.WriteLine("At least it is not Monday");
      break;
    case DayOfWeek.Wednesday:
      Console.WriteLine("A fine day.");
      break;
    case DayOfWeek.Thursday:
      Console.WriteLine("Almost Friday...");
      break;
    case DayOfWeek.Friday:
      Console.WriteLine("Yes, Friday rules!");
      break;
    case DayOfWeek.Saturday:
      Console.WriteLine("Great day indeed.");
      break;
  }
  Console.WriteLine();
}
```

Falling through from one `case` statement to another `case` statement is not allowed, but what if multiple `case` statements should produce the same result? Fortunately, they can be combined, as the following code snippet demonstrates:

```
case DayOfWeek.Saturday:
case DayOfWeek.Sunday:
  Console.WriteLine("It's the weekend!");
  break;
```

If any code were included between the case statements, the compiler would throw an error. As long as they are consecutive statements, as shown earlier, case statements can be combined to share common code.

In addition to the return and break statements shown in the previous code samples, the switch statement also supports using a goto to exit a case condition and execute another case statement. While this is supported, it is pretty universally thought of as an anti-pattern and not generally used. Here is an example of using the goto statement in a switch block:

```
static void SwitchWithGoto()
{
  var foo = 5;
  switch (foo)
  {
    case 1:
      //do something
      goto case 2;
    case 2:
      //do something else
      break;
    case 3:
      //yet another action
      goto default;
    default:
      //default action
      break;
  }
}
```

Performing switch Statement Pattern Matching (New 7.0, Updated 9.0)

Prior to C# 7, match expressions in switch statements were limited to comparing a variable to constant values, sometimes referred to as the *constant pattern*. In C# 7, switch statements can also employ the *type pattern*, where case statements can evaluate the *type* of the variable being checked and case expressions are no longer limited to constant values. The rule that each case statement must be terminated with a return or break still applies; however, goto statements are not supported using the type pattern.

■ **Note** If you are new to object-oriented programming, this section might be a little confusing. It will all come together in Chapter 6, when you revisit the new pattern matching features of C# 7 in the context of classes and base classes. For now, just understand that there is a powerful new way to write switch statements.

Add another method named ExecutePatternMatchingSwitch() and add the following code:

```
static void ExecutePatternMatchingSwitch()
{
  Console.WriteLine("1 [Integer (5)], 2 [String (\"Hi\")], 3 [Decimal (2.5)]");
  Console.Write("Please choose an option: ");
  string userChoice = Console.ReadLine();
  object choice;
  //This is a standard constant pattern switch statement to set up the example
  switch (userChoice)
  {
    case "1":
      choice = 5;
      break;
    case "2":
      choice = "Hi";
      break;
    case "3":
      choice = 2.5M;
      break;
    default:
      choice = 5;
      break;
  }
  //This is new the pattern matching switch statement
  switch (choice)
  {
    case int i:
      Console.WriteLine("Your choice is an integer.");
      break;
    case string s:
      Console.WriteLine("Your choice is a string.");
      break;
    case decimal d:
      Console.WriteLine("Your choice is a decimal.");
      break;
    default:
      Console.WriteLine("Your choice is something else");
      break;
  }
  Console.WriteLine();
}
```

The first switch statement is using the standard constant pattern and is included merely to set up this (trivial) example. In the second switch statement, the variable is typed as object and, based on the input from the user, can be parsed into an int, string, or decimal data type. Based on the *type* of the variable, different case statements are matched. In addition to checking the data type, a variable is assigned in each of the case statements (except for the default case). Update the code to the following to use the values in the variables:

```
//This is new the pattern matching switch statement
switch (choice)
{
  case int i:
    Console.WriteLine("Your choice is an integer {0}.",i);
    break;
  case string s:
    Console.WriteLine("Your choice is a string. {0}", s);
    break;
  case decimal d:
    Console.WriteLine("Your choice is a decimal. {0}", d);
    break;
  default:
    Console.WriteLine("Your choice is something else");
    break;
}
```

In addition to evaluating on the type of the match expression, `when` clauses can be added to the `case` statements to evaluate conditions on the variable. In this example, in addition to checking the type, the value of the converted type is also checked for a match:

```
static void ExecutePatternMatchingSwitchWithWhen()
{
  Console.WriteLine("1 [C#], 2 [VB]");
  Console.Write("Please pick your language preference: ");

  object langChoice = Console.ReadLine();
  var choice = int.TryParse(langChoice.ToString(), out int c) ? c : langChoice;

  switch (choice)
  {
    case int i when i == 2:
    case string s when s.Equals("VB", StringComparison.OrdinalIgnoreCase):
      Console.WriteLine("VB: OOP, multithreading, and more!");
      break;
    case int i when i == 1:
    case string s when s.Equals("C#", StringComparison.OrdinalIgnoreCase):
      Console.WriteLine("Good choice, C# is a fine language.");
      break;
    default:
      Console.WriteLine("Well...good luck with that!");
      break;
  }
  Console.WriteLine();
}
```

This adds a new dimension to the `switch` statement as the order of the `case` statements is now significant. With the constant pattern, each case statement had to be unique. With the type pattern, this is no longer the case. For example, the following code will match every integer in the first case statement and will never execute the second or the third (in fact, the following code will fail to compile):

```
switch (choice)
{
  case int i:
    //do something
    break;
  case int i when i == 0:
    //do something
    break;
  case int i when i == -1:
    // do something
    break;
}
```

With the initial release of C# 7, there was a small glitch with pattern matching when using generic types. This has been resolved with C# 7.1. Generic types will be covered in Chapter 10.

■ **Note** All of the pattern matching improvement in C# 9.0 previously demonstrated are also available for use in `switch` statements.

Using switch Expressions (New 8.0)

New in C# 8 are `switch` expressions, allowing the assignment of a variable in a concise statement. Consider the C# 7 version of this method that takes in a color and returns the hex value for the color name:

```
static string FromRainbowClassic(string colorBand)
{
  switch (colorBand)
  {
    case "Red":
      return "#FF0000";
    case "Orange":
      return "#FF7F00";
    case "Yellow":
      return "#FFFF00";
    case "Green":
      return "#00FF00";
    case "Blue":
      return "#0000FF";
    case "Indigo":
      return "#4B0082";
    case "Violet":
      return "#9400D3";
    default:
      return "#FFFFFF";
  };
}
```

With the new switch expressions in C# 8, the previous method can be written as follows, which is much more concise:

```
static string FromRainbow(string colorBand)
{
  return colorBand switch
  {
    "Red" => "#FF0000",
    "Orange" => "#FF7F00",
    "Yellow" => "#FFFF00",
    "Green" => "#00FF00",
    "Blue" => "#0000FF",
    "Indigo" => "#4B0082",
    "Violet" => "#9400D3",
    _ => "#FFFFFF",
  };
}
```

There is a lot to unpack in that example, from the lambda (=>) statements to the discard (_). These will all be covered in later chapters, as will this example, in further detail.

There is one more example before finishing the topic of switch expressions, and it involved tuples. Tuples are covered in detail in Chapter 4, so for now think of a tuple as a simple construct holding more than one value and defined with parentheses, like this tuple that holds a string and an int:

```
(string, int)
```

In the following example, the two values passed into the RockPaperScissors method are converted to a tuple, and then the switch expression evaluates the two values in a single expression. This pattern allows for comparing more than one value during a switch statement.

```
//Switch expression with Tuples
static string RockPaperScissors(string first, string second)
{
  return (first, second) switch
  {
    ("rock", "paper") => "Paper wins.",
    ("rock", "scissors") => "Rock wins.",
    ("paper", "rock") => "Paper wins.",
    ("paper", "scissors") => "Scissors wins.",
    ("scissors", "rock") => "Rock wins.",
    ("scissors", "paper") => "Scissors wins.",
    (_, _) => "Tie.",
  };
}
```

To call this method, add the following lines of code to the top-level statements:

```
Console.WriteLine(RockPaperScissors("paper","rock"));
Console.WriteLine(RockPaperScissors("scissors","rock"));
```

This example will be revisited in Chapter 4 when tuples are introduced.

■ **Note** Property patterns were also introduced in C# 8.0 and are covered in Chapter 4.

Summary

The goal of this chapter was to expose you to numerous core aspects of the C# programming language. You examined the commonplace constructs in any application you may be interested in building. After examining the role of an application object, you learned that every C# executable program must have a type defining a `Main()` method, either explicitly or through the use of top-level statements. This method serves as the program's entry point.

Next, you dove into the details of the built-in data types of C# and came to understand that each data type keyword (e.g., `int`) is really a shorthand notation for a full-blown type in the `System` namespace (`System.Int32`, in this case). Given this, each C# data type has a number of built-in members. Along the same vein, you also learned about the role of *widening* and *narrowing*, as well as the role of the `checked` and `unchecked` keywords.

The chapter wrapped up by covering the role of implicit typing using the `var` keyword. As discussed, the most useful place for implicit typing is when working with the LINQ programming model. Finally, you quickly examined the various iteration and decision constructs supported by C#.

Now that you understand some of the basic nuts and bolts, the next chapter (Chapter 4) will complete your examination of core language features. After that, you will be well prepared to examine the object-oriented features of C# beginning in Chapter 5.

CHAPTER 4

Core C# Programming Constructs, Part 2

This chapter picks up where Chapter 3 left off and completes your investigation of the core aspects of the C# programming language. You will start with an investigation of the details behind manipulating arrays using the syntax of C# and get to know the functionality contained within the related `System.Array` class type.

Next, you will examine various details regarding the construction of C# methods, exploring the `out`, `ref`, and `params` keywords. Along the way, you will also examine the role of optional and named parameters. I finish the discussion on methods with a look at *method overloading*.

Next, this chapter discusses the construction of enumeration and structure types, including a detailed examination of the distinction between a *value type* and a *reference type*. This chapter wraps up by examining the role of *nullable* data types and the related operators.

After you have completed this chapter, you will be in a perfect position to learn the object-oriented capabilities of C#, beginning in Chapter 5.

Understanding C# Arrays

As I would guess you are already aware, an *array* is a set of data items, accessed using a numerical index. More specifically, an array is a set of contiguous data points of the same type (an array of `int`s, an array of `string`s, an array of `SportsCar`s, etc.). Declaring, filling, and accessing an array with C# are all quite straightforward. To illustrate, create a new Console Application project named FunWithArrays that contains a helper method named `SimpleArrays();` as follows:

```
Console.WriteLine("***** Fun with Arrays *****");
SimpleArrays();
Console.ReadLine();

static void SimpleArrays()
{
  Console.WriteLine("=> Simple Array Creation.");
  // Create and fill an array of 3 integers
  int[] myInts = new int[3];
  // Create a 100 item string array, indexed 0 - 99
  string[] booksOnDotNet = new string[100];
  Console.WriteLine();
}
```


A. Troelsen and P. Japikse, *Pro C# 10 with .NET 6*, https://doi.org/10.1007/978-1-4842-7869-7_4

Look closely at the previous code comments. When declaring a C# array using this syntax, the number used in the array declaration represents the total number of items, not the upper bound. Also note that the lower bound of an array always begins at 0. Thus, when you write `int[] myInts = new int[3]`, you end up with an array holding three elements, indexed at positions 0, 1, and 2.

After you have defined an array variable, you are then able to fill the elements index by index, as shown here in the updated `SimpleArrays()` method:

```
static void SimpleArrays()
{
  Console.WriteLine("=> Simple Array Creation.");
  // Create and fill an array of 3 Integers
  int[] myInts = new int[3];
  myInts[0] = 100;
  myInts[1] = 200;
  myInts[2] = 300;

  // Now print each value.
  foreach(int i in myInts)
  {
    Console.WriteLine(i);
  }
  Console.WriteLine();
}
```

■ **Note** Do be aware that if you declare an array but do not explicitly fill each index, each item will be set to the default value of the data type (e.g., an array of `bool`s will be set to `false` or an array of `int`s will be set to 0).

Looking at the C# Array Initialization Syntax

In addition to filling an array element by element, you can fill the items of an array using C# *array initialization syntax*. To do so, specify each array item within the scope of curly brackets ({}). This syntax can be helpful when you are creating an array of a known size and want to quickly specify the initial values. For example, consider the following alternative array declarations:

```
static void ArrayInitialization()
{
  Console.WriteLine("=> Array Initialization.");

  // Array initialization syntax using the new keyword.
  string[] stringArray = new string[]
    { "one", "two", "three" };
  Console.WriteLine("stringArray has {0} elements", stringArray.Length);

  // Array initialization syntax without using the new keyword.
  bool[] boolArray = { false, false, true };
  Console.WriteLine("boolArray has {0} elements", boolArray.Length);

  // Array initialization with new keyword and size.
```

```
  int[] intArray = new int[4] { 20, 22, 23, 0 };
  Console.WriteLine("intArray has {0} elements", intArray.Length);
  Console.WriteLine();
}
```

Notice that when you make use of this "curly-bracket" syntax, you do not need to specify the size of the array (seen when constructing the stringArray variable), given that this will be inferred by the number of items within the scope of the curly brackets. Also notice that the use of the new keyword is optional (shown when constructing the boolArray type).

In the case of the intArray declaration, again recall the numeric value specified represents the number of elements in the array, not the value of the upper bound. If there is a mismatch between the declared size and the number of initializers (whether you have too many or too few initializers), you are issued a compile-time error. The following is an example:

```
// OOPS! Mismatch of size and elements!
int[] intArray = new int[2] { 20, 22, 23, 0 };
```

Understanding Implicitly Typed Local Arrays

In Chapter 3, you learned about the topic of implicitly typed local variables. Recall that the var keyword allows you to define a variable, whose underlying type is determined by the compiler. In a similar vein, the var keyword can be used to define *implicitly typed local arrays*. Using this technique, you can allocate a new array variable without specifying the type contained within the array itself (note you must use the new keyword when using this approach).

```
static void DeclareImplicitArrays()
{
  Console.WriteLine("=> Implicit Array Initialization.");

  // a is really int[].
  var a = new[] { 1, 10, 100, 1000 };
  Console.WriteLine("a is a: {0}", a.ToString());

  // b is really double[].
  var b = new[] { 1, 1.5, 2, 2.5 };
  Console.WriteLine("b is a: {0}", b.ToString());

  // c is really string[].
  var c = new[] { "hello", null, "world" };
  Console.WriteLine("c is a: {0}", c.ToString());
  Console.WriteLine();
}
```

Of course, just as when you allocate an array using explicit C# syntax, the items in the array's initialization list must be of the same underlying type (e.g., all ints, all strings, or all SportsCars). Unlike what you might be expecting, an implicitly typed local array does not default to System.Object; thus, the following generates a compile-time error:

```
// Error! Mixed types!
var d = new[] { 1, "one", 2, "two", false };
```

Defining an Array of Objects

In most cases, when you define an array, you do so by specifying the explicit type of item that can be within the array variable. While this seems quite straightforward, there is one notable twist. As you will come to understand in Chapter 6, `System.Object` is the ultimate base class to every type (including fundamental data types) in the .NET Core type system. Given this fact, if you were to define an array of `System.Object` data types, the subitems could be anything at all. Consider the following `ArrayOfObjects()` method:

```
static void ArrayOfObjects()
{
  Console.WriteLine("=> Array of Objects.");

  // An array of objects can be anything at all.
  object[] myObjects = new object[4];
  myObjects[0] = 10;
  myObjects[1] = false;
  myObjects[2] = new DateTime(1969, 3, 24);
  myObjects[3] = "Form & Void";
  foreach (object obj in myObjects)
  {
    // Print the type and value for each item in array.
    Console.WriteLine("Type: {0}, Value: {1}", obj.GetType(), obj);
  }
  Console.WriteLine();
}
```

Here, as you are iterating over the contents of `myObjects`, you print the underlying type of each item using the `GetType()` method of `System.Object`, as well as the value of the current item. Without going into too much detail regarding `System.Object.GetType()` at this point in the text, simply understand that this method can be used to obtain the fully qualified name of the item (Chapter 17 examines the topic of type information and reflection services in detail). The following output shows the result of calling `ArrayOfObjects()`:

```
=> Array of Objects.

Type: System.Int32, Value: 10
Type: System.Boolean, Value: False
Type: System.DateTime, Value: 3/24/1969 12:00:00 AM
Type: System.String, Value: Form & Void
```

Working with Multidimensional Arrays

In addition to the single dimension arrays you have seen thus far, C# supports two varieties of multidimensional arrays. The first of these is termed a *rectangular array*, which is simply an array of multiple dimensions, where each row is of the same length. To declare and fill a multidimensional rectangular array, proceed as follows:

```
static void RectMultidimensionalArray()
{
  Console.WriteLine("=> Rectangular multidimensional array.");
  // A rectangular MD array.
  int[,] myMatrix;
```

```
  myMatrix = new int[3,4];

  // Populate (3 * 4) array.
  for(int i = 0; i < 3; i++)
  {
    for(int j = 0; j < 4; j++)
    {
      myMatrix[i, j] = i * j;
    }
  }

  // Print (3 * 4) array.
  for(int i = 0; i < 3; i++)
  {
    for(int j = 0; j < 4; j++)
    {
      Console.Write(myMatrix[i, j] + "\t");
    }
    Console.WriteLine();
  }
  Console.WriteLine();
}
```

The second type of multidimensional array is termed a *jagged array*. As the name implies, jagged arrays contain some number of inner arrays, each of which may have a different upper limit. Here is an example:

```
static void JaggedMultidimensionalArray()
{
  Console.WriteLine("=> Jagged multidimensional array.");
  // A jagged MD array (i.e., an array of arrays).
  // Here we have an array of 5 different arrays.
  int[][] myJagArray = new int[5][];

  // Create the jagged array.
  for (int i = 0; i < myJagArray.Length; i++)
  {
    myJagArray[i] = new int[i + 7];
  }

  // Print each row (remember, each element is defaulted to zero!).
  for(int i = 0; i < 5; i++)
  {
    for(int j = 0; j < myJagArray[i].Length; j++)
    {
      Console.Write(myJagArray[i][j] + " ");
    }
    Console.WriteLine();
  }
  Console.WriteLine();
}
```

The output of calling each of the RectMultidimensionalArray() and JaggedMultidimensionalArray() methods is shown next:

```
=> Rectangular multidimensional array:

0       0       0       0
0       1       2       3
0       2       4       6

=> Jagged multidimensional array:

0 0 0 0 0 0 0
0 0 0 0 0 0 0 0
0 0 0 0 0 0 0 0 0
0 0 0 0 0 0 0 0 0 0
0 0 0 0 0 0 0 0 0 0 0
```

Using Arrays As Arguments or Return Values

After you have created an array, you are free to pass it as an argument or receive it as a member return value. For example, the following PrintArray() method takes an incoming array of ints and prints each member to the console, while the GetStringArray() method populates an array of strings and returns it to the caller:

```
static void PrintArray(int[] myInts)
{
  for(int i = 0; i < myInts.Length; i++)
  {
    Console.WriteLine("Item {0} is {1}", i, myInts[i]);
  }
}

static string[] GetStringArray()
{
  string[] theStrings = {"Hello", "from", "GetStringArray"};
  return theStrings;
}
```

These methods can be invoked as you would expect.

```
static void PassAndReceiveArrays()
{
  Console.WriteLine("=> Arrays as params and return values.");
  // Pass array as parameter.
  int[] ages = {20, 22, 23, 0} ;
  PrintArray(ages);

  // Get array as return value.
  string[] strs = GetStringArray();
  foreach(string s in strs)
```

```
    {
      Console.WriteLine(s);
    }

    Console.WriteLine();
  }
```

At this point, you should feel comfortable with the process of defining, filling, and examining the contents of a C# array variable. To complete the picture, let's now examine the role of the `System.Array` class.

Using the System.Array Base Class

Every array you create gathers much of its functionality from the `System.Array` class. Using these common members, you can operate on an array using a consistent object model. Table 4-1 gives a rundown of some of the more interesting members (be sure to check the documentation for full details).

Table 4-1. *Select Members of System.Array*

Member of Array Class	Meaning in Life
`Clear()`	This static method sets a range of elements in the array to empty values (`0` for numbers, `null` for object references, `false` for Booleans).
`CopyTo()`	This method is used to copy elements from the source array into the destination array.
`Length`	This property returns the number of items within the array.
`Rank`	This property returns the number of dimensions of the current array.
`Reverse()`	This static method reverses the contents of a one-dimensional array.
`Sort()`	This static method sorts a one-dimensional array of intrinsic types. If the elements in the array implement the `IComparer` interface, you can also sort your custom types (see Chapters 8 and 10).

Let's see some of these members in action. The following helper method makes use of the static `Reverse()` and `Clear()` methods to pump out information about an array of `string` types to the console:

```
static void SystemArrayFunctionality()
{
  Console.WriteLine("=> Working with System.Array.");
  // Initialize items at startup.
  string[] gothicBands = {"Tones on Tail", "Bauhaus", "Sisters of Mercy"};

  // Print out names in declared order.
  Console.WriteLine("-> Here is the array:");
  for (int i = 0; i < gothicBands.Length; i++)
  {
    // Print a name.
    Console.Write(gothicBands[i] + ", ");
  }
  Console.WriteLine("\n");
```

```
  // Reverse them...
  Array.Reverse(gothicBands);
  Console.WriteLine("-> The reversed array");

  // ... and print them.
  for (int i = 0; i < gothicBands.Length; i++)
  {
    // Print a name.
    Console.Write(gothicBands[i] + ", ");
  }
  Console.WriteLine("\n");

  // Clear out all but the first member.
  Console.WriteLine("-> Cleared out all but one...");
  Array.Clear(gothicBands, 1, 2);

  for (int i = 0; i < gothicBands.Length; i++)
  {
    // Print a name.
    Console.Write(gothicBands[i] + ", ");
  }
  Console.WriteLine();
}
```

If you invoke this method, you will get the output shown here:

```
=> Working with System.Array.

-> Here is the array:
Tones on Tail, Bauhaus, Sisters of Mercy,

-> The reversed array
Sisters of Mercy, Bauhaus, Tones on Tail,

-> Cleared out all but one...
Sisters of Mercy, , ,
```

Notice that many members of `System.Array` are defined as static members and are, therefore, called at the class level (e.g., the `Array.Sort()` and `Array.Reverse()` methods). Methods such as these are passed in the array you want to process. Other members of `System.Array` (such as the `Length` property) are bound at the object level; thus, you can invoke the member directly on the array.

Using Indices and Ranges (New 8.0, Updated 10.0)

To simplify working with sequences (including arrays), C# 8 introduces two new types and two new operators for use when working with arrays.

- `System.Index` represents an index into a sequence.
- `System.Range` represents a subrange of indices.

- The index from end operator (^) specifies that the index is relative to the end of the sequence.
- The range operator (..) specifies the start and end of a range as its operands.

■ **Note** Indices and ranges can be used with arrays, strings, Span<T>, ReadOnlySpan<T>, and (added in .NET 6/C# 10) IEnumerable<T>.

As you have already seen, arrays are indexed beginning with zero (0). The end of a sequence is the length of the sequence – 1. The previous for loop that printed the gothicBands array can be updated to the following:

```
for (int i = 0; i < gothicBands.Length; i++)
{
  Index idx = i;
  // Print a name
  Console.Write(gothicBands[idx] + ", ");
}
```

The index from end operator lets you specify how many positions from the end of sequence, starting with the length. Remember that the last item in a sequence is one less than the actual length, so ^0 would cause an error. The following code prints the array in reverse:

```
for (int i = 1; i <= gothicBands.Length; i++)
{
  Index idx = ^i;
  // Print a name
  Console.Write(gothicBands[idx] + ", ");
}
```

The range operator specifies a start and end index and allows for access to a subsequence within a list. The start of the range is inclusive, and the end of the range is exclusive. For example, to pull out the first two members of the array, create ranges from 0 (the first member) to 2 (one more than the desired index position).

```
foreach (var itm in gothicBands[0..2])
{
  // Print a name
  Console.Write(itm + ", ");
}
Console.WriteLine("\n");
```

Ranges can also be passed to a sequence using the new Range data type, as shown here:

```
Range r = 0..2; //the end of the range is exclusive
foreach (var itm in gothicBands[r])
{
  // Print a name
  Console.Write(itm + ", ");
}
Console.WriteLine("\n");
```

Ranges can be defined using integers or Index variables. The same result will occur with the following code:

```
Index idx1 = 0;
Index idx2 = 2;
Range r = idx1..idx2; //the end of the range is exclusive
foreach (var itm in gothicBands[r])
{
  // Print a name
  Console.Write(itm + ", ");
}
Console.WriteLine("\n");
```

If the beginning of the range is left off, the beginning of the sequence is used. If the end of the range is left off, the length of the range is used. This does not cause an error, since the value at the end of the range is exclusive. For the previous example of three items in an array, all the ranges represent the same subset.

```
gothicBands[..]
gothicBands[0..^0]
gothicBands[0..3]
```

The ElementAt() extension method (in the System.Linq namespace) retrieves the element from the array at the specified location. New in .NET 6/C# 10, using the index from end operator is supported to get an element the specified distance from the end of the array. The following code gets the second-to-last band from the list:

```
var band = gothicBands.ElementAt(^2);
Console.WriteLine(band);
```

■ **Note** Support for using Index and Range parameters has been added to LINQ. See Chapter 13 for more information.

Understanding Methods

Let's examine the details of defining methods. Methods are defined by an access modifier and return type (or void for no return type) and may or may not take parameters. A method that returns a value to the caller is commonly referred to as a *function*, while methods that do not return a value are commonly referred to as *methods*.

■ **Note** Access modifiers for methods (and classes) are covered in Chapter 5. Method parameters are covered in the next section.

At this point in the text, each of your methods has the following basic format:

```
// Recall that static methods can be called directly
// without creating a class instance.
// static returnType MethodName(parameter list) { /* Implementation */ }
```

```
static int Add(int x, int y)
{
  return x + y;
}
```

As you will see over the next several chapters, methods can be implemented within the scope of classes, structures, or (new in C# 8) interfaces.

Understanding Expression-Bodied Members

You already learned about simple methods that return values, such as the Add() method. C# 6 introduced expression-bodied members that shorten the syntax for single-line methods. For example, Add() can be rewritten using the following syntax:

```
static int Add(int x, int y) => x + y;
```

This is what is commonly referred to as *syntactic sugar*, meaning that the generated IL is no different. It is just another way to write the method. Some find it easier to read, and others do not, so the choice is yours (or your team's) which style you prefer.

■ **Note** Don't be alarmed by the => operator. This is a lambda operation, which is covered in detail in Chapter 12. That chapter also explains exactly *how* expression-bodied members work. For now, just consider them a shortcut to writing single-line statements.

Understanding Local Functions (New 7.0, Updated 9.0)

A feature introduced in C# 7.0 is the ability to create methods within methods, referred to officially as *local functions*. A local function is a function declared inside another function, must be private, with C# 8.0 can be static (see the next section), and does not support overloading. Local functions do support nesting: a local function can have a local function declared inside it.

To see how this works, create a new Console Application project named FunWithLocalFunctions. As an example, let's say you want to extend the Add() example used previously to include validation of the inputs. There are many ways to accomplish this, and one simple way is to add the validation directly into the Add() method. Let's go with that and update the previous example to the following (the comment representing validation logic):

```
static int Add(int x, int y)
{
  //Do some validation here
  return x + y;
}
```

As you can see, there are no big changes. There is just a comment indicating that real code should do something. What if you wanted to separate the actual reason for the method (returning the sum of the arguments) from the validation of the arguments? You could create additional methods and call them from the Add() method. But that would require creating another method just for use by one other method. Maybe that's overkill. Local functions allow you to do the validation first and then encapsulate the real goal of the method defined inside the AddWrapper() method, as shown here:

```
static int AddWrapper(int x, int y)
{
  //Do some validation here
  return Add();

  int Add()
  {
    return x + y;
  }
}
```

The contained Add() method can be called only from the wrapping AddWrapper() method. So, the question I am sure you are thinking is, "What did this buy me?" The answer for this specific example, quite simply, is little (if anything). But what if AddWrapper() needed to execute the Add() function from multiple places? Now you should start to see the benefit of having a local function for code reuse that is not exposed outside of where it is needed. You will see even more benefit gained with local functions when we cover custom iterator methods (Chapter 8) and asynchronous methods (Chapter 15).

■ **Note** The AddWrapper() local function is an example of local function with a nested local function. Recall that functions declared in top-level statements are created as local functions. The Add() local function is in the AddWrapper() local function. This capability typically is not used outside of teaching examples, but if you ever need to nest local functions, you know that C# supports it.

C# 9.0 updated local functions to allow for adding attributes to a local function, its parameters, and its type parameters, as in the following example (do not worry about the NotNullWhen attribute, which will be covered later in this chapter):

```
#nullable enable
private static void Process(string?[] lines, string mark)
{
    foreach (var line in lines)
    {
        if (IsValid(line))
        {
            // Processing logic...
        }
    }

    bool IsValid([NotNullWhen(true)] string? line)
    {
        return !string.IsNullOrEmpty(line) && line.Length >= mark.Length;
    }
}
```

Understanding Static Local Functions (New 8.0)

An improvement to local functions that was introduced in C# 8 is the ability to declare a local function as static. In the previous example, the local Add() function was referencing the variables from the main function directly. This could cause unexpected side effects, since the local function can change the values of the variables.

To see this in action, create a new method called AddWrapperWithSideEffect(), as shown here:

```
static int AddWrapperWithSideEffect(int x, int y)
{
  //Do some validation here
  return Add();

  int Add()
  {
    x += 1;
    return x + y;
  }
}
```

Of course, this example is so simple, it probably would not happen in real code. To prevent this type of mistake, add the static modifier to the local function. This prevents the local function from accessing the parent method variables directly, and this causes the compiler exception CS8421, "A static local function cannot contain a reference to '<variable name>.'"

The improved version of the previous method is shown here:

```
static int AddWrapperWithStatic(int x, int y)
{
  //Do some validation here
  return Add(x,y);

  static int Add(int x, int y)
  {
    return x + y;
  }
}
```

Understanding Method Parameters

Method parameters are used to pass data into a method call. Over the next several sections, you will learn the details of how methods (and their callers) treat parameters.

Understanding Method Parameter Modifiers

The default way a parameter is sent into a function is *by value*. Simply put, if you do not mark an argument with a parameter modifier, a copy of the data is passed into the function. As explained later in this chapter, exactly *what* is copied will depend on whether the parameter is a value type or a reference type.

While the definition of a method in C# is quite straightforward, you can use a handful of methods to control how arguments are passed to a method, as listed in Table 4-2.

Table 4-2. *C# Parameter Modifiers*

Parameter Modifier	Meaning in Life
(None)	If a value type parameter is not marked with a modifier, it is assumed to be passed by value, meaning the called method receives a copy of the original data. Reference types without a modifier are passed in by reference.
`out`	Output parameters must be assigned by the method being called and, therefore, are passed by reference. If the called method fails to assign output parameters, you are issued a compiler error.
`ref`	The value is initially assigned by the caller and may be optionally modified by the called method (as the data is also passed by reference). No compiler error is generated if the called method fails to assign a `ref` parameter.
`in`	New in C# 7.2, the `in` modifier indicates that a `ref` parameter is read-only by the called method.
`params`	This parameter modifier allows you to send in a variable number of arguments as a single logical parameter. A method can have only a single `params` modifier, and it must be the final parameter of the method. You might not need to use the `params` modifier all too often; however, be aware that numerous methods within the base class libraries do make use of this C# language feature.

To illustrate the use of these keywords, create a new Console Application project named FunWithMethods. Now, let's walk through the role of each keyword.

Understanding the Default Parameter-Passing Behavior

When a parameter does not have a modifier, the behavior for value types is to pass in the parameter by value and for reference types is to pass in the parameter by reference.

■ **Note** Value types and reference types are covered later in this chapter.

The Default Behavior for Value Types

The default way a value type parameter is sent into a function is *by value*. Simply put, if you do not mark the argument with a modifier, a copy of the data is passed into the function. Add the following method to the `Program.cs` file that operates on two numerical data types passed by value:

```
// Value type arguments are passed by value by default.
static int Add(int x, int y)
{
  int ans = x + y;
  // Caller will not see these changes
  // as you are modifying a copy of the
  // original data.
  x = 10000;
  y = 88888;
  return ans;
}
```

Numerical data falls under the category of *value types*. Therefore, if you change the values of the parameters within the scope of the member, the caller is blissfully unaware, given that you are changing the values on a *copy* of the caller's original data.

```
Console.WriteLine("***** Fun with Methods *****\n");

// Pass two variables in by value.
int x = 9, y = 10;
Console.WriteLine("Before call: X: {0}, Y: {1}", x, y);
Console.WriteLine("Answer is: {0}", Add(x, y));
Console.WriteLine("After call: X: {0}, Y: {1}", x, y);
Console.ReadLine();
```

As you would hope, the values of x and y remain identical before and after the call to Add(), as shown in the following output, as the data points were sent in by value. Thus, any changes on these parameters within the Add() method are not seen by the caller, as the Add() method is operating on a copy of the data.

```
***** Fun with Methods *****

Before call: X: 9, Y: 10
Answer is: 19
After call: X: 9, Y: 10
```

The Default Behavior for Reference Types

The default way a reference type parameter is sent into a function is *by reference for its properties, but by value for itself*. This is covered in detail later in this chapter, after the discussion of value types and reference types.

■ **Note** Even though the string data type is technically a reference type, as discussed in Chapter 3, it's a special case. When a string parameter does not have a modifier, it is passed in *by value*.

Using the out Modifier (Updated 7.0)

Next, you have the use of *output parameters*. Methods that have been defined to take output parameters (via the out keyword) are under obligation to assign them to an appropriate value before exiting the method scope (if you fail to do so, you will receive compiler errors).

To illustrate, here is an alternative version of the Add() method that returns the sum of two integers using the C# out modifier (note the physical return value of this method is now void):

```
// Output parameters must be assigned by the called method.
static void AddUsingOutParam(int x, int y, out int ans)
{
  ans = x + y;
}
```

Calling a method with output parameters also requires the use of the out modifier. However, the local variables that are passed as output variables are not required to be assigned before passing them in as output arguments (if you do so, the original value is lost after the call). The reason the compiler allows you to send in seemingly unassigned data is because the method being called *must* make an assignment. To call the updated Add method, create a variable of type int, and use the out modifier in the call, like this:

```
int ans;
AddUsingOutParam(90, 90, out ans);
```

Starting with C# 7.0, out parameters do not need to be declared before using them. In other words, they can be declared inside the method call, like this:

```
AddUsingOutParam(90, 90, out int ans);
```

The following code is an example of calling a method with an inline declaration of the out parameter:

```
Console.WriteLine("***** Fun with Methods *****");

// No need to assign initial value to local variables
// used as output parameters, provided the first time
// you use them is as output arguments.
// C# 7 allows for out parameters to be declared in the method call
AddUsingOutParam(90, 90, out int ans);
Console.WriteLine("90 + 90 = {0}", ans);
Console.ReadLine();
```

The previous example is intended to be illustrative in nature; you really have no reason to return the value of your summation using an output parameter. However, the C# out modifier does serve a useful purpose: it allows the caller to obtain multiple outputs from a single method invocation.

```
// Returning multiple output parameters.
static void FillTheseValues(out int , out string b, out bool c)
{
  a = 9;
  b = "Enjoy your string.";
  c = true;
}
```

The caller would be able to invoke the FillTheseValues() method. Remember that you must use the out modifier when you invoke the method, as well as when you implement the method.

```
Console.WriteLine("***** Fun with Methods *****");
FillTheseValues(out int i, out string str, out bool b);

Console.WriteLine("Int is: {0}", i);
Console.WriteLine("String is: {0}", str);
Console.WriteLine("Boolean is: {0}", b);
Console.ReadLine();
```

■ **Note** C# 7 also introduced tuples, which are another way to return multiple values out of a method call. You will learn more about that later in this chapter.

Always remember that a method that defines output parameters must assign the parameter to a valid value before exiting the method scope. Therefore, the following code will result in a compiler error, as the output parameter has not been assigned within the method scope:

```
static void ThisWontCompile(out int a)
{
  Console.WriteLine("Error! Forgot to assign output arg!");
}
```

Discarding out Parameters (New 7.0)

If you do not care about the value of an out parameter, you can use a discard as a placeholder. Discards are temporary, dummy variables that are intentionally unused. They are unassigned, do not have a value, and might not even allocate any memory. This can provide a performance benefit as well as make your code more readable. Discards can be used with out parameters, with tuples (later in this chapter), with pattern matching (Chapters 6 and 8), or even as stand-alone variables.

For example, if you want to get the value for the int in the previous example but do not care about the second two parameters, you can write the following code:

```
//This only gets the value for a, and ignores the other two parameters
FillTheseValues(out int a, out _, out _);
```

Note that the called method is still doing the work setting the values for all three parameters; it is just that the last two parameters are being *discarded* when the method call returns.

The out Modifier in Constructors and Initializers (New 7.3)

C# 7.3 extended the allowable locations for using the out parameter. In addition to methods, parameters for constructors, field and property initializers, and query clauses can all be decorated with the out modifier. Examples of these will be examined later in this book.

Using the ref Modifier

Now consider the use of the C# ref parameter modifier. Reference parameters are necessary when you want to allow a method to operate on (and usually change the values of) various data points declared in the caller's scope (such as a sorting or swapping routine). Note the distinction between output and reference parameters:

- Output parameters do not need to be initialized before they are passed to the method. The reason for this is that the method must assign output parameters before exiting.
- Reference parameters must be initialized before they are passed to the method. The reason for this is that you are passing a reference to an existing variable. If you do not assign it to an initial value, that would be the equivalent of operating on an unassigned local variable.

Let's check out the use of the ref keyword by way of a method that swaps two string variables (of course, any two data types could be used here, including int, bool, float, etc.).

```
// Reference parameters.
public static void SwapStrings(ref string s1, ref string s2)
{
  string tempStr = s1;
  s1 = s2;
  s2 = tempStr;
}
```

This method can be called as follows:

```
Console.WriteLine("***** Fun with Methods *****");

string str1 = "Flip";
string str2 = "Flop";
Console.WriteLine("Before: {0}, {1} ", str1, str2);
SwapStrings(ref str1, ref str2);
Console.WriteLine("After: {0}, {1} ", str1, str2);
Console.ReadLine();
```

Here, the caller has assigned an initial value to local string data (`str1` and `str2`). After the call to `SwapStrings()` returns, `str1` now contains the value `"Flop"`, while `str2` reports the value `"Flip"`.

```
Before: Flip, Flop

After: Flop, Flip
```

Using the in Modifier (New 7.2)

The `in` modifier passes a value by reference (for both value and reference types) and prevents the called method from modifying the values. This clearly states a design intent in your code, as well as potentially reducing memory pressure. When value types are passed by value, they are copied (internally) by the called method. If the object is large (such as a large struct), the extra overhead of making a copy for local use can be significant. Also, even when reference types are passed without a modifier, they can be modified by the called method. Both issues can be resolved using the `in` modifier.

Revisiting the `Add()` method from earlier, there are two lines of code that modify the parameters, but do not affect the values for the calling method. The values are not affected because the `Add()` method makes a copy of the variables `x` and `y` to use locally. While the calling method does not have any adverse side effects, what if the `Add()` method was changed to the following code?

```
static int Add2(int x,int y)
{
  x = 10000;
  y = 88888;
  int ans = x + y;
  return ans;
}
```

Running this code then returns 98888, regardless of the numbers sent into the method. This is obviously a problem. To correct this, update the method to the following:

```
static int AddReadOnly(in int x,in int y)
{
  //Error CS8331 Cannot assign to variable 'in int' because it is a readonly variable
  //x = 10000;
  //y = 88888;
  int ans = x + y;
  return ans;
}
```

When the code attempts to change the values of the parameters, the compiler raises the CS8331 error, indicating that the values cannot be modified because of the in modifier.

Using the params Modifier

C# supports the use of *parameter arrays* using the params keyword. The params keyword allows you to pass into a method a variable number of identically typed parameters (or classes related by inheritance) as a *single logical parameter*. As well, arguments marked with the params keyword can be processed if the caller sends in a strongly typed array or a comma-delimited list of items. Yes, this can be confusing! To clear things up, assume you want to create a function that allows the caller to pass in any number of arguments and return the calculated average.

If you were to prototype this method to take an array of doubles, this would force the caller to first define the array, then fill the array, and finally pass it into the method. However, if you define CalculateAverage() to take a params of double[] data types, the caller can simply pass a comma-delimited list of doubles. The list of doubles will be packaged into an array of doubles behind the scenes.

```
// Return average of "some number" of doubles.
static double CalculateAverage(params double[] values)
{
  Console.WriteLine("You sent me {0} doubles.", values.Length);

  double sum = 0;
  if(values.Length == 0)
  {
    return sum;
  }
  for (int i = 0; i < values.Length; i++)
  {
    sum += values[i];
  }
  return (sum / values.Length);
}
```

This method has been defined to take a parameter array of doubles. What this method is in fact saying is "Send me any number of doubles (including zero), and I'll compute the average." Given this, you can call CalculateAverage() in any of the following ways:

```
Console.WriteLine("***** Fun with Methods *****");

// Pass in a comma-delimited list of doubles...
double average;
average = CalculateAverage(4.0, 3.2, 5.7, 64.22, 87.2);
Console.WriteLine("Average of data is: {0}", average);
```

```
// ...or pass an array of doubles.
double[] data = { 4.0, 3.2, 5.7 };
average = CalculateAverage(data);
Console.WriteLine("Average of data is: {0}", average);

// Average of 0 is 0!
Console.WriteLine("Average of data is: {0}", CalculateAverage());
Console.ReadLine();
```

If you did not make use of the params modifier in the definition of CalculateAverage(), the first invocation of this method would result in a compiler error, as the compiler would be looking for a version of CalculateAverage() that took five double arguments.

■ **Note** To avoid any ambiguity, C# demands a method support only a single params argument, which must be the final argument in the parameter list.

As you might guess, this technique is nothing more than a convenience for the caller, given that the array is created by the .NET Core Runtime as necessary. By the time the array is within the scope of the method being called, you can treat it as a full-blown .NET Core array that contains all the functionality of the System.Array base class library type. Consider the following output:

```
You sent me 5 doubles.

Average of data is: 32.864
You sent me 3 doubles.
Average of data is: 4.3
You sent me 0 doubles.
Average of data is: 0
```

Defining Optional Parameters

C# allows you to create methods that can take *optional arguments*. This technique allows the caller to invoke a single method while omitting arguments deemed unnecessary, provided the caller is happy with the specified defaults.

To illustrate working with optional arguments, assume you have a method named EnterLogData(), which defines a single optional parameter.

```
static void EnterLogData(string message, string owner = "Programmer")
{
  Console.WriteLine("Error: {0}", message);
  Console.WriteLine("Owner of Error: {0}", owner);
}
```

Here, the final string argument has been assigned the default value of "Programmer" via an assignment within the parameter definition. Given this, you can call EnterLogData() in two ways.

```
Console.WriteLine("***** Fun with Methods *****");
...
EnterLogData("Oh no! Grid can't find data");
EnterLogData("Oh no! I can't find the payroll data", "CFO");

Console.ReadLine();
```

Because the first invocation of EnterLogData() did not specify a second string argument, you would find that the programmer is the one responsible for losing data for the grid, while the CFO misplaced the payroll data (as specified by the second argument in the second method call).

One important thing to be aware of is that the value assigned to an optional parameter must be known at compile time and cannot be resolved at runtime (if you attempt to do so, you will receive compile-time errors!). To illustrate, assume you want to update EnterLogData() with the following extra optional parameter:

```
// Error! The default value for an optional arg must be known
// at compile time!
static void EnterLogData(string message, string owner = "Programmer", DateTime timeStamp =
DateTime.Now)
{
  Console.WriteLine("Error: {0}", message);
  Console.WriteLine("Owner of Error: {0}", owner);
  Console.WriteLine("Time of Error: {0}", timeStamp);
}
```

This will not compile because the value of the Now property of the DateTime class is resolved at runtime, not compile time.

■ **Note** To avoid ambiguity, optional parameters must always be placed at the *end* of a method signature. It is a compiler error to have optional parameters listed before nonoptional parameters.

Using Named Arguments (Updated 7.2)

Another language feature found in C# is support for *named arguments*. Named arguments allow you to invoke a method by specifying parameter values in any order you choose. Thus, rather than passing parameters solely by position (as you will do in most cases), you can choose to specify each argument by name using a colon operator. To illustrate the use of named arguments, assume you have added the following method to the Program.cs file:

```
static void DisplayFancyMessage(ConsoleColor textColor,
  ConsoleColor backgroundColor, string message)
{
  // Store old colors to restore after message is printed.
  ConsoleColor oldTextColor = Console.ForegroundColor;
  ConsoleColor oldbackgroundColor = Console.BackgroundColor;
  // Set new colors and print message.
  Console.ForegroundColor = textColor;
  Console.BackgroundColor = backgroundColor;
  Console.WriteLine(message);
```

```
  // Restore previous colors.
  Console.ForegroundColor = oldTextColor;
  Console.BackgroundColor = oldbackgroundColor;
}
```

Now, the way DisplayFancyMessage() was written, you would expect the caller to invoke this method by passing two ConsoleColor variables followed by a string type. However, using named arguments, the following calls are completely fine:

```
Console.WriteLine("***** Fun with Methods *****");

DisplayFancyMessage(message: "Wow! Very Fancy indeed!",
  textColor: ConsoleColor.DarkRed,
  backgroundColor: ConsoleColor.White);

DisplayFancyMessage(backgroundColor: ConsoleColor.Green,
  message: "Testing...",
  textColor: ConsoleColor.DarkBlue);
Console.ReadLine();
```

The rules for using named arguments were updated slightly with C# 7.2. Prior to 7.2, if you begin to invoke a method using positional parameters, you must list them before any named parameters. With 7.2 and later versions of C#, named and unnamed parameters can be mingled if the parameters are in the correct position.

■ **Note** Just because you can mix and match named arguments with positional arguments in C# 7.2 and later, it's not considered a good idea. Just because you can does not mean you should!

The following code is an example:

```
// This is OK, as positional args are listed before named args.
DisplayFancyMessage(ConsoleColor.Blue,
  message: "Testing...",
  backgroundColor: ConsoleColor.White);

// This is OK, all arguments are in the correct order
DisplayFancyMessage(textColor: ConsoleColor.White, backgroundColor:ConsoleColor.Blue,
"Testing...");

// This is an ERROR, as positional args are listed after named args.
DisplayFancyMessage(message: "Testing...",
  backgroundColor: ConsoleColor.White,
  ConsoleColor.Blue);
```

This restriction aside, you might still be wondering when you would ever want to use this language feature. After all, if you need to specify three arguments to a method, why bother flipping around their positions?

Well, as it turns out, if you have a method that defines optional arguments, this feature can be helpful. Assume DisplayFancyMessage() has been rewritten to now support optional arguments, as you have assigned fitting defaults.

```
static void DisplayFancyMessage(ConsoleColor textColor = ConsoleColor.Blue,
  ConsoleColor backgroundColor = ConsoleColor.White,
  string message = "Test Message")
{
   ...
}
```

Given that each argument has a default value, named arguments allow the caller to specify only the parameters for which they do not want to receive the defaults. Therefore, if the caller wants the value "Hello!" to appear in blue text surrounded by a white background, they can simply specify the following:

```
DisplayFancyMessage(message: "Hello!");
```

Or, if the caller wants to see "Test Message" print out with a green background containing blue text, they can invoke the following:

```
DisplayFancyMessage(backgroundColor: ConsoleColor.Green);
```

As you can see, optional arguments and named parameters tend to work hand in hand. To wrap up your examination of building C# methods, I need to address the topic of *method overloading*.

Understanding Method Overloading

Like other modern object-oriented languages, C# allows a method to be *overloaded*. Simply put, when you define a set of identically named methods that differ by the number (or type) of parameters, the method in question is said to be *overloaded*.

To understand why overloading is so useful, consider life as an old-school Visual Basic 6.0 (VB6) developer. Assume you are using VB6 to build a set of methods that return the sum of various incoming data types (Integers, Doubles, etc.). Given that VB6 does not support method overloading, you would be required to define a unique set of methods that essentially do the same thing (return the sum of the arguments).

```
' VB6 code examples.
Public Function AddInts(ByVal x As Integer, ByVal y As Integer) As Integer
  AddInts = x + y
End Function

Public Function AddDoubles(ByVal x As Double, ByVal y As Double) As Double
  AddDoubles = x + y
End Function

Public Function AddLongs(ByVal x As Long, ByVal y As Long) As Long
  AddLongs = x + y
End Function
```

Not only can code such as this become tough to maintain, but the caller must now be painfully aware of the name of each method. Using overloading, you can allow the caller to call a single method named Add(). Again, the key is to ensure that each version of the method has a distinct set of arguments (methods differing only by return type are not unique enough).

■ **Note** As will be explained in Chapter 10, it is possible to build generic methods that take the concept of overloading to the next level. Using generics, you can define *type placeholders* for a method implementation that are specified at the time you invoke the member in question.

To check this out firsthand, create a new Console Application project named FunWithMethodOverloading. Add a new class named AddOperations.cs, and update the code to the following:

```
namespace FunWithMethodOverloading;
// C# code.
// Overloaded Add() method.

public static class AddOperations
{
  // Overloaded Add() method.
  public static int Add(int x, int y)
  {
    return x + y;
  }
  public static double Add(double x, double y)
  {
    return x + y;
  }
  public static long Add(long x, long y)
  {
    return x + y;
  }
}
```

Replace the code in the Program.cs file with the following:

```
using static FunWithMethodOverloading.AddOperations;

Console.WriteLine("***** Fun with Method Overloading *****\n");

// Calls int version of Add()
Console.WriteLine(Add(10, 10));

// Calls long version of Add() (using the new digit separator)
Console.WriteLine(Add(900_000_000_000, 900_000_000_000));

// Calls double version of Add()
Console.WriteLine(Add(4.3, 4.4));

Console.ReadLine();
```

■ **Note** The `using static` statement will be covered in Chapter 5. For now, consider it a keyboard shortcut for using methods containing a static class named AddOperations in the FunWithMethodOverloading namespace.

The top-level statements called three different versions of the Add method, each using a different data type.

Both Visual Studio and Visual Studio Code help when calling overloaded methods to boot. When you type in the name of an overloaded method (such as your good friend Console.WriteLine()), IntelliSense will list each version of the method in question. Note that you can cycle through each version of an overloaded method using the up and down arrow keys, as indicated in Figure 4-1 (Visual Studio) and Figure 4-2 (Visual Studio Code).

***Figure 4-1.** Visual Studio IntelliSense for overloaded methods*

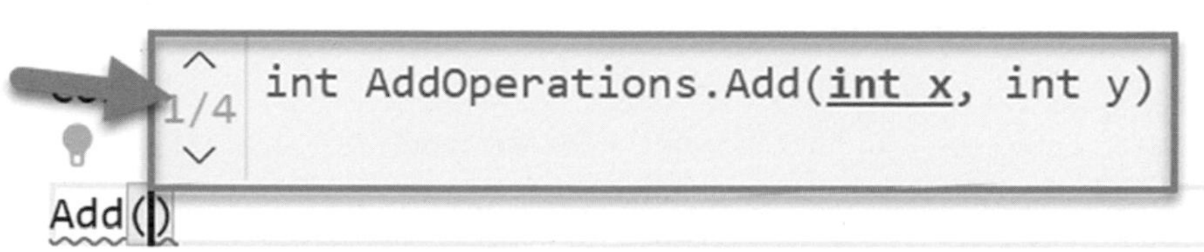

***Figure 4-2.** Visual Studio Code IntelliSense for overloaded methods*

If your overload has optional parameters, then the compiler will pick the method that is the best match for the calling code, based on named and/or positional arguments. Add the following method:

```
static int Add(int x, int y, int z = 0)
{
  return x + (y*z);
}
```

If the optional argument is not passed in by the caller, the compiler will match the first signature (the one without the optional parameter). While there is a rule set for method location, it is generally not a good idea to create methods that differ only on the optional parameters.

Finally, in, ref, and out are not considered as part of the signature for method overloading when more than one modifier is used. In other words, the following overloads will throw a compiler error:

```
static int Add(ref int x) { /* */ }
static int Add(out int x) { /* */ }
```

However, if only one method uses in, ref, or out, the compiler can distinguish between the signatures. So, this is allowed:

```
static int Add(ref int x) { /* */ }
static int Add(int x) { /* */ }
```

That wraps up the initial examination of building methods using the syntax of C#. Next, let's check out how to build and manipulate enumerations and structures.

Checking Parameters for Null (Updated 10.0)

If a method parameter is nullable (e.g., a reference type–like `string`) and required by the method body, it is considered a good programming practice to check that the parameter is not `null` before using it. If it is null, the method should throw an `ArgumentNullException`. Consider the following update to the `EnterLogData()` method that does just that (change is in bold):

```
static void EnterLogData(string message, string owner = "Programmer")
{
  if (message == null)
  {
    throw new ArgumentNullException(message);
  }
  Console.WriteLine("Error: {0}", message);
  Console.WriteLine("Owner of Error: {0}", owner);
}
```

Introduced in C# 10, the `ArgumentNullException` has an extension method to do this in one line of code:

```
static void EnterLogData(string message, string owner = "Programmer")
{
  ArgumentNullException.ThrowIfNull(message);
  Console.WriteLine("Error: {0}", message);
  Console.WriteLine("Owner of Error: {0}", owner);
}
```

■ **Note** Exceptions are covered in Chapter 7, and extension methods are covered in Chapter 11.

Enabling nullable reference types (covered later in this chapter) helps to ensure required reference types are not null.

Understanding the enum Type

Recall from Chapter 1 that the .NET Core type system is composed of classes, structures, enumerations, interfaces, and delegates. To begin exploration of these types, let's check out the role of the *enumeration* (or simply, `enum`) using a new Console Application project named FunWithEnums.

■ **Note** Do not confuse the term *enum* with *enumerator*; they are completely different concepts. An enum is a custom data type of name-value pairs. An enumerator is a class or structure that implements a .NET Core interface named `IEnumerable`. Typically, this interface is implemented on collection classes, as well as the `System.Array` class. As you will see in Chapter 8, objects that support `IEnumerable` can work within the `foreach` loop.

When building a system, it is often convenient to create a set of symbolic names that map to known numerical values. For example, if you are creating a payroll system, you might want to refer to the type of employees using constants such as vice president, manager, contractor, and grunt. C# supports the notion of custom enumerations for this very reason. For example, here is an enumeration named EmpTypeEnum (you can define this in the same file as your top-level statements, if it is placed at the end of the file):

```
Console.WriteLine("**** Fun with Enums *****\n");
Console.ReadLine();

//local functions go here:

// A custom enumeration.
enum EmpTypeEnum
{
  Manager,      // = 0
  Grunt,        // = 1
  Contractor,   // = 2
  VicePresident // = 3
}
```

■ **Note** By convention, enum types are usually suffixed with Enum. This is not necessary but makes for more readable code.

The EmpTypeEnum enumeration defines four named constants, corresponding to discrete numerical values. By default, the first element is set to the value zero (0), followed by an n+1 progression. You are free to change the initial value as you see fit. For example, if it made sense to number the members of EmpTypeEnum as 102 through 105, you could do so as follows:

```
// Begin with 102.
enum EmpTypeEnum
{
  Manager = 102,
  Grunt,        // = 103
  Contractor,   // = 104
  VicePresident // = 105
}
```

Enumerations do not necessarily need to follow a sequential ordering and do not need to have unique values. If (for some reason or another) it makes sense to establish your EmpTypeEnum as shown here, the compiler continues to be happy:

```
// Elements of an enumeration need not be sequential!
enum EmpTypeEnum
{
  Manager = 10,
  Grunt = 1,
  Contractor = 100,
  VicePresident = 9
}
```

Controlling the Underlying Storage for an enum

By default, the storage type used to hold the values of an enumeration is a `System.Int32` (the C# `int`); however, you are free to change this to your liking. C# enumerations can be defined in a similar manner for any of the core system types (`byte`, `short`, `int`, or `long`). For example, if you want to set the underlying storage value of `EmpTypeEnum` to be a `byte` rather than an `int`, you can write the following:

```
// This time, EmpTypeEnum maps to an underlying byte.
enum EmpTypeEnum : byte
{
  Manager = 10,
  Grunt = 1,
  Contractor = 100,
  VicePresident = 9
}
```

Changing the underlying type of an enumeration can be helpful if you are building a .NET Core application that will be deployed to a low-memory device and need to conserve memory wherever possible. Of course, if you do establish your enumeration to use a `byte` as storage, each value must be within its range! For example, the following version of `EmpTypeEnum` will result in a compiler error, as the value 999 cannot fit within the range of a byte:

```
// Compile-time error! 999 is too big for a byte!
enum EmpTypeEnum : byte
{
  Manager = 10,
  Grunt = 1,
  Contractor = 100,
  VicePresident = 999
}
```

Declaring enum Variables

Once you have established the range and storage type of your enumeration, you can use it in place of so-called magic numbers. Because enumerations are nothing more than a user-defined data type, you can use them as function return values, method parameters, local variables, and so forth. Assume you have a method named `AskForBonus()`, taking an `EmpTypeEnum` variable as the sole parameter. Based on the value of the incoming parameter, you will print out a fitting response to the pay bonus request.

```
Console.WriteLine("**** Fun with Enums *****");
// Make an EmpTypeEnum variable.
EmpTypeEnum emp = EmpTypeEnum.Contractor;
AskForBonus(emp);
Console.ReadLine();

// Enums as parameters.
static void AskForBonus(EmpTypeEnum e)
{
  switch (e)
  {
    case EmpTypeEnum.Manager:
```

```
      Console.WriteLine("How about stock options instead?");
      break;
    case EmpTypeEnum.Grunt:
      Console.WriteLine("You have got to be kidding...");
      break;
    case EmpTypeEnum.Contractor:
      Console.WriteLine("You already get enough cash...");
      break;
    case EmpTypeEnum.VicePresident:
      Console.WriteLine("VERY GOOD, Sir!");
      break;
  }
}
```

Notice that when you are assigning a value to an enum variable, you must scope the enum name (EmpTypeEnum) to the value (Grunt). Because enumerations are a fixed set of name-value pairs, it is illegal to set an enum variable to a value that is not defined directly by the enumerated type.

```
static void ThisMethodWillNotCompile()
{
  // Error! SalesManager is not in the EmpTypeEnum enum!
  EmpTypeEnum emp = EmpTypeEnum.SalesManager;

  // Error! Forgot to scope Grunt value to EmpTypeEnum enum!
  emp = Grunt;
}
```

Using the System.Enum Type

The interesting thing about .NET Core enumerations is that they gain functionality from the System.Enum class type. This class defines several methods that allow you to interrogate and transform a given enumeration. One helpful method is the static Enum.GetUnderlyingType(), which, as the name implies, returns the data type used to store the values of the enumerated type (System.Byte in the case of the current EmpTypeEnum declaration).

```
Console.WriteLine("**** Fun with Enums *****");
...

// Print storage for the enum.
Console.WriteLine("EmpTypeEnum uses a {0} for storage",
  Enum.GetUnderlyingType(emp.GetType()));
Console.ReadLine();
```

The Enum.GetUnderlyingType() method requires you to pass in a System.Type as the first parameter. As fully examined in Chapter 17, Type represents the metadata description of a given .NET Core entity.

One possible way to obtain metadata (as shown previously) is to use the GetType() method, which is common to all types in the .NET Core base class libraries. Another approach is to use the C# typeof operator. One benefit of doing so is that you do not need to have a variable of the entity you want to obtain a metadata description of.

```
// This time use typeof to extract a Type.
Console.WriteLine("EmpTypeEnum uses a {0} for storage",
    Enum.GetUnderlyingType(typeof(EmpTypeEnum)));
```

Dynamically Discovering an enum's Name-Value Pairs

Beyond the `Enum.GetUnderlyingType()` method, all C# enumerations support a method named `ToString()`, which returns the string name of the current enumeration's value. The following code is an example:

```
EmpTypeEnum emp = EmpTypeEnum.Contractor;
...
// Prints out "emp is a Contractor".
Console.WriteLine("emp is a {0}.", emp.ToString());
Console.ReadLine();
```

If you are interested in discovering the value of a given enumeration variable, rather than its name, you can simply cast the enum variable against the underlying storage type. The following is an example:

```
Console.WriteLine("**** Fun with Enums *****");
EmpTypeEnum emp = EmpTypeEnum.Contractor;
...
// Prints out "Contractor = 100".
Console.WriteLine("{0} = {1}", emp.ToString(), (byte)emp);
Console.ReadLine();
```

■ **Note** The static `Enum.Format()` method provides a finer level of formatting options by specifying a desired format flag. Consult the documentation for a full list of formatting flags.

`System.Enum` also defines another static method named `GetValues()`. This method returns an instance of `System.Array`. Each item in the array corresponds to a member of the specified enumeration. Consider the following method, which will print out each name-value pair within any enumeration you pass in as a parameter:

```
// This method will print out the details of any enum.
static void EvaluateEnum(System.Enum e)
{
  Console.WriteLine("=> Information about {0}", e.GetType().Name);

  Console.WriteLine("Underlying storage type: {0}",
    Enum.GetUnderlyingType(e.GetType()));

  // Get all name-value pairs for incoming parameter.
  Array enumData = Enum.GetValues(e.GetType());
  Console.WriteLine("This enum has {0} members.", enumData.Length);

  // Now show the string name and associated value, using the D format
  // flag (see Chapter 3).
  for(int i = 0; i < enumData.Length; i++)
```

```
  {
    Console.WriteLine("Name: {0}, Value: {0:D}",
      enumData.GetValue(i));
  }
}
```

To test this new method, update your code to create variables of several enumeration types declared in the System namespace (as well as an EmpTypeEnum enumeration for good measure). The following code is an example:

```
Console.WriteLine("**** Fun with Enums *****");
...
EmpTypeEnum e2 = EmpTypeEnum.Contractor;

// These types are enums in the System namespace.
DayOfWeek day = DayOfWeek.Monday;
ConsoleColor cc = ConsoleColor.Gray;

EvaluateEnum(e2);
EvaluateEnum(day);
EvaluateEnum(cc);
Console.ReadLine();
```

Some partial output is shown here:

```
=> Information about DayOfWeek

Underlying storage type: System.Int32
This enum has 7 members.
Name: Sunday, Value: 0
Name: Monday, Value: 1
Name: Tuesday, Value: 2
Name: Wednesday, Value: 3
Name: Thursday, Value: 4
Name: Friday, Value: 5
Name: Saturday, Value: 6
```

As you will see over the course of this text, enumerations are used extensively throughout the .NET Core base class libraries. When you make use of any enumeration, always remember that you can interact with the name-value pairs using the members of System.Enum.

Using Enums, Flags, and Bitwise Operations

Bitwise operations provide a fast mechanism for operating on binary numbers at the bit level. Table 4-3 contains the C# bitwise operators, what they do, and an example of each.

Table 4-3. Bitwise Operations

Operator	Operation	Example
& (AND)	Copies a bit if it exists in both operands	0110 & 0100 = 0100 (4)
| (OR)	Copies a bit if it exists in both operands	0110 | 0100 = 0110 (6)
^ (XOR)	Copies a bit if it exists in one but not both operands	0110 ^ 0100 = 0010 (2)
~ (ones' compliment)	Flips the bits	~0110 = -7 (due to overflow)
<< (left shift)	Shifts the bits left	0110 << 1 = 1100 (12)
>> (right shift)	Shifts the bits right	0110 >> 1 = 0011 (3)

To show these in action, create a new Console Application project named FunWithBitwiseOperations. Update the `Program.cs` file to the following code:

```
using FunWithBitwiseOperations;
Console.WriteLine("===== Fun wih Bitwise Operations");
Console.WriteLine("6 & 4 = {0} | {1}", 6 & 4, Convert.ToString((6 & 4),2));
Console.WriteLine("6 | 4 = {0} | {1}", 6 | 4, Convert.ToString((6 | 4),2));
Console.WriteLine("6 ^ 4 = {0} | {1}", 6 ^ 4, Convert.ToString((6 ^ 4),2));
Console.WriteLine("6 << 1  = {0} | {1}", 6 << 1, Convert.ToString((6 << 1),2));
Console.WriteLine("6 >> 1 = {0} | {1}", 6 >> 1, Convert.ToString((6 >> 1),2));
Console.WriteLine("~6 = {0} | {1}", ~6, Convert.ToString(~((short)6),2));
Console.WriteLine("Int.MaxValue {0}", Convert.ToString((int.MaxValue),2));
Console.readLine();
```

When you execute the code, you will see the following result:

```
===== Fun wih Bitwise Operations
6 & 4 = 4 | 100
6 | 4 = 6 | 110
6 ^ 4 = 2 | 10
6 << 1  = 12 | 1100
6 >> 1 = 3 | 11
~6 =  -7 | 11111111111111111111111111111001
Int.MaxValue 1111111111111111111111111111111
```

Now that you know the basics of bitwise operations, it is time to apply them to enums. Add a new file named `ContactPreferenceEnum.cs` and update the code to the following:

```
namespace FunWithBitwiseOperations
{
  [Flags]
  public enum ContactPreferenceEnum
  {
    None = 1,
    Email = 2,
    Phone = 4,
    Ponyexpress = 6
  }
}
```

Notice the Flags attribute. This allows multiple values from an enum to be combined into a single variable. For example, Email and Phone can be combined like this:

```
ContactPreferenceEnum emailAndPhone = ContactPreferenceEnum.Email |
ContactPreferenceEnum.Phone;
```

This allows you to check if one of the values exists in the combined value. For example, if you want to check to see which ContactPreference value is in emailAndPhone variable, you can use the following code:

```
Console.WriteLine("None? {0}", (emailAndPhone | ContactPreferenceEnum.None) == emailAndPhone);
Console.WriteLine("Email? {0}", (emailAndPhone | ContactPreferenceEnum.Email) == emailAndPhone);
Console.WriteLine("Phone? {0}", (emailAndPhone | ContactPreferenceEnum.Phone) == emailAndPhone);
Console.WriteLine("Text? {0}", (emailAndPhone | ContactPreferenceEnum.Text) == emailAndPhone);
```

When executed, the following is presented to the console window:

```
None? False
Email? True
Phone? True
Text? False
```

Understanding the Structure

Now that you understand the role of enumeration types, let's examine the use of .NET Core *structures* (or simply *structs*). Structure types are well suited for modeling mathematical, geometrical, and other "atomic" entities in your application. A structure (such as an enumeration) is a user-defined type; however, structures are not simply a collection of name-value pairs. Rather, structures are types that can contain any number of data fields and members that operate on these fields.

■ **Note** If you have a background in OOP, you can think of a structure as a "lightweight class type," given that structures provide a way to define a type that supports encapsulation but cannot be used to build a family of related types. They can't inherit from other class or structure types and can't be the base of a class. Inheritance is covered in Chapter 5. Structures can implement interfaces, which are covered in Chapter 8. When you need to build a family of related types through inheritance, you will need to make use of class types.

On the surface, the process of defining and using structures is simple, but as they say, the devil is in the details. To begin understanding the basics of structure types, create a new project named FunWithStructures. In C#, structures are defined using the struct keyword. Define a new structure named Point, which defines two member variables of type int and a set of methods to interact with said data.

```
struct Point
{
  // Fields of the structure.
  public int X;
  public int Y;

  // Add 1 to the (X, Y) position.
  public void Increment()
```

```
  {
    X++; Y++;
  }

  // Subtract 1 from the (X, Y) position.
  public void Decrement()
  {
    X--; Y--;
  }

  // Display the current position.
  public void Display()
  {
    Console.WriteLine("X = {0}, Y = {1}", X, Y);
  }
}
```

Here, you have defined your two integer fields (X and Y) using the public keyword, which is an access control modifier (Chapter 5 continues this discussion). Declaring data with the public keyword ensures the caller has direct access to the data from a given Point variable (via the dot operator).

■ **Note** It is typically considered bad style to define public data within a class or structure. Rather, you will want to define *private* data, which can be accessed and changed using *public* properties. These details will be examined in Chapter 5.

Here is code that takes the Point type out for a test-drive:

```
Console.WriteLine("***** A First Look at Structures *****\n");

// Create an initial Point.
Point myPoint;
myPoint.X = 349;
myPoint.Y = 76;
myPoint.Display();

// Adjust the X and Y values.
myPoint.Increment();
myPoint.Display();
Console.ReadLine();
```

The output is as you would expect.

```
***** A First Look at Structures *****

X = 349, Y = 76
X = 350, Y = 77
```

There are some rules regarding structures. First, a structure can't inherit from other class or structure types and can't be the base of a class. Structures can implement interfaces.

Creating Structure Variables

When you want to create a structure variable, you have a variety of options. Here, you simply create a Point variable and assign each piece of public field data before invoking its members. If you do *not* assign each piece of public field data (X and Y in this case) before using the structure, you will receive a compiler error.

```
// Error! Did not assign Y value.
Point p1;
p1.X = 10;
p1.Display();

// OK! Both fields assigned before use.
Point p2;
p2.X = 10;
p2.Y = 10;
p2.Display();
```

As an alternative, you can create structure variables using the C# new keyword, which will invoke the structure's *default constructor*. By definition, a default constructor does not take any arguments. The benefit of invoking the default constructor of a structure is that each piece of field data is automatically set to its default value.

```
// Set all fields to default values
// using the default constructor.
Point p1 = new Point();

// Prints X=0,Y=0.
p1.Display();
```

Structure Constructors (Updated 10.0)

It is also possible to design a structure with a *custom constructor*. This allows you to specify the values of field data upon variable creation, rather than having to set each data member field by field. Chapter 5 will provide a detailed examination of constructors; however, to illustrate, update the Point structure with the following code:

```
struct Point
{
  // Fields of the structure.
  public int X;
  public int Y;

  // A custom constructor.
  public Point(int xPos, int yPos)
  {
    X = xPos;
    Y = yPos;
  }
...
}
```

With this, you could now create Point variables, as follows:

```
// Call custom constructor.
Point p2 = new Point(50, 60);

// Prints X=50,Y=60.
p2.Display();
```

Prior to C# 10, you could not declare a parameterless (i.e., default) constructor on a structure, as it was provided in the implementation of structure types. Now you can create Point variables, as follows:

```
// Call custom constructor.
Point p2 = new Point(50, 60);

// Prints X=50,Y=60.
p2.Display();
```

Regardless of which constructor you choose to add, prior to C# 10, you could not declare a parameterless (i.e., default) constructor on a structure, as it was provided in the implementation of structure types. Now, this is possible, as long as all value types are assigned a value before the code in the constructor end. With this, you can now update the Point structure to the following:

```
struct Point
{
//omitted for brevity
  //Parameterless constructor
  public Point()
  {
    X = 0;
    Y= 0;
  }
    // A custom constructor.
  public Point(int xPos, int yPos)
  {
    X = xPos;
    Y = yPos;
  }
}
```

■ **Note** C# 10 and .NET 6 introduce the record struct, which will be covered in Chapter 5.

Using Field Initializers (New 10.0)

New in C# 10, structure fields can be initialized when declared. Update the code to the following, which initializes X with a value of 5, and Y with a value of 7:

```
struct Point
{
    // Fields of the structure.
    public int X = 5;
```

```
    public int Y = 7;
//omitted for brevity
}
```

With this update, the parameterless constructor no longer needs to initialize the X and Y fields:

```
struct Point
{
  //omitted for brevity
  //Parameterless constructor
  public Point() { }
  //omitted for brevity
}
```

Using Read-Only Structs (New 7.2)

Structs can also be marked as read-only if there is a need for them to be *immutable*. Immutable objects must be set up at construction and because they cannot be changed, can be more performant. When declaring a struct as read-only, all the properties must also be read-only. But you might ask, how can a property be set (as all properties must be on a struct) if it is read-only? The answer is that the value must be set during the construction of the struct.

Update the point class to the following example:

```
readonly struct ReadOnlyPoint
{
  // Fields of the structure.
  public int X {get; }
  public int Y { get; }

  // Display the current position and name.
  public void Display()
  {
    Console.WriteLine($"X = {X}, Y = {Y}");
  }

  public ReadOnlyPoint(int xPos, int yPos)
  {
    X = xPos;
    Y = yPos;
  }
}
```

The Increment and Decrement methods have been removed since the variables are read-only. Notice also the two properties, X and Y. Instead of setting them up as fields, they are created as read-only automatic properties. Automatic properties are covered in Chapter 5.

Using Read-Only Members (New 8.0)

New in C# 8.0, you can declare individual fields of a struct as `readonly`. This is more granular than making the entire struct read-only. The `readonly` modifier can be applied to methods, properties, and property accessors. Add the following struct code to your file, outside of the `Program.cs` file:

```
struct PointWithReadOnly
{
  // Fields of the structure.
  public int X;
  public readonly int Y;
  public readonly string Name;

  // Display the current position and name.
  public readonly void Display()
  {
    Console.WriteLine($"X = {X}, Y = {Y}, Name = {Name}");
  }

  // A custom constructor.
  public PointWithReadOnly(int xPos, int yPos, string name)
  {
    X = xPos;
    Y = yPos;
    Name = name;
  }
}
```

To use this new struct, add the following to the top-level statements:

```
PointWithReadOnly p3 =
  new PointWithReadOnly(50,60,"Point w/RO");
p3.Display();
```

Using ref Structs (New 7.2)

Also added in C# 7.2, the `ref` modifier can be used when defining a struct. This requires all instances of the struct to be stack allocated and cannot be assigned as a property of another class. The technical reason for this is that `ref` structs cannot referenced from the heap. The difference between the stack and the heap is covered in the next section.

These are some additional limitations of `ref` structs:

- They cannot be assigned to a variable of type object or dynamic, and they cannot be an interface type.
- They cannot implement interfaces.
- They cannot be used as a property of a non-`ref` struct.
- They cannot be used in async methods, iterators, lambda expressions, or local functions.

The following code, which creates a simple struct and then attempts to create a property in that struct typed to a `ref` struct, will not compile:

```
struct NormalPoint
{
  //This does not compile
  public PointWithRef PropPointer { get; set; }
}
```

Note that the `readonly` and `ref` modifiers can be combined to gain the benefits and restrictions of both.

Using Disposable ref Structs (New 8.0)

As covered in the previous section, `ref` structs (and read-only `ref` structs) cannot implement an interface and therefore cannot implement `IDisposable`. New in C# 8.0, `ref` structs and read-only `ref` structs can be made disposable by adding a `public void Dispose()` method.

Add the following struct definition to the `Program.cs` file:

```
ref struct DisposableRefStruct
{
  public int X;
  public readonly int Y;
  public readonly void Display()
  {
    Console.WriteLine($"X = {X}, Y = {Y}");
  }
  // A custom constructor.
  public DisposableRefStruct(int xPos, int yPos)
  {
    X = xPos;
    Y = yPos;
    Console.WriteLine("Created!");
  }
  public void Dispose()
  {
    //clean up any resources here
    Console.WriteLine("Disposed!");
  }
}
```

Next, add the following to the end of the top-level statements to create and dispose of the new struct:

```
var s = new DisposableRefStruct(50, 60);
s.Display();
s.Dispose();
```

■ **Note** Object lifetime and disposing of objects are covered in depth in Chapter 9.

To deepen your understanding of stack and heap allocation, you need to explore the distinction between a .NET Core value type and a .NET Core reference type.

Understanding Value Types and Reference Types

■ **Note** The following discussion of value types and reference types assumes that you have a background in object-oriented programming. If this is not the case, you might want to skip to the "Understanding C# Nullable Types" section of this chapter and return to this section after you have read Chapters 5 and 6.

Unlike arrays, strings, or enumerations, C# structures do not have an identically named representation in the .NET Core library (i.e., there is no `System.Structure` class) but are implicitly derived from `System.ValueType`. The role of `System.ValueType` is to ensure that the derived type (e.g., any structure) is allocated on the *stack*, rather than the garbage-collected *heap*. Simply put, data allocated on the stack can be created and destroyed quickly, as its lifetime is determined by the defining scope. Heap-allocated data, on the other hand, is monitored by the .NET Core garbage collector and has a lifetime that is determined by many factors, which will be examined in Chapter 9.

Functionally, the only purpose of `System.ValueType` is to override the virtual methods defined by `System.Object` to use value-based versus reference-based semantics. As you might know, overriding is the process of changing the implementation of a virtual (or possibly abstract) method defined within a base class. The base class of `ValueType` is `System.Object`. In fact, the instance methods defined by `System.ValueType` are identical to those of `System.Object`.

```
// Structures and enumerations implicitly extend System.ValueType.
public abstract class ValueType : object
{
  public virtual bool Equals(object obj);
  public virtual int GetHashCode();
  public Type GetType();
  public virtual string ToString();
}
```

Given that value types are using value-based semantics, the lifetime of a structure (which includes all numerical data types [`int`, `float`], as well as any `enum` or structure) is predictable. When a structure variable falls out of the defining scope, it is removed from memory immediately.

```
// Local structures are popped off
// the stack when a method returns.
static void LocalValueTypes()
{
  // Recall! "int" is really a System.Int32 structure.
  int i = 0;

  // Recall! Point is a structure type.
  Point p = new Point();
} // "i" and "p" popped off the stack here!
```

Using Value Types, Reference Types, and the Assignment Operator

When you assign one value type to another, a member-by-member copy of the field data is achieved. In the case of a simple data type such as System.Int32, the only member to copy is the numerical value. However, in the case of your Point, the X and Y values are copied into the new structure variable. To illustrate, create a new Console Application project named FunWithValueAndReferenceTypes and then copy your previous Point definition into your new namespace. Next, add the following local function to your top-level statements:

```
// Assigning two intrinsic value types results in
// two independent variables on the stack.
static void ValueTypeAssignment()
{
  Console.WriteLine("Assigning value types\n");

  Point p1 = new Point(10, 10);
  Point p2 = p1;

  // Print both points.
  p1.Display();
  p2.Display();

  // Change p1.X and print again. p2.X is not changed.
  p1.X = 100;
  Console.WriteLine("\n=> Changed p1.X\n");
  p1.Display();
  p2.Display();
}
```

Here, you have created a variable of type Point (named p1) that is then assigned to another Point (p2). Because Point is a value type, you have two copies of the Point type on the stack, each of which can be independently manipulated. Therefore, when you change the value of p1.X, the value of p2.X is unaffected.

```
Assigning value types

X = 10, Y = 10
X = 10, Y = 10
=> Changed p1.X
X = 100, Y = 10
X = 10, Y = 10
```

In stark contrast to value types, when you apply the assignment operator to reference types (meaning all class instances), you are redirecting what the reference variable points to in memory. To illustrate, create a new class type named PointRef that has the same members as the Point structures, beyond renaming the constructor to match the class name.

```
// Classes are always reference types.
class PointRef
{
  // Same members as the Point structure...
  // Be sure to change your constructor name to PointRef!
```

```
  public PointRef(int xPos, int yPos)
  {
    X = xPos;
    Y = yPos;
  }
}
```

Now, use your PointRef type within the following new method. Note that beyond using the PointRef class, rather than the Point structure, the code is identical to the ValueTypeAssignment() method.

```
static void ReferenceTypeAssignment()
{
  Console.WriteLine("Assigning reference types\n");
  PointRef p1 = new PointRef(10, 10);
  PointRef p2 = p1;

  // Print both point refs.
  p1.Display();
  p2.Display();

  // Change p1.X and print again.
  p1.X = 100;
  Console.WriteLine("\n=> Changed p1.X\n");
  p1.Display();
  p2.Display();
}
```

In this case, you have two references pointing to the same object on the managed heap. Therefore, when you change the value of X using the p1 reference, p2.X reports the same value. Assuming you have called this new method, your output should look like the following:

```
Assigning reference types

X = 10, Y = 10
X = 10, Y = 10
=> Changed p1.X
X = 100, Y = 10
X = 100, Y = 10
```

Using Value Types Containing Reference Types

Now that you have a better feeling for the basic differences between value types and reference types, let's examine a more complex example. Assume you have the following reference (class) type that maintains an informational string that can be set using a custom constructor:

```
class ShapeInfo
{
  public string InfoString;
  public ShapeInfo(string info)
  {
```

```
    InfoString = info;
  }
}
```

Now assume that you want to contain a variable of this class type within a value type named Rectangle. To allow the caller to set the value of the inner ShapeInfo member variable, you also provide a custom constructor. Here is the complete definition of the Rectangle type:

```
struct Rectangle
{
  // The Rectangle structure contains a reference type member.
  public ShapeInfo RectInfo;

  public int RectTop, RectLeft, RectBottom, RectRight;

  public Rectangle(string info, int top, int left, int bottom, int right)
  {
    RectInfo = new ShapeInfo(info);
    RectTop = top; RectBottom = bottom;
    RectLeft = left; RectRight = right;
  }

  public void Display()
  {
    Console.WriteLine("String = {0}, Top = {1}, Bottom = {2}, " +
      "Left = {3}, Right = {4}",
        RectInfo.InfoString, RectTop, RectBottom, RectLeft, RectRight);
  }
}
```

At this point, you have contained a reference type within a value type. The million-dollar question now becomes "What happens if you assign one Rectangle variable to another?" Given what you already know about value types, you would be correct in assuming that the integer data (which is indeed a structure, System.Int32) should be an independent entity for each Rectangle variable. But what about the internal reference type? Will the object's *state* be fully copied, or will the reference to that object be copied? To answer this question, define the following method and invoke it:

```
static void ValueTypeContainingRefType()
{
  // Create the first Rectangle.
  Console.WriteLine("-> Creating r1");
  Rectangle r1 = new Rectangle("First Rect", 10, 10, 50, 50);

  // Now assign a new Rectangle to r1.
  Console.WriteLine("-> Assigning r2 to r1");
  Rectangle r2 = r1;

  // Change some values of r2.
  Console.WriteLine("-> Changing values of r2");
  r2.RectInfo.InfoString = "This is new info!";
  r2.RectBottom = 4444;
```

```
  // Print values of both rectangles.
  r1.Display();
  r2.Display();
}
```

The output is shown here:

```
-> Creating r1

-> Assigning r2 to r1
-> Changing values of r2
String = This is new info!, Top = 10, Bottom = 50, Left = 10, Right = 50
String = This is new info!, Top = 10, Bottom = 4444, Left = 10, Right = 50
```

As you can see, when you change the value of the informational string using the `r2` reference, the `r1` reference displays the same value. By default, when a value type contains other reference types, assignment results in a copy of the references. In this way, you have two independent structures, each of which contains a reference pointing to the same object in memory (i.e., a shallow copy). When you want to perform a deep copy, where the state of internal references is fully copied into a new object, one approach is to implement the `ICloneable` interface (as you will do in Chapter 8).

Passing Reference Types by Value

As covered earlier in the chapter, reference types or value types can be passed as parameters to methods. However, passing a reference type (e.g., a class) by reference is quite different from passing it by value. To understand the distinction, assume you have a simple `Person` class defined in a new Console Application project named FunWithRefTypeValTypeParams, defined as follows:

```
class Person
{
  public string personName;
  public int personAge;

  // Constructors.
  public Person(string name, int age)
  {
    personName = name;
    personAge = age;
  }
  public Person(){}

  public void Display()
  {
    Console.WriteLine("Name: {0}, Age: {1}", personName, personAge);
  }
}
```

Now, what if you create a method that allows the caller to send in the `Person` object by value (note the lack of parameter modifiers, such as `out` or `ref`)?

```
static void SendAPersonByValue(Person p)
{
  // Change the age of "p"?
  p.personAge = 99;

  // Will the caller see this reassignment?
  p = new Person("Nikki", 99);
}
```

Notice how the SendAPersonByValue() method attempts to reassign the incoming Person reference to a new Person object, as well as change some state data. Now let's test this method using the following code:

```
// Passing ref-types by value.
Console.WriteLine("***** Passing Person object by value *****");
Person fred = new Person("Fred", 12);
Console.WriteLine("\nBefore by value call, Person is:");
fred.Display();

SendAPersonByValue(fred);
Console.WriteLine("\nAfter by value call, Person is:");
fred.Display();
Console.ReadLine();
```

The following is the output of this call:

```
***** Passing Person object by value *****

Before by value call, Person is:
Name: Fred, Age: 12

After by value call, Person is:
Name: Fred, Age: 99
```

As you can see, the value of personAge has been modified. This behavior, discussed earlier, should make more sense now that you understand the way reference types work. Given that you were able to change the state of the incoming Person, what was copied? The answer: a copy of the reference to the caller's object. Therefore, as the SendAPersonByValue() method is pointing to the same object as the caller, it is possible to alter the object's state data. What is not possible is to reassign what the reference *is pointing to*.

Passing Reference Types by Reference

Now assume you have a SendAPersonByReference() method, which passes a reference type by reference (note the ref parameter modifier).

```
static void SendAPersonByReference(ref Person p)
{
  // Change some data of "p".
  p.personAge = 555;

  // "p" is now pointing to a new object on the heap!
  p = new Person("Nikki", 999);
}
```

As you might expect, this allows complete flexibility of how the callee is able to manipulate the incoming parameter. Not only can the callee change the state of the object, but if it so chooses, it may also reassign the reference to a new Person object. Now ponder the following updated code:

```
// Passing ref-types by ref.
Console.WriteLine("***** Passing Person object by reference *****");
...

Person mel = new Person("Mel", 23);
Console.WriteLine("Before by ref call, Person is:");
mel.Display();

SendAPersonByReference(ref mel);
Console.WriteLine("After by ref call, Person is:");
mel.Display();
Console.ReadLine();
```

Notice the following output:

```
***** Passing Person object by reference *****

Before by ref call, Person is:
Name: Mel, Age: 23
After by ref call, Person is:
Name: Nikki, Age: 999
```

As you can see, an object named Mel returns after the call as an object named Nikki, as the method was able to change what the incoming reference pointed to in memory. The golden rule to keep in mind when passing reference types is the following:

- If a reference type is passed by reference, the callee may change the values of the object's state data, as well as the object it is referencing.
- If a reference type is passed by value, the callee may change the values of the object's state data but *not* the object it is referencing.

Final Details Regarding Value Types and Reference Types

To wrap up this topic, consider the information in Table 4-4, which summarizes the core distinctions between value types and reference types.

Table 4-4. *Value Types and Reference Types Comparison*

Intriguing Question	Value Type	Reference Type
Where are objects allocated?	Allocated on the stack.	Allocated on the managed heap.
How is a variable represented?	Value type variables are local copies.	Reference type variables are pointing to the memory occupied by the allocated instance.

(*continued*)

Table 4-4. *(continued)*

Intriguing Question	Value Type	Reference Type
What is the base type?	Implicitly extends `System.ValueType`.	Can derive from any other type (except `System.ValueType`), if that type is not "sealed" (more details on this in Chapter 6).
Can this type function as a base to other types?	No. Value types are always sealed and cannot be inherited from.	Yes. If the type is not sealed, it may function as a base to other types.
What is the default parameter-passing behavior?	Variables are passed by value (i.e., a copy of the variable is passed into the called function).	For reference types, the reference is copied by value.
Can this type override `System.Object.Finalize()`?	No.	Yes, indirectly (more details on this in Chapter 9).
Can I define constructors for this type?	Yes, but the default constructor is reserved (i.e., your custom constructors must all have arguments).	But of course!
When do variables of this type die?	When they fall out of the defining scope.	When the object is garbage collected (see Chapter 9).

Despite their differences, value types and reference types both can implement interfaces and may support any number of fields, methods, overloaded operators, constants, properties, and events.

Understanding C# Nullable Types

Let's examine the role of the *nullable data type* using a Console Application project named FunWithNullableValueTypes. As you know, C# data types have a fixed range and are represented as a type in the `System` namespace. For example, the `System.Boolean` data type can be assigned a value from the set `{true, false}`. Now, recall that all the numerical data types (as well as the `Boolean` data type) are *value types*. Value types can never be assigned the value of `null`, as that is used to establish an empty object reference.

```
// Compiler errors!
// Value types cannot be set to null!
bool myBool = null;
int myInt = null;
```

C# supports the concept of *nullable data types*. Simply put, a nullable type can represent all the values of its underlying type, plus the value `null`. Thus, if you declare a nullable `bool`, it could be assigned a value from the set `{true, false, null}`. This can be extremely helpful when working with relational databases, given that it is quite common to encounter undefined columns in database tables. Without the concept of a nullable data type, there is no convenient manner in C# to represent a numerical data point with no value.

To define a nullable variable type, the question mark symbol (`?`) is suffixed to the underlying data type. Like a non-nullable variable, local nullable variables must be assigned an initial value before you can use them.

```
static void LocalNullableVariables()
{
  // Define some local nullable variables.
  int? nullableInt = 10;
  double? nullableDouble = 3.14;
  bool? nullableBool = null;
  char? nullableChar = 'a';
  int?[] arrayOfNullableInts = new int?[10];
}
```

Using Nullable Value Types

In C#, the ? suffix notation is a shorthand for creating an instance of the generic System.Nullable<T> structure type. It is also used for creating nullable reference types (covered in the next section), although the behavior is a bit different. While you will not examine generics until Chapter 10, it is important to understand that the System.Nullable<T> type provides a set of members that all nullable types can make use of.

For example, you can programmatically discover whether the nullable variable indeed has been assigned a null value using the HasValue property or the != operator. The assigned value of a nullable type may be obtained directly or via the Value property. In fact, given that the ? suffix is just a shorthand for using Nullable<T>, you could implement your LocalNullableVariables() method as follows:

```
static void LocalNullableVariablesUsingNullable()
{
  // Define some local nullable types using Nullable<T>.
  Nullable<int> nullableInt = 10;
  Nullable<double> nullableDouble = 3.14;
  Nullable<bool> nullableBool = null;
  Nullable<char> nullableChar = 'a';
  Nullable<int>[] arrayOfNullableInts = new Nullable<int>[10];
}
```

As stated, nullable data types can be particularly useful when you are interacting with databases, given that columns in a data table may be intentionally empty (e.g., undefined). To illustrate, assume the following class, which simulates the process of accessing a database that has a table containing two columns that may be null. Note that the GetIntFromDatabase() method is not assigning a value to the nullable integer member variable, while GetBoolFromDatabase() is assigning a valid value to the bool? member.

```
class DatabaseReader
{
  // Nullable data field.
  public int? numericValue = null;
  public bool? boolValue = true;

  // Note the nullable return type.
  public int? GetIntFromDatabase()
  { return numericValue; }

  // Note the nullable return type.
  public bool? GetBoolFromDatabase()
  { return boolValue; }
}
```

Now, examine the following code, which invokes each member of the DatabaseReader class and discovers the assigned values using the HasValue and Value members, as well as using the C# equality operator (not equal, to be exact):

```
Console.WriteLine("***** Fun with Nullable Value Types *****\n");
DatabaseReader dr = new DatabaseReader();

// Get int from "database".
int? i = dr.GetIntFromDatabase();
if (i.HasValue)
{
  Console.WriteLine("Value of 'i' is: {0}", i.Value);
}
else
{
  Console.WriteLine("Value of 'i' is undefined.");
}
// Get bool from "database".
bool? b = dr.GetBoolFromDatabase();
if (b != null)
{
  Console.WriteLine("Value of 'b' is: {0}", b.Value);
}
else
{
  Console.WriteLine("Value of 'b' is undefined.");
}
Console.ReadLine();
```

Using Nullable Reference Types (New 8.0, Updated 10.0)

A significant feature added with C# 8 is support for nullable reference types. In fact, the change is so significant that the .NET Framework could not be updated to support this new feature, which is one of the reasons for only supporting C# 8 in .NET Core 3.0 and above.

When you create a new project in .NET Core 3.0/3.1 or .NET 5, reference types work the same way that they did with C# 7. This is to prevent breaking billions of lines of code that exist in the pre–C# 8 ecosystem. Developers must opt in to enable nullable reference types in their applications.

C# 10 and .NET 6 (and above) change the default and enable nullable reference types in all of the project templates.

Nullable reference types follow many of the same rules as nullable value types. Non-nullable reference types must be assigned a non-null value at initialization and cannot later be changed to a null value. Nullable reference types can be null, but still must be assigned something before first use (either an actual instance of something or the value of null).

Nullable reference types use the same symbol (?) to indicate that they are nullable. However, this is not a shorthand for using System.Nullable<T>, as only value types can be used in place of T. As a reminder, generics and constraints are covered in Chapter 10.

Opting in for Nullable Reference Types (Updated 10.0)

Support for nullable reference types is controlled by setting a nullable context. This can be as big as an entire project (by updating the project file) or as small as a few lines (by using compiler directives). There are also two contexts that can be set:

- *Nullable annotation context*: This enables/disables the nullable annotation (?) for nullable reference types.
- *Nullable warning context*: This enables/disables the compiler warnings for nullable reference types.

To see these in action, create a new console application named FunWithNullableReferenceTypes. Open the project file (if you are using Visual Studio, double-click the project name in Solution Explorer or right-click the project name and select Edit Project File). As mentioned previously, in C# 10, every new project defaults to enabling nullable reference types. Notice the `<Nullable>` node in the project file listing (all the available options are shown in Table 4-5):

```
<Project Sdk="Microsoft.NET.Sdk">
  <PropertyGroup>
    <OutputType>Exe</OutputType>
    <TargetFramework>net6.0</TargetFramework>
    <ImplicitUsings>enable</ImplicitUsings>
    <Nullable>enable</Nullable>
  </PropertyGroup>
</Project>
```

Table 4-5. *Values for Nullable in Project Files*

Value	Meaning in Life
`enable`	Nullable annotations are enabled, and nullable warnings are enabled.
`warnings`	Nullable annotations are disabled, and nullable warnings are enabled.
`annotations`	Nullable annotations are enabled, and nullable warnings are disabled.
`disable`	Nullable annotations are disabled, and nullable warnings are disabled.

As one would expect, the `<Nullable>` element in the project file affects the entire project. To control smaller parts of the project, use the compiler directives shown in Table 4-6.

Table 4-6. *Values for #nullable Compiler Directive*

Value	Meaning in Life
`enable`	Annotations are enabled, and warnings are enabled.
`disable`	Annotations are disabled, and warnings are disabled.
`restore`	Restores all settings to the project settings.
`disable warnings`	Warnings are disabled, and annotations are unaffected.
`enable warnings`	Warnings are enabled, and annotations are unaffected.

(*continued*)

Table 4-6. (*continued*)

Value	Meaning in Life
`restore warnings`	Warnings reset to project settings; annotations are unaffected.
`disable annotations`	Annotations are disabled, and warnings are unaffected.
`enable annotations`	Annotations are enabled, and warnings are unaffected.
`restore annotations`	Annotations are reset to project settings; warnings are unaffected.

■ **Note** As mentioned, with the introduction of C# 10/.NET 6, nullable reference types (NRTs) are enabled by default. For the rest of this book, the code samples all have NRTs *disabled* unless specifically called out in the example. This is not to say you shouldn't use NRTs—that is a decision you need to make based on your project's requirements. I have disabled them to keep the examples in this book focused on the specific teaching goal.

Nullable Reference Types in Action

Largely because of the significance of the change, nullable types only throw errors when used improperly. Add the following class to the `Program.cs` file:

```
public class TestClass
{
  public string Name { get; set; }
  public int Age { get; set; }
}
```

As you can see, this is just a normal class. The nullability comes in when you use this class in your code. Take the following declarations:

```
string? nullableString = null;
TestClass? myNullableClass = null;
```

The project file setting makes the entire project a nullable context. The nullable context allows the declarations of the `string` and `TestClass` types to use the nullable annotation (?). The following line of code generates a warning (CS8600) due to the assignment of a null to a non-nullable type in a nullable context:

```
//Warning CS8600 Converting null literal or possible null value to non-nullable type
TestClass myNonNullableClass = myNullableClass;
```

For finer control of where the nullable contexts are in your project, you can use compiler directives (as discussed earlier) to enable or disable the context. The following code turns off the nullable context (set at the project level) and then reenables it by restoring the project settings:

```
#nullable disable
TestClass anotherNullableClass = null;
//Warning CS8632 The annotation for nullable reference types
//should only be used in code within a '#nullable' annotations
```

```
TestClass? badDefinition = null;
//Warning CS8632 The annotation for nullable reference types
//should only be used in code within a '#nullable' annotations
string? anotherNullableString = null;
#nullable restore
```

Add the previous example method EnterLogData() into the top-level statements of our current project:

```
static void EnterLogData(string message, string owner = "Programmer")
{
  ArgumentNullException.ThrowIfNull(message);
  Console.WriteLine("Error: {0}", message);
  Console.WriteLine("Owner of Error: {0}", owner);
}
```

Since this project has nullable reference types enabled, the message and owner parameters are not nullable. The owner parameter has a default value set, so it will never be null. However, the message parameter does not have a default value set, so calling it like this will raise a compiler warning:

```
EnterLogData(null);
//Warning CS8625 Cannot convert null literal to non-nullable reference type.
```

Chances are you won't explicitly pass in a null value, but more likely you might pass in a variable that happens to be null:

```
string? msg = null;
EnterLogData(msg);
//Warning CS8604 Possible null reference argument for parameter 'message' in
//      'void EnterLogData(string message, string owner = "Programmer")'.
```

This doesn't solve the problem of null values passed into a method, but it does provide some level of compile-time checking of your code.

As a final note, the nullable reference types do not have the HasValue and Value properties, as those are supplied by System.Nullable<T>.

Migration Considerations

When migrating your code from C# 7 to C# 8, C# 9, or C# 10 and you want to make use of nullable reference types, you can use a combination of the project setting and compiler directives to work through your code. A common practice is to start by enabling warnings and disabling nullable annotations for the entire project. Then, as you clean up areas of code, use the compiler directives to gradually enable the annotations. Remember that with C# 10, nullable reference types are enabled by default in project templates.

Change Nullable Warnings to Errors

When you are ready to commit to nullable reference types, you can configure the nullable warnings as errors. The easiest way to do this for a project is to add the following into the project file:

```
<PropertyGroup>
  <WarningsAsErrors>CS8604,CS8625</WarningsAsErrors>
</PropertyGroup>
```

In fact, if you want to treat all warnings related to nullable reference types to errors, you can use the following syntax:

```
<PropertyGroup>
  <WarningsAsErrors>Nullable</WarningsAsErrors>
</PropertyGroup>
```

■ **Note** You can change the severity of any warning to an error, not just those regarding nullable reference types. You can also change all warnings to errors by using `<TreatWarningsAsErrors>true</TreatWarningsAsErrors>` instead of the `WarningsAsErrors` node in your project file.

Operating on Nullable Types

C# provides several operators for working with nullable types. The next sections code the null-coalescing operator, the null-coalescing assignment operator, and the null conditional operator. For these examples, go back to the FunWithNullableValueTypes project.

The Null-Coalescing Operator

The next aspect to be aware of is any variable that might have a `null` value can make use of the C# `??` operator, which is formally termed the *null-coalescing operator*. This operator allows you to assign a value to a nullable type if the retrieved value is in fact `null`. For this example, assume you want to assign a local nullable integer to 100 if the value returned from `GetIntFromDatabase()` is `null` (of course, this method is programmed to always return `null`, but I am sure you get the general idea). Move back to the FunWithNullableValueTypes project (and set it as the startup project), and enter the following code:

```
Console.WriteLine("***** Fun with Nullable Value Types *****\n");
DatabaseReader dr = new DatabaseReader();

// If the value from GetIntFromDatabase() is null,
// assign local variable to 100.
int myData = dr.GetIntFromDatabase() ?? 100;
Console.WriteLine("Value of myData: {0}", myData);
Console.ReadLine();
```

The benefit of using the `??` operator is that it provides a more compact version of a traditional `if/else` condition. However, if you want, you could have authored the following functionally equivalent code to ensure that if a value comes back as `null`, it will indeed be set to the value 100:

```
// Longhand notation not using ?? syntax.
int? moreData = dr.GetIntFromDatabase();
if (!moreData.HasValue)
{
  moreData = 100;
}
Console.WriteLine("Value of moreData: {0}", moreData);
```

The Null-Coalescing Assignment Operator (New 8.0)

Building on the null-coalescing operator, C# 8 introduced the *null-coalescing assignment operator* (??=). This operator assigns the left-hand side to the right-hand side only if the left-hand side is null. For example, enter the following code:

```
//Null-coalescing assignment operator
int? nullableInt = null;
nullableInt ??= 12;
nullableInt ??= 14;
Console.WriteLine(nullableInt);
```

The nullableInt variable is initialized to null. The next line assigns the value of 12 to the variable since the left-hand side is indeed null. The next line does *not* assign 14 to the variable since it is not null.

The Null Conditional Operator

When you are writing software, it is common to check incoming parameters, which are values returned from type members (methods, properties, indexers), against the value null. For example, let's assume you have a method that takes a string array as a single parameter. To be safe, you might want to test for null before proceeding. In that way, you will not get a runtime error if the array is empty. The following would be a traditional way to perform such a check:

```
static void TesterMethod(string[] args)
{
  // We should check for null before accessing the array data!
  if (args != null)
  {
    Console.WriteLine($"You sent me {args.Length} arguments.");
  }
}
```

Here, you use a conditional scope to ensure that the Length property of the string array will not be accessed if the array is null. If the caller failed to make an array of data and called your method like so, you are still safe and will not trigger a runtime error:

```
TesterMethod(null);
```

C# includes the null conditional operator token (a question mark placed after a variable type but before an access operator) to simplify the previous error checking. Rather than explicitly building a conditional statement to check for null, you can now write the following:

```
static void TesterMethod(string[] args)
{
  // We should check for null before accessing the array data!
  Console.WriteLine($"You sent me {args?.Length} arguments.");
}
```

In this case, you are not using a conditional statement. Rather, you are suffixing the ? operator directly after the string array variable. If the variable is null, its call to the Length property will not throw a runtime error. If you want to print an actual value, you could leverage the null-coalescing operator to assign a default value as so:

```
Console.WriteLine($"You sent me {args?.Length ?? 0} arguments.");
```

There are some additional areas of coding where the C# 6.0 `null` conditional operator will be quite handy, especially when working with delegates and events. Those topics are addressed later in the book (see Chapter 12), and you will see many more examples.

Understanding Tuples (New/Updated 7.0)

To wrap up this chapter, let's examine the role of tuples using a Console Application project named FunWithTuples. As mentioned earlier in this chapter, one way to use `out` parameters is to retrieve more than one value from a method call. Another way is to use a light construct called a *tuple*.

Tuples are lightweight data structures that contain multiple fields. They were added to the language in C# 6, but in an extremely limited way. There was also a potentially significant problem with the C# 6 implementation: each field is implemented as a reference type, potentially creating memory and/or performance problems (from boxing/unboxing).

■ **Note** *Boxing* occurs when a value type is stored as a reference variable (stored on the heap), and *unboxing* is when the value type is returned to a value type variable (stored on the stack). Boxing and unboxing and their performance implications are covered in depth in Chapter 10.

In C# 7, tuples use the new `ValueTuple` data type instead of reference types, potentially saving significant memory. The `ValueTuple` data type creates different structs based on the number of properties for a tuple. An additional feature added in C# 7 is that each property in a tuple can be assigned a specific name (just like variables), greatly enhancing the usability.

These are two important considerations for tuples:

- The fields are not validated.
- You cannot define your own methods.

They are really designed to just be a lightweight data transport mechanism.

Getting Started with Tuples

Enough theory. Let's write some code! To create a tuple, simply enclose the values to be assigned to the tuple in parentheses, as follows:

```
("a", 5, "c")
```

Notice that they do not all have to be the same data type. The parenthetical construct is also used to assign the tuple to a variable (or you can use the `var` keyword and the compiler will assign the data types for you). To assign the previous example to a variable, the following two lines achieve the same thing. The `values` variable will be a tuple with two `string` properties and an `int` property sandwiched in between.

```
(string, int, string) values = ("a", 5, "c");
var values = ("a", 5, "c");
```

By default, the compiler assigns each property the name ItemX, where X represents the one-based position in the tuple. For the previous example, the property names are Item1, Item2, and Item3. Accessing them is done as follows:

```
Console.WriteLine($"First item: {values.Item1}");
Console.WriteLine($"Second item: {values.Item2}");
Console.WriteLine($"Third item: {values.Item3}");
```

Specific names can also be added to each property in the tuple on either the right side or the left side of the statement. While it is not a compiler error to assign names on both sides of the statement, if you do, the right side will be ignored, and only the left-side names are used. The following two lines of code show setting the names on the left and the right to achieve the same end:

```
(string FirstLetter, int TheNumber, string SecondLetter) valuesWithNames = ("a", 5, "c");
var valuesWithNames2 = (FirstLetter: "a", TheNumber: 5, SecondLetter: "c");
```

Now the properties on the tuple can be accessed using the field names as well as the ItemX notation, as shown in the following code:

```
Console.WriteLine($"First item: {valuesWithNames.FirstLetter}");
Console.WriteLine($"Second item: {valuesWithNames.TheNumber}");
Console.WriteLine($"Third item: {valuesWithNames.SecondLetter}");
//Using the item notation still works!
Console.WriteLine($"First item: {valuesWithNames.Item1}");
Console.WriteLine($"Second item: {valuesWithNames.Item2}");
Console.WriteLine($"Third item: {valuesWithNames.Item3}");
```

Note that when setting the names on the right, you must use the keyword var to declare the variable. Setting the data types specifically (even without custom names) triggers the compiler to use the left side, assign the properties using the ItemX notation, and ignore any of the custom names set on the right. The following two examples ignore the Custom1 and Custom2 names:

```
(int, int) example = (Custom1:5, Custom2:7);
(int Field1, int Field2) example = (Custom1:5, Custom2:7);
```

It is also important to call out that the custom field names exist only at compile time and are not available when inspecting the tuple at runtime using reflection (reflection is covered in Chapter 17).

Tuples can also be nested as tuples inside of tuples. Since each property in a tuple is a data type and a tuple is a data type, the following code is perfectly legitimate:

```
Console.WriteLine("=> Nested Tuples");
var nt = (5, 4, ("a", "b"));
```

Using Inferred Variable Names (Updated 7.1)

An update to tuples in C# 7.1 is the ability for C# to infer the variable names of tuples, as shown here:

```
Console.WriteLine("=> Inferred Tuple Names");
var foo = new {Prop1 = "first", Prop2 = "second"};
var bar = (foo.Prop1, foo.Prop2);
Console.WriteLine($"{bar.Prop1};{bar.Prop2}");
```

Understanding Tuple Equality/Inequality (New 7.3)

An added feature in C# 7.3 is the tuple equality (==) and inequality (!=). When testing for inequality, the comparison operators will perform implicit conversions on data types within the tuples, including comparing nullable and non-nullable tuples and/or properties. That means the following tests work perfectly, despite the difference between int/long:

```
Console.WriteLine("=> Tuples Equality/Inequality");
// lifted conversions
var left = (a: 5, b: 10);
(int? a, int? b) nullableMembers = (5, 10);
Console.WriteLine(left == nullableMembers); // Also true
// converted type of left is (long, long)
(long a, long b) longTuple = (5, 10);
Console.WriteLine(left == longTuple); // Also true
// comparisons performed on (long, long) tuples
(long a, int b) longFirst = (5, 10);
(int a, long b) longSecond = (5, 10);
Console.WriteLine(longFirst == longSecond); // Also true
```

Tuples that contain tuples can also be compared, but only if they have the same shape. You cannot compare one tuple of three int properties with another tuple of two ints and a tuple.

Understanding Tuples as Method Return Values

Earlier in this chapter, out parameters were used to return more than one value from a method call. There are additional ways to do this, such as creating a class or structure specifically to return the values. But if this class or struct is to be used as a data transport for only one method, that is extra work and extra code that does not need to be developed. Tuples are perfectly suited for this task, are lightweight, and are easy to declare and use.

This is one of the examples from the out parameter section. It returns three values but requires three parameters passed in as transport mechanisms for the calling code.

```
static void FillTheseValues(out int a, out string b, out bool c)
{
  a = 9;
  b = "Enjoy your string.";
  c = true;
}
```

By using a tuple, you can remove the parameters and still get the three values back.

```
static (int a,string b,bool c) FillTheseValues()
{
  return (9,"Enjoy your string.",true);
}
```

Calling this method is as simple as calling any other method.

```
var samples = FillTheseValues();
Console.WriteLine($"Int is: {samples.a}");
```

```
Console.WriteLine($"String is: {samples.b}");
Console.WriteLine($"Boolean is: {samples.c}");
```

Perhaps a better example is deconstructing a full name into its individual parts (first, middle, last). The following code takes in a full name and returns a tuple with the different parts:

```
static (string first, string middle, string last) SplitNames(string fullName)
{
  //do what is needed to split the name apart
  return ("Philip", "F", "Japikse");
}
```

Understanding Discards with Tuples

Following up on the SplitNames() example, suppose you know that you need only the first and last names and do not care about the middle. By providing variable names for the values you want returned and filling in the unneeded values with an underscore (_) placeholder, you can refine the return value like this:

```
var (first, _, last) = SplitNames("Philip F Japikse");
Console.WriteLine($"{first}:{last}");
```

The middle name value of the tuple is discarded.

Understanding Tuple Pattern Matching switch Expressions (New 8.0)

Now that you have a thorough understanding of tuples, it is time to revisit the switch expression with tuples from Chapter 3. Here is the example again:

```
//Switch expression with Tuples
static string RockPaperScissors(string first, string second)
{
  return (first, second) switch
  {
    ("rock", "paper") => "Paper wins.",
    ("rock", "scissors") => "Rock wins.",
    ("paper", "rock") => "Paper wins.",
    ("paper", "scissors") => "Scissors wins.",
    ("scissors", "rock") => "Rock wins.",
    ("scissors", "paper") => "Scissors wins.",
    (_, _) => "Tie.",
  };
}
```

In this example, the two parameters are converted into a tuple as they are passed into the switch expression. The relevant values are represented in the switch expression, and any other cases are handled by the final tuple, which is composed of two discards.

The RockPaperScissors() method signature could also be written to take in a tuple, like this:

```
static string RockPaperScissors(
  (string first, string second) value)
```

```
{
  return value switch
  {
    //omitted for brevity
  };
}
```

Deconstructing Tuples (Updated 10.0)

Deconstructing is the term given when separating out the properties of a tuple to be used individually. The SplitNames() example did just that. The first and last variables were accessed independently from any tuple construct. The variables can be initialized while deconstructing the tuple, or they can be pre-initialized. The following examples show both patterns:

```
(int X, int Y) myTuple = (4,5);
int x = 0;
int y = 0;
(x,y) = myTuple;
Console.WriteLine($"X is: {x}");
Console.WriteLine($"Y is: {y}");
(int x1, int y1) = myTuple;
Console.WriteLine($"x1 is: {x}");
Console.WriteLine($"y1 is: {y}");
```

New in C# 10, the assignment and declaration can be mixed, as the following shows:

```
int x2 = 0;
(x2, int y2) = myTuple;
Console.WriteLine($"x2 is: {x}");
Console.WriteLine($"y2 is: {y}");
```

There is another use for this pattern that can be helpful, and that is deconstructing custom types. Take a shorter version of the Point structure used earlier in this chapter. A new method named Deconstruct() has been added to return the individual properties of the Point instance as a tuple with properties named XPos and YPos.

```
struct Point
{
  // Fields of the structure.
  public int X;
  public int Y;

  // A custom constructor.
  public Point(int XPos, int YPos)
  {
    X = XPos;
    Y = YPos;
  }

  public (int XPos, int YPos) Deconstruct() => (X, Y);
}
```

Notice the new Deconstruct() method, shown in bold in the previous code listing. This method can be named anything, but by convention it is typically named Deconstruct(). This allows a single method call to get the individual values of the structure by returning a tuple.

```
Point p = new Point(7,5);
var pointValues = p.Deconstruct();
Console.WriteLine($"X is: {pointValues.XPos}");
Console.WriteLine($"Y is: {pointValues.YPos}");
```

Deconstructing Tuples with Positional Pattern Matching (New 8.0)

When tuples have an accessible Deconstruct() method, the deconstruction can happen implicitly without having to call the Deconstruct() method. The following code shows this implicit deconstruction:

```
Point p2 = new Point(8,3);
int xp2 = 0;
int yp2 = 0;
(xp2,yp2) = p2;
Console.WriteLine($"XP2 is: {xp2}");
Console.WriteLine($"YP2 is: {yp2}");
```

Additionally, the deconstruction can be used in a tuple-based switch expression. Using the Point example, the following code uses the generated tuple and uses those values for the when clause of each expression:

```
static string GetQuadrant1(Point p)
{
  return p.Deconstruct() switch
  {
    (0, 0) => "Origin",
    var (x, y) when x > 0 && y > 0 => "One",
    var (x, y) when x < 0 && y > 0 => "Two",
    var (x, y) when x < 0 && y < 0 => "Three",
    var (x, y) when x > 0 && y < 0 => "Four",
    var (_, _) => "Border",
  };
}
```

If the Deconstruct() method is defined with two out parameters, then the switch expression will automatically deconstruct the point. Add another Deconstruct method to the Point as follows:

```
public void Deconstruct(out int XPos, out int YPos)
  => (XPos,YPos)=(X, Y);
```

Now you can update (or add a new) GetQuadrant() method to this:

```
static string GetQuadrant2(Point p)
{
  return p switch
  {
    (0, 0) => "Origin",
```

```
    var (x, y) when x > 0 && y > 0 => "One",
    var (x, y) when x < 0 && y > 0 => "Two",
    var (x, y) when x < 0 && y < 0 => "Three",
    var (x, y) when x > 0 && y < 0 => "Four",
    var (_, _) => "Border",
  };
}
```

The change is very subtle (and is highlighted in bold). Instead of calling `p.Deconstruct()`, just the `Point` variable is used in the `switch` expression.

Summary

This chapter began with an examination of arrays. Then, we discussed the C# keywords that allow you to build custom methods. Recall that by default parameters are passed by value; however, you may pass a parameter by reference if you mark it with `ref` or `out`. You also learned about the role of optional or named parameters and how to define and invoke methods taking parameter arrays.

After you investigated the topic of method overloading, the bulk of this chapter examined several details regarding how enumerations and structures are defined in C# and represented within the .NET Core base class libraries. Along the way, you examined several details regarding value types and reference types, including how they respond when passing them as parameters to methods and how to interact with nullable data types and variables that might be `null` (e.g., reference type variables and nullable value type variables) using the ?, ??, and ??= operators.

The final section of the chapter investigated a long-anticipated feature in C#, tuples. After getting an understanding of what they are and how they work, you used them to return multiple values from methods as well as to deconstruct custom types.

In Chapter 5, you will begin to dig into the details of object-oriented development.

PART III

Object Oriented Programming with C#

CHAPTER 5

Understanding Encapsulation

In Chapters 3 and 4, you investigated a number of core syntactical constructs that are commonplace to any .NET Core application you might be developing. Here, you will begin your examination of the object-oriented capabilities of C#. The first order of business is to examine the process of building well-defined class types that support any number of *constructors*. After you understand the basics of defining classes and allocating objects, the remainder of this chapter will examine the role of *encapsulation*. Along the way, you will learn how to define class properties and come to understand the details of the `static` keyword, object initialization syntax, read-only fields, constant data, and partial classes.

Introducing the C# Class Type

As far as the .NET platform is concerned, one of the most fundamental programming constructs is the *class type*. Formally, a class is a user-defined type that is composed of field data (often called *member variables*) and members that operate on this data (such as constructors, properties, methods, events, etc.). Collectively, the set of field data represents the "state" of a class instance (otherwise known as an *object*). The power of object-oriented languages, such as C#, is that by grouping data and related functionality in a unified class definition, you are able to model your software after entities in the real world.

To get the ball rolling, create a new C# Console Application project named SimpleClassExample. Next, insert a new class file (named `Car.cs`) into your project. In this new file, add the following file-scoped namespace:

```
namespace SimpleClassExample;
```

A class is defined in C# using the `class` keyword. Here is the simplest possible declaration (make sure to add the class declaration after the `SimpleClassExample` namespace):

```
class Car
{
}
```

After you have defined a class type, you will need to consider the set of member variables that will be used to represent its state. For example, you might decide that cars maintain an `int` data type to represent the current speed and a `string` data type to represent the car's friendly pet name. Given these initial design notes, update your `Car` class as follows:

```
class Car
{
  // The 'state' of the Car.
  public string petName;
  public int currSpeed;
}
```


A. Troelsen and P. Japikse, *Pro C# 10 with .NET 6*, https://doi.org/10.1007/978-1-4842-7869-7_5

Notice that these member variables are declared using the public access modifier. Public members of a class are directly accessible once an object of this type has been created. Recall the term *object* is used to describe an instance of a given class type created using the new keyword.

■ **Note** Field data of a class should seldom (if ever) be defined as public. To preserve the integrity of your state data, it is a far better design to define data as private (or possibly protected) and allow controlled access to the data via properties (as shown later in this chapter). However, to keep this first example as simple as possible, public data fits the bill.

After you have defined the set of member variables representing the state of the class, the next design step is to establish the members that model its behavior. For this example, the Car class will define one method named SpeedUp() and another named PrintState(). Update your class as so:

```
class Car
{
  // The 'state' of the Car.
  public string petName;
  public int currSpeed;

// The functionality of the Car.
// Using the expression-bodied member syntax
// covered in Chapter 4
public void PrintState()
  => Console.WriteLine("{0} is going {1} MPH.", petName, currSpeed);

public void SpeedUp(int delta)
  => currSpeed += delta;
}
```

PrintState() is more or less a diagnostic function that will simply dump the current state of a given Car object to the command window. SpeedUp() will increase the speed of the Car object by the amount specified by the incoming int parameter. Now, update your top-level statements in the Program.cs file with the following code:

```
using SimplClassExample;

Console.WriteLine("***** Fun with Class Types *****\n");

// Allocate and configure a Car object.
Car myCar = new Car();
myCar.petName = "Henry";
myCar.currSpeed = 10;

// Speed up the car a few times and print out the
// new state.
for (int i = 0; i <= 10; i++)
{
  myCar.SpeedUp(5);
  myCar.PrintState();
}
Console.ReadLine();
```

After you run your program, you will see that the Car variable (myCar) maintains its current state throughout the life of the application, as shown in the following output:

```
***** Fun with Class Types *****

Henry is going 15 MPH.
Henry is going 20 MPH.
Henry is going 25 MPH.
Henry is going 30 MPH.
Henry is going 35 MPH.
Henry is going 40 MPH.
Henry is going 45 MPH.
Henry is going 50 MPH.
Henry is going 55 MPH.
Henry is going 60 MPH.
Henry is going 65 MPH.
```

Allocating Objects with the new Keyword

As shown in the previous code example, objects must be allocated into memory using the new keyword. If you do not use the new keyword and attempt to use your class variable in a subsequent code statement, you will receive a compiler error. For example, the following top-level statement will not compile:

```
Console.WriteLine("***** Fun with Class Types *****\n");
// Compiler error! Forgot to use 'new' to create object!
Car myCar;
myCar.petName = "Fred";
```

To correctly create an object using the new keyword, you may define and allocate a Car object on a single line of code.

```
Console.WriteLine("***** Fun with Class Types *****\n");
Car myCar = new Car();
myCar.petName = "Fred";
```

As an alternative, if you want to define and allocate a class instance on separate lines of code, you may do so as follows:

```
Console.WriteLine("***** Fun with Class Types *****\n");
Car myCar;
myCar = new Car();
myCar.petName = "Fred";
```

Here, the first code statement simply declares a reference to a yet-to-be-determined Car object. It is not until you assign a reference to an object that this reference points to a valid object in memory.

In any case, at this point you have a trivial class that defines a few points of data and some basic operations. To enhance the functionality of the current Car class, you need to understand the role of *constructors*.

Understanding Constructors

Given that objects have state (represented by the values of an object's member variables), a programmer will typically want to assign relevant values to the object's field data before use. Currently, the Car class demands that the petName and currSpeed fields be assigned on a field-by-field basis. For the current example, this is not too problematic, given that you have only two public data points. However, it is not uncommon for a class to have dozens of fields to contend with. Clearly, it would be undesirable to author 20 initialization statements to set 20 points of data!

Thankfully, C# supports the use of *constructors*, which allow the state of an object to be established at the time of creation. A constructor is a special method of a class that is called indirectly when creating an object using the new keyword. However, unlike a "normal" method, constructors never have a return value (not even void) and are always named identically to the class they are constructing.

Understanding the Role of the Default Constructor

Every C# class is provided with a "freebie" *default constructor* that you can redefine if need be. By definition, a default constructor never takes arguments. After allocating the new object into memory, the default constructor ensures that all field data of the class is set to an appropriate default value (see Chapter 3 for information regarding the default values of C# data types).

If you are not satisfied with these default assignments, you may redefine the default constructor to suit your needs. To illustrate, update your C# Car class as follows:

```
class Car
{
  // The 'state' of the Car.
  public string petName;
  public int currSpeed;

  // A custom default constructor.
  public Car()
  {
    petName = "Chuck";
    currSpeed = 10;
  }
...
}
```

In this case, you are forcing all Car objects to begin life named Chuck at a rate of 10 MPH. With this, you are able to create a Car object set to these default values as follows:

```
Console.WriteLine("***** Fun with Class Types *****\n");

// Invoking the default constructor.
Car chuck = new Car();

// Prints "Chuck is going 10 MPH."
chuck.PrintState();
...
```

Defining Custom Constructors

Typically, classes define additional constructors beyond the default. In doing so, you provide the object user with a simple and consistent way to initialize the state of an object directly at the time of creation. Ponder the following update to the Car class, which now supports a total of three constructors:

```
class Car
{
  // The 'state' of the Car.
  public string petName;
  public int currSpeed;

  // A custom default constructor.
  public Car()
  {
    petName = "Chuck";
    currSpeed = 10;
  }

  // Here, currSpeed will receive the
  // default value of an int (zero).
  public Car(string pn)
  {
    petName = pn;
  }

  // Let caller set the full state of the Car.
  public Car(string pn, int cs)
  {
    petName = pn;
    currSpeed = cs;
  }
...
}
```

Keep in mind that what makes one constructor different from another (in the eyes of the C# compiler) is the number of and/or type of constructor arguments. Recall from Chapter 4, when you define a method of the same name that differs by the number or type of arguments, you have *overloaded* the method. Thus, the Car class has overloaded the constructor to provide a number of ways to create an object at the time of declaration. In any case, you are now able to create Car objects using any of the public constructors. Here is an example:

```
Console.WriteLine("***** Fun with Class Types *****\n");

// Make a Car called Chuck going 10 MPH.
Car chuck = new Car();
chuck.PrintState();

// Make a Car called Mary going 0 MPH.
Car mary = new Car("Mary");
mary.PrintState();
```

```
// Make a Car called Daisy going 75 MPH.
Car daisy = new Car("Daisy", 75);
daisy.PrintState();
...
```

Constructors As Expression-Bodied Members (New 7.0)

C# 7 added additional uses for the expression-bodied member style. Constructors, finalizers, and get/set accessors on properties and indexers now accept the new syntax. With this in mind, the previous constructors can be written like this:

```
// Here, currSpeed will receive the
// default value of an int (zero).
public Car(string pn) => petName = pn;
```

The second custom constructor cannot be converted to an expression since expression-bodied members must be one-line methods.

Constructors with out Parameters (New 7.3)

Constructors (as well as field and property initializers, covered later) can use out parameters starting with C# 7.3. For a trivial example of this, add the following constructor to the Car class:

```
public Car(string pn, int cs, out bool inDanger)
{
  petName = pn;
  currSpeed = cs;
  if (cs > 100)
  {
    inDanger = true;
  }
  else
  {
    inDanger = false;
  }
}
```

All of the rules of out parameters must be followed. In this example, the inDanger parameter must be assigned a value before the conclusion of the constructor.

Understanding the Default Constructor Revisited

As you have just learned, all classes are provided with a free default constructor. Insert a new file into your project named Motorcycle.cs, and add the following to define a Motorcycle class:

```
namespace SimpleClassExample;
class Motorcycle
{
  public void PopAWheely()
```

```
  {
    Console.WriteLine("Yeeeeee Haaaaaeewww!");
  }
}
```

Now you are able to create an instance of the Motorcycle type via the default constructor out of the box.

```
Console.WriteLine("***** Fun with Class Types *****\n");
Motorcycle mc = new Motorcycle();
mc.PopAWheely();
...
```

However, as soon as you define a custom constructor with any number of parameters, the default constructor is silently removed from the class and is no longer available. Think of it this way: if you do not define a custom constructor, the C# compiler grants you a default to allow the object user to allocate an instance of your type with the field data set to the correct default values. However, when you define a unique constructor, the compiler assumes you have taken matters into your own hands.

Therefore, if you want to allow the object user to create an instance of your type with the default constructor, as well as your custom constructor, you must *explicitly* redefine the default. To this end, understand that in a vast majority of cases, the implementation of the default constructor of a class is intentionally empty, as all you require is the ability to create an object with default values. Consider the following update to the Motorcycle class:

```
class Motorcycle
{
  public int driverIntensity;

  public void PopAWheely()
  {
    for (int i = 0; i <= driverIntensity; i++)
    {
      Console.WriteLine("Yeeeeee Haaaaaeewww!");
    }
  }

  // Put back the default constructor, which will
  // set all data members to default values.
  public Motorcycle() {}

  // Our custom constructor.
  public Motorcycle(int intensity)
  {
    driverIntensity = intensity;
  }
}
```

■ **Note** Now that you better understand the role of class constructors, here is a nice shortcut. Both Visual Studio and Visual Studio Code provide the ctor code snippet. When you type ctor and press the Tab key, the IDE will automatically define a custom default constructor. You can then add custom parameters and implementation logic. Give it a try.

Understanding the Role of the this Keyword

C# supplies a this keyword that provides access to the current class instance. One possible use of the this keyword is to resolve scope ambiguity, which can arise when an incoming parameter is named identically to a data field of the class. However, you could simply adopt a naming convention that does not result in such ambiguity; to illustrate this use of the this keyword, update your Motorcycle class with a new string field (named name) to represent the driver's name. Next, add a method named SetDriverName() implemented as follows:

```
class Motorcycle
{
  public int driverIntensity;

  // New members to represent the name of the driver.
  public string name;
  public void SetDriverName(string name) => name = name;
...
}
```

Although this code will compile, the C# compiler will display a warning message informing you that you have assigned a variable back to itself! To illustrate, update your code to call SetDriverName() and then print out the value of the name field. You might be surprised to find that the value of the name field is an empty string!

```
// Make a Motorcycle with a rider named Tiny?
Motorcycle c = new Motorcycle(5);
c.SetDriverName("Tiny");
c.PopAWheely();
Console.WriteLine("Rider name is {0}", c.name); // Prints an empty name value!
```

The problem is that the implementation of SetDriverName() is assigning the incoming parameter *back to itself* given that the compiler assumes name is referring to the variable currently in the method scope rather than the name field at the class scope. To inform the compiler that you want to set the current object's name data field to the incoming name parameter, simply use this to resolve the ambiguity.

```
public void SetDriverName(string name) => this.name = name;
```

If there is no ambiguity, you are not required to make use of the this keyword when accessing data fields or members. For example, if you rename the string data member from name to driverName (which will also require you to update your top-level statements), the use of this is optional as there is no longer a scope ambiguity.

```
class Motorcycle
{
  public int driverIntensity;
  public string driverName;

  public void SetDriverName(string name)
  {
    // These two statements are functionally the same.
    driverName = name;
```

```
    this.driverName = name;
  }
...
}
```

Even though there is little to be gained when using this in unambiguous situations, you might still find this keyword useful when implementing class members, as IDEs such as Visual Studio and Visual Studio Code will enable IntelliSense when this is specified. This can be helpful when you have forgotten the name of a class member and want to quickly recall the definition.

■ **Note** A common naming convention is to start private (or internal) class-level variable names with an underscore (e.g., _driverName) so IntelliSense shows all of your variables at the top of the list. In our trivial example, all of the fields are public, so this naming convention would not apply. Through the rest of the book, you will see private and internal variables named with a leading underscore.

Chaining Constructor Calls Using this

Another use of the this keyword is to design a class using a technique termed *constructor chaining*. This design pattern is helpful when you have a class that defines multiple constructors. Given that constructors often validate the incoming arguments to enforce various business rules, it can be quite common to find redundant validation logic within a class's constructor set. Consider the following updated Motorcycle:

```
class Motorcycle
{
  public int driverIntensity;
  public string driverName;

  public Motorcycle() { }

  // Redundant constructor logic!
  public Motorcycle(int intensity)
  {
    if (intensity > 10)
    {
      intensity = 10;
    }
    driverIntensity = intensity;
  }

  public Motorcycle(int intensity, string name)
  {
    if (intensity > 10)
    {
      intensity = 10;
    }
```

```
    driverIntensity = intensity;
    driverName = name;
  }
...
}
```

Here (perhaps in an attempt to ensure the safety of the rider) each constructor is ensuring that the intensity level is never greater than 10. While this is all well and good, you do have redundant code statements in two constructors. This is less than ideal, as you are now required to update code in multiple locations if your rules change (e.g., if the intensity should not be greater than 5 rather than 10).

One way to improve the current situation is to define a method in the `Motorcycle` class that will validate the incoming argument(s). If you were to do so, each constructor could make a call to this method before making the field assignment(s). While this approach does allow you to isolate the code you need to update when the business rules change, you are now dealing with the following redundancy:

```
class Motorcycle
{
   public int driverIntensity;
   public string driverName;

   // Constructors.
   public Motorcycle() { }

   public Motorcycle(int intensity)
   {
     SetIntensity(intensity);
   }

   public Motorcycle(int intensity, string name)
   {
     SetIntensity(intensity);
     driverName = name;
   }

   public void SetIntensity(int intensity)
   {
     if (intensity > 10)
     {
       intensity = 10;
     }
     driverIntensity = intensity;
   }
...
}
```

A cleaner approach is to designate the constructor that takes the *greatest number of arguments* as the "master constructor" and have its implementation perform the required validation logic. The remaining constructors can make use of the `this` keyword to forward the incoming arguments to the master constructor and provide any additional parameters as necessary. In this way, you need to worry only about maintaining a single constructor for the entire class, while the remaining constructors are basically empty.

Here is the final iteration of the Motorcycle class (with one additional constructor for the sake of illustration). When chaining constructors, note how the this keyword is "dangling" off the constructor's declaration (via a colon operator) outside the scope of the constructor itself.

```
class Motorcycle
{
   public int driverIntensity;
   public string driverName;

   // Constructor chaining.
   public Motorcycle() {}
   public Motorcycle(int intensity)
     : this(intensity, "") {}
   public Motorcycle(string name)
     : this(0, name) {}

   // This is the 'master' constructor that does all the real work.
   public Motorcycle(int intensity, string name)
   {
     if (intensity > 10)
     {
       intensity = 10;
     }
     driverIntensity = intensity;
     driverName = name;
   }
...
}
```

Understand that using the this keyword to chain constructor calls is never mandatory. However, when you make use of this technique, you do tend to end up with a more maintainable and concise class definition. Again, using this technique, you can simplify your programming tasks, as the real work is delegated to a single constructor (typically the constructor that has the most parameters), while the other constructors simply "pass the buck."

■ **Note** Recall from Chapter 4 that C# supports optional parameters. If you use optional parameters in your class constructors, you can achieve the same benefits as constructor chaining with less code. You will see how to do so in just a moment.

Observing Constructor Flow

On a final note, do know that once a constructor passes arguments to the designated master constructor (and that constructor has processed the data), the constructor invoked originally by the caller will finish executing any remaining code statements. To clarify, update each of the constructors of the Motorcycle class with a fitting call to Console.WriteLine().

```
class Motorcycle
{
  public int driverIntensity;
  public string driverName;

  // Constructor chaining.
  public Motorcycle()
  {
    Console.WriteLine("In default constructor");
  }

  public Motorcycle(int intensity)
     : this(intensity, "")
  {
    Console.WriteLine("In constructor taking an int");
  }

  public Motorcycle(string name)
     : this(0, name)
  {
    Console.WriteLine("In constructor taking a string");
  }

  // This is the 'main' constructor that does all the real work.
  public Motorcycle(int intensity, string name)
  {
    Console.WriteLine("In main constructor");
    if (intensity > 10)
    {
      intensity = 10;
    }
    driverIntensity = intensity;
    driverName = name;
  }
...
}
```

Now, ensure your top-level statements exercise a Motorcycle object as follows:

```
Console.WriteLine("***** Fun with class Types *****\n");

// Make a Motorcycle.
Motorcycle c = new Motorcycle(5);
c.SetDriverName("Tiny");
c.PopAWheely();
Console.WriteLine("Rider name is {0}", c.driverName);
Console.ReadLine();
```

With this, ponder the output from the previous code:

```
***** Fun with Motorcycles *****
In main constructor
In constructor taking an int
Yeeeeee Haaaaaeewww!
Yeeeeee Haaaaaeewww!
Yeeeeee Haaaaaeewww!
Yeeeeee Haaaaaeewww!
Yeeeeee Haaaaaeewww!
Yeeeeee Haaaaaeewww!
Rider name is Tiny
```

As you can see, the flow of constructor logic is as follows:

- You create your object by invoking the constructor requiring a single `int`.
- This constructor forwards the supplied data to the master constructor and provides any additional startup arguments not specified by the caller.
- The master constructor assigns the incoming data to the object's field data.
- Control is returned to the constructor originally called and executes any remaining code statements.

The nice thing about using constructor chaining is that this programming pattern will work with any version of the C# language and .NET platform. However, if you are targeting .NET 4.0 and higher, you can further simplify your programming tasks by making use of optional arguments as an alternative to traditional constructor chaining.

Revisiting Optional Arguments

In Chapter 4, you learned about optional and named arguments. Recall that optional arguments allow you to define supplied default values to incoming arguments. If the caller is happy with these defaults, they are not required to specify a unique value; however, they may do so to provide the object with custom data. Consider the following version of `Motorcycle`, which now provides a number of ways to construct objects using a *single* constructor definition:

```
class Motorcycle
{
  // Single constructor using optional args.
  public Motorcycle(int intensity = 0, string name = "")
  {
     if (intensity > 10)
     {
       intensity = 10;
     }
     driverIntensity = intensity;
     driverName = name;
  }
...
}
```

With this one constructor, you are now able to create a new Motorcycle object using zero, one, or two arguments. Recall that named argument syntax allows you to essentially skip over acceptable default settings (see Chapter 3).

```
static void MakeSomeBikes()
{
   // driverName = "", driverIntensity = 0
   Motorcycle m1 = new Motorcycle();
   Console.WriteLine("Name= {0}, Intensity= {1}",
     m1.driverName, m1.driverIntensity);

   // driverName = "Tiny", driverIntensity = 0
   Motorcycle m2 = new Motorcycle(name:"Tiny");
   Console.WriteLine("Name= {0}, Intensity= {1}",
     m2.driverName, m2.driverIntensity);

   // driverName = "", driverIntensity = 7
   Motorcycle m3 = new Motorcycle(7);
   Console.WriteLine("Name= {0}, Intensity= {1}",
     m3.driverName, m3.driverIntensity);
}
```

In any case, at this point you are able to define a class with field data (aka member variables) and various operations such as methods and constructors. Next up, let's formalize the role of the static keyword.

Understanding the static Keyword

A C# class may define any number of *static members*, which are declared using the static keyword. When you do so, the member in question must be invoked directly from the class level, rather than from an object reference variable. To illustrate the distinction, consider your good friend System.Console. As you have seen, you do not invoke the WriteLine() method from the object level, as shown here:

```
// Compiler error! WriteLine() is not an object level method!
Console c = new Console();
c.WriteLine("I can't be printed...");
```

Instead, simply prefix the class name to the static WriteLine() member.

```
// Correct! WriteLine() is a static method.
Console.WriteLine("Much better! Thanks...");
```

Simply put, static members are items that are deemed (by the class designer) to be so commonplace that there is no need to create an instance of the class before invoking the member. While any class can define static members, they are quite commonly found within *utility classes*. By definition, a utility class is a class that does not maintain any object-level state and is not created with the new keyword. Rather, a utility class exposes all functionality as class-level (aka static) members.

For example, if you were to use the Visual Studio Object Browser (via the View ➤ Object Browser menu item) to view the System namespace, you would see that all the members of the Console, Math, Environment, and GC classes (among others) expose all their functionality via static members. These are but a few utility classes found within the .NET Core base class libraries.

Again, be aware that static members are not only found in utility classes; they can be part of any class definition at all. Just remember that static members promote a given item to the class level rather than the object level. As you will see over the next few sections, the `static` keyword can be applied to the following:

- Data of a class
- Methods of a class
- Properties of a class
- A constructor
- The entire class definition
- In conjunction with the C# `using` keyword

Let's see each of our options, beginning with the concept of static data.

■ **Note** You will examine the role of static properties later in this chapter while examining the properties themselves.

Defining Static Field Data

Most of the time when designing a class, you define data as instance-level data or, said another way, as nonstatic data. When you define instance-level data, you know that every time you create a new object, the object maintains its own independent copy of the data. In contrast, when you define *static* data of a class, the memory is shared by all objects of that category.

To see the distinction, create a new Console Application project named StaticDataAndMembers. Now, insert a file into your project named `SavingsAccount.cs`, and in that file create a new class named `SavingsAccount`. Begin by defining an instance-level variable (to model the current balance) and a custom constructor to set the initial balance.

```
namespace StaticDataAndMembers;
// A simple savings account class.
class SavingsAccount
{
  // Instance-level data.
  public double currBalance;
  public SavingsAccount(double balance)
  {
    currBalance = balance;
  }
}
```

When you create `SavingsAccount` objects, memory for the `currBalance` field is allocated for each object. Thus, you could create five different `SavingsAccount` objects, each with their own unique balance. Furthermore, if you change the balance on one account, the other objects are not affected.

Static data, on the other hand, is allocated once and shared among all objects of the same class category. Add a static variable named `currInterestRate` to the `SavingsAccount` class, which is set to a default value of 0.04.

```
// A simple savings account class.
class SavingsAccount
{
   // A static point of data.
   public static double currInterestRate = 0.04;

   // Instance-level data.
   public double currBalance;

   public SavingsAccount(double balance)
   {
     currBalance = balance;
   }
}
```

Create three instances of SavingsAccount in top-level statements, as follows:

```
using StaticDataAndMembers;

  Console.WriteLine("***** Fun with Static Data *****\n");
  SavingsAccount s1 = new SavingsAccount(50);
  SavingsAccount s2 = new SavingsAccount(100);
  SavingsAccount s3 = new SavingsAccount(10000.75);
  Console.ReadLine();
```

The in-memory data allocation would look something like Figure 5-1.

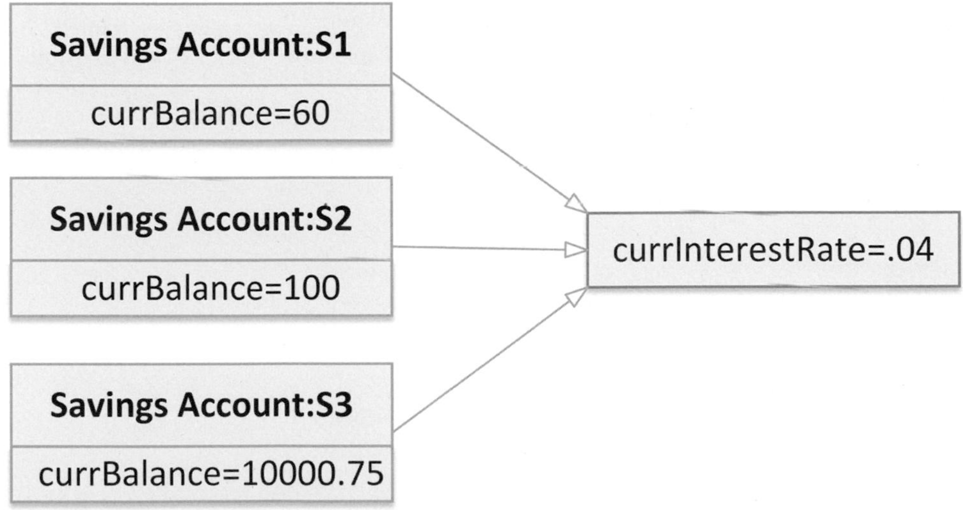

Figure 5-1. *Static data is allocated once and shared among all instances of the class*

Here, the assumption is that all saving accounts should have the same interest rate. Because static data is shared by all objects of the same category, if you were to change it in any way, all objects will "see" the new value the next time they access the static data, as they are all essentially looking at the same memory location. To understand how to change (or obtain) static data, you need to consider the role of static methods.

Defining Static Methods

Let's update the SavingsAccount class to define two static methods. The first static method (GetInterestRate()) will return the current interest rate, while the second static method (SetInterestRate()) will allow you to change the interest rate.

```
// A simple savings account class.
class SavingsAccount
{
  // Instance-level data.
  public double currBalance;

  // A static point of data.
  public static double currInterestRate = 0.04;

  public SavingsAccount(double balance)
  {
    currBalance = balance;
  }

  // Static members to get/set interest rate.
  public static void SetInterestRate(double newRate)
    => currInterestRate = newRate;

  public static double GetInterestRate()
    => currInterestRate;
}
```

Now, observe the following usage:

```
using StaticDataAndMembers;

Console.WriteLine("***** Fun with Static Data *****\n");
SavingsAccount s1 = new SavingsAccount(50);
SavingsAccount s2 = new SavingsAccount(100);

// Print the current interest rate.
Console.WriteLine("Interest Rate is: {0}", SavingsAccount.GetInterestRate());

// Make new object, this does NOT 'reset' the interest rate.
SavingsAccount s3 = new SavingsAccount(10000.75);
Console.WriteLine("Interest Rate is: {0}", SavingsAccount.GetInterestRate());

Console.ReadLine();
```

The output of the previous code is shown here:

```
***** Fun with Static Data *****
Interest Rate is: 0.04
Interest Rate is: 0.04
```

As you can see, when you create new instances of the SavingsAccount class, the value of the static data is not reset, as the CoreCLR will allocate the static data into memory exactly one time. After that point, all objects of type SavingsAccount operate on the same value for the static currInterestRate field.

When designing any C# class, one of your design challenges is to determine which pieces of data should be defined as static members and which should not. While there are no hard-and-fast rules, remember that a static data field is shared by all objects of that type. Therefore, if you are defining a point of data that *all* objects should share between them, static is the way to go.

Consider what would happen if the interest rate variable were *not* defined using the static keyword. This would mean every SavingsAccount object would have its own copy of the currInterestRate field. Now, assume you created 100 SavingsAccount objects and needed to change the interest rate. That would require you to call the SetInterestRate() method 100 times! Clearly, this would not be a useful way to model "shared data." Again, static data is perfect when you have a value that should be common to all objects of that category.

■ **Note** It is a compiler error for a static member to reference nonstatic members in its implementation. On a related note, it is an error to use the this keyword on a static member because this implies an object!

Defining Static Constructors

A typical constructor is used to set the value of an object's instance-level data at the time of creation. However, what would happen if you attempted to assign the value of a static point of data in a typical constructor? You might be surprised to find that the value is reset each time you create a new object.

To illustrate, assume you have updated the SavingsAccount class constructor as follows (also note you are no longer assigning the currInterestRate field inline):

```
class SavingsAccount
{
  public double currBalance;
  public static double currInterestRate;

  // Notice that our constructor is setting
  // the static currInterestRate value.
  public SavingsAccount(double balance)
  {
    currInterestRate = 0.04; // This is static data!
    currBalance = balance;
  }
...
}
```

Now, assume you have authored the following code in the top-level statements:

```
// Make an account.
SavingsAccount s1 = new SavingsAccount(50);

// Print the current interest rate.
Console.WriteLine("Interest Rate is: {0}", SavingsAccount.GetInterestRate());
```

```
// Try to change the interest rate via property.
SavingsAccount.SetInterestRate(0.08);

// Make a second account.
SavingsAccount s2 = new SavingsAccount(100);

// Should print 0.08...right??
Console.WriteLine("Interest Rate is: {0}", SavingsAccount.GetInterestRate());
Console.ReadLine();
```

If you executed the previous code, you would see that the currInterestRate variable is reset each time you create a new SavingsAccount object, and it is always set to 0.04. Clearly, setting the value of static data in a normal instance-level constructor sort of defeats the whole purpose. Every time you make a new object, the class-level data is reset. One approach to setting a static field is to use member initialization syntax, as you did originally.

```
class SavingsAccount
{
  public double currBalance;

  // A static point of data.
  public static double currInterestRate = 0.04;
...
}
```

This approach will ensure the static field is assigned only once, regardless of how many objects you create. However, what if the value for your static data needed to be obtained at runtime? For example, in a typical banking application, the value of an interest rate variable would be read from a database or external file. Performing such tasks usually requires a method scope such as a constructor to execute the code statements.

For this reason, C# allows you to define a static constructor, which allows you to safely set the values of your static data. Consider the following update to your class:

```
class SavingsAccount
{
  public double currBalance;
  public static double currInterestRate;

  public SavingsAccount(double balance)
  {
    currBalance = balance;
  }

   // A static constructor!
   static SavingsAccount()
   {
     Console.WriteLine("In static constructor!");
     currInterestRate = 0.04;
   }
...
}
```

Simply put, a static constructor is a special constructor that is an ideal place to initialize the values of static data when the value is not known at compile time (e.g., you need to read in the value from an external file, read in the value from a database, generate a random number, or whatnot). If you were to rerun the previous code, you would find the output you expect. Note that the message "In static constructor!" prints only one time, as the CoreCLR calls all static constructors before the first use (and never calls them again for that instance of the application).

```
***** Fun with Static Data *****
In static constructor!
Interest Rate is: 0.04
Interest Rate is: 0.08
```

Here are a few points of interest regarding static constructors:

- A given class may define only a single static constructor. In other words, the static constructor cannot be overloaded.
- A static constructor does not take an access modifier and cannot take any parameters.
- A static constructor executes exactly one time, regardless of how many objects of the type are created.
- The runtime invokes the static constructor when it creates an instance of the class or before accessing the first static member invoked by the caller.
- The static constructor executes before any instance-level constructors.

Given this modification, when you create new `SavingsAccount` objects, the value of the static data is preserved, as the static member is set only one time within the static constructor, regardless of the number of objects created.

Defining Static Classes

It is also possible to apply the `static` keyword directly on the class level. When a class has been defined as static, it is not creatable using the new keyword, and it can contain only members or data fields marked with the `static` keyword. If this is not the case, you receive compiler errors.

■ **Note** Recall that a class (or structure) that exposes only static functionality is often termed a *utility class*. When designing a utility class, it is good practice to apply the `static` keyword to the class definition.

At first glance, this might seem like a fairly odd feature, given that a class that cannot be created does not appear all that helpful. However, if you create a class that contains nothing but static members and/or constant data, the class has no need to be allocated in the first place! To illustrate, create a new class named `TimeUtilClass` and define it as follows:

```
namespace StaticDataAndMembers;
// Static classes can only
// contain static members!
static class TimeUtilClass
```

```
{
  public static void PrintTime()
    => Console.WriteLine(DateTime.Now.ToShortTimeString());

  public static void PrintDate()
    => Console.WriteLine(DateTime.Today.ToShortDateString());
}
```

Given that this class has been defined with the `static` keyword, you cannot create an instance of the `TimeUtilClass` using the `new` keyword. Rather, all functionality is exposed from the class level. To test this class, add the following to the top-level statements:

```
// These compile just fine.
TimeUtilClass.PrintDate();
TimeUtilClass.PrintTime();

// Compiler error! Can't create instance of static classes!
TimeUtilClass u = new TimeUtilClass();

Console.ReadLine();
```

Importing Static Members via the C# using Keyword

C# 6 added support for importing static members with the `using` keyword. To illustrate, consider the C# file currently defining the utility class. Because you are making calls to the `WriteLine()` method of the `Console` class, as well as the `Now` and `Today` properties of the `DateTime` class, you must have a `using` statement for the `System` namespace. Since the members of these classes are all static, you could alter your code file with the following static `using` directives:

```
// Import the static members of Console and DateTime.
using static System.Console;
using static System.DateTime;
```

With these "static imports," the remainder of your code file is able to directly use the static members of the `Console` and `DateTime` classes, without the need to prefix the defining class. For example, you could update your utility class like so:

```
static class TimeUtilClass
{
  public static void PrintTime()
    => WriteLine(Now.ToShortTimeString());

  public static void PrintDate()
    => WriteLine(Today.ToShortDateString());
}
```

A more realistic example of code simplification with importing static members might involve a C# class that is making substantial use of the `System.Math` class (or some other utility class). Since this class has nothing but static members, it could be somewhat easier to have a static `using` statement for this type and then directly call into the members of the `Math` class in your code file.

However, be aware that overuse of static `import` statements could result in potential confusion. First, what if multiple classes define a `WriteLine()` method? The compiler is confused and so are others reading your code. Second, unless developers are familiar with the .NET Core code libraries, they might not know that `WriteLine()` is a member of the `Console` class. Unless people were to notice the set of static imports at the top of a C# code file, they might be quite unsure where this method is actually defined. For these reasons, I will limit the use of static `using` statements in this text.

In any case, at this point in the chapter, you should feel comfortable defining simple class types containing constructors, fields, and various static (and nonstatic) members. Now that you understand the basics of class construction, you can formally investigate the three pillars of object-oriented programming.

Defining the Pillars of OOP

All object-oriented languages (C#, Java, C++, Visual Basic, etc.) must contend with these three core principles, often called the *pillars* of object-oriented programming (OOP):

- *Encapsulation*: How does this language hide an object's internal implementation details and preserve data integrity?
- *Inheritance*: How does this language promote code reuse?
- *Polymorphism*: How does this language let you treat related objects in a similar way?

Before digging into the details of each pillar, it is important that you understand their basic roles. Here is an overview of each pillar, which will be examined in full detail over the remainder of this chapter and the next.

■ **Note** The examples in this section are contained in the OopExamples project of the chapter's code samples.

Understanding the Role of Encapsulation

The first pillar of OOP is called *encapsulation*. This trait boils down to the language's ability to hide unnecessary implementation details from the object user. For example, assume you are using a class named `DatabaseReader`, which has two primary methods, named `Open()` and `Close()`.

```
// Assume this class encapsulates the details of opening and closing a database.
DatabaseReader dbReader = new DatabaseReader();
dbReader.Open(@"C:\AutoLot.mdf");

// Do something with data file and close the file.
dbReader.Close();
```

The fictitious `DatabaseReader` class encapsulates the inner details of locating, loading, manipulating, and closing a data file. Programmers love encapsulation, as this pillar of OOP keeps coding tasks simpler. There is no need to worry about the numerous lines of code that are working behind the scenes to carry out the work of the `DatabaseReader` class. All you do is create an instance and send the appropriate messages (e.g., "Open the file named `AutoLot.mdf` located on my C drive").

Closely related to the notion of encapsulating programming logic is the idea of data protection. Ideally, an object's state data should be specified using either the `private`, `internal`, or `protected` keyword. In this way, the outside world must ask politely in order to change or obtain the underlying value. This is a good thing, as publicly declared data points can easily become corrupted (ideally by accident rather than intent!). You will formally examine this aspect of encapsulation in just a bit.

Understanding the Role of Inheritance

The next pillar of OOP, *inheritance*, boils down to the language's ability to allow you to build new class definitions based on existing class definitions. In essence, inheritance allows you to extend the behavior of a base (or *parent*) class by inheriting core functionality into the derived subclass (also called a *child class*). Figure 5-2 shows a simple example.

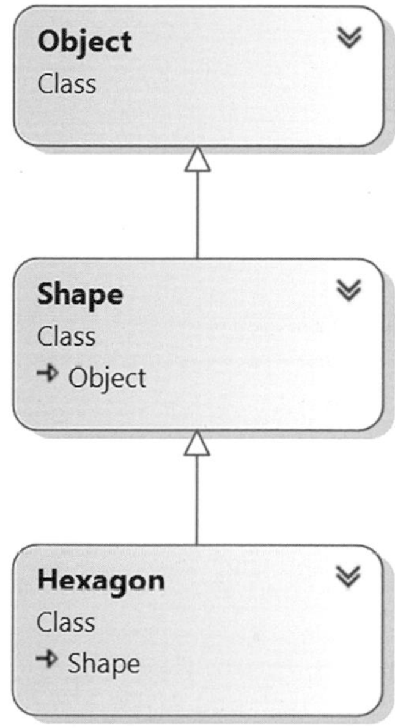

Figure 5-2. *The "is-a" relationship*

You can read the diagram in Figure 5-2 as "A Hexagon is-a Shape that is-an Object." When you have classes related by this form of inheritance, you establish *"is-a" relationships* between types. The "is-a" relationship is termed *inheritance*.

Here, you can assume that Shape defines some number of members that are common to all descendants (maybe a value to represent the color to draw the shape and other values to represent the height and width). Given that the Hexagon class extends Shape, it inherits the core functionality defined by Shape and `Object`, as well as defines additional hexagon-related details of its own (whatever those may be).

■ **Note** Under the .NET/.NET Core platforms, `System.Object` is always the topmost parent in any class hierarchy, which defines some general functionality for all types (fully described in Chapter 6).

There is another form of code reuse in the world of OOP: the containment/delegation model also known as the *"has-a" relationship* or aggregation. This form of reuse is not used to establish parent-child relationships. Rather, the "has-a" relationship allows one class to define a member variable of another class and expose its functionality (if required) to the object user indirectly.

For example, assume you are again modeling an automobile. You might want to express the idea that a car "has-a" radio. It would be illogical to attempt to derive the `Car` class from a `Radio` or vice versa (a `Car` "is-a" `Radio`? I think not!). Rather, you have two independent classes working together, where the `Car` class creates and exposes the `Radio`'s functionality.

```
namespace OopExamples;
class Radio
{
  public void Power(bool turnOn)
  {
    Console.WriteLine("Radio on: {0}", turnOn);
  }
}

namespace OopExamples;
class Car
{
  // Car 'has-a' Radio.
  private Radio myRadio = new Radio();
  public void TurnOnRadio(bool onOff)
  {
    // Delegate call to inner object.
    myRadio.Power(onOff);
  }
}
```

Notice that the object user has no clue that the Car class is using an inner Radio object.

```
using OopExamples;

Console.WriteLine("--- Fun with OOP examples ---");

// Call is forwarded to Radio internally.
Car viper = new Car();
viper.TurnOnRadio(false);
```

Understanding the Role of Polymorphism

The final pillar of OOP is *polymorphism*. This trait captures a language's ability to treat related objects in a similar manner. Specifically, this tenant of an object-oriented language allows a base class to define a set of members (formally termed the *polymorphic interface*) that are available to all descendants. A class's polymorphic interface is constructed using any number of *virtual* or *abstract* members (see Chapter 6 for full details).

In a nutshell, a *virtual member* is a member in a base class that defines a default implementation that may be changed (or more formally speaking, *overridden*) by a derived class. In contrast, an *abstract method* is a member in a base class that does not provide a default implementation but does provide a signature. When a class derives from a base class defining an abstract method, it *must* be overridden by a derived type. In either case, when derived types override the members defined by a base class, they are essentially redefining how they respond to the same request.

To preview polymorphism, let's provide some details behind the shapes hierarchy shown in Figure 5-3. Assume that the Shape class has defined a virtual method named Draw() that takes no parameters. Given that every shape needs to render itself in a unique manner, subclasses such as Hexagon and Circle are free to override this method to their own liking (see Figure 5-3).

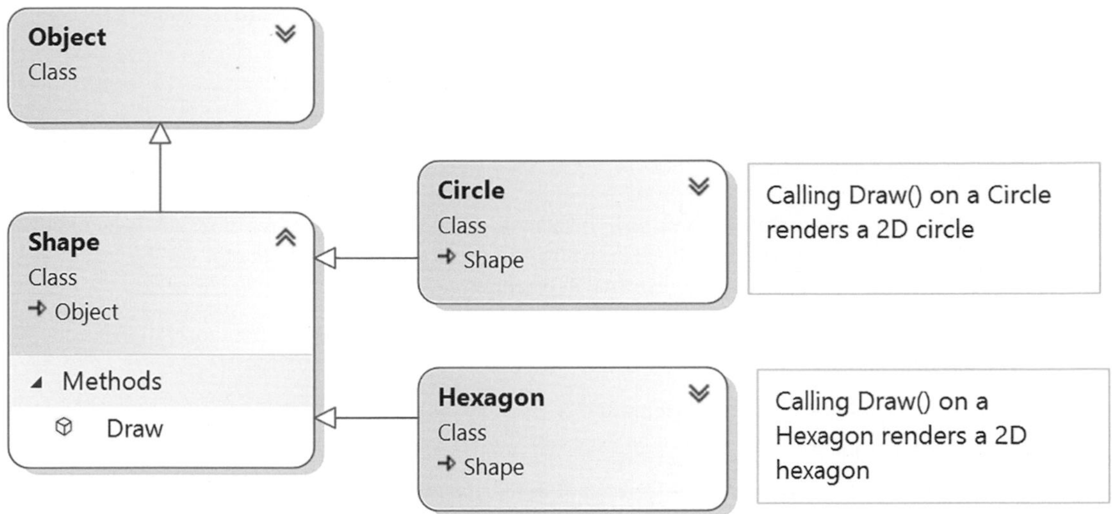

Figure 5-3. *Classical polymorphism*

After a polymorphic interface has been designed, you can begin to make various assumptions in your code. For example, given that Hexagon and Circle derive from a common parent (Shape), an array of Shape types could contain anything deriving from this base class. Furthermore, given that Shape defines a polymorphic interface to all derived types (the Draw() method in this example), you can assume each member in the array has this functionality.

Consider the following code, which instructs an array of Shape-derived types to render themselves using the Draw() method:

```
Shape[] myShapes = new Shape[3];
myShapes[0] = new Hexagon();
myShapes[1] = new Circle();
myShapes[2] = new Hexagon();

foreach (Shape s in myShapes)
{
  // Use the polymorphic interface!
  s.Draw();
}
Console.ReadLine();
```

This wraps up our brisk overview of the pillars of OOP. Now that you have the theory in your mind, the remainder of this chapter explores further details of how encapsulation is handled under C#, starting with a look at access modifiers. Chapter 6 will tackle the details of inheritance and polymorphism.

Understanding C# Access Modifiers (Updated 7.2)

When working with encapsulation, you must always consider which aspects of a type are visible to various parts of your application. Specifically, types (classes, interfaces, structures, enumerations, and delegates) as well as their members (properties, methods, constructors, and fields) are defined using a specific keyword to control how “visible” the item is to other parts of your application. Although C# defines numerous keywords to control access, they differ on where they can be successfully applied (type or member). Table 5-1 documents the role of each access modifier and where it may be applied.

Table 5-1. *C# Access Modifiers*

C# Access Modifier	May Be Applied To	Meaning in Life
`public`	Types or type members	Public items have no access restrictions. A public member can be accessed from an object, as well as any derived class. A public type can be accessed from other external assemblies.
`private`	Type members or nested types	Private items can be accessed only by the class (or structure) that defines the item.
`protected`	Type members or nested types	Protected items can be used by the class that defines it and any child class. They cannot be accessed from outside the inheritance chain.
`internal`	Types or type members	Internal items are accessible only within the current assembly. Other assemblies can be explicitly granted permission to see the internal items.
`protected internal`	Type members or nested types	When the `protected` and `internal` keywords are combined on an item, the item is accessible within the defining assembly, within the defining class, and by derived classes inside or outside of the defining assembly.
`private protected (new 7.2)`	Type members or nested types	When the `private` and `protected` keywords are combined on an item, the item is accessible within the defining class and by derived classes in the same assembly.

In this chapter, you are concerned only with the `public` and `private` keywords. Later chapters will examine the role of the `internal` and `protected internal` modifiers (useful when you build code libraries and unit tests) and the `protected` modifier (useful when you are creating class hierarchies).

Using the Default Access Modifiers

By default, type members are *implicitly private*, while types are *implicitly internal*. Thus, the following class definition is automatically set to `internal`, while the type's default constructor is automatically set to `private` (however, as you would suspect, there are few times you would want a private class constructor):

```
// An internal class with a private default constructor.
class Radio
{
  Radio(){}
}
```

If you want to be explicit, you could add these keywords yourself with no ill effect (beyond a few additional keystrokes).

```
// An internal class with a private default constructor.
internal class Radio
{
  private Radio(){}
}
```

To allow other parts of a program to invoke members of an object, you must define them with the public keyword (or possibly with the protected keyword, which you will learn about in the next chapter). As well, if you want to expose the Radio to external assemblies (again, useful when building larger solutions or code libraries), you will need to add the public modifier.

```
// A public class with a public default constructor.
public class Radio
{
  public Radio(){}
}
```

Using Access Modifiers and Nested Types

As mentioned in Table 5-1, the private, protected, protected internal, and private protected access modifiers can be applied to a *nested type*. Chapter 6 will examine nesting in detail. What you need to know at this point, however, is that a nested type is a type declared directly within the scope of class or structure. By way of example, here is a private enumeration (named CarColor) nested within a public class (named SportsCar):

```
namespace OopExamples;
public class SportsCar
{
  // OK! Nested types can be marked private.
  private enum CarColor
  {
    Red, Green, Blue
  }
}
```

Here, it is permissible to apply the private access modifier on the nested type. However, non-nested types (such as the SportsCar) can be defined only with the public or internal modifier. Therefore, the following class definition is illegal:

```
// Error! Non-nested types cannot be marked private!
private class SportsCar
{}
```

Understanding the First Pillar: C#'s Encapsulation Services

The concept of encapsulation revolves around the notion that an object's data should not be directly accessible from an object instance. Rather, class data is defined as private. If the object user wants to alter the state of an object, it does so indirectly using public members. To illustrate the need for encapsulation services, assume you have created the following class definition:

```
// A class with a single public field.
class Book
{
  public int numberOfPages;
}
```

The problem with public data is that the data itself has no ability to "understand" whether the current value to which it is assigned is valid with regard to the current business rules of the system. As you know, the upper range of a C# `int` is quite large (2,147,483,647). Therefore, the compiler allows the following assignment:

```
// Humm. That is one heck of a mini-novel!
Book miniNovel = new Book();
miniNovel.numberOfPages = 30_000_000;
```

Although you have not overflowed the boundaries of an `int` data type, it should be clear that a mini-novel with a page count of 30,000,000 pages is a bit unreasonable. As you can see, public fields do not provide a way to trap logical upper (or lower) limits. If your current system has a business rule that states a book must be between 1 and 1,000 pages, you are at a loss to enforce this programmatically. Because of this, public fields typically have no place in a production-level class definition.

■ **Note** To be more specific, members of a class that represent an object's state should not be marked as public. As you will see later in this chapter, public constants and public read-only fields are quite useful.

Encapsulation provides a way to preserve the integrity of an object's state data. Rather than defining public fields (which can easily foster data corruption), you should get in the habit of defining *private data*, which is indirectly manipulated using one of two main techniques.

- You can define a pair of public accessor (get) and mutator (set) methods.
- You can define a public property.

Whichever technique you choose, the point is that a well-encapsulated class should protect its data and hide the details of how it operates from the prying eyes of the outside world. This is often termed *black-box programming*. The beauty of this approach is that an object is free to change how a given method is implemented under the hood. It does this without breaking any existing code making use of it, provided that the parameters and return values of the method remain constant.

Encapsulation Using Traditional Accessors and Mutators

Over the remaining pages in this chapter, you will be building a fairly complete class that models a general employee. To get the ball rolling, create a new Console Application project named EmployeeApp and create a new class file named `Employee.cs`. Update the `Employee` class with the following namespace, fields, methods, and constructors:

```
namespace EmployeeApp;
class Employee
{
  // Field data.
  private string _empName;
  private int _empId;
  private float _currPay;

  // Constructors.
  public Employee() {}
  public Employee(string name, int id, float pay)
```

```
  {
    _empName = name;
    _empId = id;
    _currPay = pay;
  }

  // Methods.
  public void GiveBonus(float amount) => _currPay += amount;
  public void DisplayStats()
  {
    Console.WriteLine("Name: {0}", _empName);
    Console.WriteLine("ID: {0}", _empId);
    Console.WriteLine("Pay: {0}", _currPay);
  }
}
```

Notice that the fields of the Employee class are currently defined using the private keyword. Given this, the _empName, _empId, and _currPay fields are not directly accessible from an object variable. Therefore, the following logic in your code would result in compiler errors:

```
Employee emp = new Employee();
// Error! Cannot directly access private members
// from an object!
emp._empName = "Marv";
```

If you want the outside world to interact with a worker's full name, a traditional approach is to define an accessor (get method) and a mutator (set method). The role of a get method is to return to the caller the current value of the underlying state data. A set method allows the caller to change the current value of the underlying state data, as long as the defined business rules are met.

To illustrate, let's encapsulate the empName field. To do so, add the following public methods to the Employee class. Notice that the SetName() method performs a test on the incoming data to ensure the string is 15 characters or less. If it is not, an error prints to the console and returns without making a change to the empName field.

■ **Note** If this were a production-level class, you would probably also check the character length for an employee's name within your constructor logic. Ignore this detail for the time being, as you will clean up this code in just a bit when you examine property syntax.

```
class Employee
{
  // Field data.
  private string _empName;
  ...

  // Accessor (get method).
  public string GetName() => _empName;

  // Mutator (set method).
  public void SetName(string name)
```

```
  {
    // Do a check on incoming value
    // before making assignment.
    if (name.Length > 15)
    {
      Console.WriteLine("Error! Name length exceeds 15 characters!");
    }
    else
    {
      _empName = name;
    }
  }
}
```

This technique requires two uniquely named methods to operate on a single data point. To test your new methods, update your code method as follows:

```
using EmployeeApp;

Console.WriteLine("***** Fun with Encapsulation *****\n");

Employee emp = new Employee("Marvin", 456, 30_000);
emp.GiveBonus(1000);
emp.DisplayStats();

// Use the get/set methods to interact with the object's name.
emp.SetName("Marv");
Console.WriteLine("Employee is named: {0}", emp.GetName());
Console.ReadLine();
```

Because of the code in your SetName() method, if you attempted to specify more than 15 characters (see the following), you would find the hard-coded error message printed to the console:

```
// Longer than 15 characters! Error will print to console.
Employee emp2 = new Employee();
emp2.SetName("Xena the warrior princess");

Console.ReadLine();
```

So far, so good. You have encapsulated the private empName field using two public methods named GetName() and SetName(). If you were to further encapsulate the data in the Employee class, you would need to add various additional methods (such as GetID(), SetID(), GetCurrentPay(), SetCurrentPay()). Each of the mutator methods could also have various lines of code to check for additional business rules. While this could certainly be done, the C# language has a useful alternative notation to encapsulate class data.

Encapsulation Using Properties

Although you can encapsulate a piece of field data using traditional get and set methods, .NET Core languages prefer to enforce data encapsulation state data using *properties*. First, understand that properties are just a container for "real" accessor and mutator methods, named get and set, respectively. Therefore, as a class designer, you are still able to perform any internal logic necessary before making the value assignment (e.g., uppercase the value, scrub the value for illegal characters, check the bounds of a numerical value, etc.).

Here is the updated Employee class, now enforcing encapsulation of each field using property syntax rather than traditional get and set methods:

```
class Employee
{
  // Field data.
  private string _empName;
  private int _empId;
  private float _currPay;
  // Properties!
  public string Name
  {
    get { return _empName; }
    set
    {
      if (value.Length > 15)
      {
        Console.WriteLine("Error! Name length exceeds 15 characters!");
      }
      else
      {
        _empName = value;
      }
    }
  }
  // We could add additional business rules to the sets of these properties;
  // however, there is no need to do so for this example.
  public int Id
  {
    get { return _empId; }
    set { _empId = value; }
  }
  public float Pay
  {
    get { return _currPay; }
    set { _currPay = value; }
  }
...
}
```

A C# property is composed by defining a get scope (accessor) and set scope (mutator) directly within the property itself. Notice that the property specifies the type of data it is encapsulating by what appears to be a return value. Also take note that, unlike a method, properties do not make use of parentheses (not even empty parentheses) when being defined. Consider the following commentary on your current Id property:

```
// The 'int' represents the type of data this property encapsulates.
public int Id // Note lack of parentheses.
{
  get { return _empId; }
  set { _empID = value; }
}
```

Within a set scope of a property, you use a token named value, which is used to represent the incoming value used to assign the property by the caller. This token is *not* a true C# keyword but is what is known as a *contextual keyword*. When the token value is within the set scope of the property, it always represents the value being assigned by the caller, and it will always be the same underlying data type as the property itself. Thus, notice how the Name property can still test the range of the string as so:

```
public string Name
{
  get { return _empName; }
  set
  {
    // Here, value is really a string.
    if (value.Length > 15)
    {   Console.WriteLine("Error! Name length exceeds 15 characters!");
    }
    else
    {
      empName = value;
    }
  }
}
```

After you have these properties in place, it appears to the caller that it is getting and setting a *public point* of data; however, the correct get and set block is called behind the scenes to preserve encapsulation.

```
using EmployeeApp;

Console.WriteLine("***** Fun with Encapsulation *****\n");
Employee emp = new Employee("Marvin", 456, 30000);
emp.GiveBonus(1000);
emp.DisplayStats();

// Reset and then get the Name property.
emp.Name = "Marv";
Console.WriteLine("Employee is named: {0}", emp.Name);
Console.ReadLine();
```

Properties (as opposed to accessor and mutator methods) also make your types easier to manipulate, in that properties are able to respond to the intrinsic operators of C#. To illustrate, assume that the Employee class type has an internal private member variable representing the age of the employee. Here is the relevant update (notice the use of constructor chaining):

```
class Employee
{
...
   // New field and property.
   private int _empAge;
   public int Age
   {
     get { return _empAge; }
     set { _empAge = value; }
   }
```

```
    // Updated constructors.
    public Employee() {}
    public Employee(string name, int id, float pay)
    :this(name, 0, id, pay){}

    public Employee(string name, int age, int id, float pay)
    {
      _empName = name;
      _empId = id;
      _empAge = age;
      _currPay = pay;
    }

    // Updated DisplayStats() method now accounts for age.
    public void DisplayStats()
    {
      Console.WriteLine("Name: {0}", _empName);
      Console.WriteLine("ID: {0}", _empId);
      Console.WriteLine("Age: {0}", _empAge);
      Console.WriteLine("Pay: {0}", _currPay);
    }
}
```

Now assume you have created an Employee object named joe. On his birthday, you want to increment the age by one. Using traditional accessor and mutator methods, you would need to write code such as the following:

```
Employee joe = new Employee();
joe.SetAge(joe.GetAge() + 1);
```

However, if you encapsulate empAge using a property named Age, you are able to simply write this:

```
Employee joe = new Employee();
joe.Age++;
```

Properties As Expression-Bodied Members (New 7.0)

As mentioned previously, property get and set accessors can also be written as expression-bodied members. The rules and syntax are the same: single-line methods can be written using the new syntax. So, the Age property could be written like this:

```
public int Age
{
  get => empAge;
  set => empAge = value;
}
```

Both syntaxes compile down to the same IL, so which syntax you use is completely up to you. In this text, you will see a mix of both styles to keep visibility on them, not because I am adhering to a specific code style.

Using Properties Within a Class Definition

Properties, specifically the set portion of a property, are common places to package up the business rules of your class. Currently, the Employee class has a Name property that ensures the name is no more than 15 characters. The remaining properties (ID, Pay, and Age) could also be updated with any relevant logic.

While this is well and good, also consider what a class constructor typically does internally. It will take the incoming parameters, check for valid data, and then make assignments to the internal private fields. Currently, your master constructor does *not* test the incoming string data for a valid range, so you could update this member as so:

```
public Employee(string name, int age, int id, float pay)
{
  // Humm, this seems like a problem...
  if (name.Length > 15)
  {
    Console.WriteLine("Error! Name length exceeds 15 characters!");
  }
  else
  {
    _empName = name;
  }
  _empId = id;
  _empAge = age;
  _currPay = pay;
}
```

I am sure you can see the problem with this approach. The Name property and your master constructor are performing the same error checking. If you were also making checks on the other data points, you would have a good deal of duplicate code. To streamline your code and isolate all of your error checking to a central location, you will do well if you *always* use properties within your class whenever you need to get or set the values. Consider the following updated constructor:

```
public Employee(string name, int age, int id, float pay)
{
   // Better! Use properties when setting class data.
   // This reduces the amount of duplicate error checks.
   Name = name;
   Age = age;
   ID = id;
   Pay = pay;
}
```

Beyond updating constructors to use properties when assigning values, it is good practice to use properties throughout a class implementation to ensure your business rules are always enforced. In many cases, the only time when you directly refer to the underlying private piece of data is within the property itself. With this in mind, here is your updated Employee class:

```
class Employee
{
   // Field data.
   private string _empName;
   private int _empId;
```

```
    private float _currPay;
    private int _empAge;
    // Constructors.
    public Employee() { }
    public Employee(string name, int id, float pay)
      :this(name, 0, id, pay){}
    public Employee(string name, int age, int id, float pay)
    {
      Name = name;
      Age = age;
      ID = id;
      Pay = pay;
    }
    // Methods.
    public void GiveBonus(float amount) => Pay += amount;

    public void DisplayStats()
    {
      Console.WriteLine("Name: {0}", Name);
      Console.WriteLine("ID: {0}", Id);
      Console.WriteLine("Age: {0}", Age);
      Console.WriteLine("Pay: {0}", Pay);
    }

    // Properties as before...
...
}
```

Read-Only Properties

When encapsulating data, you might want to configure a *read-only property*. To do so, simply omit the set block. For example, assume you have a new property named SocialSecurityNumber, which encapsulates a private string variable named empSSN. If you want to make this a read-only property, you could write this:

```
public string SocialSecurityNumber
{
  get { return _empSSN; }
}
```

Properties that only have a getter can also be simplified using expression body members. The following line is equivalent to the previous code block:

```
public string SocialSecurityNumber => _empSSN;
```

Now assume your class constructor has a new parameter to let the caller set the SSN of the object. Since the SocialSecurityNumber property is read-only, you cannot set the value as so:

```
public Employee(string name, int age, int id, float pay, string ssn)
{
   Name = name;
   Age = age;
```

```
    ID = id;
    Pay = pay;

    // OOPS! This is no longer possible if the property is read only.
    SocialSecurityNumber = ssn;
}
```

Unless you are willing to redesign the property as read-write (which you will do soon), your only choice with read-only properties would be to use the underlying empSSN member variable within your constructor logic as so:

```
public Employee(string name, int age, int id, float pay, string ssn)
{
    ...
    // Check incoming ssn parameter as required and then set the value.
    empSSN = ssn;
}
```

Write-Only Properties

If you want to configure your property as a *write-only property*, omit the get block, like this:

```
public int Id
{
  set { _empId = value; }
}
```

Mixing Private and Public Get/Set Methods on Properties

When defining properties, the access level for the get and set methods can be different. Revisiting the Social Security number, if the goal is to prevent the modification of the number from *outside* the class, then declare the get method as public but the set method as private, like this:

```
public string SocialSecurityNumber
{
  get => _empSSN;
  private set => _empSSN = value;
}
```

Note that this changes the property from read-only to read-write. The difference is that the write is hidden from anything outside the defining class.

Revisiting the static Keyword: Defining Static Properties

Earlier in this chapter, you examined the role of the static keyword. Now that you understand the use of C# property syntax, you can formalize static properties. In the StaticDataAndMembers project created earlier in this chapter, your SavingsAccount class had two public static methods to get and set the interest rate. However, it would be more standard to wrap this data point in a static property. Here is an example (note the use of the static keyword):

```
// A simple savings account class.
class SavingsAccount
{
   // Instance-level data.
   public double currBalance;

   // A static point of data.
   private static double _currInterestRate = 0.04;

   // A static property.
   public static double InterestRate
   {
     get { return _currInterestRate; }
     set { _currInterestRate = value; }
   }
...
}
```

If you want to use this property in place of the previous static methods, you could update your code as so:

```
// Print the current interest rate via property.
Console.WriteLine("Interest Rate is: {0}", SavingsAccount.InterestRate);
```

Pattern Matching with Property Patterns (New 8.0)

The property pattern matches an expression when an expression result is non-null and every nested pattern matches the corresponding property or field of the expression result. In other words, the property pattern enables you to match on properties of an object. To set up the example, add a new file (EmployeePayTypeEnum.cs) to the EmployeeApp project for an enumeration of employee pay types, as follows:

```
namespace EmployeeApp;
public enum EmployeePayTypeEnum
{
  Hourly,
  Salaried,
  Commission
}
```

Update the Employee class with a property for the pay type and initialize it from the constructor. The relevant code changes are listed here:

```
private EmployeePayTypeEnum _payType;
public EmployeePayTypeEnum PayType
{
  get => _payType;
  set => _payType = value;
}
public Employee(string name, int id, float pay, string empSsn)
  : this(name,0,id,pay, empSsn, EmployeePayTypeEnum.Salaried)
```

```
{
}
public Employee(string name, int age, int id,
  float pay, string empSsn, EmployeePayTypeEnum payType)
{
  Name = name;
  Id = id;
  Age = age;
  Pay = pay;
  SocialSecurityNumber = empSsn;
  PayType = payType;
}
```

Now that all of the pieces are in place, the GiveBonus() method can be updated based on the pay type of the employee. Commissioned employees get 10 percent of the bonus, hourly get the equivalent of 40 hours of the prorated bonus, and salaried get the entered amount. The updated GiveBonus() method is listed here:

```
public void GiveBonus(float amount)
{
  Pay = this switch
  {
    {PayType: EmployeePayTypeEnum.Commission }
      => Pay += .10F * amount,
    {PayType: EmployeePayTypeEnum.Hourly }
      => Pay += 40F * amount/2080F,
    {PayType: EmployeePayTypeEnum.Salaried }
      => Pay += amount,
    _ => Pay+=0
  };
}
```

As with other switch statements that use pattern matching, either there must be a catchall case statement or the switch statement must throw an exception if none of the case statements is met.

To test this, add the following code to the top-level statements:

```
Employee emp = new Employee("Marvin",45,123,1000,"111-11-1111",EmployeePayTypeEnum.
Salaried);
Console.WriteLine(emp.Pay);
emp.GiveBonus(100);
Console.WriteLine(emp.Pay);
```

More than one property can be used in the pattern. Suppose you wanted to make sure each of the employees getting a bonus was older than the age of 18. You can update the method to the following:

```
public void GiveBonus(float amount)
{
  Pay = this switch
  {
    {Age: >= 18, PayType: EmployeePayTypeEnum.Commission }
      => Pay += .10F * amount,
    { Age: >= 18, PayType: EmployeePayTypeEnum.Hourly }
```

```
        => Pay += 40F * amount/2080F,
      { Age: >= 18, PayType: EmployeePayTypeEnum.Salaried }
        => Pay += amount,
      _ => Pay+=0
    };
}
```

Property patterns can be nested to navigate down the property chain. To demonstrate this, add a `public` property for the `HireDate`, like this:

```
private DateTime _hireDate;
public DateTime HireDate
{
  get => _hireDate;
  set => _hireDate = value;
}
```

Next, update the `switch` statement to check to make sure each employee's hire year was after 2020 to qualify for the bonus:

```
public void GiveBonus(float amount)
{
  Pay = this switch
  {
    {Age: >= 18, PayType: EmployeePayTypeEnum.Commission , HireDate: { Year: > 2020 }}
      => Pay += .10F * amount,
    { Age: >= 18, PayType: EmployeePayTypeEnum.Hourly , HireDate: { Year: > 2020 } }
      => Pay += 40F * amount/2080F,
    { Age: >= 18, PayType: EmployeePayTypeEnum.Salaried , HireDate: { Year: > 2020 } }
      => Pay += amount,
    _ => Pay+=0
  };
}
```

Extended Property Patterns (New 10.0)

New in C# 10, extended property patterns can be used instead of nesting downstream properties. This update cleans up the previous example, as shown here:

```
public void GiveBonus(float amount)
{
  Pay = this switch
  {
    { Age: >= 18, PayType: EmployeePayTypeEnum.Commission, HireDate.Year: > 2020 }
        => Pay += .10F * amount,
    { Age: >= 18, PayType: EmployeePayTypeEnum.Hourly, HireDate.Year: > 2020  }
        => Pay += 40F * amount / 2080F,
    { Age: >= 18, PayType: EmployeePayTypeEnum.Salaried, HireDate.Year: > 2020  }
        => Pay += amount,
    _ => Pay += 0
  };
}
```

Understanding Automatic Properties

When you are building properties to encapsulate your data, it is common to find that the set scopes have code to enforce business rules of your program. However, in some cases, you may not need any implementation logic beyond simply getting and setting the value. This means you can end up with a lot of code looking like the following:

```
// An Employee Car type using standard property
// syntax.
class Car
{
   private string carName = "";
   public string PetName
   {
     get { return carName; }
     set { carName = value; }
   }
}
```

In these cases, it can become rather verbose to define private backing fields and simple property definitions multiple times. By way of an example, if you are modeling a class that requires nine private points of field data, you end up authoring nine related properties that are little more than thin wrappers for encapsulation services.

To streamline the process of providing simple encapsulation of field data, you may use *automatic property syntax*. As the name implies, this feature will offload the work of defining a private backing field and the related C# property member to the compiler using a new bit of syntax. To illustrate, create a new Console Application project named AutoProps and add a new class file named `Car.cs`. Now, consider this reworking of the `Car` class, which uses this syntax to quickly create three properties:

```
namespace AutoProps;
class Car
{
   // Automatic properties! No need to define backing fields.
   public string PetName { get; set; }
   public int Speed { get; set; }
   public string Color { get; set; }
}
```

■ **Note** Visual Studio and Visual Studio Code provide the `prop` code snippet. If you type `prop` inside a class definition and press the Tab key twice, the IDE will generate starter code for a new automatic property. You can then use the Tab key to cycle through each part of the definition to fill in the details. Give it a try!

When defining automatic properties, you simply specify the access modifier, underlying data type, property name, and empty `get`/`set` scopes. At compile time, your type will be provided with an autogenerated private backing field and a fitting implementation of the `get`/`set` logic.

■ **Note** The name of the autogenerated private backing field is not visible within your C# code base. The only way to see it is to make use of a tool such as `ildasm.exe`.

Since C# version 6, it is possible to define a "read-only automatic property" by omitting the `set` scope. Read-only auto properties can be set only in the constructor. However, it is not possible to define a write-only property. To solidify, consider the following:

```
// Read-only property? This is OK!
public int MyReadOnlyProp { get; }

// Write only property? Error!
public int MyWriteOnlyProp { set; }
```

Interacting with Automatic Properties

Because the compiler will define the private backing field at compile time (and given that these fields are not directly accessible in C# code), the class-defining automatic properties will always need to use property syntax to get and set the underlying value. This is important to note because many programmers make direct use of the private fields *within* a class definition, which is not possible in this case. For example, if the `Car` class were to provide a `DisplayStats()` method, it would need to implement this method using the property name.

```
class Car
{
   // Automatic properties!
   public string PetName { get; set; }
   public int Speed { get; set; }
   public string Color { get; set; }

   public void DisplayStats()
   {
     Console.WriteLine("Car Name: {0}", PetName);
     Console.WriteLine("Speed: {0}", Speed);
     Console.WriteLine("Color: {0}", Color);
   }
}
```

When you are using an object defined with automatic properties, you will be able to assign and obtain the values using the expected property syntax.

```
using AutoProps;

Console.WriteLine("***** Fun with Automatic Properties *****\n");

Car c = new Car();
c.PetName = "Frank";
c.Speed = 55;
c.Color = "Red";

Console.WriteLine("Your car is named {0}? That's odd...",
  c.PetName);
c.DisplayStats();

Console.ReadLine();
```

Automatic Properties and Default Values

When you use automatic properties to encapsulate numerical or Boolean data, you are able to use the autogenerated type properties straightaway within your code base, as the hidden backing fields will be assigned a safe default value (`false` for Booleans and `0` for numerical data). However, be aware that if you use automatic property syntax to wrap another class variable, the hidden private reference type will also be set to a default value of `null` (which can prove problematic if you are not careful).

Let's insert into your current project a new class file named `Garage.cs`, which makes use of two automatic properties (of course, a real garage class might maintain a collection of `Car` objects; however, ignore that detail here).

```
namespace AutoProps;
class Garage
{
  // The hidden int backing field is set to zero!
  public int NumberOfCars { get; set; }

  // The hidden Car backing field is set to null!
  public Car MyAuto { get; set; }
}
```

Given C#'s default values for field data, you would be able to print out the value of `NumberOfCars` as is (as it is automatically assigned the value of zero), but if you directly invoke `MyAuto`, you will receive a "null reference exception" at runtime, as the `Car` member variable used in the background has not been assigned to a new object.

```
...
Garage g = new Garage();

// OK, prints default value of zero.
Console.WriteLine("Number of Cars: {0}", g.NumberOfCars);

// Runtime error! Backing field is currently null!
Console.WriteLine(g.MyAuto.PetName);
Console.ReadLine();
```

To solve this problem, you could update the class constructors to ensure the object comes to life in a safe manner. Here is an example:

```
class Garage
{
   // The hidden backing field is set to zero!
   public int NumberOfCars { get; set; }
   // The hidden backing field is set to null!
   public Car MyAuto { get; set; }
   // Must use constructors to override default
   // values assigned to hidden backing fields.
   public Garage()
   {
     MyAuto = new Car();
     NumberOfCars = 1;
   }
```

```
    public Garage(Car car, int number)
    {
      MyAuto = car;
      NumberOfCars = number;
    }
}
```

With this modification, you can now place a Car object into the Garage object as so:

```
using AutoProps;

Console.WriteLine("***** Fun with Automatic Properties *****\n");

// Make a car.
Car c = new Car();
c.PetName = "Frank";
c.Speed = 55;
c.Color = "Red";
c.DisplayStats();

// Put car in the garage.
Garage g = new Garage();
g.MyAuto = c;
Console.WriteLine("Number of Cars in garage: {0}", g.NumberOfCars);
Console.WriteLine("Your car is named: {0}", g.MyAuto.PetName);

Console.ReadLine();
```

Initializing Automatic Properties

While the previous approach works, since the release of C# 6, you are provided with a language feature that can simplify how an automatic property receives its initial value assignment. Recall from the onset of this chapter, a data field of a class can be directly assigned an initial value upon declaration. Here is an example:

```
class Car
{
  private int numberOfDoors = 2;
}
```

In a similar manner, C# now allows you to assign an initial value to the underlying backing field generated by the compiler. This alleviates you from the hassle of adding code statements in class constructors to ensure property data comes to life as intended.

Here is an updated version of the Garage class that is initializing automatic properties to fitting values. Note you no longer need to add logic to your default class constructor to make safe assignments. In this iteration, you are directly assigning a new Car object to the MyAuto property.

```
class Garage
{
    // The hidden backing field is set to 1.
    public int NumberOfCars { get; set; } = 1;
```

```
    // The hidden backing field is set to a new Car object.
    public Car MyAuto { get; set; } = new Car();

    public Garage(){}
    public Garage(Car car, int number)
    {
        MyAuto = car;
        NumberOfCars = number;
    }
}
```

As you may agree, automatic properties are a nice feature of the C# programming language, as you can define a number of properties for a class using a streamlined syntax. Be aware of course that if you are building a property that requires additional code beyond getting and setting the underlying private field (such as data validation logic, writing to an event log, communicating with a database, etc.), you will be required to define a "normal" .NET Core property type by hand. C# automatic properties never do more than provide simple encapsulation for an underlying piece of (compiler-generated) private data.

Understanding Object Initialization

As shown throughout this chapter, a constructor allows you to specify startup values when creating a new object. On a related note, properties allow you to get and set underlying data in a safe manner. When you are working with other people's classes, including the classes found within the .NET Core base class library, it is not too uncommon to discover that there is not a single constructor that allows you to set every piece of underlying state data. Given this point, a programmer is typically forced to pick the best constructor possible, after which the programmer makes assignments using a handful of provided properties.

Looking at the Object Initialization Syntax

To help streamline the process of getting an object up and running, C# offers *object initializer syntax*. Using this technique, it is possible to create a new object variable and assign a slew of properties and/or public fields in a few lines of code. Syntactically, an object initializer consists of a comma-delimited list of specified values, enclosed by the { and } tokens. Each member in the initialization list maps to the name of a public field or public property of the object being initialized.

To see this syntax in action, create a new Console Application project named ObjectInitializers. Now, consider a simple class named Point, created using automatic properties (which is not mandatory for object initialization syntax but helps you write some concise code).

```
class Point
{
   public int X { get; set; }
   public int Y { get; set; }

   public Point(int xVal, int yVal)
   {
     X = xVal;
     Y = yVal;
   }
   public Point() { }

   public void DisplayStats()
```

```
  {
    Console.WriteLine("[{0}, {1}]", X, Y);
  }
}
```

Now consider how you can make Point objects using any of the following approaches:

```
using ObjectInitializers;

Console.WriteLine("***** Fun with Object Init Syntax *****\n");

// Make a Point by setting each property manually.
Point firstPoint = new Point();
firstPoint.X = 10;
firstPoint.Y = 10;
firstPoint.DisplayStats();

// Or make a Point via a custom constructor.
Point anotherPoint = new Point(20, 20);
anotherPoint.DisplayStats();

// Or make a Point using object init syntax.
Point finalPoint = new Point { X = 30, Y = 30 };
finalPoint.DisplayStats();
Console.ReadLine();
```

The final Point variable is not making use of a custom constructor (as one might do traditionally) but is rather setting values to the public X and Y properties. Behind the scenes, the type's default constructor is invoked, followed by setting the values to the specified properties. To this end, object initialization syntax is just shorthand notation for the syntax used to create a class variable using a default constructor and to set the state data property by property.

■ **Note** It's important to remember that the object initialization process is using the property setter implicitly. If the property setter is marked `private`, this syntax cannot be used.

Using init-Only Setters (New 9.0)

A new feature added in C# 9.0 is `init`-only setters. These setters enable a property to have its value set during initialization, but after construction is complete on the object, the property becomes read-only. These types of properties are call *immutable*. Add a new class file named `ReadOnlyPointAfterCreation.cs` to your project, and add the following code:

```
namespace ObjectInitializers;
class PointReadOnlyAfterCreation
{
  public int X { get; init; }
  public int Y { get; init; }
```

```
  public void DisplayStats()
  {
    Console.WriteLine("InitOnlySetter: [{0}, {1}]", X, Y);
  }
  public PointReadOnlyAfterCreation(int xVal, int yVal)
  {
    X = xVal;
    Y = yVal;
  }
  public PointReadOnlyAfterCreation() { }
}
```

Use the following code to take this new class for a test-drive:

```
//Make readonly point after construction
PointReadOnlyAfterCreation firstReadonlyPoint = new PointReadOnlyAfterCreation(20, 20);
firstReadonlyPoint.DisplayStats();

// Or make a Point using object init syntax.
PointReadOnlyAfterCreation secondReadonlyPoint = new PointReadOnlyAfterCreation { X = 30,
Y = 30 };
secondReadonlyPoint.DisplayStats();
```

Notice nothing has changed from the code that you wrote for the `Point` class, except of course the class name. The difference is that the values for `X` or `Y` cannot be modified once the class is created. For example, the following code will not compile:

```
//The next two lines will not compile
secondReadonlyPoint.X = 10;
secondReadonlyPoint.Y = 10;
```

Calling Custom Constructors with Initialization Syntax

The previous examples initialized `Point` types by implicitly calling the default constructor on the type.

```
// Here, the default constructor is called implicitly.
Point finalPoint = new Point { X = 30, Y = 30 };
```

If you want to be clear about this, it is permissible to explicitly call the default constructor as follows:

```
// Here, the default constructor is called explicitly.
Point finalPoint = new Point() { X = 30, Y = 30 };
```

Be aware that when you are constructing a type using initialization syntax, you are able to invoke *any* constructor defined by the class. Your `Point` type currently defines a two-argument constructor to set the (*x, y*) position. Therefore, the following `Point` declaration results in an `X` value of `100` and a `Y` value of `100`, regardless of the fact that the constructor arguments specified the values `10` and `16`:

```
// Calling a custom constructor.
Point pt = new Point(10, 16) { X = 100, Y = 100 };
```

Given the current definition of your Point type, calling the custom constructor while using initialization syntax is not terribly useful (and more than a bit verbose). However, if your Point type provides a new constructor that allows the caller to establish a color (via a custom enum named PointColor), the combination of custom constructors and object initialization syntax becomes clear.

Add a new class named PointColorEnum.cs to your project, and add the following code to create an enum for the color:

```
namespace ObjectInitializers;
enum PointColorEnum
{
  LightBlue,
  BloodRed,
  Gold
}
```

Now, update the Point class as follows:

```
class Point
{
   public int X { get; set; }
   public int Y { get; set; }
   public PointColorEnum Color{ get; set; }

   public Point(int xVal, int yVal)
   {
     X = xVal;
     Y = yVal;
     Color = PointColorEnum.Gold;
   }

   public Point(PointColorEnum ptColor)
   {
     Color = ptColor;
   }

   public Point() : this(PointColorEnum.BloodRed){ }

   public void DisplayStats()
   {
     Console.WriteLine("[{0}, {1}]", X, Y);
     Console.WriteLine("Point is {0}", Color);
   }
}
```

With this new constructor, you can now create a gold point (positioned at 90, 20) as follows:

```
// Calling a more interesting custom constructor with init syntax.
Point goldPoint = new Point(PointColorEnum.Gold){ X = 90, Y = 20 };
goldPoint.DisplayStats();
```

Initializing Data with Initialization Syntax

As briefly mentioned earlier in this chapter (and fully examined in Chapter 6), the "has-a" relationship allows you to compose new classes by defining member variables of existing classes. For example, assume you now have a Rectangle class, which makes use of the Point type to represent its upper-left/bottom-right coordinates. Since automatic properties set all fields of class variables to null, you will implement this new class using "traditional" property syntax.

```
namespace ObjectInitializers;
class Rectangle
{
  private Point topLeft = new Point();
  private Point bottomRight = new Point();

  public Point TopLeft
  {
    get { return topLeft; }
    set { topLeft = value; }
  }
  public Point BottomRight
  {
    get { return bottomRight; }
    set { bottomRight = value; }
  }

  public void DisplayStats()
  {
    Console.WriteLine("[TopLeft: {0}, {1}, {2} BottomRight: {3}, {4}, {5}]",
        topLeft.X, topLeft.Y, topLeft.Color,
        bottomRight.X, bottomRight.Y, bottomRight.Color);
  }
}
```

Using object initialization syntax, you could create a new Rectangle variable and set the inner Points as follows:

```
// Create and initialize a Rectangle.
Rectangle myRect = new Rectangle
{
   TopLeft = new Point { X = 10, Y = 10 },
   BottomRight = new Point { X = 200, Y = 200}
};
```

Again, the benefit of object initialization syntax is that it basically decreases the number of keystrokes (assuming there is not a suitable constructor). Here is the traditional approach to establishing a similar Rectangle:

```
// Old-school approach.
Rectangle r = new Rectangle();
Point p1 = new Point();
p1.X = 10;
p1.Y = 10;
```

```
r.TopLeft = p1;
Point p2 = new Point();
p2.X = 200;
p2.Y = 200;
r.BottomRight = p2;
```

While you might feel object initialization syntax can take a bit of getting used to, once you get comfortable with the code, you will be quite pleased at how quickly you can establish the state of a new object with minimal fuss and bother.

Working with Constant and Read-Only Field Data

Sometimes you need a property that you do not want changed at all, also known as *immutable*, either from the time it was compiled or after it was set during construction. We have already explored one example with `init`-only setters. Now we will examine constants and read-only fields.

Understanding Constant Field Data

C# offers the `const` keyword to define constant data, which can never change after the initial assignment. As you might guess, this can be helpful when you are defining a set of known values for use in your applications that are logically connected to a given class or structure.

Assume you are building a utility class named `MyMathClass` that needs to define a value for pi (which you will assume to be 3.14 for simplicity). Begin by creating a new Console Application project named ConstData and add a file named `MyMathClass.cs`. Given that you would not want to allow other developers to change this value in code, pi could be modeled with the following constant:

```
//MyMathClass.cs
namespace ConstData;
class MyMathClass
{
  public const double PI = 3.14;
}
```

Update the code in the `Program.cs` file to match this:

```
using ConstData;

Console.WriteLine("***** Fun with Const *****\n");
Console.WriteLine("The value of PI is: {0}", MyMathClass.PI);
// Error! Can't change a constant!
// MyMathClass.PI = 3.1444;

Console.ReadLine();
```

Notice that you are referencing the constant data defined by `MyMathClass` using a class name prefix (i.e., `MyMathClass.PI`). This is because constant fields of a class are implicitly *static*. However, it is permissible to define and access a local constant variable within the scope of a method or property. Here is an example:

```
static void LocalConstStringVariable()
{
   // A local constant data point can be directly accessed.
```

```
    const string fixedStr = "Fixed string Data";
    Console.WriteLine(fixedStr);

    // Error!
    // fixedStr = "This will not work!";
}
```

Regardless of where you define a constant piece of data, the one point to always remember is that the initial value assigned to the constant must be specified at the time you define the constant. Assigning the value of pi in a class constructor, as shown in the following code, produces a compilation error:

```
class MyMathClass
{
    // Try to set PI in constructor?
    public const double PI;

    public MyMathClass()
    {
      // Not possible- must assign at time of declaration.
      PI = 3.14;
    }
}
```

The reason for this restriction has to do with the fact that the value of constant data must be known at compile time. Constructors (or any other method), as you know, are invoked at runtime.

Constant Interpolated Strings (New 10.0)

Introduced in C# 10, `const string` values can use string interpolation in their assignment statements as long as all of the components that are used are also `const strings`. As a trivial example, add the following code to the top-level statements:

```
Console.WriteLine("=> Constant String Interpolation:");
const string foo = "Foo";
const string bar = "Bar";
const string foobar = $"{foo}{bar}";
Console.WriteLine(foobar);
```

Understanding Read-Only Fields

Closely related to constant data is the notion of *read-only field data* (which should not be confused with a read-only property). Like a constant, a read-only field cannot be changed after the initial assignment or you will receive a compile-time error. However, unlike a constant, the value assigned to a read-only field can be determined at runtime and, therefore, can legally be assigned within the scope of a constructor but nowhere else.

This can be helpful when you do not know the value of a field until runtime, perhaps because you need to read an external file to obtain the value but want to ensure that the value will not change after that point. For the sake of illustration, assume the following update to `MyMathClass`:

```
class MyMathClass
{
   // Read-only fields can be assigned in constructors,
   // but nowhere else.
   public readonly double PI;

   public MyMathClass ()
   {
     PI = 3.14;
   }
}
```

Again, any attempt to make assignments to a field marked `readonly` outside the scope of a constructor results in a compiler error.

```
class MyMathClass
{
   public readonly double PI;
   public MyMathClass ()
   {
     PI = 3.14;
   }

   // Error!
   public void ChangePI()
   { PI = 3.14444;}
}
```

Understanding Static Read-Only Fields

Unlike a constant field, read-only fields are not implicitly static. Thus, if you want to expose `PI` from the class level, you must explicitly use the `static` keyword. If you know the value of a static read-only field at compile time, the initial assignment looks similar to that of a constant (however, in this case, it would be easier to simply use the `const` keyword in the first place, as you are assigning the data field at the time of declaration).

```
class MyMathClass
{
   public static readonly double PI = 3.14;
}

//Program.cs
using ConstData;

Console.WriteLine("***** Fun with Const *****");
Console.WriteLine("The value of PI is: {0}", MyMathClass.PI);
Console.ReadLine();
```

However, if the value of a static read-only field is not known until runtime, you must use a static constructor as described earlier in this chapter.

```
class MyMathClass
{
   public static readonly double PI;

   static MyMathClass()
   { PI = 3.14; }
}
```

Understanding Partial Classes

When working with classes, it is important to understand the role of the C# `partial` keyword. The partial keyword allows for a single class to be partitioned across multiple code files. When you scaffold Entity Framework Core classes from a database, the created classes are all created as partial classes. This way, any code that you have written to augment those files is not overwritten, presuming your code is in separate class files marked with the `partial` keyword. Another reason is that maybe your class has grown over time into something difficult to manage, and as an intermediate step toward refactoring that class, you can split it up into partials.

In C#, you can partition a single class across multiple code files to isolate the boilerplate code from more readily useful (and complex) members. To illustrate where partial classes could be useful, open the EmployeeApp project you created previously in this chapter in Visual Studio or Visual Studio Code and then open the `Employee.cs` file for editing. As you recall, this single file contains code of all aspects of the class.

```
class Employee
{
   // Field Data

   // Constructors

   // Methods

   // Properties
}
```

Using partial classes, you could choose to move (for example) the properties, constructors, and field data into a new file named `Employee.Core.cs` (the name of the file is irrelevant). The first step is to add the `partial` keyword to the current class definition and cut the code to be placed into the new file.

```
// Employee.cs
partial class Employee
{
   // Methods

   // Properties
}
```

Next, assuming you have inserted a new class file into your project, you can move the data fields and properties to the new file using a simple cut-and-paste operation. In addition, you *must* add the `partial` keyword to this aspect of the class definition. Here is an example:

```
// Employee.Core.cs
partial class Employee
{
  // Field data

  // Properties
}
```

■ **Note** Remember that each of the partial classes must be marked with the `partial` keyword!

After you compile the modified project, you should see no difference whatsoever. The whole idea of a partial class is realized only during design time. After the application has been compiled, there is just a single, unified class within the assembly. The only requirement when defining partial types is that the type's name (`Employee` in this case) is identical and defined within the same .NET Core namespace.

Recall from the discussion of top-level statements, any methods in top-level statements must be a local function. The top-level statements are implicitly defined in a `partial Program` class, allowing for the creation of another partial `Program` class to hold regular methods.

Create a new console application named FunWithPartials and add a new class file named `Program.Partial.cs`. Update the code to the following:

```
public partial class Program
{
  public static string SayHello() =>  return "Hello";
}
```

Now you can call that method from your top-level statements in the `Program.cs` file, like this:

```
Console.WriteLine(SayHello());
```

Which method you use is a matter of preference.

Records (New 9.0)

New in C# 9.0, *record types* are a special reference type that provide synthesized methods for equality using value semantics and data encapsulation. Record types can be created with immutable or standard properties. To start experimenting with records, create a new console application named FunWithRecords. Consider the following `Car` class, modified from the examples earlier in the chapter:

```
class Car
{
  public string Make { get; set; }
  public string Model { get; set; }
  public string Color { get; set; }

  public Car() {}

  public Car(string make, string model, string color)
  {
    Make = make;
```

```
    Model = model;
    Color = color;
  }
}
```

As you well know by now, once you create an instance of this class, you can change any of the properties at run time. If the properties for the previous Car class need to be immutable, you can change its property definitions to use init-only setters, like this:

```
public string Make { get; init; }
public string Model { get; init; }
public string Color { get; init; }
```

To exercise this new class, the following code creates two instances of the Car class, one through object initialization and the other through the custom constructor. Update the Program.cs file to the following:

```
using FunWithRecords;

Console.WriteLine("Fun with Records!");

//Use object initialization
Car myCar = new Car
{
    Make = "Honda",
    Model = "Pilot",
    Color = "Blue"
};
Console.WriteLine("My car: ");
DisplayCarStats(myCar);
Console.WriteLine();
//Use the custom constructor
Car anotherMyCar = new Car("Honda", "Pilot", "Blue");
Console.WriteLine("Another variable for my car: ");
DisplayCarStats(anotherMyCar);
Console.WriteLine();

//Compile error if property is changed
//myCar.Color = "Red";

Console.ReadLine();

static void DisplayCarStats(Car c)
{
  Console.WriteLine("Car Make: {0}", c.Make);
  Console.WriteLine("Car Model: {0}", c.Model);
  Console.WriteLine("Car Color: {0}", c.Color);
}
```

As expected, both methods of object creation work, properties get displayed, and trying to change a property after construction raises a compilation error.

Immutable Record Types with Standard Property Syntax

Creating an immutable Car record type using standard property syntax is similar to creating classes with immutable properties. To see this in action, add a new file named (CarRecord.cs) to your project and add the following code:

```
record CarRecord
{
  public string Make { get; init; }
  public string Model { get; init; }
  public string Color { get; init; }

  public CarRecord () {}
  public CarRecord (string make, string model, string color)
  {
    Make = make;
    Model = model;
    Color = color;
  }
}
```

■ **Note** Record types allow using the class keyword to help distinguish them from record structs, but the keyword is optional. Therefore record class and record mean the same thing.

You can confirm that the behavior is the same as the Car class with init-only settings by running the following code in Program.cs:

```
using FunWithRecords;

Console.WriteLine("*************** RECORDS *********************");
//Use object initialization
CarRecord myCarRecord = new CarRecord
{
    Make = "Honda",
    Model = "Pilot",
    Color = "Blue"
};
Console.WriteLine("My car: ");
DisplayCarRecordStats(myCarRecord);
Console.WriteLine();

//Use the custom constructor
CarRecord anotherMyCarRecord = new CarRecord("Honda", "Pilot", "Blue");
Console.WriteLine("Another variable for my car: ");
Console.WriteLine(anotherMyCarRecord.ToString());
Console.WriteLine();

//Compile error if property is changed
//myCarRecord.Color = "Red";
```

```
Console.ReadLine();

static void DisplayCarStats(Car c)
{
    Console.WriteLine("Car Make: {0}", c.Make);
    Console.WriteLine("Car Model: {0}", c.Model);
    Console.WriteLine("Car Color: {0}", c.Color);
}
```

While we have not covered equality (next section) or inheritance (next chapter) with records, this first look at records does not seem like much of a benefit. The current `Car` example includes all of the plumbing code that we have come to expect. With one notable difference on the output: the `ToString()` method is fancied up for record types, as shown in this following sample output:

```
*************** RECORDS *********************
My car:
CarRecord { Make = Honda, Model = Pilot, Color = Blue }
Another variable for my car:
CarRecord { Make = Honda, Model = Pilot, Color = Blue }
```

Immutable Record Types with Positional Syntax

Consider this updated (and much abbreviated) definition for the `Car` record:

```
record CarRecord(string Make, string Model, string Color);
```

Referred to as a *positional record type*, the constructor defines the properties on the record, and all of the other plumbing code has been removed. There are three considerations when using this syntax: the first is that you cannot use object initialization of record types using the compact definition syntax, the second is that the record must be constructed with the properties in the correct position, and the third is that the casing of the properties in the constructor is directly translated to the casing of the properties on the record type.

We can confirm that the Make, Model, and Color are all `init`-only properties on the `Car` record by looking at an abbreviated listing of the IL. Notice that there are backing fields for each of the parameters passed into the constructor, and each has the `private` and `initonly` modifiers.

```
.class private auto ansi beforefieldinit FunWithRecords.CarRecord
  extends [System.Runtime]System.Object
  implements class [System.Runtime]System.IEquatable`1<class FunWithRecords.CarRecord>
{
  .field private initonly string '<Make>k__BackingField'
  .field private initonly string '<Model>k__BackingField'
  .field private initonly string '<Color>k__BackingField'
...
}
```

When using the positional syntax, record types provide a primary constructor that matches the positional parameters on the record declaration.

Deconstructing Mutable Record Types

Record types using positional parameters also provide a Deconstruct() method with an out parameter for each positional parameter in the declaration. The following code creates a new record using the supplied constructor and then deconstructs the properties into separate variables:

```
CarRecord myCarRecord = new CarRecord("Honda", "Pilot", "Blue");
myCarRecord.Deconstruct(out string make, out string model, out string color);
Console.WriteLine($"Make: {make} Model: {model} Color: {color}");
```

Note that while the public properties on the record match the casing of the declaration, the out variables in the Deconstruct() method only have to match the *position* of the parameters. Changing the names of the variables in the Deconstruct() method still returns Make, Model, and Color, in that order:

```
myCarRecord.Deconstruct(out string a, out string b, out string c);
Console.WriteLine($"Make: {a} Model: {b} Color: {c}");
```

The tuple syntax can also be used when deconstructing records. Note the following addition to the example:

```
var (make2, model2, color2) = myCarRecord;
Console.WriteLine($"Make: {make2} Model: {model2} Color: {color2}");
```

Mutable Record Types

C# also supports mutable record types by using standard (not init-only) setters. The following is an example of this:

```
record CarRecord
{
  public string Make { get; set; }
  public string Model { get; set; }
  public string Color { get; set; }

  public CarRecord() {}
  public CarRecord(string make, string model, string color)
  {
    Make = make;
    Model = model;
    Color = color;
  }
}
```

While this syntax is supported, the record types are intended to be used for immutable data models.

Value Equality with Record Types

In the Car class example, the two Car instances were created with the same data. One *might* think that these two classes are equal, as the following line of code tests:

```
Console.WriteLine($"Cars are the same? {myCar.Equals(anotherMyCar)}");
```

However, they are not equal. Recall that record types are a specialized type of class, and classes are *reference types*. For two reference types to be equal, they have to point to the same object in memory. As a further test, check to see if the two Car objects point to the same object:

```
Console.WriteLine($"Cars are the same reference? {ReferenceEquals(myCar, anotherMyCar)}");
```

Running the program again produces this (abbreviated) result:

```
Cars are the same? False
CarRecords are the same? False
```

Record types behave differently. Record types implicitly override Equals, ==, and !=, and two record types are considered equal if the hold the same values and are the same type, just as if the instances are value types. Consider the following code and the subsequent results:

```
Console.WriteLine($"CarRecords are the same? {myCarRecord.Equals(anotherMyCarRecord)}");
Console.WriteLine($"CarRecords are the same reference? {ReferenceEquals(myCarRecord,another
MyCarRecord)}");
Console.WriteLine($"CarRecords are the same? {myCarRecord == anotherMyCarRecord}");
Console.WriteLine($"CarRecords are not the same? {myCarRecord != anotherMyCarRecord}");
```

```
/*************** RECORDS *********************/
My car:
CarRecord { Make = Honda, Model = Pilot, Color = Blue }
Another variable for my car:
CarRecord { Make = Honda, Model = Pilot, Color = Blue }

CarRecords are the same? True
CarRecords are the same reference? false
CarRecords are the same? True
CarRecords are not the same? False
```

Notice that they are considered equal, even though the variables point to two different variables in memory.

Copying Record Types Using with Expressions

With record types, assigning a record type instance to a new variable creates a pointer to the same reference, which is the same behavior as classes. The following code demonstrates this:

```
CarRecord carRecordCopy = anotherMyCarRecord;
Console.WriteLine("Car Record copy results");
Console.WriteLine($"CarRecords are the same? {carRecordCopy.Equals(anotherMyCarRecord)}");
Console.WriteLine($"CarRecords are the same? {ReferenceEquals(carRecordCopy,
anotherMyCarRecord)}");
```

When executed, both tests return true, proving that they are the same in value and reference.

To create a true copy of a record with one or more properties modified (referred to as *nondestructive mutation*), C# 9.0 introduces with expressions. In the with construct, any properties that need to be updated are specified with their new values, and any properties not listed are shallow copied exactly. Examine the following example:

```
CarRecord ourOtherCar = myCarRecord with {Model = "Odyssey"};
Console.WriteLine("My copied car:");
Console.WriteLine(ourOtherCar.ToString());

Console.WriteLine("Car Record copy using with expression results");
Console.WriteLine($"CarRecords are the same? {ourOtherCar.Equals(myCarRecord)}");
Console.WriteLine($"CarRecords are the same? {ReferenceEquals(ourOtherCar, myCarRecord)}");
```

The code creates a new instance of the CarRecord type, copying the Make and Color values of the myCarRecord instance and setting Model to the string Odyssey. The results of this code is shown here:

```
/*************** RECORDS *********************/
My copied car:
CarRecord { Make = Honda, Model = Odyssey, Color = Blue }

Car Record copy using with expression results
CarRecords are the same? False
CarRecords are the same? False
```

Using with expressions, you can easily take complex record types into new record type instances with updated property values.

Record Structs (New 10.0)

New in C# 10.0, *record structs* are the value type equivalent of record types. Record structs can also use positional parameters or standard property syntax and provide value equality, nondestructive mutation, and built-in display formatting. To start experimenting with records, create a new console application named FunWithRecordStructs. One major difference between record structs and records is that a record struct is mutable by default. To make a record struct immutable, you must use add the readonly modifier.

Mutable Record Structs

To create a record struct, let's revisit our friend the Point struct. The following shows how to create two different record struct types, one using the positional syntax and the other using standard properties:

```
public record struct Point(double X, double Y, double Z);

public record struct PointWithPropertySyntax()
{
  public double X { get; set; } = default;
  public double Y { get; set; } = default;
  public double Z { get; set; } = default;
```

```
  public PointWithPropertySyntax(double x, double y, double z) : this()
  {
    X = x;
    Y = y;
    Z = z;
  }
};
```

The following code demonstrates the mutability of the two record struct types as well as the improved ToString() method:

```
Console.WriteLine("***** Fun With Record Structs *****");
var rs = new Point(2, 4, 6);
Console.WriteLine(rs.ToString());
rs.X = 8;
Console.WriteLine(rs.ToString());

var rs2 = new PointWithPropertySyntax(2, 4, 6);
Console.WriteLine(rs2.ToString());
rs2.X = 8;
Console.WriteLine(rs2.ToString());
```

Immutable Record Structs

The previous two record struct examples can be made immutable by adding the readonly keyword:

```
public readonly record struct ReadOnlyPoint(double X, double Y, double Z);

public readonly record struct ReadOnlyPointWithPropertySyntax()
{
    public double X { get; init; } = default;
    public double Y { get; init; } = default;
    public double Z { get; init; } = default;

    public ReadOnlyPointWithPropertySyntax(double x, double y, double z) : this()
    {
        X = x;
        Y = y;
        Z = z;
    }
};
```

You can confirm that they are now immutable (enforced by the compiler) with the following code:

```
var rors = new ReadOnlyPoint(2, 4, 6);
//Compiler Error:
//rors.X = 8;
```

```
var rors2 = new ReadOnlyPointWithPropertySyntax(2, 4, 6);
//Compiler Error:
//rors2.X = 8;
```

Value equality and copying using `with` expressions work the same as record types.

Deconstructing Record Structs

Like record types, record structs that use positional syntax also provide a `Deconstruct()` method. The behavior is the same as mutable and immutable record structs. The following code creates a new record using the supplied constructor and then deconstructs the properties into separate variables:

```
Console.WriteLine("Deconstruction: ");
var (x1, y1, z1) = rs;
Console.WriteLine($"X: {x1} Y: {y1} Z: {z1}");
var (x2, y2, z2) = rors;
Console.WriteLine($"X: {x2} Y: {y2} Z: {z2}");
rs.Deconstruct(out double x3,out double y3,out double z3);
Console.WriteLine($"X: {x3} Y: {y3} Z: {z3}");
rors.Deconstruct(out double x4,out double y4,out double z4);
Console.WriteLine($"X: {x4} Y: {y4} Z: {z4}");
```

Summary

The point of this chapter was to introduce you to the role of the C# class type and the new C# 9.0 record type. As you have seen, classes can take any number of *constructors* that enable the object user to establish the state of the object upon creation. This chapter also illustrated several class design techniques (and related keywords). The `this` keyword can be used to obtain access to the current object. The `static` keyword allows you to define fields and members that are bound at the class (not object) level. The `const` keyword, `readonly` modifier, and `init`-only setters allow you to define a point of data that can never change after the initial assignment or object construction. Record types are a special type of class that are immutable (by default) and behave like value types when comparing a record type with another instance of the same record type. Record structs are value types that are mutable (by default) and provide the same equality and nondestructive mutation capabilities as record types.

The bulk of this chapter dug into the details of the first pillar of OOP: encapsulation. You learned about the access modifiers of C# and the role of type properties, object initialization syntax, and partial classes. With this behind you, you are now able to turn to the next chapter where you will learn to build a family of related classes using inheritance and polymorphism.

CHAPTER 6

Understanding Inheritance and Polymorphism

Chapter 5 examined the first pillar of OOP: encapsulation. At that time, you learned how to build a single well-defined class type with constructors and various members (fields, properties, methods, constants, and read-only fields). This chapter will focus on the remaining two pillars of OOP: inheritance and polymorphism.

First, you will learn how to build families of related classes using *inheritance*. As you will see, this form of code reuse allows you to define common functionality in a parent class that can be leveraged, and possibly altered, by child classes. Along the way, you will learn how to establish a *polymorphic interface* into class hierarchies using virtual and abstract members, as well as the role of explicit casting.

The chapter will wrap up by examining the role of the ultimate parent class in the .NET base class libraries: `System.Object`.

Understanding the Basic Mechanics of Inheritance

Recall from Chapter 5 that inheritance is an aspect of OOP that facilitates code reuse. Specifically speaking, code reuse comes in two flavors: inheritance (the "is-a" relationship) and the containment/delegation model (the "has-a" relationship). Let's begin this chapter by examining the classical inheritance model of the "is-a" relationship.

When you establish "is-a" relationships between classes, you are building a dependency between two or more class types. The basic idea behind classical inheritance is that new classes can be created using existing classes as a starting point. To begin with a simple example, create a new Console Application project named `BasicInheritance`. Now assume you have designed a class named `Car` that models some basic details of an automobile.

```
namespace BasicInheritance;
// A simple base class.
class Car
{
  public readonly int MaxSpeed;
  private int _currSpeed;

  public Car(int max)
  {
    MaxSpeed = max;
  }
```


A. Troelsen and P. Japikse, *Pro C# 10 with .NET 6*, https://doi.org/10.1007/978-1-4842-7869-7_6

```
  public Car()
  {
    MaxSpeed = 55;
  }
  public int Speed
  {
    get { return _currSpeed; }
    set
    {
      _currSpeed = value;
      if (_currSpeed > MaxSpeed)
      {
        _currSpeed = MaxSpeed;
      }
    }
  }
}
```

Notice that the Car class is using encapsulation services to control access to the private currSpeed field using a public property named Speed. At this point, you can exercise your Car type as follows:

```
using BasicInheritance;

Console.WriteLine("***** Basic Inheritance *****\n");
// Make a Car object, set max speed and current speed.
Car myCar = new Car(80) {Speed = 50};

// Print current speed.
Console.WriteLine("My car is going {0} MPH", myCar.Speed);
Console.ReadLine();
```

Specifying the Parent Class of an Existing Class

Now assume you want to build a new class named MiniVan. Like a basic Car, you want to define the MiniVan class to support data for a maximum speed, a current speed, and a property named Speed to allow the object user to modify the object's state. Clearly, the Car and MiniVan classes are related; in fact, it can be said that a MiniVan "*is-a*" type of Car. The "is-a" relationship (formally termed *classical inheritance*) allows you to build new class definitions that extend the functionality of an existing class.

The existing class that will serve as the basis for the new class is termed a *base class, superclass*, or *parent class*. The role of a base class is to define all the common data and members for the classes that extend it. The extending classes are formally termed *derived* or *child* classes. In C#, you make use of the colon operator on the class definition to establish an "is-a" relationship between classes. Assume you have authored the following new MiniVan class:

```
namespace BasicInheritance;
// MiniVan "is-a" Car.
class MiniVan : Car
{
}
```

Currently, this new class has not defined any members whatsoever. So, what have you gained by extending your MiniVan from the Car base class? Simply put, MiniVan objects now have access to each public member defined within the parent class.

■ **Note** Although constructors are typically defined as public, a derived class never inherits the constructors of a parent class. Constructors are used to construct only the class that they are defined within, although they can be called by a derived class through constructor chaining. This will be covered shortly.

Given the relation between these two class types, you can now make use of the MiniVan class like so:

```
Console.WriteLine("***** Basic Inheritance *****\n");
.
// Now make a MiniVan object.
MiniVan myVan = new MiniVan {Speed = 10};
Console.WriteLine("My van is going {0} MPH", myVan.Speed);
Console.ReadLine();
```

Again, notice that although you have not added any members to the MiniVan class, you have direct access to the public Speed property of your parent class and have thus reused code. This is a far better approach than creating a MiniVan class that has the same members as Car, such as a Speed property. If you did duplicate code between these two classes, you would need to now maintain two bodies of code, which is certainly a poor use of your time.

Always remember that inheritance preserves encapsulation; therefore, the following code results in a compiler error, as private members can never be accessed from an object reference:

```
Console.WriteLine("***** Basic Inheritance *****\n");
...
// Make a MiniVan object.
MiniVan myVan = new MiniVan();
myVan.Speed = 10;
Console.WriteLine("My van is going {0} MPH", myVan.Speed);
// Error! Can't access private members!
myVan._currSpeed = 55;
Console.ReadLine();
```

On a related note, if the MiniVan defined its own set of members, it would still not be able to access any private member of the Car base class. Remember, private members can be accessed *only* by the class that defines it. For example, the following method in MiniVan would result in a compiler error:

```
// MiniVan derives from Car.
class MiniVan : Car
{
  public void TestMethod()
  {
    // OK! Can access public members
    // of a parent within a derived type.
    Speed = 10;
```

```
    // Error! Cannot access private
    // members of parent within a derived type.
    _currSpeed = 10;
  }
}
```

Regarding Multiple Base Classes

Speaking of base classes, it is important to keep in mind that C# demands that a given class have exactly *one* direct base class. It is not possible to create a class type that directly derives from two or more base classes (this technique, which is supported in unmanaged C++, is known as *multiple inheritance*, or simply *MI*). If you attempted to create a class that specifies two direct parent classes, as shown in the following code, you would receive compiler errors:

```
// Illegal! C# does not allow
// multiple inheritance for classes!
class WontWork
  : BaseClassOne, BaseClassTwo
{}
```

As you will see in Chapter 8, the .NET Core platform does allow a given class, or structure, to implement any number of discrete interfaces. In this way, a C# type can exhibit a number of behaviors while avoiding the complexities associated with MI. Using this technique, you can build sophisticated interface hierarchies that model complex behaviors (again, see Chapter 8).

Using the sealed Keyword

C# supplies another keyword, `sealed`, that prevents inheritance from occurring. When you mark a class as `sealed`, the compiler will not allow you to derive from this type. For example, assume you have decided that it makes no sense to further extend the `MiniVan` class.

```
// The MiniVan class cannot be extended!
sealed class MiniVan : Car
{
}
```

If you (or a teammate) were to attempt to derive from this class, you would receive a compile-time error.

```
// Error! Cannot extend
// a class marked with the sealed keyword!
class DeluxeMiniVan
  : MiniVan
{
}
```

Most often, sealing a class makes the best sense when you are designing a utility class. For example, the `System` namespace defines numerous sealed classes, such as the `String` class. Thus, just like the `MiniVan`, if you attempt to build a new class that extends `System.String`, you will receive a compile-time error.

```
// Another error! Cannot extend
// a class marked as sealed!
class MyString
  : String
{
}
```

■ **Note** In Chapter 4, you learned that C# structures are always implicitly sealed (see Table 4-3). Therefore, you can never derive one structure from another structure, a class from a structure, or a structure from a class. Structures can be used to model only stand-alone, atomic, user-defined data types. If you want to leverage the "is-a" relationship, you must use classes.

As you would guess, there are many more details to inheritance that you will come to know during the remainder of this chapter. For now, simply keep in mind that the colon operator allows you to establish base/derived class relationships, while the `sealed` keyword prevents subsequent inheritance from occurring.

Revisiting Visual Studio Class Diagrams

In Chapter 2, I briefly mentioned that Visual Studio allows you to establish base/derived class relationships visually at design time. To leverage this aspect of the IDE, your first step is to include a new class diagram file into your current project. To do so, access the Project ➤ Add New Item menu option and click the Class Diagram icon (in Figure 6-1, I renamed the file from `ClassDiagram1.cd` to `Cars.cd`).

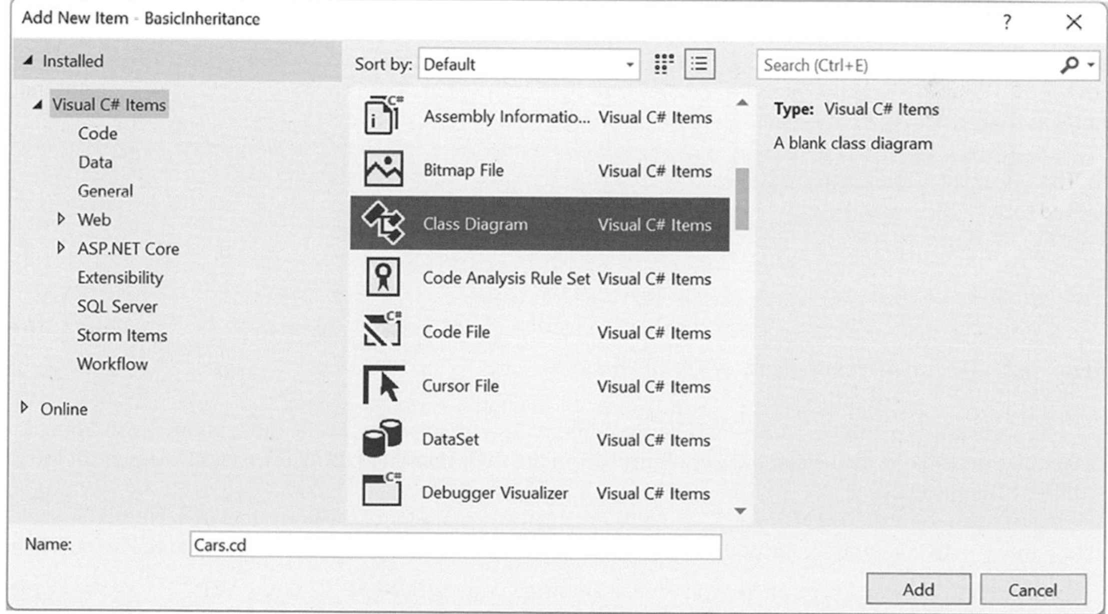

***Figure 6-1.** Inserting a new class diagram*

After you click the Add button, you will be presented with a blank designer surface. To add types to a class designer, simply drag each file from the Solution Explorer window onto the surface. Also recall that if you delete an item from the visual designer (simply by selecting it and pressing the Delete key), this will not destroy the associated source code but simply remove the item off the designer surface. Figure 6-2 shows the current class hierarchy.

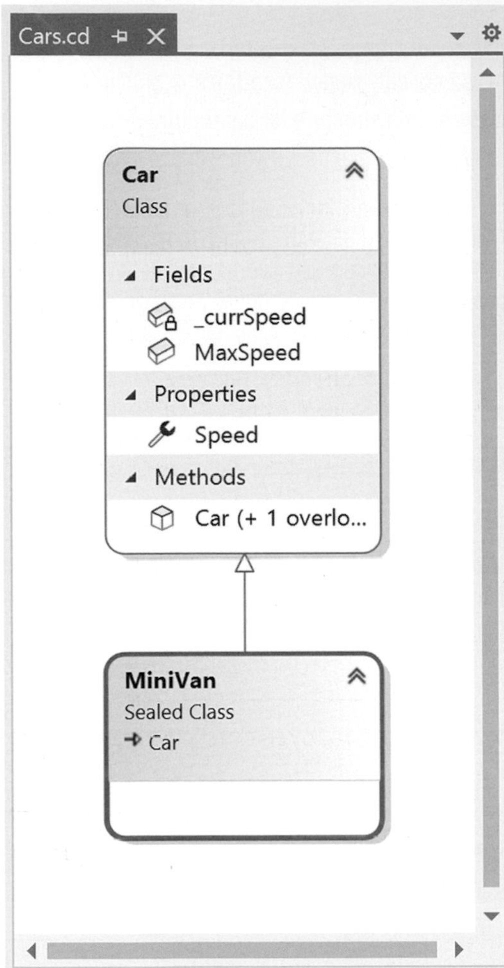

Figure 6-2. *The visual class designer of Visual Studio*

Beyond simply displaying the relationships of the types within your current application, recall from Chapter 2 that you can also create new types and populate their members using the Class Designer toolbox and Class Details window.

If you want to make use of these visual tools during the remainder of the book, feel free. However, always make sure you analyze the generated code so you have a solid understanding of what these tools have done on your behalf.

Understanding the Second Pillar of OOP: The Details of Inheritance

Now that you have seen the basic syntax of inheritance, let's create a more complex example and get to know the numerous details of building class hierarchies. To do so, you will be reusing the Employee class you designed in Chapter 5. To begin, create a new C# Console Application project named Employees.

Next, copy the Employee.cs, Employee.Core.cs, and EmployeePayTypeEnum.cs files you created in the EmployeeApp example from Chapter 5 into the Employees project.

■ **Note** Prior to .NET Core, the files needed to be referenced in the .csproj file to use them in a C# project. With .NET Core, all the files in the current directory structure are automatically included in your project. Simply copying the two files from the other project into the current project directory is enough to have them included in your project.

Before you start to build some derived classes, you have two details to attend to. Because the original Employee class was created in a project named EmployeeApp, the class has been wrapped within an identically named .NET Core namespace. Chapter 16 will examine namespaces in detail; however, for simplicity, rename the current namespace (in all three file locations) to Employees to match your new project name.

```
// Be sure to change the namespace name in both C# files!
namespace Employees;
partial class Employee
{...}
```

■ **Note** If you removed the default constructor during the changes to the Employee class in Chapter 5, make sure to add it back into the class.

The second detail is to remove any of the commented code from the different iterations of the Employee class from the Chapter 5 example.

■ **Note** As a sanity check, compile and run your new project by entering dotnet run in a command prompt (in your project's directory) or pressing Ctrl+F5 if you are using Visual Studio. The program will not do anything at this point; however, this will ensure you do not have any compiler errors.

Your goal is to create a family of classes that model various types of employees in a company. Assume you want to leverage the functionality of the Employee class to create two new classes (SalesPerson and Manager). The new SalesPerson class "is-an" Employee (as is a Manager). Remember that under the classical inheritance model, base classes (such as Employee) are used to define general characteristics that are common to all descendants. Subclasses (such as SalesPerson and Manager) extend this general functionality while adding more specific functionality.

For your example, you will assume that the Manager class extends Employee by recording the number of stock options, while the SalesPerson class maintains the number of sales made. Insert a new class file (Manager.cs) that defines the Manager class with the following automatic property:

```
namespace Employees;
// Managers need to know their number of stock options.
class Manager : Employee
{
  public int StockOptions { get; set; }
}
```

Next, add another new class file (SalesPerson.cs) that defines the SalesPerson class with a fitting automatic property.

```
namespace Employees;
// Salespeople need to know their number of sales.
class SalesPerson : Employee
{
  public int SalesNumber { get; set; }
}
```

Now that you have established an "is-a" relationship, SalesPerson and Manager have automatically inherited all public members of the Employee base class. To illustrate, update your top-level statements as follows:

```
using Employees;
// Create a subclass object and access base class functionality.
Console.WriteLine("***** The Employee Class Hierarchy *****\n");
SalesPerson fred = new SalesPerson
{
  Age = 31, Name = "Fred", SalesNumber = 50
};
```

Calling Base Class Constructors with the base Keyword

Currently, SalesPerson and Manager can be created only using the "freebie" default constructor (see Chapter 5). With this in mind, assume you have added a new seven-argument constructor to the Manager type, which is invoked as follows:

```
...
// Assume Manager has a constructor matching this signature:
// (string fullName, int age, int empId,
// float currPay, string ssn, int numbOfOpts)
Manager chucky = new Manager("Chucky", 50, 92, 100000, "333-23-2322", 9000);
```

If you look at the parameter list, you can clearly see that most of these arguments should be stored in the member variables defined by the Employee base class. To do so, you might implement this custom constructor on the Manager class as follows:

```
public Manager(string fullName, int age, int empId,
        float currPay, string ssn, int numbOfOpts)
{
  // This property is defined by the Manager class.
  StockOptions = numbOfOpts;

  // Assign incoming parameters using the
  // inherited properties of the parent class.
  Id = empId;
  Age = age;
  Name = fullName;
  Pay = currPay;
  PayType = EmployeePayTypeEnum.Salaried;
  // OOPS! This would be a compiler error,
  // if the SSN property were read-only!
  SocialSecurityNumber = ssn;
}
```

The first issue with this approach is that if you defined any property as read-only (e.g., the SocialSecurityNumber property), you are unable to assign the incoming string parameter to this field, as shown in the final code statement of this custom constructor.

The second issue is that you have indirectly created a rather inefficient constructor, given that under C#, unless you say otherwise, the default constructor of a base class is called automatically before the logic of the derived constructor is executed. After this point, the current implementation accesses numerous public properties of the Employee base class to establish its state. Thus, you have really made eight hits (six inherited properties and two constructor calls) during the creation of a Manager object!

To help optimize the creation of a derived class, you will do well to implement your subclass constructors to explicitly call an appropriate custom base class constructor, rather than the default. In this way, you are able to reduce the number of calls to inherited initialization members (which saves processing time). First, ensure your Employee parent class has the following six-argument constructor:

```
// Add to the Employee base class.
public Employee(string name, int age, int id, float pay, string empSsn, EmployeePay
TypeEnum payType)
{
  Name = name;
  Id = id;
  Age = age;
  Pay = pay;
  SocialSecurityNumber = empSsn;
  PayType = payType;
}
```

Now, let's retrofit the custom constructor of the Manager type to call this constructor using the base keyword.

```
public Manager(string fullName, int age, int empId, float currPay, string ssn, int
numbOfOpts)
  : base(fullName, age, empId, currPay, ssn, EmployeePayTypeEnum.Salaried)
```

```
{
  // This property is defined by the Manager class.
  StockOptions = numbOfOpts;
}
```

Here, the base keyword is hanging off the constructor signature (much like the syntax used to chain constructors on a single class using the this keyword, as was discussed in Chapter 5), which always indicates a derived constructor is passing data to the immediate parent constructor. In this situation, you are explicitly calling the six-parameter constructor defined by Employee and saving yourself unnecessary calls during the creation of the child class. Additionally, you added a specific behavior to the Manager class, in that the pay type is always set to Salaried. The custom SalesPerson constructor looks almost identical, with the exception that the pay type is set to Commission.

```
// As a general rule, all subclasses should explicitly call an appropriate
// base class constructor.
public SalesPerson(string fullName, int age, int empId,
  float currPay, string ssn, int numbOfSales)
  : base(fullName, age, empId, currPay, ssn, EmployeePayTypeEnum.Commission)
{
  // This belongs with us!
  SalesNumber = numbOfSales;
}
```

■ **Note** You may use the base keyword whenever a subclass wants to access a public or protected member defined by a parent class. Use of this keyword is not limited to constructor logic. You will see examples using base in this manner during the examination of polymorphism, later in this chapter.

Finally, recall that once you add a custom constructor to a class definition, the default constructor is silently removed. Therefore, be sure to redefine the default constructor for the SalesPerson and Manager types. Here's an example:

```
// Add back the default ctor
// in the Manager class as well.
public SalesPerson() {}
```

Keeping Family Secrets: The protected Keyword

As you already know, public items are directly accessible from anywhere, while private items can be accessed only by the class that has defined them. Recall from Chapter 5 that C# takes the lead of many other modern object languages and provides an additional keyword to define member accessibility: protected.

When a base class defines protected data or protected members, it establishes a set of items that can be accessed directly by any descendant. If you want to allow the SalesPerson and Manager child classes to directly access the data sector defined by Employee, you can update the original Employee class definition (in the EmployeeCore.cs file) as follows:

```
// Protected state data.
partial class Employee
```

```
{
  // Derived classes can now directly access this information.
  protected string EmpName;
  protected int EmpId;
  protected float CurrPay;
  protected int EmpAge;
  protected string EmpSsn;
  protected EmployeePayTypeEnum EmpPayType;...
}
```

■ **Note** Convention is that protected members are named PascalCased (EmpName) and not underscore-camelCase (_empName). This is not a requirement of the language, but a common code style. If you decide to update the names as I have done here, make sure to rename all of the backing methods in your properties to match the PascalCased protected properties.

The benefit of defining protected members in a base class is that derived types no longer have to access the data indirectly using public methods or properties. The possible downfall, of course, is that when a derived type has direct access to its parent's internal data, it is possible to accidentally bypass existing business rules found within public properties. When you define protected members, you are creating a level of trust between the parent class and the child class, as the compiler will not catch any violation of your type's business rules.

Finally, understand that as far as the object user is concerned, protected data is regarded as private (as the user is "outside" the family). Therefore, the following is illegal:

```
// Error! Can't access protected data from client code.
Employee emp = new Employee();
emp.empName = "Fred";
```

■ **Note** Although protected field data can break encapsulation, it is quite safe (and useful) to define protected methods. When building class hierarchies, it is common to define a set of methods that are only for use by derived types and are not intended for use by the outside world.

Adding a sealed Class

Recall that a *sealed* class cannot be extended by other classes. As mentioned, this technique is most often used when you are designing a utility class. However, when building class hierarchies, you might find that a certain branch in the inheritance chain should be "capped off," as it makes no sense to further extend the lineage. For example, assume you have added yet another class to your program (PtSalesPerson) that extends the existing SalesPerson type. Figure 6-3 shows the current update.

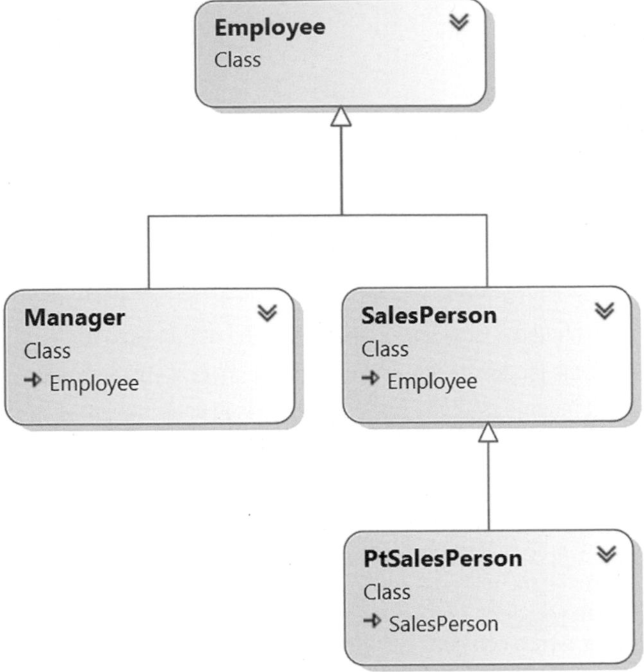

Figure 6-3. *The PtSalesPerson class*

PtSalesPerson is a class representing, of course, a part-time salesperson. For the sake of argument, let's say you want to ensure that no other developer is able to subclass from PTSalesPerson. To prevent others from extending a class, use the sealed keyword.

```
namespace Employees;
sealed class PtSalesPerson : SalesPerson
{
  public PtSalesPerson(string fullName, int age, int empId,
    float currPay, string ssn, int numbOfSales)
      : base(fullName, age, empId, currPay, ssn, numbOfSales)
  {
  }
  // Assume other members here...
}
```

Understanding Inheritance with Record Types (New 9.0)

The new C# 9.0 record types also support inheritance. To explore this, place your work in the Employees project on hold and create a new console app named RecordInheritance.

Inheritance for Record Types with Standard Properties

Add two new files named Car.cs and MiniVan.cs, and add the following record defining code into their respective files:

```
//Car.cs
namespace RecordInheritance;
//Car record type
public record Car
{
  public string Make { get; init; }
  public string Model { get; init; }
  public string Color { get; init; }

  public Car(string make, string model, string color)
  {
    Make = make;
    Model = model;
    Color = color;
  }
}

//MiniVan.cs
namespace RecordInheritance;
//MiniVan record type
public sealed record MiniVan : Car
{
  public int Seating { get; init; }
  public MiniVan(string make, string model, string color, int seating) :
  base(make, model, color)
  {
    Seating = seating;
  }
}
```

Notice that there isn't much difference between these examples using record types and the previous examples using classes. The sealed access modifier on the record type prevents other record types from deriving from the sealed record types. Although not used in the listed examples, the protected access modifier on properties and methods behave the same as with class inheritance. You will also find the remaining topics in this chapter work with inherited record types. This is because record types are just a special type of class (as detailed in Chapter 5).

Record types also include implicit casts to their base class, as shown in the following code:

```
using RecordInheritance;

Console.WriteLine("Record type inheritance!");

Car c = new Car("Honda","Pilot","Blue");
MiniVan m = new MiniVan("Honda", "Pilot", "Blue",10);
Console.WriteLine($"Checking MiniVan is-a Car:{m is Car}");
```

As one would expect, the output from the check m is that Car returns true, as the following output shows:

```
Record type inheritance!
Checking minvan is-a car:True
```

It's important to note that even though record types are specialized classes, you cannot cross-inherit between classes and records. To be clear, classes cannot inherit from record types, and record types cannot inherit from classes. Consider the following code, and notice that the last two examples won't compile:

```
namespace RecordInheritance;
public class TestClass { }
public record TestRecord { }

//Classes cannot inherit records
// public class Test2 : TestRecord { }

//Records types cannot inherit from classes
// public record Test2 : TestClass {  }
```

Inheritance for Record Types with Positional Parameters

Inheritance also works with positional record types. The derived record declares positional parameters for all of the parameters in the base record. The derived record doesn't hide them but uses them from the base record. The derived record only creates and initializes properties that are not on the base record.

To see this in action, create a new file named PositionalRecordTypes.cs in your project. Add the following code into your file:

```
namespace RecordInheritance;
public record PositionalCar (string Make, string Model, string Color);
public record PositionalMiniVan (string Make, string Model, string Color, int seating)
  : PositionalCar(Make, Model, Color);

public record MotorCycle(string Make, string Model);
public record Scooter(string Make, string Model) : MotorCycle(Make,Model);
public record FancyScooter(string Make, string Model, string FancyColor)
  : Scooter(Make, Model);
```

Add the following code to show what you already know to be true: that the positional record types work exactly the same as record types:

```
PositionalCar pc = new PositionalCar("Honda", "Pilot", "Blue");
PositionalMiniVan pm = new PositionalMiniVan("Honda", "Pilot", "Blue", 10);
Console.WriteLine($"Checking PositionalMiniVan is-a PositionalCar:{pm is PositionalCar}");
```

Nondestructive Mutation with Inherited Record Types

When creating new record type instances using the `with` expression, the resulting record type is the same runtime type of the operand. Take the following example:

```
MotorCycle mc = new FancyScooter("Harley", "Lowrider","Gold");
Console.WriteLine($"mc is a FancyScooter: {mc is FancyScooter}");
MotorCycle mc2 = mc with { Make = "Harley", Model = "Lowrider" };
Console.WriteLine($"mc2 is a FancyScooter: {mc2 is FancyScooter}");
```

In both of these examples, the runtime type of the instances is `FancyScooter`, not `MotorCycle`:

```
Record type inheritance!
mc is a FancyScooter: True
mc2 is a FancyScooter: True
```

Equality with Inherited Record Types

Recall from Chapter 5 that record types use value semantics to determine equality. One additional detail regarding record types is that the *type* of the record is part of the equality consideration. Take into consideration the `MotorCycle` and `Scooter` types from earlier:

```
public record MotorCycle(string Make, string Model);
public record Scooter(string Make, string Model) : MotorCycle(Make,Model);
```

Ignoring the fact that typically inherited classes extend base classes, these simple examples define two different record types that have the same properties. When creating instances with the same values for the properties, they fail the equality test due to being different types. Take the following code and results, for example:

```
MotorCycle mc3 = new MotorCycle("Harley","Lowrider");
Scooter sc = new Scooter("Harley", "Lowrider");
Console.WriteLine($"MotorCycle and Scooter are equal: {Equals(mc3,sc)}");
```

```
Record type inheritance!
MotorCycle and Scooter are equal: False
```

The reason for the two not being equal is that the equality check with record types uses the *runtime* type, not the *declared* type. The following example further illustrates this:

```
MotorCycle mc3 = new MotorCycle("Harley","Lowrider");
MotorCycle scMotorCycle = new Scooter("Harley", "Lowrider");
Console.WriteLine($"MotorCycle and Scooter Motorcycle are equal: {Equals(mc3,scMotorCycle)}");
```

Notice that both the mc3 and scMotorCycle variables are declared as MotorCycle record types. Despite this, the types are not equal, since the runtime types are different:

```
Record type inheritance!
MotorCycle and Scooter Motorcycle are equal: False
```

Deconstructor Behavior with Inherited Record Types

The Deconstruct() method of a derived record returns the values of all positional properties of the declared, compile-time type. In this first example, the FancyColor property is not deconstructed because the compile-time type is MotorCycle:

```
MotorCycle mc = new FancyScooter("Harley", "Lowrider","Gold");
var (make1, model1) = mc; //doesn't deconstruct FancyColor
var (make2, model2, fancyColor2) = (FancyScooter)mc;
```

However, if the variable is cast to the derived type, then all of the positional properties of the derived type are deconstructed, as shown here:

```
MotorCycle mc = new FancyScooter("Harley", "Lowrider","Gold");
var (make2, model2, fancyColor2) = (FancyScooter)mc;
```

Programming for Containment/Delegation

Recall that code reuse comes in two flavors. You have just explored the classical "is-a" relationship. Before you examine the third pillar of OOP (polymorphism), let's examine the "has-a" relationship (also known as the *containment/delegation model* or *aggregation*). Returning to the Employees project, create a new file named BenefitPackage.cs and add the code to model an employee benefits package, as follows:

```
namespace Employees;
// This new type will function as a contained class.
class BenefitPackage
{
  // Assume we have other members that represent
  // dental/health benefits, and so on.
  public double ComputePayDeduction()
  {
    return 125.0;
  }
}
```

Obviously, it would be rather odd to establish an "is-a" relationship between the BenefitPackage class and the employee types. (Employee "is-a" BenefitPackage? I don't think so.) However, it should be clear that some sort of relationship between the two could be established. In short, you would like to express the idea that each employee "has-a" BenefitPackage. To do so, you can update the Employee class definition as follows:

```
// Employees now have benefits.
partial class Employee
{
  // Contain a BenefitPackage object.
  protected BenefitPackage EmpBenefits = new BenefitPackage();
...
}
```

At this point, you have successfully contained another object. However, exposing the functionality of the contained object to the outside world requires delegation. *Delegation* is simply the act of adding public members to the containing class that use the contained object's functionality.

For example, you could update the Employee class to expose the contained empBenefits object using a custom property, as well as make use of its functionality internally using a new method named GetBenefitCost().

```
partial class Employee
{
  // Contain a BenefitPackage object.
  protected BenefitPackage EmpBenefits = new BenefitPackage();

  // Expose certain benefit behaviors of object.
  public double GetBenefitCost()
     => EmpBenefits.ComputePayDeduction();

  // Expose object through a custom property.
  public BenefitPackage Benefits
  {
    get { return EmpBenefits; }
    set { EmpBenefits = value; }
  }
}
```

In the following updated code, notice how you can interact with the internal BenefitsPackage type defined by the Employee type:

```
Console.WriteLine("***** The Employee Class Hierarchy *****\n");
...
Manager chucky = new Manager("Chucky", 50, 92, 100000, "333-23-2322", 9000);
double cost = chucky.GetBenefitCost();
Console.WriteLine($"Benefit Cost: {cost}");
Console.ReadLine();
```

Understanding Nested Type Definitions

Chapter 5 briefly mentioned the concept of nested types, which is a spin on the "has-a" relationship you have just examined. In C# (as well as other .NET languages), it is possible to define a type (enum, class, interface, struct, or delegate) directly within the scope of a class or structure. When you have done so, the nested (or "inner") type is considered a member of the nesting (or "outer") class and in the eyes of the runtime can be manipulated like any other member (fields, properties, methods, and events). The syntax used to nest a type is quite straightforward.

```
public class OuterClass
{
  // A public nested type can be used by anybody.
  public class PublicInnerClass {}

  // A private nested type can only be used by members
  // of the containing class.
  private class PrivateInnerClass {}
}
```

Although the syntax is fairly clear, understanding why you would want to do this might not be readily apparent. To understand this technique, ponder the following traits of nesting a type:

- Nested types allow you to gain complete control over the access level of the inner type because they may be declared privately (recall that non-nested classes cannot be declared using the `private` keyword).
- Because a nested type is a member of the containing class, it can access private members of the containing class.
- Often, a nested type is useful only as a helper for the outer class and is not intended for use by the outside world.

When a type nests another class type, it can create member variables of the type, just as it would for any point of data. However, if you want to use a nested type from outside the containing type, you must qualify it by the scope of the nesting type. Consider the following code:

```
// Create and use the public inner class. OK!
OuterClass.PublicInnerClass inner;
inner = new OuterClass.PublicInnerClass();

// Compiler Error! Cannot access the private class.
OuterClass.PrivateInnerClass inner2;
inner2 = new OuterClass.PrivateInnerClass();
```

To use this concept within the employee's example, assume you have now nested the `BenefitPackage` directly within the `Employee` class type.

```
partial class Employee
{
  public class BenefitPackage
  {
    // Assume we have other members that represent
    // dental/health benefits, and so on.
    public double ComputePayDeduction()
    {
      return 125.0;
    }
  }
...
}
```

The nesting process can be as "deep" as you require. For example, assume you want to create an enumeration named BenefitPackageLevel, which documents the various benefit levels an employee may choose. To programmatically enforce the tight connection between Employee, BenefitPackage, and BenefitPackageLevel, you could nest the enumeration as follows:

```
// Employee nests BenefitPackage.
public partial class Employee
{
  // BenefitPackage nests BenefitPackageLevel.
  public class BenefitPackage
  {
    public enum BenefitPackageLevel
    {
      Standard, Gold, Platinum
    }

    public double ComputePayDeduction()
    {
      return 125.0;
    }
  }
...
}
```

Because of the nesting relationships, note how you are required to make use of this enumeration:

```
...
// Define my benefit level.
Employee.BenefitPackage.BenefitPackageLevel myBenefitLevel =
    Employee.BenefitPackage.BenefitPackageLevel.Platinum;
```

Excellent! At this point, you have been exposed to a number of keywords (and concepts) that allow you to build hierarchies of related types via classical inheritance, containment, and nested types. If the details aren't crystal clear right now, don't sweat it. You will be building a number of additional hierarchies over the remainder of this book. Next up, let's examine the final pillar of OOP: polymorphism.

Understanding the Third Pillar of OOP: C#'s Polymorphic Support

Recall that the Employee base class defined a method named GiveBonus(), which was originally implemented as follows (before updating it to use the property pattern):

```
public partial class Employee
{
  public void GiveBonus(float amount) => _currPay += amount;
...
}
```

Because this method has been defined with the public keyword, you can now give bonuses to salespeople and managers (as well as part-time salespeople).

```
Console.WriteLine("***** The Employee Class Hierarchy *****\n");

// Give each employee a bonus?
Manager chucky = new Manager("Chucky", 50, 92, 100000, "333-23-2322", 9000);
chucky.GiveBonus(300);
chucky.DisplayStats();
Console.WriteLine();

SalesPerson fran = new SalesPerson("Fran", 43, 93, 3000, "932-32-3232", 31);
fran.GiveBonus(200);
fran.DisplayStats();
Console.ReadLine();
```

The problem with the current design is that the publicly inherited GiveBonus() method operates identically for all subclasses. Ideally, the bonus of a salesperson or part-time salesperson should consider the number of sales. Perhaps managers should gain additional stock options in conjunction with a monetary bump in salary. Given this, you are suddenly faced with an interesting question: "How can related types respond differently to the same request?" Again, glad you asked!

Using the virtual and override Keywords

Polymorphism provides a way for a subclass to define its own version of a method defined by its base class, using the process termed *method overriding*. To retrofit your current design, you need to understand the meaning of the virtual and override keywords. If a base class wants to define a method that *may be* (but does not have to be) overridden by a subclass, it must mark the method with the virtual keyword.

```
partial class Employee
{
  // This method can now be "overridden" by a derived class.
  public virtual void GiveBonus(float amount)
  {
    Pay += amount;
  }
...
}
```

■ **Note** Methods that have been marked with the virtual keyword are (not surprisingly) termed *virtual methods.*

When a subclass wants to change the implementation details of a virtual method, it does so using the override keyword. For example, SalesPerson and Manager could override GiveBonus() as follows (assume that PTSalesPerson will not override GiveBonus() and, therefore, simply inherits the version defined by SalesPerson):

```
//SalesPerson.cs
namespace Employees;
```

```
class SalesPerson : Employee
{
...
  // A salesperson's bonus is influenced by the number of sales.
  public override void GiveBonus(float amount)
  {
    int salesBonus = 0;
    if (SalesNumber >= 0 && SalesNumber <= 100)
    {
      salesBonus = 10;
    }
    else
    {
      if (SalesNumber >= 101 && SalesNumber <= 200)
      {
        salesBonus = 15;
      }
      else
      {
        salesBonus = 20;
      }
    }
    base.GiveBonus(amount * salesBonus);
  }
}

//Manager.cs
namespace Employees;
class Manager : Employee
{
...
  public override void GiveBonus(float amount)
  {
    base.GiveBonus(amount);
    Random r = new Random();
    StockOptions += r.Next(500);
  }
}
```

Notice how each overridden method is free to leverage the default behavior using the base keyword. In this way, you have no need to completely reimplement the logic behind GiveBonus() but can reuse (and possibly extend) the default behavior of the parent class.

Also assume that the current DisplayStats() method of the Employee class has been declared virtually.

```
public virtual void DisplayStats()
{
    Console.WriteLine("Name: {0}", Name);
    Console.WriteLine("Id: {0}", Id);
    Console.WriteLine("Age: {0}", Age);
    Console.WriteLine("Pay: {0}", Pay);
    Console.WriteLine("SSN: {0}", SocialSecurityNumber);
}
```

By doing so, each subclass can override this method to account for displaying the number of sales (for salespeople) and current stock options (for managers). For example, consider Manager's version of the DisplayStats() method (the SalesPerson class would implement DisplayStats() in a similar manner to show the number of sales).

```
//Manager.cs
public override void DisplayStats()
{
  base.DisplayStats();
  Console.WriteLine("Number of Stock Options: {0}", StockOptions);
}
//SalesPerson.cs
public override void DisplayStats()
{
  base.DisplayStats();
  Console.WriteLine("Number of Sales: {0}", SalesNumber);
}
```

Now that each subclass can interpret what these virtual methods mean for itself, each object instance behaves as a more independent entity.

```
Console.WriteLine("***** The Employee Class Hierarchy *****\n");

// A better bonus system!
Manager chucky = new Manager("Chucky", 50, 92, 100000, "333-23-2322", 9000);
chucky.GiveBonus(300);
chucky.DisplayStats();
Console.WriteLine();

SalesPerson fran = new SalesPerson("Fran", 43, 93, 3000, "932-32-3232", 31);
fran.GiveBonus(200);
fran.DisplayStats();
Console.ReadLine();
```

The following output shows a possible test run of your application thus far:

```
***** The Employee Class Hierarchy *****
Name: Chucky
ID: 92
Age: 50
Pay: 100300
SSN: 333-23-2322
Number of Stock Options: 9337

Name: Fran
ID: 93
Age: 43
Pay: 5000
SSN: 932-32-3232
Number of Sales: 31
```

Overriding Virtual Members with Visual Studio/Visual Studio Code

As you might have already noticed, when you are overriding a member, you must recall the type of every parameter—not to mention the method name and parameter-passing conventions (ref, out, and params). Both Visual Studio and Visual Studio Code have a helpful feature that you can make use of when overriding a virtual member. If you type the word override within the scope of a class type (then hit the spacebar), IntelliSense will automatically display a list of all the overridable members defined in your parent classes, excluding methods already overridden.

When you select a member and hit the Enter key, the IDE responds by automatically filling in the method stub on your behalf. Note that you also receive a code statement that calls your parent's version of the virtual member (you are free to delete this line if it is not required). For example, if you used this technique when overriding the DisplayStats() method, you might find the following autogenerated code:

```
public override void DisplayStats()
{
  base.DisplayStats();
}
```

Sealing Virtual Members (Updated 10.0)

Recall that the sealed keyword can be applied to a class type to prevent other types from extending its behavior via inheritance. As you might remember, you sealed PtSalesPerson because you assumed it made no sense for other developers to extend this line of inheritance any further.

On a related note, sometimes you might not want to seal an entire class but simply want to prevent derived types from overriding particular virtual methods. For example, assume you do not want part-time salespeople to obtain customized bonuses. To prevent the PTSalesPerson class from overriding the virtual GiveBonus() method, you could effectively seal this method in the SalesPerson class as follows:

```
// SalesPerson has sealed the GiveBonus() method!
class SalesPerson : Employee
{
...
  public override sealed void GiveBonus(float amount)
  {
    ...
  }
}
```

Here, SalesPerson has indeed overridden the virtual GiveBonus() method defined in the Employee class; however, it has explicitly marked it as sealed. Thus, if you attempted to override this method in the PtSalesPerson class, you would receive compile-time errors, as shown in the following code:

```
sealed class PTSalesPerson : SalesPerson
{
...
  // Compiler error! Can't override this method
  // in the PTSalesPerson class, as it was sealed.
  public override void GiveBonus(float amount)
  {
  }
}
```

New in C# 10, the ToString() method for a record can be sealed, preventing the compiler from synthesizing a ToString() method for any derived record types. Returning to the CarRecord from Chapter 5, notice the sealed ToString() method:

```
public record CarRecord
{
  public string Make { get; init; }
  public string Model { get; init; }
  public string Color { get; init; }

  public CarRecord() {}
  public CarRecord(string make, string model, string color)
  {
    Make = make;
    Model = model;
    Color = color;
  }
  public sealed override string ToString() => $"The is a {Color} {Make} {Model}";
}
```

Understanding Abstract Classes

Currently, the Employee base class has been designed to supply various data members for its descendants, as well as supply two virtual methods (GiveBonus() and DisplayStats()) that may be overridden by a given descendant. While this is all well and good, there is a rather odd byproduct of the current design; you can directly create instances of the Employee base class.

```
// What exactly does this mean?
Employee X = new Employee();
```

In this example, the only real purpose of the Employee base class is to define common members for all subclasses. In all likelihood, you did not intend anyone to create a direct instance of this class, reason being that the Employee type itself is too general of a concept. For example, if I were to walk up to you and say "I'm an employee," I would bet your first question to me would be "What *kind* of employee are you? Are you a consultant, trainer, admin assistant, copy editor, or White House aide?"

Given that many base classes tend to be rather nebulous entities, a far better design for this example is to prevent the ability to directly create a new Employee object in code. In C#, you can enforce this programmatically by using the abstract keyword in the class definition, thus creating an *abstract base class*.

```
// Update the Employee class as abstract
// to prevent direct instantiation.
abstract partial class Employee
{
  ...
}
```

With this, if you now attempt to create an instance of the Employee class, you are issued a compile-time error.

```
// Error! Cannot create an instance of an abstract class!
Employee X = new Employee();
```

At first glance, it might seem strange to define a class that you cannot directly create an instance of. Recall, however, that base classes (abstract or not) are useful, in that they contain all the common data and functionality of derived types. Using this form of abstraction, you are able to model that the "idea" of an employee is completely valid; it is just not a concrete entity. Also understand that although you cannot *directly* create an instance of an abstract class, it is still assembled in memory when derived classes are created. Thus, it is perfectly fine (and common) for abstract classes to define any number of constructors that are called *indirectly* when derived classes are allocated.

At this point, you have constructed a fairly interesting employee hierarchy. You will add a bit more functionality to this application later in this chapter when examining C# casting rules. Until then, Figure 6-4 illustrates the crux of your current design.

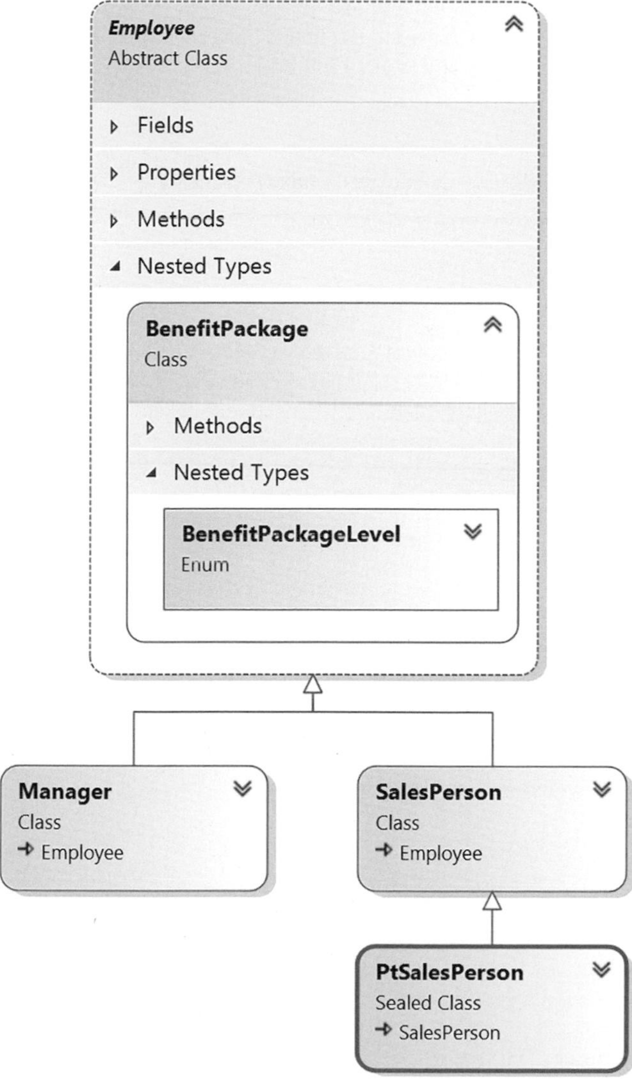

Figure 6-4. *The employee hierarchy*

Understanding the Polymorphic Interface

When a class has been defined as an abstract base class (via the `abstract` keyword), it may define any number of *abstract members*. Abstract members can be used whenever you want to define a member that does *not* supply a default implementation but *must* be accounted for by each derived class. By doing so, you enforce a *polymorphic interface* on each descendant, leaving them to contend with the task of providing the details behind your abstract methods.

Simply put, an abstract base class's polymorphic interface simply refers to its set of virtual and abstract methods. This is much more interesting than first meets the eye because this trait of OOP allows you to build easily extendable and flexible software applications. To illustrate, you will be implementing (and slightly modifying) the hierarchy of shapes briefly examined in Chapter 5 during the overview of the pillars of OOP. To begin, create a new C# Console Application project named Shapes.

In Figure 6-5, notice that the `Hexagon` and `Circle` types each extend the `Shape` base class. Like any base class, `Shape` defines a number of members (a `PetName` property and `Draw()` method, in this case) that are common to all descendants.

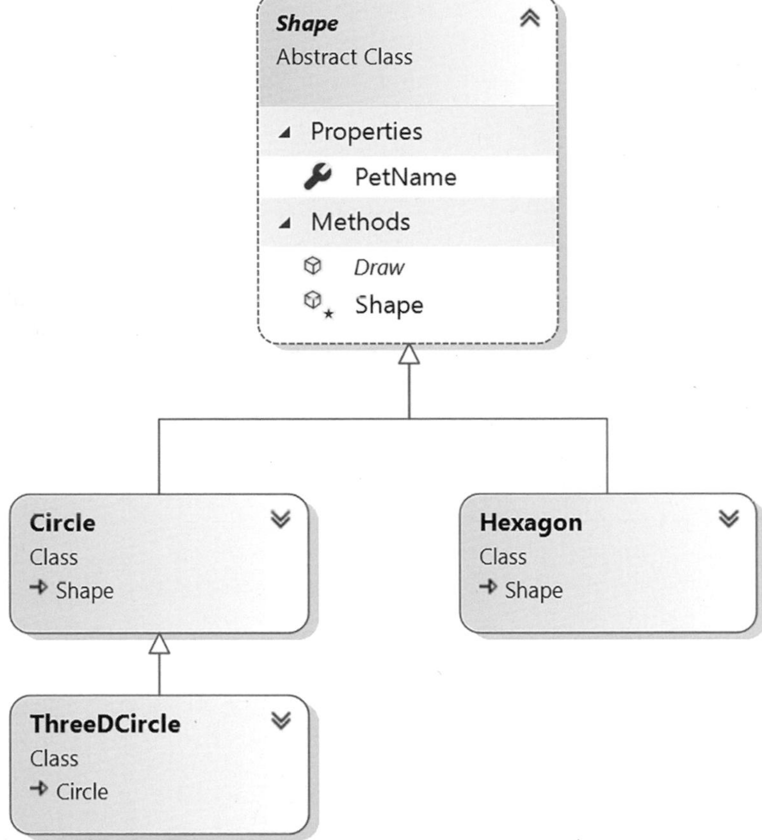

Figure 6-5. *The shapes hierarchy*

Much like the employee hierarchy, you should be able to tell that you don't want to allow the object user to create an instance of Shape directly, as it is too abstract of a concept. Again, to prevent the direct creation of the Shape type, you could define it as an abstract class. As well, given that you want the derived types to respond uniquely to the Draw() method, let's mark it as virtual and define a default implementation. Notice that the constructor is marked as protected so it can be called only from derived classes.

```
// The abstract base class of the hierarchy.
namespace Shapes;
abstract class Shape
{
  protected Shape(string name = "NoName")
  {
    PetName = name;
  }

  public string PetName { get; set; }

  // A single virtual method.
  public virtual void Draw()
  {
    Console.WriteLine("Inside Shape.Draw()");
  }
}
```

Notice that the virtual Draw() method provides a default implementation that simply prints out a message that informs you that you are calling the Draw() method within the Shape base class. Now recall that when a method is marked with the virtual keyword, the method provides a default implementation that all derived types automatically inherit. If a child class so chooses, it *may* override the method but does not *have* to. Given this, consider the following implementation of the Circle and Hexagon types:

```
//Circle.cs
namespace Shapes;
// Circle DOES NOT override Draw().
class Circle : Shape
{
  public Circle() {}
  public Circle(string name) : base(name){}
}

//Hexagon.cs
namespace Shapes;
// Hexagon DOES override Draw().
class Hexagon : Shape
{
  public Hexagon() {}
  public Hexagon(string name) : base(name){}
  public override void Draw()
  {
    Console.WriteLine("Drawing {0} the Hexagon", PetName);
  }
}
```

The usefulness of abstract methods becomes crystal clear when you once again remember that subclasses are *never required* to override virtual methods (as in the case of `Circle`). Therefore, if you create an instance of the Hexagon and `Circle` types, you'd find that Hexagon understands how to "draw" itself correctly or at least print out an appropriate message to the console. `Circle`, however, is more than a bit confused.

```
using Shapes;
Console.WriteLine("***** Fun with Polymorphism *****\n");

Hexagon hex = new Hexagon("Beth");
hex.Draw();
Circle cir = new Circle("Cindy");
// Calls base class implementation!
cir.Draw();
Console.ReadLine();
```

Now consider the following output of the previous code:

```
***** Fun with Polymorphism *****
Drawing Beth the Hexagon
Inside Shape.Draw()
```

Clearly, this is not an intelligent design for the current hierarchy. To force each child class to override the `Draw()` method, you can define `Draw()` as an abstract method of the Shape class, which by definition means you provide no default implementation whatsoever. To mark a method as abstract in C#, you use the `abstract` keyword. Notice that abstract members do not provide any implementation whatsoever.

```
abstract class Shape
{
  // Force all child classes to define how to be rendered.
  public abstract void Draw();
  ...
}
```

■ **Note** Abstract methods can be defined only in abstract classes. If you attempt to do otherwise, you will be issued a compiler error.

Methods marked with `abstract` are pure protocol. They simply define the name, return type (if any), and parameter set (if required). Here, the abstract Shape class informs the derived types that "I have a method named `Draw()` that takes no arguments and returns nothing. If you derive from me, you figure out the details."

Given this, you are now obligated to override the `Draw()` method in the `Circle` class. If you do not, `Circle` is also assumed to be a non-creatable abstract type that must be adorned with the `abstract` keyword (which is obviously not useful in this example). Here is the code update:

```
// If we did not implement the abstract Draw() method, Circle would also be
// considered abstract, and would have to be marked abstract!
class Circle : Shape
```

```
{
  public Circle() {}
  public Circle(string name) : base(name) {}
  public override void Draw()
  {
    Console.WriteLine("Drawing {0} the Circle", PetName);
  }
}
```

The short answer is that you can now assume that anything deriving from Shape does indeed have a unique version of the Draw() method. To illustrate the full story of polymorphism, consider the following code:

```
Console.WriteLine("***** Fun with Polymorphism *****\n");

// Make an array of Shape-compatible objects.
Shape[] myShapes = {new Hexagon(), new Circle(), new Hexagon("Mick"),
  new Circle("Beth"), new Hexagon("Linda")};

// Loop over each item and interact with the
// polymorphic interface.
foreach (Shape s in myShapes)
{
  s.Draw();
}
Console.ReadLine();
```

Here is the output from the modified code:

```
***** Fun with Polymorphism *****
Drawing NoName the Hexagon
Drawing NoName the Circle
Drawing Mick the Hexagon
Drawing Beth the Circle
Drawing Linda the Hexagon
```

This code illustrates polymorphism at its finest. Although it is not possible to *directly* create an instance of an abstract base class (the Shape), you are able to freely store references to any subclass with an abstract base variable. Therefore, when you are creating an array of Shapes, the array can hold any object deriving from the Shape base class (if you attempt to place Shape-incompatible objects into the array, you receive a compiler error).

Given that all items in the myShapes array do indeed derive from Shape, you know they all support the same "polymorphic interface" (or said more plainly, they all have a Draw() method). As you iterate over the array of Shape references, it is at runtime that the underlying type is determined. At this point, the correct version of the Draw() method is invoked in memory.

This technique also makes it simple to safely extend the current hierarchy. For example, assume you derived more classes from the abstract Shape base class (Triangle, Square, etc.). Because of the polymorphic interface, the code within your foreach loop would not have to change in the slightest, as the compiler enforces that only Shape-compatible types are placed within the myShapes array.

Understanding Member Shadowing

C# provides a facility that is the logical opposite of method overriding, termed *shadowing*. Formally speaking, if a derived class defines a member that is identical to a member defined in a base class, the derived class has shadowed the parent's version. In the real world, the possibility of this occurring is the greatest when you are subclassing from a class you (or your team) did not create yourself (such as when you purchase a third-party software package).

For the sake of illustration, assume you receive a class named ThreeDCircle from a co-worker (or classmate) that defines a subroutine named Draw() taking no arguments.

```
namespace Shapes;
class ThreeDCircle
{
  public void Draw()
  {
    Console.WriteLine("Drawing a 3D Circle");
  }
}
```

You figure that ThreeDCircle "is-a" Circle, so you derive from your existing Circle type.

```
class ThreeDCircle : Circle
{
  public void Draw()
  {
    Console.WriteLine("Drawing a 3D Circle");
  }
}
```

After you recompile, you find the following warning:

```
'ThreeDCircle.Draw()' hides inherited member 'Circle.Draw()'. To make the current member
override that implementation, add the override keyword. Otherwise add the new keyword.
```

The problem is that you have a derived class (ThreeDCircle) that contains a method that is identical to an inherited method. To address this issue, you have a few options. You could simply update the child's version of Draw() using the override keyword (as suggested by the compiler). With this approach, the ThreeDCircle type is able to extend the parent's default behavior as required. However, if you don't have access to the code defining the base class (again, as would be the case in many third-party libraries), you would be unable to modify the Draw() method as a virtual member, as you don't have access to the code file!

As an alternative, you can include the new keyword to the offending Draw() member of the derived type (ThreeDCircle, in this example). Doing so explicitly states that the derived type's implementation is intentionally designed to effectively ignore the parent's version (again, in the real world, this can be helpful if external software somehow conflicts with your current software).

```
// This class extends Circle and hides the inherited Draw() method.
class ThreeDCircle : Circle
{
  // Hide any Draw() implementation above me.
  public new void Draw()
```

```
  {
    Console.WriteLine("Drawing a 3D Circle");
  }
}
```

You can also apply the new keyword to any member type inherited from a base class (field, constant, static member, or property). As a further example, assume that ThreeDCircle wants to hide the inherited PetName property.

```
class ThreeDCircle : Circle
{
  // Hide the PetName property above me.
  public new string PetName { get; set; }

  // Hide any Draw() implementation above me.
  public new void Draw()
  {
    Console.WriteLine("Drawing a 3D Circle");
  }
}
```

Finally, be aware that it is still possible to trigger the base class implementation of a shadowed member using an explicit cast, as described in the next section. The following code shows an example:

```
...
// This calls the Draw() method of the ThreeDCircle.
ThreeDCircle o = new ThreeDCircle();
o.Draw();

// This calls the Draw() method of the parent!
((Circle)o).Draw();
Console.ReadLine();
```

Understanding Base Class/Derived Class Casting Rules

Now that you can build a family of related class types, you need to learn the rules of class *casting operations*. To do so, let's return to the employee hierarchy created earlier in this chapter and add some new methods to the Program.cs file (if you are following along, open the Employees project). As described later in this chapter, the ultimate base class in the system is System.Object. Therefore, everything "is-an" Object and can be treated as such. Given this fact, it is legal to store an instance of any type within an object variable.

```
static void CastingExamples()
{
  // A Manager "is-a" System.Object, so we can
  // store a Manager reference in an object variable just fine.
  object frank = new Manager("Frank Zappa", 9, 3000, 40000, "111-11-1111", 5);
}
```

In the Employees project, Managers, SalesPerson, and PtSalesPerson types all extend Employee, so you can store any of these objects in a valid base class reference. Therefore, the following statements are also legal:

```
static void CastingExamples()
{
  // A Manager "is-a" System.Object, so we can
  // store a Manager reference in an object variable just fine.
  object frank = new Manager("Frank Zappa", 9, 3000, 40000, "111-11-1111", 5);

  // A Manager "is-an" Employee too.
  Employee moonUnit = new Manager("MoonUnit Zappa", 2, 3001, 20000, "101-11-1321", 1);

  // A PtSalesPerson "is-a" SalesPerson.
  SalesPerson jill = new PtSalesPerson("Jill", 834, 3002, 100000, "111-12-1119", 90);
}
```

The first law of casting between class types is that when two classes are related by an "is-a" relationship, it is always safe to store a derived object within a base class reference. Formally, this is called an *implicit cast*, as "it just works" given the laws of inheritance. This leads to some powerful programming constructs. For example, assume you have defined a new method within your current Program.cs file.

```
static void GivePromotion(Employee emp)
{
  // Increase pay...
  // Give new parking space in company garage...

  Console.WriteLine("{0} was promoted!", emp.Name);
}
```

Because this method takes a single parameter of type Employee, you can effectively pass any descendant from the Employee class into this method directly, given the "is-a" relationship.

```
static void CastingExamples()
{
  // A Manager "is-a" System.Object, so we can
  // store a Manager reference in an object variable just fine.
  object frank = new Manager("Frank Zappa", 9, 3000, 40000, "111-11-1111", 5);

  // A Manager "is-an" Employee too.
  Employee moonUnit = new Manager("MoonUnit Zappa", 2, 3001, 20000, "101-11-1321", 1);
  GivePromotion(moonUnit);

  // A PTSalesPerson "is-a" SalesPerson.
  SalesPerson jill = new PtSalesPerson("Jill", 834, 3002, 100000, "111-12-1119", 90);
  GivePromotion(jill);
}
```

The previous code compiles given the implicit cast from the base class type (Employee) to the derived type. However, what if you also wanted to promote Frank Zappa (currently stored in a general System.Object reference)? If you pass the frank object directly into this method, you will find a compiler error as follows:

```
object frank = new Manager("Frank Zappa", 9, 3000, 40000, "111-11-1111", 5);
// Error!
GivePromotion(frank);
```

The problem is that you are attempting to pass in a variable that is not declared as an Employee but a more general System.Object. Given that object is higher up the inheritance chain than Employee, the compiler will not allow for an implicit cast, in an effort to keep your code as type-safe as possible.

Even though you can figure out that the object reference is pointing to an Employee-compatible class in memory, the compiler cannot, as that will not be known until runtime. You can satisfy the compiler by performing an *explicit cast*. This is the second law of casting: you can, in such cases, explicitly downcast using the C# casting operator. The basic template to follow when performing an explicit cast looks something like the following:

```
(ClassIWantToCastTo)referenceIHave
```

Thus, to pass the object variable into the GivePromotion() method, you can author the following code:

```
// OK!
GivePromotion((Manager)frank);
```

Using the C# as Keyword

Be aware that explicit casting is evaluated at *runtime*, not compile time. For the sake of argument, assume your Employees project had a copy of the Hexagon class created earlier in this chapter. For simplicity, you can add the following class to the current project:

```
namespace Shapes;
class Hexagon
{
  public void Draw()
  {
    Console.WriteLine("Drawing a hexagon!");
  }
}
```

Although casting the Employee object to a shape object makes absolutely no sense, code such as the following could compile without error:

```
// Ack! You can't cast frank to a Hexagon, but this compiles fine!
object frank = new Manager();
Hexagon hex = (Hexagon)frank;
```

However, you would receive a runtime error, or, more formally, a *runtime exception*. Chapter 7 will examine the full details of structured exception handling; however, it is worth pointing out, for the time being, that when you are performing an explicit cast, you can trap the possibility of an invalid cast using the try and catch keywords (again, see Chapter 7 for full details).

```
// Catch a possible invalid cast.
object frank = new Manager();
Hexagon hex;
try
{
  hex = (Hexagon)frank;
}
catch (InvalidCastException ex)
{
  Console.WriteLine(ex.Message);
}
```

Obviously, this is a contrived example; you would never bother casting between these types in this situation. However, assume you have an array of System.Object types, only a few of which contain Employee-compatible objects. In this case, you would like to determine whether an item in an array is compatible to begin with and, if so, perform the cast.

C# provides the as keyword to quickly determine at runtime whether a given type is compatible with another. When you use the as keyword, you are able to determine compatibility by checking against a null return value. Consider the following:

```
// Use "as" to test compatibility.
object[] things = new object[4];
things[0] = new Hexagon();
things[1] = false;
things[2] = new Manager();
things[3] = "Last thing";

foreach (object item in things)
{
  Hexagon h = item as Hexagon;
  if (h == null)
  {
    Console.WriteLine("Item is not a hexagon");
  }
  else
  {
    h.Draw();
  }
}
```

Here, you loop over each item in the array of objects, checking each one for compatibility with the Hexagon class. If (and only if!) you find a Hexagon-compatible object, you invoke the Draw() method. Otherwise, you simply report the items are not compatible.

Using the C# is Keyword (Updated 7.0, 9.0)

In addition to the as keyword, the C# language provides the is keyword to determine whether two items are compatible. Unlike the as keyword, however, the is keyword returns false, rather than a null reference, if the types are incompatible. Currently, the GivePromotion() method has been designed to take any possible type derived from Employee. Consider the following update, which now checks to see exactly which "type of employee" has been passed in:

```
static void GivePromotion(Employee emp)
{
  Console.WriteLine("{0} was promoted!", emp.Name);
  if (emp is SalesPerson)
  {
    Console.WriteLine("{0} made {1} sale(s)!", emp.Name, ((SalesPerson)emp).SalesNumber);
    Console.WriteLine();
  }
  else if (emp is Manager)
  {
    Console.WriteLine("{0} had {1} stock options...", emp.Name, ((Manager)emp).StockOptions);
    Console.WriteLine();
  }
}
```

Here, you are performing a runtime check to determine what the incoming base class reference is actually pointing to in memory. After you determine whether you received a SalesPerson or Manager type, you are able to perform an explicit cast to gain access to the specialized members of the class. Also notice that you are not required to wrap your casting operations within a try/catch construct, as you know that the cast is safe if you enter either if scope, given your conditional check.

New in C# 7.0, the is keyword can also assign the converted type to a variable if the cast works. This cleans up the preceding method by preventing the "double-cast" problem. In the preceding example, the first cast is done when checking to see whether the type matches, and if it does, then the variable has to be cast again. Consider this update to the preceding method:

```
static void GivePromotion(Employee emp)
{
  Console.WriteLine("{0} was promoted!", emp.Name);
  //Check if is SalesPerson, assign to variable s
  if (emp is SalesPerson s)
  {
    Console.WriteLine("{0} made {1} sale(s)!", s.Name, s.SalesNumber);
    Console.WriteLine();
  }
  //Check if is Manager, if it is, assign to variable m
  else if (emp is Manager m)
  {
    Console.WriteLine("{0} had {1} stock options...", m.Name, m.StockOptions);
    Console.WriteLine();
  }
}
```

C# 9.0 introduced additional pattern matching capabilities (covered in Chapter 3). These updated pattern matches can be used with the `is` keyword. For example, to check if the employee is not a `Manager` and not a `SalesPerson`, use the following code:

```
if (emp is not Manager and not SalesPerson)
{
  Console.WriteLine("Unable to promote {0}. Wrong employee type", emp.Name);
  Console.WriteLine();
}
```

Discards with the is Keyword (New 7.0)

The `is` keyword can also be used in conjunction with the discard variable placeholder. If you want to create a catchall in your `if` or `switch` statement, you can do so as follows:

```
if (obj is var _)
{
//do something
}
```

This will match everything, so be careful about the order in which you use the comparer with the discard. The updated `GivePromotion()` method is shown here:

```
if (emp is SalesPerson s)
{
  Console.WriteLine("{0} made {1} sale(s)!", s.Name, s.SalesNumber);
  Console.WriteLine();
}
//Check if is Manager, if it is, assign to variable m
else if (emp is Manager m)
{
  Console.WriteLine("{0} had {1} stock options...", m.Name, m.StockOptions);
  Console.WriteLine();
}
else if (emp is var _)
{
  Console.WriteLine("Unable to promote {0}. Wrong employee type", emp.Name);
  Console.WriteLine();
}
```

The final `if` statement will catch any `Employee` instance that is not a `Manager`, `SalesPerson`, or `PtSalesPerson`. Remember that you can downcast to a base class, so the `PtSalesPerson` *will* register as a `SalesPerson`.

Revisiting Pattern Matching (New 7.0)

Chapter 3 introduced the C# 7 feature of pattern matching along with the updates that came with C# 9.0. Now that you have a firm understanding of casting, it's time for a better example. The preceding example can now be cleanly updated to use a pattern matching `switch` statement, as follows:

```
static void GivePromotion(Employee emp)
{
  Console.WriteLine("{0} was promoted!", emp.Name);
  switch (emp)
  {
    case SalesPerson s:
      Console.WriteLine("{0} made {1} sale(s)!", emp.Name, s.SalesNumber);
      break;
    case Manager m:
      Console.WriteLine("{0} had {1} stock options...", emp.Name, m.StockOptions);
      break;
  }
  Console.WriteLine();
}
```

When adding a `when` clause to the `case` statement, the full definition of the object *as it is cast* is available for use. For example, the `SalesNumber` property exists only on the `SalesPerson` class and not the `Employee` class. If the cast in the first `case` statement succeeds, the variable `s` will hold an instance of a `SalesPerson` class, so the `case` statement could be updated to the following:

```
case SalesPerson s when s.SalesNumber > 5:
```

These new additions to the `is` and `switch` statements provide nice improvements that help reduce the amount of code to perform matching, as the previous examples demonstrated.

Discards with switch Statements (New 7.0)

Discards can also be used in `switch` statements, as shown in the following code:

```
switch (emp)
{
  case SalesPerson s when s.SalesNumber > 5:
    Console.WriteLine("{0} made {1} sale(s)!", emp.Name, s.SalesNumber);
    break;
  case Manager m:
    Console.WriteLine("{0} had {1} stock options...", emp.Name, m.StockOptions);
    break;
  case Employee _:
    Console.WriteLine("Unable to promote {0}. Wrong employee type", emp.Name);
    break;
}
```

Every type coming in is already an Employee, so the final case statement is always true. However, as discussed when pattern matching was introduced in Chapter 3, once a match is made, the switch statement is exited. This demonstrates the importance of getting the order correct. If the final statement was moved to the top, no Employee would ever be promoted.

Understanding the Super Parent Class: System.Object

To wrap up this chapter, I'd like to examine the details of the super parent class: Object. As you were reading the previous section, you might have noticed that the base classes in your hierarchies (Car, Shape, Employee) never explicitly specify their parent classes.

```
// Who is the parent of Car?
class Car
{...}
```

In the .NET Core universe, every type ultimately derives from a base class named System.Object, which can be represented by the C# object keyword (lowercase *o*). The Object class defines a set of common members for every type in the framework. In fact, when you do build a class that does not explicitly define its parent, the compiler automatically derives your type from Object. If you want to be clear in your intentions, you are free to define classes that derive from Object as follows (however, again, there is no need to do so):

```
// Here we are explicitly deriving from System.Object.
class Car : object
{...}
```

Like any class, System.Object defines a set of members. In the following formal C# definition, note that some of these items are declared virtual, which specifies that a given member may be overridden by a subclass, while others are marked with static (and are therefore called at the class level):

```
public class Object
{
  // Virtual members.
  public virtual bool Equals(object obj);
  protected virtual void Finalize();
  public virtual int GetHashCode();
  public virtual string ToString();

  // Instance-level, nonvirtual members.
  public Type GetType();
  protected object MemberwiseClone();

  // Static members.
  public static bool Equals(object objA, object objB);
  public static bool ReferenceEquals(object objA, object objB);
}
```

Table 6-1 offers a rundown of the functionality provided by some of the methods you're most likely to use.

Table 6-1. *Core Members of System.Object*

Instance Method of Object Class	Meaning in Life
`Equals()`	By default, this method returns `true` only if the items being compared refer to the same item in memory. Thus, `Equals()` is used to compare object references, not the state of the object. Typically, this method is overridden to return `true` only if the objects being compared have the same internal state values (i.e., value-based semantics). Be aware that if you override `Equals()`, you should also override `GetHashCode()`, as these methods are used internally by `Hashtable` types to retrieve subobjects from the container. Also recall from Chapter 4 that the `ValueType` class overrides this method for all structures, so they work with value-based comparisons.
`Finalize()`	For the time being, you can understand this method (when overridden) is called to free any allocated resources before the object is destroyed. I talk more about the CoreCLR garbage collection services in Chapter 9.
`GetHashCode()`	This method returns an `int` that identifies a specific object instance.
`ToString()`	This method returns a string representation of this object, using the `<namespace>.<type name>` format (termed the *fully qualified name*). This method will often be overridden by a subclass to return a tokenized string of name-value pairs that represent the object's internal state, rather than its fully qualified name.
`GetType()`	This method returns a `Type` object that fully describes the object you are currently referencing. In short, this is a runtime type identification (RTTI) method available to all objects (discussed in greater detail in Chapter 17).
`MemberwiseClone()`	This method exists to return a member-by-member copy of the current object, which is often used when cloning an object (see Chapter 8).

To illustrate some of the default behavior provided by the `Object` base class, create a final C# Console Application project named ObjectOverrides. Insert a new C# class type that contains the following empty class definition for a type named `Person`:

```
namespace ObjectOverrides;
// Remember! Person extends Object.
class Person
{
}
```

Now, update your top-level statements to interact with the inherited members of `System.Object` as follows:

```
using ObjectOverrides;
Console.WriteLine("***** Fun with System.Object *****\n");
Person p1 = new Person();

// Use inherited members of System.Object.
Console.WriteLine("ToString: {0}", p1.ToString());
Console.WriteLine("Hash code: {0}", p1.GetHashCode());
Console.WriteLine("Type: {0}", p1.GetType());
```

```
// Make some other references to p1.
Person p2 = p1;
object o = p2;
// Are the references pointing to the same object in memory?
if (o.Equals(p1) && p2.Equals(o))
{
  Console.WriteLine("Same instance!");
}
Console.ReadLine();
}
```

Here is the output of the current code:

```
***** Fun with System.Object *****
ToString: ObjectOverrides.Person
Hash code: 58225482
Type: ObjectOverrides.Person
Same instance!
```

Notice how the default implementation of ToString() returns the fully qualified name of the current type (ObjectOverrides.Person). As you will see later during the examination of building custom namespaces in Chapter 15, every C# project defines a "root namespace," which has the same name of the project itself. Here, you created a project named ObjectOverrides; thus, the Person type and the Program.cs file have both been placed within the ObjectOverrides namespace.

The default behavior of Equals() is to test whether two variables are pointing to the same object in memory. Here, you create a new Person variable named p1. At this point, a new Person object is placed on the managed heap. p2 is also of type Person. However, you are not creating a *new* instance but rather assigning this variable to reference p1. Therefore, p1 and p2 are both pointing to the same object in memory, as is the variable o (of type object, which was thrown in for good measure). Given that p1, p2, and o all point to the same memory location, the equality test succeeds.

Although the canned behavior of System.Object can fit the bill in a number of cases, it is quite common for your custom types to override some of these inherited methods. To illustrate, update the Person class to support some properties representing an individual's first name, last name, and age, each of which can be set by a custom constructor.

```
namespace ObjectOverrides;
// Remember! Person extends Object.
class Person
{
  public string FirstName { get; set; } = "";
  public string LastName { get; set; } = "";
  public int Age { get; set; }

  public Person(string fName, string lName, int personAge)
  {
    FirstName = fName;
    LastName = lName;
    Age = personAge;
  }
  public Person(){}
}
```

Overriding System.Object.ToString( )

Many classes (and structures) that you create can benefit from overriding ToString() to return a string textual representation of the type's current state. This can be quite helpful for purposes of debugging (among other reasons). How you choose to construct this string is a matter of personal choice; however, a recommended approach is to separate each name-value pair with semicolons and wrap the entire string within square brackets (many types in the .NET Core base class libraries follow this approach). Consider the following overridden ToString() for your Person class:

```
public override string ToString() => $"[First Name: {FirstName}; Last Name: {LastName};
Age: {Age}]";
```

This implementation of ToString() is quite straightforward, given that the Person class has only three pieces of state data. However, always remember that a proper ToString() override should also account for any data defined *up the chain of inheritance.*

When you override ToString() for a class extending a custom base class, the first order of business is to obtain the ToString() value from your parent using the base keyword. After you have obtained your parent's string data, you can append the derived class's custom information.

Overriding System.Object.Equals( )

Let's also override the behavior of Object.Equals() to work with value-based semantics. Recall that, by default, Equals() returns true only if the two objects being compared reference the same object instance in memory. For the Person class, it may be helpful to implement Equals() to return true if the two variables being compared contain the same state values (e.g., first name, last name, and age).

First, notice that the incoming argument of the Equals() method is a general System.Object. Given this, your first order of business is to ensure the caller has indeed passed in a Person object and, as an extra safeguard, to make sure the incoming parameter is not a null reference.

After you have established the caller has passed you an allocated Person, one approach to implement Equals() is to perform a field-by-field comparison against the data of the incoming object to the data of the current object.

```
public override bool Equals(object obj)
{
  if (!(obj is Person temp))
  {
    return false;
  }
  if (temp.FirstName == this.FirstName
      && temp.LastName == this.LastName
      && temp.Age == this.Age)
  {
    return true;
  }
  return false;
}
```

Here, you are examining the values of the incoming object against the values of your internal values (note the use of the this keyword). If the names and age of each are identical, you have two objects with the same state data and, therefore, return true. Any other possibility results in returning false.

While this approach does indeed work, you can certainly imagine how labor intensive it would be to implement a custom Equals() method for nontrivial types that may contain dozens of data fields. One common shortcut is to leverage your own implementation of ToString(). If a class has a prim-and-proper implementation of ToString() that accounts for all field data up the chain of inheritance, you can simply perform a comparison of the object's string data (checking for null).

```
// No need to cast "obj" to a Person anymore,
// as everything has a ToString() method.
public override bool Equals(object obj)
  => obj?.ToString() == ToString();
```

Notice in this case that you no longer need to check whether the incoming argument is of the correct type (a Person, in this example), as everything in .NET supports a ToString() method. Even better, you no longer need to perform a property-by-property equality check, as you are now simply testing the value returned from ToString().

Overriding System.Object.GetHashCode()

When a class overrides the Equals() method, you should also override the default implementation of GetHashCode(). Simply put, a *hash code* is a numerical value that represents an object as a particular state. For example, if you create two string variables that hold the value Hello, you will obtain the same hash code. However, if one of the string objects were in all lowercase (hello), you would obtain different hash codes.

By default, System.Object.GetHashCode() uses your object's current location in memory to yield the hash value. However, if you are building a custom type that you intend to store in a Hashtable type (within the System.Collections namespace), you should always override this member, as the Hashtable will be internally invoking Equals() and GetHashCode() to retrieve the correct object.

■ **Note** To be more specific, the System.Collections.Hashtable class calls GetHashCode() internally to gain a general idea where the object is located, but a subsequent (internal) call to Equals() determines the exact match.

Although you are not going to place your Person into a System.Collections.Hashtable in this example, for completion let's override GetHashCode(). There are many algorithms that can be used to create a hash code—some fancy, others not so fancy. Most of the time, you are able to generate a hash code value by leveraging the System.String's GetHashCode() implementation.

Given that the String class already has a solid hash code algorithm that is using the character data of the String to compute a hash value, if you can identify a piece of field data on your class that should be unique for all instances (such as a Social Security number), simply call GetHashCode() on that point of field data. Thus, if the Person class defined an SSN property, you could author the following code:

```
// Assume we have an SSN property as so.
class Person
{
  public string SSN {get; } = "";
  public Person(string fName, string lName, int personAge, string ssn)
  {
```

```
    FirstName = fName;
    LastName = lName;
    Age = personAge;
    SSN = ssn;
  }
  // Return a hash code based on unique string data.
  public override int GetHashCode() => SSN.GetHashCode();
}
```

If you use a read-write property for the basis of the hash code, you will receive a warning. Once an object is created, the hash code should be immutable. In the previous example, the SSN property has only a get method, which makes the property read-only, and can be set only in the constructor.

If you cannot find a single point of unique string data but you have overridden ToString() (which satisfies the read-only convention), call GetHashCode() on your own string representation.

```
// Return a hash code based on the person's ToString() value.
public override int GetHashCode() => ToString().GetHashCode();
```

Testing Your Modified Person Class

Now that you have overridden the virtual members of Object, update the top-level statements to test your updates.

```
...
// NOTE: We want these to be identical to test
// the Equals() and GetHashCode() methods.
Person p1 = new Person("Homer", "Simpson", 50, "111-11-1111");
Person p2 = new Person("Homer", "Simpson", 50, "111-11-1111");
// Get stringified version of objects.
Console.WriteLine("p1.ToString() = {0}", p1.ToString());
Console.WriteLine("p2.ToString() = {0}", p2.ToString());

// Test overridden Equals().
Console.WriteLine("p1 = p2?: {0}", p1.Equals(p2));

// Test hash codes.
//still using the hash of the SSN
Console.WriteLine("Same hash codes?: {0}", p1.GetHashCode() == p2.GetHashCode());
Console.WriteLine();

// Change age of p2 and test again.
p2.Age = 45;
Console.WriteLine("p1.ToString() = {0}", p1.ToString());
Console.WriteLine("p2.ToString() = {0}", p2.ToString());
Console.WriteLine("p1 = p2?: {0}", p1.Equals(p2));
//still using the hash of the SSN
Console.WriteLine("Same hash codes?: {0}", p1.GetHashCode() == p2.GetHashCode());
Console.ReadLine();
```

The output is shown here:

```
***** Fun with System.Object *****
p1.ToString() = [First Name: Homer; Last Name: Simpson; Age: 50]
p2.ToString() = [First Name: Homer; Last Name: Simpson; Age: 50]
p1 = p2?: True
Same hash codes?: True

p1.ToString() = [First Name: Homer; Last Name: Simpson; Age: 50]
p2.ToString() = [First Name: Homer; Last Name: Simpson; Age: 45]
p1 = p2?: False
Same hash codes?: True
```

Using the Static Members of System.Object

In addition to the instance-level members you have just examined, `System.Object` does define two static members that also test for value-based or reference-based equality. Consider the following code:

```
static void StaticMembersOfObject()
{
  // Static members of System.Object.
  Person p3 = new Person("Sally", "Jones", 4);
  Person p4 = new Person("Sally", "Jones", 4);
  Console.WriteLine("P3 and P4 have same state: {0}", object.Equals(p3, p4));
  Console.WriteLine("P3 and P4 are pointing to same object: {0}",
    object.ReferenceEquals(p3, p4));
}
```

Here, you are able to simply send in two objects (of any type) and allow the `System.Object` class to determine the details automatically.

The output (when called from the top-level statements) is shown here:

```
***** Fun with System.Object *****
P3 and P4 have the same state: True
P3 and P4 are pointing to the same object: False
```

Summary

This chapter explored the role and details of inheritance and polymorphism. Over these pages you were introduced to numerous new keywords and tokens to support each of these techniques. For example, recall that the colon token is used to establish the parent class of a given type. Parent types are able to define any number of virtual and/or abstract members to establish a polymorphic interface. Derived types override such members using the `override` keyword.

In addition to building numerous class hierarchies, this chapter also examined how to explicitly cast between base and derived types and wrapped up by diving into the details of the cosmic parent class in the .NET base class libraries: `System.Object`.

CHAPTER 7

Understanding Structured Exception Handling

In this chapter, you will learn how to handle runtime anomalies in your C# code through the use of *structured exception handling*. Not only will you examine the C# keywords that allow you to handle such matters (`try`, `catch`, `throw`, `finally`, `when`), but you will also come to understand the distinction between application-level and system-level exceptions, as well as the role of the `System.Exception` base class. This discussion will lead into the topic of building custom exceptions and, finally, to a quick look at some exception-centric debugging tools of Visual Studio.

Ode to Errors, Bugs, and Exceptions

Despite what our (sometimes inflated) egos may tell us, no programmer is perfect. Writing software is a complex undertaking, and given this complexity, it is quite common for even the best software to ship with various *problems*. Sometimes the problem is caused by bad code (such as overflowing the bounds of an array). Other times, a problem is caused by bogus user input that has not been accounted for in the application's code base (e.g., a phone number input field assigned to the value `Chucky`). Now, regardless of the cause of the problem, the end result is that the application does not work as expected. To help frame the upcoming discussion of structured exception handling, allow me to provide definitions for three commonly used anomaly-centric terms.

- *Bugs*: These are, simply put, errors made by the programmer. For example, suppose you are programming with unmanaged C++. If you fail to delete dynamically allocated memory, resulting in a memory leak, you have a bug.
- *User errors*: User errors, on the other hand, are typically caused by the individual running your application, rather than by those who created it. For example, an end user who enters a malformed string into a text box could very well generate an error *if* you fail to handle this faulty input in your code base.
- *Exceptions*: Exceptions are typically regarded as runtime anomalies that are difficult, if not impossible, to account for while programming your application. Possible exceptions include attempting to connect to a database that no longer exists, opening a corrupted XML file, or trying to contact a machine that is currently offline. In each of these cases, the programmer (or end user) has little control over these "exceptional" circumstances.

A. Troelsen and P. Japikse, *Pro C# 10 with .NET 6*, https://doi.org/10.1007/978-1-4842-7869-7_7

Given these definitions, it should be clear that .NET structured *exception* handling is a technique for dealing with runtime *exceptions*. However, even for the bugs and user errors that have escaped your view, the runtime will often generate a corresponding exception that identifies the problem at hand. By way of a few examples, the .NET base class libraries define numerous exceptions, such as `FormatException`, `IndexOutOfRangeException`, `FileNotFoundException`, `ArgumentOutOfRangeException`, and so forth.

Within the .NET nomenclature, an *exception* accounts for bugs, bogus user input, and runtime errors, even though programmers may view each of these as a distinct issue. However, before I get too far ahead of myself, let's formalize the role of structured exception handling and check out how it differs from traditional error-handling techniques.

■ **Note** To make the code examples used in this book as clean as possible, I will not catch every possible exception that may be thrown by a given method in the base class libraries. In your production-level projects, you should, of course, make liberal use of the techniques presented in this chapter.

The Role of .NET Exception Handling

Prior to .NET, error handling under the Windows operating system was a confused mishmash of techniques. Many programmers rolled their own error-handling logic within the context of a given application. For example, a development team could define a set of numerical constants that represented known error conditions and make use of them as method return values. By way of an example, consider the following partial C code:

```
/* A very C-style error trapping mechanism. */
#define E_FILENOTFOUND 1000

int UseFileSystem()
{
  // Assume something happens in this function
  // that causes the following return value.
  return E_FILENOTFOUND;
}

void main()
{
  int retVal = UseFileSystem();
  if(retVal == E_FILENOTFOUND)
    printf("Cannot find file...");
}
```

This approach is less than ideal, given that the constant `E_FILENOTFOUND` is little more than a numerical value and is far from being a helpful agent regarding how to deal with the problem. Ideally, you would like to wrap the error's name, a descriptive message, and other helpful information about this error condition into a single, well-defined package (which is exactly what happens under structured exception handling). In addition to a developer's ad hoc techniques, the Windows API defines hundreds of error codes that come by way of `#defines`, `HRESULTs`, and far too many variations on the simple Boolean (`bool`, `BOOL`, `VARIANT_BOOL`, etc.).

The obvious problem with these older techniques is the tremendous lack of symmetry. Each approach is more or less tailored to a given technology, a given language, and perhaps even a given project. To put an end to this madness, the .NET platform provides a standard technique to send and trap runtime errors: structured exception handling. The beauty of this approach is that developers now have a unified approach to error handling, which is common to all languages targeting the .NET platform. Therefore, the way in which a C# programmer handles errors is syntactically similar to that of a VB programmer, or a C++ programmer using C++/CLI.

As an added bonus, the syntax used to throw and catch exceptions across assemblies and machine boundaries is identical. For example, if you use C# to build a ASP.NET Core RESTful service, you can throw a JSON fault to a remote caller, using the same keywords that allow you to throw an exception between methods in the same application.

Another bonus of .NET exceptions is that rather than receiving a cryptic numerical value, exceptions are objects that contain a human-readable description of the problem, as well as a detailed snapshot of the call stack that triggered the exception in the first place. Furthermore, you are able to give the end user help-link information that points the user to a URL that provides details about the error, as well as custom programmer-defined data.

The Building Blocks of .NET Exception Handling

Programming with structured exception handling involves the use of four interrelated entities.

- A class type that represents the details of the exception
- A member that *throws* an instance of the exception class to the caller under the correct circumstances
- A block of code on the caller's side that invokes the exception-prone member
- A block of code on the caller's side that will process (or *catch*) the exception, should it occur

The C# programming language offers five keywords (`try`, `catch`, `throw`, `finally`, and `when`) that allow you to throw and handle exceptions. The object that represents the problem at hand is a class extending `System.Exception` (or a descendent thereof). Given this fact, let's check out the role of this exception-centric base class.

The System.Exception Base Class

All exceptions ultimately derive from the `System.Exception` base class, which in turn derives from `System.Object`. Here is the main definition of this class (note that some of these members are virtual and may thus be overridden by derived classes):

```
public class Exception : ISerializable
{
  // Public constructors
  public Exception(string message, Exception innerException);
  public Exception(string message);
  public Exception();
...
  // Methods
  public virtual Exception GetBaseException();
  public virtual void GetObjectData(SerializationInfo info,
    StreamingContext context);
```

```
  // Properties
  public virtual IDictionary Data { get; }
  public virtual string HelpLink { get; set; }
  public int HResult {get;set;}
  public Exception InnerException { get; }
  public virtual string Message { get; }
  public virtual string Source { get; set; }
  public virtual string StackTrace { get; }
  public MethodBase TargetSite { get; }
}
```

As you can see, many of the properties defined by System.Exception are read-only in nature. This is because derived types will typically supply default values for each property. For example, the default message of the IndexOutOfRangeException type is "Index was outside the bounds of the array."

Table 7-1 describes the most important members of System.Exception.

Table 7-1. *Core Members of the System.Exception Type*

System.Exception Property	Meaning in Life
Data	This read-only property retrieves a collection of key-value pairs (represented by an object implementing IDictionary) that provide additional, programmer-defined information about the exception. By default, this collection is empty.
HelpLink	This property gets or sets a URL to a help file or website describing the error in full detail.
InnerException	This read-only property can be used to obtain information about the previous exceptions that caused the current exception to occur. The previous exceptions are recorded by passing them into the constructor of the most current exception.
Message	This read-only property returns the textual description of a given error. The error message itself is set as a constructor parameter.
Source	This property gets or sets the name of the assembly, or the object, that threw the current exception.
StackTrace	This read-only property contains a string that identifies the sequence of calls that triggered the exception. As you might guess, this property is useful during debugging or if you want to dump the error to an external error log.
TargetSite	This read-only property returns a MethodBase object, which describes numerous details about the method that threw the exception (invoking ToString() will identify the method by name).

The Simplest Possible Example

To illustrate the usefulness of structured exception handling, you need to create a class that will throw an exception under the correct (or one might say *exceptional*) circumstances. Assume you have created a new C# Console Application project (named SimpleException) that defines two class types (Car and Radio) associated by the "has-a" relationship. The Radio type defines a single method that turns the radio's power on or off.

```
namespace SimpleException;
class Radio
{
  public void TurnOn(bool on)
  {
    Console.WriteLine(on ? "Jamming..." : "Quiet time...");
  }
}
```

In addition to leveraging the Radio class via containment/delegation, the Car class (shown next) is defined in such a way that if the user accelerates a Car object beyond a predefined maximum speed (specified using a constant member variable named MaxSpeed), its engine explodes, rendering the Car unusable (captured by a private bool member variable named _carIsDead).

Beyond these points, the Car type has a few properties to represent the current speed and a user-supplied "pet name," as well as various constructors to set the state of a new Car object. Here is the complete definition (with code comments):

```
namespace SimpleException;
class Car
{
  // Constant for maximum speed.
  public const int MaxSpeed = 100;

  // Car properties.
  public int CurrentSpeed {get; set;} = 0;
  public string PetName {get; set;} = "";

  // Is the car still operational?
  private bool _carIsDead;

  // A car has-a radio.
  private readonly Radio _theMusicBox = new Radio();

  // Constructors.
  public Car() {}
  public Car(string name, int speed)
  {
    CurrentSpeed = speed;
    PetName = name;
  }

  public void CrankTunes(bool state)
  {
    // Delegate request to inner object.
    _theMusicBox.TurnOn(state);
  }

  // See if Car has overheated.
  public void Accelerate(int delta)
  {
    if (_carIsDead)
```

```
    {
      Console.WriteLine("{0} is out of order...", PetName);
    }
    else
    {
      CurrentSpeed += delta;
      if (CurrentSpeed > MaxSpeed)
      {
        Console.WriteLine("{0} has overheated!", PetName);
        CurrentSpeed = 0;
        _carIsDead = true;
      }
      else
      {
        Console.WriteLine("=> CurrentSpeed = {0}",
          CurrentSpeed);
      }
    }
  }
}
```

Next, update your Program.cs file to force a Car object to exceed the predefined maximum speed (set to 100, in the Car class), as shown here:

```
using System.Collections;
using SimpleException;

Console.WriteLine("***** Simple Exception Example *****");
Console.WriteLine("=> Creating a car and stepping on it!");
Car myCar = new Car("Zippy", 20);
myCar.CrankTunes(true);

for (int i = 0; i < 10; i++)
{
  myCar.Accelerate(10);
}
Console.ReadLine();
```

When executing the code, you would see the following output:

```
***** Simple Exception Example *****
=> Creating a car and stepping on it!
Jamming...
=> CurrentSpeed = 30
=> CurrentSpeed = 40
=> CurrentSpeed = 50
=> CurrentSpeed = 60
=> CurrentSpeed = 70
=> CurrentSpeed = 80
=> CurrentSpeed = 90
```

```
=> CurrentSpeed = 100
Zippy has overheated!
Zippy is out of order...
```

Throwing a General Exception

Now that you have a functional Car class, I'll demonstrate the simplest way to throw an exception. The current implementation of Accelerate() simply displays an error message if the caller attempts to speed up the Car beyond its upper limit.

To retrofit this method to throw an exception if the user attempts to speed up the automobile after it has met its maker, you want to create and configure a new instance of the System.Exception class, setting the value of the read-only Message property via the class constructor. When you want to send the exception object back to the caller, use the C# throw() statement. Here is the relevant code update to the Accelerate() method:

```
// This time, throw an exception if the user speeds up beyond MaxSpeed.
public void Accelerate(int delta)
{
  if (_carIsDead)
  {
    Console.WriteLine("{0} is out of order...", PetName);
  }
  else
  {
    CurrentSpeed += delta;
    if (CurrentSpeed >= MaxSpeed)
    {
      CurrentSpeed = 0;
      _carIsDead = true;

      // Use the "throw" keyword to raise an exception.
      throw new Exception($"{PetName} has overheated!");
    }
    Console.WriteLine("=> CurrentSpeed = {0}", CurrentSpeed);
  }
}
```

Before examining how a caller would catch this exception, let's look at a few points of interest. First, when you are throwing an exception, it is always up to you to decide exactly what constitutes the error in question and when an exception should be thrown. Here, you are making the assumption that if the program attempts to increase the speed of a Car object beyond the maximum, a System.Exception object should be thrown to indicate the Accelerate() method cannot continue (which may or may not be a valid assumption; this will be a judgment call on your part based on the application you are creating).

Alternatively, you could implement Accelerate() to recover automatically without needing to throw an exception in the first place. By and large, exceptions should be thrown only when a more terminal condition has been met (e.g., not finding a necessary file, failing to connect to a database, and the like) and not used as a logic flow mechanism. Deciding exactly what justifies throwing an exception is a design issue you must always contend with. For the current purposes, assume that asking a doomed automobile to increase its speed is cause to throw an exception.

Second, notice how the final else was removed from the method. When an exception is thrown (either by the framework or by manually using a throw() statement), control is returned to the calling method (or by the catch block in a try catch). This eliminates the need for the final else. Whether you leave it in for readability is up to you and your coding standards.

In any case, if you were to rerun the application at this point using the previous logic in the top-level statements, the exception would eventually be thrown. As shown in the following output, the result of not handling this error is less than ideal, given you receive a verbose error dump followed by the program's termination (with your specific file path and line numbers):

```
 ***** Simple Exception Example *****
=> Creating a car and stepping on it!
Jamming...
=> CurrentSpeed = 30
=> CurrentSpeed = 40
=> CurrentSpeed = 50
=> CurrentSpeed = 60
=> CurrentSpeed = 70
=> CurrentSpeed = 80
=> CurrentSpeed = 90
=> CurrentSpeed = 100

Unhandled exception. System.Exception: Zippy has overheated!
   at SimpleException.Car.Accelerate(Int32 delta) in [path to file]\Car.cs:line 52
   at SimpleException.Program.Main(String[] args) in [path to file]\Program.cs:line 16
```

Catching Exceptions

■ **Note** For those coming to C# from a Java background, understand that type members are not prototyped with the set of exceptions they may throw (in other words, .NET Core does not support checked exceptions). For better or for worse, you are not required to handle every exception thrown from a given member.

Because the Accelerate() method now throws an exception, the caller needs to be ready to handle the exception, should it occur. When you are invoking a method that may throw an exception, you make use of a try/catch block. After you have caught the exception object, you are able to invoke the members of the exception object to extract the details of the problem.

What you do with this data is largely up to you. You might want to log this information to a report file, write the data to the event log, email a system administrator, or display the problem to the end user. Here, you will simply dump the contents to the console window:

```
// Speed up past the car's max speed to
// trigger the exception.
try
{
  for(int i = 0; i < 10; i++)
  {
```

```
    myCar. Accelerate(10);
  }
}
catch(Exception e)
{
  // Handle the thrown exception.
  Console.WriteLine("\n*** Error! ***");
  Console.WriteLine("Method: {0}", e.TargetSite);
  Console.WriteLine("Message: {0}", e.Message);
  Console.WriteLine("Source: {0}", e.Source);
}
// The error has been handled, processing continues with the next statement.
Console.WriteLine("\n***** Out of exception logic *****");
Console.ReadLine();
```

In essence, a `try` block is a section of statements that may throw an exception during execution. If an exception is detected, the flow of program execution is sent to the appropriate `catch` block. On the other hand, if the code within a `try` block does not trigger an exception, the `catch` block is skipped entirely, and all is right with the world. The following output shows a test run of this program:

```
***** Simple Exception Example *****
=> Creating a car and stepping on it!
Jamming...
=> CurrentSpeed = 30
=> CurrentSpeed = 40
=> CurrentSpeed = 50
=> CurrentSpeed = 60
=> CurrentSpeed = 70
=> CurrentSpeed = 80
=> CurrentSpeed = 90
=> CurrentSpeed = 100

*** Error! ***
Method: Void Accelerate(Int32)
Message: Zippy has overheated!
Source: SimpleException

***** Out of exception logic *****
```

As you can see, after an exception has been handled, the application is free to continue from the point after the `catch` block. In some circumstances, a given exception could be critical enough to warrant the termination of the application. However, in a good number of cases, the logic within the exception handler will ensure the application can continue on its merry way (although it could be slightly less functional, such as not being able to connect to a remote data source).

Throw As Expression (New 7.0)

Prior to C# 7, `throw()` was a statement, which meant you could throw an exception only where statements are allowed. With C# 7.0 and later, `throw()` is available as an expression as well and can be called anywhere expressions are allowed.

Configuring the State of an Exception

Currently, the System.Exception object configured within the Accelerate() method simply establishes a value exposed to the Message property (via a constructor parameter). As shown previously in Table 7-1, however, the Exception class also supplies a number of additional members (TargetSite, StackTrace, HelpLink, and Data) that can be useful in further qualifying the nature of the problem. To spruce up the current example, let's examine further details of these members on a case-by-case basis.

The TargetSite Property

The System.Exception.TargetSite property allows you to determine various details about the method that threw a given exception. As shown in the previous code example, printing the value of TargetSite will display the return type, name, and parameter types of the method that threw the exception. However, TargetSite does not return just a vanilla-flavored string but rather a strongly typed System.Reflection.MethodBase object. This type can be used to gather numerous details regarding the offending method, as well as the class that defines the offending method. To illustrate, assume the previous catch logic has been updated as follows:

```
...
// TargetSite actually returns a MethodBase object.
catch(Exception e)
{
  Console.WriteLine("\n*** Error! ***");
  Console.WriteLine("Member name: {0}", e.TargetSite);
  Console.WriteLine("Class defining member: {0}", e.TargetSite.DeclaringType);
  Console.WriteLine("Member type: {0}", e.TargetSite.MemberType);
  Console.WriteLine("Message: {0}", e.Message);
  Console.WriteLine("Source: {0}", e.Source);
}
Console.WriteLine("\n***** Out of exception logic *****");
Console.ReadLine();
```

This time, you use the MethodBase.DeclaringType property to determine the fully qualified name of the class that threw the error (SimpleException.Car, in this case) as well as the MemberType property of the MethodBase object to identify the type of member (such as a property versus a method) where this exception originated. In this case, the catch logic will display the following:

```
*** Error! ***
Member name: Void Accelerate(Int32)
Class defining member: SimpleException.Car
Member type: Method
Message: Zippy has overheated!
Source: SimpleException
```

The StackTrace Property

The `System.Exception.StackTrace` property allows you to identify the series of calls that resulted in the exception. Be aware that you never set the value of `StackTrace`, as it is established automatically at the time the exception is created. To illustrate, assume you have once again updated your `catch` logic.

```
catch(Exception e)
{
  ...
  Console.WriteLine("Stack: {0}", e.StackTrace);
}
```

If you were to run the program, you would find the following stack trace is printed to the console (your line numbers and file paths may differ, of course):

```
Stack: at SimpleException.Car.Accelerate(Int32 delta)
in [path to file]\car.cs:line 57 at <Program>$.<Main>$(String[] args)
in [path to file]\Program.cs:line 20
```

The `string` returned from `StackTrace` documents the sequence of calls that resulted in the throwing of this exception. Notice how the bottommost line number of this `string` identifies the first call in the sequence, while the topmost line number identifies the exact location of the offending member. Clearly, this information can be quite helpful during the debugging or logging of a given application, as you are able to "follow the flow" of the error's origin.

The HelpLink Property

While the `TargetSite` and `StackTrace` properties allow programmers to gain an understanding of a given exception, this information is of little use to the end user. As you have already seen, the `System.Exception.Message` property can be used to obtain human-readable information that can be displayed to the current user. In addition, the `HelpLink` property can be set to point the user to a specific URL or standard help file that contains more detailed information.

By default, the value managed by the `HelpLink` property is an empty string. Update the exception using object initialization to provide a more interesting value. Here are the relevant updates to the `Car.Accelerate()` method:

```
public void Accelerate(int delta)
{
  if (_carIsDead)
  {
    Console.WriteLine("{0} is out of order...", PetName);
  }
  else
  {
    CurrentSpeed += delta;
    if (CurrentSpeed >= MaxSpeed)
    {
      CurrentSpeed = 0;
      _carIsDead = true;
```

```
        // Use the "throw" keyword to raise an exception and
        // return to the caller.
        throw new Exception($"{PetName} has overheated!")
        {
          HelpLink = "http://www.CarsRUs.com"
        };
      }
      Console.WriteLine("=> CurrentSpeed = {0}", CurrentSpeed);
    }
}
```

The catch logic could now be updated to print this help-link information as follows:

```
catch(Exception e)
{
  ...
  Console.WriteLine("Help Link: {0}", e.HelpLink);
}
```

The Data Property

The Data property of System.Exception allows you to fill an exception object with relevant auxiliary information (such as a timestamp). The Data property returns an object implementing an interface named IDictionary, defined in the System.Collections namespace. Chapter 8 examines the role of interface-based programming, as well as the System.Collections namespace. For the time being, just understand that dictionary collections allow you to create a set of values that are retrieved using a specific key. Observe the next update to the Car.Accelerate() method:

```
public void Accelerate(int delta)
{
  if (_carIsDead)
  {
    Console.WriteLine("{0} is out of order...", PetName);
  }
  else
  {
    CurrentSpeed += delta;
    if (CurrentSpeed >= MaxSpeed)
    {
      Console.WriteLine("{0} has overheated!", PetName);
      CurrentSpeed = 0;
      _carIsDead = true;
      // Use the "throw" keyword to raise an exception
      // and return to the caller.
      throw new Exception($"{PetName} has overheated!")
      {
        HelpLink = "http://www.CarsRUs.com",
        Data = {
          {"TimeStamp",$"The car exploded at {DateTime.Now}"},
          {"Cause","You have a lead foot."}
        }
```

```
      };
    }
    Console.WriteLine("=> CurrentSpeed = {0}", CurrentSpeed);
  }
}
```

To successfully enumerate over the key-value pairs, make sure you added a `using` directive for the `System.Collections` namespace since you will use a `DictionaryEntry` type in the file containing the class implementing your top-level statements.

```
using System.Collections;
```

Next, you need to update the `catch` logic to test that the value returned from the `Data` property is not `null` (the default value). After that, you use the `Key` and `Value` properties of the `DictionaryEntry` type to print the custom data to the console.

```
catch (Exception e)
{
...
  Console.WriteLine("\n-> Custom Data:");
  foreach (DictionaryEntry de in e.Data)
  {
    Console.WriteLine("-> {0}: {1}", de.Key, de.Value);
  }
}
```

With this, here's the final output you'd see:

```
***** Simple Exception Example *****
=> Creating a car and stepping on it!
Jamming...
=> CurrentSpeed = 30
=> CurrentSpeed = 40
=> CurrentSpeed = 50
=> CurrentSpeed = 60
=> CurrentSpeed = 70
=> CurrentSpeed = 80
=> CurrentSpeed = 90
*** Error! ***
Member name: Void Accelerate(Int32)
Class defining member: SimpleException.Car
Member type: Method
Message: Zippy has overheated!
Source: SimpleException
Stack: at SimpleException.Car.Accelerate(Int32 delta) ...
       at SimpleException.Program.Main(String[] args) ...
Help Link: http://www.CarsRUs.com
```

```
-> Custom Data:
-> TimeStamp: The car exploded at 3/15/2020 16:22:59
-> Cause: You have a lead foot.

***** Out of exception logic *****
```

The Data property is useful in that it allows you to pack in custom information regarding the error at hand, without requiring the building of a new class type to extend the Exception base class. As helpful as the Data property may be, however, it is still common for developers to build strongly typed exception classes, which handle custom data using strongly typed properties.

This approach allows the caller to catch a specific exception-derived type, rather than having to dig into a data collection to obtain additional details. To understand how to do this, you need to examine the distinction between system-level and application-level exceptions.

System-Level Exceptions (System.SystemException)

The .NET base class libraries define many classes that ultimately derive from System.Exception. For example, the System namespace defines core exception objects such as ArgumentOutOfRangeException, IndexOutOfRangeException, StackOverflowException, and so forth. Other namespaces define exceptions that reflect the behavior of that namespace. For example, System.Drawing.Printing defines printing exceptions, System.IO defines input/output-based exceptions, System.Data defines database-centric exceptions, and so forth.

Exceptions that are thrown by the .NET platform are (appropriately) called *system exceptions*. These exceptions are generally regarded as nonrecoverable, fatal errors. System exceptions derive directly from a base class named System.SystemException, which in turn derives from System.Exception (which derives from System.Object).

```
public class SystemException : Exception
{
  // Various constructors.
}
```

Given that the System.SystemException type does not add any functionality beyond a set of custom constructors, you might wonder why SystemException exists in the first place. Simply put, when an exception type derives from System.SystemException, you are able to determine that the .NET runtime is the entity that has thrown the exception, rather than the code base of the executing application. You can verify this quite simply using the is keyword.

```
// True! NullReferenceException is-a SystemException.
NullReferenceException nullRefEx = new NullReferenceException();
Console.WriteLine(
  "NullReferenceException is-a SystemException? : {0}",
  nullRefEx is SystemException);
```

Application-Level Exceptions (System.ApplicationException)

Given that all .NET exceptions are class types, you are free to create your own application-specific exceptions. However, because the System.SystemException base class represents exceptions thrown from the runtime, you might naturally assume that you should derive your custom exceptions from the System.Exception type. You could do this, but you could instead derive from the System.ApplicationException class.

```
public class ApplicationException : Exception
{
  // Various constructors.
}
```

Like SystemException, ApplicationException does not define any additional members beyond a set of constructors. Functionally, the only purpose of System.ApplicationException is to identify the source of the error. When you handle an exception deriving from System.ApplicationException, you can assume the exception was raised by the code base of the executing application, rather than by the .NET Core base class libraries or .NET runtime engine.

Building Custom Exceptions, Take 1

While you can always throw instances of System.Exception to signal a runtime error (as shown in the first example), it is sometimes advantageous to build a *strongly typed exception* that represents the unique details of your current problem. For example, assume you want to build a custom exception (named CarIsDeadException) to represent the error of speeding up a doomed automobile. The first step is to derive a new class from System.Exception/System.ApplicationException (by convention, all exception class names end with the Exception suffix).

■ **Note** As a rule, all custom exception classes should be defined as public classes (recall that the default access modifier of a non-nested type is internal). The reason is that exceptions are often passed outside of assembly boundaries and should therefore be accessible to the calling code base.

Create a new Console Application project named CustomException, copy the previous Car.cs and Radio.cs files into your new project, and change the namespace that defines the Car and Radio types from SimpleException to CustomException. Next, add a new file named CarIsDeadException.cs and add the following class definition:

```
namespace CustomException;
// This custom exception describes the details of the car-is-dead condition.
// (Remember, you can also simply extend Exception.)
public class CarIsDeadException : ApplicationException
{
}
```

As with any class, you are free to include any number of custom members that can be called within the catch block of the calling logic. You are also free to override any virtual members defined by your parent classes. For example, you could implement CarIsDeadException by overriding the virtual Message property.

As well, rather than populating a data dictionary (via the Data property) when throwing the exception, the constructor allows the sender to pass in a timestamp and reason for the error. Finally, the timestamp data and cause of the error can be obtained using strongly typed properties.

```
public class CarIsDeadException : ApplicationException
{
  private string _messageDetails = String.Empty;
  public DateTime ErrorTimeStamp {get; set;}
  public string CauseOfError {get; set;}

  public CarIsDeadException(){}
  public CarIsDeadException(string message, string cause, DateTime time)
  {
    _messageDetails = message;
    CauseOfError = cause;
    ErrorTimeStamp = time;
  }

  // Override the Exception.Message property.
  public override string Message
    => $"Car Error Message: {_messageDetails}";
}
```

Here, the `CarIsDeadException` class maintains a private field (`_messageDetails`) that represents data regarding the current exception, which can be set using a custom constructor. Throwing this exception from the `Accelerate()` method is straightforward. Simply allocate, configure, and throw a `CarIsDeadException` type rather than a `System.Exception`.

```
// Throw the custom CarIsDeadException.
public void Accelerate(int delta)
{
...
  throw new CarIsDeadException(
    $"{PetName} has overheated!",
      "You have a lead foot", DateTime.Now)
  {
    HelpLink = "http://www.CarsRUs.com",
  };
...
}
```

To catch this incoming exception, your `catch` scope can now be updated to catch a specific `CarIsDeadException` type (however, given that `CarIsDeadException` "is-a" `System.Exception`, it is still permissible to catch a `System.Exception` as well).

```
using CustomException;

Console.WriteLine("***** Fun with Custom Exceptions *****\n");
Car myCar = new Car("Rusty", 90);

try
{
  // Trip exception.
  myCar.Accelerate(50);
}
catch (CarIsDeadException e)
```

```
{
  Console.WriteLine(e.Message);
  Console.WriteLine(e.ErrorTimeStamp);
  Console.WriteLine(e.CauseOfError);
}
Console.ReadLine();
```

So, now that you understand the basic process of building a custom exception, it's time to build on that knowledge.

Building Custom Exceptions, Take 2

The current CarIsDeadException type has overridden the virtual System.Exception.Message property to configure a custom error message and has supplied two custom properties to account for additional bits of data. In reality, however, you are not required to override the virtual Message property, as you could simply pass the incoming message to the parent's constructor as follows:

```
public class CarIsDeadException : ApplicationException
{
  public DateTime ErrorTimeStamp { get; set; }
  public string CauseOfError { get; set; }

  public CarIsDeadException() { }

  // Feed message to parent constructor.
  public CarIsDeadException(string message, string cause, DateTime time)
    :base(message)
  {
    CauseOfError = cause;
    ErrorTimeStamp = time;
  }
}
```

Notice that this time you have *not* defined a string variable to represent the message and have *not* overridden the Message property. Rather, you are simply passing the parameter to your base class constructor. With this design, a custom exception class is little more than a uniquely named class deriving from System.ApplicationException (with additional properties if appropriate), devoid of any base class overrides.

Don't be surprised if most (if not all) of your custom exception classes follow this simple pattern. Many times, the role of a custom exception is not necessarily to provide additional functionality beyond what is inherited from the base classes but to supply a *strongly named type* that clearly identifies the nature of the error so the client can provide different handler logic for different types of exceptions.

Building Custom Exceptions, Take 3

If you want to build a truly prim-and-proper custom exception class, you want to make sure your custom exception does the following:

- Derives from Exception/ApplicationException
- Defines a default constructor

- Defines a constructor that sets the inherited Message property
- Defines a constructor to handle "inner exceptions"

To complete your examination of building custom exceptions, here is the final iteration of CarIsDeadException, which accounts for each of these special constructors (the properties would be as shown in the previous example):

```
public class CarIsDeadException : ApplicationException
{
  private string _messageDetails = String.Empty;
  public DateTime ErrorTimeStamp {get; set;}
  public string CauseOfError {get; set;}

  public CarIsDeadException(){}
  public CarIsDeadException(string cause, DateTime time) : this(cause,time,string.Empty)
  {
  }
  public CarIsDeadException(string cause, DateTime time, string message) :
  this(cause,time,message, null)
  {
  }

  public CarIsDeadException(string cause, DateTime time, string message, System.
  Exception inner)
    : base(message, inner)
  {
    CauseOfError = cause;
    ErrorTimeStamp = time;
  }
}
```

With this update to your custom exception, update the Accelerate() method to the following:

```
throw new CarIsDeadException("You have a lead foot",
  DateTime.Now,$"{PetName} has overheated!")
{
  HelpLink = "http://www.CarsRUs.com",
};
```

Given that building custom exceptions that adhere to .NET Core best practices really differ by only their name, you will be happy to know that Visual Studio provides a code snippet template named Exception that will autogenerate a new exception class that adheres to .NET best practices. To activate it, type exc in the editor and hit the Tab key (in Visual Studio, hit the Tab key twice).

Processing Multiple Exceptions

In its simplest form, a try block has a single catch block. In reality, though, you often run into situations where the statements within a try block could trigger *numerous* possible exceptions. Create a new C# Console Application project named ProcessMultipleExceptions; copy the Car.cs, Radio.cs, and CarIsDeadException.cs files from the previous CustomException example into the new project, and update your namespace names accordingly.

Now, update Car's Accelerate() method to also throw a predefined base class library ArgumentOutOfRangeException if you pass an invalid parameter (which you can assume is any value less than zero). Note the constructor of this exception class takes the name of the offending argument as the first string, followed by a message describing the error.

```
// Test for invalid argument before proceeding.
public void Accelerate(int delta)
{
  if (delta < 0)
  {
    throw new ArgumentOutOfRangeException(nameof(delta),
      "Speed must be greater than zero");
  }
  ...
}
```

■ **Note** The nameof() operator returns a string representing the name of the object, in this example the variable delta. This is a safer way to refer to C# objects, methods, and variables when the string version is required.

The catch logic could now specifically respond to each type of exception.

```
using ProcessMultipleExceptions;

Console.WriteLine("***** Handling Multiple Exceptions *****\n");
Car myCar = new Car("Rusty", 90);
try
{
  // Trip Arg out of range exception.
  myCar.Accelerate(-10);
}
catch (CarIsDeadException e)
{
  Console.WriteLine(e.Message);
}
catch (ArgumentOutOfRangeException e)
{
  Console.WriteLine(e.Message);
}
Console.ReadLine();
```

When you are authoring multiple catch blocks, you must be aware that when an exception is thrown, it will be processed by the first appropriate catch. To illustrate exactly what the "first appropriate" catch means, assume you retrofitted the previous logic with an additional catch scope that attempts to handle all exceptions beyond CarIsDeadException and ArgumentOutOfRangeException by catching a general System. Exception as follows:

```
// This code will not compile!
Console.WriteLine("***** Handling Multiple Exceptions *****\n");
Car myCar = new Car("Rusty", 90);

try
{
  // Trigger an argument out of range exception.
  myCar.Accelerate(-10);
}
catch(Exception e)
{
  // Process all other exceptions?
  Console.WriteLine(e.Message);
}
catch (CarIsDeadException e)
{
  Console.WriteLine(e.Message);
}
catch (ArgumentOutOfRangeException e)
{
  Console.WriteLine(e.Message);
}
Console.ReadLine();
```

This exception handling logic generates compile-time errors. The problem is that the first `catch` block can handle *anything* derived from `System.Exception` (given the "is-a" relationship), including the `CarIsDeadException` and `ArgumentOutOfRangeException` types. Therefore, the final two `catch` blocks are unreachable!

The rule of thumb to keep in mind is to make sure your `catch` blocks are structured such that the first catch is the most specific exception (i.e., the most derived type in an exception-type inheritance chain), leaving the final `catch` for the most general (i.e., the base class of a given exception inheritance chain, in this case `System.Exception`).

Thus, if you want to define a `catch` block that will handle any errors beyond `CarIsDeadException` and `ArgumentOutOfRangeException`, you could write the following:

```
// This code compiles just fine.
Console.WriteLine("***** Handling Multiple Exceptions *****\n");
Car myCar = new Car("Rusty", 90);
try
{
  // Trigger an argument out of range exception.
  myCar.Accelerate(-10);
}
catch (CarIsDeadException e)
{
  Console.WriteLine(e.Message);
}
catch (ArgumentOutOfRangeException e)
{
  Console.WriteLine(e.Message);
}
```

```
// This will catch any other exception
// beyond CarIsDeadException or
// ArgumentOutOfRangeException.
catch (Exception e)
{
  Console.WriteLine(e.Message);
}
Console.ReadLine();
```

■ **Note** Where at all possible, always favor catching specific exception classes, rather than a general `System.Exception`. Though it might appear to make life simple in the short term (you may think "Ah! This catches all the other things I don't care about."), in the long term you could end up with strange runtime crashes, as a more serious error was not directly dealt with in your code. Remember, a final `catch` block that deals with `System.Exception` tends to be very general indeed.

General catch Statements

C# also supports a "general" `catch` scope that does not explicitly receive the exception object thrown by a given member.

```
// A generic catch.
Console.WriteLine("***** Handling Multiple Exceptions *****\n");
Car myCar = new Car("Rusty", 90);
try
{
  myCar.Accelerate(90);
}
catch
{
  Console.WriteLine("Something bad happened...");
}
Console.ReadLine();
```

Obviously, this is not the most informative way to handle exceptions since you have no way to obtain meaningful data about the error that occurred (such as the method name, call stack, or custom message). Nevertheless, C# does allow for such a construct, which can be helpful when you want to handle all errors in a general fashion.

Rethrowing Exceptions

When you catch an exception, it is permissible for the logic in a `try` block to *rethrow* the exception up the call stack to the previous caller. To do so, simply use `throw()` within a `catch` block. This passes the exception up the chain of calling logic, which can be helpful if your `catch` block is only able to partially handle the error at hand.

```
// Passing the buck.
...
try
{
  // Speed up car logic...
}
catch(CarIsDeadException e)
{
  // Do any partial processing of this error and pass the buck.
  throw;
}
...
```

Be aware that, in this example code, the ultimate receiver of CarIsDeadException is the .NET runtime because it is the top-level statements rethrowing the exception. Because of this, your end user is presented with a system-supplied error dialog box. Typically, you would only rethrow a partial handled exception to a caller that has the ability to handle the incoming exception more gracefully.

Notice as well that you are not explicitly rethrowing the CarIsDeadException object but rather making use of throw() with no argument. You're not creating a new exception object; you're just rethrowing the original exception object (with all its original information). Doing so preserves the context of the original target.

Inner Exceptions

As you might suspect, it is entirely possible to trigger an exception at the time you are handling another exception. For example, assume you are handling a CarIsDeadException within a particular catch scope and during the process you attempt to record the stack trace to a file on your C: drive named carErrors.txt (the implicit global using statements grant you access to the System.IO namespace and its I/O-centric types).

```
catch(CarIsDeadException e)
{
  // Attempt to open a file named carErrors.txt on the C drive.
  FileStream fs = File.Open(@"C:\carErrors.txt", FileMode.Open);
  ...
}
```

Now, if the specified file is not located on your C: drive, the call to File.Open() results in a FileNotFoundException! Later in this book, you will learn all about the System.IO namespace where you'll discover how to programmatically determine whether a file exists on the hard drive before attempting to open the file in the first place (thereby avoiding the exception altogether). However, to stay focused on the topic of exceptions, assume the exception has been raised.

When you encounter an exception while processing another exception, best practice states that you should record the new exception object as an "inner exception" within a new object of the same type as the initial exception. (That was a mouthful!) The reason you need to allocate a new object of the exception being handled is that the only way to document an inner exception is via a constructor parameter. Consider the following code:

```
//Update the exception handler
catch (CarIsDeadException e)
{
```

```
  try
  {
    FileStream fs = File.Open(@"C:\carErrors.txt", FileMode.Open);
    ...
  }
  catch (Exception e2)
  {
    //This causes a compile error-InnerException is read only
    //e.InnerException = e2;
    // Throw an exception that records the new exception,
    // as well as the message of the first exception.
    throw new CarIsDeadException( e.CauseOfError, e.ErrorTimeStamp, e.Message, e2);  }
}
```

Notice, in this case, I have passed in the `FileNotFoundException` object as the fourth parameter to the `CarIsDeadException` constructor. After you have configured this new object, you throw it up the call stack to the next caller, which in this case would be the top-level statements.

Given that there is no "next caller" after the top-level statements to catch the exception, you would be again presented with an error dialog box. Much like the act of rethrowing an exception, recording inner exceptions is usually useful only when the caller has the ability to gracefully catch the exception in the first place. If this is the case, the caller's `catch` logic can use the `InnerException` property to extract the details of the inner exception object.

The finally Block

A `try/catch` scope may also define an optional `finally` block. The purpose of a `finally` block is to ensure that a set of code statements will *always* execute, exception (of any type) or not. To illustrate, assume you want to always power down the car's radio before exiting the program, regardless of any handled exception.

```
Console.WriteLine("***** Handling Multiple Exceptions *****\n");
Car myCar = new Car("Rusty", 90);
myCar.CrankTunes(true);
try
{
  // Speed up car logic.
}
catch(CarIsDeadException e)
{
  // Process CarIsDeadException.
}
catch(ArgumentOutOfRangeException e)
{
  // Process ArgumentOutOfRangeException.
}
catch(Exception e)
{
  // Process any other Exception.
}
```

```
finally
{
  // This will always occur. Exception or not.
  myCar.CrankTunes(false);
}
Console.ReadLine();
```

If you did not include a finally block, the radio would not be turned off if an exception were encountered (which might or might not be problematic). In a more real-world scenario, when you need to dispose of objects, close a file, or detach from a database (or whatever), a finally block ensures a location for proper cleanup.

Exception Filters

C# 6 introduced a new clause that can be placed on a catch scope, via the when keyword. When you add this clause, you have the ability to ensure that the statements within a catch block are executed only if some condition in your code holds true. This expression must evaluate to a Boolean (true or false) and can be obtained by using a simple code statement in the when definition itself or by calling an additional method in your code. In a nutshell, this approach allows you to add "filters" to your exception logic.

Consider the following modified exception logic. I have added a when clause to the CarIsDeadException handler to ensure the catch block is never executed on a Friday (a contrived example, but who wants their automobile to break down right before the weekend?). Notice that the single Boolean statement in the when clause must be wrapped in parentheses.

```
catch (CarIsDeadException e) when (e.ErrorTimeStamp.DayOfWeek != DayOfWeek.Friday)
{
  // This new line will only print if the when clause evaluates to true.
  Console.WriteLine("Catching car is dead!");

  Console.WriteLine(e.Message);
}
```

While this example is very contrived, a more realistic use for using an exception filter is to catch SystemExceptions. For example, suppose your code is saving data to the database, a general exception is thrown. By examining the message and exception data, you can create specific handlers based on what caused the exception.

Debugging Unhandled Exceptions Using Visual Studio

Visual Studio supplies a number of tools that help you debug unhandled exceptions. Assume you have increased the speed of a Car object beyond the maximum but this time did not bother to wrap your call within a try block.

```
Car myCar = new Car("Rusty", 90);
myCar.Accelerate(100);
```

If you start a debugging session within Visual Studio (using the Debug ➤ Start Debugging menu selection), Visual Studio automatically breaks at the time the uncaught exception is thrown. Better yet, you are presented with a window (see Figure 7-1) displaying the value of the Message property.

```
catch (CarIsDeadException e) //when (e.ErrorTimeStamp.D...
{
    Console.WriteLine(e.Message);
    try
    {
        FileStream fs = File.Open(@"C:\carErrors.txt",
    }
    catch (Exception e2)
    {
        // This causes a compile error - InnerException
        // e.InnerException = e2;
        // Throw an exception that records the new exce
        // as well as the message of the first exceptio...
        throw new CarIsDeadException(e.CauseOfError, e.ErrorTimeStamp, e.Message, e2);
    }
    //Rethrow the exception to the caller
    throw;
}
```


***Figure 7-1.** Debugging unhandled custom exceptions with Visual Studio*

■ **Note** If you fail to handle an exception thrown by a method in the .NET base class libraries, the Visual Studio debugger breaks at the statement that called the offending method.

If you click the View Detail link, you will find the details regarding the state of the object (see Figure 7-2).

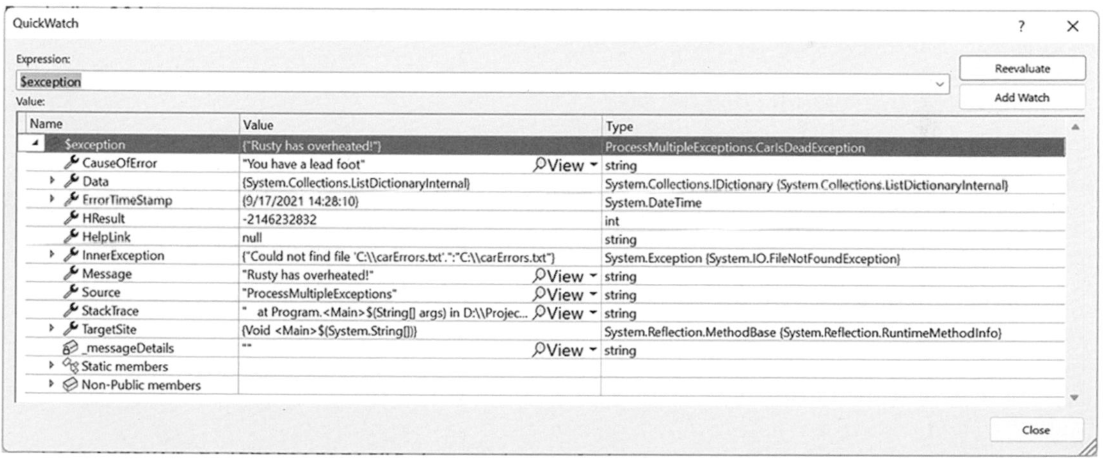

***Figure 7-2.** Viewing exception details*

Summary

In this chapter, you examined the role of structured exception handling. When a method needs to send an error object to the caller, it will allocate, configure, and throw a specific `System.Exception`-derived type via `throw()`. The caller is able to handle any possible incoming exceptions using the C# `catch` keyword and an optional `finally` scope. Since C# 6.0, the ability to create exception filters using the optional `when` keyword was added, and C# 7 has expanded the locations from where you can throw exceptions.

When you are creating your own custom exceptions, you ultimately create a class type deriving from `System.ApplicationException`, which denotes an exception thrown from the currently executing application. In contrast, error objects deriving from `System.SystemException` represent critical (and fatal) errors thrown by the .NET runtime. Last but not least, this chapter illustrated various tools within Visual Studio that can be used to create custom exceptions (according to .NET best practices) as well as debug exceptions.

CHAPTER 8

Working with Interfaces

This chapter builds upon your current understanding of object-oriented development by examining the topic of interface-based programming. Here, you will learn how to define and implement interfaces and come to understand the benefits of building types that support multiple behaviors. Along the way, you will look at several related topics, such as obtaining interface references, implementing explicit interfaces, and constructing interface hierarchies. You will also examine several standard interfaces defined within the .NET Core base class libraries. Also covered are the new features introduced in C# 8 regarding interfaces, including default interface methods, static members, and access modifiers. As you will see, your custom classes and structures are free to implement these predefined interfaces to support several useful behaviors, such as object cloning, object enumeration, and object sorting.

Understanding Interface Types

To begin this chapter, allow me to provide a formal definition of the *interface type*, which has changed with the introduction of C# 8.0. Prior to C# 8.0, an interface is nothing more than a named set of *abstract members*. Recall from Chapter 6 that abstract methods are pure protocol, in that they do not provide a default implementation. The specific members defined by an interface depend on the exact behavior it is modeling. Said another way, an interface expresses a *behavior* that a given class or structure may choose to support. Furthermore, as you will see in this chapter, a class or structure can support as many interfaces as necessary, thereby supporting (in essence) multiple behaviors.

The default interface methods feature, introduced in C# 8.0, allows for interface methods to contain an implementation that may or may not be overridden by the implementing class. More on this later in this chapter.

As you might guess, the .NET Core base class libraries ship with numerous predefined interface types that are implemented by various classes and structures. For example, as you will see in Chapter 20, ADO.NET ships with multiple data providers that allow you to communicate with a particular database management system. Thus, under ADO.NET, you have numerous connection objects to choose from (`SqlConnection`, `OleDbConnection`, `OdbcConnection`, etc.). In addition, third-party database vendors (as well as numerous open source projects) provide .NET libraries to communicate with a wide number of other databases (MySQL, Oracle, etc.), all of which contain objects implementing these interfaces.

Although each connection class has a unique name, is defined within a different namespace, and (in some cases) is bundled within a different assembly, all connection classes implement a common interface named `IDbConnection`.

```
// The IDbConnection interface defines a common
// set of members supported by all connection objects.
public interface IDbConnection : IDisposable
{
```


A. Troelsen and P. Japikse, *Pro C# 10 with .NET 6*, https://doi.org/10.1007/978-1-4842-7869-7_8

```
    // Methods
    IDbTransaction BeginTransaction();
    IDbTransaction BeginTransaction(IsolationLevel il);
    void ChangeDatabase(string databaseName);
    void Close();
    IDbCommand CreateCommand();
    void Open();
    // Properties
    string ConnectionString { get; set;}
    int ConnectionTimeout { get; }
    string Database { get; }
    ConnectionState State { get; }
}
```

■ **Note** By convention, .NET interface names are prefixed with a capital letter *I*. When you are creating your own custom interfaces, it is considered a best practice to do the same.

Do not concern yourself with the details of what these members do at this point. Simply understand that the IDbConnection interface defines a set of members that are common to all ADO.NET connection classes. Given this, you are guaranteed that every connection object supports members such as Open(), Close(), CreateCommand(), and so forth. Furthermore, given that interface members are always abstract, each connection object is free to implement these methods in its own unique manner.

As you work through the remainder of this book, you will be exposed to dozens of interfaces that ship with the .NET Core base class libraries. As you will see, these interfaces can be implemented on your own custom classes and structures to define types that integrate tightly within the framework. As well, once you understand the usefulness of the interface type, you will certainly find reasons to build your own.

Interface Types vs. Abstract Base Classes

Given your work in Chapter 6, the interface type might seem somewhat like an abstract base class. Recall that when a class is marked as abstract, it *may* define any number of abstract members to provide a polymorphic interface to all derived types. However, even when a class does define a set of abstract members, it is also free to define any number of constructors, field data, nonabstract members (with implementation), and so on. Interfaces (prior to C# 8.0) contain *only* member definitions. Now, with C# 8, interfaces can contain member definitions (like abstract members), members with default implementations (like virtual methods), and static members. There are only two real differences: interfaces cannot have nonstatic constructors, and a class can implement multiple interfaces. More on this second point next.

The polymorphic interface established by an abstract parent class suffers from one major limitation, in that *only derived types* support the members defined by the abstract parent. However, in larger software systems, it is common to develop multiple class hierarchies that have no common parent beyond System.Object. Given that abstract members in an abstract base class apply only to derived types, you have no way to configure types in different hierarchies to support the same polymorphic interface. To begin, create a new Console Application project named CustomInterfaces. Add the following abstract class to the project:

```
namespace CustomInterfaces;
public abstract class CloneableType
{
  // Only derived types can support this
  // "polymorphic interface." Classes in other
```

```
  // hierarchies have no access to this abstract
  // member.
  public abstract object Clone();
}
```

Given this definition, only members that extend CloneableType can support the Clone() method. If you create a new set of classes that do not extend this base class, you cannot gain this polymorphic interface. Also, recall that C# does not support multiple inheritance for classes. Therefore, if you wanted to create a MiniVan that "is-a" Car and "is-a" CloneableType, you are unable to do so.

```
// Nope! Multiple inheritance is not possible in C#
// for classes.
public class MiniVan : Car, CloneableType
{
}
```

As you might guess, interface types come to the rescue. After an interface has been defined, it can be implemented by any class or structure, in any hierarchy, and within any namespace or any assembly (written in any .NET Core programming language). As you can see, interfaces are *highly* polymorphic. Consider the standard .NET Core interface named ICloneable, defined in the System namespace. This interface defines a single method named Clone().

```
public interface ICloneable
{
  object Clone();
}
```

If you examine the .NET Core base class libraries, you will find that many seemingly unrelated types (System.Array, System.Data.SqlClient.SqlConnection, System.OperatingSystem, System.String, etc.) all implement this interface. Although these types have no common parent (other than System.Object), you can treat them polymorphically via the ICloneable interface type.

To get started, clear out the Program.cs code and add the following:

```
using CustomInterfaces;

Console.WriteLine("***** A First Look at Interfaces *****\n");
CloneableExample();
```

Next, add the following local function named CloneMe() to your top-level statements. This function takes an ICloneable interface parameter, which accepts any object that implements this interface. Here is the function code:

```
static void CloneableExample()
{
  // All of these classes support the ICloneable interface.
  string myStr = "Hello";
  OperatingSystem unixOS = new OperatingSystem(PlatformID.Unix, new Version());

  // Therefore, they can all be passed into a method taking ICloneable.
  CloneMe(myStr);
```

```
  CloneMe(unixOS);
  static void CloneMe(ICloneable c)
  {
    // Clone whatever we get and print out the name.
    object theClone = c.Clone();
    Console.WriteLine("Your clone is a: {0}", theClone.GetType().Name);
  }
}
```

When you run this application, the class name of each class prints to the console via the `GetType()` method you inherit from `System.Object`. As will be explained in detail in Chapter 17, this method allows you to understand the composition of any type at runtime. In any case, the output of the previous program is shown next:

```
***** A First Look at Interfaces *****
Your clone is a: String
Your clone is a: OperatingSystem
```

Another limitation of abstract base classes is that *each derived type* must contend with the set of abstract members and provide an implementation. To see this problem, recall the shapes hierarchy you defined in Chapter 6. Assume you defined a new abstract method in the Shape base class named `GetNumberOfPoints()`, which allows derived types to return the number of points required to render the shape.

```
namespace CustomInterfaces;
abstract class Shape
{
...
  // Every derived class must now support this method!
  public abstract byte GetNumberOfPoints();
}
```

Clearly, the only class that has any points in the first place is Hexagon. However, with this update, *every* derived class (`Circle`, `Hexagon`, and `ThreeDCircle`) must now provide a concrete implementation of this function, even if it makes no sense to do so. Again, the interface type provides a solution. If you define an interface that represents the behavior of "having points," you can simply plug it into the Hexagon type, leaving `Circle` and `ThreeDCircle` untouched.

■ **Note** The changes to interfaces in C# 8 are probably the most significant changes to an existing language feature that I can recall. As described earlier, the new interface capabilities move them significantly closer to the functionality of abstract classes, with the added ability for a class to implement multiple interfaces. My advice is to tread carefully in these waters and use common sense. Just because you can do something does not mean that you should.

Defining Custom Interfaces

Now that you better understand the overall role of interface types, let's see an example of defining and implementing custom interfaces. Copy the `Shape.cs`, `Hexagon.cs`, `Circle.cs`, and `ThreeDCircle.cs` files from the Shapes solution you created in Chapter 6. After you have done so, rename the namespace that defines your shape-centric types to `CustomInterfaces` (simply to avoid having to import namespace definitions in your new project). Now, insert a new file into your project named `IPointy.cs`.

At a syntactic level, an interface is defined using the C# `interface` keyword. Unlike a class, interfaces never specify a base class (not even `System.Object`; however, as you will see later in this chapter, an interface can specify base interfaces). Prior to C# 8.0, the members of an interface never specify an access modifier (as all interface members are implicitly public and abstract). New in C# 8.0, private, internal, protected, and even static members can also be defined. More on this later. To get the ball rolling, here is a custom interface defined in C#:

```
namespace CustomInterfaces;
// This interface defines the behavior of "having points."
public interface IPointy
{
  // Implicitly public and abstract.
  byte GetNumberOfPoints();
}
```

Interfaces in C# 8 cannot define data fields or nonstatic constructors. Hence, the following version of `IPointy` will result in various compiler errors:

```
// Ack! Errors abound!
public interface IPointy
{
  // Error! Interfaces cannot have data fields!
  public int numbOfPoints;
  // Error! Interfaces do not have nonstatic constructors!
  public IPointy() { numbOfPoints = 0;}
}
```

In any case, this initial `IPointy` interface defines a single method. Interface types are also able to define any number of property prototypes. For example, we could update the `IPointy` interface to use a read-write property (commented out) and a read-only property. The `Points` property replaces the `GetNumberOfPoints()` method.

```
// The pointy behavior as a read-only property.
public interface IPointy
{
  // Implicitly public and abstract.
  //byte GetNumberOfPoints();

  // A read-write property in an interface would look like:
  //string PropName { get; set; }

  // while a read-only property in an interface would be:
   byte Points { get; }
}
```

■ **Note** Interface types can also contain event (see Chapter 12) and indexer (see Chapter 11) definitions.

Interface types are quite useless on their own, as you cannot allocate interface types as you would a class or structure.

```
// Ack! Illegal to allocate interface types.
IPointy p = new IPointy(); // Compiler error!
```

Interfaces do not bring much to the table until they are implemented by a class or structure. Here, IPointy is an interface that expresses the behavior of "having points." The idea is simple: some classes in the shapes hierarchy have points (such as the Hexagon), while others (such as the Circle) do not.

Implementing an Interface

When a class (or structure) chooses to extend its functionality by supporting interfaces, it does so using a comma-delimited list in the type definition. Be aware that the direct base class must be the first item listed after the colon operator. When your class type derives directly from System.Object, you are free to simply list the interface (or interfaces) supported by the class, as the C# compiler will extend your types from System.Object if you do not say otherwise. On a related note, given that structures always derive from System.ValueType (see Chapter 4), simply list each interface directly after the structure definition. Ponder the following examples:

```
// This class derives from System.Object and
// implements a single interface.
public class Pencil : IPointy
{...}

// This class also derives from System.Object
// and implements a single interface.
public class SwitchBlade : object, IPointy
{...}

// This class derives from a custom base class
// and implements a single interface.
public class Fork : Utensil, IPointy
{...}

// This struct implicitly derives from System.ValueType and
// implements two interfaces.
public struct PitchFork : ICloneable, IPointy
{...}
```

Understand that implementing an interface is an all-or-nothing proposition for interface items that do not include a default implementation. The supporting type is not able to selectively choose which members it will implement. Given that the IPointy interface defines a single read-only property, this is not too much of a burden. However, if you are implementing an interface that defines ten members (such as the IDbConnection interface shown earlier), the type is now responsible for fleshing out the details of all ten abstract members.

For this example, insert a new class type named Triangle that "is-a" Shape and supports IPointy. Note that the implementation of the read-only Points property (implemented using the expression-bodied member syntax) simply returns the correct number of points (three).

```
namespace CustomInterfaces;
// New Shape derived class named Triangle.
class Triangle : Shape, IPointy
{
  public Triangle() { }
  public Triangle(string name) : base(name) { }
  public override void Draw()
  {
    Console.WriteLine("Drawing {0} the Triangle", PetName);
  }

  // IPointy implementation.
  //public byte Points
  //{
    //    get { return 3; }
  //}
  public byte Points => 3;
}
```

Now, update your existing Hexagon type to also support the IPointy interface type.

```
namespace CustomInterfaces;
// Hexagon now implements IPointy.
class Hexagon : Shape, IPointy
{
  public Hexagon(){ }
  public Hexagon(string name) : base(name){ }
  public override void Draw()
  {
    Console.WriteLine("Drawing {0} the Hexagon", PetName);
  }

  // IPointy implementation.
  public byte Points => 6;
}
```

To sum up the story so far, the Visual Studio class diagram shown in Figure 8-1 illustrates IPointy-compatible classes using the popular "lollipop" notation. Notice again that Circle and ThreeDCircle do not implement IPointy, as this behavior makes no sense for these classes.

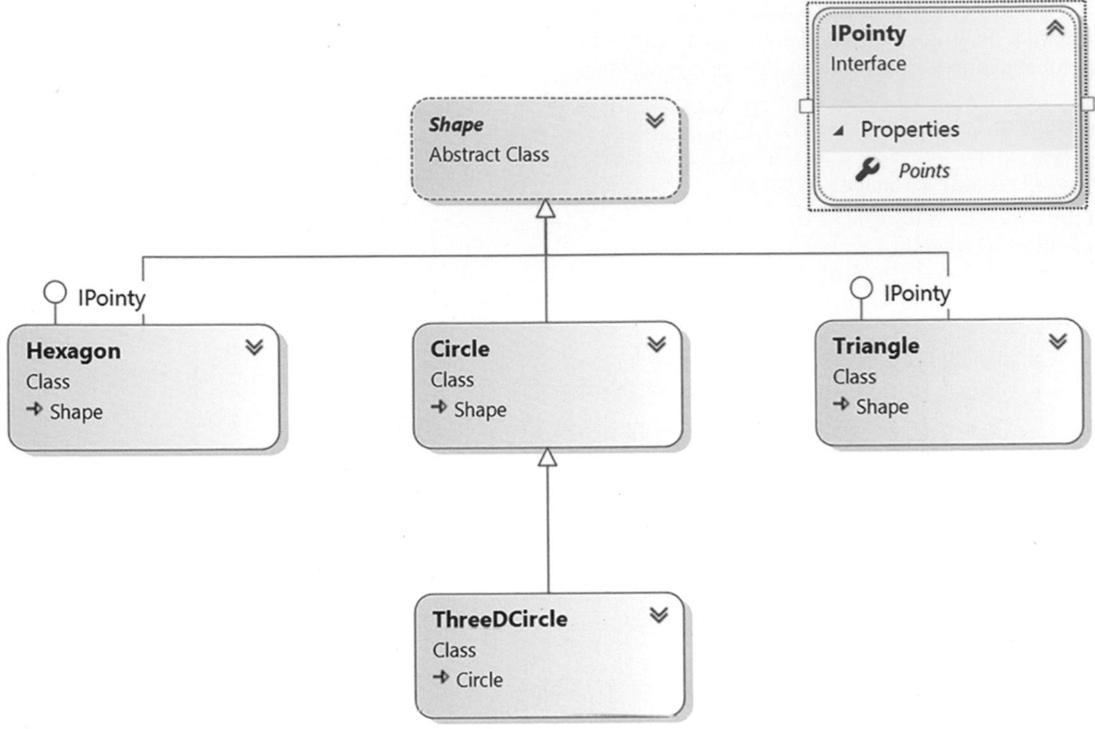

Figure 8-1. *The shapes hierarchy, now with interfaces*

■ **Note** To display or hide interface names in the class designer, right-click the interface icon and select the Collapse or Expand option.

Invoking Interface Members at the Object Level

Now that you have some classes that support the `IPointy` interface, the next question is how you interact with the new functionality. The most straightforward way to interact with functionality supplied by a given interface is to invoke the members directly from the object level (provided the interface members are not implemented explicitly; you can find more details later in the section "Explicit Interface Implementation"). For example, consider the following code:

```
using CustomInterfaces;

Console.WriteLine("***** Fun with Interfaces *****\n");
// Call Points property defined by IPointy.
Hexagon hex = new Hexagon();
Console.WriteLine("Points: {0}", hex.Points);
Console.ReadLine();
```

This approach works fine in this case, given that you understand the Hexagon type has implemented the interface in question and, therefore, has a Points property. Other times, however, you might not be able to determine which interfaces are supported by a given type. For example, suppose you have an array containing 50 Shape-compatible types, only some of which support IPointy. Obviously, if you attempt to invoke the Points property on a type that has not implemented IPointy, you will receive an error. So, how can you dynamically determine whether a class or structure supports the correct interface?

One way to determine at runtime whether a type supports a specific interface is to use an explicit cast. If the type does not support the requested interface, you receive an InvalidCastException. To handle this possibility gracefully, use structured exception handling as in the following example:

```
...
// Catch a possible InvalidCastException.
Circle c = new Circle("Lisa");
IPointy itfPt = null;
try
{
  itfPt = (IPointy)c;
  Console.WriteLine(itfPt.Points);
}
catch (InvalidCastException e)
{
  Console.WriteLine(e.Message);
}
Console.ReadLine();
```

While you could use try/catch logic and hope for the best, it would be ideal to determine which interfaces are supported before invoking the interface members in the first place. Let's see two ways of doing so.

Obtaining Interface References: The as Keyword

You can determine whether a given type supports an interface by using the as keyword, introduced in Chapter 6. If the object can be treated as the specified interface, you are returned a reference to the interface in question. If not, you receive a null reference. Therefore, be sure to check against a null value before proceeding.

```
...
// Can we treat hex2 as IPointy?
Hexagon hex2 = new Hexagon("Peter");
IPointy itfPt2 = hex2 as IPointy;
if(itfPt2 != null)
{
  Console.WriteLine("Points: {0}", itfPt2.Points);
}
else
{
   Console.WriteLine("OOPS! Not pointy...");
}
Console.ReadLine();
```

Notice that when you use the as keyword, you have no need to use try/catch logic; if the reference is not null, you know you are calling on a valid interface reference.

Obtaining Interface References: The is Keyword (Updated 7.0)

You may also check for an implemented interface using the `is` keyword (also first discussed in Chapter 6). If the object in question is not compatible with the specified interface, you are returned the value `false`. If you supply a variable name in the statement, the type is assigned into the variable, eliminating the need to do the type check and perform a cast. The previous example is updated here:

```
Console.WriteLine("***** Fun with Interfaces *****\n");
...
if(hex2 is IPointy itfPt3)
{
  Console.WriteLine("Points: {0}", itfPt3.Points);
}
else
{
  Console.WriteLine("OOPS! Not pointy...");
}
 Console.ReadLine();
```

Default Implementations (New 8.0)

As mentioned earlier, C# 8.0 added the ability for interface methods and properties to have a default implementation. Add a new interface named `IRegularPointy` to represent a regularly shaped polygon. The code is shown here:

```
namespace CustomInterfaces;
interface IRegularPointy : IPointy
{
  int SideLength { get; set; }
  int NumberOfSides { get; set; }
  int Perimeter => SideLength * NumberOfSides;
}
```

Add a new class named `Square.cs` to the project, inherit the Shape base class, and implement the `IRegularPointy` interface, as follows:

```
namespace CustomInterfaces;
class Square: Shape,IRegularPointy
{
  public Square() { }
  public Square(string name) : base(name) { }
  //Draw comes from the Shape base class
  public override void Draw()
  {
    Console.WriteLine("Drawing a square");
  }

  //This comes from the IPointy interface
  public byte Points => 4;
```

```
  //These come from the IRegularPointy interface
  public int SideLength { get; set; }
  public int NumberOfSides { get; set; }
  //Note that the Perimeter property is not implemented
}
```

Here we have unwittingly introduced the first "catch" of using default implementations in interfaces. The Perimeter property, defined on the IRegularPointy interface, is not defined in the Square class, making it inaccessible from an instance of Square. To see this in action, create a new instance of a Square class and output the relevant values to the console, like this:

```
Console.WriteLine("\n***** Fun with Interfaces *****\n");
...
var sq = new Square("Boxy")
  {NumberOfSides = 4, SideLength = 4};
sq.Draw();
//This won't compile
//Console.WriteLine($"{sq.PetName} has {sq.NumberOfSides} of length {sq.SideLength} and a
perimeter of {sq.Perimeter}");
```

Instead, the Square instance must be explicitly cast to the IRegularPointy interface (since that is where the implementation lives), and then the Perimeter property can be accessed. Update the code to the following:

```
Console.WriteLine($"{sq.PetName} has {sq.NumberOfSides} of length {sq.SideLength} and a
perimeter of {((IRegularPointy)sq).Perimeter}");
```

One option to get around this problem is to always code to the interface of a type. Change the definition of the Square instance to IRegularPointy instead of Square, like this:

```
IRegularPointy sq = new Square("Boxy") {NumberOfSides = 4, SideLength = 4};
```

The problem with this approach (in our case) is that the Draw() method and PetName property are not defined on the interface, causing compilation errors.

While this is a trivial example, it does demonstrate one of the problems with default interfaces. Before using this feature in your code, make sure you measure the implications of the calling code having to know where the implementation exists.

Static Constructors and Members (New 8.0)

Another addition to interfaces in C# 8.0 is the ability to have static constructors and members, which function the same as static members on class definitions but are defined on interfaces. Update the IRegularPointy interface with an example static property and a static constructor.

```
interface IRegularPointy : IPointy
{
  int SideLength { get; set; }
  int NumberOfSides { get; set; }
  int Perimeter => SideLength * NumberOfSides;
```

```
  //Static members are also allowed in C# 8
  static string ExampleProperty { get; set; }

  static IRegularPointy() => ExampleProperty = "Foo";
}
```

Static constructors must be parameterless and can only access static properties and methods. To access the interface static property, add the following code to the top-level statements:

```
Console.WriteLine($"Example property: {IRegularPointy.ExampleProperty}");
IRegularPointy.ExampleProperty = "Updated";
Console.WriteLine($"Example property: {IRegularPointy.ExampleProperty}");
```

Notice how the static property must be invoked from the interface and not an instance variable.

Interfaces as Parameters

Given that interfaces are valid types, you may construct methods that take interfaces as parameters, as illustrated by the CloneMe() method earlier in this chapter. For the current example, assume you have defined another interface named IDraw3D.

```
namespace CustomInterfaces;
// Models the ability to render a type in stunning 3D.
public interface IDraw3D
{
  void Draw3D();
}
```

Next, assume that two of your three shapes (ThreeDCircle and Hexagon) have been configured to support this new behavior.

```
// Circle supports IDraw3D.
class ThreeDCircle : Circle, IDraw3D
{
...
  public void Draw3D()
    =>  Console.WriteLine("Drawing Circle in 3D!"); }
}

// Hexagon supports IPointy and IDraw3D.
class Hexagon : Shape, IPointy, IDraw3D
{
...
  public void Draw3D()
    => Console.WriteLine("Drawing Hexagon in 3D!");
}
```

Figure 8-2 presents the updated Visual Studio class diagram.

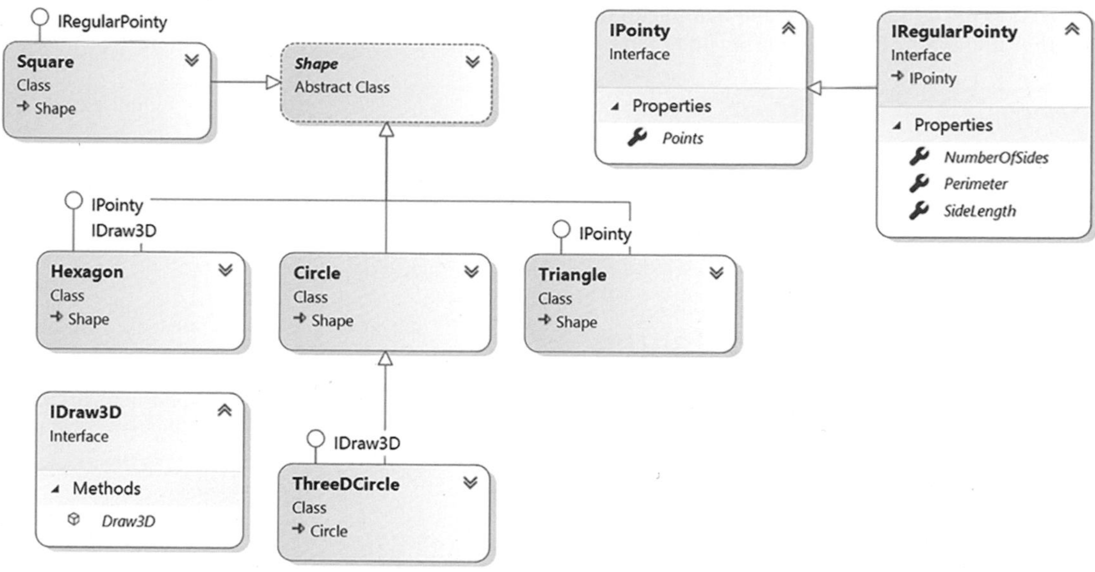

Figure 8-2. *The updated shapes hierarchy*

If you now define a method taking an IDraw3D interface as a parameter, you can effectively send in any object implementing IDraw3D. If you attempt to pass in a type not supporting the necessary interface, you receive a compile-time error. Consider the following method defined within your Program.cs file:

```
// I'll draw anyone supporting IDraw3D.
static void DrawIn3D(IDraw3D itf3d)
{
  Console.WriteLine("-> Drawing IDraw3D compatible type");
  itf3d.Draw3D();
}
```

You could now test whether an item in the Shape array supports this new interface and, if so, pass it into the DrawIn3D() method for processing.

```
Console.WriteLine("***** Fun with Interfaces *****\n");
...
Shape[] myShapes = { new Hexagon(), new Circle(),
  new Triangle("Joe"), new Circle("JoJo") } ;
for(int i = 0; i < myShapes.Length; i++)
{
  // Can I draw you in 3D?
  if (myShapes[i] is IDraw3D s)
  {
    DrawIn3D(s);
  }
}
```

Here is the output of the updated application. Notice that only the Hexagon object prints out in 3D, as the other members of the Shape array do not implement the IDraw3D interface.

```
***** Fun with Interfaces *****
...
-> Drawing IDraw3D compatible type
Drawing Hexagon in 3D!
```

Interfaces as Return Values

Interfaces can also be used as method return values. For example, you could write a method that takes an array of Shape objects and returns a reference to the first item that supports IPointy.

```
// This method returns the first object in the
// array that implements IPointy.
static IPointy FindFirstPointyShape(Shape[] shapes)
{
  foreach (Shape s in shapes)
  {
    if (s is IPointy ip)
    {
      return ip;
    }
  }
  return null;
}
```

You could interact with this method as follows:

```
Console.WriteLine("***** Fun with Interfaces *****\n");
...
// Make an array of Shapes.
Shape[] myShapes = { new Hexagon(), new Circle(),
                  new Triangle("Joe"), new Circle("JoJo")};

// Get first pointy item.
IPointy firstPointyItem = FindFirstPointyShape(myShapes);
// To be safe, use the null conditional operator.
Console.WriteLine("The item has {0} points",
 firstPointyItem?.Points);
```

Arrays of Interface Types

Recall that the same interface can be implemented by numerous types, even if they are not within the same class hierarchy and do not have a common parent class beyond System.Object. This can yield some powerful programming constructs. For example, assume you have developed three new class types within your current project that model kitchen utensils (via Knife and Fork classes) and another modeling gardening equipment (à la PitchFork). The relevant code for the classes is shown here, and the updated class diagram is shown in Figure 8-3:

```
//Fork.cs
namespace CustomInterfaces;
class Fork : IPointy
{
  public byte Points => 4;
}
//PitchFork.cs
namespace CustomInterfaces;
class PitchFork : IPointy
{
  public byte Points => 3;
}
//Knife.cs.cs
namespace CustomInterfaces;
class Knife : IPointy
{
  public byte Points => 1;
}
```

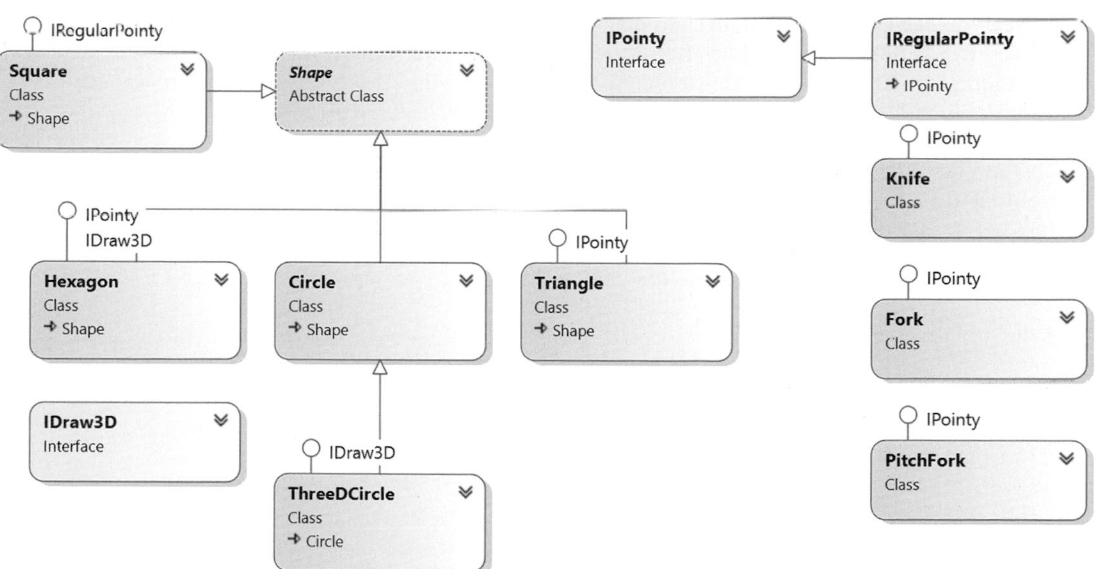

Figure 8-3. *Recall that interfaces can be "plugged into" any type in any part of a class hierarchy.*

If you defined the PitchFork, Fork, and Knife types, you could now define an array of IPointy-compatible objects. Given that these members all support the same interface, you can iterate through the array and treat each item as an IPointy-compatible object, regardless of the overall diversity of the class hierarchies.

```
...
// This array can only contain types that
// implement the IPointy interface.
IPointy[] myPointyObjects = {new Hexagon(), new Knife(),
  new Triangle(), new Fork(), new PitchFork()};

foreach(IPointy i in myPointyObjects)
{
  Console.WriteLine("Object has {0} points.", i.Points);
}
Console.ReadLine();
```

Just to highlight the importance of this example, remember this: when you have an array of a given interface, the array can contain any class or structure that implements that interface.

Implementing Interfaces Using Visual Studio or Visual Studio Code

Although interface-based programming is a powerful technique, implementing interfaces may entail a healthy amount of typing. Given that interfaces are a named set of abstract members, you are required to type in the definition and implementation for *each* interface method on *each* type that supports the behavior. Therefore, if you want to support an interface that defines a total of five methods and three properties, you need to account for all eight members (or else you will receive compiler errors).

As you would hope, Visual Studio and Visual Studio Code both support various tools that make the task of implementing interfaces less burdensome. By way of a simple test, insert a final class into your current project named `PointyTestClass`. When you add an interface such as `IPointy` (or any interface for that matter) to a class type, you might have noticed that when you complete typing the interface's name (or when you position the mouse cursor on the interface name in the code window), Visual Studio and Visual Studio Code both add a lightbulb, which can also be invoked with the Ctrl+period (.) key combination. When you click the lightbulb, you will be presented with a drop-down list that allows you to implement the interface (see Figures 8-4 and 8-5).

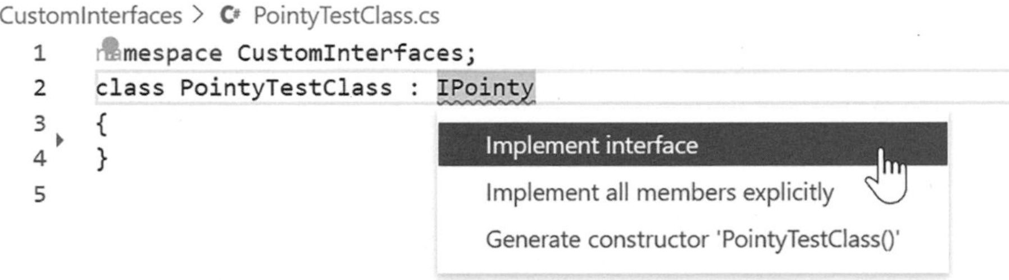

Figure 8-4. *Implementing interfaces automatically using Visual Studio Code*

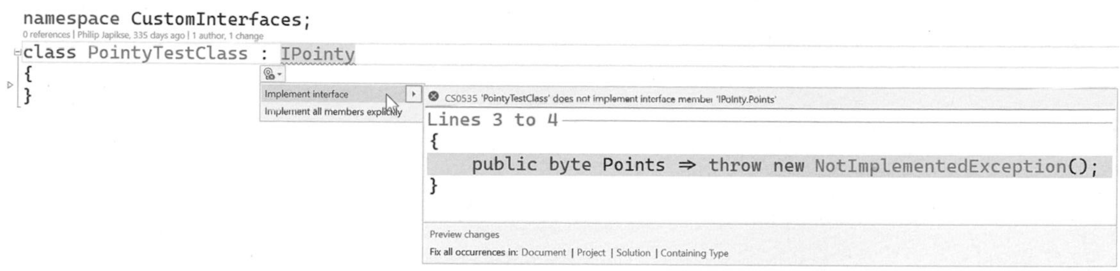

```
namespace CustomInterfaces;
0 references | Philip Japikse, 335 days ago | 1 author, 1 change
class PointyTestClass : IPointy
{
}
```

Implement interface
Implement all members explicitly

CS0535 'PointyTestClass' does not implement interface member 'IPointy.Points'

```
Lines 3 to 4
{
    public byte Points => throw new NotImplementedException();
}
```

Preview changes
Fix all occurrences in: Document | Project | Solution | Containing Type

Figure 8-5. *Implementing interfaces automatically using Visual Studio*

Notice you are presented with two options, the second of which (explicit interface implementation) will be examined in the next section. For the time being, select the first option, and you will see that Visual Studio/Visual Studio Code has generated stub code for you to update. (Note that the default implementation throws a `System.NotImplementedException`, which can obviously be deleted.)

```
namespace CustomInterfaces;
class PointyTestClass : IPointy
{
  public byte Points => throw new NotImplementedException();
}
```

■ **Note** Visual Studio /Visual Studio Code also supports extract interface refactoring, available from the Extract Interface option of the Quick Actions menu. This allows you to pull out a new interface definition from an existing class definition. For example, you might be halfway through writing a class when it dawns on you that you can generalize the behavior into an interface (and thereby open the possibility of alternative implementations).

Explicit Interface Implementation

As shown earlier in this chapter, a class or structure can implement any number of interfaces. Given this, there is always the possibility you might implement interfaces that contain identical members and, therefore, have a name clash to contend with. To illustrate various manners in which you can resolve this issue, create a new Console Application project named InterfaceNameClash. Now design three interfaces that represent various locations to which an implementing type could render its output.

```
namespace InterfaceNameClash;
// Draw image to a form.
public interface IDrawToForm
{
  void Draw();
}

namespace InterfaceNameClash;
// Draw to buffer in memory.
public interface IDrawToMemory
```

```
{
  void Draw();
}

namespace InterfaceNameClash;
// Render to the printer.
public interface IDrawToPrinter
{
  void Draw();
}
```

Notice that each interface defines a method named Draw(), with the identical signature. If you now want to support each of these interfaces on a single class type named Octagon, the compiler will allow the following definition:

```
namespace InterfaceNameClash;
class Octagon : IDrawToForm, IDrawToMemory, IDrawToPrinter
{
 public void Draw()
 {
    // Shared drawing logic.
    Console.WriteLine("Drawing the Octagon...");
  }
}
```

Although the code compiles cleanly, you do have a possible problem. Simply put, providing a single implementation of the Draw() method does not allow you to take unique courses of action based on which interface is obtained from an Octagon object. For example, the following code will invoke the same Draw() method, regardless of which interface you obtain:

```
using InterfaceNameClash;

Console.WriteLine("***** Fun with Interface Name Clashes *****\n");
Octagon oct = new Octagon();

// Both of these invocations call the
// same Draw() method!

// Shorthand notation if you don't need
// the interface variable for later use.
((IDrawToPrinter)oct).Draw();

// Could also use the "is" keyword.
if (oct is IDrawToMemory dtm)
{
  dtm.Draw();
}

Console.ReadLine();
```

Clearly, the sort of code required to render the image to a window is quite different from the code needed to render the image to a networked printer or a region of memory. When you implement several interfaces that have identical members, you can resolve this sort of name clash using *explicit interface implementation* syntax. Consider the following update to the Octagon type:

```
class Octagon : IDrawToForm, IDrawToMemory, IDrawToPrinter
{
   // Explicitly bind Draw() implementations
   // to a given interface.
   void IDrawToForm.Draw()
   {
     Console.WriteLine("Drawing to form...");
   }
   void IDrawToMemory.Draw()
   {
     Console.WriteLine("Drawing to memory...");
   }
   void IDrawToPrinter.Draw()
   {
     Console.WriteLine("Drawing to a printer...");
   }
}
```

As you can see, when explicitly implementing an interface member, the general pattern breaks down to this:

```
returnType InterfaceName.MethodName(params){}
```

Note that when using this syntax, you do not supply an access modifier; explicitly implemented members are automatically private. For example, the following is illegal syntax:

```
// Error! No access modifier!
public void IDrawToForm.Draw()
{
   Console.WriteLine("Drawing to form...");
}
```

Because explicitly implemented members are always implicitly private, these members are no longer available from the object level. In fact, if you were to apply the dot operator to an Octagon type, you would find that IntelliSense does not show you any of the Draw() members. As expected, you must use explicit casting to access the required functionality. The previous code in the top-level statements is already using explicit casting, so it works with explicit interfaces.

```
Console.WriteLine("***** Fun with Interface Name Clashes *****\n");
Octagon oct = new Octagon();

// We now must use casting to access the Draw()
// members.
IDrawToForm itfForm = (IDrawToForm)oct;
itfForm.Draw();
```

```
// Shorthand notation if you don't need
// the interface variable for later use.
((IDrawToPrinter)oct).Draw();

// Could also use the "is" keyword.
if (oct is IDrawToMemory dtm)
{
  dtm.Draw();
}
Console.ReadLine();
```

While this syntax is quite helpful when you need to resolve name clashes, you can use explicit interface implementation simply to hide more "advanced" members from the object level. In this way, when the object user applies the dot operator, the user will see only a subset of the type's overall functionality. However, those who require the more advanced behaviors can extract the desired interface via an explicit cast.

Designing Interface Hierarchies

Interfaces can be arranged in an interface hierarchy. Like a class hierarchy, when an interface extends an existing interface, it inherits the abstract members defined by the parent (or parents). Prior to C# 8, derived interfaces never inherit true implementation. Rather, a derived interface simply extends its own definition with additional abstract members. In C# 8, derived interfaces inherit the default implementations as well as extend the definition and potentially add new default implementations.

Interface hierarchies can be useful when you want to extend the functionality of an existing interface without breaking existing code bases. To illustrate, create a new Console Application project named InterfaceHierarchy. Now, let's design a new set of rendering-centric interfaces such that `IDrawable` is the root of the family tree.

```
namespace InterfaceHierarchy;
public interface IDrawable
{
  void Draw();
}
```

Given that `IDrawable` defines a basic drawing behavior, you could now create a derived interface that extends this interface with the ability to render in modified formats. Here is an example:

```
namespace InterfaceHierarchy;
public interface IAdvancedDraw : IDrawable
{
  void DrawInBoundingBox(int top, int left, int bottom, int right);
  void DrawUpsideDown();
}
```

Given this design, if a class were to implement `IAdvancedDraw`, it would now be required to implement every member defined up the chain of inheritance (specifically, the `Draw()`, `DrawInBoundingBox()`, and `DrawUpsideDown()` methods).

```
namespace InterfaceHierarchy;
public class BitmapImage : IAdvancedDraw
{
  public void Draw()
  {
    Console.WriteLine("Drawing...");
  }
  public void DrawInBoundingBox(int top, int left, int bottom, int right)
  {
    Console.WriteLine("Drawing in a box...");
  }
  public void DrawUpsideDown()
  {
    Console.WriteLine("Drawing upside down!");
  }
}
```

Now, when you use the `BitmapImage`, you can invoke each method at the object level (as they are all `public`), as well as extract a reference to each supported interface explicitly via casting.

```
using InterfaceHierarchy;

Console.WriteLine("***** Simple Interface Hierarchy *****");

// Call from object level.
BitmapImage myBitmap = new BitmapImage();
myBitmap.Draw();
myBitmap.DrawInBoundingBox(10, 10, 100, 150);
myBitmap.DrawUpsideDown();

// Get IAdvancedDraw explicitly.
if (myBitmap is IAdvancedDraw iAdvDraw)
{
  iAdvDraw.DrawUpsideDown();
}
Console.ReadLine();
```

Interface Hierarchies with Default Implementations (New 8.0)

When interface hierarchies also include default implementations, downstream interfaces can choose to carry the implementation from the base interface or create a new default implementation. Update the `IDrawable` interface to the following:

```
public interface IDrawable
{
  void Draw();
  int TimeToDraw() => 5;
}
```

Next, update the top-level statements to the following:

```
Console.WriteLine("***** Simple Interface Hierarchy *****");
...
if (myBitmap is IAdvancedDraw iAdvDraw)
{
  iAdvDraw.DrawUpsideDown();
  Console.WriteLine($"Time to draw: {iAdvDraw.TimeToDraw()}");
}
Console.ReadLine();
```

Not only does this code compile, but it outputs a value of 5 for the `TimeToDraw()` method. This is because default implementations automatically carry forward to descendant interfaces. Casting the `BitMapImage` to the `IAdvancedDraw` interface provides access to the `TimeToDraw()` method, even though the `BitMapImage` instance does not have access to the default implementation. To prove this, enter the following code and see the compile error:

```
//This does not compile
myBitmap.TimeToDraw();
```

If a downstream interface wants to provide its own default implementation, it must hide the upstream implementation. For example, if the `IAdvancedDraw TimeToDraw()` method takes 15 units to draw, update the interface to the following definition:

```
public interface IAdvancedDraw : IDrawable
{
  void DrawInBoundingBox(
    int top, int left, int bottom, int right);
  void DrawUpsideDown();
  new int TimeToDraw() => 15;
}
```

Of course, the `BitMapImage` class is also free to implement the `TimeToDraw()` method. Unlike the `IAdvancedDraw TimeToDraw()` method, the class only needs to ***implement*** the method, not hide it.

```
public class BitmapImage : IAdvancedDraw
{
...
  public int TimeToDraw() => 12;
}
```

When casting the `BitmapImage` instance to either the `IAdvancedDraw` or `IDrawable` interface, the method on the instance still is executed. Add this code to the top-level statements:

```
//Always calls method on instance:
Console.WriteLine("***** Calling Implemented TimeToDraw *****");
Console.WriteLine($"Time to draw: {myBitmap.TimeToDraw()}");
Console.WriteLine($"Time to draw: {((IDrawable) myBitmap).TimeToDraw()}");
Console.WriteLine($"Time to draw: {((IAdvancedDraw) myBitmap).TimeToDraw()}");
```

Here are the results:

```
***** Simple Interface Hierarchy *****
...
***** Calling Implemented TimeToDraw *****
Time to draw: 12
Time to draw: 12
Time to draw: 12
```

Multiple Inheritance with Interface Types

Unlike class types, an interface can extend multiple base interfaces, allowing you to design some powerful and flexible abstractions. Create a new Console Application project named MiInterfaceHierarchy. Here is another collection of interfaces that model various rendering and shape abstractions. Notice that the `IShape` interface is extending both `IDrawable` and `IPrintable`.

```
//IDrawable.cs
namespace MiInterfaceHierarchy;
// Multiple inheritance for interface types is A-okay.
interface IDrawable
{
  void Draw();
}

//IPrintable.cs
namespace MiInterfaceHierarchy;
interface IPrintable
{
  void Print();
  void Draw(); // <-- Note possible name clash here!
}

//IShape.cs
namespace MiInterfaceHierarchy;
// Multiple interface inheritance. OK!
interface IShape : IDrawable, IPrintable
{
  int GetNumberOfSides();
}
```

Figure 8-6 illustrates the current interface hierarchy.

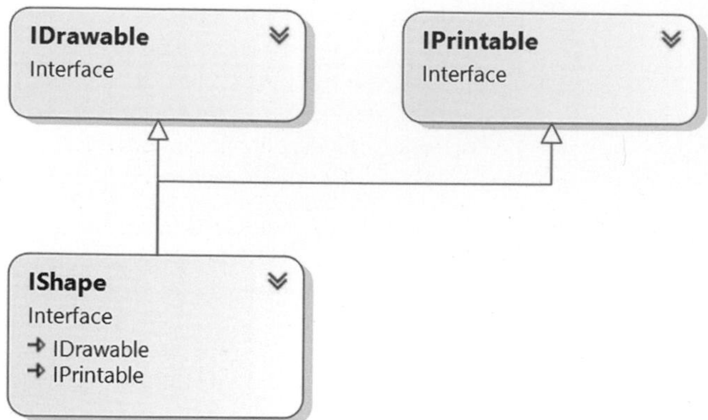

Figure 8-6. *Unlike classes, interfaces can extend multiple interface types*

At this point, the million-dollar question is "If you have a class supporting IShape, how many methods will it be required to implement?" The answer: it depends. If you want to provide a simple implementation of the Draw() method, you need to provide only three members, as shown in the following Rectangle type:

```
namespace MiInterfaceHierarchy;
class Rectangle : IShape
{
  public int GetNumberOfSides() => 4;
  public void Draw() => Console.WriteLine("Drawing...");
  public void Print() => Console.WriteLine("Printing...");
}
```

If you would rather have specific implementations for each Draw() method (which in this case would make the most sense), you can resolve the name clash using explicit interface implementation, as shown in the following Square type:

```
namespace MiInterfaceHierarchy;
class Square : IShape
{
  // Using explicit implementation to handle member name clash.
  void IPrintable.Draw()
  {
    // Draw to printer ...
  }
  void IDrawable.Draw()
  {
    // Draw to screen ...
  }
  public void Print()
  {
    // Print ...
  }

  public int GetNumberOfSides() => 4;
}
```

Ideally, at this point you feel more comfortable with the process of defining and implementing custom interfaces using the C# syntax. To be honest, interface-based programming can take a while to get comfortable with, so if you are in fact still scratching your head just a bit, this is a perfectly normal reaction.

Do be aware, however, that interfaces are a fundamental aspect of the .NET Core Framework. Regardless of the type of application you are developing (web-based, desktop GUIs, data access libraries, etc.), working with interfaces will be part of the process. To summarize the story thus far, remember that interfaces can be extremely useful in the following cases:

- You have a single hierarchy where only a subset of the derived types supports a common behavior.
- You need to model a common behavior that is found across multiple hierarchies with no common parent class beyond `System.Object`.

Now that you have drilled into the specifics of building and implementing custom interfaces, the remainder of this chapter examines several predefined interfaces contained within the .NET Core base class libraries. As you will see, you can implement standard .NET Core interfaces on your custom types to ensure they integrate into the framework seamlessly.

The IEnumerable and IEnumerator Interfaces

To begin examining the process of implementing existing .NET Core interfaces, let's first look at the role of `IEnumerable` and `IEnumerator`. Recall that C# supports a keyword named `foreach` that allows you to iterate over the contents of any array type.

```
// Iterate over an array of items.
int[] myArrayOfInts = {10, 20, 30, 40};

foreach(int i in myArrayOfInts)
{
  Console.WriteLine(i);
}
```

While it might seem that only array types can use this construct, the truth of the matter is any type supporting a method named `GetEnumerator()` can be evaluated by the `foreach` construct. To illustrate, begin by creating a new Console Application project named CustomEnumerator. Next, copy the `Car.cs` and `Radio.cs` files defined in the SimpleException example of Chapter 7 into the new project. Make sure to update the namespaces for the classes to `CustomEnumerator`.

Now, insert a new class named `Garage` that stores a set of `Car` objects within a `System.Array`.

```
using System.Collections;

namespace CustomEnumerator;
// Garage contains a set of Car objects.
public class Garage
{
  private Car[] carArray = new Car[4];

  // Fill with some Car objects upon startup.
  public Garage()
  {
    carArray[0] = new Car("Rusty", 30);
```

```
      carArray[1] = new Car("Clunker", 55);
      carArray[2] = new Car("Zippy", 30);
      carArray[3] = new Car("Fred", 30);
    }
  }
```

Ideally, it would be convenient to iterate over the Garage object's subitems using the foreach construct, just like an array of data values. Update the Program.cs file to the following:

```
using System.Collections;
using CustomEnumerator;

// This seems reasonable ...
Console.WriteLine("***** Fun with IEnumerable / IEnumerator *****\n");
Garage carLot = new Garage();

// Hand over each car in the collection?
foreach (Car c in carLot)
{
  Console.WriteLine("{0} is going {1} MPH",
    c.PetName, c.CurrentSpeed);
}
Console.ReadLine();
```

Sadly, the compiler informs you that the Garage class does not implement a method named GetEnumerator(). This method is formalized by the IEnumerable interface, which is found lurking within the System.Collections namespace.

■ **Note** In Chapter 10, you will learn about the role of generics and the System.Collections.Generic namespace. As you will see, this namespace contains generic versions of IEnumerable/IEnumerator that provide a more type-safe way to iterate over items.

Classes or structures that support this behavior advertise that they can expose contained items to the caller (in this example, the foreach keyword itself). Here is the definition of this standard interface:

```
// This interface informs the caller
// that the object's items can be enumerated.
public interface IEnumerable
{
   IEnumerator GetEnumerator();
}
```

As you can see, the GetEnumerator() method returns a reference to yet another interface named System.Collections.IEnumerator. This interface provides the infrastructure to allow the caller to traverse the internal objects contained by the IEnumerable-compatible container.

```
// This interface allows the caller to
// obtain a container's items.
public interface IEnumerator
```

```
{
   bool MoveNext ();  // Advance the internal position of the cursor.
   object Current { get;}  // Get the current item (read-only property).
   void Reset (); // Reset the cursor before the first member.
}
```

If you want to update the Garage type to support these interfaces, you could take the long road and implement each method manually. While you are certainly free to provide customized versions of GetEnumerator(), MoveNext(), Current, and Reset(), there is a simpler way. As the System.Array type (as well as many other collection classes) already implements IEnumerable and IEnumerator, you can simply delegate the request to the System.Array as follows (note you will need to import the System.Collections namespace into your code file):

```
using System.Collections;
namespace CustomEnumerator;
public class Garage : IEnumerable
{
  // System.Array already implements IEnumerator!
  private Car[] carArray = new Car[4];

  public Garage()
  {
    carArray[0] = new Car("FeeFee", 200);
    carArray[1] = new Car("Clunker", 90);
    carArray[2] = new Car("Zippy", 30);
    carArray[3] = new Car("Fred", 30);
  }

  // Return the array object's IEnumerator.
  public IEnumerator GetEnumerator()
    => carArray.GetEnumerator();
}
```

After you have updated your Garage type, you can safely use the type within the C# foreach construct. Furthermore, given that the GetEnumerator() method has been defined publicly, the object user could also interact with the IEnumerator type.

```
// Manually work with IEnumerator.
IEnumerator carEnumerator = carLot.GetEnumerator();
carEnumerator.MoveNext();
Car myCar = (Car)i.Current;
Console.WriteLine("{0} is going {1} MPH", myCar.PetName, myCar.CurrentSpeed);
```

However, if you prefer to hide the functionality of IEnumerable from the object level, simply make use of explicit interface implementation.

```
// Return the array object's IEnumerator.
IEnumerator IEnumerable.GetEnumerator()
  => return carArray.GetEnumerator();
```

By doing so, the casual object user will not find the Garage's GetEnumerator() method, while the foreach construct will obtain the interface in the background when necessary.

Building Iterator Methods with the yield Keyword

There is an alternative way to build types that work with the foreach loop via *iterators*. Simply put, an *iterator* is a member that specifies how a container's internal items should be returned when processed by foreach. To illustrate, create a new Console Application project named CustomEnumeratorWithYield and insert the Car, Radio, and Garage types from the previous example (again, renaming your namespace definitions to the current project). Now, retrofit the current Garage type as follows:

```
public class Garage : IEnumerable
{
...
  // Iterator method.

  public IEnumerator GetEnumerator()
  {
    foreach (Car c in carArray)
    {
      yield return c;
    }
  }
}
```

Notice that this implementation of GetEnumerator() iterates over the subitems using internal foreach logic and returns each Car to the caller using the yield return syntax. The yield keyword is used to specify the value (or values) to be returned to the caller's foreach construct. When the yield return statement is reached, the current location in the container is stored, and execution is restarted from this location the next time the iterator is called.

Iterator methods are not required to use the foreach keyword to return its contents. It is also permissible to define this iterator method as follows:

```
public IEnumerator GetEnumerator()
{
   yield return carArray[0];
   yield return carArray[1];
   yield return carArray[2];
   yield return carArray[3];
}
```

In this implementation, notice that the GetEnumerator() method is explicitly returning a new value to the caller with each pass through. Doing so for this example makes little sense, given that if you were to add more objects to the carArray member variable, your GetEnumerator() method would now be out of sync. Nevertheless, this syntax can be useful when you want to return local data from a method for processing by the foreach syntax.

Guard Clauses with Local Functions (New 7.0)

None of the code in the GetEnumerator() method is executed until the first time that the items are iterated over (or any element is accessed). That means if there is an exception prior to the yield statement, it will not get thrown when the method is first called, but only when the first MoveNext() is called.

To test this, update the GetEnumerator method to this:

```
public IEnumerator GetEnumerator()
{
  //This will not get thrown until MoveNext() is called
  throw new Exception("This won't get called");
  foreach (Car c in carArray)
  {
    yield return c;
  }
}
```

If you were to call the function like this and do *nothing else*, the exception will never be thrown:

```
using System.Collections;
...
Console.WriteLine("***** Fun with the Yield Keyword *****\n");
Garage carLot = new Garage();
IEnumerator carEnumerator = carLot.GetEnumerator();

Console.ReadLine();
```

It is not until MoveNext() is called that the code will execute, and the exception is thrown. Depending on the needs of your program, that might be perfectly fine. But it might not. Your GetEnumerator method might have a *guard clause* that needs to execute when the method is first called. For example, suppose that the list is gathered from a database. You might want to check that the database connection can be opened at the time the method is *called*, not when the list is iterated over. Or you might want to check the input parameters to the Iterator method (covered next) for validity.

Recall from Chapter 4 the C# 7 local function feature; local functions are private functions inside other functions. By moving the yield return into a local function that is returned from the main body of the method, the code in the top-level statements (before the local function is returned) is executed immediately. The local function is executed when MoveNext() is called.

Update the method to this:

```
public IEnumerator GetEnumerator()
{
  //This will get thrown immediately
  throw new Exception("This will get called");

  return ActualImplementation();

  //this is the local function and the actual IEnumerator implementation
  IEnumerator ActualImplementation()
  {
    foreach (Car c in carArray)
    {
      yield return c;
    }
  }
}
```

Test this by updating the calling code to this:

```
Console.WriteLine("***** Fun with the Yield Keyword *****\n");
Garage carLot = new Garage();
try
{
  //Error at this time
  var carEnumerator = carLot.GetEnumerator();
}
catch (Exception e)
{
  Console.WriteLine($"Exception occurred on GetEnumerator");
}
Console.ReadLine();
```

With the update to the `GetEnumerator()` method, the exception is thrown immediately instead of when `MoveNext()` is called.

Building a Named Iterator

It is also interesting to note that the `yield` keyword can technically be used within any method, regardless of its name. These methods (which are technically called *named iterators*) are also unique in that they can take any number of arguments. When building a named iterator, be aware that the method will return the `IEnumerable` interface, rather than the expected `IEnumerator`-compatible type. To illustrate, you could add the following method to the `Garage` type (using a local function to encapsulate the iteration functionality):

```
public IEnumerable GetTheCars(bool returnReversed)
{
  //do some error checking here
  return ActualImplementation();

  IEnumerable ActualImplementation()
  {
    // Return the items in reverse.
    if (returnReversed)
    {
      for (int i = carArray.Length; i != 0; i--)
      {
        yield return carArray[i - 1];
      }
    }
    else
    {
      // Return the items as placed in the array.
      foreach (Car c in carArray)
      {
        yield return c;
      }
    }
  }
}
```

Notice that the new method allows the caller to obtain the subitems in sequential order, as well as in reverse order, if the incoming parameter has the value `true`. You could now interact with your new method as follows (be sure to comment out the `throw new` exception statement in the `GetEnumerator()` method):

```
Console.WriteLine("***** Fun with the Yield Keyword *****\n");
Garage carLot = new Garage();

// Get items using GetEnumerator().
foreach (Car c in carLot)
{
  Console.WriteLine("{0} is going {1} MPH",
    c.PetName, c.CurrentSpeed);
}

Console.WriteLine();

// Get items (in reverse!) using named iterator.
foreach (Car c in carLot.GetTheCars(true))
{
  Console.WriteLine("{0} is going {1} MPH",
    c.PetName, c.CurrentSpeed);
}
Console.ReadLine();
```

As you might agree, named iterators are helpful constructs, in that a single custom container can define multiple ways to request the returned set.

So, to wrap up this look at building enumerable objects, remember that for your custom types to work with the C# `foreach` keyword, the container must define a method named `GetEnumerator()`, which has been formalized by the `IEnumerable` interface type. The implementation of this method is typically achieved by simply delegating it to the internal member that is holding onto the subobjects; however, it is also possible to use the `yield return` syntax to provide multiple "named iterator" methods.

The ICloneable Interface

As you might recall from Chapter 6, `System.Object` defines a method named `MemberwiseClone()`. This method is used to obtain a *shallow copy* of the current object. Object users do not call this method directly, as it is protected. However, a given object may call this method itself during the *cloning* process. To illustrate, create a new Console Application project named `CloneablePoint` that defines a class named `Point`.

```
namespace CloneablePoint;
// A class named Point.
public class Point
{
  public int X {get; set;}
  public int Y {get; set;}

  public Point(int xPos, int yPos) { X = xPos; Y = yPos;}
  public Point(){}
```

```
  // Override Object.ToString().
  public override string ToString() => $"X = {X}; Y = {Y}";
}
```

Given what you already know about reference types and value types (see Chapter 4), you are aware that if you assign one reference variable to another, you have two references pointing to the same object in memory. Thus, the following assignment operation results in two references to the same Point object on the heap; modifications using either reference affect the same object on the heap:

```
using CloneablePoint;
Console.WriteLine("***** Fun with Object Cloning *****\n");
// Two references to same object!
Point p1 = new Point(50, 50);
Point p2 = p1;
p2.X = 0;
Console.WriteLine(p1);
Console.WriteLine(p2);
Console.ReadLine();
```

When you want to give your custom type the ability to return an identical copy of itself to the caller, you may implement the standard ICloneable interface. As shown at the start of this chapter, this type defines a single method named Clone().

```
public interface ICloneable
{
  object Clone();
}
```

Obviously, the implementation of the Clone() method varies among your classes. However, the basic functionality tends to be the same: copy the values of your member variables into a new object instance of the same type and return it to the user. To illustrate, ponder the following update to the Point class:

```
// The Point now supports "clone-ability."
public class Point : ICloneable
{
  public int X { get; set; }
  public int Y { get; set; }

  public Point(int xPos, int yPos) { X = xPos; Y = yPos; }
  public Point() { }

  // Override Object.ToString().
  public override string ToString() => $"X = {X}; Y = {Y}";

  // Return a copy of the current object.
  public object Clone() => new Point(this.X, this.Y);
}
```

In this way, you can create exact stand-alone copies of the Point type, as illustrated by the following code:

```
Console.WriteLine("***** Fun with Object Cloning *****\n");
...
// Notice Clone() returns a plain object type.
// You must perform an explicit cast to obtain the derived type.
Point p3 = new Point(100, 100);
Point p4 = (Point)p3.Clone();

// Change p4.X (which will not change p3.X).
p4.X = 0;

// Print each object.
Console.WriteLine(p3);
Console.WriteLine(p4);
Console.ReadLine();
```

While the current implementation of `Point` fits the bill, you can streamline things just a bit. Because the `Point` type does not contain any internal reference type variables, you could simplify the implementation of the `Clone()` method as follows:

```
// Copy each field of the Point member by member.
public object Clone() => this.MemberwiseClone();
```

Be aware, however, that if the `Point` did contain any reference type member variables, `MemberwiseClone()` would copy the references to those objects (i.e., a *shallow copy*). If you want to support a true *deep copy*, you will need to create a new instance of any reference type variables during the cloning process. Let's see an example next.

A More Elaborate Cloning Example

Now assume the `Point` class contains a reference type member variable of type `PointDescription`. This class maintains a point's friendly name as well as an identification number expressed as a `System.Guid` (a globally unique identifier [GUID] is a statistically unique 128-bit number). Here is the implementation:

```
namespace CloneablePoint;
// This class describes a point.
public class PointDescription
{
  public string PetName {get; set;}
  public Guid PointID {get; set;}

  public PointDescription()
  {
    PetName = "No-name";
    PointID = Guid.NewGuid();
  }
}
```

The initial updates to the `Point` class itself included modifying `ToString()` to account for these new bits of state data, as well as defining and creating the `PointDescription` reference type. To allow the outside world to establish a pet name for the `Point`, you also update the arguments passed into the overloaded constructor.

```
public class Point : ICloneable
{
  public int X { get; set; }
  public int Y { get; set; }
  public PointDescription desc = new PointDescription();

  public Point(int xPos, int yPos, string petName)
  {
    X = xPos; Y = yPos;
    desc.PetName = petName;
  }
  public Point(int xPos, int yPos)
  {
    X = xPos; Y = yPos;
  }
  public Point() { }

  // Override Object.ToString().
  public override string ToString()
     => $"X = {X}; Y = {Y}; Name = {desc.PetName};\nID = {desc.PointID}\n";

  // Return a copy of the current object.
  public object Clone() => this.MemberwiseClone();
}
```

Notice that you did not yet update your Clone() method. Therefore, when the object user asks for a clone using the current implementation, a shallow (member-by-member) copy is achieved. To illustrate, assume you have updated the calling code as follows:

```
Console.WriteLine("***** Fun with Object Cloning *****\n");
...
Console.WriteLine("Cloned p3 and stored new Point in p4");
Point p3 = new Point(100, 100, "Jane");
Point p4 = (Point)p3.Clone();

Console.WriteLine("Before modification:");
Console.WriteLine("p3: {0}", p3);
Console.WriteLine("p4: {0}", p4);
p4.desc.PetName = "My new Point";
p4.X = 9;

Console.WriteLine("\nChanged p4.desc.petName and p4.X");
Console.WriteLine("After modification:");
Console.WriteLine("p3: {0}", p3);
Console.WriteLine("p4: {0}", p4);
Console.ReadLine();
```

Notice in the following output that while the value types have indeed been changed, the internal reference types maintain the same values, as they are "pointing" to the same objects in memory (specifically, note that the pet name for both objects is now "My new Point").

```
***** Fun with Object Cloning *****
Cloned p3 and stored new Point in p4
Before modification:
p3: X = 100; Y = 100; Name = Jane;
ID = 133d66a7-0837-4bd7-95c6-b22ab0434509

p4: X = 100; Y = 100; Name = Jane;
ID = 133d66a7-0837-4bd7-95c6-b22ab0434509

Changed p4.desc.petName  and p4.X
After modification:
p3: X = 100; Y = 100; Name = My new Point;
ID = 133d66a7-0837-4bd7-95c6-b22ab0434509

p4: X = 9; Y = 100; Name = My new Point;
ID = 133d66a7-0837-4bd7-95c6-b22ab0434509
```

To have your Clone() method make a complete deep copy of the internal reference types, you need to configure the object returned by MemberwiseClone() to account for the current point's name (the System.Guid type is in fact a structure, so the numerical data is indeed copied). Here is one possible implementation:

```
// Now we need to adjust for the PointDescription member.
public object Clone()
{
  // First get a shallow copy.
  Point newPoint = (Point)this.MemberwiseClone();

  // Then fill in the gaps.
  PointDescription currentDesc = new PointDescription();
  currentDesc.PetName = this.desc.PetName;
  newPoint.desc = currentDesc;
  return newPoint;
}
```

If you rerun the application once again and view the output (shown next), you see that the Point returned from Clone() does copy its internal reference type member variables (note the pet name is now unique for both p3 and p4).

```
***** Fun with Object Cloning *****
Cloned p3 and stored new Point in p4
Before modification:
p3: X = 100; Y = 100; Name = Jane;
ID = 51f64f25-4b0e-47ac-ba35-37d263496406

p4: X = 100; Y = 100; Name = Jane;
ID = 0d3776b3-b159-490d-b022-7f3f60788e8a
```

```
Changed p4.desc.petName  and p4.X
After modification:
p3: X = 100; Y = 100; Name = Jane;
ID = 51f64f25-4b0e-47ac-ba35-37d263496406

p4: X = 9; Y = 100; Name = My new Point;
ID = 0d3776b3-b159-490d-b022-7f3f60788e8a
```

To summarize the cloning process, if you have a class or structure that contains nothing but value types, implement your Clone() method using MemberwiseClone(). However, if you have a custom type that maintains other reference types, you might want to create a new object that considers each reference type member variable to get a "deep copy."

The IComparable Interface

The System.IComparable interface specifies a behavior that allows an object to be sorted based on some specified key. Here is the formal definition:

```
// This interface allows an object to specify its
// relationship between other like objects.
public interface IComparable
{
  int CompareTo(object o);
}
```

■ **Note** The generic version of this interface (IComparable<T>) provides a more type-safe manner to handle comparisons between objects. You will examine generics in Chapter 10.

Create a new Console Application project named ComparableCar, copy the Car and Radio classes from the SimpleException example in Chapter 7, and rename the namespace for each file to ComparableCar. Update the Car class by adding a new property to represent a unique ID for each car and a modified constructor:

```
using System.Collections;

namespace ComparableCar;
public class Car
{
.
  public int CarID {get; set;}
  public Car(string name, int currSp, int id)
  {
    CurrentSpeed = currSp;
    PetName = name;
    CarID = id;
  }
...
}
```

Now assume you have an array of Car objects as follows in your top-level statements:

```
global using System.Collections;

using ComparableCar;
Console.WriteLine("***** Fun with Object Sorting *****\n");

// Make an array of Car objects.
Car[] myAutos = new Car[5];
myAutos[0] = new Car("Rusty", 80, 1);
myAutos[1] = new Car("Mary", 40, 234);
myAutos[2] = new Car("Viper", 40, 34);
myAutos[3] = new Car("Mel", 40, 4);
myAutos[4] = new Car("Chucky", 40, 5);

Console.ReadLine();
```

The System.Array class defines a static method named Sort(). When you invoke this method on an array of intrinsic types (int, short, string, etc.), you can sort the items in the array in numeric/alphabetic order, as these intrinsic data types implement IComparable. However, what if you were to send an array of Car types into the Sort() method as follows?

```
// Sort my cars? Not yet!
Array.Sort(myAutos);
```

If you run this test, you would get a runtime exception, as the Car class does not support the necessary interface. When you build custom types, you can implement IComparable to allow arrays of your types to be sorted. When you flesh out the details of CompareTo(), it will be up to you to decide what the baseline of the ordering operation will be. For the Car type, the internal CarID seems to be the logical candidate.

```
// The iteration of the Car can be ordered
// based on the CarID.
public class Car : IComparable
{
...
  // IComparable implementation.
  int IComparable.CompareTo(object obj)
  {
    if (obj is Car temp)
    {
      if (this.CarID > temp.CarID)
      {
        return 1;
      }
      if (this.CarID < temp.CarID)
      {
        return -1;
      }
      return 0;
    }
    throw new ArgumentException("Parameter is not a Car!");
  }
}
```

As you can see, the logic behind CompareTo() is to test the incoming object against the current instance based on a specific point of data. The return value of CompareTo() is used to discover whether this type is less than, greater than, or equal to the object it is being compared with (see Table 8-1).

Table 8-1. *CompareTo Return Values*

Return Value	Description
Any number less than zero	This instance comes before the specified object in the sort order.
Zero	This instance is equal to the specified object.
Any number greater than zero	This instance comes after the specified object in the sort order.

You can streamline the previous implementation of CompareTo() given that the C# int data type (which is just a shorthand notation for System.Int32) implements IComparable. You could implement the Car's CompareTo() as follows:

```
int IComparable.CompareTo(object obj)
{
  if (obj is Car temp)
  {
    return this.CarID.CompareTo(temp.CarID);
  }
  throw new ArgumentException("Parameter is not a Car!");
}
```

In either case, so that your Car type understands how to compare itself to like objects, you can write the following user code:

```
// Exercise the IComparable interface.
// Make an array of Car objects.
...
// Display current array.
Console.WriteLine("Here is the unordered set of cars:");
foreach(Car c in myAutos)
{
  Console.WriteLine("{0} {1}", c.CarID, c.PetName);
}

// Now, sort them using IComparable!
Array.Sort(myAutos);
Console.WriteLine();

// Display sorted array.
Console.WriteLine("Here is the ordered set of cars:");
foreach(Car c in myAutos)
{
  Console.WriteLine("{0} {1}", c.CarID, c.PetName);
}
Console.ReadLine();
```

Here is the output from the previous code listing:

```
***** Fun with Object Sorting *****
Here is the unordered set of cars:
1 Rusty
234 Mary
34 Viper
4 Mel
5 Chucky

Here is the ordered set of cars:
1 Rusty
4 Mel
5 Chucky
34 Viper
234 Mary
```

Specifying Multiple Sort Orders with IComparer

In this version of the Car type, you used the car's ID as the base for the sort order. Another design might have used the pet name of the car as the basis for the sorting algorithm (to list cars alphabetically). Now, what if you wanted to build a Car that could be sorted by ID *as well as* by pet name? If this is the type of behavior you are interested in, you need to make friends with another standard interface named IComparer, defined within the System.Collections namespace as follows:

```
// A general way to compare two objects.
interface IComparer
{
  int Compare(object o1, object o2);
}
```

■ **Note** The generic version of this interface (IComparer<T>) provides a more type-safe manner to handle comparisons between objects. You will examine generics in Chapter 10.

Unlike the IComparable interface, IComparer is typically *not* implemented on the type you are trying to sort (i.e., the Car). Rather, you implement this interface on any number of helper classes, one for each sort order (pet name, car ID, etc.). Currently, the Car type already knows how to compare itself against other cars based on the internal car ID. Therefore, allowing the object user to sort an array of Car objects by pet name will require an additional helper class that implements IComparer. Here is the code:

```
namespace ComparableCar;
// This helper class is used to sort an array of Cars by pet name.
public class PetNameComparer : IComparer
{
  // Test the pet name of each object.
  int IComparer.Compare(object o1, object o2)
  {
```

```
    if (o1 is Car t1 && o2 is Car t2)
    {
      return string.Compare(t1.PetName, t2.PetName,
        StringComparison.OrdinalIgnoreCase);
    }
    else
    {
      throw new ArgumentException("Parameter is not a Car!");
    }
  }
}
```

The object user code can use this helper class. `System.Array` has several overloaded `Sort()` methods, one that just happens to take an object implementing `IComparer`.

```
...
// Now sort by pet name.
Array.Sort(myAutos, new PetNameComparer());

// Dump sorted array.
Console.WriteLine("Ordering by pet name:");
foreach(Car c in myAutos)
{
  Console.WriteLine("{0} {1}", c.CarID, c.PetName);
}
...
```

Custom Properties and Custom Sort Types

It is worth pointing out that you can use a custom static property to help the object user along when sorting your `Car` types by a specific data point. Assume the `Car` class has added a static read-only property named `SortByPetName` that returns an instance of an object implementing the `IComparer` interface (`PetNameComparer`, in this case; be sure to import `System.Collections`).

```
// We now support a custom property to return
// the correct IComparer interface.
public class Car : IComparable
{
...
  // Property to return the PetNameComparer.
  public static IComparer SortByPetName
    => (IComparer)new PetNameComparer();}
```

The object user code can now sort by pet name using a strongly associated property, rather than just "having to know" to use the stand-alone `PetNameComparer` class type.

```
// Sorting by pet name made a bit cleaner.
Array.Sort(myAutos, Car.SortByPetName);
```

Ideally, at this point you not only understand how to define and implement your own interfaces but also understand their usefulness. To be sure, interfaces are found within every major .NET Core namespace, and you will continue working with various standard interfaces in the remainder of this book.

Summary

An interface can be defined as a named collection of *abstract members*. It is common to regard an interface as a behavior that may be supported by a given type. When two or more classes implement the same interface, you can treat each type the same way (interface-based polymorphism) even if the types are defined within unique class hierarchies.

C# provides the `interface` keyword to allow you to define a new interface. As you have seen, a type can support as many interfaces as necessary using a comma-delimited list. Furthermore, it is permissible to build interfaces that derive from multiple base interfaces.

In addition to building your custom interfaces, the .NET Core libraries define several standard (i.e., framework-supplied) interfaces. As you have seen, you are free to build custom types that implement these predefined interfaces to gain several desirable traits such as cloning, sorting, and enumerating.

CHAPTER 9

■ ■ ■

Understanding Object Lifetime

At this point in the book, you have learned a great deal about how to build custom class types using C#. Now you will see how the runtime manages allocated class instances (aka objects) via *garbage collection* (*GC*). C# programmers never directly deallocate a managed object from memory (recall there is no `delete` keyword in the C# language). Rather, .NET Core objects are allocated to a region of memory termed the *managed heap*, where they will be automatically destroyed by the garbage collector "sometime in the future."

After you have looked at the core details of the collection process, you'll learn how to programmatically interact with the garbage collector using the `System.GC` class type (which is something you will typically not be required to do for a majority of your projects). Next, you'll examine how the virtual `System.Object.Finalize()` method and `IDisposable` interface can be used to build classes that release internal *unmanaged resources* in a predictable and timely manner.

You will also delve into some functionality of the garbage collector introduced in .NET 4.0, including background garbage collections and lazy instantiation using the generic `System.Lazy<>` class. By the time you have completed this chapter, you will have a solid understanding of how .NET Core objects are managed by the runtime.

Classes, Objects, and References

To frame the topics covered in this chapter, it is important to further clarify the distinction between classes, objects, and reference variables. Recall that a class is nothing more than a blueprint that describes how an instance of this type will look and feel in memory. Classes, of course, are defined within a code file (which in C# takes a `*.cs` extension by convention). Consider the following simple `Car` class defined within a new C# Console Application project named SimpleGC:

```
namespace SimpleGC;
// Car.cs
public class Car
{
  public int CurrentSpeed {get; set;}
  public string PetName {get; set;}

  public Car(){}
  public Car(string name, int speed)
  {
    PetName = name;
    CurrentSpeed = speed;
  }
```


A. Troelsen and P. Japikse, *Pro C# 10 with .NET 6*, https://doi.org/10.1007/978-1-4842-7869-7_9

```
  public override string ToString()
    => $"{PetName} is going {CurrentSpeed} MPH";

}
```

After a class has been defined, you may allocate any number of objects using the C# new keyword. Understand, however, that the new keyword returns a *reference* to the object on the heap, not the actual object. If you declare the reference variable as a local variable in a method scope, it is stored on the stack for further use in your application. When you want to invoke members on the object, apply the C# dot operator to the stored reference, like so:

```
using SimpleGC;
Console.WriteLine("***** GC Basics *****");

// Create a new Car object on the managed heap.
// We are returned a reference to the object
// ("refToMyCar").
Car refToMyCar = new Car("Zippy", 50);

// The C# dot operator (.) is used to invoke members
// on the object using our reference variable.
Console.WriteLine(refToMyCar.ToString());
Console.ReadLine();
```

Figure 9-1 illustrates the class, object, and reference relationship.

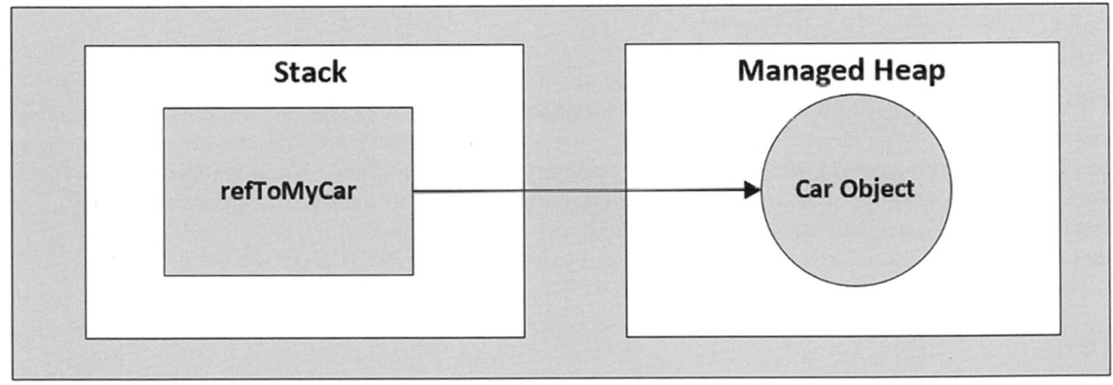

Figure 9-1. *References to objects on the managed heap*

■ **Note** Recall from Chapter 4 that structures are *value types* that are always allocated directly on the stack and are never placed on the .NET Core managed heap. Heap allocation occurs only when you are creating instances of classes.

The Basics of Object Lifetime

When you are building your C# applications, you are correct to assume that the .NET Core runtime environment will take care of the managed heap without your direct intervention. In fact, the golden rule of .NET Core memory management is simple.

■ **Rule** Allocate a class instance onto the managed heap using the new keyword and forget about it.

Once instantiated, the garbage collector will destroy an object when it is no longer needed. The next obvious question, of course, is "How does the garbage collector determine when an object is no longer needed?" The short (i.e., incomplete) answer is that the garbage collector removes an object from the heap only if it is *unreachable* by any part of your code base. Assume you have a method in your `Program.cs` file that allocates a local `Car` object as follows:

```
static void MakeACar()
{
  // If myCar is the only reference to the Car object, it *may* be destroyed when this
  method returns.
  Car myCar = new Car();
}
```

Notice that this `Car` reference (`myCar`) has been created directly within the `MakeACar()` method and has not been passed outside of the defining scope (via a return value or `ref/out` parameters). Thus, once this method call completes, the `myCar` reference is no longer reachable, and the associated `Car` object is now a candidate for garbage collection. Understand, however, that you can't guarantee that this object will be reclaimed from memory immediately after `MakeACar()` has completed. All you can assume at this point is that when the runtime performs the next garbage collection, the `myCar` object could be safely destroyed.

As you will most certainly discover, programming in a garbage-collected environment greatly simplifies your application development. In stark contrast, C++ programmers are painfully aware that if they fail to manually delete heap-allocated objects, memory leaks are never far behind. In fact, tracking down memory leaks is one of the most time-consuming (and tedious) aspects of programming in unmanaged environments. By allowing the garbage collector to take charge of destroying objects, the burden of memory management has been lifted from your shoulders and placed onto those of the runtime.

The CIL of new

When the C# compiler encounters the new keyword, it emits a CIL `newobj` instruction into the method implementation. If you compile the current example code and investigate the resulting assembly using `ildasm.exe`, you'd find the following CIL statements within the `MakeACar()` method:

```
.method assembly hidebysig static
        void  '<<Main>$>g__MakeACar|0_0'() cil managed
{
    // Code size       8 (0x8)
    .maxstack  1
    .locals init (class SimpleGC.Car V_0)
    IL_0000: nop
```

```
    IL_0001: newobj      instance void SimpleGC.Car::.ctor()
    IL_0006: stloc.0
    IL_0007: ret
  } // end of method '<Program>$'::'<<Main>$>g__MakeACar|0_0'
```

Before you examine the exact rules that determine when an object is removed from the managed heap, let's check out the role of the CIL `newobj` instruction in a bit more detail. First, understand that the managed heap is more than just a random chunk of memory accessed by the runtime. The .NET Core garbage collector is quite a tidy housekeeper of the heap, given that it will compact empty blocks of memory (when necessary) for the purposes of optimization.

To aid in this endeavor, the managed heap maintains a pointer (commonly referred to as the *next object pointer* or *new object pointer*) that identifies exactly where the next object will be located. That said, the `newobj` instruction tells the runtime to perform the following core operations:

1. Calculate the total amount of memory required for the object to be allocated (including the memory required by the data members and the base classes).
2. Examine the managed heap to ensure that there is indeed enough room to host the object to be allocated. If there is, the specified constructor is called, and the caller is ultimately returned a reference to the new object in memory, whose address just happens to be identical to the last position of the next object pointer.
3. Finally, before returning the reference to the caller, advance the next object pointer to point to the next available slot on the managed heap.

Figure 9-2 illustrates the basic process.

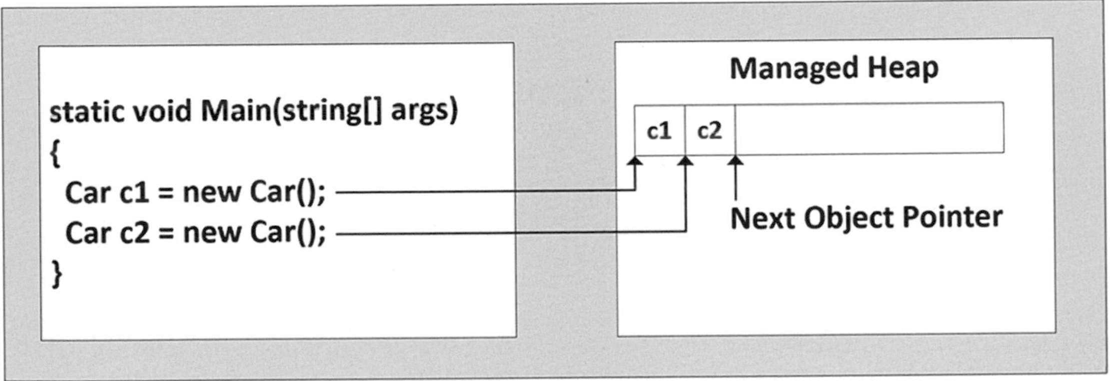

Figure 9-2. *The details of allocating objects onto the managed heap*

As your application is busy allocating objects, the space on the managed heap may eventually become full. When processing the `newobj` instruction, if the runtime determines that the managed heap does not have sufficient memory to allocate the requested type, it will perform a garbage collection in an attempt to free up memory. Thus, the next rule of garbage collection is also quite simple.

■ **Rule** If the managed heap does not have sufficient memory to allocate a requested object, a garbage collection will occur.

Exactly *how* this garbage collection occurs, however, depends on which type of garbage collection your application uses. You'll look at the differences a bit later in this chapter.

Setting Object References to null

C/C++ programmers often set pointer variables to null to ensure they are no longer referencing unmanaged memory. Given this, you might wonder what the end result is of assigning object references to null under C#. For example, assume the MakeACar() subroutine has now been updated as follows:

```
static void MakeACar()
{
  Car myCar = new Car();
  myCar = null;
}
```

When you assign object references to null, the compiler generates CIL code that ensures the reference (myCar, in this example) no longer points to any object. If you once again made use of ildasm.exe to view the CIL code of the modified MakeACar(), you would find the ldnull opcode (which pushes a null value on the virtual execution stack) followed by a stloc.0 opcode (which sets the null reference on the variable).

```
.method assembly hidebysig static
        void  '<<Main>$>g__MakeACar|0_0'() cil managed
{
  // Code size       10 (0xa)
  .maxstack  1
  .locals init (class SimpleGC.Car V_0)
  IL_0000: nop
  IL_0001: newobj     instance void SimpleGC.Car::.ctor()
  IL_0006: stloc.0
  IL_0007: ldnull
  IL_0008: stloc.0
  IL_0009: ret
} // end of method '<Program>$'::'<<Main>$>g__MakeACar|0_0'
```

What you must understand, however, is that assigning a reference to null does not in any way force the garbage collector to fire up at that exact moment and remove the object from the heap. The only thing you have accomplished is explicitly clipping the connection between the reference and the object it previously pointed to. Given this point, setting references to null under C# is far less consequential than doing so in other C-based languages; however, doing so will certainly not cause any harm.

Determining If an Object Is Live

Now, back to the topic of how the garbage collector determines when an object is no longer needed. The garbage collector uses the following information to determine whether an object is live:

- *Stack roots*: Stack variables provided by the compiler and stack walker
- *Garbage collection handles*: Handles that point to managed objects that can be referenced from code or the runtime
- *Static data*: Static objects in application domains that can reference other objects

During a garbage collection process, the runtime will investigate objects on the managed heap to determine whether they are still reachable by the application. To do so, the runtime will build an *object graph*, which represents each reachable object on the heap. Object graphs are explained in some detail during the discussion of object serialization in Chapter 19. For now, just understand that object graphs are used to document all reachable objects. As well, be aware that the garbage collector will never graph the same object twice, thus avoiding the nasty circular reference count found in COM programming.

Assume the managed heap contains a set of objects named A, B, C, D, E, F, and G. During garbage collection, these objects (as well as any internal object references they may contain) are examined. After the graph has been constructed, unreachable objects (which you can assume are objects C and F) are marked as garbage. Figure 9-3 diagrams a possible object graph for the scenario just described (you can read the directional arrows using the phrase *depends on* or *requires*; for example, E depends on G and B, A depends on nothing, etc.).

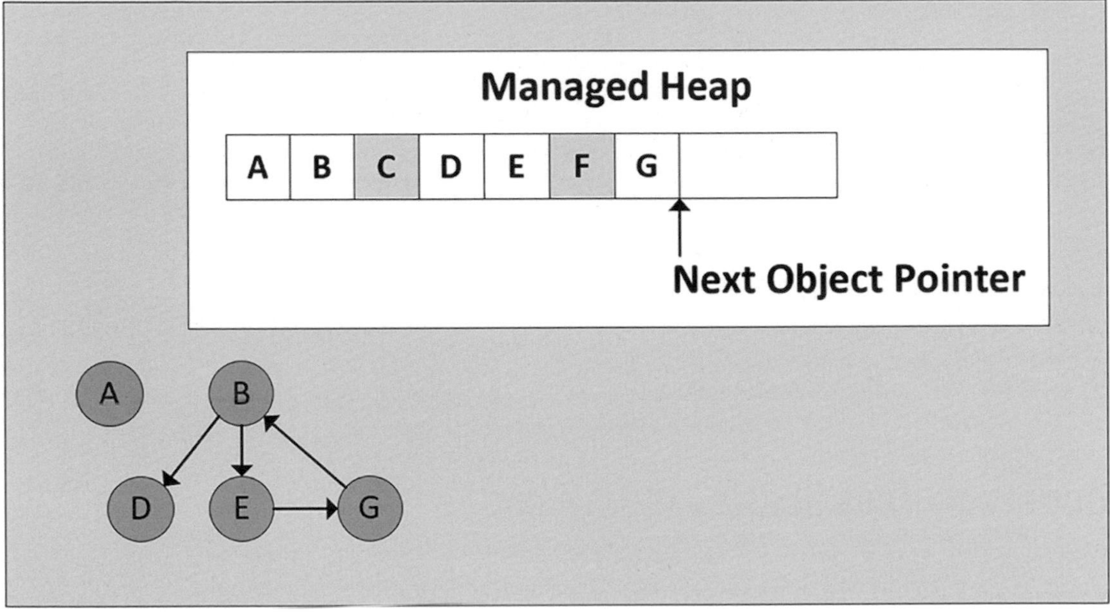

Figure 9-3. *Object graphs are constructed to determine which objects are reachable by application roots*

After objects have been marked for termination (C and F in this case, as they are not accounted for in the object graph), they are swept from memory. At this point, the remaining space on the heap is compacted, which in turn causes the runtime to modify the set of underlying pointers to refer to the correct memory location (this is done automatically and transparently). Last but not least, the next object pointer is readjusted to point to the next available slot. Figure 9-4 illustrates the resulting readjustment.

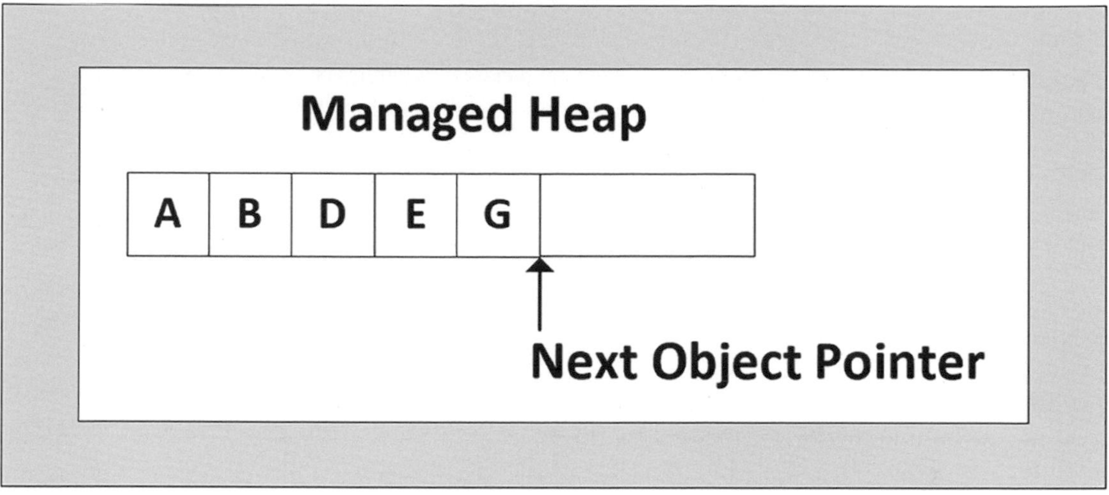

Figure 9-4. A clean and compacted heap

■ **Note** Strictly speaking, the garbage collector uses two distinct heaps, one of which is specifically used to store large objects. This heap is less frequently consulted during the collection cycle, given possible performance penalties involved with relocating large objects. In .NET Core, the large heap can be compacted on demand or when optional hard limits for absolute or percentage memory usage is reached.

Understanding Object Generations

When the runtime is attempting to locate unreachable objects, it does not literally examine every object placed on the managed heap. Doing so, obviously, would involve considerable time, especially in larger (i.e., real-world) applications.

To help optimize the process, each object on the heap is assigned to a specific "generation." The idea behind generations is simple: the longer an object has existed on the heap, the more likely it is to stay there. For example, the class that defined the main window of a desktop application will be in memory until the program terminates. Conversely, objects that have only recently been placed on the heap (such as an object allocated within a method scope) are likely to be unreachable rather quickly. Given these assumptions, each object on the heap belongs to a collection in one of the following generations:

- *Generation 0*: Identifies a newly allocated object that has never been marked for collection (with the exception of large objects, which are initially placed in a generation 2 collection). Most objects are reclaimed for garbage collection in generation 0 and do now survive to generation 1.
- *Generation 1*: Identifies an object that has survived a garbage collection. This generation also serves as a buffer between short-lived objects and long-lived objects.
- *Generation 2*: Identifies an object that has survived more than one sweep of the garbage collector or a significantly large object that started in a generation 2 collection.

■ **Note** Generations 0 and 1 are termed *ephemeral generations*. As explained in the next section, you will see that the garbage collection process does treat ephemeral generations differently.

The garbage collector will investigate all generation 0 objects first. If marking and sweeping (or said more plainly, getting rid of) these objects results in the required amount of free memory, any surviving objects are promoted to generation 1. To see how an object's generation affects the collection process, ponder Figure 9-5, which diagrams how a set of surviving generation 0 objects (A, B, and E) are promoted once the required memory has been reclaimed.

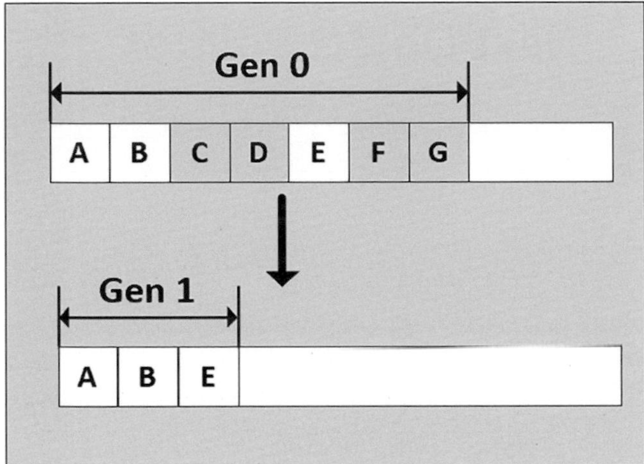

Figure 9-5. *Generation 0 objects that survive a garbage collection are promoted to generation 1*

If all generation 0 objects have been evaluated but additional memory is still required, generation 1 objects are then investigated for reachability and collected accordingly. Surviving generation 1 objects are then promoted to generation 2. If the garbage collector *still* requires additional memory, generation 2 objects are evaluated. At this point, if a generation 2 object survives a garbage collection, it remains a generation 2 object, given the predefined upper limit of object generations.

The bottom line is that by assigning a generational value to objects on the heap, newer objects (such as local variables) will be removed quickly, while older objects (such as a program's main window) are not "bothered" as often.

Garbage collection is triggered when the system has low physical memory, when memory allocated on the managed heap rises above an acceptable threshold, or when `GC.Collect()` is called in the application code.

If this all seems a bit wonderful and better than having to manage memory yourself, remember that the process of garbage collection is not without some cost. The timing of garbage collection and what gets collected when are typically out of the developers' controls, although garbage collection can certainly be influenced for good or bad. And when garbage collection is executing, CPU cycles are being used and can affect the performance of the application. The next sections examine the different types of garbage collection.

Ephemeral Generations and Segments

As mentioned earlier, generations 0 and 1 are short-lived and are known as *ephemeral generations*. These generations are allocated in a memory segment known as the *ephemeral segment*. As garbage collection occurs, new segments acquired by the garbage collection become new ephemeral segments, and the segment containing objects surviving past generation 1 becomes the new generation 2 segment.

The size of the ephemeral segment varies on a number of factors, such as the garbage collection type (covered next) and the bitness of the system. Table 9-1 shows the different sizes of the ephemeral segments.

Table 9-1. *Ephemeral Segment Sizes*

Garbage Collection Type	32-bit	64-bit
Workstation	16 MB	256 MB
Server	64 MB	4 GB
Server with > 4 logical CPUs	32 MB	2 GB
Server with > 8 logical CPUs	16 MB	1 GB

Garbage Collection Types

There are two types of garbage collection provided by the runtime:

- *Workstation garbage collection*: This is designed for client applications and is the default for stand-alone applications. Workstation GC can be background (covered next) or nonconcurrent.
- *Server garbage collection*: This is designed for server applications that require high throughput and scalability. Server GC can be background or nonconcurrent, just like workstation GC.

■ **Note** The names are indicative of the default settings for workstation and server applications, but the method of garbage collection is configurable through the machine's `runtimeconfig.json` or system environment variables. Unless the computer has only one processor, then it will always use workstation garbage collection.

Workstation GC occurs on the same thread that triggered the garbage collection and remains at the same priority as when it was triggered. This can cause competition with other threads in the application.

Server GC occurs on multiple dedicated threads that are set to the `THREAD_PRIORITY_HIGHEST` priority level (threading is covered in Chapter 15). Each CPU gets a dedicated heap and dedicated thread to perform garbage collection. This can lead to server garbage collection becoming very resource intensive.

Background Garbage Collection

Beginning with .NET 4.0 (and continuing in .NET Core), the garbage collector is able to deal with thread suspension when it cleans up objects on the managed heap, using *background garbage collection*. Despite its name, this does not mean that all garbage collection now takes place on additional background threads of execution. Rather, if a background garbage collection is taking place for objects living in a nonephemeral generation, the .NET Core runtime is now able to collect objects on the ephemeral generations using a dedicated background thread.

On a related note, the .NET 4.0 and higher garbage collection have been improved to further reduce the amount of time a given thread involved with garbage collection details must be suspended. The end result of these changes is that the process of cleaning up unused objects living in generation 0 or generation 1 has been optimized and can result in better runtime performance of your programs (which is really important for real-time systems that require a small, and predictable, GC stop time).

Do understand, however, that the introduction of this new garbage collection model has no effect on how you build your .NET Core applications. For all practical purposes, you can simply allow the garbage collector to perform its work without your direct intervention (and be happy that the folks at Microsoft are improving the collection process in a transparent manner).

The System.GC Type

The `mscorlib.dll` assembly provides a class type named `System.GC` that allows you to programmatically interact with the garbage collector using a set of static members. Now, do be aware that you will seldom (if ever) need to make use of this class directly in your code. Typically, the only time you will use the members of `System.GC` is when you are creating classes that make internal use of *unmanaged resources*. This could be the case if you are building a class that makes calls into the Windows C-based API using the .NET Core platform invocation protocol or perhaps because of some very low-level and complicated COM interop logic. Table 9-2 provides a rundown of some of the more interesting members (consult the .NET Framework SDK documentation for complete details).

Table 9-2. *Select Members of the System.GC Type*

System.GC Member	Description
`AddMemoryPressure()` `RemoveMemoryPressure()`	Allows you to specify a numerical value that represents the calling object's "urgency level" regarding the garbage collection process. Be aware that these methods should alter pressure *in tandem* and, thus, never remove more pressure than the total amount you have added.
`Collect()`	Forces the GC to perform a garbage collection. This method has been overloaded to specify a generation to collect, as well as the mode of collection (via the `GCCollectionMode` enumeration).
`CollectionCount()`	Returns a numerical value representing how many times a given generation has been swept.
`GetGeneration()`	Returns the generation to which an object currently belongs.
`GetTotalMemory()`	Returns the estimated amount of memory (in bytes) currently allocated on the managed heap. A Boolean parameter specifies whether the call should wait for garbage collection to occur before returning.
`MaxGeneration`	Returns the maximum number of generations supported on the target system. Under Microsoft's .NET 4.0, there are three possible generations: 0, 1, and 2.
`SuppressFinalize()`	Sets a flag indicating that the specified object should not have its `Finalize()` method called.
`WaitForPendingFinalizers()`	Suspends the current thread until all finalizable objects have been finalized. This method is typically called directly after invoking `GC.Collect()`.

To illustrate how the System.GC type can be used to obtain various garbage collection–centric details, update your top-level statements of the SimpleGC project to the following, which makes use of several members of GC:

```
Console.WriteLine("***** Fun with System.GC *****");

// Print out estimated number of bytes on heap.
Console.WriteLine("Estimated bytes on heap: {0}",
  GC.GetTotalMemory(false));

// MaxGeneration is zero based, so add 1 for display
// purposes.
Console.WriteLine("This OS has {0} object generations.\n",
 (GC.MaxGeneration + 1));

Car refToMyCar = new Car("Zippy", 100);
Console.WriteLine(refToMyCar.ToString());

// Print out generation of refToMyCar object.
Console.WriteLine("Generation of refToMyCar is: {0}",
  GC.GetGeneration(refToMyCar));
Console.ReadLine();
```

After running this, you should see output similar to this:

```
***** Fun with System.GC *****

Estimated bytes on heap: 75760
This OS has 3 object generations.

Zippy is going 100 MPH
Generation of refToMyCar is: 0
```

You will explore more of the methods from Table 9-2 in the next section.

Forcing a Garbage Collection

Again, the whole purpose of the garbage collector is to manage memory on your behalf. However, in some rare circumstances, it may be beneficial to programmatically force a garbage collection using GC.Collect(). Here are two common situations where you might consider interacting with the collection process:

- Your application is about to enter a block of code that you don't want interrupted by a possible garbage collection.
- Your application has just finished allocating an extremely large number of objects, and you want to remove as much of the acquired memory as soon as possible.

If you determine it could be beneficial to have the garbage collector check for unreachable objects, you could explicitly trigger a garbage collection, as follows:

```
...
// Force a garbage collection and wait for
// each object to be finalized.
GC.Collect();
GC.WaitForPendingFinalizers();
...
```

When you manually force a garbage collection, you should always make a call to `GC.WaitForPendingFinalizers()`. With this approach, you can rest assured that all *finalizable objects* (described in the next section) have had a chance to perform any necessary cleanup before your program continues. Under the hood, `GC.WaitForPendingFinalizers()` will suspend the calling thread during the collection process. This is a good thing, as it ensures your code does not invoke methods on an object currently being destroyed!

The `GC.Collect()` method can also be supplied a numerical value that identifies the oldest generation on which a garbage collection will be performed. For example, to instruct the runtime to investigate only generation 0 objects, you would write the following:

```
...
// Only investigate generation 0 objects.
GC.Collect(0);
GC.WaitForPendingFinalizers();
...
```

As well, the `Collect()` method can be passed in a value of the `GCCollectionMode` enumeration as a second parameter, to fine-tune exactly how the runtime should force the garbage collection. This enum defines the following values:

```
public enum GCCollectionMode
{
  Default,  // Forced is the current default.
  Forced,   // Tells the runtime to collect immediately!
  Optimized // Allows the runtime to determine whether the current time is optimal to
reclaim objects.
}
```

As with any garbage collection, calling `GC.Collect()` promotes surviving generations. To illustrate, assume that your top-level statements have been updated as follows:

```
Console.WriteLine("***** Fun with System.GC *****");

// Print out estimated number of bytes on heap.
Console.WriteLine("Estimated bytes on heap: {0}",
  GC.GetTotalMemory(false));

// MaxGeneration is zero based.
Console.WriteLine("This OS has {0} object generations.\n",
  (GC.MaxGeneration + 1));
Car refToMyCar = new Car("Zippy", 100);
Console.WriteLine(refToMyCar.ToString());
```

```
// Print out generation of refToMyCar.
Console.WriteLine("\nGeneration of refToMyCar is: {0}",
  GC.GetGeneration(refToMyCar));

// Make a ton of objects for testing purposes.
object[] tonsOfObjects = new object[50000];
for (int i = 0; i < 50000; i++)
{
  tonsOfObjects[i] = new object();
}

// Collect only gen 0 objects.
Console.WriteLine("Force Garbage Collection");
GC.Collect(0, GCCollectionMode.Forced);
GC.WaitForPendingFinalizers();

// Print out generation of refToMyCar.
Console.WriteLine("Generation of refToMyCar is: {0}",
  GC.GetGeneration(refToMyCar));

// See if tonsOfObjects[9000] is still alive.
if (tonsOfObjects[9000] != null)
{
  Console.WriteLine("Generation of tonsOfObjects[9000] is: {0}", GC.GetGeneration(
  tonsOfObjects[9000]));
}
else
{
  Console.WriteLine("tonsOfObjects[9000] is no longer alive.");
}

// Print out how many times a generation has been swept.
Console.WriteLine("\nGen 0 has been swept {0} times",
  GC.CollectionCount(0));
Console.WriteLine("Gen 1 has been swept {0} times",
  GC.CollectionCount(1));
Console.WriteLine("Gen 2 has been swept {0} times",
  GC.CollectionCount(2));
Console.ReadLine();
```

Here, I have purposely created a large array of object types (50,000 to be exact) for testing purposes. Here is the output from the program:

```
***** Fun with System.GC *****

Estimated bytes on heap: 75760
This OS has 3 object generations.

Zippy is going 100 MPH
Generation of refToMyCar is: 0
Forcing Garbage Collection
```

```
Generation of refToMyCar is: 1
Generation of tonsOfObjects[9000] is: 1

Gen 0 has been swept 1 times
Gen 1 has been swept 0 times
Gen 2 has been swept 0 times
```

At this point, I hope you feel more comfortable regarding the details of object lifetime. In the next section, you'll examine the garbage collection process a bit further by addressing how you can build *finalizable objects*, as well as *disposable objects*. Be aware that the following techniques are typically necessary only if you are building C# classes that maintain internal unmanaged resources.

Building Finalizable Objects

In Chapter 6, you learned that the supreme base class of .NET Core, `System.Object`, defines a virtual method named `Finalize()`. The default implementation of this method does nothing whatsoever.

```
// System.Object
public class Object
{
  ...
  protected virtual void Finalize() {}
}
```

When you override `Finalize()` for your custom classes, you establish a specific location to perform any necessary cleanup logic for your type. Given that this member is defined as protected, it is not possible to directly call an object's `Finalize()` method from a class instance via the dot operator. Rather, the *garbage collector* will call an object's `Finalize()` method (if supported) before removing the object from memory.

■ **Note** It is illegal to override `Finalize()` on structure types. This makes perfect sense given that structures are value types, which are never allocated on the heap to begin with and, therefore, are not garbage collected! However, if you create a structure that contains unmanaged resources that need to be cleaned up, you can implement the `IDisposable` interface (described shortly). Remember from Chapter 4 that `ref` structs and read-only `ref` structs can't implement an interface but can implement a `Dispose()` method.

Of course, a call to `Finalize()` will (eventually) occur during a "natural" garbage collection or possibly when you programmatically force a collection via `GC.Collect()`. In prior versions of .NET (not .NET Core), each object's finalizer is called on application shutdown. In .NET Core, there isn't any way to force the finalizer to be executed, even when the app is shut down.

Now, despite what your developer instincts may tell you, the vast majority of your C# classes will not require any explicit cleanup logic or a custom finalizer. The reason is simple: if your classes are just making use of other managed objects, everything will eventually be garbage collected. The only time you would need to design a class that can clean up after itself is when you are using *unmanaged* resources (such as raw OS file handles, raw unmanaged database connections, chunks of unmanaged memory, or other unmanaged resources). Under the .NET Core platform, unmanaged resources are obtained by directly calling into the API of the operating system using Platform Invocation Services (PInvoke) or as a result of some elaborate COM interoperability scenarios. Given this, consider the next rule of garbage collection.

■ **Rule** The only compelling reason to override `Finalize()` is if your C# class is using unmanaged resources via PInvoke or complex COM interoperability tasks (typically via various members defined by the `System.Runtime.InteropServices.Marshal` type). The reason is that under these scenarios you are manipulating memory that the runtime cannot manage.

Overriding System.Object.Finalize()

In the rare case that you do build a C# class that uses unmanaged resources, you will obviously want to ensure that the underlying memory is released in a predictable manner. Suppose you have created a new C# Console Application project named SimpleFinalize and inserted a class named `MyResourceWrapper` that uses an unmanaged resource (whatever that might be) and you want to override `Finalize()`. The odd thing about doing so in C# is that you can't do it using the expected `override` keyword.

```
namespace SimpleFinalize;
class MyResourceWrapper
{
  // Compile-time error!
  protected override void Finalize(){ }
}
```

Rather, when you want to configure your custom C# class types to override the `Finalize()` method, you make use of (C++-like) destructor syntax to achieve the same effect. The reason for this alternative form of overriding a virtual method is that when the C# compiler processes the finalizer syntax, it automatically adds a good deal of required infrastructure within the implicitly overridden `Finalize()` method (shown in just a moment).

C# finalizers look similar to constructors, in that they are named identically to the class they are defined within. In addition, finalizers are prefixed with a tilde symbol (~). Unlike a constructor, however, a finalizer never takes an access modifier (they are implicitly protected), never takes parameters, and can't be overloaded (only one finalizer per class).

The following is a custom finalizer for `MyResourceWrapper` that will issue a system beep when invoked. Obviously, this example is only for instructional purposes. A real-world finalizer would do nothing more than free any unmanaged resources and would *not* interact with other managed objects, even those referenced by the current object, as you can't assume they are still alive at the point the garbage collector invokes your `Finalize()` method.

```
// Override System.Object.Finalize() via finalizer syntax.
class MyResourceWrapper
{
    // Clean up unmanaged resources here.
    // Beep when destroyed (testing purposes only!)
  ~MyResourceWrapper() => Console.Beep();
}
```

If you were to examine this C# destructor using `ildasm.exe`, you would see that the compiler inserts some necessary error-checking code. First, the code statements within the scope of your `Finalize()` method are placed within a `try` block (see Chapter 7). The related `finally` block ensures that your base classes' `Finalize()` method will always execute, regardless of any exceptions encountered within the `try` scope.

```
.method family hidebysig virtual instance void
Finalize() cil managed
{
  .override [System.Runtime]System.Object::Finalize
  // Code size       17 (0x11)
  .maxstack  1
  .try
  {
    IL_0000:  call  void [System.Console]System.Console::Beep()
    IL_0005: nop
    IL_0006: leave.s    IL_0010
  }  // end .try
  finally
  {
    IL_0008:  ldarg.0
    IL_0009:  call instance void [System.Runtime]System.Object::Finalize()
    IL_000e:  nop
    IL_000f:  endfinally
  }  // end handler
  IL_0010:  ret
} // end of method MyResourceWrapper::Finalize
```

If you then tested the MyResourceWrapper type, you would find that a system beep occurs when the finalizer executes.

```
using SimpleFinalize;

Console.WriteLine("***** Fun with Finalizers *****\n");
Console.WriteLine("Hit return to create the objects ");
Console.WriteLine("then force the GC to invoke Finalize()");
//Depending on the power of your system,
//you might need to increase these values
CreateObjects(1_000_000);
//Artificially inflate the memory pressure
GC.AddMemoryPressure(2147483647);
GC.Collect(0, GCCollectionMode.Forced);
GC.WaitForPendingFinalizers();
Console.ReadLine();

static void CreateObjects(int count)
{
  MyResourceWrapper[] tonsOfObjects =
    new MyResourceWrapper[count];
  for (int i = 0; i < count; i++)
  {
    tonsOfObjects[i] = new MyResourceWrapper();
  }
  tonsOfObjects = null;
}
```

■ **Note** The only way to guarantee that this small console app will force a garbage collection in .NET Core is to create a huge amount of the objects in memory and then set them to `null`. If you run this sample app, make sure to hit the Ctrl+C key combination to stop the program execution and all of the beeping!

Detailing the Finalization Process

It's important to always remember that the role of the `Finalize()` method is to ensure that a .NET Core object can clean up unmanaged resources when it is garbage collected. Thus, if you are building a class that does not make use of unmanaged memory (by far the most common case), finalization is of little use. In fact, if at all possible, you should design your types to avoid supporting a `Finalize()` method for the simple reason that finalization takes time.

When you allocate an object onto the managed heap, the runtime automatically determines whether your object supports a custom `Finalize()` method. If so, the object is marked as *finalizable*, and a pointer to this object is stored on an internal queue named the *finalization queue*. The finalization queue is a table maintained by the garbage collector that points to every object that must be finalized before it is removed from the heap.

When the garbage collector determines it is time to free an object from memory, it examines each entry on the finalization queue and copies the object off the heap to yet another managed structure termed the *finalization reachable table* (often abbreviated as *freachable* and pronounced "eff-reachable"). At this point, a separate thread is spawned to invoke the `Finalize()` method for each object on the freachable table *at the next garbage collection*. Given this, it will take, at the least, two garbage collections to truly finalize an object.

The bottom line is that while finalization of an object does ensure an object can clean up unmanaged resources, it is still nondeterministic in nature and, because of the extra behind-the-curtains processing, considerably slower.

Building Disposable Objects

As you have seen, finalizers can be used to release unmanaged resources when the garbage collector kicks in. However, given that many unmanaged objects are "precious items" (such as raw database or file handles), it could be valuable to release them as soon as possible instead of relying on a garbage collection to occur. As an alternative to overriding `Finalize()`, your class could implement the `IDisposable` interface, which defines a single method named `Dispose()` as follows:

```
public interface IDisposable
{
  void Dispose();
}
```

When you do implement the `IDisposable` interface, the assumption is that when the *object user* is finished using the object, the object user manually calls `Dispose()` before allowing the object reference to drop out of scope. In this way, an object can perform any necessary cleanup of unmanaged resources without incurring the hit of being placed on the finalization queue and without waiting for the garbage collector to trigger the class's finalization logic.

■ **Note** Non-ref structures and class types both can implement IDisposable (unlike overriding Finalize(), which is reserved for class types), as the object user (not the garbage collector) invokes the Dispose() method. Disposable ref structs were covered in Chapter 4.

To illustrate the use of this interface, create a new C# Console Application project named SimpleDispose. Here is an updated MyResourceWrapper class that now implements IDisposable, rather than overriding System.Object.Finalize():

```
namespace SimpleDispose;
// Implementing IDisposable.
class MyResourceWrapper : IDisposable
{
  // The object user should call this method
  // when they finish with the object.
  public void Dispose()
  {
    // Clean up unmanaged resources...
    // Dispose other contained disposable objects...
    // Just for a test.
    Console.WriteLine("***** In Dispose! *****");
  }
}
```

Notice that a Dispose() method not only is responsible for releasing the type's unmanaged resources but can also call Dispose() on any other contained disposable methods. Unlike with Finalize(), it is perfectly safe to communicate with other managed objects within a Dispose() method. The reason is simple: the garbage collector has no clue about the IDisposable interface and will never call Dispose(). Therefore, when the object user calls this method, the object is still living a productive life on the managed heap and has access to all other heap-allocated objects. The calling logic, shown here, is straightforward:

```
using SimpleDispose;
Console.WriteLine("***** Fun with Dispose *****\n");
// Create a disposable object and call Dispose()
// to free any internal resources.
MyResourceWrapper rw = new MyResourceWrapper();
rw.Dispose();
Console.ReadLine();
```

Of course, before you attempt to call Dispose() on an object, you will want to ensure the type supports the IDisposable interface. While you will typically know which base class library types implement IDisposable by consulting the documentation, a programmatic check can be accomplished using the is or as keyword discussed in Chapter 6.

```
Console.WriteLine("***** Fun with Dispose *****\n");
MyResourceWrapper rw = new MyResourceWrapper();
if (rw is IDisposable)
{
  rw.Dispose();
}
Console.ReadLine();
```

This example exposes yet another rule regarding memory management.

■ **Rule** It is a good idea to call Dispose() on any object you directly create if the object supports IDisposable. The assumption you should make is that if the class designer chose to support the Dispose() method, the type has some cleanup to perform. If you forget, memory will eventually be cleaned up (so don't panic), but it could take longer than necessary.

There is one caveat to the previous rule. A number of types in the base class libraries that do implement the IDisposable interface provide a (somewhat confusing) alias to the Dispose() method, in an attempt to make the disposal-centric method sound more natural for the defining type. By way of an example, while the System.IO.FileStream class implements IDisposable (and therefore supports a Dispose() method), it also defines the following Close() method that is used for the same purpose:

```
static void DisposeFileStream()
{
  FileStream fs = new FileStream("myFile.txt", FileMode.OpenOrCreate);

  // Confusing, to say the least!
  // These method calls do the same thing!
  fs.Close();
  fs.Dispose();
}
```

While it does feel more natural to "close" a file rather than "dispose" of one, this doubling up of cleanup methods can be confusing. For the few types that do provide an alias, just remember that if a type implements IDisposable, calling Dispose() is always a safe course of action.

Reusing the C# using Keyword

When you are handling a managed object that implements IDisposable, it is quite common to make use of structured exception handling to ensure the type's Dispose() method is called in the event of a runtime exception, like so:

```
Console.WriteLine("***** Fun with Dispose *****\n");
MyResourceWrapper rw = new MyResourceWrapper ();
try
{
  // Use the members of rw.
}
finally
{
  // Always call Dispose(), error or not.
  rw.Dispose();
}
```

While this is a fine example of defensive programming, the truth of the matter is that few developers are thrilled by the prospects of wrapping every disposable type within a `try/finally` block just to ensure the `Dispose()` method is called. To achieve the same result in a much less obtrusive manner, C# supports a special bit of syntax that looks like this:

```
Console.WriteLine("***** Fun with Dispose *****\n");
// Dispose() is called automatically when the using scope exits.
using(MyResourceWrapper rw = new MyResourceWrapper())
{
  // Use rw object.
}
```

If you looked at the following CIL code of the top-level statements using `ildasm.exe`, you would find the `using` syntax does indeed expand to `try/finally` logic, with the expected call to `Dispose()`:

```
.method private hidebysig static void
    '<Main>$'(string[] args) cil managed
{
...
  .try
  {
  } // end .try
  finally
  {
      IL_0019:  callvirt   instance void [System.Runtime]System.IDisposable::Dispose()
  } // end handler
} // end of method '<Program>$'::'<Main>$'
```

■ **Note** If you attempt to "use" an object that does not implement `IDisposable`, you will receive a compiler error.

While this syntax does remove the need to manually wrap disposable objects within `try/finally` logic, the C# `using` keyword unfortunately now has a double meaning (importing namespaces and invoking a `Dispose()` method). Nevertheless, when you are working with types that support the `IDisposable` interface, this syntactical construct will ensure that the object "being used" will automatically have its `Dispose()` method called once the `using` block has exited.

Also, be aware that it is possible to declare multiple objects *of the same type* within a `using` scope. As you would expect, the compiler will inject code to call `Dispose()` on each declared object.

```
// Use a comma-delimited list to declare multiple objects to dispose.
using(MyResourceWrapper rw = new MyResourceWrapper(), rw2 = new MyResourceWrapper())
{
  // Use rw and rw2 objects.
}
```

Using Declarations (New 8.0)

New in C# 8.0 is the addition of *using declarations*. A using declaration is a variable declaration preceded by the using keyword. This is functionally the same as the syntax covered in the last question, with the exception of the explicit code block marked by braces ({}).

Add the following method to your class:

```
private static void UsingDeclaration()
{
  //This variable will be in scope until the end of the method
  using var rw = new MyResourceWrapper();
  //Do something here
  Console.WriteLine("About to dispose.");
  //Variable is disposed at this point.
}
```

Next, add the following call to the top-level statements:

```
Console.WriteLine("***** Fun with Dispose *****\n");
...
Console.WriteLine("Demonstrate using declarations");
UsingDeclaration();
Console.ReadLine();
```

If you examine the new method with ILDASM, you will (as you might expect) find the same code as before.

```
.method private hidebysig static
  void  UsingDeclaration() cil managed
{
...
  .try
  {
...
  } // end .try
  finally
  {
    IL_0018: callvirt instance void
      [System.Runtime]System.IDisposable::Dispose()
...
  } // end handler
  IL_001f: ret
} // end of method Program::UsingDeclaration
```

This new feature is essentially compiler magic, saving a few keystrokes. Be careful when using it, as the new syntax is not as explicit as the previous syntax.

Building Finalizable and Disposable Types

At this point, you have seen two different approaches to constructing a class that cleans up internal unmanaged resources. On the one hand, you can use a finalizer. Using this technique, you have the peace of mind that comes with knowing the object cleans itself up when garbage collected (whenever that may be) without the need for user interaction. On the other hand, you can implement `IDisposable` to provide a way for the object user to clean up the object as soon as it is finished. However, if the caller forgets to call `Dispose()`, the unmanaged resources may be held in memory indefinitely.

As you might suspect, it is possible to blend both techniques into a single class definition. By doing so, you gain the best of both models. If the object user does remember to call `Dispose()`, you can inform the garbage collector to bypass the finalization process by calling `GC.SuppressFinalize()`. If the object user forgets to call `Dispose()`, the object will eventually be finalized and have a chance to free up the internal resources. The good news is that the object's internal unmanaged resources will be freed one way or another.

Here is the next iteration of `MyResourceWrapper`, which is now finalizable and disposable, defined in a C# Console Application project named `FinalizableDisposableClass`:

```
namespace FinalizableDisposableClass;
// A sophisticated resource wrapper.
public class MyResourceWrapper : IDisposable
{
  // The garbage collector will call this method if the object user forgets to call
  Dispose().
  ~MyResourceWrapper()
  {
    // Clean up any internal unmanaged resources.
    // Do **not** call Dispose() on any managed objects.
  }
  // The object user will call this method to clean up resources ASAP.
  public void Dispose()
  {
    // Clean up unmanaged resources here.
    // Call Dispose() on other contained disposable objects.
    // No need to finalize if user called Dispose(), so suppress finalization.
    GC.SuppressFinalize(this);
  }
}
```

Notice that this `Dispose()` method has been updated to call `GC.SuppressFinalize()`, which informs the runtime that it is no longer necessary to call the destructor when this object is garbage collected, given that the unmanaged resources have already been freed via the `Dispose()` logic.

A Formalized Disposal Pattern

The current implementation of `MyResourceWrapper` does work fairly well; however, you are left with a few minor drawbacks. First, the `Finalize()` and `Dispose()` methods each have to clean up the same unmanaged resources. This could result in duplicate code, which can easily become a nightmare to maintain. Ideally, you would define a private helper function that is called by either method.

Next, you'd like to make sure that the `Finalize()` method does not attempt to dispose of any managed objects, while the `Dispose()` method should do so. Finally, you'd also like to be certain the object user can safely call `Dispose()` multiple times without error. Currently, the `Dispose()` method has no such safeguards.

To address these design issues, Microsoft defined a formal, prim-and-proper disposal pattern that strikes a balance between robustness, maintainability, and performance. Here is the final (and annotated) version of MyResourceWrapper, which makes use of this official pattern:

```
class MyResourceWrapper : IDisposable
{
  // Used to determine if Dispose() has already been called.
  private bool disposed = false;

  public void Dispose()
  {
    // Call our helper method.
    // Specifying "true" signifies that the object user triggered the cleanup.
    CleanUp(true);

    // Now suppress finalization.
    GC.SuppressFinalize(this);
  }

  private void CleanUp(bool disposing)
  {
    // Be sure we have not already been disposed!
    if (!this.disposed)
    {

      // If disposing equals true, dispose all managed resources.
      if (disposing)
      {
        // Dispose managed resources.
      }
      // Clean up unmanaged resources here.
    }
    disposed = true;
  }
  ~MyResourceWrapper()
  {
    // Call our helper method.
    // Specifying "false" signifies that the GC triggered the cleanup.
    CleanUp(false);
  }
}
```

Notice that MyResourceWrapper now defines a private helper method named CleanUp(). By specifying true as an argument, you indicate that the object user has initiated the cleanup, so you should clean up all managed *and* unmanaged resources. However, when the garbage collector initiates the cleanup, you specify false when calling CleanUp() to ensure that internal disposable objects are *not* disposed (as you can't assume they are still in memory!). Last but not least, the bool member variable (disposed) is set to true before exiting CleanUp() to ensure that Dispose() can be called numerous times without error.

■ **Note** After an object has been "disposed," it's still possible for the client to invoke members on it, as it is still in memory. Therefore, a robust resource wrapper class would also need to update each member of the class with additional coding logic that says, in effect, "If I am disposed, do nothing and return from the member."

To test the final iteration of MyResourceWrapper, update your Program.cs file to the following:

```
using FinalizableDisposableClass;

Console.WriteLine("***** Dispose() / Destructor Combo Platter *****");

// Call Dispose() manually. This will not call the finalizer.
MyResourceWrapper rw = new MyResourceWrapper();
rw.Dispose();

// Don't call Dispose(). This will trigger the finalizer when the object gets GCd.
MyResourceWrapper rw2 = new MyResourceWrapper();
```

Notice that you are explicitly calling Dispose() on the rw object, so the destructor call is suppressed. However, you have "forgotten" to call Dispose() on the rw2 object; no worries—the finalizer will still execute when the object is garbage collected.

That concludes your investigation of how the runtime manages your objects via garbage collection. While there are additional (somewhat esoteric) details regarding the collection process I haven't covered here (such as weak references and object resurrection), you are now in a perfect position for further exploration on your own. To wrap up this chapter, you will examine a programming feature called *lazy instantiation* of objects.

Understanding Lazy Object Instantiation

When you are creating classes, you might occasionally need to account for a particular member variable in code, which might never actually be needed, in that the object user might not call the method (or property) that makes use of it. Fair enough. However, this can be problematic if the member variable in question requires a large amount of memory to be instantiated.

For example, assume you are writing a class that encapsulates the operations of a digital music player. In addition to the expected methods, such as Play(), Pause(), and Stop(), you also want to provide the ability to return a collection of Song objects (via a class named AllTracks), which represents every single digital music file on the device.

If you'd like to follow along, create a new Console Application project named LazyObjectInstantiation, and define the following class types:

```
//Song.cs
namespace LazyObjectInstantiation;
// Represents a single song.
class Song
{
  public string Artist { get; set; }
  public string TrackName { get; set; }
  public double TrackLength { get; set; }
}
```

```
//AllTracks.cs
namespace LazyObjectInstantiation;
// Represents all songs on a player.
class AllTracks
{
  // Our media player can have a maximum
  // of 10,000 songs.
  private Song[] _allSongs = new Song[10000];

  public AllTracks()
  {
    // Assume we fill up the array
    // of Song objects here.
    Console.WriteLine("Filling up the songs!");
  }
}

//MediaPlayer.cs
namespace LazyObjectInstantiation;
// The MediaPlayer has-an AllTracks object.
class MediaPlayer
{
  // Assume these methods do something useful.
  public void Play() { /* Play a song */ }
  public void Pause() { /* Pause the song */ }
  public void Stop() { /* Stop playback */ }
  private AllTracks _allSongs = new AllTracks();

  public AllTracks GetAllTracks()
  {
    // Return all of the songs.
    return _allSongs;
  }
}
```

The current implementation of MediaPlayer assumes that the object user will want to obtain a list of songs via the GetAllTracks() method. Well, what if the object user does *not* need to obtain this list? In the current implementation, the AllTracks member variable will still be allocated, thereby creating 10,000 Song objects in memory, as follows:

```
using LazyObjectInstantiation;

Console.WriteLine("***** Fun with Lazy Instantiation *****\n");

// This caller does not care about getting all songs,
// but indirectly created 10,000 objects!
MediaPlayer myPlayer = new MediaPlayer();
myPlayer.Play();

Console.ReadLine();
```

Clearly, you would rather not create 10,000 objects that nobody will use, as that will add a good deal of stress to the .NET Core garbage collector. While you could manually add some code to ensure the _allSongs object is created only if used (perhaps using the factory method design pattern), there is an easier way.

The base class libraries provide a useful generic class named Lazy<>, defined in the System namespace of mscorlib.dll. This class allows you to define data that will *not* be created unless your code base actually uses it. As this is a generic class, you must specify the type of item to be created on first use, which can be any type with the .NET Core base class libraries or a custom type you have authored yourself. To enable lazy instantiation of the AllTracks member variable, you can simply update the MediaPlayer code to this:

```
// The MediaPlayer has-an Lazy<AllTracks> object.
class MediaPlayer
{
...
  private Lazy<AllTracks> _allSongs = new Lazy<AllTracks>();
  public AllTracks GetAllTracks()
  {
    // Return all of the songs.
    return _allSongs.Value;
  }
}
```

Beyond the fact that you are now representing the AllTracks member variable as a Lazy<> type, notice that the implementation of the previous GetAllTracks() method has also been updated. Specifically, you must use the read-only Value property of the Lazy<> class to obtain the actual stored data (in this case, the AllTracks object that is maintaining the 10,000 Song objects).

With this simple update, notice how the following updated code will indirectly allocate the Song objects only if GetAllTracks() is indeed called:

```
Console.WriteLine("***** Fun with Lazy Instantiation *****\n");

// No allocation of AllTracks object here!
MediaPlayer myPlayer = new MediaPlayer();
myPlayer.Play();

// Allocation of AllTracks happens when you call GetAllTracks().
MediaPlayer yourPlayer = new MediaPlayer();
AllTracks yourMusic = yourPlayer.GetAllTracks();

Console.ReadLine();
```

■ **Note** Lazy object instantiation is useful not only to decrease allocation of unnecessary objects. You can also use this technique if a given member has expensive creation code, such as invoking a remote method, communicating with a relational database, etc.

Customizing the Creation of the Lazy Data

When you declare a Lazy<> variable, the actual internal data type is created using the default constructor, like so:

```
// Default constructor of AllTracks is called when the Lazy<>
// variable is used.
private Lazy<AllTracks> _allSongs = new Lazy<AllTracks>();
```

While this might be fine in some cases, what if the AllTracks class had some additional constructors and you want to ensure the correct one is called? Furthermore, what if you have some extra work to do (beyond simply creating the AllTracks object) when the Lazy<> variable is made? As luck would have it, the Lazy<> class allows you to specify a generic delegate as an optional parameter, which will specify a method to call during the creation of the wrapped type.

The generic delegate in question is of type System.Func<>, which can point to a method that returns the same data type being created by the related Lazy<> variable and can take up to 16 arguments (which are typed using generic type parameters). In most cases, you will not need to specify any parameters to pass to the method pointed to by Func<>. Furthermore, to greatly simplify the use of the required Func<>, I recommend using a lambda expression (see Chapter 12 to learn or review the delegate/lambda relationship).

With this in mind, the following is a final version of MediaPlayer that adds a bit of custom code when the wrapped AllTracks object is created. Remember, this method must return a new instance of the type wrapped by Lazy<> before exiting, and you can use any constructor you choose (here, you are still invoking the default constructor of AllTracks).

```
class MediaPlayer
{
...
  // Use a lambda expression to add additional code
  // when the AllTracks object is made.
  private Lazy<AllTracks> _allSongs =
    new Lazy<AllTracks>( () =>
      {
        Console.WriteLine("Creating AllTracks object!");
        return new AllTracks();
      }
  );

  public AllTracks GetAllTracks()
  {
    // Return all of the songs.
    return _allSongs.Value;
  }
}
```

Sweet! I hope you can see the usefulness of the Lazy<> class. Essentially, this generic class allows you to ensure expensive objects are allocated only when the object user requires them.

Summary

The point of this chapter was to demystify the garbage collection process. As you saw, the garbage collector will run only when it is unable to acquire the necessary memory from the managed heap (or when the developer calls GC.Collect()). When a collection does occur, you can rest assured that Microsoft's collection algorithm has been optimized by the use of object generations, secondary threads for the purpose of object finalization, and a managed heap dedicated to hosting large objects.

This chapter also illustrated how to programmatically interact with the garbage collector using the System.GC class type. As mentioned, the only time you will really need to do so is when you are building finalizable or disposable class types that operate on unmanaged resources.

Recall that finalizable types are classes that have provided a destructor (effectively overriding the Finalize() method) to clean up unmanaged resources at the time of garbage collection. Disposable objects, on the other hand, are classes (or non-ref structures) that implement the IDisposable interface, which should be called by the object user when it is finished using said objects. Finally, you learned about an official "disposal" pattern that blends both approaches.

This chapter wrapped up with a look at a generic class named Lazy<>. As you saw, you can use this class to delay the creation of an expensive (in terms of memory consumption) object until the caller actually requires it. By doing so, you can help reduce the number of objects stored on the managed heap and also ensure expensive objects are created only when actually required by the caller.

PART IV

Advanced C# Programming

CHAPTER 10

Collections and Generics

Any application you create with the .NET Core platform will need to contend with the issue of maintaining and manipulating a set of data points in memory. These data points can come from any variety of locations including a relational database, a local text file, an XML document, a web service call, or perhaps user-provided input.

When the .NET platform was first released, programmers frequently used the classes of the `System.Collections` namespace to store and interact with bits of data used within an application. In .NET 2.0, the C# programming language was enhanced to support a feature termed *generics*; with this change, a new namespace was introduced in the base class libraries: `System.Collections.Generic`.

This chapter will provide you with an overview of the various collection (generic and nongeneric) namespaces and types found within the .NET Core base class libraries. As you will see, generic containers are often favored over their nongeneric counterparts because they typically provide greater type safety and performance benefits. After you have learned how to create and manipulate the generic items found in the framework, the remainder of this chapter will examine how to build your own generic methods and generic types. As you do this, you will learn about the role of *constraints* (and the corresponding C# `where` keyword), which allow you to build extremely type-safe classes.

The Motivation for Collection Classes

The most primitive container you could use to hold application data is undoubtedly the array. As you saw in Chapter 4, C# arrays allow you to define a set of identically typed items (including an array of `System.Objects`, which essentially represents an array of any type of data) of a fixed upper limit. Also recall from Chapter 4 that all C# array variables gather a good deal of functionality from the `System.Array` class. By way of a quick review, consider the following code, which creates an array of textual data and manipulates its contents in various ways:

```
// Make an array of string data.
string[] strArray = {"First", "Second", "Third" };

// Show number of items in array using Length property.
Console.WriteLine("This array has {0} items.", strArray.Length);
Console.WriteLine();

// Display contents using enumerator.
foreach (string s in strArray)
{
  Console.WriteLine("Array Entry: {0}", s);
}
```


A. Troelsen and P. Japikse, *Pro C# 10 with .NET 6*, https://doi.org/10.1007/978-1-4842-7869-7_10

```
Console.WriteLine();

// Reverse the array and print again.
Array.Reverse(strArray);
foreach (string s in strArray)
{
  Console.WriteLine("Array Entry: {0}", s);
}

Console.ReadLine();
```

While basic arrays can be useful to manage small amounts of fixed-size data, there are many other times where you require a more flexible data structure, such as a dynamically growing and shrinking container or a container that can hold objects that meet only a specific criterion (e.g., only objects deriving from a specific base class or only objects implementing a particular interface). When you make use of a simple array, always remember they are created with a "fixed size." If you make an array of three items, you get only three items; therefore, the following code will result in a runtime exception (an `IndexOutOfRangeException`, to be exact):

```
// Make an array of string data.
string[] strArray = { "First", "Second", "Third" };

// Try to add a new item at the end?? Runtime error!
strArray[3] = "new item?";
...
```

■ **Note** It is actually possible to change the size of an array using the generic `Resize()<T>` method. However, this will result in a copy of the data into a new array object and could be inefficient.

To help overcome the limitations of a simple array, the .NET Core base class libraries ship with a number of namespaces containing *collection classes*. Unlike a simple C# array, collection classes are built to dynamically resize themselves on the fly as you insert or remove items. Moreover, many of the collection classes offer increased type safety and are highly optimized to process the contained data in a memory-efficient manner. As you read this chapter, you will quickly notice that a collection class can belong to one of two broad categories.

- Nongeneric collections (primarily found in the `System.Collections` namespace)
- Generic collections (primarily found in the `System.Collections.Generic` namespace)

Nongeneric collections are typically designed to operate on `System.Object` types and are, therefore, loosely typed containers (however, some nongeneric collections do operate on only a specific type of data, such as `string` objects). In contrast, generic collections are much more type-safe, given that you must specify the "type of type" they contain upon creation. As you will see, the telltale sign of any generic item is the "type parameter" marked with angled brackets (e.g., `List<T>`). You will examine the details of generics (including the many benefits they provide) a bit later in this chapter. For now, let's examine some of the key nongeneric collection types in the `System.Collections` and `System.Collections.Specialized` namespaces.

The System.Collections Namespace

When the .NET platform was first released, programmers frequently used the nongeneric collection classes found within the System.Collections namespace, which contains a set of classes used to manage and organize large amounts of in-memory data. Table 10-1 documents some of the more commonly used collection classes of this namespace and the core interfaces they implement.

Table 10-1. *Useful Types of System.Collections*

System.Collections Class	Meaning in Life	Key Implemented Interfaces
ArrayList	Represents a dynamically sized collection of objects listed in sequential order	IList, ICollection, IEnumerable, and ICloneable
BitArray	Manages a compact array of bit values, which are represented as Booleans, where true indicates that the bit is on (1) and false indicates the bit is off (0)	ICollection, IEnumerable, and ICloneable
Hashtable	Represents a collection of key-value pairs that are organized based on the hash code of the key	IDictionary, ICollection, IEnumerable, and ICloneable
Queue	Represents a standard first-in, first-out (FIFO) collection of objects	ICollection, IEnumerable, and ICloneable
SortedList	Represents a collection of key-value pairs that are sorted by the keys and are accessible by key and by index	IDictionary, ICollection, IEnumerable, and ICloneable
Stack	A last-in, first-out (LIFO) stack providing push and pop (and peek) functionality	ICollection, IEnumerable, and ICloneable

The interfaces implemented by these collection classes provide huge insights into their overall functionality. Table 10-2 documents the overall nature of these key interfaces, some of which you worked with firsthand in Chapter 8.

Table 10-2. *Key Interfaces Supported by Classes of System.Collections*

System.Collections Interface	Meaning in Life
ICollection	Defines general characteristics (e.g., size, enumeration, and thread safety) for all nongeneric collection types
ICloneable	Allows the implementing object to return a copy of itself to the caller
IDictionary	Allows a nongeneric collection object to represent its contents using key-value pairs
IEnumerable	Returns an object implementing the IEnumerator interface (see next table entry)
IEnumerator	Enables foreach-style iteration of collection items
IList	Provides behavior to add, remove, and index items in a sequential list of objects

An Illustrative Example: Working with the ArrayList

Based on your experience, you might have some firsthand experience using (or implementing) some of these classic data structures such as stacks, queues, and lists. If this is not the case, I will provide some further details on their differences when you examine their generic counterparts a bit later in this chapter. Until then, here is example code using an ArrayList object:

```
// You must import System.Collections to access the ArrayList.
using System.Collections;
ArrayList strArray = new ArrayList();
strArray.AddRange(new string[] { "First", "Second", "Third" });

// Show number of items in ArrayList.
System.Console.WriteLine("This collection has {0} items.", strArray.Count);
System.Console.WriteLine();

// Add a new item and display current count.
strArray.Add("Fourth!");
System.Console.WriteLine("This collection has {0} items.", strArray.Count);

// Display contents.
foreach (string s in strArray)
{
  System.Console.WriteLine("Entry: {0}", s);
}
System.Console.WriteLine();
```

Notice that you can add (or remove) items on the fly and the container automatically resizes itself accordingly.

As you would guess, the ArrayList class has many useful members beyond the Count property and AddRange() and Add() methods, so be sure you consult the .NET Core documentation for full details. On a related note, the other classes of System.Collections (Stack, Queue, etc.) are also fully documented in the .NET Core help system.

However, it is important to point out that a majority of your .NET Core projects will most likely *not* make use of the collection classes in the System.Collections namespace! To be sure, these days it is far more common to make use of the generic counterpart classes found in the System.Collections.Generic namespace. Given this point, I won't comment on (or provide code examples for) the remaining nongeneric classes found in System.Collections.

A Survey of System.Collections.Specialized Namespace

System.Collections is not the only .NET Core namespace that contains nongeneric collection classes. The System.Collections.Specialized namespace defines a number of (pardon the redundancy) specialized collection types. Table 10-3 documents some of the more useful types in this particular collection-centric namespace, all of which are nongeneric.

Table 10-3. *Useful Classes of System.Collections.Specialized*

System.Collections. Specialized Type	Meaning in Life
`HybridDictionary`	This class implements `IDictionary` by using a `ListDictionary` while the collection is small and then switching to a `Hashtable` when the collection gets large.
`ListDictionary`	This class is useful when you need to manage a small number of items (ten or so) that can change over time. This class makes use of a singly linked list to maintain its data.
`StringCollection`	This class provides an optimal way to manage large collections of string data.
`BitVector32`	This class provides a simple structure that stores Boolean values and small integers in 32 bits of memory.

Beyond these concrete class types, this namespace also contains many additional interfaces and abstract base classes that you can use as a starting point for creating custom collection classes. While these "specialized" types might be just what your projects require in some situations, I won't comment on their usage here. Again, in many cases, you will likely find that the `System.Collections.Generic` namespace provides classes with similar functionality and additional benefits.

■ **Note** There are two additional collection-centric namespaces (`System.Collections.ObjectModel` and `System.Collections.Concurrent`) in the .NET Core base class libraries. You will examine the former namespace later in this chapter, after you are comfortable with the topic of generics. `System.Collections.Concurrent` provides collection classes well suited to a multithreaded environment (see Chapter 15 for information on multithreading).

The Problems of Nongeneric Collections

While it is true that many successful .NET and .NET Core applications have been built over the years using these nongeneric collection classes (and interfaces), history has shown that using these types can result in a number of issues.

The first issue is that using the `System.Collections` and `System.Collections.Specialized` classes can result in some poorly performing code, especially when you are manipulating numerical data (e.g., value types). As you'll see momentarily, the CoreCLR must perform a number of memory transfer operations when you store structures in any nongeneric collection class prototyped to operate on `System.Objects`, which can hurt runtime execution speed.

The second issue is that most of the nongeneric collection classes are not type-safe because (again) they were developed to operate on `System.Objects`, and they could therefore contain anything at all. If a developer needed to create a highly type-safe collection (e.g., a container that can hold objects implementing only a certain interface), the only real choice was to create a new collection class by hand. Doing so was not too labor intensive, but it was a tad on the tedious side.

Before you look at how to use generics in your programs, you'll find it helpful to examine the issues of nongeneric collection classes a bit closer; this will help you better understand the problems generics intended to solve in the first place. If you want to follow along, create a new Console Application project named IssuesWithNonGenericCollections. Next, make sure you import the `System.Collections` namespace to the top of the `Program.cs` file and clear out the rest of the code.

```
using System.Collections;
```

The Issue of Performance

As you might recall from Chapter 4, the .NET Core platform supports two broad categories of data: value types and reference types. Given that .NET Core defines two major categories of types, you might occasionally need to represent a variable of one category as a variable of the other category. To do so, C# provides a simple mechanism, termed *boxing*, to store the data in a value type within a reference variable. Assume that you have created a local variable of type `int` in a method called `SimpleBoxUnboxOperation`. If, during the course of your application, you were to represent this value type as a reference type, you would *box* the value, as follows:

```
static void SimpleBoxUnboxOperation()
{
  // Make a ValueType (int) variable.
  int myInt = 25;

  // Box the int into an object reference.
  object boxedInt = myInt;
}
```

Boxing can be formally defined as the process of explicitly assigning a value type to a `System.Object` variable. When you box a value, the CoreCLR allocates a new object on the heap and copies the value type's value (25, in this case) into that instance. What is returned to you is a reference to the newly allocated heap-based object.

The opposite operation is also permitted through *unboxing*. Unboxing is the process of converting the value held in the object reference back into a corresponding value type on the stack. Syntactically speaking, an unboxing operation looks like a normal casting operation. However, the semantics are quite different. The CoreCLR begins by verifying that the receiving data type is equivalent to the boxed type, and if so, it copies the value back into a local stack-based variable. For example, the following unboxing operations work successfully, given that the underlying type of the `boxedInt` is indeed an `int`:

```
static void SimpleBoxUnboxOperation()
{
  // Make a ValueType (int) variable.
  int myInt = 25;

  // Box the int into an object reference.
  object boxedInt = myInt;

  // Unbox the reference back into a corresponding int.
  int unboxedInt = (int)boxedInt;
}
```

When the C# compiler encounters boxing/unboxing syntax, it emits CIL code that contains the box/unbox op codes. If you were to examine your compiled assembly using `ildasm.exe`, you would find the following:

```
.method assembly hidebysig static
    void  '<<Main>$>g__SimpleBoxUnboxOperation|0_0'() cil managed
{
  .maxstack  1
  .locals init (int32 V_0, object V_1, int32 V_2)
    IL_0000:  nop
    IL_0001:  ldc.i4.s   25
    IL_0003:  stloc.0
    IL_0004:  ldloc.0
    IL_0005:  box        [System.Runtime]System.Int32
    IL_000a:  stloc.1
    IL_000b:  ldloc.1
    IL_000c:  unbox.any  [System.Runtime]System.Int32
    IL_0011:  stloc.2
    IL_0012:  ret
  } // end of method '<Program>$'::'<<Main>$>g__SimpleBoxUnboxOperation|0_0'
```

Remember that unlike when performing a typical cast, you *must* unbox into an appropriate data type. If you attempt to unbox a piece of data into the incorrect data type, an `InvalidCastException` exception will be thrown. To be perfectly safe, you should wrap each unboxing operation in `try`/`catch` logic; however, this would be quite labor intensive to do for every unboxing operation. Consider the following code update, which will throw an error because you're attempting to unbox the boxed `int` into a `long`:

```
static void SimpleBoxUnboxOperation()
{
  // Make a ValueType (int) variable.
  int myInt = 25;

  // Box the int into an object reference.
  object boxedInt = myInt;

  // Unbox in the wrong data type to trigger
  // runtime exception.
  try
  {
    long unboxedLong = (long)boxedInt;
  }
  catch (InvalidCastException ex)
  {
    Console.WriteLine(ex.Message);
  }
}
```

At first glance, boxing/unboxing might seem like a rather uneventful language feature that is more academic than practical. After all, you will seldom need to store a local value type in a local `object` variable, as shown here. However, it turns out that the boxing/unboxing process is quite helpful because it allows you to assume everything can be treated as a `System.Object`, while the CoreCLR takes care of the memory-related details on your behalf.

Let's look at a practical use of these techniques. We will examine the System.Collections.ArrayList class and use it to hold onto a batch of numeric (stack-allocated) data. The relevant members of the ArrayList class are listed as follows. Notice that they are prototyped to operate on System.Object data. Now consider the Add(), Insert(), and Remove() methods, as well as the class indexer.

```
public class ArrayList : IList, ICloneable
{
...
  public virtual int Add(object? value);
  public virtual void Insert(int index, object? value);
  public virtual void Remove(object? obj);
  public virtual object? this[int index] {get; set; }
}
```

ArrayList has been built to operate on objects, which represent data allocated on the heap, so it might seem strange that the following code compiles and executes without throwing an error:

```
static void WorkWithArrayList()
{
  // Value types are automatically boxed when
  // passed to a method requesting an object.
  ArrayList myInts = new ArrayList();
  myInts.Add(10);
  myInts.Add(20);
  myInts.Add(35);
}
```

Although you pass in numerical data directly into methods requiring an object, the runtime automatically boxes the stack-based data on your behalf. Later, if you want to retrieve an item from the ArrayList using the type indexer, you must unbox the heap-allocated object into a stack-allocated integer using a casting operation. Remember that the indexer of the ArrayList is returning System.Objects, not System.Int32s.

```
static void WorkWithArrayList()
{
  // Value types are automatically boxed when
  // passed to a member requesting an object.
  ArrayList myInts = new ArrayList();
  myInts.Add(10);
  myInts.Add(20);
  myInts.Add(35);

  // Unboxing occurs when an object is converted back to
  // stack-based data.
  int i = (int)myInts[0];

  // Now it is reboxed, as WriteLine() requires object types!
  Console.WriteLine("Value of your int: {0}", i);
}
```

Again, note that the stack-allocated `System.Int32` is boxed prior to the call to `ArrayList.Add()`, so it can be passed in the required `System.Object`. Also note that the `System.Object` is unboxed back into a `System.Int32` once it is retrieved from the `ArrayList` via the casting operation, only to be boxed *again* when it is passed to the `Console.WriteLine()` method, as this method is operating on `System.Object` variables.

Boxing and unboxing are convenient from a programmer's viewpoint, but this simplified approach to stack/heap memory transfer comes with the baggage of performance issues (in both speed of execution and code size) and a lack of type safety. To understand the performance issues, ponder these steps that must occur to box and unbox a simple integer:

1. A new object must be allocated on the managed heap.
2. The value of the stack-based data must be transferred into that memory location.
3. When unboxed, the value stored on the heap-based object must be transferred back to the stack.
4. The now unused object on the heap will (eventually) be garbage collected.

Although this particular `WorkWithArrayList()` method won't cause a major bottleneck in terms of performance, you could certainly feel the impact if an `ArrayList` contained thousands of integers that your program manipulates on a somewhat regular basis. In an ideal world, you could manipulate stack-based data in a container without any performance issues. Ideally, it would be nice if you did not have to bother plucking data from this container using `try/catch` scopes (this is exactly what generics let you achieve).

The Issue of Type Safety

I touched on the issue of type safety when covering unboxing operations. Recall that you must unbox your data into the same data type it was declared as before boxing. However, there is another aspect of type safety you must keep in mind in a generic-free world: the fact that a majority of the classes of `System.Collections` can typically hold anything whatsoever because their members are prototyped to operate on `System.Objects`. For example, this method builds an `ArrayList` of random bits of unrelated data:

```
static void ArrayListOfRandomObjects()
{
  // The ArrayList can hold anything at all.
  ArrayList allMyObjects = new ArrayList();
  allMyObjects.Add(true);
  allMyObjects.Add(new OperatingSystem(PlatformID.MacOSX, new Version(10, 0)));
  allMyObjects.Add(66);
  allMyObjects.Add(3.14);
}
```

In some cases, you will require an extremely flexible container that can hold literally anything (as shown here). However, most of the time you desire a *type-safe* container that can operate only on a particular type of data point. For example, you might need a container that can hold only database connections, bitmaps, or `IPointy`-compatible objects.

Prior to generics, the only way you could address this issue of type safety was to create a custom (strongly typed) collection class manually. Assume you want to create a custom collection that can contain only objects of type `Person`.

```
namespace IssuesWithNonGenericCollections;
public class Person
{
  public int Age {get; set;}
  public string FirstName {get; set;}
  public string LastName {get; set;}

  public Person(){}
  public Person(string firstName, string lastName, int age)
  {
    Age = age;
    FirstName = firstName;
    LastName = lastName;
  }

  public override string ToString()
  {
    return $"Name: {FirstName} {LastName}, Age: {Age}";
  }
}
```

To build a collection that can hold only Person objects, you could define a System.Collections.ArrayList member variable within a class named PersonCollection and configure all members to operate on strongly typed Person objects, rather than on System.Object types. Here is a simple example (a production-level custom collection could support many additional members and might extend an abstract base class from the System.Collections or System.Collections.Specialized namespace):

```
using System.Collections;
namespace IssuesWithNonGenericCollections;
public class PersonCollection : IEnumerable
{
  private ArrayList arPeople = new ArrayList();

  // Cast for caller.
  public Person GetPerson(int pos) => (Person)arPeople[pos];

  // Insert only Person objects.
  public void AddPerson(Person p)
  {
    arPeople.Add(p);
  }

  public void ClearPeople()
  {
    arPeople.Clear();
  }

  public int Count => arPeople.Count;

  // Foreach enumeration support.
  IEnumerator IEnumerable.GetEnumerator() => arPeople.GetEnumerator();
}
```

Notice that the PersonCollection class implements the IEnumerable interface, which allows a foreach-like iteration over each contained item. Also notice that your GetPerson() and AddPerson() methods have been prototyped to operate only on Person objects, not bitmaps, strings, database connections, nor other items. With these types defined, you are now assured of type safety, given that the C# compiler will be able to determine any attempt to insert an incompatible data type. Update the using statements in Program.cs to the following and add the UserPersonCollection() method to the end of your current code:

```
using System.Collections;
using IssuesWithNonGenericCollections;
//Top level statements in Program.cs
static void UsePersonCollection()
{
  Console.WriteLine("***** Custom Person Collection *****\n");
  PersonCollection myPeople = new PersonCollection();
  myPeople.AddPerson(new Person("Homer", "Simpson", 40));
  myPeople.AddPerson(new Person("Marge", "Simpson", 38));
  myPeople.AddPerson(new Person("Lisa", "Simpson", 9));
  myPeople.AddPerson(new Person("Bart", "Simpson", 7));
  myPeople.AddPerson(new Person("Maggie", "Simpson", 2));

  // This would be a compile-time error!
  // myPeople.AddPerson(new Car());

  foreach (Person p in myPeople)
  {
    Console.WriteLine(p);
  }
}
```

While custom collections do ensure type safety, this approach leaves you in a position where you must create an (almost identical) custom collection for each unique data type you want to contain. Thus, if you need a custom collection that can operate only on classes deriving from the Car base class, you need to build a highly similar collection class.

```
using System.Collections;
public class CarCollection : IEnumerable
{
  private ArrayList arCars = new ArrayList();

  // Cast for caller.
  public Car GetCar(int pos) => (Car) arCars[pos];

  // Insert only Car objects.
  public void AddCar(Car c)
  {
    arCars.Add(c);
  }

  public void ClearCars()
  {
    arCars.Clear();
  }
```

```
  public int Count => arCars.Count;

  // Foreach enumeration support.
  IEnumerator IEnumerable.GetEnumerator() => arCars.GetEnumerator();
}
```

However, a custom collection class does nothing to solve the issue of boxing/unboxing penalties. Even if you were to create a custom collection named IntCollection that you designed to operate only on System.Int32 items, you would have to allocate some type of object to hold the data (e.g., System.Array and ArrayList).

```
using System.Collections;
public class IntCollection : IEnumerable
{
  private ArrayList arInts = new ArrayList();

  // Get an int (performs unboxing!).
  public int GetInt(int pos) => (int)arInts[pos];

  // Insert an int (performs boxing)!
  public void AddInt(int i)
  {
    arInts.Add(i);
  }

  public void ClearInts()
  {
    arInts.Clear();
  }

  public int Count => arInts.Count;

  IEnumerator IEnumerable.GetEnumerator() => arInts.GetEnumerator();
}
```

Regardless of which type you might choose to hold the integers, you cannot escape the boxing dilemma using nongeneric containers.

A First Look at Generic CollectionsT

When you use generic collection classes, you rectify all the previous issues, including boxing/unboxing penalties and a lack of type safety. Also, the need to build a custom (generic) collection class becomes quite rare. Rather than having to build unique classes that can contain people, cars, and integers, you can use a generic collection class and specify the type of type.

Consider the following method (added to the bottom of Program.cs), which uses the generic List<T> class (in the System.Collections.Generic namespace) to contain various types of data in a strongly typed manner (don't fret the details of generic syntax at this time):

```
static void UseGenericList()
{
  Console.WriteLine("***** Fun with Generics *****\n");

  // This List<> can hold only Person objects.
  List<Person> morePeople = new List<Person>();
  morePeople.Add(new Person ("Frank", "Black", 50));
  Console.WriteLine(morePeople[0]);

  // This List<> can hold only integers.
  List<int> moreInts = new List<int>();
  moreInts.Add(10);
  moreInts.Add(2);
  int sum = moreInts[0] + moreInts[1];

  // Compile-time error! Can't add Person object
  // to a list of ints!
  // moreInts.Add(new Person());
}
```

The first `List<T>` object can contain only `Person` objects. Therefore, you do not need to perform a cast when plucking the items from the container, which makes this approach more type-safe. The second `List<T>` can contain only integers, all of which are allocated on the stack; in other words, there is no hidden boxing or unboxing as you found with the nongeneric `ArrayList`. Here is a short list of the benefits generic containers provide over their nongeneric counterparts:

- Generics provide better performance because they do not result in boxing or unboxing penalties when storing value types.
- Generics are type-safe because they can contain only the type of type you specify.
- Generics greatly reduce the need to build custom collection types because you specify the "type of type" when creating the generic container.

The Role of Generic Type Parameters

You can find generic classes, interfaces, structures, and delegates throughout the .NET Core base class libraries, and these might be part of any .NET Core namespace. Also be aware that generics have far more uses than simply defining a collection class. To be sure, you will see many different generics used in the remainder of this book for various reasons.

■ **Note** Only classes, structures, interfaces, and delegates can be written generically; enum types cannot.

When you see a generic item listed in the .NET Core documentation or the Visual Studio Object Browser, you will notice a pair of angled brackets with a letter or other token sandwiched within. Figure 10-1 shows the Visual Studio Object Browser displaying a number of generic items located within the `System.Collections.Generic` namespace, including the highlighted `List<T>` class.

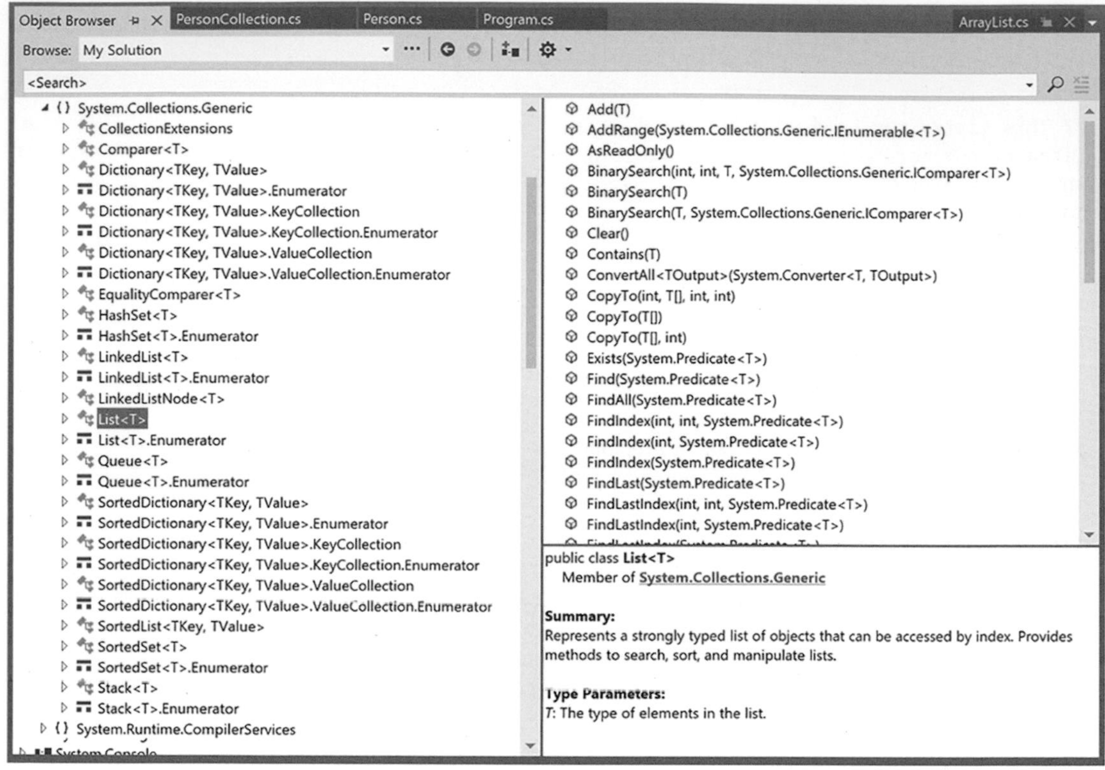

Figure 10-1. *Generic items supporting type parameters*

Formally speaking, you call these tokens *type parameters*; however, in more user-friendly terms, you can simply call them *placeholders*. You can read the symbol `<T>` as "of T." Thus, you can read `IEnumerable<T>` as "`IEnumerable` of T" or, to say it another way, "`IEnumerable` of type T."

■ **Note** The name of a type parameter (placeholder) is irrelevant, and it is up to the developer who created the generic item. However, typically *T* is used to represent types, *TKey* or *K* is used for keys, and *TValue* or *V* is used for values.

When you create a generic object, implement a generic interface, or invoke a generic member, it is up to you to supply a value to the type parameter. You'll see many examples in this chapter and throughout the remainder of the text. However, to set the stage, let's see the basics of interacting with generic types and members.

Specifying Type Parameters for Generic Classes/Structures

When you create an instance of a generic class or structure, you specify the type parameter when you declare the variable and when you invoke the constructor. As you saw in the preceding code example, `UseGenericList()` defined two `List<T>` objects.

```
// This List<> can hold only Person objects.
List<Person> morePeople = new List<Person>();
// This List<> can hold only integers.
List<int> moreInts = new List<int>();
```

You can read the first line in the preceding snippet as "a List<> of T, where T is of type Person." Or, more simply, you can read it as "a list of person objects." After you specify the type parameter of a generic item, it cannot be changed (remember, generics are all about type safety). When you specify a type parameter for a generic class or structure, all occurrences of the placeholder(s) are now replaced with your supplied value.

If you were to view the full declaration of the generic List<T> class using the Visual Studio Object Browser, you would see that the placeholder T is used throughout the definition of the List<T> type. Here is a partial listing:

```
// A partial listing of the List<T> class.
namespace System.Collections.Generic;
  public class List<T> : IList<T>, IList, IReadOnlyList<T>
  {
...
  public void Add(T item);
  public void AddRange(IEnumerable<T> collection);
  public ReadOnlyCollection<T> AsReadOnly();
  public int BinarySearch(T item);
  public bool Contains(T item);
  public void CopyTo(T[] array);
  public int FindIndex(System.Predicate<T> match);
  public T FindLast(System.Predicate<T> match);
  public bool Remove(T item);
  public int RemoveAll(System.Predicate<T> match);
  public T[] ToArray();
  public bool TrueForAll(System.Predicate<T> match);
  public T this[int index] { get; set; }
}
```

When you create a List<T> specifying Person objects, it is as if the List<T> type were defined as follows:

```
namespace System.Collections.Generic;
public class List<Person>
  : IList<Person>, IList, IReadOnlyList<Person>
{
...
  public void Add(Person item);
  public void AddRange(IEnumerable<Person> collection);
  public ReadOnlyCollection<Person> AsReadOnly();
  public int BinarySearch(Person item);
  public bool Contains(Person item);
  public void CopyTo(Person[] array);
  public int FindIndex(System.Predicate<Person> match);
  public Person FindLast(System.Predicate<Person> match);
  public bool Remove(Person item);
  public int RemoveAll(System.Predicate<Person> match);
  public Person[] ToArray();
```

```
  public bool TrueForAll(System.Predicate<Person> match);
  public Person this[int index] { get; set; }
}
```

Of course, when you create a generic List<T> variable, the compiler does not literally create a new implementation of the List<T> class. Rather, it will address only the members of the generic type you actually invoke.

Specifying Type Parameters for Generic Members

It is fine for a nongeneric class or structure to support generic properties. In these cases, you would also need to specify the placeholder value at the time you invoke the method. For example, System.Array supports several generic methods. Specifically, the nongeneric static Sort() method now has a generic counterpart named Sort<T>(). Consider the following code snippet, where T is of type int:

```
int[] myInts = { 10, 4, 2, 33, 93 };

// Specify the placeholder to the generic
// Sort<>() method.
Array.Sort<int>(myInts);

foreach (int i in myInts)
{
  Console.WriteLine(i);
}
```

Specifying Type Parameters for Generic Interfaces

It is common to implement generic interfaces when you build classes or structures that need to support various framework behaviors (e.g., cloning, sorting, and enumeration). In Chapter 8, you learned about a number of nongeneric interfaces, such as IComparable, IEnumerable, IEnumerator, and IComparer. Recall that the nongeneric IComparable interface was defined like this:

```
public interface IComparable
{
  int CompareTo(object obj);
}
```

In Chapter 8, you also implemented this interface on your Car class to enable sorting in a standard array. However, the code required several runtime checks and casting operations because the parameter was a general System.Object.

```
public class Car : IComparable
{
...
  // IComparable implementation.
  int IComparable.CompareTo(object obj)
  {
    if (obj is Car temp)
```

```
    {
      return this.CarID.CompareTo(temp.CarID);
    }
    throw new ArgumentException("Parameter is not a Car!");
  }
}
```

Now assume you use the generic counterpart of this interface.

```
public interface IComparable<T>
{
  int CompareTo(T obj);
}
```

In this case, your implementation code will be cleaned up considerably.

```
public class Car : IComparable<Car>
{
...
  // IComparable<T> implementation.
  int IComparable<Car>.CompareTo(Car obj)
  {
    if (this.CarID > obj.CarID)
    {
      return 1;
    }
    if (this.CarID < obj.CarID)
    {
      return -1;
    }
    return 0;
  }
}
```

Here, you do not need to check whether the incoming parameter is a `Car` because it can *only* be a `Car`! If someone were to pass in an incompatible data type, you would get a compile-time error. Now that you have a better handle on how to interact with generic items, as well as the role of type parameters (aka placeholders), you're ready to examine the classes and interfaces of the `System.Collections.Generic` namespace.

The System.Collections.Generic Namespace

When you are building a .NET Core application and need a way to manage in-memory data, the classes of `System.Collections.Generic` will most likely fit the bill. At the opening of this chapter, I briefly mentioned some of the core nongeneric interfaces implemented by the nongeneric collection classes. Not too surprisingly, the `System.Collections.Generic` namespace defines generic replacements for many of them.

In fact, you can find a number of the generic interfaces that extend their nongeneric counterparts. This might seem odd; however, by doing so, implementing classes will also support the legacy functionally found in their nongeneric siblings. For example, `IEnumerable<T>` extends `IEnumerable`. Table 10-4 documents the core generic interfaces you'll encounter when working with the generic collection classes.

Table 10-4. *Key Interfaces Supported by Classes of System.Collections.Generic*

System.Collections.Generic Interface	Meaning in Life
`ICollection<T>`	Defines general characteristics (e.g., size, enumeration, and thread safety) for all generic collection types.
`IComparer<T>`	Defines a way to compare to objects.
`IDictionary<TKey, TValue>`	Allows a generic collection object to represent its contents using key-value pairs.
`IEnumerable<T>/` `IAsyncEnumerable<T>`	Returns the `IEnumerator<T>` interface for a given object. `IAsyncEnumerable` (new in C# 8.0) is covered in Chapter 15.
`IEnumerator<T>`	Enables `foreach`-style iteration over a generic collection.
`IList<T>`	Provides behavior to add, remove, and index items in a sequential list of objects.
`ISet<T>`	Provides the base interface for the abstraction of sets.

The `System.Collections.Generic` namespace also defines several classes that implement many of these key interfaces. Table 10-5 describes some commonly used classes of this namespace, the interfaces they implement, and their basic functionality.

Table 10-5. *Classes of System.Collections.Generic*

Generic Class	Supported Key Interfaces	Meaning in Life
`Dictionary<TKey, TValue>`	`ICollection<T>`, `IDictionary<TKey, TValue>`, `IEnumerable<T>`	This represents a generic collection of keys and values.
`LinkedList<T>`	`ICollection<T>`, `IEnumerable<T>`	This represents a doubly linked list.
`List<T>`	`ICollection<T>`, `IEnumerable<T>`, `IList<T>`	This is a dynamically resizable sequential list of items.
`Queue<T>`	`ICollection` (not a typo; this is the nongeneric collection interface), `IEnumerable<T>`	This is a generic implementation of a first-in, first-out list.
`SortedDictionary<TKey, TValue>`	`ICollection<T>`, `IDictionary<TKey, TValue>`, `IEnumerable<T>`	This is a generic implementation of a sorted set of key-value pairs.
`SortedSet<T>`	`ICollection<T>`, `IEnumerable<T>`, `ISet<T>`	This represents a collection of objects that is maintained in sorted order with no duplication.
`Stack<T>`	`ICollection` (not a typo; this is the nongeneric collection interface), `IEnumerable<T>`	This is a generic implementation of a last-in, first-out list.

The `System.Collections.Generic` namespace also defines many auxiliary classes and structures that work in conjunction with a specific container. For example, the `LinkedListNode<T>` type represents a node within a generic `LinkedList<T>`, the `KeyNotFoundException` exception is raised when attempting to grab an item from a container using a nonexistent key, and so forth. Be sure to consult the .NET Core documentation for full details of the System.Collections.Generic namespace.

In any case, your next task is to learn how to use some of these generic collection classes. Before you do, however, allow me to illustrate a C# language feature (first introduced in .NET 3.5) that simplifies the way you populate generic (and nongeneric) collection containers with data.

Understanding Collection Initialization Syntax

In Chapter 4, you learned about *object initialization syntax*, which allows you to set properties on a new variable at the time of construction. Closely related to this is *collection initialization syntax*. This C# language feature makes it possible to populate many containers (such as ArrayList or List<T>) with items by using syntax similar to what you use to populate a basic array. Create a new .NET Core Console application named FunWithCollectionInitialization. Clear out the generated code in Program.cs and add the following using statements:

```
using System.Collections;
using System.Drawing;
```

■ **Note** You can apply collection initialization syntax only to classes that support an Add() method, which is formalized by the ICollection<T>/ICollection interfaces.

Consider the following examples:

```
// Init a standard array.
int[] myArrayOfInts = { 0, 1, 2, 3, 4, 5, 6, 7, 8, 9 };

// Init a generic List<> of ints.
List<int> myGenericList = new List<int> { 0, 1, 2, 3, 4, 5, 6, 7, 8, 9 };

// Init an ArrayList with numerical data.
ArrayList myList = new ArrayList { 0, 1, 2, 3, 4, 5, 6, 7, 8, 9 };
```

If your container is managing a collection of classes or a structure, you can blend object initialization syntax with collection initialization syntax to yield some functional code. You might recall the Point class from Chapter 5, which defined two properties named X and Y. If you wanted to build a generic List<T> of Point objects, you could write the following:

```
List<Point> myListOfPoints = new List<Point>
{
  new Point { X = 2, Y = 2 },
  new Point { X = 3, Y = 3 },
  new Point { X = 4, Y = 4 }
};

foreach (var pt in myListOfPoints)
{
  Console.WriteLine(pt);
}
```

Again, the benefit of this syntax is that you save yourself numerous keystrokes. While the nested curly brackets can become difficult to read if you don't mind your formatting, imagine the amount of code that would be required to fill the following List<T> of Rectangles if you did not have collection initialization syntax.

```
List<Rectangle> myListOfRects = new List<Rectangle>
{
  new Rectangle {
    Height = 90, Width = 90,
    Location = new Point { X = 10, Y = 10 }},
  new Rectangle {
    Height = 50,Width = 50,
    Location = new Point { X = 2, Y = 2 }},
};
foreach (var r in myListOfRects)
{
  Console.WriteLine(r);
}
```

Working with the List<T> Class

Create a new Console Application project named FunWithGenericCollections. Add a new file, named Person.cs, and add the following code (which is the same code as the previous Person class):

```
namespace FunWithGenericCollections;
public class Person
{
  public int Age {get; set;}
  public string FirstName {get; set;}
  public string LastName {get; set;}

  public Person(){}
  public Person(string firstName, string lastName, int age)
  {
    Age = age;
    FirstName = firstName;
    LastName = lastName;
  }

  public override string ToString()
  {
    return $"Name: {FirstName} {LastName}, Age: {Age}";
  }
}
```

Clear out the generated code in Program.cs and add the following using statement:

```
using FunWithGenericCollections;
```

The first generic class you will examine is List<T>, which you've already seen once or twice in this chapter. The List<T> class is bound to be your most frequently used type in the System.Collections.Generic namespace because it allows you to resize the contents of the container dynamically. To illustrate the basics of this type, ponder the following method in your Program.cs file, which leverages List<T> to manipulate the set of Person objects shown earlier in this chapter; you might recall that these Person objects defined three properties (Age, FirstName, and LastName) and a custom ToString() implementation:

```
static void UseGenericList()
{
  // Make a List of Person objects, filled with
  // collection/object init syntax.
  List<Person> people = new List<Person>()
  {
    new Person {FirstName= "Homer", LastName="Simpson", Age=47},
    new Person {FirstName= "Marge", LastName="Simpson", Age=45},
    new Person {FirstName= "Lisa", LastName="Simpson", Age=9},
    new Person {FirstName= "Bart", LastName="Simpson", Age=8}
  };

  // Print out # of items in List.
  Console.WriteLine("Items in list: {0}", people.Count);

  // Enumerate over list.
  foreach (Person p in people)
  {
    Console.WriteLine(p);
  }

  // Insert a new person.
  Console.WriteLine("\n->Inserting new person.");
  people.Insert(2, new Person { FirstName = "Maggie", LastName = "Simpson", Age = 2 });
  Console.WriteLine("Items in list: {0}", people.Count);

  // Copy data into a new array.
  Person[] arrayOfPeople = people.ToArray();
  foreach (Person p in arrayOfPeople)
  {
    Console.WriteLine("First Names: {0}", p.FirstName);
  }
}
```

Here, you use collection initialization syntax to populate your List<T> with objects, as a shorthand notation for calling Add() *multiple* times. After you print out the number of items in the collection (as well as enumerate over each item), you invoke Insert(). As you can see, Insert() allows you to plug a new item into the List<T> at a specified index.

Finally, notice the call to the ToArray() method, which returns an array of Person objects based on the contents of the original List<T>. From this array, you loop over the items again using the array's indexer syntax. If you call this method from your top-level statements, you get the following output:

```
***** Fun with Generic Collections *****
Items in list: 4
Name: Homer Simpson, Age: 47
Name: Marge Simpson, Age: 45
Name: Lisa Simpson, Age: 9
Name: Bart Simpson, Age: 8

->Inserting new person.
Items in list: 5
First Names: Homer
First Names: Marge
First Names: Maggie
First Names: Lisa
First Names: Bart
```

The List<T> class defines many additional members of interest, so be sure to consult the documentation for more information. Next, let's look at a few more generic collections, specifically Stack<T>, Queue<T>, and SortedSet<T>. This should get you in a great position to understand your basic choices regarding how to hold your custom application data.

Working with the Stack<T> Class

The Stack<T> class represents a collection that maintains items using a last-in, first-out manner. As you might expect, Stack<T> defines members named Push() and Pop() to place items onto or remove items from the stack. The following method creates a stack of Person objects:

```
static void UseGenericStack()
{
  Stack<Person> stackOfPeople = new();
  stackOfPeople.Push(new Person { FirstName = "Homer", LastName = "Simpson", Age = 47 });
  stackOfPeople.Push(new Person { FirstName = "Marge", LastName = "Simpson", Age = 45 });
  stackOfPeople.Push(new Person { FirstName = "Lisa", LastName = "Simpson", Age = 9 });

  // Now look at the top item, pop it, and look again.
  Console.WriteLine("First person is: {0}", stackOfPeople.Peek());
  Console.WriteLine("Popped off {0}", stackOfPeople.Pop());
  Console.WriteLine("\nFirst person is: {0}", stackOfPeople.Peek());
  Console.WriteLine("Popped off {0}", stackOfPeople.Pop());
  Console.WriteLine("\nFirst person item is: {0}", stackOfPeople.Peek());
  Console.WriteLine("Popped off {0}", stackOfPeople.Pop());

  try
  {
    Console.WriteLine("\nnFirst person is: {0}", stackOfPeople.Peek());
    Console.WriteLine("Popped off {0}", stackOfPeople.Pop());
  }
  catch (InvalidOperationException ex)
```

```
  {
    Console.WriteLine("\nError! {0}", ex.Message);
  }
}
```

Here, you build a stack that contains three people, added in the order of their first names: Homer, Marge, and Lisa. As you peek into the stack, you will always see the object at the top first; therefore, the first call to Peek() reveals the third Person object. After a series of Pop() and Peek() calls, the stack eventually empties, at which time additional Peek() and Pop() calls raise a system exception. You can see the output for this here:

```
***** Fun with Generic Collections *****
First person is: Name: Lisa Simpson, Age: 9
Popped off Name: Lisa Simpson, Age: 9

First person is: Name: Marge Simpson, Age: 45
Popped off Name: Marge Simpson, Age: 45

First person item is: Name: Homer Simpson, Age: 47
Popped off Name: Homer Simpson, Age: 47

Error! Stack empty.
```

Working with the Queue<T> Class

Queues are containers that ensure items are accessed in a first-in, first-out manner. Sadly, we humans are subject to queues all day long: lines at the bank, lines at the movie theater, and lines at the morning coffeehouse. When you need to model a scenario in which items are handled on a first-come, first-served basis, you will find the Queue<T> class fits the bill. In addition to the functionality provided by the supported interfaces, Queue defines the key members shown in Table 10-6.

Table 10-6. *Members of the Queue<T> Type*

Select Member of Queue<T>	Meaning in Life
Dequeue()	Removes and returns the object at the beginning of the Queue<T>
Enqueue()	Adds an object to the end of the Queue<T>
Peek()	Returns the object at the beginning of the Queue<T> without removing it

Now let's put these methods to work. You can begin by leveraging your Person class again and building a Queue<T> object that simulates a line of people waiting to order coffee.

```
static void UseGenericQueue()
{
  // Make a Q with three people.
  Queue<Person> peopleQ = new();
  peopleQ.Enqueue(new Person {FirstName= "Homer", LastName="Simpson", Age=47});
```

```
  peopleQ.Enqueue(new Person {FirstName= "Marge", LastName="Simpson", Age=45});
  peopleQ.Enqueue(new Person {FirstName= "Lisa", LastName="Simpson", Age=9});

  // Peek at first person in Q.
  Console.WriteLine("{0} is first in line!", peopleQ.Peek().FirstName);

  // Remove each person from Q.
  GetCoffee(peopleQ.Dequeue());
  GetCoffee(peopleQ.Dequeue());
  GetCoffee(peopleQ.Dequeue());
  // Try to de-Q again?
  try
  {
    GetCoffee(peopleQ.Dequeue());
  }
  catch(InvalidOperationException e)
  {
    Console.WriteLine("Error! {0}", e.Message);
  }
  //Local helper function
  static void GetCoffee(Person p)
  {
    Console.WriteLine("{0} got coffee!", p.FirstName);
  }
}
```

Here, you insert three items into the `Queue<T>` class using its `Enqueue()` method. The call to `Peek()` allows you to view (but not remove) the first item currently in the `Queue`. Finally, the call to `Dequeue()` removes the item from the line and sends it into the `GetCoffee()` helper function for processing. Note that if you attempt to remove items from an empty queue, a runtime exception is thrown. Here is the output you receive when calling this method:

```
***** Fun with Generic Collections *****
Homer is first in line!
Homer got coffee!
Marge got coffee!
Lisa got coffee!
Error! Queue empty.
```

Working with the PriorityQueue<TElement, TPriority> Class (New 10)

Introduced in .NET 6/C# 10, the `PriorityQueue` works just like the `Queue<T>` except that each queued item is given a priority. When items are dequeued, they are removed from lowest to highest priority. The following updates the previous `Queue` example to use a `PriorityQueue`:

```
static void UsePriorityQueue()
{
    Console.WriteLine("* Fun with Generic Priority Queues *\n");

    PriorityQueue<Person, int> peopleQ = new();
    peopleQ.Enqueue(new Person { FirstName = "Lisa", LastName = "Simpson", Age = 9 }, 1);
    peopleQ.Enqueue(new Person { FirstName = "Homer", LastName = "Simpson", Age = 47 }, 3);
    peopleQ.Enqueue(new Person { FirstName = "Marge", LastName = "Simpson", Age = 45 }, 3);
    peopleQ.Enqueue(new Person { FirstName = "Bart", LastName = "Simpson", Age = 12 }, 2);

    while (peopleQ.Count > 0)
    {
        Console.WriteLine(peopleQ.Dequeue().FirstName); //Displays Lisa
        Console.WriteLine(peopleQ.Dequeue().FirstName); //Displays Bart
        Console.WriteLine(peopleQ.Dequeue().FirstName); //Displays either Marge or Homer
        Console.WriteLine(peopleQ.Dequeue().FirstName); //Displays the other priority 3 item
    }
}
```

If more than one item is set to the current lowest priority, the order of dequeuing is not guaranteed. As shown in code sample, the third call to Dequeue() will return either Homer or Marge, as they are both set to a priority of three. The fourth call will then return the other person. If exact order matters, you must ensure values for each priority are unique.

Working with the SortedSet<T> Class

The SortedSet<T> class is useful because it automatically ensures that the items in the set are sorted when you insert or remove items. However, you do need to inform the SortedSet<T> class exactly *how* you want it to sort the objects, by passing in as a constructor argument an object that implements the generic IComparer<T> interface.

Begin by creating a new class named SortPeopleByAge, which implements IComparer<T>, where T is of type Person. Recall that this interface defines a single method named Compare(), where you can author whatever logic you require for the comparison. Here is a simple implementation of this class:

```
namespace FunWithGenericCollections;
class SortPeopleByAge : IComparer<Person>
{
  public int Compare(Person firstPerson, Person secondPerson)
  {
    if (firstPerson?.Age > secondPerson?.Age)
    {
        return 1;
    }
    if (firstPerson?.Age < secondPerson?.Age)
    {
      return -1;
    }
    return 0;
  }
}
```

Now add the following new method that demonstrates using SortedSet<Person>:

```
static void UseSortedSet()
{
  // Make some people with different ages.
  SortedSet<Person> setOfPeople = new SortedSet<Person>(new SortPeopleByAge())
  {
    new Person {FirstName= "Homer", LastName="Simpson", Age=47},
    new Person {FirstName= "Marge", LastName="Simpson", Age=45},
    new Person {FirstName= "Lisa", LastName="Simpson", Age=9},
    new Person {FirstName= "Bart", LastName="Simpson", Age=8}
  };

  // Note the items are sorted by age!
  foreach (Person p in setOfPeople)
  {
    Console.WriteLine(p);
  }
    Console.WriteLine();

  // Add a few new people, with various ages.
  setOfPeople.Add(new Person { FirstName = "Saku", LastName = "Jones", Age = 1 });
  setOfPeople.Add(new Person { FirstName = "Mikko", LastName = "Jones", Age = 32 });

  // Still sorted by age!
  foreach (Person p in setOfPeople)
  {
    Console.WriteLine(p);
  }
}
```

When you run your application, the listing of objects is now always ordered based on the value of the Age property, regardless of the order you inserted or removed objects.

```
***** Fun with Generic Collections *****
Name: Bart Simpson, Age: 8
Name: Lisa Simpson, Age: 9
Name: Marge Simpson, Age: 45
Name: Homer Simpson, Age: 47

Name: Saku Jones, Age: 1
Name: Bart Simpson, Age: 8
Name: Lisa Simpson, Age: 9
Name: Mikko Jones, Age: 32
Name: Marge Simpson, Age: 45
Name: Homer Simpson, Age: 47
```

Working with the Dictionary<TKey, TValue> Class

Another handy generic collection is the Dictionary<TKey,TValue> type, which allows you to hold any number of objects that may be referred to via a unique key. Thus, rather than obtaining an item from a List<T> using a numerical identifier (e.g., "Give me the second object"), you could use the unique text key (e.g., "Give me the object I keyed as Homer").

Like other collection objects, you can populate a Dictionary<TKey,TValue> by calling the generic Add() method manually. However, you can also fill a Dictionary<TKey,TValue> using collection initialization syntax. Do be aware that when you are populating this collection object, key names must be unique. If you mistakenly specify the same key multiple times, you will receive a runtime exception.

Consider the following method that fills a Dictionary<K,V> with various objects. Notice when you create the Dictionary<TKey,TValue> object, you specify the key type (TKey) and underlying object type (TValue) as constructor arguments. In this example, you are using a string data type as the key and a Person type as the value. Also note that you can combine object initialization syntax with collection initialization syntax.

```
private static void UseDictionary()
{
    // Populate using Add() method
    Dictionary<string, Person> peopleA = new Dictionary<string, Person>();
    peopleA.Add("Homer", new Person { FirstName = "Homer", LastName = "Simpson", Age
    = 47 });
    peopleA.Add("Marge", new Person { FirstName = "Marge", LastName = "Simpson", Age
    = 45 });
    peopleA.Add("Lisa", new Person { FirstName = "Lisa", LastName = "Simpson", Age = 9 });

    // Get Homer.
    Person homer = peopleA["Homer"];
    Console.WriteLine(homer);

    // Populate with initialization syntax.
    Dictionary<string, Person> peopleB = new Dictionary<string, Person>()
    {
        { "Homer", new Person { FirstName = "Homer", LastName = "Simpson", Age = 47 } },
        { "Marge", new Person { FirstName = "Marge", LastName = "Simpson", Age = 45 } },
        { "Lisa", new Person { FirstName = "Lisa", LastName = "Simpson", Age = 9 } }
    };

    // Get Lisa.
    Person lisa = peopleB["Lisa"];
    Console.WriteLine(lisa);
}
```

It is also possible to populate a Dictionary<TKey,TValue> using a related initialization syntax that is specific to this type of container (not surprisingly termed *dictionary initialization*). Similar to the syntax used to populate the personB object in the previous code example, you still define an initialization scope for the collection object; however, you can use the indexer to specify the key and assign this to a new object as so:

```
// Populate with dictionary initialization syntax.
Dictionary<string, Person> peopleC = new Dictionary<string, Person>()
{
    ["Homer"] = new Person { FirstName = "Homer", LastName = "Simpson", Age = 47 },
    ["Marge"] = new Person { FirstName = "Marge", LastName = "Simpson", Age = 45 },
    ["Lisa"] = new Person { FirstName = "Lisa", LastName = "Simpson", Age = 9 }
};
```

The System.Collections.ObjectModel Namespace

Now that you understand how to work with the major generic classes, we will briefly examine an additional collection-centric namespace, System.Collections.ObjectModel. This is a relatively small namespace, which contains a handful of classes. Table 10-7 documents the two classes that you should most certainly be aware of.

***Table 10-7.** Useful Members of System.Collections.ObjectModel*

System.Collections. ObjectModel Type	Meaning in Life
ObservableCollection<T>	Represents a dynamic data collection that provides notifications when items get added, when items get removed, or when the whole list is refreshed
ReadOnlyObservable Collection<T>	Represents a read-only version of ObservableCollection<T>

The ObservableCollection<T> class is useful, in that it has the ability to inform external objects when its contents have changed in some way (as you might guess, working with ReadOnlyObservableCollection <T> is similar but read-only in nature).

Working with ObservableCollection<T>

Create a new Console Application project named FunWithObservableCollections and import the System.Collections.ObjectModel namespace into your initial C# code file. In many ways, working with ObservableCollection<T> is identical to working with List<T>, given that both of these classes implement the same core interfaces. What makes the ObservableCollection<T> class unique is that this class supports an event named CollectionChanged. This event will fire whenever a new item is inserted, a current item is removed (or relocated), or the entire collection is modified.

Like any event, CollectionChanged is defined in terms of a delegate, which in this case is NotifyCollectionChangedEventHandler. This delegate can call any method that takes an object as the first parameter and takes a NotifyCollectionChangedEventArgs as the second. Consider the following code, which populates an observable collection containing Person objects and wires up the CollectionChanged event:

```
using System.Collections.ObjectModel;
using System.Collections.Specialized;
using FunWithObservableCollections;
```

```
// Make a collection to observe
//and add a few Person objects.
ObservableCollection<Person> people = new ObservableCollection<Person>()
{
  new Person{ FirstName = "Peter", LastName = "Murphy", Age = 52 },
  new Person{ FirstName = "Kevin", LastName = "Key", Age = 48 },
};

// Wire up the CollectionChanged event.
people.CollectionChanged += people_CollectionChanged;

static void people_CollectionChanged(object sender,
    System.Collections.Specialized.NotifyCollectionChangedEventArgs e)
{
  throw new NotImplementedException();
}
```

The incoming `NotifyCollectionChangedEventArgs` parameter defines two important properties, `OldItems` and `NewItems`, which will give you a list of items that were currently in the collection before the event fired and the new items that were involved in the change. However, you will want to examine these lists only under the correct circumstances. Recall that the `CollectionChanged` event can fire when items are added, removed, relocated, or reset. To discover which of these actions triggered the event, you can use the `Action` property of `NotifyCollectionChangedEventArgs`. The `Action` property can be tested against any of the following members of the `NotifyCollectionChangedAction` enumeration:

```
public enum NotifyCollectionChangedAction
{
  Add = 0,
  Remove = 1,
  Replace = 2,
  Move = 3,
  Reset = 4,
}
```

Here is an implementation of the `CollectionChanged` event handler that will traverse the old and new sets when an item has been inserted into or removed from the collection at hand (notice the `using` for `System.Collections.Specialized`):

```
using System.Collections.Specialized;
...
static void people_CollectionChanged(object sender,
  NotifyCollectionChangedEventArgs e)
{
  // What was the action that caused the event?
  Console.WriteLine("Action for this event: {0}", e.Action);

  // They removed something.
  if (e.Action == NotifyCollectionChangedAction.Remove)
  {
    Console.WriteLine("Here are the OLD items:");
    foreach (Person p in e.OldItems)
```

```
      {
        Console.WriteLine(p.ToString());
      }
      Console.WriteLine();
    }

    // They added something.
    if (e.Action == NotifyCollectionChangedAction.Add)
    {
      // Now show the NEW items that were inserted.
      Console.WriteLine("Here are the NEW items:");
      foreach (Person p in e.NewItems)
      {
        Console.WriteLine(p.ToString());
      }
    }
  }
```

Now, update your calling code to add and remove an item.

```
// Now add a new item.
people.Add(new Person("Fred", "Smith", 32));
// Remove an item.
people.RemoveAt(0);
```

When you run the program, you will see output similar to the following:

```
Action for this event: Add
Here are the NEW items:
Name: Fred Smith, Age: 32

Action for this event: Remove
Here are the OLD items:
Name: Peter Murphy, Age: 52
```

That wraps up the examination of the various collection-centric namespaces. To conclude the chapter, you will now examine how you can build your own custom generic methods and custom generic types.

Creating Custom Generic Methods

While most developers typically use the existing generic types within the base class libraries, it is also possible to build your own generic members and custom generic types. Let's look at how to incorporate custom generics into your own projects. The first step is to build a generic swap method. Begin by creating a new console application named CustomGenericMethods.

When you build custom generic methods, you achieve a supercharged version of traditional method overloading. In Chapter 2, you learned that overloading is the act of defining multiple versions of a single method, which differ by the number of, or type of, parameters.

While overloading is a useful feature in an object-oriented language, one problem is that you can easily end up with a ton of methods that essentially do the same thing. For example, assume you need to build some methods that can switch two pieces of data using a simple swap routine. You might begin by authoring a new static class with a method that can operate on integers, like this:

```
namespace CustomGenericMethods;
static class SwapFunctions
{
  // Swap two integers.
  static void Swap(ref int a, ref int b)
  {
    int temp = a;
    a = b;
    b = temp;
  }
}
```

So far, so good. But now assume you also need to swap two Person objects; this would require authoring a new version of Swap().

```
// Swap two Person objects.
static void Swap(ref Person a, ref Person b)
{
  Person temp = a;
  a = b;
  b = temp;
}
```

No doubt, you can see where this is going. If you also needed to swap floating-point numbers, bitmaps, cars, buttons, etc., you would have to build even more methods, which would become a maintenance nightmare. You could build a single (nongeneric) method that operated on object parameters, but then you face all the issues you examined earlier in this chapter, including boxing, unboxing, a lack of type safety, explicit casting, and so on.

Whenever you have a group of overloaded methods that differ only by incoming arguments, this is your clue that generics could make your life easier. Consider the following generic Swap<T>() method that can swap any two Ts:

```
// This method will swap any two items.
// as specified by the type parameter <T>.
static void Swap<T>(ref T a, ref T b)
{
  Console.WriteLine("You sent the Swap() method a {0}", typeof(T));
  T temp = a;
  a = b;
  b = temp;
}
```

Notice how a generic method is defined by specifying the type parameters after the method name but before the parameter list. Here, you state that the Swap<T>() method can operate on any two parameters of type <T>. To spice things up a bit, you also print out the type name of the supplied placeholder to the console using C#'s typeof() operator. Now consider the following calling code, which swaps integers and strings:

```
Console.WriteLine("***** Fun with Custom Generic Methods *****\n");

// Swap 2 ints.
int a = 10, b = 90;
Console.WriteLine("Before swap: {0}, {1}", a, b);
SwapFunctions.Swap<int>(ref a, ref b);
Console.WriteLine("After swap: {0}, {1}", a, b);
Console.WriteLine();

// Swap 2 strings.
string s1 = "Hello", s2 = "There";
Console.WriteLine("Before swap: {0} {1}!", s1, s2);
SwapFunctions.Swap<string>(ref s1, ref s2);
Console.WriteLine("After swap: {0} {1}!", s1, s2);

Console.ReadLine();
```

The output looks like this:

```
***** Fun with Custom Generic Methods *****
Before swap: 10, 90
You sent the Swap() method a System.Int32
After swap: 90, 10

Before swap: Hello There!
You sent the Swap() method a System.String
After swap: There Hello!
```

The major benefit of this approach is that you have only one version of Swap<T>() to maintain, yet it can operate on any two items of a given type in a type-safe manner. Better yet, stack-based items stay on the stack, while heap-based items stay on the heap!

Inference of Type Parameters

When you invoke generic methods such as Swap<T>, you can optionally omit the type parameter if (and only if) the generic method requires arguments because the compiler can infer the type parameter based on the member parameters. For example, you could swap two System.Boolean values by adding the following code to your top-level statements:

```
// Compiler will infer System.Boolean.
bool b1 = true, b2 = false;
Console.WriteLine("Before swap: {0}, {1}", b1, b2);
SwapFunctions.Swap(ref b1, ref b2);
Console.WriteLine("After swap: {0}, {1}", b1, b2);
```

Even though the compiler can discover the correct type parameter based on the data type used to declare b1 and b2, you should get in the habit of always specifying the type parameter explicitly.

```
SwapFunctions.Swap<bool>(ref b1, ref b2);
```

This makes it clear to your fellow programmers that this method is indeed generic. Moreover, inference of type parameters works only if the generic method has at least one parameter. For example, assume you have the following generic method in your `Program.cs` file:

```
static void DisplayBaseClass<T>()
{
  // BaseType is a method used in reflection,
  // which will be examined in Chapter 17
  Console.WriteLine("Base class of {0} is: {1}.", typeof(T), typeof(T).BaseType);
}
```

In this case, you must supply the type parameter upon invocation.

```
...
// Must supply type parameter if
// the method does not take params.
DisplayBaseClass<int>();
DisplayBaseClass<string>();

// Compiler error! No params? Must supply placeholder!
// DisplayBaseClass();
Console.ReadLine();
```

Of course, generic methods do not need to be static as they are in these examples. All rules and options for nongeneric methods also apply.

Creating Custom Generic Structures and Classes

Now that you understand how to define and invoke generic methods, it's time to turn your attention to the construction of a generic structure (the process of building a generic class is identical) within a new Console Application project named GenericPoint. Assume you have built a generic `Point` structure that supports a single type parameter that represents the underlying storage for the (*x, y*) coordinates. The caller can then create `Point<T>` types as follows:

```
// Point using ints.
Point<int> p = new Point<int>(10, 10);

// Point using double.
Point<double> p2 = new Point<double>(5.4, 3.3);

// Point using strings.
Point<string> p3 = new Point<string>("""",""3"");
```

Creating a point using strings might seem a bit odd at first, but consider the case of imaginary numbers. Then it might make sense to use strings for the values of `X` and `Y` of a point. Regardless, it demonstrates the power of generics. Here is the complete definition of `Point<T>`:

```
namespace GenericPoint;
// A generic Point structure.
public struct Point<T>
```

```
{
  // Generic state data.
  private T _xPos;
  private T _yPos;

  // Generic constructor.
  public Point(T xVal, T yVal)
  {
    _xPos = xVal;
    _yPos = yVal;
  }

  // Generic properties.
  public T X
  {
    get => _xPos;
    set => _xPos = value;
  }

  public T Y
  {
    get => _yPos;
    set => _yPos = value;
  }

  public override string ToString() => $"[{_xPos}, {_yPos}]";
}
```

As you can see, `Point<T>` leverages its type parameter in the definition of the field data, constructor arguments, and property definitions.

Default Value Expressions with Generics

With the introduction of generics, the C# `default` keyword has been given a dual identity. In addition to its use within a `switch` construct, it can be used to set a type parameter to its default value. This is helpful because a generic type does not know the actual placeholders up front, which means it cannot safely assume what the default value will be. The defaults for a type parameter are as follows:

- Numeric values have a default value of `0`.
- Reference types have a default value of `null`.
- Fields of a structure are set to `0` (for value types) or `null` (for reference types).

To reset an instance of `Point<T>`, you could set the `X` and `Y` values to `0` directly. This assumes the caller will supply only numerical data. What about the `string` version? This is where the `default(T)` syntax comes in handy. The default keyword resets a variable to the default value for the variable's data type. Add a method called `ResetPoint()` as follows:

```
// Reset fields to the default value of the type parameter.
// The "default" keyword is overloaded in C#.
// When used with generics, it represents the default
```

```
// value of a type parameter.
public void ResetPoint()
{
  _xPos = default(T);
  _yPos = default(T);
}
```

Now that you have the ResetPoint() method in place, you can fully exercise the methods of Point<T> struct.

```
using GenericPoint;

Console.WriteLine("***** Fun with Generic Structures *****\n");
// Point using ints.
Point<int> p = new Point<int>(10, 10);
Console.WriteLine("p.ToString()={0}", p.ToString());
p.ResetPoint();
Console.WriteLine("p.ToString()={0}", p.ToString());
Console.WriteLine();

// Point using double.
Point<double> p2 = new Point<double>(5.4, 3.3);
Console.WriteLine("p2.ToString()={0}", p2.ToString());
p2.ResetPoint();
Console.WriteLine("p2.ToString()={0}", p2.ToString());
Console.WriteLine();

// Point using strings.
Point<string> p3 = new Point<string>("i", "3i");
Console.WriteLine("p3.ToString()={0}", p3.ToString());
p3.ResetPoint();
Console.WriteLine("p3.ToString()={0}", p3.ToString());
Console.ReadLine();
```

Here is the output:

```
***** Fun with Generic Structures *****
p.ToString()=[10, 10]
p.ToString()=[0, 0]

p2.ToString()=[5.4, 3.3]
p2.ToString()=[0, 0]

p3.ToString()=[i, 3i]
p3.ToString()=[, ]
```

Default Literal Expressions (New 7.1)

In addition to setting the default value of a property, C# 7.1 introduced default literal expressions. This eliminates the need for specifying the type of the variable in the default statement. Update the ResetPoint() method to the following:

```
public void ResetPoint()
{
  _xPos = default;
  _yPos = default;
}
```

The default expression isn't limited to simple variables but can also be applied to complex types. For example, to create and initialize the Point structure, you can write the following:

```
Point<string> p4 = default;
Console.WriteLine("p4.ToString()={0}", p4.ToString());
Console.WriteLine();
Point<int> p5 = default;
Console.WriteLine("p5.ToString()={0}", p5.ToString());
```

Pattern Matching with Generics (New 7.1)

Another update in C# 7.1 is the ability to pattern match on generics. Take the following method, which checks the Point instance for the data type that it is based on (arguably incomplete, but enough to show the concept):

```
static void PatternMatching<T>(Point<T> p)
{
  switch (p)
  {
    case Point<string> pString:
      Console.WriteLine("Point is based on strings");
      return;
    case Point<int> pInt:
      Console.WriteLine("Point is based on ints");
      return;
  }
}
```

To exercise the pattern matching code, update the top-level statements to the following:

```
Point<string> p4 = default;
Point<int> p5 = default;
PatternMatching(p4);
PatternMatching(p5);
```

Constraining Type Parameters

As this chapter illustrates, any generic item has at least one type parameter that you need to specify at the time you interact with the generic type or member. This alone allows you to build some type-safe code; however, you can also use the where keyword to get extremely specific about what a given type parameter must look like.

Using this keyword, you can add a set of constraints to a given type parameter, which the C# compiler will check at compile time. Specifically, you can constrain a type parameter as described in Table 10-8.

Table 10-8. *Possible Constraints for Generic Type Parameters*

Generic Constraint	Meaning in Life
where T : struct	The type parameter <T> must have System.ValueType in its chain of inheritance (i.e., <T> must be a structure).
where T : class	The type parameter <T> must not have System.ValueType in its chain of inheritance (i.e., <T> must be a reference type).
where T : new()	The type parameter <T> must have a default constructor. This is helpful if your generic type must create an instance of the type parameter because you cannot assume you know the format of custom constructors. Note that this constraint must be listed last on a multiconstrained type.
where T : NameOfBaseClass	The type parameter <T> must be derived from the class specified by NameOfBaseClass.
where T : NameOfInterface	The type parameter <T> must implement the interface specified by NameOfInterface. You can separate multiple interfaces as a comma-delimited list.

Unless you need to build some extremely type-safe custom collections, you might never need to use the where keyword in your C# projects. Regardless, the following handful of (partial) code examples illustrate how to work with the where keyword.

Examples of Using the where Keyword

Begin by assuming that you have created a custom generic class, and you want to ensure that the type parameter has a default constructor. This could be useful when the custom generic class needs to create instances of the T because the default constructor is the only constructor that is potentially common to all types. Also, constraining T in this way lets you get compile-time checking; if T is a reference type, the programmer remembered to redefine the default in the class definition (you might recall that the default constructor is removed in classes when you define your own).

```
// MyGenericClass derives from object, while
// contained items must have a default ctor.
public class MyGenericClass<T> where T : new()
{
  ...
}
```

Notice that the where clause specifies which type parameter is being constrained, followed by a colon operator. After the colon operator, you list each possible constraint (in this case, a default constructor). Here is another example:

```
// MyGenericClass derives from object, while
// contained items must be a class implementing IDrawable
// and must support a default ctor.
public class MyGenericClass<T> where T : class, IDrawable, new()
{
  ...
}
```

In this case, T has three requirements. It must be a reference type (not a structure), as marked with the class token. Second, T must implement the IDrawable interface. Third, it must also have a default constructor. Multiple constraints are listed in a comma-delimited list; however, you should be aware that the new() constraint must always be listed last! Thus, the following code will not compile:

```
// Error! new() constraint must be listed last!
public class MyGenericClass<T> where T : new(), class, IDrawable
{
  ...
}
```

If you ever create a custom generic collection class that specifies multiple type parameters, you can specify a unique set of constraints for each, using separate where clauses.

```
// <K> must extend SomeBaseClass and have a default ctor,
// while <T> must be a structure and implement the
// generic IComparable interface.
public class MyGenericClass<K, T> where K : SomeBaseClass, new()
  where T : struct, IComparable<T>
{
  ...
}
```

You will rarely encounter cases where you need to build a complete custom generic collection class; however, you can use the where keyword on generic methods as well. For example, if you want to specify that your generic Swap<T>() method can operate only on structures, you will update the method like this:

```
// This method will swap any structure, but not classes.
static void Swap<T>(ref T a, ref T b) where T : struct
{
  ...
}
```

Note that if you were to constrain the Swap() method in this manner, you would no longer be able to swap string objects (as is shown in the sample code) because string is a reference type.

The Lack of Operator Constraints

I want to make one more comment about generic methods and constraints as this chapter ends. It might come as a surprise to you to find out that when creating generic methods, you will get a compiler error if you apply any C# operators (+, -, *, ==, etc.) on the type parameters. For example, imagine the usefulness of a class that can add, subtract, multiply, and divide generic types.

```
// Compiler error! Cannot apply
// operators to type parameters!
public class BasicMath<T>
{
  public T Add(T arg1, T arg2)
  { return arg1 + arg2; }
  public T Subtract(T arg1, T arg2)
  { return arg1 - arg2; }
  public T Multiply(T arg1, T arg2)
  { return arg1 * arg2; }
  public T Divide(T arg1, T arg2)
  { return arg1 / arg2; }
}
```

Unfortunately, the preceding BasicMath class will not compile. While this might seem like a major restriction, you need to remember that generics are generic. Of course, the numerical data can work with the binary operators of C#. However, for the sake of argument, if <T> were a custom class or structure type, the compiler could assume the class supports the +, -, *, and / operators. Ideally, C# would allow a generic type to be constrained by supported operators, as in this example:

```
// Illustrative code only!
public class BasicMath<T> where T : operator +, operator -,
  operator *, operator /
{
  public T Add(T arg1, T arg2)
  { return arg1 + arg2; }
  public T Subtract(T arg1, T arg2)
  { return arg1 - arg2; }
  public T Multiply(T arg1, T arg2)
  { return arg1 * arg2; }
  public T Divide(T arg1, T arg2)
  { return arg1 / arg2; }
}
```

Alas, operator constraints are not supported under the current version of C#. However, it is possible (albeit it requires a bit more work) to achieve the desired effect by defining an interface that supports these operators (C# interfaces can define operators!) and then specifying an interface constraint of the generic class. In any case, this wraps up this book's initial look at building custom generic types. In Chapter 12, I will pick up the topic of generics once again while examining the delegate type.

Summary

This chapter began by examining the nongeneric collection types of `System.Collections` and `System.Collections.Specialized`, including the various issues associated with many nongeneric containers, such as a lack of type safety and the runtime overhead of boxing and unboxing operations. As mentioned, for these very reasons, modern-day .NET programs will typically make use of the generic collection classes found in `System.Collections.Generic` and `System.Collections.ObjectModel`.

As you have seen, a generic item allows you to specify placeholders (type parameters) at the time of object creation (or invocation, in the case of generic methods). While you will most often simply use the generic types provided in the .NET base class libraries, you will also be able to create your own generic types (and generic methods). When you do so, you have the option of specifying any number of constraints (using the `where` keyword) to increase the level of type safety and ensure that you perform operations on types of a *known quantity* that are guaranteed to exhibit certain basic capabilities.

As a final note, remember that generics are found in numerous locations within the .NET base class libraries. Here, you focused specifically on generic collections. However, as you work through the remainder of this book (and when you dive into the platform on your own terms), you will certainly find generic classes, structures, and delegates located in a given namespace. As well, be on the lookout for generic members of a nongeneric class!

CHAPTER 11

Advanced C# Language Features

In this chapter, you'll deepen your understanding of the C# programming language by examining several more advanced topics. To begin, you'll learn how to implement and use an *indexer method*. This C# mechanism enables you to build custom types that provide access to internal subitems using an array-like syntax. After you learn how to build an indexer method, you'll see how to overload various operators (+, -, <, >, etc.) and how to create custom explicit and implicit conversion routines for your types (and you'll learn why you might want to do this).

Next, you'll examine topics that are particularly useful when working with LINQ-centric APIs (though you can use them outside of the context of LINQ)—specifically extension methods and anonymous types.

To wrap things up, you'll learn how to create an "unsafe" code context to directly manipulate unmanaged pointers. While it is certainly true that using pointers in C# applications is an infrequent activity, understanding how to do so can be helpful in some circumstances that involve complex interoperability scenarios.

Understanding Indexer Methods

As a programmer, you are certainly familiar with the process of accessing individual items contained within a simple array using the index operator ([ ]). Here's an example:

```
// Loop over incoming command-line arguments
// using index operator.
for(int i = 0; i < args.Length; i++)
{
  Console.WriteLine("Args: {0}", args[i]);
}

// Declare an array of local integers.
int[] myInts = { 10, 9, 100, 432, 9874};

// Use the index operator to access each element.
for(int j = 0; j < myInts.Length; j++)
{
  Console.WriteLine("Index {0}  = {1} ", j,  myInts[j]);
}
Console.ReadLine();
```


A. Troelsen and P. Japikse, *Pro C# 10 with .NET 6*, https://doi.org/10.1007/978-1-4842-7869-7_11

This code is by no means a major news flash. However, the C# language provides the capability to design custom classes and structures that may be indexed just like a standard array, by defining an *indexer method*. This feature is most useful when you are creating custom collection classes (generic or nongeneric).

Before examining how to implement a custom indexer, let's begin by seeing one in action. Assume you have added support for an indexer method to the custom PersonCollection type developed in Chapter 10 (specifically, the IssuesWithNonGenericCollections project). While you have not yet added the indexer, observe the following usage within a new Console Application project named SimpleIndexer:

```
using System.Data;
using SimpleIndexer;

// Indexers allow you to access items in an array-like fashion.
Console.WriteLine("***** Fun with Indexers *****\n");

PersonCollection myPeople = new PersonCollection();

// Add objects with indexer syntax.
myPeople[0] = new Person("Homer", "Simpson", 40);
myPeople[1] = new Person("Marge", "Simpson", 38);
myPeople[2] = new Person("Lisa", "Simpson", 9);
myPeople[3] = new Person("Bart", "Simpson", 7);
myPeople[4] = new Person("Maggie", "Simpson", 2);

// Now obtain and display each item using indexer.
for (int i = 0; i < myPeople.Count; i++)
{
  Console.WriteLine("Person number: {0}", i);
  Console.WriteLine("Name: {0} {1}",
    myPeople[i].FirstName, myPeople[i].LastName);
  Console.WriteLine("Age: {0}", myPeople[i].Age);
  Console.WriteLine();
}
```

As you can see, indexers allow you to manipulate the internal collection of subobjects just like a standard array. Now for the big question: how do you configure the PersonCollection class (or any custom class or structure) to support this functionality? An indexer is represented as a slightly modified C# property definition. In its simplest form, an indexer is created using the this[] syntax. Here is the required update for the PersonCollection class:

```
using System.Collections;

namespace SimpleIndexer;
// Add the indexer to the existing class definition.
public class PersonCollection : IEnumerable
{
  private ArrayList arPeople = new ArrayList();
...
  // Custom indexer for this class.
  public Person this[int index]
```

```
  {
    get => (Person)arPeople[index];
    set => arPeople.Insert(index, value);
  }
}
```

Apart from using the this keyword with the brackets, the indexer looks just like any other C# property declaration. For example, the role of the get scope is to return the correct object to the caller. Here, you are doing so by delegating the request to the indexer of the ArrayList object, as this class also supports an indexer. The set scope oversees adding new Person objects; this is achieved by calling the Insert() method of the ArrayList.

Indexers are yet another form of syntactic sugar, given that this functionality can also be achieved using "normal" public methods such as AddPerson() or GetPerson(). Nevertheless, when you support indexer methods on your custom collection types, they integrate well into the fabric of the .NET base class libraries.

While creating indexer methods is quite commonplace when you are building custom collections, do remember that generic types give you this functionality out of the box. Consider the following method, which uses a generic List<T> of Person objects. Note that you can simply use the indexer of List<T> directly. Here's an example:

```
static void UseGenericListOfPeople()
{
  List<Person> myPeople = new List<Person>();
  myPeople.Add(new Person("Lisa", "Simpson", 9));
  myPeople.Add(new Person("Bart", "Simpson", 7));

  // Change first person with indexer.
  myPeople[0] = new Person("Maggie", "Simpson", 2);

  // Now obtain and display each item using indexer.
  for (int i = 0; i < myPeople.Count; i++)
  {
    Console.WriteLine("Person number: {0}", i);
    Console.WriteLine("Name: {0} {1}", myPeople[i].FirstName, myPeople[i].LastName);
    Console.WriteLine("Age: {0}", myPeople[i].Age);
    Console.WriteLine();
  }
}
```

Indexing Data Using String Values

The current PersonCollection class defined an indexer that allowed the caller to identify subitems using a numerical value. Understand, however, that this is not a requirement of an indexer method. Suppose you'd prefer to contain the Person objects using a System.Collections.Generic.Dictionary<TKey, TValue> rather than an ArrayList. Given that Dictionary types allow access to the contained types using a key (such as a person's first name), you could define an indexer as follows:

```
using System.Collections;
namespace SimpleIndexer;
public class PersonCollectionStringIndexer : IEnumerable
{
  private Dictionary<string, Person> listPeople = new Dictionary<string, Person>();
```

```
  // This indexer returns a person based on a string index.
  public Person this[string name]
  {
    get => (Person)listPeople[name];
    set => listPeople[name] = value;
  }
  public void ClearPeople()
  {
    listPeople.Clear();
  }

  public int Count => listPeople.Count;

  IEnumerator IEnumerable.GetEnumerator() => listPeople.GetEnumerator();
}
```

The caller would now be able to interact with the contained Person objects, as shown here:

```
Console.WriteLine("***** Fun with Indexers *****\n");

PersonCollectionStringIndexer myPeopleStrings =
  new PersonCollectionStringIndexer();

myPeopleStrings["Homer"] =
  new Person("Homer", "Simpson", 40);
myPeopleStrings["Marge"] =
  new Person("Marge", "Simpson", 38);

// Get "Homer" and print data.
Person homer = myPeopleStrings["Homer"];
Console.ReadLine();
```

Again, if you were to use the generic Dictionary<TKey, TValue> type directly, you'd gain the indexer method functionality out of the box, without building a custom, nongeneric class supporting a string indexer. Nevertheless, do understand that the data type of any indexer will be based on how the supporting collection type allows the caller to retrieve subitems.

Overloading Indexer Methods

Indexer methods may be overloaded on a single class or structure. Thus, if it makes sense to allow the caller to access subitems using a numerical index *or* a string value, you might define multiple indexers for a single type. By way of example, in ADO.NET (.NET's native database-access API), the DataSet class supports a property named Tables, which returns to you a strongly typed DataTableCollection type. As it turns out, DataTableCollection defines *three* indexers to get and set DataTable objects—one by ordinal position and the others by a friendly string moniker and optional containing namespace, as shown here:

```
public sealed class DataTableCollection : InternalDataCollectionBase
{
...
  // Overloaded indexers!
  public DataTable this[int index] { get; }
```

```
  public DataTable this[string name] { get; }
  public DataTable this[string name, string tableNamespace] { get; }
}
```

It is common for types in the base class libraries to support indexer methods. So be aware, even if your current project does not require you to build custom indexers for your classes and structures, that many types already support this syntax.

Indexers with Multiple Dimensions

You can also create an indexer method that takes multiple parameters. Assume you have a custom collection that stores subitems in a 2D array. If this is the case, you may define an indexer method as follows:

```
public class SomeContainer
{
  private int[,] my2DintArray = new int[10, 10];

  public int this[int row, int column]
  {  /* get or set value from 2D array */  }
}
```

Again, unless you are building a highly stylized custom collection class, you won't have much need to build a multidimensional indexer. Still, once again ADO.NET showcases how useful this construct can be. The ADO.NET DataTable is essentially a collection of rows and columns, much like a piece of graph paper or the general structure of a Microsoft Excel spreadsheet.

While DataTable objects are typically populated on your behalf using a related "data adapter," the following code illustrates how to manually create an in-memory DataTable containing three columns (for the first name, last name, and age of each record). Notice how once you have added a single row to the DataTable, you use a multidimensional indexer to drill into each column of the first (and only) row. (If you are following along, you'll need to import the System.Data namespace into your code file.)

```
static void MultiIndexerWithDataTable()
{
  // Make a simple DataTable with 3 columns.
  DataTable myTable = new DataTable();
  myTable.Columns.Add(new DataColumn("FirstName"));
  myTable.Columns.Add(new DataColumn("LastName"));
  myTable.Columns.Add(new DataColumn("Age"));

  // Now add a row to the table.
  myTable.Rows.Add("Mel", "Appleby", 60);

  // Use multidimension indexer to get details of first row.
  Console.WriteLine("First Name: {0}", myTable.Rows[0][0]);
  Console.WriteLine("Last Name: {0}", myTable.Rows[0][1]);
  Console.WriteLine("Age : {0}", myTable.Rows[0][2]);
}
```

Do be aware that you'll take a rather deep dive into ADO.NET beginning with Chapter 20, so if some of the previous code seems unfamiliar, fear not. The main point of this example is that indexer methods can support multiple dimensions and, if used correctly, can simplify the way you interact with contained subobjects in custom collections.

Indexer Definitions on Interface Types

Indexers can be defined on a given .NET interface type to allow supporting types to provide a custom implementation. Here is a simple example of an interface that defines a protocol for obtaining string objects using a numerical indexer:

```
public interface IStringContainer
{
  string this[int index] { get; set; }
}
```

With this interface definition, any class or structure that implements this interface must now support a read-write indexer that manipulates subitems using a numerical value. Here is a partial implementation of such a class:

```
class SomeClass : IStringContainer
{
  private List<string> myStrings = new List<string>();

  public string this[int index]
  {
    get => myStrings[index];
    set => myStrings.Insert(index, value);
  }
}
```

That wraps up the first major topic of this chapter. Now let's examine a language feature that lets you build custom classes or structures that respond uniquely to the intrinsic operators of C#. Next, allow me to introduce the concept of *operator overloading*.

Understanding Operator Overloading

C#, like any programming language, has a canned set of tokens that are used to perform basic operations on intrinsic types. For example, you know that the + operator can be applied to two integers to yield a larger integer.

```
// The + operator with ints.
int a = 100;
int b = 240;
int c = a + b; // c is now 340
```

Once again, this is no major news flash, but have you ever stopped and noticed how the same + operator can be applied to most intrinsic C# data types? For example, consider this code:

```
// + operator with strings.
```

```
string s1 = "Hello";
string s2 = " world!";
string s3 = s1 + s2;  // s3 is now "Hello World!"
```

The + operator functions in specific ways based on the supplied data types (strings or integers, in this case). When the + operator is applied to numerical types, the result is the summation of the operands. However, when the + operator is applied to string types, the result is string concatenation.

The C# language gives you the capability to build custom classes and structures that also respond uniquely to the same set of basic tokens (such as the + operator). While not every possible C# operator can be overloaded, many can, as shown in Table 11-1.

Table 11-1. *Overloadability of C# Operators*

C# Operator	Overloadability
+, -, !, ~, ++, --, true, false	These unary operators can be overloaded. C# demands that if true or false is overloaded, both must be overloaded.
+, -, *, /, %, &, |, ^, <<, >>	These binary operators can be overloaded.
==, !=, <, >, <=, >=	These comparison operators can be overloaded. C# demands that "like" operators (i.e., < and >, <= and >=, == and !=) are overloaded together.
[]	The [] operator cannot be overloaded. As you saw earlier in this chapter, however, the indexer construct provides the same functionality.
()	The () operator cannot be overloaded. As you will see later in this chapter, however, custom conversion methods provide the same functionality.
+=, -=, *=, /=, %=, &=, |=, ^=, <<=, >>=	Shorthand assignment operators cannot be overloaded; however, you receive them as a freebie when you overload the related binary operator.

Overloading Binary Operators

To illustrate the process of overloading binary operators, assume the following simple Point class is defined in a new Console Application project named OverloadedOps:

```
namespace OverloadedOps;
// Just a simple, everyday C# class.
public class Point
{
  public int X {get; set;}
  public int Y {get; set;}

  public Point(int xPos, int yPos)
  {
    X = xPos;
    Y = yPos;
  }
  public override string ToString()
    => $"[{this.X}, {this.Y}]";
}
```

Now, logically speaking, it makes sense to "add" Points together. For example, if you added together two Point variables, you should receive a new Point that is the summation of the X and Y values. Of course, it might also be helpful to subtract one Point from another. Ideally, you would like to be able to author the following code:

```
using OverloadedOps;

// Adding and subtracting two points?
Console.WriteLine("***** Fun with Overloaded Operators *****\n");

// Make two points.
Point ptOne = new Point(100, 100);
Point ptTwo = new Point(40, 40);
Console.WriteLine("ptOne = {0}", ptOne);
Console.WriteLine("ptTwo = {0}", ptTwo);
// Add the points to make a bigger point?
Console.WriteLine("ptOne + ptTwo: {0} ", ptOne + ptTwo);

// Subtract the points to make a smaller point?
  Console.WriteLine("ptOne - ptTwo: {0} ", ptOne - ptTwo);
  Console.ReadLine();
```

However, as your Point now stands, you will receive compile-time errors, as the Point type does not know how to respond to the + or - operator. To equip a custom type to respond uniquely to intrinsic operators, C# provides the operator keyword, which you can use only in conjunction with the static keyword. When you overload a binary operator (such as + and -), you will most often pass in two arguments that are the same type as the defining class (a Point in this example), as illustrated in the following code update:

```
// A more intelligent Point type.
public class Point
{
...
  // Overloaded operator +.
  public static Point operator + (Point p1, Point p2)
    => new Point(p1.X + p2.X, p1.Y + p2.Y);

  // Overloaded operator -.
  public static Point operator - (Point p1, Point p2)
    => new Point(p1.X - p2.X, p1.Y - p2.Y);
}
```

The logic behind operator + is simply to return a new Point object based on the summation of the fields of the incoming Point parameters. Thus, when you write pt1 + pt2, under the hood you can envision the following hidden call to the static operator + method:

```
// Pseudo-code: Point p3 = Point.operator+ (p1, p2)
Point p3 = p1 + p2;
```

Likewise, p1-p2 maps to the following:

```
// Pseudo-code: Point p4 = Point.operator- (p1, p2)
Point p4 = p1 - p2;
```

With this update, your program now compiles, and you find you can add and subtract Point objects, as shown in the following output:

```
***** Fun with Overloaded Operators *****
ptOne = [100, 100]
ptTwo = [40, 40]
ptOne + ptTwo: [140, 140]
ptOne - ptTwo: [60, 60]
```

When you are overloading a binary operator, you are not required to pass in two parameters of the same type. If it makes sense to do so, one of the arguments can differ. For example, here is an overloaded operator + that allows the caller to obtain a new Point that is based on a numerical adjustment:

```
public class Point
{
...
  public static Point operator + (Point p1, int change)
    => new Point(p1.X + change, p1.Y + change);

  public static Point operator + (int change, Point p1)
    => new Point(p1.X + change, p1.Y + change);
}
```

Notice that you need *both* versions of the method if you want the arguments to be passed in either order (i.e., you can't just define one of the methods and expect the compiler to automatically support the other one). You are now able to use these new versions of operator + as follows:

```
// Prints [110, 110].
Point biggerPoint = ptOne + 10;
Console.WriteLine("ptOne + 10 = {0}", biggerPoint);

// Prints [120, 120].
Console.WriteLine("10 + biggerPoint = {0}", 10 + biggerPoint);
Console.WriteLine();
```

What of the += and -= Operators?

If you are coming to C# from a C++ background, you might lament the loss of overloading the shorthand assignment operators (+=, -=, etc.). Don't despair. In terms of C#, the shorthand assignment operators are automatically simulated if a type overloads the related binary operator. Thus, given that the Point structure has already overloaded the + and - operators, you can write the following:

```
// Overloading binary operators results in a freebie shorthand operator.
...
// Freebie +=
Point ptThree = new Point(90, 5);
Console.WriteLine("ptThree = {0}", ptThree);
Console.WriteLine("ptThree += ptTwo: {0}", ptThree += ptTwo);
```

```
// Freebie -=
Point ptFour = new Point(0, 500);
Console.WriteLine("ptFour = {0}", ptFour);
Console.WriteLine("ptFour -= ptThree: {0}", ptFour -= ptThree);
Console.ReadLine();
```

Overloading Unary Operators

C# also allows you to overload various unary operators, such as ++ and --. When you overload a unary operator, you also must use the static keyword with the operator keyword; however, in this case, you simply pass in a single parameter that is the same type as the defining class/structure. For example, if you were to update the Point with the following overloaded operators:

```
public class Point
{
...
  // Add 1 to the X/Y values for the incoming Point.
  public static Point operator ++(Point p1)
    => new Point(p1.X+1, p1.Y+1);

  // Subtract 1 from the X/Y values for the incoming Point.
  public static Point operator --(Point p1)
    => new Point(p1.X-1, p1.Y-1);
}
```

you could increment and decrement Point's x and y values like this:

```
...
// Applying the ++ and -- unary operators to a Point.
Point ptFive = new Point(1, 1);
Console.WriteLine("++ptFive = {0}", ++ptFive);  // [2, 2]
Console.WriteLine("--ptFive = {0}", --ptFive);  // [1, 1]

// Apply same operators as postincrement/decrement.
Point ptSix = new Point(20, 20);
Console.WriteLine("ptSix++ = {0}", ptSix++);    // [20, 20]
Console.WriteLine("ptSix-- = {0}", ptSix--);    // [21, 21]
Console.ReadLine();
```

Notice in the preceding code example you are applying the custom ++ and -- operators in two different manners. In C++, it is possible to overload pre- and post-increment/decrement operators separately. This is not possible in C#. However, the return value of the increment/decrement is automatically handled "correctly" free of charge (i.e., for an overloaded ++ operator, pt++ has the value of the unmodified object as its value within an expression, while ++pt has the new value applied before use in the expression).

Overloading Equality Operators

As you might recall from Chapter 6, System.Object.Equals() can be overridden to perform value-based (rather than referenced-based) comparisons between reference types. If you choose to override Equals() (and the often-related System.Object.GetHashCode() method), it is trivial to overload the equality operators (== and !=). To illustrate, here is the updated Point type:

```
// This incarnation of Point also overloads the == and != operators.
public class Point
{
...
  public override bool Equals(object o)
    => o.ToString() == this.ToString();

  public override int GetHashCode()
    => this.ToString().GetHashCode();

  // Now let's overload the == and != operators.
  public static bool operator ==(Point p1, Point p2)
    => p1.Equals(p2);

  public static bool operator !=(Point p1, Point p2)
    => !p1.Equals(p2);
}
```

Notice how the implementation of operator == and operator != simply makes a call to the overridden Equals() method to get the bulk of the work done. Given this, you can now exercise your Point class as follows:

```
// Make use of the overloaded equality operators.
...
Console.WriteLine("ptOne == ptTwo : {0}", ptOne == ptTwo);
Console.WriteLine("ptOne != ptTwo : {0}", ptOne != ptTwo);
Console.ReadLine();
```

As you can see, it is quite intuitive to compare two objects using the well-known == and != operators, rather than making a call to Object.Equals(). If you do overload the equality operators for a given class, keep in mind that C# demands that if you override the == operator, you *must* also override the != operator (if you forget, the compiler will let you know).

Overloading Comparison Operators

In Chapter 8, you learned how to implement the IComparable interface to compare the relationship between two like objects. You can, in fact, also overload the comparison operators (<, >, <=, and >=) for the same class. As with the equality operators, C# demands that if you overload <, you must also overload >. The same holds true for the <= and >= operators. If the Point type overloaded these comparison operators, the object user could now compare Points, as follows:

```
// Using the overloaded < and > operators.
...
Console.WriteLine("ptOne < ptTwo : {0}", ptOne < ptTwo);
Console.WriteLine("ptOne > ptTwo : {0}", ptOne > ptTwo);
Console.ReadLine();
```

Assuming you have implemented the IComparable interface (or better yet, the generic equivalent), overloading the comparison operators is trivial. Here is the updated class definition:

```
// Point is also comparable using the comparison operators.
public class Point : IComparable<Point>
{
...
  public int CompareTo(Point other)
  {
    if (this.X > other.X && this.Y > other.Y)
    {
      return 1;
    }
    if (this.X < other.X && this.Y < other.Y)
    {
      return -1;
    }
    return 0;
  }
  public static bool operator <(Point p1, Point p2)
    => p1.CompareTo(p2) < 0;

  public static bool operator >(Point p1, Point p2)
    => p1.CompareTo(p2) > 0;

  public static bool operator <=(Point p1, Point p2)
    => p1.CompareTo(p2) <= 0;

  public static bool operator >=(Point p1, Point p2)
    => p1.CompareTo(p2) >= 0;
}
```

Final Thoughts Regarding Operator Overloading

As you have seen, C# provides the capability to build types that can respond uniquely to various intrinsic, well-known operators. Now, before you go and retrofit all your classes to support such behavior, you must be sure that the operators you are about to overload make some sort of logical sense in the world at large.

For example, let's say you overloaded the multiplication operator for the MiniVan class. What exactly would it mean to multiply two MiniVan objects? Not much. In fact, it would be confusing for teammates to see the following use of MiniVan objects:

```
// Huh?! This is far from intuitive...
MiniVan newVan = myVan * yourVan;
```

Overloading operators is generally useful only when you're building atomic data types. Vectors, matrices, text, points, shapes, sets, etc., make good candidates for operator overloading. People, managers, cars, database connections, and web pages do not. As a rule of thumb, if an overloaded operator makes it *harder* for the user to understand a type's functionality, don't do it. Use this feature wisely.

Understanding Custom Type Conversions

Let's now examine a topic closely related to operator overloading: custom type conversions. To set the stage for the discussion, let's quickly review the notion of explicit and implicit conversions between numerical data and related class types.

Recall: Numerical Conversions

In terms of the intrinsic numerical types (sbyte, int, float, etc.), an *explicit conversion* is required when you attempt to store a larger value in a smaller container, as this could result in a loss of data. Basically, this is your way to tell the compiler, "Leave me alone, I know what I am trying to do." Conversely, an *implicit conversion* happens automatically when you attempt to place a smaller type in a destination type that will not result in a loss of data.

```
int a = 123;
long b = a;       // Implicit conversion from int to long.
int c = (int) b;  // Explicit conversion from long to int.
```

Recall: Conversions Among Related Class Types

As shown in Chapter 6, class types may be related by classical inheritance (the "is-a" relationship). In this case, the C# conversion process allows you to cast up and down the class hierarchy. For example, a derived class can always be implicitly cast to a base type. However, if you want to store a base class type in a derived variable, you must perform an explicit cast, like so:

```
// Two related class types.
class Base{}
class Derived : Base{}

// Implicit cast between derived to base.
Base myBaseType;
myBaseType = new Derived();
// Must explicitly cast to store base reference
// in derived type.
Derived myDerivedType = (Derived)myBaseType;
```

This explicit cast works because the Base and Derived classes are related by classical inheritance and myBaseType is constructed as an instance of Derived. However, if myBaseType is an instance of Base, the cast throws an InvalidCastException. If there is any doubt that the cast will fail, you should use the as keyword, as discussed in Chapter 6. Here is the sample reworked to demonstrate this:

```
// Implicit cast between derived to base.
Base myBaseType2 = new();
// Throws InvalidCastException
//Derived myDerivedType2 = (Derived)myBaseType2 as Derived;
//No exception, myDerivedType2 is null
Derived myDerivedType2 = myBaseType2 as Derived;
```

However, what if you have two class types in *different hierarchies* with no common parent (other than `System.Object`) that require conversions? Given that they are not related by classical inheritance, typical casting operations offer no help (and you would get a compiler error to boot!).

On a related note, consider value types (structures). Assume you have two structures named `Square` and `Rectangle`. Given that structures cannot leverage classic inheritance (as they are always sealed), you have no natural way to cast between these seemingly related types.

While you could create helper methods in the structures (such as `Rectangle.ToSquare()`), C# lets you build custom conversion routines that allow your types to respond to the `()` casting operator. Therefore, if you configured the structures correctly, you would be able to use the following syntax to explicitly convert between them as follows:

```
// Convert a Rectangle to a Square!
Rectangle rect = new Rectangle
{
  Width = 3;
  Height = 10;
}
Square sq = (Square)rect;
```

Creating Custom Conversion Routines

Begin by creating a new Console Application project named CustomConversions. C# provides two keywords, `explicit` and `implicit`, that you can use to control how your types respond during an attempted conversion. Assume you have the following structure definitions:

```
namespace CustomConversions;
public struct Rectangle
{
  public int Width {get; set;}
  public int Height {get; set;}

  public Rectangle(int w, int h)
  {
    Width = w;
    Height = h;
  }

  public void Draw()
  {
    for (int i = 0; i < Height; i++)
    {
      for (int j = 0; j < Width; j++)
```

```
        {
          Console.Write("*");
        }
        Console.WriteLine();
      }
    }

    public override string ToString()
      => $"[Width = {Width}; Height = {Height}]";
}

namespace CustomConversions;
  public struct Square
  {
    public int Length {get; set;}
    public Square(int l) : this()
    {
      Length = l;
    }

    public void Draw()
    {
      for (int i = 0; i < Length; i++)
      {
        for (int j = 0; j < Length; j++)
        {
          Console.Write("*");
        }
        Console.WriteLine();
      }
    }

    public override string ToString() => $"[Length = {Length}]";

    // Rectangles can be explicitly converted into Squares.
    public static explicit operator Square(Rectangle r)
    {
      Square s = new Square {Length = r.Height};
      return s;
    }
  }
}
```

Notice that this iteration of the Square type defines an explicit conversion operator. Like the process of overloading an operator, conversion routines make use of the C# `operator` keyword, in conjunction with the `explicit` or `implicit` keyword, and must be defined as `static`. The incoming parameter is the entity you are converting *from*, while the operator type is the entity you are converting *to*.

In this case, the assumption is that a square (being a geometric pattern in which all sides are of equal length) can be obtained from the height of a rectangle. Thus, you are free to convert a `Rectangle` into a `Square`, as follows:

```
using CustomConversions;

Console.WriteLine("***** Fun with Conversions *****\n");
// Make a Rectangle.
Rectangle r = new Rectangle(15, 4);
Console.WriteLine(r.ToString());
r.Draw();

Console.WriteLine();

// Convert r into a Square,
// based on the height of the Rectangle.
Square s = (Square)r;
Console.WriteLine(s.ToString());
s.Draw();
Console.ReadLine();
```

You can see the output here:

```
***** Fun with Conversions *****
[Width = 15; Height = 4]

***************
***************
***************
***************

[Length = 4]
****
****
****
****
```

While it may not be all that helpful to convert a Rectangle into a Square within the same scope, assume you have a function that has been designed to take Square parameters.

```
// This method requires a Square type.
static void DrawSquare(Square sq)
{
  Console.WriteLine(sq.ToString());
  sq.Draw();
}
```

Using your explicit conversion operation on the Square type, you can now pass in Rectangle types for processing using an explicit cast, like so:

```
...
// Convert Rectangle to Square to invoke method.
Rectangle rect = new Rectangle(10, 5);
DrawSquare((Square)rect);
Console.ReadLine();
```

Additional Explicit Conversions for the Square Type

Now that you can explicitly convert Rectangles into Squares, let's examine a few additional explicit conversions. Given that a square is symmetrical on all sides, it might be helpful to provide an explicit conversion routine that allows the caller to cast from an integer type into a Square (which, of course, will have a side length equal to the incoming integer). Likewise, what if you were to update Square such that the caller can cast *from* a Square into an int? Here is the calling logic:

```
...
// Converting an int to a Square.
Square sq2 = (Square)90;
Console.WriteLine("sq2 = {0}", sq2);

// Converting a Square to an int.
int side = (int)sq2;
Console.WriteLine("Side length of sq2 = {0}", side);
Console.ReadLine();
```

and here is the update to the Square class:

```
public struct Square
{
...
  public static explicit operator Square(int sideLength)
  {
    Square newSq = new Square {Length = sideLength};
    return newSq;
  }

  public static explicit operator int (Square s) => s.Length;
}
```

To be honest, converting from a Square into an integer may not be the most intuitive (or useful) operation (after all, chances are you could just pass such values to a constructor). However, it does point out an important fact regarding custom conversion routines: the compiler does not care what you convert to or from, if you have written syntactically correct code.

Thus, as with overloading operators, just because you *can* create an explicit cast operation for a given type does not mean you *should*. Typically, this technique will be most helpful when you're creating structure types, given that they are unable to participate in classical inheritance (where casting comes for free).

Defining Implicit Conversion Routines

So far, you have created various custom *explicit* conversion operations. However, what about the following *implicit* conversion?

```
...
Square s3 = new Square {Length = 83};

// Attempt to make an implicit cast?
Rectangle rect2 = s3;

Console.ReadLine();
```

This code will not compile, given that you have not provided an implicit conversion routine for the Rectangle type. Now here is the catch: it is illegal to define explicit and implicit conversion functions on the same type if they do not differ by their return type or parameter set. This might seem like a limitation; however, the second catch is that when a type defines an *implicit* conversion routine, it is legal for the caller to make use of the *explicit* cast syntax!

Confused? To clear things up, let's add an implicit conversion routine to the Rectangle structure using the C# implicit keyword (note that the following code assumes the width of the resulting Rectangle is computed by multiplying the side of the Square by 2):

```
public struct Rectangle
{
...
  public static implicit operator Rectangle(Square s)
  {
    Rectangle r = new Rectangle
    {
      Height = s.Length,
      Width = s.Length * 2 // Assume the length of the new Rectangle with (Length x 2).
    };
    return r;
  }
}
```

With this update, you are now able to convert between types, as follows:

```
...
// Implicit cast OK!
Square s3 = new Square { Length= 7};

Rectangle rect2 = s3;
Console.WriteLine("rect2 = {0}", rect2);

// Explicit cast syntax still OK!
Square s4 = new Square {Length = 3};
Rectangle rect3 = (Rectangle)s4;

Console.WriteLine("rect3 = {0}", rect3);
Console.ReadLine();
```

That wraps up your look at defining custom conversion routines. As with overloaded operators, remember that this bit of syntax is simply a shorthand notation for "normal" member functions, and in this light, it is always optional. When used correctly, however, custom structures can be used more naturally, as they can be treated as true class types related by inheritance.

Understanding Extension Methods

.NET 3.5 introduced the concept of *extension methods*, which allow you to add new methods or properties to a class or structure, without modifying the original type in any direct manner. So, where might this be helpful? Consider the following possibilities.

First, say you have a given class that is in production. It becomes clear over time that this class should support a handful of new members. If you modify the current class definition directly, you risk the possibility of breaking backward compatibility with older code bases making use of it, as they might not have been compiled with the latest and greatest class definition. One way to ensure backward compatibility is to create a new derived class from the existing parent; however, now you have two classes to maintain. As we all know, code maintenance is the least glamorous part of a software engineer's job description.

Now consider this situation. Let's say you have a structure (or maybe a sealed class) and want to add new members so that it behaves polymorphically in your system. Since structures and sealed classes cannot be extended, your only choice is to add the members to the type, once again risking breaking backward compatibility!

Using extension methods, you can modify types without subclassing and without modifying the type directly. The catch is that the new functionality is offered to a type only if the extension methods have been referenced for use in your current project.

Defining Extension Methods

When you define extension methods, the first restriction is that they must be defined within a static class (see Chapter 5); therefore, each extension method must be declared with the `static` keyword. The second point is that all extension methods are marked as such by using the `this` keyword as a modifier on the first (and only the first) parameter of the method in question. The "`this` qualified" parameter represents the item being extended.

To illustrate, create a new Console Application project named ExtensionMethods. Now, assume you are authoring a class named `MyExtensions` that defines two extension methods. The first method allows any `object` to use a new method named `DisplayDefiningAssembly()` that makes use of types in the `System.Reflection` namespace to display the name of the assembly containing the type in question.

■ **Note** You will formally examine the reflection API in Chapter 17. If you are new to the topic, simply understand that reflection allows you to discover the structure of assemblies, types, and type members at runtime.

The second extension method, named `ReverseDigits()`, allows any `int` to obtain a new version of itself where the value is reversed digit by digit. For example, if an integer with the value 1234 called `ReverseDigits()`, the integer returned is set to the value 4321. Consider the following class implementation (be sure to import the `System.Reflection` namespace if you are following along):

```
using System.Reflection;

namespace MyExtensionMethods;
static class MyExtensions
{
  // This method allows any object to display the assembly
  // it is defined in.
  public static void DisplayDefiningAssembly(this object obj)
  {
    Console.WriteLine("{0} lives here: => {1}\n",
      obj.GetType().Name,
      Assembly.GetAssembly(obj.GetType()).GetName().Name);
  }
```

```
    // This method allows any integer to reverse its digits.
    // For example, 56 would return 65.
    public static int ReverseDigits(this int i)
    {
      // Translate int into a string, and then
      // get all the characters.
      char[] digits = i.ToString().ToCharArray();

      // Now reverse items in the array.
      Array.Reverse(digits);

      // Put back into string.
      string newDigits = new string(digits);

      // Finally, return the modified string back as an int.
      return int.Parse(newDigits);
    }
}
```

Again, note how the first parameter of each extension method has been qualified with the `this` keyword, before defining the parameter type. It is always the case that the first parameter of an extension method represents the type being extended. Given that `DisplayDefiningAssembly()` has been prototyped to extend `System.Object`, every type now has this new member, as `Object` is the parent to all types in the .NET platform. However, `ReverseDigits()` has been prototyped to extend only integer types; therefore, if anything other than an integer attempts to invoke this method, you will receive a compile-time error.

■ **Note** Understand that a given extension method can have multiple parameters, but *only* the first parameter can be qualified with `this`. The additional parameters would be treated as normal incoming parameters for use by the method.

Invoking Extension Methods

Now that you have these extension methods in place, consider the following code example that applies the extension method to various types in the base class libraries:

```
using MyExtensionMethods;

Console.WriteLine("***** Fun with Extension Methods *****\n");

// The int has assumed a new identity!
int myInt = 12345678;
myInt.DisplayDefiningAssembly();

// So has the DataSet!
System.Data.DataSet d = new System.Data.DataSet();
d.DisplayDefiningAssembly();
```

```
// Use new integer functionality.
Console.WriteLine("Value of myInt: {0}", myInt);
Console.WriteLine("Reversed digits of myInt: {0}",
  myInt.ReverseDigits());

Console.ReadLine();
```

Here is the output:

```
***** Fun with Extension Methods *****
Int32 lives here: => System.Private.CoreLib

DataSet lives here: => System.Data.Common

Value of myInt: 12345678
Reversed digits of myInt: 87654321
```

Importing Extension Methods

When you define a class containing extension methods, it will no doubt be defined within a namespace. If this namespace is different from the namespace using the extension methods, you will need to make use of the expected C# `using` keyword. When you do, your code file has access to all extension methods for the type being extended. This is important to remember because if you do not explicitly import the correct namespace, the extension methods are not available for that C# code file.

In effect, although it can appear on the surface that extension methods are global in nature, they are in fact limited to the namespaces that define them or the namespaces that import them. Recall that you wrapped the `MyExtensions` class into a namespace named `MyExtensionMethods`, as follows:

```
namespace MyExtensionMethods;
static class MyExtensions
{
  ...
}
```

To use the extension methods in the class, you need to explicitly import the `MyExtensionMethods` namespace, as we did in the top-level statements used to exercise the examples.

Extending Types Implementing Specific Interfaces

At this point, you have seen how to extend classes (and, indirectly, structures that follow the same syntax) with new functionality via extension methods. It is also possible to define an extension method that can only extend a class or structure that implements the correct interface. For example, you could say something to the effect of "If a class or structure implements `IEnumerable<T>`, then that type gets the following new members." Of course, it is possible to demand that a type support any interface at all, including your own custom interfaces.

To illustrate, create a new Console Application project named InterfaceExtensions. The goal here is to add a new method to any type that implements `IEnumerable`, which would include any array and many nongeneric collection classes (recall from Chapter 10 that the generic `IEnumerable<T>` interface extends the nongeneric `IEnumerable` interface). Add the following extension class to your new project:

```
namespace InterfaceExtensions;
static class AnnoyingExtensions
{
  public static void PrintDataAndBeep(
    this System.Collections.IEnumerable iterator)
  {
    foreach (var item in iterator)
    {
      Console.WriteLine(item);
      Console.Beep();
    }
  }
}
```

Given that the `PrintDataAndBeep()` method can be used by any class or structure that implements `IEnumerable`, you could test via the following code:

```
using InterfaceExtensions;

Console.WriteLine("***** Extending Interface Compatible Types *****\n");

// System.Array implements IEnumerable!
string[] data =
  { "Wow", "this", "is", "sort", "of", "annoying",
      "but", "in", "a", "weird", "way", "fun!"};
data.PrintDataAndBeep();

Console.WriteLine();

// List<T> implements IEnumerable!
List<int> myInts = new List<int>() {10, 15, 20};
myInts.PrintDataAndBeep();

Console.ReadLine();
```

That wraps up your examination of C# extension methods. Remember that this language feature can be useful whenever you want to extend the functionality of a type but do not want to subclass (or cannot subclass if the type is sealed), for the purposes of polymorphism. As you will see later in the text, extension methods play a key role for LINQ APIs. In fact, you will see that under the LINQ APIs, one of the most common items being extended is a class or structure implementing (surprise!) the generic version of `IEnumerable`.

Extension Method GetEnumerator Support (New 9.0)

Prior to C# 9.0, to use `foreach` on a class, the `GetEnumerator()` method had to be defined on that class directly. With C# 9.0, the `foreach` method will examine extension methods on the class and, if a `GetEnumerator()` method is found, will use that method to get the `IEnumerator` for that class. To see this in action, add a new Console application named ForEachWithExtensionMethods, and add simplified versions of the `Car` and `Garage` classes from Chapter 8.

```
//Car.cs
namespace ForEachWithExtensionMethods;
class Car
{
  // Car properties.
  public int CurrentSpeed {get; set;} = 0;
  public string PetName {get; set;} = "";

  // Constructors.
  public Car() {}
  public Car(string name, int speed)
  {
    CurrentSpeed = speed;
    PetName = name;
  }

  // See if Car has overheated.
}

//Garage.cs
namespace ForEachWithExtensionMethods;
class Garage
{
  public Car[] CarsInGarage { get; set; }

  // Fill with some Car objects upon startup.
  public Garage()
  {
    CarsInGarage = new Car[4];
    CarsInGarage[0] = new Car("Rusty", 30);
    CarsInGarage[1] = new Car("Clunker", 55);
    CarsInGarage[2] = new Car("Zippy", 30);
    CarsInGarage[3] = new Car("Fred", 30);
  }

}
```

Note that the `Garage` class does not implement `IEnumerable`, nor does it have a `GetEnumerator()` method. The `GetEnumerator()` method is added through the `GarageExtensions` class, shown here:

```
using System.Collections;

namespace ForEachWithExtensionMethods;
```

```
static class GarageExtensions
{
  public static IEnumerator GetEnumerator(this Garage g)
      => g.CarsInGarage.GetEnumerator();
}
```

The code to test this new feature is the same code used to test the `GetEnumerator()` method in Chapter 8. Update `Program.cs` to the following:

```
using ForEachWithExtensionMethods;

Console.WriteLine("***** Support for Extension Method GetEnumerator *****\n");
Garage carLot = new Garage();

// Hand over each car in the collection?
foreach (Car c in carLot)
{
    Console.WriteLine("{0} is going {1} MPH",
        c.PetName, c.CurrentSpeed);
}
```

You will see that the code works, printing to the console the list of cars and their speed.

```
***** Support for Extension Method GetEnumerator *****

Rusty is going 30 MPH
Clunker is going 55 MPH
Zippy is going 30 MPH
Fred is going 30 MPH
```

> **Note** There is a potential drawback to this new feature, in that classes that were never meant to be `foreach`ed could now be `foreach`ed.

Understanding Anonymous Types

As an object-oriented programmer, you know the benefits of defining classes to represent the state and functionality of a given item you are attempting to model. To be sure, whenever you need to define a class that is intended to be reused across projects and that provides numerous bits of functionality through a set of methods, events, properties, and custom constructors, creating a new C# class is common practice.

However, there are other times when you want to define a class simply to model a set of encapsulated (and somehow related) data points without any associated methods, events, or other specialized functionality. Furthermore, what if this type is to be used by only a handful of methods in your program? It would be rather a bother to define a full class definition as shown next when you know full well this class will be used in only a handful of places. To accentuate this point, here is the rough outline of what you might need to do when you need to create a "simple" data type that follows typical value-based semantics:

```
class SomeClass
{
  // Define a set of private member variables...

  // Make a property for each member variable...

  // Override ToString() to account for key member variables...

  // Override GetHashCode() and Equals() to work with value-based equality...
}
```

As you can see, it is not necessarily so simple. Not only do you need to author a fair amount of code, but you have another class to maintain in your system. For temporary data such as this, it would be useful to whip up a custom data type on the fly. For example, let's say you need to build a custom method that receives a set of incoming parameters. You would like to take these parameters and use them to create a new data type for use in this method scope. Further, you would like to quickly print out this data using the typical `ToString()` method and perhaps use other members of `System.Object`. You can do this very thing using anonymous type syntax.

Defining an Anonymous Type

When you define an anonymous type, you do so by using the `var` keyword (see Chapter 3) in conjunction with object initialization syntax (see Chapter 5). You must use the `var` keyword because the compiler will automatically generate a new class definition at compile time (and you never see the name of this class in your C# code). The initialization syntax is used to tell the compiler to create private backing fields and (read-only) properties for the newly created type.

To illustrate, create a new Console Application project named AnonymousTypes. Now, add the following method to your `Program.cs` file, which composes a new type, on the fly, using the incoming parameter data:

```
static void BuildAnonymousType( string make, string color, int currSp )
{
  // Build anonymous type using incoming args.
  var car = new { Make = make, Color = color, Speed = currSp };

  // Note you can now use this type to get the property data!
   Console.WriteLine("You have a {0} {1} going {2} MPH", car.Color, car.Make, car.Speed);

  // Anonymous types have custom implementations of each virtual
  // method of System.Object. For example:
  Console.WriteLine("ToString() == {0}", car.ToString());
}
```

Note that an anonymous type can also be created inline in addition to wrapping the code in a function, as shown here:

```
Console.WriteLine("***** Fun with Anonymous Types *****\n");

// Make an anonymous type representing a car.
var myCar = new { Color = "Bright Pink", Make = "Saab", CurrentSpeed = 55 };
```

```
// Now show the color and make.
Console.WriteLine("My car is a {0} {1}.", myCar.Color, myCar.Make);

// Now call our helper method to build anonymous type via args.
BuildAnonymousType("BMW", "Black", 90);

Console.ReadLine();
```

So, at this point, simply understand that anonymous types allow you to quickly model the "shape" of data with little overhead. This technique is little more than a way to whip up a new data type on the fly, which supports bare-bones encapsulation via properties and acts according to value-based semantics. To understand that last point, let's see how the C# compiler builds out anonymous types at compile time and, specifically, how it overrides the members of `System.Object`.

The Internal Representation of Anonymous Types

All anonymous types are automatically derived from `System.Object` and, therefore, support each of the members provided by this base class. Given this, you could invoke `ToString()`, `GetHashCode()`, `Equals()`, or `GetType()` on the implicitly typed `myCar` object. Assume your `Program.cs` file defines the following static helper function:

```
static void ReflectOverAnonymousType(object obj)
{
  Console.WriteLine("obj is an instance of: {0}",
    obj.GetType().Name);
  Console.WriteLine("Base class of {0} is {1}",
    obj.GetType().Name, obj.GetType().BaseType);
  Console.WriteLine("obj.ToString() == {0}", obj.ToString());
  Console.WriteLine("obj.GetHashCode() == {0}",
    obj.GetHashCode());
  Console.WriteLine();
}
```

Now assume you invoke this method, passing in the `myCar` object as the parameter, like so:

```
Console.WriteLine("***** Fun with Anonymous Types *****\n");

// Make an anonymous type representing a car.
var myCar = new {Color = "Bright Pink", Make = "Saab",
  CurrentSpeed = 55};

// Reflect over what the compiler generated.
ReflectOverAnonymousType(myCar);
...

Console.ReadLine();
```

The output will look like the following:

```
***** Fun with Anonymous Types *****
obj is an instance of: <>f__AnonymousType0`3
Base class of <>f__AnonymousType0`3 is System.Object
obj.ToString() = { Color = Bright Pink, Make = Saab, CurrentSpeed = 55 }
obj.GetHashCode() = -564053045
```

First, notice that, in this example, the myCar object is of type <>f__AnonymousType0`3 (your name may differ). Remember that the assigned type name is completely determined by the compiler and is not directly accessible in your C# code base.

Perhaps most important, notice that each name-value pair defined using the object initialization syntax is mapped to an identically named read-only property and a corresponding private init-only backing field. The following C# code approximates the compiler-generated class used to represent the myCar object (which again can be verified using ildasm.exe):

```
.class private sealed '<>f__AnonymousType0'3'<'<Color>j__TPar',
  '<Make>j__TPar', <CurrentSpeed>j__TPar>'
  extends [Systcm.Runtime][System.Object]
{
  // init-only fields.
  private initonly <Color>j__TPar <Color>i__Field;
  private initonly <CurrentSpeed>j__TPar <CurrentSpeed>i__Field;
  private initonly <Make>j__TPar <Make>i__Field;

  // Default constructor.
  public <>f__AnonymousTypc0(<Color>j__TPar Color,
    <Make>j__TPar Make, <CurrentSpeed>j__TPar CurrentSpeed);
  // Overridden methods.
  public override bool Equals(object value);
  public override int GetHashCode();
  public override string IoString();

  // Read-only properties.
  <Color>j__TPar Color { get; }
  <CurrentSpeed>j__TPar CurrentSpeed { get; }
  <Make>j__TPar Make { get; }
}
```

The Implementation of ToString() and GetHashCode()

All anonymous types automatically derive from System.Object and are provided with an overridden version of Equals(), GetHashCode(), and ToString(). The ToString() implementation simply builds a string from each name-value pair. Here's an example:

```
public override string ToString()
{
  StringBuilder builder = new StringBuilder();
  builder.Append("{ Color = ");
```

```
    builder.Append(this.<Color>i__Field);
    builder.Append(", Make = ");
    builder.Append(this.<Make>i__Field);
    builder.Append(", CurrentSpeed = ");
    builder.Append(this.<CurrentSpeed>i__Field);
    builder.Append(" }");
    return builder.ToString();
}
```

The GetHashCode() implementation computes a hash value using each anonymous type's member variables as input to the System.Collections.Generic.EqualityComparer<T> type. Using this implementation of GetHashCode(), two anonymous types will yield the same hash value if they have the same set of properties that have been assigned the same values. Given this implementation, anonymous types are well suited to be contained within a Hashtable container.

The Semantics of Equality for Anonymous Types

While the implementation of the overridden ToString() and GetHashCode() methods is straightforward, you might be wondering how the Equals() method has been implemented. For example, if you were to define two "anonymous cars" variables that specify the same name-value pairs, would these two variables be considered equal? To see the results firsthand, update your Program.cs class with the following new method:

```
static void EqualityTest()
{
  // Make 2 anonymous classes with identical name/value pairs.
  var firstCar = new { Color = "Bright Pink", Make = "Saab",
    CurrentSpeed = 55 };
  var secondCar = new { Color = "Bright Pink", Make = "Saab",
    CurrentSpeed = 55 };

  // Are they considered equal when using Equals()?
  if (firstCar.Equals(secondCar))
  {
    Console.WriteLine("Same anonymous object!");
  }
  else
  {
    Console.WriteLine("Not the same anonymous object!");
  }

  // Are they considered equal when using ==?
  if (firstCar == secondCar)
  {
    Console.WriteLine("Same anonymous object!");
  }
  else
  {
    Console.WriteLine("Not the same anonymous object!");
  }
```

```
  // Are these objects the same underlying type?
  if (firstCar.GetType().Name == secondCar.GetType().Name)
  {
    Console.WriteLine("We are both the same type!");
  }
  else
  {
    Console.WriteLine("We are different types!");
  }

  // Show all the details.
  Console.WriteLine();
  ReflectOverAnonymousType(firstCar);
  ReflectOverAnonymousType(secondCar);
}
```

When you call this method, the output might be somewhat surprising.

```
My car is a Bright Pink Saab.
You have a Black BMW going 90 MPH
ToString() == { Make = BMW, Color = Black, Speed = 90 }

Same anonymous object!
Not the same anonymous object!
We are both the same type!

obj is an instance of: <>f__AnonymousType0`3
Base class of <>f__AnonymousType0`3 is System.Object
obj.ToString() == { Color = Bright Pink, Make = Saab, CurrentSpeed = 55 }
obj.GetHashCode() == -925496951

obj is an instance of: <>f__AnonymousType0`3
Base class of <>f__AnonymousType0`3 is System.Object
obj.ToString() == { Color = Bright Pink, Make = Saab, CurrentSpeed = 55 }
obj.GetHashCode() == -925496951
```

When you run this test code, you will see that the first conditional test where you call Equals() returns true and, therefore, the message "Same anonymous object!" prints out to the screen. This is because the compiler-generated Equals() method uses value-based semantics when testing for equality (e.g., checking the value of each field of the objects being compared).

However, the second conditional test, which makes use of the C# equality operator (==), prints out "Not the same anonymous object!" This might seem at first glance to be a bit counterintuitive. This result is because anonymous types do *not* receive overloaded versions of the C# equality operators (== and !=). Given this, when you test for equality of anonymous types using the C# equality operators (rather than the Equals() method), the *references*, not the values maintained by the objects, are being tested for equality.

Finally, in the final conditional test (where you examine the underlying type name), you find that the anonymous types are instances of the same compiler-generated class type (in this example, <>f__AnonymousType0`3) because firstCar and secondCar have the same properties (Color, Make, and CurrentSpeed).

This illustrates an important but subtle point: the compiler will generate a new class definition only when an anonymous type contains *unique* names of the anonymous type. Thus, if you declare identical anonymous types (again, meaning the same names) within the same assembly, the compiler generates only a single anonymous type definition.

Anonymous Types Containing Anonymous Types

It is possible to create an anonymous type that is composed of other anonymous types. For example, assume you want to model a purchase order that consists of a timestamp, a price point, and the automobile purchased. Here is a new (slightly more sophisticated) anonymous type representing such an entity:

```
// Make an anonymous type that is composed of another.
var purchaseItem = new {
  TimeBought = DateTime.Now,
  ItemBought = new {Color = "Red", Make = "Saab", CurrentSpeed = 55},
  Price = 34.000};

ReflectOverAnonymousType(purchaseItem);
```

At this point, you should understand the syntax used to define anonymous types, but you might still be wondering exactly where (and when) to use this new language feature. To be blunt, anonymous type declarations should be used sparingly, typically only when making use of the LINQ technology set (see Chapter 13). You would never want to abandon the use of strongly typed classes/structures simply for the sake of doing so, given anonymous types' numerous limitations, which include the following:

- You don't control the name of the anonymous type.
- Anonymous types always extend `System.Object`.
- The fields and properties of an anonymous type are always read-only.
- Anonymous types cannot support events, custom methods, custom operators, or custom overrides.
- Anonymous types are always implicitly sealed.
- Anonymous types are always created using the default constructor.

However, when programming with the LINQ technology set, you will find that in many cases this syntax can be helpful when you want to quickly model the overall *shape* of an entity rather than its functionality.

Working with Pointer Types

And now for the final topic of the chapter, which most likely will be the least used of all C# features for most of your .NET projects.

■ **Note** In the examples that follow, I'm assuming you have some background in C++ pointer manipulation. If this is not true, feel free to skip this topic entirely. Using pointers will not be a common task for most C# applications.

In Chapter 4, you learned that the .NET platform defines two major categories of data: value types and reference types. Truth be told, however, there is a third category: *pointer types*. To work with pointer types, you get specific operators and keywords that allow you to bypass the .NET Runtime's memory management scheme and take matters into your own hands (see Table 11-2).

Table 11-2. *Pointer-centric C# Operators and Keywords*

Operator/Keyword	Meaning in Life
`*`	This operator is used to create a pointer variable (i.e., a variable that represents a direct location in memory). As in C++, this same operator is used for pointer indirection.
`&`	This operator is used to obtain the address of a variable in memory.
`->`	This operator is used to access fields of a type that is represented by a pointer (the unsafe version of the C# dot operator).
`[]`	This operator (in an unsafe context) allows you to index the slot pointed to by a pointer variable (if you're a C++ programmer, you will recall the interplay between a pointer variable and the [] operator).
`++, --`	In an unsafe context, the increment and decrement operators can be applied to pointer types.
`+, -`	In an unsafe context, the addition and subtraction operators can be applied to pointer types.
`==, !=, <, >, <=, =>`	In an unsafe context, the comparison and equality operators can be applied to pointer types.
`Stackalloc`	In an unsafe context, the `stackalloc` keyword can be used to allocate C# arrays directly on the stack.
`Fixed`	In an unsafe context, the `fixed` keyword can be used to temporarily fix a variable so that its address can be found.

Now, before digging into the details, let me again point out that you will *seldom if ever* need to make use of pointer types. Although C# does allow you to drop down to the level of pointer manipulations, understand that the .NET runtime has absolutely no clue of your intentions. Thus, if you mismanage a pointer, you are the one in charge of dealing with the consequences. Given these warnings, when exactly would you need to work with pointer types? There are two common situations.

- You are looking to optimize select parts of your application by directly manipulating memory outside the management of the .NET 5 Runtime.
- You are calling methods of a C-based `.dll` or COM server that demand pointer types as parameters. Even in this case, you can often bypass pointer types in favor of the `System.IntPtr` type and members of the `System.Runtime.InteropServices.Marshal` type.

When you decide to make use of this C# language feature, you are required to inform the C# compiler of your intentions by enabling your project to support "unsafe code." Create a new Console Application project named UnsafeCode, and set the project to support unsafe code by adding the following to the `UnsafeCode.csproj` file:

```
<PropertyGroup>
  <AllowUnsafeBlocks>true</AllowUnsafeBlocks>
</PropertyGroup>
```

Visual Studio 2022 provides a GUI to set this property. Access your project's property page, navigate to the Build tab, and then select the "Allow unsafe code" box. See Figure 11-1.

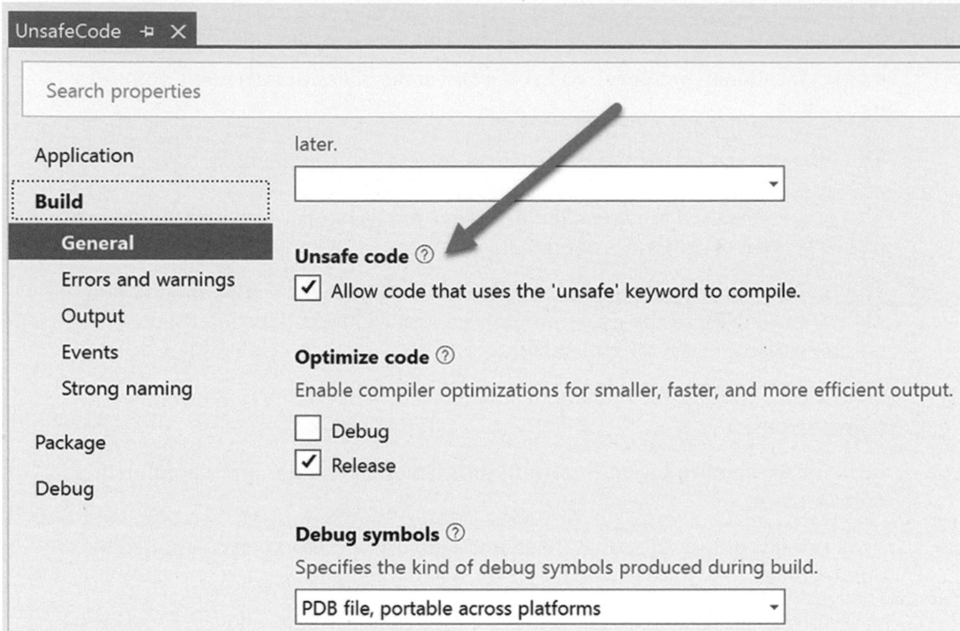

Figure 11-1. *Enabling unsafe code using Visual Studio 2022*

To select the build configuration for the settings, hover over the check box or to the left side of the "Unsafe code" label, and a gear will appear. Click the gear to select where the setting will be applied. See Figure 11-2.

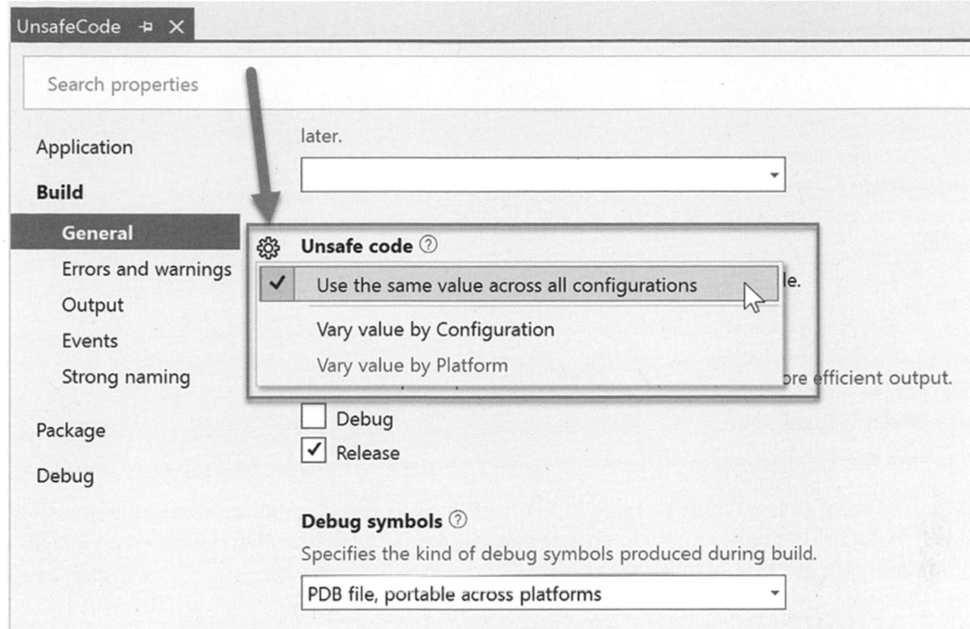

Figure 11-2. *Specifying the configuration(s) for the unsafe code setting*

The unsafe Keyword

When you want to work with pointers in C#, you must specifically declare a block of "unsafe code" using the `unsafe` keyword (any code that is not marked with the `unsafe` keyword is considered "safe" automatically). For example, the following `Program.cs` file declares a scope of unsafe code within the safe top-level statements:

```
using UnsafeCode;

Console.WriteLine("***** Calling method with unsafe code *****");

unsafe
{
  // Work with pointer types here!
}
// Can't work with pointers here!
```

In addition to declaring a scope of unsafe code within a method, you can build structures, classes, type members, and parameters that are "unsafe." Here are a few examples to gnaw on (no need to define the `Node` or `Node2` types in your current project):

```
// This entire structure is "unsafe" and can
// be used only in an unsafe context.
unsafe struct Node
{
```

```
  public int Value;
  public Node* Left;
  public Node* Right;
}

// This struct is safe, but the Node2* members
// are not. Technically, you may access "Value" from
// outside an unsafe context, but not "Left" and "Right".
public struct Node2
{
  public int Value;

  // These can be accessed only in an unsafe context!
  public unsafe Node2* Left;
  public unsafe Node2* Right;
}
```

Methods (static or instance level) may be marked as unsafe as well. For example, assume you know that a static method will make use of pointer logic. To ensure that this method can be called only from an unsafe context, you could define the method as follows:

```
static unsafe void SquareIntPointer(int* myIntPointer)
{
  // Square the value just for a test.
  *myIntPointer *= *myIntPointer;
}
```

The configuration of your method demands that the caller invoke SquareIntPointer() as follows:

```
  unsafe
  {
    int myInt = 10;

    // OK, because we are in an unsafe context.
    SquareIntPointer(&myInt);
    Console.WriteLine("myInt: {0}", myInt);
  }

  int myInt2 = 5;

  // Compiler error! Must be in unsafe context!
  SquareIntPointer(&myInt2);
  Console.WriteLine("myInt: {0}", myInt2);
```

If you would rather not force the caller to wrap the invocation within an unsafe context, you could wrap all the top-level statements with an unsafe block. If you are using a Main() method as entry point, you can update Main() with the unsafe keyword. In this case, the following code would compile:

```
static unsafe void Main(string[] args)
{
  int myInt2 = 5;
```

```
  SquareIntPointer(&myInt2);
  Console.WriteLine("myInt: {0}", myInt2);
}
```

If you run this version of the code, you will see the following output:

```
myInt: 25
```

■ **Note** It is important to note that the term *unsafe* was chosen for a reason. Directly accessing the stack and working with pointers can cause unexpected issues with your application as well as the machine it is running on. If you have to work with unsafe code, be extra diligent.

Working with the * and & Operators

After you have established an unsafe context, you are then free to build pointers to data types using the * operator and obtain the address of what is being pointed to using the & operator. Unlike in C or C++, in C# the * operator is applied to the underlying type only, not as a prefix to each pointer variable name. For example, consider the following code, which illustrates both the correct and incorrect ways to declare pointers to integer variables:

```
// No! This is incorrect under C#!
int *pi, *pj;

// Yes! This is the way of C#.
int* pi, pj;
```

Consider the following unsafe method:

```
static unsafe void PrintValueAndAddress()
{
  int myInt;

  // Define an int pointer, and
  // assign it the address of myInt.
  int* ptrToMyInt = &myInt;

  // Assign value of myInt using pointer indirection.
  *ptrToMyInt = 123;

  // Print some stats.
  Console.WriteLine("Value of myInt {0}", myInt);
  Console.WriteLine("Address of myInt {0:X}", (int)&ptrToMyInt);
}
```

If you run this method from the unsafe block, you will see the following output:

```
**** Print Value And Address ****
Value of myInt 123
Address of myInt 90F7E698
```

An Unsafe (and Safe) Swap Function

Of course, declaring pointers to local variables simply to assign their value (as in the previous example) is never required and not altogether useful. To illustrate a more practical example of unsafe code, assume you want to build a swap function using pointer arithmetic.

```
unsafe static void UnsafeSwap(int* i, int* j)
{
  int temp = *i;
  *i = *j;
  *j = temp;
}
```

Very C-like, don't you think? However, given your work previously, you should be aware that you could write the following safe version of your swap algorithm using the C# `ref` keyword:

```
static void SafeSwap(ref int i, ref int j)
{
  int temp = i;
  i = j;
  j = temp;
}
```

The functionality of each method is identical, thus reinforcing the point that direct pointer manipulation is not a mandatory task under C#. Here is the calling logic using safe top level statements, with an unsafe context:

```
Console.WriteLine("***** Calling method with unsafe code *****");

// Values for swap.
int i = 10, j = 20;

// Swap values "safely."
Console.WriteLine("\n***** Safe swap *****");
Console.WriteLine("Values before safe swap: i = {0}, j = {1}", i, j);
SafeSwap(ref i, ref j);
Console.WriteLine("Values after safe swap: i = {0}, j = {1}", i, j);

// Swap values "unsafely."
Console.WriteLine("\n***** Unsafe swap *****");
Console.WriteLine("Values before unsafe swap: i = {0}, j = {1}", i, j);
unsafe { UnsafeSwap(&i, &j); }

Console.WriteLine("Values after unsafe swap: i = {0}, j = {1}", i, j);
Console.ReadLine();
```

Field Access via Pointers (the -> Operator)

Now assume you have defined a simple, safe Point structure, as follows:

```
struct Point
{
  public int x;
  public int y;

  public override string ToString() => $"({x}, {y})";
}
```

If you declare a pointer to a Point type, you will need to make use of the pointer field-access operator (represented by ->) to access its public members. As shown in Table 11-2, this is the unsafe version of the standard (safe) dot operator (.). In fact, using the pointer indirection operator (*), it is possible to dereference a pointer to (once again) apply the dot operator notation. Check out the unsafe method:

```
static unsafe void UsePointerToPoint()
{
  // Access members via pointer.
  Point;
  Point* p = &point;
  p->x = 100;
  p->y = 200;
  Console.WriteLine(p->ToString());

  // Access members via pointer indirection.
  Point point2;
  Point* p2 = &point2;
  (*p2).x = 100;
  (*p2).y = 200;
  Console.WriteLine((*p2).ToString());
}
```

The stackalloc Keyword

In an unsafe context, you may need to declare a local variable that allocates memory directly from the call stack (and is, therefore, not subject to .NET garbage collection). To do so, C# provides the stackalloc keyword, which is the C# equivalent to the _alloca function of the C runtime library. Here is a simple example:

```
static unsafe string UnsafeStackAlloc()
{
  char* p = stackalloc char[52];
  for (int k = 0; k < 52; k++)
  {
    p[k] = (char)(k + 65)k;
  }
  return new string(p);
}
```

Pinning a Type via the fixed Keyword

As you saw in the previous example, allocating a chunk of memory within an unsafe context may be facilitated via the `stackalloc` keyword. By the very nature of this operation, the allocated memory is cleaned up as soon as the allocating method has returned (as the memory is acquired from the stack). However, assume a more complex example. During our examination of the `->` operator, you created a value type named `Point`. Like all value types, the allocated memory is popped off the stack once the executing scope has terminated. For the sake of argument, assume `Point` was instead defined as a *reference* type, like so:

```
class PointRef // <= Renamed and retyped.
{
  public int x;
  public int y;
  public override string ToString() => $"({x}, {y})";
}
```

As you are aware, if the caller declares a variable of type `Point`, the memory is allocated on the garbage-collected heap. The burning question then becomes "What if an unsafe context wants to interact with this object (or any object on the heap)?" Given that garbage collection can occur at any moment, imagine the problems encountered when accessing the members of `Point` at the very point in time a sweep of the heap is underway. Theoretically, it is possible that the unsafe context is attempting to interact with a member that is no longer accessible or has been repositioned on the heap after surviving a generational sweep (which is an obvious problem).

To lock a reference type variable in memory from an unsafe context, C# provides the `fixed` keyword. The `fixed` statement sets a pointer to a managed type and "pins" that variable during the execution of the code. Without `fixed`, pointers to managed variables would be of little use, since garbage collection could relocate the variables unpredictably. (In fact, the C# compiler will not allow you to set a pointer to a managed variable except in a `fixed` statement.)

Thus, if you create a `PointRef` object and want to interact with its members, you must write the following code (or receive a compiler error):

```
unsafe static void UseAndPinPoint()
{
  PointRef pt = new PointRef
  {
    x = 5,
    y = 6
  };

  // Pin pt in place so it will not
  // be moved or GC-ed.
  fixed (int* p = &pt.x)
  {
    // Use int* variable here!
  }

  // pt is now unpinned, and ready to be GC-ed once
  // the method completes.
  Console.WriteLine ("Point is: {0}", pt);
}
```

In a nutshell, the fixed keyword allows you to build a statement that locks a reference variable in memory, such that its address remains constant for the duration of the statement (or scope block). Any time you interact with a reference type from within the context of unsafe code, pinning the reference is a must.

The sizeof Keyword

The final unsafe-centric C# keyword to consider is sizeof. As in C++, the C# sizeof keyword is used to obtain the size in bytes of an *intrinsic data type*, but not a custom type, unless within an unsafe context. For example, the following method does not need to be declared "unsafe" as all arguments to the sizeof keyword are intrinsic types:

```
static void UseSizeOfOperator()
{
  Console.WriteLine("The size of short is {0}.", sizeof(short));
  Console.WriteLine("The size of int is {0}.", sizeof(int));
  Console.WriteLine("The size of long is {0}.", sizeof(long));
}
```

However, if you want to get the size of your custom Point structure, you need to update this method as so (note the unsafe keyword has been added):

```
unsafe static void UseSizeOfOperator()
{
...
  unsafe {
    Console.WriteLine("The size of Point is {0}.", sizeof(Point));
  }
}
```

That wraps up the look at some of the more advanced features of the C# programming language. To make sure we are all on the same page here, I again must say that most of your .NET projects might never need to directly use these features (especially pointers). Nevertheless, as you will see in later chapters, some topics are quite useful, if not required, when working with the LINQ APIs, most notably extension methods and anonymous types.

Summary

The purpose of this chapter was to deepen your understanding of the C# programming language. First, you investigated various advanced type construction techniques (indexer methods, overloaded operators, and custom conversion routines).

Next, you examined the role of extension methods and anonymous types. As you'll see in some detail in Chapter 13, these features are useful when working with LINQ-centric APIs (though you can use them anywhere in your code, should they be useful). Recall that anonymous methods allow you to quickly model the "shape" of a type, while extension methods allow you to tack on new functionality to types, without the need to subclass.

You spent the remainder of this chapter examining a small set of lesser-known keywords (sizeof, unsafe, etc.) and during the process learned how to work with raw pointer types. As stated throughout the examination of pointer types, most of your C# applications will never need to use them.

CHAPTER 12

Delegates, Events, and Lambda Expressions

Up to this point in the text, most of the applications you have developed added various bits of code to `Program.cs` as top-level statements, which, in some way or another, sent requests *to* a given object. However, many applications require that an object be able to communicate *back to* the entity that created it using a callback mechanism. While callback mechanisms can be used in any application, they are especially critical for graphical user interfaces in that controls (such as a button) need to invoke external methods under the correct circumstances (when the button is clicked, when the mouse enters the button surface, etc.).

Under the .NET platform, the *delegate* type is the preferred means of defining and responding to callbacks within applications. Essentially, the .NET delegate type is a type-safe object that "points to" a method or a list of methods that can be invoked later. Unlike a traditional C++ function pointer, however, delegates are classes that have built-in support for multicasting.

Note In prior versions of .NET, delegates exposed asynchronous method invocation with `BeginInvoke()/EndInvoke()`. While these are still generated by the compiler, they are not supported under .NET. This is because the `IAsyncResult()/BeginInvoke()` pattern used by delegates has been replaced by the task-based async pattern. For more on asynchronous execution, see Chapter 15.

In this chapter, you will learn how to create and manipulate delegate types, and then you'll investigate the C# `event` keyword, which streamlines the process of working with delegate types. Along the way, you will also examine several delegate-centric and event-centric language features of C#, including anonymous methods and method group conversions.

I wrap up this chapter by examining *lambda expressions*. Using the C# lambda operator (`=>`), you can specify a block of code statements (and the parameters to pass to those code statements) wherever a strongly typed delegate is required. As you will see, a lambda expression is little more than an anonymous method in disguise and provides a simplified approach to working with delegates. In addition, this same operation (as of .NET Framework 4.6 and later) can be used to implement a single-statement method or property using a concise syntax.

A. Troelsen and P. Japikse, *Pro C# 10 with .NET 6*, https://doi.org/10.1007/978-1-4842-7869-7_12

Understanding the Delegate Type

Before formally defining delegates, let's gain a bit of perspective. Historically, the Windows API made frequent use of C-style function pointers to create entities termed *callback functions*, or simply *callbacks*. Using callbacks, programmers were able to configure one function to report back to (call back) another function in the application. With this approach, Windows developers were able to handle button clicking, mouse moving, menu selecting, and general bidirectional communications between two entities in memory.

In the .NET and .NET Core (and .NET 5+) Frameworks, callbacks are accomplished in a type-safe and object-oriented manner using *delegates*. A delegate is a type-safe object that points to another method (or possibly a list of methods) in the application, which can be invoked later. Specifically, a delegate maintains three important pieces of information.

- The *address* of the method on which it makes calls
- The *parameters* (if any) of this method
- The *return type* (if any) of this method

■ **Note** .NET delegates can point to either static or instance methods.

After a delegate object has been created and given the necessary information, it may dynamically invoke the method(s) it points to at runtime.

Defining a Delegate Type in C#

When you want to create a delegate type in C#, you use the `delegate` keyword. The name of your delegate type can be whatever you desire. However, you must define the delegate to match the signature of the method(s) it will point to. For example, the following delegate type (named `BinaryOp`) can point to any method that returns an integer and takes two integers as input parameters (you will build and use this delegate yourself a bit later in this chapter, so hang tight for now):

```
// This delegate can point to any method,
// taking two integers and returning an integer.
public delegate int BinaryOp(int x, int y);
```

When the C# compiler processes delegate types, it automatically generates a sealed class deriving from `System.MulticastDelegate`. This class (in conjunction with its base class, `System.Delegate`) provides the necessary infrastructure for the delegate to hold onto a list of methods to be invoked later. For example, if you were to examine the `BinaryOp` delegate using `ildasm.exe`, you would find some of the details as shown here (you will build this full example in just a moment if you want to check for yourself):

```
// -------------------------------------------------------
//      TypDefName:BinaryOp
//      Extends   : System.MulticastDelegate
//      Method #1
//      -------------------------------------------------------
//              MethodName: .ctor
//              ReturnType: Void
//              2 Arguments
//                      Argument #1:  Object
```

```
//                    Argument #2:  I
//            2 Parameters
//                    (1) ParamToken :Name : object flags: [none]
//                    (2) ParamToken : Name : method flags: [none]
//    Method #2
//    -------------------------------------------------------
//            MethodName: Invoke
//            ReturnType: I4
//            2 Arguments
//                    Argument #1:  I4
//                    Argument #2:  I4
//            2 Parameters
//                    (1) ParamToken : Name : x flags: [none]
//                    (2) ParamToken : Name : y flags: [none] //
//    Method #3
//    -------------------------------------------------------
//            MethodName: BeginInvoke
//            ReturnType: Class System.IAsyncResult
//            4 Arguments
//                    Argument #1:  I4
//                    Argument #2:  I4
//                    Argument #3:  Class System.AsyncCallback
//                    Argument #4:  Object
//            4 Parameters
//                    (1) ParamToken : Name : x flags: [none]
//                    (2) ParamToken : Name : y flags: [none]
//                    (3) ParamToken : Name : callback flags: [none]
//                    (4) ParamToken : Name : object flags: [none]
//
//    Method #4
//    -------------------------------------------------------
//            MethodName: EndInvoke
//            ReturnType: I4 (int32)
//            1 Arguments
//                    Argument #1:  Class System.IAsyncResult
//            1 Parameters
//                    (1) ParamToken : Name : result flags: [none]
```

As you can see, the compiler-generated BinaryOp class defines three public methods. Invoke() is the key method in .NET, as it is used to invoke each method maintained by the delegate object in a *synchronous* manner, meaning the caller must wait for the call to complete before continuing its way. Strangely enough, the synchronous Invoke() method may not need to be called explicitly from your C# code. As you will see in just a bit, Invoke() is called behind the scenes when you use the appropriate C# syntax.

■ **Note** While BeginInvoke() and EndInvoke() are generated, they are not supported when running your code under .NET Core or .NET 5+. This can be frustrating, since you will not receive a compiler error but a runtime error if you use them.

Now, how exactly does the compiler know how to define the Invoke() method? To understand the process, here is the crux of the compiler-generated BinaryOp class type (bold italic marks the items specified by the defined delegate type):

```
sealed class BinaryOp : System.MulticastDelegate
{
  public int Invoke(int x, int y);
...
}
```

First, notice that the parameters and return type defined for the Invoke() method exactly match the definition of the BinaryOp delegate.

Let's see another example. Assume you have defined a delegate type that can point to any method returning a string and receiving three System.Boolean input parameters.

```
public delegate string MyDelegate (bool a, bool b, bool c);
```

This time, the compiler-generated class breaks down as follows:

```
sealed class MyDelegate : System.MulticastDelegate
{
  public string Invoke(bool a, bool b, bool c);
...
}
```

Delegates can also "point to" methods that contain any number of out or ref parameters (as well as array parameters marked with the params keyword). For example, assume the following delegate type:

```
public delegate string MyOtherDelegate(
  out bool a, ref bool b, int c);
```

The signature of the Invoke() method looks as you would expect.

To summarize, a C# delegate type definition results in a sealed class with a compiler-generated method whose parameter and return types are based on the delegate's declaration. The following pseudocode approximates the basic pattern:

```
// This is only pseudo-code!
public sealed class DelegateName : System.MulticastDelegate
{
  public delegateReturnValue Invoke(allDelegateInputRefAndOutParams);
}
```

The System.MulticastDelegate and System.Delegate Base Classes

So, when you build a type using the C# delegate keyword, you are indirectly declaring a class type that derives from System.MulticastDelegate. This class provides descendants with access to a list that contains the addresses of the methods maintained by the delegate object, as well as several additional methods (and a few overloaded operators) to interact with the invocation list. Here are some select members of System.MulticastDelegate:

```
public abstract class MulticastDelegate : Delegate
{
  // Returns the list of methods "pointed to."
  public sealed override Delegate[] GetInvocationList();

  // Overloaded operators.
  public static bool operator ==
    (MulticastDelegate d1, MulticastDelegate d2);
  public static bool operator !=
    (MulticastDelegate d1, MulticastDelegate d2);

  // Used internally to manage the list of methods maintained by the delegate.
  private IntPtr _invocationCount;
  private object _invocationList;
}
```

System.MulticastDelegate obtains additional functionality from its parent class, System.Delegate. Here is a partial snapshot of the class definition:

```
public abstract class Delegate : ICloneable, ISerializable
{
  // Methods to interact with the list of functions.
  public static Delegate Combine(params Delegate[] delegates);
  public static Delegate Combine(Delegate a, Delegate b);
  public static Delegate Remove(
    Delegate source, Delegate value);
  public static Delegate RemoveAll(
    Delegate source, Delegate value);

  // Overloaded operators.
  public static bool operator ==(Delegate d1, Delegate d2);
  public static bool operator !=(Delegate d1, Delegate d2);

  // Properties that expose the delegate target.
  public MethodInfo Method { get; }
  public object Target { get; }
}
```

Now, understand that you can never directly derive from these base classes in your code (it is a compiler error to do so). Nevertheless, when you use the delegate keyword, you have indirectly created a class that "is-a" MulticastDelegate. Table 12-1 documents the core members common to all delegate types.

Table 12-1. Select Members of System.MulticastDelegate/System.Delegate

Member	Meaning in Life
`Method`	This property returns a `System.Reflection.MethodInfo` object that represents details of a static method maintained by the delegate.
`Target`	If the method to be called is defined at the object level (rather than a static method), `Target` returns an object that represents the method maintained by the delegate. If the value returned from `Target` equals `null`, the method to be called is a static member.
`Combine()`	This static method adds a method to the list maintained by the delegate. In C#, you trigger this method using the overloaded += operator as a shorthand notation.
`GetInvocationList()`	This method returns an array of `System.Delegate` objects, each representing a method that may be invoked.
`Remove() / RemoveAll()`	These static methods remove a method (or all methods) from the delegate's invocation list. In C#, the `Remove()` method can be called indirectly using the overloaded -= operator.

The Simplest Possible Delegate Example

To be sure, delegates can cause some confusion when encountered for the first time. Thus, to get the ball rolling, let's look at a simple Console Application program (named SimpleDelegate) that uses the `BinaryOp` delegate type you've seen previously. Here is the complete code, with analysis to follow:

```
//SimpleMath.cs
namespace SimpleDelegate;
// This class contains methods BinaryOp will
// point to.
public class SimpleMath
{
  public static int Add(int x, int y) => x + y;
  public static int Subtract(int x, int y) => x - y;
}

//Program.cs
using SimpleDelegate;

Console.WriteLine("***** Simple Delegate Example *****\n");

// Create a BinaryOp delegate object that
// "points to" SimpleMath.Add().
BinaryOp b = new BinaryOp(SimpleMath.Add);

// Invoke Add() method indirectly using delegate object.
Console.WriteLine("10 + 10 is {0}", b(10, 10));
Console.ReadLine();
```

```
//Additional type definitions must be placed at the end of the
// top-level statements
// This delegate can point to any method,
// taking two integers and returning an integer.
public delegate int BinaryOp(int x, int y);
```

■ **Note** Recall from Chapter 3 that additional type declarations (in this example the `BinaryOp` delegate) must come after *all* top-level statements.

Again, notice the format of the `BinaryOp` delegate type declaration; it specifies that `BinaryOp` delegate objects can point to any method taking two integers and returning an integer (the actual name of the method pointed to is irrelevant). Here, you have created a class named `SimpleMath`, which defines two static methods that match the pattern defined by the `BinaryOp` delegate.

When you want to assign the target method to a given delegate object, simply pass in the name of the method to the delegate's constructor.

```
// Create a BinaryOp delegate object that
// "points to" SimpleMath.Add().
BinaryOp b = new BinaryOp(SimpleMath.Add);
```

At this point, you can invoke the member pointed to using a syntax that looks like a direct function invocation.

```
// Invoke() is really called here!
Console.WriteLine("10 + 10 is {0}", b(10, 10));
```

Under the hood, the runtime calls the compiler-generated `Invoke()` method on your `MulticastDelegate`-derived class. You can verify this for yourself if you open your assembly in `ildasm.exe` and examine the CIL code within the `Main()` method.

```
.method private hidebysig static void '<Main>$'(string[] args) cil managed
{
...
  callvirt   instance int32 BinaryOp::Invoke(int32, int32)
}
```

C# does not require you to explicitly call `Invoke()` within your code base. Because `BinaryOp` can point to methods that take two arguments, the following code statement is also permissible:

```
Console.WriteLine("10 + 10 is {0}", b.Invoke(10, 10));
```

Recall that .NET delegates are *type-safe*. Therefore, if you attempt to create a delegate object pointing to a method that does not match the pattern, you receive a compile-time error. To illustrate, assume the `SimpleMath` class now defines an additional method named `SquareNumber()`, which takes a single integer as input.

```
public class SimpleMath
{
  public static int SquareNumber(int a) => a * a;
}
```

Given that the BinaryOp delegate can point *only* to methods that take two integers and return an integer, the following code is illegal and will not compile:

```
// Compiler error! Method does not match delegate pattern!
BinaryOp b2 = new BinaryOp(SimpleMath.SquareNumber);
```

Investigating a Delegate Object

Let's spice up the current example by creating a static method (named DisplayDelegateInfo()) within the Program.cs file. This method will print out the names of the methods maintained by a delegate object, as well as the name of the class defining the method. To do this, you will iterate over the System.Delegate array returned by GetInvocationList(), invoking each object's Target and Method properties.

```
static void DisplayDelegateInfo(Delegate delObj)
{
  // Print the names of each member in the
  // delegate's invocation list.
  foreach (Delegate d in delObj.GetInvocationList())
  {
    Console.WriteLine("Method Name: {0}", d.Method);
    Console.WriteLine("Type Name: {0}", d.Target);
  }
}
```

Assuming you have updated your Main() method to call this new helper method, as shown here:

```
BinaryOp b = new BinaryOp(SimpleMath.Add);
DisplayDelegateInfo(b);
```

you would find the output shown next:

```
***** Simple Delegate Example *****
Method Name: Int32 Add(Int32, Int32)
Type Name:
10 + 10 is 20
```

Notice that the name of the target class (SimpleMath) is currently *not* displayed when calling the Target property. The reason has to do with the fact that your BinaryOp delegate is pointing to a *static method* and, therefore, there is no object to reference! However, if you update the Add() and Subtract() methods to be non-static (simply by deleting the static keywords), you could create an instance of the SimpleMath class and specify the methods to invoke using the object reference.

```
using SimpleDelegate;

Console.WriteLine("***** Simple Delegate Example *****\n");

// Delegates can also point to instance methods as well.
SimpleMath m = new SimpleMath();
BinaryOp b = new BinaryOp(m.Add);
```

```
// Show information about this object.
DisplayDelegateInfo(b);

Console.WriteLine("10 + 10 is {0}", b(10, 10));
Console.ReadLine();
```

In this case, you would find the output shown here:

```
***** Simple Delegate Example *****
Method Name: Int32 Add(Int32, Int32)
Type Name: SimpleDelegate.SimpleMath
10 + 10 is 20
```

Sending Object State Notifications Using Delegates

Clearly, the previous SimpleDelegate example was intended to be purely illustrative in nature, given that there would be no compelling reason to define a delegate simply to add two numbers. To provide a more realistic use of delegate types, let's use delegates to define a `Car` class that can inform external entities about its current engine state. To do so, you will take the following steps:

1. Define a new delegate type that will be used to send notifications to the caller.
2. Declare a member variable of this delegate in the `Car` class.
3. Create a helper function on the `Car` that allows the caller to specify the method to call back on.
4. Implement the `Accelerate()` method to invoke the delegate's invocation list under the correct circumstances.

To begin, create a new Console Application project named CarDelegate. Now, define a new `Car` class that looks initially like this:

```
namespace CarDelegate;
public class Car
{
  // Internal state data.
  public int CurrentSpeed { get; set; }
  public int MaxSpeed { get; set; } = 100;
  public string PetName { get; set; }

  // Is the car alive or dead?
  private bool _carIsDead;

  // Class constructors.
  public Car() {}
  public Car(string name, int maxSp, int currSp)
  {
    CurrentSpeed = currSp;
    MaxSpeed = maxSp;
```

```
    PetName = name;
  }
}
```

Now, consider the following updates, which address the first three points:

```
public class Car
{
  ...
  // 1) Define a delegate type.
  public delegate void CarEngineHandler(string msgForCaller);

  // 2) Define a member variable of this delegate.
  private CarEngineHandler _listOfHandlers;

  // 3) Add registration function for the caller.
  public void RegisterWithCarEngine(CarEngineHandler methodToCall)
  {
    _listOfHandlers = methodToCall;
  }
}
```

Notice in this example that you define the delegate types directly within the scope of the Car class, which is certainly not necessary but does help enforce the idea that the delegate works naturally with this class. The delegate type, CarEngineHandler, can point to any method taking a single string as input and void as a return value.

Next, note that you declare a private member variable of your delegate type (named _listOfHandlers) and a helper function (named RegisterWithCarEngine()) that allows the caller to assign a method to the delegate's invocation list.

■ **Note** Strictly speaking, you could have defined your delegate member variable as public, therefore avoiding the need to create additional registration methods. However, by defining the delegate member variable as private, you are enforcing encapsulation services and providing a more type-safe solution. You'll revisit the risk of public delegate member variables later in this chapter when you look at the C# event keyword.

At this point, you need to create the Accelerate() method. Recall, the point here is to allow a Car object to send engine-related messages to any subscribed listener. Here is the update:

```
// 4) Implement the Accelerate() method to invoke the delegate's
//    invocation list under the correct circumstances.
public void Accelerate(int delta)
{
  // If this car is "dead," send dead message.
  if (_carIsDead)
  {
    _listOfHandlers?.Invoke("Sorry, this car is dead...");
  }
  else
  {
```

```
      CurrentSpeed += delta;
      // Is this car "almost dead"?
      if (10 == (MaxSpeed - CurrentSpeed))
      {
        _listOfHandlers?.Invoke("Careful buddy! Gonna blow!");
      }
      if (CurrentSpeed >= MaxSpeed)
      {
        _carIsDead = true;
      }
      else
      {
        Console.WriteLine("CurrentSpeed = {0}", CurrentSpeed);
      }
    }
  }
```

Notice that you are using the null propagation syntax when attempting to invoke the methods maintained by the listOfHandlers member variable. The reason is that it will be the job of the caller to allocate these objects by calling the RegisterWithCarEngine() helper method. If the caller does not call this method and you attempt to invoke the delegate's invocation list, you will trigger a NullReferenceException at runtime. Now that you have the delegate infrastructure in place, observe the updates to the Program.cs file, shown here:

```
using CarDelegate;

Console.WriteLine("** Delegates as event enablers **\n");

// First, make a Car object.
Car c1 = new Car("SlugBug", 100, 10);

// Now, tell the car which method to call
// when it wants to send us messages.
c1.RegisterWithCarEngine(
  new Car.CarEngineHandler(OnCarEngineEvent));

// Speed up (this will trigger the events).
Console.WriteLine("***** Speeding up *****");
for (int i = 0; i < 6; i++)
{
  c1.Accelerate(20);
}
Console.ReadLine();

// This is the target for incoming events.
static void OnCarEngineEvent(string msg)
{
  Console.WriteLine("\n*** Message From Car Object ***");
  Console.WriteLine("=> {0}", msg);
  Console.WriteLine("********************\n");
}
```

The code begins by simply making a new Car object. Since you are interested in hearing about the engine events, the next step is to call your custom registration function, RegisterWithCarEngine(). Recall that this method expects to be passed an instance of the nested CarEngineHandler delegate, and as with any delegate, you specify a “method to point to” as a constructor parameter. The trick in this example is that the method in question is located back in the Program.cs file! Again, notice that the OnCarEngineEvent() method is a dead-on match to the related delegate, in that it takes a string as input and returns void. Consider the output of the current example:

```
***** Delegates as event enablers *****
***** Speeding up *****
CurrentSpeed = 30
CurrentSpeed = 50
CurrentSpeed = 70

***** Message From Car Object *****
=> Careful buddy! Gonna blow!
***********************************
CurrentSpeed = 90
***** Message From Car Object *****
=> Sorry, this car is dead...
***********************************
```

Enabling Multicasting

Recall that .NET delegates have the built-in ability to *multicast*. In other words, a delegate object can maintain a list of methods to call, rather than just a single method. When you want to add multiple methods to a delegate object, you simply use the overloaded += operator, rather than a direct assignment. To enable multicasting on the Car class, you could update the RegisterWithCarEngine() method, like so:

```
public class Car
{
  // Now with multicasting support!
  // Note we are now using the += operator, not
  // the assignment operator (=).
  public void RegisterWithCarEngine(
    CarEngineHandler methodToCall)
  {
    _listOfHandlers += methodToCall;
  }
...
}
```

When you use the += operator on a delegate object, the compiler resolves this to a call on the static Delegate.Combine() method. In fact, you could call Delegate.Combine() directly; however, the += operator offers a simpler alternative. There is no need to modify your current RegisterWithCarEngine() method, but here is an example of using Delegate.Combine() rather than the += operator:

```
public void RegisterWithCarEngine( CarEngineHandler methodToCall )
{
  if (_listOfHandlers == null)
  {
    _listOfHandlers = methodToCall;
  }
  else
  {
    _listOfHandlers =
      Delegate.Combine(_listOfHandlers, methodToCall)
        as CarEngineHandler;
  }
}
```

In any case, the caller can now register multiple targets for the same callback notification. Here, the second handler prints the incoming message in uppercase, just for display purposes:

```
Console.WriteLine("***** Delegates as event enablers *****\n");

// First, make a Car object.
Car c1 = new Car("SlugBug", 100, 10);

// Register multiple targets for the notifications.
c1.RegisterWithCarEngine(
  new Car.CarEngineHandler(OnCarEngineEvent));
c1.RegisterWithCarEngine(
  new Car.CarEngineHandler(OnCarEngineEvent2));

// Speed up (this will trigger the events).
Console.WriteLine("***** Speeding up *****");
for (int i = 0; i < 6; i++)
{
  c1.Accelerate(20);
}
Console.ReadLine();

// We now have TWO methods that will be called by the Car
// when sending notifications.
static void OnCarEngineEvent(string msg)
{
  Console.WriteLine("\n*** Message From Car Object ***");
  Console.WriteLine("=> {0}", msg);
  Console.WriteLine("********************************\n");
}

static void OnCarEngineEvent2(string msg)
{
  Console.WriteLine("=> {0}", msg.ToUpper());
}
```

Removing Targets from a Delegate's Invocation List

The Delegate class also defines a static Remove() method that allows a caller to dynamically remove a method from a delegate object's invocation list. This makes it simple to allow the caller to "unsubscribe" from a given notification at runtime. While you could call Delegate.Remove() directly in code, C# developers can use the -= operator as a convenient shorthand notation. Let's add a new method to the Car class that allows a caller to remove a method from the invocation list.

```
public class Car
{
...
  public void UnRegisterWithCarEngine(CarEngineHandler methodToCall)
  {
    _listOfHandlers -= methodToCall;
  }
}
```

With the current updates to the Car class, you could stop receiving the engine notification on the second handler by updating the calling code as follows:

```
Console.WriteLine("***** Delegates as event enablers *****\n");

// First, make a Car object.
Car c1 = new Car("SlugBug", 100, 10);
c1.RegisterWithCarEngine(
  new Car.CarEngineHandler(OnCarEngineEvent));

// This time, hold onto the delegate object,
// so we can unregister later.
Car.CarEngineHandler handler2 =
  new Car.CarEngineHandler(OnCarEngineEvent2);
c1.RegisterWithCarEngine(handler2);

// Speed up (this will trigger the events).
Console.WriteLine("***** Speeding up *****");
for (int i = 0; i < 6; i++)
{
  c1.Accelerate(20);
}

// Unregister from the second handler.
c1.UnRegisterWithCarEngine(handler2);

// We won't see the "uppercase" message anymore!
Console.WriteLine("***** Speeding up *****");
for (int i = 0; i < 6; i++)
{
  c1.Accelerate(20);
}

Console.ReadLine();
```

One difference in this code is that this time you are creating a Car.CarEngineHandler object and storing it in a local variable so you can use this object to unregister with the notification later. Thus, the second time you speed up the Car object, you no longer see the uppercase version of the incoming message data, as you have removed this target from the delegate's invocation list.

Method Group Conversion Syntax

In the previous CarDelegate example, you explicitly created instances of the Car.CarEngineHandler delegate object to register and unregister with the engine notifications.

```
Console.WriteLine("***** Delegates as event enablers *****\n");

Car c1 = new Car("SlugBug", 100, 10);
c1.RegisterWithCarEngine(new Car.CarEngineHandler(OnCarEngineEvent));

Car.CarEngineHandler handler2 =
  new Car.CarEngineHandler(OnCarEngineEvent2);
c1.RegisterWithCarEngine(handler2);
...
```

To be sure, if you need to call any of the inherited members of MulticastDelegate or Delegate, manually creating a delegate variable is the most straightforward way of doing so. However, in most cases, you don't really need to hang onto the delegate object. Rather, you typically need to use the delegate object only to pass in the method name as a constructor parameter.

As a simplification, C# provides a shortcut termed *method group conversion*. This feature allows you to supply a direct method name, rather than a delegate object, when calling methods that take delegates as arguments.

■ **Note** As you will see later in this chapter, you can also use method group conversion syntax to simplify how you register with a C# event.

To illustrate, consider the following updates to the Program.cs file, which uses method group conversion to register and unregister from the engine notifications:

```
...
Console.WriteLine("***** Method Group Conversion *****\n");
Car c2 = new Car();

// Register the simple method name.
c2.RegisterWithCarEngine(OnCarEngineEvent);

Console.WriteLine("***** Speeding up *****");
for (int i = 0; i < 6; i++)
{
  c2.Accelerate(20);
}
```

```
// Unregister the simple method name.
c2.UnRegisterWithCarEngine(OnCarEngineEvent);

// No more notifications!
for (int i = 0; i < 6; i++)
{
  c2.Accelerate(20);
}

Console.ReadLine();
```

Notice that you are not directly allocating the associated delegate object but rather simply specifying a method that matches the delegate's expected signature (a method returning `void` and taking a single `string`, in this case). Understand that the C# compiler is still ensuring type safety. Thus, if the `OnCarEngineEvent()` method did not take a `string` and return `void`, you would be issued a compiler error.

Understanding Generic Delegates

In Chapter 10, I mentioned that C# allows you to define generic delegate types. For example, assume you want to define a delegate type that can call any method returning `void` and receiving a single parameter. If the argument in question may differ, you could model this using a type parameter. To illustrate, consider the following code within a new Console Application project named GenericDelegate:

```
Console.WriteLine("***** Generic Delegates *****\n");

// Register targets.
MyGenericDelegate<string> strTarget =
  new MyGenericDelegate<string>(StringTarget);
strTarget("Some string data");

//Using the method group conversion syntax
MyGenericDelegate<int> intTarget = IntTarget;
intTarget(9);
Console.ReadLine();

static void StringTarget(string arg)
{
  Console.WriteLine("arg in uppercase is: {0}", arg.ToUpper());
}

static void IntTarget(int arg)
{
  Console.WriteLine("++arg is: {0}", ++arg);
}
  // This generic delegate can represent any method
  // returning void and taking a single parameter of type T.
  public delegate void MyGenericDelegate<T>(T arg);
```

Notice that `MyGenericDelegate<T>` defines a single type parameter that represents the argument to pass to the delegate target. When creating an instance of this type, you are required to specify the value of the type parameter, as well as the name of the method the delegate will invoke. Thus, if you specified a string type, you send a string value to the target method.

```
// Create an instance of MyGenericDelegate<T>
// with string as the type parameter.
MyGenericDelegate<string> strTarget = StringTarget;
strTarget("Some string data");
```

Given the format of the `strTarget` object, the `StringTarget()` method must now take a single string as a parameter.

```
static void StringTarget(string arg)
{
  Console.WriteLine(
    "arg in uppercase is: {0}", arg.ToUpper());
}
```

The Generic Action<> and Func<> Delegates

Over the course of this chapter, you have seen that when you want to use delegates to enable callbacks in your applications, you typically follow the steps shown here:

1. Define a custom delegate that matches the format of the method being pointed to.
2. Create an instance of your custom delegate, passing in a method name as a constructor argument.
3. Invoke the method indirectly, via a call to `Invoke()` on the delegate object.

When you take this approach, you typically end up with several custom delegates that might never be used beyond the current task at hand (e.g., `MyGenericDelegate<T>`, `CarEngineHandler`, etc.). While it may certainly be the case that you do indeed need to have a custom, uniquely named delegate type for your project, other times the exact *name* of the delegate type is irrelevant. In many cases, you simply want "some delegate" that takes a set of arguments and possibly has a return value other than `void`. In these cases, you can use the framework's built-in `Action<>` and `Func<>` delegate types. To illustrate their usefulness, create a new Console Application project named ActionAndFuncDelegates.

The generic `Action<>` delegate is defined in the `System` namespace, and you can use this generic delegate to "point to" a method that takes up to *16 arguments* (that ought to be enough!) and returns `void`. Now recall, because `Action<>` is a generic delegate, you will need to specify the underlying types of each parameter as well.

Update your `Program.cs` file to define a new static method that takes three (or so) unique parameters. Here's an example:

```
// This is a target for the Action<> delegate.
static void DisplayMessage(string msg, ConsoleColor txtColor, int printCount)
{
  // Set color of console text.
  ConsoleColor previous = Console.ForegroundColor;
  Console.ForegroundColor = txtColor;
```

```
  for (int i = 0; i < printCount; i++)
  {
    Console.WriteLine(msg);
  }

  // Restore color.
  Console.ForegroundColor = previous;
}
```

Now, rather than building a custom delegate manually to pass the program's flow to the DisplayMessage() method, you can use the out-of-the-box Action<> delegate, as so:

```
Console.WriteLine("***** Fun with Action and Func *****");

// Use the Action<> delegate to point to DisplayMessage.
Action<string, ConsoleColor, int> actionTarget =
  DisplayMessage;
actionTarget("Action Message!", ConsoleColor.Yellow, 5);

Console.ReadLine();
```

As you can see, using the Action<> delegate saves you the bother of defining a custom delegate type. However, recall that the Action<> delegate type can point only to methods that take a void return value. If you want to point to a method that does have a return value (and don't want to bother writing the custom delegate yourself), you can use Func<>.

The generic Func<> delegate can point to methods that (like Action<>) take up to 16 parameters and a custom return value. To illustrate, add the following new method to the Program.cs file:

```
// Target for the Func<> delegate.
static int Add(int x, int y)
{
  return x + y;
}
```

Earlier in the chapter, I had you build a custom BinaryOp delegate to "point to" addition and subtraction methods. However, you can simplify your efforts using a version of Func<> that takes a total of three type parameters. Be aware that the *final* type parameter of Func<> is *always* the return value of the method. Just to solidify that point, assume the Program.cs file also defines the following method:

```
static string SumToString(int x, int y)
{
  return (x + y).ToString();
}
```

Now, the calling code can call each of these methods, as so:

```
Func<int, int, int> funcTarget = Add;
int result = funcTarget.Invoke(40, 40);
Console.WriteLine("40 + 40 = {0}", result);
```

```
Func<int, int, string> funcTarget2 = SumToString;
string sum = funcTarget2(90, 300);
Console.WriteLine(sum);
```

In any case, given that Action<> and Func<> can save you the step of manually defining a custom delegate, you might be wondering if you should use them all the time. The answer, like so many aspects of programming, is "it depends." In many cases, Action<> and Func<> will be the preferred course of action (no pun intended). However, if you need a delegate that has a custom name that you feel helps better capture your problem domain, building a custom delegate is as simple as a single code statement. You'll see both approaches as you work over the remainder of this text.

■ **Note** Many important .NET APIs make considerable use of Action<> and Func<> delegates, including the parallel programming framework and LINQ (among others).

That wraps up our initial look at the delegate type. Next, let's move on to the related topic of the C# event keyword.

Understanding C# Events

Delegates are interesting constructs, in that they enable objects in memory to engage in a two-way conversation. However, working with delegates in the raw can entail the creation of some boilerplate code (defining the delegate, declaring necessary member variables, creating custom registration and unregistration methods to preserve encapsulation, etc.).

Moreover, when you use delegates in the raw as your application's callback mechanism, if you do not define a class's delegate member variables as private, the caller will have direct access to the delegate objects. In this case, the caller could reassign the variable to a new delegate object (effectively deleting the current list of functions to call), and, worse yet, the caller would be able to directly invoke the delegate's invocation list. To demonstrate this problem, create a new Console Application named PublicDelegateProblem and add the following reworking (and simplification) of the Car class from the previous CarDelegate example:

```
namespace PublicDelegateProblem;
public class Car
{
  public delegate void CarEngineHandler(string msgForCaller);

  // Now a public member!
  public CarEngineHandler ListOfHandlers;

  // Just fire out the Exploded notification.
  public void Accelerate(int delta)
  {
    if (ListOfHandlers != null)
    {
      ListOfHandlers("Sorry, this car is dead...");
    }
  }
}
```

Notice that you no longer have private delegate member variables encapsulated with custom registration methods. Because these members are indeed public, the caller can directly access the listOfHandlers member variable and reassign this type to new CarEngineHandler objects and invoke the delegate whenever it so chooses.

```
using PublicDelegateProblem;

Console.WriteLine("***** Agh! No Encapsulation! *****\n");
// Make a Car.
Car myCar = new Car();
// We have direct access to the delegate!
myCar.ListOfHandlers = CallWhenExploded;
myCar.Accelerate(10);

// We can now assign to a whole new object...
// confusing at best.
myCar.ListOfHandlers = CallHereToo;
myCar.Accelerate(10);

// The caller can also directly invoke the delegate!
myCar.ListOfHandlers.Invoke("hee, hee, hee...");
Console.ReadLine();

static void CallWhenExploded(string msg)
{
  Console.WriteLine(msg);
}

static void CallHereToo(string msg)
{
  Console.WriteLine(msg);
}
```

Exposing public delegate members breaks encapsulation, which not only can lead to code that is hard to maintain (and debug) but could also open your application to possible security risks! Here is the output of the current example:

```
***** Agh! No Encapsulation! *****
Sorry, this car is dead...
Sorry, this car is dead...
hee, hee, hee...
```

Obviously, you would not want to give other applications the power to change what a delegate is pointing to or to invoke the members without your permission. Given this, it is common practice to declare private delegate member variables.

The C# event Keyword

As a shortcut, so you don't have to build custom methods to add or remove methods to a delegate's invocation list, C# provides the event keyword. When the compiler processes the event keyword, you are automatically provided with registration and un-registration methods, as well as any necessary member variables for your delegate types. These delegate member variables are *always* declared private, and, therefore, they are not directly exposed from the object firing the event. To be sure, the event keyword can be used to simplify how a custom class sends out notifications to external objects.

Defining an event is a two-step process. First, you need to define a delegate type (or reuse an existing one) that will hold the list of methods to be called when the event is fired. Next, you declare an event (using the C# event keyword) in terms of the related delegate type.

To illustrate the event keyword, create a new console application named CarEvents. In this iteration of the Car class, you will define two events named AboutToBlow and Exploded. These events are associated to a single delegate type named CarEngineHandler. Here are the initial updates to the Car class:

```
namespace CarEvents;
public class Car
{
...
  // This delegate works in conjunction with the
  // Car's events.
  public delegate void CarEngineHandler(string msgForCaller);

  // This car can send these events.
  public event CarEngineHandler Exploded;
  public event CarEngineHandler AboutToBlow;
 ...
}
```

Sending an event to the caller is as simple as specifying the event by name, along with any required parameters as defined by the associated delegate. To ensure that the caller has indeed registered with the event, you will want to check the event against a null value before invoking the delegate's method set. With these points in mind, here is the new iteration of the Car's Accelerate() method:

```
public void Accelerate(int delta)
{
  // If the car is dead, fire Exploded event.
  if (_carIsDead)
  {
    Exploded?.Invoke("Sorry, this car is dead...");
  }
  else
  {
    CurrentSpeed += delta;

    // Almost dead?
    if (10 == MaxSpeed - CurrentSpeed)
    {
      AboutToBlow?.Invoke("Careful buddy! Gonna blow!");
    }

    // Still OK!
    if (CurrentSpeed >= MaxSpeed)
    {
      _carIsDead = true;
```

```
    }
    else
    {
      Console.WriteLine("CurrentSpeed = {0}", CurrentSpeed);
    }
  }
}
```

With this, you have configured the car to send two custom events without having to define custom registration functions or declare delegate member variables. You will see the usage of this new automobile in just a moment, but first let's check the event architecture in a bit more detail.

Events Under the Hood

When the compiler processes the C# event keyword, it generates two hidden methods, one having an add_ prefix and the other having a remove_ prefix. Each prefix is followed by the name of the C# event. For example, the Exploded event results in two hidden methods named add_Exploded() and remove_Exploded(). If you were to check out the CIL instructions behind add_AboutToBlow(), you would find a call to the Delegate.Combine() method. Consider the partial CIL code:

```
.method public hidebysig specialname instance void  add_AboutToBlow(
  class [System.Runtime]System.EventHandler`1<class CarEvents.CarEventArgs> 'value')
  cil managed
  {
...
    IL_000b: call class [System.Runtime]System.Delegate [System.Runtime]System.
    Delegate::Combine(class [System.Runtime]System.Delegate, class [System.Runtime]System.
    Delegate)
...
  } // end of method Car::add_AboutToBlow
```

As you would expect, remove_AboutToBlow() will call Delegate.Remove() on your behalf.

```
.method public hidebysig specialname instance void  remove_AboutToBlow (
  class [System.Runtime]System.EventHandler`1<class CarEvents.CarEventArgs> 'value')
  cil managed
  {
...
    IL_000b:  call class [System.Runtime]System.Delegate [System.Runtime]System.
    Delegate::Remove(class [System.Runtime]System.Delegate, class [System.Runtime]System.
    Delegate)
...
}
```

Finally, the CIL code representing the event itself uses the .addon and .removeon directives to map the names of the correct add_XXX() and remove_XXX() methods to invoke.

```
.event class [System.Runtime]System.EventHandler`1<class CarEvents.CarEventArgs> AboutToBlow
{
  .addon instance void CarEvents.Car::add_AboutToBlow(
```

```
    class [System.Runtime]System.EventHandler`1<class CarEvents.CarEventArgs>)
  .removeon instance void CarEvents.Car::remove_AboutToBlow(
    class [System.Runtime]System.EventHandler`1<class CarEvents.CarEventArgs>)
} // end of event Car::AboutToBlow
```

Now that you understand how to build a class that can send C# events (and are aware that events are little more than a typing time-saver), the next big question is how to listen to the incoming events on the caller's side.

Listening to Incoming Events

C# events also simplify the act of registering the caller-side event handlers. Rather than having to specify custom helper methods, the caller simply uses the += and -= operators directly (which triggers the correct `add_XXX()` or `remove_XXX()` method in the background). When you want to register with an event, follow the pattern shown here:

```
// NameOfObject.NameOfEvent +=
//    new RelatedDelegate(functionToCall);
//
Car.CarEngineHandler d =
  new Car.CarEngineHandler(CarExplodedEventHandler);
myCar.Exploded += d;
```

When you want to detach from a source of events, use the -= operator, using the following pattern:

```
// NameOfObject.NameOfEvent -=
//  new RelatedDelegate(functionToCall);
//
myCar.Exploded -= d;
```

Note that you can also use the method group conversion syntax with events as well:

```
Car.CarEngineHandler d = CarExplodedEventHandler;
myCar.Exploded += d;
```

Given these very predictable patterns, here is the refactored calling code, now using the C# event registration syntax:

```
Console.WriteLine("***** Fun with Events *****\n");
Car c1 = new Car("SlugBug", 100, 10);

// Register event handlers.
c1.AboutToBlow += CarIsAlmostDoomed;
c1.AboutToBlow += CarAboutToBlow;

Car.CarEngineHandler d = CarExploded;
c1.Exploded += d;
```

```
Console.WriteLine("***** Speeding up *****");
for (int i = 0; i < 6; i++)
{
  c1.Accelerate(20);
}

// Remove CarExploded method
// from invocation list.
c1.Exploded -= d;

Console.WriteLine("\n***** Speeding up *****");
for (int i = 0; i < 6; i++)
{
  c1.Accelerate(20);
}
Console.ReadLine();

static void CarAboutToBlow(string msg)
{
  Console.WriteLine(msg);
}

static void CarIsAlmostDoomed(string msg)
{
  Console.WriteLine("=> Critical Message from Car: {0}", msg);
}

static void CarExploded(string msg)
{
  Console.WriteLine(msg);
}
```

Simplifying Event Registration Using Visual Studio

Visual Studio helps with the process of registering event handlers. When you apply the += syntax during event registration, you will find an IntelliSense window displayed, inviting you to hit the Tab key to autocomplete the associated delegate instance (see Figure 12-1), which is captured using *method group conversion syntax.*

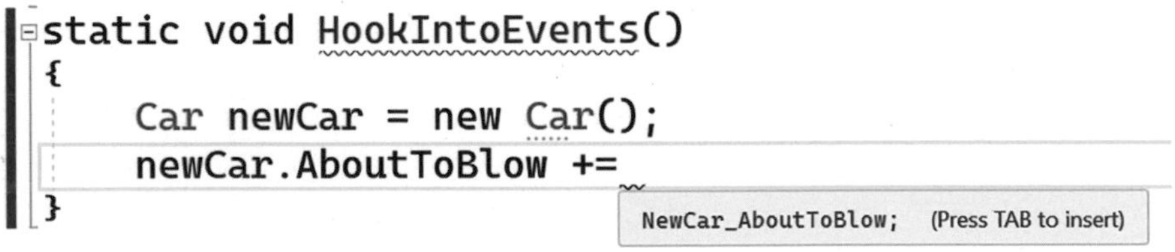

```
static void HookIntoEvents()
{
    Car newCar = new Car();
    newCar.AboutToBlow +=
}
```

NewCar_AboutToBlow; (Press TAB to insert)

Figure 12-1. *Delegate selection IntelliSense*

After you hit the Tab key, the IDE will generate the new method automatically, as shown in Figure 12-2.

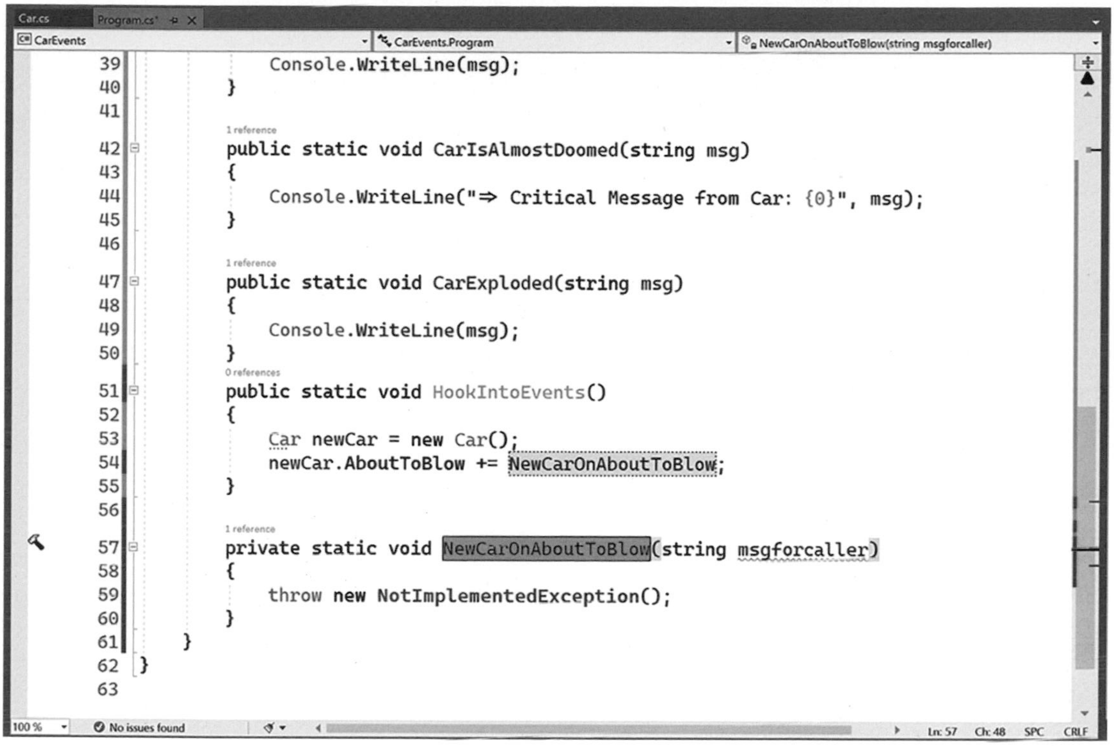

```
        Console.WriteLine(msg);
    }

    public static void CarIsAlmostDoomed(string msg)
    {
        Console.WriteLine("=> Critical Message from Car: {0}", msg);
    }

    public static void CarExploded(string msg)
    {
        Console.WriteLine(msg);
    }
    public static void HookIntoEvents()
    {
        Car newCar = new Car();
        newCar.AboutToBlow += NewCarOnAboutToBlow;
    }

    private static void NewCarOnAboutToBlow(string msgforcaller)
    {
        throw new NotImplementedException();
    }
  }
}
```

Figure 12-2. *Delegate target format IntelliSense*

Note the stub code is in the correct format of the delegate target (note that this method has been declared static because the event was registered within a static method).

```
static void NewCar_AboutToBlow(string msg)
{
  throw new NotImplementedException();
}
```

IntelliSense is available to all .NET events, your custom events, and all the events in the base class libraries. This IDE feature is a massive time-saver, given that it saves you from having to search the help system to figure out both the correct delegate to use with an event and the format of the delegate target method.

Creating Custom Event Arguments

Truth be told, there is one final enhancement you could make to the current iteration of the `Car` class that mirrors Microsoft's recommended event pattern. As you begin to explore the events sent by a given type in the base class libraries, you will find that the first parameter of the underlying delegate is a `System.Object`, while the second parameter is a descendant of `System.EventArgs`.

The System.Object argument represents a reference to the object that sent the event (such as the Car), while the second parameter represents information regarding the event at hand. The System.EventArgs base class represents an event that is not sending any custom information.

```
public class EventArgs
{
  public static readonly EventArgs Empty;
  public EventArgs();
}
```

For simple events, you can pass an instance of EventArgs directly. However, when you want to pass along custom data, you should build a suitable class deriving from EventArgs. For this example, assume you have a class named CarEventArgs, which maintains a string representing the message sent to the receiver.

```
namespace CarEvents;
public class CarEventArgs : EventArgs
{
  public readonly string msg;
  public CarEventArgs(string message)
  {
    msg = message;
  }
}
```

With this, you would now update the CarEngineHandler delegate type definition as follows (the events would be unchanged):

```
public class Car
{
  public delegate void CarEngineHandler(object sender, CarEventArgs e);
...
}
```

Here, when firing the events from within the Accelerate() method, you would now need to supply a reference to the current Car (via the this keyword) and an instance of the CarEventArgs type. For example, consider the following partial update:

```
public void Accelerate(int delta)
{
  // If the car is dead, fire Exploded event.
  if (carIsDead)
  {
    Exploded?.Invoke(this, new CarEventArgs("Sorry, this car is dead..."));
  }
...
}
```

On the caller's side, all you would need to do is update your event handlers to receive the incoming parameters and obtain the message via the read-only field. Here's an example:

```
static void CarAboutToBlow(object sender, CarEventArgs e)
```

```
{
  Console.WriteLine($"{sender} says: {e.msg}");
}
```

If the receiver wants to interact with the object that sent the event, you can explicitly cast the System.Object. From this reference, you can make use of any public member of the object that sent the event notification.

```
static void CarAboutToBlow(object sender, CarEventArgs e)
{
  // Just to be safe, perform a
  // runtime check before casting.
  if (sender is Car c)
  {
    Console.WriteLine(
      $"Critical Message from {c.PetName}: {e.msg}");
  }
}
```

The Generic EventHandler<T> Delegate

Given that so many custom delegates take an object as the first parameter and an EventArgs descendant as the second, you could further streamline the previous example by using the generic EventHandler<T> type, where T is your custom EventArgs type. Consider the following update to the Car type (notice how you no longer need to define a custom delegate type at all):

```
public class Car
{
...
  public event EventHandler<CarEventArgs> Exploded;
  public event EventHandler<CarEventArgs> AboutToBlow;
}
```

The calling code could then use EventHandler<CarEventArgs> anywhere you previously specified CarEventHandler (or, once again, use method group conversion).

```
Console.WriteLine("***** Prim and Proper Events *****\n");

// Make a car as usual.
Car c1 = new Car("SlugBug", 100, 10);

// Register event handlers.
c1.AboutToBlow += CarIsAlmostDoomed;
c1.AboutToBlow += CarAboutToBlow;

EventHandler<CarEventArgs> d = CarExploded;
c1.Exploded += d;
...
```

Great! At this point, you have seen the core aspects of working with delegates and events in the C# language. While you could use this information for just about all your callback needs, you will wrap up this chapter with a look at some final simplifications, specifically anonymous methods and lambda expressions.

Understanding C# Anonymous Methods

As you have seen, when a caller wants to listen to incoming events, it must define a custom method in a class (or structure) that matches the signature of the associated delegate. Here's an example:

```
SomeType t = new SomeType();

// Assume "SomeDelegate" can point to methods taking no
// args and returning void.
t.SomeEvent += new SomeDelegate(MyEventHandler);

// Typically only called by the SomeDelegate object.
static void MyEventHandler()
{
  // Do something when event is fired.
}
```

When you think about it, however, methods such as `MyEventHandler()` are seldom intended to be called by any part of the program other than the invoking delegate. As far as productivity is concerned, it is a bit of a bother (though in no way a showstopper) to manually define a separate method to be called by the delegate object.

To address this point, it is possible to associate an event directly to a block of code statements at the time of event registration. Formally, such code is termed an *anonymous method*. To illustrate the syntax, first create a new Console Application named AnonymousMethods, and copy the `Car.cs` and `CarEventArgs.cs` classes from the CarEvents project into the new project (making sure to change their namespaces to `AnonymousMethods`). Update the `Program.cs` file's code to match the following, which handles the events sent from the `Car` class using anonymous methods, rather than specifically named event handlers:

```
using AnonymousMethods;

Console.WriteLine("***** Anonymous Methods *****\n");
Car c1 = new Car("SlugBug", 100, 10);

// Register event handlers as anonymous methods.
c1.AboutToBlow += delegate
{
  Console.WriteLine("Eek! Going too fast!");
};

c1.AboutToBlow += delegate(object sender, CarEventArgs e)
{
  Console.WriteLine("Message from Car: {0}", e.msg);
};

c1.Exploded += delegate(object sender, CarEventArgs e)
{
```

```
  Console.WriteLine("Fatal Message from Car: {0}", e.msg);
};

// This will eventually trigger the events.
for (int i = 0; i < 6; i++)
{
  c1.Accelerate(20);
}
Console.ReadLine();
```

■ **Note** The final curly bracket of an anonymous method must be terminated by a semicolon. If you fail to do so, you are issued a compilation error.

Again, notice that the calling code no longer needs to define specific static event handlers such as `CarAboutToBlow()` or `CarExploded()`. Rather, the unnamed (aka anonymous) methods are defined inline at the time the caller is handling the event using the += syntax. The basic syntax of an anonymous method matches the following pseudocode:

```
SomeType t = new SomeType();
t.SomeEvent += delegate (optionallySpecifiedDelegateArgs)
{ /* statements */ };
```

When handling the first `AboutToBlow` event within the previous code sample, notice that you are not specifying the arguments passed from the delegate.

```
c1.AboutToBlow += delegate
{
  Console.WriteLine("Eek! Going too fast!");
};
```

Strictly speaking, you are not required to receive the incoming arguments sent by a specific event. However, if you want to make use of the possible incoming arguments, you will need to specify the parameters prototyped by the delegate type (as shown in the second handling of the `AboutToBlow` and `Exploded` events). Here's an example:

```
c1.AboutToBlow += delegate(object sender, CarEventArgs e)
{
  Console.WriteLine("Critical Message from Car: {0}", e.msg);
};
```

Accessing Local Variables

Anonymous methods are interesting, in that they can access the local variables of the method that defines them. Formally speaking, such variables are termed *outer variables* of the anonymous method. The following important points about the interaction between an anonymous method scope and the scope of the defining method should be mentioned:

- An anonymous method cannot access `ref` or `out` parameters of the defining method.

- An anonymous method cannot have a local variable with the same name as a local variable in the outer method.
- An anonymous method can access instance variables (or static variables, as appropriate) in the outer class scope.
- An anonymous method can declare local variables with the same name as outer class member variables (the local variables have a distinct scope and hide the outer class member variables).

Assume your top-level statements define a local integer named `aboutToBlowCounter`. Within the anonymous methods that handle the `AboutToBlow` event, you will increment this counter by one and print out the tally before the statements complete.

```
Console.WriteLine("***** Anonymous Methods *****\n");
int aboutToBlowCounter = 0;

// Make a car as usual.
Car c1 = new Car("SlugBug", 100, 10);

// Register event handlers as anonymous methods.
c1.AboutToBlow += delegate
{
  aboutToBlowCounter++;
  Console.WriteLine("Eek! Going too fast!");
};

c1.AboutToBlow += delegate(object sender, CarEventArgs e)
{
  aboutToBlowCounter++;
  Console.WriteLine("Critical Message from Car: {0}", e.msg);
};
...
// This will eventually trigger the events.
for (int i = 0; i < 6; i++)
{
  c1.Accelerate(20);
}

Console.WriteLine("AboutToBlow event was fired {0} times.",
  aboutToBlowCounter);
Console.ReadLine();
```

After you run this updated code, you will find the final `Console.WriteLine()` reports the `AboutToBlow` event was fired twice.

Using static with Anonymous Methods (New 9.0)

The previous example demonstrated anonymous methods interacting with variables declared outside of the scope of the method itself. While this might be what you intend, it breaks encapsulation and could introduce unintended side effects into your program. Recall from Chapter 4 that local functions can be isolated from the containing code by setting them as static, as in the following example:

```
static int AddWrapperWithStatic(int x, int y)
{
  //Do some validation here
  return Add(x,y);
  static int Add(int x, int y)
  {
    return x + y;
  }
}
```

New in C# 9.0, anonymous methods can also be marked as static to preserve encapsulation and ensure that the method cannot introduce any side effects into the containing code. For example, see the updated anonymous method here:

```
c1.AboutToBlow += static delegate
{
  //This causes a compile error because it is marked static
  aboutToBlowCounter++;
  Console.WriteLine("Eek! Going too fast!");
};
```

The preceding code will not compile due to the anonymous methods attempting to access the variable declared outside its scope. To remove the compile error, comment out (or remove) the line that updates the counter:

```
c1.AboutToBlow += static delegate
{
  //aboutToBlowCounter++;
  Console.WriteLine("Eek! Going too fast!");
};
```

Discards with Anonymous Methods (New 9.0)

Discards, introduced in Chapter 3, have been updated in C# 9.0 for use as input parameters for anonymous methods, with a catch. Because the underscore (_) was a legal variable identifier in previous versions of C#, there must be two or more discards used with the anonymous method to be treated as discards.

For example, the following code created a delegate for a Func that takes two integers and returns another. This implementation ignores any variables passed in and returns 42:

```
Console.WriteLine("******** Discards with Anonymous Methods ********");

Func<int,int,int> constant = delegate (int _, int _) {return 42;};
Console.WriteLine("constant(3,4)={0}",constant(3,4));
```

Understanding Lambda Expressions

To conclude your look at the .NET event architecture, you will examine C# *lambda expressions*. As just explained, C# supports the ability to handle events "inline" by assigning a block of code statements directly to an event using anonymous methods, rather than building a stand-alone method to be called by the underlying delegate. Lambda expressions are nothing more than a concise way to author anonymous methods and ultimately simplify how you work with the .NET delegate type.

To set the stage for your examination of lambda expressions, create a new Console Application project named LambdaExpressions. To begin, consider the `FindAll()` method of the generic `List<T>` class. This method can be called when you need to extract a subset of items from the collection and is prototyped like so:

```
// Method of the System.Collections.Generic.List<T>
public List<T> FindAll(Predicate<T> match)
```

As you can see, this method returns a new `List<T>` that represents the subset of data. Also notice that the sole parameter to `FindAll()` is a generic delegate of type `System.Predicate<T>`. This delegate type can point to any method returning a `bool` and takes a single type parameter as the only input parameter.

```
// This delegate is used by FindAll() method
// to extract out the subset.
public delegate bool Predicate<T>(T obj);
```

When you call `FindAll()`, each item in the `List<T>` is passed to the method pointed to by the `Predicate<T>` object. The implementation of said method will perform some calculations to see whether the incoming data matches the necessary criteria and will return `true` or `false`. If this method returns `true`, the item will be added to the new `List<T>` that represents the subset (got all that?).

Before you see how lambda expressions can simplify working with `FindAll()`, let's work the problem out in longhand notation, using the delegate objects directly. Add a method (named `TraditionalDelegateSyntax()`) within your `Program.cs` file that interacts with the `System.Predicate<T>` type to discover the even numbers in a `List<T>` of integers.

```
using LambdaExpressions;

Console.WriteLine("***** Fun with Lambdas *****\n");
TraditionalDelegateSyntax();
Console.ReadLine();

static void TraditionalDelegateSyntax()
{
  // Make a list of integers.
  List<int> list = new List<int>();
  list.AddRange(new int[] { 20, 1, 4, 8, 9, 44 });

  // Call FindAll() using traditional delegate syntax.
  Predicate<int> callback = IsEvenNumber;
  List<int> evenNumbers = list.FindAll(callback);

  Console.WriteLine("Here are your even numbers:");
  foreach (int evenNumber in evenNumbers)
  {
```

```
    Console.Write("{0}\t", evenNumber);
  }
  Console.WriteLine();
}

// Target for the Predicate<> delegate.
static bool IsEvenNumber(int i)
{
  // Is it an even number?
  return (i % 2) == 0;
}
```

Here, you have a method (`IsEvenNumber()`) that oversees testing the incoming integer parameter to see whether it is even or odd via the C# modulo operator, %. If you execute your application, you will find the numbers 20, 4, 8, and 44 print to the console.

While this traditional approach to working with delegates behaves as expected, the `IsEvenNumber()` method is invoked only in limited circumstances—specifically when you call `FindAll()`, which leaves you with the baggage of a full method definition. While you could make this a local function, if you were to instead use an anonymous method, your code would clean up considerably. Consider the following new method of the `Program.cs` file:

```
static void AnonymousMethodSyntax()
{
  // Make a list of integers.
  List<int> list = new List<int>();
  list.AddRange(new int[] { 20, 1, 4, 8, 9, 44 });

  // Now, use an anonymous method.
  List<int> evenNumbers =
    list.FindAll(delegate(int i) { return (i % 2) == 0; } );

  Console.WriteLine("Here are your even numbers:");
  foreach (int evenNumber in evenNumbers)
  {
    Console.Write("{0}\t", evenNumber);
  }
  Console.WriteLine();
}
```

In this case, rather than directly creating a `Predicate<T>` delegate object and then authoring a stand-alone method, you can inline a method anonymously. While this is a step in the right direction, you are still required to use the `delegate` keyword (or a strongly typed `Predicate<T>`), and you must ensure that the parameter list is a dead-on match.

```
List<int> evenNumbers = list.FindAll(
  delegate(int i)
  {
    return (i % 2) == 0;
  }
);
```

Lambda expressions can be used to simplify the call to FindAll() even more. When you use lambda syntax, there is no trace of the underlying delegate object whatsoever. Consider the following new method to the Program.cs file:

```
static void LambdaExpressionSyntax()
{
  // Make a list of integers.
  List<int> list = new List<int>();
  list.AddRange(new int[] { 20, 1, 4, 8, 9, 44 });

  // Now, use a C# lambda expression.
  List<int> evenNumbers = list.FindAll(i => (i % 2) == 0);

  Console.WriteLine("Here are your even numbers:");
  foreach (int evenNumber in evenNumbers)
  {
    Console.Write("{0}\t", evenNumber);
  }
  Console.WriteLine();
}
```

In this case, notice the rather strange statement of code passed into the FindAll() method, which is in fact a lambda expression. In this iteration of the example, there is no trace whatsoever of the Predicate<T> delegate (or the delegate keyword, for that matter). All you have specified is the lambda expression.

```
i => (i % 2) == 0
```

Before I break this syntax down, first understand that lambda expressions can be used anywhere you would have used an anonymous method or a strongly typed delegate (typically with far fewer keystrokes). Under the hood, the C# compiler translates the expression into a standard anonymous method making use of the Predicate<T> delegate type (which can be verified using ildasm.exe or reflector.exe). Specifically, the following code statement:

```
// This lambda expression...
List<int> evenNumbers = list.FindAll(i => (i % 2) == 0);
```

is compiled into the following approximate C# code:

```
// ...becomes this anonymous method.
List<int> evenNumbers = list.FindAll(delegate (int i)
{
  return (i % 2) == 0;
});
```

Dissecting a Lambda Expression

A lambda expression is written by first defining a parameter list, followed by the => token (C#'s token for the lambda operator found in the *lambda calculus*), followed by a set of statements (or a single statement) that will process these arguments. From a high level, a lambda expression can be understood as follows:

```
ArgumentsToProcess => StatementsToProcessThem
```

Within the LambdaExpressionSyntax() method, things break down like so:

```
// "i" is our parameter list.
// "(i % 2) == 0" is our statement set to process "i".
List<int> evenNumbers = list.FindAll(i => (i % 2) == 0);
```

The parameters of a lambda expression can be explicitly or implicitly typed. Currently, the underlying data type representing the i parameter (an integer) is determined implicitly. The compiler can figure out that i is an integer based on the context of the overall lambda expression and the underlying delegate. However, it is also possible to explicitly define the type of each parameter in the expression by wrapping the data type and variable name in a pair of parentheses, as follows:

```
// Now, explicitly state the parameter type.
List<int> evenNumbers = list.FindAll((int i) => (i % 2) == 0);
```

As you have seen, if a lambda expression has a single, implicitly typed parameter, the parentheses may be omitted from the parameter list. If you want to be consistent regarding your use of lambda parameters, you can *always* wrap the parameter list within parentheses, leaving you with this expression:

```
List<int> evenNumbers = list.FindAll((i) => (i % 2) == 0);
```

Finally, notice that currently the expression has not been wrapped in parentheses (you have of course wrapped the modulo statement to ensure it is executed first before the test for equality). Lambda expressions do allow for the statement to be wrapped as follows:

```
// Now, wrap the expression as well.
List<int> evenNumbers = list.FindAll((i) => ((i % 2) == 0));
```

Now that you have seen the various ways to build a lambda expression, how can you read this lambda statement in human-friendly terms? Leaving the raw mathematics behind, the following explanation fits the bill:

```
// My list of parameters (in this case, a single integer named i)
// will be processed by the expression (i % 2) == 0.
List<int> evenNumbers = list.FindAll((i) => ((i % 2) == 0));
```

Processing Arguments Within Multiple Statements

The first lambda expression was a single statement that ultimately evaluated to a Boolean. However, as you know, many delegate targets must perform several code statements. For this reason, C# allows you to build lambda expressions containing multiple statements by specifying a code block using the standard curly braces. Consider the following example update to the LambdaExpressionSyntax() method:

```
static void LambdaExpressionSyntax()
{
  // Make a list of integers.
  List<int> list = new List<int>();
  list.AddRange(new int[] { 20, 1, 4, 8, 9, 44 });

  // Now process each argument within a group of
  // code statements.
  List<int> evenNumbers = list.FindAll((i) =>
```

```
  {
    Console.WriteLine("value of i is currently: {0}", i);
    bool isEven = ((i % 2) == 0);
    return isEven;
  });

  Console.WriteLine("Here are your even numbers:");
  foreach (int evenNumber in evenNumbers)
  {
    Console.Write("{0}\t", evenNumber);
  }
  Console.WriteLine();
}
```

In this case, the parameter list (again, a single integer named i) is being processed by a set of code statements. Beyond the calls to Console.WriteLine(), the modulo statement has been broken into two code statements for increased readability. Assuming each of the methods you've looked at in this section is called from within your top-level statements:

```
Console.WriteLine("***** Fun with Lambdas *****\n");
TraditionalDelegateSyntax();
AnonymousMethodSyntax();
Console.WriteLine();
LambdaExpressionSyntax();
Console.ReadLine();
```

you will find the following output:

```
***** Fun with Lambdas *****
Here are your even numbers:
20      4       8       44
Here are your even numbers:
20      4       8       44
value of i is currently: 20
value of i is currently: 1
value of i is currently: 4
value of i is currently: 8
value of i is currently: 9
value of i is currently: 44
Here are your even numbers:
20      4       8       44
```

Lambda Expressions with Multiple (or Zero) Parameters

The lambda expressions you have seen in this chapter so far processed a single parameter. This is not a requirement, however, as a lambda expression may process multiple arguments (or none). To illustrate the first scenario of multiple arguments, add the following incarnation of the SimpleMath type:

```
public class SimpleMath
```

```
{
  public delegate void MathMessage(string msg, int result);
  private MathMessage _mmDelegate;

  public void SetMathHandler(MathMessage target)
  {
    _mmDelegate = target;
  }

  public void Add(int x, int y)
  {
    _mmDelegate?.Invoke("Adding has completed!", x + y);
  }
}
```

Notice that the MathMessage delegate type is expecting two parameters. To represent them as a lambda expression, the code might be written as follows:

```
// Register with delegate as a lambda expression.
SimpleMath m = new SimpleMath();
m.SetMathHandler((msg, result) =>
  {Console.WriteLine("Message: {0}, Result: {1}", msg, result);});

// This will execute the lambda expression.
m.Add(10, 10);
Console.ReadLine();
```

Here, you are leveraging type inference, as the two parameters have not been strongly typed for simplicity. However, you could call SetMathHandler(), as follows:

```
m.SetMathHandler((string msg, int result) =>
  {Console.WriteLine("Message: {0}, Result: {1}", msg, result);});
```

Finally, if you are using a lambda expression to interact with a delegate taking no parameters at all, you may do so by supplying a pair of empty parentheses as the parameter. Thus, assuming you have defined the following delegate type:

```
public delegate string VerySimpleDelegate();
```

you could handle the result of the invocation as follows:

```
// Prints "Enjoy your string!" to the console.
VerySimpleDelegate d = new VerySimpleDelegate( () => {return "Enjoy your string!";} );
Console.WriteLine(d());
```

Using the new expression syntax, the previous line can be written like this:

```
VerySimpleDelegate d2 =
  new VerySimpleDelegate(() => "Enjoy your string!");
```

which can also be shortened to this:

```
VerySimpleDelegate d3 = () => "Enjoy your string!";
```

Using static with Lambda Expressions (New 9.0)

Since lambda expressions are shorthand for delegates, it is understandable that lambda also support the `static` keyword (with C# 9.0) as well as discards (covered in the next section). Add the following to your top-level statements:

```
var outerVariable = 0;

Func<int, int, bool> DoWork = (x,y) =>
{
  outerVariable++;
  return true;
};
DoWork(3,4);
Console.WriteLine("Outer variable now = {0}", outerVariable);
```

When this code is executed, it outputs the following:

```
***** Fun with Lambdas *****

Outer variable now = 1
```

If you update the lambda to static, you will receive a compile error since the expression is trying to update a variable declared in an outer scope.

```
var outerVariable = 0;

Func<int, int, bool> DoWork = static (x,y) =>
{
 //Compile error since it's accessing an outer variable
  //outerVariable++;
  return true;
};
```

Discards with Lambda Expressions (New 9.0)

As with delegates (and C# 9.0), input variables to a lambda expression can be replaced with discards if the input variables aren't needed. The same catch applies as with delegates. Since the underscore (_) was a legal variable identifier in previous versions of C#, they must be two or more discards used with the lambda expression.

```
var outerVariable = 0;

Func<int, int, bool> DoWork = (x,y) =>
```

```
{
  outerVariable++;
  return true;
};
DoWork(_,_);
Console.WriteLine("Outer variable now = {0}", outerVariable);
```

Retrofitting the CarEvents Example Using Lambda Expressions

Given that the whole reason for lambda expressions is to provide a clean, concise manner to define an anonymous method (and therefore indirectly a manner to simplify working with delegates), let's retrofit the CarEventArgs project created earlier in this chapter. Here is a simplified version of that project's `Program.cs` file, which makes use of lambda expression syntax (rather than the raw delegates) to hook into each event sent from the `Car` object:

```
using CarEventsWithLambdas;

Console.WriteLine("***** More Fun with Lambdas *****\n");

// Make a car as usual.
Car c1 = new Car("SlugBug", 100, 10);

// Hook into events with lambdas!
c1.AboutToBlow += (sender, e)
  => { Console.WriteLine(e.msg);};
c1.Exploded += (sender, e) => { Console.WriteLine(e.msg); };

// Speed up (this will generate the events).
Console.WriteLine("\n***** Speeding up *****");
for (int i = 0; i < 6; i++)
{
  c1.Accelerate(20);
}
Console.ReadLine();
```

Lambdas and Expression-Bodied Members (Updated 7.0)

Now that you understand lambda expressions and how they work, it should be much clearer how expression-bodied members work under the covers. As mentioned in Chapter 4, as of C# 6, it is permissible to use the => operator to simplify member implementations. Specifically, if you have a method or property (in addition to a custom operator or conversion routine; see Chapter 11) that consists of exactly a single line of code in the implementation, you are not required to define a scope via curly bracket. You can instead leverage the lambda operator and write an expression-bodied member. In C# 7, you can also use this syntax for class constructors, finalizers (covered in Chapter 9), and `get` and `set` accessors on property members.

Be aware, however, this new shortened syntax can be used anywhere at all, even when your code has nothing to do with delegates or events. So, for example, if you were to build a trivial class to add two numbers, you might write the following:

```
class SimpleMath
{
  public int Add(int x, int y)
  {
    return x + y;
  }

  public void PrintSum(int x, int y)
  {
    Console.WriteLine(x + y);
  }
}
```

Alternatively, you could now write code like the following:

```
class SimpleMath
{
  public int Add(int x, int y) =>  x + y;
  public void PrintSum(int x, int y) => Console.WriteLine(x + y);
}
```

Ideally, at this point, you can see the overall role of lambda expressions and understand how they provide a “functional manner” to work with anonymous methods and delegate types. Although the lambda operator (=>) might take a bit to get used to, always remember a lambda expression can be broken down to the following simple equation:

```
ArgumentsToProcess =>
{
  //StatementsToProcessThem
}
```

Or, if using the => operator to implement a single-line type member, it would be like this:

```
TypeMember => SingleCodeStatement
```

It is worth pointing out that the LINQ programming model also makes substantial use of lambda expressions to help simplify your coding efforts. You will examine LINQ beginning in Chapter 13.

Summary

In this chapter, you examined several ways in which multiple objects can partake in a bidirectional conversation. First, you looked at the C# `delegate` keyword, which is used to indirectly construct a class derived from `System.MulticastDelegate`. As you saw, a delegate object maintains the method to call when told to do so.

You then examined the C# `event` keyword, which, when used in conjunction with a delegate type, can simplify the process of sending your event notifications to waiting callers. As shown via the resulting CIL, the .NET event model maps to hidden calls on the `System.Delegate/System.MulticastDelegate` types. In this light, the C# `event` keyword is purely optional, in that it simply saves you some typing time. As well, you have seen that the C# 6.0 null conditional operator simplifies how you safely fire events to any interested party.

This chapter also explored a C# language feature termed *anonymous methods*. Using this syntactic construct, you can directly associate a block of code statements to a given event. As you have seen, anonymous methods are free to ignore the parameters sent by the event and have access to the "outer variables" of the defining method. You also examined a simplified way to register events using *method group conversion*.

Finally, you wrapped things up by looking at the C# *lambda operator*, `=>`. As shown, this syntax is a great shorthand notation for authoring anonymous methods, where a stack of arguments can be passed into a group of statements for processing. Any method in the .NET platform that takes a delegate object as an argument can be substituted with a related lambda expression, which will typically simplify your code base quite a bit.

CHAPTER 13

LINQ to Objects

Regardless of the type of application you are creating using the .NET platform, your program will certainly need to access some form of data as it executes. To be sure, data can be found in numerous locations including XML files, relational databases, in-memory collections, and primitive arrays. Historically speaking, based on the location of said data, programmers needed to use different and unrelated APIs. The Language Integrated Query (LINQ) technology set, introduced initially in .NET 3.5, provides a concise, symmetrical, and strongly typed manner to access a wide variety of data stores. In this chapter, you will begin your investigation of LINQ by focusing on LINQ to Objects.

Before you dive into LINQ to Objects proper, the first part of this chapter quickly reviews the key C# programming constructs that enable LINQ. As you work through this chapter, you will find that implicitly typed local variables, object initialization syntax, lambda expressions, extension methods, and anonymous types will be quite useful (if not occasionally mandatory).

After this supporting infrastructure is reviewed, the remainder of the chapter will introduce you to the LINQ programming model and its role in the .NET platform. Here, you will come to learn the role of query operators and query expressions, which allow you to define statements that will interrogate a data source to yield the requested result set. Along the way, you will build numerous LINQ examples that interact with data contained within arrays as well as various collection types (both generic and nongeneric) and understand the assemblies, namespaces, and types that represent the LINQ to Objects API.

Note The information in this chapter is the foundation for future sections and chapters of this book, including Parallel LINQ (Chapter 15) and Entity Framework Core (Chapters 21 through 23).

LINQ-Specific Programming Constructs

From a high level, LINQ can be understood as a strongly typed query language, embedded directly into the grammar of C#. Using LINQ, you can build any number of expressions that have a look and feel like that of a database SQL query. However, a LINQ query can be applied to any number of data stores, including stores that have nothing to do with a literal relational database.

Note Although LINQ queries can look similar to SQL queries, the syntax is *not* identical. In fact, many LINQ queries seem to be the exact opposite format of a similar database query! If you attempt to map LINQ directly to SQL, you will surely become frustrated. To keep your sanity, I recommend you try your best to regard LINQ queries as unique statements, which just "happen to look" like SQL.

A. Troelsen and P. Japikse, *Pro C# 10 with .NET 6*, https://doi.org/10.1007/978-1-4842-7869-7_13

When LINQ was first introduced to the .NET platform in version 3.5, the C# and VB languages were each expanded with many new programming constructs used to support the LINQ technology set. Specifically, the C# language uses the following core LINQ-centric features:

- Implicitly typed local variables
- Object/collection initialization syntax
- Lambda expressions
- Extension methods
- Anonymous types

These features have already been explored in detail within various chapters of the text. However, to get the ball rolling, let's quickly review each feature in turn, just to make sure we are all in the proper mindset.

■ **Note** Because the following sections are reviews of material covered elsewhere in the book, I have not included a C# code project for this content.

Implicit Typing of Local Variables

In Chapter 3, you learned about the var keyword of C#. This keyword allows you to define a local variable without explicitly specifying the underlying data type. The variable, however, is strongly typed, as the compiler will determine the correct data type based on the initial assignment. Recall this code example from Chapter 3:

```
static void DeclareImplicitVars()
{
  // Implicitly typed local variables.
  var myInt = 0;
  var myBool = true;
  var myString = "Time, marches on...";

  // Print out the underlying type.
  Console.WriteLine("myInt is a: {0}", myInt.GetType().Name);
  Console.WriteLine("myBool is a: {0}",
    myBool.GetType().Name);
  Console.WriteLine("myString is a: {0}",
    myString.GetType().Name);
}
```

This language feature is helpful, and often mandatory, when using LINQ. As you will see during this chapter, many LINQ queries will return a sequence of data types, which are not known until compile time. Given that the underlying data type is not known until the application is compiled, you obviously can't declare a variable explicitly!

Object and Collection Initialization Syntax

Chapter 5 explored the role of object initialization syntax, which allows you to create a class or structure variable and to set any number of its public properties in one fell swoop. The result is a compact (yet still easy on the eyes) syntax that can be used to get your objects ready for use. Also recall from Chapter 10, the C# language allows you to use a similar syntax to initialize collections of objects. Consider the following code snippet, which uses collection initialization syntax to fill a List<T> of Rectangle objects, each of which maintains two Point objects to represent an (x,y) position:

```
List<Rectangle> myListOfRects = new List<Rectangle>
{
  new Rectangle {TopLeft = new Point { X = 10, Y = 10 },
                 BottomRight = new Point { X = 200, Y = 200}},
  new Rectangle {TopLeft = new Point { X = 2, Y = 2 },
                 BottomRight = new Point { X = 100, Y = 100}},
  new Rectangle {TopLeft = new Point { X = 5, Y = 5 },
                 BottomRight = new Point { X = 90, Y = 75}}
};
```

While you are never required to use collection/object initialization syntax, doing so results in a more compact code base. Furthermore, this syntax, when combined with implicit typing of local variables, allows you to declare an anonymous type, which is useful when creating a LINQ projection. You'll learn about LINQ projections later in this chapter.

Lambda Expressions

The C# lambda operator (=>) was fully explored in Chapter 12. Recall that this operator allows you to build a lambda expression, which can be used any time you invoke a method that requires a strongly typed delegate as an argument. Lambdas greatly simplify how you work with delegates in that they reduce the amount of code you must author by hand. Recall that a lambda expression can be broken down into the following usage:

```
( ArgumentsToProcess ) => { StatementsToProcessThem }
```

In Chapter 12, I walked you through how to interact with the FindAll() method of the generic List<T> class using three different approaches. After working with the raw Predicate<T> delegate and a C# anonymous method, you eventually arrived at the following (extremely concise) iteration with this lambda expression:

```
static void LambdaExpressionSyntax()
{
  // Make a list of integers.
  List<int> list = new List<int>();
  list.AddRange(new int[] { 20, 1, 4, 8, 9, 44 });

  // C# lambda expression.
  List<int> evenNumbers = list.FindAll(i => (i % 2) == 0);

  Console.WriteLine("Here are your even numbers:");
  foreach (int evenNumber in evenNumbers)
  {
```

```
    Console.Write("{0}\t", evenNumber);
  }
  Console.WriteLine();
}
```

Lambdas will be useful when working with the underlying object model of LINQ. As you will soon find out, the C# LINQ query operators are simply a shorthand notation for calling true-blue methods on a class named `System.Linq.Enumerable`. These methods typically require delegates (the `Func<>` delegate in particular) as parameters, which are used to process your data to yield the correct result set. Using lambdas, you can streamline your code and allow the compiler to infer the underlying delegate.

Extension Methods

C# extension methods allow you to tack on new functionality to existing classes without the need to subclass. As well, extension methods allow you to add new functionality to sealed classes and structures, which could never be subclassed in the first place. Recall from Chapter 11, when you author an extension method, the first parameter is qualified with the `this` keyword and marks the type being extended. Also recall that extension methods must always be defined within a static class and must, therefore, also be declared using the `static` keyword. Here's an example:

```
namespace MyExtensions;
static class ObjectExtensions
{
  // Define an extension method to System.Object.
  public static void DisplayDefiningAssembly(this object obj)
  {
    Console.WriteLine("{0} lives here:\n\t->{1}\n", obj.GetType().Name,
      Assembly.GetAssembly(obj.GetType()));
  }
}
```

To use this extension, an application must import the namespace defining the extension (and possibly add a reference to the external assembly). At this point, simply import the defining namespace and code away.

```
// Since everything extends System.Object, all classes and structures
// can use this extension.
int myInt = 12345678;
myInt.DisplayDefiningAssembly();

System.Data.DataSet d = new System.Data.DataSet();
d.DisplayDefiningAssembly();
```

When you are working with LINQ, you will seldom, if ever, be required to manually build your own extension methods. However, as you create LINQ query expressions, you will be making use of numerous extension methods already defined by Microsoft. In fact, each C# LINQ query operator is a shorthand notation for making a manual call on an underlying extension method, typically defined by the `System.Linq.Enumerable` utility class.

Anonymous Types

The final C# language feature I'd like to quickly review is that of anonymous types, which were explored in Chapter 11. This feature can be used to quickly model the "shape" of data by allowing the compiler to generate a new class definition at compile time, based on a supplied set of name-value pairs. Recall that this type will be composed using value-based semantics, and each virtual method of `System.Object` will be overridden accordingly. To define an anonymous type, declare an implicitly typed variable and specify the data's shape using object initialization syntax.

```
// Make an anonymous type that is composed of another.
var purchaseItem = new {
  TimeBought = DateTime.Now,
  ItemBought =
    new {Color = "Red", Make = "Saab", CurrentSpeed = 55},
  Price = 34.000};
```

LINQ makes frequent use of anonymous types when you want to project new forms of data on the fly. For example, assume you have a collection of `Person` objects and want to use LINQ to obtain information on the age and Social Security number of each. Using a LINQ projection, you can allow the compiler to generate a new anonymous type that contains your information.

Understanding the Role of LINQ

That wraps up the quick review of the C# language features that allow LINQ to work its magic. However, why have LINQ in the first place? Well, as software developers, it is hard to deny that a significant amount of programming time is spent obtaining and manipulating data. When speaking of "data," it is easy to immediately envision information contained within relational databases. However, another popular location for data is within XML documents or simple text files.

Data can be found in numerous places beyond these two common homes for information. For instance, say you have an array or generic `List<T>` type containing 300 integers and you want to obtain a subset that meets a given criterion (e.g., only the odd or even members in the container, only prime numbers, only nonrepeating numbers greater than 50). Or perhaps you are making use of the reflection APIs and need to obtain only metadata descriptions for each class deriving from a parent class within an array of Types. Indeed, data is *everywhere*.

Prior to .NET 3.5, interacting with a flavor of data required programmers to use very diverse APIs. Consider, for example, Table 13-1, which illustrates several common APIs used to access various types of data (I'm sure you can think of many other examples).

Table 13-1. *Ways to Manipulate Various Types of Data*

The Data You Want	How to Obtain It
Relational data	`System.Data.dll`, `System.Data.SqlClient.dll`, etc.
XML document data	`System.Xml.dll`
Metadata tables	The `System.Reflection` namespace
Collections of objects	`System.Array` and the `System.Collections`/`System.Collections.Generic` namespaces

Of course, nothing is wrong with these approaches to data manipulation. In fact, you can (and will) certainly make direct use of ADO.NET, the XML namespaces, reflection services, and the various collection types. However, the basic problem is that each of these APIs is an island unto itself, which offers little in the way of integration. True, it is possible (for example) to save an ADO.NET `DataSet` as XML and then manipulate it via the `System.Xml` namespaces, but nonetheless, data manipulation remains rather asymmetrical.

The LINQ API is an attempt to provide a consistent, symmetrical way programmers can obtain and manipulate "data" in the broad sense of the term. Using LINQ, you can create directly within the C# programming language constructs called *query expressions*. These query expressions are based on numerous query operators that have been intentionally designed to look and feel similar (but not quite identical) to a SQL expression.

The twist, however, is that a query expression can be used to interact with numerous types of data—even data that has nothing to do with a relational database. Strictly speaking, "LINQ" is the term used to describe this overall approach to data access. However, based on where you are applying your LINQ queries, you will encounter various terms, such as the following:

- *LINQ to Objects*: This term refers to the act of applying LINQ queries to arrays and collections.
- *LINQ to XML*: This term refers to the act of using LINQ to manipulate and query XML documents.
- *LINQ to Entities*: This aspect of LINQ allows you to make use of LINQ queries within the ADO.NET Entity Framework (EF) Core API.
- *Parallel LINQ (aka PLINQ)*: This allows for parallel processing of data returned from a LINQ query.

Today, LINQ is an integral part of the .NET base class libraries, managed languages, and Visual Studio itself.

LINQ Expressions Are Strongly Typed

It is also important to point out that a LINQ query expression (unlike a traditional SQL statement) is *strongly typed*. Therefore, the C# compiler will keep you honest and make sure that these expressions are syntactically well formed. Tools such as Visual Studio and Visual Studio Code can use metadata for useful features such as IntelliSense, autocompletion, and so forth.

The Core LINQ Assemblies

The LINQ assemblies are contained in the `System.Linq` namespace, which is provided by the .NET Framework as an implicit global `using`.

Applying LINQ Queries to Primitive Arrays

To begin examining LINQ to Objects, let's build an application that will apply LINQ queries to various array objects. Create a Console Application project named LinqOverArray and define a static helper method within the `Program.cs` file named `QueryOverStrings()`. In this method, create a `string` array containing six or so items of your liking (here, I listed a batch of video games in my library). Make sure to have at least two entries that contain numerical values and a few that have embedded spaces.

```
static void QueryOverStrings()
{
  // Assume we have an array of strings.
  string[] currentVideoGames = {"Morrowind", "Uncharted 2", "Fallout 3", "Daxter", "System
  Shock 2"};
}
```

Now, update Program.cs to invoke QueryOverStrings().

```
Console.WriteLine("***** Fun with LINQ to Objects *****\n");
QueryOverStrings();
Console.ReadLine();
```

When you have any array of data, it is common to extract a subset of items based on a given requirement. Maybe you want to obtain only the subitems that contain a number (e.g., System Shock 2, Uncharted 2, and Fallout 3), have some number of characters, or don't contain embedded spaces (e.g., Morrowind or Daxter). While you could certainly perform such tasks using members of the System.Array type and a bit of elbow grease, LINQ query expressions can greatly simplify the process.

Going on the assumption that you want to obtain from the array only items that contain an embedded blank space and you want these items listed in alphabetical order, you could build the following LINQ query expression:

```
static void QueryOverStrings()
{
  // Assume we have an array of strings.
  string[] currentVideoGames = {"Morrowind", "Uncharted 2", "Fallout 3", "Daxter", "System
  Shock 2"};

  // Build a query expression to find the items in the array
  // that have an embedded space.
  IEnumerable<string> subset =
    from g in currentVideoGames
    where g.Contains(" ")
    orderby g
    select g;

  // Print out the results.
  foreach (string s in subset)
  {
    Console.WriteLine("Item: {0}", s);
  }
}
```

Notice that the query expression created here makes use of the from, in, where, orderby, and select LINQ query operators. You will dig into the formalities of query expression syntax later in this chapter. However, even now you should be able to read this statement roughly as "Give me the items inside of currentVideoGames that contain a space, ordered alphabetically."

Here, each item that matches the search criteria has been given the name g (as in "game"); however, any valid C# variable name would do.

```
IEnumerable<string> subset =
  from game in currentVideoGames
  where game.Contains(" ")
  orderby game
  select game;
```

Notice that the returned sequence is held in a variable named subset, typed as a type that implements the generic version of IEnumerable<T>, where T is of type System.String (after all, you are querying an array of strings). After you obtain the result set, you then simply print out each item using a standard foreach construct. If you run your application, you will find the following output:

```
***** Fun with LINQ to Objects *****
Item: Fallout 3
Item: System Shock 2
Item: Uncharted 2
```

Once Again, Using Extension Methods

The LINQ syntax used earlier (and the rest of this chapter) is referred to as LINQ *query expressions*, which is a format that is like SQL but slightly different. There is another syntax that uses extension methods that will be the syntax used in most of the examples in this book.

Create a new method named QueryOverStringsWithExtensionMethods() and enter the following code:

```
static void QueryOverStringsWithExtensionMethods()
{
  // Assume we have an array of strings.
  string[] currentVideoGames = {"Morrowind", "Uncharted 2", "Fallout 3", "Daxter", "System
  Shock 2"};

  // Build a query expression to find the items in the array
  // that have an embedded space.
  IEnumerable<string> subset =
    currentVideoGames.Where(g => g.Contains(" ")).OrderBy(g => g).Select(g => g);

  // Print out the results.
  foreach (string s in subset)
  {
    Console.WriteLine("Item: {0}", s);
  }
}
```

Everything is the same as the previous method, except for the line in bold. This is using the extension method syntax. This syntax uses lambda expressions within each method to define the operation. For example, the lambda in the Where() method defines the condition (where a value contains a space). Just as in the query expression syntax, the letter used to indicate the value being evaluated in the lambda is arbitrary; I could have used v for video games.

While the results are the same (running this method produces the same output as the previous method using the query expression), you will see soon that the *type* of the result set is slightly different. For most (if not practically all) scenarios, this difference doesn't cause any issues, and the formats can be used interchangeably.

Once Again, Without LINQ

To be sure, LINQ is never mandatory. If you so choose, you could have found the same result set by forgoing LINQ altogether and making use of programming primitives such as `if` statements and `for` loops. Here is a method that yields the same result as the `QueryOverStrings()` method but in a much more verbose manner:

```
static void QueryOverStringsLongHand()
{
  // Assume we have an array of strings.
  string[] currentVideoGames = {"Morrowind", "Uncharted 2", "Fallout 3", "Daxter", "System
  Shock 2"};

  string[] gamesWithSpaces = new string[5];

  for (int i = 0; i < currentVideoGames.Length; i++)
  {
    if (currentVideoGames[i].Contains(" "))
    {
      gamesWithSpaces[i] = currentVideoGames[i];
    }
  }

  // Now sort them.
  Array.Sort(gamesWithSpaces);

  // Print out the results.
  foreach (string s in gamesWithSpaces)
  {
    if( s != null)
    {
      Console.WriteLine("Item: {0}", s);
    }
  }
  Console.WriteLine();
}
```

While I am sure you can think of ways to tweak the previous method, the fact remains that LINQ queries can be used to radically simplify the process of extracting new subsets of data from a source. Rather than building nested loops, complex `if/else` logic, temporary data types, and so on, the C# compiler will perform the dirty work on your behalf, once you create a fitting LINQ query.

Reflecting Over a LINQ Result Set

Now, assume the `Program.cs` file defines an additional helper function named `ReflectOverQueryResults()` that will print out various details of the LINQ result set (note the parameter is a `System.Object` to account for multiple types of result sets).

```
static void ReflectOverQueryResults(object resultSet, string queryType = "Query Expressions")
{
  Console.WriteLine($"***** Info about your query using {queryType} *****");
  Console.WriteLine("resultSet is of type: {0}", resultSet.GetType().Name);
  Console.WriteLine("resultSet location: {0}", resultSet.GetType().Assembly.GetName().Name);
}
```

Update the core of the QueryOverStrings() method to the following:

```
// Build a query expression to find the items in the array
// that have an embedded space.
IEnumerable<string> subset =
  from g in currentVideoGames
  where g.Contains(" ")
  orderby g
  select g;

ReflectOverQueryResults(subset);

// Print out the results.
foreach (string s in subset)
{
  Console.WriteLine("Item: {0}", s);
}
```

When you run the application, you will see the subset variable is really an instance of the generic OrderedEnumerable<TElement, TKey> type (represented as OrderedEnumerable`2), which is an internal abstract type residing in the System.Linq.dll assembly.

```
***** Info about your query using Query Expressions*****
resultSet is of type: OrderedEnumerable`2
resultSet location: System.Linq
```

Make the same change to the QueryOverStringsWithExtensionMethods() method, except for adding "Extension Methods" for the second parameter.

```
// Build a query expression to find the items in the array
// that have an embedded space.
IEnumerable<string> subset =
  currentVideoGames
    .Where(g => g.Contains(" "))
    .OrderBy(g => g)
    .Select(g => g);

ReflectOverQueryResults(subset,"Extension Methods");

// Print out the results.
foreach (string s in subset)
{
  Console.WriteLine("Item: {0}", s);
}
```

When you run the application, you will see the subset variable is an instance of type SelectIPartitionIterator. If you remove Select(g=>g) from the query, you will be back to having an instance of type OrderedEnumerable<TElement, TKey>. What does this all mean? For most developers, not much (if anything). They both derive from IEnumerable<T>, both can be iterated over in the same manner, and both can create a list or an array from their values.

```
***** Info about your query using Extension Methods *****
resultSet is of type: SelectIPartitionIterator`2
resultSet location: System.Linq
```

LINQ and Implicitly Typed Local Variables

While the current sample program makes it relatively easy to determine that the result set can be captured as an enumeration of the `string` object (e.g., `IEnumerable<string>`), I would guess that it is *not* clear that `subset` is really of type `OrderedEnumerable<TElement, TKey>`.

Given that LINQ result sets can be represented using a good number of types in various LINQ-centric namespaces, it would be tedious to define the proper type to hold a result set, because in many cases the underlying type may not be obvious or even directly accessible from your code base (and as you will see, in some cases the type is generated at compile time).

To further accentuate this point, consider the following additional helper method defined within the `Program.cs` file:

```
static void QueryOverInts()
{
  int[] numbers = {10, 20, 30, 40, 1, 2, 3, 8};

  // Print only items less than 10.
  IEnumerable<int> subset = from i in numbers where i < 10 select i;

  foreach (int i in subset)
  {
    Console.WriteLine("Item: {0}", i);
  }
  ReflectOverQueryResults(subset);
}
```

In this case, the `subset` variable is a completely different underlying type. This time, the type implementing the `IEnumerable<int>` interface is a low-level class named `WhereArrayIterator<T>`.

```
Item: 1
Item: 2
Item: 3
Item: 8

***** Info about your query *****
resultSet is of type: WhereArrayIterator`1
resultSet location: System.Linq
```

Given that the exact underlying type of a LINQ query is certainly not obvious, these first examples have represented the query results as an `IEnumerable<T>` variable, where `T` is the type of data in the returned sequence (`string`, `int`, etc.). However, this is still rather cumbersome. To add insult to injury, given that `IEnumerable<T>` extends the nongeneric `IEnumerable` interface, it would also be permissible to capture the result of a LINQ query as follows:

```
System.Collections.IEnumerable subset =
  from i in numbers
  where i < 10
  select i;
```

Thankfully, implicit typing cleans things up considerably when working with LINQ queries.

```
static void QueryOverInts()
{
  int[] numbers = {10, 20, 30, 40, 1, 2, 3, 8};

  // Use implicit typing here...
  var subset = from i in numbers where i < 10 select i;

  // ...and here.
  foreach (var i in subset)
  {
    Console.WriteLine("Item: {0} ", i);
  }
  ReflectOverQueryResults(subset);
}
```

As a rule of thumb, you will always want to make use of implicit typing when capturing the results of a LINQ query. Just remember, however, that (in most cases) the *real* return value is a type implementing the generic `IEnumerable<T>` interface.

Exactly what this type is under the covers (`OrderedEnumerable<TElement, TKey>`, `WhereArrayIterator<T>`, etc.) is irrelevant and not necessary to discover. As shown in the previous code example, you can simply use the `var` keyword within a `foreach` construct to iterate over the fetched data.

LINQ and Extension Methods

Although the current example does not have you author any extension methods directly, you are in fact using them seamlessly in the background. LINQ query expressions can be used to iterate over data containers that implement the generic `IEnumerable<T>` interface. However, the `System.Array` class type (used to represent the array of strings and array of integers) does *not* implement this contract.

```
// The System.Array type does not seem to implement the
// correct infrastructure for query expressions!
public abstract class Array : ICloneable, IList,
  IStructuralComparable, IStructuralEquatable
{
  ...
}
```

While `System.Array` does not directly implement the `IEnumerable<T>` interface, it indirectly gains the required functionality of this type (as well as many other LINQ-centric members) via the static `System.Linq.Enumerable` class type.

This utility class defines a good number of generic extension methods (such as `Aggregate<T>()`, `First<T>()`, `Max<T>()`, etc.), which `System.Array` (and other types) acquires in the background. Thus, if you apply the dot operator on the `currentVideoGames` local variable, you will find a good number of members *not* found within the formal definition of `System.Array`.

The Role of Deferred Execution

Another important point regarding LINQ query expressions is that when they return a sequence, they are not actually evaluated until you iterate over the resulting sequence. Formally speaking, this is termed *deferred execution*. The benefit of this approach is that you can apply the same LINQ query multiple times to the same container and rest assured you are obtaining the latest and greatest results. Consider the following update to the QueryOverInts() method:

```
static void QueryOverInts()
{
  int[] numbers = { 10, 20, 30, 40, 1, 2, 3, 8 };

  // Get numbers less than ten.
  var subset = from i in numbers where i < 10 select i;

  // LINQ statement evaluated here!
  foreach (var i in subset)
  {
    Console.WriteLine("{0} < 10", i);
  }
  Console.WriteLine();
  // Change some data in the array.
  numbers[0] = 4;

  // Evaluated again!
  foreach (var j in subset)
  {
    Console.WriteLine("{0} < 10", j);
  }

  Console.WriteLine();
  ReflectOverQueryResults(subset);
}
```

■ **Note** When a LINQ statement is selecting a single element (using First/FirstOrDefault, Single/SingleOrDefault, or any of the aggregation methods), the query is executed immediately. First, FirstOrDefault, Single, and SingleOrDefault are covered in the next section. The aggregation methods are covered later in this chapter.

If you were to execute the program yet again, you would find the following output. Notice that the second time you iterate over the requested sequence, you find an additional member, as you set the first item in the array to be a value less than ten.

```
1 < 10
2 < 10
3 < 10
8 < 10
```

```
4 < 10
1 < 10
2 < 10
3 < 10
8 < 10
```

One useful aspect of Visual Studio is that if you set a breakpoint before the evaluation of a LINQ query, you can view the contents during a debugging session. Simply locate your mouse cursor over the LINQ result set variable (`subset` in Figure 13-1). When you do, you will be given the option of evaluating the query at that time by expanding the Results View option.

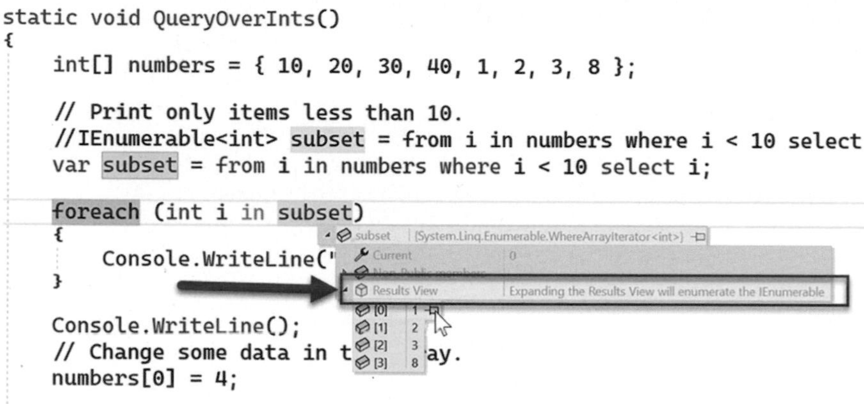

```
static void QueryOverInts()
{
    int[] numbers = { 10, 20, 30, 40, 1, 2, 3, 8 };

    // Print only items less than 10.
    //IEnumerable<int> subset = from i in numbers where i < 10 select i;
    var subset = from i in numbers where i < 10 select i;

    foreach (int i in subset)
    {
        Console.WriteLine('
    }

    Console.WriteLine();
    // Change some data in t    ay.
    numbers[0] = 4;
```


Figure 13-1. *Debugging LINQ expressions*

DefaultIfEmpty (New 10.0)

New to C# 10, the `DefaultIfEmpty()` method returns the elements of the sequence or a default value if the sequence is empty. The query execution is deferred until the list is iterated. The following example shows `DefaultIfEmpty()` in action:

```
static void DefaultWhenEmpty()
{
  Console.WriteLine("Default When Empty");
  int[] numbers = { 10, 20, 30, 40, 1, 2, 3, 8 };

  //Returns all of the numbers
  foreach (var i in numbers.DefaultIfEmpty(-1))
  {
    Console.Write($"{i},");
  }
  Console.WriteLine();
  //Returns -1 since the sequence is empty
  foreach (var i in (from i in numbers where i > 99 select i).DefaultIfEmpty(-1))
  {
```

```
        Console.Write($"{i},");
    }
    Console.WriteLine();
}
```

The Role of Immediate Execution

When you need to evaluate a LINQ expression resulting in a sequence from outside the confines of `foreach` logic, you can call any number of extension methods defined by the `Enumerable` type such as `ToArray<T>()`, `ToDictionary<TSource,TKey>()`, and `ToList<T>()`. These methods will cause a LINQ query to execute at the exact moment you call one of the extension methods to obtain a snapshot of the data. After you have done so, the snapshot of data may be independently manipulated.

Additionally, if you are seeking only a single element, the query is executed immediately. `First()` returns the first member of the sequence (and should always be used with an `OrderBy()` or `OrderByDescending()`). `FirstOrDefault()` returns the default value for the type of item in the list if there aren't any to return, such as when the original sequence is empty or the `Where()` clause filters out all elements. `Single()` also returns the first member of the sequence (based on the `Orderby()`/`OrderByDescending()`, or element order if there isn't an ordering clause). Like its similarly named counterpart, `SingleOrDefault()` returns the default value for the element type if there aren't any items in the sequence (or all records are filtered out by a `where` clause). If no records are returned, `First()` and `Single()` throw an exception that no records were returned, while `FirstOrDefault()` and `SingleOrDefault()` simply return null. The difference between `First()`/`FirstOrDefault()` and `Single()`/`SingleOr()` is that `Single()`/`SingleOrDefault()` will throw an exception if more than one element is returned from the query.

```
static void ImmediateExecution()
{
    Console.WriteLine();
    Console.WriteLine("Immediate Execution");
    int[] numbers = { 10, 20, 30, 40, 1, 2, 3, 8 };

    //get the first element in sequence order
    int number = (from i in numbers select i).First();
    Console.WriteLine("First is {0}", number);

    //get the first in query order
    number = (from i in numbers orderby i select i).First();
    Console.WriteLine("First is {0}", number);

    //get the one element  that matches the query
    number = (from i in numbers where i > 30 select i).Single();
    Console.WriteLine("Single is {0}", number);

  //Return null if nothing is returned
    number = (from i in numbers where i > 99 select i).FirstOrDefault();
    number = (from i in numbers where i > 99 select i).SingleOrDefault();
    try
    {
        //Throw an exception if no records returned
        number = (from i in numbers where i > 99 select i).First();
    }
```

```
    catch (Exception ex)
    {
        Console.WriteLine("An exception occurred: {0}", ex.Message);
    }

    try
    {
        //Throw an exception if no records returned
        number = (from i in numbers where i > 99 select i).Single();
    }
    catch (Exception ex)
    {
        Console.WriteLine("An exception occurred: {0}", ex.Message);
    }

    try
    {
        //Throw an exception if more than one element passes the query
        number = (from i in numbers where i > 10 select i).Single();
    }
    catch (Exception ex)
    {
        Console.WriteLine("An exception occurred: {0}", ex.Message);
    }
  // Get data RIGHT NOW as int[].
  int[] subsetAsIntArray =
    (from i in numbers where i < 10 select i).ToArray<int>();

  // Get data RIGHT NOW as List<int>.
  List<int> subsetAsListOfInts =
    (from i in numbers where i < 10 select i).ToList<int>();
}
```

Notice that the entire LINQ expression is wrapped within parentheses to cast it into the correct underlying type (whatever that might be) to call the extension methods of Enumerable.

Also recall from Chapter 10 that when the C# compiler can unambiguously determine the type parameter of a generic, you are not required to specify the type parameter. Thus, you could also call ToArray() (or ToList() for that matter) as follows:

```
int[] subsetAsIntArray =
  (from i in numbers where i < 10 select i).ToArray();
```

The usefulness of immediate execution is obvious when you need to return the results of a LINQ query to an external caller. And, as luck would have it, this happens to be the next topic of this chapter.

Set Default for [First/Last/Single]OrDefault Methods (New 10)

The FirstOrDefault(), SingleOrDefault(), and LastOrDefault() methods have been updated in .NET 6/C# 10 to allow specification of the default value when the query doesn't return any elements. The base version of these methods automatically sets the default value (0 for a number, null for class, etc.). Now you can programmatically set the default when no record is returned.

Take the following trivial example. The sample LINQ query doesn't return any records. Instead of returning the default value of zero, each of the methods returns a different negative number.

```
static void SettingDefaults()
{
  int[] numbers = Array.Empty<int>();
  var query = from i in numbers where i>100 select i;
  var number = query.FirstOrDefault(-1);
  Console.WriteLine(number);
  number = query.SingleOrDefault(-2);
  Console.WriteLine(number);
  number = query.LastOrDefault(-3);
  Console.WriteLine(number);
}
```

Returning the Result of a LINQ Query

It is possible to define a field within a class (or structure) whose value is the result of a LINQ query. To do so, however, you cannot use implicit typing (as the var keyword cannot be used for fields), and the target of the LINQ query cannot be instance-level data; therefore, it must be static. Given these limitations, you will seldom need to author code like the following:

```
class LINQBasedFieldsAreClunky
{
  private static string[] currentVideoGames =
    {"Morrowind", "Uncharted 2",
    "Fallout 3", "Daxter", "System Shock 2"};

  // Can't use implicit typing here! Must know type of subset!
  private IEnumerable<string> subset =
    from g in currentVideoGames
    where g.Contains(" ")
    orderby g
    select g;

  public void PrintGames()
  {
    foreach (var item in subset)
    {
      Console.WriteLine(item);
    }
  }
}
```

Often, LINQ queries are defined within the scope of a method or property. Moreover, to simplify your programming, the variable used to hold the result set will be stored in an implicitly typed local variable using the var keyword. Now, recall from Chapter 3 that implicitly typed variables cannot be used to define parameters, return values, or fields of a class or structure.

Given this point, you might wonder exactly how you could return a query result to an external caller. The answer is: it depends. If you have a result set consisting of strongly typed data, such as an array of strings or a List<Car>, you could abandon the use of the var keyword and use a proper IEnumerable<T> or IEnumerable type (again, as IEnumerable<T> extends IEnumerable). Consider the following example for a new console application named LinqRetValues:

```
Console.WriteLine("***** LINQ Return Values *****\n");
IEnumerable<string> subset = GetStringSubset();

foreach (string item in subset)
{
  Console.WriteLine(item);
}

Console.ReadLine();

static IEnumerable<string> GetStringSubset()
{
  string[] colors = {"Light Red", "Green", "Yellow", "Dark Red", "Red", "Purple"};
  // Note subset is an IEnumerable<string>-compatible object.
  IEnumerable<string> theRedColors = from c in colors where c.Contains("Red") select c;
  return theRedColors;
}
```

The results are as expected.

```
Light Red
Dark Red
Red
```

Returning LINQ Results via Immediate Execution

This example works as expected, only because the return value of GetStringSubset() and the LINQ query within this method has been strongly typed. If you used the var keyword to define the subset variable, it would be permissible to return the value *only* if the method is still prototyped to return IEnumerable<string> (and if the implicitly typed local variable is in fact compatible with the specified return type).

Because it is a bit inconvenient to operate on IEnumerable<T>, you could use immediate execution. For example, rather than returning IEnumerable<string>, you could simply return a string[], if you transform the sequence to a strongly typed array. Consider this new method of the Program.cs file, which does this very thing:

```
static string[] GetStringSubsetAsArray()
{
  string[] colors = {"Light Red", "Green", "Yellow", "Dark Red", "Red", "Purple"};

  var theRedColors = from c in colors where c.Contains("Red") select c;

  // Map results into an array.
  return theRedColors.ToArray();
}
```

With this, the caller can be blissfully unaware that their result came from a LINQ query and simply work with the array of strings as expected. Here's an example:

```
foreach (string item in GetStringSubsetAsArray())
{
  Console.WriteLine(item);
}
```

Immediate execution is also critical when attempting to return to the caller the results of a LINQ projection. You'll examine this topic a bit later in the chapter. Next up, let's look at how to apply LINQ queries to generic and nongeneric collection objects.

Applying LINQ Queries to Collection Objects

Beyond pulling results from a simple array of data, LINQ query expressions can also manipulate data within members of the System.Collections.Generic namespace, such as the List<T> type. Create a new Console Application project named LinqOverCollections, and define a basic Car class that maintains a current speed, color, make, and pet name, as shown in the following code:

```
namespace LinqOverCollections;
class Car
{
  public string PetName {get; set;} = "";
  public string Color {get; set;} = "";
  public int Speed {get; set;}
  public string Make {get; set;} = "";
}
```

Now, within your top-level statements, define a local List<T> variable of type Car, and make use of object initialization syntax to fill the list with a handful of new Car objects.

```
using System.Collections;
using LinqOverCollections;

Console.WriteLine("***** LINQ over Generic Collections *****\n");

// Make a List<> of Car objects.
List<Car> myCars = new List<Car>() {
  new Car{ PetName = "Henry", Color = "Silver", Speed = 100, Make = "BMW"},
  new Car{ PetName = "Daisy", Color = "Tan", Speed = 90, Make = "BMW"},
  new Car{ PetName = "Mary", Color = "Black", Speed = 55, Make = "VW"},
  new Car{ PetName = "Clunker", Color = "Rust", Speed = 5, Make = "Yugo"},
  new Car{ PetName = "Melvin", Color = "White", Speed = 43, Make = "Ford"}
};

Console.ReadLine();
```

Accessing Contained Subobjects

Applying a LINQ query to a generic container is no different from doing so with a simple array, as LINQ to Objects can be used on any type implementing IEnumerable<T>. This time, your goal is to build a query expression to select only the Car objects within the myCars list, where the speed is greater than 55.

After you get the subset, you will print out the name of each Car object by calling the PetName property. Assume you have the following helper method (taking a List<Car> parameter), which is called from the top-level statements:

```
static void GetFastCars(List<Car> myCars)
{
  // Find all Car objects in the List<>, where the Speed is
  // greater than 55.
  var fastCars = from c in myCars where c.Speed > 55 select c;

  foreach (var car in fastCars)
  {
    Console.WriteLine("{0} is going too fast!", car.PetName);
  }
}
```

Notice that your query expression is grabbing only those items from the List<T> where the Speed property is greater than 55. If you run the application, you will find that Henry and Daisy are the only two items that match the search criteria.

If you want to build a more complex query, you might want to find only the BMWs that have a Speed value greater than 90. To do so, simply build a compound Boolean statement using the C# && operator.

```
static void GetFastBMWs(List<Car> myCars)
  {
  // Find the fast BMWs!
  var fastCars = from c in myCars where c.Speed > 90 && c.Make == "BMW" select c;
  foreach (var car in fastCars)
  {
    Console.WriteLine("{0} is going too fast!", car.PetName);
  }
}
```

In this case, the only pet name printed out is Henry.

Applying LINQ Queries to Nongeneric Collections

Recall that the query operators of LINQ are designed to work with any type implementing IEnumerable<T> (either directly or via extension methods). Given that System.Array has been provided with such necessary infrastructure, it might surprise you that the legacy (nongeneric) containers within System.Collections have not. Thankfully, it is still possible to iterate over data contained within nongeneric collections using the generic Enumerable.OfType<T>() extension method.

When calling OfType<T>() from a nongeneric collection object (such as the ArrayList), simply specify the type of item within the container to extract a compatible IEnumerable<T> object. In code, you can store this data point using an implicitly typed variable.

Consider the following new method, which fills an ArrayList with a set of Car objects (be sure to import the System.Collections namespace into your Program.cs file):

```
static void LINQOverArrayList()
{
  Console.WriteLine("***** LINQ over ArrayList *****");

  // Here is a nongeneric collection of cars.
  ArrayList myCars = new ArrayList() {
    new Car{ PetName = "Henry", Color = "Silver", Speed = 100, Make = "BMW"},
    new Car{ PetName = "Daisy", Color = "Tan", Speed = 90, Make = "BMW"},
    new Car{ PetName = "Mary", Color = "Black", Speed = 55, Make = "VW"},
    new Car{ PetName = "Clunker", Color = "Rust", Speed = 5, Make = "Yugo"},
    new Car{ PetName = "Melvin", Color = "White", Speed = 43, Make = "Ford"}
  };

  // Transform ArrayList into an IEnumerable<T>-compatible type.
  var myCarsEnum = myCars.OfType<Car>();

  // Create a query expression targeting the compatible type.
  var fastCars = from c in myCarsEnum where c.Speed > 55 select c;
  foreach (var car in fastCars)
  {
    Console.WriteLine("{0} is going too fast!", car.PetName);
  }
}
```

Like the previous examples, this method, when called from the top-level statements, will display only the names Henry and Daisy, based on the format of the LINQ query.

Filtering Data Using OfType<T>()

As you know, nongeneric types can contain any combination of items, as the members of these containers (again, such as the ArrayList) are prototyped to receive System.Objects. For example, assume an ArrayList contains a variety of items, only a subset of which are numerical. If you want to obtain a subset that contains only numerical data, you can do so using OfType<T>() since it filters out each element whose type is different from the given type during the iterations.

```
static void OfTypeAsFilter()
{
  // Extract the ints from the ArrayList.
  ArrayList myStuff = new ArrayList();
  myStuff.AddRange(new object[] { 10, 400, 8, false, new Car(), "string data" });
  var myInts = myStuff.OfType<int>();

  // Prints out 10, 400, and 8.
  foreach (int i in myInts)
  {
    Console.WriteLine("Int value: {0}", i);
  }
}
```

At this point, you have had a chance to apply LINQ queries to arrays, generic collections, and nongeneric collections. These containers held both C# primitive types (integers, string data) as well as custom classes. The next task is to learn about many additional LINQ operators that can be used to build more complex and useful queries.

Investigating the C# LINQ Query Operators

C# defines a good number of query operators out of the box. Table 13-2 documents some of the more commonly used query operators. In addition to the partial list of operators shown in Table 13-2, the `System.Linq.Enumerable` class provides a set of methods that do not have a direct C# query operator shorthand notation but are instead exposed as extension methods. These generic methods can be called to transform a result set in various manners (`Reverse<>()`, `ToArray<>()`, `ToList<>()`, etc.). Some are used to extract singletons from a result set, others perform various set operations (`Distinct<>()`, `Union<>()`, `Intersect<>()`, etc.), and still others aggregate results (`Count<>()`, `Sum<>()`, `Min<>()`, `Max<>()`, etc.).

Table 13-2. *Common LINQ Query Operators*

Query Operators	Meaning in Life
`from`, `in`	Used to define the backbone for any LINQ expression, which allows you to extract a subset of data from a fitting container.
`where`	Used to define a restriction for which items to extract from a container.
`select`	Used to select a sequence from the container.
`join`, `on`, `equals`, `into`	Performs joins based on specified key. Remember, these "joins" do not need to have anything to do with data in a relational database.
`orderby`, `ascending`, `descending`	Allows the resulting subset to be ordered in ascending or descending order.
`groupby`	Yields a subset with data grouped by a specified value.

To begin digging into more intricate LINQ queries, create a new Console Application project named FunWithLinqExpressions. Next, you need to define an array or collection of some sample data. For this project, you will make an array of `ProductInfo` objects, defined in the following code:

```
namespace FunWithLinqExpressions;
class ProductInfo
{
  public string Name {get; set;} = "";
  public string Description {get; set;} = "";
  public int NumberInStock {get; set;} = 0;

  public override string ToString()
    => $"Name={Name}, Description={Description}, Number in Stock={NumberInStock}";
}
```

Now populate an array with a batch of `ProductInfo` objects within your calling code.

```
Console.WriteLine("***** Fun with Query Expressions *****\n");

// This array will be the basis of our testing...
ProductInfo[] itemsInStock = new[] {
  new ProductInfo{ Name = "Mac's Coffee", Description = "Coffee with TEETH",
  NumberInStock = 24},
  new ProductInfo{ Name = "Milk Maid Milk", Description = "Milk cow's love",
  NumberInStock = 100},
```

```
    new ProductInfo{ Name = "Pure Silk Tofu", Description = "Bland as Possible",
    NumberInStock = 120},
    new ProductInfo{ Name = "Crunchy Pops", Description = "Cheezy, peppery goodness",
    NumberInStock = 2},
    new ProductInfo{ Name = "RipOff Water", Description = "From the tap to your wallet",
    NumberInStock = 100},
    new ProductInfo{ Name = "Classic Valpo Pizza", Description = "Everyone loves
    pizza!",  NumberInStock = 73}
  };

  // We will call various methods here!
  Console.ReadLine();
```

Basic Selection Syntax

Because the syntactical correctness of a LINQ query expression is validated at compile time, you need to remember that the ordering of these operators is critical. In the simplest terms, every LINQ query expression is built using the from, in, and select operators. Here is the general template to follow:

```
var result =
  from matchingItem in container
  select matchingItem;
```

The item after the from operator represents an item that matches the LINQ query criteria, which can be named anything you choose. The item after the in operator represents the data container to search (an array, collection, XML document, etc.).

Here is a simple query, doing nothing more than selecting every item in the container (similar in behavior to a database Select * SQL statement). Consider the following:

```
static void SelectEverything(ProductInfo[] products)
{
  // Get everything!
  Console.WriteLine("All product details:");
  var allProducts = from p in products select p;

  foreach (var prod in allProducts)
  {
    Console.WriteLine(prod.ToString());
  }
}
```

To be honest, this query expression is not entirely useful, given that your subset is identical to that of the data in the incoming parameter. If you want, you could extract only the Name values of each car using the following selection syntax:

```
static void ListProductNames(ProductInfo[] products)
{
  // Now get only the names of the products.
  Console.WriteLine("Only product names:");
  var names = from p in products select p.Name;
```

```
  foreach (var n in names)
  {
    Console.WriteLine("Name: {0}", n);
  }
}
```

Obtaining Subsets of Data

To obtain a specific subset from a container, you can use the where operator. When doing so, the general template now becomes the following code:

```
var result =
  from item
  in container
  where BooleanExpression
  select item;
```

Notice that the where operator expects an expression that resolves to a Boolean. For example, to extract from the ProductInfo[] argument only the items that have more than 25 items on hand, you could author the following code:

```
static void GetOverstock(ProductInfo[] products)
{
  Console.WriteLine("The overstock items!");

  // Get only the items where we have more than
  // 25 in stock.
  var overstock =
    from p
    in products
    where p.NumberInStock > 25
    select p;

  foreach (ProductInfo c in overstock)
  {
    Console.WriteLine(c.ToString());
  }
}
```

As shown earlier in this chapter, when you are building a where clause, it is permissible to make use of any valid C# operators to build complex expressions. For example, recall this query that extracts only the BMWs going at least 100 MPH:

```
// Get BMWs going at least 100 MPH.
var onlyFastBMWs =
  from c
  in myCars
  where c.Make == "BMW" && c.Speed >= 100
  select c;
```

Paging Data

If you need to get a certain number of records, you can use the Take()/TakeWhile()/TakeLast() and Skip()/SkipWhile()/SkipLast() methods. The first set of methods returns the specified number of records (Take()), all of the records where the condition is true (TakeWhile()), or the last specified number of records (TakeLast()). The second set of methods passes over the specified number of records (Skip()), skips all of the records where the condition is true (SkipWhile()), or skips the last specified number of records (SkipLast()).

These methods are exposed through the IEnumerable interface, so while you can't use the paging operators on the LINQ statements directly, you can use them on the result of the LINQ statement.

Begin by creating a new method named PagingWithLinq(). The first example will take the first three records from the list and then pass the result to a local function for display. The paging methods (like the where clause) participate in deferred execution, so the return type is also an IEnumerable<T>. Here is the method with the first example and local helper function:

```
static void PagingWithLINQ(ProductInfo[] products)
{
  Console.WriteLine("Paging Operations");

  IEnumerable<ProductInfo> list = (from p in products select p).Take(3);
  OutputResults("The first 3",list);

  static void OutputResults(string message, IEnumerable<ProductInfo> products)
  {
    Console.WriteLine(message);
    foreach (ProductInfo c in products)
    {
      Console.WriteLine(c.ToString());
    }
  }
}
```

The TakeWhile() method takes records as long as a condition is true. The condition is passed into the method as a lambda expression, like this:

```
list = (from p in products select p).TakeWhile(x=>x.NumberInStock>20);
OutputResults("All while number in stock > 20",list);
```

The preceding code returns the first three in the list, as the fourth record ("Crunchy Pops") has only two items in stock. It's important to note that the method stops taking records when the condition fails, even though there are two more items that would have passed the condition. If you need to take all the items into consideration, then add an orderby clause to the list before calling TakeWhile().

The TakeLast() method takes the last specified number of records.

```
list = (from p in products select p).TakeLast(2);
OutputResults("The last 2",list);
```

The Skip() and SkipWhile() methods work in the same manner, only skipping records instead of taking records. The next example skips the first three records and then returns the rest:

```
list = (from p in products select p).Skip(3);
OutputResults("Skipping the first 3",list);
```

To skip the records where the number in stock is greater than 20, use the following code. Note that the same issue of sorting exists with SkipWhile() as TakeWhile(). Both methods are best used when the records are sorted accordingly.

```
list = (from p in products select p).SkipWhile(x=>x.NumberInStock>20);
OutputResults("Skip while number in stock > 20",list);
```

The SkipLast() method takes all but the last specified number of records:

```
list = (from p in products select p).SkipLast(2);
OutputResults("All but the last 2",list);
```

These methods can be combined to truly "page" the data. To skip three records and take two, execute the following code:

```
list = (from p in products select p).Skip(3).Take(2);
OutputResults("Skip 3 take 2",list);
```

Paging Data with Ranges (New 10.0)

Support for using ranges in the Take() method has been added in .NET 6/C# 10, enabling paging without needing the Take() and Skip() methods used together. Note that the TakeWhile() and SkipWhile() methods have not been updated to accept ranges.

Here is a new method named PagingWithRanges() that repeats the calls to Take() and Skip() from the previous example, using ranges to retrieve the same data:

```
static void PagingWithRanges(ProductInfo[] products)
{
    Console.WriteLine("Paging Operations");

    IEnumerable<ProductInfo> list = (from p in products select p).Take(..3);
    OutputResults("The first 3",list);

    list = (from p in products select p).Take(3..);
    OutputResults("Skipping the first 3",list);

    list = (from p in products select p).Take(^2..);
    OutputResults("The last 2",list);

    list = (from p in products select p).Take(3..5);
    OutputResults("Skip 3 take 2",list);

    list = (from p in products select p).Take(..^2);
    OutputResults("Skip the last 2",list);

    static void OutputResults(string message, IEnumerable<ProductInfo> products)
    {
        Console.WriteLine(message);
        foreach (ProductInfo c in products)
        {
```

```
            Console.WriteLine(c.ToString());
        }
    }
}
```

Paging Data with Chunks (New 10.0)

Chunk() is another new method for paging has been added in .NET 6/C# 10. This method takes one parameter (size) and then splits the source into an Enumerable of Enumerables. For example, if we take the ProductInfo list and apply Chunk(2), the return value is a list of three lists, each inner list containing two records. If the list can't be split evenly, the last list will hold fewer records.

Here is a new method named PagingWithChunks() that demonstrates the Chunk() method:

```
static void PagingWithChunks(ProductInfo[] products)
{
  Console.WriteLine("Chunking Operations");

  IEnumerable<ProductInfo[]> chunks = products.Chunk(size:2);
  var counter = 0;
  foreach (var chunk in chunks)
  {
    OutputResults($"Chunk #{++counter}",chunk);
  }
  static void OutputResults(string message, IEnumerable<ProductInfo> products)
  {
    Console.WriteLine(message);
    foreach (ProductInfo c in products)
    {
      Console.WriteLine(c.ToString());
    }
  }
}
```

Projecting New Data Types

It is also possible to project new forms of data from an existing data source. Let's assume you want to take the incoming ProductInfo[] parameter and obtain a result set that accounts only for the name and description of each item. To do so, you can define a select statement that dynamically yields a new anonymous type.

```
static void GetNamesAndDescriptions(ProductInfo[] products)
{
  Console.WriteLine("Names and Descriptions:");
  var nameDesc =
    from p
    in products
    select new { p.Name, p.Description };

  foreach (var item in nameDesc)
  {
```

```
    // Could also use Name and Description properties
    // directly.
    Console.WriteLine(item.ToString());
  }
}
```

Always remember that when you have a LINQ query that makes use of a projection, you have no way of knowing the underlying data type, as this is determined at compile time. In these cases, the var keyword is mandatory. As well, recall that you cannot create methods with implicitly typed return values. Therefore, the following method would not compile:

```
static var GetProjectedSubset(ProductInfo[] products)
{
  var nameDesc =
    from p in products select new { p.Name, p.Description };
  return nameDesc; // Nope!
}
```

When you need to return projected data to a caller, one approach is to transform the query result into a System.Array object using the ToArray() extension method. Thus, if you were to update your query expression as follows:

```
// Return value is now an Array.
static Array GetProjectedSubset(ProductInfo[] products)
{
  var nameDesc =
    from p in products select new { p.Name, p.Description };

  // Map set of anonymous objects to an Array object.
  return nameDesc.ToArray();
}
```

you could invoke and process the data as follows:

```
Array objs = GetProjectedSubset(itemsInStock);
foreach (object o in objs)
{
  Console.WriteLine(o); // Calls ToString() on each anonymous object.
}
```

Note that you must use a literal System.Array object and cannot use the C# array declaration syntax, given that you don't know the underlying type because you are operating on a compiler-generated anonymous class! Also note that you are not specifying the type parameter to the generic ToArray<T>() method, as you once again don't know the underlying data type until compile time, which is too late for your purposes.

The obvious problem is that you lose any strong typing, as each item in the Array object is assumed to be of type Object. Nevertheless, when you need to return a LINQ result set that is the result of a projection operation to an anonymous type, transforming the data into an Array type (or another suitable container via other members of the Enumerable type) is mandatory.

Projecting to Different Data Types

In addition to projecting into anonymous types, you can project the results of your LINQ query into another concrete type. This allows for static typing and using IEnumerable<T> as the result set. To start, create a smaller version of the ProductInfo class.

```
namespace FunWithLinqExpressions;
class ProductInfoSmall
{
  public string Name {get; set;} = "";
  public string Description {get; set;} = "";
  public override string ToString()
    => $"Name={Name}, Description={Description}";
}
```

The next change is to project the query results into a collection of ProductInfoSmall objects, instead of anonymous types. Add the following method to your class:

```
static void GetNamesAndDescriptionsTyped(
  ProductInfo[] products)
{
  Console.WriteLine("Names and Descriptions:");
  IEnumerable<ProductInfoSmall> nameDesc =
    from p
    in products
    select new ProductInfoSmall
      { Name=p.Name, Description=p.Description };

  foreach (ProductInfoSmall item in nameDesc)
  {
    Console.WriteLine(item.ToString());
  }
}
```

With LINQ projections, you have choices for which method you use (anonymous or strong-typed objects). Which decision you make depends entirely on your business need.

Obtaining Counts Using Enumerable

When you are projecting new batches of data, you may need to discover exactly how many items have been returned into the sequence. Any time you need to determine the number of items returned from a LINQ query expression, simply use the Count() extension method of the Enumerable class. For example, the following method will find all string objects in a local array that have a length greater than six characters:

```
static void GetCountFromQuery()
{
  string[] currentVideoGames = {"Morrowind", "Uncharted 2", "Fallout 3", "Daxter", "System
  Shock 2"};

  // Get count from the query.
  int numb =  (from g in currentVideoGames where g.Length > 6 select g).Count();
```

```
  // Print out the number of items.
  Console.WriteLine("{0} items honor the LINQ query.", numb);
}
```

Obtaining Nonenumerated Counts (New 10.0)

Introduced in .NET 6/C# 10, the `TryGetNonEnumeratedCount()` method attempts to get the total count of an `IEnumerable` without actually enumerating the list. If the list must be enumerated over to get the count, the method fails.

The following code demonstrates an “easy” count that doesn’t cause a performance issue by enumerating the entire list:

```
static void GetUnenumeratedCount(ProductInfo[] products)
{
  Console.WriteLine("Get Unenumeratord Count");
  IEnumerable<ProductInfo> query = from p in products select p;
  var result = query.TryGetNonEnumeratedCount(out int count);
  if (result)
  {
    Console.WriteLine($"Total count:{count}");
  }
  else
  {
    Console.WriteLine("Try Get Count Failed");
  }
}
```

The following updated code fails when calling the `GetProducts()` local function, since the `yield return` must be enumerated:

```
static void GetUnenumeratedCount(ProductInfo[] products)
{
  Console.WriteLine("Get Unenumeratord Count");
  //omitted for brevity
  var newResult = GetProduct(products).TryGetNonEnumeratedCount(out int newCount);
  if (newResult)
  {
    Console.WriteLine($"Total count:{newCount}");
  }
  else
  {
    Console.WriteLine("Try Get Count Failed");
  }
  static IEnumerable<ProductInfo> GetProduct(ProductInfo[] products)
  {
    for (int i = 0;i < products.Count();i++)
    {
      yield return products[i];
    }
  }
}
```

Reversing Result Sets

You can reverse the items within a result set quite simply using the Reverse() extension method of the Enumerable class. For example, the following method selects all items from the incoming ProductInfo[] parameter, in reverse:

```
static void ReverseEverything(ProductInfo[] products)
{
  Console.WriteLine("Product in reverse:");
  var allProducts = from p in products select p;
  foreach (var prod in allProducts.Reverse())
  {
    Console.WriteLine(prod.ToString());
  }
}
```

Sorting Expressions

As you have seen in this chapter's initial examples, a query expression can take an orderby operator to sort items in the subset by a specific value. By default, the order will be ascending; thus, ordering by a string would be alphabetical, ordering by numerical data would be lowest to highest, and so forth. If you need to view the results in descending order, simply include the descending operator. Ponder the following method:

```
static void AlphabetizeProductNames(ProductInfo[] products)
{
  // Get names of products, alphabetized.
  var subset = from p in products orderby p.Name select p;

  Console.WriteLine("Ordered by Name:");
  foreach (var p in subset)
  {
    Console.WriteLine(p.ToString());
  }
}
```

Although ascending order is the default, you can make your intentions clear by using the ascending operator.

```
var subset = from p in products orderby p.Name ascending select p;
```

If you want to get the items in descending order, you can do so via the descending operator.

```
var subset = from p in products orderby p.Name descending select p;
```

LINQ As a Better Venn Diagramming Tool

The Enumerable class supports a set of extension methods that allows you to use two (or more) LINQ queries as the basis to find unions, differences, concatenations, and intersections of data. First, consider the Except() extension method, which will return a LINQ result set that contains the difference between two containers, which, in this case, is the value Yugo.

```
static void DisplayDiff()
{
  List<string> myCars =
    new List<string> {"Yugo", "Aztec", "BMW"};
  List<string> yourCars =
    new List<string>{"BMW", "Saab", "Aztec" };

  var carDiff =
    (from c in myCars select c)
    .Except(from c2 in yourCars select c2);

  Console.WriteLine("Here is what you don't have, but I do:");
  foreach (string s in carDiff)
  {
    Console.WriteLine(s); // Prints Yugo.
  }
}
```

The `Intersect()` method will return a result set that contains the common data items in a set of containers. For example, the following method returns the sequence `Aztec` and `BMW`:

```
static void DisplayIntersection()
{
  List<string> myCars = new List<string> { "Yugo", "Aztec", "BMW" };
  List<string> yourCars = new List<string> { "BMW", "Saab", "Aztec" };

  // Get the common members.
  var carIntersect =
    (from c in myCars select c)
    .Intersect(from c2 in yourCars select c2);

  Console.WriteLine("Here is what we have in common:");
  foreach (string s in carIntersect)
  {
    Console.WriteLine(s); // Prints Aztec and BMW.
  }
}
```

The `Union()` method, as you would guess, returns a result set that includes all members of a batch of LINQ queries. Like any proper union, you will not find repeating values if a common member appears more than once. Therefore, the following method will print out the values `Yugo`, `Aztec`, `BMW`, and `Saab`:

```
static void DisplayUnion()
{
  List<string> myCars =
    new List<string> { "Yugo", "Aztec", "BMW" };
  List<string> yourCars =
    new List<string> { "BMW", "Saab", "Aztec" };

  // Get the union of these containers.
  var carUnion =
```

```
    (from c in myCars select c)
    .Union(from c2 in yourCars select c2);

  Console.WriteLine("Here is everything:");
  foreach (string s in carUnion)
  {
    Console.WriteLine(s); // Prints all common members.
  }
}
```

Finally, the `Concat()` extension method returns a result set that is a direct concatenation of LINQ result sets. For example, the following method prints out the results `Yugo`, `Aztec`, `BMW`, `BMW`, `Saab`, and `Aztec`:

```
static void DisplayConcat()
{
  List<string> myCars =
    new List<string> { "Yugo", "Aztec", "BMW" };
  List<string> yourCars =
    new List<string> { "BMW", "Saab", "Aztec" };

  var carConcat =
    (from c in myCars select c)
    .Concat(from c2 in yourCars select c2);

  // Prints:
  // Yugo Aztec BMW BMW Saab Aztec.
  foreach (string s in carConcat)
  {
    Console.WriteLine(s);
  }
}
```

Venn Diagramming with Selectors (New 10.0)

A new set of methods was introduced in .NET 6/C# 10 that adds the ability to use a selector when finding unions, differences, and intersections of data. The selectors use a specific property of the objects in the lists to determine the action to perform.

The `ExceptBy()` extension method uses the selector to remove the records from the first set where the value of the selector exists in the second set. The following method creates two lists of tuples and uses the `Age` property for the selector. Both `Claire` and `Pat` have the same age as `Lindsey`, but `Age` values for `Francis` and `Ashley` are not in the second list. So the result of the `ExceptBy()` extension method is `Francis` and `Ashley`:

```
static void DisplayDiffBySelector()
{
  var first = new (string Name, int Age)[] { ("Francis", 20), ("Lindsey", 30),
  ("Ashley", 40) };
  var second = new (string Name, int Age)[] { ("Claire", 30), ("Pat", 30), ("Drew", 33) };
  var result = first.ExceptBy(second.Select(x=>x.Age), product => product.Age); // }
  Console.WriteLine("Except for by selector:");
  foreach (var item in result)
```

```
  {
    Console.WriteLine(item); // { ("Francis", 20), ("Ashley", 40) }
  }
}
```

The IntersectBy() method will return a result set that contains the common data items in a set of containers based on the selector. The following method returns the tuple Lindsey. Note that even though Claire and Pat also have the same Age value as Lindsey, they are not returned since the IntersectBy() method returns only one result per selector value.

```
static void DisplayIntersectionBySelector()
{
  var first = new (string Name, int Age)[] { ("Francis", 20), ("Lindsey", 30),
  ("Ashley", 40) };
  var second = new (string Name, int Age)[] { ("Claire", 30), ("Pat", 30), ("Drew", 33) };
  var result = first.IntersectBy(second.Select(x=>x.Age), person => person.Age);
  Console.WriteLine("Intersection by selector:");
  foreach (var item in result)
  {
    Console.WriteLine(item); // { ("Lindsey", 30) }
  }
}
```

Reversing the call between the first and second lists still produces one result, which is the first tuple in the second list with the selector value of 30.

```
var result = second.IntersectBy(first.Select(x=>x.Age), person => person.Age);
// returns ("Claire",30)
```

The UnionBy() method returns a result set that includes all the values for the selector, and the first member of the combined lists that have a value that matches the list. In the following method, notice that while each of the Age values is represented in the result, Claire and Pat are not, since their Age is already represented by Lindsey:

```
static void DisplayUnionBySelector()
{
    var first = new (string Name, int Age)[] { ("Francis", 20), ("Lindsey", 30),
    ("Ashley", 40) };
    var second = new (string Name, int Age)[] { ("Claire", 30), ("Pat", 30), ("Drew", 33) };
    var result = first.UnionBy(second, person => person.Age);
    Console.WriteLine("Union by selector:");
    foreach (var item in result)
    {
        Console.WriteLine(item); // { ("Francis", 20), ("Lindsey", 30), ("Ashley", 40),
        ("Drew", 33) };
    }
}
```

These new methods, ExceptBy(), IntersectBy(), and UnionBy(), add a lot of power to your list arsenal, but as you saw, they might not always do what you expect them to do.

Removing Duplicates

When you call the Concat() extension method, you could very well end up with redundant entries in the fetched result, which could be exactly what you want in some cases. However, in other cases, you might want to remove duplicate entries in your data. To do so, simply call the Distinct() extension method, as shown here:

```
static void DisplayConcatNoDups()
{
  List<string> myCars =
    new List<String> { "Yugo", "Aztec", "BMW" };
  List<string> yourCars =
    new List<String> { "BMW", "Saab", "Aztec" };

  var carConcat =
    (from c in myCars select c)
    .Concat(from c2 in yourCars select c2);

  // Prints:
  // Yugo Aztec BMW Saab.
  foreach (string s in carConcat.Distinct())
  {
    Console.WriteLine(s);
  }
}
```

Removing Duplicates with Selectors (New 10.0)

Another new method in .NET 6/C# 10 for working with lists is the DistinctBy() method. This method, like its cousins UnionBy(), IntersectBy(), and ExceptBy(), uses a selector to perform its function. The following example gets the distinct records by Age. Notice that the final list only includes Lindsey of the three tuples that have 30 for their Age value. The accepted tuple is the one that appears first in the list.

```
static void DisplayConcatNoDupsBySelector()
{
    var first = new (string Name, int Age)[] { ("Francis", 20), ("Lindsey", 30),
    ("Ashley", 40) };
    var second = new (string Name, int Age)[] { ("Claire", 30), ("Pat", 30), ("Drew", 33) };
    var result = first.Concat(second).DistinctBy(x=>x.Age);
    Console.WriteLine("Distinct by selector:");
    foreach (var item in result)
    {
        Console.WriteLine(item); // { ("Francis", 20), ("Lindsey", 30), ("Ashley", 40),
        ("Drew", 33) };
    }
}
```

LINQ Aggregation Operations

LINQ queries can also be designed to perform various aggregation operations on the result set. The Count() extension method is one such aggregation example. Other possibilities include obtaining an average, maximum, minimum, or sum of values using the Max(), Min(), Average(), or Sum() members of the Enumerable class. Here is a simple example:

```
static void AggregateOps()
{
  double[] winterTemps = { 2.0, -21.3, 8, -4, 0, 8.2 };

  // Various aggregation examples.
  Console.WriteLine("Max temp: {0}",
    (from t in winterTemps select t).Max());

  Console.WriteLine("Min temp: {0}",
    (from t in winterTemps select t).Min());

  Console.WriteLine("Average temp: {0}",
    (from t in winterTemps select t).Average());

  Console.WriteLine("Sum of all temps: {0}",
    (from t in winterTemps select t).Sum());
}
```

Aggregation with Selectors (New 10.0)

Two new aggregate functions introduced in .NET 6/C# 10 are MaxBy() and MinBy(). Using the ProductInfo list from earlier, here is a method that gets the max and min, using the NumberInStock property:

```
static void AggregateOpsBySelector(ProductInfo[] products)
{
  Console.WriteLine("Max by In Stock: {0}", products.MaxBy(x=>x.NumberInStock));
  Console.WriteLine("Min temp: {0}", products.MinBy(x=>x.NumberInStock));
}
```

The Internal Representation of LINQ Query Statements

While this is not a complete LINQ reference, the previous examples in this chapter should give you enough knowledge to feel comfortable with the process of building LINQ query expressions. You will see further examples later in this text, especially in the Entity Framework Core chapters. To wrap up your first look at LINQ, the remainder of this chapter will dive into the details between the C# LINQ query operators and the underlying object model.

At this point, you have been introduced to the process of building query expressions using various C# query operators (such as from, in, where, orderby, and select). Also, you discovered that some functionality of the LINQ to Objects API can be accessed only when calling extension methods of the Enumerable class. The truth of the matter, however, is that when LINQ queries are compiled, the C# compiler translates all C# LINQ operators into calls on methods of the Enumerable class.

A great many of the methods of Enumerable have been prototyped to take delegates as arguments. Many methods require a generic delegate named Func<>, which was introduced to you during your examination of generic delegates in Chapter 10. Consider the Where() method of Enumerable, which is called on your behalf when you use the C# where LINQ query operator.

```
// Overloaded versions of the Enumerable.Where<T>() method.
// Note the second parameter is of type System.Func<>.
public static IEnumerable<TSource> Where<TSource>(
  this IEnumerable<TSource> source,
  System.Func<TSource,int,bool> predicate)

public static IEnumerable<TSource> Where<TSource>(
  this IEnumerable<TSource> source,
  System.Func<TSource,bool> predicate)
```

The Func<> delegate (as the name implies) represents a pattern for a given function with a set of up to 16 arguments and a return value. If you were to examine this type using the Visual Studio Object Browser, you would notice various forms of the Func<> delegate. Here's an example:

```
// The various formats of the Func<> delegate.
public delegate TResult Func<T1,T2,T3,T4,TResult>(T1 arg1, T2 arg2, T3 arg3, T4 arg4)

public delegate TResult Func<T1,T2,T3,TResult>(T1 arg1, T2 arg2, T3 arg3)

public delegate TResult Func<T1,T2,TResult>(T1 arg1, T2 arg2)

public delegate TResult Func<T1,TResult>(T1 arg1)

public delegate TResult Func<TResult>()
```

Given that many members of System.Linq.Enumerable demand a delegate as input, when invoking them, you can either manually create a new delegate type and author the necessary target methods, use a C# anonymous method, or define a proper lambda expression. Regardless of which approach you take, the result is identical.

While it is true that using C# LINQ query operators is far and away the simplest way to build a LINQ query expression, let's walk through each of these possible approaches, just so you can see the connection between the C# query operators and the underlying Enumerable type.

Building Query Expressions with Query Operators (Revisited)

To begin, create a new Console Application project named LinqUsingEnumerable. The Program.cs file will define a series of static helper methods (each of which is called within the top-level statements) to illustrate the various manners in which you can build LINQ query expressions.

The first method, QueryStringsWithOperators(), offers the most straightforward way to build a query expression and is identical to the code shown in the LinqOverArray example earlier in this chapter.

```
static void QueryStringWithOperators()
{
  Console.WriteLine("***** Using Query Operators *****");

  string[] currentVideoGames = {"Morrowind", "Uncharted 2", "Fallout 3", "Daxter", "System
  Shock 2"};
```

```
  var subset = from game in currentVideoGames
    where game.Contains(" ") orderby game select game;

  foreach (string s in subset)
  {
    Console.WriteLine("Item: {0}", s);
  }
}
```

The obvious benefit of using C# query operators to build query expressions is that the Func<> delegates and calls on the Enumerable type are abstracted away from your code, as it is the job of the C# compiler to perform this translation. To be sure, building LINQ expressions using various query operators (from, in, where, or orderby) is the most common and straightforward approach.

Building Query Expressions Using the Enumerable Type and Lambda Expressions

Keep in mind that the LINQ query operators used here are simply shorthand versions for calling various extension methods defined by the Enumerable type. Consider the following QueryStringsWithEnumerableAndLambdas() method, which is processing the local string array now making direct use of the Enumerable extension methods:

```
static void QueryStringsWithEnumerableAndLambdas()
{
  Console.WriteLine("***** Using Enumerable / Lambda Expressions *****");

  string[] currentVideoGames = {"Morrowind", "Uncharted 2", "Fallout 3", "Daxter", "System
  Shock 2"};

  // Build a query expression using extension methods
  // granted to the Array via the Enumerable type.
  var subset = currentVideoGames
    .Where(game => game.Contains(" "))
    .OrderBy(game => game).Select(game => game);

  // Print out the results.
  foreach (var game in subset)
  {
    Console.WriteLine("Item: {0}", game);
  }
  Console.WriteLine();
}
```

Here, you begin by calling the Where() extension method on the currentVideoGames string array. Recall that the Array class receives this via an extension method granted by Enumerable. The Enumerable.Where() method requires a System.Func<T1, TResult> delegate parameter. The first type parameter of this delegate represents the IEnumerable<T>-compatible data to process (an array of strings in this case), while the second type parameter represents the method result data, which is obtained from a single statement fed into the lambda expression.

The return value of the Where() method is hidden from view in this code example, but under the covers you are operating on an Enumerable type. From this object, you call the generic OrderBy() method, which also requires a Func<> delegate parameter. This time, you are simply passing each item in turn via a fitting lambda expression. The result of calling OrderBy() is a new ordered sequence of the initial data.

Finally, you call the Select() method off the sequence returned from OrderBy(), which results in the final set of data that is stored in an implicitly typed variable named subset.

To be sure, this "longhand" LINQ query is a bit more complex to tease apart than the previous C# LINQ query operator example. Part of the complexity is, no doubt, due to the chaining together of calls using the dot operator. Here is the same query, with each step broken into discrete chunks (as you might guess, you could break down the overall query in various manners):

```
static void QueryStringsWithEnumerableAndLambdas2()
{
  Console.WriteLine("***** Using Enumerable / Lambda Expressions *****");

  string[] currentVideoGames = {"Morrowind", "Uncharted 2", "Fallout 3", "Daxter", "System
  Shock 2"};

  // Break it down!
  var gamesWithSpaces = currentVideoGames.Where(game => game.Contains(" "));
  var orderedGames = gamesWithSpaces.OrderBy(game => game);
  var subset = orderedGames.Select(game => game);

  foreach (var game in subset)
  {
    Console.WriteLine("Item: {0}", game);
  }
  Console.WriteLine();
}
```

As you might agree, building a LINQ query expression using the methods of the Enumerable class directly is much more verbose than making use of the C# query operators. As well, given that the methods of Enumerable require delegates as parameters, you will typically need to author lambda expressions to allow the input data to be processed by the underlying delegate target.

Building Query Expressions Using the Enumerable Type and Anonymous Methods

Given that C# lambda expressions are simply shorthand notations for working with anonymous methods, consider the third query expression created within the QueryStringsWithAnonymousMethods() helper function, shown here:

```
static void QueryStringsWithAnonymousMethods()
{
  Console.WriteLine("***** Using Anonymous Methods *****");

  string[] currentVideoGames = {"Morrowind", "Uncharted 2", "Fallout 3", "Daxter", "System
  Shock 2"};

  // Build the necessary Func<> delegates using anonymous methods.
```

```
  Func<string, bool> searchFilter = delegate(string game) { return game.Contains(" "); };
  Func<string, string> itemToProcess = delegate(string s) { return s; };

  // Pass the delegates into the methods of Enumerable.
  var subset = currentVideoGames.Where(searchFilter).OrderBy(itemToProcess).
  Select(itemToProcess);

  // Print out the results.
  foreach (var game in subset)
  {
    Console.WriteLine("Item: {0}", game);
  }
  Console.WriteLine();
}
```

This iteration of the query expression is even more verbose, because you are manually creating the `Func<>` delegates used by the `Where()`, `OrderBy()`, and `Select()` methods of the `Enumerable` class. On the plus side, the anonymous method syntax does keep all the delegate processing contained within a single method definition. Nevertheless, this method is functionally equivalent to the `QueryStringsWithEnumerableAndLambdas()` and `QueryStringsWithOperators()` methods created in the previous sections.

Building Query Expressions Using the Enumerable Type and Raw Delegates

Finally, if you want to build a query expression using the *verbose approach*, you could avoid the use of lambdas/anonymous method syntax and directly create delegate targets for each `Func<>` type. Here is the final iteration of your query expression, modeled within a new class type named `VeryComplexQueryExpression`:

```
class VeryComplexQueryExpression
{
  public static void QueryStringsWithRawDelegates()
  {
    Console.WriteLine("***** Using Raw Delegates *****");
    string[] currentVideoGames = {"Morrowind", "Uncharted 2", "Fallout 3", "Daxter", "System
    Shock 2"};

    // Build the necessary Func<> delegates.
    Func<string, bool> searchFilter =
      new Func<string, bool>(Filter);
    Func<string, string> itemToProcess =
      new Func<string,string>(ProcessItem);

    // Pass the delegates into the methods of Enumerable.
    var subset =
      currentVideoGames
       .Where(searchFilter)
       .OrderBy(itemToProcess)
       .Select(itemToProcess);
```

```
    // Print out the results.
    foreach (var game in subset)
    {
      Console.WriteLine("Item: {0}", game);
    }
    Console.WriteLine();
  }

  // Delegate targets.
  public static bool Filter(string game)
  {
    return game.Contains(" ");
  }
  public static string ProcessItem(string game)
  {
    return game;
  }
}
```

You can test this iteration of your string-processing logic by calling this method within the top-level statements of the Program.cs file, as follows:

```
VeryComplexQueryExpression.QueryStringsWithRawDelegates();
```

If you were to now run the application to test each possible approach, it should not be too surprising that the output is identical, regardless of the path taken. Keep the following points in mind regarding how LINQ query expressions are represented under the covers:

- Query expressions are created using various C# query operators.
- Query operators are simply shorthand notations for invoking extension methods defined by the System.Linq.Enumerable type.
- Many methods of Enumerable require delegates (Func<> in particular) as parameters.
- Any method requiring a delegate parameter can instead be passed a lambda expression.
- Lambda expressions are simply anonymous methods in disguise (which greatly improve readability).
- Anonymous methods are shorthand notations for allocating a raw delegate and manually building a delegate target method.

Whew! That might have been a bit deeper under the hood than you wanted to go, but I hope this discussion has helped you understand what the user-friendly C# query operators are doing behind the scenes.

Summary

LINQ is a set of related technologies attempting to provide a single, symmetrical manner to interact with diverse forms of data. As explained over the course of this chapter, LINQ can interact with any type implementing the IEnumerable<T> interface, including simple arrays as well as generic and nongeneric collections of data.

As you have seen, working with LINQ technologies is accomplished using several C# language features. For example, given that LINQ query expressions can return any number of result sets, it is common to make use of the `var` keyword to represent the underlying data type. Lambda expressions, object initialization syntax, and anonymous types can all be used to build functional and compact LINQ queries.

More importantly, you have seen how the C# LINQ query operators are simply shorthand notations for making calls on static members of the `System.Linq.Enumerable` type. As shown, most members of `Enumerable` operate on `Func<T>` delegate types, which can take literal method addresses, anonymous methods, or lambda expressions as input to evaluate the query.

CHAPTER 14

Processes, AppDomains, and Load Contexts

In this chapter, you'll drill deep into the details of how an assembly is hosted by the runtime and come to understand the relationship between processes, application domains, and object contexts.

In a nutshell, *application domains* (or simply *AppDomains*) are logical subdivisions within a given process that host a set of related .NET Core assemblies. As you will see, an AppDomain is further subdivided into *contextual boundaries*, which are used to group like-minded .NET Core objects. Using the notion of context, the runtime can ensure that objects with special requirements are handled appropriately.

While it is true that many of your day-to-day programming tasks might not involve directly working with processes, AppDomains, or object contexts, understanding these topics is important when working with numerous .NET Core APIs, including multithreading, parallel processing, and object serialization.

The Role of a Windows Process

The concept of a "process" existed within Windows-based operating systems well before the release of the .NET/.NET Core platforms. In simple terms, a *process* is a running program. However, formally speaking, a process is an operating system–level concept used to describe a set of resources (such as external code libraries and the primary thread) and the necessary memory allocations used by a running application. For each .NET Core application loaded into memory, the OS creates a separate and isolated process for use during its lifetime.

Using this approach to application isolation, the result is a much more robust and stable runtime environment, given that the failure of one process does not affect the functioning of another. Furthermore, data in one process cannot be directly accessed by another process, unless you use specific tools such as `System.IO.Pipes` or the `MemoryMappedFile` class. Given these points, you can regard the process as a fixed, safe boundary for a running application.

Every Windows process is assigned a unique process identifier (PID) and may be independently loaded and unloaded by the OS as necessary (as well as programmatically). As you might be aware, the Processes tab of the Windows Task Manager utility (activated via the Ctrl+Shift+Esc keystroke combination on Windows) allows you to view various statistics regarding the processes running on a given machine. The Details tab allows you to view the assigned PID and image name (see Figure 14-1).

A. Troelsen and P. Japikse, *Pro C# 10 with .NET 6*, https://doi.org/10.1007/978-1-4842-7869-7_14

Task Manager

File Options View

Processes | Performance | App history | Startup | Users | Details | Services

Name	PID	Status	User name	CPU	Memory (ac...	UAC virtualizati...
AcroRd32.exe	37956	Running	japik	00	1,276 K	Disabled
AcroRd32.exe	37176	Running	japik	00	33,856 K	Disabled
Adobe CEF Helper.exe	21904	Running	japik	00	16,820 K	Disabled
Adobe Desktop Servi...	21840	Running	japik	00	34,568 K	Disabled
Adobe Installer.exe	14400	Running	japik	00	528 K	Not allowed
AdobeCollabSync.exe	11820	Running	japik	00	644 K	Disabled
AdobeCollabSync.exe	27404	Running	japik	00	1,852 K	Disabled
AdobeIPCBroker.exe	1500	Running	japik	00	2,700 K	Disabled
AdobeUpdateService....	5860	Running	SYSTEM	00	712 K	Not allowed
aesm_service.exe	12180	Running	SYSTEM	00	768 K	Not allowed
AGMService.exe	5892	Running	SYSTEM	00	592 K	Not allowed
AGSService.exe	5900	Running	SYSTEM	00	1,732 K	Not allowed
ApplicationFrameHos...	13452	Running	japik	00	12,140 K	Disabled
armsvc.exe	5848	Running	SYSTEM	00	412 K	Not allowed
audiodg.exe	8188	Running	LOCAL SERV...	00	5,272 K	Not allowed
backgroundTaskHost....	51380	Suspended	japik	00	0 K	Disabled
BCClipboard.exe	7604	Running	japik	00	800 K	Disabled
browser_broker.exe	23380	Running	japik	00	396 K	Disabled
caller64.exe	25016	Running	japik	00	468 K	Disabled
CCLibrary.exe	22564	Running	japik	00	40 K	Disabled
CCXProcess.exe	7720	Running	japik	00	68 K	Disabled

Fewer details

End task

Figure 14-1. *The Windows Task Manager*

The Role of Threads

Every Windows process contains an initial "thread" that functions as the entry point for the application. Chapter 15 examines the details of building multithreaded applications under the .NET Core platform; however, to facilitate the topics presented here, you need a few working definitions. First, a *thread* is a path of execution within a process. Formally speaking, the first thread created by a process's entry point is termed the *primary thread*. Any .NET Core program (console application, Windows service, WPF application, etc.) marks its entry point with the `Main()` method or a file containing top-level statements (which gets converted to a `Program` class and `Main()` method, as demonstrated earlier in this book). When this code is invoked, the primary thread is created automatically.

Processes that contain a single primary thread of execution are intrinsically *thread-safe*, given that there is only one thread that can access the data in the application at a given time. However, a single-threaded process (especially one that is GUI based) will often appear a bit unresponsive to the user if this single thread is performing a complex operation (such as printing out a lengthy text file, performing a mathematically intensive calculation, or attempting to connect to a remote server located thousands of miles away).

Given this potential drawback of single-threaded applications, the operating systems that are supported by .NET Core (as well as the .NET Core platform) make it possible for the primary thread to spawn additional secondary threads (also termed *worker threads*) using a handful of API functions such as `CreateThread()`. Each thread (primary or secondary) becomes a unique path of execution in the process and has concurrent access to all shared points of data within the process.

As you might have guessed, developers typically create additional threads to help improve the program's overall responsiveness. Multithreaded processes provide the illusion that numerous activities are happening at the same time. For example, an application may spawn a worker thread to perform a labor-intensive unit of work (again, such as printing a large text file). As this secondary thread is churning away, the main thread is still responsive to user input, which gives the entire process the potential of delivering greater performance. However, this may not actually be the case: using too many threads in a single process can actually *degrade* performance, as the CPU must switch between the active threads in the process (which takes time).

On some machines, multithreading is most commonly an illusion provided by the OS. Machines that host a single (nonhyperthreaded) CPU do not have the ability to literally handle multiple threads at the same time. Rather, a single CPU will execute one thread for a unit of time (called a *time slice*) based in part on the thread's priority level. When a thread's time slice is up, the existing thread is suspended to allow another thread to perform its business. For a thread to remember what was happening before it was kicked out of the way, each thread is given the ability to write to Thread Local Storage (TLS) and is provided with a separate call stack, as illustrated in Figure 14-2.

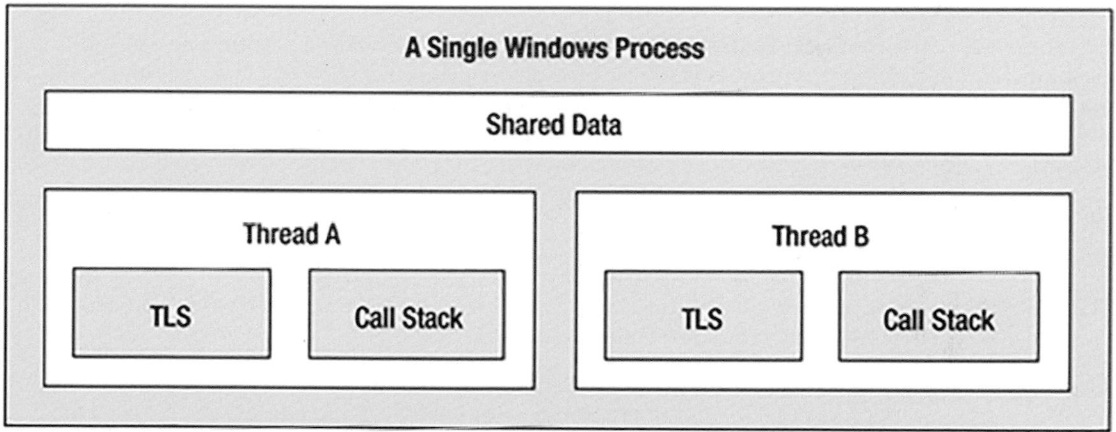

Figure 14-2. *The Windows process/thread relationship*

If the subject of threads is new to you, don't sweat the details. At this point, just remember that a thread is a unique path of execution within a Windows process. Every process has a primary thread (created via the executable's entry point) and may contain additional threads that have been programmatically created.

Interacting with Processes Using .NET Core

Although processes and threads are nothing new, the way you interact with these primitives under the .NET Core platform has changed quite a bit (for the better). To pave the way to understanding the world of building multithreaded assemblies (see Chapter 15), let's begin by checking out how to interact with processes using the .NET Core base class libraries.

The `System.Diagnostics` namespace defines several types that allow you to programmatically interact with processes and various diagnostic-related types such as the system event log and performance counters. In this chapter, you are concerned with only the process-centric types defined in Table 14-1.

Table 14-1. *Select Members of the System.Diagnostics Namespace*

Process-Centric Types of the System.Diagnostics Namespace	Meaning in Life
`Process`	The `Process` class provides access to local and remote processes and allows you to programmatically start and stop processes.
`ProcessModule`	This type represents a module (`*.dll` or `*.exe`) that is loaded into a process. Understand that the `ProcessModule` type can represent *any* module—COM-based, .NET-based, or traditional C-based binaries.
`ProcessModuleCollection`	This provides a strongly typed collection of `ProcessModule` objects.
`ProcessStartInfo`	This specifies a set of values used when starting a process via the `Process.Start()` method.
`ProcessThread`	This type represents a thread within a given process. Be aware that `ProcessThread` is a type used to diagnose a process's thread set and is not used to spawn new threads of execution within a process.
`ProcessThreadCollection`	This provides a strongly typed collection of `ProcessThread` objects.

The `System.Diagnostics.Process` class allows you to analyze the processes running on a given machine (local or remote). The `Process` class also provides members that allow you to programmatically start and terminate processes, view (or modify) a process's priority level, and obtain a list of active threads and/or loaded modules within a given process. Table 14-2 lists some of the key properties of `System.Diagnostics.Process`.

Table 14-2. *Select Properties of the Process Type*

Property	Meaning in Life
`ExitTime`	This property gets the timestamp associated with the process that has terminated (represented with a `DateTime` type).
`Handle`	This property returns the handle (represented by an `IntPtr`) associated to the process by the OS. This can be useful when building .NET applications that need to communicate with unmanaged code.
`Id`	This property gets the PID for the associated process.
`MachineName`	This property gets the name of the computer the associated process is running on.
`MainWindowTitle`	`MainWindowTitle` gets the caption of the main window of the process (if the process does not have a main window, you receive an empty `string`).
`Modules`	This property provides access to the strongly typed `ProcessModuleCollection` type, which represents the set of modules (`*.dll` or `*.exe`) loaded within the current process.
`ProcessName`	This property gets the name of the process (which, as you would assume, is the name of the application itself).
`Responding`	This property gets a value indicating whether the user interface of the process is responding to user input (or is currently "hung").
`StartTime`	This property gets the time that the associated process was started (via a `DateTime` type).
`Threads`	This property gets the set of threads that are running in the associated process (represented via a collection of `ProcessThread` objects).

In addition to the properties just examined, System.Diagnostics.Process also defines a few useful methods (see Table 14-3).

Table 14-3. *Select Methods of the Process Type*

Method	Meaning in Life
CloseMainWindow()	This method closes a process that has a user interface by sending a close message to its main window.
GetCurrentProcess()	This static method returns a new Process object that represents the currently active process.
GetProcesses()	This static method returns an array of new Process objects running on a given machine.
Kill()	This method immediately stops the associated process.
Start()	This method starts a process.

Enumerating Running Processes

To illustrate the process of manipulating Process objects (pardon the redundancy), create a C# Console Application project named ProcessManipulator. Next, define the following static helper method within the Program.cs file:

```
static void ListAllRunningProcesses()
{
  // Get all the processes on the local machine, ordered by
  // PID.
  var runningProcs =
    from proc
    in Process.GetProcesses(".")
    orderby proc.Id
    select proc;

  // Print out PID and name of each process.
  foreach(var p in runningProcs)
  {
    string info = $"-> PID: {p.Id}\tName: {p.ProcessName}";
    Console.WriteLine(info);
  }
  Console.WriteLine("************************************\n");
}
```

The static Process.GetProcesses() method returns an array of Process objects that represent the running processes on the target machine (the dot notation shown here represents the local computer). After you have obtained the array of Process objects, you are able to invoke any of the members listed in Tables 14-2 and 14-3. Here, you are simply displaying the PID and the name of each process, ordered by PID. Update the top-level statements as follows:

```
using System.Diagnostics;

Console.WriteLine("***** Fun with Processes *****\n");
ListAllRunningProcesses();
Console.ReadLine();
```

When you run the application, you will see the names and PIDs for all processes on your local computer. Here is some partial output from my current machine (your output will most likely be different):

```
***** Fun with Processes *****
-> PID: 0       Name: Idle
-> PID: 4       Name: System
-> PID: 104     Name: Secure System
-> PID: 176     Name: Registry
-> PID: 908     Name: svchost
-> PID: 920     Name: smss
-> PID: 1016    Name: csrss
-> PID: 1020    Name: NVDisplay.Container
-> PID: 1104    Name: wininit
-> PID: 1112    Name: csrss
************************************
```

Investigating a Specific Process

In addition to obtaining a complete list of all running processes on a given machine, the static `Process.GetProcessById()` method allows you to obtain a single `Process` object via the associated PID. If you request access to a nonexistent PID, an `ArgumentException` exception is thrown. For example, if you were interested in obtaining a `Process` object representing a process with the PID of 30592, you could write the following code:

```
// If there is no process with the PID of 30592, a runtime exception will be thrown.
static void GetSpecificProcess()
{
  Process theProc = null;
  try
  {
    theProc = Process.GetProcessById(30592);
    Console.WriteLine(theProc?.ProcessName);
  }
  catch(ArgumentException ex)
  {
    Console.WriteLine(ex.Message);
  }
}
```

At this point, you have learned how to get a list of all processes, as well as a specific process on a machine via a PID lookup. While it is somewhat useful to discover PIDs and process names, the `Process` class also allows you to discover the set of current threads and libraries used within a given process. Let's see how to do so.

Investigating a Process's Thread Set

The set of threads is represented by the strongly typed `ProcessThreadCollection` collection, which contains some number of individual `ProcessThread` objects. To illustrate, add the following additional static helper function to your current application:

```
static void EnumThreadsForPid(int pID)
{
  Process theProc = null;
  try
  {
    theProc = Process.GetProcessById(pID);
  }
  catch(ArgumentException ex)
  {
    Console.WriteLine(ex.Message);
    return;
  }

  // List out stats for each thread in the specified process.
  Console.WriteLine(
    "Here are the threads used by: {0}", theProc.ProcessName);
  ProcessThreadCollection theThreads = theProc.Threads;

  foreach(ProcessThread pt in theThreads)
  {
    string info =
       $"-> Thread ID: {pt.Id}\tStart Time: {pt.StartTime.ToShortTimeString()}\tPriority:
       {pt.PriorityLevel}";
    Console.WriteLine(info);
  }
  Console.WriteLine("************************************\n");
}
```

As you can see, the `Threads` property of the `System.Diagnostics.Process` type provides access to the `ProcessThreadCollection` class. Here, you are printing the assigned thread ID, start time, and priority level of each thread in the process specified by the client. Now, update your program's top-level statements to prompt the user for a PID to investigate, as follows:

```
...
// Prompt user for a PID and print out the set of active threads.
Console.WriteLine("***** Enter PID of process to investigate *****");
Console.Write("PID: ");
string pID = Console.ReadLine();
int theProcID = int.Parse(pID);

EnumThreadsForPid(theProcID);
Console.ReadLine();
```

When you run your program, you can now enter the PID of any process on your machine and see the threads used in the process. The following output shows a partial list of the threads used by PID 3804 on my machine, which happens to be hosting Edge:

```
***** Enter PID of process to investigate *****
PID: 3804
Here are the threads used by: msedge
-> Thread ID: 3464      Start Time: 01:20 PM    Priority: Normal
-> Thread ID: 19420     Start Time: 01:20 PM    Priority: Normal
-> Thread ID: 17780     Start Time: 01:20 PM    Priority: Normal
-> Thread ID: 22380     Start Time: 01:20 PM    Priority: Normal
-> Thread ID: 27580     Start Time: 01:20 PM    Priority: -4
...
************************************
```

The ProcessThread type has additional members of interest beyond Id, StartTime, and PriorityLevel. Table 14-4 documents some members of interest.

Table 14-4. *Select Members of the ProcessThread Type*

Member	Meaning in Life
CurrentPriority	Gets the current priority of the thread
Id	Gets the unique identifier of the thread
IdealProcessor	Sets the preferred processor for this thread to run on
PriorityLevel	Gets or sets the priority level of the thread
ProcessorAffinity	Sets the processors on which the associated thread can run
StartAddress	Gets the memory address of the function that the operating system called that started this thread
StartTime	Gets the time that the operating system started the thread
ThreadState	Gets the current state of this thread
TotalProcessorTime	Gets the total amount of time that this thread has spent using the processor
WaitReason	Gets the reason that the thread is waiting

Before you read any further, be aware that the ProcessThread type is *not* the entity used to create, suspend, or kill threads under the .NET Core platform. Rather, ProcessThread is a vehicle used to obtain diagnostic information for the active Windows threads within a running process. Again, you will investigate how to build multithreaded applications using the System.Threading namespace in Chapter 15.

Investigating a Process's Module Set

Next up, let's check out how to iterate over the number of loaded modules that are hosted within a given process. When talking about processes, a *module* is a general term used to describe a given *.dll (or the *.exe itself) that is hosted by a specific process. When you access the ProcessModuleCollection via the Process.Modules property, you can enumerate over *all modules* hosted within a process: .NET Core-based,

COM-based, or traditional C-based libraries. Ponder the following additional helper function that will enumerate the modules in a specific process based on the PID:

```
static void EnumModsForPid(int pID)
{
  Process theProc = null;
  try
  {
    theProc = Process.GetProcessById(pID);
  }
  catch(ArgumentException ex)
  {
    Console.WriteLine(ex.Message);
    return;
  }

  Console.WriteLine("Here are the loaded modules for: {0}",
    theProc.ProcessName);
  ProcessModuleCollection theMods = theProc.Modules;
  foreach(ProcessModule pm in theMods)
  {
    string info = $"-> Mod Name: {pm.ModuleName}";
    Console.WriteLine(info);
  }
  Console.WriteLine("************************************\n");
}
```

To see some possible output, let's check out the loaded modules for the process hosting the current example program (ProcessManipulator). To do so, run the application, identify the PID assigned to ProcessManipulator.exe (via the Task Manager), and pass this value to the EnumModsForPid() method. Once you do, you might be surprised to see the list of *.dlls used for a simple Console Application project (GDI32.dll, USER32.dll, ole32.dll, etc.). The following output is a partial listing of modules loaded (edited for brevity):

```
Here are (some of) the loaded modules for: ProcessManipulator
Here are the loaded modules for: ProcessManipulator
-> Mod Name: ProcessManipulator.exe
-> Mod Name: ntdll.dll
-> Mod Name: KERNEL32.DLL
-> Mod Name: KERNELBASE.dll
-> Mod Name: USER32.dll
-> Mod Name: win32u.dll
-> Mod Name: GDI32.dll
-> Mod Name: gdi32full.dll
-> Mod Name: msvcp_win.dll
-> Mod Name: ucrtbase.dll
-> Mod Name: SHELL32.dll
-> Mod Name: ADVAPI32.dll
-> Mod Name: msvcrt.dll
-> Mod Name: sechost.dll
-> Mod Name: RPCRT4.dll
```

```
-> Mod Name: IMM32.DLL
-> Mod Name: hostfxr.dll
-> Mod Name: hostpolicy.dll
-> Mod Name: coreclr.dll
-> Mod Name: ole32.dll
-> Mod Name: combase.dll
-> Mod Name: OLEAUT32.dll
-> Mod Name: bcryptPrimitives.dll
-> Mod Name: System.Private.CoreLib.dll
...
************************************
```

Starting and Stopping Processes Programmatically

The final aspects of the `System.Diagnostics.Process` class examined here are the `Start()` and `Kill()` methods. As you can gather by their names, these members provide a way to programmatically launch and terminate a process, respectively. For example, consider the following static `StartAndKillProcess()` helper method.

> **Note** Depending on your operating system's security settings, you might need to be running with Administrator rights to start new processes.

```
static void StartAndKillProcess()
{
  Process proc = null;

  // Launch Edge, and go to Facebook!
  try
  {
    proc = Process.Start(@"C:\Program Files (x86)\Microsoft\Edge\Application\msedge.exe",
    "www.facebook.com");
  }
  catch (InvalidOperationException ex)
  {
    Console.WriteLine(ex.Message);
  }

  Console.Write("--> Hit enter to kill {0}...",
    proc.ProcessName);
  Console.ReadLine();

  // Kill all of the msedge.exe processes.
  try
  {
    foreach (var p in Process.GetProcessesByName("MsEdge"))
    {
      p.Kill(true);
    }
```

```
  }
  catch (InvalidOperationException ex)
  {
    Console.WriteLine(ex.Message);
  }
}
```

The static Process.Start() method has been overloaded a few times. At a minimum, you will need to specify the path and filename of the process you want to launch. This example uses a variation of the Start() method that allows you to specify any additional arguments to pass into the program's entry point, in this case, the web page to load.

After you call the Start() method, you are returned a reference to the newly activated process. When you want to terminate the process, simply call the instance-level Kill() method. In this example, since Microsoft Edge launches a lot of processes, you are looping through to kill all the launched processes. You are also wrapping the calls to Start() and Kill() within a try/catch block to handle any InvalidOperationException errors. This is especially important when calling the Kill() method, as this error will be raised if the process has already been terminated prior to calling Kill().

■ **Note** When using the .NET Framework (prior to .NET Core), the Process.Start() method allowed for either the full path and filename or the operating system shortcut (e.g., msedge) of the process to start. With .NET Core and the cross-platform support, you must specify the full path and filename. Operating system associations can be leveraged using the ProcessStartInfo, covered in the next two sections.

Controlling Process Startup Using the ProcessStartInfo Class

The Process.Start() method also allows you to pass in a System.Diagnostics.ProcessStartInfo type to specify additional bits of information regarding how a given process should come to life. Here is a partial definition of ProcessStartInfo (see the documentation for full details):

```
public sealed class ProcessStartInfo : object
{
  public ProcessStartInfo();
  public ProcessStartInfo(string fileName);
  public ProcessStartInfo(string fileName, string arguments);
  public string Arguments { get; set; }
  public bool CreateNoWindow { get; set; }
  public StringDictionary EnvironmentVariables { get; }
  public bool ErrorDialog { get; set; }
  public IntPtr ErrorDialogParentHandle { get; set; }
  public string FileName { get; set; }
  public bool LoadUserProfile { get; set; }
  public SecureString Password { get; set; }
  public bool RedirectStandardError { get; set; }
  public bool RedirectStandardInput { get; set; }
  public bool RedirectStandardOutput { get; set; }
  public Encoding StandardErrorEncoding { get; set; }
  public Encoding StandardOutputEncoding { get; set; }
  public bool UseShellExecute { get; set; }
```

```
  public string Verb { get; set; }
  public string[] Verbs { get; }
  public ProcessWindowStyle WindowStyle { get; set; }
  public string WorkingDirectory { get; set; }
}
```

To illustrate how to fine-tune your process startup, here is a modified version of StartAndKillProcess(), which will load Microsoft Edge and navigate to www.facebook.com, using the Windows association MsEdge:

```
static void StartAndKillProcess()
{
  Process proc = null;

  // Launch Microsoft Edge, and go to Facebook, with maximized window.
  try
  {
    ProcessStartInfo startInfo = new
      ProcessStartInfo("MsEdge", "www.facebook.com");
    startInfo.UseShellExecute = true;
    proc = Process.Start(startInfo);
  }
  catch (InvalidOperationException ex)
  {
    Console.WriteLine(ex.Message);
  }
...
}
```

In .NET Core, the UseShellExecute property defaults to false, while in prior versions of .NET, the UseShellExecute property defaults to true. This is the reason that the previous version of Process.Start(), shown here, no longer works without using ProcessStartInfo and setting the UseShellExecute property to true:

```
Process.Start("msedge")
```

Leveraging OS Verbs with ProcessStartInfo

In addition to using the OS shortcuts to launch applications, you can also take advantage of file associations with ProcessStartInfo. On Windows, if you right-click a Word document, there are options to edit or print the document. Let's use the ProcessStartInfo to determine the verbs available and then use them to manipulate the process.

Create a new method with the following code:

```
static void UseApplicationVerbs()
{
  int i = 0;
  //adjust this path and name to a document on your machine
  ProcessStartInfo si =
    new ProcessStartInfo(@"..\TestPage.docx");
  foreach (var verb in si.Verbs)
```

```
  {
    Console.WriteLine($"  {i++}. {verb}");
  }
  si.WindowStyle = ProcessWindowStyle.Maximized;
  si.Verb = "Edit";
  si.UseShellExecute = true;
  Process.Start(si);
}
```

When you run this code, the first part prints out all the available verbs for a Word document, as the following shows:

```
***** Fun with Processes *****
  0. Edit
  1. OnenotePrintto
  2. Open
  3. OpenAsReadOnly
  4. Print
  5. Printto
  6. ViewProtected
```

After setting `WindowStyle` to maximized, the verb is set to `Edit`, which opens the document in edit mode. If you set the verb to `Print`, the document will be sent straight to the printer.

Now that you understand the role of Windows processes and how to interact with them from C# code, you are ready to investigate the concept of a .NET application domain.

■ **Note** The directory in which the application runs is dependent on how you run the sample application. If you use the CLI command `dotnet run`, the current directory is the same as where the project file is located. If you are using Visual Studio, the current directory will be the directory of the compiled assembly, which is `.\bin\debug\net6.0`. You will need to adjust the path to the Word document accordingly.

Understanding .NET Application Domains

Under the .NET and .NET Core platforms, executables are not hosted directly within a Windows process, as is the case in traditional unmanaged applications. Rather, .NET and .NET Core executables are hosted by a logical partition within a process called an *application domain*. This partition of a traditional Windows process offers several benefits, some of which are as follows:

- AppDomains are a key aspect of the OS-neutral nature of the .NET Core platform, given that this logical division abstracts away the differences in how an underlying OS represents a loaded executable.
- AppDomains are far less expensive in terms of processing power and memory than a full-blown process. Thus, the CoreCLR can load and unload application domains much quicker than a formal process and can drastically improve scalability of server applications.

AppDomains are fully and completely isolated from other AppDomains within a process. Given this fact, be aware that an application running in one AppDomain is unable to obtain data of any kind (global variables or static fields) within another AppDomain, unless they use a distributed programming protocol.

■ **Note** Support for AppDomains is changed in .NET Core. In .NET Core, there is exactly one AppDomain. Creation of new AppDomains is no longer supported because they require runtime support and are generally expensive to create. The `ApplicationLoadContext` (covered later in this chapter) provides assembly isolation in .NET Core.

The System.AppDomain Class

The `AppDomain` class is largely deprecated with .NET Core. While most of the remaining support is designed to make migrating from .NET 4.x to .NET Core easier, the remaining features can still provide value, as covered in the next two sections.

Interacting with the Default Application Domain

Your application has access to the default application domain using the static `AppDomain.CurrentDomain` property. After you have this access point, you can use the methods and properties of `AppDomain` to perform some runtime diagnostics.

To learn how to interact with the default application domain, begin by creating a new Console Application project named DefaultAppDomainApp and disable nullability in the project file. Now, update your `Program.cs` file with the following logic, which will simply display some details about the default application domain, using a number of members of the `AppDomain` class:

```
using System.Reflection;
using System.Runtime.Loader;

Console.WriteLine("***** Fun with the default AppDomain *****\n");
DisplayDADStats();
Console.ReadLine();

static void DisplayDADStats()
{
  // Get access to the AppDomain for the current thread.
  AppDomain defaultAD = AppDomain.CurrentDomain;
  // Print out various stats about this domain.
  Console.WriteLine("Name of this domain: {0}",
    defaultAD.FriendlyName);
  Console.WriteLine("ID of domain in this process: {0}",
    defaultAD.Id);
  Console.WriteLine("Is this the default domain?: {0}",
    defaultAD.IsDefaultAppDomain());
  Console.WriteLine("Base directory of this domain: {0}",
    defaultAD.BaseDirectory);
  Console.WriteLine("Setup Information for this domain:");
  Console.WriteLine("\t Application Base: {0}",
```

```
    defaultAD.SetupInformation.ApplicationBase);
  Console.WriteLine("\t Target Framework: {0}",
    defaultAD.SetupInformation.TargetFrameworkName);
}
```

The output of this example is shown here:

```
***** Fun with the default AppDomain *****
Name of this domain: DefaultAppDomainApp
ID of domain in this process: 1
Is this the default domain?: True
Base directory of this domain: C:\GitHub\Books\csharp8-wf\Code\Chapter_14\
DefaultAppDomainApp\DefaultAppDomainApp\bin\Debug\net6.0\
Setup Information for this domain:
  Application Base: C:\GitHub\Books\csharp8-wf\Code\Chapter_14\DefaultAppDomainApp\
DefaultAppDomainApp\bin\Debug\net6.0\
  Target Framework: .NETCoreApp,Version=v5.0
```

Notice that the name of the default application domain will be identical to the name of the executable that is contained within it (`DefaultAppDomainApp.exe`, in this example). Also notice that the base directory value, which will be used to probe for externally required private assemblies, maps to the current location of the deployed executable.

Enumerating Loaded Assemblies

It is also possible to discover all the loaded .NET Core assemblies within a given application domain using the instance-level `GetAssemblies()` method. This method will return to you an array of `Assembly` objects (covered in Chapter 17). To do this, you must have added the `System.Reflection` namespace to your code file (as you did earlier in this section).

To illustrate, define a new method named `ListAllAssembliesInAppDomain()` within the `Program.cs` file. This helper method will obtain all loaded assemblies and print the friendly name and version of each.

```
static void ListAllAssembliesInAppDomain()
{
  // Get access to the AppDomain for the current thread.
  AppDomain defaultAD = AppDomain.CurrentDomain;

  // Now get all loaded assemblies in the default AppDomain.
  Assembly[] loadedAssemblies = defaultAD.GetAssemblies();
  Console.WriteLine("***** Here are the assemblies loaded in {0} *****\n",
    defaultAD.FriendlyName);
  foreach(Assembly a in loadedAssemblies)
  {
    Console.WriteLine($"-> Name, Version: {a.GetName().Name}:{a.GetName().Version}" );
  }
}
```

Assuming you have updated your top-level statements to call this new member, you will see that the application domain hosting your executable is currently using the following .NET Core libraries:

```
***** Here are the assemblies loaded in DefaultAppDomainApp *****
-> Name, Version: System.Private.CoreLib:5.0.0.0
-> Name, Version: DefaultAppDomainApp:1.0.0.0
-> Name, Version: System.Runtime:5.0.0.0
-> Name, Version: System.Console:5.0.0.0
-> Name, Version: System.Threading:5.0.0.0
-> Name, Version: System.Text.Encoding.Extensions:5.0
```

Now understand that the list of loaded assemblies can change at any time as you author new C# code. For example, assume you have updated your `ListAllAssembliesInAppDomain()` method to make use of a LINQ query, which will order the loaded assemblies by name, as follows:

```
static void ListAllAssembliesInAppDomain()
{
  // Get access to the AppDomain for the current thread.
  AppDomain defaultAD = AppDomain.CurrentDomain;

  // Now get all loaded assemblies in the default AppDomain.
  var loadedAssemblies =
    defaultAD.GetAssemblies().OrderBy(x=>x.GetName().Name);
  Console.WriteLine("***** Here are the assemblies loaded in {0} *****\n",
  defaultAD.FriendlyName);
  foreach(Assembly a in loadedAssemblies)
  {
    Console.WriteLine($"-> Name, Version: {a.GetName().Name}:{a.GetName().Version}" );
  }
}
```

If you were to run the program once again, you would see that `System.Linq.dll` has also been loaded into memory.

```
** Here are the assemblies loaded in DefaultAppDomainApp **
-> Name, Version: DefaultAppDomainApp:1.0.0.0
-> Name, Version: System.Console:5.0.0.0
-> Name, Version: System.Linq:5.0.0.0
-> Name, Version: System.Private.CoreLib:5.0.0.0
-> Name, Version: System.Runtime:5.0.0.0
-> Name, Version: System.Text.Encoding.Extensions:5.0.0.0
-> Name, Version: System.Threading:5.0.0
```

Assembly Isolation with Application Load Contexts

As you have just seen, AppDomains are logical partitions used to host .NET Core assemblies. Additionally, an application domain may be further subdivided into numerous load context boundaries. Conceptually, a load context creates a scope for loading, resolving, and potentially unloading a set of assemblies. In a nutshell, a .NET Core load context provides a way for a single AppDomain to establish a "specific home" for a given object.

■ **Note** While understanding processes and application domains is quite important, most .NET Core applications will never demand that you work with object contexts. I've included this overview material just to paint a more complete picture.

The AssemblyLoadContext class provides the capability to load additional assemblies into their own contexts. To demonstrate, first add a class library project named ClassLibary1 and add it to your current solution. Using the .NET Core CLI, execute the following commands in the directory containing your current solution:

```
dotnet new classlib -lang c# -n ClassLibrary1 -o .\ClassLibrary1 -f net6.0
dotnet sln .\Chapter14_AllProjects.sln add .\ClassLibrary1
```

Next, add a reference from the DefaultAppDomainApp to the ClassLibrary1 project by executing the following CLI command:

```
dotnet add DefaultAppDomainApp reference ClassLibrary1
```

If you are using Visual Studio, right-click the solution node in Solution Explorer, select Add ➤ New Project, and add a .NET Core class library named ClassLibrary1. This creates the project and adds it to your solution. Next, add a reference to this new project by right-clicking the DefaultAppDomainApp project and selecting Add ➤ Project Reference. Select the Projects ➤ Solution option in the left rail, and select the ClassLibrary1 check box, as shown in Figure 14-3.

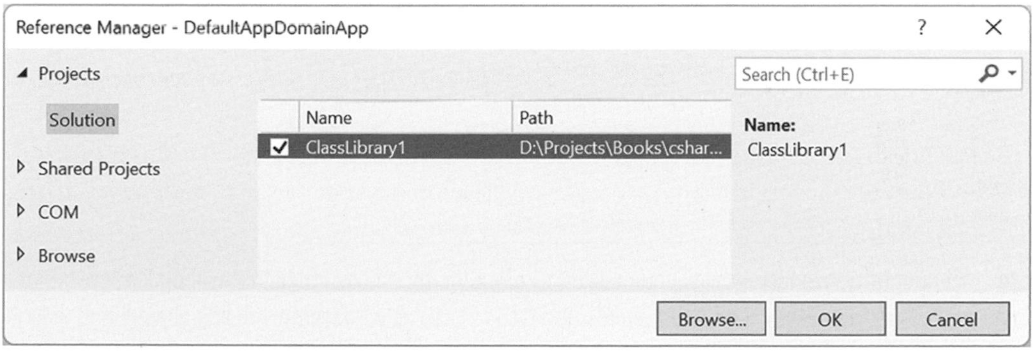

Figure 14-3. *Adding the project reference in Visual Studio*

In this new class library, add a Car class, as follows:

```
namespace ClassLibrary1;
public class Car
{
  public string PetName { get; set; }
  public string Make { get; set; }
  public int Speed { get; set; }
}
```

With this new assembly in place, make sure the following using statements are at the top of the Program.cs file in the DefaultAppDomainApp project:

```
using System.Reflection;
using System.Runtime.Loader;
```

The next method in the DefaultAppDomainApp top level statements is the LoadAdditionalAssembliesDifferentContexts() method, shown here:

```
static void LoadAdditionalAssembliesDifferentContexts()
{
  var path =
   Path.Combine(AppDomain.CurrentDomain.BaseDirectory,
             "ClassLibrary1.dll");
  AssemblyLoadContext lc1 =
    new AssemblyLoadContext("NewContext1",false);
  var cl1 = lc1.LoadFromAssemblyPath(path);
  var c1 = cl1.CreateInstance("ClassLibrary1.Car");

  AssemblyLoadContext lc2 =
    new AssemblyLoadContext("NewContext2",false);
  var cl2 = lc2.LoadFromAssemblyPath(path);
  var c2 = cl2.CreateInstance("ClassLibrary1.Car");
  Console.WriteLine("*** Loading Additional Assemblies in Different Contexts ***");
  Console.WriteLine($"Assembly1 Equals(Assembly2) {cl1.Equals(cl2)}");
  Console.WriteLine($"Assembly1 == Assembly2 {cl1 == cl2}");
  Console.WriteLine($"Class1.Equals(Class2) {c1.Equals(c2)}");
  Console.WriteLine($"Class1 == Class2 {c1 == c2}");
}
```

The first line uses the static Path.Combine method to build up the directory for the ClassLibrary1 assembly.

■ **Note** You might be wondering why you created a reference for an assembly that will be loaded dynamically. This is to make sure that when the project builds, the ClassLibrary1 assembly builds as well and is in the same directory as the DefaultAppDomainApp. This is merely a convenience for this example. There is no need to reference an assembly that you will load dynamically.

Next, the code creates a new AssemblyLoadContext with the name NewContext1 (the first parameter of the method) and does not support unloading (the second parameter). This LoadContext is used to load the ClassLibrary1 assembly and then create an instance of a Car class. If some of this code is new to you, it will be explained more fully in Chapter 18. The process is repeated with a new AssemblyLoadContext, and then the assemblies and classes are compared for equality. When you run this new method, you will see the following output:

```
*** Loading Additional Assemblies in Different Contexts ***
Assembly1 Equals(Assembly2) False
```

```
Assembly1 == Assembly2 False
Class1.Equals(Class2) False
Class1 ==8 Class2 False
```

This demonstrates that the same assembly has been loaded twice into the app domain. The classes are also different, as should be expected.

Next, add a new method that will load the assembly from the same `AssemblyLoadContext`.

```
static void LoadAdditionalAssembliesSameContext()
{
  var path =
   Path.Combine(AppDomain.CurrentDomain.BaseDirectory,
              "ClassLibrary1.dll");
  AssemblyLoadContext lc1 =
    new AssemblyLoadContext(null,false);
  var cl1 = lc1.LoadFromAssemblyPath(path);
  var c1 = cl1.CreateInstance("ClassLibrary1.Car");
  var cl2 = lc1.LoadFromAssemblyPath(path);
  var c2 = cl2.CreateInstance("ClassLibrary1.Car");
  Console.WriteLine("*** Loading Additional Assemblies in Same Context ***");
  Console.WriteLine($"Assembly1.Equals(Assembly2) {cl1.Equals(cl2)}");
  Console.WriteLine($"Assembly1 == Assembly2 {cl1 == cl2}");
  Console.WriteLine($"Class1.Equals(Class2) {c1.Equals(c2)}");
  Console.WriteLine($"Class1 == Class2 {c1 == c2}");
}
```

The main difference in this code is that only one `AssemblyLoadContext` is created. Now, when the `ClassLibrary1` assembly is loaded twice, the second assembly is simply a pointer to the first instance of the assembly. Running the code produces the following output:

```
*** Loading Additional Assemblies in Same Context ***
Assembly1.Equals(Assembly2) True
Assembly1 == Assembly2 True
Class1.Equals(Class2) False
Class1 == Class2 False
```

Summarizing Processes, AppDomains, and Load Contexts

At this point, you should have a much better idea about how a .NET Core assembly is hosted by the runtime. If the previous pages have seemed to be a bit too low level for your liking, fear not. For the most part, .NET Core automatically deals with the details of processes, application domains, and load contexts on your behalf. The good news, however, is that this information provides a solid foundation for understanding multithreaded programming under the .NET Core platform.

Summary

The point of this chapter was to examine exactly how a .NET Core application is hosted by the .NET Core platform. As you have seen, the long-standing notion of a Windows process has been altered under the hood to accommodate the needs of the CoreCLR. A single process (which can be programmatically manipulated via the `System.Diagnostics.Process` type) is now composed of an application domain, which represents isolated and independent boundaries within a process.

An application domain is capable of hosting and executing any number of related assemblies. Furthermore, a single application domain can contain any number of load contexts for further assembly isolation. Using this additional level of type isolation, the CoreCLR can ensure that special-need objects are handled correctly.

CHAPTER 15

Multithreaded, Parallel, and Async Programming

Nobody enjoys working with an application that is sluggish during its execution. Moreover, nobody enjoys starting a task in an application (perhaps initiated by clicking a toolbar item) that prevents other parts of the program from being as responsive as possible. Before the release of .NET (and .NET Core), building applications that had the ability to perform multiple tasks typically required authoring complex C++ code that used the Windows threading APIs. Thankfully, the .NET/.NET Core platform provides several ways for you to build software that can perform complex operations on unique paths of execution, with far fewer pain points.

This chapter begins by defining the overall nature of a "multithreaded application." Next, you will be introduced to the original threading namespace that has shipped since .NET 1.0, specifically `System.Threading`. Here, you will examine numerous types (`Thread`, `ThreadStart`, etc.) that allow you to explicitly create additional threads of execution and synchronize your shared resources, which helps ensure that multiple threads can share data in a nonvolatile manner.

The remaining parts of this chapter will examine three more recent techniques .NET Core developers can use to build multithreaded software, specifically the Task Parallel Library (TPL), Parallel LINQ (PLINQ), and the relatively new (as of C# 6) intrinsic asynchronous keywords of C# (`async` and `await`). As you will see, these features can dramatically simplify how you can build responsive multithreaded software applications.

The Process/AppDomain/Context/Thread Relationship

In Chapter 14, a *thread* was defined as a path of execution within an executable application. While many .NET Core applications can live happy and productive single-threaded lives, an assembly's primary thread (spawned by the runtime when the application's entry point executes) may create secondary threads of execution at any time to perform additional units of work. By creating additional threads, you can build more responsive (but not necessarily faster executing on single-core machines) applications.

The `System.Threading` namespace was released with .NET 1.0 and offers one approach to build multithreaded applications. The `Thread` class is perhaps the core type, as it represents a given thread. If you want to programmatically obtain a reference to the thread currently executing a given member, simply call the static `Thread.CurrentThread` property, like so:

```
static void ExtractExecutingThread()
{
  // Get the thread currently
  // executing this method.
  Thread currThread = Thread.CurrentThread;
}
```


A. Troelsen and P. Japikse, *Pro C# 10 with .NET 6*, https://doi.org/10.1007/978-1-4842-7869-7_15

Recall that with .NET Core, there is only a single AppDomain. Even though extra AppDomain's cannot be created, an application's AppDomain can have numerous threads executing within it at any given time. To get a reference to the AppDomain that is hosting the application, call the static `Thread.GetDomain()` method, like so:

```
static void ExtractAppDomainHostingThread()
{
  // Obtain the AppDomain hosting the current thread.
  AppDomain ad = Thread.GetDomain();
}
```

A single thread may also be moved into an execution context at any given time, and it may be relocated within a new execution context at the whim of the .NET Core Runtime. When you want to obtain the current execution context a thread happens to be executing in, use the static `Thread.CurrentThread.ExecutionContext` property, like so:

```
static void ExtractCurrentThreadExecutionContext()
{
  // Obtain the execution context under which the
  // current thread is operating.
  ExecutionContext ctx =
    Thread.CurrentThread.ExecutionContext;
}
```

Again, the .NET Core Runtime oversees moving threads into (and out of) execution contexts. As a .NET Core developer, you can usually remain blissfully unaware where a given thread ends up. Nevertheless, you should be aware of the various ways of obtaining the underlying primitives.

The Problem of Concurrency

One of the many "joys" (read: painful aspects) of multithreaded programming is that you have little control over how the underlying operating system or the runtime uses its threads. For example, if you craft a block of code that creates a new thread of execution, you cannot guarantee that the thread executes immediately. Rather, such code only instructs the OS/Runtime to execute the thread as soon as possible (which is typically when the thread scheduler gets around to it).

Furthermore, given that threads can be moved between application and contextual boundaries as required by the runtime, you must be mindful of which aspects of your application are *thread-volatile* (e.g., subject to multithreaded access) and which operations are *atomic* (thread-volatile operations are the dangerous ones!).

To illustrate the problem, assume a thread is invoking a method of a specific object. Now assume that this thread is instructed by the thread scheduler to suspend its activity to allow another thread to access the same method of the same object.

If the original thread was not finished with its operation, the second incoming thread may be viewing an object in a partially modified state. At this point, the second thread is basically reading bogus data, which is sure to give way to extremely odd (and hard to find) bugs, which are even harder to replicate and debug.

Atomic operations, on the other hand, are always safe in a multithreaded environment. Sadly, there are few operations in the .NET Core base class libraries that are guaranteed to be atomic. Even the act of assigning a value to a member variable is not atomic! Unless the .NET Core documentation specifically says an operation is atomic, you must assume it is thread-volatile and take precautions.

The Role of Thread Synchronization

At this point, it should be clear that multithreaded programs are in themselves quite volatile, as numerous threads can operate on the shared resources at (more or less) the same time. To protect an application's resources from possible corruption, .NET Core developers must use any number of threading primitives (such as locks, monitors, and the `[Synchronization]` attribute or language keyword support) to control access among the executing threads.

Although the .NET Core platform cannot make the difficulties of building robust multithreaded applications completely disappear, the process has been simplified considerably. Using types defined within the `System.Threading` namespace, the Task Parallel Library, and the C# `async` and `await` language keywords, you can work with multiple threads with minimal fuss and bother.

Before diving into the `System.Threading` namespace, the TPL, and the C# `async` and `await` keywords, you will begin by examining how the .NET Core delegate type can be used to invoke a method in an asynchronous manner. While it is most certainly true that since .NET 4.6 the new C# `async` and `await` keywords offer a simpler alternative to asynchronous delegates, it is still important that you know how to interact with code using this approach (trust me, there is a ton of code in production that uses asynchronous delegates).

The System.Threading Namespace

Under the .NET and .NET Core platforms, the `System.Threading` namespace provides types that enable the direct construction of multithreaded applications. In addition to providing types that allow you to interact with a .NET Core Runtime thread, this namespace defines types that allow access to the .NET Core Runtime-maintained thread pool, a simple (non-GUI-based) `Timer` class, and numerous types used to provide synchronized access to shared resources. Table 15-1 lists some of the important members of this namespace. (Be sure to consult the .NET Core SDK documentation for full details.)

Table 15-1. *Core Types of the System.Threading Namespace*

Type	Meaning in Life
`Interlocked`	This type provides atomic operations for variables that are shared by multiple threads.
`Monitor`	This type provides the synchronization of threading objects using locks and wait/signals. The C# `lock` keyword uses a `Monitor` object under the hood.
`Mutex`	This synchronization primitive can be used for synchronization between application domain boundaries.
`ParameterizedThreadStart`	This delegate allows a thread to call methods that take any number of arguments.
`Semaphore`	This type allows you to limit the number of threads that can access a resource concurrently.
`Thread`	This type represents a thread that executes within the .NET Core Runtime. Using this type, you can spawn additional threads in the originating AppDomain.
`ThreadPool`	This type allows you to interact with the .NET Core Runtime-maintained thread pool within a given process.

(*continued*)

Table 15-1. *(continued)*

Type	Meaning in Life
`ThreadPriority`	This enum represents a thread's priority level (`Highest`, `Normal`, etc.).
`ThreadStart`	This delegate is used to specify the method to call for a given thread. Unlike the `ParameterizedThreadStart` delegate, targets of `ThreadStart` must always have the same prototype.
`ThreadState`	This enum specifies the valid states a thread may take (`Running`, `Aborted`, etc.).
`Timer`	This type provides a mechanism for executing a method at specified intervals.
`TimerCallback`	This delegate type is used in conjunction with `Timer` types.

The System.Threading.Thread Class

The most primitive of all types in the `System.Threading` namespace is `Thread`. This class represents an object-oriented wrapper around a given path of execution within an AppDomain. This type also defines several methods (both static and instance level) that allow you to create new threads within the current AppDomain, as well as to suspend, stop, and destroy a thread. Consider the list of key static members in Table 15-2.

Table 15-2. *Key Static Members of the Thread Type*

Static Member	Meaning in Life
`ExecutionContext`	This read-only property returns information relevant to the logical thread of execution, including security, call, synchronization, localization, and transaction contexts.
`CurrentThread`	This read-only property returns a reference to the currently running thread.
`Sleep()`	This method suspends the current thread for a specified time.

The `Thread` class also supports several instance-level members, some of which are shown in Table 15-3.

Table 15-3. *Select Instance-Level Members of the Thread Type*

Instance-Level Member	Meaning in Life
`IsAlive`	Returns a Boolean that indicates whether this thread has been started (and has not yet terminated or aborted).
`IsBackground`	Gets or sets a value indicating whether this thread is a "background thread" (more details in just a moment).
`Name`	Allows you to establish a friendly text name of the thread.
`Priority`	Gets or sets the priority of a thread, which may be assigned a value from the `ThreadPriority` enumeration.

(continued)

Table 15-3. (*continued*)

Instance-Level Member	Meaning in Life
`ThreadState`	Gets the state of this thread, which may be assigned a value from the `ThreadState` enumeration.
`Abort()`	Instructs the .NET Core Runtime to terminate the thread as soon as possible.
`Interrupt()`	Interrupts (e.g., wakes) the current thread from a suitable wait period.
`Join()`	Blocks the calling thread until the specified thread (the one on which `Join()` is called) exits.
`Resume()`	Resumes a thread that has been previously suspended.
`Start()`	Instructs the .NET Core Runtime to execute the thread ASAP.
`Suspend()`	Suspends the thread. If the thread is already suspended, a call to `Suspend()` has no effect.

■ **Note** Aborting or suspending an active thread is generally considered a bad idea. When you do so, there is a chance (however small) that a thread could "leak" its workload when disturbed or terminated.

Obtaining Statistics About the Current Thread of Execution

Recall that the entry point of an executable assembly (i.e., the top-level statements or the `Main()` method) runs on the primary thread of execution. To illustrate the basic use of the `Thread` type, assume you have a new Console Application project named ThreadStats. As you know, the static `Thread.CurrentThread` property retrieves a `Thread` object that represents the currently executing thread. Once you have obtained the current thread, you are able to print out various statistics, like so:

```
Console.WriteLine("***** Primary Thread stats *****\n");

// Obtain and name the current thread.
Thread primaryThread = Thread.CurrentThread;
primaryThread.Name = "ThePrimaryThread";

// Print out some stats about this thread.
Console.WriteLine("ID of current thread: {0}",
  primaryThread.ManagedThreadId);
Console.WriteLine("Thread Name: {0}",
  primaryThread.Name);
Console.WriteLine("Has thread started?: {0}",
  primaryThread.IsAlive);
Console.WriteLine("Priority Level: {0}",
  primaryThread.Priority);
Console.WriteLine("Thread State: {0}",
  primaryThread.ThreadState);
Console.ReadLine();
```

Here is the current output:

```
***** Primary Thread stats *****
ID of current thread: 1
Thread Name: ThePrimaryThread
Has thread started?: True
Priority Level: Normal
Thread State: Running
```

The Name Property

Notice that the Thread class supports a property called Name. If you do not set this value, Name will return an empty string. However, once you assign a friendly string moniker to a given Thread object, you can greatly simplify your debugging endeavors. If you are using Visual Studio, you may access the Threads window during a debugging session (select Debug ➤ Windows ➤ Threads when the program is running). As you can see from Figure 15-1, you can quickly identify the thread you want to diagnose.

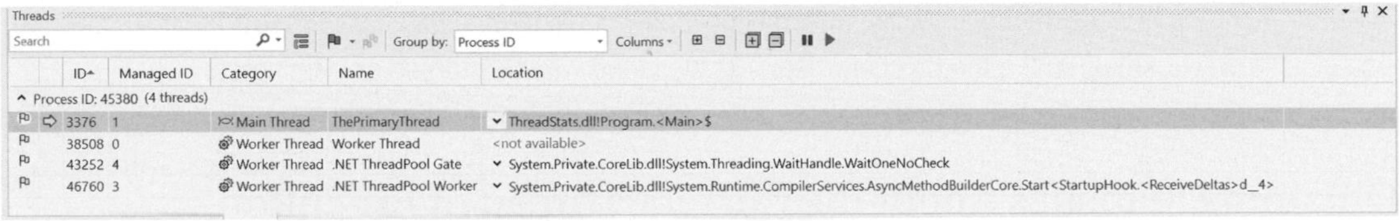

Figure 15-1. *Debugging a thread with Visual Studio*

The Priority Property

Next, notice that the Thread type defines a property named Priority. By default, all threads have a priority level of Normal. However, you can change this at any point in the thread's lifetime using the Priority property and the related System.Threading.ThreadPriority enumeration, like so:

```
public enum ThreadPriority
{
  Lowest,
  BelowNormal,
  Normal, // Default value.
  AboveNormal,
  Highest
}
```

If you were to assign a thread's priority level to a value other than the default (ThreadPriority.Normal), understand that you would have no direct control over when the thread scheduler switches between threads. A thread's priority level offers a hint to the .NET Core Runtime regarding the importance of the thread's activity. Thus, a thread with the value ThreadPriority.Highest is not necessarily guaranteed to be given the highest precedence.

Again, if the thread scheduler is preoccupied with a given task (e.g., synchronizing an object, switching threads, or moving threads), the priority level will most likely be altered accordingly. However, all things being equal, the .NET Core Runtime will read these values and instruct the thread scheduler how to best allocate time slices. Threads with an identical thread priority should each receive the same amount of time to perform their work.

In most cases, you will seldom (if ever) need to directly alter a thread's priority level. In theory, it is possible to jack up the priority level on a set of threads, thereby preventing lower-priority threads from executing at their required levels (so use caution).

Manually Creating Secondary Threads

When you want to programmatically create additional threads to carry on some unit of work, follow this predictable process when using the types of the `System.Threading` namespace:

1. Create a method to be the entry point for the new thread.
2. Create a new `ParameterizedThreadStart` (or `ThreadStart`) delegate, passing the address of the method defined in step 1 to the constructor.
3. Create a `Thread` object, passing the `ParameterizedThreadStart`/`ThreadStart` delegate as a constructor argument.
4. Establish any initial thread characteristics (name, priority, etc.).
5. Call the `Thread.Start()` method. This starts the thread at the method referenced by the delegate created in step 2 as soon as possible.

As stated in step 2, you may use two distinct delegate types to "point to" the method that the secondary thread will execute. The `ThreadStart` delegate can point to any method that takes no arguments and returns nothing. This delegate can be helpful when the method is designed to simply run in the background without further interaction.

The limitation of `ThreadStart` is that you are unable to pass in parameters for processing. However, the `ParameterizedThreadStart` delegate type allows a single parameter of type `System.Object`. Given that anything can be represented as a `System.Object`, you can pass in any number of parameters via a custom class or structure. Do note, however, that the `ThreadStart` and `ParameterizedThreadStart` delegates can only point to methods that return `void`.

Working with the ThreadStart Delegate

To illustrate the process of building a multithreaded application (as well as to demonstrate the usefulness of doing so), assume you have a Console Application project named SimpleMultiThreadApp that allows the end user to choose whether the application will perform its duties using the single primary thread or whether it will split its workload using two separate threads of execution.

Assuming you have imported the `System.Threading` namespace, your first step is to define a method to perform the work of the (possible) secondary thread. To keep focused on the mechanics of building multithreaded programs, this method will simply print out a sequence of numbers to the console window, pausing for approximately two seconds with each pass. Here is the full definition of the `Printer` class:

```
namespace SimpleMultiThreadApp;
public class Printer
{
  public void PrintNumbers()
  {
    // Display Thread info.
    Console.WriteLine("-> {0} is executing PrintNumbers()",
      Thread.CurrentThread.Name);
```

```
    // Print out numbers.
    Console.Write("Your numbers: ");
    for(int i = 0; i < 10; i++)
    {
      Console.Write("{0}, ", i);
      Thread.Sleep(2000);
    }
    Console.WriteLine();
  }
}
```

Now, within Program.cs, you will add top-level statements to first prompt the user to determine whether one or two threads will be used to perform the application's work. If the user requests a single thread, you will simply invoke the PrintNumbers() method within the primary thread. However, if the user specifies two threads, you will create a ThreadStart delegate that points to PrintNumbers(), pass this delegate object into the constructor of a new Thread object, and call Start() to inform the .NET Core Runtime this thread is ready for processing. Here is the complete implementation:

```
using SimpleMultiThreadApp;

Console.WriteLine("***** The Amazing Thread App *****\n");
Console.Write("Do you want [1] or [2] threads? ");
string threadCount = Console.ReadLine();

// Name the current thread.
Thread primaryThread = Thread.CurrentThread;
primaryThread.Name = "Primary";

// Display Thread info.
Console.WriteLine("-> {0} is executing Main()",
Thread.CurrentThread.Name);

// Make worker class.
Printer p = new Printer();

switch(threadCount)
{
  case "2":
    // Now make the thread.
    Thread backgroundThread =
      new Thread(new ThreadStart(p.PrintNumbers));
    backgroundThread.Name = "Secondary";
    backgroundThread.Start();
    break;
  case "1":
    p.PrintNumbers();
    break;
  default:
    Console.WriteLine("I don't know what you want...you get 1 thread.");
    goto case "1";
}
```

```
// Do some additional work.
Console.WriteLine("This is on the main thread, and we are finished.");
Console.ReadLine();
```

Now, if you run this program with a single thread, you will find that the final console output will not display the message until the entire sequence of numbers has printed to the console. As you are explicitly pausing for approximately two seconds after each number is printed, this will result in a less-than-stellar end-user experience. However, if you select two threads, the message box displays instantly, given that a unique Thread object is responsible for printing the numbers to the console.

Working with the ParameterizedThreadStart Delegate

Recall that the ThreadStart delegate can point only to methods that return void and take no arguments. While this might fit the bill in some cases, if you want to pass data to the method executing on the secondary thread, you will need to use the ParameterizedThreadStart delegate type. To illustrate, create a new Console Application project named AddWithThreads. Now, given that ParameterizedThreadStart can point to any method taking a System.Object parameter, you will create a custom type containing the numbers to be added, like so:

```
namespace AddWithThreads;
class AddParams
{
  public int a, b;

  public AddParams(int numb1, int numb2)
  {
    a = numb1;
    b = numb2;
  }
}
```

Next, create a method in the Program.cs file that will take an AddParams parameter and print the sum of the two numbers involved, as follows:

```
void Add(object data)
{
  if (data is AddParams ap)
  {
    Console.WriteLine("ID of thread in Add(): {0}",
      Environment.CurrentManagedThreadId);

    Console.WriteLine("{0} + {1} is {2}",
      ap.a, ap.b, ap.a + ap.b);
  }
}
```

The code within Program.cs is straightforward. Simply use ParameterizedThreadStart rather than ThreadStart, like so:

```
using AddWithThreads;

Console.WriteLine("***** Adding with Thread objects *****");
Console.WriteLine("ID of thread in Main(): {0}",
  Environment.CurrentManagedThreadId);

// Make an AddParams object to pass to the secondary thread.
AddParams ap = new AddParams(10, 10);
Thread t = new Thread(new ParameterizedThreadStart(Add));
t.Start(ap);

// Force a wait to let other thread finish.
Thread.Sleep(5);
Console.ReadLine();
```

The AutoResetEvent Class

In these first few examples, there is not a clean way to know when the secondary thread has completed its work. In the last example, Sleep was called with an arbitrary time to let the other thread finish. One simple and thread-safe way to force a thread to wait until another is completed is to use the AutoResetEvent class. In the thread that needs to wait, create an instance of this class and pass in false to the constructor to signify you have not yet been notified. Then, at the point at which you are willing to wait, call the WaitOne() method. Here is the update to the Program.cs class, which will do this very thing using a static-level AutoResetEvent member variable:

```
AutoResetEvent _waitHandle = new AutoResetEvent(false);

Console.WriteLine("***** Adding with Thread objects *****");
Console.WriteLine("ID of thread in Main(): {0}",
  Environment.CurrentManagedThreadId);
AddParams ap = new AddParams(10, 10);
Thread t = new Thread(new ParameterizedThreadStart(Add));
t.Start(ap);

// Wait here until you are notified!
_waitHandle.WaitOne();
Console.WriteLine("Other thread is done!");

Console.ReadLine();
...
```

When the other thread is completed with its workload, it will call the Set() method on the same instance of the AutoResetEvent type.

```
void Add(object data)
{
  if (data is AddParams ap)
  {
```

```
    Console.WriteLine("ID of thread in Add(): {0}",
      Environment.CurrentManagedThreadId);

    Console.WriteLine("{0} + {1} is {2}",
      ap.a, ap.b, ap.a + ap.b);

    // Tell other thread we are done.
    _waitHandle.Set();
  }
}
```

Foreground Threads and Background Threads

Now that you have seen how to programmatically create new threads of execution using the System.Threading namespace, let's formalize the distinction between foreground threads and background threads:

- *Foreground threads* can prevent the current application from terminating. The .NET Core Runtime will not shut down an application (which is to say, unload the hosting AppDomain) until all foreground threads have ended.
- *Background threads* (sometimes called *daemon threads*) are viewed by the .NET Core Runtime as expendable paths of execution that can be ignored at any point in time (even if they are currently laboring over some unit of work). Thus, if all foreground threads have terminated, all background threads are automatically killed when the application domain unloads.

It is important to note that foreground and background threads are *not* synonymous with primary and worker threads. By default, every thread you create via the Thread.Start() method is automatically a foreground thread. Again, this means that the AppDomain will not unload until all threads of execution have completed their units of work. In most cases, this is exactly the behavior you require.

For the sake of argument, however, assume that you want to invoke Printer.PrintNumbers() on a secondary thread that should behave as a background thread. Again, this means the method pointed to by the Thread type (via the ThreadStart or ParameterizedThreadStart delegate) should be able to halt safely as soon as all foreground threads are done with their work. Configuring such a thread is as simple as setting the IsBackground property to true.

Create a new Console Application named BackgroundThreads and copy the Printer.cs file into the new project. Update the namespace of the Printer class to BackgroundThreads, like this:

```
namespace BackgroundThreads;
public class Printer
{
...
}
```

Update the Program.cs file to match the following:

```
using BackgroundThreads;

Console.WriteLine("***** Background Threads *****\n");
Printer p = new Printer();
Thread bgroundThread =
  new Thread(new ThreadStart(p.PrintNumbers));
```

```
// This is now a background thread.
bgroundThread.IsBackground = true;
bgroundThread.Start();
```

Notice that this code is *not* making a call to `Console.ReadLine()` to force the console to remain visible until you press the Enter key. Thus, when you run the application, it will shut down immediately because the `Thread` object has been configured as a background thread. Given that the entry point into an application (either top-level statements as shown here or a `Main()` method) triggers the creation of the primary *foreground* thread, as soon as the logic in the entry point completes, the AppDomain unloads before the secondary thread can complete its work.

However, if you comment out the line that sets the `IsBackground` property, you will find that each number prints to the console, as all foreground threads must finish their work before the AppDomain is unloaded from the hosting process.

For the most part, configuring a thread to run as a background type can be helpful when the worker thread in question is performing a noncritical task that is no longer needed when the main task of the program is finished. For example, you could build an application that pings an email server every few minutes for new emails, updates current weather conditions, or performs some other noncritical task.

The Issue of Concurrency

When you build multithreaded applications, your program needs to ensure that any piece of shared data is protected against the possibility of numerous threads changing its value. Given that all threads in an AppDomain have concurrent access to the shared data of the application, imagine what might happen if multiple threads were accessing the same point of data. As the thread scheduler will force threads to suspend their work at random, what if thread A is kicked out of the way before it has fully completed its work? Thread B is now reading unstable data.

To illustrate the problem of concurrency, let's build another Console Application project named MultiThreadedPrinting. This application will once again use the `Printer` class created previously, but this time the `PrintNumbers()` method will force the current thread to pause for a randomly generated amount of time.

```
namespace MultiThreadedPrinting;
public class Printer
{
  public void PrintNumbers()
  {
    // Display Thread info.
    Console.WriteLine("-> {0} is executing PrintNumbers()",
      Thread.CurrentThread.Name);

    // Print out numbers.
    for (int i = 0; i < 10; i++)
    {
      // Put thread to sleep for a random amount of time.
      Random r = new Random();
      Thread.Sleep(1000 * r.Next(5));
      Console.Write("{0}, ", i);
    }
    Console.WriteLine();
  }
}
```

The calling code is responsible for creating an array of ten (uniquely named) Thread objects, each of which is making calls on the *same instance* of the Printer object as follows:

```
using MultiThreadedPrinting;

Console.WriteLine("*****Synchronizing Threads *****\n");

Printer p = new Printer();

// Make 10 threads that are all pointing to the same
// method on the same object.
Thread[] threads = new Thread[10];
for (int i = 0; i < 10; i++)
{
  threads[i] = new Thread(new ThreadStart(p.PrintNumbers))
  {
    Name = $"Worker thread #{i}"
  };
}
// Now start each one.
foreach (Thread t in threads)
{
  t.Start();
}
Console.ReadLine();
```

Before looking at some test runs, let's recap the problem. The primary thread within this AppDomain begins life by spawning ten secondary worker threads. Each worker thread is told to make calls on the PrintNumbers() method on the *same* Printer instance. Given that you have taken no precautions to lock down this object's shared resources (the console), there is a good chance that the current thread will be kicked out of the way before the PrintNumbers() method is able to print the complete results. Because you do not know exactly when (or if) this might happen, you are bound to get unpredictable results. For example, you might find the output shown here:

```
*****Synchronizing Threads *****
-> Worker thread #3 is executing PrintNumbers()
-> Worker thread #0 is executing PrintNumbers()
-> Worker thread #1 is executing PrintNumbers()
-> Worker thread #2 is executing PrintNumbers()
-> Worker thread #4 is executing PrintNumbers()
-> Worker thread #5 is executing PrintNumbers()
-> Worker thread #6 is executing PrintNumbers()
-> Worker thread #7 is executing PrintNumbers()
-> Worker thread #8 is executing PrintNumbers()
-> Worker thread #9 is executing PrintNumbers()
0, 0, 0, 0, 1, 0, 1, 0, 1, 0, 0, 0, 1, 0, 1, 1, 2, 3, 1, 2, 2, 2, 1, 2, 1, 1, 2, 2, 3, 3, 4,
3, 3, 2, 2, 3, 4, 3, 4, 5, 4, 5, 4, 4, 3, 6, 7, 2, 3, 4, 4, 4, 5, 6, 5, 3, 5, 8, 9,
6, 7, 4, 5, 6, 6, 5, 5, 5, 8, 5, 6, 7, 8, 7, 7, 6, 6, 6, 8, 9,
8, 7, 7, 7, 7, 9,
6, 8, 9,
8, 9,
```

```
9, 9,

8, 8, 7, 8, 9,
9,
9,
```

Now run the application a few more times and examine the output. It will most likely be different each time.

■ **Note** If you are unable to generate unpredictable outputs, increase the number of threads from 10 to 100 (for example) or introduce another call to `Thread.Sleep()` within your program. Eventually, you will encounter the concurrency issue.

There are clearly some problems here. As each thread is telling the `Printer` to print the numerical data, the thread scheduler is happily swapping threads in the background. The result is inconsistent output. What you need is a way to programmatically enforce synchronized access to the shared resources. As you would guess, the `System.Threading` namespace provides several synchronization-centric types. The C# programming language also provides a keyword for the very task of synchronizing shared data in multithreaded applications.

Synchronization Using the C# lock Keyword

The first technique you can use to synchronize access to shared resources is the C# `lock` keyword. This keyword allows you to define a scope of statements that must be synchronized between threads. By doing so, incoming threads cannot interrupt the current thread, thus preventing it from finishing its work. The `lock` keyword requires you to specify a *token* (an object reference) that must be acquired by a thread to enter within the lock scope. When you are attempting to lock down a *private* instance-level method, you can simply pass in a reference to the current type, as follows:

```
private void SomePrivateMethod()
{
  // Use the current object as the thread token.
  lock(this)
  {
    // All code within this scope is thread safe.
  }
}
```

However, if you are locking down a region of code within a *public* member, it is safer (and a best practice) to declare a private `object` member variable to serve as the lock token, like so:

```
public class Printer
{
  // Lock token.
  private object threadLock = new object();

  public void PrintNumbers()
  {
```

```
      // Use the lock token.
      lock (threadLock)
      {
        ...
      }
    }
}
```

In any case, if you examine the PrintNumbers() method, you can see that the shared resource the threads are competing to gain access to is the console window. Scope all interactions with the Console type within a lock scope, as follows:

```
public void PrintNumbers()
{
  // Use the private object lock token.
  lock (threadLock)
  {
    // Display Thread info.
    Console.WriteLine("-> {0} is executing PrintNumbers()",
      Thread.CurrentThread.Name);
    // Print out numbers.
    Console.Write("Your numbers: ");
    for (int i = 0; i < 10; i++)
    {
      Random r = new Random();
      Thread.Sleep(1000 * r.Next(5));
      Console.Write("{0}, ", i);
    }
    Console.WriteLine();
  }
}
```

When doing this, you have effectively designed a method that will allow the current thread to complete its task. Once a thread enters into a lock scope, the lock token (in this case, a reference to the current object) is inaccessible by other threads until the lock is released after the lock scope has exited. Thus, if thread A has obtained the lock token, other threads are unable to enter *any scope* that uses the same lock token until thread A relinquishes the lock token.

■ **Note** If you are attempting to lock down code in a static method, simply declare a private static object member variable to serve as the lock token.

If you now run the application, you can see that each thread has ample opportunity to finish its business.

```
*****Synchronizing Threads *****
-> Worker thread #0 is executing PrintNumbers()
Your numbers: 0, 1, 2, 3, 4, 5, 6, 7, 8, 9,
-> Worker thread #1 is executing PrintNumbers()
Your numbers: 0, 1, 2, 3, 4, 5, 6, 7, 8, 9,
```

```
-> Worker thread #3 is executing PrintNumbers()
Your numbers: 0, 1, 2, 3, 4, 5, 6, 7, 8, 9,
-> Worker thread #2 is executing PrintNumbers()
Your numbers: 0, 1, 2, 3, 4, 5, 6, 7, 8, 9,
-> Worker thread #4 is executing PrintNumbers()
Your numbers: 0, 1, 2, 3, 4, 5, 6, 7, 8, 9,
-> Worker thread #5 is executing PrintNumbers()
Your numbers: 0, 1, 2, 3, 4, 5, 6, 7, 8, 9,
-> Worker thread #7 is executing PrintNumbers()
Your numbers: 0, 1, 2, 3, 4, 5, 6, 7, 8, 9,
-> Worker thread #6 is executing PrintNumbers()
Your numbers: 0, 1, 2, 3, 4, 5, 6, 7, 8, 9,
-> Worker thread #8 is executing PrintNumbers()
Your numbers: 0, 1, 2, 3, 4, 5, 6, 7, 8, 9,
-> Worker thread #9 is executing PrintNumbers()
Your numbers: 0, 1, 2, 3, 4, 5, 6, 7, 8, 9,
```

Synchronization Using the System.Threading.Monitor Type

The C# `lock` statement is a shorthand notation for working with the `System.Threading.Monitor` class. Once processed by the C# compiler, a lock scope resolves to the following (which you can verify using `ildasm.exe`):

```
public void PrintNumbers()
{
  Monitor.Enter(threadLock);
  try
  {
    // Display Thread info.
    Console.WriteLine("-> {0} is executing PrintNumbers()",
      Thread.CurrentThread.Name);

    // Print out numbers.
    Console.Write("Your numbers: ");
    for (int i = 0; i < 10; i++)
    {
      Random r = new Random();
      Thread.Sleep(1000 * r.Next(5));
      Console.Write("{0}, ", i);
    }
    Console.WriteLine();
  }
  finally
  {
    Monitor.Exit(threadLock);
  }
}
```

First, notice that the `Monitor.Enter()` method is the ultimate recipient of the thread token you specified as the argument to the `lock` keyword. Next, all code within a lock scope is wrapped within a `try` block. The corresponding `finally` block ensures that the thread token is released (via the `Monitor.Exit()` method), regardless of any possible runtime exception. If you were to modify the MultiThreadPrinting program to make direct use of the `Monitor` type (as just shown), you would find the output is identical.

Now, given that the `lock` keyword seems to require less code than making explicit use of the `System.Threading.Monitor` type, you might wonder about the benefits of using the `Monitor` type directly. The short answer is control. If you use the `Monitor` type, you can instruct the active thread to wait for some duration of time (via the static `Monitor.Wait()` method), inform waiting threads when the current thread is completed (via the static `Monitor.Pulse()` and `Monitor.PulseAll()` methods), and so on.

As you would expect, in a great number of cases, the C# `lock` keyword will fit the bill. However, if you are interested in checking out additional members of the `Monitor` class, consult the .NET Core documentation.

Synchronization Using the System.Threading.Interlocked Type

Although it is always hard to believe, until you look at the underlying CIL code, assignments and simple arithmetic operations are *not atomic*. For this reason, the `System.Threading` namespace provides a type that allows you to operate on a single point of data atomically with less overhead than with the `Monitor` type. The `Interlocked` class defines the key static members shown in Table 15-4.

Table 15-4. *Select Static Members of the System.Threading.Interlocked Type*

Member	Meaning in Life
`CompareExchange()`	Safely tests two values for equality and, if equal, exchanges one of the values with a third
`Decrement()`	Safely decrements a value by 1
`Exchange()`	Safely swaps two values
`Increment()`	Safely increments a value by 1

Although it might not seem like it from the onset, the process of atomically altering a single value is quite common in a multithreaded environment. Assume you have code that increments an integer member variable named `intVal`. Rather than writing synchronization code such as the following:

```
int intVal = 5;
object myLockToken = new();
lock(myLockToken)
{
  intVal++;
}
```

you can simplify your code via the static `Interlocked.Increment()` method. Simply pass in the variable to increment by reference. Do note that the `Increment()` method not only adjusts the value of the incoming parameter but also returns the new value.

```
intVal = Interlocked.Increment(ref intVal);
```

In addition to `Increment()` and `Decrement()`, the `Interlocked` type allows you to atomically assign numerical and object data. For example, if you want to assign the value of a member variable to the value 83, you can avoid the need to use an explicit lock statement (or explicit Monitor logic) and use the Interlocked.Exchange() method, like so:

```
var myInt = 27;
Interlocked.Exchange(ref myInt, 83);
Console.WriteLine(myInt);
```

Finally, if you want to test two values for equality and change the point of comparison in a thread-safe manner, you can leverage the Interlocked.CompareExchange() method as follows:

```
// If the value of i is currently 83, change myInt  to 99.
Interlocked.CompareExchange(ref myInt, 99, 83);
```

Programming with Timer Callbacks

Many applications have the need to call a specific method during regular intervals of time. For example, you might have an application that needs to display the current time on a status bar via a given helper function. As another example, you might want to have your application call a helper function every so often to perform noncritical background tasks such as checking for new email messages. For situations such as these, you can use the System.Threading.Timer type in conjunction with a related delegate named TimerCallback.

To illustrate, assume you have a Console Application project (TimerApp) that will print the current time every second until the user presses a key to terminate the application. The first obvious step is to write the method that will be called by the Timer type.

```
Console.WriteLine("***** Working with Timer type *****\n");
Console.ReadLine();

static void PrintTime(object state)
{
  Console.WriteLine("Time is: {0}",
    DateTime.Now.ToLongTimeString());
}
```

Notice the PrintTime() method has a single parameter of type System.Object and returns void. This is not optional, given that the TimerCallback delegate can only call methods that match this signature. The value passed into the target of your TimerCallback delegate can be any type of object (in the case of the email example, this parameter might represent the name of the Microsoft Exchange Server to interact with during the process). Also note that given that this parameter is indeed a System.Object, you can pass in multiple arguments using a System.Array or custom class/structure.

The next step is to configure an instance of the TimerCallback delegate and pass it into the Timer object. In addition to configuring a TimerCallback delegate, the Timer constructor allows you to specify the optional parameter information to pass into the delegate target (defined as a System.Object), the interval to poll the method, and the amount of time to wait (in milliseconds) before making the first call. Here is an example:

```
Console.WriteLine("***** Working with Timer type *****\n");

// Create the delegate for the Timer type.
TimerCallback timeCB = new TimerCallback(PrintTime);

// Establish timer settings.
```

```
Timer t = new Timer(
  timeCB,     // The TimerCallback delegate object.
  null,       // Any info to pass into the called method (null for no info).
  0,          // Amount of time to wait before starting (in milliseconds).
  1000);      // Interval of time between calls (in milliseconds).

Console.WriteLine("Hit Enter key to terminate...");
Console.ReadLine();
```

In this case, the PrintTime() method will be called roughly every second and will pass in no additional information to said method. Here is the output:

```
***** Working with Timer type *****
Hit key to terminate...
Time is: 6:51:48 PM
Time is: 6:51:49 PM
Time is: 6:51:50 PM
Time is: 6:51:51 PM
Time is: 6:51:52 PM
Press any key to continue . . .
```

If you did want to send in some information for use by the delegate target, simply substitute the null value of the second constructor parameter with the appropriate information, like so:

```
// Establish timer settings.
Timer t = new Timer(timeCB, "Hello From C# 10.0", 0, 1000);
```

You can then obtain the incoming data as follows:

```
static void PrintTime(object state)
{
  Console.WriteLine("Time is: {0}, Param is: {1}",
    DateTime.Now.ToLongTimeString(), state.ToString());
}
```

Using a Stand-Alone Discard (New 7.0)

In the previous example, the Timer variable is not used in any execution path, so it can be replaced with a discard, as follows:

```
  _ = new Timer(
    timeCB,  // The TimerCallback delegate object.
    "Hello from C# 10.0",     // Any info to pass into the called method
            // (null for no info).
    0,      // Amount of time to wait before starting
            //(in milliseconds).
    1000);  // Interval of time between calls
            //(in milliseconds).
```

Understanding the ThreadPool

The next thread-centric topic you will examine in this chapter is the role of the runtime thread pool. There is a cost with starting a new thread, so for purposes of efficiency, the thread pool holds onto created (but inactive) threads until needed. To allow you to interact with this pool of waiting threads, the System.Threading namespace provides the ThreadPool class type.

If you want to queue a method call for processing by a worker thread in the pool, you can use the ThreadPool.QueueUserWorkItem() method. This method has been overloaded to allow you to specify an optional System.Object for custom state data in addition to an instance of the WaitCallback delegate.

```
public static class ThreadPool
{
  ...
  public static bool QueueUserWorkItem(WaitCallback callBack);
  public static bool QueueUserWorkItem(WaitCallback callBack,
                                       object state);
}
```

The WaitCallback delegate can point to any method that takes a System.Object as its sole parameter (which represents the optional state data) and returns nothing. Note that if you do not provide a System.Object when calling QueueUserWorkItem(), the .NET Core Runtime automatically passes a null value. To illustrate queuing methods for use by the .NET Core Runtime thread pool, ponder the following program (in a console application called ThreadPoolApp), which uses the Printer type once again (make sure to update the namespace to ThreadPoolApp). In this case, however, you are not manually creating an array of Thread objects; rather, you are assigning members of the pool to the PrintNumbers() method.

```
using ThreadPoolApp;

Console.WriteLine("***** Fun with the .NET Core Runtime Thread Pool *****\n");

Console.WriteLine("Main thread started. ThreadID = {0}",
  Environment.CurrentManagedThreadId);

Printer p = new Printer();

WaitCallback workItem = new WaitCallback(PrintTheNumbers);

// Queue the method ten times.
for (int i = 0; i < 10; i++)
{
  ThreadPool.QueueUserWorkItem(workItem, p);
}
Console.WriteLine("All tasks queued");
Console.ReadLine();

static void PrintTheNumbers(object state)
{
  Printer task = (Printer)state;
  task.PrintNumbers();
}
```

At this point, you might be wondering if it would be advantageous to use the .NET Core Runtime–maintained thread pool rather than explicitly creating `Thread` objects. Consider these benefits of leveraging the thread pool:

- The thread pool manages threads efficiently by minimizing the number of threads that must be created, started, and stopped.
- By using the thread pool, you can focus on your business problem rather than the application's threading infrastructure.

However, using manual thread management is preferred in some cases. Here is an example:

- If you require foreground threads or must set the thread priority. Pooled threads are *always* background threads with default priority (`ThreadPriority.Normal`).
- If you require a thread with a fixed identity to abort it, suspend it, or discover it by name.

That wraps up your investigation of the `System.Threading` namespace. To be sure, understanding the topics presented thus far in the chapter (especially during your examination of concurrency issues) will be extremely valuable when creating a multithreaded application. Given this foundation, you will now turn your attention to several new thread-centric topics that were introduced in .NET 4.0 and carried forward to .NET Core. To begin, you will examine the role of an alternative threading model, the Task Parallel Library.

Parallel Programming Using the Task Parallel Library

At this point in the chapter, you have examined the `System.Threading` namespace objects that allow you to build multithreaded software. Beginning with the release of .NET 4.0, Microsoft introduced a new approach to multithreaded application development using a parallel programming library termed the *Task Parallel Library* (TPL). Using the types of `System.Threading.Tasks`, you can build fine-grained, scalable parallel code without having to work directly with threads or the thread pool.

This is not to say, however, that you will not use the types of `System.Threading` when you use the TPL. Both threading toolkits can work together quite naturally. This is especially true in that the `System.Threading` namespace still provides most of the synchronization primitives you examined previously (`Monitor`, `Interlocked`, etc.). However, you will quite likely find that you will favor working with the TPL rather than the original `System.Threading` namespace, given that the same set of tasks can be performed in a more straightforward manner.

The System.Threading.Tasks Namespace

Collectively speaking, the types of `System.Threading.Tasks` are referred to as the *Task Parallel Library*. The TPL will automatically distribute your application's workload across available CPUs dynamically, using the runtime thread pool. The TPL handles the partitioning of the work, thread scheduling, state management, and other low-level details. The result is that you can maximize the performance of your .NET Core applications while being shielded from many of the complexities of directly working with threads.

The Role of the Parallel Class

A key class of the TPL is `System.Threading.Tasks.Parallel`. This class contains methods that allow you to iterate over a collection of data (specifically, an object implementing `IEnumerable<T>`) in a parallel fashion, mainly through two primary static methods, `Parallel.For()` and `Parallel.ForEach()`, each of which defines numerous overloaded versions.

These methods allow you to author a body of code statements that will be processed in a parallel manner. In concept, these statements are the same sort of logic you would write in a normal looping construct (via the `for` or `foreach` C# keyword). The benefit is that the `Parallel` class will pluck threads from the thread pool (and manage concurrency) on your behalf.

Both methods require you to specify an `IEnumerable`- or `IEnumerable<T>`-compatible container that holds the data you need to process in a parallel manner. The container could be a simple array, a nongeneric collection (such as `ArrayList`), a generic collection (such as `List<T>`), or the results of a LINQ query.

In addition, you will need to use the `System.Func<T>` and `System.Action<T>` delegates to specify the target method that will be called to process the data. You have already encountered the `Func<T>` delegate in Chapter 13, during your investigation of LINQ to Objects. Recall that `Func<T>` represents a method that can have a given return value and a varied number of arguments. The `Action<T>` delegate is like `Func<T>`, in that it allows you to point to a method taking some number of parameters. However, `Action<T>` specifies a method that can only return `void`.

While you could call the `Parallel.For()` and `Parallel.ForEach()` methods and pass a strongly typed `Func<T>` or `Action<T>` delegate object, you can simplify your programming by using a fitting C# anonymous method or lambda expression.

Data Parallelism with the Parallel Class

The first way to use the TPL is to perform *data parallelism*. Simply put, this term refers to the task of iterating over an array or collection in a parallel manner using the `Parallel.For()` or `Parallel.ForEach()` method. Assume you need to perform some labor-intensive file I/O operations. Specifically, you need to load a large number of `*.jpg` files into memory, flip them upside down, and save the modified image data to a new location.

In this example, you will see how to perform the same overall task using a graphical user interface, so you can examine the use of "anonymous delegates" to allow secondary threads to update the primary user interface thread (aka the UI thread).

■ **Note** When you are building a multithreaded graphical user interface (GUI) application, secondary threads can never directly access user interface controls. The reason is that controls (buttons, text boxes, labels, progress bars, etc.) have thread affinity with the thread that created them. In the following example, I will illustrate one way to allow secondary threads to access UI items in a thread-safe manner. You will see a more simplified approach when you examine the C# `async` and `await` keywords.

To illustrate, create a new Windows Presentation Foundation application (the template is abbreviated to WPF App (.NET Core)) named DataParallelismWithForEach. To create the project using the CLI and add it to the chapter's solution, enter the following command:

```
dotnet new wpf -lang c# -n DataParallelismWithForEach -o .\DataParallelismWithForEach -f
net6.0
dotnet sln .\Chapter15_AllProjects.sln add .\DataParallelismWithForEach
```

■ **Note** Windows Presentation Foundation (WPF) is Windows only in this version of .NET Core and will be covered in detail in Chapters 24–28. If you have not worked with WPF or you don't have access to a Windows machine, everything you need for this example is listed here. If you would rather just follow along with a completed solution, you can find DataParallelismWithForEach in the `Chapter 15` folder of the GitHub repo. WPF development works with Visual Studio Code, although there is no designer support. For a richer development experience, I suggest you use Visual Studio 2022 for the WPF examples in this chapter.

At the time of this writing, the WPF project templates do not add support for global implicit `using` statements. Update the main `PropertyGroup` in the `DataParallelismWithForEach.csproj` file to the following, which also disables nullable reference types (updates in bold):

```
<PropertyGroup>
  <OutputType>WinExe</OutputType>
  <TargetFramework>net6.0-windows</TargetFramework>
  <ImplicitUsings>enable</ImplicitUsings>
  <Nullable>disable</Nullable>
  <UseWPF>true</UseWPF>
</PropertyGroup>
```

Double-click the `MainWindow.xaml` file in Solution Explorer, and replace the XAML with the following:

```
<Window x:Class="DataParallelismWithForEach.MainWindow"
        xmlns="http://schemas.microsoft.com/winfx/2006/xaml/presentation"
        xmlns:x="http://schemas.microsoft.com/winfx/2006/xaml"
        xmlns:d="http://schemas.microsoft.com/expression/blend/2008"

        xmlns:mc="http://schemas.openxmlformats.org/markup-compatibility/2006"

        xmlns:local="clr-namespace:DataParallelismWithForEach"
        mc:Ignorable="d"
        Title="Fun with TPL" Height="400" Width="800">
  <Grid>
    <Grid.RowDefinitions>
      <RowDefinition Height="Auto"/>
      <RowDefinition Height="*"/>
      <RowDefinition Height="Auto"/>
    </Grid.RowDefinitions>
    <Label Grid.Row="0" Grid.Column="0">
      Feel free to type here while the images are processed...
    </Label>
    <TextBox Grid.Row="1" Grid.Column="0"  Margin="10,10,10,10"/>
    <Grid Grid.Row="2" Grid.Column="0">
      <Grid.ColumnDefinitions>
        <ColumnDefinition Width="Auto"/>
        <ColumnDefinition Width="*"/>
        <ColumnDefinition Width="Auto"/>
      </Grid.ColumnDefinitions>
            <Button Name="cmdCancel" Grid.Row="0" Grid.Column="0" Margin="10,10,0,10"
            Click="cmdCancel_Click">
                Cancel
```

```
            </Button>
            <Button Name="cmdProcess" Grid.Row="0" Grid.Column="2" Margin="0,10,10,10"
                    Click="cmdProcess_Click">
                Click to Flip Your Images!
            </Button>
    </Grid>
  </Grid>
</Window>
```

Again, do not worry about what the markup means or how it works; you will spend plenty of time with WPF later in this book. The GUI of the application consists of a multiline `TextBox` and a single `Button` (named `cmdProcess`). The purpose of the text area is to allow you to enter data while the work is being performed in the background, thus illustrating the nonblocking nature of the parallel task.

For this example, an additional NuGet package (`System.Drawing.Common`) is required. To add it to your project, enter the following line (all on one line) in the command line (in the same directory as your solution file) or Package Manager Console in Visual Studio:

```
dotnet add DataParallelismWithForEach package System.Drawing.Common
```

Open the `MainWindow.xaml.cs` file (double-click it in Visual Studio—you might have to expand the arrow by `MainWindow.xaml`), and add the following `using` statements to the top of the file:

```
using System.Drawing;
using System.Windows;
using System.IO;
```

■ **Note** You should update the string passed into the following `Directory.GetFiles()` method call to point to a path on your computer that has some image files (such as a personal folder of family pictures). I have included some sample images (that ship with the Windows operating system) in the chapter's sample code for your convenience.

```
public partial class MainWindow : Window
{
  public MainWindow()
  {
    InitializeComponent();
  }

  private void cmdCancel_Click(object sender, EventArgs e)
  {
    // This will be updated shortly
  }

  private void cmdProcess_Click(object sender, EventArgs e)
  {
    this.Title = $"Starting...";
    ProcessFiles();
    this.Title = "Processing Complete";
  }
```

```
  private void ProcessFiles()
  {
    // Load up all *.jpg files, and make a new folder for the
    //   modified data.
    //Get the directory path where the file is executing
    //For VS 2022 debugging, the current directory will be <projectdirectory>\bin\debug\
    net6.0-windows
    //For VS Code or "dotnet run", the current directory will be <projectdirectory>
    var basePath = Directory.GetCurrentDirectory();
    var pictureDirectory =
      Path.Combine(basePath, "TestPictures");
    var outputDirectory =
      Path.Combine(basePath, "ModifiedPictures");
    //Clear out any existing files
    if (Directory.Exists(outputDirectory))
    {
      Directory.Delete(outputDirectory, true);
    }
    Directory.CreateDirectory(outputDirectory);
    string[] files = Directory.GetFiles(pictureDirectory,
       "*.jpg", SearchOption.AllDirectories);

    // Process the image data in a blocking manner.
    foreach (string currentFile in files)
    {
      string filename = Path.GetFileName(currentFile);
      // Print out the ID of the thread processing the current image.
       this.Title = $"Processing {filename} on thread {Environment.CurrentManagedThreadId}";
      using (Bitmap bitmap = new Bitmap(currentFile))
      {
        bitmap.RotateFlip(RotateFlipType.Rotate180FlipNone);
        bitmap.Save(Path.Combine(outputDirectory, filename));
      }
    }
  }
}
```

Note If you receive an error that `Path` is an ambiguous reference between `System.IO.Path` and `System.Windows.Shapes.Path`, either remove the `using` for `System.Windows.Shapes` or add `System.IO` to `Path`: `System.IO.Path.Combine(...)`.

Notice that the `ProcessFiles()` method will rotate each `*.jpg` file under the specified directory. Currently, all the work is happening on the primary thread of the executable. Therefore, when the button to process the files is clicked, the program will appear to hang. Furthermore, the caption of the window will also report that the same primary thread is processing the file, as we have only a single thread of execution.

To process the files on as many CPUs as possible, you can rewrite the current `foreach` loop to use `Parallel.ForEach()`. Recall that this method has been overloaded numerous times; however, in the simplest form, you must specify the `IEnumerable<T>`-compatible object that contains the items to process (that would be the `files` string array) and an `Action<T>` delegate that points to the method that will perform the work.

Here is the relevant update, using the C# lambda operator in place of a literal `Action<T>` delegate object. Notice that you are currently *commenting out* the line of code that displayed the ID of the thread executing the current image file. See the next section to find out the reason why.

```
// Process the image data in a parallel manner!
Parallel.ForEach(files, currentFile =>
  {
    string filename = Path.GetFileName(currentFile);

      // This code statement is now a problem! See next section.
      // this.Title = $"Processing {filename} on thread
      //      {Environment.CurrentManagedThreadId}";

    using (Bitmap bitmap = new Bitmap(currentFile))
    {
      bitmap.RotateFlip(RotateFlipType.Rotate180FlipNone);
      bitmap.Save(Path.Combine(outputDirectory, filename));
    }
  }
);
```

Accessing UI Elements on Secondary Threads

You will notice that I have commented out the previous line of code that updated the caption of the main window with the ID of the currently executing thread. As noted previously, GUI controls have "thread affinity" with the thread that created them. If secondary threads attempt to access a control they did not directly create, it will cause a runtime exception. However, this isn't guaranteed to happen, and exceptions might not be raised. Threading issues depend on a lot of different variables and are typically intermittent and very hard to reproduce.

■ **Note** Let me reiterate the previous point: when you debug a multithreaded application, you can sometimes catch errors that arise when a secondary thread is "touching" a control created on the primary thread. However, oftentimes when you run the application, the application could appear to run correctly (or it might error straightaway). Until you take precautions (examined next), your application has the potential of raising a runtime error under such circumstances.

One approach that you can use to allow these secondary threads to access the controls in a thread-safe manner is yet another delegate-centric technique, specifically an *anonymous delegate*. The `Control` parent class in WPF defines a `Dispatcher` object, which manages the work items for a thread. This object has a method named `Invoke()`, which takes a `System.Delegate` as input. You can call this method when you are in a coding context involving secondary threads to provide a thread-safe manner to update the UI of the given control. Now, while you could write all the required delegate code directly, most developers use expression syntax as a simple alternative. Here is the relevant update to the content with the previously commented-out code statement:

```
// Eek! This will not work anymore!
//this.Title = $"Processing {filename} on thread {Environment.CurrentManagedThreadId}";
```

```
// Invoke on the Form object, to allow secondary threads to access controls
// in a thread-safe manner.
Dispatcher?.Invoke(() =>
{
  this.Title = $"Processing {filename}";
});
using (Bitmap bitmap = new Bitmap(currentFile))
{
  bitmap.RotateFlip(RotateFlipType.Rotate180FlipNone);
  bitmap.Save(Path.Combine(outputDirectory, filename));
}
```

Now, if you run the program, the TPL will indeed distribute the workload to multiple threads from the thread pool, using as many CPUs as possible. However, since the `Title` is always updated from the main thread, the `Title` update code no longer displays the current thread, and you will not see anything if you type in the text box until all the images have been processed! The reason is that the primary UI thread is still blocked, waiting for all the other threads to finish up their business.

The Task Class

The `Task` class allows you to easily invoke a method on a secondary thread and can be used as a simple alternative to using asynchronous delegates. Update the `Click` handler of your `Button` control as so:

```
private void cmdProcess_Click(object sender, EventArgs e)
{
  this.Title = $"Starting...";
  // Start a new "task" to process the files.
  Task.Factory.StartNew(() => ProcessFiles());
  //Can also be written this way
  //Task.Factory.StartNew(ProcessFiles);

}
```

The `Factory` property of `Task` returns a `TaskFactory` object. When you call its `StartNew()` method, you pass in an `Action<T>` delegate (here, hidden away with a fitting lambda expression) that points to the method to invoke in an asynchronous manner. With this small update, you will now find that the window's title will show which thread from the thread pool is processing a given file, and better yet, the text area is able to receive input, as the UI thread is no longer blocked.

Handling Cancellation Request

One improvement you can make to the current example is to provide a way for the user to stop the processing of the image data, via a second (aptly named) Cancel button. Thankfully, the `Parallel.For()` and `Parallel.ForEach()` methods both support cancellation with *cancellation tokens*. When you invoke methods on `Parallel`, you can pass in a `ParallelOptions` object, which in turn contains a `CancellationTokenSource` object.

First, define the following new private member variable in your Form-derived class of type CancellationTokenSource named _cancelToken:

```
public partial class MainWindow :Window
{
  // New Window-level variable.
  private CancellationTokenSource _cancelToken = new CancellationTokenSource();
...
}
```

Update the Cancel button Click event to the following code:

```
private void cmdCancel_Click(object sender, EventArgs e)
{
  // This will be used to tell all the worker threads to stop!
  _cancelToken.Cancel();
}
```

Now, the real modifications need to occur within the ProcessFiles() method. Consider the final implementation:

```
private void ProcessFiles()
{
  // Use ParallelOptions instance to store the CancellationToken.
  ParallelOptions parOpts = new ParallelOptions();
  parOpts.CancellationToken = _cancelToken.Token;
  parOpts.MaxDegreeOfParallelism = System.Environment.ProcessorCount;

  // Load up all *.jpg files, and make a new folder for the modified data.
  string[] files = Directory.GetFiles(@".\TestPictures", "*.jpg", SearchOption.
  AllDirectories);
  string outputDirectory = @".\ModifiedPictures";
  Directory.CreateDirectory(outputDirectory);

  try
  {
    // Process the image data in a parallel manner!
    Parallel.ForEach(files, parOpts, currentFile =>
    {
      parOpts
         .CancellationToken.ThrowIfCancellationRequested();

      string filename = Path.GetFileName(currentFile);
      Dispatcher?.Invoke(() =>
      {
        this.Title =
          $"Processing {filename} on thread {Environment.CurrentManagedThreadId}";
      });
      using (Bitmap bitmap = new Bitmap(currentFile))
      {
        bitmap.RotateFlip(RotateFlipType.Rotate180FlipNone);
```

```
        bitmap.Save(Path.Combine(outputDirectory, filename));
      }
    });
    Dispatcher?.Invoke(()=>this.Title = "Done!");
  }
  catch (OperationCanceledException ex)
  {
    Dispatcher?.Invoke(()=>this.Title = ex.Message);
  }
}
```

Notice that you begin the method by configuring a `ParallelOptions` object, setting the `CancellationToken` property to use the `CancellationTokenSource` token. Also note that when you call the `Parallel.ForEach()` method, you pass in the `ParallelOptions` object as the second parameter.

Within the scope of the looping logic, you make a call to `ThrowIfCancellationRequested()` on the token, which will ensure if the user clicks the Cancel button, all threads will stop, and you will be notified via a runtime exception. When you catch the `OperationCanceledException` error, you will set the text of the main window to the error message.

■ **Note** New in C# 10, there is a new `async` method on the `Parallel` class named `ForEachAsync()`. This is covered later in this chapter.

Task Parallelism Using the Parallel Class

In addition to data parallelism, the TPL can also be used to easily fire off any number of asynchronous tasks using the `Parallel.Invoke()` method. This approach is a bit more straightforward than using members from `System.Threading`; however, if you require more control over the way tasks are executed, you could forgo use of `Parallel.Invoke()` and use the `Task` class directly, as you did in the previous example.

To illustrate task parallelism, create a new console application called MyEBookReader and be sure the `System.Text` and `System.Net` namespaces are imported at the top of `Program.cs` (this example is a modification of a useful example in the .NET Core documentation). Here, you will fetch a publicly available ebook from Project Gutenberg (`www.gutenberg.org`) and then perform a set of lengthy tasks in parallel.

The book is downloaded in the `GetBook()` method, shown here:

```
using System.Net;
using System.Text;

string _theEBook = "";
GetBook();
Console.WriteLine("Downloading book...");
Console.ReadLine();

void GetBook()
{
  //NOTE: The WebClient is obsolete.
  //We will revisit this example using HttpClient when we discuss async/await
  using WebClient wc = new WebClient();
  wc.DownloadStringCompleted += (s, eArgs) =>
```

```
  {
    _theEBook = eArgs.Result;
    Console.WriteLine("Download complete.");
    GetStats();
  };

  // The Project Gutenberg EBook of A Tale of Two Cities, by Charles Dickens
  // You might have to run it twice if you've never visited the site before, since the first
  // time you visit there is a message box that pops up, and breaks this code.
  wc.DownloadStringAsync(new Uri("http://www.gutenberg.org/files/98/98-0.txt"));
}
```

The WebClient class is a member of System.Net. This class provides methods for sending data to and receiving data from a resource identified by a URI. As it turns out, many of these methods have an asynchronous version, such as DownloadStringAsync(). This method will spin up a new thread from the .NET Core Runtime thread pool automatically. When the WebClient is done obtaining the data, it will fire the DownloadStringCompleted event, which you are handling here using a C# lambda expression. If you were to call the synchronous version of this method (DownloadString()), the "Downloading" message would not show until the download was complete.

■ **Note** The WebClient is obsolete and has been replaced by the HttpClient. We will revisit this example using the HttpClient class in the "Async Calls with Async/Await" section of this chapter.

Next, the GetStats() method is implemented to extract the individual words contained in the theEBook variable and then pass the string array to a few helper functions for processing as follows:

```
void GetStats()
{
  // Get the words from the ebook.
  string[] words = _theEBook.Split(new char[]
    { ' ', '\u000A', ',', '.', ';', ':', '-', '?', '/' },
    StringSplitOptions.RemoveEmptyEntries);

  // Now, find the ten most common words.
  string[] tenMostCommon = FindTenMostCommon(words);

  // Get the longest word.
  string longestWord = FindLongestWord(words);

  // Now that all tasks are complete, build a string to show all stats.
  StringBuilder bookStats = new StringBuilder("Ten Most Common Words are:\n");
  foreach (string s in tenMostCommon)
  {
    bookStats.AppendLine(s);
  }

  bookStats.AppendFormat("Longest word is: {0}", longestWord);
  bookStats.AppendLine();
  Console.WriteLine(bookStats.ToString(), "Book info");
}
```

The FindTenMostCommon() method uses a LINQ query to obtain a list of string objects that occur most often in the string array, while FindLongestWord() locates, well, the longest word.

```
string[] FindTenMostCommon(string[] words)
{
    var frequencyOrder = from word in words
                         where word.Length > 6
                         group word by word into g
                         orderby g.Count() descending
                         select g.Key;
    string[] commonWords = (frequencyOrder.Take(10)).ToArray();
    return commonWords;
}
string FindLongestWord(string[] words)
{
    return (from w in words orderby w.Length descending select w).FirstOrDefault();
}
```

If you were to run this project, performing all the tasks could take a significant amount of time, based on the CPU count of your machine and overall processor speed. Eventually, you should see the output shown here:

```
Downloading book...
Download complete.
Ten Most Common Words are:
Defarge
himself
Manette
through
nothing
business
another
looking
prisoner
Cruncher
Longest word is: undistinguishable
```

You can help ensure that your application uses all available CPUs on the host machine by invoking the FindTenMostCommon() and FindLongestWord() methods in parallel. To do so, modify your GetStats() method as so:

```
void GetStats()
{
  // Get the words from the ebook.
  string[] words = _theEBook.Split(
    new char[] { ' ', '\u000A', ',', '.', ';', ':', '-', '?', '/' },
    StringSplitOptions.RemoveEmptyEntries);
  string[] tenMostCommon = null;
  string longestWord = string.Empty;
```

```
    Parallel.Invoke(
      () =>
      {
        // Now, find the ten most common words.
        tenMostCommon = FindTenMostCommon(words);
      },
      () =>
      {
        // Get the longest word.
        longestWord = FindLongestWord(words);
      });

    // Now that all tasks are complete, build a string to show all stats.
    ...
}
```

The `Parallel.Invoke()` method expects a parameter array of `Action<>` delegates, which you have supplied indirectly using lambda expressions. Again, while the output is identical, the benefit is that the TPL will now use all possible processors on the machine to invoke each method in parallel if possible.

Parallel LINQ Queries (PLINQ)

To wrap up your look at the TPL, be aware that there is another way you can incorporate parallel tasks into your .NET Core applications. If you choose, you can use a set of extension methods that allow you to construct a LINQ query that will perform its workload in parallel (if possible). Fittingly, LINQ queries that are designed to run in parallel are termed *PLINQ queries*.

Like parallel code authored using the `Parallel` class, PLINQ has the option of ignoring your request to process the collection in parallel if need be. The PLINQ framework has been optimized in numerous ways, which includes determining whether a query would, in fact, perform faster in a synchronous manner.

At runtime, PLINQ analyzes the overall structure of the query, and if the query is likely to benefit from parallelization, it will run concurrently. However, if parallelizing a query would hurt performance, PLINQ just runs the query sequentially. If PLINQ has a choice between a potentially expensive parallel algorithm or an inexpensive sequential algorithm, it chooses the sequential algorithm by default.

The necessary extension methods are found within the `ParallelEnumerable` class of the `System.Linq` namespace. Table 15-5 documents some useful PLINQ extensions.

Table 15-5. *Select Members of the ParallelEnumerable Class*

Member	Meaning in Life
`AsParallel()`	Specifies that the rest of the query should be parallelized, if possible
`WithCancellation()`	Specifies that PLINQ should periodically monitor the state of the provided cancellation token and cancel execution if it is requested
`WithDegreeOfParallelism()`	Specifies the maximum number of processors that PLINQ should use to parallelize the query
`ForAll()`	Enables results to be processed in parallel without first merging back to the consumer thread, as would be the case when enumerating a LINQ result using the `foreach` keyword

To see PLINQ in action, create a console application named PLINQDataProcessingWithCancellation. When processing starts, the program will fire off a new Task, which executes a LINQ query that investigates a large array of integers, looking for only the items where x % 3 == 0 is true. Here is a *nonparallel* version of the query:

```
Console.WriteLine("Start any key to start processing");
Console.ReadKey();

Console.WriteLine("Processing");
Task.Factory.StartNew(ProcessIntData);
Console.ReadLine();

void ProcessIntData()
{
  // Get a very large array of integers.
  int[] source = Enumerable.Range(1, 10_000_000).ToArray();
  // Find the numbers where num % 3 == 0 is true, returned
  // in descending order.
  int[] modThreeIsZero = (
    from num in source
    where num % 3 == 0
    orderby num descending
    select num).ToArray();
  Console.WriteLine($"Found { modThreeIsZero.Count()} numbers that match query!");
}
```

Opting in to a PLINQ Query

If you want to inform the TPL to execute this query in parallel (if possible), you will want to use the AsParallel() extension method as so:

```
int[] modThreeIsZero = (
  from num in source.AsParallel()
  where num % 3 == 0
  orderby num descending select num).ToArray();
```

Notice how the overall format of the LINQ query is identical to what you saw in previous chapters. However, by including a call to AsParallel(), the TPL will attempt to pass the workload off to any available CPU.

Cancelling a PLINQ Query

It is also possible to use a CancellationTokenSource object to inform a PLINQ query to stop processing under the correct conditions (typically because of user intervention). Declare a class-level CancellationTokenSource object named _cancelToken and update the top-level statements method to take input from the user. Here is the relevant code update:

```
CancellationTokenSource _cancelToken =
  new CancellationTokenSource();
```

```
do
{
  Console.WriteLine("Start any key to start processing");
  Console.ReadKey();
  Console.WriteLine("Processing");
  Task.Factory.StartNew(ProcessIntData);
  Console.Write("Enter Q to quit: ");
  string answer = Console.ReadLine();
  // Does user want to quit?
  if (answer.Equals("Q",
    StringComparison.OrdinalIgnoreCase))
  {
    _cancelToken.Cancel();
    break;
  }
}
while (true);

Console.ReadLine();
```

Now, inform the PLINQ query that it should be on the lookout for an incoming cancellation request by chaining on the WithCancellation() extension method and passing in the token. In addition, you will want to wrap this PLINQ query in a proper try/catch scope and deal with the possible exception. Here is the final version of the ProcessIntData() method:

```
void ProcessIntData()
{
  // Get a very large array of integers.
  int[] source = Enumerable.Range(1, 10_000_000).ToArray();
  // Find the numbers where num % 3 == 0 is true, returned
  // in descending order.
  int[] modThreeIsZero = null;
  try
  {
    modThreeIsZero = (from num in source.AsParallel().WithCancellation(_cancelToken.Token)
            where num % 3 == 0
            orderby num descending
            select num).ToArray();
    Console.WriteLine();
    Console.WriteLine($"Found {modThreeIsZero.Count()} numbers that match query!");
  }
  catch (OperationCanceledException ex)
  {
    Console.WriteLine(ex.Message);
  }
}
```

When running this, you will want to hit Q and enter quickly to see the message from the cancellation token. On my development machine, I had less than one second to quit before it finished on its own. You can add a call to Thread.Sleep() to make it easier to cancel the process:

```
try
{
  Thread.Sleep(3000);
  modThreeIsZero = (from num in source.AsParallel().WithCancellation(_cancelToken.Token)
      where num % 3 == 0
      orderby num descending
      select num).ToArray();
  Console.WriteLine();
  Console.WriteLine($"Found {modThreeIsZero.Count()} numbers that match query!");
}
```

Async Calls Using the async/await Pattern

I have covered a lot of material in this (rather lengthy) chapter. To be sure, building, debugging, and understanding complex multithreaded applications are challenging in any framework. While the TPL, PLINQ, and the delegate type can simplify matters to some extent (especially when compared to other platforms and languages), developers are still required to know the ins and outs of various advanced techniques.

Since the release of .NET 4.5, the C# programming language has been updated with two new keywords that further simplify the process of authoring asynchronous code. In contrast to all the examples in this chapter, when you use the new async and await keywords, the compiler will generate a good deal of threading code on your behalf, using numerous members of the System.Threading and System.Threading.Tasks namespaces.

A First Look at the C# async and await Keywords (Updated 7.1, 9.0)

The async keyword of C# is used to qualify that a method, lambda expression, or anonymous method should be called in an asynchronous manner *automatically*. Yes, it is true. Simply by marking a method with the async modifier, the .NET Core Runtime will create a new thread of execution to handle the task at hand. Furthermore, when you are calling an async method, the await keyword will *automatically* pause the current thread from any further activity until the task is complete, leaving the calling thread free to continue.

To illustrate, create a console application named FunWithCSharpAsync and add a method named DoWork(), which forces the calling thread to wait for five seconds. Here is the story thus far:

```
Console.WriteLine(" Fun With Async ===>");
Console.WriteLine(DoWork());
Console.WriteLine("Completed");
Console.ReadLine();

static string DoWork()
{
  Thread.Sleep(5_000);
  return "Done with work!";
}
```

Now, given your work in this chapter, you know that if you were to run the program, you would need to wait five seconds before anything else can happen. If this were a graphical application, the entire screen would be locked until the work was completed.

If you were to use any of the previous techniques shown in this chapter to make your program more responsive, you would have a good deal of work ahead of you. However, since .NET 4.5, you can author the following C# code base:

```
...
string message = await DoWorkAsync();
Console.WriteLine(message);
...

static async Task<string> DoWorkAsync()
{
  return await Task.Run(() =>
  {
    Thread.Sleep(5_000);
    return "Done with work!";
  });
}
```

If you are using a `Main()` method as your entry point (instead of top-level statements), you need to mark the method as async, introduced in C# 7.1.

```
static async Task Main(string[] args)
{
...
string message = await DoWorkAsync();
Console.WriteLine(message);
...
}
```

■ **Note** The ability to decorate the `Main()` method with `async` is new as of C# 7.1. Top-level statements, added in C# 9.0, are implicitly `async`.

Notice the `await` keyword *before* naming the method that will be called in an asynchronous manner. This is important: if you decorate a method with the `async` keyword but do not have at least one internal `await`-centric method call, you have essentially built a synchronous method call (in fact, you will be given a compiler warning to this effect).

Now, notice that you are required to use the `Task` class from the `System.Threading.Tasks` namespace to refactor your `Main()` (if you are using `Main()`) and `DoWork()` methods (the latter is added as `DoWorkAsync()`). Basically, rather than returning a specific return value straightaway (a `string` object in the current example), you return a `Task<T>` object, where the generic type parameter `T` is the underlying, actual return value. If the method does not have a return value (as in the `Main()` method), then instead of `Task<T>` you just use `Task`.

The implementation of `DoWorkAsync()` now directly returns a `Task<T>` object, which is the return value of `Task.Run()`. The `Run()` method takes a `Func<>` or `Action<>` delegate, and as you know by this point in the text, you can simplify your life by using a lambda expression. Basically, your new version of `DoWorkAsync()` is essentially saying the following:

> *When you call me, I will run a new task. This task will cause the calling thread to sleep for five seconds, and when it is done, it gives me a string return value. I will put this string in a new Task<string> object and return it to the caller.*

Having translated this new implementation of DoWorkAsync() into more natural (poetic) language, you gain some insight into the real role of the await token. This keyword will always modify a method that returns a Task object. When the flow of logic reaches the await token, the calling thread is suspended in this method until the call completes. If this were a graphical application, the user could continue to use the UI while the DoWorkAsync() method executes.

SynchronizationContext and async/await

The official definition of the SynchronizationContext is a base class that provides free-threaded context with no synchronization. While that initial definition is not very descriptive, the official documentation goes on to say:

> *The purpose of the synchronization model implemented by this class is to allow the internal asynchronous/synchronous operations of the common language runtime to behave properly with different synchronization models.*

That statement, along with what you know about multithreading, sheds light on the matter. Recall that GUI applications (WinForms, WPF) do not allow secondary threads to access controls directly but must delegate that access. We have already seen the Dispatcher object in the WPF example. For the console applications that did not use WPF, this restriction is not in place. These are the different synchronization models that are referred to. With that in mind, let's dig deeper into the SynchronizationContext.

The SynchonizationContext is a type that provides a virtual post method, which takes a delegate to be executed asynchronously. This provides a pattern for frameworks to appropriately handle asynchronous requests (dispatching for WPF/WinForms, directly executing for non-GUI applications, etc.). It provides a way to queue a unit of work to a context and keeps count of outstanding async operations.

As we discussed earlier, when a delegate is queued to run asynchronously, it is scheduled to run on a separate thread. This detail is handled by the .NET Core Runtime. This is typically done using the .NET Core Runtime managed thread pool but can be overridden with a custom implementation.

While this plumbing work can be manually managed through code, the async/await pattern does most of the heavy lifting. When an async method is awaited, it leverages the SynchronizationContext and TaskScheduler implementations of the target framework. For example, if you are using async/await in a WPF application, the WPF framework manages the dispatching of the delegate and calling back into the state machine when the awaited task completes in order to safely update controls.

The Role of ConfigureAwait

Now that you understand the SynchronizationContext a little better, it is time to cover the role of the ConfigureAwait() method. By default, awaiting a Task will result in a synchronization context being utilized. When developing GUI applications (WinForms, WPF), this is the behavior that you want. However, if you are writing non-GUI application code, the overhead of queuing the original context when not needed can potentially cause performance issues in your application.

To see this in action, update your top-level statements to the following:

```
Console.WriteLine(" Fun With Async ===>");
//Console.WriteLine(DoWork());
string message = await DoWorkAsync();
```

```
Console.WriteLine($"0 - {message}");

string message1 = await DoWorkAsync().ConfigureAwait(false);
Console.WriteLine($"1 - {message1}");
```

The original code block is using the SynchronizationContext supplied by the framework (in this case, the .NET Core Runtime). It is equivalent to calling ConfigureAwait(true). The second example ignores the current context and scheduler.

Guidance from the .NET Core team suggests that when developing application code (WinForms, WPF, etc.), leave the default behavior in place. If you are writing nonapplication code (e.g., library code), then use ConfigureAwait(false). The one exception for this is ASP.NET Core (covered starting with Chapter 29). ASP.NET Core does not create a custom SynchronizationContext; therefore, ConfigureAwait(false) does not provide the benefit when using other frameworks.

Naming Conventions for Asynchronous Methods

Of course, you noticed the name change from DoWork() to DoWorkAsync(), but why the change? Let's say that the new version of the method was still named DoWork(); however, the calling code has been implemented as so:

```
//Oops! No await keyword here!
string message = DoWork();
```

Notice you did indeed mark the method with the async keyword, but you neglected to use the await keyword as a decorator before calling the DoWork() method call. At this point, you will have compiler errors, as the return value of DoWork() is a Task object, which you are attempting to assign directly to a string variable. Remember, the await token extracts the internal return value contained in the Task object. Since you have not used this token, you have a type mismatch.

■ **Note** An "awaitable" method is simply a method that returns a Task or Task<T>.

Given that methods that return Task objects can now be called in a nonblocking manner via the async and await tokens, the recommendation is to name any method returning a Task with an Async suffix. In this way, developers who know the naming convention receive a visual reminder that the await keyword is required, if they intend to invoke the method within an asynchronous context.

■ **Note** Event handlers for GUI controls (such as a button Click handler) as well as action methods in MVC-style apps that use the async/await keywords do not follow this naming convention (by convention—pardon the redundancy!).

Async Methods That Don't Return Data

Currently, your DoWorkAsync() method is returning a Task<string>, which contains "real data" for the caller that will be obtained transparently via the await keyword. However, what if you want to build an asynchronous method that doesn't return anything? While there are two ways to do this, there is really only one right way to do it. First, let's look at the problems with defining an async void method.

Async Void Methods

The following is an example of an async method that uses void as the return type instead of Task:

```
static async void MethodReturningVoidAsync()
{
  await Task.Run(() =>
      {
          /* Do some work here... */
          Thread.Sleep(4_000);
      });
  Console.WriteLine("Fire and forget void method completed");
}
```

If you were to call this method, it would run on its own without blocking the main thread. The following code will show the "Completed" message before the message from the MethodReturningVoidAsync() method:

```
MethodReturningVoidAsync();
Console.WriteLine("Completed");
Console.ReadLine();
```

While this might seem like a viable option for "fire and forget" scenarios, there is a larger problem. If the method throws an exception, it has nowhere to go except to the synchronization context of the calling method. Update the method to the following:

```
static async void MethodReturningVoidAsync()
{
    await Task.Run(() =>
    {
      /* Do some work here... */
      Thread.Sleep(4_000);
      throw new Exception("Something bad happened");
    });
    Console.WriteLine("Fire and forget void method completed");
}
```

To be safe, wrap the call to this method in a try-catch block, and run the program again:

```
try
{
  MethodReturningVoidAsync();
}
catch (Exception e)
{
  Console.WriteLine(e);
}
```

Not only does the catch block not catch the exception, but the exception is placed on the threading execution context. So, while this might seem like a good idea for "fire and forget" scenarios, you better hope there isn't an exception thrown in the async void method or your whole application might come crashing down.

Async Void Methods Using Task

The better way is to have your method use Task instead of void. Update the method to the following:

```
static async Task MethodReturningVoidTaskAsync()
{
    await Task.Run(() =>
    {
        /* Do some work here... */
        Thread.Sleep(4_000);
    });
    Console.WriteLine("Void method completed");
}
```

If you call with method without the await keyword, the same result will happen as in the previous example:

```
MethodReturningVoidTaskAsync();
Console.WriteLine("Void method complete");
```

Update the MethodReturningVoidTaskAsync() to throw an exception:

```
static async Task MethodReturningVoidTaskAsync()
{
    await Task.Run(() =>
    {
        /* Do some work here... */
        Thread.Sleep(4_000);
        throw new Exception("Something bad happened");
    });
    Console.WriteLine("Void method completed");
}
```

Now wrap the call to this method in a try-catch block:

```
try
{
    MethodReturningVoidTaskAsync();
}
catch (Exception ex)
{
    Console.WriteLine(ex);
}
```

When you run the program and the exception is thrown, two interesting things happen. The first is that the whole program doesn't crash, and the second is that the catch block doesn't catch the exception. When an exception is thrown out of a Task/Task<T> method, the exception is captured and placed on the Task object. When using await, the Exception (or AggregateException) is available to handle.

Update the calling code to await the method, and the catch block will now work as expected:

```
try
{
    await MethodReturningVoidTaskAsync();
}
catch (Exception ex)
{
    Console.WriteLine(ex);
}
```

To sum it up, you should avoid creating async void methods and use async Task methods. Whether or not you await them becomes a business decision, but either way, at least you won't crash your app!

Async Methods with Multiple Awaits

It is completely permissible for a single async method to have multiple await contexts within its implementation. The following example shows this in action:

```
static async Task MultipleAwaits()
{
    await Task.Run(() => { Thread.Sleep(2_000); });
    Console.WriteLine("Done with first task!");

    await Task.Run(() => { Thread.Sleep(2_000); });
    Console.WriteLine("Done with second task!");

    await Task.Run(() => { Thread.Sleep(2_000); });
    Console.WriteLine("Done with third task!");
}
```

Again, here each task is not doing much more than suspending the current thread for a spell; however, any unit of work could be represented by these tasks (calling a web service, reading a database, etc.).

Another option is to not await each task but await them all together and return when all of the tasks are completed. This is a more likely scenario, where there are three things (check email, update server, download files) that must be completed in a batch, but can be done in parallel. Here is the code updated using the Task.WhenAll() method:

```
static async Task MultipleAwaitsAsync()
{
  await Task.WhenAll(Task.Run(() =>
  {
    Thread.Sleep(2_000);
    Console.WriteLine("Done with first task!");
  }), Task.Run(() =>
  {
    Thread.Sleep(1_000);
    Console.WriteLine("Done with second task!");
  }), Task.Run(() =>
```

```
  {
    Thread.Sleep(1_000);
    Console.WriteLine("Done with third task!");
  }));
}
```

When you run the program now, you see that the three tasks fire in order of the lowest Sleep time.

```
Fun With Async ===>
Done with second task!
Done with third task!
Done with first task!
Completed
```

There is also a WhenAny(), which signals that one of the tasks have completed. The method returns the first task that completed. To demonstrate WhenAny(), change the last line of the MultipleAwaitsAsync to this:

```
await Task.WhenAny(Task.Run(() =>
{
  Thread.Sleep(2_000);
  Console.WriteLine("Done with first task!");
}), Task.Run(() =>
{
  Thread.Sleep(1_000);
  Console.WriteLine("Done with second task!");
}), Task.Run(() =>
{
  Thread.Sleep(1_000);
  Console.WriteLine("Done with third task!");
}));
```

When you do this, the output changes to this:

```
Fun With Async ===>
Done with second task!
Completed
Done with third task!
Done with first task!
```

Each of these methods also works with an array of tasks. To demonstrate this, create a new method named MultipleAwaitsTake2Async(). In this method, create a List<Task>, add the three tasks to it, and then call Task.WhenAll() or Task.WhenAny():

```
static async Task MultipleAwaitsTake2()
{
  var tasks = new List<Task>();
  tasks.Add(Task.Run(() =>
  {
```

```
    Thread.Sleep(2_000);
    Console.WriteLine("Done with first task!");
  }));
  tasks.Add(Task.Run(() =>
  {
    Thread.Sleep(1_000);
    Console.WriteLine("Done with second task!");
  }));
  tasks.Add(Task.Run(() =>
  {
    Thread.Sleep(1_000);
    Console.WriteLine("Done with third task!");
  }));
  //await Task.WhenAny(tasks);
  await Task.WhenAll(tasks);
}
```

Calling Async Methods from Synchronous Methods

Each of the previous examples used the `async` keyword to return the thread to calling code while the `async` method executes. In review, you can use the `await` keyword only in a method marked `async`. What if you cannot (or do not want to) mark a method `async`?

Fortunately, there are ways to call async methods when in a synchronous context. Unfortunately, most of them are bad. The first option is to simply forego the `await` keyword, allowing the original thread to continue execution while the `async` method runs on a separate thread, never returning to the caller. This behaves like the previous example of calling async Task methods. Any values returned from the method are lost, and exceptions are swallowed.

This might fit your needs, but if it doesn't, you have three choices. The first is to simply use the `Result` property on the `Task<T>` or the `Wait()` method on `Task` methods. If the method fails, any exceptions are wrapped in an `AggregateException`, potentially complicating error handling. You can also call `GetAwaiter().GetResult()`. This behaves in the same way as the `Wait()` and `Result` calls, with the small difference of not wrapping exceptions into an `AggregateException`. While the `GetAwaiter().GetResult()` methods work on both methods with a return value and methods without a return value, they are marked in the documentation as "not for external use," which means they might change or go away at some point in the future.

While those two options seem harmless replacements for using `await` in an async method, there is a more serious issue with using them. Calling either `Wait()`, `Result`, or `GetAwaiter().GetResult()` blocks the calling thread, processes the `async` method on another thread, then returns back to the calling thread, tying up two threads to get the work performed. Worse yet, each of these can cause deadlocks, especially if the calling thread is from the UI of the application.

To help discover and correct improper async/await code (and naming conventions), add the `Microsoft.VisualStudio.Threading.Analyzers` package to the project. This package adds analyzers that will provide compiler warnings when improper threading code is discovered, including bad naming conventions. To see this in action, add the following code to the top level statements:

```
_ = DoWorkAsync().Result;
_ = DoWorkAsync().GetAwaiter().GetResult();
```

This causes the following compiler warning:

```
VSTHRD002   Synchronously waiting on tasks or awaiters may cause deadlocks. Use await or
JoinableTaskFactory.Run instead.
```

Not only is there a compiler warning, but the recommended solution is also provided! To use the `JoinableTaskFactory` class, you need to add the `Microsoft.VisualStudio.Threading` NuGet package and the following using statement to the top of the Program.cs file:

```
using Microsoft.VisualStudio.Threading;
```

The `JoinableTaskFactory` needs a `JoinableTaskContext` in the constructor:

```
JoinableTaskFactory joinableTaskFactory = new JoinableTaskFactory(new JoinableTaskContext());
```

With this in place, you can use the Run() method to safely execute an async method, such as the `DoWork()` method, from a synchronous context:

```
string message2 = joinableTaskFactory.Run(async () => await DoWorkAsync());
```

As you know, the `DoWork()` method returns Task<string>, and that value is indeed returned from the `Run()` method. You can also call methods that just return `Task`, as follows:

```
joinableTaskFactory.Run(async () =>
{
  await MethodReturningVoidTaskAsync();
  await SomeOtherAsyncMethod();
});
```

■ **Note** Even though the packages have VisualStudio in the name, the packages do not depend on Visual Studio. They are .NET packages that can be used with or without Visual Studio installed.

Await in catch and finally Blocks

C# 6 introduced the ability to place await calls in `catch` and `finally` blocks. The method itself must be async to do this. The following code example demonstrates the capability:

```
static async Task<string> MethodWithTryCatch()
{
  try
  {
    //Do some work
    return "Hello";
  }
  catch (Exception ex)
  {
    await LogTheErrors();
    throw;
  }
```

```
  finally
  {
    await DoMagicCleanUp();
  }
}
```

Generalized Async Return Types (New 7.0)

Prior to C# 7, the only return options for async methods were Task, Task<T>, and void. C# 7 enables additional return types, if they follow the async pattern. One concrete example is ValueTask. To see this in action, create code like this:

```
static async ValueTask<int> ReturnAnInt()
{
  await Task.Delay(1_000);
  return 5;
}
```

The same rules apply for ValueTask as for Task, since ValueTask is just a Task for value types instead of forcing allocation of an object on the heap.

Local Functions with async/await (New 7.0)

Local functions were introduced in Chapter 4 and used throughout this book. They can also be beneficial for async methods. To demonstrate the benefit, you need to first see the problem. Add a new method named MethodWithProblems() and add the following code:

```
static async Task MethodWithProblems(int firstParam, int secondParam)
{
  Console.WriteLine("Enter");
  await Task.Run(() =>
  {
    //Call long running method
    Thread.Sleep(4_000);
    Console.WriteLine("First Complete");
    //Call another long running method that fails because
    //the second parameter is out of range
    Console.WriteLine("Something bad happened");
  });
}
```

The scenario is that the second long-running task fails because of invalid input data. You can (and should) add checks to the beginning of the method, but since the entire method is asynchronous, there is no guarantee when the checks will be executed. It would be better for the checks to happen right away before the calling code moves on. In the following update, the checks are done in a synchronous manner, and then the private function is executed asynchronously:

```
static async Task MethodWithProblemsFixed(int firstParam, int secondParam)
{
  Console.WriteLine(“Enter”);
```

```
  if (secondParam < 0)
  {
    Console.WriteLine("Bad data");
    return;
  }

  await actualImplementation();

  async Task actualImplementation()
  {
    await Task.Run(() =>
    {
      //Call long running method
      Thread.Sleep(4_000);
      Console.WriteLine("First Complete");
      //Call another long running method that fails because
      //the second parameter is out of range
      Console.WriteLine("Something bad happened");
    });
  }
}
```

Cancelling async/await Operations

Cancellation is also possible with the async/await pattern and much simpler than with Parallel.ForEach. To demonstrate, we will use the same WPF project from earlier in the chapter. You can either reuse that project or add a new WPF app (.NET Core) to the solution and add the System.Drawing.Common package to the project by executing the following CLI commands:

```
dotnet new wpf -lang c# -n PictureHandlerWithAsyncAwait -o .\PictureHandlerWithAsyncAwait -f net6.0
dotnet sln .\Chapter15_AllProjects.sln add .\PictureHandlerWithAsyncAwait
dotnet add PictureHandlerWithAsyncAwait package System.Drawing.Common
```

If you are using Visual Studio, do this by right-clicking the solution name in Solution Explorer, selecting Add ➤ Project, and naming it PictureHandlerWithAsyncAwait. Make sure to set the new project as the startup project by right-clicking the new project name and selecting Set as StartUp Project from the context menu. Add the System.Drawing.Common NuGet package.

```
dotnet add PictureHandlerWithAsyncAwait package System.Drawing.Common
```

Replace the XAML to match the previous WPF project (DataParallelismWithForEach), except change the title to Picture Handler with Async/Await. Also make sure to update the main PropertyGroup in the project file to disable nullable reference types.

```
<PropertyGroup>
  <OutputType>WinExe</OutputType>
  <TargetFramework>net6.0-windows</TargetFramework>
  <ImplicitUsings>enable</ImplicitUsings>
  <Nullable>disable</Nullable>
  <UseWPF>true</UseWPF>
</PropertyGroup>
```

In the MainWindow.xaml.cs file, make sure that the following using statements are in place:

```
using System.IO;
using System.Windows;
using System.Drawing;
```

Next, add a class-level variable for the CancellationToken and add the Cancel button event handler:

```
private CancellationTokenSource _cancelToken = null;
private void cmdCancel_Click(object sender, EventArgs e)
{
  _cancelToken.Cancel();
}
```

The process is the same as the previous example: get the picture directory, create the output directory, and get the picture files, rotate them, and save them to the new directory. Instead of using Parallel.ForEach(), this new version will use async methods to do the work, and the method signatures accept a CancellationToken as a parameter. Enter the following code:

```
private async void cmdProcess_Click(object sender, EventArgs e)
{
  _cancelToken = new CancellationTokenSource();
  var basePath = Directory.GetCurrentDirectory();
  var pictureDirectory =
    Path.Combine(basePath, "TestPictures");
  var outputDirectory =
    Path.Combine(basePath, "ModifiedPictures");
  //Clear out any existing files
  if (Directory.Exists(outputDirectory))
  {
    Directory.Delete(outputDirectory, true);
  }
  Directory.CreateDirectory(outputDirectory);
  string[] files = Directory.GetFiles(
    pictureDirectory, "*.jpg", SearchOption.AllDirectories);
  try
  {
    foreach(string file in files)
    {
      try
      {
        await ProcessFileAsync(file, outputDirectory,_cancelToken.Token);
      }
      catch (OperationCanceledException ex)
      {
        Console.WriteLine(ex);
        throw;
      }
    }
  }
  catch (OperationCanceledException ex)
```

```
  {
    Console.WriteLine(ex);
    throw;
  }
  catch (Exception ex)
  {
    Console.WriteLine(ex);
    throw;
  }
  _cancelToken = null;
  this.Title = "Processing complete";
}
```

After the initial setup, the code loops through the files and calls `ProcessFileAsync()` asynchronously for each file. The call to `ProcessFileAsync()` is wrapped in a `try/catch` block, and the `CancellationToken` is passed into the `ProcessFile()` method. If `Cancel()` is executed on the `CancellationTokenSource` (such as when the user clicks the Cancel button), an `OperationCanceledException` is thrown.

■ **Note** The `try/catch` code can be anywhere in the calling chain (as you shall soon see). Whether to place it at the first call or in the asynchronous method itself is a matter of pure preference and application needs.

The final method to add is the `ProcessFileAsync()` method.

```
private async Task ProcessFileAsync(string currentFile,
  string outputDirectory, CancellationToken token)
{
  string filename = Path.GetFileName(currentFile);
  using (Bitmap bitmap = new Bitmap(currentFile))
  {
    try
    {
      await Task.Run(() =>
      {
        Dispatcher?.Invoke(() =>
        {
          this.Title = $"Processing {filename}";
        });
        bitmap.RotateFlip(RotateFlipType.Rotate180FlipNone);
        bitmap.Save(Path.Combine(outputDirectory, filename));
      }
      ,token);
    }
    catch (OperationCanceledException ex)
    {
      Console.WriteLine(ex);
      throw;
    }
  }
}
```

This method uses another overload of the Task.Run command, taking in the CancellationToken as a parameter. The Task.Run command is wrapped in a try/catch block (just like the calling code) in case the user clicks the Cancel button.

Cancelling async/await operations with WaitAsync() (New 10.0)

New in C# 10.0, async calls can be cancelled with a cancellation token and/or after a time limit has been reached by using the WaitAsync() method. The following examples (located in the FunWithCSharpAsync project in this chapter's code) show all three variations of this new feature:

```
CancellationTokenSource tokenSource = new CancellationTokenSource();
_ = await DoWorkAsync().WaitAsync(TimeSpan.FromSeconds(10));
_ = await DoWorkAsync().WaitAsync(tokenSource.Token);
_ = await DoWorkAsync().WaitAsync(TimeSpan.FromSeconds(10), tokenSource.Token);
```

Cancelling async/await operations in Synchronous Calls

The Wait() method can also take a cancellation token when calling async methods from a non-async method. This can be used with or without a timeout specified. When used with a timeout, the timeout must be in milliseconds:

```
CancellationTokenSource tokenSource = new CancellationTokenSource();
MethodReturningTaskOfVoidAsync().Wait(tokenSource.Token);
MethodReturningTaskOfVoidAsync().Wait(10000,tokenSource.Token);
```

You can also use the JoinableTaskFactory and the new WaitAsync() method when calling from synchronous code:

```
JoinableTaskFactory joinableTaskFactory2 = new JoinableTaskFactory(new
JoinableTaskContext());
CancellationTokenSource tokenSource2 = new CancellationTokenSource();
joinableTaskFactory2.Run(async () =>
{
  await MethodReturningVoidTaskAsync().WaitAsync(tokenSource.Token);
  await MethodReturningVoidTaskAsync().WaitAsync(TimeSpan.
  FromSeconds(10),tokenSource.Token);
});
```

Asynchronous Streams (New 8.0)

New in C# 8.0, streams (covered in greater detail in Chapter 19) can be created and consumed asynchronously. A method that returns an asynchronous stream

- Is declared with the async modifier
- Returns an IAsyncEnumerable<T>
- Contains yield return statements (covered in Chapter 8) to return successive elements in the asynchronous stream

Take the following example:

```
public static async IAsyncEnumerable<int> GenerateSequence()
{
  for (int i = 0; i < 20; i++)
  {
    await Task.Delay(100);
    yield return i;
  }
}
```

The method is declared as async, returns an `IAsyncEnumerable<int>`, and uses the `yield return` to return integers in from a sequence. To call this method, add the following to your calling code:

```
await foreach (var number in GenerateSequence())
{
  Console.WriteLine(number);
}
```

The Parallel.ForEachAsync() Method (New 10.0)

New in C# 10, the `Parallel` class has a new `ForEachAsync()` method, which is (as the name suggests) async and also provides an async method for the body. Back in the DataParallelismWithForEach project, create a new async method named `ProcessFilesAsync()` and copy the code from the `ProcessFiles()` method.

Once the code is copied, replace the previous call to `Parallel.ForEach()` with `await Parallel.ForEachAsync()`. The first two parameters (`files`, `parOpts`) are the same in both calls. The change is in the body, which takes two parameters, the `currentFile` and the cancellation `token`:

```
//Old code:
//Parallel.ForEach(files, parOpts, currentFile =>
//New code:
await Parallel.ForEachAsync(files, parOpts, async (currentFile, token) =>
```

The cancellation token that is passed into the body is the same cancellation token as the one in the `ParallelOptions` instance. This means we can check the `token` parameter for requested cancellation requests instead of the one on the `ParallelOptions` instance:

```
//Old code:
//parOpts.CancellationToken.ThrowIfCancellationRequested();
//New code:
token.ThrowIfCancellationRequested();
```

The complete method is shown here:

```
private async Task ProcessFilesAsync()
{
  // Load up all *.jpg files, and make a new folder for the modified data.
  var basePath = Directory.GetCurrentDirectory();
  var pictureDirectory = Path.Combine(basePath, "TestPictures");
  var outputDirectory = Path.Combine(basePath, "ModifiedPictures");
  //Clear out any existing files
```

```
  if (Directory.Exists(outputDirectory))
  {
    Directory.Delete(outputDirectory, true);
  }
  Directory.CreateDirectory(outputDirectory);
  string[] files = Directory.GetFiles(pictureDirectory, "*.jpg", SearchOption.
  AllDirectories);
  // Use ParallelOptions instance to store the CancellationToken.
  ParallelOptions parOpts = new ParallelOptions();
  parOpts.CancellationToken = _cancelToken.Token;
  parOpts.MaxDegreeOfParallelism = System.Environment.ProcessorCount;
  try
  {
    // Process the image data in a parallel manner!
    await Parallel.ForEachAsync(files, parOpts, async (currentFile,token) =>
    {
      token.ThrowIfCancellationRequested();
      string filename = Path.GetFileName(currentFile);
      Dispatcher?.Invoke(() =>
        {
          this.Title = $"Processing {filename} on thread {Environment.
          CurrentManagedThreadId}";
        }
    );
    using (Bitmap bitmap = new Bitmap(currentFile))
    {
      bitmap.RotateFlip(RotateFlipType.Rotate180FlipNone);
      bitmap.Save(Path.Combine(outputDirectory, filename));
    }
    Thread.Sleep(2000);
    });
    Dispatcher?.Invoke(() => this.Title = "Done!");
  }
  catch (OperationCanceledException ex)
  {
    Dispatcher?.Invoke(() => this.Title = ex.Message);
  }
}
```

The final change is to call this new method when the button is clicked:

```
private void cmdProcess_Click(object sender, EventArgs e)
{
  this.Title = $"Starting...";
  ProcessFilesAsync().Wait();
}
```

Update the Book Reader App with async/await

Now that you understand the async/await pattern, let's update the Book Reader app to use the HttpClient instead of the WebClient. Create a new method named GetBookAsync().

```
async Task GetBookAsync()
{
    HttpClient client = new HttpClient();
    _theEBook = await client.GetStringAsync("http://www.gutenberg.org/files/98/98-0.txt");
    Console.WriteLine("Download complete.");
    GetStats();
}
```

After creating a new instance of the `HttpClient` class, the code calls the `GetStringAsync()` method to make an HTTP Get call to retrieve the text from the website. As you can see, the `HttpClient` provides a much more concise way to make HTTP calls. The `HttpClient` class will be explored in much more detail in the chapters that cover ASP.NET Core.

Wrapping Up async and await

This section contained a lot of examples; here are the key points of this section:

- Methods (as well as lambda expressions or anonymous methods) can be marked with the `async` keyword to enable the method to do work in a nonblocking manner.
- Methods (as well as lambda expressions or anonymous methods) marked with the `async` keyword will run synchronously until the `await` keyword is encountered.
- A single `async` method can have multiple `await` contexts.
- When the `await` expression is encountered, the calling thread is suspended until the awaited task is complete. In the meantime, control is returned to the caller of the method.
- The `await` keyword will hide the returned `Task` object from view, appearing to directly return the underlying return value. Methods with no return value simply return `void`.
- Parameter checking and other error handling should be done in the main section of the method, with the actual async portion moved to a private function.
- For stack variables, the `ValueTask` is more efficient than the `Task` object, which might cause boxing and unboxing.
- As a naming convention, methods that are to be called asynchronously should be marked with the `Async` suffix.

Summary

This chapter began by examining the role of the `System.Threading` namespace. As you learned, when an application creates additional threads of execution, the result is that the program in question can carry out numerous tasks at (what appears to be) the same time. You also examined several manners in which you can protect thread-sensitive blocks of code to ensure that shared resources do not become unusable units of bogus data.

This chapter then examined some new models for working with multithreaded development introduced with .NET 4.0, specifically the Task Parallel Library and PLINQ. I wrapped things up by covering the role of the `async` and `await` keywords. As you have seen, these keywords are using many types of the TPL framework in the background; however, the compiler does most of the work to create the complex threading and synchronization code on your behalf.

PART V

Programming with .NET Core Assemblies

CHAPTER 16

Building and Configuring Class Libraries

For most of the examples so far in this book, you have created "stand-alone" executable applications, in which all the programming logic was packaged within a single assembly (*.dll) and executed using dotnet.exe (or a copy of dotnet.exe named after the assembly). These assemblies were using little more than the .NET base class libraries. While some simple .NET programs may be constructed using nothing more than the base class libraries, chances are it will be commonplace for you (or your teammates) to isolate reusable programming logic into *custom* class libraries (*.dll files) that can be shared among applications.

In this chapter, you'll start by learning the details of partitioning types into .NET namespaces. After this, you will take a deep look at class libraries in .NET, the difference between a .NET and .NET Standard, application configuration, publishing .NET console applications, and packaging your libraries into reusable NuGet packages.

Defining Custom Namespaces (Updated 10.0)

Before diving into the aspects of library deployment and configuration, the first task is to learn the details of packaging your custom types into .NET namespaces. Up to this point in the text, you've been building small test programs that leverage existing namespaces in the .NET universe (System, in particular). However, when you build larger applications with many types, it can be helpful to group your related types into custom namespaces. In C#, this is accomplished using the namespace keyword. Explicitly defining custom namespaces is even more important when creating shared assemblies, as other developers will need to reference the library and import your custom namespaces to use your types. Custom namespaces also prevent name collisions by segregating your custom classes from other custom classes that might have the same name.

To investigate the issues firsthand, begin by creating a new .NET Console Application project named CustomNamespaces. Now, assume you are developing a collection of geometric classes named Square, Circle, and Hexagon. Given their similarities, you would like to group them into a unique namespace called CustomNamespaces.MyShapes within the CustomNamespaces.exe assembly.

Guidance While you are free to use any name you choose for your namespaces, the naming convention is typically similar to CompanyName.ProductName.AssemblyName.Path.

A. Troelsen and P. Japikse, *Pro C# 10 with .NET 6*, https://doi.org/10.1007/978-1-4842-7869-7_16

While the C# compiler has no problems with a single C# code file containing multiple types, this can be problematic when working in a team environment. If you are working on the `Circle` class and your co-worker needs to work on the Hexagon class, you would have to take turns working in the monolithic file or face difficult-to-resolve (well, at least time-consuming) merge conflicts.

A better approach is to place each class in its own file with a namespace definition. To ensure each type is packaged into the same logical group, simply wrap the given class definitions in the same namespace scope. The following example uses the pre–C# 10 namespace syntax, where each namespace declaration wrapped its contents with an opening and closing curly brace, like so:

```
// Circle.cs
namespace CustomNamespaces.MyShapes
{
  // Circle class
  public class Circle { /* Interesting methods... */ }
}
// Hexagon.cs
namespace CustomNamespaces.MyShapes
{
  // Hexagon class
  public class Hexagon { /* More interesting methods... */ }
}
// Square.cs
namespace CustomNamespaces.MyShapes
{
  // Square class
  public class Square { /* Even more interesting methods...*/}
}
```

One of the updates in C# 10 is the addition of file-scoped namespaces. This eliminates the need for opening and closing curly braces wrapping the contents. Simply declare the namespace, and everything that comes after that namespace declaration is included in the namespace. The following code sample produces the same result as the example with the namespaces wrapping their contents:

```
// Circle.cs
namespace CustomNamespaces.MyShapes;
// Circle class
public class Circle { /* Interesting methods... */ }
// Hexagon.cs
namespace CustomNamespaces.MyShapes;
// Hexagon class
public class Hexagon { /* More interesting methods... */ }
// Square.cs
namespace CustomNamespaces.MyShapes;
// Square class
public class Square { /* Even more interesting methods...*/}
```

This change by the C# team (along with global using statements and implicit global using statements) has eliminated a lot of the boilerplate code that was necessary in versions of C# prior to C# 10. In fact, as I updated the book for this version, I was able to remove on average two pages per chapter, just by removing the (now) unnecessary `using` statements and curly braces!

Notice how the CustomNamespaces.MyShapes namespace acts as the conceptual "container" of these classes. When another namespace (such as CustomNamespaces) wants to use types in a separate namespace, you use the using keyword, just as you would when using namespaces of the .NET base class libraries, as follows:

```
// Make use of types defined the MyShapes namespace.
using CustomNamespaces.MyShapes;

Hexagon h = new Hexagon();
Circle c = new Circle();
Square s = new Square();
```

For this example, the assumption is that the C# files that define the CustomNamespaces.MyShapes namespace are part of the same Console Application project; in other words, all the files are compiled into a single assembly. If you defined the CustomNamespaces.MyShapes namespace within an external assembly, you would also need to add a reference to that library before you could compile successfully. You'll learn all the details of building applications that use external libraries during this chapter.

Resolving Name Clashes with Fully Qualified Names

Technically speaking, you are not required to use the C# using keyword when referring to types defined in external namespaces. You could use the *fully qualified name* of the type, which, as you may recall from Chapter 1, is the type's name prefixed with the defining namespace. Here's an example:

```
// Note we are not importing CustomNamespaces.MyShapes anymore!
CustomNamespaces.MyShapes.Hexagon h = new CustomNamespaces.MyShapes.Hexagon();
CustomNamespaces.MyShapes.Circle c = new CustomNamespaces.MyShapes.Circle();
CustomNamespaces.MyShapes.Square s = new CustomNamespaces.MyShapes.Square();
```

Typically, there is no need to use a fully qualified name. Not only does it require a greater number of keystrokes, it also makes no difference whatsoever in terms of code size or execution speed. In fact, in CIL code, types are *always* defined with the fully qualified name. In this light, the C# using keyword is simply a typing time-saver.

However, fully qualified names can be helpful (and sometimes necessary) to avoid potential name clashes when using multiple namespaces that contain identically named types. Assume you have a new namespace termed CustomNamespaces.My3DShapes, which defines the following three classes, capable of rendering a shape in stunning 3D:

```
// Another shape-centric namespace.
//Circle.cs
namespace CustomNamespaces.My3DShapes;
// 3D Circle class.
public class Circle { }
//Hexagon.cs
namespace CustomNamespaces.My3DShapes;
// 3D Hexagon class.
public class Hexagon { }
//Square.cs
namespace CustomNamespaces.My3DShapes;
// 3D Square class.
public class Square { }
```

If you update the top-level statements as shown next, you are issued several compile-time errors, because both namespaces define identically named classes:

```
// Ambiguities abound!
using CustomNamespaces.MyShapes;
using CustomNamespaces.My3DShapes;

// Which namespace do I reference?
Hexagon h = new Hexagon(); // Compiler error!
Circle c = new Circle();   // Compiler error!
Square s = new Square();   // Compiler error!
```

The ambiguity can be resolved using the type's fully qualified name, like so:

```
// We have now resolved the ambiguity.
CustomNamespaces.My3DShapes.Hexagon h = new CustomNamespaces.My3DShapes.Hexagon();
CustomNamespaces.My3DShapes.Circle c = new CustomNamespaces.My3DShapes.Circle();
CustomNamespaces.MyShapes.Square s = new CustomNamespaces.MyShapes.Square();
```

Resolving Name Clashes with Aliases

The C# `using` keyword also lets you create an alias for a type's fully qualified name. When you do so, you define a token that is substituted for the type's full name at compile time. Defining aliases provides a second way to resolve name clashes. Here's an example:

```
using MyShapes;
using My3DShapes;

// Resolve the ambiguity for a type using a custom alias.
using The3DHexagon = My3DShapes.Hexagon;

// This is really creating a My3DShapes.Hexagon class.
The3DHexagon h2 = new The3DHexagon();
...
```

There is another (more commonly used) `using` syntax that lets you create an alias for a namespace instead of a type. For example, you could alias the `CustomNamespaces.My3DShapes` namespace, and create an instance of the 3D Hexagon as follows:

```
using ThreeD = CustomNamespaces.My3DShapes;
ThreeD.Hexagon h2 = new ThreeD.Hexagon();
```

■ **Note** Be aware that overuse of C# aliases for types can result in a confusing code base. If other programmers on your team are unaware of your custom aliases for types, they could have difficulty locating the real types in the project(s).

Creating Nested Namespaces

When organizing your types, you are free to define namespaces within other namespaces. The base class libraries do so in numerous places to provide deeper levels of type organization. For example, the IO namespace is nested within System to yield System.IO. In fact, you already created nested namespaces in the previous example. The multipart namespaces (CustomNamespaces.MyShapes and CustomNamespaces.My3DShapes) are nested under the root namespace, CustomNamespaces.

As you have seen already throughout this book, the .NET project templates add the initial code for console applications in a file named Program.cs. This file contains a namespace named after the project and a single class, Program. This base namespace is referred to as the *root* namespace. In our current example, the root namespace created by the .NET template is CustomNamespaces. To nest the MyShapes and My3DShapes namespaces inside the root namespace, there are three options. The first is to simply nest the namespace keyword, like this (using pre-C# 10 syntax):

```
namespace CustomNamespaces
{
  namespace MyShapes
  {
    // Circle class
    public class Circle
    {
      /* Interesting methods... */
    }
  }
}
```

The second option, using C# 10 (and later), uses a file-scoped namespace followed by a block-scoped namespace for the nested namespace:

```
namespace CustomNamespaces;
namespace MyShapes
{
  // Circle class
  public class Circle
  {
    /* Interesting methods... */
  }
}
```

The third option (and more commonly used) is to use "dot notation" in the namespace definition, as we did with the previous class examples:

```
namespace CustomNamespaces.MyShapes;
// Circle class
public class Circle
{
  /* Interesting methods... */
}
```

Namespaces do not have to directly contain any types. This allows developers to use namespaces to provide a further level of scope.

■ **Guidance** A common practice is to group files in a namespace by directory. Where a file lives in the directory structure has no impact on namespaces. However, it does make the namespace structure clearer to other developers. Therefore, many developers and code linting tools expect the namespaces to match the folder structures.

Change the Root Namespace Using Visual Studio 2022

As mentioned, when you create a new C# project using Visual Studio (or the .NET CLI), the name of your application's root namespace will be identical to the project name. From this point on, when you use Visual Studio to insert new code files using the Project ➤ Add New Item menu selection, types will automatically be wrapped within the root namespace and have directory path appended. If you want to change the name of the root namespace, simply access the "Default namespace" option using the Application/General tab of the project's properties window (see Figure 16-1).

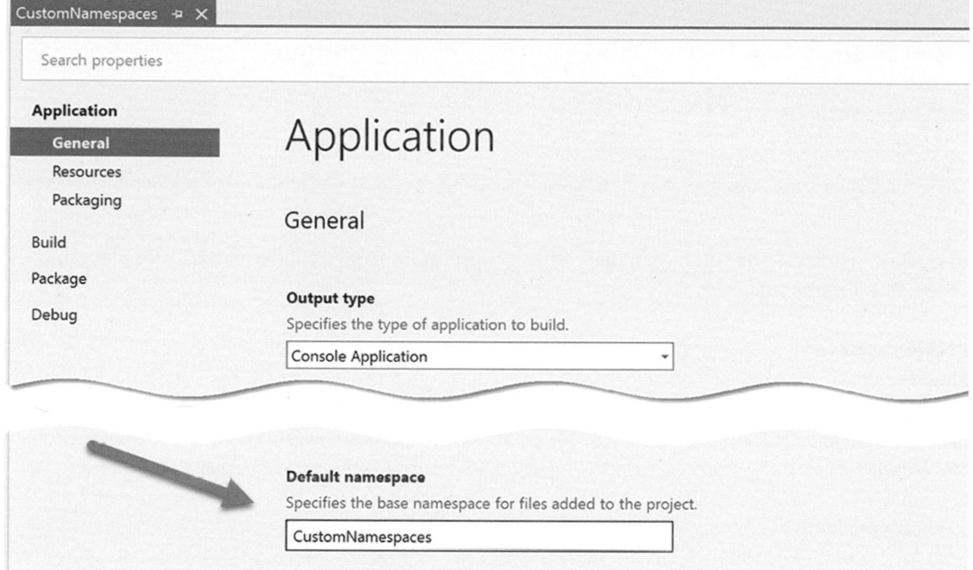

Figure 16-1. *Configuring the default/root namespace*

■ **Note** The Visual Studio property pages still refer to the root namespace as the *Default* namespace. You will see next why I refer to it as the *root* namespace.

Change the Root Namespace Using the Project File

If not using Visual Studio (or even with Visual Studio), you can also configure the root namespace by updating the project (`*.csproj`) file. With .NET projects, editing the project file in Visual Studio is as easy as double-clicking the project file in Solution Explorer (or right-clicking the project file in Solution Explorer and selecting "Edit project file"). Once the file is open, update the main PropertyGroup by adding the RootNamespace node, like this:

```
<Project Sdk="Microsoft.NET.Sdk">

  <PropertyGroup>
    <OutputType>Exe</OutputType>
    <TargetFramework>net6.0</TargetFramework>
    <ImplicitUsings>enable</ImplicitUsings>
    <Nullable>disable</Nullable>
    <RootNamespace>CustomNamespaces2</RootNamespace>
  </PropertyGroup>

</Project>
```

So far, so good. Now that you have seen some details regarding how to package your custom types into well-organized namespaces, let's quickly review the benefits and format of the .NET assembly. After this, you will delve into the details of creating, deploying, and configuring your custom class libraries.

The Role of .NET Assemblies

.NET applications are constructed by piecing together any number of *assemblies*. Simply put, an assembly is a versioned, self-describing binary file hosted by the .NET Runtime. Now, despite that .NET assemblies have the same file extensions (*.exe or *.dll) as previous Windows binaries, they have little in common under the hood with those files. Before unpacking that last statement, let's consider some of the benefits provided by the assembly format.

Assemblies Promote Code Reuse

As you have built your Console Application projects over the previous chapters, it might have seemed that *all* the applications' functionality was contained within the executable assembly you were constructing. Your applications were leveraging numerous types contained within the always-accessible .NET base class libraries.

As you might know, a *code library* (also termed a *class library*) is a *.dll that contains types intended to be used by external applications. When you are creating executable assemblies, you will no doubt be leveraging numerous system-supplied and custom code libraries as you create your application. Do be aware, however, that a code library need not take a *.dll file extension. It is perfectly possible (although certainly not common) for an executable assembly to use types defined within an external executable file. In this light, a referenced *.exe can also be considered a code library.

Regardless of how a code library is packaged, the .NET platform allows you to reuse types in a language-independent manner. For example, you could create a code library in C# and reuse that library in any other .NET programming language. It is possible not only to allocate types across languages but also to derive from them. A base class defined in C# could be extended by a class authored in Visual Basic. Interfaces defined in F# can be implemented by structures defined in C# and so forth. The point is that when you begin to break apart a single monolithic executable into numerous .NET assemblies, you achieve a *language-neutral* form of code reuse.

Assemblies Establish a Type Boundary

Recall that a type's *fully qualified name* is composed by prefixing the type's namespace (e.g., `System`) to its name (e.g., `Console`). Strictly speaking, however, the assembly in which a type resides further establishes a type's identity. For example, if you have two uniquely named assemblies (say, `MyCars.dll` and `YourCars.dll`) that both define a namespace (`CarLibrary`) containing a class named `SportsCar`, they are considered unique types in the .NET universe.

Assemblies Are Versionable Units

.NET assemblies are assigned a four-part numerical version number of the form *<major>.<minor>.<build>.<revision>*. (If you do not explicitly provide a version number, the assembly is automatically assigned a version of 1.0.0.0, given the default .NET project settings.) This number allows multiple versions of the same assembly to coexist in harmony on a single machine.

Assemblies Are Self-Describing

Assemblies are regarded as *self-describing*, in part because they record in the assembly's *manifest* every external assembly they must be able to access to function correctly. Recall from Chapter 1 that a manifest is a blob of metadata that describes the assembly itself (name, version, required external assemblies, etc.).

In addition to manifest data, an assembly contains metadata that describes the composition (member names, implemented interfaces, base classes, constructors, etc.) of every contained type. Because an assembly is documented in such detail, the .NET Runtime does *not* consult the Windows system registry to resolve its location (quite the radical departure from Microsoft's legacy COM programming model). This separation from the registry is one of the factors that enables .NET applications to run on other operating systems besides Windows as well as supporting multiple versions of .NET on the same machine.

As you will discover during this chapter, the .NET Runtime makes use of an entirely new scheme to resolve the location of external code libraries.

Understanding the Format of a .NET Assembly

Now that you've learned about several benefits provided by the .NET assembly, let's shift gears and get a better idea of how an assembly is composed under the hood. Structurally speaking, a .NET assembly (`*.dll` or `*.exe`) consists of the following elements:

- An operating system (e.g., Windows) file header
- A CLR file header
- CIL code
- Type metadata
- An assembly manifest
- Optional embedded resources

While the first two elements (the operating system and CLR headers) are blocks of data you can typically always ignore, they do deserve some brief consideration. Here's an overview of each element.

Installing the C++ Profiling Tools

The next few sections use a utility call `dumpbin.exe`, and it ships with the C++ profiling tools. To install them, type *C++ profiling tools* in the quick search bar, and click the prompt to install the tools, as shown in Figure 16-2.

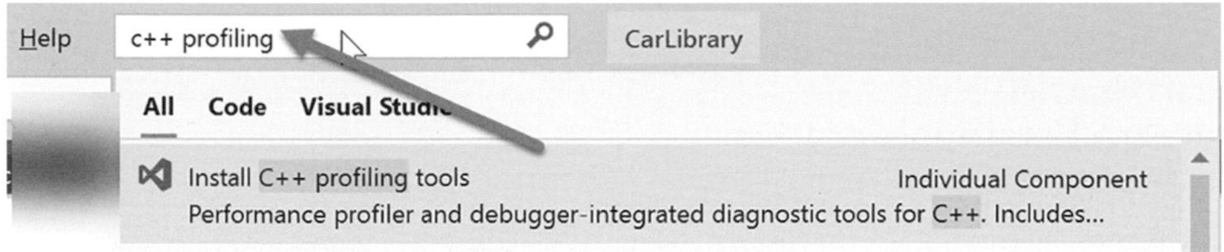

Figure 16-2. *Installing the C++ profiling tools from Quick Launch*

This will bring up the Visual Studio installer with the tools selected. Alternatively, you can launch the Visual Studio installer yourself and select the components shown in Figure 16-3.

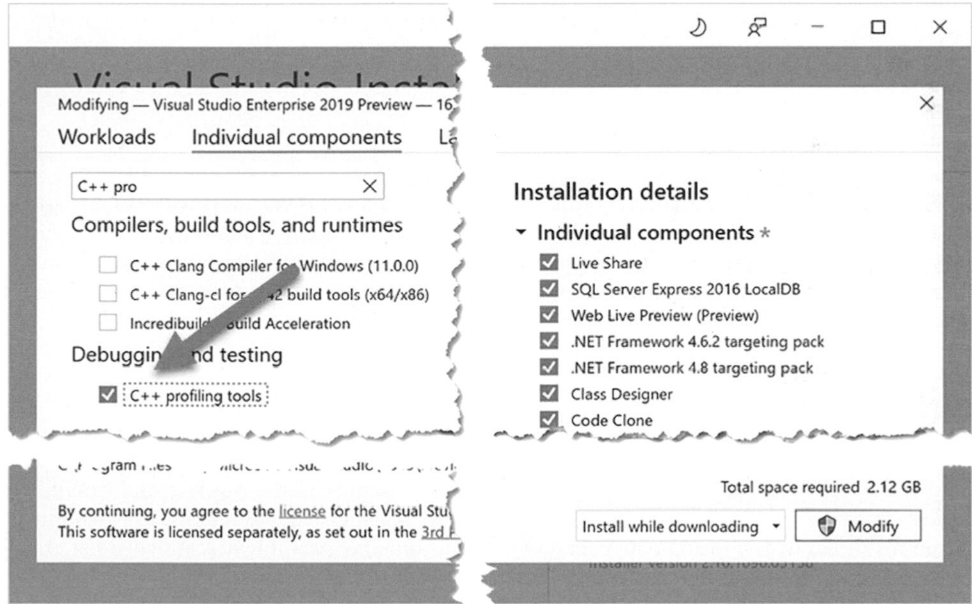

Figure 16-3. *Installing the C++ profiling tools*

The Operating System (Windows) File Header

The operating system file header establishes the fact that the assembly can be loaded and manipulated by the target operating system (in the following example, Windows). This header data also identifies the kind of application (console-based, GUI-based, or `*.dll` code library) to be hosted by the operating system.

Open the CarLibrary.dll file (in the book's repo or created later in this chapter) using the dumpbin.exe utility (via the developer command prompt) with the /headers flag as so:

```
dumpbin /headers CarLibrary.dll
```

This displays the assembly's operating system header information (shown in the following when built for Windows). Here is the (partial) Windows header information for CarLibrary.dll:

```
Dump of file carlibrary.dll
PE signature found
File Type: DLL

FILE HEADER VALUES
       14C machine (x86)
         3 number of sections
  877429B3 time date stamp
         0 file pointer to symbol table
         0 number of symbols
        E0 size of optional header
      2022 characteristics
             Executable
             Application can handle large (>2GB) addresses
             DLL
...
```

Now, remember that most .NET programmers will never need to concern themselves with the format of the header data embedded in a .NET assembly. Unless you happen to be building a new .NET language compiler (where you *would* care about such information), you are free to remain blissfully unaware of the grimy details of the header data. Do be aware, however, that this information is used under the covers when the operating system loads the binary image into memory.

The CLR File Header

The CLR header is a block of data that all .NET assemblies must support (and do support, courtesy of the C# compiler) to be hosted by the .NET Runtime. In a nutshell, this header defines numerous flags that enable the runtime to understand the layout of the managed file. For example, flags exist that identify the location of the metadata and resources within the file, the version of the runtime the assembly was built against, the value of the (optional) public key, and so forth. Execute dumpbin.exe again with the /clrheader flag.

```
dumpbin /clrheader CarLibrary.dll
```

You are presented with the internal CLR header information for a given .NET assembly, as shown here:

```
Dump of file CarLibrary.dll
File Type: DLL

  clr Header:

    48 cb
  2.05 runtime version
```

```
2158 [ B7C] RVA [size] of MetaData Directory
   1 flags
       IL Only
   0 entry point token
   0 [    0] RVA [size] of Resources Directory
   0 [    0] RVA [size] of StrongNameSignature Directory
   0 [    0] RVA [size] of CodeManagerTable Directory
   0 [    0] RVA [size] of VTableFixups Directory
   0 [    0] RVA [size] of ExportAddressTableJumps Directory
   0 [    0] RVA [size] of ManagedNativeHeader Directory

 Summary

       2000 .reloc
       2000 .rsrc
       2000 .text
```

Again, as a .NET developer, you will not need to concern yourself with the gory details of an assembly's CLR header information. Just understand that every .NET assembly contains this data, which is used behind the scenes by the .NET Runtime as the image data loads into memory. Now turn your attention to some information that is much more useful in your day-to-day programming tasks.

CIL Code, Type Metadata, and the Assembly Manifest

At its core, an assembly contains CIL code, which, as you recall, is a platform- and CPU-agnostic intermediate language. At runtime, the internal CIL is compiled on the fly using a just-in-time (JIT) compiler, according to platform- and CPU-specific instructions. Given this design, .NET assemblies can indeed execute on a variety of architectures, devices, and operating systems. (Although you can live a happy and productive life without understanding the details of the CIL programming language, Chapter 18 offers an introduction to the syntax and semantics of CIL.)

An assembly also contains metadata that completely describes the format of the contained types, as well as the format of external types referenced by this assembly. The .NET Runtime uses this metadata to resolve the location of types (and their members) within the binary, lay out types in memory, and facilitate remote method invocations. You'll check out the details of the .NET metadata format in Chapter 17 during your examination of reflection services.

An assembly must also contain an associated *manifest* (also referred to as *assembly metadata*). The manifest documents each *module* within the assembly, establishes the version of the assembly, and documents any *external* assemblies referenced by the current assembly. As you will see over the course of this chapter, the CLR makes extensive use of an assembly's manifest during the process of locating external assembly references.

Optional Assembly Resources

Finally, a .NET assembly may contain any number of embedded resources, such as application icons, image files, sound clips, or string tables. In fact, the .NET platform supports *satellite assemblies* that contain nothing but localized resources. This can be useful if you want to partition your resources based on a specific culture (English, German, etc.) for the purposes of building international software. The topic of building satellite assemblies is outside the scope of this text. Consult the .NET documentation for information on satellite assemblies and localization if you are interested.

Class Libraries vs. Console Applications

So far in this book, the examples were almost exclusively .NET Console applications. If you are reading this book as a current .NET Framework developer, these are like .NET console applications, with the main difference being the configuration process (to be covered later) and, of course, that they run on .NET Core. Console applications have a single-entry point (either a specified `Main()` method or top-level statements), can interact with the console, and can be launched directly from the operating system. Another difference between .NET Framework and .NET console applications is that console applications in .NET are launched using the .NET Application Host (`dotnet.exe`).

Class libraries, on the other hand, don't have an entry point and therefore cannot be launched directly. They are used to encapsulate logic, custom types, and so on, and they are referenced by other class libraries and/or console applications. In other words, class libraries are used to contain the things talked about in "The Role of .NET Assemblies" section.

.NET Standard vs. .NET (Core) Class Libraries

.NET (including .NET Core/.NET 5/.NET 6) class libraries run on .NET Core, and .NET Framework class libraries run on the .NET Framework. While it's pretty straightforward, there is a problem with this. Assume you have a large .NET Framework code base in your organization, with (potentially) years of development behind you and your team. There is probably a significant amount of shared code leveraged by the applications you and your team have built over the years. Perhaps it's centralized logging, reporting, or domain-specific functionality.

Now you (and your organization) want to move to the new .NET for all new development. What about all that shared code? The effort to rewrite all of your legacy code into .NET 6 assemblies could be significant, and until all of your applications were moved to .NET 6, you would have to support two versions (one in .NET Framework and one in .NET 6). That would bring productivity to a screeching halt.

Fortunately, the builders of .NET (Core) thought through this scenario. .NET Standard is a new type of class library project that was introduced with .NET Core 1.0 and can be referenced by .NET Framework as well as .NET (Core) applications. Before you get your hopes up, though, there is a catch with .NET 5 and .NET 6. More on that shortly.

Each .NET Standard version defines a common set of APIs that must be supported by all .NET versions (.NET, .NET Core, Xamarin, etc.) to conform to the standard. For example, if you were to build a class library as a .NET Standard 2.0 project, it can be referenced by .NET 4.61+ and .NET Core 2.0+ (plus various versions of Xamarin, Mono, Universal Windows Platform, and Unity).

This means you could move the code from your .NET Framework class libraries into .NET Standard 2.0 class libraries, and they can be shared by .NET (Core) and .NET Framework applications. That's much better than supporting duplicate copies of the same code, one for each framework.

Now for the catch. Each .NET Standard version represents the lowest common denominator for the frameworks that it supports. That means the lower the version, the less that you can do in your class library. While .NET Framework and .NET 6 projects can reference a .NET Standard 2.0 library, you cannot use a significant number of C# 8.0 features in a .NET Standard 2.0 library, and you can't use any new features from C# 9.0 or later. You must use .NET Standard 2.1 for full C# 8.0+ support. And .NET 4.8 (the latest/last version of the original .NET Framework) only goes up to .NET Standard 2.0.

It's still a good mechanism for leveraging existing code in newer applications up to and including .NET Core 3.1, but not a silver bullet. With the unification of the frameworks (.NET, Xamarin, Mon, etc.) with .NET 6, the usefulness of .NET Standard is slowly fading into the past.

Configuring Applications with Configuration Files

While it is possible to keep all the information needed by your .NET application in the source code, being able to change certain values at runtime is vitally important in most applications of significance. One of the more common options is to use one or more configuration files shipped (or deployed) along with your application's executable.

The .NET Framework relied mostly on XML files named app.config (or web.config for ASP.NET applications) for configuration. While XML-based configuration files can still be used, the most common method for configuring .NET applications is with JavaScript Object Notation (JSON) files..

■ **Note** If you are not familiar with JSON, it is a name-value pair format where each object is enclosed in curly braces. Values can also be objects using the same name-value pair format. Chapter 20 covers working with JSON files in depth.

To illustrate the process, create a new .NET Console application named FunWithConfiguration and add the following package reference to your project:

```
dotnet new console -lang c# -n FunWithConfiguration -o .\FunWithConfiguration -f net6.0
dotnet add FunWithConfiguration package Microsoft.Extensions.Configuration
dotnet add FunWithConfiguration package Microsoft.Extensions.Configuration.Binder
dotnet add FunWithConfiguration package Microsoft.Extensions.Configuration.Json
```

This adds a reference for configuration subsystem, the JSON file-based .NET configuration subsystem, and the binding extensions for configuration into your project. Start by adding a new JSON file into your project named appsettings.json. Update the project file to make sure the file is always copied to the output directory when the project is built.

```
<ItemGroup>
  <None Update="appsettings.json">
    <CopyToOutputDirectory>Always</CopyToOutputDirectory>
  </None>
</ItemGroup>
```

Finally, update the appsettings.json file to match the following:

```
{
  "CarName": "Suzy"
}
```

The final step to adding the configuration into your app is to read in the configuration file and get the CarName value. Update the Program.cs file to the following:

```
using Microsoft.Extensions.Configuration;

IConfiguration config = new ConfigurationBuilder()
    .SetBasePath(Directory.GetCurrentDirectory())
    .AddJsonFile("appsettings.json", true, true)
    .Build();
```

The new configuration system starts with a ConfigurationBuilder. The path that the configuration build will start to look for the files being added is set with the SetBasePath() method. Then the configuration file is added with the AddJsonFile() method, which takes three parameters. The first parameter is the path and name of the file. Since this file is in the same location as the base path, there isn't any path information in the string, just the filename. The second parameter sets whether the file is optional (true) or required (false), and the final parameter determines if the configuration should use a file watcher to look for any changes in the file (true) or to ignore any changes during runtime (false). The final step is to build the configuration into an instance of IConfiguration using the Build() method. This instance provides access to all the configured values.

■ **Note** File watchers are covered in Chapter 20.

Once you have an instance of IConfiguration, you can get the values from the configuration files much the same way as calling the ConfigurationManager in .NET 4.8. Add the following to the bottom of the Main() method, and when you run the app, you will see the value written to the console:

```
Console.WriteLine($"My car's name is {config["CarName"]}");
```

If the request name doesn't exist in the configuration, the result will be null. The following code still runs without an exception; it just doesn't display a name in the first line and displays True in the second line:

```
Console.WriteLine($"My car's name is {config["CarName2"]}");
Console.WriteLine($"CarName2 is null? {config["CarName2"] == null}");
```

There is also a GetValue() method (and its generic version GetValue<T>()) that can retrieve primitive values from the configuration. The following example shows both of these methods to get the CarName:

```
Console.WriteLine($"My car's name is {config.GetValue(typeof(string),"CarName")}");
Console.WriteLine($"My car's name is {config.GetValue<string>("CarName")}");
```

These methods return the default value (e.g., null for reference types, 0 for numeric types) if the name requested doesn't exist. The following code returns 0 for the CarName2 property:

```
Console.WriteLine($"My car's name is {config.GetValue<int>("CarName2")}");
```

These methods will throw an exception if the value found for the name can't be intrinsically cast to the requested datatype. For example, trying to cast the CarName property to an int will throw an InvalidOperationException as shown by the following code:

```
try
{
  Console.WriteLine($"My car's name is {config.GetValue<int>("CarName")}");
}
catch (InvalidOperationException ex)
{
  Console.WriteLine($"An exception occurred: {ex.Message}");
}
```

■ **Note** The GetValue() method is designed to work with primitive types. For complex types, use the Bind() or Get()/Get<T>() methods, covered in the "Working with Objects" section.

Multiple Configuration Files

More than one configuration file can be added into the configuration system. When more than one file is used, the configuration properties are additive, unless any names of the name-value pairs conflict. When there is a name conflict, the last one in wins. To see this in action, add another file named appsettings.development.json, and set the project to always copy it to the output directory.

```
<ItemGroup>
  <None Update="appsettings.development.json">
    <CopyToOutputDirectory>Always</CopyToOutputDirectory>
   </None>
</ItemGroup>
```

Update the JSON to the following:

```
{
  "CarName": "Logan"
}
```

Now update the code that creates the instance of the IConfiguration interface to the following (update in bold):

```
IConfiguration config = new ConfigurationBuilder()
    .SetBasePath(Directory.GetCurrentDirectory())
    .AddJsonFile("appsettings.json", true, true)
    .AddJsonFile("appsettings.development.json", true, true)
    .Build();
```

When you run this program, you will see the name of the car is indeed Logan, and not Suzy.

Working with Objects (Updated 10.0)

Our sample JSON file so far is extremely simple with a single name-value pair. In real-world projects, application configuration is usually more complex than a single property. Update the appsettings.development.json file to the following, which adds a new Car object to the JSON:

```
{
  "CarName": "Suzy",
  "Car": {
    "Make":"Honda",
    "Color": "Blue",
    "PetName":"Dad's Taxi"
  }
}
```

To access multilevel JSON values, the key used for searching is the hierarchy of the JSON, with each level separated by colons (:). For example, the key for the Car object's Make property is Car:Make. Update the top-level statements to the following to get all the Car properties and display them:

```
Console.Write($"My car object is a {config["Car:Color"]} ");
Console.WriteLine($"{config["Car:Make"]} named {config["Car:PetName"]}");
```

Instead of traversing the hierarchy of names, entire sections can be retrieved using the GetSection() method. Once you have the section, you can then get the values from the section using the simple name format, as shown in the following example:

```
IConfigurationSection section = config.GetSection("Car");
Console.Write($"My car object is a {section["Color"]} ");
Console.WriteLine($"{section["Make"]} named {section["PetName"]}");
```

As a final note for working with objects, you can use the Bind() method to bind configuration values to an existing instance of an object or the Get() method to create a new object instance. These are similar to the GetValue() method but work with nonprimitive types. To get started, create a simple Car class at the end of the top-level statements:

```
public class Car
{
  public string Make {get;set;}
  public string Color {get;set;}
  public string PetName { get; set; }
}
```

Next, create a new instance of a Car class, and then call Bind() on the section passing in the Car instance:

```
var c = new Car();
section.Bind(c);
Console.Write($"My car object is a {c.Color} ");
Console.WriteLine($"{c.Make} named {c.PetName}");
```

If the section isn't configured, the Bind() method will not update the instance but will leave all of the properties as they existed prior to the call to Bind(). The following will leave the Color set to Red and the remaining properties null:

```
var notFoundCar = new Car { Color = "Red"};
config.GetSection("Car2").Bind(notFoundCar);
Console.Write($"My car object is a {notFoundCar.Color} ");
Console.WriteLine($"{notFoundCar.Make} named {notFoundCar.PetName}");
```

The Get() method creates a new instance of the specified type from a section of the configuration. The non-generic version of the method returns an object type, so the return value must be cast to the specific type before being used. Here is an example using the Get() method to create an instance of the Car class from the Car section of the configuration:

```
var carFromGet = config.GetSection(nameof(Car)).Get(typeof(Car)) as Car;
Console.Write($"My car object (using Get()) is a {carFromGet.Color} ");
Console.WriteLine($"{carFromGet.Make} named {carFromGet.PetName}");
```

If the named section isn't found, the Get() method returns null:

```
var notFoundCarFromGet = config.GetSection("Car2").Get(typeof(Car));
Console.WriteLine($"The not found car is null? {notFoundCarFromGet == null}");
```

The generic version returns an instance of the specified type without having to perform a cast. If the section isn't found, the method returns null.

```
//Returns a Car instance
var carFromGet2 = config.GetSection(nameof(Car)).Get<Car>();
Console.Write($"My car object (using Get()) is a {carFromGet.Color} ");
Console.WriteLine($"{carFromGet.Make} named {carFromGet.PetName}");

//Returns null
var notFoundCarFromGet2 = config.GetSection("Car2").Get<Car>();
Console.WriteLine($"The not found car is null? {notFoundCarFromGet2 == null}");
```

The Bind() and Get()/Get<T>() methods use reflection (covered in the next chapter) to match the names of the public properties on the class to the names in the configuration section in a case-insensitive manner. For example, if you update appsettings.development.json to the following (notice the casing change of the petName property), the previous code will still work:

```
{
  "CarName": "Suzy",
  "Car": {
    "Make":"Honda",
    "Color": "Blue",
    "petName":"Dad's Taxi"
  }
}
```

If a property in the configuration doesn't exist in the class (or the name is spelled differently), then that particular configuration value (by default) is ignored. If you update the JSON to the following, the Make and Color properties are populated, but the PetName property on the Car object isn't:

```
{
  "CarName": "Suzy",
  "Car": {
    "Make":"Honda",
    "Color": "Blue",
    "PetNameForCar":"Dad's Taxi"
  }
}
```

The Bind(), Get() and Get<T>() methods can optionally take an Action<BinderOptions> to further refine the process of updating (Bind()) or instantiating (Get()/Get<T>()) class instances. The BinderOptions class is listed here:

```
public class BinderOptions
{
  public bool BindNonPublicProperties { get; set; } //Defaults to false
  public bool ErrorOnUnknownConfiguration { get; set; } //Defaults to false
}
```

If the ErrorOnUnknownConfiguration option is set to true, then an InvalidOperationException will be thrown if the configuration contains a name that doesn't exist on the model. With the renamed configuration value (PetNameForCar), the following call throws the exception listed in the code sample:

```
try
{
  _ = config.GetSection(nameof(Car)).Get<Car>(t=>t.ErrorOnUnknownConfiguration=true);
}
catch (InvalidOperationException ex)
{
    Console.WriteLine($"An exception occurred: {ex.Message}");
}
/*
Error message: 'ErrorOnUnknownConfiguration' was set on the provided BinderOptions, but the
following properties were not found on the instance of Car: 'PetNameForCar'
*/
```

The other option allows for binding non-public properties. By default, both properties are false. If non-public properties should be bound from the configuration, set the BindNonPublicProperties, like this:

```
var carFromGet3 = config.GetSection(nameof(Car)).Get<Car>(t=>t.BindNonPublicPropert
ies=true);
```

New in C# 10, the GetRequiredSection() method will throw an exception if the section isn't configured. For example, the following code will throw an exception since there isn't a Car2 section in the configuration:

```
try
{
  config.GetRequiredSection("Car2").Bind(notFoundCar);
}
catch (InvalidOperationException ex)
{
  Console.WriteLine($"An exception occurred: {ex.Message}");
}
```

Additional Configuration Options

In addition to using file-based configuration, there are options to use environment variables, Azure Key Vault, command-line arguments, and many more. Many of these are used intrinsically in ASP.NET Core, as you will see later in this book. You can also reference the .NET documentation for more information on using other methods for configuring applications.

Building and Consuming a .NET Class Library

To begin exploring the world of .NET class libraries, you'll first create a `*.dll` assembly (named `CarLibrary`) that contains a small set of public types. If you are working in Visual Studio, name the solution file something meaningful (different than `CarLibrary`). You will add two projects into the solution later in this section. If you are working in Visual Studio Code, you don't need to have a solution, although most developers find it useful to group related projects into a single solution.

As a reminder, you can create and manage solutions and projects through the .NET Command Line Interface (CLI). Use the following command to create the solution and class library:

```
dotnet new sln -n Chapter16_AllProjects
dotnet new classlib -lang c# -n CarLibrary -o .\CarLibrary -f net6.0
dotnet sln .\Chapter16_AllProjects.sln add .\CarLibrary
```

The first command creates an empty solution file named `Chapter16_AllProjects` (`-n`) in the current directory. The next command creates a new .NET 6.0 (`-f`) class library named `CarLibrary` (`-n`) in the subdirectory named `CarLibrary` (`-o`). The output (`-o`) location is optional. If left off, the project will be created in a subdirectory with the same name as the project name. The final command adds the new project to the solution.

■ **Note** The .NET CLI has a good help system. To get help for any command, add `-h` to the command. For example, to see all templates, type `dotnet new -h`. To get more information about creating a class library, type `dotnet new classlib -h`.

Now that you have created your project and solution, you can open it in Visual Studio (or Visual Studio Code) to begin building the classes. After opening the solution, delete the autogenerated file `Class1.cs`.

The design of your automobile library begins with the `EngineStateEnum` and `MusicMediaEnum` enums. Add two files to your project named `MusicMediaEnum.cs` and `EngineStateEnum.cs` and add the following code to each file, respectively:

```
//MusicMediaEnum.cs
namespace CarLibrary;
// Which type of music player does this car have?
public enum MusicMediaEnum
{
  MusicCd,
  MusicTape,
  MusicRadio,
  MusicMp3
}
//EngineStateEnum.cs
namespace CarLibrary;
// Represents the state of the engine.
public enum EngineStateEnum
{
  EngineAlive,
  EngineDead
}
```

Next, insert a new C# class file into your project, named Car.cs, that will hold an abstract base class named Car. This class defines various state data via automatic property syntax. This class also has a single abstract method named TurboBoost(), which uses the EngineStateEnum enumeration to represent the current condition of the car's engine. Update the file to the following code:

```
namespace CarLibrary;
// The abstract base class in the hierarchy.
public abstract class Car
{
  public string PetName {get; set;}
  public int CurrentSpeed {get; set;}
  public int MaxSpeed {get; set;}

  protected EngineStateEnum State = EngineStateEnum.EngineAlive;
  public EngineStateEnum EngineState => State;
  public abstract void TurboBoost();

  protected Car(){}
  protected Car(string name, int maxSpeed, int currentSpeed)
  {
    PetName = name;
    MaxSpeed = maxSpeed;
    CurrentSpeed = currentSpeed;
  }
}
```

Now assume you have two direct descendants of the Car type named MiniVan and SportsCar. Each overrides the abstract TurboBoost() method by displaying an appropriate message via console message. Insert two new C# class files into your project, named MiniVan.cs and SportsCar.cs, respectively. Update the code in each file with the relevant code.

```
//SportsCar.cs
namespace CarLibrary;
public class SportsCar : Car
{
  public SportsCar(){ }
  public SportsCar(
    string name, int maxSpeed, int currentSpeed)
    : base (name, maxSpeed, currentSpeed){ }

  public override void TurboBoost()
  {
    Console.WriteLine("Ramming speed! Faster is better...");
  }
}

//MiniVan.cs
namespace CarLibrary;
public class MiniVan : Car
{
  public MiniVan(){ }
```

```
  public MiniVan(
    string name, int maxSpeed, int currentSpeed)
    : base (name, maxSpeed, currentSpeed){ }

  public override void TurboBoost()
  {
    // Minivans have poor turbo capabilities!
    State = EngineStateEnum.EngineDead;
    Console.WriteLine("Eek! Your engine block exploded!");
  }
}
```

Exploring the Manifest

Before using `CarLibrary.dll` from a client application, let's check out how the code library is composed under the hood. Assuming you have compiled this project, run `ildasm.exe` against the compiled assembly. If you don't have `ildasm.exe` (covered earlier in this book), it is also located in the Chapter 16 directory of this book's repository.

```
ildasm /METADATA /out=CarLibrary.il .\CarLibrary\bin\Debug\net6.0\CarLibrary.dll
```

The `Manifest` section of the disassembled results starts with `//Metadata version: 4.0.30319`. Immediately following is the list of all external assemblies required by the class library, as shown here:

```
// Metadata version: v4.0.30319
.assembly extern System.Runtime
{
  .publickeytoken = (B0 3F 5F 7F 11 D5 0A 3A )
  .ver 6:0:0:0
}
.assembly extern System.Console
{
  .publickeytoken = (B0 3F 5F 7F 11 D5 0A 3A )
  .ver 6:0:0:0
}
```

Each `.assembly extern` block is qualified by the `.publickeytoken` and `.ver` directives. The `.publickeytoken` instruction is present only if the assembly has been configured with a *strong name*. The `.ver` token defines the numerical version identifier of the referenced assembly.

■ **Note** Prior versions of the .NET Framework relied heavily on strong naming, which involved using a public/private key combination. This was required on Windows for an assembly to be added into the Global Assembly Cache, but its need has severely diminished with the advent of .NET Core.

After the external references, you will find a number of `.custom` tokens that identify assembly-level attributes (some system generated, but also copyright information, company name, assembly version, etc.). Here is a (very) partial listing of this chunk of manifest data:

```
.assembly CarLibrary
{
...
  .custom instance void ... TargetFrameworkAttribute ...
  .custom instance void ... AssemblyCompanyAttribute ...
  .custom instance void ... AssemblyConfigurationAttribute ...
  .custom instance void ... AssemblyFileVersionAttribute ...
  .custom instance void ... AssemblyProductAttribute ...
  .custom instance void ... AssemblyTitleAttribute ...
```

These settings can be set either using the Visual Studio property pages or editing the project file and adding in the correct elements. To edit the package properties in Visual Studio 2022, right-click the project in Solution Explorer, select Properties, and navigate to the Package menu in the left rail of the window. This brings up the dialog shown in Figure 16-4. For the sake of brevity, Figure 16-4 is only part of the dialog.

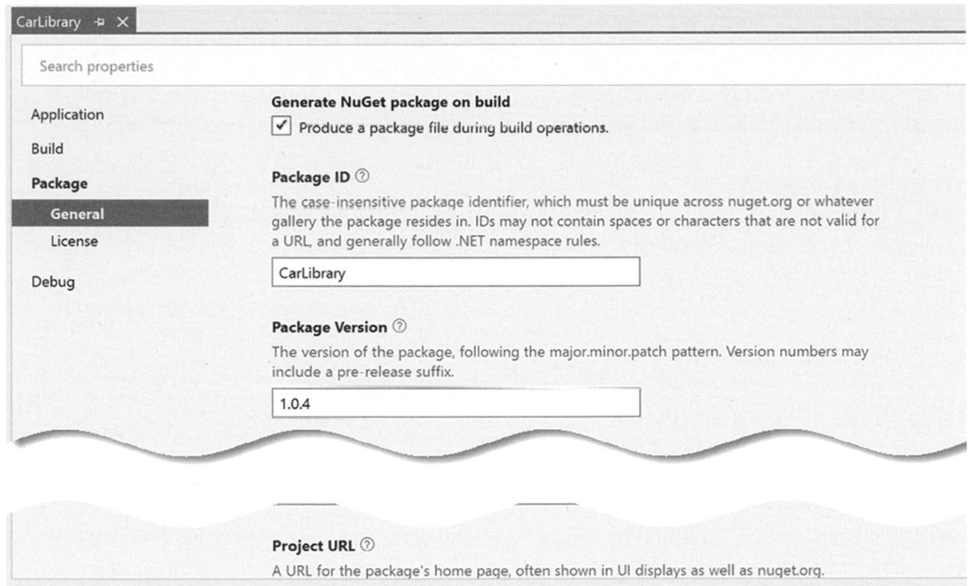

Figure 16-4. *Editing assembly information using Visual Studio 2022's Properties window*

■ **Note** There are three different version fields in the Package screen. The Assembly version and the File version use the same schema, which is based on semantic versioning (`https://semver.org`). The first number is the *major* build version, the second is the *minor* build version, and the third is the *patch* number. The fourth number is usually used to indicate a build number. The *package version* number should adhere to semantic versioning, with just the `{major}.{minor}.{patch}` placeholders used. Semantic versioning allows for an alphanumeric extension to the version, which is separated by a dash instead of a period (e.g., 1.0.0-rc). This denotes noncomplete versions, such as betas and release candidates.

A package version sets the NuGet package version (NuGet packaging is covered in more detail later in this chapter). The Assembly version is used by .NET during build and runtime to locate, link, and load assemblies. The File version is used only by Windows Explorer, and it not used by .NET.

Another way to add the metadata to your assembly is directly in the `*.csproj` project file. The following update to the main PropertyGroup in the project file does the same thing as filling in the form shown in Figure 16-4. Notice that the package version is simply called Version in the project file.

```
<PropertyGroup>
  <TargetFramework>net6.0</TargetFramework>
  <ImplicitUsings>enable</ImplicitUsings>
  <Nullable>disable</Nullable>
  <Copyright>Copyright 2021</Copyright>
  <Authors>Phil Japikse</Authors>
  <Company>Apress</Company>
  <Product>Pro C# 10.0</Product>
  <PackageId>CarLibrary</PackageId>
  <Description>This is an awesome library for cars.</Description>
  <AssemblyVersion>1.0.0.1</AssemblyVersion>
  <FileVersion>1.0.0.2</FileVersion>
  <Version>1.0.3</Version>
</PropertyGroup>
```

■ **Note** The rest of the entries from Figure 16-4 (and the project file listing) are used when generating NuGet packages from your assembly. This is covered later in the chapter.

Exploring the CIL

Recall that an assembly does not contain platform-specific instructions; rather, it contains platform-agnostic Common Intermediate Language (CIL) instructions. When the .NET Runtime loads an assembly into memory, the underlying CIL is compiled (using the JIT compiler) into instructions that can be understood by the target platform. For example, the TurboBoost() method of the SportsCar class is represented by the following CIL:

```
.method public hidebysig virtual
   instance void  TurboBoost() cil managed
{
  .maxstack  8
  IL_0000:  nop
  IL_0001:  ldstr "Ramming speed! Faster is better..."
  IL_0006:  call  void [System.Console]System.Console::WriteLine(string)
  IL_000b:  nop
  IL_000c:  ret
}
// end of method SportsCar::TurboBoost
```

As with the other CIL examples in this book, most .NET developers don't need to be deeply concerned with the details. Chapter 18 provides more details on its syntax and semantics, which can be helpful when you are building more complex applications that require advanced services, such as runtime construction of assemblies.

Exploring the Type Metadata

Before you build some applications that use your custom .NET library, examine the metadata for the types within the `CarLibrary.dll` assembly. For an example, here is the `TypeDef` for the `EngineStateEnum`:

```
TypeDef #2
-------------------------------------------------------
 TypDefName: CarLibrary.EngineStateEnum
 Flags     : [Public] [AutoLayout] [Class] [Sealed] [AnsiClass]
 Extends   : [TypeRef] System.Enum
 Field #1
 -------------------------------------------------------
  Field Name: value__
  Flags     : [Public] [SpecialName] [RTSpecialName]
  CallCnvntn: [FIELD]
  Field type:  I4

 Field #2
 -------------------------------------------------------
  Field Name: EngineAlive
  Flags     : [Public] [Static] [Literal] [HasDefault]
 DefltValue: (I4) 0
  CallCnvntn: [FIELD]
  Field type:  ValueClass CarLibrary.EngineStateEnum

 Field #3
 -------------------------------------------------------
  Field Name: EngineDead
  Flags     : [Public] [Static] [Literal] [HasDefault]
 DefltValue: (I4) 1
  CallCnvntn: [FIELD]
  Field type:  ValueClass CarLibrary.EngineStateEnum
```

As explained in the next chapter, an assembly's metadata is an important element of the .NET platform and serves as the backbone for numerous technologies (object serialization, late binding, extendable applications, etc.). In any case, now that you have looked inside the `CarLibrary.dll` assembly, you can build some client applications that use your types.

Building a C# Client Application

Because each of the CarLibrary project types has been declared using the `public` keyword, other .NET applications are able to use them as well. Recall that you may also define types using the C# `internal` keyword (in fact, this is the default C# access mode for classes). Internal types can be used only by the assembly in which they are defined. External clients can neither see nor create types marked with the `internal` keyword.

■ **Note** The exception to the internal rule is when an assembly explicitly allows access to another assembly using the `InternalsVisibleTo` attribute, covered shortly.

To use your library's functionality, create a new C# Console Application project named CSharpCarClient in the same solution as CarLibrary. You can do this using Visual Studio (right-click the solution and select Add ➤ New Project) or using the command line (three lines, each executed separately).

```
dotnet new console -lang c# -n CSharpCarClient -o .\CSharpCarClient -f net6.0
dotnet add CSharpCarClient reference CarLibrary
dotnet sln .\Chapter16_AppRojects.sln add .\CSharpCarClient
```

The previous commands created the console application, added a project reference to the CarLibrary project for the new project, and added it to your solution.

■ **Note** The add `reference` command creates a *project* reference. This is convenient for development, as CSharpCarClient will always be using the latest version of CarLibrary. You can also reference an assembly *directly*. Direct references are created by referencing the compiled class library.

If you still have the solution open in Visual Studio, you'll notice that the new project shows up in Solution Explorer without any intervention on your part.

The final change to make is to right-click CSharpCarClient in Solution Explorer and select "Set as Startup Project." If you are not using Visual Studio, you can run the new project by executing `dotnet run` in the project directory.

■ **Note** You can set the project reference in Visual Studio as well by right-clicking the CSharpCarClient project in Solution Explorer, selecting Add ➤ Reference, and selecting the CarLibrary project from the project's node.

At this point, you can build your client application to use the external types. Update the `Program.cs` file as follows:

```
// Don't forget to import the CarLibrary namespace!
using CarLibrary;

Console.WriteLine("***** C# CarLibrary Client App *****");
// Make a sports car.
SportsCar viper = new SportsCar("Viper", 240, 40);
viper.TurboBoost();

// Make a minivan.
MiniVan mv = new MiniVan();
mv.TurboBoost();

Console.WriteLine("Done. Press any key to terminate");
Console.ReadLine();
```

This code looks just like the code of the other applications developed thus far in the book. The only point of interest is that the C# client application is now using types defined within a separate custom library. Run your program and verify that you see the display of messages.

You might be wondering exactly what happened when you referenced the CarLibrary project. When a *project reference* is made, the solution build order is adjusted so that dependent projects (CarLibrary in this example) build first, and then the output from that build is copied into the output directory of the parent project (CSharpCarLibrary). The compiled client library references the compiled class library. When the client project is rebuilt, so is the dependent library, and the new version is once again copied to the target folder.

■ **Note** If you are using Visual Studio, you can click the Show All Files button in Solution Explorer, and you can see all the output files and verify that the compiled CarLibrary is there. If you are using Visual Studio Code, navigate to the `bin/debug/net6.0` directory in the Explorer tab.

When a *direct reference* instead of a *project reference* is made, the compiled library is also copied to the output directory of the client library, but at the time the reference is made. Without the project reference in place, the projects can be built independently of each other, and the files could become out of sync. In short, if you are developing dependent libraries (as is usually the case with real software projects), it is best to reference the project and not the project output.

Building a Visual Basic Client Application

Recall that the .NET platform allows developers to share compiled code across programming languages. To illustrate the language-agnostic attitude of the .NET platform, let's create another Console Application project (VisualBasicCarClient), this time using Visual Basic (note that each of commands is a one-line command).

```
dotnet new console -lang vb -n VisualBasicCarClient -o .\VisualBasicCarClient -f net6.0
dotnet add VisualBasicCarClient reference CarLibrary
dotnet sln .\Chapter16_AllProjects.sln add VisualBasicCarClient
```

Like C#, Visual Basic allows you to list each namespace used within the current file. However, Visual Basic uses the `Imports` keyword rather than the C# `using` keyword, so add the following `Imports` statement within the `Program.vb` code file:

```
Imports CarLibrary
Module Program
  Sub Main()
  End Sub
End Module
```

Notice that the `Main()` method is defined within a Visual Basic module type. In a nutshell, modules are a Visual Basic notation for defining a class that can contain only static methods (much like a C# static class). In any case, to exercise the `MiniVan` and `SportsCar` types using the syntax of Visual Basic, update your `Main()` method as follows:

```
Sub Main()
  Console.WriteLine("***** VB CarLibrary Client App *****")
  ' Local variables are declared using the Dim keyword.
```

```
  Dim myMiniVan As New MiniVan()
  myMiniVan.TurboBoost()

  Dim mySportsCar As New SportsCar()
  mySportsCar.TurboBoost()
  Console.ReadLine()
End Sub
```

When you compile and run your application (make sure to set VisualBasicCarClient as the startup project if you are using Visual Studio), you will once again find a series of message boxes displayed. Furthermore, this new client application has its own local copy of `CarLibrary.dll` located under the `bin\Debug\net6.0` folder.

Cross-Language Inheritance in Action

An enticing aspect of .NET development is the notion of *cross-language inheritance*. To illustrate, let's create a new Visual Basic class that derives from `SportsCar` (which was authored using C#). First, add a new class file named `PerformanceCar.vb` to your current Visual Basic application. Update the initial class definition by deriving from the `SportsCar` type using the `Inherits` keyword. Then, override the abstract `TurboBoost()` method using the `Overrides` keyword, like so:

```
Imports CarLibrary
' This VB class is deriving from the C# SportsCar.
Public Class PerformanceCar
  Inherits SportsCar
  Public Overrides Sub TurboBoost()
    Console.WriteLine("Zero to 60 in a cool 4.8 seconds...")
  End Sub
End Class
```

To test this new class type, update the module's `Main()` method as follows:

```
Sub Main()
...
  Dim dreamCar As New PerformanceCar()

  ' Use Inherited property.
  dreamCar.PetName = "Hank"
  dreamCar.TurboBoost()
  Console.ReadLine()
End Sub
```

Notice that the `dreamCar` object can invoke any public member (such as the `PetName` property) found up the chain of inheritance, although the base class was defined in a completely different language and in a completely different assembly! The ability to extend classes across assembly boundaries in a language-independent manner is a natural aspect of the .NET development cycle. This makes it easy to use compiled code written by individuals who would rather not build their shared code with C#.

Exposing internal Types to Other Assemblies

As mentioned earlier, internal classes are visible only to other objects in the assembly where they are defined. The exception to this is when visibility is explicitly granted to another project.

Begin by adding a new class named MyInternalClass to the CarLibrary project, and update the code to the following:

```
namespace CarLibrary;
internal class MyInternalClass
{
}
```

■ **Note** Why expose internal types at all? This is usually done for unit and integration testing. Developers want to be able to test their code but not necessarily expose it beyond the borders of the assembly.

Using an Assembly Attribute

Chapter 17 will cover attributes in depth, but for now open the Car.cs class in the CarLibrary project, and add the following attribute and using statement:

```
using System.Runtime.CompilerServices;
[assembly:InternalsVisibleTo("CSharpCarClient")]
namespace CarLibrary;
```

The InternalsVisibleTo attribute takes the name of the project that can see into the class that has the attribute set. Note that other projects cannot "ask" for this permission; it must be granted by the project holding the internal types.

■ **Note** Previous versions of the .NET Framework allowed you to place assembly-level attributes into the AssemblyInfo.cs class, which still exists in .NET but is autogenerated and not meant for developer consumption.

Now you can update the CSharpCarClient project by adding the following code to the top-level statements:

```
var internalClassInstance = new MyInternalClass();
```

This works perfectly. Now try to do the same thing in the VisualBasicCarClient Main method.

```
'Will not compile
'Dim internalClassInstance = New MyInternalClass()
```

Because the VisualBasicCarClient library was not granted permission to see the internals, the previous line of code will not compile.

Using the Project File

Another way to accomplish the same thing is to use the updated capabilities in the .NET project file. Comment out the attribute you just added and open the project file for CarLibrary. Add the following ItemGroup in the project file:

```
<ItemGroup>
  <AssemblyAttribute Include="System.Runtime.CompilerServices.InternalsVisibleToAttribute">
    <_Parameter1>CSharpCarClient</_Parameter1>
  </AssemblyAttribute>
</ItemGroup>
```

This accomplishes the same thing as using the attribute on a class and, in my opinion, is a better solution, since other developers will see it right in the project file instead of having to know where to look throughout the project.

NuGet and .NET Core

NuGet is the package manager for the .NET Framework and .NET (Core). It is a mechanism to share software in a format that .NET applications understand and is the default mechanism for loading .NET and its related framework pieces (ASP.NET Core, EF Core, etc.). Many organizations package their standard assemblies for cross-cutting concerns (like logging and error reporting) into NuGet packages for consumption into their line-of-business applications.

Packaging Assemblies with NuGet

To see this in action, we will turn the CarLibrary into a NuGet package and then reference it from the two client applications.

The NuGet Package properties can be accessed from the project's property pages. Right-click the CarLibrary project and select Properties. Navigate to the Package page and see the values that we entered before to customize the assembly. There are additional properties that can be set for the NuGet package (i.e., license agreement acceptance and project information such as URL and repository location).

■ **Note** All of the values in the Visual Studio Package page UI can be entered into the project file manually, but you need to know the keywords. It helps to use Visual Studio at least once to fill everything out, and then you can edit the project file by hand. You can also find all the allowable properties in the .NET documentation.

For this example, we don't need to set any additional properties except to select the "Generate NuGet package on build" check box or update the project file with the following:

```
<PropertyGroup>
  <TargetFramework>net6.0</TargetFramework>
  <ImplicitUsings>enable</ImplicitUsings>
  <Nullable>disable</Nullable>
  <Copyright>Copyright 2021</Copyright>
  <Authors>Phil Japikse</Authors>
  <Company>Apress</Company>
```

```
  <Product>Pro C# 10.0</Product>
  <PackageId>CarLibrary</PackageId>
  <Description>This is an awesome library for cars.</Description>
  <AssemblyVersion>1.0.0.1</AssemblyVersion>
  <FileVersion>1.0.0.2</FileVersion>
  <Version>1.0.0.3</Version>
  <GeneratePackageOnBuild>true</GeneratePackageOnBuild>
</PropertyGroup>
```

This will cause the package to be rebuilt every time the software is built. By default, the package will be created in the bin/Debug or bin/Release folder, depending on which configuration is selected.

Packages can also be created from the command line, and the CLI provides more options than Visual Studio. For example, to build the package and place it in a directory called Publish, enter the following commands (in the CarLibrary project directory). The first command builds the assembly, and the second packages up the NuGet package.

```
dotnet build -c Release
dotnet pack -o .\Publish -c Release
```

The CarLibrary.1.0.3.nupkg file is now in the Publish directory. To see its contents, open the file with any zip utility (such as 7-Zip), and you can see the entire content, which includes the assembly, but also additional metadata.

Referencing NuGet Packages

You might be wondering where the packages that were added in the previous examples came from. The location of NuGet packages is controlled by an XML-based file named NuGet.Config. On Windows, this file is in the %appdata%\NuGet directory. This is the main file. Open it, and you will see several package sources.

```
<?xml version="1.0" encoding="utf-8"?>
<configuration>
  <packageSources>
    <add key="nuget.org" value="https://api.nuget.org/v3/index.json" protocolVersion="3" />
    <add key="Microsoft Visual Studio Offline Packages" value="C:\Program Files (x86)\
    Microsoft SDKs\NuGetPackages\" />
  </packageSources>
</configuration>
```

The previous file listing shows two sources. The first points to NuGet.org, which is the largest NuGet package repository in the world. The second is on your local drive and is used by Visual Studio as a cache of packages.

The important item to note is that NuGet.Config files are *additive* by default. To add additional sources without changing the list for the entire system, you can add additional NuGet.Config files. Each file is valid for the directory that it's placed in as well as any subdirectory. Add a new file named NuGet.Config into the solution directory, and update the contents to this:

```
<?xml version="1.0" encoding="utf-8"?>
<configuration>
    <packageSources>
        <add key="local-packages" value=".\CarLibrary\Publish" />
    </packageSources>
</configuration>
```

You can also reset the list of packages by adding `<clear/>` into the `<packageSources>` node, like this:

```
<?xml version="1.0" encoding="utf-8"?>
<configuration>
  <packageSources>
    <clear />
    <add key="local-packages" value=".\CarLibrary\Publish" />
    <add key="NuGet" value="https://api.nuget.org/v3/index.json" />
  </packageSources>
</configuration>
```

■ **Note** If you are using Visual Studio, you will have to restart the IDE before the updated `nuget.config` settings take effect.

Remove the project references from the CSharpCarClient and VisualBasicCarClient projects, and then add package references like this (from the solution directory):

```
dotnet add CSharpCarClient package CarLibrary
dotnet add VisualBasicCarClient package CarLibrary
```

Once the references are set, build the solution and look at the output in the target directories (`bin\Debug\new6.0`), and you will see the `CarLibrary.dll` in the directory and not the `CarLibrary.nupkg` file. This is because .NET unpacks the contents and adds in the assemblies contained as direct references.

Now set one of the clients as the startup project and run the application, and it works exactly like before.

Next, update the version number of CarLibrary to 1.0.0.4, and repackage it. In the `Publish` directory, there are now two CarLibrary NuGet packages. If you rerun the `add package` commands, the project will be updated to use the new version. If the older version was preferred, the `add package` command allows for adding version numbers for a specific package.

Publishing Console Applications (Updated .NET 5/6)

Now that you have your C# CarClient application (and its related CarLibrary assembly), how do you get it out to your users? Packaging up your application and its related dependencies is referred to as *publishing*. Publishing .NET Framework applications required the framework to be installed on the target machine, and then it was a simple copy of the application executable and related files to run your application on another machine.

As you might expect, .NET applications can also be published in a similar manner, which is referred to as a *framework-dependent* deployment. However, .NET applications can also be published as a *self-contained* application, which doesn't require .NET to be installed at all!

When publishing applications as self-contained, you must specify the target runtime identifier (RID) in the project file or through the command-line options. The runtime identifier is used to package your application for a specific operating system. When a runtime identifier is specified, the publish process defaults to self-contained. For a full list of available runtime identifiers (RIDs), see the .NET RID Catalog at `https://docs.microsoft.com/en-us/dotnet/core/rid-catalog`.

Applications can be published directly from Visual Studio or by using the .NET CLI. The command for the CLI is `dotnet publish`. To see all the options, use `dotnet publish -h`. Table 16-1 explores the common options used when publishing from the command line.

Table 16-1. *Some Options for Application Publishing*

<table>
<tr><th>Option</th><th>Meaning in Life</th></tr>
<tr><td>--use-current-runtime</td><td>Use current runtime as the target runtime.</td></tr>
<tr><td>-o, --output <OUTPUT_DIR></td><td>The output directory to place the published artifacts in.</td></tr>
<tr><td>--self-contained</td><td>Publish the .NET Runtime with your application so the runtime doesn't need to be installed on the target machine. The default is true if a runtime identifier is specified.</td></tr>
<tr><td>--no-self-contained</td><td>Publish your application as a framework-dependent application without the .NET Runtime. A supported .NET Runtime must be installed to run your application.</td></tr>
<tr><td>-r <RUNTIME_IDENTIFIER>--runtime <RUNTIME_IDENTIFIER></td><td>The target runtime to publish for. This is used when creating a self-contained deployment. The default is to publish a framework-dependent application.</td></tr>
<tr><td>-c debug | release--configuration debug | release</td><td>The configuration to publish for. The default for most projects is debug.</td></tr>
<tr><td>-v, --verbosity <d|detailed|diag|diagnostic|m|minimal|n|normal|q|quiet></td><td>Set the MSBuild verbosity level. Allowed values are q/quiet, m/minimal, n/normal, d/detailed, and diag/diagnostic.</td></tr>
</table>

Publishing Framework-Dependent Applications

When a runtime identifier isn't specified, framework-dependent deployment is the default for the dotnet publish command. To package your application and the required files, all you need to execute with the CLI is the following command:

```
dotnet publish
```

■ **Note** The publish command uses the default configuration for your project, which is typically debug.

This places your application and its supporting files (six files in total) into the bin\Debug\net6.0\publish directory. Examining the files that were added to that directory, you see two *.dll files (CarLibrary.dll and CSharpCarClient.dll) that contain all the application code. As a reminder, the CSharpCarClient.exe file is a packaged version of dotnet.exe that is configured to launch CSharpCarClient.dll. The CSharpCarClient.deps.json file lists all the dependencies for the application, and the CSharpCarClient.runtimeconfig.json file specifies the target framework (net6.0) and the framework version. The last file is the debug file for the CSharpCarClient.

To create a release version (which will be placed in the bin\release\net6.0\publish directory), enter the following command:

```
dotnet publish -c release
```

Publishing Self-Contained Applications

Like framework-dependent deploys, self-contained deployments include all your application code and referenced assemblies, but also include the .NET Runtime files required by your application. To publish your application as a self-contained deployment, you must include a runtime identifier in the command (or in your project file). Enter the following CLI command that places the output into a folder named `selfcontained`. If you are on a Mac or Linux machine, select `osx-x64` or `linux-x64` instead of `win-x64`.

```
dotnet publish  -r win-x64 -c release -o selfcontained
```

■ **Note** New in .NET 6, the `--self-contained true` option is no longer necessary. If a runtime identifier is specified, the `publish` command will use the self-contained process.

This places your application and its supporting files (226 files in total) into the `selfcontained` directory. If you copied these files to another computer that matches the runtime identifier, you can run the application even if the .NET 6 Runtime isn't installed.

Publishing Self-Contained Applications as a Single File

In most situations, deploying 226 files (for an application that prints a few lines of text) is probably not the most effective way to get your application out to users. Fortunately, .NET 5 greatly improved the ability to publish your application and the cross-platform runtime files into a single file. This process is improved again with .NET 6, eliminating the need to have the native libraries exist outside of the single EXE, which was necessary in .NET 5 for Windows publishing.

The following command creates a single-file, self-contained deployment package for 64-bit Windows operating systems and places the resulting files in a folder named `singlefile`.

```
dotnet publish -r win-x64 -c release -o singlefile --self-contained
true -p:PublishSingleFile=true
```

When you examine files that were created, you will find a single executable (`CSharpCarClient.exe`) and a debug file (`CSharpCarClient.pdb`). While the previous publish process produced a large number of smaller files, the single file version of `CSharpCarClient.exe` clocks in at 60 MB! Creating the single file publication packed all of the 226 files into the new single file. What was made up for in file count reduction was traded for in file size.

To include the debug symbols file in the single file (to truly make it a single file), update your command to the following:

```
dotnet publish -r win-x64 -c release -o singlefile -p:PublishSingleFile=
true -p:DebugType=embedded
```

Now you have one file that contains everything, but it's still quite large. One option that might help with file size is compression. The output can be compressed to save space, but this will most likely affect the startup time of your application even more. To enable compression, use the following command (all on one line):

```
dotnet publish -c release -r win-x64 -o singlefilecompressed -p:PublishSingleFile=
true -p:DebugType=embedded  -p:EnableCompressionInSingleFile=true
```

The .NET team has been working on file trimming during the publication process for the past few releases, and with .NET 6, it's out of preview and ready to be used. The file trimming process determines what can be removed from the runtime based on what your application uses. Part of the reason this process is now live is because the team has been annotating the runtime itself to remove the false warnings that were prevalent in .NET 5. New in .NET 6, the trimming process doesn't just look for assemblies that can be removed; it also looks for unused members. Use the following command to trim the single file output (all on one line):

```
dotnet publish -c release -r win-x64 -o singlefilecompressedandtrimmed -p:
PublishSingleFile=true -p:DebugType=embedded  -p:EnableCompressionInSingleFile=
true -p:PublishTrimmed=true
```

The final step in this journey is to publish your app in a ready-to-run state. This can improve startup time since some of the JIT compilation is done ahead of time (AOT), during the publish process.

```
dotnet publish -c release -r win-x64 -o singlefilefinal -p:PublishSingleFile=
true -p:DebugType=embedded  -p:EnableCompressionInSingleFile=true -p:PublishTrimmed=
true -p:PublishReadyToRun=true
```

The final size of our application is 11 MB, far less than the 60 MB that we started with.

As a final note, all of these settings can be configured in the project file for your application, like this:

```
<PropertyGroup>
  <OutputType>Exe</OutputType>
  <TargetFramework>net6.0</TargetFramework>
  <ImplicitUsings>enable</ImplicitUsings>
  <Nullable>disable</Nullable>
  <PublishSingleFile>true</PublishSingleFile>
  <SelfContained>true</SelfContained>
  <RuntimeIdentifier>win-x64</RuntimeIdentifier>
  <PublishTrimmed>true</PublishTrimmed>
  <DebugType>embedded</DebugType>
  <EnableCompressionInSinglefile>true</EnableCompressionInSinglefile>
  <PublishReadyToRun>true</PublishReadyToRun>
</PropertyGroup>
```

With those values set in the project file, the command line becomes much shorter:

```
dotnet publish -c release -o singlefilefinal2
```

How .NET Locates Assemblies

So far in this book, all the assemblies that you have built were directly related (except for the NuGet example you just completed). You added either a project reference or a direct reference between projects. In these cases (as well as the NuGet example), the dependent assembly was copied directly into the target directory of the client application. Locating the dependent assembly isn't an issue, since they reside on the disk right next to the application that needs them.

But what about the .NET Framework? How are those located? Previous versions of .NET installed the framework files into the Global Assembly Cache (GAC), and all .NET Framework applications knew how to locate the framework files.

However, the GAC prevents the side-by-side capabilities in .NET Core, so there isn't a single repository of runtime and framework files. Instead, the files that make up the framework are installed together in `C:\Program Files\dotnet` (on Windows), separated by version. Based on the version of the application (as specified in the `.csproj` file), the necessary runtime and framework files are loaded for an application from the specified version's directory.

Specifically, when a version of the runtime is started, the runtime host provides a set of *probing paths* that it will use to find an application's dependencies. There are five probing properties (each of them optional), as listed in Table 16-2.

Table 16-2. *Application Probing Properties*

Option	Meaning in Life
TRUSTED_PLATFORM_ASSEMBLIES	List of platform and application assembly file paths
PLATFORM_RESOURCE_ROOTS	List of directory paths to search for satellite resource assemblies
NATIVE_DLL_SEARCH_DIRECTORIES	List of directory paths to search for unmanaged (native) libraries
APP_PATHS	List of directory paths to search for managed assemblies
APP_NI_PATHS	List of directory paths to search for native images of managed assemblies

To see the default paths for these, create a new .NET Console application named FunWithProbingPaths. Update the Program.cs file to the following top-level statements:

```
Console.WriteLine("*** Fun with Probing Paths ***");
Console.WriteLine($"TRUSTED_PLATFORM_ASSEMBLIES: ");
//Use ':' on non-Windows platforms
var list = AppContext.GetData("TRUSTED_PLATFORM_ASSEMBLIES")
            .ToString().Split(';');
foreach (var dir in list)
{
  Console.WriteLine(dir);
}
Console.WriteLine();
Console.WriteLine($"PLATFORM_RESOURCE_ROOTS: {AppContext.GetData ("PLATFORM_RESOURCE_ROOTS")}");
Console.WriteLine();
Console.WriteLine($"NATIVE_DLL_SEARCH_DIRECTORIES: {AppContext.GetData ("NATIVE_DLL_SEARCH_
DIRECTORIES")}");
Console.WriteLine();
Console.WriteLine($"APP_PATHS: {AppContext.GetData("APP_PATHS")}");
Console.WriteLine();
Console.WriteLine($"APP_NI_PATHS: {AppContext.GetData("APP_NI_PATHS")}");
Console.WriteLine();
Console.ReadLine();
```

When you run this app, you will see most of the values come from the TRUSTED_PLATFORM_ASSEMBLIES variable. In addition to the assembly that is created for this project in the target directory, you will see a list of base class libraries from the current runtime directory, C:\Program Files\dotnet\shared\Microsoft.NETCore.App\6.0.0 (your version number might be different).

Each of the files directly referenced by your application is added to the list as well as any runtime files that are required for your application. The list of runtime libraries is populated by one or more *.deps.json files that are loaded with the .NET Runtime. There are several in the installation directory for the SDK (used for building the software) and the runtime (used for running the software). With our simple example, the only file used is Microsoft.NETCore.App.deps.json.

As your application grows in complexity, so will the list of files in TRUSTED_PLATFORM_ASSEMBLIES. For example, if you add a reference to the Microsoft.EntityFrameworkCore package, the list of required assemblies grows. To demonstrate this, enter the following command in Package Manager Console (in the same directory as the `*.csproj` file):

```
dotnet add package Microsoft.EntityFrameworkCore
```

Once you have added the package, rerun the application, and notice how many more files are listed. Even though you added only one new reference, the `Microsoft.EntityFrameworkCore` package has its dependencies, which get added into the trusted file list.

Summary

This chapter examined the role of .NET class libraries (aka .NET `*.dlls`). As you have seen, class libraries are .NET binaries that contain logic intended to be reused across a variety of projects.

You learned the details of partitioning types into .NET namespaces and the difference between a .NET and .NET Standard, got started with application configuration, and dove deep into the composition of class libraries. Next you learned how to publish .NET console applications. Finally, you learned how to package your applications using NuGet.

CHAPTER 17

Type Reflection, Late Binding, Attribute, and Dynamic Types

As shown in Chapter 16, assemblies are the basic unit of deployment in the .NET universe. Using the integrated Object Browser of Visual Studio (and numerous other IDEs), you can examine the types within a project's referenced set of assemblies. Furthermore, external tools such as `ildasm.exe` allow you to peek into the underlying CIL code, type metadata, and assembly manifest for a given .NET binary. In addition to this design-time investigation of .NET assemblies, you are also able to *programmatically* obtain this same information using the `System.Reflection` namespace. To this end, the first task of this chapter is to define the role of reflection and the necessity of .NET metadata.

The next sections of the chapter examine several closely related topics, which hinge upon reflection services. For example, you will learn how a .NET client may employ dynamic loading and late binding to activate types it has no compile-time knowledge of. You will also learn how to insert custom metadata into your .NET assemblies using system-supplied and custom attributes. To put all of these (seemingly esoteric) topics into perspective, the chapter closes by demonstrating how to build several "snap-in objects" that you can plug into an extendable console application.

In this chapter, you will also be introduced to the C# `dynamic` keyword and understand how loosely typed calls are mapped to the correct in-memory object using the Dynamic Language Runtime (DLR). After you understand the services provided by the DLR, you will see examples of using dynamic types to streamline how you can perform late-bound method calls (via reflection services) and to easily communicate with legacy COM libraries.

Note Don't confuse the C# `dynamic` keyword with the concept of a *dynamic assembly* (see Chapter 18). While you could use the `dynamic` keyword when building a dynamic assembly, these are ultimately two independent concepts.

The Necessity of Type Metadata

The ability to fully describe types (classes, interfaces, structures, enumerations, and delegates) using metadata is a key element of the .NET platform. Many .NET technologies, such as object serialization, require the ability to discover the format of types at runtime. Furthermore, cross-language interoperability, numerous compiler services, and an IDE's IntelliSense capabilities all rely on a concrete description of *type*.

A. Troelsen and P. Japikse, *Pro C# 10 with .NET 6*, https://doi.org/10.1007/978-1-4842-7869-7_17

Recall that the `ildasm.exe` utility allows you to view an assembly's type metadata. In the generated `CarLibrary.il` file (from Chapter 16), navigate to the `METAINFO` section to see all the CarLibrary's metadata. A small snippet is included here:

```
// ==== M E T A I N F O ===

// ===========================================================
// ScopeName : CarLibrary.dll
// MVID      : {DF92DBD2-2C47-4CF8-B25E-7319F1351625}
// ===========================================================
// Global functions
// -------------------------------------------------------
//
// Global fields
// -------------------------------------------------------
//
// Global MemberRefs
// -------------------------------------------------------
//
// TypeDef #1
// -------------------------------------------------------
//   TypDefName: CarLibrary.Car
//   Flags     : [Public] [AutoLayout] [Class] [Abstract] [AnsiClass] [BeforeFieldInit]
//   Extends   : [TypeRef] System.Object
//   Field #1
//   -------------------------------------------------------
//       Field Name: <PetName>k__BackingField
//       Flags     : [Private]
//     CallCnvntn : [FIELD]
//     Field type :  String
...
```

As you can see, the .NET type metadata is verbose (the actual binary format is much more compact). In fact, if I were to list the entire metadata description representing the `CarLibrary.dll` assembly, it would span several pages. Given that this act would be a woeful waste of paper, let's just glimpse into some key metadata descriptions of the `CarLibrary.dll` assembly.

■ **Note** Don't be too concerned with the exact syntax of every piece of .NET metadata in the next few sections. The bigger point to absorb is that .NET metadata is very descriptive and lists each internally defined (and externally referenced) type found within a given code base.

Viewing (Partial) Metadata for the EngineStateEnum Enumeration

Each type defined within the current assembly is documented using a `TypeDef #n` token (where `TypeDef` is short for *type definition*). If the type being described uses a type defined within a separate .NET assembly, the referenced type is documented using a `TypeRef #n` token (where `TypeRef` is short for *type reference*). A `TypeRef` token is a pointer (if you will) to the referenced type's full metadata definition in an external assembly. In a nutshell, .NET metadata is a set of tables that clearly mark all type definitions (`TypeDefs`) and referenced types (`TypeRefs`), all of which can be examined using `ildasm.exe`.

As far as CarLibrary.dll goes, one TypeDef is the metadata description of the CarLibrary.EngineStateEnum enumeration (your number may differ; TypeDef numbering is based on the order in which the C# compiler processes the file).

```
// TypeDef #2
// -------------------------------------------------------
//   TypDefName: CarLibrary.EngineStateEnum
//   Flags     : [Public] [AutoLayout] [Class] [Sealed] [AnsiClass]
//   Extends   : [TypeRef] System.Enum
//   Field #1
//   -------------------------------------------------------
//     Field Name: value__
//     Flags     : [Public] [SpecialName] [RTSpecialName]
//     CallCnvntn: [FIELD]
//     Field type:  I4
//
//   Field #2
//   -------------------------------------------------------
//     Field Name: EngineAlive
//     Flags     : [Public] [Static] [Literal] [HasDefault]
//     DefltValue: (I4) 0
//     CallCnvntn: [FIELD]
//     Field type:  ValueClass CarLibrary.EngineStateEnum
//
//   Field #3 (04000007)
//   -------------------------------------------------------
//      Field Name: EngineDead (04000007)
//      Flags     : [Public] [Static] [Literal] [HasDefault]  (00008056)
//      DefltValue: (I4) 1
//      CallCnvntn: [FIELD]
//      Field type:  ValueClass CarLibrary.EngineStateEnum
...
```

Here, the TypDefName token is used to establish the name of the given type, which in this case is the custom CarLibrary.EngineStateEnum enum. The Extends metadata token is used to document the base type of a given .NET type (in this case, the referenced type, System.Enum). Each field of an enumeration is marked using the Field #n token.

■ **Note** While they look like typos, TypDefName does not have the *e* and DefltValue does not have the *au* one would expect.

Viewing (Partial) Metadata for the Car Type

Here is a partial dump of the Car class that illustrates the following:

- How fields are defined in terms of .NET metadata
- How methods are documented via .NET metadata
- How an automatic property is represented in .NET metadata

```
// TypeDef #1
// -------------------------------------------------------
//   TypDefName: CarLibrary.Car
//   Flags     : [Public] [AutoLayout] [Class] [Abstract] [AnsiClass] [BeforeFieldInit]
//   Extends   : [TypeRef] System.Object
//   Field #1
//   -------------------------------------------------------
//     Field Name: <PetName>k__BackingField
//     Flags     : [Private]
//     CallCnvntn: [FIELD]
//     Field type:  String
...
//  Method #1
// -------------------------------------------------------
//    MethodName: get_PetName
//    Flags     : [Public] [HideBySig] [ReuseSlot] [SpecialName]
//    RVA       : 0x00002050
//    ImplFlags : [IL] [Managed]
//    CallCnvntn: [DEFAULT]
//    hasThis
//    ReturnType: String
//    No arguments.
...
//   Method #2
//   -------------------------------------------------------
//     MethodName: set_PetName
//     Flags     : [Public] [HideBySig] [ReuseSlot] [SpecialName]
//     RVA       : 0x00002058
//     ImplFlags : [IL] [Managed]
//     CallCnvntn: [DEFAULT]
//     hasThis
//     ReturnType: Void
//     1 Arguments
//       Argument #1:  String
//     1 Parameters
//       (1) ParamToken : Name : value flags: [none]
...

//   Property #1
//   -------------------------------------------------------
//     Prop.Name : PetName
//     Flags     : [none]
//     CallCnvntn: [PROPERTY]
//     hasThis
//     ReturnType: String
//     No arguments.
//     DefltValue:
//     Setter    : set_PetName
//     Getter    : get_PetName
//     0 Others
...
```

First, note that the Car class metadata marks the type's base class (System.Object) and includes various flags that describe how this type was constructed (e.g., [Public], [Abstract], and whatnot). Methods (such as the Car's constructor) are described by their parameters, return value, and name.

Note how an automatic property results in a compiler-generated private backing field (which was named <PetName>k__BackingField) and two compiler-generated methods (in the case of a read-write property) named, in this example, get_PetName() and set_PetName(). Finally, the actual property is mapped to the internal get/set methods using the .NET metadata Getter/Setter tokens.

Examining a TypeRef

Recall that an assembly's metadata will describe not only the set of internal types (Car, EngineStateEnum, etc.) but also any external types the internal types reference. For example, given that CarLibrary.dll has defined two enumerations, you find a TypeRef block for the System.Enum type, as follows:

```
// TypeRef #19
// -------------------------------------------------------
// Token:             0x01000013
// ResolutionScope:   0x23000001
// TypeRefName:        System.Enum
```

Documenting the Defining Assembly

The CarLibrary.il file also allows you to view the .NET metadata that describes the assembly itself using the Assembly token. The following is a partial dump of the manifest of CarLibrary.dll. Note that the version matches the assembly version set for the library.

```
// Assembly
// -------------------------------------------------------
//    Token: 0x20000001
//    Name : CarLibrary
//    Public Key    :
//    Hash Algorithm : 0x00008004
//    Version: 1.0.0.1
//    Major Version: 0x00000001
//    Minor Version: 0x00000000
//    Build Number: 0x00000000
//    Revision Number: 0x00000001
//    Locale: <null>
//    Flags : [none] (00000000)
```

Documenting Referenced Assemblies

In addition to the Assembly token and the set of TypeDef and TypeRef blocks, .NET metadata also makes use of AssemblyRef #n tokens to document each external assembly. Given that each .NET assembly references the System.Runtime base class library assembly, you will find an AssemblyRef for the System.Runtime assembly, as shown in the following code:

```
// AssemblyRef #1
// -------------------------------------------------------
//    Token: 0x23000001
//    Public Key or Token: b0 3f 5f 7f 11 d5 0a 3a
//    Name: System.Runtime
//    Version: 6.0.0.0
//    Major Version: 0x00000006
//    Minor Version: 0x00000000
//    Build Number: 0x00000000
//    Revision Number: 0x00000000
//    Locale: <null>
//    HashValue Blob:
//    Flags: [none] (00000000)
```

Documenting String Literals

The final point of interest regarding .NET metadata is the fact that every string literal in your code base is documented under the `User Strings` token.

```
// User Strings
// -------------------------------------------------------
// 70000001 : (23) L"CarLibrary Version 2.0!"
// 70000031 : (13) L"Quiet time..."
// 7000004d : (11) L"Jamming {0}"
// 70000065 : (32) L"Eek! Your engine block exploded!"
// 700000a7 : (34) L"Ramming speed! Faster is better..."
```

■ **Note** As illustrated in the previous metadata listing, always be aware that all strings are clearly documented in the assembly metadata. This could have huge security consequences if you were to use string literals to represent passwords, credit card numbers, or other sensitive information.

The next question on your mind may be (in the best-case scenario) "How can I leverage this information in my applications?" or (in the worst-case scenario) "Why should I care about metadata?" To address both points of view, allow me to introduce .NET reflection services. Be aware that the usefulness of the topics presented over the pages that follow may be a bit of a head-scratcher until this chapter's endgame. So, hang tight.

■ **Note** You will also find a number of `CustomAttribute` tokens displayed by the `METAINFO` section, which documents the attributes applied within the code base. You will learn about the role of .NET attributes later in this chapter.

Understanding Reflection

In the .NET universe, *reflection* is the process of runtime type discovery. Using reflection services, you can programmatically obtain the same metadata information generated by `ildasm.exe` using a friendly object model. For example, through reflection, you can obtain a list of all types contained within a given `*.dll` or `*.exe` assembly, including the methods, fields, properties, and events defined by a given type. You can also dynamically discover the set of interfaces supported by a given type, the parameters of a method, and other related details (base classes, namespace information, manifest data, etc.).

Like any namespace, `System.Reflection` (which is defined in `System.Runtime.dll`) contains several related types. Table 17-1 lists some of the core items you should be familiar with.

Table 17-1. *A Sampling of Members of the System.Reflection Namespace*

Type	Meaning in Life
`Assembly`	This abstract class contains members that allow you to load, investigate, and manipulate an assembly.
`AssemblyName`	This class allows you to discover numerous details behind an assembly's identity (version information, culture information, etc.).
`EventInfo`	This abstract class holds information for a given event.
`FieldInfo`	This abstract class holds information for a given field.
`MemberInfo`	This is the abstract base class that defines common behaviors for the `EventInfo`, `FieldInfo`, `MethodInfo`, and `PropertyInfo` types.
`MethodInfo`	This abstract class contains information for a given method.
`Module`	This abstract class allows you to access a given module within a multifile assembly.
`ParameterInfo`	This class holds information for a given parameter.
`PropertyInfo`	This abstract class holds information for a given property.

To understand how to leverage the `System.Reflection` namespace to programmatically read .NET metadata, you need to first come to terms with the `System.Type` class.

The System.Type Class

The `System.Type` class defines members that can be used to examine a type's metadata, a great number of which return types from the `System.Reflection` namespace. For example, `Type.GetMethods()` returns an array of `MethodInfo` objects, `Type.GetFields()` returns an array of `FieldInfo` objects, and so on. The complete set of members exposed by `System.Type` is quite expansive; however, Table 17-2 offers a partial snapshot of the members supported by `System.Type` (see the .NET documentation for full details).

Table 17-2. Select Members of System.Type

Member	Meaning in Life
IsAbstract IsArray IsClass IsCOMObject IsEnum IsGenericTypeDefinition IsGenericParameter IsInterface IsPrimitive IsNestedPrivate IsNestedPublic IsSealed IsValueType	These properties (among others) allow you to discover a number of basic traits about the Type you are referring to (e.g., if it is an abstract entity, an array, a nested class, etc.).
GetConstructors() GetEvents() GetFields() GetInterfaces() GetMembers() GetMethods() GetNestedTypes() GetProperties()	These methods (among others) allow you to obtain an array representing the items (interface, method, property, etc.) you are interested in. Each method returns a related array (e.g., GetFields() returns a FieldInfo array, GetMethods() returns a MethodInfo array, etc.). Be aware that each of these methods has a singular form (e.g., GetMethod(), GetProperty(), etc.) that allows you to retrieve a specific item by name, rather than an array of all related items.
FindMembers()	This method returns a MemberInfo array based on search criteria.
GetType()	This static method returns a Type instance given a string name.
InvokeMember()	This method allows "late binding" for a given item. You'll learn about late binding later in this chapter.

Obtaining a Type Reference Using System.Object.GetType()

You can obtain an instance of the Type class in a variety of ways. However, the one thing you cannot do is directly create a Type object using the new keyword, as Type is an abstract class. Recall that System.Object defines a method named GetType(), which returns an instance of the Type class that represents the metadata for the current object.

```
// Obtain type information using a SportsCar instance.
SportsCar sc = new SportsCar();
Type t = sc.GetType();
```

Obviously, this approach will work only if you have compile-time knowledge of the type you want to reflect over (SportsCar in this case) and currently have an instance of the type in memory. Given this restriction, it should make sense that tools such as ildasm.exe do not obtain type information by directly calling System.Object.GetType() for each type since that ildasm.exe was not compiled against your custom assemblies.

Obtaining a Type Reference Using typeof()

The next way to obtain type information is using the C# `typeof` operator, like so:

```
// Get the type using typeof.
Type t = typeof(SportsCar);
```

Unlike `System.Object.GetType()`, the `typeof` operator is helpful, in that you do not need to first create an object instance to extract type information. However, your code base must still have compile-time knowledge of the type you are interested in examining, as `typeof` expects the strongly typed name of the type.

Obtaining a Type Reference Using System.Type.GetType()

To obtain type information in a more flexible manner, you may call the static `GetType()` member of the `System.Type` class and specify the fully qualified string name of the type you are interested in examining. Using this approach, you do *not* need to have compile-time knowledge of the type you are extracting metadata from, given that `Type.GetType()` takes an instance of the omnipresent `System.String`.

■ **Note** When I say you do not need compile-time knowledge when calling `Type.GetType()`, I am referring to the fact that this method can take any string value whatsoever (rather than a strongly typed variable). Of course, you would still need to know the name of the type in a "stringified" format!

The `Type.GetType()` method has been overloaded to allow you to specify two Boolean parameters, one of which controls whether an exception should be thrown if the type cannot be found, and the other of which establishes the case sensitivity of the string. To illustrate, ponder the following:

```
// Obtain type information using the static Type.GetType() method
// (don't throw an exception if SportsCar cannot be found and ignore case).
Type t = Type.GetType("CarLibrary.SportsCar", false, true);
```

In the previous example, notice that the string you are passing into `GetType()` makes no mention of the assembly containing the type. In this case, the assumption is that the type is defined within the currently executing assembly. However, when you want to obtain metadata for a type within an external assembly, the string parameter is formatted using the type's fully qualified name, followed by a comma, followed by the friendly name (the assembly name without any version information) of the assembly containing the type, like so:

```
// Obtain type information for a type within an external assembly.
Type t = Type.GetType("CarLibrary.SportsCar, CarLibrary");
```

As well, do know that the string passed into `Type.GetType()` may specify a plus token (+) to denote a *nested type*. Assume you want to obtain type information for an enumeration (`SpyOptions`) nested within a class named `JamesBondCar`. To do so, you would write the following:

```
// Obtain type information for a nested enumeration
// within the current assembly.
Type t = Type.GetType("CarLibrary.JamesBondCar+SpyOptions");
```

Building a Custom Metadata Viewer

To illustrate the basic process of reflection (and the usefulness of System.Type), let's create a Console Application project named MyTypeViewer. This program will display details of the methods, properties, fields, and supported interfaces (in addition to some other points of interest) for any type within System.Runtime.dll (recall all .NET applications have automatic access to this framework class library) or a type within MyTypeViewer itself. Once the application has been created, be sure to import the System.Reflection namespace.

```
// Need to import this namespace to do any reflection!
using System.Reflection;
```

Reflecting on Methods

Several static methods will be added to the Program.cs file, each of which takes a single System.Type parameter and returns void. First you have ListMethods(), which (as you might guess) prints the name of each method defined by the incoming type. Notice how Type.GetMethods() returns an array of System.Reflection.MethodInfo objects, which can be enumerated with a standard foreach loop, as follows:

```
// Display method names of type.
static void ListMethods(Type t)
{
  Console.WriteLine("***** Methods *****");
  MethodInfo[] mi = t.GetMethods();
  foreach(MethodInfo m in mi)
  {
    Console.WriteLine("->{0}", m.Name);
  }
  Console.WriteLine();
}
```

Here, you are simply printing the name of the method using the MethodInfo.Name property. As you might guess, MethodInfo has many additional members that allow you to determine whether the method is static, virtual, generic, or abstract. As well, the MethodInfo type allows you to obtain the method's return value and parameter set. You'll spruce up the implementation of ListMethods() in just a bit.

If you wanted, you could also build a fitting LINQ query to enumerate the names of each method. Recall from Chapter 13, LINQ to Objects allows you to build strongly typed queries that can be applied to in-memory object collections. As a good rule of thumb, whenever you find blocks of looping or decision programming logic, you could make use of a related LINQ query. For example, you could rewrite the previous method with LINQ like this:

```
static void ListMethods(Type t)
{
  Console.WriteLine("***** Methods *****");
  var methodNames = from n in t.GetMethods() orderby n.Name select n.Name;
// Using LINQ extensions:
// var methodNames = t.GetMethods().OrderBy(m=>m.Name).Select(m=>m.Name);
  foreach (var name in methodNames)
  {
```

```
    Console.WriteLine("->{0}", name);
  }
  Console.WriteLine();
}
```

Reflecting on Fields and Properties

The implementation of ListFields() is similar. The only notable difference is the call to Type.GetFields() and the resulting FieldInfo array. Again, to keep things simple, you are printing out only the name of each field using a LINQ query.

```
// Display field names of type.
static void ListFields(Type t)
{
  Console.WriteLine("***** Fields *****");
  //  var fieldNames = from f in t.GetFields() orderby f.Name select f.Name;
var fieldNames = t.GetFields().OrderBy(m=>m.Name).Select(x=>x.Name);
  foreach (var name in fieldNames)
  {
    Console.WriteLine("->{0}", name);
  }
  Console.WriteLine();
}
```

The logic to display a type's properties is similar.

```
// Display property names of type.
static void ListProps(Type t)
{
  Console.WriteLine("***** Properties *****");
  var propNames = from p in t.GetProperties() orderby p.Name select p.Name;
  //var propNames = t.GetProperties().Select(p=>p.Name);
  foreach (var name in propNames)
  {
    Console.WriteLine("->{0}", name);
  }
  Console.WriteLine();
}
```

Reflecting on Implemented Interfaces

Next, you will author a method named ListInterfaces() that will print the names of any interfaces supported on the incoming type. The only point of interest here is that the call to GetInterfaces() returns an array of System.Types! This should make sense given that interfaces are, indeed, types.

```
// Display implemented interfaces.
static void ListInterfaces(Type t)
{
  Console.WriteLine("***** Interfaces *****");
```

```
  var ifaces = from i in t.GetInterfaces() orderby i.Name select i;
  //var ifaces = t.GetInterfaces().OrderBy(i=>i.Name);
  foreach(Type i in ifaces)
  {
    Console.WriteLine("->{0}", i.Name);
  }
}
```

■ **Note** Be aware that a majority of the "get" methods of `System.Type` (`GetMethods()`, `GetInterfaces()`, etc.) have been overloaded to allow you to specify values from the `BindingFlags` enumeration. This provides a greater level of control on exactly what should be searched for (e.g., only static members, only public members, include private members, etc.). Consult the documentation for details.

Displaying Various Odds and Ends

Last but not least, you have one final helper method that will simply display various statistics (indicating whether the type is generic, what the base class is, whether the type is sealed, etc.) regarding the incoming type.

```
// Just for good measure.
static void ListVariousStats(Type t)
{
  Console.WriteLine("***** Various Statistics *****");
  Console.WriteLine("Base class is: {0}", t.BaseType);
  Console.WriteLine("Is type abstract? {0}", t.IsAbstract);
  Console.WriteLine("Is type sealed? {0}", t.IsSealed);
  Console.WriteLine("Is type generic? {0}", t.IsGenericTypeDefinition);
  Console.WriteLine("Is type a class type? {0}", t.IsClass);
  Console.WriteLine();
}
```

Adding the Top-Level Statements

The top-level statements of the `Program.cs` file prompts the user for the fully qualified name of a type. Once you obtain this string data, you pass it into the `Type.GetType()` method and send the extracted `System.Type` into each of your helper methods. This process repeats until the user presses Q to terminate the application.

```
Console.WriteLine("***** Welcome to MyTypeViewer *****");
string typeName = "";

do
{
  Console.WriteLine("\nEnter a type name to evaluate");
  Console.Write("or enter Q to quit: ");

  // Get name of type.
  typeName = Console.ReadLine();
```

```
  // Does user want to quit?
  if (typeName.Equals("Q",StringComparison.OrdinalIgnoreCase))
  {
    break;
  }

  // Try to display type.
  try
  {
    Type t = Type.GetType(typeName);
    Console.WriteLine("");
    ListVariousStats(t);
    ListFields(t);
    ListProps(t);
    ListMethods(t);
    ListInterfaces(t);
  }
  catch
  {
    Console.WriteLine("Sorry, can't find type");
  }
} while (true);
```

At this point, MyTypeViewer.exe is ready to take a test-drive. For example, run your application and enter the following fully qualified names (be aware that Type.GetType() requires case-sensitive string names):

- System.Int32
- System.Collections.ArrayList
- System.Threading.Thread
- System.Void
- System.Math

For example, here is some partial output when specifying System.Math:

```
***** Welcome to MyTypeViewer *****
Enter a type name to evaluate
or enter Q to quit: System.Math

***** Various Statistics *****
Base class is: System.Object
Is type abstract? True
Is type sealed? True
Is type generic? False
Is type a class type? True

***** Fields *****
->E
->PI
->Tau
```

```
***** Properties *****

***** Methods *****
->Abs
->Abs
...
->Acos
->Asin
->Atan
->Atan2
->Ceiling
->Cos
...
```

Notice the repeated listing for Abs. This is because there will be at least one overload for the Abs() method. The code will be expanded to show the parameters and return types shortly.

Reflecting on Static Types

If you enter System.Console in the previous method, an exception will be thrown in the first helper method because the value for t will be null. Static types cannot be loaded using the Type.GetType(typeName) method. Instead, you must use another mechanism, the typeof function from System.Type. Update the program to handle the System.Console special case like this:

```
Type t = Type.GetType(typeName);
if (t == null && typeName.Equals("System.Console",
         StringComparison.OrdinalIgnoreCase))
{
  t = typeof(System.Console);
}
```

Reflecting on Generic Types

When you call Type.GetType() to obtain metadata descriptions of generic types, you must make use of a special syntax involving a "backtick" character (`) followed by a numerical value that represents the number of type parameters the type supports. For example, if you want to print out the metadata description of System.Collections.Generic.List<T>, you need to pass the following string into your application:

```
System.Collections.Generic.List`1
```

Here, you are using the numerical value of 1, given that List<T> has only one type parameter. However, if you want to reflect over Dictionary<TKey, TValue>, supply the value 2, like so:

```
System.Collections.Generic.Dictionary`2
```

Reflecting on Method Parameters and Return Values

So far, so good! Next, we will make a minor enhancement to the current application. Specifically, you will update the ListMethods() helper function to list not only the name of a given method but also the return type and incoming parameter types. The MethodInfo type provides the ReturnType property and GetParameters()

method for these tasks. In the following modified code, notice that you are building a string that contains the type and name of each parameter using a nested foreach loop (without the use of LINQ):

```
static void ListMethods(Type t)
{
  Console.WriteLine("***** Methods *****");
  MethodInfo[] mi = t.GetMethods().OrderBy(m=>m.Name).ToArray();
  foreach (MethodInfo m in mi)
  {
    // Get return type.
    string retVal = m.ReturnType.FullName;
    string paramInfo = "( ";
    // Get params.
    foreach (ParameterInfo pi in m.GetParameters())
    {
      paramInfo += string.Format("{0} {1} ", pi.ParameterType, pi.Name);
    }
    paramInfo += " )";

    // Now display the basic method sig.
    Console.WriteLine("->{0} {1} {2}", retVal, m.Name, paramInfo);
  }
  Console.WriteLine();
}
```

If you now run this updated application, you will find that the methods of a given type are much more detailed and the mystery of the repeated methods is solved. If you enter System.Math into the program, both of the Abs() methods (and all other methods) will display the return type and the parameter(s).

```
***** Methods *****
 ->System.Double Abs ( System.Double value  )
 ->System.Single Abs ( System.Single value  )
```

The current implementation of ListMethods() is helpful, in that you can directly investigate each parameter and method return type using the System.Reflection object model. As an extreme shortcut, be aware that all of the XXXInfo types (MethodInfo, PropertyInfo, EventInfo, etc.) have overridden ToString() to display the signature of the item requested. Thus, you could also implement ListMethods() as follows (once again using LINQ, where you simply select all MethodInfo objects, rather than only the Name values):

```
static void ListMethods(Type t)
{
  Console.WriteLine("***** Methods *****");
  var methods = t.GetMethods().OrderBy(m=>m.Name);
  foreach (var m in methods)
  {
    Console.WriteLine("->{0}", m);
  }
  Console.WriteLine();
}
```

Interesting stuff, huh? Clearly, the `System.Reflection` namespace and `System.Type` class allow you to reflect over many other aspects of a type beyond what `MyTypeViewer` is currently displaying. As you would hope, you can obtain a type's events, get the list of any generic parameters for a given member, and glean dozens of other details.

Nevertheless, at this point you have created a (somewhat capable) object browser. The major limitation with this specific example is that you have no way to reflect beyond the current assembly (`MyTypeViewer`) or assemblies in the base class libraries that are always referenced. This begs the question "How can I build applications that can load (and reflect over) assemblies not referenced at compile time?" Glad you asked.

Dynamically Loading Assemblies

There will be times when you need to load assemblies on the fly programmatically, even if there is no record of said assembly in the manifest. Formally speaking, the act of loading external assemblies on demand is known as a *dynamic load*.

`System.Reflection` defines a class named `Assembly`. Using this class, you can dynamically load an assembly, as well as discover properties about the assembly itself. In essence, the `Assembly` class provides methods that allow you to programmatically load assemblies off disk.

To illustrate dynamic loading, create a new Console Application project named ExternalAssemblyReflector. Your task is to construct code that prompts for the name of an assembly (minus any extension) to load dynamically. You will pass the `Assembly` reference into a helper method named `DisplayTypes()`, which will simply print the names of each class, interface, structure, enumeration, and delegate it contains. The code is refreshingly simple.

```
using System.Reflection;

Console.WriteLine("***** External Assembly Viewer *****");
string asmName = "";
Assembly asm = null;
do
{
  Console.WriteLine("\nEnter an assembly to evaluate");
  Console.Write("or enter Q to quit: ");
  // Get name of assembly.
  asmName = Console.ReadLine();
  // Does user want to quit?
  if (asmName.Equals("Q",StringComparison.OrdinalIgnoreCase))
  {
    break;
  }

  // Try to load assembly.
  try
  {
    asm = Assembly.LoadFrom(asmName);
    DisplayTypesInAsm(asm);
  }
  catch
  {
    Console.WriteLine("Sorry, can't find assembly.");
  }
```

```
} while (true);

static void DisplayTypesInAsm(Assembly asm)
{
  Console.WriteLine("\n***** Types in Assembly *****");
  Console.WriteLine("->{0}", asm.FullName);
  Type[] types = asm.GetTypes();
  foreach (Type t in types)
  {
    Console.WriteLine("Type: {0}", t);
  }
  Console.WriteLine("");
}
```

If you want to reflect over `CarLibrary.dll`, you will need to copy the `CarLibrary.dll` binary (from the previous chapter) to the project directory (if using Visual Studio Code) or to the `\bin\Debug\net6.0` directory (if using Visual Studio) of the ExternalAssemblyReflector application to run this program. Enter **CarLibrary** (the extension is optional) when prompted, and the output will look like this:

```
***** External Assembly Viewer *****
Enter an assembly to evaluate
or enter Q to quit: CarLibrary

***** Types in Assembly *****
->CarLibrary, Version=1.0.0.1, Culture=neutral, PublicKeyToken=null
Type: CarLibrary.Car
Type: CarLibrary.EngineStateEnum
Type: CarLibrary.MiniVan
Type: CarLibrary.MusicMediaEnum
Type: CarLibrary.MyInternalClass
Type: CarLibrary.SportsCar
```

The `LoadFrom` method can also take an absolute path to the assembly you want to view (e.g., `C:\MyApp\MyAsm.dll`). With this method, you can pass in a full path to your Console Application project. Thus, if `CarLibrary.dll` was located under `C:\MyCode`, you could enter **C:\MyCode\CarLibrary** (the extension is still optional).

Reflecting on Framework Assemblies

The `Assembly.Load()` method has several overloads. One variation allows you to specify a culture value (for localized assemblies), as well as a version number and public key token value (for framework assemblies). Collectively speaking, the set of items identifying an assembly is termed the *display name*. The format of a display name is a comma-delimited string of name-value pairs that begins with the friendly name of the assembly, followed by optional qualifiers (that may appear in any order). Here is the template to follow (optional items appear in parentheses):

```
Name (,Version = major.minor.build.revision) (,Culture = culture token) (,PublicKeyToken=
public key token)
```

When you are crafting a display name, the convention PublicKeyToken=null indicates that binding and matching against a nonstrongly named assembly is required. Additionally, Culture="" indicates matching against the default culture of the target machine. Here is an example:

```
// Load version 1.0.0.1 of CarLibrary using the default culture.
Assembly a =
  Assembly.Load("CarLibrary, Version=1.0.0.1, PublicKeyToken=null, Culture=\"\"");
// The quotes must be escaped with back slashes in C#
```

Also be aware that the System.Reflection namespace supplies the AssemblyName type, which allows you to represent the preceding string information in a handy object variable. Typically, this class is used in conjunction with System.Version, which is a wrapper around an assembly's version number. Once you have established the display name, it can then be passed into the overloaded Assembly.Load() method, like so:

```
// Make use of AssemblyName to define the display name.
AssemblyName asmName;
asmName = new AssemblyName();
asmName.Name = "CarLibrary";
Version v = new Version("1.0.0.1");
asmName.Version = v;
Assembly a = Assembly.Load(asmName);
```

To load a .NET Framework assembly (not .NET), the Assembly.Load() parameter should specify a PublicKeyToken value. With .NET, it's not required, due to the diminished use of strong naming. For example, assume you have a new Console Application project named FrameworkAssemblyViewer that has a reference to the Microsoft.EntityFrameworkCore package. As a reminder, this can all be done with the .NET command-line interface (CLI).

```
dotnet new console -lang c# -n FrameworkAssemblyViewer -o .\FrameworkAssemblyViewer -f net6.0
dotnet sln .\Chapter17_AllProjects.sln add .\FrameworkAssemblyViewer
dotnet add .\FrameworkAssemblyViewer package Microsoft.EntityFrameworkCore -v 6.0.0
```

Recall that when you reference another assembly, a copy of that assembly is copied into the output directory of the referencing project. Build the project using the CLI.

```
dotnet build
```

With the project created, EntityFrameworkCode referenced, and the project built, you can now load it and inspect it. Given that the number of types in this assembly is quite large, the following application prints out only the names of public enums, using a simple LINQ query:

```
using System.Reflection;

Console.WriteLine("***** The Framework Assembly Reflector App *****\n");

// Load Microsoft.EntityFrameworkCore.dll
var displayName =
  "Microsoft.EntityFrameworkCore, Version=6.0.0.0, Culture=neutral, PublicKeyToken=a
  db9793829ddae60";
  Assembly asm = Assembly.Load(displayName);
  DisplayInfo(asm);
  Console.WriteLine("Done!");
```

```
  Console.ReadLine();

static void DisplayInfo(Assembly a)
{
  AssemblyName asmNameInfo = a.GetName();
  Console.WriteLine("***** Info about Assembly *****");
  Console.WriteLine($"Asm Name: {asmNameInfo.Name}");
  Console.WriteLine($"Asm Version: {asmNameInfo.Version}");
  Console.WriteLine($"Asm Culture: {asmNameInfo.CultureInfo.DisplayName}");

  Console.WriteLine("\nHere are the public enums:");
  // Use a LINQ query to find the public enums.
  var publicEnums = a.GetTypes().Where(p=>p.IsEnum && p.IsPublic);
  foreach (var pe in publicEnums)
  {
    Console.WriteLine(pe);
  }
}
```

At this point, you should understand how to use some of the core members of the `System.Reflection` namespace to discover metadata at runtime. Of course, you likely will not need to build custom object browsers often (if ever). However, reflection services are the foundation for many common programming activities, including late binding.

Understanding Late Binding

Simply put, *late binding* is a technique in which you can create an instance of a given type and invoke its members at runtime without having hard-coded compile-time knowledge of its existence. When you are building an application that binds late to a type in an external assembly, you have no reason to set a reference to the assembly; therefore, the caller's manifest has no direct listing of the assembly.

At first glance, it is not easy to see the value of late binding. It is true that if you can "bind early" to an object (e.g., add an assembly reference and allocate the type using the C# `new` keyword), you should opt to do so. For one reason, early binding allows you to determine errors at compile time, rather than at runtime. Nevertheless, late binding does have a critical role in any extendable application you may be building. You will have a chance to build such an "extendable" program later in this chapter, in the section "Building an Extendable Application." Until then, let's examine the role of the `Activator` class.

The System.Activator Class

The `System.Activator` class is the key to the .NET late-binding process. For the next example, you are interested only in the `Activator.CreateInstance()` method, which is used to create an instance of a type through late binding. This method has been overloaded numerous times to provide a good deal of flexibility. The simplest variation of the `CreateInstance()` member takes a valid Type object that describes the entity you want to allocate into memory on the fly.

Create a new Console Application project named LateBindingApp and update the `Program.cs` file as follows:

```
using System.Reflection;

// This program will load an external library,
// and create an object using late binding.
```

```
Console.WriteLine("***** Fun with Late Binding *****");
// Try to load a local copy of CarLibrary.
Assembly a = null;
try
{
  a = Assembly.LoadFrom("CarLibrary");
}
catch(FileNotFoundException ex)
{
  Console.WriteLine(ex.Message);
  return;
}
if(a != null)
{
  CreateUsingLateBinding(a);
}
Console.ReadLine();

static void CreateUsingLateBinding(Assembly asm)
{
  try
  {
    // Get metadata for the Minivan type.
    Type miniVan = asm.GetType("CarLibrary.MiniVan");

    // Create a Minivan instance on the fly.
    object obj = Activator.CreateInstance(miniVan);
    Console.WriteLine("Created a {0} using late binding!", obj);
  }
  catch(Exception ex)
  {
    Console.WriteLine(ex.Message);
  }
}
```

Now, before you run this application, you will need to manually place a copy of `CarLibrary.dll` into the project file folder (or `bin\Debug\net6.0` folder if you are using Visual Studio) of this new application.

■ **Note** Don't add a reference to `CarLibrary.dll` for this example! The whole point of late binding is that you are trying to create an object that is not known at compile time.

Notice that the `Activator.CreateInstance()` method returns a `System.Object` rather than a strongly typed `MiniVan`. Therefore, if you apply the dot operator on the `obj` variable, you will fail to see any members of the `MiniVan` class. At first glance, you might assume you can remedy this problem with an explicit cast, like so:

```
// Cast to get access to the members of MiniVan?
// Nope! Compiler error!
object obj = (MiniVan)Activator.CreateInstance(minivan);
```

However, because your program has not added a reference to CarLibrary.dll, you cannot use the C# using keyword to import the CarLibrary namespace, and therefore, you cannot use a MiniVan type during the casting operation! Remember that the whole point of late binding is to create instances of objects for which there is no compile-time knowledge. Given this, how can you invoke the underlying methods of the MiniVan object stored in the System.Object reference? The answer, of course, is by using reflection.

Invoking Methods with No Parameters

Assume you want to invoke the TurboBoost() method of the MiniVan. As you recall, this method will set the state of the engine to "dead" and display an informational message. The first step is to obtain a MethodInfo object for the TurboBoost() method using Type.GetMethod(). From the resulting MethodInfo, you are then able to call MiniVan.TurboBoost using Invoke(). MethodInfo.Invoke() requires you to send in all parameters that are to be given to the method represented by MethodInfo. These parameters are represented by an array of System.Object types (as the parameters for a given method could be any number of various entities).

Given that TurboBoost() does not require any parameters, you can simply pass null (meaning "this method has no parameters"). Update your CreateUsingLateBinding() method as follows (updates in bold):

```
static void CreateUsingLateBinding(Assembly asm)
{
  try
  {
    // Get metadata for the Minivan type.
    Type miniVan = asm.GetType("CarLibrary.MiniVan");

    // Create the Minivan on the fly.
    object obj = Activator.CreateInstance(miniVan);
    Console.WriteLine($"Created a {obj} using late binding!");

    // Get info for TurboBoost.
    MethodInfo mi = miniVan.GetMethod("TurboBoost");

    // Invoke method ('null' for no parameters).
    mi.Invoke(obj, null);
  }
  catch(Exception ex)
  {
    Console.WriteLine(ex.Message);
  }
}
```

At this point, you will see the message in the console that your engine exploded.

Invoking Methods with Parameters

When you want to use late binding to invoke a method requiring parameters, you should package up the arguments as a loosely typed array of objects. The version of the Car class that has a radio and has the following method:

```
public void TurnOnRadio(bool musicOn, MusicMediaEnum mm)
    => MessageBox.Show(musicOn ? $"Jamming {mm}" : "Quiet time...");
```

This method takes two parameters: a Boolean representing if the automobile's music system should be turned on or off and an enum representing the type of music player. Recall this enum was structured as so:

```
public enum MusicMediaEnum
{
  musicCd,     // 0
  musicTape,   // 1
  musicRadio,  // 2
  musicMp3     // 3
}
```

Here is a new method of the `Program.cs` file, which invokes `TurnOnRadio()`. Notice that you are using the underlying numerical values of the `MusicMediaEnum` enumeration to specify a "radio" media player.

```
static void InvokeMethodWithArgsUsingLateBinding(Assembly asm)
{
  try
  {
    // First, get a metadata description of the sports car.
    Type sport = asm.GetType("CarLibrary.SportsCar");

    // Now, create the sports car.
    object obj = Activator.CreateInstance(sport);
    // Invoke TurnOnRadio() with arguments.
    MethodInfo mi = sport.GetMethod("TurnOnRadio");
    mi.Invoke(obj, new object[] { true, 2 });
  }
  catch (Exception ex)
  {
    Console.WriteLine(ex.Message);
  }
}
```

Ideally, at this point, you can see the relationships among reflection, dynamic loading, and late binding. To be sure, the reflection API provides many additional features beyond what has been covered here, but you should be in good shape to dig into more details if you are interested.

Again, you still might wonder exactly *when* you should use these techniques in your own applications. The extendable app later in this chapter should shed light on this issue; however, the next topic under investigation is the role of .NET attributes.

Understanding the Role of .NET Attributes

As illustrated at the beginning of this chapter, one role of a .NET compiler is to generate metadata descriptions for all defined and referenced types. In addition to this standard metadata contained within any assembly, the .NET platform provides a way for programmers to embed additional metadata into an assembly using *attributes*. In a nutshell, attributes are nothing more than code annotations that can be applied to a given type (class, interface, structure, etc.), member (property, method, etc.), assembly, or module.

.NET attributes are class types that extend the abstract `System.Attribute` base class. As you explore the .NET namespaces, you will find many predefined attributes that you are able to use in your applications. Furthermore, you are free to build custom attributes to further qualify the behavior of your types by creating a new type deriving from Attribute. The .NET base class library provides attributes in various namespaces. Table 17-3 gives a snapshot of some—but by *absolutely* no means all—predefined attributes.

Table 17-3. *A Tiny Sampling of Predefined Attributes*

Attribute	Meaning in Life
[CLSCompliant]	Enforces the annotated item to conform to the rules of the Common Language Specification (CLS). Recall that CLS-compliant types are guaranteed to be used seamlessly across all .NET programming languages.
[DllImport]	Allows .NET code to make calls to any unmanaged C- or C++-based code library, including the API of the underlying operating system.
[Obsolete]	Marks a deprecated type or member. If other programmers attempt to use such an item, they will receive a compiler warning describing the error of their ways.

Understand that when you apply attributes in your code, the embedded metadata is essentially useless until another piece of software explicitly reflects over the information. If this is not the case, the blurb of metadata embedded within the assembly is ignored and completely harmless.

Attribute Consumers

As you would guess, the .NET Framework ships with numerous utilities that are indeed on the lookout for various attributes. The C# compiler (csc.exe) itself has been preprogrammed to discover the presence of various attributes during the compilation cycle. For example, if the C# compiler encounters the [CLSCompliant] attribute, it will automatically check the attributed item to ensure it is exposing only CLS-compliant constructs. By way of another example, if the C# compiler discovers an item attributed with the [Obsolete] attribute, it will display a compiler warning.

In addition to development tools, numerous methods in the .NET base class libraries are preprogrammed to reflect over specific attributes. Chapter 19 introduces XML and JSON serialization, both of which use attributes to control the serialization process.

Finally, you are free to build applications that are programmed to reflect over your own custom attributes, as well as any attribute in the .NET base class libraries. By doing so, you are essentially able to create a set of "keywords" that are understood by a specific set of assemblies.

Applying Attributes in C#

To illustrate the process of applying attributes in C#, create a new Console Application project named ApplyingAttributes and add a reference to the System.Text.Json NuGet package. Update the Program.cs file to include the following global using statements:

```
global using System.Text.Json.Serialization;
global using System.Xml.Serialization;
```

Assume you want to build a class named Motorcycle that can be persisted to JSON format. If you have a field that should not be exported to JSON, you can apply the [JsonIgnore] attribute.

```
namespace ApplyingAttributes;
public class Motorcycle
{
```

```
  [JsonIgnore]
  public float weightOfCurrentPassengers;
  // These fields are still serializable.
  public bool hasRadioSystem;
  public bool hasHeadSet;
  public bool hasSissyBar;
}
```

■ **Note** An attribute applies to the "very next" item.

At this point, do not concern yourself with the actual process of object serialization (again, Chapter 19 examines the details). Just notice that when you want to apply an attribute, the name of the attribute is sandwiched between square brackets.

As you might guess, a single item can be attributed with multiple attributes. Assume you have a legacy C# class type (HorseAndBuggy) that was attributed to have a custom XML namespace. The code base has changed over time, and the class is now considered obsolete for current development. Rather than deleting the class definition from your code base (and risk breaking existing software), you can mark the class with the [Obsolete] attribute. To apply multiple attributes to a single item, simply use a comma-delimited list, like so:

```
namespace ApplyingAttributes;
[XmlRoot(Namespace = "http://www.MyCompany.com"), Obsolete("Use another vehicle!")]
public class HorseAndBuggy
{
  // ...
}
```

As an alternative, you can also apply multiple attributes on a single item by stacking each attribute as follows:

```
[XmlRoot(Namespace = "http://www.MyCompany.com")]
[Obsolete("Use another vehicle!")]
public class HorseAndBuggy
{
  // ...
}
```

C# Attribute Shorthand Notation

If you were consulting the .NET documentation, you might have noticed that the actual class name of the [Obsolete] attribute is ObsoleteAttribute, not Obsolete. As a naming convention, all .NET attributes (including custom attributes you may create yourself) are suffixed with the Attribute token. However, to simplify the process of applying attributes, the C# language does not require you to type in the Attribute suffix. Given this, the following iteration of the HorseAndBuggy type is identical to the previous example (it just involves a few more keystrokes):

```
[XmlRootAttribute(Namespace = "http://www.MyCompany.com")]
[ObsoleteAttribute("Use another vehicle!")]
public class HorseAndBuggy
```

```
{
  // ...
}
```

Be aware that this is a courtesy provided by C#. Not all .NET languages support this shorthand attribute syntax.

Specifying Constructor Parameters for Attributes

Notice that the [Obsolete] attribute can accept what appears to be a constructor parameter. If you view the formal definition of the [Obsolete] attribute, you will find that this class indeed provides a constructor receiving a System.String.

```
public sealed class ObsoleteAttribute : Attribute
{
  public ObsoleteAttribute();
  public ObsoleteAttribute(string? message);
  public ObsoleteAttribute(string? message, bool error);
  public string? Message { get; }
  public bool IsError { get; }
  public string DiagnosticId { get; set; }
  public string UrlFormat { get; set; }
}
```

Understand that when you supply constructor parameters to an attribute, the attribute is *not* allocated into memory until the parameters are reflected upon by another type or an external tool. The string data defined at the attribute level is simply stored within the assembly as a blurb of metadata.

The Obsolete Attribute in Action

Now that HorseAndBuggy has been marked as obsolete, if you were to allocate an instance of this type:

```
using ApplyingAttributes;

Console.WriteLine("Hello World!");
HorseAndBuggy mule = new HorseAndBuggy();
```

you would find that a compiler warning is issued. The warning is specifically CS0618, and the message includes the information passed into the attribute.

```
'HorseAndBuggy' is obsolete: 'Use another vehicle!'
```

Visual Studio and Visual Studio Code also help with IntelliSense, which gets their information through reflection. Figure 17-1 shows the results of the Obsolete attribute in Visual Studio through IntelliSense, and Figure 17-2 shows the more detailed messaging in the Visual Studio code editor. Note that both use the term *deprecated* instead of *obsolete*.

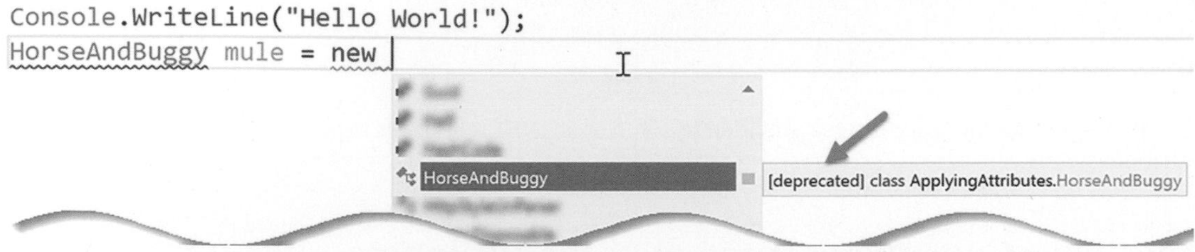

Figure 17-1. *Attributes in action in Visual Studio*

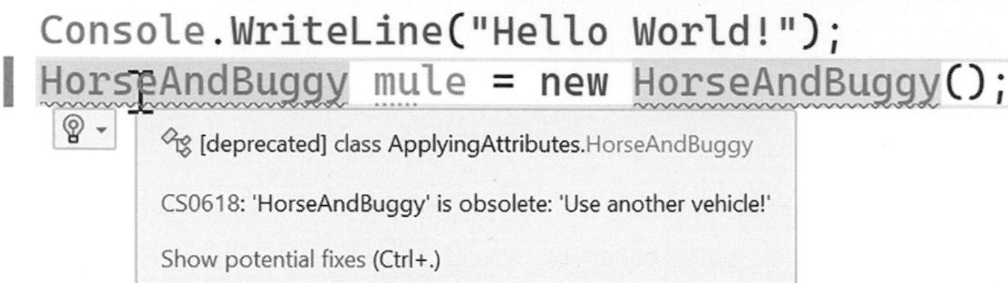

Figure 17-2. *Hovering over Obsolete types in the Visual Studio editor window*

Figure 17-3 and Figure 17-4 show the results of the `Obsolete` attribute in Visual Studio Code.

Figure 17-3. *Attributes in action in Visual Studio Code*

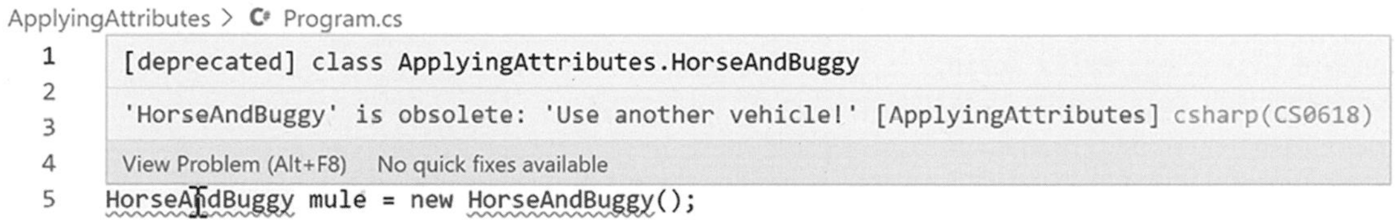

ApplyingAttributes > C# Program.cs

```
[deprecated] class ApplyingAttributes.HorseAndBuggy
'HorseAndBuggy' is obsolete: 'Use another vehicle!' [ApplyingAttributes] csharp(CS0618)
View Problem (Alt+F8)    No quick fixes available
HorseAndBuggy mule = new HorseAndBuggy();
```

Figure 17-4. *Hovering over Obsolete types in the Visual Studio Code editor*

Ideally, at this point, you should understand the following key points regarding .NET attributes:

- Attributes are classes that derive from `System.Attribute`.
- Attributes result in embedded metadata.
- Attributes are basically useless until another agent (including IDEs) reflects upon them.
- Attributes are applied in C# using square brackets.

Next up, let's examine how you can build your own custom attributes and a piece of custom software that reflects over the embedded metadata.

Building Custom Attributes

The first step in building a custom attribute is to create a new class deriving from `System.Attribute`. Keeping in step with the automobile theme used throughout this book, assume you have created a new C# Class Library project named AttributedCarLibrary.

This assembly will define a handful of vehicles, each of which is described using a custom attribute named `VehicleDescriptionAttribute`, as follows:

```
namespace AttributedCarLibrary;
// A custom attribute.
public sealed class VehicleDescriptionAttribute :Attribute
{
  public string Description { get; set; }

  public VehicleDescriptionAttribute(string description)
    => Description = description;
  public VehicleDescriptionAttribute(){ }
}
```

As you can see, `VehicleDescriptionAttribute` maintains a piece of string data using an automatic property (`Description`). Beyond the fact that this class derived from `System.Attribute`, there is nothing unique to this class definition.

■ **Note** For security reasons, it is considered a .NET best practice to design all custom attributes as sealed. In fact, both Visual Studio and Visual Studio Code provide a code snippet named `Attribute` that will scaffold a new `System.Attribute`-derived class into your code window. You can expand any snippet by typing its name and pressing the Tab key.

Applying Custom Attributes

Given that `VehicleDescriptionAttribute` is derived from `System.Attribute`, you are now able to annotate your vehicles as you see fit. For testing purposes, add the following classes to your new class library:

```
//Motorcycle.cs
namespace AttributedCarLibrary;
// Assign description using a "named property."
[VehicleDescription(Description = "My rocking Harley")]
public class Motorcycle
{
}

//HorseAndBuggy.cs
namespace AttributedCarLibrary;
[Obsolete ("Use another vehicle!")]
```

```
[VehicleDescription("The old gray mare, she ain't what she used to be...")]
public class HorseAndBuggy
{
}

//Winnebago.cs
namespace AttributedCarLibrary;
[VehicleDescription("A very long, slow, but feature-rich auto")]
public class Winnebago
{
}
```

Named Property Syntax

Notice that the description of Motorcycle is assigned a description using a new bit of attribute syntax termed a *named property*. In the constructor of the first [VehicleDescription] attribute, you set the underlying string data by using the Description property. If this attribute is reflected upon by an external agent, the value is fed into the Description property (named property syntax is legal only if the attribute supplies a writable .NET property).

In contrast, the HorseAndBuggy and Winnebago types are not using named property syntax and are simply passing the string data via the custom constructor. In any case, once you compile the AttributedCarLibrary assembly, you can use ildasm.exe to view the injected metadata descriptions for your type. For example, the following shows the embedded description of the Winnebago class:

```
// CustomAttribute #1
// -------------------------------------------------------
//   CustomAttribute Type: 06000005
//   CustomAttributeName: AttributedCarLibrary.VehicleDescriptionAttribute :: instance void
     .ctor(class System.String)
//   Length: 45
//   Value : 01 00 28 41 20 76 65 72  79 20 6c 6f 6e 67 2c 20 >  (A very long, <
//         : 73 6c 6f 77 2c 20 62 75  74 20 66 65 61 74 75 72 >slow, but feature<
//         : 65 2d 72 69 63 68 20 61  75 74 6f 00 00          >e-rich auto     <
//   ctor args: ("A very long, slow, but feature-rich auto")
```

Restricting Attribute Usage

By default, custom attributes can be applied to just about any aspect of your code (methods, classes, properties, etc.). Thus, if it made sense to do so, you could use VehicleDescription to qualify methods, properties, or fields (among other things).

```
[VehicleDescription("A very long, slow, but feature-rich auto")]
public class Winnebago
{
  [VehicleDescription("My rocking CD player")]
  public void PlayMusic(bool On)
  {
    ...
  }
}
```

In some cases, this is exactly the behavior you require. Other times, however, you may want to build a custom attribute that can be applied only to select code elements. If you want to constrain the scope of a custom attribute, you will need to apply the [AttributeUsage] attribute on the definition of your custom attribute. The [AttributeUsage] attribute allows you to supply any combination of values (via an OR operation) from the AttributeTargets enumeration, like so:

```
// This enumeration defines the possible targets of an attribute.
public enum AttributeTargets
{
  All, Assembly, Class, Constructor,
  Delegate, Enum, Event, Field, GenericParameter,
  Interface, Method, Module, Parameter,
  Property, ReturnValue, Struct
}
```

Furthermore, [AttributeUsage] also allows you to optionally set a named property (AllowMultiple) that specifies whether the attribute can be applied more than once on the same item (the default is false). As well, [AttributeUsage] allows you to establish whether the attribute should be inherited by derived classes using the Inherited named property (the default is true).

To establish that the [VehicleDescription] attribute can be applied only once on a class or structure, you can update the VehicleDescriptionAttribute definition as follows:

```
// This time, we are using the AttributeUsage attribute
// to annotate our custom attribute.
[AttributeUsage(AttributeTargets.Class | AttributeTargets.Struct, Inherited = false)]
public sealed class VehicleDescriptionAttribute : System.Attribute
{
...
}
```

With this, if a developer attempted to apply the [VehicleDescription] attribute on anything other than a class or structure, they are issued a compile-time error.

Assembly-Level Attributes

It is also possible to apply attributes on all types within a given assembly using the [assembly:] tag. For example, assume you want to ensure that every public member of every public type defined within your assembly is CLS compliant. To do so, simply add the following assembly-level attribute at the top of any C# source code file, like this (outside of any namespace declarations):

```
[assembly: CLSCompliant]
namespace AttributedCarLibrary;
...
```

■ **Note** All assembly-level or module-level attributes must be listed outside the scope of any namespace scope.

Using a Separate File for Assembly Attributes

Another approach is to add a new file to your project named similar to AssemblyAttributes.cs (any name will work, but that name conveys the purpose of the file) and place your assembly-level attributes in that file. In the .NET Framework, it was recommended to use AssemblyInfo.cs; however, with .NET (Core), that file can't be used. Placing the attributes in a separate file will make it easier for other developers to find the attributes applied to the project.

■ **Note** There are two significant changes in .NET. The first is that the AssemblyInfo.cs file is now autogenerated from the project properties and is not meant for developer use. The second (and related) change is that many of the prior assembly-level attributes (Version, Company, etc.) have been replaced with properties in the project file.

Create a new file named AssemblyAttributes.cs and update it to match the following:

```
// List "using" statements first.

// Now list any assembly- or module-level attributes.
// Enforce CLS compliance for all public types in this
// assembly.
[assembly: CLSCompliant(true)]
```

If you now add a bit of code that falls outside the CLS specification (such as an exposed point of unsigned data), you will be issued a compiler warning.

```
// Ulong types don't jibe with the CLS.
public class Winnebago
{
  public ulong notCompliant;
}
```

Using the Project File for Assembly Attributes

As shown in Chapter 16 with InternalsVisibleToAttribute, assembly attributes can also be added to the project file. There is a catch, in that only single-string parameter attributes can be used this way. This is true for the properties that can be set on the Package tab in the project properties.

■ **Note** At the time of this writing, there is an active discussion on the MSBuild GitHub repo regarding adding capability for nonstring parameters support. This would enable the CLSCompliant attribute to be added using the project file instead of a *.cs file.

Go ahead and set some of the properties (such as Authors, Description) by right-clicking the project in Solution Explorer, selecting Properties, and then clicking Package. Also, add InternalsVisibleToAttribute as you did in Chapter 16. Your project file will now look something like this:

```
<Project Sdk="Microsoft.NET.Sdk">

  <PropertyGroup>
    <TargetFramework>net6.0</TargetFramework>
    <ImplicitUsings>enable</ImplicitUsings>
    <Nullable>disable</Nullable>
    <Authors>Philip Japikse</Authors>
    <Company>Apress</Company>
    <Description>This is a simple car library with attributes</Description>
  </PropertyGroup>
</Project>
```

After you compile your project, navigate to the \obj\Debug\net6.0 directory, and look for the AttributedCarLibrary.AssemblyInfo.cs file. Open that, and you will see those properties as attributes (unfortunately, not very readable in this format).

```
using System;
using System.Reflection;

[assembly: System.Runtime.CompilerServices.InternalsVisibleToAttribute("CSharpCarClient")]
[assembly: System.Reflection.AssemblyCompanyAttribute("Philip Japikse")]
[assembly: System.Reflection.AssemblyConfigurationAttribute("Debug")]
[assembly: System.Reflection.AssemblyDescriptionAttribute("This is a sample car library with
           attributes")]
[assembly: System.Reflection.AssemblyFileVersionAttribute("1.0.0.0")]
[assembly: System.Reflection.AssemblyInformationalVersionAttribute("1.0.0")]
[assembly: System.Reflection.AssemblyProductAttribute("AttributedCarLibrary")]
[assembly: System.Reflection.AssemblyTitleAttribute("AttributedCarLibrary")]
[assembly: System.Reflection.AssemblyVersionAttribute("1.0.0.0")]
```

As a final closing remark on assembly attributes, you can turn off the generation of the AssemblyInfo.cs class if you want to manage the process yourself.

Reflecting on Attributes Using Early Binding

Remember that an attribute is quite useless until another piece of software reflects over its values. Once a given attribute has been discovered, that piece of software can take whatever course of action necessary. Now, like any application, this "other piece of software" could discover the presence of a custom attribute using either early binding or late binding. If you want to make use of early binding, you'll require the client application to have a compile-time definition of the attribute in question (VehicleDescriptionAttribute, in this case). Given that the AttributedCarLibrary assembly has defined this custom attribute as a public class, early binding is the best option.

To illustrate the process of reflecting on custom attributes, add a new C# Console Application project named VehicleDescriptionAttributeReader to the solution. Next, add a reference to the AttributedCarLibrary project. Using the CLI, execute these commands (each command must be on its own line):

```
dotnet new console -lang c# -n VehicleDescriptionAttributeReader -o .\
VehicleDescriptionAttributeReader -f net6.0
dotnet sln .\Chapter17_AllProjects.sln add .\VehicleDescriptionAttributeReader
dotnet add VehicleDescriptionAttributeReader reference .\AttributedCarLibrary
```

Update the Program.cs file with the following code:

```
using AttributedCarLibrary;

Console.WriteLine("***** Value of VehicleDescriptionAttribute *****\n");
ReflectOnAttributesUsingEarlyBinding();
Console.ReadLine();

static void ReflectOnAttributesUsingEarlyBinding()
{
  // Get a Type representing the Winnebago.
  Type t = typeof(Winnebago);

  // Get all attributes on the Winnebago.
  object[] customAtts = t.GetCustomAttributes(false);

  // Print the description.
  foreach (VehicleDescriptionAttribute v in customAtts)
  {
    Console.WriteLine("-> {0}\n", v.Description);
  }
}
```

The Type.GetCustomAttributes() method returns an object array that represents all the attributes applied to the member represented by the Type (the Boolean parameter controls whether the search should extend up the inheritance chain). Once you have obtained the list of attributes, iterate over each VehicleDescriptionAttribute class, and print out the value obtained by the Description property.

Reflecting on Attributes Using Late Binding

The previous example used early binding to print out the vehicle description data for the Winnebago type. This was possible because the VehicleDescriptionAttribute class type was defined as a public member in the AttributedCarLibrary assembly. It is also possible to make use of dynamic loading and late binding to reflect over attributes.

Add a new project called VehicleDescriptionAttributeReaderLateBinding to the solution, set it as the startup project, and copy AttributedCarLibrary.dll to the project's folder (or \bin\Debug\net6.0 if using Visual Studio). Now, update your Program.cs file as follows:

```
using System.Reflection;

Console.WriteLine("***** Value of VehicleDescriptionAttribute *****\n");
```

```
ReflectAttributesUsingLateBinding();
Console.ReadLine();

static void ReflectAttributesUsingLateBinding()
{
  try
  {
    // Load the local copy of AttributedCarLibrary.
    Assembly asm = Assembly.LoadFrom("AttributedCarLibrary");

    // Get type info of VehicleDescriptionAttribute.
    Type vehicleDesc =
      asm.GetType("AttributedCarLibrary.VehicleDescriptionAttribute");

    // Get type info of the Description property.
     PropertyInfo propDesc = vehicleDesc.GetProperty("Description");

    // Get all types in the assembly.
     Type[] types = asm.GetTypes();

    // Iterate over each type and obtain any VehicleDescriptionAttributes.
    foreach (Type t in types)
    {
      object[] objs = t.GetCustomAttributes(vehicleDesc, false);

      // Iterate over each VehicleDescriptionAttribute and print
      // the description using late binding.
      foreach (object o in objs)
      {
        Console.WriteLine("-> {0}: {1}\n", t.Name,
          propDesc.GetValue(o, null));
      }
    }
  }
  catch (Exception ex)
  {
    Console.WriteLine(ex.Message);
  }
}
```

If you were able to follow along with the examples in this chapter, this code should be (more or less) self-explanatory. The only point of interest is the use of the PropertyInfo.GetValue() method, which is used to trigger the property's accessor. Here is the output of the current example:

```
***** Value of VehicleDescriptionAttribute *****
-> Motorcycle: My rocking Harley

-> HorseAndBuggy: The old gray mare, she ain't what she used to be...

-> Winnebago: A very long, slow, but feature-rich auto
```

Putting Reflection, Late Binding, and Custom Attributes in Perspective

Even though you have seen numerous examples of these techniques in action, you may still be wondering when to make use of reflection, dynamic loading, late binding, and custom attributes in your programs. To be sure, these topics can seem a bit on the academic side of programming (which may or may not be a bad thing, depending on your point of view). To help map these topics to a real-world situation, you need a solid example. Assume for the moment that you are on a programming team that is building an application with the following requirement:

> The product must be extendable using additional third-party tools.

What exactly is meant by *extendable*? Well, consider the Visual Studio or Visual Studio Code IDEs. When this application was developed, various "hooks" were inserted into the code base to allow other software vendors to "snap" (or plug in) custom modules into the IDE. Obviously, the Visual Studio/Visual Studio Code development teams had no way to set references to external .NET assemblies that had not been developed yet (thus, no early binding), so how exactly would an application provide the required hooks? Here is one possible way to solve this problem:

1. First, an extendable application must provide some input mechanism to allow the user to specify the module to plug in (such as a dialog box or command-line flag). This requires *dynamic loading*.
2. Second, an extendable application must be able to determine whether the module supports the correct functionality (such as a set of required interfaces) to be plugged into the environment. This requires *reflection*.
3. Finally, an extendable application must obtain a reference to the required infrastructure (such as a set of interface types) and invoke the members to trigger the underlying functionality. This may require *late binding*.

Simply put, if the extendable application has been preprogrammed to query for specific interfaces, it is able to determine at runtime whether the type can be activated. Once this verification test has been passed, the type in question may support additional interfaces that provide a polymorphic fabric to their functionality. This is the exact approach taken by the Visual Studio team and, despite what you might be thinking, is not at all difficult!

Building an Extendable Application

In the sections that follow, I will take you through an example that illustrates the process of building an application that can be augmented by the functionality of external assemblies. To serve as a road map, the extendable application entails the following assemblies:

- `CommonSnappableTypes.dll`: This assembly contains type definitions that will be used by each snap-in object and will be directly referenced by the Windows Forms application.
- `CSharpSnapIn.dll`: A snap-in written in C#, which leverages the types of `CommonSnappableTypes.dll`.
- `VBSnapIn.dll`: A snap-in written in Visual Basic, which leverages the types of `CommonSnappableTypes.dll`.
- `MyExtendableApp.exe`: A console application that may be extended by the functionality of each snap-in.

This application will use dynamic loading, reflection, and late binding to dynamically gain the functionality of assemblies it has no prior knowledge of.

■ **Note** You might be thinking to yourself, "My boss has never asked me to build a console application," and you are probably correct! Line-of-business applications built with C# usually fall into the category of smart client (WinForms or WPF), web applications/RESTful services (ASP.NET Core), or headless processes (Azure Functions, Windows services, etc.). We are using console applications to focus on the specific concepts of the example, in this case dynamic loading, reflection, and late binding. Later in this book, you will explore "real" user-facing applications using WPF and ASP.NET Core.

Building the Multiproject ExtendableApp Solution

Up to this point in this book, most of the applications have been stand-alone projects, with a few exceptions (like the previous one). This was done to keep the examples simple and focused. However, in real-world development, you typically work with multiple projects together in a solution.

Creating the Solution and Projects with the CLI

To get started using the CLI, enter the following commands to create a new solution, the class libraries and console application, and the project references:

```
dotnet new sln -n Chapter17_ExtendableApp

dotnet new classlib -lang c# -n CommonSnappableTypes -o .\CommonSnappableTypes -f net6.0
dotnet sln .\Chapter17_ExtendableApp.sln add .\CommonSnappableTypes

dotnet new classlib -lang c# -n CSharpSnapIn -o .\CSharpSnapIn -f net6.0
dotnet sln .\Chapter17_ExtendableApp.sln add .\CSharpSnapIn
dotnet add CSharpSnapin reference CommonSnappableTypes

dotnet new classlib -lang vb -n VBSnapIn -o .\VBSnapIn -f net6.0
dotnet sln .\Chapter17_ExtendableApp.sln add .\VBSnapIn
dotnet add VBSnapIn reference CommonSnappableTypes

dotnet new console -lang c# -n MyExtendableApp -o .\MyExtendableApp -f net6.0
dotnet sln .\Chapter17_ExtendableApp.sln add .\MyExtendableApp
dotnet add MyExtendableApp reference CommonSnappableTypes
```

Adding PostBuild Events into the Project Files

When projects are built (either from Visual Studio or from the command line), there are events that can be hooked into. For example, we want to copy the two snap-in assemblies into the console app project directory (when debugging with `dotnet run`) and the console app output directory (when debugging with Visual Studio) after every successful build. To do this, we are going to take advantage of several built-in macros.

If you are using Visual Studio, copy this block of markup into the `CSharpSnapIn.csproj` and `VBSnapIn.vbproj` files, which copies the compiled assembly into the `MyExtendableApp` output directory (`MyExtendableApp\bin\debug\net6.0`):

```
<Target Name="PostBuild" AfterTargets="PostBuildEvent">
    <Exec Command="copy $(TargetPath) $(SolutionDir)MyExtendableApp\$(OutDir)$(TargetFile
    Name) /Y " />
</Target>
```

If you are using Visual Studio Code, copy this block of markup into the `CSharpSnapIn.csproj` and `VBSnapIn.vbproj` files, which copies the compiled assembly into the `MyExtendableApp` project directory:

```
<Target Name="PostBuild" AfterTargets="PostBuildEvent">
    <Exec Command="copy $(TargetPath) $(ProjectDir)..\MyExtendableApp\$(TargetFileName)
     /Y " />
</Target>
```

Now when each project is built, its assembly is copied into the `MyExtendableApp`'s target directory as well.

Creating the Solution and Projects with Visual Studio

Recall that, by default, Visual Studio names the solution the same as the first project created in that solution. However, you can easily change the name of the solution, as shown in Figure 17-5.

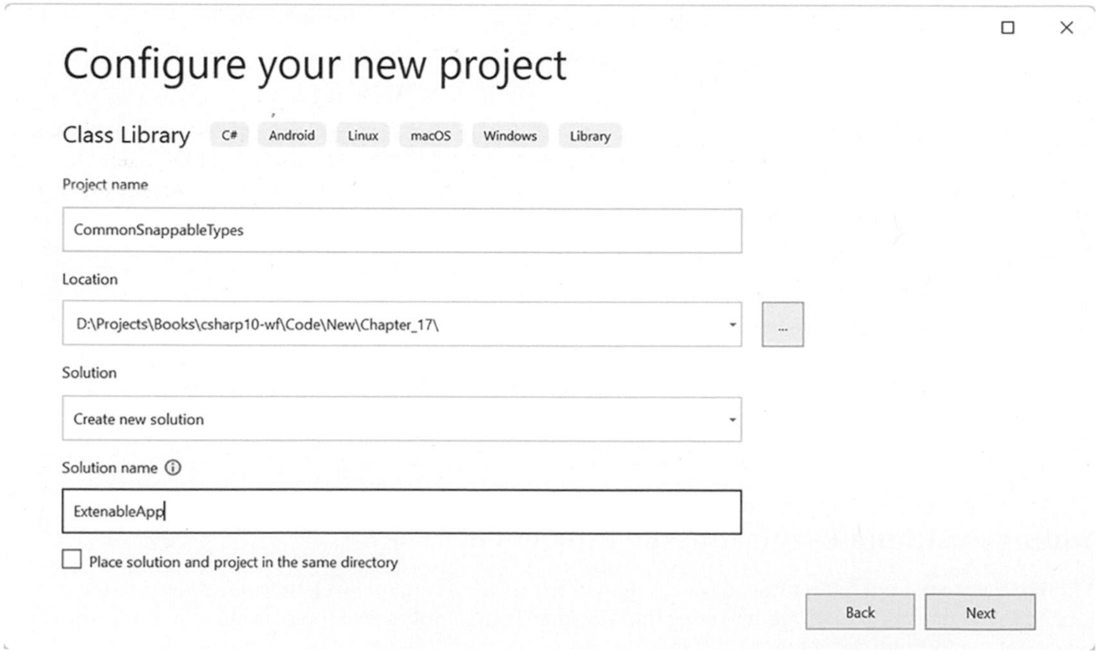

Figure 17-5. *Creating the CommonSnappableTypes project and the ExtendableApp solution*

To create the ExtendableApp solution, start by selecting File ➤ New Project to load the New Project dialog. Select Class Library and enter the name **CommonSnappableTypes**. Before you click OK, enter the solution name **ExtendableApp**, as shown in Figure 17-5.

To add another project into the solution, right-click the solution name (ExtendableApp) in Solution Explorer (or click File ➤ Add ➤ New Project) and select Add ➤ New Project. When adding another project into an existing solution, the Add New Project dialog box is a little different now; the solution options are no longer there, so you will see just the project information (name and location). Name the Class Library project CSharpSnapIn and click Create.

Next, add a reference to the CommonSnappableTypes project from the CSharpSnapIn project. To do this in Visual Studio, right-click the CSharpSnapIn project and select Add ➤ Project Reference. In the Reference Manager dialog, select Projects ➤ Solution from the left (if not already selected) and select the box next to CommonSnappableTypes.

Repeat the process for a new Visual Basic class library (`VBSnapIn`) that references the CommonSnappableTypes project.

The final project to add is a .NET Console app named MyExtendableApp. Add a reference to the CommonSnappableTypes project and set the console app as the startup project for the solution. To do this, right-click the `MyExtendableApp` project in Solution Explorer and select Set as StartUp Project.

■ **Note** If you right-click the ExtendableApp solution instead of one of the projects, the context menu option displayed is Set StartUp Projects. In addition to having just one project execute when you click Run, you can set up multiple projects to execute. This will be demonstrated in later chapters.

Setting Project Build Dependencies

When Visual Studio is given the command to run a solution, the startup projects and all referenced projects are built if any changes are detected; however, any unreferenced projects are *not* built. This can be changed by setting project dependencies. To do this, right-click the solution in Solution Explorer, select Project Build Order, and, in the resulting dialog, select the Dependencies tab and change the project to MyExtendableApp.

Notice that the CommonSnappableTypes project is already selected and the check box is disabled. This is because it is referenced directly. Select the CSharpSnapIn and VBSnapIn project check boxes as well, as shown in Figure 17-6.

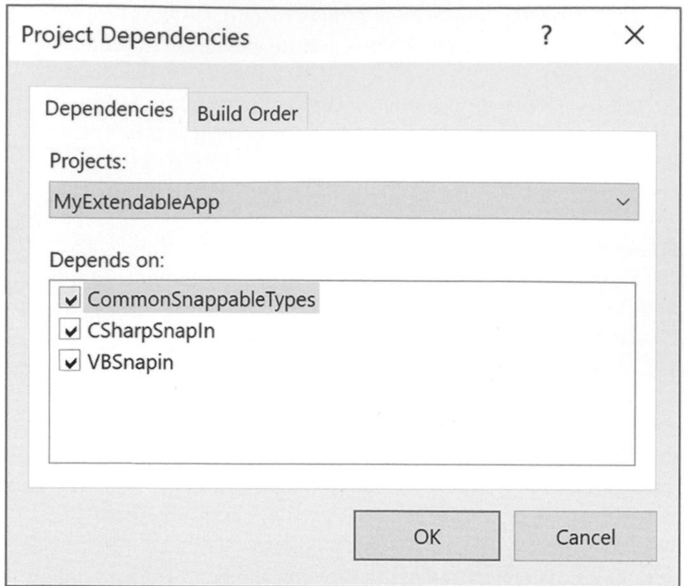

Figure 17-6. *Accessing the Project Build Order context menu*

Now, each time the MyExtendableApp project is built, the CSharpSnapIn and VBSnapIn projects build as well.

Adding PostBuild Events

Open the project properties for the CSharpSnapIn (right-click Solution Explorer and select Properties) and navigate to the Build Events page (C#). Click the Edit Post-build button and then click Macros>>. Here you can see the macros available for use, and they all refer to paths and/or filenames. The advantage of using these macros in build events is that they are machine independent and work on the relative paths. For example, I am working in a directory called `c-sharp-wf\code\chapter17`. You might be (and probably are) using a different directory. By using the macros, MSBuild will always use the correct path relative to the `*.csproj` files.

In the PostBuild box, enter the following (over two lines):

```
copy $(TargetPath) $(SolutionDir)MyExtendableApp\$(OutDir)$(TargetFileName) /Y
copy $(TargetPath) $(SolutionDir)MyExtendableApp\$(TargetFileName) /Y
```

Do the same for the VBSnapIn project, except the property page is called Compile, and from there you can click the Build Events button.

After you have added these post-build event commands, each assembly will be copied into the MyExtendableApp's project and output directories each time they are compiled.

Building CommonSnappableTypes.dll

In the CommonSnappableTypes project, delete the default Class1.cs file, add a new interface file named IAppFunctionality.cs, and update the file to the following:

```
namespace CommonSnappableTypes;
public interface IAppFunctionality
{
  void DoIt();
}
```

Add a class file named CompanyInfoAttribute.cs and update it to the following:

```
namespace CommonSnappableTypes;
[AttributeUsage(AttributeTargets.Class)]
public sealed class CompanyInfoAttribute : System.Attribute
{
  public string CompanyName { get; set; }
  public string CompanyUrl { get; set; }
}
```

The IAppFunctionality interface provides a polymorphic interface for all snap-ins that can be consumed by the extendable application. Given that this example is purely illustrative, you supply a single method named DoIt().

The CompanyInfoAttribute type is a custom attribute that can be applied on any class type that wants to be snapped into the container. As you can tell by the definition of this class, [CompanyInfo] allows the developer of the snap-in to provide some basic details about the component's point of origin.

Building the C# Snap-In

In the CSharpSnapIn project, delete the Class1.cs file and add a new file named CSharpModule.cs. Update the code to match the following:

```
using CommonSnappableTypes;

namespace CSharpSnapIn;
[CompanyInfo(CompanyName = "FooBar", CompanyUrl = "www.FooBar.com")]
public class CSharpModule : IAppFunctionality
{
  void IAppFunctionality.DoIt()
  {
    Console.WriteLine("You have just used the C# snap-in!");
  }
}
```

Notice that I chose to make use of explicit interface implementation (see Chapter 8) when supporting the IAppFunctionality interface. This is not required; however, the idea is that the only part of the system that needs to directly interact with this interface type is the hosting application. By explicitly implementing this interface, the DoIt() method is not directly exposed from the CSharpModule type.

Building the Visual Basic Snap-In

Moving on to the VBSnapIn project, delete the `Class1.vb` file and add a new file named `VBSnapIn.vb`. The code is (again) intentionally simple.

```
Imports CommonSnappableTypes

<CompanyInfo(CompanyName:="Chucky's Software", CompanyUrl:="www.ChuckySoft.com")>
Public Class VBSnapIn
  Implements IAppFunctionality

  Public Sub DoIt() Implements CommonSnappableTypes.IAppFunctionality.DoIt
    Console.WriteLine("You have just used the VB snap in!")
  End Sub
End Class
```

Notice that applying attributes in the syntax of Visual Basic requires angle brackets (< >) rather than square brackets ([ ]). Also notice that the `Implements` keyword is used to implement interface types on a given class or structure.

Adding the Code for the ExtendableApp

The final project to update is the C# console application (`MyExtendableApp`). After adding the MyExtendableApp console application to the solution and setting it as the startup project, add a reference to the CommonSnappableTypes project but *not* the `CSharpSnapIn.dll` or `VBSnapIn.dll` project.

Begin by updating the `using` statements at the top of the `Program.cs` class to the following:

```
using System.Reflection;
using CommonSnappableTypes;
```

The `LoadExternalModule()` method performs the following tasks:

- Dynamically loads the selected assembly into memory
- Determines whether the assembly contains any types implementing `IAppFunctionality`
- Creates the type using late binding

If a type implementing `IAppFunctionality` is found, the `DoIt()` method is called and then sent to the `DisplayCompanyData()` method to output additional information from the reflected type.

```
static void LoadExternalModule(string assemblyName)
{
  Assembly theSnapInAsm = null;
  try
  {
    // Dynamically load the selected assembly.
    theSnapInAsm = Assembly.LoadFrom(assemblyName);
  }
  catch (Exception ex)
  {
```

```
    Console.WriteLine($"An error occurred loading the snapin: {ex.Message}");
    return;
  }

  // Get all IAppFunctionality compatible classes in assembly.
  var theClassTypes = theSnapInAsm
      .GetTypes()
      .Where(t => t.IsClass && (t.GetInterface("IAppFunctionality") != null))
      .ToList();
  if (!theClassTypes.Any())
  {
    Console.WriteLine("Nothing implements IAppFunctionality!");
  }

  // Now, create the object and call DoIt() method.
  foreach (Type t in theClassTypes)
  {
    // Use late binding to create the type.
    IAppFunctionality itfApp = (IAppFunctionality) theSnapInAsm.CreateInstance
    (t.FullName, true);
    itfApp?.DoIt();
    // Show company info.
    DisplayCompanyData(t);
  }
}
```

The final task is to display the metadata provided by the [CompanyInfo] attribute. Create the DisplayCompanyData() method as follows. Notice this method takes a single System.Type parameter.

```
static void DisplayCompanyData(Type t)
{
  // Get [CompanyInfo] data.
  var compInfo = t
    .GetCustomAttributes(false)
    .Where(ci => (ci is CompanyInfoAttribute));
  // Show data.
  foreach (CompanyInfoAttribute c in compInfo)
  {
    Console.WriteLine($"More info about {c.CompanyName} can be found at {c.CompanyUrl}");
  }
}
```

Finally, update the top-level statements to the following:

```
Console.WriteLine("***** Welcome to MyTypeViewer *****");
string typeName = "";
do
{
  Console.WriteLine("\nEnter a snapin to load");
  Console.Write("or enter Q to quit: ");
```

```
  // Get name of type.
  typeName = Console.ReadLine();

  // Does user want to quit?
  if (typeName.Equals("Q", StringComparison.OrdinalIgnoreCase))
  {
    break;
  }
  // Try to display type.
  try
  {
    LoadExternalModule(typeName);
  }
  catch (Exception ex)
  {
    Console.WriteLine("Sorry, can't find snapin");
  }
}
while (true);
```

That wraps up the example application. When you run the application, type in either VBSnapIn or CSharpSnapIn and see the program in action. Note that while C# is case sensitive, when using reflection, case doesn't matter. Both CSharpSnapIn and csharpsnapin work the equally as well.

This concludes our look at late binding. Next up is exploring dynamics in C#.

The Role of the C# dynamic Keyword

In Chapter 3, you learned about the var keyword, which allows you to define local variables in such a way that the underlying data type is determined at compile time, based on the initial assignment (recall that this is termed *implicit typing*). Once this initial assignment has been made, you have a strongly typed variable, and any attempt to assign an incompatible value will result in a compiler error.

To begin your investigation into the C# dynamic keyword, create a new Console Application project named DynamicKeyword. Now, add the following method in your Program.cs file, and verify that the final code statement will indeed trigger a compile-time error if uncommented:

```
static void ImplicitlyTypedVariable()
{
  // a is of type List<int>.
  var a = new List<int> {90};
  // This would be a compile-time error!
  // a = "Hello";
}
```

As you saw in Chapter 13, implicit typing is useful with LINQ, as many LINQ queries return enumerations of anonymous classes (via projections) that you cannot directly declare in your C# code. However, even in such cases, the implicitly typed variable is, in fact, strongly typed. In the previous example, the variable a is strongly typed to be List<int>.

On a related note, as you learned in Chapter 6, System.Object is the topmost parent class in the .NET Core Framework and can represent anything at all. If you declare a variable of type object, you have a strongly typed piece of data; however, what it points to in memory can differ based on your assignment of the reference. To gain access to the members the object reference is pointing to in memory, you need to perform an explicit cast.

Assume you have a simple class named Person that defines two automatic properties (FirstName and LastName) both encapsulating a string:

```
//Person.cs
namespace DynamicKeyword;
class Person
{
  public string FirstName { get; set; } = "";
  public string LastName { get; set; } = "";
}
```

Now, observe the following code:

```
static void UseObjectVariable()
{
  // Create a new instance of the Person class
  // and assign it to a variable of type System.Object
  object o = new Person() { FirstName = "Mike", LastName = "Larson" };

  // Must cast object as Person to gain access
  // to the Person properties.
  Console.WriteLine("Person's first name is {0}", ((Person)o).FirstName);
}
```

Now, back to the dynamic keyword. From a high level, you can consider the dynamic keyword a specialized form of System.Object, in that any value can be assigned to a dynamic data type. At first glance, this can appear horribly confusing, as it appears you now have three ways to define data whose underlying type is not directly indicated in your code base. For example, this method

```
static void PrintThreeStrings()
{
  var s1 = "Greetings";
  object s2 = "From";
  dynamic s3 = "Minneapolis";

  Console.WriteLine("s1 is of type: {0}", s1.GetType());
  Console.WriteLine("s2 is of type: {0}", s2.GetType());
  Console.WriteLine("s3 is of type: {0}", s3.GetType());
}
```

would print out the following if invoked from your top-level statements:

```
s1 is of type: System.String
s2 is of type: System.String
s3 is of type: System.String
```

What makes a dynamic variable vastly different from a variable declared implicitly or via a System.Object reference is that it is *not strongly typed*. Said another way, dynamic data is not *statically typed*. As far as the C# compiler is concerned, a data point declared with the dynamic keyword can be assigned any initial value at all and can be reassigned to any new (and possibly unrelated) value during its lifetime. Consider the following method and the resulting output:

```
static void ChangeDynamicDataType()
{
  // Declare a single dynamic data point
  // named "t".
  dynamic t = "Hello!";
  Console.WriteLine("t is of type: {0}", t.GetType());

  t = false;
  Console.WriteLine("t is of type: {0}", t.GetType());

  t = new List<int>();
  Console.WriteLine("t is of type: {0}", t.GetType());
}
```

```
t is of type: System.String
t is of type: System.Boolean
t is of type: System.Collections.Generic.List`1[System.Int32]
```

At this point in your investigation, do be aware that the previous code would compile and execute identically if you were to declare the `t` variable as a `System.Object`. However, as you will soon see, the `dynamic` keyword offers many additional features.

Calling Members on Dynamically Declared Data

Given that a dynamic variable can take on the identity of any type on the fly (just like a variable of type `System.Object`), the next question on your mind might be about calling members on the dynamic variable (properties, methods, indexers, register with events, etc.). Syntactically speaking, it will look no different. Just apply the dot operator to the dynamic data variable, specify a public member, and supply any arguments (if required).

However (and this is a very big "however"), the validity of the members you specify will not be checked by the compiler! Remember, unlike a variable defined as a `System.Object`, dynamic data is not statically typed. It is not until runtime that you will know whether the dynamic data you invoked supports a specified member, whether you passed in the correct parameters, whether you spelled the member correctly, and so on. Thus, as strange as it might seem, the following method compiles perfectly:

```
static void InvokeMembersOnDynamicData()
{
  dynamic textData1 = "Hello";
  Console.WriteLine(textData1.ToUpper());

  // You would expect compiler errors here!
  // But they compile just fine.
  Console.WriteLine(textData1.toupper());
  Console.WriteLine(textData1.Foo(10, "ee", DateTime.Now));
}
```

Notice the second call to WriteLine() attempts to call a method named toupper() on the dynamic data point (note the incorrect casing—it should be ToUpper()). As you can see, textData1 is of type string, and therefore, you know it does not have a method of this name in all lowercase letters. Furthermore, string certainly does not have a method named Foo() that takes int, string, and DateTime objects!

Nevertheless, the C# compiler is satisfied. However, if you invoke this method from within Main(), you will get runtime errors like the following output:

```
Unhandled Exception: Microsoft.CSharp.RuntimeBinder.RuntimeBinderException:
'string' does not contain a definition for 'toupper'
```

Another obvious distinction between calling members on dynamic data and strongly typed data is that when you apply the dot operator to a piece of dynamic data, you will *not* see the expected Visual Studio IntelliSense. The IDE will allow you to enter any member name you could dream up. This means you need to be extremely careful when you are typing C# code on such data points. Any misspelling or incorrect capitalization of a member will throw a runtime error, specifically an instance of the RuntimeBinderException class.

The RuntimeBinderException represents an error that will be thrown if you attempt to invoke a member on a dynamic data type that does not actually exist (as in the case of the toupper() and Foo() methods). This same error will be raised if you specify the wrong parameter data to a member that does exist.

Because dynamic data is so volatile, whenever you are invoking members on a variable declared with the C# dynamic keyword, you could wrap the calls within a proper try/catch block and handle the error in a graceful manner, like so:

```
static void InvokeMembersOnDynamicData()
{
  dynamic textData1 = "Hello";

  try
  {
    Console.WriteLine(textData1.ToUpper());
    Console.WriteLine(textData1.toupper());
    Console.WriteLine(textData1.Foo(10, "ee", DateTime.Now));
  }
  catch (Microsoft.CSharp.RuntimeBinder.RuntimeBinderException ex)
  {
    Console.WriteLine(ex.Message);
  }
}
```

If you call this method again, you will find the call to ToUpper() (note the capital *T* and *U*) works correctly; however, you then find the error data displayed to the console.

```
HELLO
'string' does not contain a definition for 'toupper'
```

Of course, the process of wrapping all dynamic method invocations in a try/catch block is rather tedious. If you watch your spelling and parameter passing, this is not required. However, catching exceptions is handy when you might not know in advance if a member will be present on the target type.

The Scope of the dynamic Keyword

Recall that implicitly typed data (declared with the var keyword) is possible only for local variables in a member scope. The var keyword can never be used as a return value, a parameter, or a member of a class/structure. This is not the case with the dynamic keyword, however. Consider the following class definition:

```
namespace DynamicKeyword;
class VeryDynamicClass
{
  // A dynamic field.
  private static dynamic _myDynamicField;

  // A dynamic property.
  public dynamic DynamicProperty { get; set; }

  // A dynamic return type and a dynamic parameter type.
  public dynamic DynamicMethod(dynamic dynamicParam)
  {
    // A dynamic local variable.
    dynamic dynamicLocalVar = "Local variable";

    int myInt = 10;

    if (dynamicParam is int)
    {
      return dynamicLocalVar;
    }
    else
    {
      return myInt;
    }
  }
}
```

You could now invoke the public members as expected; however, as you are operating on dynamic methods and properties, you cannot be completely sure what the data type will be! While the VeryDynamicClass definition might not be useful in a real-world application, it does illustrate the scope of where you can apply this C# keyword.

Limitations of the dynamic Keyword

While a great many things can be defined using the dynamic keyword, there are some limitations regarding its usage. While they are not showstoppers, do know that a dynamic data item cannot make use of lambda expressions or C# anonymous methods when calling a method. For example, the following code will always result in errors, even if the target method does indeed take a delegate parameter that takes a string value and returns void:

```
dynamic a = GetDynamicObject();

// Error! Methods on dynamic data can't use lambdas!
a.Method(arg => Console.WriteLine(arg));
```

To circumvent this restriction, you will need to work with the underlying delegate directly, using the techniques described in Chapter 12. Another limitation is that a dynamic point of data cannot understand any extension methods (see Chapter 11). Unfortunately, this would also include any of the extension methods that come from the LINQ APIs. Therefore, a variable declared with the `dynamic` keyword has limited use within LINQ to Objects and other LINQ technologies.

```
dynamic a = GetDynamicObject();
// Error! Dynamic data can't find the Select() extension method!
var data = from d in a select d;
```

Practical Uses of the dynamic Keyword

Given that dynamic data is not strongly typed, not checked at compile time, has no ability to trigger IntelliSense, and cannot be the target of a LINQ query, you are absolutely correct to assume that using the `dynamic` keyword just for the sake of doing so is a poor programming practice.

However, in a few circumstances, the `dynamic` keyword can radically reduce the amount of code you need to author by hand. Specifically, if you are building a .NET application that makes heavy use of late binding (via reflection), the `dynamic` keyword can save you typing time. As well, if you are building a .NET application that needs to communicate with legacy COM libraries (such as Microsoft Office products), you can greatly simplify your code base via the `dynamic` keyword. By way of a final example, web applications built using ASP.NET Core frequently use the `ViewBag` type, which can also be accessed in a simplified manner using the `dynamic` keyword.

■ **Note** COM interaction is strictly a Windows paradigm and removes the cross-platform capabilities of your application.

Like any "shortcut," you need to weigh the pros and cons. The use of the `dynamic` keyword is a trade-off between brevity of code and type safety. While C# is a strongly typed language at its core, you can opt in (or opt out) of dynamic behaviors on a call-by-call basis. Always remember that you never need to use the `dynamic` keyword. You could always get to the same end result by authoring alternative code by hand (and typically much more of it).

The Role of the Dynamic Language Runtime

Now that you better understand what "dynamic data" is about, let's learn how it is processed. Since the release of .NET 4.0, the Common Language Runtime (CLR) was supplemented with a complementary runtime environment named the Dynamic Language Runtime. The concept of a "dynamic runtime" is certainly not new. In fact, many programming languages such as JavaScript, LISP, Ruby, and Python have used it for years. In a nutshell, a dynamic runtime allows a dynamic language the ability to discover types completely at runtime with no compile-time checks.

■ **Note** While a lot of the DLR was ported to .NET Core (starting with 3.0), feature parity between the DLR in .NET 6 and .NET 4.8 hasn't been achieved.

If you have a background in strongly typed languages (including C#, without dynamic types), the notion of such a runtime might seem undesirable. After all, you typically want to receive compile-time errors, not runtime errors, wherever possible. Nevertheless, dynamic languages/runtimes do provide some interesting features, including the following:

- An extremely flexible code base. You can refactor code without making numerous changes to data types.
- A simple way to interoperate with diverse object types built in different platforms and programming languages.
- A way to add or remove members to a type, in memory, at runtime.

One role of the DLR is to enable various dynamic languages to run with the .NET Runtime and give them a way to interoperate with other .NET code. These languages live in a dynamic universe, where type is discovered solely at runtime. And yet, these languages have access to the richness of the .NET base class libraries. Even better, their code bases can interoperate with C# (or vice versa), thanks to the inclusion of the `dynamic` keyword.

■ **Note** This chapter will not address how the DLR can be used to integrate with dynamic languages.

The Role of Expression Trees

The DLR makes use of *expression trees* to capture the meaning of a dynamic call in neutral terms. For example, take the following C# code:

```
dynamic d = GetSomeData();
d.SuperMethod(12);
```

In this example, the DLR will automatically build an expression tree that says, in effect, "Call the method named `SuperMethod` on object `d`, passing in the number `12` as an argument." This information (formally termed the *payload*) is then passed to the correct runtime binder, which again could be the C# dynamic binder or even (as explained shortly) legacy COM objects.

From here, the request is mapped into the required call structure for the target object. The nice thing about these expression trees (beyond that you do not need to manually create them) is that this allows you to write a fixed C# code statement and not worry about what the underlying target actually is.

Dynamic Runtime Lookup of Expression Trees

As explained, the DLR will pass the expression trees to a target object; however, this dispatching will be influenced by a few factors. If the dynamic data type is pointing in memory to a COM object, the expression tree is sent to a low-level COM interface named `IDispatch`. As you might know, this interface was COM's way of incorporating its own set of dynamic services. COM objects, however, can be used in a .NET application without the use of the DLR or C# `dynamic` keyword. Doing so, however (as you will see), tends to result in much more complex C# coding.

If the dynamic data is not pointing to a COM object, the expression tree may be passed to an object implementing the `IDynamicObject` interface. This interface is used behind the scenes to allow a language, such as IronRuby, to take a DLR expression tree and map it to Ruby specifics.

Finally, if the dynamic data is pointing to an object that is *not* a COM object and does *not* implement `IDynamicObject`, the object is a normal, everyday .NET object. In this case, the expression tree is dispatched to the C# runtime binder for processing. The process of mapping the expression tree to .NET specifics involves reflection services.

After the expression tree has been processed by a given binder, the dynamic data will be resolved to the real in-memory data type, after which the correct method is called with any necessary parameters. Now, let's look at a few practical uses of the DLR, beginning with the simplification of late-bound .NET calls.

Simplifying Late-Bound Calls Using Dynamic Types

One instance where you might decide to use the `dynamic` keyword is when you are working with reflection services, specifically when making late-bound method calls. Earlier in this chapter, you saw a few examples of when this type of method call can be useful, most commonly when you are building some type of extensible application. At that time, you learned how to use the `Activator.CreateInstance()` method to create an `object`, for which you have no compile-time knowledge of (beyond its display name). You can then make use of the types of the `System.Reflection` namespace to invoke members via late binding. Recall the earlier example:

```
static void CreateUsingLateBinding(Assembly asm)
{
  try
  {
    // Get metadata for the Minivan type.
    Type miniVan = asm.GetType("CarLibrary.MiniVan");

    // Create the Minivan on the fly.
    object obj = Activator.CreateInstance(miniVan);

    // Get info for TurboBoost.
    MethodInfo mi = miniVan.GetMethod("TurboBoost");

    // Invoke method ("null" for no parameters).
    mi.Invoke(obj, null);
  }
  catch (Exception ex)
  {
    Console.WriteLine(ex.Message);
  }
}
```

While this code works as expected, you might agree it is a bit clunky. You must manually make use of the `MethodInfo` class, manually query the metadata, and so forth. The following is a version of this same method, now using the C# `dynamic` keyword and the DLR:

```
static void InvokeMethodWithDynamicKeyword(Assembly asm)
{
  try
  {
    // Get metadata for the Minivan type.
    Type miniVan = asm.GetType("CarLibrary.MiniVan");

    // Create the Minivan on the fly and call method!
    dynamic obj = Activator.CreateInstance(miniVan);
    obj.TurboBoost();
  }
```

```
  catch (Exception ex)
  {
    Console.WriteLine(ex.Message);
  }
}
```

By declaring the obj variable using the dynamic keyword, the heavy lifting of reflection is done on your behalf, courtesy of the DRL.

Leveraging the dynamic Keyword to Pass Arguments

The usefulness of the DLR becomes even more obvious when you need to make late-bound calls on methods that take parameters. When you use "longhand" reflection calls, arguments need to be packaged up as an array of objects, which are passed to the Invoke() method of MethodInfo.

To illustrate using a fresh example, begin by creating a new C# Console Application project named LateBindingWithDynamic. Next, add a Class Library project named MathLibrary. Rename the initial Class1.cs file of the MathLibrary project to SimpleMath.cs, and implement the class like so:

```
namespace MathLibrary;
public class SimpleMath
{
  public int Add(int x, int y)
  {
    return x + y;
  }
}
```

If you are using Visual Studio, update the MathLibrary.csproj file with the following (to copy the compiled assembly to the LateBindingWithDynamic target directory):

```
<Target Name="PostBuild" AfterTargets="PostBuildEvent">
    <Exec Command="copy $(TargetPath) $(SolutionDir)LateBindingWithDynamic\$(OutDir)$(Target
    FileName) /Y" />
</Target>
```

If you are using Visual Studio Code, update the MathLibrary.csproj file with the following (to copy the compiled assembly to the LateBindingWithDynamic project directory):

```
<Target Name="PostBuild" AfterTargets="PostBuildEvent">
    <Exec Command="copy $(TargetPath) $(ProjectDir)..\LateBindingWithDynamic\$(TargetFile
    Name) /Y" />
</Target>
```

Now, back in the LateBindingWithDynamic project and the Program.cs file, update the using statements to the following:

```
using System.Reflection;
using Microsoft.CSharp.RuntimeBinder;
```

Next, add the following method to the Program.cs file, which invokes the Add() method using typical reflection API calls:

```
static void AddWithReflection()
{
  Assembly asm = Assembly.LoadFrom("MathLibrary");
  try
  {
    // Get metadata for the SimpleMath type.
    Type math = asm.GetType("MathLibrary.SimpleMath");

    // Create a SimpleMath on the fly.
    object obj = Activator.CreateInstance(math);

    // Get info for Add.
    MethodInfo mi = math.GetMethod("Add");

    // Invoke method (with parameters).
    object[] args = { 10, 70 };
    Console.WriteLine("Result is: {0}", mi.Invoke(obj, args));
  }
  catch (Exception ex)
  {
    Console.WriteLine(ex.Message);
  }
}
```

Now, consider the simplification of the previous logic with the dynamic keyword, via the following new method:

```
static void AddWithDynamic()
{
  Assembly asm = Assembly.LoadFrom("MathLibrary");

  try
  {
    // Get metadata for the SimpleMath type.
    Type math = asm.GetType("MathLibrary.SimpleMath");

    // Create a SimpleMath on the fly.
    dynamic obj = Activator.CreateInstance(math);

    // Note how easily we can now call Add().
    Console.WriteLine("Result is: {0}", obj.Add(10, 70));
  }
  catch (RuntimeBinderException ex)
  {
    Console.WriteLine(ex.Message);
  }
}
```

Not too shabby! If you call both methods, you will see identical output. However, when using the `dynamic` keyword, you saved yourself quite a bit of work. With dynamically defined data, you no longer need to manually package up arguments as an array of objects, query the assembly metadata, or set other such details. If you are building an application that makes heavy use of dynamic loading/late binding, I am sure you can see how these code savings would add up over time.

Summary

Reflection is an interesting aspect of a robust object-oriented environment. In the world of .NET, the keys to reflection services revolve around the `System.Type` class and the `System.Reflection` namespace. As you have seen, reflection is the process of placing a type under the magnifying glass at runtime to understand the who, what, where, when, why, and how of a given item.

Late binding is the process of creating an instance of a type and invoking its members without prior knowledge of the specific names of said members. Late binding is often a direct result of *dynamic loading*, which allows you to load a .NET assembly into memory programmatically. As shown during this chapter's extendable application example, this is a powerful technique used by tool builders as well as tool consumers.

This chapter also examined the role of attribute-based programming. When you adorn your types with attributes, the result is the augmentation of the underlying assembly metadata.

The `dynamic` keyword allows you to define data whose identity is not known until runtime. When processed by the Dynamic Language Runtime, the automatically created "expression tree" will be passed to the correct dynamic language binder, where the payload will be unpackaged and sent to the correct object member.

Using dynamic data and the DLR, complex C# programming tasks can be radically simplified, especially the act of incorporating COM libraries into your .NET applications.

While these features can certainly simplify your code, always remember that dynamic data makes your C# code much less type-safe and open to runtime errors. Be sure you weigh the pros and cons of using dynamic data in your C# projects, and test accordingly!

CHAPTER 18

Understanding CIL and the Role of Dynamic Assemblies

When you are building a full-scale .NET application, you will most certainly use C# (or a similar managed language such as Visual Basic), given its inherent productivity and ease of use. However, as you learned in the beginning of this book, the role of a managed compiler is to translate `*.cs` code files into terms of CIL code, type metadata, and an assembly manifest. As it turns out, CIL is a full-fledged .NET programming language, with its own syntax, semantics, and compiler (`ilasm.exe`).

In this chapter, you will be given a tour of .NET's mother tongue. Here, you will understand the distinction between a CIL *directive*, CIL *attribute*, and CIL *opcode*. You will then learn about the role of round-trip engineering of a .NET Core assembly and various CIL programming tools. The remainder of the chapter will then walk you through the basics of defining namespaces, types, and members using the grammar of CIL. The chapter will wrap up with an examination of the role of the `System.Reflection.Emit` namespace and explain how it is possible to construct an assembly (with CIL instructions) dynamically at runtime.

Of course, few programmers will ever need to work with raw CIL code on a day-to-day basis. Therefore, I will start this chapter by examining a few reasons why getting to know the syntax and semantics of this low-level .NET language might be worth your while.

Motivations for Learning the Grammar of CIL

When you build a .NET assembly using your managed language of choice (C#, VB, F#, etc.), the associated compiler translates your source code into terms of CIL. Like any programming language, CIL provides numerous structural and implementation-centric tokens. Given that CIL is just another .NET programming language, it should come as no surprise that it is possible to build your .NET assemblies directly using CIL and the CIL compiler (`ilasm.exe`).

A. Troelsen and P. Japikse, *Pro C# 10 with .NET 6*, https://doi.org/10.1007/978-1-4842-7869-7_18

■ **Note** As covered in Chapter 1, neither `ildasm.exe` nor `ilasm.exe` ships with the .NET Runtime. There are two options for getting these tools. The first is to compile the .NET Runtime from the source located at `https://github.com/dotnet/runtime`. The second, and easier, method is to pull down the desired version from `www.nuget.org`. The URL for ILDasm on NuGet is `https://www.nuget.org/packages/Microsoft.NETCore.ILDAsm/`, and for `ILAsm.exe` it is `https://www.nuget.org/packages/Microsoft.NETCore.ILAsm/`. Make sure to select the correct version (for this book you need version 6.0.0 or greater). Add the ILDasm and ILAsm NuGet packages to your project with the following commands: dotnet add package Microsoft.NETCore.ILDAsm --version 6.0.0dotnet add package Microsoft.NETCore.ILAsm --version 6.0.0

This does not actually add `ILDasm.exe` or `ILAsm.exe` into your project but places them in your package folder (on Windows): %userprofile%\.nuget\packages\microsoft.netcore.ilasm\6.0.0\runtimes\native\%userprofile%\.nuget\packages\microsoft.netcore.ildasm\6.0.0\runtimes\native\

I have also included the 6.0.0 version of both programs in this book's GitHub repo.

Now while it is true that few (if any!) programmers would choose to build an entire .NET application directly with CIL, CIL is still an extremely interesting intellectual pursuit. Simply put, the more you understand the grammar of CIL, the better able you are to move into the realm of advanced .NET development. By way of some concrete examples, individuals who possess an understanding of CIL are capable of the following:

- Disassembling an existing .NET assembly, editing the CIL code, and recompiling the updated code base into a modified .NET binary. For example, there are some scenarios where you might need to modify the CIL to interoperate with some advanced COM features.
- Building dynamic assemblies using the `System.Reflection.Emit` namespace. This API allows you to generate an in-memory .NET assembly, which can optionally be persisted to disk. This is a useful technique for the tool builders of the world who need to generate assemblies on the fly.
- Understanding aspects of the Common Type System (CTS) that are not supported by higher-level managed languages but do exist at the level of CIL. To be sure, CIL is the only .NET language that allows you to access every aspect of the CTS. For example, using raw CIL, you can define global-level members and fields (which are not permissible in C#).

Again, to be perfectly clear, if you choose *not* to concern yourself with the details of CIL code, you are still able to gain mastery of C# and the .NET base class libraries. In many ways, knowledge of CIL is analogous to a C (and C++) programmer's understanding of assembly language. Those who know the ins and outs of the low-level "goo" can create rather advanced solutions for the task at hand and gain a deeper understanding of the underlying programming (and runtime) environment. So, if you are up for the challenge, let's begin to examine the details of CIL.

■ **Note** This chapter is not intended to be a comprehensive treatment of the syntax and semantics of CIL. We are really just skimming the surface. If you want (or need) to get deeper into CIL, consult the documentation.

Examining CIL Directives, Attributes, and Opcodes

When you begin to investigate low-level languages such as CIL, you are guaranteed to find new (and often intimidating sounding) names for familiar concepts. For example, the previous chapters showed CIL examples that contained the following set of items:

```
{new, public, this, base, get, set, explicit, unsafe, enum, operator, partial}
```

After reading the chapters leading up to this in this text, you understand them to be keywords of the C# language. However, if you look more closely at the members of this set, you might be able to see that while each item is indeed a C# keyword, it has radically different semantics. For example, the `enum` keyword defines a `System.Enum`-derived type, while the `this` and `base` keywords allow you to reference the current object or the object's parent class, respectively. The `unsafe` keyword is used to establish a block of code that cannot be directly monitored by the CLR, while the `operator` keyword allows you to build a hidden (specially named) method that will be called when you apply a specific C# operator (such as the plus sign).

In stark contrast to a higher-level language such as C#, CIL does not just simply define a general set of keywords per se. Rather, the token set understood by the CIL compiler is subdivided into the following three broad categories based on semantics:

- CIL directives
- CIL attributes
- CIL operation codes (opcodes)

Each category of CIL token is expressed using a particular syntax, and the tokens are combined to build a valid .NET assembly.

The Role of CIL Directives

First up, there is a set of well-known CIL tokens that are used to describe the overall structure of a .NET assembly. These tokens are called *directives*. CIL directives are used to inform the CIL compiler how to define the namespaces(s), type(s), and member(s) that will populate an assembly.

Directives are represented syntactically using a single dot (`.`) prefix (e.g., `.namespace`, `.class`, `.publickeytoken`, `.method`, `.assembly`, etc.). Thus, if your `*.il` file (the conventional extension for a file containing CIL code) has a single `.namespace` directive and three `.class` directives, the CIL compiler will generate an assembly that defines a single .NET Core namespace containing three .NET class types.

The Role of CIL Attributes

In many cases, CIL directives in and of themselves are not descriptive enough to fully express the definition of a given .NET type or type member. Given this fact, many CIL directives can be further specified with various CIL *attributes* to qualify how a directive should be processed. For example, the `.class` directive can be adorned with the `public` attribute (to establish the type visibility), the `extends` attribute (to explicitly specify the type's base class), and the `implements` attribute (to list the set of interfaces supported by the type).

■ **Note** Don't confuse a .NET attribute (see Chapter 17) with that of a CIL attribute, which are two very different concepts.

The Role of CIL Opcodes

Once a .NET assembly, namespace, and type set have been defined in terms of CIL using various directives and related attributes, the final remaining task is to provide the type's implementation logic. This is a job for *operation codes*, or simply *opcodes*. In the tradition of other low-level languages, many CIL opcodes tend to be cryptic and completely unpronounceable by us mere humans. For example, if you need to load a `string` variable into memory, you do not use a friendly opcode named `LoadString` but rather `ldstr`.

Now, to be fair, some CIL opcodes do map quite naturally to their C# counterparts (e.g., `box`, `unbox`, `throw`, and `sizeof`). As you will see, the opcodes of CIL are always used within the scope of a member's implementation, and unlike CIL directives, they are never written with a dot prefix.

The CIL Opcode/CIL Mnemonic Distinction

As just explained, opcodes such as `ldstr` are used to implement the members of a given type. However, tokens such as `ldstr` are *CIL mnemonics* for the actual *binary CIL opcodes*. To clarify the distinction, assume you have authored the following method in C# in a .NET Console Application named FirstSamples:

```
int Add(int x, int y)
{
  return x + y;
}
```

The act of adding two numbers is expressed in terms of the CIL opcode `0X58`. In a similar vein, subtracting two numbers is expressed using the opcode `0X59`, and the act of allocating a new object on the managed heap is achieved using the `0X73` opcode. Given this reality, understand that the "CIL code" processed by a JIT compiler is nothing more than blobs of binary data.

Thankfully, for each binary opcode of CIL, there is a corresponding mnemonic. For example, the `add` mnemonic can be used rather than `0X58`, `sub` rather than `0X59`, and `newobj` rather than `0X73`. Given this opcode/mnemonic distinction, realize that CIL decompilers such as `ildasm.exe` translate an assembly's binary opcodes into their corresponding CIL mnemonics. For example, here would be the CIL presented by `ildasm.exe` for the previous C# `Add()` method (your exact output may differ based on your version of .NET Core):

```
.method /*06000002*/ assembly hidebysig static int32
      '<<Main>$>g__Add|0_0'(int32 x, int32 y) cil managed
// SIG: 00 02 08 08 08
{
  // Method begins at RVA 0x2060
  // Code size       9 (0x9)
  .maxstack  2
  .locals /*11000001*/ init (int32 V_0)
  IL_0000:  /* 00   |                  */ nop
  IL_0001:  /* 02   |                  */ ldarg.0
  IL_0002:  /* 03   |                  */ ldarg.1
  IL_0003:  /* 58   |                  */ add
  IL_0004:  /* 0A   |                  */ stloc.0
  IL_0005:  /* 2B   | 00               */ br.s       IL_0007
  IL_0007:  /* 06   |                  */ ldloc.0
  IL_0008:  /* 2A   |                  */ ret
} // end of method '<Program>$'::'<<Main>$>g__Add|0_0'
```

Unless you are building some extremely low-level .NET software (such as a custom managed compiler), you will never need to concern yourself with the literal numeric binary opcodes of CIL. For all practical purposes, when .NET programmers speak about "CIL opcodes," they are referring to the set of friendly string token mnemonics (as I have done within this text and will do for the remainder of this chapter) rather than the underlying numerical values.

Pushing and Popping: The Stack-Based Nature of CIL

Higher-level .NET languages (such as C#) attempt to hide low-level CIL grunge from view as much as possible. One aspect of .NET development that is particularly well hidden is that CIL is a stack-based programming language. Recall from the examination of the collection namespaces (see Chapter 10) that the `Stack<T>` class can be used to push a value onto a stack as well as pop the topmost value off the stack for use. Of course, CIL developers do not use an object of type `Stack<T>` to load and unload the values to be evaluated; however, the same pushing and popping mindset still applies.

Formally speaking, the entity used to hold a set of values to be evaluated is termed the *virtual execution stack*. As you will see, CIL provides several opcodes that are used to push a value onto the stack; this process is termed *loading*. As well, CIL defines additional opcodes that transfer the topmost value on the stack into memory (such as a local variable) using a process termed *storing*.

In the world of CIL, it is impossible to access a point of data directly, including locally defined variables, incoming method arguments, or field data of a type. Rather, you are required to explicitly load the item onto the stack, only to then pop it off for later use (keep this point in mind, as it will help explain why a given block of CIL code can look a bit redundant).

■ **Note** Recall that CIL is not directly executed but compiled on demand. During the compilation of CIL code, many of these implementation redundancies are optimized away. Furthermore, if you enable the code optimization option for your current project (using the Build tab of the Visual Studio Project Properties window or adding `<Optimize>true</Optimize>` into the main property group of the project file), the compiler will also remove various CIL redundancies.

To understand how CIL leverages a stack-based processing model, consider a simple C# method, `PrintMessage()`, which takes no arguments and returns `void`. Within the implementation of this method, you will simply print the value of a local string variable to the standard output stream, like so:

```
void PrintMessage()
{
  string myMessage = "Hello.";
  Console.WriteLine(myMessage);
}
```

If you were to examine how the C# compiler translates this method in terms of CIL, you would first find that the `PrintMessage()` method defines a storage slot for a local variable using the `.locals` directive. The local string is then loaded and stored in this local variable using the `ldstr` (load string) and `stloc.0` opcodes (which can be read as "store the current value in a local variable at storage slot zero").

The value (again, at index 0) is then loaded into memory using the `ldloc.0` ("load the local argument at index 0") opcode for use by the `System.Console.WriteLine()` method invocation (specified using the `call` opcode). Finally, the function returns via the `ret` opcode. Here is the (annotated) CIL code for the `PrintMessage()` method (note that I have removed the nop opcodes from this listing, for brevity):

```
.method assembly hidebysig static void
       '<<Main>$>g__PrintMessage|0_1'() cil managed
{
  // Method begins at RVA 0x2064
  // Code size       13 (0xd)
  .maxstack  1
  // Define a local string variable (at index 0).
  .locals init (string V_0)
  // Load a string onto the stack with the value "Hello."
  IL_0000:  ldstr      "Hello."
  // Store string value on the stack in the local variable.
  IL_0005:  stloc.0
  // Load the value at index 0.
  IL_0006:  ldloc.0
  // Call method with current value.
  IL_0007:  call       void System.Console::WriteLine(string)
  IL_000c:  ret
} // end of method '<Program>$'::'<<Main>$>g__PrintMessage|0_1'
```

■ **Note** As you can see, CIL supports code comments using the double-slash syntax (as well as the `/*...*/` syntax, for that matter). As in C#, code comments are completely ignored by the CIL compiler.

Now that you have the basics of CIL directives, attributes, and opcodes, let's see a practical use of CIL programming, beginning with the topic of round-trip engineering.

Understanding Round-Trip Engineering

You are aware of how to use `ildasm.exe` to view the CIL code generated by the C# compiler (see Chapter 1). Once you have the CIL code at your disposal, you are free to edit and recompile the code base using the CIL compiler, `ilasm.exe`.

Formally speaking, this technique is termed *round-trip engineering*, and it can be useful under select circumstances, such as the following:

- You need to modify an assembly for which you no longer have the source code.
- You are working with a less-than-perfect .NET language compiler that has emitted ineffective (or flat-out incorrect) CIL code, and you want to modify the code base.
- You are constructing a COM interoperability library and want to account for some COM IDL attributes that have been lost during the conversion process (such as the COM `[helpstring]` attribute).

To illustrate the process of round-tripping, begin by creating a new C# .NET Core Console application named RoundTrip. Update the Program.cs file to the following:

```
// A simple C# console app.
Console.WriteLine("Hello CIL code!");
Console.ReadLine();
```

Compile your program using the .NET Core CLI.dotnet build

■ **Note** Recall from Chapter 1 that all .NET Core assemblies (class libraries or console apps) by default are compiled to assemblies that have a *.dll extension and are executed using dotnet.exe. New in .NET Core 3.0 (and newer), the dotnet.exe file is copied into the output directory and renamed to match the assembly name. So, while it *looks* like your project was compiled to RoundTrip.exe, it was compiled to RoundTrip.dll with dotnet.exe copied to RoundTrip.exe along with the required command-line arguments needed to execute Roundtrip.dll. If you publish as a single file (covered in Chapter 16), then RoundTrip.exe contains even more than just your code.

Next execute ildasm.exe against RoundTrip.dll using the following command (executed from the solution folder level):

```
ildasm /all /METADATA /out=.\RoundTrip\RoundTrip.il .\RoundTrip\bin\Debug\net6.0\
RoundTrip.dll
```

The previous command output just about everything contained in the assembly, including the file headers, hex commands as comments, all metadata, and much more. If you want a more concise file to work with when examining IL code, you can drop the /all and /METADATA options. However, for these examples, you need all of the extra information.

■ **Note** ildasm.exe will also generate a *.res file when dumping the contents of an assembly to file. These resource files can be ignored (and deleted) throughout this chapter, as you will not be using them. This file contains some low-level CLR security information (among other things).

Now you can view RoundTrip.il using Visual Studio, Visual Studio Code, or your text editor of choice. First, notice that the *.il file opens by declaring each externally referenced assembly that the current assembly is compiled against. If your class library used additional types within other referenced assemblies (beyond System.Runtime and System.Console), you would find additional .assembly extern directives.

```
.assembly extern System.Runtime
{
  .publickeytoken = (B0 3F 5F 7F 11 D5 0A 3A )
  .ver 6:0:0:0
}
.assembly extern System.Console
{
  .publickeytoken = (B0 3F 5F 7F 11 D5 0A 3A )
  .ver 6:0:0:0
}
```

Next, you find the formal definition of your RoundTrip.dll assembly, described using various CIL directives (such as .module, .imagebase, etc.).

```
.assembly RoundTrip
{
...
  .hash algorithm 0x00008004
  .ver 1:0:0:0
}
.module RoundTrip.dll
.imagebase 0x00400000
.file alignment 0x00000200
.stackreserve 0x00100000
.subsystem 0x0003       // WINDOWS_CUI
.corflags 0x00000001    //  ILONLY
```

After documenting the externally referenced assemblies and defining the current assembly, you find a definition of the Program type, created from the top-level statements. Note that the .class directive has various attributes (many of which are optional) such as extends, shown here, which marks the base class of the type:

```
.class private abstract auto ansi sealed beforefieldinit '<Program>$'
  extends [System.Runtime]System.Object
{ ... }
```

The bulk of the CIL code represents the implementation of the class's default constructor and the autogenerated Main() method, both of which are defined (in part) with the .method directive. Once the members have been defined using the correct directives and attributes, they are implemented using various opcodes.

```
.method private hidebysig static void  '<Main>$'(string[] args) cil managed
{
  .entrypoint
  // Code size       18 (0x12)
  .maxstack  8
  IL_0000:  ldstr      "Hello CIL code!"
  IL_0005:  call       void [System.Console]System.Console::WriteLine(string)
  IL_000a:  nop
  IL_000b:  call       string [System.Console]System.Console::ReadLine()
  IL_0010:  pop
  IL_0011:  ret
} // end of method '<Program>$'::'<Main>$'
```

It is critical to understand that when interacting with .NET Core types (such as System.Console) in CIL, you will *always* need to use the type's fully qualified name. Furthermore, the type's fully qualified name must *always* be prefixed with the friendly name of the defining assembly (in square brackets), as in the following two lines from the generated Main() method:

```
IL_0005:  call   void [System.Console]System.Console::WriteLine(string)
IL_000b:  call  string [System.Console]System.Console::ReadLine()
```

The Role of CIL Code Labels

One thing you certainly have noticed is that each line of implementation code is prefixed with a token of the form `IL_XXX:` (e.g., `IL_0000:`, `IL_0001:`, etc.). These tokens are called *code labels* and may be named in any manner you choose (provided they are not duplicated within the same member scope). When you dump an assembly to file using `ildasm.exe`, it will automatically generate code labels that follow an `IL_XXX:` naming convention. However, you may change them to reflect a more descriptive marker. Here is an example:

```
.method private hidebysig static void Main(string[] args) cil managed
{
  .entrypoint
  .maxstack 8
  Load_String: ldstr "Hello CIL code!"
  PrintToConsole: call void [System.Console]System.Console::WriteLine(string)
  Nothing_2: nop
  WaitFor_KeyPress: call string [System.Console]System.Console::ReadLine()
  RemoveValueFromStack: pop
  Leave_Function: ret
}
```

The truth of the matter is that most code labels are completely optional. The only time code labels are truly mandatory is when you are authoring CIL code that makes use of various branching or looping constructs, as you specify where to direct the flow of logic via these code labels. For the current example, you can remove these autogenerated labels altogether with no ill effect, like so:

```
.method private hidebysig static void Main(string[] args) cil managed
{
  .entrypoint
  .maxstack 8
  ldstr "Hello CIL code!"
  call void [System.Console]System.Console::WriteLine(string)
  nop
  call string [System.Console]System.Console::ReadLine()
  pop
  ret
}
```

Interacting with CIL: Modifying an *.il File

Now that you have a better understanding of how a basic CIL file is composed, let's complete the round-tripping experiment. The goal here is quite simple: change the message that is output to the console. You can do more, such as add assembly references or create new classes and methods, but we will keep it simple.

To make the change, you need to alter the current implementation of the top-level statements, created as the `<Main>$` method. Locate this method within the `*.il` file and change the message to "Hello from altered CIL Code!"

In effect, you have just updated the CIL code to correspond to the following C# class definition:

```
static void Main(string[] args)
{
  Console.WriteLine("Hello from altered CIL code!");
  Console.ReadLine();
}
```

There are two ways to create compile .NET assemblies using an `*.il` file. Using the IL project type provides more flexibility but is a bit more involved. The second simply uses `ILASM.EXE` to create a `*.dll` file from the IL file. We will explore using `ILASM.EXE` first.

Compiling CIL Code with ILASM.EXE

Start by creating a new directory on your machine (in the samples on GitHub, I named the new directory `RoundTrip2`). In this directory, copy in the updated `RoundTrip.il` file. Also copy the `RoundTrip.runtimeconfig.json` file from the `RoundTrip\bin\Debug\.net6.0` folder. This file is needed for executables created using `ILASM.EXE` to configure the target framework moniker and the target framework. For reference, the contents of the file are listed here:

```
{
  "runtimeOptions": {
    "tfm": "net6.0",
    "framework": {
      "name": "Microsoft.NETCore.App",
      "version": "6.0.0-preview.3.21201.4"
    }
  }
}
```

Finally, compile the assembly with the following command from the `RoundTrip2` directory (update the path to `ILASM.EXE` as necessary):

```
..\..\ilasm /DLL RoundTrip.il /X64
```

To execute the program, use the CLI, like this:

```
dotnet RoundTrip.dll
```

Sure enough, you will see the updated message displaying in the console window.

Compiling CIL Code with Microsoft.NET.Sdk.il Projects

As you just saw, compiling IL with `ILASM.EXE` is a bit limited. A much more powerful way is to create a project that uses the `Microsoft.NET.Sdk.IL` project type. Unfortunately, at the time of this writing, this project type is not included in the standard project templates, so manual intervention is required. Begin by creating a new directory named `RoundTrip3` and copying the modified `RoundTrip.il` file into the new directory.

■ **Note** At the time of this writing, Visual Studio does directly support the `*.ilproj` project type. While there are some extensions in the marketplace, I can't recommend for or against using them. Visual Studio Code supports all of the code in this section.

In this directory, create a global.json file. The global.json file applies to the current directory and all subdirectories below the file. It is used to define which SDK version you will use when running .NET Core CLI commands. Update the files to the following:

```
{
  "msbuild-sdks": {
    "Microsoft.NET.Sdk.IL": "6.0.0"
  }
}
```

The next step is to create the project file. Create a file named RoundTrip.ilproj and update it to the following:

```
<Project Sdk="Microsoft.NET.Sdk.IL">
  <PropertyGroup>
    <OutputType>Exe</OutputType>
    <TargetFramework>net6.0</TargetFramework>
    <MicrosoftNetCoreIlasmVersion>6.0.0</MicrosoftNetCoreIlasmVersion>
    <ProduceReferenceAssembly>false</ProduceReferenceAssembly>
  </PropertyGroup>
</Project>
```

Finally, copy in your updated RoundTrip.il file into the directory. Compile the assembly using the .NET Core CLI:

```
dotnet build
```

You will find the resulting files in the usual bin\debug\net6.0 folder. At this point, you can run your new application by executing RoundTrip.exe, just as if you built it using a standard C# console application template.

In addition to a better resulting experience, the IL project can take advantage of producing single-file assemblies, as was covered in Chapter 16. Update the project file to the following:

```
<Project Sdk="Microsoft.NET.Sdk.IL">
  <PropertyGroup>
    <OutputType>Exe</OutputType>
    <TargetFramework>net6.0</TargetFramework>
    <MicrosoftNetCoreIlasmVersion>6.0.0-preview.3.21201.4</MicrosoftNetCoreIlasmVersion>
    <ProduceReferenceAssembly>false</ProduceReferenceAssembly>
    <PublishSingleFile>true</PublishSingleFile>
    <SelfContained>true</SelfContained>
    <RuntimeIdentifier>win-x64</RuntimeIdentifier>
    <PublishReadyToRun>true</PublishReadyToRun>
    <PublishTrimmerd>true</PublishTrimmed>
  </PropertyGroup>
</Project>
```

Now you can publish as a stand-alone file just like a C# project. Use the publish command to see this in action:

```
dotnet publish -r win-x64 -p:PublishSingleFile=true -c release -o singlefile --self-
contained true
```

While the output of this simple example is not all that spectacular, it does illustrate one practical use of programming in CIL: round-tripping.

Understanding CIL Directives and Attributes

Now that you have seen how to convert .NET Core assemblies into IL and compile IL into assemblies, you can get down to the business of checking out the syntax and semantics of CIL itself. The next sections will walk you through the process of authoring a custom namespace containing a set of types. However, to keep things simple, these types will not contain any implementation logic for their members (yet). After you understand how to create empty types, you can then turn your attention to the process of defining "real" members using CIL opcodes.

Specifying Externally Referenced Assemblies in CIL

In a new directory named CILTypes, copy the global.json file from the previous example. Create a new project file named CILTypes.ilproj, and update it to the following:

```
<Project Sdk="Microsoft.NET.Sdk.IL">
  <PropertyGroup>
    <TargetFramework>net6.0</TargetFramework>
    <MicrosoftNetCoreIlasmVersion>6.0.0</MicrosoftNetCoreIlasmVersion>
    <ProduceReferenceAssembly>false</ProduceReferenceAssembly>
  </PropertyGroup>
</Project>
```

Next, create a new file named CILTypes.il using your editor of choice. The first task a CIL project will require is to list the set of external assemblies used by the current assembly. For this example, you will only use types found within System.Runtime.dll. To do so, the .assembly directive will be qualified using the external attribute. When you are referencing a strongly named assembly, such as System.Runtime.dll, you will want to specify the .publickeytoken and .ver directives as well, like so:

```
.assembly extern System.Runtime
{
  .publickeytoken = (B0 3F 5F 7F 11 D5 0A 3A )
  .ver 6:0:0:0
}
.assembly extern System.Runtime.Extensions
{
  .publickeytoken = (B0 3F 5F 7F 11 D5 0A 3A )
  .ver 6:0:0:0
}
.assembly extern mscorlib
```

```
{
  .publickeytoken = (B7 7A 5C 56 19 34 E0 89)
  .ver 6:0:0:0
}
```

Defining the Current Assembly in CIL

The next order of business is to define the assembly you are interested in building using the `.assembly` directive. At the simplest level, an assembly can be defined by specifying the friendly name of the binary, like so:

```
// Our assembly.
.assembly CILTypes { }
```

While this indeed defines a new .NET Core assembly, you will typically place additional directives within the scope of the assembly declaration. For this example, update your assembly definition to include a version number of 1.0.0.0 using the `.ver` directive (note that each numerical identifier is separated by *colons*, not the C#-centric dot notation), as follows:

```
// Our assembly.
.assembly CILTypes
{
  .ver 1:0:0:0
}
```

Given that the `CILTypes` assembly is a single-file assembly, you will finish up the assembly definition using the following single `.module` directive, which marks the official name of your .NET binary, `CILTypes.dll`:

```
.assembly CILTypes
{
  .ver 1:0:0:0
}
// The module of our single-file assembly.
.module CILTypes.dll
```

In addition to `.assembly` and `.module` are CIL directives that further qualify the overall structure of the .NET binary you are composing. Table 18-1 lists a few of the more common assembly-level directives.

Table 18-1. *Additional Assembly-Centric Directives*

Directive	Meaning in Life
`.mresources`	If your assembly uses internal resources (such as bitmaps or string tables), this directive is used to identify the name of the file that contains the resources to be embedded.
`.subsystem`	This CIL directive is used to establish the preferred UI that the assembly wants to execute within. For example, a value of 2 signifies that the assembly should run within a GUI application, whereas a value of 3 denotes a console executable.

Defining Namespaces in CIL

Now that you have defined the look and feel of your assembly (and the required external references), you can create a .NET Core namespace (MyNamespace) using the .namespace directive, like so:

```
// Our assembly has a single namespace.
.namespace MyNamespace {}
```

Like C#, CIL namespace definitions can be nested within further namespaces. There is no need to define a root namespace here; however, for the sake of argument, assume you want to create the following root namespace named MyCompany:

```
.namespace MyCompany
{
  .namespace MyNamespace {}
}
```

Like C#, CIL allows you to define a nested namespace as follows:

```
// Defining a nested namespace.
.namespace MyCompany.MyNamespace {}
```

Defining Class Types in CIL

Empty namespaces are not remarkably interesting, so let's now check out the process of defining a class type using CIL. Not surprisingly, the .class directive is used to define a new class. However, this simple directive can be adorned with numerous additional attributes, to further qualify the nature of the type. To illustrate, add a public class to your namespace named MyBaseClass. As in C#, if you do not specify an explicit base class, your type will automatically be derived from System.Object.

```
.namespace MyNamespace
{
  // System.Object base class assumed.
  .class public MyBaseClass {}
}
```

When you are building a class type that derives from any class other than System.Object, you use the extends attribute. Whenever you need to reference a type defined within the same assembly, CIL demands that you also use the fully qualified name (however, if the base type is within the same assembly, you can omit the assembly's friendly name prefix). Therefore, the following attempt to extend MyBaseClass results in a compiler error:

```
// This will not compile!
.namespace MyNamespace
{
  .class public MyBaseClass {}

  .class public MyDerivedClass
    extends MyBaseClass {}
}
```

To correctly define the parent class of MyDerivedClass, you must specify the full name of MyBaseClass as follows:

```
// Better!
.namespace MyNamespace
{
  .class public MyBaseClass {}

  .class public MyDerivedClass
    extends MyNamespace.MyBaseClass {}
}
```

In addition to the public and extends attributes, a CIL class definition may take numerous additional qualifiers that control the type's visibility, field layout, and so on. Table 18-2 illustrates some (but not all) of the attributes that may be used in conjunction with the .class directive.

Table 18-2. *Various Attributes Used in Conjunction with the .class Directive*

Attributes	Meaning in Life
public, private, nested assembly, nested famandassem, nested family, nested famorassem, nested public, nested private	CIL defines various attributes that are used to specify the visibility of a given type. As you can see, raw CIL offers numerous possibilities other than those offered by C#. Refer to ECMA 335 for details if you are interested.
abstract, sealed	These two attributes may be tacked onto a .class directive to define an abstract class or sealed class, respectively.
auto, sequential, explicit	These attributes are used to instruct the CLR how to lay out field data in memory. For class types, the default layout flag (auto) is appropriate. Changing this default can be helpful if you need to use P/Invoke to call into unmanaged C code.
extends, implements	These attributes allow you to define the base class of a type (via extends) or implement an interface on a type (via implements).

Defining and Implementing Interfaces in CIL

As odd as it might seem, interface types are defined in CIL using the .class directive. However, when the .class directive is adorned with the interface attribute, the type is realized as a CTS interface type. Once an interface has been defined, it may be bound to a class or structure type using the CIL implements attribute, like so:

```
.namespace MyNamespace
{
  // An interface definition.
  .class public interface IMyInterface {}

  // A simple base class.
  .class public MyBaseClass {}

  // MyDerivedClass now implements IMyInterface,
  // and extends MyBaseClass.
```

```
  .class public MyDerivedClass
    extends MyNamespace.MyBaseClass
    implements MyNamespace.IMyInterface {}
}
```

■ **Note** The extends clause must precede the implements clause. As well, the implements clause can incorporate a comma-separated list of interfaces.

As you recall from Chapter 10, interfaces can function as the base interface to other interface types to build interface hierarchies. However, contrary to what you might be thinking, the extends attribute cannot be used to derive interface A from interface B. The extends attribute is used only to qualify a type's base class. When you want to extend an interface, you will use the implements attribute yet again. Here is an example:

```
// Extending interfaces in terms of CIL.
.class public interface IMyInterface {}

.class public interface IMyOtherInterface
  implements MyNamespace.IMyInterface {}
```

Defining Structures in CIL

The .class directive can be used to define a CTS structure if the type extends System.ValueType. As well, the .class directive must be qualified with the sealed attribute (given that structures can never be a base structure to other value types). If you attempt to do otherwise, ilasm.exe will issue a compiler error.

```
// A structure definition is always sealed.
.class public sealed MyStruct
  extends [System.Runtime]System.ValueType{}
```

Do be aware that CIL provides a shorthand notation to define a structure type. If you use the value attribute, the new type will derive the type from [System.Runtime]System.ValueType automatically. Therefore, you could define MyStruct as follows:

```
// Shorthand notation for declaring a structure.
.class public sealed value MyStruct{}
```

Defining Enums in CIL

.NET Core enumerations (as you recall) derive from System.Enum, which is a System.ValueType (and therefore must also be sealed). When you want to define an enum in terms of CIL, simply extend [System.Runtime]System.Enum, like so:

```
// An enum.
.class public sealed MyEnum
  extends [System.Runtime]System.Enum{}
```

Like a structure definition, enumerations can be defined with a shorthand notation using the enum attribute. Here is an example:

```
// Enum shorthand.
.class public sealed enum MyEnum{}
```

You will see how to specify the name-value pairs of an enumeration in just a moment.

Defining Generics in CIL

Generic types also have a specific representation in the syntax of CIL. Recall from Chapter 10 that a given generic type or generic member may have one or more type parameters. For example, the List<T> type has a single type parameter, while Dictionary<TKey, TValue> has two. In terms of CIL, the number of type parameters is specified using a backward-leaning single tick (`), followed by a numerical value representing the number of type parameters. Like C#, the actual value of the type parameters is encased within angled brackets.

■ **Note** On US keyboards, you can usually find the ` character on the key above the Tab key (and to the left of the 1 key).

For example, assume you want to create a List<T> variable, where T is of type System.Int32. In C#, you would type the following:

```
void SomeMethod()
{
  List<int> myInts = new List<int>();
}
```

In CIL, you would author the following (which could appear in any CIL method scope):

```
// In C#: List<int> myInts = new List<int>();
newobj instance void class [System.Collections]
  System.Collections.Generic.List`1<int32>::.ctor()
```

Notice that this generic class is defined as List`1<int32>, as List<T> has a single type parameter. However, if you needed to define a Dictionary<string, int> type, you would do so as follows:

```
// In C#: Dictionary<string, int> d = new Dictionary<string, int>();

newobj instance void class [System.Collections]
  System.Collections.Generic.Dictionary`2<string,int32>
  ::.ctor()
```

As another example, if you have a generic type that uses another generic type as a type parameter, you would author CIL code such as the following:

```
// In C#: List<List<int>> myInts = new List<List<int>>();
newobj instance void class [mscorlib]
  System.Collections.Generic.List`1<class
    [System.Collections]
    System.Collections.Generic.List`1<int32>>
    ::.ctor()
```

Compiling the CILTypes.il File

Even though you have not yet added any members or implementation code to the types you have defined, you are able to compile this `*.il` file into a .NET Core DLL assembly (which you must do, as you have not specified a `Main()` method). Open a command prompt and enter the following command:

```
dotnet build
```

After you have done so, you can now open your compiled assembly into `ildasm.exe` to verify the creation of each type. To understand how to populate a type with content, you first need to examine the fundamental data types of CIL.

.NET Base Class Library, C#, and CIL Data Type Mappings

Table 18-3 illustrates how a .NET base class type maps to the corresponding C# keyword and how each C# keyword maps into raw CIL. As well, Table 18-3 documents the shorthand constant notations used for each CIL type. As you will see in just a moment, these constants are often referenced by numerous CIL opcodes.

Table 18-3. *Mapping .NET Base Class Types to C# Keywords and C# Keywords to CIL*

.NET Core Base Class Type	C# Keyword	CIL Representation	CIL Constant Notation
`System.SByte`	`sbyte`	`int8`	`I1`
`System.Byte`	`byte`	`unsigned int8`	`U1`
`System.Int16`	`short`	`int16`	`I2`
`System.UInt16`	`ushort`	`unsigned int16`	`U2`
`System.Int32`	`int`	`int32`	`I4`
`System.UInt32`	`uint`	`unsigned int32`	`U4`
`System.Int64`	`long`	`int64`	`I8`
`System.UInt64`	`ulong`	`unsigned int64`	`U8`
`System.Char`	`char`	`char`	`CHAR`
`System.Single`	`float`	`float32`	`R4`
`System.Double`	`double`	`float64`	`R8`
`System.Boolean`	`bool`	`bool`	`BOOLEAN`
`System.String`	`string`	`string`	N/A
`System.Object`	`object`	`object`	N/A
`System.Void`	`void`	`void`	`VOID`

■ **Note** The `System.IntPtr` and `System.UIntPtr` types map to native `int` and native `unsigned int` (many COM interoperability and P/Invoke scenarios use these extensively).

Defining Type Members in CIL

As you are already aware, .NET types may support various members. Enumerations have some set of name-value pairs. Structures and classes may have constructors, fields, methods, properties, static members, and so on. Over the course of this book's first 18 chapters, you have already seen partial CIL definitions for the items previously mentioned, but nevertheless, here is a quick recap of how various members map to CIL primitives.

Defining Field Data in CIL

Enumerations, structures, and classes can all support field data. In each case, the `.field` directive will be used. For example, let's breathe some life into the skeleton `MyEnum` enumeration and define the following three name-value pairs (note the values are specified within parentheses):

```
.class public sealed enum MyEnum
{
  .field public static literal valuetype
   MyNamespace.MyEnum A = int32(0)
  .field public static literal valuetype
   MyNamespace.MyEnum B = int32(1)
  .field public static literal valuetype
   MyNamespace.MyEnum C = int32(2)
}
```

Fields that reside within the scope of a .NET Core `System.Enum` derived type are qualified using the `static` and `literal` attributes. As you would guess, these attributes set up the field data to be a fixed value accessible from the type itself (e.g., `MyEnum.A`).

■ **Note** The values assigned to an enum value may also be in hexadecimal with a `0x` prefix.

Of course, when you want to define a point of field data within a class or structure, you are not limited to a point of public static literal data. For example, you could update `MyBaseClass` to support two points of private, instance-level field data, set to default values.

```
.class public MyBaseClass
{
  .field private string stringField = "hello!"
  .field private int32 intField = int32(42)
}
```

As in C#, class field data will automatically be initialized to an appropriate default value. If you want to allow the object user to supply custom values at the time of creation for each of these points of private field data, you (of course) need to create custom constructors.

Defining Type Constructors in CIL

The CTS supports both instance-level and class-level (static) constructors. In terms of CIL, instance-level constructors are represented using the `.ctor` token, while a static-level constructor is expressed via `.cctor` (class constructor). Both CIL tokens must be qualified using the `rtspecialname` (return type special name) and `specialname` attributes. Simply put, these attributes are used to identify a specific CIL token that can be treated in unique ways by a given .NET language. For example, in C#, constructors do not define a return type; however, in terms of CIL, the return value of a constructor is indeed `void`.

```
.class public MyBaseClass
{
  .field private string stringField
  .field private int32 intField

  .method public hidebysig specialname rtspecialname
    instance void .ctor(string s, int32 i) cil managed
  {
    // TODO: Add implementation code...
  }
}
```

Note that the `.ctor` directive has been qualified with the `instance` attribute (as it is not a static constructor). The `cil managed` attributes denote that the scope of this method contains CIL code, rather than unmanaged code, which may be used during platform invocation requests.

Defining Properties in CIL

Properties and methods also have specific CIL representations. By way of an example, if `MyBaseClass` were updated to support a public property named `TheString`, you would author the following CIL (note again the use of the `specialname` attribute):

```
.class public MyBaseClass
{
...
  .method public hidebysig specialname
    instance string get_TheString() cil managed
  {
    // TODO: Add implementation code...
  }

  .method public hidebysig specialname
    instance void set_TheString(string 'value') cil managed
  {
    // TODO: Add implementation code...
  }

  .property instance string TheString()
  {
    .get instance string
      MyNamespace.MyBaseClass::get_TheString()
    .set instance void
```

```
      MyNamespace.MyBaseClass::set_TheString(string)
  }
}
```

In terms of CIL, a property maps to a pair of methods that take get_ and set_ prefixes. The .property directive makes use of the related .get and .set directives to map property syntax to the correct "specially named" methods.

■ **Note** Notice that the incoming parameter to the set method of a property is placed in single quotation marks, which represents the name of the token to use on the right side of the assignment operator within the method scope.

Defining Member Parameters

In a nutshell, specifying arguments in CIL is (more or less) identical to doing so in C#. For example, each argument is defined by specifying its data type, followed by the parameter name. Furthermore, like C#, CIL provides a way to define input, output, and pass-by-reference parameters. As well, CIL allows you to define a parameter array argument (aka the C# params keyword), as well as optional parameters.

To illustrate the process of defining parameters in raw CIL, assume you want to build a method that takes an int32 (by value), an int32 (by reference), an [mscorlib]System.Collection.ArrayList, and a single output parameter (of type int32). In terms of C#, this method would look something like the following:

```
public static void MyMethod(int inputInt,
  ref int refInt, ArrayList ar, out int outputInt)
{
  outputInt = 0; // Just to satisfy the C# compiler...
}
```

If you were to map this method into CIL terms, you would find that C# reference parameters are marked with an ampersand (&) suffixed to the parameter's underlying data type (int32&).

Output parameters also use the & suffix, but they are further qualified using the CIL [out] token. Also notice that if the parameter is a reference type (in this case, the [mscorlib]System.Collections.ArrayList type), the class token is prefixed to the data type (not to be confused with the .class directive!).

```
.method public hidebysig static void MyMethod(int32 inputInt,
  int32& refInt,
  class [System.Runtime.Extensions]System.Collections.ArrayList ar,
  [out] int32& outputInt) cil managed
{
  ...
}
```

Examining CIL Opcodes

The final aspect of CIL code you will examine in this chapter has to do with the role of various operational codes (opcodes). Recall that an opcode is simply a CIL token used to build the implementation logic for a given member. The complete set of CIL opcodes (which is large) can be grouped into the following broad categories:

- Opcodes that control program flow
- Opcodes that evaluate expressions
- Opcodes that access values in memory (via parameters, local variables, etc.)

To provide some insight to the world of member implementation via CIL, Table 18-4 defines some of the more useful opcodes that are related to member implementation logic, grouped by related functionality.

Table 18-4. *Various Implementation-Specific CIL Opcodes*

Opcodes	Meaning in Life
`add`, `sub`, `mul`, `div`, `rem`	These CIL opcodes allow you to add, subtract, multiply, and divide two values (`rem` returns the remainder of a division operation).
`and`, `or`, `not`, `xor`	These CIL opcodes allow you to perform bit-wise operations on two values.
`ceq`, `cgt`, `clt`	These CIL opcodes allow you to compare two values on the stack in various manners. Here are some examples: `ceq`: Compare for equality `cgt`: Compare for greater than `clt`: Compare for less than
`box`, `unbox`	These CIL opcodes are used to convert between reference types and value types.
`Ret`	This CIL opcode is used to exit a method and return a value to the caller (if necessary).
`beq`, `bgt`, `ble`, `blt`, `switch`	These CIL opcodes (in addition to many other related opcodes) are used to control branching logic within a method. Here are some examples: `beq`: Break to code label if equal `bgt`: Break to code label if greater than `ble`: Break to code label if less than or equal to `blt`: Break to code label if less than All the branch-centric opcodes require that you specify a CIL code label to jump to if the result of the test is true.
`Call`	This CIL opcode is used to call a member on a given type.
`newarr`, `newobj`	These CIL opcodes allow you to allocate a new array or new object type into memory (respectively).

The next broad category of CIL opcodes (a subset of which is shown in Table 18-5) is used to load (push) arguments onto the virtual execution stack. Note how these load-specific opcodes take a `ld` (load) prefix.

Table 18-5. The Primary Stack-Centric Opcodes of CIL

Opcode	Meaning in Life
ldarg (with numerous variations)	Loads a method's argument onto the stack. In addition to the general ldarg (which works in conjunction with a given index that identifies the argument), there are numerous other variations. For example, ldarg opcodes that have a numerical suffix (ldarg.0) hard-code which argument to load. As well, variations of the ldarg opcode allow you to hard-code the data type using the CIL constant notation shown in Table 18-4 (ldarg_I4, for an int32), as well as the data type and value (ldarg_I4_5, to load an int32 with the value of 5).
ldc (with numerous variations)	Loads a constant value onto the stack.
ldfld (with numerous variations)	Loads the value of an instance-level field onto the stack.
ldloc (with numerous variations)	Loads the value of a local variable onto the stack.
Ldobj	Obtains all the values gathered by a heap-based object and places them on the stack.
Ldstr	Loads a string value onto the stack.

In addition to the set of load-specific opcodes, CIL provides numerous opcodes that *explicitly* pop the topmost value off the stack. As shown over the first few examples in this chapter, popping a value off the stack typically involves storing the value into temporary local storage for further use (such as a parameter for an upcoming method invocation). Given this, note how many opcodes that pop the current value off the virtual execution stack take an st (store) prefix. Table 18-6 hits the highlights.

Table 18-6. Various Pop-Centric Opcodes

Opcode	Meaning in Life
Pop	Removes the value currently on top of the evaluation stack but does not bother to store the value
Starg	Stores the value on top of the stack into the method argument at a specified index
stloc (with numerous variations)	Pops the current value from the top of the evaluation stack and stores it in a local variable list at a specified index
Stobj	Copies a value of a specified type from the evaluation stack into a supplied memory address
Stsfld	Replaces the value of a static field with a value from the evaluation stack

Do be aware that various CIL opcodes will *implicitly* pop values off the stack to perform the task at hand. For example, if you are attempting to subtract two numbers using the sub opcode, it should be clear that sub will have to pop off the next two available values before it can perform the calculation. Once the calculation is complete, the result of the value (surprise, surprise) is pushed onto the stack once again.

The .maxstack Directive

When you write method implementations using raw CIL, you need to be mindful of a special directive named .maxstack. As its name suggests, .maxstack establishes the maximum number of variables that may be pushed onto the stack at any given time during the execution of the method. The good news is that the .maxstack directive has a default value (8), which should be safe for a vast majority of methods you might be authoring. However, if you want to be explicit, you can manually calculate the number of local variables on the stack and define this value explicitly, like so:

```
.method public hidebysig instance void
  Speak() cil managed
{
  // During the scope of this method, exactly
  // 1 value (the string literal) is on the stack.
  .maxstack 1
  ldstr "Hello there..."
  call void [mscorlib]System.Console::WriteLine(string)
  ret
}
```

Declaring Local Variables in CIL

Let's first check out how to declare a local variable. Assume you want to build a method in CIL named MyLocalVariables() that takes no arguments and returns void. Within the method, you want to define three local variables of types System.String, System.Int32, and System.Object. In C#, this member would appear as follows (recall that locally scoped variables do not receive a default value and should be set to an initial state before further use):

```
public static void MyLocalVariables()
{
  string myStr = "CIL code is fun!";
  int myInt = 33;
  object myObj = new object();
}
```

If you were to construct MyLocalVariables() directly in CIL, you could author the following:

```
.method public hidebysig static void
  MyLocalVariables() cil managed
{
  .maxstack 8
  // Define three local variables.
  .locals init (string myStr, int32 myInt, object myObj)
  // Load a string onto the virtual execution stack.
  ldstr "CIL code is fun!"
```

```
  // Pop off current value and store in local variable [0].
  stloc.0

  // Load a constant of type "i4"
  // (shorthand for int32) set to the value 33.
  ldc.i4.s 33
  // Pop off current value and store in local variable [1].
  stloc.1

  // Create a new object and place on stack.
  newobj instance void [mscorlib]System.Object::.ctor()
  // Pop off current value and store in local variable [2].
  stloc.2
  ret
}
```

The first step taken to allocate local variables in raw CIL is to use the `.locals` directive, which is paired with the `init` attribute. Each variable is identified by its data type and an optional variable name. After the local variables have been defined, you load a value onto the stack (using the various load-centric opcodes) and store the value within the local variable (using the various storage-centric opcodes).

Mapping Parameters to Local Variables in CIL

You have already seen how to declare local variables in raw CIL using the `.locals init` directive; however, you have yet to see exactly how to map incoming parameters to local methods. Consider the following static C# method:

```
public static int Add(int a, int b)
{
  return a + b;
}
```

This innocent-looking method has a lot to say in terms of CIL. First, the incoming arguments (a and b) must be pushed onto the virtual execution stack using the `ldarg` (load argument) opcode. Next, the `add` opcode will be used to pop the next two values off the stack and find the summation and store the value on the stack yet again. Finally, this sum is popped off the stack and returned to the caller via the `ret` opcode. If you were to disassemble this C# method using `ildasm.exe`, you would find numerous additional tokens injected by the build process, but the crux of the CIL code is quite simple.

```
.method public hidebysig static int32 Add(int32 a,
  int32 b) cil managed
{
  .maxstack 2
  ldarg.0 // Load "a" onto the stack.
  ldarg.1 // Load "b" onto the stack.
  add     // Add both values.
  ret
}
```

The Hidden this Reference

Notice that the two incoming arguments (a and b) are referenced within the CIL code using their indexed position (index 0 and index 1), given that the virtual execution stack begins indexing at position 0.

One thing to be mindful of when you are examining or authoring CIL code is that every nonstatic method that takes incoming arguments automatically receives an implicit additional parameter, which is a reference to the current object (like the C# `this` keyword). Given this, if the `Add()` method were defined as *nonstatic*, like so:

```
// No longer static!
public int Add(int a, int b)
{
  return a + b;
}
```

Then the incoming a and b arguments are loaded using `ldarg.1` and `ldarg.2` (rather than the expected `ldarg.0` and `ldarg.1` opcodes). Again, the reason is that slot 0 contains the implicit `this` reference. Consider the following pseudocode:

```
// This is JUST pseudocode!
.method public hidebysig static int32 AddTwoIntParams(
  MyClass_HiddenThisPointer this, int32 a, int32 b) cil managed
{
  ldarg.0 // Load MyClass_HiddenThisPointer onto the stack.
  ldarg.1 // Load "a" onto the stack.
  ldarg.2 // Load "b" onto the stack.
...
}
```

Representing Iteration Constructs in CIL

Iteration constructs in the C# programming language are represented using the `for`, `foreach`, `while`, and `do` keywords, each of which has a specific representation in CIL. Consider the following classic `for` loop:

```
public static void CountToTen()
{
  for(int i = 0; i < 10; i++)
  {
  }
}
```

Now, as you may recall, the `br` opcodes (`br`, `blt`, etc.) are used to control a break in flow when some condition has been met. In this example, you have set up a condition in which the `for` loop should break out of its cycle when the local variable `i` is equal to or greater than the value of 10. With each pass, the value of 1 is added to `i`, at which point the test condition is yet again evaluated.

Also recall that when you use any of the CIL branching opcodes, you will need to define a specific code label (or two) that marks the location to jump to when the condition is indeed true. Given these points, ponder the following (edited) CIL code generated via `ildasm.exe` (including the autogenerated code labels):

```
.method public hidebysig static void CountToTen() cil managed
{
  .maxstack 2
```

```
  .locals init (int32 V_0, bool V_1)
  IL_0000: ldc.i4.0      // Load this value onto the stack.
  IL_0001: stloc.0       // Store this value at index "0".
  IL_0002: br.s IL_0007 // Jump to IL_0008.
  IL_0003: ldloc.0       // Load value of variable at index 0.
  IL_0004: ldc.i4.1      // Load the value "1" on the stack.
  IL_0005: add   // Add current value on the stack at index 0.
  IL_0006: stloc.0
  IL_0007: ldloc.0       // Load value at index "0".
  IL_0008: ldc.i4.s 10  // Load value of "10" onto the stack.
  IL_0009: clt           // check less than value on the stack
  IL_000a: stloc.1       // Store result at index "1"
  IL_000b: ldloc.1       // Load value at index "1"
  IL_000c: brtrue.s IL_0003 // if true jump back to IL_0003
  IL_000d: ret
}
```

In a nutshell, this CIL code begins by defining the local `int32` and loading it onto the stack. At this point, you jump back and forth between code labels `IL_0008` and `IL_0004`, each time bumping the value of `i` by 1 and testing to see whether `i` is still less than the value 10. If so, you exit the method.

The Final Word on CIL

Now that you see the process for creating an executable from an `*.IL` file, you are probably thinking "that is an awful lot of work" and then wondering "what's the benefit?" For the vast majority, you will never create a .NET Core executable from IL. However, being able to understand IL can be helpful if you are trying to dig into an assembly that you do not have the source code for.

There are also commercial projects that can take a .NET assembly and reverse engineer it into source code. If you have ever used one of these tools, now you know how they work!

Understanding Dynamic Assemblies

To be sure, the process of building a complex .NET application in CIL would be quite the labor of love. On the one hand, CIL is an extremely expressive programming language that allows you to interact with all the programming constructs allowed by the CTS. On the other hand, authoring raw CIL is tedious, error-prone, and painful. While it is true that knowledge is power, you might indeed wonder just how important it is to commit the laws of CIL syntax to memory. The answer is "it depends." To be sure, most of your .NET programming endeavors will not require you to view, edit, or author CIL code. However, with the CIL primer behind you, you are now ready to investigate the world of dynamic assemblies (as opposed to static assemblies) and the role of the `System.Reflection.Emit` namespace.

The first question you may have is "What exactly is the difference between static and dynamic assemblies?" By definition, *static assemblies* are .NET binaries loaded directly from disk storage, meaning they are located somewhere in a physical file (or possibly a set of files in the case of a multifile assembly) at the time the CLR requests them. As you might guess, every time you compile your C# source code, you end up with a static assembly.

A *dynamic assembly*, on the other hand, is created in memory, on the fly, using the types provided by the `System.Reflection.Emit` namespace. The `System.Reflection.Emit` namespace makes it possible to create an assembly and its modules, type definitions, and CIL implementation logic at *runtime*. After you have done so, you are then free to save your in-memory binary to disk. This, of course, results in a new static assembly. To be sure, the process of building a dynamic assembly using the System.Reflection.Emit namespace does require some level of understanding regarding the nature of CIL opcodes.

Although creating dynamic assemblies is an advanced (and uncommon) programming task, they can be useful under various circumstances. Here is an example:

- You are building a .NET programming tool that needs to generate assemblies on demand based on user input.
- You are building a program that needs to generate proxies to remote types on the fly, based on the obtained metadata.
- You want to load a static assembly and dynamically insert new types into the binary image.

Let's check out the types within System.Reflection.Emit.

Exploring the System.Reflection.Emit Namespace

Creating a dynamic assembly requires you to have some familiarity with CIL opcodes, but the types of the System.Reflection.Emit namespace hide the complexity of CIL as much as possible. For example, rather than specifying the necessary CIL directives and attributes to define a class type, you can simply use the TypeBuilder class. Likewise, if you want to define a new instance-level constructor, you have no need to emit the specialname, rtspecialname, or .ctor token; rather, you can use the ConstructorBuilder. Table 18-7 documents the key members of the System.Reflection.Emit namespace.

Table 18-7. *Select Members of the System.Reflection.Emit Namespace*

Members	Meaning in Life
AssemblyBuilder	Used to create an assembly (*.dll or *.exe) at runtime. *.exes must call the ModuleBuilder.SetEntryPoint() method to set the method that is the entry point to the module. If no entry point is specified, a *.dll will be generated.
ModuleBuilder	Used to define the set of modules within the current assembly.
EnumBuilder	Used to create a .NET enumeration type.
TypeBuilder	May be used to create classes, interfaces, structures, and delegates within a module at runtime.
MethodBuilder LocalBuilder PropertyBuilder FieldBuilder ConstructorBuilder CustomAttributeBuilder ParameterBuilder EventBuilder	Used to create type members (such as methods, local variables, properties, constructors, and attributes) at runtime.
ILGenerator	Emits CIL opcodes into a given type member.
OpCodes	Provides numerous fields that map to CIL opcodes. This type is used in conjunction with the various members of System.Reflection.Emit.ILGenerator.

In general, the types of the System.Reflection.Emit namespace allow you to represent raw CIL tokens programmatically during the construction of your dynamic assembly. You will see many of these members in the example that follows; however, the ILGenerator type is worth checking out straightaway.

The Role of the System.Reflection.Emit.ILGenerator

As its name implies, the ILGenerator type's role is to inject CIL opcodes into a given type member. However, you cannot directly create ILGenerator objects, as this type has no public constructors; rather, you receive an ILGenerator type by calling specific methods of the builder-centric types (such as the MethodBuilder and ConstructorBuilder types). Here is an example:

```
// Obtain an ILGenerator from a ConstructorBuilder
// object named "myCtorBuilder".
ConstructorBuilder myCtorBuilder = helloWorldClass.DefineConstructor(
          MethodAttributes.Public,
          CallingConventions.Standard,
          constructorArgs);
ILGenerator myCILGen = myCtorBuilder.GetILGenerator();
```

Once you have an ILGenerator in your hands, you are then able to emit the raw CIL opcodes using any number of methods. Table 18-8 documents some (but not all) methods of ILGenerator.

Table 18-8. *Various Methods of ILGenerator*

Method	Meaning in Life
BeginCatchBlock()	Begins a catch block
BeginExceptionBlock()	Begins an exception scope for an exception
BeginFinallyBlock()	Begins a finally block
BeginScope()	Begins a lexical scope
DeclareLocal()	Declares a local variable
DefineLabel()	Declares a new label
Emit()	Is overloaded numerous times to allow you to emit CIL opcodes
EmitCall()	Pushes a call or callvirt opcode into the CIL stream
EmitWriteLine()	Emits a call to Console.WriteLine() with different types of values
EndExceptionBlock()	Ends an exception block
EndScope()	Ends a lexical scope
ThrowException()	Emits an instruction to throw an exception
UsingNamespace()	Specifies the namespace to be used in evaluating locals and watches for the current active lexical scope

The key method of ILGenerator is Emit(), which works in conjunction with the System.Reflection.Emit.OpCodes class type. As mentioned earlier in this chapter, this type exposes a good number of read-only fields that map to raw CIL opcodes. The full set of these members is documented within online help, and you will see various examples in the pages that follow.

Emitting a Dynamic Assembly

To illustrate the process of defining a .NET Core assembly at runtime, let's walk through the process of creating a single-file dynamic assembly. Within this assembly is a class named HelloWorld. The HelloWorld class supports a default constructor and a custom constructor that is used to assign the value of a private member variable (theMessage) of type string. In addition, HelloWorld supports a public instance method named SayHello(), which prints a greeting to the standard I/O stream, and another instance method named GetMsg(), which returns the internal private string. In effect, you are going to programmatically generate the following class type:

```
// This class will be created at runtime
// using System.Reflection.Emit.
public class HelloWorld
{
  private string theMessage;
  HelloWorld() {}
  HelloWorld(string s) {theMessage = s;}

  public string GetMsg() {return theMessage;}
  public void SayHello()
  {
    System.Console.WriteLine("Hello from the HelloWorld class!");
  }
}
```

Assume you have created a new Console Application project named DynamicAsmBuilder and you add the System.Reflection.Emit NuGet package. Next, import the System.Reflection and System.Reflection.Emit namespaces. Define a static method named CreateMyAsm() in the Program.cs file. This single method oversees the following:

- Defining the characteristics of the dynamic assembly (name, version, etc.)
- Implementing the HelloClass type
- Returning the AssemblyBuilder to the calling method

Here is the complete code, with analysis to follow:

```
static AssemblyBuilder CreateMyAsm()
{
  // Establish general assembly characteristics.
  AssemblyName assemblyName = new AssemblyName
  {
    Name = "MyAssembly",
    Version = new Version("1.0.0.0")
  };

  // Create new assembly.
  var builder = AssemblyBuilder.DefineDynamicAssembly(
    assemblyName,AssemblyBuilderAccess.Run);

  // Define the name of the module.
  ModuleBuilder module =
```

```
  builder.DefineDynamicModule("MyAssembly");
// Define a public class named "HelloWorld".
TypeBuilder helloWorldClass =
  module.DefineType("MyAssembly.HelloWorld",
  TypeAttributes.Public);

// Define a private String variable named "theMessage".
FieldBuilder msgField = helloWorldClass.DefineField(
  "theMessage",
  Type.GetType("System.String"),
  attributes: FieldAttributes.Private);

// Create the custom ctor.
Type[] constructorArgs = new Type[1];
constructorArgs[0] = typeof(string);
ConstructorBuilder constructor =
  helloWorldClass.DefineConstructor(
    MethodAttributes.Public,
    CallingConventions.Standard,
    constructorArgs);
ILGenerator constructorIl = constructor.GetILGenerator();
constructorIl.Emit(OpCodes.Ldarg_0);
Type objectClass = typeof(object);
ConstructorInfo superConstructor =
  objectClass.GetConstructor(new Type[0]);
constructorIl.Emit(OpCodes.Call, superConstructor);
constructorIl.Emit(OpCodes.Ldarg_0);
constructorIl.Emit(OpCodes.Ldarg_1);
constructorIl.Emit(OpCodes.Stfld, msgField);
constructorIl.Emit(OpCodes.Ret);

// Create the default constructor.
helloWorldClass.DefineDefaultConstructor(
  MethodAttributes.Public);
// Now create the GetMsg() method.
MethodBuilder getMsgMethod = helloWorldClass.DefineMethod(
  "GetMsg",
  MethodAttributes.Public,
  typeof(string),
  null);
ILGenerator methodIl = getMsgMethod.GetILGenerator();
methodIl.Emit(OpCodes.Ldarg_0);
methodIl.Emit(OpCodes.Ldfld, msgField);
methodIl.Emit(OpCodes.Ret);

// Create the SayHello method.
MethodBuilder sayHiMethod = helloWorldClass.DefineMethod(
  "SayHello", MethodAttributes.Public, null, null);
methodIl = sayHiMethod.GetILGenerator();
methodIl.EmitWriteLine("Hello from the HelloWorld class!");
methodIl.Emit(OpCodes.Ret);
```

```
  // "Bake" the class HelloWorld.
  // (Baking is the formal term for emitting the type.)
  helloWorldClass.CreateType();

  return builder;
}
```

Emitting the Assembly and Module Set

The method body begins by establishing the minimal set of characteristics about your assembly, using the AssemblyName and Version types (defined in the System.Reflection namespace). Next, you obtain an AssemblyBuilder type via the static AssemblyBuilder.DefineDynamicAssembly() method.

When calling DefineDynamicAssembly(), you must specify the access mode of the assembly you want to define, the most common values of which are shown in Table 18-9.

Table 18-9. *Common Values of the AssemblyBuilderAccess Enumeration*

Value	Meaning in Life
RunAndCollect	The assembly will be immediately unloaded, and its memory is reclaimed once it is no longer accessible.
Run	This represents that a dynamic assembly can be executed in memory but not saved to disk.

The next task is to define the module set (and its name) for your new assembly. Once the DefineDynamicModule() method has returned, you are provided with a reference to a valid ModuleBuilder type.

```
// Create new assembly.
var builder = AssemblyBuilder.DefineDynamicAssembly(
  assemblyName,AssemblyBuilderAccess.Run);
```

The Role of the ModuleBuilder TypeC

ModuleBuilder is the key type used during the development of dynamic assemblies. As you would expect, ModuleBuilder supports several members that allow you to define the set of types contained within a given module (classes, interfaces, structures, etc.) as well as the set of embedded resources (string tables, images, etc.) contained within. Table 18-10 describes two of the creation-centric methods. (Do note that each method will return to you a related type that represents the type you want to construct.)

Table 18-10. *Select Members of the ModuleBuilder Type*

Method	Meaning in Life
DefineEnum()	Used to emit a .NET enum definition
DefineType()	Constructs a TypeBuilder, which allows you to define value types, interfaces, and class types (including delegates)

The key member of the ModuleBuilder class to be aware of is DefineType(). In addition to specifying the name of the type (via a simple string), you will also use the System.Reflection.TypeAttributes enum to describe the format of the type itself. Table 18-11 lists some (but not all) of the key members of the TypeAttributes enumeration.

Table 18-11. *Select Members of the TypeAttributes Enumeration*

Member	Meaning in Life
Abstract	Specifies that the type is abstract
Class	Specifies that the type is a class
Interface	Specifies that the type is an interface
NestedAssembly	Specifies that the class is nested with assembly visibility and is thus accessible only by methods within its assembly
NestedFamANDAssem	Specifies that the class is nested with assembly and family visibility and is thus accessible only by methods lying in the intersection of its family and assembly
NestedFamily	Specifies that the class is nested with family visibility and is thus accessible only by methods within its own type and any subtypes
NestedFamORAssem	Specifies that the class is nested with family or assembly visibility and is thus accessible only by methods lying in the union of its family and assembly
NestedPrivate	Specifies that the class is nested with private visibility
NestedPublic	Specifies that the class is nested with public visibility
NotPublic	Specifies that the class is not public
Public	Specifies that the class is public
Sealed	Specifies that the class is concrete and cannot be extended
Serializable	Specifies that the class can be serialized

Emitting the HelloClass Type and the String Member Variable

Now that you have a better understanding of the role of the ModuleBuilder.CreateType() method, let's examine how you can emit the public HelloWorld class type and the private string variable.

```
// Define a public class named "HelloWorld".
TypeBuilder helloWorldClass =
  module.DefineType("MyAssembly.HelloWorld",
  TypeAttributes.Public);

// Define a private String variable named "theMessage".
FieldBuilder msgField = helloWorldClass.DefineField(
  "theMessage",
  Type.GetType("System.String"),
  attributes: FieldAttributes.Private);
```

Notice how the TypeBuilder.DefineField() method provides access to a FieldBuilder type. The TypeBuilder class also defines other methods that provide access to other "builder" types. For example, DefineConstructor() returns a ConstructorBuilder, DefineProperty() returns a PropertyBuilder, and so forth.

Emitting the Constructors

As mentioned earlier, the TypeBuilder.DefineConstructor() method can be used to define a constructor for the current type. However, when it comes to implementing the constructor of HelloClass, you need to inject raw CIL code into the constructor body, which is responsible for assigning the incoming parameter to the internal private string. To obtain an ILGenerator type, you call the GetILGenerator() method from the respective "builder" type you have reference to (in this case, the ConstructorBuilder type).

The Emit() method of the ILGenerator class is the entity in charge of placing CIL into a member implementation. Emit() itself makes frequent use of the OpCodes class type, which exposes the opcode set of CIL using read-only fields. For example, OpCodes.Ret signals the return of a method call, OpCodes.Stfld makes an assignment to a member variable, and OpCodes.Call is used to call a given method (in this case, the base class constructor). That said, ponder the following constructor logic:

```
// Create the custom ctor taking single string arg.
Type[] constructorArgs = new Type[1];
constructorArgs[0] = typeof(string);
ConstructorBuilder constructor =
  helloWorldClass.DefineConstructor(
    MethodAttributes.Public,
    CallingConventions.Standard,
    constructorArgs);
//Emit the necessary CIL into the ctor
ILGenerator constructorIl = constructor.GetILGenerator();
constructorIl.Emit(OpCodes.Ldarg_0);
Type objectClass = typeof(object);
ConstructorInfo superConstructor =
  objectClass.GetConstructor(new Type[0]);
constructorIl.Emit(OpCodes.Call, superConstructor);
//Load this pointer onto the stack
constructorIl.Emit(OpCodes.Ldarg_0);
constructorIl.Emit(OpCodes.Ldarg_1);
//Load argument on virtual stack and store in msdField
constructorIl.Emit(OpCodes.Stfld, msgField);
constructorIl.Emit(OpCodes.Ret);
```

Now, as you are aware, as soon as you define a custom constructor for a type, the default constructor is silently removed. To redefine the no-argument constructor, simply call the DefineDefaultConstructor() method of the TypeBuilder type as follows:

```
// Create the default ctor.
helloWorldClass.DefineDefaultConstructor(
  MethodAttributes.Public);
```

Emitting the SayHello() Method

Finally, let's examine the process of emitting the SayHello() method. The first task is to obtain a MethodBuilder type from the helloWorldClass variable. After you do this, you define the method and obtain the underlying ILGenerator to inject the CIL instructions, like so:

```
// Create the SayHello method.
MethodBuilder sayHiMethod = helloWorldClass.DefineMethod(
  "SayHello", MethodAttributes.Public, null, null);
methodIl = sayHiMethod.GetILGenerator();

//Write to the console
methodIl.EmitWriteLine("Hello from the HelloWorld class!");
methodIl.Emit(OpCodes.Ret);
```

Here you have established a public method (`MethodAttributes.Public`) that takes no parameters and returns nothing (marked by the null entries contained in the `DefineMethod()` call). Also note the `EmitWriteLine()` call. This helper member of the `ILGenerator` class automatically writes a line to the standard output with minimal fuss and bother.

Using the Dynamically Generated Assembly

Now that you have the logic in place to create your assembly, all that is needed is to execute the generated code. The logic in the calling code calls the `CreateMyAsm()` method, getting a reference to the created AssemblyBuilder.

Next, you will exercise some late binding (see Chapter 17) to create an instance of the `HelloWorld` class and interact with its members. Update your top-level statements as follows:

```
using System.Reflection;
using System.Reflection.Emit;

Console.WriteLine("***** The Amazing Dynamic Assembly Builder App *****");
// Create the assembly builder using our helper f(x).
AssemblyBuilder builder = CreateMyAsm();

// Get the HelloWorld type.
Type hello = builder.GetType("MyAssembly.HelloWorld");

// Create HelloWorld instance and call the correct ctor.
Console.Write("-> Enter message to pass HelloWorld class: ");
string msg = Console.ReadLine();
object[] ctorArgs = new object[1];
ctorArgs[0] = msg;
object obj = Activator.CreateInstance(hello, ctorArgs);

// Call SayHello and show returned string.
Console.WriteLine("-> Calling SayHello() via late binding.");
MethodInfo mi = hello.GetMethod("SayHello");
mi.Invoke(obj, null);

// Invoke method.
mi = hello.GetMethod("GetMsg");
Console.WriteLine(mi.Invoke(obj, null));
```

In effect, you have just created a .NET Core assembly that is able to create and execute .NET Core assemblies at runtime! That wraps up the examination of CIL and the role of dynamic assemblies. I hope this chapter has deepened your understanding of the .NET Core type system, the syntax and semantics of CIL, and how the C# compiler processes your code at compile time.

Summary

This chapter provided an overview of the syntax and semantics of CIL. Unlike higher-level managed languages such as C#, CIL does not simply define a set of keywords but provides directives (used to define the structure of an assembly and its types), attributes (which further qualify a given directive), and opcodes (which are used to implement type members).

You were introduced to a few CIL-centric programming tools and learned how to alter the contents of a .NET assembly with new CIL instructions using round-trip engineering. After this point, you spent time learning how to establish the current (and referenced) assembly, namespaces, types, and members. I wrapped up with a simple example of building a .NET code library and executable using little more than CIL, command-line tools, and a bit of elbow grease.

Finally, you took an introductory look at the process of creating a *dynamic assembly*. Using the `System.Reflection.Emit` namespace, it is possible to define a .NET Core assembly in memory at runtime. As you have seen firsthand, using this API requires you to know the semantics of CIL code in some detail. While the need to build dynamic assemblies is certainly not a common task for most .NET Core applications, it can be useful for those of you who need to build support tools and other programming utilities.

PART VI

File Handling, Object Serialization, and Data Access

CHAPTER 19

File I/O and Object Serialization

When you create desktop applications, the ability to save information between user sessions is commonplace. This chapter examines several I/O-related topics as seen through the eyes of the .NET Framework. The first order of business is to explore the core types defined in the `System.IO` namespace and learn how to modify a machine's directory and file structure programmatically. The next task is to explore various ways to read from and write to character-based, binary-based, string-based, and memory-based data stores.

After you learn how to manipulate files and directories using the core I/O types, you will examine the related topic of *object serialization*. You can use object serialization to persist and retrieve the state of an object to (or from) any `System.IO.Stream`-derived type.

Note To ensure you can run each of the examples in this chapter, start Visual Studio with administrative rights (just right-click the Visual Studio icon and select Run as Administrator). If you do not do so, you may encounter runtime security exceptions when accessing the computer file system.

Exploring the System.IO Namespace

In the framework of .NET Core, the `System.IO` namespace is the region of the base class libraries devoted to file-based (and memory-based) input and output (I/O) services. Like any namespace, `System.IO` defines a set of classes, interfaces, enumerations, structures, and delegates, most of which you can find in `mscorlib.dll`. In addition to the types contained within `mscorlib.dll`, the `System.dll` assembly defines additional members of the `System.IO` namespace.

Many of the types within the `System.IO` namespace focus on the programmatic manipulation of physical directories and files. However, additional types provide support to read data from and write data to string buffers, as well as raw memory locations. Table 19-1 outlines the core (nonabstract) classes, providing a road map of the functionality in `System.IO`.

A. Troelsen and P. Japikse, *Pro C# 10 with .NET 6*, https://doi.org/10.1007/978-1-4842-7869-7_19

Table 19-1. *Key Members of the System.IO Namespace*

Nonabstract I/O Class Type	Meaning in Life
`BinaryReader` `BinaryWriter`	These classes allow you to store and retrieve primitive data types (integers, Booleans, strings, and whatnot) as a binary value.
`BufferedStream`	This class provides temporary storage for a stream of bytes that you can commit to storage later.
`Directory` `DirectoryInfo`	You use these classes to manipulate a machine's directory structure. The `Directory` type exposes functionality using *static members*, while the `DirectoryInfo` type exposes similar functionality from a valid *object reference*.
`DriveInfo`	This class provides detailed information regarding the drives that a given machine uses.
`File` `FileInfo`	You use these classes to manipulate a machine's set of files. The `File` type exposes functionality using *static members*, while the `FileInfo` type exposes similar functionality from a valid *object reference*.
`FileStream`	This class gives you random file access (e.g., seeking capabilities) with data represented as a stream of bytes.
`FileSystemWatcher`	This class allows you to monitor the modification of external files in a specified directory.
`MemoryStream`	This class provides random access to streamed data stored in memory rather than in a physical file.
`Path`	This class performs operations on `System.String` types that contain file or directory path information in a platform-neutral manner.
`StreamWriter` `StreamReader`	You use these classes to store (and retrieve) textual information to (or from) a file. These types do not support random file access.
`StringWriter` `StringReader`	Like the `StreamReader`/`StreamWriter` classes, these classes also work with textual information. However, the underlying storage is a string buffer rather than a physical file.

In addition to these concrete class types, `System.IO` defines several enumerations, as well as a set of abstract classes (e.g., `Stream`, `TextReader`, and `TextWriter`), that define a shared polymorphic interface to all descendants. You will read about many of these types in this chapter.

The Directory(Info) and File(Info) Types

`System.IO` provides four classes that allow you to manipulate individual files, as well as interact with a machine's directory structure. The first two types, `Directory` and `File`, expose creation, deletion, copying, and moving operations using various static members. The closely related `FileInfo` and `DirectoryInfo` types expose similar functionality as instance-level methods (therefore, you must allocate them with the `new` keyword). The `Directory` and `File` classes directly extend `System.Object`, while `DirectoryInfo` and `FileInfo` derive from the abstract `FileSystemInfo` type.

FileInfo and DirectoryInfo typically serve as better choices for obtaining full details of a file or directory (e.g., time created or read/write capabilities) because their members tend to return strongly typed objects. In contrast, the Directory and File class members tend to return simple string values rather than strongly typed objects. This is only a guideline, however; in many cases, you can get the same work done using File/FileInfo or Directory/DirectoryInfo.

The Abstract FileSystemInfo Base Class

The DirectoryInfo and FileInfo types receive many behaviors from the abstract FileSystemInfo base class. For the most part, you use the members of the FileSystemInfo class to discover general characteristics (such as time of creation, various attributes, etc.) about a given file or directory. Table 19-2 lists some core properties of interest.

Table 19-2. *FileSystemInfo Properties*

Property	Meaning in Life
Attributes	Gets or sets the attributes associated with the current file that are represented by the FileAttributes enumeration (e.g., is the file or directory read-only, encrypted, hidden, or compressed?)
CreationTime	Gets or sets the time of creation for the current file or directory
Exists	Determines whether a given file or directory exists
Extension	Retrieves a file's extension
FullName	Gets the full path of the directory or file
LastAccessTime	Gets or sets the time the current file or directory was last accessed
LastWriteTime	Gets or sets the time when the current file or directory was last written to
Name	Obtains the name of the current file or directory

FileSystemInfo also defines the Delete() method. This is implemented by derived types to delete a given file or directory from the hard drive. Also, you can call Refresh() prior to obtaining attribute information to ensure that the statistics regarding the current file (or directory) are not outdated.

Working with the DirectoryInfo Type

The first creatable I/O-centric type you will examine is the DirectoryInfo class. This class contains a set of members used for creating, moving, deleting, and enumerating over directories and subdirectories. In addition to the functionality provided by its base class (FileSystemInfo), DirectoryInfo offers the key members detailed in Table 19-3.

Table 19-3. *Key Members of the DirectoryInfo Type*

Member	Meaning in Life
`Create()` `CreateSubdirectory()`	Creates a directory (or set of subdirectories) when given a path name
`Delete()`	Deletes a directory and all its contents
`GetDirectories()`	Returns an array of `DirectoryInfo` objects that represent all subdirectories in the current directory
`GetFiles()`	Retrieves an array of `FileInfo` objects that represent a set of files in the given directory
`MoveTo()`	Moves a directory and its contents to a new path
`Parent`	Retrieves the parent directory of this directory
`Root`	Gets the root portion of a path

You begin working with the `DirectoryInfo` type by specifying a particular directory path as a constructor parameter. Use the dot (`.`) notation if you want to obtain access to the current working directory (the directory of the executing application). Here are some examples:

```
// Bind to the current working directory.
DirectoryInfo dir1 = new DirectoryInfo(".");
// Bind to C:\Windows,
// using a verbatim string.
DirectoryInfo dir2 = new DirectoryInfo(@"C:\Windows");
```

In the second example, you assume that the path passed into the constructor (`C:\Windows`) already exists on the physical machine. However, if you attempt to interact with a nonexistent directory, a `System.IO.DirectoryNotFoundException` is thrown. Thus, if you specify a directory that is not yet created, you need to call the `Create()` method before proceeding, like so:

```
// Bind to a nonexistent directory, then create it.
DirectoryInfo dir3 = new DirectoryInfo(@"C:\MyCode\Testing");
dir3.Create();
```

The path syntax used in the previous example is Windows-centric. If you are developing .NET applications for different platforms, you should use the `Path.VolumeSeparatorChar` and `Path.DirectorySeparatorChar` constructs, which will yield the appropriate characters based on the platform. Update the previous code to the following:

```
DirectoryInfo dir3 = new DirectoryInfo(
$@"C{Path.VolumeSeparatorChar}{Path.DirectorySeparatorChar}MyCode{Path.DirectorySeparator
Char}Testing");
```

After you create a `DirectoryInfo` object, you can investigate the underlying directory contents using any of the properties inherited from `FileSystemInfo`. To see this in action, create a new Console Application project named DirectoryApp and update your C# file to import `System` and `System.IO`. Update your `Program.cs` file with the following new static method that creates a new `DirectoryInfo` object mapped to `C:\Windows` (adjust your path if need be), which displays several interesting statistics:

```
Console.WriteLine("***** Fun with Directory(Info) *****\n");
ShowWindowsDirectoryInfo();
Console.ReadLine();

static void ShowWindowsDirectoryInfo()
{
  // Dump directory information. If you are not on Windows, plug in another directory
  DirectoryInfo dir = new DirectoryInfo($@"C{Path.VolumeSeparatorChar}{Path.
DirectorySeparatorChar}Windows");
  Console.WriteLine("***** Directory Info *****");
  Console.WriteLine("FullName: {0}", dir.FullName);
  Console.WriteLine("Name: {0}", dir.Name);
  Console.WriteLine("Parent: {0}", dir.Parent);
  Console.WriteLine("Creation: {0}", dir.CreationTime);
  Console.WriteLine("Attributes: {0}", dir.Attributes);
  Console.WriteLine("Root: {0}", dir.Root);
  Console.WriteLine("**************************\n");
}
```

While your output might differ, you should see something like the following:

```
***** Fun with Directory(Info) *****
***** Directory Info *****
FullName: C:\Windows
Name: Windows
Parent:
Creation: 3/19/2019 00:37:22
Attributes: Directory
Root: C:\
**************************
```

■ **Note** If you are not on a Windows machine, the output from these samples will show a different directory separator.

Enumerating Files with the DirectoryInfo Type

In addition to obtaining basic details of an existing directory, you can extend the current example to use some methods of the `DirectoryInfo` type. First, you can leverage the `GetFiles()` method to obtain information about all `*.jpg` files located in the `C:\Windows\Web\Wallpaper` directory (update this directory if necessary to one that has images on your machine).

The GetFiles() method returns an array of FileInfo objects, each of which exposes details of a particular file (you will learn the full details of the FileInfo type later in this chapter). Create the following static method in the Program.cs file:

```
static void DisplayImageFiles()
{
  DirectoryInfo dir = new
DirectoryInfo($@"C{Path.VolumeSeparatorChar}{Path.DirectorySeparatorChar}Windows{Path.
DirectorySeparatorChar}Web{Path.DirectorySeparatorChar}Wallpaper");
  // Get all files with a *.jpg extension.
  FileInfo[] imageFiles =
    dir.GetFiles("*.jpg", SearchOption.AllDirectories);

  // How many were found?
  Console.WriteLine("Found {0} *.jpg files\n", imageFiles.Length);

  // Now print out info for each file.
  foreach (FileInfo f in imageFiles)
  {
    Console.WriteLine("***************************");
    Console.WriteLine("File name: {0}", f.Name);
    Console.WriteLine("File size: {0}", f.Length);
    Console.WriteLine("Creation: {0}", f.CreationTime);
    Console.WriteLine("Attributes: {0}", f.Attributes);
    Console.WriteLine("***************************\n");
  }
}
```

Notice that you specify a search option when you call GetFiles(); you do this to look within all subdirectories of the root. After you run the application, you will see a listing of all files that match the search pattern.

Creating Subdirectories with the DirectoryInfo Type

You can programmatically extend a directory structure using the DirectoryInfo.CreateSubdirectory() method. This method can create a single subdirectory, as well as multiple nested subdirectories, in a single function call. This method illustrates how to do so, extending the directory structure of the application execution directory (denoted with the .) with some custom subdirectories:

```
static void ModifyAppDirectory()
{
  DirectoryInfo dir = new DirectoryInfo(".");

  // Create \MyFolder off application directory.
  dir.CreateSubdirectory("MyFolder");

  // Create \MyFolder2\Data off application directory.
  dir.CreateSubdirectory(
    $@"MyFolder2{Path.DirectorySeparatorChar}Data");
}
```

You are not required to capture the return value of the CreateSubdirectory() method, but you should be aware that a DirectoryInfo object representing the newly created item is passed back on successful execution. Consider the following update to the previous method:

```
static void ModifyAppDirectory()
{
  DirectoryInfo dir = new DirectoryInfo(".");

  // Create \MyFolder off initial directory.
  dir.CreateSubdirectory("MyFolder");

  // Capture returned DirectoryInfo object.
  DirectoryInfo myDataFolder = dir.CreateSubdirectory(
    $@"MyFolder2{Path.DirectorySeparatorChar}Data");

  // Prints path to ..\MyFolder2\Data.
  Console.WriteLine("New Folder is: {0}", myDataFolder);
}
```

If you call this method from the top-level statements and examine your Windows directory using Windows Explorer, you will see that the new subdirectories are present and accounted for.

Working with the Directory Type

You have seen the DirectoryInfo type in action; now you are ready to learn about the Directory type. For the most part, the static members of Directory mimic the functionality provided by the instance-level members defined by DirectoryInfo. Recall, however, that the members of Directory typically return string data rather than strongly typed FileInfo/DirectoryInfo objects.

Now let's look at some functionality of the Directory type. This final helper function displays the names of all drives mapped to the current computer (using the Directory.GetLogicalDrives() method) and uses the static Directory.Delete() method to remove the \MyFolder and \MyFolder2\Data subdirectories created previously.

```
static void FunWithDirectoryType()
{
  // List all drives on current computer.
  string[] drives = Directory.GetLogicalDrives();
  Console.WriteLine("Here are your drives:");
  foreach (string s in drives)
  {
    Console.WriteLine("--> {0} ", s);
  }

  // Delete what was created.
  Console.WriteLine("Press Enter to delete directories");
  Console.ReadLine();
  try
  {
    Directory.Delete("MyFolder");
```

```
    // The second parameter specifies whether you
    // wish to destroy any subdirectories.
    Directory.Delete("MyFolder2", true);
  }
  catch (IOException e)
  {
    Console.WriteLine(e.Message);
  }
}
```

Working with the DriveInfo Class Type

The System.IO namespace provides a class named DriveInfo. Like Directory.GetLogicalDrives(), the static DriveInfo.GetDrives() method allows you to discover the names of a machine's drives. Unlike Directory.GetLogicalDrives(), however, DriveInfo provides numerous other details (e.g., the drive type, available free space, and volume label). Consider the following Program.cs file defined within a new Console Application project named DriveInfoApp:

```
// Get info regarding all drives.
DriveInfo[] myDrives = DriveInfo.GetDrives();
// Now print drive stats.
foreach(DriveInfo d in myDrives)
{
  Console.WriteLine("Name: {0}", d.Name);
  Console.WriteLine("Type: {0}", d.DriveType);

  // Check to see whether the drive is mounted.
  if(d.IsReady)
  {
    Console.WriteLine("Free space: {0}", d.TotalFreeSpace);
    Console.WriteLine("Format: {0}", d.DriveFormat);
    Console.WriteLine("Label: {0}", d.VolumeLabel);
  }
  Console.WriteLine();
}
Console.ReadLine();
```

Here is some possible output:

```
***** Fun with DriveInfo *****
Name: C:\
Type: Fixed
Free space: 284131119104
Format: NTFS
Label: OS
```

```
Name: M:\
Type: Network
Free space: 4711871942656
Format: NTFS
Label: DigitalMedia
```

At this point, you have investigated some core behaviors of the Directory, DirectoryInfo, and DriveInfo classes. Next, you will learn how to create, open, close, and destroy the files that populate a given directory.

Working with the FileInfo Class

As shown in the previous DirectoryApp example, the FileInfo class allows you to obtain details regarding existing files on your hard drive (e.g., time created, size, and file attributes) and aids in the creation, copying, moving, and destruction of files. In addition to the set of functionalities inherited by FileSystemInfo, you can find some core members unique to the FileInfo class, which are described in Table 19-4.

Table 19-4. *FileInfo Core Members*

Member	Meaning in Life
AppendText()	Creates a StreamWriter object (described later) that appends text to a file
CopyTo()	Copies an existing file to a new file
Create()	Creates a new file and returns a FileStream object (described later) to interact with the newly created file
CreateText()	Creates a StreamWriter object that writes a new text file
Delete()	Deletes the file to which a FileInfo instance is bound
Directory	Gets an instance of the parent directory
DirectoryName	Gets the full path to the parent directory
Length	Gets the size of the current file
MoveTo()	Moves a specified file to a new location, providing the option to specify a new filename
Name	Gets the name of the file
Open()	Opens a file with various read/write and sharing privileges
OpenRead()	Creates a read-only FileStream object
OpenText()	Creates a StreamReader object (described later) that reads from an existing text file
OpenWrite()	Creates a write-only FileStream object

Note that a majority of the methods of the FileInfo class return a specific I/O-centric object (e.g., FileStream and StreamWriter) that allows you to begin reading and writing data to (or reading from) the associated file in a variety of formats. You will check out these types in just a moment; however, before you see a working example, you will find it helpful to examine various ways to obtain a file handle using the FileInfo class type.

The FileInfo.Create() Method

The next set of examples are all in a Console Application named SimpleFileIO. One way you can create a file handle is to use the `FileInfo.Create()` method, like so:

```
Console.WriteLine("***** Simple IO with the File Type *****\n");
//Change to a folder on your machine that you have read/write access to, or run as
administrator
var fileName = $@"C{Path.VolumeSeparatorChar}{Path.DirectorySeparatorChar}temp{Path.
DirectorySeparatorChar}Test.dat";
// Make a new file on the C drive.
FileInfo f = new FileInfo(fileName);
FileStream fs = f.Create();

// Use the FileStream object...

// Close down file stream.
fs.Close();
```

■ **Note** These examples might require running Visual Studio as an Administrator, depending on your user permissions and system configuration.

Notice that the `FileInfo.Create()` method returns a `FileStream` object, which exposes synchronous and asynchronous write/read operations to/from the underlying file (more details on that in a moment). Be aware that the `FileStream` object returned by `FileInfo.Create()` grants full read/write access to all users.

Also notice that after you finish with the current `FileStream` object, you must ensure you close the handle to release the underlying unmanaged stream resources. Given that `FileStream` implements `IDisposable`, you can use the C# `using` scope to allow the compiler to generate the teardown logic (see Chapter 8 for details), like so:

```
var fileName = $@"C{Path.VolumeSeparatorChar}{Path.DirectorySeparatorChar}Test.dat";
...
//wrap the file stream in a using statement
// Defining a using scope for file I/O
FileInfo f1 = new FileInfo(fileName);
using (FileStream fs1 = f1.Create())
{
  // Use the FileStream object...
}
f1.Delete();
```

■ **Note** Almost all of these examples in this chapter include `using` statements. I could have used the new using declaration syntax but chose not to in this rewrite to keep the examples focused on the `System.IO` components that we are examining.

The FileInfo.Open() Method

You can use the FileInfo.Open() method to open existing files, as well as to create new files with far more precision than you can with FileInfo.Create(). This works because Open() typically takes several parameters to qualify exactly how to iterate the file you want to manipulate. Once the call to Open() completes, you are returned a FileStream object. Consider the following logic:

```
var fileName = $@"C{Path.VolumeSeparatorChar}{Path.DirectorySeparatorChar}Test.dat";
...
// Make a new file via FileInfo.Open().
FileInfo f2 = new FileInfo(fileName);
using(FileStream fs2 = f2.Open(FileMode.OpenOrCreate,
  FileAccess.ReadWrite, FileShare.None))
{
  // Use the FileStream object...
}
f2.Delete();
```

This version of the overloaded Open() method requires three parameters. The first parameter of the Open() method specifies the general flavor of the I/O request (e.g., make a new file, open an existing file, and append to a file), which you specify using the FileMode enumeration (see Table 19-5 for details), like so:

```
public enum FileMode
{
  CreateNew,
  Create,
  Open,
  OpenOrCreate,
  Truncate,
  Append
}
```

Table 19-5. *Members of the FileMode Enumeration*

Member	Meaning in Life
CreateNew	Informs the OS to make a new file. If it already exists, an IOException is thrown.
Create	Informs the OS to make a new file. If it already exists, it will be overwritten.
Open	Opens an existing file. If the file does not exist, a FileNotFoundException is thrown.
OpenOrCreate	Opens the file if it exists; otherwise, a new file is created.
Truncate	Opens an existing file and truncates the file to 0 bytes in size.
Append	Opens a file, moves to the end of the file, and begins write operations (you can use this flag only with a write-only stream). If the file does not exist, a new file is created.

You use the second parameter of the Open() method, a value from the FileAccess enumeration, to determine the read/write behavior of the underlying stream, as follows:

```
public enum FileAccess
{
  Read,
  Write,
  ReadWrite
}
```

Finally, the third parameter of the Open() method, FileShare, specifies how to share the file among other file handlers. Here are the core names:

```
public enum FileShare
{
  None,
  Read,
  Write,
  ReadWrite,
  Delete,
  Inheritable
}
```

The FileInfo.OpenRead() and FileInfo.OpenWrite() Methods

The FileInfo.Open() method allows you to obtain a file handle in a flexible manner, but the FileInfo class also provides members named OpenRead() and OpenWrite(). As you might imagine, these methods return a properly configured read-only or write-only FileStream object, without the need to supply various enumeration values. Like FileInfo.Create() and FileInfo.Open(), OpenRead() and OpenWrite() return a FileStream object.

Note that the OpenRead() method requires the file to already exist. The following code creates the file and then closes the FileStream so it can be used by the OpenRead() method:

```
f3.Create().Close();
```

Here are the full examples:

```
var fileName = $@"C{Path.VolumeSeparatorChar}{Path.DirectorySeparatorChar}Test.dat";
...
// Get a FileStream object with read-only permissions.
FileInfo f3 = new FileInfo(fileName);
//File must exist before using OpenRead
f3.Create().Close();
using(FileStream readOnlyStream = f3.OpenRead())
{
  // Use the FileStream object...
}
f3.Delete();
```

```
// Now get a FileStream object with write-only permissions.
FileInfo f4 = new FileInfo(fileName);
using(FileStream writeOnlyStream = f4.OpenWrite())
{
  // Use the FileStream object...
}
f4.Delete();
```

The FileInfo.OpenText() Method

Another open-centric member of the FileInfo type is OpenText(). Unlike Create(), Open(), OpenRead(), or OpenWrite(), the OpenText() method returns an instance of the StreamReader type, rather than a FileStream type. Assuming you have a file named boot.ini on your C: drive, the following snippet gives you access to its contents:

```
var fileName = $@"C{Path.VolumeSeparatorChar}{Path.DirectorySeparatorChar}Test.dat";
...
// Get a StreamReader object.
//If not on a Windows machine, change the file name accordingly
FileInfo f5 = new FileInfo(fileName);
//File must exist before using OpenText
f5.Create().Close();
using(StreamReader sreader = f5.OpenText())
{
  // Use the StreamReader object...
}
f5.Delete();
```

As you will see shortly, the StreamReader type provides a way to read character data from the underlying file.

The FileInfo.CreateText() and FileInfo.AppendText() Methods

The final two FileInfo methods of interest at this point are CreateText() and AppendText(). Both return a StreamWriter object, as shown here:

```
var fileName = $@"C{Path.VolumeSeparatorChar}{Path.DirectorySeparatorChar}Test.dat";
...
FileInfo f6 = new FileInfo(fileName);
using(StreamWriter swriter = f6.CreateText())
{
  // Use the StreamWriter object...
}
f6.Delete();
FileInfo f7 = new FileInfo(fileName);
using(StreamWriter swriterAppend = f7.AppendText())
{
  // Use the StreamWriter object...
}
f7.Delete();
```

As you might guess, the StreamWriter type provides a way to write character data to the underlying file.

Working with the File Type

The File type uses several static members to provide functionality almost identical to that of the FileInfo type. Like FileInfo, File supplies AppendText(), Create(), CreateText(), Open(), OpenRead(), OpenWrite(), and OpenText() methods. In many cases, you can use the File and FileInfo types interchangeably. Note that OpenText() and OpenRead() require the file to already exist. To see this in action, you can simplify each of the previous FileStream examples by using the File type instead, like so:

```
var fileName = $@"C{Path.VolumeSeparatorChar}{Path.DirectorySeparatorChar}Test.dat";
...
//Using File instead of FileInfo
using (FileStream fs8 = File.Create(fileName))
{
  // Use the FileStream object...
}
File.Delete(fileName);
// Make a new file via FileInfo.Open().
using(FileStream fs9 =  File.Open(fileName,
  FileMode.OpenOrCreate, FileAccess.ReadWrite,
  FileShare.None))
{
  // Use the FileStream object...
}
// Get a FileStream object with read-only permissions.
using(FileStream readOnlyStream = File.OpenRead(fileName))
{}
File.Delete(fileName);
// Get a FileStream object with write-only permissions.
using(FileStream writeOnlyStream = File.OpenWrite(fileName))
{}
// Get a StreamReader object.
using(StreamReader sreader = File.OpenText(fileName))
{}
File.Delete(fileName);
// Get some StreamWriters.
using(StreamWriter swriter = File.CreateText(fileName))
{}
File.Delete(fileName);

using(StreamWriter swriterAppend =
  File.AppendText(fileName))
{}
File.Delete(fileName);
```

Additional File-centric Members

The File type also supports a few members, shown in Table 19-6, which can greatly simplify the processes of reading and writing textual data.

Table 19-6. *Methods of the File Type*

Method	Meaning in Life
`ReadAllBytes()`	Opens the specified file, returns the binary data as an array of bytes, and then closes the file
`ReadAllLines()`	Opens a specified file, returns the character data as an array of strings, and then closes the file
`ReadAllText()`	Opens a specified file, returns the character data as a `System.String`, and then closes the file
`WriteAllBytes()`	Opens the specified file, writes out the byte array, and then closes the file
`WriteAllLines()`	Opens a specified file, writes out an array of strings, and then closes the file
`WriteAllText()`	Opens a specified file, writes the character data from a specified string, and then closes the file

You can use these methods of the `File` type to read and write batches of data in only a few lines of code. Even better, each of these members automatically closes the underlying file handle. For example, the following code persists the string data into a new file on the `C:` drive (and reads it into memory) with minimal fuss:

```
Console.WriteLine("***** Simple I/O with the File Type *****\n");
string[] myTasks = {
  "Fix bathroom sink", "Call Dave",
  "Call Mom and Dad", "Play Xbox One"};

// Write out all data to file on C drive.
File.WriteAllLines(@"tasks.txt", myTasks);

// Read it all back and print out.
foreach (string task in File.ReadAllLines(@"tasks.txt"))
{
  Console.WriteLine("TODO: {0}", task);
}
Console.ReadLine();
File.Delete("tasks.txt");
```

The lesson here is that when you want to obtain a file handle quickly, the `File` type will save you some keystrokes. However, one benefit of creating a `FileInfo` object first is that you can investigate the file using the members of the abstract `FileSystemInfo` base class.

The Abstract Stream Class

At this point, you have seen many ways to obtain `FileStream`, `StreamReader`, and `StreamWriter` objects, but you have yet to read data from or write data to a file using these types. To understand how to do this, you will need to familiarize yourself with the concept of a *stream*. In the world of I/O manipulation, a *stream* represents a chunk of data flowing between a source and a destination. Streams provide a common way to interact with a *sequence of bytes*, regardless of what kind of device (e.g., file, network connection, or printer) stores or displays the bytes in question.

The abstract System.IO.Stream class defines several members that provide support for synchronous and asynchronous interactions with the storage medium (e.g., an underlying file or memory location).

■ **Note** The concept of a stream is not limited to file I/O. To be sure, the .NET libraries provide stream access to networks, memory locations, and other stream-centric abstractions.

Again, Stream descendants represent data as a raw stream of bytes; therefore, working directly with raw streams can be quite cryptic. Some Stream-derived types support *seeking*, which refers to the process of obtaining and adjusting the current position in the stream. Table 19-7 helps you understand the functionality provided by the Stream class by describing its core members.

Table 19-7. *Abstract Stream Members*

Member	Meaning in Life
CanRead CanWrite CanSeek	Determines whether the current stream supports reading, seeking, and/or writing.
Close()	Closes the current stream and releases any resources (such as sockets and file handles) associated with the current stream. Internally, this method is aliased to the Dispose() method; therefore, *closing a stream* is functionally equivalent to *disposing a stream*.
Flush()	Updates the underlying data source or repository with the current state of the buffer and then clears the buffer. If a stream does not implement a buffer, this method does nothing.
Length	Returns the length of the stream in bytes.
Position	Determines the position in the current stream.
Read() ReadByte() ReadAsync()	Reads a sequence of bytes (or a single byte) from the current stream and advances the current position in the stream by the number of bytes read.
Seek()	Sets the position in the current stream.
SetLength()	Sets the length of the current stream.
Write() WriteByte() WriteAsync()	Writes a sequence of bytes (or a single byte) to the current stream and advances the current position in this stream by the number of bytes written.

Working with FileStreams

The FileStream class provides an implementation for the abstract Stream members in a manner appropriate for file-based streaming. It is a primitive stream; it can read or write only a single byte or an array of bytes. However, you will not often need to interact directly with the members of the FileStream type. Instead, you will probably use various *stream wrappers*, which make it easier to work with textual data or .NET types. Nevertheless, you will find it helpful to experiment with the synchronous read/write capabilities of the FileStream type.

Assume you have a new Console Application project named FileStreamApp (and verify that the System.Text namespace is imported into your initial C# code file). Your goal is to write a simple text message to a new file named myMessage.dat. However, given that FileStream can operate only on raw bytes, you will be required to encode the System.String type into a corresponding byte array. Fortunately, the System.Text namespace defines a type named Encoding that provides members that encode and decode strings to (or from) an array of bytes.

Once encoded, the byte array is persisted to file with the FileStream.Write() method. To read the bytes back into memory, you must reset the internal position of the stream (using the Position property) and call the ReadByte() method. Finally, you display the raw byte array and the decoded string to the console. Here is the complete code:

```
using System.Text;

// Don't forget to import the System.Text namespaces.
Console.WriteLine("***** Fun with FileStreams *****\n");

// Obtain a FileStream object.
using(FileStream fStream = File.Open("myMessage.dat",
  FileMode.Create))
{
  // Encode a string as an array of bytes.
  string msg = "Hello!";
  byte[] msgAsByteArray = Encoding.Default.GetBytes(msg);

  // Write byte[] to file.
  fStream.Write(msgAsByteArray, 0, msgAsByteArray.Length);

  // Reset internal position of stream.
  fStream.Position = 0;

  // Read the types from file and display to console.
  Console.Write("Your message as an array of bytes: ");
  byte[] bytesFromFile = new byte[msgAsByteArray.Length];
  for (int i = 0; i < msgAsByteArray.Length; i++)
  {
    bytesFromFile[i] = (byte)fStream.ReadByte();
    Console.Write(bytesFromFile[i]);
  }

  // Display decoded messages.
  Console.Write("\nDecoded Message: ");
  Console.WriteLine(Encoding.Default.GetString(bytesFromFile));
  Console.ReadLine();
}
File.Delete("myMessage.dat");
```

This example populates the file with data, but it also punctuates the major downfall of working directly with the FileStream type: it demands to operate on raw bytes. Other Stream-derived types operate in a similar manner. For example, if you want to write a sequence of bytes to a region of memory, you can allocate a MemoryStream.

As mentioned previously, the System.IO namespace provides several *reader* and *writer* types that encapsulate the details of working with Stream-derived types.

Working with StreamWriters and StreamReaders

The `StreamWriter` and `StreamReader` classes are useful whenever you need to read or write character-based data (e.g., strings). Both work by default with Unicode characters; however, you can change this by supplying a properly configured `System.Text.Encoding` object reference. To keep things simple, assume that the default Unicode encoding fits the bill.

`StreamReader` derives from an abstract type named `TextReader`, as does the related `StringReader` type (discussed later in this chapter). The `TextReader` base class provides a limited set of functionalities to each of these descendants; specifically, it provides the ability to read and peek into a character stream.

The `StreamWriter` type (as well as `StringWriter`, which you will examine later in this chapter) derives from an abstract base class named `TextWriter`. This class defines members that allow derived types to write textual data to a given character stream.

To aid in your understanding of the core writing capabilities of the `StreamWriter` and `StringWriter` classes, Table 19-8 describes the core members of the abstract `TextWriter` base class.

Table 19-8. *Core Members of TextWriter*

Member	Meaning in Life
`Close()`	This method closes the writer and frees any associated resources. In the process, the buffer is automatically flushed (again, this member is functionally equivalent to calling the `Dispose()` method).
`Flush()`	This method clears all buffers for the current writer and causes any buffered data to be written to the underlying device; however, it does not close the writer.
`NewLine`	This property indicates the newline constant for the derived writer class. The default line terminator for the Windows OS is a carriage return, followed by a line feed (`\r\n`).
`Write()` `WriteAsync()`	This overloaded method writes data to the text stream without a newline constant.
`WriteLine()` `WriteLineAsync()`	This overloaded method writes data to the text stream with a newline constant.

■ **Note** The last two members of the `TextWriter` class probably look familiar to you. If you recall, the `System.Console` type has `Write()` and `WriteLine()` members that push textual data to the standard output device. In fact, the `Console.In` property wraps a `TextReader`, and the `Console.Out` property wraps a `TextWriter`.

The derived `StreamWriter` class provides an appropriate implementation for the `Write()`, `Close()`, and `Flush()` methods, and it defines the additional `AutoFlush` property. When set to `true`, this property forces `StreamWriter` to flush all data every time you perform a write operation. Be aware that you can gain better performance by setting `AutoFlush` to `false`, provided you always call `Close()` when you finish writing with a `StreamWriter`.

Writing to a Text File

To see the `StreamWriter` type in action, create a new Console Application project named StreamWriterReaderApp. The following code creates a new file named `reminders.txt` in the current execution folder, using the `File.CreateText()` method. Using the obtained `StreamWriter` object, you can add some textual data to the new file.

```
Console.WriteLine("***** Fun with StreamWriter / StreamReader *****\n");

// Get a StreamWriter and write string data.
using(StreamWriter writer = File.CreateText("reminders.txt"))
{
  writer.WriteLine("Don't forget Mother's Day this year...");
  writer.WriteLine("Don't forget Father's Day this year...");
  writer.WriteLine("Don't forget these numbers:");
  for(int i = 0; i < 10; i++)
  {
    writer.Write(i + " ");
  }

  // Insert a new line.
  writer.Write(writer.NewLine);
}
Console.WriteLine("Created file and wrote some thoughts...");
Console.ReadLine();
//File.Delete("reminders.txt");
```

After you run this program, you can examine the contents of this new file. You will find this file in the root directory of your project (Visual Studio Code) or under the `bin\Debug\net6.0` folder (Visual Studio) because you did not specify an absolute path at the time you called `CreateText()` and the file location defaults to the current execution directory of the assembly.

Reading from a Text File

Next, you will learn to read data from a file programmatically by using the corresponding `StreamReader` type. Recall that this class derives from the abstract `TextReader`, which offers the functionality described in Table 19-9.

Table 19-9. *TextReader Core Members*

Member	Meaning in Life
`Peek()`	Returns the next available character (expressed as an integer) without changing the position of the reader. A value of `-1` indicates you are at the end of the stream.
`Read()` `ReadAsync()`	Reads data from an input stream.
`ReadBlock()` `ReadBlockAsync()`	Reads a specified maximum number of characters from the current stream and writes the data to a buffer, beginning at a specified index.
`ReadLine()` `ReadLineAsync()`	Reads a line of characters from the current stream and returns the data as a string (a `null` string indicates EOF).
`ReadToEnd()` `ReadToEndAsync()`	Reads all characters from the current position to the end of the stream and returns them as a single string.

If you now extend the current sample application to use a StreamReader, you can read in the textual data from the reminders.txt file, as shown here:

```
Console.WriteLine("***** Fun with StreamWriter / StreamReader *****\n");
...
// Now read data from file.
Console.WriteLine("Here are your thoughts:\n");
using(StreamReader sr = File.OpenText("reminders.txt"))
{
  string input = null;
  while ((input = sr.ReadLine()) != null)
  {
    Console.WriteLine (input);
  }
}
Console.ReadLine();
```

After you run the program, you will see the character data in reminders.txt displayed to the console.

Directly Creating StreamWriter/StreamReader Types

One of the confusing aspects of working with the types within System.IO is that you can often achieve an identical result using different approaches. For example, you have already seen that you can use the CreateText() method to obtain a StreamWriter with the File or FileInfo type. It so happens that you can work with StreamWriters and StreamReaders another way: by creating them directly. For example, you could retrofit the current application as follows:

```
Console.WriteLine("***** Fun with StreamWriter / StreamReader *****\n");

// Get a StreamWriter and write string data.
using(StreamWriter writer = new StreamWriter("reminders.txt"))
{
  ...
}

// Now read data from file.
using(StreamReader sr = new StreamReader("reminders.txt"))
{
  ...
}
```

Although it can be a bit confusing to see so many seemingly identical approaches to file I/O, keep in mind that the result is greater flexibility. In any case, you are now ready to examine the role of the StringWriter and StringReader classes, given that you have seen how to move character data to and from a given file using the StreamWriter and StreamReader types.

Working with StringWriters and StringReaders

You can use the `StringWriter` and `StringReader` types to treat textual information as a stream of in-memory characters. This can prove helpful when you would like to append character-based information to an underlying buffer. The following Console Application project (named StringReaderWriterApp) illustrates this by writing a block of string data to a `StringWriter` object, rather than to a file on the local hard drive (do not forget to import `System.Text`):

```
using System.Text;

  Console.WriteLine("***** Fun with StringWriter / StringReader *****\n");

// Create a StringWriter and emit character data to memory.
using(StringWriter strWriter = new StringWriter())
{
  strWriter.WriteLine("Don't forget Mother's Day this year...");
  // Get a copy of the contents (stored in a string) and dump
  // to console.
  Console.WriteLine("Contents of StringWriter:\n{0}", strWriter);
}
Console.ReadLine();
```

`StringWriter` and `StreamWriter` both derive from the same base class (`TextWriter`), so the writing logic is similar. However, given the nature of `StringWriter`, you should also be aware that this class allows you to use the following `GetStringBuilder()` method to extract a `System.Text.StringBuilder` object:

```
using (StringWriter strWriter = new StringWriter())
{
  strWriter.WriteLine("Don't forget Mother's Day this year...");
  Console.WriteLine("Contents of StringWriter:\n{0}", strWriter);

  // Get the internal StringBuilder.
  StringBuilder sb = strWriter.GetStringBuilder();
  sb.Insert(0, "Hey!! ");
  Console.WriteLine("-> {0}", sb.ToString());
  sb.Remove(0, "Hey!! ".Length);
  Console.WriteLine("-> {0}", sb.ToString());
}
```

When you want to read from a stream of character data, you can use the corresponding `StringReader` type, which (as you would expect) functions identically to the related `StreamReader` class. In fact, the `StringReader` class does nothing more than override the inherited members to read from a block of character data, rather than from a file, as shown here:

```
using (StringWriter strWriter = new StringWriter())
{
  strWriter.WriteLine("Don't forget Mother's Day this year...");
  Console.WriteLine("Contents of StringWriter:\n{0}", strWriter);
```

```
  // Read data from the StringWriter.
  using (StringReader strReader = new StringReader(strWriter.ToString()))
  {
    string input = null;
    while ((input = strReader.ReadLine()) != null)
    {
      Console.WriteLine(input);
    }
  }
}
```

Working with BinaryWriters and BinaryReaders

The final writer/reader sets you will examine in this section are `BinaryReader` and `BinaryWriter`. Both derive directly from `System.Object`. These types allow you to read and write discrete data types to an underlying stream in a compact binary format. The `BinaryWriter` class defines a highly overloaded `Write()` method to place a data type in the underlying stream. In addition to the `Write()` member, `BinaryWriter` provides additional members that allow you to get or set the `Stream`-derived type; it also offers support for random access to the data (see Table 19-10).

Table 19-10. *BinaryWriter Core Members*

Member	Meaning in Life
`BaseStream`	This read-only property provides access to the underlying stream used with the `BinaryWriter` object.
`Close()`	This method closes the binary stream.
`Flush()`	This method flushes the binary stream.
`Seek()`	This method sets the position in the current stream.
`Write()`	This method writes a value to the current stream.

The `BinaryReader` class complements the functionality offered by `BinaryWriter` with the members described in Table 19-11.

Table 19-11. *BinaryReader Core Members*

Member	Meaning in Life
`BaseStream`	This read-only property provides access to the underlying stream used with the `BinaryReader` object.
`Close()`	This method closes the binary reader.
`PeekChar()`	This method returns the next available character without advancing the position in the stream.
`Read()`	This method reads a given set of bytes or characters and stores them in the incoming array.
`ReadXXXX()`	The `BinaryReader` class defines numerous read methods that grab the next type from the stream (e.g., `ReadBoolean()`, `ReadByte()`, and `ReadInt32()`).

The following example (a Console Application project named BinaryWriterReader with using `System.IO`) writes some data types to a new `*.dat` file:

```
Console.WriteLine("***** Fun with Binary Writers / Readers *****\n");

// Open a binary writer for a file.
FileInfo f = new FileInfo("BinFile.dat");
using(BinaryWriter bw = new BinaryWriter(f.OpenWrite()))
{
  // Print out the type of BaseStream.
  // (System.IO.FileStream in this case).
  Console.WriteLine("Base stream is: {0}", bw.BaseStream);

  // Create some data to save in the file.
  double aDouble = 1234.67;
  int anInt = 34567;
  string aString = "A, B, C";

  // Write the data.
  bw.Write(aDouble);
  bw.Write(anInt);
  bw.Write(aString);
}
Console.WriteLine("Done!");
Console.ReadLine();
```

Notice how the `FileStream` object returned from `FileInfo.OpenWrite()` is passed to the constructor of the `BinaryWriter` type. Using this technique makes it easy to *layer in* a stream before writing out the data. Note that the constructor of `BinaryWriter` takes any `Stream`-derived type (e.g., `FileStream`, `MemoryStream`, or `BufferedStream`). Thus, writing binary data to memory instead is as simple as supplying a valid `MemoryStream` object.

To read the data out of the `BinFile.dat` file, the `BinaryReader` type provides several options. Here, you call various read-centric members to pluck each chunk of data from the file stream:

```
...
FileInfo f = new FileInfo("BinFile.dat");
...
// Read the binary data from the stream.
using(BinaryReader br = new BinaryReader(f.OpenRead()))
{
  Console.WriteLine(br.ReadDouble());
  Console.WriteLine(br.ReadInt32());
  Console.WriteLine(br.ReadString());
}
Console.ReadLine();
```

Watching Files Programmatically

Now that you have a better handle on the use of various readers and writers, you will look at the role of the `FileSystemWatcher` class. This type can be quite helpful when you want to monitor (or "watch") files on your system programmatically. Specifically, you can instruct the `FileSystemWatcher` type to monitor files for any of the actions specified by the `System.IO.NotifyFilters` enumeration.

```
public enum NotifyFilters
{
  Attributes, CreationTime,
  DirectoryName, FileName,
  LastAccess, LastWrite,
  Security, Size
}
```

To begin working with the `FileSystemWatcher` type, you need to set the `Path` property to specify the name (and location) of the directory that contains the files you want to monitor, as well as the `Filter` property that defines the file extensions of the files you want to monitor.

At this point, you may choose to handle the `Changed`, `Created`, and `Deleted` events, all of which work in conjunction with the `FileSystemEventHandler` delegate. This delegate can call any method matching the following pattern:

```
// The FileSystemEventHandler delegate must point
// to methods matching the following signature.
void MyNotificationHandler(object source, FileSystemEventArgs e)
```

You can also handle the `Renamed` event using the `RenamedEventHandler` delegate type, which can call methods that match the following signature:

```
// The RenamedEventHandler delegate must point
// to methods matching the following signature.
void MyRenamedHandler(object source, RenamedEventArgs e)
```

Next, let's look at the process of watching a file. The following Console Application project (named MyDirectoryWatcher and with a `using` for `System.IO`) monitors the `*.txt` files in the `bin\debug\net6.0` directory and prints messages when files are created, deleted, modified, or renamed:

```
Console.WriteLine("***** The Amazing File Watcher App *****\n");
// Establish the path to the directory to watch.
FileSystemWatcher watcher = new FileSystemWatcher();
try
{
  watcher.Path = @".";
}
catch(ArgumentException ex)
{
  Console.WriteLine(ex.Message);
  return;
}
```

```
// Set up the things to be on the lookout for.
watcher.NotifyFilter = NotifyFilters.LastAccess
  | NotifyFilters.LastWrite
  | NotifyFilters.FileName
  | NotifyFilters.DirectoryName;

// Only watch text files.
watcher.Filter = "*.txt";

// Add event handlers.
// Specify what is done when a file is changed, created, or deleted.
watcher.Changed += (s, e) =>
  Console.WriteLine($"File: {e.FullPath} {e.ChangeType}!");
watcher.Created += (s, e) =>
  Console.WriteLine($"File: {e.FullPath} {e.ChangeType}!");
watcher.Deleted += (s, e) =>
  Console.WriteLine($"File: {e.FullPath} {e.ChangeType}!");
// Specify what is done when a file is renamed.
watcher.Renamed += (s, e) =>
  Console.WriteLine($"File: {e.OldFullPath} renamed to {e.FullPath}");
// Begin watching the directory.
watcher.EnableRaisingEvents = true;

// Wait for the user to quit the program.
Console.WriteLine(@"Press 'q' to quit app.");
// Raise some events.
using (var sw = File.CreateText("Test.txt"))
{
  sw.Write("This is some text");
}
File.Move("Test.txt","Test2.txt");
File.Delete("Test2.txt");

while(Console.Read()!='q');
```

When you run this program, the last lines will create, change, rename, and then delete a text file, raising the events along the way. You can also navigate to the project directory (Visual Studio Code) or the bin\debug\net6.0 directory (Visual Studio) and play with files (with the *.txt extension) and raise additional events.

```
***** The Amazing File Watcher App *****
Press 'q' to quit app.
File: .\Test.txt Created!
File: .\Test.txt Changed!
File: .\Test.txt renamed to .\Test2.txt
File: .\Test2.txt Deleted!
```

That wraps up this chapter's look at fundamental I/O operations within the .NET platform. While you will certainly use these techniques in many of your applications, you might also find that *object serialization* services can greatly simplify how you persist large amounts of data.

Understanding Object Serialization

The term *serialization* describes the process of persisting (and possibly transferring) the state of an object into a stream (e.g., file stream or memory stream). The persisted data sequence contains all the necessary information you need to reconstruct (or *deserialize*) the public state of the object for use later. Using this technology makes it trivial to save vast amounts of data. In many cases, saving application data using serialization services results in less code than using the readers/writers you find in the `System.IO` namespace.

For example, assume you want to create a GUI-based desktop application that provides a way for end users to save their preferences (e.g., window color and font size). To do this, you might define a class named `UserPrefs` that encapsulates 20 or so pieces of field data. Now, if you were to use a `System.IO.BinaryWriter` type, you would need to save each field of the `UserPrefs` object *manually*. Likewise, if you were to load the data from a file back into memory, you would need to use a `System.IO.BinaryReader` and (once again) *manually* read in each value to reconfigure a new `UserPrefs` object.

This is all doable, but you can save yourself time by using either eXtensible Markup Language (XML) or JavaScript Object Notation (JSON) serialization. Each of these formats enables representing the public state of an object in a single block of text that is usable across platforms and programming languages. Doing this means that you can persist the entire public state of the object with only a few lines of code.

■ **Note** The `BinaryFormatter` type, covered in previous editions of this book, is a high security risk, and you should stop using it immediately (`http://aka.ms/binaryformatter`). More secure alternatives include using `BinaryReaders/BinaryWriters` in conjunction with XML or JSON serialization.

.NET object serialization makes it easy to persist objects; however, the processes used behind the scenes are quite sophisticated. For example, when an object is persisted to a stream, all associated public data (e.g., base class data and contained objects) is automatically serialized as well. Therefore, if you attempt to persist a derived class, all public data up the chain of inheritance comes along for the ride. As you will see, you use an object graph to represent a set of interrelated objects.

Finally, understand that you can persist an object graph into *any* `System.IO.Stream`-derived type. All that matters is that the sequence of data correctly represents the state of objects within the graph.

The Role of Object Graphs

As mentioned previously, the .NET Runtime will account for all related objects to ensure that public data is persisted correctly when an object is serialized. This set of related objects is referred to as an *object graph*. Object graphs provide a simple way to document how a set of items refer to each other. Object graphs are *not* denoting OOP *is-a* or *has-a* relationships. Rather, you can read the arrows in an object diagram as "requires" or "depends on."

Each object in an object graph is assigned a unique numerical value. Keep in mind that the numbers assigned to the members in an object graph are arbitrary and have no real meaning to the outside world. Once you assign all objects a numerical value, the object graph can record each object's set of dependencies.

For example, assume you have created a set of classes that model some automobiles (of course). You have a base class named `Car`, which *has-a* `Radio`. Another class named `JamesBondCar` extends the `Car` base type. Figure 19-1 shows a possible object graph that models these relationships.

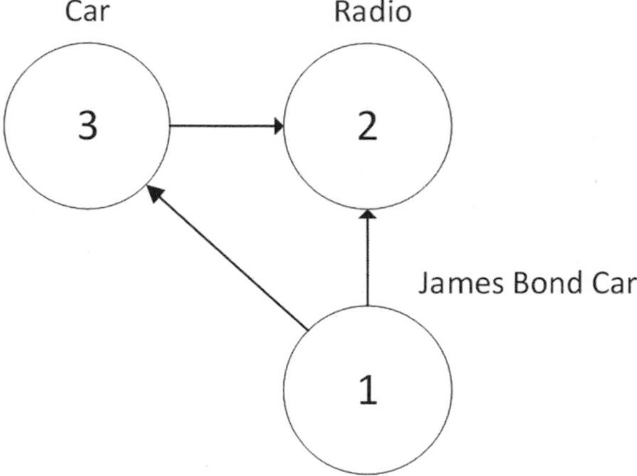

Figure 19-1. *A simple object graph*

When reading object graphs, you can use the phrase *depends on* or *refers to* when connecting the arrows. Thus, in Figure 19-1, you can see that the Car refers to the Radio class (given the *has-a* relationship). JamesBondCar refers to Car (given the *is-a* relationship), as well as to Radio (it inherits this protected member variable).

Of course, the CLR does not paint pictures in memory to represent a graph of related objects. Rather, the relationship documented in Figure 19-1 is represented by a mathematical formula that looks something like this:

```
[Car 3, ref 2], [Radio 2], [JamesBondCar 1, ref 3, ref 2]
```

If you parse this formula, you can see that object 3 (the Car) has a dependency on object 2 (the Radio). Object 2, the Radio, is a lone wolf and requires nobody. Finally, object 1 (the JamesBondCar) has a dependency on object 3, as well as object 2. In any case, when you serialize or deserialize an instance of JamesBondCar, the object graph ensures that the Radio and Car types also participate in the process.

The beautiful thing about the serialization process is that the graph representing the relationships among your objects is established automatically behind the scenes. As you will see later in this chapter, however, you can become more involved in the construction of a given object graph by customizing the serialization process using attributes.

Creating the Sample Types and Top-Level Statements

Create a new Console Application project named SimpleSerialize. Update the Program.cs file to the following:

```
global using System.Text.Json;
global using System.Text.Json.Serialization;
global using System.Xml;
global using System.Xml.Serialization;

using SimpleSerialize;

Console.WriteLine("***** Fun with Object Serialization *****\n");
```

Next, add a new class named Radio.cs, and update the code to the following:

```
namespace SimpleSerialize;

public class Radio
{
  public bool HasTweeters;
  public bool HasSubWoofers;
  public List<double> StationPresets;
  public string RadioId = "XF-552RR6";
  public override string ToString()
  {
    var presets = string.Join(",", StationPresets.Select(i => i.ToString()).ToList());
    return $"HasTweeters:{HasTweeters} HasSubWoofers:{HasSubWoofers} Station Presets:{presets}";
  }
}
```

Next, add a class named Car.cs, and update the code to match this listing:

```
namespace SimpleSerialize;
public class Car
{
  public Radio TheRadio = new Radio();
  public bool IsHatchBack;
  public override string ToString()
    => $"IsHatchback:{IsHatchBack} Radio:{TheRadio.ToString()}";
}
```

Next, add another class named JamesBondCar.cs and use the following code for this class:

```
namespace SimpleSerialize;
public class JamesBondCar : Car
{
  public bool CanFly;
  public bool CanSubmerge;
  public override string ToString()
    => $"CanFly:{CanFly}, CanSubmerge:{CanSubmerge} {base.ToString()}";
}
```

The final class, Person.cs, is shown here:

```
namespace SimpleSerialize;

public class Person
{
  // A public field.
  public bool IsAlive = true;
  // A private field.
  private int PersonAge = 21;
  // Public property/private data.
  private string _fName = string.Empty;
```

```
  public string FirstName
  {
    get { return _fName; }
    set { _fName = value; }
  }
  public override string ToString() =>
  $"IsAlive:{IsAlive} FirstName:{FirstName} Age:{PersonAge} ";
}
```

Finally, add the following code to the Program.cs file in the starter code (preserving the using statements added earlier):

```
Console.WriteLine("***** Fun with Object Serialization *****\n");
var theRadio = new Radio
{
    StationPresets = new() { 89.3, 105.1, 97.1 },
    HasTweeters = true
};
// Make a JamesBondCar and set state.
JamesBondCar jbc = new()
{
    CanFly = true,
    CanSubmerge = false,
    TheRadio = new()
    {
        StationPresets = new() { 89.3, 105.1, 97.1 },
        HasTweeters = true
    }
};

List<JamesBondCar> myCars = new()
{
    new JamesBondCar { CanFly = true, CanSubmerge = true, TheRadio = theRadio },
    new JamesBondCar { CanFly = true, CanSubmerge = false, TheRadio = theRadio },
    new JamesBondCar { CanFly = false, CanSubmerge = true, TheRadio = theRadio },
    new JamesBondCar { CanFly = false, CanSubmerge = false, TheRadio = theRadio },
};

Person p = new Person
{
    FirstName = "James",
    IsAlive = true
};
```

Now you are all set up to explore XML and JSON serialization.

Extensible Markup Language (XML)

One of the original goals of XML was to represent an object (or set of objects) in human- and machine-readable format. An XML document is a single file that contains the item(s) being serialized. To conform to the standard (and be usable by software systems that support XML), the document opens with an

XML declaration defining the version and optionally the encoding. The next line is the root element and contains the XML namespaces. All the data is contained between the opening and closing tags for the root element.

For example, the Person class can be represented in XML as shown in the following sample. You can see the XML declaration and the root element (Person), as well as additional *markup* for the properties. Optionally, properties can be represented using attributes.

```
<?xml version="1.0"?>
<Person xmlns:xsi="http://www.w3.org/2001/XMLSchema-instance"
     xmlns:xsd="http://www.w3.org/2001/XMLSchema">
  <IsAlive>true</IsAlive>
  <FirstName>James</FirstName>
</Person>
```

If you have a list of objects, such as a list of JamesBondCar objects, the structure is the same. In the following example, the root element is not a JamesBondCar, but an array of JamesBondCar. Then each JamesBondCar in the array is contained within the root element. The following example shows the attribute syntax for the CanFly and CanSubmerge properties:

```
<?xml version="1.0"?>
<ArrayOfJamesBondCar xmlns:xsi="http://www.w3.org/2001/XMLSchema-instance"
    xmlns:xsd="http://www.w3.org/2001/XMLSchema">
  <JamesBondCar CanFly="true" CanSubmerge="true">
    <TheRadio xmlns="http://www.MyCompany.com">
      <HasTweeters>false</HasTweeters>
      <HasSubWoofers>false</HasSubWoofers>
      <RadioId>XF-552RR6</RadioId>
      <StationPresets>
        <double>89.3</double>
        <double>105.1</double>
        <double>97.1</double>
      </StationPresets>
    </TheRadio>
    <IsHatchBack xmlns="http://www.MyCompany.com">false</IsHatchBack>
  </JamesBondCar>
  <JamesBondCar CanFly="true" CanSubmerge="false">
    <TheRadio xmlns="http://www.MyCompany.com">
      <HasTweeters>false</HasTweeters>
      <HasSubWoofers>false</HasSubWoofers>
      <RadioId>XF-552RR6</RadioId>
      <StationPresets>
        <double>89.3</double>
        <double>105.1</double>
        <double>97.1</double>
      </StationPresets>
    </TheRadio>
    <IsHatchBack xmlns="http://www.MyCompany.com">false</IsHatchBack>
  </JamesBondCar>
</ArrayOfJamesBondCar>
```

Serializing and Deserializing with the XmlSerializer

The System.Xml namespace provides the System.Xml.Serialization.XmlSerializer. You can use this formatter to persist the *public* state of a given object as pure XML. Note that the XmlSerializer requires you to declare the type that will be serialized (or deserialized).

Controlling the Generated XML Data

If you have a background in XML technologies, you know that it is often critical to ensure the data within an XML document conforms to a set of rules that establishes the *validity* of the data. Understand that a *valid* XML document does not have anything to do with the syntactic well-being of the XML elements (e.g., all opening elements must have a closing element). Rather, valid documents conform to agreed-upon formatting rules (e.g., field X must be expressed as an attribute and not a subelement), which are typically defined by an XML schema or document-type definition (DTD) file.

By default, XmlSerializer serializes all public fields/properties as XML elements, rather than as XML attributes. If you want to control how the XmlSerializer generates the resulting XML document, you can decorate types with any number of additional .NET attributes from the System.Xml.Serialization namespace. Table 19-12 documents some (but not all) of the .NET attributes that influence how XML data is encoded to a stream.

Table 19-12. *Select Attributes of the System.Xml.Serialization Namespace*

.NET Attribute	Meaning in Life
[XmlAttribute]	You can use this .NET attribute on a public field or property in a class to tell XmlSerializer to serialize the data as an XML attribute (rather than as a subelement).
[XmlElement]	The field or property will be serialized as an XML element named as you so choose.
[XmlEnum]	This attribute provides the element name of an enumeration member.
[XmlRoot]	This attribute controls how the root element will be constructed (namespace and element name).
[XmlText]	The property or field will be serialized as XML text (i.e., the content between the start tag and the end tag of the root element).
[XmlType]	This attribute provides the name and namespace of the XML type.

Of course, you can use many other .NET attributes to control how the XmlSerializer generates the resulting XML document. For full details, look up the System.Xml.Serialization namespace in the .NET documentation.

■ **Note** The XmlSerializer demands that all serialized types in the object graph support a default constructor (so be sure to add it back if you define custom constructors).

Serializing Objects Using the XmlSerializer

Consider the following local function added to your Program.cs file:

```
static void SaveAsXmlFormat<T>(T objGraph, string fileName)
{
  //Must declare type in the constructor of the XmlSerializer
  XmlSerializer xmlFormat = new XmlSerializer(typeof(T));
  using (Stream fStream = new FileStream(fileName,
    FileMode.Create, FileAccess.Write, FileShare.None))
  {
    xmlFormat.Serialize(fStream, objGraph);
  }
}
```

Add the following code to your top-level statements:

```
  SaveAsXmlFormat(jbc, "CarData.xml");
  Console.WriteLine("=> Saved car in XML format!");

  SaveAsXmlFormat(p, "PersonData.xml");
  Console.WriteLine("=> Saved person in XML format!");
```

If you were to look within the newly generated CarData.xml file, you would find the XML data shown here:

```
<?xml version="1.0"?>
<JamesBondCar xmlns:xsi="http://www.w3.org/2001/XMLSchema-instance"
    xmlns:xsd="http://www.w3.org/2001/XMLSchema" >
  <TheRadio>
    <HasTweeters>true</HasTweeters>
    <HasSubWoofers>false</HasSubWoofers>
    <StationPresets>
      <double>89.3</double>
      <double>105.1</double>
      <double>97.1</double>
    </StationPresets>
    <RadioId>XF-552RR6</RadioId>
  </TheRadio>
  <IsHatchBack>false</IsHatchBack>
  <CanFly>true</CanFly>
  <CanSubmerge>false</CanSubmerge>
</JamesBondCar>
```

If you want to specify a custom XML namespace that qualifies the JamesBondCar and encodes the canFly and canSubmerge values as XML attributes instead of elements, you can do so by modifying the C# definition of JamesBondCar like this:

```
[Serializable, XmlRoot(Namespace = "http://www.MyCompany.com")]
public class JamesBondCar : Car
{
  [XmlAttribute]
```

```
  public bool CanFly;
  [XmlAttribute]
  public bool CanSubmerge;
...
}
```

This yields the following XML document (note the opening <JamesBondCar> element):

```
<?xml version="1.0"""?>
<JamesBondCar xmlns:xsi="http://www.w3.org/2001/XMLSchema-instance"
  xmlns:xsd="http://www.w3.org/2001/XMLSchema"
  CanFly="true" CanSubmerge="false" xmlns="http://www.MyCompany.com">
...
</JamesBondCar>
```

Next, examine the following PersonData.xml file:

```
<?xml version="1.0"?>
<Person xmlns:xsi="http://www.w3.org/2001/XMLSchema-instance" xmlns:xsd="http://www.
w3.org/2001/XMLSchema">
  <IsAlive>true</IsAlive>
  <FirstName>James</FirstName>
</Person>
```

Notice how the PersonAge property is not serialized into the XML. This confirms that XML serialization serializes only public properties and fields.

Serializing Collections of Objects

Serializing collections works in the same manner. Add the following to your top-level statements:

```
SaveAsXmlFormat(myCars,"CarCollection.xml");
Console.WriteLine("=> Saved list of cars!");
```

The generated XML matches the example shown at the beginning of this section, with the ArrayOfJamesBondCar as the root element.

Deserializing Objects and Collections of Objects

XML deserialization is literally the opposite of serializing objects (and collections of objects). Consider the following local function to deserialize XML back into an object graph. Notice that, once again, the type to be deserialized must be passed into the constructor for the XmlSerializer:

```
static T ReadAsXmlFormat<T>(string fileName)
{
  // Create a typed instance of the XmlSerializer
  XmlSerializer xmlFormat = new XmlSerializer(typeof(T));
  using (Stream fStream = new FileStream(fileName, FileMode.Open))
  {
    T obj = default;
```

```
        obj = (T)xmlFormat.Deserialize(fStream);
        return obj;
    }
}
```

Add the following code to the top-level statements to reconstitute your XML back into objects (or list of objects):

```
JamesBondCar savedCar = ReadAsXmlFormat<JamesBondCar>("CarData.xml");
Console.WriteLine("Original Car:\t {0}",jbc.ToString());
Console.WriteLine("Read Car:\t {0}",savedCar.ToString());

List<JamesBondCar> savedCars = ReadAsXmlFormat<List<JamesBondCar>>("CarCollection.xml");
```

XML serialization is used not only for storing and retrieving data, as shown in these examples, but also for sending data between systems, especially systems developed with differing technology stacks. All modern programming languages (and many database providers) have built-in support for XML.

JavaScript Object Notation (JSON) Serialization

While XML serialization is still widely used, it has largely taken a backseat to systems using JSON to share, persist, and/or load data. JSON, like XML, is a textual representation of an object (or object graph) that is cross-platform compatible and adheres to an open standard. Systems built with a wide range of languages and tooling have built-in support for JSON.

Objects in JSON documents are designated using name-value pairs for the properties enclosed in curly braces ({}). For example, a `Person` instance when serialized to JSON produces the following document:

```
{
  "firstName": "James",
  "isAlive": true
}
```

Notice some of the key differences between the JSON and the XML representation of the same instance from the previous section. There isn't a declaration or a root name, just the properties of the serialized object. This results in a much smaller amount of text, making it a more efficient format.

The lack of the class name (`Person`) in the JSON provides additional flexibility. The sender (in this case us) might call the class `Person`, while the receiver might call the class `Human`. As long as the properties match, the JSON will be properly applied to the object.

Lists of objects are stored as JavaScript arrays using square brackets ([]). The following is a list containing two `JamesBondCar` objects:

```
[
  {
    "CanFly": true,
    "CanSubmerge": true,
    "TheRadio": {
      "StationPresets": ["89.3", "105.1", "97.1"],
      "HasTweeters": true,
```

```
      "HasSubWoofers": false,
      "RadioId": "XF-552RR6"
    },
    "IsHatchBack": false
  },
  {
    "CanFly": true,
    "CanSubmerge": false,
    "TheRadio": {
      "StationPresets": ["89.3", "105.1", "97.1"],
      "HasTweeters": true,
      "HasSubWoofers": false,
      "RadioId": "XF-552RR6"
    },
    "IsHatchBack": false
  }
]
```

Notice that the entire file is opened and closed with a square bracket, and then each object in the array is opened and closed with a curly brace. The radio presets are also a list, so they are serialized as an array of values.

Serializing and Deserializing with System.Text.Json

The `System.Text.Json` namespace provides the `System.Text.Json.JsonSerializer`. You can use this formatter to persist the *public* state of a given object as JSON.

Controlling the Generated JSON Data

By default, `JsonSerializer` serializes all public properties as JSON name-value pairs using the same name (and casing) of the object's property names. You can control many aspects of the serialization process with attributes; some of the more commonly used attributes are listed in Table 19-13.

Table 19-13. *Select Attributes of the System.Text.Json.Serialization Namespace*

.NET Attribute	Meaning in Life
`[JsonIgnore]`	The property will be ignored.
`[JsonInclude]`	The member will be included.
`[JsonPropertyName]`	This specifies the property name to be used when serializing/deserializing a member. This is commonly used to resolve character casing issues.
`[JsonConstructor]`	This indicates the constructor that should be used when deserializing JSON back into an object graph.

Serializing Objects Using the JsonSerializer

The JsonSerializer contains static Serialize methods used to convert .NET objects (including object graphs) into a string representation of the public properties. The data is represented as name-value pairs in JavaScript Object Notation. Consider the following local function added to your Program.cs file:

```
static void SaveAsJsonFormat<T>(T objGraph, string fileName)
{
  File.WriteAllText(fileName, System.Text.Json.JsonSerializer.Serialize(objGraph));
}
```

Add the following code to your top-level statements:

```
  SaveAsJsonFormat(jbc, "CarData.json");
  Console.WriteLine("=> Saved car in JSON format!");

  SaveAsJsonFormat(p, "PersonData.json");
  Console.WriteLine("=> Saved person in JSON format!");
```

When you examine the created JSON files, you might be surprised to see that the CarData.json file is empty (except for a pair of braces) and the PersonData.json file contains only the Firstname value. This is because the JsonSerializer only writes public *properties* by default, and not public fields. You will correct this in the next section.

Including Fields

To include public fields into the generated JSON, you have two options. The other method is to use the JsonSerializerOptions class to instruct the JsonSerializer to include all fields. The second is to update your classes by adding the [JsonInclude] attribute to each public field that should be included in the JSON output. Note that the first method (using the JsonSerializationOptions) will include *all* public fields in the object graph. To exclude certain public fields using this technique, you must use the JsonExclude attribute on them to be excluded.

Update the SaveAsJsonFormat method to the following:

```
static void SaveAsJsonFormat<T>(T objGraph, string fileName)
{
  var options = new JsonSerializerOptions
  {
    IncludeFields = true,
  };
  File.WriteAllText(fileName, System.Text.Json.JsonSerializer.Serialize(objGraph, options));
}
```

Instead of using the JsonSerializerOptions, you can achieve the same result by updating all public fields in the sample classes to the following (note that you can leave the Xml attributes in the classes and they will not interfere with the JsonSerializer):

```
//Radio.cs
public class Radio
{
  [JsonInclude]
```

```
  public bool HasTweeters;
  [JsonInclude]
  public bool HasSubWoofers;
  [JsonInclude]
  public List<double> StationPresets;
  [JsonInclude]
  public string RadioId = "XF-552RR6";
...
}

//Car.cs
public class Car
{
  [JsonInclude]
  public Radio TheRadio = new Radio();
  [JsonInclude]
  public bool IsHatchBack;
...
}

//JamesBondCar.cs
public class JamesBondCar : Car
{
  [XmlAttribute]
  [JsonInclude]
  public bool CanFly;
  [XmlAttribute]
  [JsonInclude]
  public bool CanSubmerge;
...
}

//Person.cs
public class Person
{
  // A public field.
  [JsonInclude]
  public bool IsAlive = true;
...
}
```

Now when you run the code using either method, all public properties *and fields* are written to the file. However, when you examine the contents, you will see that the JSON is written *minified*. Minified is a format where all insignificant whitespace and line breaks are removed. This is the default format largely due to JSON's wide use of RESTful services and reduces the size of the data packet when sending information between services over HTTP/HTTPS.

■ **Note** The field handling for serializing JSON is the same as deserializing JSON. If you chose to set the option to include fields when serializing JSON, you must also include that option when deserializing JSON.

Pretty-Print the JSON

In addition to the option to include public fields, the `JsonSerializer` can be instructed to write the JSON indented (and human readable). Update your method to the following:

```
static void SaveAsJsonFormat<T>(T objGraph, string fileName)
{
  var options = new JsonSerializerOptions
  {
    IncludeFields = true,
    WriteIndented = true
  };
  File.WriteAllText(fileName, System.Text.Json.JsonSerializer.Serialize(objGraph, options));
}
```

Now examine the `CarData.json` file; the output is much more readable.

```
{
  "canFly": true,
  "canSubmerge": false,
  "theRadio": {
    "stationPresets": [
      "89.3",
      "105.1",
      "97.1"
    ],
    "hasTweeters": true,
    "hasSubWoofers": false,
    "radioId": "XF-552RR6"
  },
  "isHatchBack": false
}
```

PascalCase or camelCase JSON

Pascal casing is a format that uses the first character capitalized and every significant part of a name capitalized as well. Camel casing, on the other hand, sets the first character to lowercase (like the word *camelCase* in the title of this section), and then every significant part of the name starts with a capital. Take the previous JSON listing. `canSubmerge` is an example of camel casing. The Pascal case version of the previous example is `CanSubmerge`.

Why does this matter? It matters because most of the popular languages are case sensitive (like C#). That means `CanSubmerge` and `canSubmerge` are two different items. As you have seen throughout this book, the generally accepted standard for naming public things in C# (classes, public properties, functions, etc.) is to use Pascal casing. However, most of the JavaScript frameworks prefer to use camel casing. This can be problematic when using .NET and C# to pass JSON data to/from non-C#/.NET RESTful services.

Fortunately, the `JsonSerializer` is customizable to handle most situations, including casing differences. If no naming policy is specified, the `JsonSerializer` will use camel casing when serializing and deserializing JSON. To change the serialization process to use Pascal casing, you need to set `PropertyNamingPolicy` to `null`, as follows:

```
static void SaveAsJsonFormat<T>(T objGraph, string fileName)
{
  JsonSerializerOptions options = new()
  {
    PropertyNamingPolicy = null,
    IncludeFields = true,
    WriteIndented = true,
  };
  File.WriteAllText(fileName, System.Text.Json.JsonSerializer.Serialize(objGraph, options));
}
```

Now, when you execute the calling code, the JSON produced is all Pascal cased.


```
{
  "CanFly": true,
  "CanSubmerge": false,
  "TheRadio": {
    "StationPresets": [
      "89.3",
      "105.1",
      "97.1"
    ],
    "HasTweeters": true,
    "HasSubWoofers": false,
    "RadioId": "XF-552RR6"
  },
  "IsHatchBack": false
}
```


When reading JSON, C# is (by default) case sensitive. The casing setting of the `PropertyNamingPolicy` is used during `Deserialization`. If the property is not set, the default (camel casing) is used. By setting the `PropertyNamingPolicy` to Pascal case, then all incoming JSON is expected to be in Pascal case. If the casing does not match, the deserialization process (covered soon) fails.

There is a third option when deserializing JSON, and that is casing indifference. By setting the `PropertyNameCaseInsensitive` option to true, then C# will deserialize `canSubmerge` as well as `CanSubmerge`. Here is the code to set the option:

```
JsonSerializerOptions options = new()
{
  PropertyNameCaseInsensitive = true,
  IncludeFields = true
};
```

Ignoring Circular References with JsonSerializer (New 10)

Introduced in .NET 6/C# 10, the System.Text.Json.JsonSerializer supports ignoring circular references when serializing an object graph. This is done by setting the ReferenceHandler to ReferenceHandler.IgnoreCycles in the JsonSerializerOptions. Here is the code to set the serializer to ignore the circular references:

```
JsonSerializerOptions options = new()
{
  ReferenceHandler = ReferenceHandler.IgnoreCycles
};
```

Table 19-14 lists the available values in the ReferenceHandler enum.

Table 19-14. *ReferenceHandler Enum Values*

Enum Value	Meaning in Life
IgnoreCycles	Circular references are not serialized, and the reference loop is replaced with a null.
Preserve	Metadata properties will be honored when deserializing JSON objects and arrays into reference types and written when serializing reference types. This is necessary to create round-trippable JSON from objects that contain cycles or duplicate references.

Number Handling with JsonSerializer

The default handling of numbers is Strict, meaning numbers will be serialized as numbers (without quotes) and deserialized as numbers (without quotes). The JsonSerializerOptions has a NumberHandling property that controls reading and writing numbers. Table 19-15 lists the available values in the JsonNumberHandling enum.

Table 19-15. *JsonNumberHandling Enum Values*

Enum Value	Meaning in Life
Strict (0)	Numbers are read from numbers and written as numbers. Quotes are not allowed nor are they generated.
AllowReadingFromString (1)	Numbers can be read from number or string tokens.
WriteAsString (2)	Numbers are written as JSON strings (with quotes).
AllowNamedFloatingPointLiterals (4)	The Nan, Infinity, and -Infinity string tokens can be read, and Single and Double values will be written as their corresponding JSON string representations.

The enum has a flags attribute, which allows a bitwise combination of its values. For example, if you want to read strings (and numbers) and write numbers as strings, you use the following option setting:

```
JsonSerializerOptions options = new()
{
...
  NumberHandling = JsonNumberHandling.AllowReadingFromString & JsonNumberHandling.WriteAsString
};
```

With this change, the JSON created for the Car class is as follows:

```
{
  "canFly": true,
  "canSubmerge": false,
  "theRadio": {
    "hasTweeters": true,
    "hasSubWoofers": false,
    "stationPresets": [
      "89.3",
      "105.1",
      "97.1"
    ],
    "radioId": "XF-552RR6"
  },
  "isHatchBack": false
}
```

JSON Property Ordering (New 10)

With the release of .NET 6/C# 10, the JsonPropertyOrder attribute controls property ordering during serialization. The smaller the number (including negative values), the earlier the property is in the resulting JSON. Properties without an order are assigned a default order of zero. Update the Person class to the following:

```
namespace SimpleSerialize;

public class Person
{
    [JsonPropertyOrder(1)]
    public bool IsAlive = true;

    private int PersonAge = 21;

    private string _fName = string.Empty;
    [JsonPropertyOrder(-1)]
    public string FirstName
    {
        get { return _fName; }
        set { _fName = value; }
    }
    public override string ToString() => $"IsAlive:{IsAlive} FirstName:{FirstName}
Age:{PersonAge} ";
}
```

With that change, the properties are serialized in the order of FirstName (-1) and then IsAlive (1). PersonAge doesn't get serialized because it's private. If it were made public, it would get the default order of zero and be placed between the other two properties.

Support for IAsyncEnumerable (New 10)

With the release of .NET 6/C# 10, the `System.Text.Json.JsonSerializer` now has support for serializing and deserializing async streams.

Streaming Serialization

To demonstrate streaming serialization, start by adding a new method that will return an `IAsyncEnumerable<int>`:

```
static async IAsyncEnumerable<int> PrintNumbers(int n)
{
  for (int i = 0; i < n; i++)
  {
    yield return i;
  }
}
```

Next, create a `Stream` from the `Console` and serialize the `IAsyncEnumerable<int>` returned from the `PrintNumbers()` function.

```
async static void SerializeAsync()
{
  Console.WriteLine("Async Serialization");
  using Stream stream = Console.OpenStandardOutput();
  var data = new { Data = PrintNumbers(3) };
  await JsonSerializer.SerializeAsync(stream, data);
  Console.WriteLine();
}
```

Streaming Deserialization

There is a new API to support streaming deserialization, `DeserializeAsyncEnumerable<T>()`. To demonstrate the use of this, add a new method that will create a new `MemoryStream` and then deserialize from the stream:

```
async static void DeserializeAsync()
{
  Console.WriteLine("Async Deserialization");
  var stream = new MemoryStream(System.Text.Encoding.UTF8.GetBytes("[0,1,2,3,4]"));
  await foreach (int item in JsonSerializer.DeserializeAsyncEnumerable<int>(stream))
  {
    Console.Write(item);
  }
  Console.WriteLine();
}
```

Potential Performance Issues Using JsonSerializerOptions

When using JsonSerializerOption, it is best to create a single instance and reuse it throughout your application. With that in mind, update your top-level statements and JSON methods to the following:

```
JsonSerializerOptions options = new()
{
    PropertyNameCaseInsensitive = true,
    //PropertyNamingPolicy = JsonNamingPolicy.CamelCase,
    PropertyNamingPolicy = null, //Pascal casing
    IncludeFields = true,
    WriteIndented = true,
    NumberHandling = JsonNumberHandling.AllowReadingFromString | JsonNumberHandling.
    WriteAsString
};
SaveAsJsonFormat(options, jbc, "CarData.json");
Console.WriteLine("=> Saved car in JSON format!");

SaveAsJsonFormat(options, p, "PersonData.json");
Console.WriteLine("=> Saved person in JSON format!");

static void SaveAsJsonFormat<T>(JsonSerializerOptions options, T objGraph, string fileName)
=> File.WriteAllText(fileName, System.Text.Json.JsonSerializer.Serialize(objGraph,
options));
```

Web Defaults for JsonSerializer

When building web applications, you can use a specialized constructor to set the following properties:

```
PropertyNameCaseInsensitive = true,
PropertyNamingPolicy = JsonNamingPolicy.CamelCase,
NumberHandling = JsonNumberHandling.AllowReadingFromString
```

You can still set additional properties or override the defaults through object initialization, like this:

```
JsonSerializerOptions options = new(JsonSerializerDefaults.Web)
{
  WriteIndented = true,
  ReferenceHandler = ReferenceHandler.IgnoreCycles
};
```

General Defaults for JsonSerializer

If you want to start off with more general settings, passing JsonSerializerDefaults.General into the constructor will set the following properties:

```
PropertyNameCaseInsensitive = false,
PropertyNamingPolicy = null, //Pascal Casing
NumberHandling = JsonNumberHandling.Strict
```

Like the web version, you can still set additional properties or override the defaults through object initialization, like this:

```
JsonSerializerOptions options = new(JsonSerializerDefaults.General)
{
  WriteIndented = true,
  ReferenceHandler = ReferenceHandler.IgnoreCycles,
  PropertyNameCaseInsensitive = true
};
```

Serializing Collections of Objects

Serializing a collection of objects into JSON is handled the same way as a single object. Add the following line to the top-level statements:

```
SaveAsJsonFormat(options, myCars, "CarCollection.json");
```

Deserializing Objects and Collections of Objects

JSON deserialization is the opposite of serialization. The following function will deserialize JSON into the type specified using the generic version of the method:

```
static T ReadAsJsonFormat<T>(JsonSerializerOptions options, string fileName) =>
  System.Text.Json.JsonSerializer.Deserialize<T>(File.ReadAllText(fileName), options);
```

Add the following code to the top-level statements to reconstitute your XML back into objects (or list of objects):

```
JamesBondCar savedJsonCar = ReadAsJsonFormat<JamesBondCar>(options, "CarData.json");
Console.WriteLine("Read Car: {0}", savedJsonCar.ToString());

List<JamesBondCar> savedJsonCars = ReadAsJsonFormat<List<JamesBondCar>>(options,
"CarCollection.json");
Console.WriteLine("Read Car: {0}", savedJsonCar.ToString());
```

Note that the type being created during the deserializing process can be a single object or a generic collection.

JsonConverters

You can take additional control of the serialization/deserialization process by adding in custom converters. Custom converters inherit from `JsonConverter<T>` (where `T` is the type that the converter operates on) and override the base `Read()` and `Write()` methods. Here are the abstract base methods to overwrite:

```
public abstract T? Read(ref Utf8JsonReader reader, Type typeToConvert, JsonSerializerOptions
options);
public abstract void Write(Utf8JsonWriter writer, T value, JsonSerializerOptions options);
```

One common scenario is converting null values in your object to an empty string in the JSON and back to a null in your object. To demonstrate this, add a new file named JsonStringNullToEmptyConverter.cs, make the class public, inherit from JsonConverter<string>, and implement the abstract members. Here is the initial code:

```
namespace SimpleSerialize
{
  public class JsonStringNullToEmptyConverter : JsonConverter<string>
  {
    public override string Read(ref Utf8JsonReader reader, Type typeToConvert,
JsonSerializerOptions options)
    {
    }

    public override void Write(Utf8JsonWriter writer, string value, JsonSerializerOptions
    options)
    {
    }
  }
}
```

In the Read method, use the Utf8JsonReader instance to read the string value for the node, and if it is null or an empty string, then return null. Otherwise, return the value read:

```
public override string Read(ref Utf8JsonReader reader, Type typeToConvert,
JsonSerializerOptions options)
{
  var value = reader.GetString();
  if (string.IsNullOrEmpty(value))
  {
    return null;
  }
  return value;
}
```

In the Write method, use the Utf8JsonWriter to write an empty string if the value is null:

```
public override void Write(Utf8JsonWriter writer, string value, JsonSerializerOptions
options)
{
  value ??= string.Empty;
  writer.WriteStringValue(value);
}
```

The final step for the custom converter is to force the serializer to process null values. By default, null values are not sent through the conversion process to improve performance. However, in this scenario, we want the null values to be processed, so override the base property HandleNull and set it to true instead of the default false value.

```
public override bool HandleNull => true;
```

The final step is to add the custom converter into the serialization options. Create a new method named `HandleNullStrings()` and add the following code:

```
static void HandleNullStrings()
{
  Console.WriteLine("Handling Null Strings");
  var options = new JsonSerializerOptions
  {
    PropertyNameCaseInsensitive = true,
    PropertyNamingPolicy = null,
    IncludeFields = true,
    WriteIndented = true,
    Converters = { new JsonStringNullToEmptyConverter() },
  };
  //Create a new object with a null string
  var radio = new Radio
  {
    HasSubWoofers = true,
    HasTweeters = true,
    RadioId = null
  };
  //serialize the object to JSON
  var json = JsonSerializer.Serialize(radio, options);
  Console.WriteLine(json);
}
```

When you call this method from the top-level statements, you can see that the `RadioId` property is indeed an empty string in the JSON instead of a `null`. The `StationPresets` values are still `null` in the JSON because the custom converter acts only on `string` types, not on `List<string>` types.

```
{
  "StationPresets": null,
  "HasTweeters": true,
  "HasSubWoofers": true,
  "RadioId": null
}
```

Summary

You began this chapter by examining the use of the `Directory(Info)` and `File(Info)` types. As you learned, these classes allow you to manipulate a physical file or directory on your hard drive. Next, you examined several classes derived from the abstract `Stream` class. Given that `Stream`-derived types operate on a raw stream of bytes, the `System.IO` namespace provides numerous reader/writer types (e.g., `StreamWriter`, `StringWriter`, and `BinaryWriter`) that simplify the process. Along the way, you also checked out the functionality provided by `DriveType`, learned how to monitor files using the `FileSystemWatcher` type, and saw how to interact with streams in an asynchronous manner.

This chapter also introduced you to the topic of object serialization services. As you have seen, the .NET platform uses an object graph to account for the full set of related objects that you want to persist to a stream. You then worked with XML and JSON serialization and deserialization.

CHAPTER 20

Data Access with ADO.NET

The .NET platform defines several namespaces that allow you to interact with relational database systems. Collectively speaking, these namespaces are known as ADO.NET. In this chapter, you will learn about the overall role of ADO.NET and the core types and namespaces, and then you will move on to the topic of ADO.NET data providers. The .NET platform supports numerous data providers (both provided as part of the .NET Framework and available from third-party sources), each of which is optimized to communicate with a specific database management system (e.g., Microsoft SQL Server, Oracle, and MySQL).

After you understand the common functionality provided by various data providers, you will then look at the data provider factory pattern. As you will see, using types within the `System.Data` namespaces (including `System.Data.Common` and database provider-specific namespaces like `Microsoft.Data.SqlClient`, `System.Data.Odbc`, and the Windows only database provider namespace `System.Data.Oledb`), you can build a single code base that can dynamically pick and choose the underlying data provider without the need to recompile or redeploy the application's code base.

Next, you will learn how to work directly with the SQL Server database provider, creating and opening connections to retrieve data, and then move on to inserting, updating, and deleting data, followed by examining the topic of database transactions. Finally, you will execute SQL Server's bulk copy feature using ADO.NET to load a list of records into the database.

Note This chapter focuses on the raw ADO.NET. Starting with Chapter 21, I cover Entity Framework (EF) Core, Microsoft's object-relational mapping (ORM) framework. Since EF Core uses ADO.NET for data access under the covers, a solid understanding of how ADO.NET works is vital when troubleshooting data access. There are also scenarios that are not solved by EF Core (such as executing a SQL bulk copy), and you will need to know ADO.NET to solve those issues.

ADO.NET vs. ADO

If you have a background in Microsoft's previous COM-based data access model (Active Data Objects [ADO]) and are just starting to work with the .NET platform, you need to understand that ADO.NET has little to do with ADO beyond the letters *A*, *D*, and *O*. While it is true that there is some relationship between the two systems (e.g., each has the concept of connection and command objects), some familiar ADO types (e.g., the `Recordset`) no longer exist. Furthermore, you can find many new types that have no direct equivalent under classic ADO (e.g., the data adapter).

A. Troelsen and P. Japikse, *Pro C# 10 with .NET 6*, https://doi.org/10.1007/978-1-4842-7869-7_20

Understanding ADO.NET Data Providers

ADO.NET does not provide a single set of objects that communicate with multiple database management systems (DBMSs). Rather, ADO.NET supports multiple *data providers*, each of which is optimized to interact with a specific DBMS. The first benefit of this approach is that you can program a specific data provider to access any unique features of a particular DBMS. The second benefit is that a specific data provider can connect directly to the underlying engine of the DBMS in question without an intermediate mapping layer standing between the tiers.

Simply put, a data provider is a set of types defined in a given namespace that understand how to communicate with a specific type of data source. Regardless of which data provider you use, each defines a set of class types that provide core functionality. Table 20-1 documents some of the core base classes and the key interfaces they implement.

Table 20-1. *The Core Objects of an ADO.NET Data Provider*

Base Class	Relevant Interfaces	Meaning in Life
`DbConnection`	`IDbConnection`	Provides the ability to connect to and disconnect from the data store. Connection objects also provide access to a related transaction object.
`DbCommand`	`IDbCommand`	Represents a SQL query or a stored procedure. Command objects also provide access to the provider's data reader object.
`DbDataReader`	`IDataReader`, `IDataRecord`	Provides forward-only, read-only access to data using a server-side cursor.
`DbDataAdapter`	`IDataAdapter`, `IDbDataAdapter`	Transfers `DataSets` between the caller and the data store. Data adapters contain a connection and a set of four internal command objects used to select, insert, update, and delete information from the data store.
`DbParameter`	`IDataParameter`, `IDbDataParameter`	Represents a named parameter within a parameterized query.
`DbTransaction`	`IDbTransaction`	Encapsulates a database transaction.

Although the specific names of these core classes will differ among data providers (e.g., `SqlConnection` versus `OdbcConnection`), each class derives from the same base class (`DbConnection`, in the case of connection objects) that implements identical interfaces (e.g., `IDbConnection`). Given this, you would be correct to assume that after you learn how to work with one data provider, the remaining providers prove quite straightforward.

■ **Note** When you refer to a connection object under ADO.NET, you're actually referring to a specific `DbConnection`-derived type; there is no class literally named *Connection*. The same idea holds true for a *command object*, *data adapter object*, and so forth. As a naming convention, the objects in a specific data provider are prefixed with the name of the related DBMS (e.g., `SqlConnection`, `SqlCommand`, and `SqlDataReader`).

Figure 20-1 shows the big picture behind ADO.NET data providers. The client assembly can be any type of .NET application: console program, Windows Forms, Windows Presentation Foundation, ASP.NET Core, .NET code library, and so on.

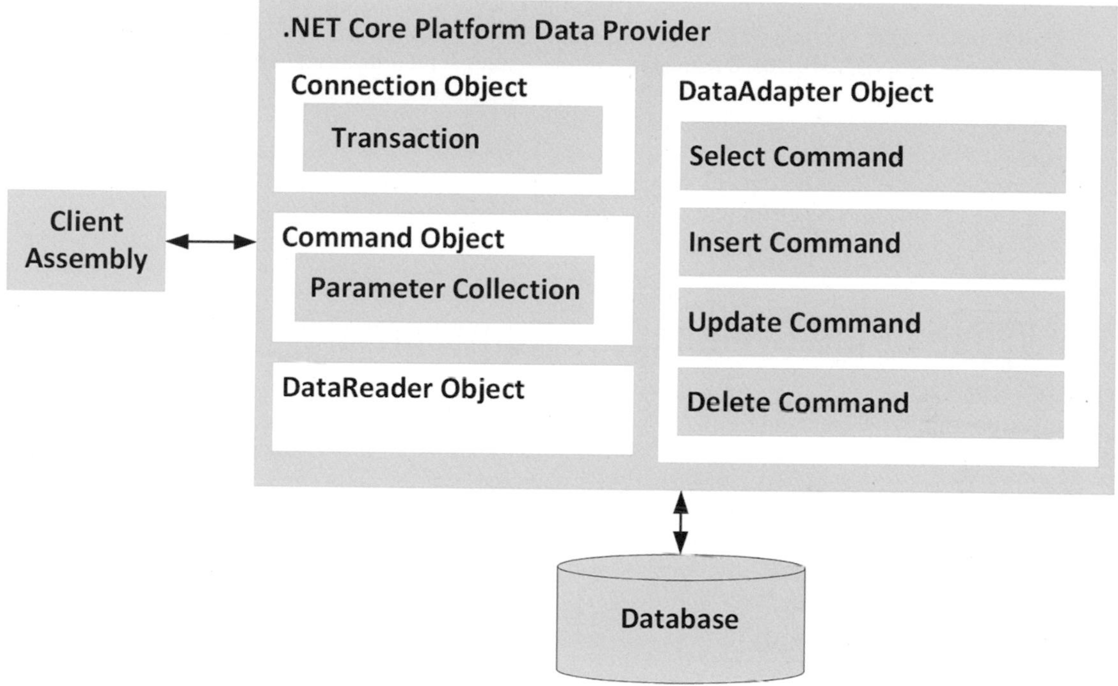

Figure 20-1. *ADO.NET data providers provide access to a given DBMS*

A data provider will supply you with other types beyond the objects shown in Figure 20-1; however, these core objects define a common baseline across all data providers.

ADO.NET Data Providers

As with all of .NET, data providers ship as NuGet packages. There are several supported by Microsoft as well as a multitude of third-party providers available. Table 20-2 documents some of the data providers supported by Microsoft.

Table 20-2. *Some of the Microsoft-Supported Data Providers*

Data Provider	Namespace/NuGet Package Name
Microsoft SQL Server	`Microsoft.Data.SqlClient`
ODBC	`System.Data.Odbc`
OLE DB (Windows only)	`System.Data.OleDb`

The Microsoft SQL Server data provider offers direct access to Microsoft SQL Server data stores—and *only* SQL Server data stores (including SQL Azure). The `Microsoft.Data.SqlClient` namespace contains the types used by the SQL Server provider.

■ **Note** While System.Data.SqlClient is still supported, all development effort for interaction with SQL Server (and SQL Azure) is focused on the new Microsoft.Data.SqlClient provider library.

The ODBC provider (System.Data.Odbc) provides access to ODBC connections. The ODBC types defined within the System.Data.Odbc namespace are typically useful only if you need to communicate with a given DBMS for which there is no custom .NET data provider. This is true because ODBC is a widespread model that provides access to several data stores.

The OLE DB data provider, which is composed of the types defined in the System.Data.OleDb namespace, allows you to access data located in any data store that supports the classic COM-based OLE DB protocol. Due to the dependence on COM, this provider will work only on the Windows operating system and should be considered deprecated in the cross-platform world of .NET.

The Types of the System.Data Namespace

Of all the ADO.NET namespaces, System.Data is the lowest common denominator. This namespace contains types that are shared among all ADO.NET data providers, regardless of the underlying data store. In addition to a number of database-centric exceptions (e.g., NoNullAllowedException, RowNotInTableException, and MissingPrimaryKeyException), System.Data contains types that represent various database primitives (e.g., tables, rows, columns, and constraints), as well as the common interfaces implemented by data provider objects. Table 20-3 lists some of the core types you should be aware of.

Table 20-3. *Core Members of the System.Data Namespace*

Type	Meaning in Life
Constraint	Represents a constraint for a given DataColumn object
DataColumn	Represents a single column within a DataTable object
DataRelation	Represents a parent-child relationship between two DataTable objects
DataRow	Represents a single row within a DataTable object
DataSet	Represents an in-memory cache of data consisting of any number of interrelated DataTable objects
DataTable	Represents a tabular block of in-memory data
DataTableReader	Allows you to treat a DataTable as a firehose cursor (forward-only, read-only data access)
DataView	Represents a customized view of a DataTable for sorting, filtering, searching, editing, and navigation
IDataAdapter	Defines the core behavior of a data adapter object
IDataParameter	Defines the core behavior of a parameter object
IDataReader	Defines the core behavior of a data reader object
IDbCommand	Defines the core behavior of a command object
IDbDataAdapter	Extends IDataAdapter to provide additional functionality of a data adapter object
IDbTransaction	Defines the core behavior of a transaction object

Your next task is to examine the core interfaces of System.Data at a high level; this can help you understand the common functionality offered by any data provider. You will also learn specific details throughout this chapter; however, for now it is best to focus on the overall behavior of each interface type.

The Role of the IDbConnection Interface

The IDbConnection type is implemented by a data provider's *connection object*. This interface defines a set of members used to configure a connection to a specific data store. It also allows you to obtain the data provider's transaction object. Here is the formal definition of IDbConnection:

```
public interface IDbConnection : IDisposable
{
  string ConnectionString { get; set; }
  int ConnectionTimeout { get; }
  string Database { get; }
  ConnectionState State { get; }

  IDbTransaction BeginTransaction();
  IDbTransaction BeginTransaction(IsolationLevel il);
  void ChangeDatabase(string databaseName);
  void Close();
  IDbCommand CreateCommand();
  void Open();
  void Dispose();
}
```

The Role of the IDbTransaction Interface

The overloaded BeginTransaction() method defined by IDbConnection provides access to the provider's *transaction object*. You can use the members defined by IDbTransaction to interact programmatically with a transactional session and the underlying data store.

```
public interface IDbTransaction : IDisposable
{
  IDbConnection Connection { get; }
  IsolationLevel IsolationLevel { get; }

  void Commit();
  void Rollback();
  void Dispose();
}
```

The Role of the IDbCommand Interface

Next up is the IDbCommand interface, which will be implemented by a data provider's *command object*. Like other data access object models, command objects allow programmatic manipulation of SQL statements, stored procedures, and parameterized queries. Command objects also provide access to the data provider's data reader type through the overloaded ExecuteReader() method.

```
public interface IDbCommand : IDisposable
{
  string CommandText { get; set; }
  int CommandTimeout { get; set; }
  CommandType CommandType { get; set; }
  IDbConnection Connection { get; set; }
  IDbTransaction Transaction { get; set; }
  IDataParameterCollection Parameters { get; }
  UpdateRowSource UpdatedRowSource { get; set; }

  void Prepare();
  void Cancel();
  IDbDataParameter CreateParameter();
  int ExecuteNonQuery();
  IDataReader ExecuteReader();
  IDataReader ExecuteReader(CommandBehavior behavior);
  object ExecuteScalar();
  void Dispose();
}
```

The Role of the IDbDataParameter and IDataParameter Interfaces

Notice that the Parameters property of IDbCommand returns a strongly typed collection that implements IDataParameterCollection. This interface provides access to a set of IDbDataParameter-compliant class types (e.g., parameter objects).

```
public interface IDbDataParameter : IDataParameter
{
//Plus members in the IDataParameter interface
  byte Precision { get; set; }
  byte Scale { get; set; }
  int Size { get; set; }
}
```

IDbDataParameter extends the IDataParameter interface to obtain the following additional behaviors:

```
public interface IDataParameter
{
  DbType DbType { get; set; }
  ParameterDirection Direction { get; set; }
  bool IsNullable { get; }
  string ParameterName { get; set; }
  string SourceColumn { get; set; }
  DataRowVersion SourceVersion { get; set; }
  object Value { get; set; }
}
```

As you will see, the functionality of the IDbDataParameter and IDataParameter interfaces allows you to represent parameters within a SQL command (including stored procedures) through specific ADO.NET parameter objects, rather than through hard-coded string literals.

The Role of the IDbDataAdapter and IDataAdapter Interfaces

You use *data adapters* to push and pull DataSets to and from a given data store. The IDbDataAdapter interface defines the following set of properties that you can use to maintain the SQL statements for the related select, insert, update, and delete operations:

```
public interface IDbDataAdapter : IDataAdapter
{
  //Plus members of IDataAdapter
  IDbCommand SelectCommand { get; set; }
  IDbCommand InsertCommand { get; set; }
  IDbCommand UpdateCommand { get; set; }
  IDbCommand DeleteCommand { get; set; }
}
```

In addition to these four properties, an ADO.NET data adapter picks up the behavior defined in the base interface, IDataAdapter. This interface defines the key function of a data adapter type: the ability to transfer DataSets between the caller and underlying data store using the Fill() and Update() methods. The IDataAdapter interface also allows you to map database column names to more user-friendly display names with the TableMappings property.

```
public interface IDataAdapter
{
  MissingMappingAction MissingMappingAction { get; set; }
  MissingSchemaAction MissingSchemaAction { get; set; }
  ITableMappingCollection TableMappings { get; }

  DataTable[] FillSchema(DataSet dataSet, SchemaType schemaType);
  int Fill(DataSet dataSet);
  IDataParameter[] GetFillParameters();
  int Update(DataSet dataSet);
}
```

The Role of the IDataReader and IDataRecord Interfaces

The next key interface to be aware of is IDataReader, which represents the common behaviors supported by a given data reader object. When you obtain an IDataReader-compatible type from an ADO.NET data provider, you can iterate over the result set in a forward-only, read-only manner.

```
public interface IDataReader : IDisposable, IDataRecord
{
  //Plus members from IDataRecord
  int Depth { get; }
  bool IsClosed { get; }
  int RecordsAffected { get; }

  void Close();
  DataTable GetSchemaTable();
  bool NextResult();
  bool Read();
  Dispose();
}
```

Finally, IDataReader extends IDataRecord, which defines many members that allow you to extract a strongly typed value from the stream, rather than casting the generic System.Object retrieved from the data reader's overloaded indexer method. Here is the IDataRecord interface definition:

```
public interface IDataRecord
{
  int FieldCount { get; }
  object this[ int i ] { get; }
  object this[ string name ] { get; }
  bool GetBoolean(int i);
  byte GetByte(int i);
  long GetBytes(int i, long fieldOffset, byte[] buffer,
    int bufferoffset, int length);
  char GetChar(int i);
  long GetChars(int i, long fieldoffset, char[] buffer,
    int bufferoffset, int length);
  IDataReader GetData(int i);
  string GetDataTypeName(int i);
  DateTime GetDateTime(int i);
  Decimal GetDecimal(int i);
  double GetDouble(int i);
  Type GetFieldType(int i);
  float GetFloat(int i);
  Guid GetGuid(int i);
  short GetInt16(int i);
  int GetInt32(int i);
  long GetInt64(int i);
  string GetName(int i);
  int GetOrdinal(string name);
  string GetString(int i);
  object GetValue(int i);
  int GetValues(object[] values);
  bool IsDBNull(int i);
}
```

■ **Note** You can use the IDataReader.IsDBNull() method to discover programmatically whether a specified field is set to null before attempting to obtain a value from the data reader (to avoid triggering a runtime exception). Also recall that C# supports nullable data types (see Chapter 4), which are ideal for interacting with data columns that could be null in the database table.

Abstracting Data Providers Using Interfaces

At this point, you should have a better idea of the common functionality found among all .NET data providers. Recall that even though the exact names of the implementing types will differ among data providers, you can program against these types in a similar manner—that is the beauty of interface-based polymorphism. For example, if you define a method that takes an IDbConnection parameter, you can pass in any ADO.NET connection object, like so:

```
public static void OpenConnection(IDbConnection cn)
{
  // Open the incoming connection for the caller.
  connection.Open();
}
```

■ **Note** Interfaces are not strictly required; you can achieve the same level of abstraction using abstract base classes (such as `DbConnection`) as parameters or return values. However, using interfaces instead of base classes is the generally accepted best practice.

The same holds true for member return values. Create a new .NET Console application named MyConnectionFactory. Add the following NuGet packages to the project (note that the `OleDb` package is valid only on Windows):

`Microsoft.Data.SqlClient`

`System.Data.Common`

`System.Data.Odbc`

`System.Data.OleDb`

Next, add a new file named `DataProviderEnum.cs` and update the code to the following:

```
namespace MyConnectionFactory;
//OleDb is Windows only and is not supported in .NET Core/.NET 5+
enum DataProviderEnum
{
  SqlServer,
#if PC
  OleDb,
#endif
  Odbc,
  None
}
```

If you are using a Windows OS on your development machine, update the project file to define the conditional compiler symbol PC.

```
<PropertyGroup>
  <DefineConstants>PC</DefineConstants>
</PropertyGroup>
```

If you are using Visual Studio, right-click the project, select Properties, and then go to the Build tab to enter the "Conditional compiler symbols" values.

The following code example allows you to obtain a specific connection object based on the value of a custom enumeration. For diagnostic purposes, you simply print the underlying connection object using reflection services.

```
using System.Data;
using System.Data.Odbc;
#if PC
  using System.Data.OleDb;
#endif
using Microsoft.Data.SqlClient;
using MyConnectionFactory;

Console.WriteLine("**** Very Simple Connection Factory *****\n");
Setup(DataProviderEnum.SqlServer);
#if PC
  Setup(DataProviderEnum.OleDb); //Not supported on macOS
#endif
Setup(DataProviderEnum.Odbc);
Setup(DataProviderEnum.None);
Console.ReadLine();

void Setup(DataProviderEnum provider)
{
  // Get a specific connection.
  IDbConnection myConnection = GetConnection(provider);
  Console.WriteLine($"Your connection is a {myConnection?.GetType().Name ?? "unrecognized
  type"}");
  // Open, use and close connection...
}

// This method returns a specific connection object
// based on the value of a DataProvider enum.
IDbConnection GetConnection(DataProviderEnum dataProvider)
  => dataProvider switch
  {
    DataProviderEnum.SqlServer => new SqlConnection(),
#if PC
    //Not supported on macOS
    DataProviderEnum.OleDb => new OleDbConnection(),
#endif
    DataProviderEnum.Odbc => new OdbcConnection(),
    _ => null,
  };
```

The benefit of working with the general interfaces of `System.Data` (or, for that matter, the abstract base classes of `System.Data.Common`) is that you have a much better chance of building a flexible code base that can evolve over time. For example, today you might be building an application that targets Microsoft SQL Server; however, it is possible your company could switch to a different database. If you build a solution that hard-codes the Microsoft SQL Server–specific types of `System.Data.SqlClient`, you will need to edit, recompile, and redeploy the code for the new database provider.

At this point, you have authored some (quite simple) ADO.NET code that allows you to create different types of provider-specific connection objects. However, obtaining a connection object is only one aspect of working with ADO.NET. To make a worthwhile data provider factory library, you would also have to account for command objects, data readers, transaction objects, and other data-centric types. Building such a code library would not necessarily be difficult, but it would require a considerable amount of code and time.

Since the release of .NET 2.0, the kind folks in Redmond have built this exact functionality directly into the .NET base class libraries. This functionality has been significantly updated for .NET Core and .NET 5+.

You will examine this formal API in just a moment; however, first you need to create a custom database to use throughout this chapter (and for many chapters to come).

Setting Up SQL Server and Azure Data Studio

As you work through this chapter, you will execute queries against a simple SQL Server test database named `AutoLot`. In keeping with the automotive theme used throughout this book, this database will contain five interrelated tables (`Inventory`, `Makes`, `Orders`, `Customers`, and `CreditRisks`) that contain various bits of data representing information for a fictional automobile sales company. Before getting into the database details, you must set up SQL Server and a SQL Server IDE.

■ **Note** If you are using a Windows-based development machine and have installed Visual Studio 2022, you also have a special instance of SQL Server Express (called LocalDb) installed, which can be used for all the examples in this book. If you are content to use that version, please skip to the section "Installing a SQL Server IDE."

Installing SQL Server

For this chapter and many of the remaining chapters in this book, you will need to have access to an instance of SQL Server. If you are using a non-Windows-based development machine and do not have an external instance of SQL Server available, or choose not to use an external SQL Server instance, you can run SQL Server inside a Docker container on your Mac- or Linux-based workstation. Docker also works on Windows machines, so you are welcome to run the examples in this book using Docker regardless of your operating system of choice.

■ **Note** Containerization is a large topic, and there just isn't space in this book to get into the deep details of containers or Docker. This book will cover just enough so you can work through the examples.

Installing SQL Server in a Docker Container

Docker Desktop can be downloaded from `www.docker.com/get-started`. Download and install the appropriate version (Windows, Mac, Linux) for your workstation (you will need a free DockerHub user account). Make sure you select Linux containers when prompted.

■ **Note** The container choice (Windows or Linux) is the operating system running inside the container, not the operating system of your workstation.

Pulling the Image and Running SQL Server 2019

Containers are based on images, and each image is a layered set that builds up the final product. To get the image needed to run SQL Server 2019 in a container, open a command window and enter the following command:

```
docker pull mcr.microsoft.com/mssql/server:2019-latest
```

Once you have the image loaded onto your machine, you need to start SQL Server. To do that, enter the following command (all on one line):

```
docker run -e "ACCEPT_EULA=Y" -e "SA_PASSWORD=P@ssw0rd" -p 5433:1433 --name AutoLot -h
AutoLotHost -d mcr.microsoft.com/mssql/server:2019-latest
```

The previous command accepts the end user license agreement, sets the password (in real life, you need to use a strong password), sets the port mapping (port 5433 on your machine maps to the default port for SQL Server, which is 1433) in the container, names the container (AutoLot), names the host (AutoLotHost), and finally informs Docker to use the previously downloaded image.

■ **Note** These are not settings you want to use for real development. For information on changing the SA password and to see a tutorial, go to https://docs.microsoft.com/en-us/sql/linux/quickstart-install-connect-docker?view=sql-server-ver15&pivots=cs1-cmd.

To confirm that it is running, enter the command docker ps -a in your command prompt. You will see output like the following (some columns omitted for brevity):

```
C:\Users\japik>docker ps -a
CONTAINER ID IMAGE                                      PORTS                    NAMES
347475cfb823 mcr.microsoft.com/mssql/server:2019-latest 0.0.0.0:5433->1433/tcp   AutoLot
```

To stop the container, enter docker stop 34747, where the numbers 34747 are the first five characters of the container ID. To restart the container, enter docker start 34747, again updating the command with the beginning of your container's ID.

■ **Note** You can also use the container's name (AutoLot in this example) with the Docker CLI commands, for example, docker start AutoLot. Be aware that the Docker commands, regardless of operating system, are case sensitive.

If you want to use the Docker Dashboard, right-click the Docker ship (in your system tray) and select Dashboard, and you should see the image running on port 5433. Hover over the image name with your mouse, and you will see the commands to stop, start, and delete (among others), as shown in Figure 20-2.

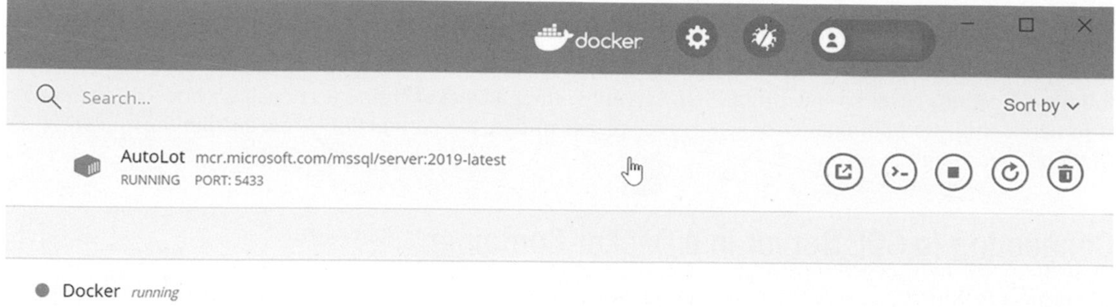

Figure 20-2. Docker Dashboard

■ **Note** To connect to SQL Server with an encrypted connection, there must be a certificate installed on the host. Follow the instructions in the docs to install a certificate in your Docker container and enable secure connections: `https://docs.microsoft.com/en-us/sql/linux/sql-server-linux-docker-container-security?view=sql-server-ver15`. For this book, we will use an unencrypted connection to SQL Server, which should not be used in real development.

Installing SQL Server 2019

A special instance of SQL Server named LocalDb is installed with Visual Studio 2022. If you choose not to use SQL Server Express LocalDB or Docker and you are using a Windows machine, you need to install SQL Server 2019 Developer Edition. SQL Server 2019 Developer Edition is free and can be downloaded from here:

```
https://www.microsoft.com/en-us/sql-server/sql-server-downloads
```

If you have another edition, you can use that instance with this book as well; you will just need to change your connection string to match your installed instance.

Installing a SQL Server IDE

Azure Data Studio is a new IDE for use with SQL Server. It is free and cross-platform, so it will work on Windows, Mac, or Linux. It can be downloaded from here:

```
https://docs.microsoft.com/en-us/sql/azure-data-studio/download-azure-data-studio
```

■ **Note** If you are using a Windows machine and prefer to use SQL Server Management Studio (SSMS), you can download the latest copy from here: `https://docs.microsoft.com/en-us/sql/ssms/download-sql-server-management-studio-ssms`.

Connecting to SQL Server

Once you have Azure Data Studio or SSMS installed, it is time to connect to your database instance. The following sections cover connecting to SQL Server in either a Docker container or using a LocalDb instance. If you are using another instance of SQL Server, please update the connection string used in the following sections accordingly.

Connecting to SQL Server in a Docker Container

To connect to your SQL Server instance running in a Docker container, first make sure it is up and running. Next, click "Create a connection" in Azure Data Studio, as shown in Figure 20-3.

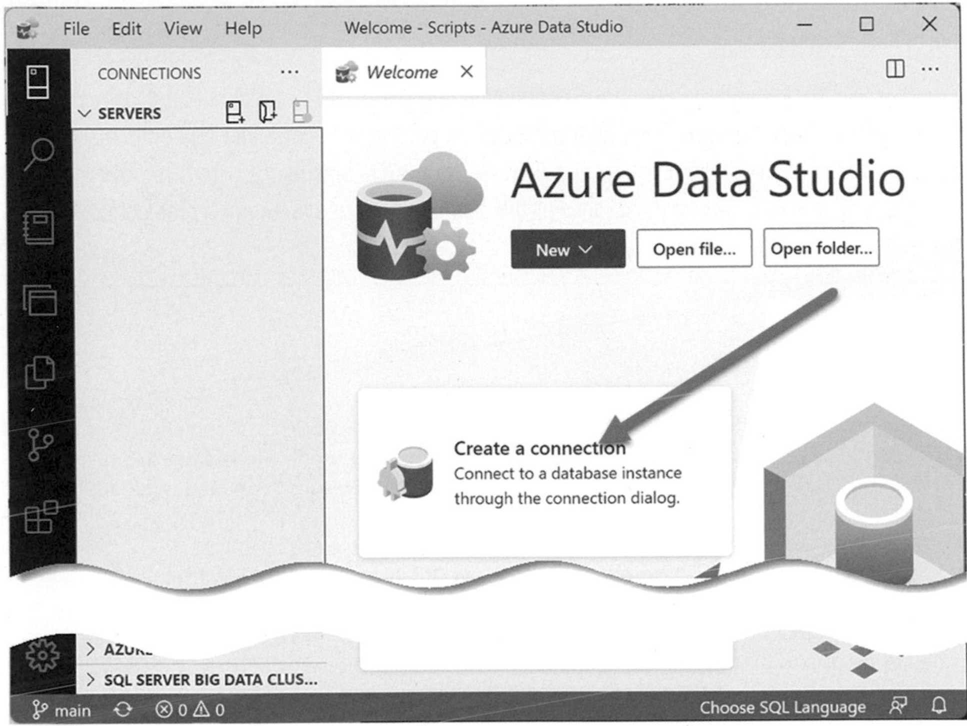

Figure 20-3. *Creating a connection in Azure Data Studio*

In the Connection Details dialog, enter **.,5433** for the Server value. The dot indicates the current host, and 5433 is the port that you indicated when creating the SQL Server instance in the Docker container. The host and the port must be separated by a comma. Enter **sa** for the username; the password is the same one that you entered when creating the SQL Server instance. The name is optional but allows you to quickly select this connection in subsequent Azure Data Studio sessions. Figure 20-4 shows these connection options.

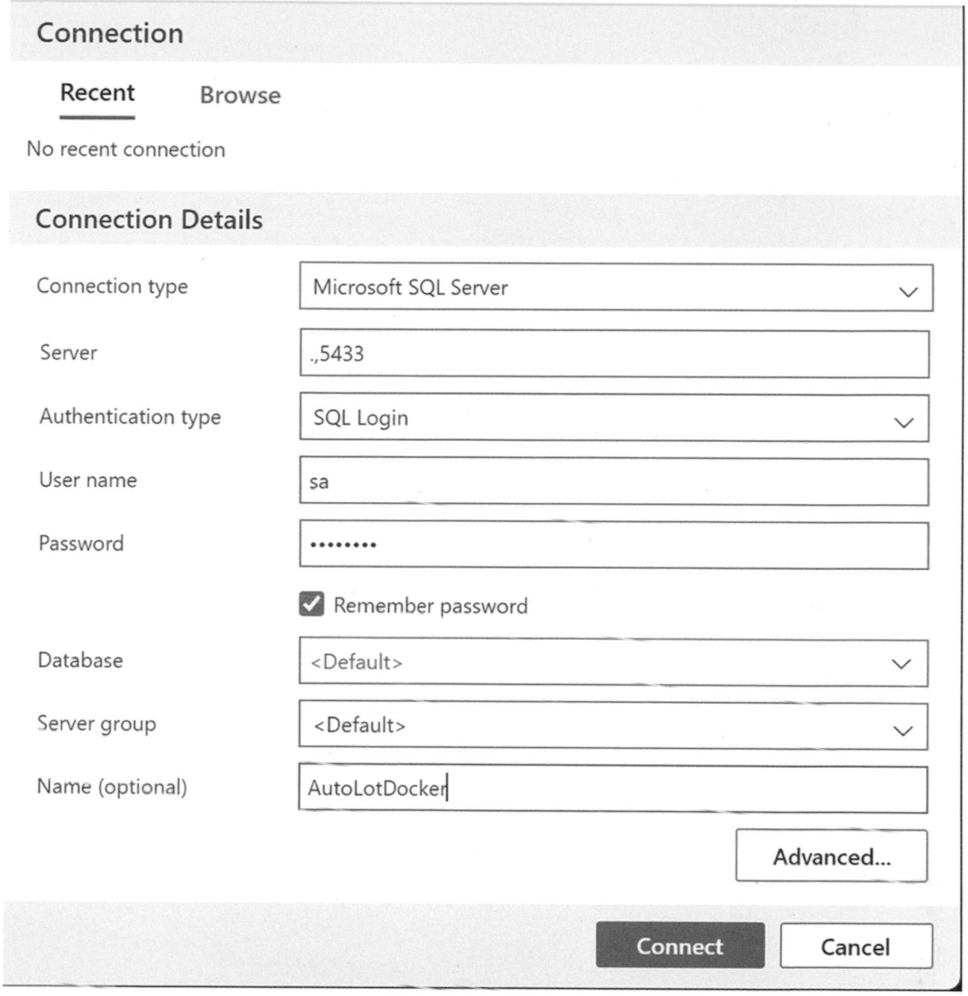

Connection

Recent Browse

No recent connection

Connection Details

Connection type Microsoft SQL Server

Server .,5433

Authentication type SQL Login

User name sa

Password ••••••••

Remember password

Database <Default>

Server group <Default>

Name (optional) AutoLotDocker

Advanced...

Connect Cancel

Figure 20-4. *Setting the connection options for Docker SQL Server*

Connecting to SQL Server LocalDb

To connect to the Visual Studio–installed version of SQL Server Express LocalDb, update the connection information to match what is shown in Figure 20-5.

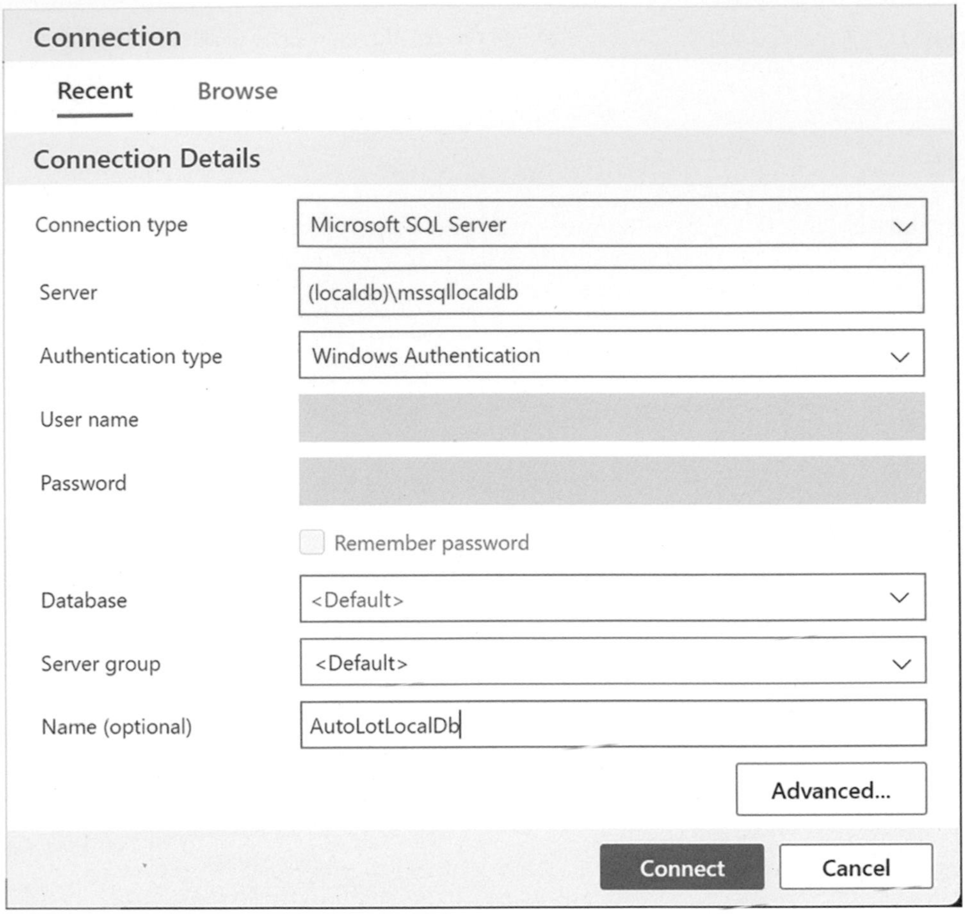

Connection

Recent Browse

Connection Details

Connection type: Microsoft SQL Server

Server: (localdb)\mssqllocaldb

Authentication type: Windows Authentication

User name

Password

Remember password

Database: <Default>

Server group: <Default>

Name (optional): AutoLotLocalDb

Advanced...

Connect Cancel

Figure 20-5. *Setting the connection options for SQL Server LocalDb*

When connecting to LocalDb, you can use Windows Authentication, since the instance is running on the same machine as Azure Data Studio and the same security context as the currently logged in user.

Connecting to Any Other SQL Server Instance

If you are connecting to any other SQL Server instance, update the connection properties accordingly.

Restoring the AutoLot Database Backup

Instead of building the database from scratch, you can use either SSMS or Azure Data Studio to restore one of the supplied backups contained in the chapter's files in the repository. There are two backups supplied: the one named `AutoLotWindows.ba_` is designed for use on a Windows machine (LocalDb, Windows Server, etc.), and the one named `AutoLotDocker.ba_` is designed for use in a Docker container.

■ **Note** Git by default ignores files with a bak extension. You will need to rename the extension from ba_ to bak before restoring the database.

Copying the Backup File to Your Container

If you are using SQL Server in a Docker container, you first must copy the backup file to the container. Fortunately, the Docker CLI provides a mechanism for working with a container's file system. First, create a new directory for the backup using the following command in a command window on your host machine:

```
docker exec -it AutoLot mkdir var/opt/mssql/backup
```

The path structure must match the container's operating system (in this case Ubuntu), even if your host machine is Windows based. Next, copy the backup to your new directory using the following command (updating the location of AutoLotDocker.bak to your local machine's relative or absolute path):

```
[Windows]
docker cp .\AutoLotDocker.bak AutoLot:var/opt/mssql/backup

[Non-Windows]
docker cp ./AutoLotDocker.bak AutoLot:var/opt/mssql/backup
```

Note that the source directory structure matches the host machine (in my example, Windows), while the target is the container name and then the directory path (in the target OS format).

Restoring the Database with SSMS

To restore the database using SSMS, right-click the Databases node in Object Explorer. Select Restore Database. Select Device and click the ellipses. This will open the Select Backup Device dialog.

Restoring the Database to SQL Server (Docker)

Keep "Backup media type" set to File, and then click Add, navigate to the AutoLotDocker.bak file in the container, and click OK. When you are back on the main restore screen, click OK, as shown in Figure 20-6.

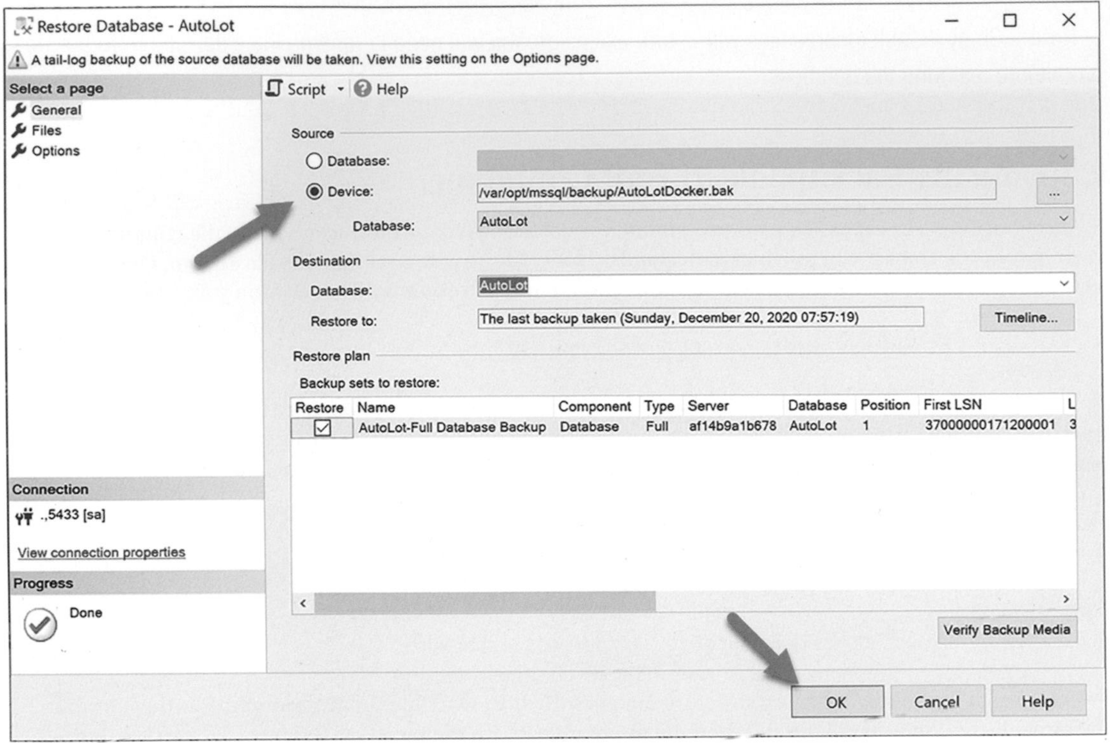

Figure 20-6. *Restoring the database with SSMS*

Restoring the Database to SQL Server (Windows)

Keep "Backup media type" set to File, and then click Add, navigate to `AutoLotWindows.bak`, and click OK. When you are back on the main restore screen, click OK, as shown in Figure 20-7.

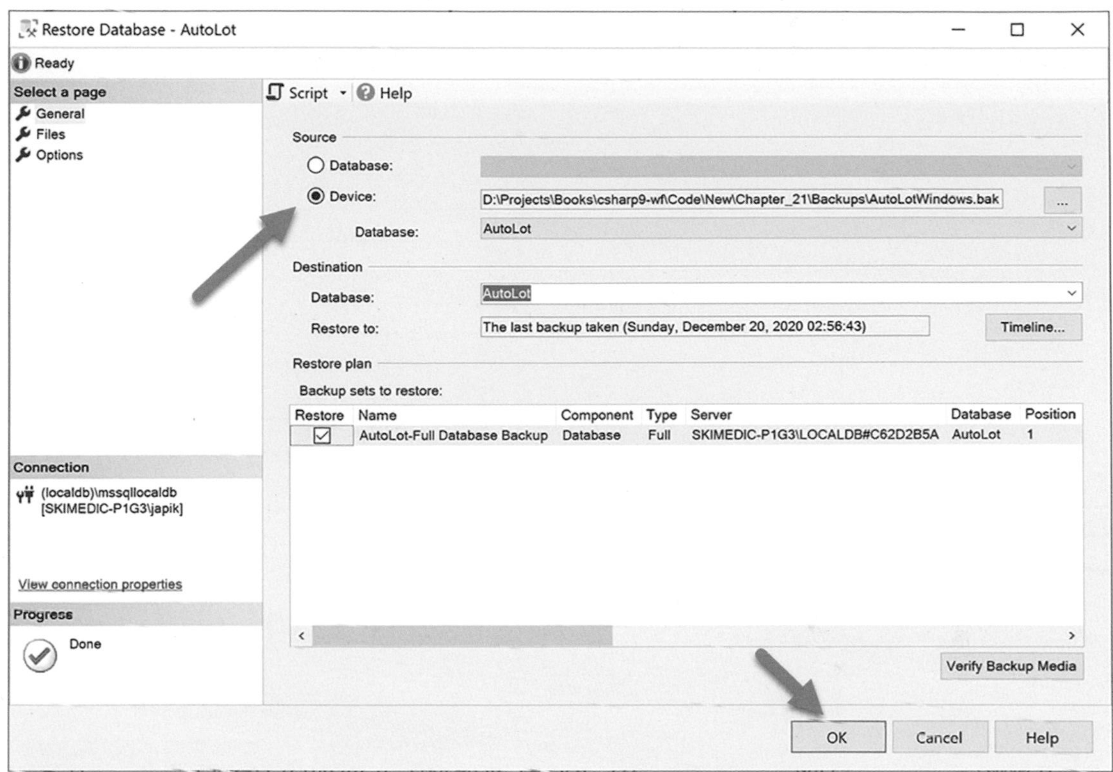

Figure 20-7. *Restoring the database with SSMS*

Restoring the Database with Azure Data Studio

To restore the database using Azure Data Studio, click View, select the Command Palette (or press Ctrl+Shift+P), and select Restore. Select "Backup file" as the "Restore from" option and then the file you just copied. The target database and related fields will be filled in for you, as shown in Figure 20-8.

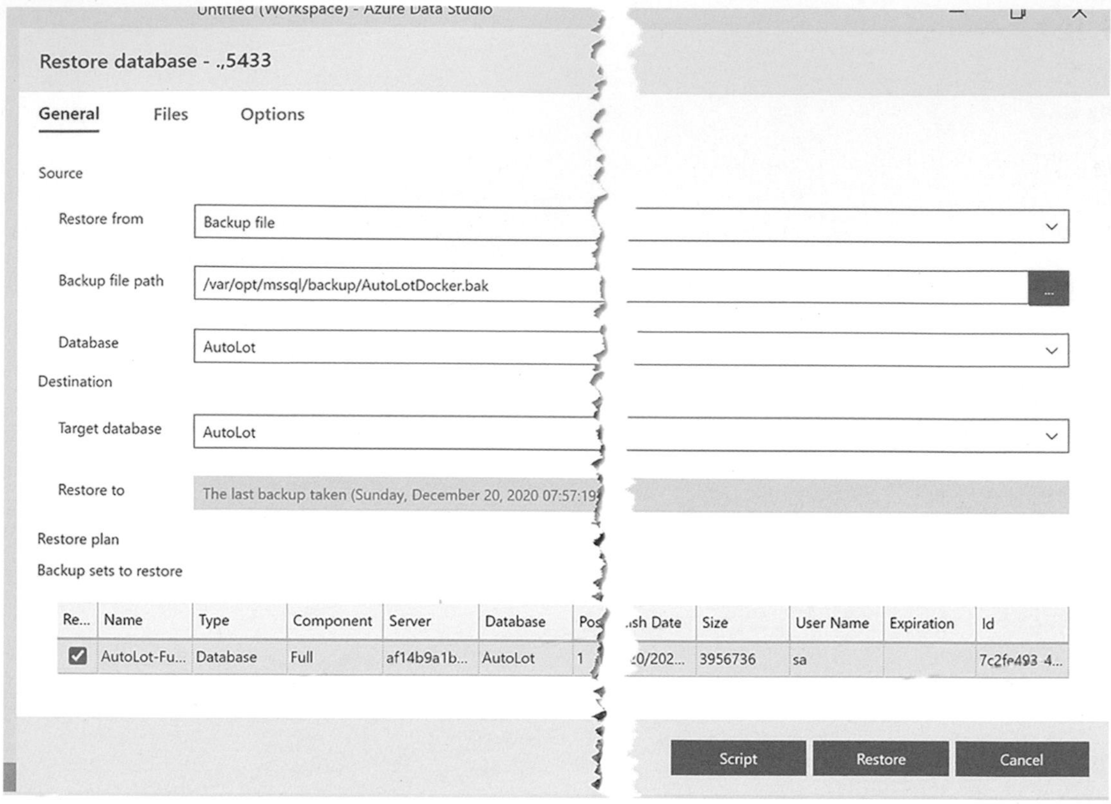

Figure 20-8. *Restoring the database to Docker using Azure Data Studio*

■ **Note** The process is the same to restore the Windows version of the backup using Azure Data Studio. Simply adjust the filename and paths.

Creating the AutoLot Database

This entire section is devoted to creating the `AutoLot` database using Azure Data Studio (or SQL Server Management Studio). If you restored the backup, you can skip ahead to the section "The ADO.NET Data Provider Factory Model."

■ **Note** All of the script files are located in a folder named `Scripts` along with this chapter's code in the Git repository.

Creating the Database

To create the AutoLot database, connect to your database server using Azure Data Studio. Open a new query by selecting File ➤ New Query (or by pressing Ctrl+N) and entering the following command text:

```
USE [master]
GO
CREATE DATABASE [AutoLot]
GO
ALTER DATABASE [AutoLot] SET RECOVERY SIMPLE
GO
```

Besides changing the recovery mode to simple, this creates the AutoLot database using the SQL Server defaults. Click Run (or press F5) to create the database.

Creating the Tables

The AutoLot database contains five tables: Inventory, Makes, Customers, Orders, and CreditRisks.

Creating the Inventory Table

With the database created, it is time to create the tables. First up is the Inventory table. Open a new query and enter the following SQL:

```
USE [AutoLot]
GO
CREATE TABLE [dbo].[Inventory](
    [Id] [int] IDENTITY(1,1) NOT NULL,
    [MakeId] [int] NOT NULL,
    [Color] [nvarchar](50) NOT NULL,
    [PetName] [nvarchar](50) NOT NULL,
    [TimeStamp] [timestamp] NULL,
 CONSTRAINT [PK_Inventory] PRIMARY KEY CLUSTERED
(
  [Id] ASC
) ON [PRIMARY]
) ON [PRIMARY]
GO
```

Click Run (or press F5) to create the table.

■ **Note** If you are not familiar with the SQL Server TimeStamp data type (that maps to a byte[] in C#), don't worry about it at this time. Just know that it is used for row-level concurrency checking and will be covered with Entity Framework Core.

Creating the Makes Table

The Inventory table stores a foreign key to the (not yet created) Makes table. Create a new query and enter the following SQL to create the Makes table:

```
USE [AutoLot]
GO
CREATE TABLE [dbo].[Makes](
  [Id] [int] IDENTITY(1,1) NOT NULL,
  [Name] [nvarchar](50) NOT NULL,
  [TimeStamp] [timestamp] NULL,
 CONSTRAINT [PK_Makes] PRIMARY KEY CLUSTERED
(
  [Id] ASC
) ON [PRIMARY]
) ON [PRIMARY]
GO
```

Click Run (or press F5) to create the table.

Creating the Customers Table

The Customers table (as the name suggests) will contain a list of customers. Create a new query and enter the following SQL commands:

```
USE [AutoLot]
GO
CREATE TABLE [dbo].[Customers](
  [Id] [int] IDENTITY(1,1) NOT NULL,
  [FirstName] [nvarchar](50) NOT NULL,
  [LastName] [nvarchar](50) NOT NULL,
  [TimeStamp] [timestamp] NULL,
 CONSTRAINT [PK_Customers] PRIMARY KEY CLUSTERED
(
  [Id] ASC
) ON [PRIMARY]
) ON [PRIMARY]
GO
```

Click Run (or press F5) to create the Customers table.

Creating the Orders Table

You will use the next table, Orders, to represent the automobile a given customer has ordered. Create a new query, enter the following code, and click Run (or press F5):

```
USE [AutoLot]
GO
CREATE TABLE [dbo].[Orders](
  [Id] [int] IDENTITY(1,1) NOT NULL,
  [CustomerId] [int] NOT NULL,
```

```
  [CarId] [int] NOT NULL,
  [TimeStamp] [timestamp] NULL,
 CONSTRAINT [PK_Orders] PRIMARY KEY CLUSTERED
(
  [Id] ASC
) ON [PRIMARY]
) ON [PRIMARY]
GO
```

Creating the CreditRisks Table

You will use your final table, CreditRisks, to represent the customers who are considered a credit risk. Create a new query, enter the following code, and click Run (or press F5):

```
USE [AutoLot]
GO
CREATE TABLE [dbo].[CreditRisks](
  [Id] [int] IDENTITY(1,1) NOT NULL,
  [FirstName] [nvarchar](50) NOT NULL,
  [LastName] [nvarchar](50) NOT NULL,
  [CustomerId] [int] NOT NULL,
  [TimeStamp] [timestamp] NULL,
 CONSTRAINT [PK_CreditRisks] PRIMARY KEY CLUSTERED
(
    [Id] ASC
) ON [PRIMARY]
) ON [PRIMARY]
GO
```

Creating the Table Relationships

This section will add the foreign key relationships between the interrelated tables.

Creating the Inventory to Makes Relationship

Open a new query, enter the following SQL, and click Run (or press F5):

```
USE [AutoLot]
GO
CREATE NONCLUSTERED INDEX [IX_Inventory_MakeId] ON [dbo].[Inventory]
(
  [MakeId] ASC
) ON [PRIMARY]
GO
ALTER TABLE [dbo].[Inventory]  WITH CHECK ADD  CONSTRAINT [FK_Make_Inventory] FOREIGN
KEY([MakeId])
REFERENCES [dbo].[Makes] ([Id])
GO
ALTER TABLE [dbo].[Inventory] CHECK CONSTRAINT [FK_Make_Inventory]
GO
```

Creating the Inventory to Orders Relationship

Open a new query, enter the following SQL, and click Run (or press F5):

```
USE [AutoLot]
GO
CREATE NONCLUSTERED INDEX [IX_Orders_CarId] ON [dbo].[Orders]
(
  [CarId] ASC
) ON [PRIMARY]
GO
ALTER TABLE [dbo].[Orders]  WITH CHECK ADD  CONSTRAINT [FK_Orders_Inventory] FOREIGN
KEY([CarId])
REFERENCES [dbo].[Inventory] ([Id])
GO
ALTER TABLE [dbo].[Orders] CHECK CONSTRAINT [FK_Orders_Inventory]
GO
```

Creating the Orders to Customers Relationship

Open a new query, enter the following SQL, and click Run (or press F5):

```
USE [AutoLot]
GO
CREATE UNIQUE NONCLUSTERED INDEX [IX_Orders_CustomerId_CarId] ON [dbo].[Orders]
(
  [CustomerId] ASC,
  [CarId] ASC
) ON [PRIMARY]
GO
ALTER TABLE [dbo].[Orders]  WITH CHECK ADD  CONSTRAINT [FK_Orders_Customers] FOREIGN
KEY([CustomerId])
REFERENCES [dbo].[Customers] ([Id])
ON DELETE CASCADE
GO
ALTER TABLE [dbo].[Orders] CHECK CONSTRAINT [FK_Orders_Customers]
GO
```

Creating the Customers to CreditRisks Relationship

Open a new query, enter the following SQL, and click Run (or press F5):

```
USE [AutoLot]
GO
CREATE NONCLUSTERED INDEX [IX_CreditRisks_CustomerId] ON [dbo].[CreditRisks]
(
  [CustomerId] ASC
) ON [PRIMARY]
GO
```

```
ALTER TABLE [dbo].[CreditRisks]  WITH CHECK ADD  CONSTRAINT [FK_CreditRisks_Customers]
FOREIGN KEY([CustomerId])
REFERENCES [dbo].[Customers] ([Id])
ON DELETE CASCADE
GO
ALTER TABLE [dbo].[CreditRisks] CHECK CONSTRAINT [FK_CreditRisks_Customers]
GO
```

■ **Note** If you are wondering why there are columns for `FirstName` and `LastName` *and* a relationship to the customer table, it's merely for demo purposes. I could think up a creative reason for it, but at the end of the day, they are used in later examples in the book.

Creating the GetPetName() Stored Procedure

Later in this chapter, you will learn how to use ADO.NET to invoke stored procedures. As you might already know, stored procedures are code routines stored within a database that do something. Like C# methods, stored procedures can return data or just operate on data without returning anything. You will add a single stored procedure that will return an automobile's pet name, based on the supplied `carId`. To do so, create a new query window and enter the following SQL command:

```
USE [AutoLot]
GO
CREATE PROCEDURE [dbo].[GetPetName]
@carID int,
@petName nvarchar(50) output
AS
SELECT @petName = PetName from dbo.Inventory where Id = @carID
GO
```

Click Run (or press F5) to create the stored procedure.

Adding Test Records

Databases are rather boring without data, and it is a good idea to have scripts that can quickly load test records into the database.

Makes Records

Create a new query and execute the following SQL statements to add records into the `Makes` table:

```
USE [AutoLot]
GO
SET IDENTITY_INSERT [dbo].[Makes] ON
INSERT INTO [dbo].[Makes] ([Id], [Name]) VALUES (1, N'VW')
INSERT INTO [dbo].[Makes] ([Id], [Name]) VALUES (2, N'Ford')
INSERT INTO [dbo].[Makes] ([Id], [Name]) VALUES (3, N'Saab')
INSERT INTO [dbo].[Makes] ([Id], [Name]) VALUES (4, N'Yugo')
```

```
INSERT INTO [dbo].[Makes] ([Id], [Name]) VALUES (5, N'BMW')
INSERT INTO [dbo].[Makes] ([Id], [Name]) VALUES (6, N'Pinto')
SET IDENTITY_INSERT [dbo].[Makes] OFF
```

Inventory Table Records

To add records to your first table, create a new query and execute the following SQL statements to add records into the Inventory table:

```
USE [AutoLot]
GO
SET IDENTITY_INSERT [dbo].[Inventory] ON
GO
INSERT INTO [dbo].[Inventory] ([Id], [MakeId], [Color], [PetName]) VALUES (1, 1, N'Black',
N'Zippy')
INSERT INTO [dbo].[Inventory] ([Id], [MakeId], [Color], [PetName]) VALUES (2, 2, N'Rust',
N'Rusty')
INSERT INTO [dbo].[Inventory] ([Id], [MakeId], [Color], [PetName]) VALUES (3, 3,
N'Black', N'Mel')
INSERT INTO [dbo].[Inventory] ([Id], [MakeId], [Color], [PetName]) VALUES (4, 4, N'Yellow',
N'Clunker')
INSERT INTO [dbo].[Inventory] ([Id], [MakeId], [Color], [PetName]) VALUES (5, 5, N'Black',
N'Bimmer')
INSERT INTO [dbo].[Inventory] ([Id], [MakeId], [Color], [PetName]) VALUES (6, 5, N'Green',
N'Hank')
INSERT INTO [dbo].[Inventory] ([Id], [MakeId], [Color], [PetName]) VALUES (7, 5, N'Pink',
N'Pinky')
INSERT INTO [dbo].[Inventory] ([Id], [MakeId], [Color], [PetName]) VALUES (8, 6, N'Black',
N'Pete')
INSERT INTO [dbo].[Inventory] ([Id], [MakeId], [Color], [PetName]) VALUES (9, 4, N'Brown',
N'Brownie')SET IDENTITY_INSERT [dbo].[Inventory] OFF
GO
```

Customer Records

To add records to the Customers table, create a new query and execute the following SQL statements:

```
USE [AutoLot]
GO
SET IDENTITY_INSERT [dbo].[Customers] ON
INSERT INTO [dbo].[Customers] ([Id], [FirstName], [LastName]) VALUES (1, N'Dave',
N'Brenner')
INSERT INTO [dbo].[Customers] ([Id], [FirstName], [LastName]) VALUES (2, N'Matt', N'Walton')
INSERT INTO [dbo].[Customers] ([Id], [FirstName], [LastName]) VALUES (3, N'Steve', N'Hagen')
INSERT INTO [dbo].[Customers] ([Id], [FirstName], [LastName]) VALUES (4, N'Pat', N'Walton')
INSERT INTO [dbo].[Customers] ([Id], [FirstName], [LastName]) VALUES (5, N'Bad',
N'Customer')
SET IDENTITY_INSERT [dbo].[Customers] OFF
```

Order Records

Now add data to your Orders table. Create a new query, enter the following SQL, and click Run (or press F5):

```
USE [AutoLot]
GO
SET IDENTITY_INSERT [dbo].[Orders] ON
INSERT INTO [dbo].[Orders] ([Id], [CustomerId], [CarId]) VALUES (1, 1, 5)
INSERT INTO [dbo].[Orders] ([Id], [CustomerId], [CarId]) VALUES (2, 2, 1)
INSERT INTO [dbo].[Orders] ([Id], [CustomerId], [CarId]) VALUES (3, 3, 4)
INSERT INTO [dbo].[Orders] ([Id], [CustomerId], [CarId]) VALUES (4, 4, 7)
SET IDENTITY_INSERT [dbo].[Orders] OFF
```

CreditRisk Records

The final step is to add data to the CreditRisks table. Create a new query, enter the following SQL, and click Run (or press F5):

```
USE [AutoLot]
GO
SET IDENTITY_INSERT [dbo].[CreditRisks] ON
INSERT INTO [dbo].[CreditRisks] ([Id], [FirstName], [LastName], [CustomerId]) VALUES (1,
N'Bad', N'Customer', 5)
SET IDENTITY_INSERT [dbo].[CreditRisks] OFF
```

With this, the AutoLot database is complete! Of course, this is a far cry from a real-world application database, but it will serve your needs for this chapter and will be added to in the Entity Framework Core chapters. Now that you have a database to test with, you can dive into the details of the ADO.NET data provider factory model.

The ADO.NET Data Provider Factory Model

The .NET data provider factory pattern allows you to build a single code base using generalized data access types. To understand the data provider factory implementation, recall from Table 20-1 that the classes within a data provider all derive from the same base classes defined within the System.Data.Common namespace.

- DbCommand: The abstract base class for all command classes
- DbConnection: The abstract base class for all connection classes
- DbDataAdapter: The abstract base class for all data adapter classes
- DbDataReader: The abstract base class for all data reader classes
- DbParameter: The abstract base class for all parameter classes
- DbTransaction: The abstract base class for all transaction classes

Each of the .NET-compliant data providers contains a class type that derives from System.Data.Common.DbProviderFactory. This base class defines several methods that retrieve provider-specific data objects. Here are the members of DbProviderFactory:

```
public abstract class DbProviderFactory
{
..public virtual bool CanCreateDataAdapter { get;};
..public virtual bool CanCreateCommandBuilder { get;};
  public virtual DbCommand CreateCommand();
  public virtual DbCommandBuilder CreateCommandBuilder();
  public virtual DbConnection CreateConnection();
  public virtual DbConnectionStringBuilder
    CreateConnectionStringBuilder();
  public virtual DbDataAdapter CreateDataAdapter();
  public virtual DbParameter CreateParameter();
  public virtual DbDataSourceEnumerator
    CreateDataSourceEnumerator();
}
```

To obtain the DbProviderFactory-derived type for your data provider, each provider provides a static property used to return the correct type. To return the SQL Server version of the DbProviderFactory, use the following code:

```
// Get the factory for the SQL data provider.
DbProviderFactory sqlFactory =
  Microsoft.Data.SqlClient.SqlClientFactory.Instance;
```

To make the program more versatile, you can create a DbProviderFactory factory that returns a specific flavor of a DbProviderFactory based on a setting in the appsettings.json file for the application. You will learn how to do this shortly; for the moment, you can obtain the associated provider-specific data objects (e.g., connections, commands, and data readers) once you have obtained the factory for your data provider.

A Complete Data Provider Factory Example

For a complete example, create a new C# Console Application project (named DataProviderFactory) that prints out the automobile inventory of the AutoLot database. For this initial example, you will hard-code the data access logic directly within the console application (to keep things simple). As you progress through this chapter, you will see better ways to do this.

Add the Microsoft.Extensions.Configuration.Json, System.Data.Common, System.Data.Odbc, System.Data.OleDb, and Microsoft.Data.SqlClient packages to the project. Next, define the PC compiler constant (if you are using a Windows OS).

```
<PropertyGroup>
  <DefineConstants>PC</DefineConstants>
</PropertyGroup>
```

Next, add a new file named DataProviderEnum.cs and update the code to the following:

```
namespace DataProviderFactory;
//OleDb is Windows only
enum DataProviderEnum
{
```

```
  SqlServer,
#if PC
  OleDb,
#endif
  Odbc
}
```

Add a new JSON file named appsettings.json to the project and update its contents to the following (update the connection strings based on your specific environment):

```
{
  "ProviderName": "SqlServer",
  //"ProviderName": "OleDb",
  //"ProviderName": "Odbc",
  "SqlServer": {
    // for localdb use @"Data Source=(localdb)\mssqllocaldb;Integrated Security=true;
    Initial Catalog=AutoLot"
    "ConnectionString": "Data Source=.,5433;User Id=sa;Password=P@ssw0rd;Initial Catalog=Aut
    oLot;Encrypt=False;"
  },
  "Odbc": {
    // for localdb use @"Driver={ODBC Driver 17 for SQL Server};Server=(localdb)\mssqllocald
    b;Database=AutoLot;Trusted_Connection=Yes";
    "ConnectionString": "Driver={ODBC Driver 17 for SQL Server};Server=localhost,5433;
    Database=AutoLot;UId=sa;Pwd=P@ssw0rd;Encrypt=False;"
  },
  "OleDb": {
    // if localdb use @"Provider=SQLNCLI11;Data Source=(localdb)\mssqllocaldb;Initial
    Catalog=AutoLot;Integrated Security=SSPI"),
    "ConnectionString": "Provider=SQLNCLI11;Data Source=.,5433;User Id=sa;Password=P@ssw0rd;
    Initial Catalog=AutoLot;Encrypt=False;"
  }
}
```

■ **Note** When using SQL Server in a Docker container that does not have a certificate installed, the connection string must be unencrypted, which is why we have the `Encrypt=False;` setting in the Docker connection strings. For real-world applications, do not use this setting; instead, make sure the container (or your SQL Server instance) has a certificate, and use `Encrypt=True;` instead.

Configure MSBuild to copy the JSON settings file to the output directory on every build. Update the project file by adding the following:

```
<ItemGroup>
  <None Update="appsettings.json">
    <CopyToOutputDirectory>Always</CopyToOutputDirectory>
  </None>
</ItemGroup>
```

■ **Note** The `CopyToOutputDirectory` is whitespace sensitive. Make sure it is all on one line without any spaces around the word *Always*.

Now that you have a proper `appsettings.json`, you can read in the provider and `connectionString` values using .NET configuration. Start by clearing out all the code in the file and adding the following `using` statements at the top of the `Program.cs` file:

```
using System.Data.Common;
using System.Data.Odbc;
#if PC
  using System.Data.OleDb;
#endif
using Microsoft.Data.SqlClient;
using Microsoft.Extensions.Configuration;
using DataProviderFactory;
```

Add the following code to the `Program.cs` file:

```
Console.WriteLine("***** Fun with Data Provider Factories *****\n");
var (provider, connectionString) = GetProviderFromConfiguration();
DbProviderFactory factory = GetDbProviderFactory(provider);
// Now get the connection object.
using (DbConnection connection = factory.CreateConnection())
{
  Console.WriteLine($"Your connection object is a: {connection.GetType().Name}");
  connection.ConnectionString = connectionString;
  connection.Open();

  // Make command object.
  DbCommand command = factory.CreateCommand();
  Console.WriteLine($"Your command object is a: {command.GetType().Name}");
  command.Connection = connection;
  command.CommandText =
    "Select i.Id, m.Name From Inventory i inner join Makes m on m.Id = i.MakeId ";

  // Print out data with data reader.
  using (DbDataReader dataReader = command.ExecuteReader())
  {
    Console.WriteLine($"Your data reader object is a: {dataReader.GetType().Name}");
    Console.WriteLine("\n***** Current Inventory *****");
    while (dataReader.Read())
    {
      Console.WriteLine($"-> Car #{dataReader["Id"]} is a {dataReader["Name"]}.");
    }
  }
}
Console.ReadLine();
```

Next, add the following code to the end of the Program.cs file. These methods read the configuration, set the DataProviderEnum to the correct value, get the connection string, and return an instance of the DbProviderFactory:

```
static DbProviderFactory GetDbProviderFactory(DataProviderEnum provider)
  => provider switch
{
  DataProviderEnum.SqlServer => SqlClientFactory.Instance,
  DataProviderEnum.Odbc => OdbcFactory.Instance,
#if PC
  DataProviderEnum.OleDb => OleDbFactory.Instance,
#endif
  _ => null
};

static (DataProviderEnum Provider, string ConnectionString)
  GetProviderFromConfiguration()
{
  IConfiguration config = new ConfigurationBuilder()
    .SetBasePath(Directory.GetCurrentDirectory())
    .AddJsonFile("appsettings.json", true, true)
    .Build();
  var providerName = config["ProviderName"];
  if (Enum.TryParse<DataProviderEnum>
    (providerName, out DataProviderEnum provider))
  {
    return (provider,config[$"{providerName}:ConnectionString"]);
  };
  throw new Exception("Invalid data provider value supplied.");
}
```

Notice that, for diagnostic purposes, you use reflection services to print the name of the underlying connection, command, and data reader. If you run this application, you will find the following current data in the Inventory table of the AutoLot database printed to the console:

```
***** Fun with Data Provider Factories *****
Your connection object is a: SqlConnection
Your command object is a: SqlCommand
Your data reader object is a: SqlDataReader

***** Current Inventory *****
-> Car #1 is a VW.
-> Car #2 is a Ford.
-> Car #3 is a Saab.
-> Car #4 is a Yugo.
-> Car #9 is a Yugo.
-> Car #5 is a BMW.
-> Car #6 is a BMW.
-> Car #7 is a BMW.
-> Car #8 is a Pinto.
```

Now change the settings file to specify a different provider. The code will pick up the related connection string and produce the same output as before, except for the type-specific information.

Of course, based on your experience with ADO.NET, you might be a bit unsure exactly what the connection, command, and data reader objects actually *do*. Do not sweat the details for the time being (quite a few pages remain in this chapter, after all!). At this point, it is enough to know that you can use the ADO.NET data provider factory model to build a single code base that can consume various data providers in a declarative manner.

A Potential Drawback with the Data Provider Factory Model

Although this is a powerful model, you must make sure that the code base uses only types and methods common to all providers through the members of the abstract base classes. Therefore, when authoring your code base, you are limited to the members exposed by DbConnection, DbCommand, and the other types of the System.Data.Common namespace.

Given this, you might find that this generalized approach prevents you from directly accessing some of the bells and whistles of a particular DBMS. If you must be able to invoke specific members of the underlying provider (e.g., SqlConnection), you can do so using an explicit cast, as in this example:

```
if (connection is SqlConnection sqlConnection)
{
  // Print out which version of SQL Server is used.
  WriteLine(sqlConnection.ServerVersion);
}
```

When doing this, however, your code base becomes a bit harder to maintain (and less flexible) because you must add a number of runtime checks. Nevertheless, if you need to build ADO.NET data access libraries in the most flexible way possible, the data provider factory model provides a great mechanism for doing so.

■ **Note** Entity Framework Core and its support for dependency injection greatly simplifies building data access libraries that need to access disparate data sources.

With this first example behind you, you can now dive into the details of working with ADO.NET.

Diving Deeper into Connections, Commands, and DataReaders

As shown in the previous example, ADO.NET allows you to interact with a database using the connection, command, and data reader objects of your data provider. Now you will create an expanded example to get a deeper understanding of these objects in ADO.NET.

In the previous example demonstrated, you need to perform the following steps when you want to connect to a database and read the records using a data reader object:

1. Allocate, configure, and open your connection object.
2. Allocate and configure a command object, specifying the connection object as a constructor argument or with the Connection property.
3. Call ExecuteReader() on the configured command class.
4. Process each record using the Read() method of the data reader.

To get the ball rolling, create a new Console Application project named AutoLot.DataReader and add the `Microsoft.Data.SqlClient` package. Here is the complete code within the `Program.cs` file (analysis will follow):

```
using Microsoft.Data.SqlClient;

Console.WriteLine("***** Fun with Data Readers *****\n");

// Create and open a connection.
using (SqlConnection connection = new SqlConnection())
{
  connection.ConnectionString =
    @" Data Source=.,5433;User Id=sa;Password=P@ssw0rd;Initial Catalog=AutoLot;Encryp
    t=False;";
    connection.Open();
   // Create a SQL command object.
  string sql =
    @"Select i.id, m.Name as Make, i.Color, i.Petname
          FROM Inventory i
          INNER JOIN Makes m on m.Id = i.MakeId";
  SqlCommand myCommand = new SqlCommand(sql, connection);

  // Obtain a data reader a la ExecuteReader().
  using (SqlDataReader myDataReader = myCommand.ExecuteReader())
  {
    // Loop over the results.
    while (myDataReader.Read())
    {
      Console.WriteLine($"-> Make: {myDataReader["Make"]}, PetName: {myDataReader
      ["PetName"]}, Color: {myDataReader["Color"]}.");
    }
  }
}
Console.ReadLine();
```

Working with Connection Objects

The first step to take when working with a data provider is to establish a session with the data source using the connection object (which, as you recall, derives from `DbConnection`). .NET connection objects are provided with a formatted *connection string*; this string contains a number of name-value pairs, separated by semicolons. You use this information to identify the name of the machine you want to connect to, the required security settings, the name of the database on that machine, and other data provider–specific information.

As you can infer from the preceding code, the `Initial Catalog` name refers to the database you want to establish a session with. The `Data Source` name identifies the name of the machine that maintains the database. I am using **.,5433**, which refers to the host machine (the period is the same as using "localhost"), and port 5433, which is the port the Docker container has mapped to the SQL Server port. If you were using a different instance, you would define the property as `machinename,port\instance`. For example, `MYSERVER\SQLSERVER2019` means `MYSERVER` is the name of the server the SQL Server is running on, the default port is being used, and `SQLSERVER2019` is the name of the instance. If the machine is local to the development, you can use a period (`.`) or the token (`localhost`) for the server name. If the SQL Server instance is the default instance, the instance name is left off. For example, if you created AutoLot on a Microsoft SQL Server installation set up as the default instance on your local computer, you would use "Data Source=localhost".

Beyond this, you can supply any number of tokens that represent security credentials. If Integrated Security is set to true, current Windows account credentials are used for authentication and authorization.

After you establish your connection string, you can use a call to Open() to establish a connection with the DBMS. In addition to the ConnectionString, Open(), and Close() members, a connection object provides a number of members that let you configure additional settings regarding your connection, such as timeout settings and transactional information. Table 20-4 lists some (but not all) members of the DbConnection base class.

Table 20-4. *Members of the DbConnection Type*

Member	Meaning in Life
BeginTransaction()	You use this method to begin a database transaction.
ChangeDatabase()	You use this method to change the database on an open connection.
ConnectionTimeout	This read-only property returns the amount of time to wait while establishing a connection before terminating and generating an error (the default value is provider dependent). If you would like to change the default, specify a Connect Timeout segment in the connection string (e.g., Connect Timeout=30).
Database	This read-only property gets the name of the database maintained by the connection object.
DataSource	This read-only property gets the location of the database maintained by the connection object.
GetSchema()	This method returns a DataTable object that contains schema information from the data source.
State	This read-only property gets the current state of the connection, which is represented by the ConnectionState enumeration.

The properties of the DbConnection type are typically read-only in nature and are useful only when you want to obtain the characteristics of a connection at runtime. When you need to override default settings, you must alter the connection string itself. For example, the following connection string sets the connection timeout setting from the default (15 seconds for SQL Server) to 30 seconds:

```
using(SqlConnection connection = new SqlConnection())
{
  connection.ConnectionString =
    @" Data Source=.,5433;User Id=sa;Password=P@ssw0rd;Initial Catalog=AutoLot;Encrypt=False
;Connect Timeout=30";
  connection.Open();
}
```

The following code outputs details about the SqlConnection that is passed into it:

```
static void ShowConnectionStatus(SqlConnection connection)
{
  // Show various stats about current connection object.
  Console.WriteLine("***** Info about your connection *****");
```

```
    Console.WriteLine($"Database location:  {connection.DataSource}");
    Console.WriteLine($"Database name: {connection.Database}");
    Console.WriteLine($"Timeout:  {connection.ConnectionTimeout}");
    Console.WriteLine($"Connection state: {connection.State}");
}
```

While most of these properties are self-explanatory, the State property is worth a special mention. You can assign this property any value of the ConnectionState enumeration, as shown here:

```
public enum ConnectionState
{
  Broken,
  Closed,
  Connecting,
  Executing,
  Fetching,
  Open
}
```

However, the only valid ConnectionState values are ConnectionState.Open, ConnectionState.Connecting, and ConnectionState.Closed (the remaining members of this enum are reserved for future use). Also, it is always safe to close a connection, even if the connection state is currently ConnectionState.Closed.

Working with ConnectionStringBuilder Objects

Working with connection strings programmatically can be cumbersome because they are often represented as string literals, which are difficult to maintain and error-prone at best. The .NET-compliant data providers support *connection string builder objects*, which allow you to establish the name-value pairs using strongly typed properties. Consider the following update to the current code:

```
var connectionStringBuilder = new SqlConnectionStringBuilder
{
  InitialCatalog = "AutoLot",
  DataSource = ".,5433",
  UserID = "sa",
  Password = "P@ssw0rd",
  ConnectTimeout = 30,
  Encrypt=false
};
  connection.ConnectionString =
    connectionStringBuilder.ConnectionString;
```

In this iteration, you create an instance of SqlConnectionStringBuilder, set the properties accordingly, and obtain the internal string using the ConnectionString property. Also note that you use the default constructor of the type. If you so choose, you can also create an instance of your data provider's connection string builder object by passing in an existing connection string as a starting point (this can be helpful when you read these values dynamically from an external source). Once you have hydrated the object with the initial string data, you can change specific name-value pairs using the related properties.

Working with Command Objects

Now that you understand better the role of the connection object, the next order of business is to check out how to submit SQL queries to the database in question. The SqlCommand type (which derives from DbCommand) is an OO representation of a SQL query, table name, or stored procedure. You specify the type of command using the CommandType property, which can take any value from the CommandType enum, as shown here:

```
public enum CommandType
{
  StoredProcedure,
  TableDirect,
  Text // Default value.
}
```

When you create a command object, you can establish the SQL query as a constructor parameter or directly by using the CommandText property. Also, when you create a command object, you need to specify the connection you want to use. Again, you can do so as a constructor parameter or by using the Connection property. Consider this code snippet:

```
// Create command object via ctor args.
string sql =
    @"Select i.id, m.Name as Make, i.Color, i.Petname
         FROM Inventory i
         INNER JOIN Makes m on m.Id = i.MakeId";
SqlCommand myCommand = new SqlCommand(sql, connection);
// Create another command object via properties.
SqlCommand testCommand = new SqlCommand();
testCommand.Connection = connection;
testCommand.CommandText = sql;
```

Realize that, at this point, you have not actually submitted the SQL query to the AutoLot database but instead prepared the state of the command object for future use. Table 20-5 highlights some additional members of the DbCommand type.

Table 20-5. *Members of the DbCommand Type*

Member	Meaning in Life
CommandTimeout	Gets or sets the time to wait while executing the command before terminating the attempt and generating an error. The default is 30 seconds.
Connection	Gets or sets the DbConnection used by this instance of the DbCommand.
Parameters	Gets the collection of DbParameter objects used for a parameterized query.
Cancel()	Cancels the execution of a command.
ExecuteReader()	Executes a SQL query and returns the data provider's DbDataReader object, which provides forward-only, read-only access for the result of the query.
ExecuteNonQuery()	Executes a SQL nonquery (e.g., an insert, update, delete, or create table).

(*continued*)

Table 20-5. *(continued)*

Member	Meaning in Life
ExecuteScalar()	A lightweight version of the ExecuteReader() method that was designed specifically for singleton queries (e.g., obtaining a record count).
Prepare()	Creates a prepared (or compiled) version of the command on the data source. As you might know, a *prepared query* executes slightly faster and is useful when you need to execute the same query multiple times (typically with different parameters each time).

Working with Data Readers

After you establish the active connection and SQL command, the next step is to submit the query to the data source. As you might guess, you have a number of ways to do this. The DbDataReader type (which implements IDataReader) is the simplest and fastest way to obtain information from a data store. Recall that data readers represent a read-only, forward-only stream of data returned one record at a time. Given this, data readers are useful only when submitting SQL selection statements to the underlying data store.

Data readers are useful when you need to iterate over large amounts of data quickly and you do not need to maintain an in-memory representation. For example, if you request 20,000 records from a table to store in a text file, it would be rather memory intensive to hold this information in a DataSet (because a DataSet holds the entire result of the query in memory at the same time).

A better approach is to create a data reader that spins over each record as rapidly as possible. Be aware, however, that data reader objects (unlike data adapter objects, which you will examine later) maintain an open connection to their data source until you explicitly close the connection.

You obtain data reader objects from the command object using a call to ExecuteReader(). The data reader represents the current record it has read from the database. The data reader has an indexer method (e.g., [] syntax in C#) that allows you to access a column in the current record. You can access the column either by name or by zero-based integer.

The following use of the data reader leverages the Read() method to determine when you have reached the end of your records (using a false return value). For each incoming record that you read from the database, you use the type indexer to print out the make, pet name, and color of each automobile. Also note that you call Close() as soon as you finish processing the records, which frees up the connection object.

```
...
// Obtain a data reader via ExecuteReader().
using(SqlDataReader myDataReader = myCommand.ExecuteReader())
{
  // Loop over the results.
  while (myDataReader.Read())
  {
    WriteLine($"-> Make: { myDataReader["Make"]}, PetName: { myDataReader["PetName"]},
    Color: { myDataReader["Color"]}.");
  }
}
ReadLine();
```

In the preceding snippet, you overload the indexer of a data reader object to take either a string (representing the name of the column) or an int (representing the column's ordinal position). Thus, you can clean up the current reader logic (and avoid hard-coded string names) with the following update (note the use of the FieldCount property):

```
while (myDataReader.Read())
{
  for (int i = 0; i < myDataReader.FieldCount; i++)
  {
    Console.Write(i != myDataReader.FieldCount - 1
      ? $"{myDataReader.GetName(i)} = {myDataReader.GetValue(i)}, "
      : $"{myDataReader.GetName(i)} = {myDataReader.GetValue(i)} ");
  }
  Console.WriteLine();
}
```

If you compile and run your project at this point, you should see a list of all automobiles in the Inventory table of the AutoLot database.

```
***** Fun with Data Readers *****

***** Info about your connection *****
Database location: .,5433
Database name: AutoLot
Timeout: 30
Connection state: Open

id = 1, Make = VW, Color = Black, Petname = Zippy
id = 2, Make = Ford, Color = Rust, Petname = Rusty
id = 3, Make = Saab, Color = Black, Petname = Mel
id = 4, Make = Yugo, Color = Yellow, Petname = Clunker
id = 5, Make = BMW, Color = Black, Petname = Bimmer
id = 6, Make = BMW, Color = Green, Petname = Hank
id = 7, Make = BMW, Color = Pink, Petname = Pinky
id = 8, Make = Pinto, Color = Black, Petname = Pete
id = 9, Make = Yugo, Color = Brown, Petname = Brownie
```

Obtaining Multiple Result Sets Using a Data Reader

Data reader objects can obtain multiple result sets using a single command object. For example, if you want to obtain all rows from the Inventory table, as well as all rows from the Customers table, you can specify both SQL SELECT statements using a semicolon delimiter, like so:

```
sql += ";Select * from Customers;";
```

■ **Note** The semicolon in the beginning is not a typo. When using multiple statements, they must be separated by semicolons. And since the initial statement did not contain one, it is added here at the beginning of the second statement.

After you obtain the data reader, you can iterate over each result set using the NextResult() method. Note that you are always returned the first result set automatically. Thus, if you want to read over the rows of each table, you can build the following iteration construct:

```
do
{
  while (myDataReader.Read())
  {
    for (int i = 0; i < myDataReader.FieldCount; i++)
    {
      Console.Write(i != myDataReader.FieldCount - 1
        ? $"{myDataReader.GetName(i)} = {myDataReader.GetValue(i)}, "
        : $"{myDataReader.GetName(i)} = {myDataReader.GetValue(i)} ");
    }
    Console.WriteLine();
  }
  Console.WriteLine();
} while (myDataReader.NextResult());
```

At this point, you should be more aware of the functionality data reader objects bring to the table. Always remember that a data reader can process only SQL `Select` statements; you cannot use them to modify an existing database table using `Insert`, `Update`, or `Delete` requests. Modifying an existing database requires additional investigation of command objects.

Working with Create, Update, and Delete Queries

The `ExecuteReader()` method extracts a data reader object that allows you to examine the results of a SQL `Select` statement using a forward-only, read-only flow of information. However, when you want to submit SQL statements that result in the modification of a given table (or any other nonquery SQL statement, such as creating tables or granting permissions), you call the `ExecuteNonQuery()` method of your command object. This single method performs inserts, updates, and deletes based on the format of your command text.

■ **Note** Technically speaking, a *nonquery* is a SQL statement that does not return a result set. Thus, `Select` statements are queries, while `Insert`, `Update`, and `Delete` statements are not. Given this, `ExecuteNonQuery()` returns an `int` that represents the number of rows affected, not a new set of records.

All the database interaction examples in this chapter so far have only opened connections and used them to retrieve data. This is just one part of working with a database; a data access framework would not be of much use unless it also fully supported Create, Read, Update, and Delete (CRUD) functionality. Next, you will learn how to do this using calls to `ExecuteNonQuery()`.

Begin by creating a new C# Class Library project named AutoLot.Dal (short for *AutoLot data access layer*), delete the default class file, and add the `Microsoft.Data.SqlClient` package to the project. Add a new class file named `GlobalUsings.cs` to the project, and update the file to the following global `using` statements:

```
global using System.Data;
global using System.Reflection;
global using Microsoft.Data.SqlClient;
```

Before building the class that will conduct the data operations, we will first create a C# class that represents a record from the `Inventory` table with its related `Make` information.

Create the Car and CarViewModel Classes

Modern data access libraries use classes (commonly called *models or entities*) that are used to represent and transport the data from the database. Additionally, classes can be used to represent a view into the data that combines two or more tables to make the data more meaningful. Entity classes are used to work with the database directory (for update statements), and view model classes are used for displaying the data in a meaningful way. You will see in the next chapter that these concepts are a foundation of object relational mappers (ORMs) like the Entity Framework Core, but for now, you are just going to create one model (for a raw inventory row) and one view model (combining an inventory row with the related data in the Makes table). Add a new folder to your project named Models, and add two new files, named Car.cs and CarViewModel.cs. Update the code to the following:

```
//Car.cs
namespace AutoLot.Dal.Models;
public class Car
{
  public int Id { get; set; }
  public int MakeId { get; set; }
  public string Color { get; set; }
  public string PetName { get; set; }
  public byte[] TimeStamp {get;set;}
}

//CarViewModel.cs
namespace AutoLot.Dal.Models;
public class CarViewModel : Car
{
  public string Make { get; set; }
}
```

These classes will be used shortly, but first, add the AutoLot.Dal.Models namespace into the GlobalUsings.cs file:

```
global using System.Data;
global using System.Reflection;
global using Microsoft.Data.SqlClient;
global using AutoLot.Dal.Models;
```

Adding the InventoryDal Class

Next, add a new folder named DataOperations. In this new folder, add a new class named InventoryDal.cs and change the class to public. This class will define various members to interact with the Inventory table of the AutoLot database.

Adding Constructors

Create a constructor that takes a string parameter (connectionString) and assigns the value to a class-level variable. Next, create a parameterless constructor that passes a default connection string to the other constructor. This enables the calling code to change the connection string from the default. The relevant code is as follows:

```
namespace AuoLot.Dal.DataOperations;
public class InventoryDal
{
  private readonly string _connectionString;
  public InventoryDal() : this(
    @"Data Source=.,5433;User Id=sa;Password=P@ssw0rd;Initial Catalog=AutoLot;Encryp
    t=False;")
  {
  }
  public InventoryDal(string connectionString)
    => _connectionString = connectionString;
}
```

Opening and Closing the Connection

Next, add a class-level variable to hold a connection that will be used by the data access code. Also, add two methods, one to open the connection (OpenConnection()) and the other to close the connection (CloseConnection()). In the CloseConnection() method, check the state of the connection, and if it is not closed, then call Close() on the connection. The code listing follows:

```
private SqlConnection _sqlConnection = null;
private void OpenConnection()
{
  _sqlConnection = new SqlConnection
  {
    ConnectionString = _connectionString
  };
  _sqlConnection.Open();
}
private void CloseConnection()
{
  if (_sqlConnection?.State != ConnectionState.Closed)
  {
    _sqlConnection?.Close();
  }
}
```

For the sake of brevity, most of the methods in the InventoryDal class will not use try/catch blocks to handle possible exceptions, nor will they throw custom exceptions to report various issues with the execution (e.g., a malformed connection string). If you were to build an industrial-strength data access library, you would absolutely want to use structured exception handling techniques (as covered in Chapter 7) to account for any runtime anomalies.

Adding IDisposable

Add the IDisposable interface to the class definition, like this:

```
public class InventoryDal : IDisposable
{
...
}
```

Next, implement the disposable pattern, calling Dispose on the SqlConnection object.

```
bool _disposed = false;
protected virtual void Dispose(bool disposing)
{
  if (_disposed)
  {
    return;
  }
  if (disposing)
  {
    _sqlConnection.Dispose();
  }
  _disposed = true;
}
public void Dispose()
{
  Dispose(true);
  GC.SuppressFinalize(this);
}
```

Adding the Selection Methods

You start by combining what you already know about Command objects, DataReaders, and generic collections to get the records from the Inventory table. As you saw earlier in this chapter, a data provider's data reader object allows for a selection of records using a read-only, forward-only mechanism using the Read() method. In this example, the CommandBehavior property on the DataReader is set to automatically close the connection when the reader is closed. The GetAllInventory() method returns a List<CarViewModel> to represent all the data in the Inventory table.

```
public List<CarViewModel> GetAllInventory()
{
  OpenConnection();
  // This will hold the records.
  List<CarViewModel> inventory = new List<CarViewModel>();

  // Prep command object.
  string sql =
    @"SELECT i.Id, i.Color, i.PetName,m.Name as Make
        FROM Inventory i
        INNER JOIN Makes m on m.Id = i.MakeId";
  using SqlCommand command =
    new SqlCommand(sql, _sqlConnection)
    {
      CommandType = CommandType.Text
    };
  command.CommandType = CommandType.Text;
  SqlDataReader dataReader =
    command.ExecuteReader(CommandBehavior.CloseConnection);
  while (dataReader.Read())
```

```
    {
      inventory.Add(new CarViewModel
      {
        Id = (int)dataReader["Id"],
        Color = (string)dataReader["Color"],
        Make = (string)dataReader["Make"],
        PetName = (string)dataReader["PetName"]
      });
    }
    dataReader.Close();
    return inventory;
  }
```

The next selection method gets a single CarViewModel based on the CarId.

```
public CarViewModel GetCar(int id)
{
  OpenConnection();
  CarViewModel car = null;
  //This should use parameters for security reasons
  string sql =
   $@"SELECT i.Id, i.Color, i.PetName,m.Name as Make
          FROM Inventory i
          INNER JOIN Makes m on m.Id = i.MakeId
          WHERE i.Id = {id}";
  using SqlCommand command =
    new SqlCommand(sql, _sqlConnection)
    {
      CommandType = CommandType.Text
    };
  SqlDataReader dataReader =
    command.ExecuteReader(CommandBehavior.CloseConnection);
  while (dataReader.Read())
  {
    car = new CarViewModel
    {
      Id = (int) dataReader["Id"],
      Color = (string) dataReader["Color"],
      Make = (string) dataReader["Make"],
      PetName = (string) dataReader["PetName"]
    };
  }
  dataReader.Close();
  return car;
}
```

■ **Note** It's generally a bad practice to accept user input into raw SQL statements as is done here. Later in this chapter, this code will be updated to use parameters.

Inserting a New Car

Inserting a new record into the Inventory table is as simple as formatting the SQL Insert statement (based on user input), opening the connection, calling the ExecuteNonQuery() using your command object, and closing the connection. You can see this in action by adding a public method to your InventoryDal type named InsertAuto() that takes three parameters that map to the nonidentity columns of the Inventory table (Color, Make, and PetName). You use these arguments to format a string type to insert the new record. Finally, use your SqlConnection object to execute the SQL statement.

```
public void InsertAuto(string color, int makeId, string petName)
{
  OpenConnection();
  // Format and execute SQL statement.
  string sql = $"Insert Into Inventory (MakeId, Color, PetName) Values ('{makeId}',
  '{color}', '{petName}')";
  // Execute using our connection.
  using (SqlCommand command = new SqlCommand(sql, _sqlConnection))
  {
    command.CommandType = CommandType.Text;
    command.ExecuteNonQuery();
  }
  CloseConnection();
}
```

This previous method takes three values for Car and works as long as the calling code passes the values in the correct order. A better method uses Car to make a strongly typed method, ensuring all the properties are passed into the method in the correct order.

Create the Strongly Type InsertCar() Method

Add another InsertAuto() method that takes Car as a parameter to your InventoryDal class, as shown here:

```
public void InsertAuto(Car car)
{
  OpenConnection();
  // Format and execute SQL statement.
  string sql = "Insert Into Inventory (MakeId, Color, PetName) Values " +
    $"('{car.MakeId}', '{car.Color}', '{car.PetName}')";

  // Execute using our connection.
  using (SqlCommand command = new SqlCommand(sql, _sqlConnection))
  {
    command.CommandType = CommandType.Text;
    command.ExecuteNonQuery();
  }
  CloseConnection();
}
```

Adding the Deletion Logic

Deleting an existing record is as simple as inserting a new record. Unlike when you created the code for InsertAuto(), this time you will learn about an important try/catch scope that handles the possibility of attempting to delete a car that is currently on order for an individual in the Customers table. The default INSERT and UPDATE options for foreign keys default to preventing the deletion of related records in linked tables. When this happens, a SqlException is thrown. A real program would handle that error intelligently; however, in this sample, you are just throwing a new exception. Add the following method to the InventoryDal class type:

```
public void DeleteCar(int id)
{
  OpenConnection();
  // Get ID of car to delete, then do so.
  string sql = $"Delete from Inventory where Id = '{id}'";
  using (SqlCommand command = new SqlCommand(sql, _sqlConnection))
  {
    try
    {
      command.CommandType = CommandType.Text;
      command.ExecuteNonQuery();
    }
    catch (SqlException ex)
    {
      Exception error = new Exception("Sorry! That car is on order!", ex);
      throw error;
    }
  }
  CloseConnection();
}
```

Adding the Update Logic

When it comes to the act of updating an existing record in the Inventory table, the first thing you must decide is what you want to allow the caller to change, whether it is the car's color, the pet name, the make, or all of these. One way to give the caller complete flexibility is to define a method that takes a string type to represent any sort of SQL statement, but that is risky at best.

Ideally, you want to have a set of methods that allow the caller to update a record in a variety of ways. However, for this simple data access library, you will define a single method that allows the caller to update the pet name of a given automobile, like so:

```
public void UpdateCarPetName(int id, string newPetName)
{
  OpenConnection();
  // Get ID of car to modify the pet name.
  string sql = $"Update Inventory Set PetName = '{newPetName}' Where Id = '{id}'";
  using (SqlCommand command = new SqlCommand(sql, _sqlConnection))
  {
    command.ExecuteNonQuery();
  }
  CloseConnection();
}
```

Working with Parameterized Command Objects

Currently, the insert, update, and delete logic for the `InventoryDal` type uses hard-coded string literals for each SQL query. With *parameterized queries*, SQL parameters are objects, rather than simple blobs of text. Treating SQL queries in a more object-oriented manner helps reduce the number of typos (given strongly typed properties); plus, parameterized queries typically execute much faster than a literal SQL string because they are parsed exactly once (rather than each time the SQL string is assigned to the `CommandText` property). Parameterized queries also help protect against SQL injection attacks (a well-known data access security issue).

To support parameterized queries, ADO.NET command objects maintain a collection of individual parameter objects. By default, this collection is empty, but you can insert any number of parameter objects that map to a *placeholder parameter* in the SQL query. When you want to associate a parameter within a SQL query to a member in the command object's parameters collection, you can prefix the SQL text parameter with the @ symbol (at least when using Microsoft SQL Server; not all DBMSs support this notation).

Specifying Parameters Using the DbParameter Type

Before you build a parameterized query, you need to familiarize yourself with the `DbParameter` type (which is the base class to a provider's specific parameter object). This class maintains a number of properties that allow you to configure the name, size, and data type of the parameter, as well as other characteristics, including the parameter's direction of travel. Table 20-6 describes some key properties of the `DbParameter` type.

Table 20-6. *Key Members of the DbParameter Type*

Property	Meaning in Life
`DbType`	Gets or sets the native data type of the parameter, represented as a CLR data type
`Direction`	Gets or sets whether the parameter is input-only, output-only, bidirectional, or a return value parameter
`IsNullable`	Gets or sets whether the parameter accepts null values
`ParameterName`	Gets or sets the name of the `DbParameter`
`Size`	Gets or sets the maximum parameter size of the data in bytes; this is useful only for textual data
`Value`	Gets or sets the value of the parameter

Now let's look at how to populate a command object's collection of `DBParameter`-compatible objects by reworking the `InventoryDal` methods to use parameters.

Update the GetCar Method

The original implementation of the `GetCar()` method used C# string interpolation when building the SQL string to retrieve the car data. To update this method, create an instance of `SqlParameter` with the appropriate values, as follows:

```
SqlParameter param = new SqlParameter
{
  ParameterName = "@carId",
  Value = id,
```

```
  SqlDbType = SqlDbType.Int,
  Direction = ParameterDirection.Input
};
```

The ParameterName value must match the name used in the SQL query (you will update that next), the type must match the database column type, and the direction is dependent on whether the parameter is used to send data *into* the query (ParameterDirection.Input) or if it is meant to return data *from* the query (ParameterDirection.Output). Parameters can also be defined as input/output or as return values (e.g., from a stored procedure).

Next, update the SQL string to use the parameter name ("@carId") instead of the C# string interpolation construct ("{id}").

```
string sql =
  @"SELECT i.Id, i.Color, i.PetName,m.Name as Make
        FROM Inventory i
        INNER JOIN Makes m on m.Id = i.MakeId
        WHERE i.Id = @CarId";
```

The final update is to add the new parameter to the Parameters collection of the command object.

```
command.Parameters.Add(param);
```

Update the DeleteCar Method

Likewise, the original implementation of the DeleteCar() method used C# string interpolation. To update this method, create an instance of SqlParameter with the appropriate values, as follows:

```
SqlParameter param = new SqlParameter
{
  ParameterName = "@carId",
  Value = id,
  SqlDbType = SqlDbType.Int,
  Direction = ParameterDirection.Input
};
```

Next, update the SQL string to use the parameter name ("@carId").

```
string sql = "Delete from Inventory where Id = @carId";
```

The final update is to add the new parameter to the Parameters collection of the command object.

```
command.Parameters.Add(param);
```

Update the UpdateCarPetName Method

This method requires two parameters, one for the car Id and the other for the new PetName. The first parameter is created just like the two previous examples (with the exception of a different variable name), and the second creates a parameter that maps to the database NVarChar type (the PetName field type from the Inventory table). Notice that a Size value is set. It is important this size matches your database field size so as to not create problems when executing the command.

```
SqlParameter paramId = new SqlParameter
{
  ParameterName = "@carId",
  Value = id,
  SqlDbType = SqlDbType.Int,
  Direction = ParameterDirection.Input
};
SqlParameter paramName = new SqlParameter
{
  ParameterName = "@petName",
  Value = newPetName,
  SqlDbType = SqlDbType.NVarChar,
  Size = 50,
  Direction = ParameterDirection.Input
};
```

Next, update the SQL string to use the parameters.

```
string sql = $"Update Inventory Set PetName = @petName Where Id = @carId";
```

The final update is to add the new parameters to the Parameters collection of the command object.

```
command.Parameters.Add(paramId);
command.Parameters.Add(paramName);
```

Update the InsertAuto Method

Add the following version of the InsertAuto() method to leverage parameter objects:

```
public void InsertAuto(Car car)
{
  OpenConnection();
  // Note the "placeholders" in the SQL query.
  string sql = "Insert Into Inventory" +
    "(MakeId, Color, PetName) Values" +
    "(@MakeId, @Color, @PetName)";

  // This command will have internal parameters.
  using (SqlCommand command = new SqlCommand(sql, _sqlConnection))
  {
    // Fill params collection.
    SqlParameter parameter = new SqlParameter
    {
      ParameterName = "@MakeId",
      Value = car.MakeId,
      SqlDbType = SqlDbType.Int,
      Direction = ParameterDirection.Input
    };
    command.Parameters.Add(parameter);

    parameter = new SqlParameter
```

```
    {
      ParameterName = "@Color",
      Value = car.Color,
      SqlDbType = SqlDbType. NVarChar,
      Size = 50,
      Direction = ParameterDirection.Input
    };
    command.Parameters.Add(parameter);

    parameter = new SqlParameter
    {
      ParameterName = "@PetName",
      Value = car.PetName,
      SqlDbType = SqlDbType. NVarChar,
      Size = 50,
      Direction = ParameterDirection.Input
    };
    command.Parameters.Add(parameter);

    command.ExecuteNonQuery();
    CloseConnection();
  }
}
```

While building a parameterized query often requires more code, the end result is a more convenient way to tweak SQL statements programmatically, as well as to achieve better overall performance. They also are extremely helpful when you want to trigger a stored procedure.

Executing a Stored Procedure

Recall that a *stored procedure* is a named block of SQL code stored in the database. You can construct stored procedures so they return a set of rows or scalar data types or do anything else that makes sense (e.g., insert, update, or delete records); you can also have them take any number of optional parameters. The end result is a unit of work that behaves like a typical method, except that it is located on a data store rather than a binary business object. Currently, your AutoLot database contains a single stored procedure named GetPetName.

Now consider the following final method (for now) of the InventoryDal type, which invokes your stored procedure:

```
public string LookUpPetName(int carId)
{
  OpenConnection();
  string carPetName;

  // Establish name of stored proc.
  using (SqlCommand command = new SqlCommand("GetPetName", _sqlConnection))
  {
    command.CommandType = CommandType.StoredProcedure;

    // Input param.
    SqlParameter param = new SqlParameter
    {
```

```
      ParameterName = "@carId",
      SqlDbType = SqlDbType.Int,
      Value = carId,
      Direction = ParameterDirection.Input
    };
    command.Parameters.Add(param);

    // Output param.
    param = new SqlParameter
    {
      ParameterName = "@petName",
      SqlDbType = SqlDbType.NVarChar,
      Size = 50,
      Direction = ParameterDirection.Output
    };
    command.Parameters.Add(param);

    // Execute the stored proc.
    command.ExecuteNonQuery();

    // Return output param.
    carPetName = (string)command.Parameters["@petName"].Value;
    CloseConnection();
  }
  return carPetName;
}
```

One important aspect of invoking a stored procedure is to keep in mind that a command object can represent a SQL statement (the default) or the name of a stored procedure. When you want to inform a command object that it will be invoking a stored procedure, you pass in the name of the procedure (as a constructor argument or by using the CommandText property) and must set the CommandType property to the value CommandType.StoredProcedure. (If you fail to do this, you will receive a runtime exception because the command object is expecting a SQL statement by default.)

Next, notice that the Direction property of the @petName parameter is set to ParameterDirection.Output. As before, you add each parameter object to the command object's parameters collection.

After the stored procedure completes with a call to ExecuteNonQuery(), you can obtain the value of the output parameter by investigating the command object's parameter collection and casting accordingly.

```
// Return output param.
carPetName = (string)command.Parameters["@petName"].Value;
```

At this point, you have an extremely simple data access library that you can use to build a client to display and edit your data. You have not yet examined how to build graphical user interfaces, so next you will test your data library from a new console application.

Creating a Console-Based Client Application

Add a new console application (named AutoLot.Client) to the AutoLot.Dal solution and add a reference to the AutoLot.Dal project. Clear out the generated code in the Program.cs file and add the following using statements to the top of the file:

```
using AutoLot.Dal.Models;
using AutoLot.Dal.DataOperations;
using AutoLot.Dal.BulkImport;
```

Next, add the following top-level statements to exercise the AutoLot.Dal code:

```
InventoryDal dal = new InventoryDal();
List<CarViewModel> list = dal.GetAllInventory();
Console.WriteLine(" ************** All Cars ************** ");
Console.WriteLine("Id\tMake\tColor\tPet Name");
foreach (var itm in list)
{
  Console.WriteLine($"{itm.Id}\t{itm.Make}\t{itm.Color}\t{itm.PetName}");
}
Console.WriteLine();
CarViewModel car = dal.GetCar(list.OrderBy(x=>x.Color).Select(x => x.Id).First());
Console.WriteLine(" ************** First Car By Color ************** ");
Console.WriteLine("CarId\tMake\tColor\tPet Name");
Console.WriteLine($"{car.Id}\t{car.Make}\t{car.Color}\t{car.PetName}");

try
{
  //This will fail because of related data in the Orders table
  dal.DeleteCar(5);
  Console.WriteLine("Car deleted.");
}
catch (Exception ex)
{
  Console.WriteLine($"An exception occurred: {ex.Message}");
}
dal.InsertAuto(new Car { Color = "Blue", MakeId = 5, PetName = "TowMonster" });
list = dal.GetAllInventory();
var newCar = list.First(x => x.PetName == "TowMonster");
Console.WriteLine(" ************** New Car ************** ");
Console.WriteLine("CarId\tMake\tColor\tPet Name");
Console.WriteLine($"{newCar.Id}\t{newCar.Make}\t{newCar.Color}\t{newCar.PetName}");
dal.DeleteCar(newCar.Id);
var petName = dal.LookUpPetName(car.Id);
Console.WriteLine(" ************** New Car ************** ");
Console.WriteLine($"Car pet name: {petName}");
Console.Write("Press enter to continue...");
Console.ReadLine();
```

Understanding Database Transactions

The next tool that we will examine is the use of database transactions. Simply put, a *transaction* is a set of database operations that succeed or fail as a collective unit. If one of the operations fails, all other operations are rolled back, as if nothing ever happened. As you might imagine, transactions are quite important to ensure that table data is safe, valid, and consistent.

Transactions are important when a database operation involves interacting with multiple tables or multiple stored procedures (or a combination of database atoms). The classic transaction example involves the process of transferring monetary funds between two bank accounts. For example, if you were to transfer $500 from your savings account into your checking account, the following steps should occur in a transactional manner:

1. The bank should remove $500 from your savings account.
2. The bank should add $500 to your checking account.

It would be an extremely bad thing if the money were removed from the savings account but not transferred to the checking account (because of some error on the bank's part) because then you would be out $500! However, if these steps are wrapped up into a database transaction, the DBMS ensures that all related steps occur as a single unit. If any part of the transaction fails, the entire operation is *rolled back* to the original state. On the other hand, if all steps succeed, the transaction is *committed.*

■ **Note** You might be familiar with the acronym ACID from looking at transactional literature. This represents the four key properties of a prim-and-proper transaction: *atomic* (all or nothing), *consistent* (data remains stable throughout the transaction), *isolated* (transactions do not interfere with other operations), and *durable* (transactions are saved and logged).

It turns out that the .NET platform supports transactions in a variety of ways. This chapter will look at the transaction object of your ADO.NET data provider (`SqlTransaction`, in the case of `Microsoft.Data.SqlClient`).

In addition to the baked-in transactional support within the .NET base class libraries, it is possible to use the SQL language of your database management system. For example, you could author a stored procedure that uses the `BEGIN TRANSACTION`, `ROLLBACK`, and `COMMIT` statements.

Key Members of an ADO.NET Transaction Object

All the transactions we will use implement the `IDbTransaction` interface. Recall from the beginning of this chapter that `IDbTransaction` defines a handful of members as follows:

```
public interface IDbTransaction : IDisposable
{
  IDbConnection Connection { get; }
  IsolationLevel IsolationLevel { get; }

  void Commit();
  void Rollback();
}
```

Notice the `Connection` property, which returns a reference to the connection object that initiated the current transaction (as you will see, you obtain a transaction object from a given connection object). You call the `Commit()` method when each of your database operations has succeeded. Doing this causes each of the pending changes to be persisted in the data store. Conversely, you can call the `Rollback()` method in the event of a runtime exception, which informs the DBMS to disregard any pending changes, leaving the original data intact.

■ **Note** The IsolationLevel property of a transaction object allows you to specify how aggressively a transaction should be guarded against the activities of other parallel transactions. By default, transactions are isolated completely until committed.

Beyond the members defined by the IDbTransaction interface, the SqlTransaction type defines an additional member named Save(), which allows you to define *save points*. This concept allows you to roll back a failed transaction up until a named point, rather than rolling back the entire transaction. Essentially, when you call Save() using a SqlTransaction object, you can specify a friendly string moniker. When you call Rollback(), you can specify this same moniker as an argument to perform an effective *partial rollback*. Calling Rollback() with no arguments causes all the pending changes to be rolled back.

Adding a Transaction Method to InventoryDal

Now let's look at how you work with ADO.NET transactions programmatically. Begin by opening the AutoLot.Dal code library project you created earlier and add a new public method named ProcessCreditRisk() to the InventoryDal class to deal with perceived credit risks. The method will look up a customer, add them to the CreditRisks table, and then update their last name by adding "(Credit Risk)" to the end.

```
public void ProcessCreditRisk(bool throwEx, int customerId)
{
  OpenConnection();
  // First, look up current name based on customer ID.
  string fName;
  string lName;
  var cmdSelect = new SqlCommand(
    "Select * from Customers where Id = @customerId",
    _sqlConnection);
  SqlParameter paramId = new SqlParameter
  {
    ParameterName = "@customerId",
    SqlDbType = SqlDbType.Int,
    Value = customerId,
    Direction = ParameterDirection.Input
  };
  cmdSelect.Parameters.Add(paramId);
  using (var dataReader = cmdSelect.ExecuteReader())
  {
    if (dataReader.HasRows)
    {
      dataReader.Read();
      fName = (string) dataReader["FirstName"];
      lName = (string) dataReader["LastName"];
    }
    else
    {
      CloseConnection();
      return;
    }
  }
```

```
  cmdSelect.Parameters.Clear();
// Create command objects that represent each step of the operation.
  var cmdUpdate = new SqlCommand(
    "Update Customers set LastName = LastName + ' (CreditRisk) ' where Id = @customerId",
    _sqlConnection);
  cmdUpdate.Parameters.Add(paramId);
  var cmdInsert = new SqlCommand(
    "Insert Into CreditRisks (CustomerId,FirstName, LastName) Values( @CustomerId, @
    FirstName, @LastName)", _sqlConnection);
  SqlParameter parameterId2 = new SqlParameter
  {
    ParameterName = "@CustomerId",
    SqlDbType = SqlDbType.Int,
    Value = customerId,
    Direction = ParameterDirection.Input
  };
  SqlParameter parameterFirstName = new SqlParameter
  {
    ParameterName = "@FirstName",
    Value = fName,
    SqlDbType = SqlDbType.NVarChar,
    Size = 50,
    Direction = ParameterDirection.Input
  };
  SqlParameter parameterLastName = new SqlParameter
  {
    ParameterName = "@LastName",
    Value = lName,
    SqlDbType = SqlDbType.NVarChar,
    Size = 50,
    Direction = ParameterDirection.Input
  };

  cmdInsert.Parameters.Add(parameterId2);
  cmdInsert.Parameters.Add(parameterFirstName);
  cmdInsert.Parameters.Add(parameterLastName);
  // We will get this from the connection object.
  SqlTransaction tx = null;
  try
  {
    tx = _sqlConnection.BeginTransaction();
    // Enlist the commands into this transaction.
    cmdInsert.Transaction = tx;
    cmdUpdate.Transaction = tx;
    // Execute the commands.
    cmdInsert.ExecuteNonQuery();
    cmdUpdate.ExecuteNonQuery();
    // Simulate error.
    if (throwEx)
    {
      throw new Exception("Sorry!  Database error! Tx failed...");
```

```
    }
    // Commit it!
    tx.Commit();
  }
  catch (Exception ex)
  {
    Console.WriteLine(ex.Message);
    // Any error will roll back transaction.  Using the new conditional access operator to
    check for null.
    tx?.Rollback();
  }
  finally
  {
    CloseConnection();
  }
}
```

Here, you use an incoming bool parameter to represent whether you will throw an arbitrary exception when you attempt to process the offending customer. This allows you to simulate an unforeseen circumstance that will cause the database transaction to fail. Obviously, you do this here only for illustrative purposes; a true database transaction method would not want to allow the caller to force the logic to fail on a whim!

Note that you use two SqlCommand objects to represent each step in the transaction you will kick off. After you obtain the customer's first and last names based on the incoming customerID parameter, you can obtain a valid SqlTransaction object from the connection object using BeginTransaction(). Next, and most importantly, you must *enlist each command object* by assigning the Transaction property to the transaction object you have just obtained. If you fail to do so, the Insert/Update logic will not be under a transactional context.

After you call ExecuteNonQuery() on each command, you throw an exception if (and only if) the value of the bool parameter is true. In this case, all pending database operations are rolled back. If you do not throw an exception, both steps will be committed to the database tables once you call Commit().

Testing Your Database Transaction

Select one of the customers you added to the Customers table (e.g., Dave Benner, Id = 1). Next, add a new method to the Program.cs file in the AutoLot.Client project named FlagCustomer().

```
void FlagCustomer()
{
  Console.WriteLine("***** Simple Transaction Example *****\n");

  // A simple way to allow the tx to succeed or not.
  bool throwEx = true;
  Console.Write("Do you want to throw an exception (Y or N): ");
  var userAnswer = Console.ReadLine();
  if (string.IsNullOrEmpty(userAnswer) || userAnswer.Equals("N",StringComparison.
  OrdinalIgnoreCase))
  {
    throwEx = false;
  }
  var dal = new InventoryDal();
```

```
  // Process customer 1 - enter the id for the customer to move.
  dal.ProcessCreditRisk(throwEx, 1);
  Console.WriteLine("Check CreditRisk table for results");
  Console.ReadLine();
}
```

If you were to run your program and elect to throw an exception, you would find that the customer's last name is *not* changed in the Customers table because the entire transaction has been rolled back. However, if you did not throw an exception, you would find that the customer's last name is updated in the Customers table and has been added to the CreditRisks table.

Executing Bulk Copies with ADO.NET

In cases where you need to load lots of records into the database, the methods shown so far would be rather inefficient. SQL Server has a feature called *bulk copy* that is designed specifically for this scenario, and it is wrapped up in ADO.NET with the SqlBulkCopy class. This section of the chapter shows how to do this with ADO.NET.

Exploring the SqlBulkCopy Class

The SqlBulkCopy class has one method, WriteToServer() (and the async version WriteToServerAsync()), that processes a list of records and writes the data to the database more efficiently than writing a series of insert statements and running them with a Command object. The WriteToServer overloads take a DataTable, a DataReader, or an array of DataRows. To keep with the theme of this chapter, you are going to use the DataReader version. For that, you need to create a custom data reader.

Creating a Custom Data Reader

You want your custom data reader to be generic and hold a list of the models that you want to import. Begin by creating a new folder in the AutoLot.Dal project named BulkImport; in the folder, create a new interface class named IMyDataReader.cs that implements IDataReader, and update the code to the following:

```
namespace AutoLot.Dal.BulkImport;
public interface IMyDataReader<T> : IDataReader
{
  List<T> Records { get; set; }
}
```

Next comes the task of implementing the custom data reader. As you have already seen, data readers have lots of moving parts. The good news for you is that, for SqlBulkCopy, you must implement only a handful of them. Create a new class named MyDataReader.cs, update the class to public and sealed, and implement IMyDataReader. Add a constructor to take in the records and set the property.

```
public sealed class MyDataReader<T> : IMyDataReader<T>
{
  public List<T> Records { get; set; }
  public MyDataReader(List<T> records)
  {
    Records = records;
```

```
  }
}
```

Have Visual Studio or Visual Studio Code implement all the methods for you (or copy them from the following code listings that follow Table 20-7), and you will have your starting point for the custom data reader. Table 20-7 details the only methods that need to be implemented for this scenario.

Table 20-7. *Key Methods of IDataReader for SqlBulkCopy*

Method	Meaning in Life
`Read`	Gets the next record; returns `true` if there is another record or returns `false` if at the end of the list
`FieldCount`	Gets the total number of fields in the data source
`GetValue`	Gets the value of a field based on the ordinal position
`GetSchemaTable`	Gets the schema information for the target table

Starting with the `Read()` method, return `false` if the reader is at the end of the list, and return `true` (and increment a class-level counter) if the reader is not at the end of the list. Add a class-level variable to hold the current index of the `List<T>` and update the `Read()` method like this:

```
public class MyDataReader<T> : IMyDataReader<T>
{
...
  private int _currentIndex = -1;
  public bool Read()
  {
    if (_currentIndex + 1 >= Records.Count)
    {
      return false;
    }
    _currentIndex++;
    return true;
  }
}
```

Each of the get methods and the `FieldCount` methods requires an intimate knowledge of the specific model to be loaded. An example of the `GetValue()` method (using the `Car` class) is as follows:

```
public object GetValue(int i)
{
  Car currentRecord = Records[_currentIndex] as Car;
  return i switch
  {
    0 => currentRecord.Id,
    1 => currentRecord.MakeId,
    2 => currentRecord.Color,
    3 => currentRecord.PetName,
    4 => currentRecord.TimeStamp,
```

```
      _ => string.Empty,
    };
}
```

The database has only four tables, but that means you still have four variations of the data reader. Imagine if you had a real production database with many more tables! You can do better than this using reflection (covered in Chapter 17) and LINQ to Objects (covered in Chapter 13).

Add readonly variables to hold the PropertyInfo values for the model as well as a dictionary that will be used to hold the field position and name for the table in SQL Server. Update the constructor to get the properties of the generic type and initialize the Dictionary. The added code is as follows:

```
private readonly PropertyInfo[] _propertyInfos;
private readonly Dictionary<int, string> _nameDictionary;

public MyDataReader(List<T> records)
{
  Records = records;
  _propertyInfos = typeof(T).GetProperties();
  _nameDictionary = new Dictionary<int,string>();
}
```

Next, update the constructor to take a SQLConnection as well as strings for the schema and table names for the table the records are going to be inserted into and add class-level variables for the values.

```
private readonly SqlConnection _connection;
private readonly string _schema;
private readonly string _tableName;
public MyDataReader(List<T> records, SqlConnection connection, string schema, string
tableName)
{
  Records = records;
  _propertyInfos = typeof(T).GetProperties();
  _nameDictionary = new Dictionary<int, string>();

  _connection = connection;
  _schema = schema;
  _tableName = tableName;
}
```

Implement the GetSchemaTable() method next. This retrieves the SQL Server information regarding the target table.

```
public DataTable GetSchemaTable()
{
  using var schemaCommand = new SqlCommand($"SELECT * FROM {_schema}.{_tableName}", _
  connection);
  using var reader = schemaCommand.ExecuteReader(CommandBehavior.SchemaOnly);
  return reader.GetSchemaTable();
}
```

Update the constructor to use the SchemaTable to construct the dictionary that contains the fields of the target table in database order.

```
public MyDataReader(List<T> records, SqlConnection connection, string schema, string
tableName)
{
...
  DataTable schemaTable = GetSchemaTable();
  for (int x = 0; x<schemaTable?.Rows.Count;x++)
  {
    DataRow col = schemaTable.Rows[x];
    var columnName = col.Field<string>("ColumnName");
    _nameDictionary.Add(x,columnName);
  }
}
```

Now, the following methods can be implemented generically, using the reflected information:

```
public int FieldCount => _propertyInfos.Length;
public object GetValue(int i)
  => _propertyInfos
      .First(x=>x.Name.Equals(_nameDictionary[i],StringComparison.OrdinalIgnoreCase))
      .GetValue(Records[_currentIndex]);
```

The remainder of the methods that must be present (but not implemented) are listed here for reference:

```
public string GetName(int i) => throw new NotImplementedException();
public int GetOrdinal(string name) => throw new NotImplementedException();
public string GetDataTypeName(int i) => throw new NotImplementedException();
public Type GetFieldType(int i) => throw new NotImplementedException();
public int GetValues(object[] values) => throw new NotImplementedException();
public bool GetBoolean(int i) => throw new NotImplementedException();
public byte GetByte(int i) => throw new NotImplementedException();
public long GetBytes(int i, long fieldOffset, byte[] buffer, int bufferoffset, int length)
  => throw new NotImplementedException();
public char GetChar(int i) => throw new NotImplementedException();
public long GetChars(int i, long fieldoffset, char[] buffer, int bufferoffset, int length)
   => throw new NotImplementedException();
public Guid GetGuid(int i) => throw new NotImplementedException();
public short GetInt16(int i) => throw new NotImplementedException();
public int GetInt32(int i) => throw new NotImplementedException();
public long GetInt64(int i) => throw new NotImplementedException();
public float GetFloat(int i) => throw new NotImplementedException();
public double GetDouble(int i)  => throw new NotImplementedException();
public string GetString(int i) => throw new NotImplementedException();
public decimal GetDecimal(int i) => throw new NotImplementedException();
public DateTime GetDateTime(int i) => throw new NotImplementedException();
public IDataReader GetData(int i) => throw new NotImplementedException();
public bool IsDBNull(int i) => throw new NotImplementedException();
object IDataRecord.this[int i] => throw new NotImplementedException();
object IDataRecord.this[string name] => throw new NotImplementedException();
```

```
public void Close() => throw new NotImplementedException();
public DataTable GetSchemaTable() => throw new NotImplementedException();
public bool NextResult() => throw new NotImplementedException();
public int Depth { get; }
public bool IsClosed { get; }
public int RecordsAffected { get; }
```

Executing the Bulk Copy

Add a new public static class named ProcessBulkImport.cs to the BulkImport folder. Add the code to handle opening and closing connections (like the code in the InventoryDal class), as follows:

```
private const string ConnectionString =
  @"Data Source=.,5433;User Id=sa;Password=P@ssw0rd;Initial Catalog=AutoLot;Encrypt=False;";
private static SqlConnection _sqlConnection = null;

private static void OpenConnection()
{
  _sqlConnection = new SqlConnection
  {
    ConnectionString = ConnectionString
  };
  _sqlConnection.Open();
}

private static void CloseConnection()
{
  if (_sqlConnection?.State != ConnectionState.Closed)
  {
    _sqlConnection?.Close();
  }
}
```

The SqlBulkCopy class requires the name (and schema, if different than dbo) to process the records. After creating a new SqlBulkCopy instance (passing in the connection object), set the DestinationTableName property. Then, create a new instance of the custom data reader holding the list to be bulk copied, and call WriteToServer(). The ExecuteBulkImport method is shown here:

```
public static void ExecuteBulkImport<T>(IEnumerable<T> records, string tableName)
{
  OpenConnection();
  using SqlConnection conn = _sqlConnection;
  SqlBulkCopy bc = new SqlBulkCopy(conn)
  {
    DestinationTableName = tableName
  };
  var dataReader = new MyDataReader<T>(records.ToList(),_sqlConnection,
  "dbo",tableName);    try
  {
    bc.WriteToServer(dataReader);
  }
```

```
    catch (Exception ex)
    {
      //Should do something here
    }
    finally
    {
      CloseConnection();
    }
  }
```

Testing the Bulk Copy

Back in the AutoLot.Client project, add a new method to the Program.cs file named DoBulkCopy(). Create a list of Car objects and pass that (and the name of the table) into the ExecuteBulkImport() method. The rest of the code displays the results of the bulk copy.

```
void DoBulkCopy()
{
  Console.WriteLine(" ************** Do Bulk Copy ************** ");
  var cars = new List<Car>
  {
    new Car() {Color = "Blue", MakeId = 1, PetName = "MyCar1"},
    new Car() {Color = "Red", MakeId = 2, PetName = "MyCar2"},
    new Car() {Color = "White", MakeId = 3, PetName = "MyCar3"},
    new Car() {Color = "Yellow", MakeId = 4, PetName = "MyCar4"}
  };
  ProcessBulkImport.ExecuteBulkImport(cars, "Inventory");
  InventoryDal dal = new InventoryDal();
  List<CarViewModel> list = dal.GetAllInventory();
  Console.WriteLine(" ************** All Cars ************** ");
  Console.WriteLine("CarId\tMake\tColor\tPet Name");
  foreach (var itm in list)
  {
    Console.WriteLine(
      $"{itm.Id}\t{itm.Make}\t{itm.Color}\t{itm.PetName}");
  }
  Console.WriteLine();
}
```

While adding four new cars does not show the merits of the work involved in using the SqlBulkCopy class, imagine trying to load *thousands* of records. I have done this with customers, and the load time has been mere seconds, where looping through each record took hours! As with everything in .NET, this is just another tool to keep in your toolbox to use when it makes the most sense.

Summary

ADO.NET is the native data access technology of the .NET platform. In this chapter, you began by learning the role of data providers, which are essentially concrete implementations of several abstract base classes (in the `System.Data.Common` namespace) and interface types (in the `System.Data` namespace). You also saw that it is possible to build a provider-neutral code base using the ADO.NET data provider factory model.

You also learned that you use connection objects, transaction objects, command objects, and data reader objects to select, update, insert, and delete records. Also, recall that command objects support an internal parameter collection, which you can use to add some type safety to your SQL queries; these also prove quite helpful when triggering stored procedures.

Next, you learned how to safeguard your data manipulation code with transactions and wrapped up the chapter with a look at using the `SqlBulkCopy` class to load large amounts of data into SQL Server using ADO.NET.

PART VII

Entity Framework Core

CHAPTER 21

Introducing Entity Framework Core

The previous chapter examined the fundamentals of ADO.NET. As you saw, ADO.NET enables .NET programmers to work with relational data. While ADO.NET is an *effective* tool for working with data, it isn't necessarily an *efficient* tool. The efficiency that I am referring to is *developer* efficiency. To help with the developer efficiency, Microsoft introduced a new framework for data access called the *Entity Framework* (or simply, *EF*) in .NET 3.5 Service Pack 1.

EF provides the capability to interact with data from relational databases using an object model that maps directly to the business objects (or domain objects) in your application. For example, rather than treating a batch of data as a collection of rows and columns, you can operate on a collection of strongly typed objects termed *entities*. These entities are held in specialized collection classes that are LINQ aware, enabling data access operations using C# code. The collection classes provide querying against the data store using the same LINQ grammar you learned about in Chapter 13.

In addition to working with your data as the application domain model (instead of a normalized database model), EF provides efficiencies such as state tracking, unit of work operations, and intrinsic transaction support.

Entity Framework Core is a complete rewrite of Entity Framework 6. It is built on top of the .NET 6 Framework, enabling EF Core to run on multiple platforms. Rewriting EF Core has enabled the team to add new features and performance improvements to EF Core that couldn't be reasonably implemented in EF 6.

Re-creating an entire framework from scratch requires a hard look at which features will be supported in the new framework and which features will be left behind. One of the features of EF 6 that is not in EF Core (and not likely to ever be added) is support for the Entity Designer. EF Core only supports what is called *code-first* development. The name is really a terrible name since it infers you can't use EF Core with an existing database. It really means "without a designer," but that wasn't the name that was chosen. EF Core can be used with existing databases that can be scaffolded into entity classes and a derived `DbContext`, or you can use EF Core to create/update your database from your entity classes and derived `DbContext`. I will cover both of these scenarios shortly.

With each release, EF Core has added more features that existed in EF 6 as well as new features that never existed in EF 6. The 3.1 release significantly shortened the list of essential features that are missing from EF Core (as compared to EF 6), and 5.0 closed the gap even more. The release of EF Core 6.0 has solidified the framework, and now, for most projects, EF Core has everything you need.

This chapter and the next three will introduce you to data access using EF Core. You will learn about the following: creating a domain model, mapping entity classes and properties to the database tables and columns, implementing change tracking, using the EF Core command-line interface (CLI) for scaffolding and migrations, as well as the role of the `DbContext` class. You will also learn about relating entities with navigation properties, transactions, and concurrency checking, just to name a few of the features explored. The fourth and final chapter on EF Core exercises the data access layer by using a series of integration tests. These tests demonstrate using EF Core for create, read, update, and delete (CRUD) operations.

By the time you complete these chapters, you will have the final version of the data access layer for our `AutoLot` database. Before we get into EF Core, let's talk about object-relational mappers in general.

A. Troelsen and P. Japikse, *Pro C# 10 with .NET 6*, https://doi.org/10.1007/978-1-4842-7869-7_21

■ **Note** Four chapters are not nearly enough to cover all of Entity Framework Core, as entire books (some the size of this one) are dedicated to just EF Core. The intent of these chapters is to give you a working knowledge to get you started using EF Core for your line-of-business applications.

Object-Relational Mappers

ADO.NET provides you with a fabric that lets you select, insert, update, and delete data with connections, commands, and data readers. While this is all well and good, these aspects of ADO.NET force you to treat the fetched data in a manner that is tightly coupled to the physical database schema. Recall, for example, when getting records from the database, you open a connection, create and execute a command object, and then use a data reader to iterate over each record using database-specific column names.

When you use ADO.NET, you must always be mindful of the physical structure of the back-end database. You must know the schema of each data table, author potentially complex SQL queries to interact with data table(s), track changes to the retrieved (or added) data, etc. This can force you to author some fairly verbose C# code because C# itself does not speak the language of the database schema directly.

To make matters worse, the way in which a physical database is usually constructed is squarely focused on database constructs such as foreign keys, views, stored procedures, and data normalization, not object-oriented programming.

Another concern for application developers is change tracking. Getting the data from the database is one step of the process, but any changes, additions, and/or deletions must be tracked by the developer so they can be persisted back to the data store.

The availability of *object-relational mapping* frameworks (commonly referred to as ORMs) in .NET greatly enhanced the data access story by managing the bulk of CRUD data access tasks for the developer. The developer creates a mapping between the .NET objects and the relational database, and the ORM manages connections, query generation, change tracking, and persisting the data. This leaves the developer free to focus on the business needs of the application.

■ **Note** It is important to remember that ORMs are not magical unicorns riding on rainbows. Every decision involves trade-offs. ORMs reduce the amount of work for developers creating data access layers but can also introduce performance and scaling issues if used improperly. Use ORMs for CRUD operations and use the power of your database for set-based operations.

Even though the different ORMs have slight differences in how they operate and how they are used, they all have essentially the same pieces and parts and strive for the same goal—to make data access operations easier. Entities are classes that are mapped to the database tables. A specialized collection type contains one or more entities. A change tracking mechanism tracks the state of the entities and any changes, additions, and/or deletions made to them, and a central construct controls operations as the ringleader.

Understanding the Role of the Entity Framework Core

Under the covers, EF Core uses the ADO.NET infrastructure you have already examined in the previous chapter. Like any ADO.NET interaction with a data store, EF Core uses an ADO.NET data provider for data store interactions. Before an ADO.NET data provider can be used by EF Core, it must be updated to fully integrate with EF Core. Due to this added functionality, you might have fewer EF Core data providers available than ADO.NET data providers.

The benefit of EF Core using the ADO.NET database provider pattern is that it enables you to combine EF Core and ADO.NET data access paradigms in the same project, augmenting your capabilities. For example, using EF Core to provide the connection, schema, and table name for bulk copy operations leverages the mapping capabilities of EF Core and the BCP functionality built into ADO.NET. This blended approach makes EF Core just another tool in your tool chest.

When you see how much of the basic data access plumbing is handled for you in a convenient and efficient manner, EF Core will most likely become your go-to mechanism for data access.

■ **Note** Many third-party databases (e.g., Oracle and MySQL) provide EF-aware data providers. If you are not using SQL Server, consult your database vendor for details or navigate to `https://docs.microsoft.com/en-us/ef/core/providers` for a list of available EF Core data providers.

EF Core best fits into the development process in forms-over-data (or API-over-data) situations. Operations on small numbers of entities using the unit of work pattern to ensure consistency is the sweet spot for EF Core. It is not very well suited for large-scale data operations such as extract-transform-load (ETL) data warehouse applications or large reporting situations.

The Building Blocks of the Entity Framework

The main components of EF Core are `DbContext`, `ChangeTracker`, the `DbSet` specialized collection type, the database providers, and the application's entities. To work through this chapter, create a new Console Application named AutoLot.Samples and add the `Microsoft.EntityFrameworkCore`, `Microsoft.EntityFrameworkCore.Design`, and `Microsoft.EntityFrameworkCore.SqlServer` packages. Remember to disable nullable reference types in the project file:

```
<PropertyGroup>
  <OutputType>Exe</OutputType>
  <TargetFramework>net6.0</TargetFramework>
  <ImplicitUsings>enable</ImplicitUsings>
  <Nullable>disable</Nullable>
</PropertyGroup>
```

The `Microsoft.EntityFrameworkCore` package provides the common functionality for EF Core. The `Microsoft.EntityFrameworkCore.SqlServer` package supplies the SQL Server data provider, and the `Microsoft.EntityFrameworkCore.Design` package is required for the EF Core command-line tools.

■ **Note** If you prefer to use the NuGet Package Manager Console to run the EF Core commands, install the `Microsoft.EntityFrameworkCore.Tools` package. This text does not cover the NuGet-style commands since the CLI works across all platforms and doesn't rely on Visual Studio.

Add a new file named `GlobalUsings.cs`, clear out the template code, and update the file to match the following:

```
global using Microsoft.EntityFrameworkCore;
global using Microsoft.EntityFrameworkCore.ChangeTracking;
global using Microsoft.EntityFrameworkCore.Design;
```

```
global using Microsoft.EntityFrameworkCore.Metadata;
global using Microsoft.EntityFrameworkCore.Metadata.Builders;

global using System.ComponentModel.DataAnnotations;
global using System.ComponentModel.DataAnnotations.Schema;
```

The DbContext Class

The DbContext class is the ringleader component of EF Core and provides access to the database through the Database property. DbContext manages the ChangeTracker instance, exposes the virtual OnModelCreating() method for access to the Fluent API, holds all the DbSet<T> properties, and supplies the SaveChanges method to persist data to the data store. It is not used directly, but through a custom class that inherits DbContext. It is in the derived class that the DbSet<T> properties are placed.

Table 21-1 shows some of the more commonly used members of DbContext.

Table 21-1. *Common Members of DbContext*

Member of DbContext	Meaning in Life
Database	Provides access to database-related information and functionality, including execution of SQL statements.
Model	The metadata about the shape of entities, the relationships between them, and how they map to the database. **Note:** This property is usually not interacted with directly.
ChangeTracker	Provides access to information and operations for entity instances this DbContext is tracking.
DbSet<T>	Not truly a member of DbContext, but properties added to the custom derived DbContext class. The properties are of type DbSet<T> and are used to query and save instances of application entities. LINQ queries against DbSet<T> properties are translated into SQL queries.
Entry()	Provides access to change tracking information and operations for the entity, such as explicitly loading related entities or changing the EntityState. Can also be called on an untracked entity to change the state to tracked.
Set<TEntity>()	Creates an instance of the DbSet<T> property that can be used to query and persist data.
SaveChanges()/SaveChangesAsync()	Saves all entity changes to the database and returns the number of records affected. Executes in a transaction (implicit or explicit).
Add()/AddRange() Update()/UpdateRange() Remove()/RemoveRange()	Methods to add, update, and remove entity instances. Changes are persisted only when SaveChanges() is executed successfully. Async versions are available as well. **Note:** While available on the derived DbContext, these methods are usually called directly on the DbSet<T> properties.
Find()	Finds an entity of a type with the given primary key values. Async versions are available as well. **Note:** While available on the derived DbContext, these methods are usually called directly on the DbSet<T> properties.

(*continued*)

Table 21-1. *(continued)*

Member of DbContext	Meaning in Life
`Attach()/AttachRange()`	Begins tracking an entity (or list of entities). Async versions are available as well. **Note:** While available on the derived `DbContext`, these methods are usually called directly on the `DbSet<T>` properties.
`SavingChanges()`	Event fired at the beginning of a call to `SaveChanges()/SaveChangesAsync()`.
`SavedChanges()`	Event fired at the end of a call to `SaveChanges()/SaveChangesAsync()`.
`SaveChangesFailed`	Event fired if a call to `SaveChanges()/SaveChangesAsync()` fails.
`OnModelCreating()`	Called when a model has been initialized, but before it's finalized. Methods from the Fluent API are placed in this method to finalize the shape of the model.
`OnConfiguring()`	A builder used to create or modify options for `DbContext`. Executes each time a `DbContext` instance is created. **Note:** It is recommended not to use this and instead use `DbContextOptions` to configure the `DbContext` instance at runtime and use an instance of `IDesignTimeDbContextFactory` at design time.

Creating a Derived DbContext

The first step in EF Core is to create a custom class that inherits from `DbContext`. Then add a constructor that accepts a strongly typed instance of `DbContextOptions` (covered next) and passes the instance through to the base class. Add a file named `ApplicationDbContext.cs` and update the code to match the following:

```
namespace AutoLot.Samples;

public class ApplicationDbContext : DbContext
{
  public ApplicationDbContext(DbContextOptions<ApplicationDbContext> options)
     : base(options)
  {
  }
}
```

This is the class that is used to access the database and work with entities, the change tracker, and all components of EF Core.

Configuring the DbContext

The `DbContext` instance is configured using an instance of the `DbContextOptions` class. The `DbContextOptions` instance is created using `DbContextOptionsBuilder`, as the `DbContextOptions` class is not meant to be directly constructed in your code. Through the `DbContextOptionsBuilder` instance, the database provider is selected (along with any provider-specific settings), and EF Core `DbContext` general options (such as logging) are set. Then the instance of the `DbContextOptions` is injected into the base `DbContext` at runtime. You will see this in action in the next section.

This dynamic configuration capability enables changing settings at runtime simply by selecting different options (e.g., MySQL instead of the SQL Server provider) and creating a new instance of your derived `DbContext`.

The Design-Time DbContext Factory

The design-time DbContext factory is a class that implements the IDesignTimeDbContextFactory<T> interface, where T is the derived DbContext class. The interface has one method, CreateDbContext(), that you must implement to create an instance of your derived DbContext. This class is not meant for production use, but only during development, and exists primarily for the EF Core command-line tools, which you will explore shortly. In the examples in this and the next chapter, it will be used to create new instances of the ApplicationDbContext.

■ **Note** It is considered bad practice to use the DbContext factory to create instances of your derived DbContext class. Remember that this is demo code meant for teaching, and using it in this way keeps the demo code cleaner. You will see how to properly instantiate your derived DbContext class in the chapters on Windows Presentation Foundation and ASP.NET Core.

The following ApplicationDbContextFactory class uses the CreateDbContext() method to create a strongly typed DbContextOptionsBuilder for the ApplicationDbContext class, sets the database provider to the SQL Server provider (using the Docker instance connection string from Chapter 20), and then creates and returns a new instance of the ApplicationDbContext:

```
namespace AutoLot.Samples;

public class ApplicationDbContextFactory : IDesignTimeDbContextFactory<ApplicationDbContext>
{
  public ApplicationDbContext CreateDbContext(string[] args)
  {
    var optionsBuilder = new DbContextOptionsBuilder<ApplicationDbContext>();
    var connectionString = @"server=.,5433;Database=AutoLotSamples;User Id=sa;Password=
    P@ssw0rd;Encrypt=False;";
    optionsBuilder.UseSqlServer(connectionString);
    Console.WriteLine(connectionString);
    return new ApplicationDbContext(optionsBuilder.Options);
  }
}
```

■ **Note** The database name used in these samples is AutoLotSamples, and not AutoLot, which was the name used in Chapter 20. The AutoLot database will be updated to its final form starting with Chapter 20.

Again, the context factory is designed for the EF Core command-line interface to create an instance of the derived DbContext class, and not for production use. The command-line interface uses the factory when performing actions such as creating or applying database migrations. One major reason that you don't want to use this in production is the hard-coded connection string. Since this is for design-time use, using a set connection string that points to the development database works perfectly.

The CreateDbContext() method takes a string array as argument. While not used in earlier versions, support for passing in arguments from the command line into the IDesignTimeDbContextFactory CreateDbContext() method was added in EF Core 5.

OnModelCreating

The base DbContext class exposes the OnModelCreating method that is used to shape your entities using the Fluent API. This will be covered in depth later in this chapter, but for now, add the following code to the ApplicationDbContext class:

```
protected override void OnModelCreating(ModelBuilder modelBuilder)
{
  // Fluent API calls go here
}
```

Saving Changes

To persist any changes (add, update, or delete) to entities, call the SaveChanges() (or SaveChangesAsync()) method on the derived DbContext. The SaveChanges()/SaveChangesAsync() methods wrap the database calls in an implicit transaction and persist them as a unit of work. Transactions are covered next, and the change tracker is covered later in this section.

Add the following global using statement to the GlobalUsings.cs file:

```
global using AutoLot.Samples;
```

Clear out any code in the Program.cs file, and update it to match the following:

```
Console.WriteLine("Fun with Entity Framework Core");

static void SampleSaveChanges()
{
    //The factory is not meant to be used like this, but it's demo code :-)
    var context = new ApplicationDbContextFactory().CreateDbContext(null);
    //make some changes
    context.SaveChanges();
}
```

There will be many examples of saving changes through the rest of this chapter (and book).

Transaction and Save Point Support

As mentioned previously, EF Core wraps each call to SaveChanges()/SaveChangesAsync() in an implicit transaction. By default, the transaction uses the isolation level of the database. For more control, you can enlist the derived DbContext into an explicit transaction instead of using the default implicit transaction. To execute in an explicit transaction, create a transaction using the Database property of the derived DbContext. Conduct your operation(s) as usual and then commit or roll back the transaction. Here is a code snippet that demonstrates this:

```
static void TransactedSaveChanges()
{
  //The factory is not meant to be used like this, but it's demo code :-)
  var context = new ApplicationDbContextFactory().CreateDbContext(null);
  using var trans = context.Database.BeginTransaction();
```

```
  try
  {
    //Create, change, delete stuff
    context.SaveChanges();
    trans.Commit();
  }
  catch (Exception ex)
  {
    trans.Rollback();
  }
}
```

Save points for EF Core transactions were introduced in EF Core 5. When SaveChanges()/SaveChangesAsync() is called and a transaction is already in progress, EF Core creates a save point in that transaction. If the call fails, the transaction is rolled back to the save point and not the beginning of the transaction. Save points can also be managed programmatically by calling CreateSavePoint() and RollbackToSavepoint() on the transaction, like this:

```
static void UsingSavePoints()
{
  //The factory is not meant to be used like this, but it's demo code :-)
  var context = new ApplicationDbContextFactory().CreateDbContext(null);
  using var trans = context.Database.BeginTransaction();
  try
  {
    //Create, change, delete stuff
    trans.CreateSavepoint("check point 1");
    context.SaveChanges();
    trans.Commit();
  }
  catch (Exception ex)
  {
    trans. RollbackToSavepoint("check point 1");
  }
}
```

Explicit Transactions and Execution Strategies

When an execution strategy is active (covered in the next chapter in the "Connection Resiliency" section), before creating an explicit transaction, you must get a reference to the current execution strategy in use. Then call the Execute() method on the strategy to create an explicit transaction.

```
static void TransactionWithExecutionStrategies()
{
  //The factory is not meant to be used like this, but it's demo code :-)
  var context = new ApplicationDbContextFactory().CreateDbContext(null);
  var strategy = context.Database.CreateExecutionStrategy();
  strategy.Execute(() =>
  {
    using var trans = context.Database.BeginTransaction();
```

```
      try
      {
        //actionToExecute();
        trans.Commit();
        Console.WriteLine("Insert succeeded");
      }
      catch (Exception ex)
      {
        trans.Rollback();
        Console.WriteLine($"Insert failed: {ex.Message}");
      }
    });
}
```

Saving/Saved Changes Events

EF Core 5 introduced three new events that are triggered by the SaveChanges()/SaveChangesAsync() methods. The SavingChanges event fires when SaveChanges() is called but before the SQL statements are executed against the data store. The SavedChanges event fires after SaveChanges() has completed. The SaveChangesFailed event fires if the call to SaveChanges() was unsuccessful. The following (trivial) code examples in the ApplicationDbContext class constructor show the events and their handlers in action:

```
public ApplicationDbContext(DbContextOptions<ApplicationDbContext> options)
    : base(options)
{
  SavingChanges += (sender, args) =>
  {
    Console.WriteLine($"Saving changes for {((DbContext)sender).Database.
GetConnectionString()}");
  };
  SavedChanges += (sender, args) =>
  {
    Console.WriteLine($"Saved {args.EntitiesSavedCount} entities");
  };
  SaveChangesFailed += (sender, args) =>
  {
    Console.WriteLine($"An exception occurred! {args.Exception.Message} entities");
  };
}
```

The DbSet<T> Class

For each entity type (T) in your object model, you add a property of type DbSet<T> to the derived DbContext class. The DbSet<T> class is a specialized collection property used to interact with the database provider to read, add, update, or delete records in the database. Each DbSet<T> provides a number of core services for the database interactions, including translating LINQ queries executed against a DbSet<T> property into database queries by the database provider. Table 21-2 describes some of the core members of the DbSet<T> class.

Table 21-2. Common Members and Extension Methods of DbSet<T>

Member of DbSet<T>	Meaning in Life
Add()/AddRange()	Begins tracking the entity/entities in the Added state. Item(s) will be added when SaveChanges() is called. Async versions are available as well.
AsAsyncEnumerable()	Returns the collection as IAsyncEnumerable<T>.
AsQueryable()	Returns the collection as IQueryable<T>.
Find()	Searches for the entity in the ChangeTracker by primary key. If not found in the change tracker, the data store is queried for the object. An async version is available as well.
Update()UpdateRange()	Begins tracking the entity/entities in the Modified state. Item(s) will be updated when SaveChanges is called. Async versions are available as well.
Remove()RemoveRange()	Begins tracking the entity/entities in the Deleted state. Item(s) will be removed when SaveChanges() is called. Async versions are available as well.
Attach()AttachRange()	Begins tracking the entity/entities. Entities with numeric primary keys defined as an identity and value equaling zero are tracked as Added. All others are tracked as Unchanged. Async versions are available as well.
FromSqlRaw() FromSqlInterpolated()	Creates a LINQ query based on a raw or interpolated string representing a SQL query. Can be combined with additional LINQ statements for server-side execution.
AsQueryable()	Returns an IQueryable<T> instance from DbSet<T>.

The DbSet<T> type implements IQueryable<T>, which enables the use of LINQ queries to retrieve records from the database. In addition to extension methods added by EF Core, DbSet<T> supports the same extension methods you learned about in Chapter 13, such as ForEach(), Select(), and All().

You will be adding the DbSet<T> properties to ApplicationDbContext in the "Entities" section.

■ **Note** Many of the methods listed in Table 21-2 are named the same as the methods in Table 21-1. The main difference is that the DbSet<T> methods already know the type to operate on and have the list of entities. The DbContext methods must determine what to act on using reflection. It is much more common to use the methods on the DbSet<T> properties rather than the more general methods on the derived DbContext.

The ChangeTracker

The ChangeTracker instance tracks the state for objects loaded into DbSet<T> within a DbContext instance. Table 21-3 lists the possible values for the state of an object.

Table 21-3. Entity State Enumeration Values

Value	Meaning in Life
Added	The entity is being tracked but does not yet exist in the database.
Deleted	The entity is being tracked and is marked for deletion from the database.
Detached	The entity is not being tracked by the change tracker.
Modified	The entry is being tracked and has been changed.
Unchanged	The entity is being tracked, exists in the database, and has not been modified.

If you need to check the state of an object, use the following code:

```
EntityState state = context.Entry(entity).State;
```

You can also programmatically change the state of an object using the same mechanism. To change the state to Deleted (for example), use the following code:

```
context.Entry(entity).State = EntityState.Deleted;
```

ChangeTracker Events

There are two events that can be raised by ChangeTracker. The first is StateChanged, and the second is Tracked. The StateChanged event fires when an entity's state is changed. It does not fire when an entity is first tracked. The Tracked event fires when an entity starts being tracked, either by being programmatically added to a DbSet<T> instance or when returned from a query.

Update the constructor for the ApplicationDbContext class to the following to specify the event handlers for the StateChanged and Tracked events:

```
public ApplicationDbContext(DbContextOptions<ApplicationDbContext> options)
  : base(options)
{
...
  ChangeTracker.StateChanged += ChangeTracker_StateChanged;
  ChangeTracker.Tracked += ChangeTracker_Tracked;
}
```

The StateChanged Event

As mentioned, the StateChanged event fires when the state of an entity changes, but not when an entity is first tracked. The OldState and NewState are exposed through the EntityStateChangedEventArgs. The following example writes to the console anytime an entity is updated:

```
private void ChangeTracker_StateChanged(object sender, EntityStateChangedEventArgs e)
{
  if (e.OldState == EntityState.Modified && e.NewState == EntityState.Unchanged)
  {
    Console.WriteLine($"An entity of type {e.Entry.Entity.GetType().Name} was updated.");
  }
}
```

The Tracked Event

The Tracked event fires when ChangeTracker starts to track an entity. The FromQuery property of the EntityTrackedEventArgs indicates if the entity was loaded via a database query or programmatically. The following example writes to the console anytime an entity is loaded from the database:

```
private void ChangeTracker_Tracked(object sender, EntityTrackedEventArgs e)
{
  if (e.FromQuery)
  {
    Console.WriteLine($"An entity of type {e.Entry.Entity.GetType().Name} was loaded from
    the database.");
  }
}
```

Resetting DbContext State

EF Core 5 added the ability to reset a derived DbContext back to its original state. The ChangeTracker.Clear() method clears out all entities from the DbSet<T> collections by setting their state to Detached. The main benefit of this is to improve performance. As with any ORM, there is some overhead that comes with instantiating a derived DbContext class. While that overhead isn't usually significant, the ability to clean up an already instantiated context could help with performance in some scenarios.

Entities

The strongly typed classes that map to database tables are officially called *entities*. The collection of entities in an application comprises a conceptual model of a physical database. Formally speaking, this model is termed an *entity data model* (EDM), usually referred to simply as the *model*. The model is mapped to the application/business domain. The entities and their properties are mapped to the tables and columns using Entity Framework Core conventions, configuration, and the Fluent API (code). Entities do not need to map directly to the database schema. You are free to structure your entity classes to fit your application needs and then map your unique entities to your database schema.

This loose coupling between the database and your entities means you can shape the entities to match your business domain, independent of the database design and structure. For example, take the simple Inventory table in the AutoLot database and the Car entity class from the previous chapter. The names are different, yet the Car entity can be mapped to the Inventory table. EF Core examines the configuration of your entities in the model to map the client-side representation of the Inventory table (in our example, the Car class) to the correct columns of the Inventory table.

The next several sections detail how EF Core conventions, data annotations, and code (using the Fluent API) map entities, properties, and the relationships between entities in the mode to the tables, columns, and foreign key relationships in your database. Each of these topics is covered in depth later in this chapter.

Entity Properties and Database Columns

When using a relational data store, EF Core uses data from a table's columns to populate an entity's properties when reading from the data store and writes from the entity's properties to a table's columns when persisting data. If the property is an automatic property, EF Core reads and writes through the getter and setter. If the property has a backing field, EF Core will read and write to the backing field instead of the public property, even if the backing field is private. While EF Core *can* read and write to private fields, there still must be a public read-write property that encapsulates the backing field.

Two scenarios where the backing field support is advantageous are when using the `INotifyPropertyChanged` pattern in Windows Presentation Foundation (WPF) applications and when database default values clash with .NET default values. Using EF Core with WPF is covered in Chapter 28, and database default values are covered later in this chapter.

Table Mapping Schemes

There are two class to table mapping schemes available in EF Core: *table-per-hierarchy* (TPH) and *table-per-type* (TPT). TPH mapping is the default and maps an inheritance hierarchy to a single table. Introduced in EF Core 5, TPT maps each class in the hierarchy to its own table.

■ **Note** Classes can also be mapped to views and raw SQL queries. These are referred to as *query types* and are covered later in this chapter.

Table Per-Hierarchy Mapping

Consider the following example, which shows the `Car` class from Chapter 20 split into two classes: a base class (`BaseEntity`) for the `Id` and `TimeStamp` properties, and the rest of the properties in the `Car` class. The code for the TPH examples are in the AutoLot.TPH project in the source for this chapter.

```
//BaseEntity.cs
namespace AutoLot.TPH.Models;

public abstract class BaseEntity
{
  public int Id { get; set; }
  public byte[] TimeStamp { get; set; }
}

//Car.cs
namespace AutoLot.TPH.Models;

public class Car : BaseEntity
{
  public string Color { get; set; }
  public string PetName { get; set; }
  public int MakeId { get; set; }
}
```

To make EF Core aware that an entity class is part of the object model, add a `DbSet<T>` property for the entity. Create an `ApplicationDbContext` class and update it to the following:

```
using Microsoft.EntityFrameworkCore;
using AutoLot.TPH.Models;

namespace AutoLot.TPH;
```

```
public class ApplicationDbContext : DbContext
{
  public ApplicationDbContext(DbContextOptions<ApplicationDbContext> options)
    : base(options) { }
  public DbSet<Car> Cars { get; set; }
}
```

Note the DbSet<T> property in the ApplicationDbContext class. This informs EF Core that the Car class maps to the Cars table in the database (more on this in the "Entity Conventions" section). Also notice that there isn't a DbSet<T> property for the BaseEntity class. This is because in the TPH scheme, the entire hierarchy becomes a *single* table. The properties of the tables up the inheritance chain are folded into the table with the DbSet<T> property. This is shown by the following SQL:

```
CREATE TABLE [dbo].[Cars](
    [Id] [INT] IDENTITY(1,1) NOT NULL,
    [Color] [NVARCHAR](MAX) NULL,
    [PetName] [NVARCHAR](MAX) NULL,
    [MakeId] [INT] NOT NULL,
    [TimeStamp] [VARBINARY](MAX) NULL,
 CONSTRAINT [PK_Cars] PRIMARY KEY CLUSTERED
(
    [Id] ASC
)
WITH (PAD_INDEX = OFF, STATISTICS_NORECOMPUTE = OFF,
IGNORE_DUP_KEY = OFF, ALLOW_ROW_LOCKS = ON, ALLOW_PAGE_LOCKS = ON,
OPTIMIZE_FOR_SEQUENTIAL_KEY = OFF) ON [PRIMARY]
) ON [PRIMARY] TEXTIMAGE_ON [PRIMARY]
```

Table-per-Type Mapping

To explore the TPT mapping scheme, the BaseEntity and Car classes can be used, even with the base class marked as abstract. Since TPH is the default, EF Core must be instructed to map each class to a table. This can be done with data annotations (shown later in this chapter) or the Fluent API. To use the TPT mapping scheme, use the following Fluent API code in the OnModelCreating() method of the ApplicationDbContext. These examples are in the AutoLot.TPT project in the chapter's code samples.

```
protected override void OnModelCreating(ModelBuilder modelBuilder)
{
  modelBuilder.Entity<BaseEntity>().ToTable("BaseEntities");
  modelBuilder.Entity<Car>().ToTable("Cars");
}
```

EF Core will create two tables, shown here. The indexes also show that the tables have a one-to-one mapping between the BaseEntities and Cars tables.

```
CREATE TABLE [dbo].[BaseEntities](
    [Id] [INT] IDENTITY(1,1) NOT NULL,
    [TimeStamp] [VARBINARY](MAX) NULL,
 CONSTRAINT [PK_BaseEntities] PRIMARY KEY CLUSTERED
```

```
(
    [Id] ASC
)WITH (PAD_INDEX = OFF, STATISTICS_NORECOMPUTE = OFF, IGNORE_DUP_KEY = OFF,
ALLOW_ROW_LOCKS = ON, ALLOW_PAGE_LOCKS = ON, OPTIMIZE_FOR_SEQUENTIAL_KEY = OFF)
ON [PRIMARY]
) ON [PRIMARY] TEXTIMAGE_ON [PRIMARY]
GO

CREATE TABLE [dbo].[Cars](
    [Id] [INT] NOT NULL,
    [Color] [NVARCHAR](MAX) NULL,
    [PetName] [NVARCHAR](MAX) NULL,
    [MakeId] [INT] NOT NULL,
 CONSTRAINT [PK_Cars] PRIMARY KEY CLUSTERED
(
    [Id] ASC
)WITH (PAD_INDEX = OFF, STATISTICS_NORECOMPUTE = OFF, IGNORE_DUP_KEY = OFF, ALLOW_ROW_LOCKS
= ON, ALLOW_PAGE_LOCKS = ON, OPTIMIZE_FOR_SEQUENTIAL_KEY = OFF) ON [PRIMARY]
) ON [PRIMARY] TEXTIMAGE_ON [PRIMARY]
GO

ALTER TABLE [dbo].[Cars]  WITH CHECK ADD  CONSTRAINT [FK_Cars_BaseEntities_Id] FOREIGN
KEY([Id])
REFERENCES [dbo].[BaseEntities] ([Id])
GO

ALTER TABLE [dbo].[Cars] CHECK CONSTRAINT [FK_Cars_BaseEntities_Id]
GO
```

■ **Note** Table-per-type mapping can have significant performance implications that should be considered before using this mapping scheme. For more information, refer to the documentation: `https://docs.microsoft.com/en-us/ef/core/performance/modeling-for-performance#inheritance-mapping`.

Navigation Properties and Foreign Keys

Navigation properties represent how entity classes relate to each other and enable code to traverse from one entity instance to another. By definition, a navigation property is any property that maps to a nonscalar type as defined by the database provider. In practice, navigation properties map to another entity (called *reference navigation properties*) or a collection of another entity (called *collection navigation properties*). On the database side, navigation properties are translated into foreign key relationships between tables. One-to-one, one-to-many, and (new in EF Core 5) many-to-many relationships are directly supported in EF Core. Entity classes can also have navigation properties that point back to themselves, representing self-referencing tables.

■ **Note** I find it helpful to consider objects with navigation properties as linked lists, and if the navigation properties are bidirectional, the objects act like doubly linked lists.

Before covering the details of navigation properties and entity relationship patterns, refer to Table 21-4. These terms are used in all three relationship patterns.

Table 21-4. *Terms Used to Describe Navigation Properties and Relationships*

Term	Meaning in Life
Principal entity	The parent of the relationship.
Dependent entity	The child of the relationship.
Principal key	The property/properties used to define the principal entity. Can be the primary key or an alternate key. Keys can be configured using a single property or multiple properties.
Foreign key	The property/properties held by the child entity to store the principal key.
Required relationship	Relationship where the foreign key value is required (non-nullable).
Optional relationship	Relationship where the foreign key value is not (nullable).

Missing Foreign Key Properties

If an entity with a reference navigation property does not have a property for the foreign key value, EF Core will create the necessary property/properties on the entity. These are known as *shadow foreign key properties* and are named in the format of `<navigation property name><principal key property name>` or `<principal entity name><principal key property name>`. This is true for all the relationship types (one-to-many, one-to-one, many-to-many). It is a much cleaner approach to build your entities with explicit foreign key property/properties than to make EF Core create them for you.

One-to-Many Relationships

To create a one-to-many relationship, the entity class on the one side (the principal) adds a collection property of the entity class that is on the many side (the dependent). The dependent entity should also have properties for the foreign key back to the principal. If not, EF Core will create shadow foreign key properties, as explained earlier.

For example, in the database created in Chapter 20, the `Makes` table (represented by the `Make` entity class) and `Inventory` table (represented by the `Car` entity class) have a one-to-many relationship.

■ **Note** For these initial examples, the `Car` class will map to a table named `Cars`. Later in this chapter the `Car` class will be mapped to the `Inventory` table.

Back in the AutoLot.Samples project, create a new folder named Models. Add the following BaseEntity.cs, Make.cs, and Car.cs files as shown in the code listing. The bold code shows the bidirectional navigation properties representing the one-to-many relationship:

```
//BaseEntity.cs
namespace AutoLot.Samples.Models;

public abstract class BaseEntity
{
  public int Id { get; set; }
  public byte[] TimeStamp { get; set; }
}

//Make.cs
namespace AutoLot.Samples.Models;

  public class Make : BaseEntity
  {
     public string Name { get; set; }
     public IEnumerable<Car> Cars { get; set; } = new List<Car>();
  }

//Car.cs
namespace AutoLot.Samples.Models;

public class Car : BaseEntity
{
  public string Color { get; set; }
  public string PetName { get; set; }
  public int MakeId { get; set; }
  public Make MakeNavigation { get; set; }
}
```

■ **Note** When scaffolding an existing database (as you will do in the next chapter), EF Core names reference navigation properties the same as the property type name (e.g., `public Make Make {get; set;}`). This can cause issues with navigation and IntelliSense, as well as make the code difficult to work with. I prefer to add the suffix `Navigation` to reference navigation properties for clarity, as shown in the previous example.

In the `Car`/`Make` example, the `Car` entity is the dependent entity (the *many* of the one-to-many), and the `Make` entity is the principal entity (the *one* of the one-to-many).

Update the `GlobalUsings.cs` file to include the new namespace for the models:

```
global using AutoLot.Samples.Models;
```

Next, add the `DbSet<Car>` and `DbSet<Make>` properties to `ApplicationDbContext`, as shown here:

```
public DbSet<Car> Cars { get; set; }
public DbSet<Make> Makes { get; set; }
```

When the database is updated using EF Core migrations, the following tables are created:

```
CREATE TABLE [dbo].[Makes](
  [Id] [int] IDENTITY(1,1) NOT NULL,
  [Name] [nvarchar](max) NULL,
  [TimeStamp] [varbinary](max) NULL,
 CONSTRAINT [PK_Makes] PRIMARY KEY CLUSTERED
(
  [Id] ASC
)WITH (PAD_INDEX = OFF, STATISTICS_NORECOMPUTE = OFF, IGNORE_DUP_KEY = OFF, ALLOW_ROW_LOCKS = ON,
ALLOW_PAGE_LOCKS = ON, OPTIMIZE_FOR_SEQUENTIAL_KEY = OFF) ON [PRIMARY]
) ON [PRIMARY] TEXTIMAGE_ON [PRIMARY]
GO

CREATE TABLE [dbo].[Cars](
  [Id] [int] IDENTITY(1,1) NOT NULL,
  [Color] [nvarchar](max) NULL,
  [PetName] [nvarchar](max) NULL,
  [TimeStamp] [varbinary](max) NULL,
  [MakeId] [int] NOT NULL,
 CONSTRAINT [PK_Cars] PRIMARY KEY CLUSTERED
(
  [Id] ASC
)WITH (PAD_INDEX = OFF, STATISTICS_NORECOMPUTE = OFF, IGNORE_DUP_KEY = OFF, ALLOW_ROW_LOCKS = ON,
ALLOW_PAGE_LOCKS = ON, OPTIMIZE_FOR_SEQUENTIAL_KEY = OFF) ON [PRIMARY]
) ON [PRIMARY] TEXTIMAGE_ON [PRIMARY]
GO

ALTER TABLE [dbo].[Cars] WITH CHECK ADD  CONSTRAINT [FK_Cars_Makes_MakeId]
  FOREIGN KEY([MakeId]) REFERENCES [dbo].[Makes] ([Id])
  ON DELETE CASCADE
GO
ALTER TABLE [dbo].[Cars] CHECK CONSTRAINT [FK_Cars_Makes_MakeId]
GO
```

Note the foreign key and check constraints created on the dependent (`Cars`) table.

■ **Note** Updating the database using EF Core migrations is covered later in this chapter. If you are already familiar with EF Core migrations or want to skip ahead to the section on EF Core CLI commands to learn about migrations before continuing on with this section, the specific commands to create these tables are here: `dotnet ef migrations add Initial -o Migrations -c AutoLot.Samples.ApplicationDbContextdotnet ef database update Initial -c AutoLot.Samples.ApplicationDbContext`

One-to-One Relationships

In one-to-one relationships, both entities have a reference navigation property to the other entity. While one-to-many relationships clearly denote the principal and dependent entity, when building one-to-one relationships, EF Core must be informed which side is the principal entity. This can be done either by having a clearly defined foreign key to the principal entity or by indicating the principal using the Fluent API. If EF Core is not informed through one of those two methods, it will choose one based on its ability to detect a foreign key. In practice, you should clearly define the dependent by adding foreign key properties. This removes any ambiguity and ensures that your tables are properly configured.

Add a new class named Radio.cs and update the code to the following:

```
namespace AutoLot.Samples.Models;

public class Radio : BaseEntity
{
  public bool HasTweeters { get; set; }
  public bool HasSubWoofers { get; set; }
  public string RadioId { get; set; }
  public int CarId { get; set; }
  public Car CarNavigation { get; set; }
}
```

Add the Radio navigation property to the Car class:

```
namespace AutoLot.Samples.Models;

public class Car : BaseEntity
{

  public Radio RadioNavigation { get; set; }
}
```

Since Radio has a foreign key to the Car class (based on convention, covered shortly), Radio is the dependent entity, and Car is the principal entity. EF Core creates the required unique index on the foreign key property in the dependent entity implicitly. If you want to change the name of the index, that can be accomplished using data annotations or the Fluent API.

Add the DbSet<Radio> property to the ApplicationDbContext class:

```
public DbSet<Car> Cars { get; set; }
public DbSet<Make> Makes { get; set; }
public DbSet<Radio> Radios { get; set; }
```

When the database is updated using the following EF Core migrations, the Cars table is unchanged, and the following Radios table is created:

```
dotnet ef migrations add Radio -o Migrations -c AutoLot.Samples.ApplicationDbContext
dotnet ef database update Radio  -c AutoLot.Samples.ApplicationDbContext
```

The following shows the added Radios table:

```
CREATE TABLE [dbo].[Radios](
  [Id] [int] IDENTITY(1,1) NOT NULL,
  [HasTweeters] [bit] NOT NULL,
  [HasSubWoofers] [bit] NOT NULL,
  [RadioId] [nvarchar](max) NULL,
  [TimeStamp] [varbinary](max) NULL,
  [CarId] [int] NOT NULL,
```

```
 CONSTRAINT [PK_Radios] PRIMARY KEY CLUSTERED
(
        [Id] ASC
)WITH (PAD_INDEX = OFF, STATISTICS_NORECOMPUTE = OFF, IGNORE_DUP_KEY = OFF, ALLOW_ROW_LOCKS = ON,
ALLOW_PAGE_LOCKS = ON, OPTIMIZE_FOR_SEQUENTIAL_KEY = OFF) ON [PRIMARY]
) ON [PRIMARY] TEXTIMAGE_ON [PRIMARY]
GO
ALTER TABLE [dbo].[Radios]  WITH CHECK ADD  CONSTRAINT [FK_Radios_Cars_CarId] FOREIGN
KEY([CarId])
REFERENCES [dbo].[Cars] ([Id])
ON DELETE CASCADE
GO
ALTER TABLE [dbo].[Radios] CHECK CONSTRAINT [FK_Radios_Cars_CarId]
GO
```

Note the foreign key and check constraints created on the dependent (Radios) table (shown in bold).

Many-to-Many Relationships

In many-to-many relationships, both entities have a collection navigation property to the other entity. This is implemented in the data store with a join table in between the two entity tables. This join table, by default, is named after the two tables using <Entity1Entity2>, but can be changed programmatically through the Fluent API. The join entity has one-to-many relationships to each of the entity tables.

Start by creating a Driver class, which will have a many-to-many relationship with the Car class. On the Driver side, this is implemented with a collection navigation property to the Car class:

```
namespace AutoLot.Samples.Models;

public class Driver : BaseEntity
{
  public string FirstName { get; set; }
  public string LastName { get; set; }
  public IEnumerable<Car> Cars { get; set; } = new List<Car>();
}
```

Add the DbSet<Driver> property to the ApplicationDbContext class:

```
public DbSet<Car> Cars { get; set; }
public DbSet<Make> Makes { get; set; }
public DbSet<Radio> Radios { get; set; }
public DbSet<Driver> Drivers { get; set; }
```

Next, update the Car class to have a collection navigation property to the new Driver class:

```
namespace AutoLot.Samples.Models;

public class Car : BaseEntity
{
  public string Color { get; set; }
  public string PetName { get; set; }
  public int MakeId { get; set; }
  public Make MakeNavigation { get; set; }
```

```
  public Radio RadioNavigation { get; set; }
  public IEnumerable<Driver> Drivers { get; set; } = new List<Driver>();
}
```

To update the database, use the following migration commands (again, migrations will be fully explained later in this chapter):

```
dotnet ef migrations add Drivers -o Migrations -c AutoLot.Samples.ApplicationDbContext
dotnet ef database update Drivers  -c AutoLot.Samples.ApplicationDbContext
```

When the database is updated, the Cars table is unchanged, and the Drivers and CarDriver tables are created. Here are the definitions for the new tables:

```
CREATE TABLE [dbo].[Drivers](
  [Id] [INT] IDENTITY(1,1) NOT NULL,
  [FirstName] [NVARCHAR](MAX) NULL,
  [LastName] [NVARCHAR](MAX) NULL,
  [TimeStamp] [VARBINARY](MAX) NULL,
 CONSTRAINT [PK_Drivers] PRIMARY KEY CLUSTERED
(
  [Id] ASC
)WITH (PAD_INDEX = OFF, STATISTICS_NORECOMPUTE = OFF, IGNORE_DUP_KEY = OFF, ALLOW_ROW_LOCKS
= ON, ALLOW_PAGE_LOCKS = ON, OPTIMIZE_FOR_SEQUENTIAL_KEY = OFF) ON [PRIMARY]
) ON [PRIMARY] TEXTIMAGE_ON [PRIMARY]
GO

CREATE TABLE [dbo].[CarDriver](
  [CarsId] [int] NOT NULL,
  [DriversId] [int] NOT NULL,
 CONSTRAINT [PK_CarDriver] PRIMARY KEY CLUSTERED
(
  [CarsId] ASC,
  [DriversId] ASC
)WITH (PAD_INDEX = OFF, STATISTICS_NORECOMPUTE = OFF, IGNORE_DUP_KEY = OFF, ALLOW_ROW_LOCKS
= ON, ALLOW_PAGE_LOCKS = ON, OPTIMIZE_FOR_SEQUENTIAL_KEY = OFF) ON [PRIMARY]
) ON [PRIMARY]
GO
ALTER TABLE [dbo].[CarDriver]  WITH CHECK ADD  CONSTRAINT [FK_CarDriver_Cars_CarsId]
  FOREIGN KEY([CarsId]) REFERENCES [dbo].[Cars] ([Id]) ON DELETE CASCADE
GO

ALTER TABLE [dbo].[CarDriver] CHECK CONSTRAINT [FK_CarDriver_Cars_CarsId]
GO

ALTER TABLE [dbo].[CarDriver]  WITH CHECK ADD  CONSTRAINT [FK_CarDriver_Drivers_DriversId]
  FOREIGN KEY([DriversId]) REFERENCES [dbo].[Drivers] ([Id]) ON DELETE CASCADE
GO

ALTER TABLE [dbo].[CarDriver] CHECK CONSTRAINT [FK_CarDriver_Drivers_DriversId]
GO
```

Note the compound primary key, the check constraints (foreign keys), and the cascade behavior are all created by EF Core to make sure the CarDriver table is configured as a proper join table.

Many-to-Many Prior to EF Core 5

The equivalent Car-Driver many-to-many relationship can be accomplished by creating the three tables explicitly and is how it must be done in EF Core versions earlier than EF Core 5. Here is an abbreviated example:

```
public class Driver
{
...
  public IEnumerable<CarDriver> CarDrivers { get; set; }
}

public class Car
{
...
  public IEnumerable<CarDriver> CarDrivers { get; set; }
}
public class CarDriver
{
  public int CarId {get;set;}
  public Car CarNavigation {get;set;}
  public int DriverId {get;set;}
  public Driver DriverNavigation {get;set;}
}
```

Cascade Behavior

Most data stores (like SQL Server) have rules controlling the behavior when a row is deleted. If the related (dependent) records should also be deleted, this is referred to as *cascade delete*. In EF Core, there are three actions that can occur when a principal entity (with dependent entities loaded into memory) is deleted.

- Dependent records are deleted.
- Dependent foreign keys are set to null.
- The dependent entity remains unchanged.

The default behavior is different between optional and required relationships. The behavior can also be configured to one of seven values, although only five are recommended for use. The behavior is configured with the DeleteBehavior enum using the Fluent API. The options available in the enumeration are listed here:

- Cascade
- ClientCascade
- ClientNoAction (not recommended for use)
- ClientSetNull
- NoAction (not recommended for use)
- SetNull
- Restrict

In EF Core, the specified behavior is triggered only after an entity is deleted and SaveChanges() is called on the derived DbContext. See the "Query Execution" section for more details about when EF Core interacts with the data store.

Optional Relationships

Recall from Table 21-4 that optional relationships are where the dependent entity *can* set the foreign key value(s) to null. For optional relationships, the default behavior is ClientSetNull. Table 21-5 shows the cascade behavior with dependent entities and the effect on database records when using SQL Server.

Table 21-5. *Cascade Behavior with Optional Relationships*

Delete Behavior	Effect on Dependents (In Memory)	Effect on Dependents (In Database)
Cascade	Entities are deleted.	Entities are deleted by the database.
ClientCascade	Entities are deleted.	For databases that do not support cascade delete, EF Core deletes the entities.
ClientSetNull (default)	Foreign key property/ properties set to null.	None.
SetNull	Foreign key property/ properties set to null.	Foreign key property/properties set to null.
Restrict	None.	None.

Required Relationships

Required relationships are where the dependent entity *cannot* set the foreign key value(s) to null. For required relationships, the default behavior is Cascade. Table 21-6 shows the cascade behavior with dependent entities and the effect on database records when using SQL Server.

Table 21-6. *Cascade Behavior with Required Relationships*

Delete Behavior	Effect on Dependents (In Memory)	Effect on Dependents (In Database)
Cascade (default)	Entities are deleted.	Entities are deleted.
ClientCascade	Entities are deleted.	For databases that do not support cascade delete, EF Core deletes the entities.
ClientSetNull	SaveChanges throws exception.	None.
SetNull	SaveChanges throws exception.	SaveChanges throws exception.
Restrict	None.	None.

Entity Conventions

There are many conventions that EF Core uses to define an entity and how it relates to the data store. The conventions are always enabled unless overruled by data annotations or code in the Fluent API. Table 21-7 lists some of the more important EF Core conventions.

Table 21-7. *Some of the EF Core Conventions*

Convention	Meaning in Life
Included tables	All classes with a DbSet property and all classes that can be reached (through navigation properties) by a DbSet class are created in the database.
Included columns	All public properties with a getter and setter (including automatic properties) are mapped to columns.
Table name	Maps to the name of the DbSet property name in the derived DbContext. If no DbSet exists, the class name is used.
Schema	Tables are created in the data store's default schema (dbo on SQL Server).
Column name	Column names are mapped to the property names of the class.
Column data type	Data types are selected based on the .NET data type and translated by the database provider (SQL Server). DateTime maps to datetime2(7), and string maps to nvarchar(max). Strings as part of a primary key map to nvarchar(450).
Column nullability	Non-nullable data types are created as Not Null persistence columns. EF Core honors C# 8 nullability.
Primary key	Properties named Id or <EntityTypeName>Id will be configured as the primary key. Keys of type short, int, long, or Guid have values controlled by the data store. Numerical values are created as Identity columns (SQL Server).
Relationships	Relationships between tables are created when there are navigation properties between two entity classes.
Foreign key	Properties named <OtherClassName>Id are foreign keys for navigation properties of type <OtherClassName>.

The previous navigation property examples all leverage EF Core conventions to build the relationships between the tables.

Mapping Properties to Columns

By convention, the public read-write properties map to columns of the same name. The data type matches the data store's equivalent of the property's CLR data type. Non-nullable properties are set to not null in the data store, and nullable properties (including nullable reference types introduced in C# 8) are set to allow null.

EF Core also supports reading and writing to property backing fields. EF Core expects the backing field to be named using one of the following conventions (in order of precedence):

- _<camel-cased property name>
- _<property name>
- m_<camel-cased property name>
- m_<property name>

If the Color property of the Car class is updated to use a backing field, it would (by convention) need to be named one of _color, _Color, m_color, or m_Color, like this:

```
private string _color;
public string Color
{
  get => _color;
  set => _color = value;
}
```

Overriding EF Core Conventions

New in EF Core 6, the conventions can be overridden using the ConfigureConventions() method. For example, if you want string properties to default to a certain size (instead of nvarchar(max)), you can add the following code into the ApplicationDbContext class:

```
protected override void ConfigureConventions(ModelConfigurationBuilder configurationBuilder)
{
  configurationBuilder.Properties<string>().HaveMaxLength(50);
}
```

When a new migration is created and executed, you will see that all of the string properties are updated to nvarchar(50).

Entity Framework Data Annotations

Data annotations are C# attributes that are used to further shape your entities. Table 21-8 lists some of the most commonly used data annotations for defining how your entity classes and properties map to database tables and fields. Data annotations override any conflicting conventions. There are many more annotations that you can use to refine the entities in the model, as you will see throughout the rest of this chapter and book.

Table 21-8. *Some Data Annotations Supported by the Entity Framework Core (*New Attributes in EF Core 6)*

Data Annotation	Meaning in Life
Table	Defines the schema and table name for the entity.
EntityTypeConfiguration*	In conjunction with the IEntityTypeConfiguration interface, allows an entity to be configured in its own class using the Fluent API. The use of this attribute is covered in the Fluent API section.
Keyless	Indicates an entity does not have a key (e.g., representing a database view).
Column	Defines the column name for the entity property.
BackingField	Specifies the C# backing field for a property.
Key	Defines the primary key for the entity. Key fields are implicitly also [Required].
Index	Placed on a class to specify a single column or multicolumn index. Allows for specifying the index is unique.

(continued)

Table 21-8. *(continued)*

Data Annotation	Meaning in Life
Owned	Declares that the class will be owned by another entity class.
Required	Declares the property as not nullable in the database.
ForeignKey	Declares a property that is used as the foreign key for a navigation property.
InverseProperty	Declares the navigation property on the other end of a relationship.
StringLength	Specifies the max length for a string property.
TimeStamp	Declares a type as a rowversion in SQL Server and adds concurrency checks to database operations involving the entity.
ConcurrencyCheck	Flags field to be used in concurrency checking when executing updates and deletes.
DatabaseGenerated	Specifies if the field is database generated or not. Takes a DatabaseGeneratedOption value of Computed, Identity, or None.
DataType	Provides for a more specific definition of a field than the intrinsic data type.
Unicode*	Maps string property to Unicode/non-Unicode database column without specifying the native datatype.
Precision*	Specifies precision and scale for the database column without specifying the native datatype.
NotMapped	Excludes the property or class in regard to database fields and tables.

The following code shows the BaseEntity class with annotations that declare the Id field as the primary key. The second data annotation on the Id property indicates that it is an Identity column in SQL Server. The TimeStamp property will be a SQL Server timestamp/rowversion property (for concurrency checking, covered later in this chapter).

```
public abstract class BaseEntity
{
  [Key, DatabaseGenerated(DatabaseGeneratedOption.Identity)]
  public int Id { get; set; }
  [Timestamp]
  public byte[] TimeStamp { get; set; }
}
```

Here is the Car class and the data annotations that shape it in the database, explained after the code sample:

```
[Table("Inventory", Schema="dbo")]
[Index(nameof(MakeId), Name = "IX_Inventory_MakeId")]
public class Car : BaseEntity
{
  private string _color;
  [Required, StringLength(50)]
  public string Color
```

```
  {
    get => _color;
    set => _color = value;
  }
  [Required, StringLength(50)]
  public string PetName { get; set; }
  public int MakeId { get; set; }
  [ForeignKey(nameof(MakeId))]
  public Make MakeNavigation { get; set; }
  public Radio RadioNavigation { get; set; }
  [InverseProperty(nameof(Driver.Cars))]
  public IEnumerable<Driver> Drivers { get; set; }
}
```

The Table attribute maps the Car class to the Inventory table in the dbo schema. The Column attribute (not shown in this example) works in a similar fashion and is used to change a column name or data type. The Index attribute creates an index on the foreign key MakeId. The two text fields (Color and PetName) are set to be Required and a max StringLength of 50 characters. The InverseProperty and ForeignKey attributes are explained in the next section.

The changes from the EF Core conventions are as follows:

- Renaming the table from Cars to Inventory.
- Changing the TimeStamp column from varbinary(max) to the SQL Server timestamp data type.
- Setting the nullability for the Color and PetName columns from null to not null.
- Explicitly setting the size of the Color and PetName columns to nvarchar(50). This was already handled when the EF Core conventions for string properties were overridden but included here for visibility.
- Renaming the index on the MakeId column.

The rest of the annotations used match the configuration defined by the EF Core conventions. To confirm the changes, we examine the table created by EF Core:

```
CREATE TABLE [dbo].[Inventory](
        [Id] [INT] IDENTITY(1,1) NOT NULL,
        [Color] [NVARCHAR](50) NOT NULL,
        [PetName] [NVARCHAR](50) NOT NULL,
        [MakeId] [INT] NOT NULL,
        [TimeStamp] [TIMESTAMP] NULL,
 CONSTRAINT [PK_Inventory] PRIMARY KEY CLUSTERED
(
        [Id] ASC
)WITH (PAD_INDEX = OFF, STATISTICS_NORECOMPUTE = OFF, IGNORE_DUP_KEY = OFF, ALLOW_ROW_LOCKS
= ON, ALLOW_PAGE_LOCKS = ON, OPTIMIZE_FOR_SEQUENTIAL_KEY = OFF) ON [PRIMARY]
) ON [PRIMARY] TEXTIMAGE_ON [PRIMARY]
GO

ALTER TABLE [dbo].[Inventory] ADD  DEFAULT (N'') FOR [Color]
GO
```

```
ALTER TABLE [dbo].[Inventory] ADD  DEFAULT (N'') FOR [PetName]
GO

ALTER TABLE [dbo].[Inventory]  WITH CHECK ADD  CONSTRAINT [FK_Inventory_Makes_MakeId]
  FOREIGN KEY([MakeId]) REFERENCES [dbo].[Makes] ([Id]) ON DELETE CASCADE
GO

ALTER TABLE [dbo].[Inventory] CHECK CONSTRAINT [FK_Inventory_Makes_MakeId]
GO
```

■ **Note** If you have been following along and running migrations with each of these changes, you might be surprised to see a failure when updating the TimeStamp column to the SQL Server timestamp data type. This is because SQL Server does not allow an existing column's datatype to be changed to the timestamp datatype from another datatype. The column must be dropped and then re-added with the new timestamp datatype. EF Core sees the column as already existing and issues an alter statement and not the paired drop/add commands that are required to make the change. To update your database, comment out the TimeStamp property on the base class, create a new migration and apply it, and then uncomment the TimeStamp property and create another migration and apply it.

Note the defaults added to the Color and PetName columns. If there was any data that had null values for either of these columns, it would cause the migration to fail. This change ensures the change to not null will succeed by placing an empty string in those columns if they were null at the time of the migration being applied.

To change the Radio's CarId property to map to a field named InventoryId, and make the RadioId required and explicitly set the size to 50, update the Radio entity to the following (note the changes in bold):

```
namespace AutoLot.Samples.Models;

[Table("Radios", Schema="dbo")]
public class Radio : BaseEntity
{
  public bool HasTweeters { get; set; }
  public bool HasSubWoofers { get; set; }
  [Required, StringLength(50)]
  public string RadioId { get; set; }
  [Column("InventoryId")]
  public int CarId { get; set; }
  [ForeignKey(nameof(CarId))]
  public Car CarNavigation { get; set; }
}
```

The migration commands and the resulting table are shown here:

```
dotnet ef migrations add UpdateRadio -o Migrations -c AutoLot.Samples.ApplicationDbContext
dotnet ef database update UpdateRadio  -c AutoLot.Samples.ApplicationDbContext

CREATE TABLE [dbo].[Radios](
        [Id] [INT] IDENTITY(1,1) NOT NULL,
```

```
        [HasTweeters] [BIT] NOT NULL,
        [HasSubWoofers] [BIT] NOT NULL,
        [RadioId] [NVARCHAR](50) NOT NULL,
        [InventoryId] [INT] NOT NULL,
        [TimeStamp] [TIMESTAMP] NULL,
 CONSTRAINT [PK_Radios] PRIMARY KEY CLUSTERED
(
        [Id] ASC
)WITH (PAD_INDEX = OFF, STATISTICS_NORECOMPUTE = OFF, IGNORE_DUP_KEY = OFF, ALLOW_ROW_LOCKS
= ON, ALLOW_PAGE_LOCKS = ON, OPTIMIZE_FOR_SEQUENTIAL_KEY = OFF) ON [PRIMARY]
) ON [PRIMARY]
GO

ALTER TABLE [dbo].[Radios] ADD  DEFAULT (N'') FOR [RadioId]
GO

ALTER TABLE [dbo].[Radios]  WITH CHECK ADD  CONSTRAINT [FK_Radios_Inventory_InventoryId]
  FOREIGN KEY([InventoryId]) REFERENCES [dbo].[Inventory] ([Id]) ON DELETE CASCADE
GO

ALTER TABLE [dbo].[Radios] CHECK CONSTRAINT [FK_Radios_Inventory_InventoryId]
GO
```

As a final step in updating our models, update the Name property on the Make entity to be required, as well as set the max length of to 50, and do the same for the FirstName and LastName properties on the Driver entity:

```
//Make.cs
namespace AutoLot.Samples.Models;

[Table("Makes", Schema="dbo")]
public class Make : BaseEntity
{
  [Required, StringLength(50)]
  public string Name { get; set; }
  [InverseProperty(nameof(Car.MakeNavigation))]
  public IEnumerable<Car> Cars { get; set; } = new List<Car>();
}
//Driver.cs
namespace AutoLot.Samples.Models;

[Table("Drivers", Schema="dbo")]
public class Driver : BaseEntity
{
  [Required, StringLength(50)]
  public string FirstName { get; set; }

  [Required, StringLength(50)]
  public string LastName { get; set; }
  [InverseProperty(nameof(Car.Drivers))]
  public IEnumerable<Car> Cars { get; set; } = new List<Car>();
}
```

Annotations and Navigation Properties

The ForeignKey annotation lets EF Core know which property is the backing field for the navigation property. By convention, <TypeName>Id would automatically be set as the foreign key property. In the preceding examples, it is explicitly set for readability. This supports different naming styles as well as having more than one foreign key to the same table. Note that in a one-to-one relationship, only the dependent entity has a foreign key.

InverseProperty informs EF Core of how the entities relate by indicating the navigation property on the other entity that navigates back to this entity. InverseProperty is required when an entity relates to another entity more than once and also (in my honest opinion) makes the code more readable.

The Fluent API

The Fluent API configures the application entities through C# code. The methods are exposed by the ModelBuilder instance available in the DbContext OnModelCreating() method. The Fluent API is the most powerful of the configuration methods and overrides any conventions or data annotations that are in conflict. Some configuration options are available only using the Fluent API, such as setting default values and cascade behavior for navigation properties.

Class and Property Methods

The Fluent API is a superset of the data annotations when shaping your individual entities. It supports all of the functionality contained in the data annotations, but has additional capabilities, such as specifying composite keys and indices, and defining computed columns.

Class and Property Mapping

The following code shows the previous Car example with the Fluent API equivalent to the data annotations used (omitting the navigation properties, which will be covered next).

```
modelBuilder.Entity<Car>(entity =>
{
  entity.ToTable("Inventory","dbo");
});
```

The following maps the CarId property of the Radio class to the InventoryId column of the Makes table:

```
modelBuilder.Entity<Radio>(entity =>
{
  entity.Property(e => e.CarId).HasColumnName("InventoryId");
});
```

Keys and Indices

To set the primary key for an entity, use the HasKey() method, as shown here:

```
modelBuilder.Entity<Car>(entity =>
{
  entity.ToTable("Inventory","dbo");
  entity.HasKey(e=>e.Id);
});
```

To set a composite key, select the properties that are in the key in the expression for the HasKey() method. For example, if the primary key for the Car entity should be the Id columns and an OrganizationId property, you would set it like this:

```
modelBuilder.Entity<Car>(entity =>
{
  entity.ToTable("Inventory","dbo");
  entity.HasKey(e=> new { e.Id, e.OrganizationId});
});
```

The process is the same for creating indices, except that it uses the HasIndex() Fluent API method. For example, to create an index named IX_Inventory_MakeId, use the following code:

```
modelBuilder.Entity<Car>(entity =>
{
  entity.ToTable("Inventory","dbo");
  entity.HasKey(e=>e.Id);
  entity.HasIndex(e => e.MakeId, "IX_Inventory_MakeId");
});
```

To make the index unique, use the IsUnique() method. The IsUnique() method takes an optional bool that defaults to true:

```
entity.HasIndex(e => e.MakeId, "IX_Inventory_MakeId").IsUnique();
```

Field Size and Nullability

Properties are configured by selecting them using the Property() method and then using additional methods to configure the property. You already saw an example of this with the mapping of the CarId property to the InventoryId column.

The IsRequired() takes an optional bool that defaults to true and defines the nullability of the database column. The HasMaxLength() method sets the size of the column. Here is the Fluent API code that sets the Color and PetName properties as required with a max length of 50 characters:

```
modelBuilder.Entity<Car>(entity =>
{
...
  entity.Property(e => e.Color)
    .IsRequired()
    .HasMaxLength(50);
  entity.Property(e => e.PetName)
    .IsRequired()
    .HasMaxLength(50);
});
```

Default Values

The Fluent API provides methods to set default values for columns. The default value can be a value type or a SQL string. For example, to set the default Color for a new Car to Black, use the following:

```
modelBuilder.Entity<Car>(entity =>
{
...
  entity.Property(e => e.Color)
  .IsRequired()
  .HasMaxLength(50)
  .HasDefaultValue("Black");
});
```

To set the value to a database function (like getdate()), use the HasDefaultValueSql() method. Presume that a DateTime property named DateBuilt has been added to the Car class:

```
public class Car : BaseEntity
{
...
  public DateTime? DateBuilt { get; set; }
}
```

The default value should be the current date using the SQL Server getdate() method. To configure this property to have this default, use the following Fluent API code:

```
modelBuilder.Entity<Car>(entity =>
{
...
  entity.Property(e => e.DateBuilt)
  .HasDefaultValueSql("getdate()");
});
```

SQL Server will use the result of the getdate() function if the DateBuilt property on the entity does not have a value when saved to the database.

A problem exists when a Boolean or numeric property has a database default value that contradicts the CLR default value. For example, if a Boolean property (such as IsDrivable) has a default set to true in the database, the database will set the value to true when inserting a record if a value isn't specified for that column. This is, of course, the expected behavior on the database side of the equation. However, the default CLR value for Boolean properties is false, which causes an issue due to how EF Core handles default values.

For example, add a bool property named IsDrivable to the Car class. If you are following along, make sure to create and apply a new migration to update the database.

```
//Car.cs
public class Car : BaseEntity
{
...
  public bool IsDrivable { get; set; }
}
```

Before discussing default values, let's examine the EF Core behavior for the Boolean datatype. Take the following code to create a new Car record with the IsDrivable set to false:

```
context.Cars.Add(new() { MakeId = 1, Color = "Rust", PetName = "Lemon", IsDrivable = false });
context.SaveChanges();
```

Here is the generated SQL for the insert:

```
exec sp_executesql N'SET NOCOUNT ON;
INSERT INTO [dbo].[Inventory] ([Color], [IsDrivable], [MakeId], [PetName], [Price])
VALUES (@p0, @p1, @p2, @p3, @p4);
SELECT [Id], [DateBuilt], [Display], [IsDeleted], [TimeStamp], [ValidFrom], [ValidTo]
FROM [dbo].[Inventory]
WHERE @@ROWCOUNT = 1 AND [Id] = scope_identity();

',N'@p0 nvarchar(50),@p1 bit,@p2 int,@p3 nvarchar(50),@p4 decimal(18,2)',@p0=N'Rust',@p1=0,
@p2=1,@p3=N'Lemon',@p4=NULL
```

Now set the default for the property's column mapping to true in the ApplicationDbContext's OnModelCreating() method (once again creating and applying a new database migration):

```
//ApplicationDbContext
protected override void OnModelCreating(ModelBuilder modelBuilder)
{
  modelBuilder.Entity<Car>(entity =>
  {
...
    entity.Property(e => e.IsDrivable).HasDefaultValue(true);
});
```

Executing the same code to insert the previous Car record generates different SQL:

```
exec sp_executesql N'SET NOCOUNT ON;
INSERT INTO [dbo].[Inventory] ([Color], [MakeId], [PetName], [Price])
VALUES (@p0, @p1, @p2, @p3);
SELECT [Id], [DateBuilt], [Display], [IsDeleted], [IsDrivable], [TimeStamp], [ValidFrom],
[ValidTo]
FROM [dbo].[Inventory]
WHERE @@ROWCOUNT = 1 AND [Id] = scope_identity();

',N'@p0 nvarchar(50),@p1 int,@p2 nvarchar(50),@p3 decimal(18,2)',@p0=N'Rust',@p1=1,
@p2=N'Lemon',@p3=NULL
```

Notice that the IsDrivable column is not included in the insert statement. EF Core knows that the IsDrivable property's value is the CLR default, and it knows that the column has a SQL Server default, so the column isn't included in the statement. Therefore, when you save a new record with IsDrivable = false, the value is ignored, and the database default will be used. This means that the value for IsDrivable will always be true!

EF Core does alert you to this problem when you create a migration. In this particular example, this warning is output:

```
The 'bool' property 'IsDrivable' on entity type 'Car' is configured with a database-
generated default. This default will always be used for inserts when the property has
the value 'false', since this is the CLR default for the 'bool' type. Consider using the
nullable 'bool?' type instead, so that the default will only be used for inserts when the
property value is 'null'.
```

One solution for this is to make your public property (and therefore the column) nullable, since the default value for a nullable value type is null, so setting a Boolean property to false works as expected. However, changing the nullability of the property might not fit the business need.

Another solution is provided by EF Core and its support for backing fields. Recall from earlier that if a backing field exists (and is identified as the backing field for the property through convention, data annotation, or Fluent API), then EF Core will use the backing field for read-write actions and not the public property.

If you update `IsDrivable` to use a nullable backing field (but keep the property non-nullable), EF Core will read-write from the backing field and not the property. The default value for a nullable `bool` is `null` and not `false`. This change now makes the property work as expected.

```
public class Car
{
...
  private bool? _isDrivable;
  public bool IsDrivable
  {
    get => _isDrivable ?? true;
    set => _isDrivable = value;
  }
}
```

The Fluent API is used to inform EF Core of the backing field.

```
modelBuilder.Entity<Car>(entity =>
{
  entity.Property(p => p.IsDrivable)
    .HasField("_isDrivable")
    .HasDefaultValue(true);
});
```

■ **Note** The `HasField()` method is not necessary in this example since the name of the backing field follows the naming conventions. I included it to show how to use the Fluent API to set it and to keep the code readable.

EF Core translates the field to the following SQL definition:

```
CREATE TABLE [dbo].[Inventory](
...
  [IsDrivable] [BIT] NOT NULL,
...
GO
ALTER TABLE [dbo].[Inventory] ADD  DEFAULT (CONVERT([BIT],(1))) FOR [IsDrivable]
GO
```

Although not shown in the previous examples, numeric properties work the same way. If you are setting a non-zero default value, the backing field (or property itself if not using a backing field) must be nullable.

As a final note, the warning will still appear even when the fields are properly configured with nullable backing fields. The warning can be suppressed; however, I recommend leaving it in place as a reminder to check to make sure the field/property is properly configured. If you want to suppress it, set the following option in the DbContextOptions:

```
options.ConfigureWarnings(wc => wc.Ignore(RelationalEventId.BoolWithDefaultWarning));
```

RowVersion/Concurrency Tokens

To set a property as the rowversion datatype, use the IsRowVersion() method. To also set the property as a concurrency token, use the IsConcurrencyToken() method. The combination of these two methods has the same effect as the [Timestamp] data annotation:

```
modelBuilder.Entity<Car>(entity =>
{
...
  entity.Property(e => e.TimeStamp)
    .IsRowVersion()
    .IsConcurrencyToken();
});
```

Concurrency checking will be covered in the next chapter.

SQL Server Sparse Columns

SQL Server sparse columns are optimized to store null values. EF Core 6 added support for sparse columns with the IsSparse() method in the Fluent API. The following code illustrates setting the fictitious IsRaceCar property to use SQl Server sparse columns:

```
modelBuilder.Entity<Car>(entity =>
{
  entity.Property(p => p.IsRaceCare).IsSparse();
});
```

Computed Columns

Columns can also be set to computed based on the capabilities of the data store. For SQL Server, two of the options are to compute the value based on the value of other fields in the same record or to use a scalar function. For example, to create a computed column on the Inventory table that combines the PetName and Color values to create a property named Display, use the HasComputedColumnSql() function.

First add the new column to the Car class:

```
public class Car : BaseEntity
{
...
   public string Display { get; set; }
}
```

Then add the Fluent API call to HasComputedColumnSql():

```
modelBuilder.Entity<Car>(entity =>
{
  entity.Property(p => p.Display)
    .HasComputedColumnSql("[PetName] + ' (' + [Color] + ')'");
});
```

Introduced in EF Core 5, the computed values can be persisted, so the value is calculated only on row creation or update. While SQL Server supports this, not all data stores do, so check the documentation of your database provider.

```
modelBuilder.Entity<Car>(entity =>
{
  entity.Property(p => p.Display)
    .HasComputedColumnSql("[PetName] + ' (' + [Color] + ')'", stored:true);

});
```

The DatabaseGenerated data annotation is often used in conjunction with the Fluent API to increase readability of the code. Here is the updated version of the Display property with the annotation included:

```
public class Car : BaseEntity
{
...
  [DatabaseGenerated(DatabaseGeneratedOption.Computed)]
   public string Display { get; set; }
}
```

Check Constraints

Check constraints are a SQL Server feature that define a condition on a row that must be true. For example, in an ecommerce system, a check constraint can be added to make sure the quantity is greater than zero or that the price is greater than the discounted price. Since we don't have any numeric values in our system, we will make a contrived constraint that prevents using the name "Lemon" in the Makes table.

Add the following to the OnModelCreating() method in the ApplicationDbContext class, which creates the check constraint preventing a Name of "Lemon" in the Makes table:

```
modelBuilder.Entity<Make>()
    .HasCheckConstraint(name:"CH_Name", sql:"[Name]<>'Lemon'",
          buildAction:c => c.HasName("CK_Check_Name"));
```

The first parameter gives the constraint a name in the model, the second is the SQL for the constraint, and the final assigns the SQL Server name for the check constraint. Here is the check constraint as defined in SQL:

```
ALTER TABLE [dbo].[Makes]  WITH CHECK ADD  CONSTRAINT [CK_Check_Name]
CHECK  (([Name]<>'Lemon'))
```

Now, when a record with the Name of "Lemon" is added to the table, a SQL exception will be thrown. Execute the following code to see the exception in action:

```
var context = new ApplicationDbContextFactory().CreateDbContext(null);
context.Makes.Add(new Make { Name = "Lemon" });
context.SaveChanges();
```

This throws the following exception:

```
The INSERT statement conflicted with the CHECK constraint "CK_Check_Name". The conflict
occurred in database "AutoLotSamples", table "dbo.Makes", column 'Name'.
```

Feel free to revert the migration for the check constraint and remove the migration, as the rest of the book doesn't use the check constraint. It was added in this section for demonstration purposes.

One-to-Many Relationships

To use the Fluent API to define one-to-many relationships, pick *one* of the entities to update. Both sides of the navigation chain are set in one block of code.

```
modelBuilder.Entity<Car>(entity =>
{
...
  entity.HasOne(d => d.MakeNavigation)
    .WithMany(p => p.Cars)
    .HasForeignKey(d => d.MakeId)
    .OnDelete(DeleteBehavior.ClientSetNull)
    .HasConstraintName("FK_Inventory_Makes_MakeId");
});
```

If you select the principal entity as the base for the navigation property configuration, the code looks like this:

```
modelBuilder.Entity<Make>(entity =>
{
...
  entity.HasMany(e=>e.Cars)
```

```
    .WithOne(c=>c.MakeNavigation)
    .HasForeignKey(c=>c.MakeId)
    .OnDelete(DeleteBehavior.ClientSetNull)
    .HasConstraintName("FK_Inventory_Makes_MakeId");
});
```

One-to-One Relationships

One-to-one relationships are configured the same way, except that the WithOne() Fluent API method is used instead of WithMany(). Also, a unique index is required on the dependent entity and will be created automatically if one is not defined. The following example explicitly creates the unique index to specify the name. Here is the code for the relationship between the Car and Radio entities using the dependent entity (Radio):

```
modelBuilder.Entity<Radio>(entity =>
{
  entity.HasIndex(e => e.CarId, "IX_Radios_CarId")
    .IsUnique();

  entity.HasOne(d => d.CarNavigation)
    .WithOne(p => p.RadioNavigation)
    .HasForeignKey<Radio>(d => d.CarId);
});
```

If the relationship is defined on a principal entity, a unique index will still be added to the dependent entity. Here is the code for the relationship between the Car and Radio entities using the principal entity for the relationship and specifying the name of the index on the dependent entity:

```
modelBuilder.Entity<Radio>(entity =>
{
  entity.HasIndex(e => e.CarId, "IX_Radios_CarId")
    .IsUnique();
});

modelBuilder.Entity<Car>(entity =>
{
  entity.HasOne(d => d.RadioNavigation)
    .WithOne(p => p.CarNavigation)
    .HasForeignKey<Radio>(d => d.CarId);
});
```

Many-to-Many Relationships

Many-to-many relationships are much more customizable with the Fluent API. The foreign key field names, index names, and cascade behavior can all be set in the statements that define the relationship. It also allows for specifying the pivot table directly, which allows for additional fields to be added and for simplified querying.

Start by adding a CarDriver entity:

```
//CarDriver.cs
namespace AutoLot.Samples.Models;

[Table("InventoryToDrivers", Schema = "dbo")]
public class CarDriver : BaseEntity
{
  public int DriverId {get;set;}
  [ForeignKey(nameof(DriverId))]
  public Driver DriverNavigation {get;set;}

  [Column("InventoryId")]
  public int CarId {get;set;}
  [ForeignKey(nameof(CarId))]
  public Car CarNavigation {get;set;}
}
```

Add a DbSet<T> for the new entity into the ApplicationDbContext:

```
public DbSet<CarDriver> CarsToDrivers {get;set;}
```

Next, update the Car entity to add a navigation property for the new CarDriver entity:

```
public class Car : BaseEntity
{
...
  [InverseProperty(nameof(CarDriver.CarNavigation))]
  public IEnumerable<CarDriver> CarDrivers { get; set; } = new List<CarDriver>();
}
```

Now, update the Driver entity for the navigation property to the CarDriver entity:

```
public class Driver : BaseEntity
{
  [InverseProperty(nameof(CarDriver.DriverNavigation))]
  public IEnumerable<CarDriver> CarDrivers { get; set; } = new List<CarDriver>();
}
```

Finally, add in the Fluent API code for the many-to-many relationship:

```
modelBuilder.Entity<Car>()
  .HasMany(p => p.Drivers)
  .WithMany(p => p.Cars)
  .UsingEntity<CarDriver>(
    j => j
        .HasOne(cd => cd.DriverNavigation)
        .WithMany(d => d.CarDrivers)
        .HasForeignKey(nameof(CarDriver.DriverId))
        .HasConstraintName("FK_InventoryDriver_Drivers_DriverId")
        .OnDelete(DeleteBehavior.Cascade),
```

```
    j => j
        .HasOne(cd => cd.CarNavigation)
        .WithMany(c => c.CarDrivers)
        .HasForeignKey(nameof(CarDriver.CarId))
        .HasConstraintName("FK_InventoryDriver_Inventory_InventoryId")
        .OnDelete(DeleteBehavior.ClientCascade),
    j =>
        {
            j.HasKey(cd => new { cd.CarId, cd.DriverId });
        });
```

Excluding Entities from Migrations

If an entity is shared between multiple DbContexts, each DbContext will create code in the migration files for creation of or changes to that entity. This causes a problem since the second migration script will fail if the changes are already present in the database. Prior to EF Core 5, the only solution was to manually edit one of the migration files to remove those changes.

In EF Core 5, a DbContext can mark an entity as excluded from migrations, letting the other DbContext become the system of record for that entity. The following code shows an entity being excluded from migrations:

```
protected override void OnModelCreating(ModelBuilder modelBuilder)
{
  modelBuilder.Entity<LogEntry>().ToTable("Logs", t => t.ExcludeFromMigrations());
}
```

Using IEntityTypeConfiguration Classes

As you might have surmised at this stage of working with the Fluent API, the OnModelCreating() method can become quite lengthy (and unwieldy) the more complex your model becomes. Introduced in EF Core 6, the IEntityTypeConfiguration interface and the EntityTypeConfiguration attribute allow for moving the Fluent API configuration for an entity into its own class. This makes for a cleaner ApplicationDbContext and supports the separation of concerns design principle.

Start by creating a new directory named Configuration in the Models directory. In this new directory, add a new file named CarConfiguration.cs, make it public, and implement the IEntityTypeConfiguration<Car> interface, like this:

```
namespace AutoLot.Samples.Models.Configuration;

public class CarConfiguration : IEntityTypeConfiguration<Car>
{
  public void Configure(EntityTypeBuilder<Car> builder)
  {
  }
}
```

Next, move the contents of the configuration for the Car entity from the OnModelCreating() method in the ApplicationDbContext into the Configure() method of the CarConfiguration class. Replace the entity variable with the builder variable so the Configure() method looks like this:

```
public void Configure(EntityTypeBuilder<Car> builder)
{
  builder.ToTable("Inventory", "dbo");
  builder.HasKey(e => e.Id);
  builder.HasIndex(e => e.MakeId, "IX_Inventory_MakeId");
  builder.Property(e => e.Color)
    .IsRequired()
    .HasMaxLength(50)
    .HasDefaultValue("Black");
  builder.Property(e => e.PetName)
    .IsRequired()
    .HasMaxLength(50);
  builder.Property(e => e.DateBuilt).HasDefaultValueSql("getdate()");
  builder.Property(e => e.IsDrivable)
    .HasField("_isDrivable")
    .HasDefaultValue(true);
  builder.Property(e => e.TimeStamp)
    .IsRowVersion()
    .IsConcurrencyToken();
  builder.Property(e => e.Display).HasComputedColumnSql("[PetName] + ' (' + [Color] + ')'",
  stored: true);
  builder.HasOne(d => d.MakeNavigation)
    .WithMany(p => p.Cars)
    .HasForeignKey(d => d.MakeId)
    .OnDelete(DeleteBehavior.ClientSetNull)
    .HasConstraintName("FK_Inventory_Makes_MakeId");
}
```

This configuration also works with the fluent many-to-many configuration between Car and Driver. It's your choice whether to add the configuration into the CarConfiguration class or create a DriverConfiguration class. For this example, move it into the CarConfiguration class at the end of the Configure() method:

```
public void Configure(EntityTypeBuilder<Car> builder)
{
...
  builder
    .HasMany(p => p.Drivers)
    .WithMany(p => p.Cars)
    .UsingEntity<CarDriver>(
      j => j
        .HasOne(cd => cd.DriverNavigation)
        .WithMany(d => d.CarDrivers)
        .HasForeignKey(nameof(CarDriver.DriverId))
        .HasConstraintName("FK_InventoryDriver_Drivers_DriverId")
        .OnDelete(DeleteBehavior.Cascade),
      j => j
        .HasOne(cd => cd.CarNavigation)
        .WithMany(c => c.CarDrivers)
        .HasForeignKey(nameof(CarDriver.CarId))
        .HasConstraintName("FK_InventoryDriver_Inventory_InventoryId")
        .OnDelete(DeleteBehavior.ClientCascade),
```

```
    j =>
      {
        j.HasKey(cd => new { cd.CarId, cd.DriverId });
      });
}
```

Update the GlobalUsings.cs file to include the new namespace for the configuration classes:

```
global using AutoLot.Samples.Models.Configuration;
```

Replace all the code in the OnModelBuilding() method (in the ApplicationDbContext.cs class) that configures the Car class and the Car to Driver many-to-many relationship with the following single line of code:

```
protected override void OnModelCreating(ModelBuilder modelBuilder)
{
  new CarConfiguration().Configure(modelBuilder.Entity<Car>());
...
}
```

The final step for the Car class is to add the EntityTypeConfiguration attribute:

```
[Table("Inventory", Schema = "dbo")]
[Index(nameof(MakeId), Name = "IX_Inventory_MakeId")]
[EntityTypeConfiguration(typeof(CarConfiguration))]
public class Car : BaseEntity
{
...
}
```

Next, repeat the same steps for the Radio Fluent API code. Create a new class named RadioConfiguration, implement the IEntityTypeConfiguration<Radio> interface, and add the code from the ApplicationDbContext OnModelBuilding() method:

```
namespace AutoLot.Samples.Models.Configuration;

public class RadioConfiguration : IEntityTypeConfiguration<Radio>
{
  public void Configure(EntityTypeBuilder<Radio> builder)
  {
    builder.Property(e => e.CarId).HasColumnName("InventoryId");
    builder.HasIndex(e => e.CarId, "IX_Radios_CarId").IsUnique();
    builder.HasOne(d => d.CarNavigation)
      .WithOne(p => p.RadioNavigation)
      .HasForeignKey<Radio>(d => d.CarId);
  }
}
```

Update the OnModelCreating() method in the ApplicationDbContext:

```
protected override void OnModelCreating(ModelBuilder modelBuilder)
{
  new CarConfiguration().Configure(modelBuilder.Entity<Car>());
  new RadioConfiguration().Configure(modelBuilder.Entity<Radio>());
}
```

Finally, add the EntityTypeConfiguration attribute to the Radio class:

```
[Table("Radios", Schema = "dbo")]
[EntityTypeConfiguration(typeof(RadioConfiguration))]
public class Radio : BaseEntity
{
...
}
```

While this didn't reduce the total number of lines of code, this new feature made the ApplicationDbContext a lot cleaner.

Conventions, Annotations, and the Fluent API, Oh My!

At this point in the chapter, you might be wondering which of the three options to use to shape your entities and their relationship to each other and the data store. The answer is all three. The conventions are always active (unless you override them with data annotations or the Fluent API). The data annotations can do almost everything the Fluent API methods can do and keep the information in the entity class themselves, which can increase code readability and support. The Fluent API is the most powerful of all three. Whether you use data annotations or the Fluent API, know that data annotations overrule the built-in conventions, and the methods of the Fluent API overrule everything.

Owned Entity Types

There will be time when two or more entities contain the same set of properties. Using a C# class as a property on an entity to define a collection of properties for another entity was first introduced in EF Core version 2.0. When types marked with the [Owned] attribute (or configured with the Fluent API) are added as a property of an entity, EF Core will add all the properties from the [Owned] entity class to the owning entity. This increases the possibility of C# code reuse.

Behind the scenes, EF Core considers this a one-to-one relation. The owned class is the dependent entity, and the owning class is the principal entity. The owned class, even though it is considered an entity, cannot exist without the owning entity. The default column names from the owned type will be formatted as NavigationPropertyName_OwnedEntityPropertyName (e.g., PersonalNavigation_FirstName). The default names can be changed using the Fluent API.

Take this Person class (notice the Owned attribute):

```
namespace AutoLot.Samples.Models;

[Owned]
public class Person
{
  [Required, StringLength(50)]
```

```
  public string FirstName { get; set; }
  [Required, StringLength(50)]
  public string LastName { get; set; }
}
```

With this in place, we can replace the FirstName and LastName properties on the Driver class with the new Person class:

```
namespace AutoLot.Samples.Models;

[Table("Drivers", Schema = "dbo")]
public class Driver : BaseEntity
{
  public Person PersonInfo {get;set;} = new Person();
  public IEnumerable<Car> Cars { get; set; } = new List<Car>();
  [InverseProperty(nameof(CarDriver.DriverNavigation))]
  public IEnumerable<CarDriver> CarDrivers { get; set; } = new List<CarDriver>();
}
```

By default, the two Person properties are mapped to columns named PersonInfo_FirstName and PersonInfo_LastName. To change this, first add a new file named DriverConfiguration.cs into the Configuration folder, and update the code to the following:

```
namespace AutoLot.Samples.Models.Configuration;

public class DriverConfiguration : IEntityTypeConfiguration<Driver>
{
  public void Configure(EntityTypeBuilder<Driver> builder)
  {
    builder.OwnsOne(o => o.PersonInfo,
      pd =>
        {
          pd.Property<string>(nameof(Person.FirstName))
            .HasColumnName(nameof(Person.FirstName))
            .HasColumnType("nvarchar(50)");
          pd.Property<string>(nameof(Person.LastName))
            .HasColumnName(nameof(Person.LastName))
            .HasColumnType("nvarchar(50)");
        });
  }
}
```

Update the ApplicationDbContext OnConfiguring() method:

```
protected override void OnModelCreating(ModelBuilder modelBuilder)
{
  new CarConfiguration().Configure(modelBuilder.Entity<Car>());
  new RadioConfiguration().Configure(modelBuilder.Entity<Radio>());
  new DriverConfiguration().Configure(modelBuilder.Entity<Driver>());
}
```

Finally, update the Driver class:

```
[Table("Drivers", Schema = "dbo")]
[EntityTypeConfiguration(typeof(DriverConfiguration))]
public class Driver : BaseEntity
{
...
}
```

The Drivers table is updated like this (note that the nullability of the FirstName and LastName columns doesn't match the Required data annotations on the Person owned entity):

```
CREATE TABLE [dbo].[Drivers](
        [Id] [INT] IDENTITY(1,1) NOT NULL,
        [FirstName] [NVARCHAR](50) NULL,
        [LastName] [NVARCHAR](50) NULL,
        [TimeStamp] [TIMESTAMP] NULL,
 CONSTRAINT [PK_Drivers] PRIMARY KEY CLUSTERED
(
        [Id] ASC
)WITH (PAD_INDEX = OFF, STATISTICS_NORECOMPUTE = OFF, IGNORE_DUP_KEY = OFF, ALLOW_ROW_LOCKS =
ON, ALLOW_PAGE_LOCKS = ON, OPTIMIZE_FOR_SEQUENTIAL_KEY = OFF) ON [PRIMARY]
) ON [PRIMARY]]
GO
```

While the Person class has the Required data annotation on both of its properties, the SQL Server columns are both set as NULL. This is due to an issue with how the migration system translates owned entities when they are used with an *optional* relationship.

To correct this, there are a couple of options. The first is to enable C# null reference types (at the project level or in the classes). This makes the PersonInfo navigation property non-nullable, which EF Core honors, and in turn EF Core then appropriately configures the columns in the owned entity. The other option is to add a Fluent API statement to make the navigation property required.

```
public class DriverConfiguration : IEntityTypeConfiguration<Driver>
{
  public void Configure(EntityTypeBuilder<Driver> builder)
  {
...
    builder.Navigation(d=>d.PersonInfo).IsRequired(true);
  }
}
```

This updates the properties of the Person owned type to be set as a not null column in SQL Server:

```
CREATE TABLE [dbo].[Drivers](
      [Id] [INT] IDENTITY(1,1) NOT NULL,
      [FirstName] [NVARCHAR](50) NOT NULL,
      [LastName] [NVARCHAR](50) NOT NULL,
      [TimeStamp] [TIMESTAMP] NULL,
```

```
 CONSTRAINT [PK_Drivers] PRIMARY KEY CLUSTERED
(
      [Id] ASC
)WITH (PAD_INDEX = OFF, STATISTICS_NORECOMPUTE = OFF,
      IGNORE_DUP_KEY = OFF, ALLOW_ROW_LOCKS = ON, ALLOW_PAGE_LOCKS = ON,
      OPTIMIZE_FOR_SEQUENTIAL_KEY = OFF) ON [PRIMARY]
) ON [PRIMARY]
GO
```

There are four limitations when using owned types:

- You cannot create a DbSet<T> for an owned type.
- You cannot call Entity<T>() with an owned type on ModelBuilder.
- Instances of an owned entity type cannot be shared between multiple owners.
- Owned entity types cannot have inheritance hierarchies.

There are additional options to explore with owned entities, including collections, table splitting, and nesting. These are all beyond the scope of this book. To find out more information, consult the EF Core documentation on owned entities here: https://docs.microsoft.com/en-us/ef/core/modeling/owned-entities.

Query Types

Query types are DbSet<T> collections that are used to represent views, a SQL statement, or tables without a primary key. Prior versions of EF Core used DbQuery<T> for these, but from EF Core 3.x on, the DbQuery type has been retired. Query types are added to the derived DbContext using DbSet<T> properties and are configured as keyless.

Query types are usually used to represent combinations of tables, such as combining the details from the Make and Inventory tables. Take this query, for example:

```
SELECT m.Id MakeId, m.Name Make,
    i.Id CarId, i.IsDrivable, i.Display, i.DateBuilt, i.Color, i.PetName
FROM dbo.Makes m
INNER JOIN dbo.Inventory i ON i.MakeId = m.Id
```

To hold the results of this query, create a new folder named ViewModels, and in that folder create a new class named CarMakeViewModel:

```
namespace AutoLot.Samples.ViewModels;

[Keyless]
public class CarMakeViewModel
{
  public int MakeId { get; set; }
  public string Make { get; set; }
  public int CarId { get; set; }
  public bool IsDrivable { get; set; }
  public string Display { get; set; }
  public DateTime DateBuilt { get; set; }
```

```
  public string Color { get; set; }
  public string PetName { get; set; }

  [NotMapped]
  public string FullDetail => $" The {Color} {Make} is named {PetName}";
  public override string ToString() => FullDetail;
}
```

The Keyless attribute instructs EF Core that this entity is a query type and will never be used for updates and is to be excluded from the change tracker when queried. Note the use of the NotMapped attribute to create a display string that combines several properties into a single, human-readable string. Update the ApplicationDbContext to include a DbSet<T> for the view model:

```
public class ApplicationDbContext : DbContext
{
...
    public DbSet<Car> Cars { get; set; }
    public DbSet<Make> Makes { get; set; }
    public DbSet<Radio> Radios { get; set; }
    public DbSet<Driver> Drivers { get; set; }
    public DbSet< CarMakeViewModel> CarMakeViewModels { get; set; }
...
}
```

Update the GlobalUsings.cs file to include the new namespace for the view model and the configuration (which will be created next):

```
global using AutoLot.Samples.ViewModels;
global using AutoLot.Samples.ViewModels.Configuration;
```

The remainder of the configuration takes place in the Fluent API. Create a new folder named Configuration under the ViewModels folder, and in that folder create a new class named CarMakeViewModelConfiguration and update the code to the following:

```
namespace AutoLot.Samples.ViewModels.Configuration;

public class CarMakeViewModelConfiguration : IEntityTypeConfiguration<CarMakeViewModel>
{
  public void Configure(EntityTypeBuilder<CarMakeViewModel> builder)
  {
  }
}
```

Update the CarMakeViewModel class to add the EntityTypeConfiguration attribute:

```
[Keyless]
[EntityTypeConfiguration(typeof(CarMakeViewModelConfiguration))]
public class CarMakeViewModel : INonPersisted
{
...
}
```

Update the OnModelCreating() method to the following:

```
protected override void OnModelCreating(ModelBuilder modelBuilder)
{
  new CarConfiguration().Configure(modelBuilder.Entity<Car>());
  new RadioConfiguration().Configure(modelBuilder.Entity<Radio>());
  new DriverConfiguration().Configure(modelBuilder.Entity<Driver>());
  new CarMakeViewModelConfiguration().Configure(modelBuilder.Entity<CarMakeViewModel>());
}
```

The following example sets the entity as keyless and maps the query type to raw SQL query. The HasNoKey() Fluent API method is not necessary if the Keyless data annotation is on the model, and vice versa, but is shown in this example for completeness):

```
  public void Configure(EntityTypeBuilder<CarMakeViewModel> builder)
  {
    builder.HasNoKey().ToSqlQuery(@"
      SELECT m.Id MakeId, m.Name Make, i.Id CarId, i.IsDrivable,
        i.DisplayName, i.DateBuilt, i.Color, i.PetName
      FROM dbo.Makes m
      INNER JOIN dbo.Inventory i ON i.MakeId = m.Id");
  }
```

Query types can also be mapped to a database view. Presuming there was a view named dbo.CarMakeView, the configuration would look like this:

```
builder.HasNoKey().ToView("CarMakeView", "dbo");
```

■ **Note** When using EF Core migrations to update your database, query types that are mapped to a view do not get created as tables. Query types that are not mapped to views are created as keyless tables.

If you don't want the view model mapped to a table in your database and don't have a view to map, use the following overload of the ToTable() method to exclude the item from migrations:

```
builder.ToTable( x => x.ExcludeFromMigrations());
```

The final mechanisms that query types can be used with are the FromSqlRaw() and FromSqlInterpolated() methods. These will be covered in detail in the next chapter, but here is a sneak peek:

```
var records = context.CarMakeViewModel.FromSqlRaw(
    @" SELECT m.Id MakeId, m.Name Make, i.Id CarId, i.IsDrivable,
        i.Display, i.DateBuilt, i.Color, i.PetName
        FROM dbo.Makes m
        INNER JOIN dbo.Inventory i ON i.MakeId = m.Id ");
```

Flexible Query/Table Mapping

EF Core 5 introduced the ability to map the same class to more than one database object. These objects can be tables, views, or functions. For example, CarViewModel from Chapter 20 can be mapped to a view that returns the make name with the Car data and the Inventory table. EF Core will then query from the view and send updates to the table.

```
modelBuilder.Entity<CarViewModel>()
  .ToTable("Inventory")
  .ToView("InventoryWithMakesView");
```

Query Execution

Data retrieval queries are created with LINQ queries written against the DbSet<T> properties. The LINQ query is changed to the database-specific language (e.g., T-SQL) by the database provider's LINQ translation engine and executed on the server side. Multirecord (or potential multirecord) LINQ queries are not executed until the query is iterated over (e.g., using a foreach) or bound to a control for display (like a data grid). This deferred execution allows building up queries in code without suffering performance issues from chattiness with the database or retrieving more records than intended.

For example, to get all yellow Car records from the database, execute the following query:

```
    //The factory is not meant to be used like this, but it's demo code :-)
var context = new ApplicationDbContextFactory().CreateDbContext(null);
var cars = context.Cars.Where(x=>x.Color == "Yellow");
```

With deferred execution, that database is not actually queried until the results are iterated over. To have the query execute immediately, use ToList().

```
var listOfCars = context.Cars.Where(x=>x.Color == "Yellow").ToList();
```

Since queries aren't executed until triggered, they can be built up over multiple lines of code. The following code sample executes the same as the previous example:

```
var query = context.Cars.AsQueryable();
query = query.Where(x=>x.Color == "Yellow");
var moreCars = query.ToList();
```

Single-record queries (such as when using First()/FirstOrDefault()) execute immediately on calling the action (such as FirstOrDefault()), and create, update, and delete statements are executed immediately when the DbContext.SaveChanges() method is executed.

■ **Note** The next chapters covers executing CRUD operations in great detail.

Mixed Client-Server Evaluation

Prior versions of EF Core introduced the ability to mix server-side and client-side execution. This meant that a C# function could be used in the middle of a LINQ statement and essentially negate what I described in the previous paragraph. The part up to the C# function would execute on the server side, but then all of the results (at that point of the query) were brought back on the client side, and then the rest of the query would execute as LINQ to Objects. This ended up causing more problems than it solved, and with the release of EF Core 3.1, this functionality was changed. Now, only the final node of a LINQ statement can execute on the client side.

Tracking vs. NoTracking Queries

When data is read from the database into a DbSet<T> instance with a primary key, the entities (by default) are tracked by the change tracker. This is typically what you want in your application. Any changes to the item can then be persisted to the database merely by calling SaveChanges() on your derived DbContext instance without any additional work on your part. Also, once an instance is tracked by the change tracker, any further calls to the database for that same item (based on the primary key) will result in an update of the item and not a duplication.

However, there might be times when you need to get some data from the database, but you don't want it to be tracked by the change tracker. The reason might be performance (tracking original and current values for a large set of records can add memory pressure), or maybe you know those records will never be changed by the part of the application that needs the data.

To load data into a DbSet<T> instance without adding the data to the ChangeTracker, add AsNoTracking() into the LINQ statement. This signals EF Core to retrieve the data without adding it into the ChangeTracker. For example, to load a Car record without adding it into the ChangeTracker, execute the following:

```
var untrackedCar = context.Cars.Where(x=>x.Id ==1).AsNoTracking();
```

This provides the benefit of not adding the potential memory pressure with a potential drawback: additional calls to retrieve the same Car will create additional copies of the record. At the expense of using more memory and having a slightly slower execution time, the query can be modified to ensure there is only one instance of the unmapped Car.

```
var untrackedWithIdResolution =
    context.Cars.Where(x=>x.Id == 1).AsNoTrackingWithIdentityResolution();
```

Query types are never tracked since they cannot be updated. The exception to this is when using flexible query/table mapping. In that case, instances are tracked by default so they can be persisted to the target table.

Code First vs. Database First

Whether you are building a new application or adding EF Core into an existing application, you will fall into one of two camps: you have an existing database that you need to work with, or you don't yet have a database and need to create one.

Code first means that you create and configure your entity classes and the derived DbContext in code and then use migrations to update the database. This is how most greenfield, or new, projects are developed. The advantage is that as you build your application, your entities evolve based on the needs of your application. The migrations keep the database in sync, so the database design evolves along with your application. This emerging design process is popular with agile development teams, as you build the right parts at the right time.

If you already have a database or prefer to have your database design drive your application, that is referred to as *database first*. Instead of creating the derived DbContext and all of the entities manually, you scaffold the classes from the database. When the database changes, you need to re-scaffold your classes to keep your code in sync with the database. Any custom code in the entities or the derived DbContext must be placed in partial classes so it doesn't get overwritten when the classes are re-scaffolded. Fortunately, the scaffolding process creates partial classes just for that reason.

Whichever method you chose, code first or database first, know that it is essentially a commitment. If you are using code first, all changes are made to the entity and context classes, and the database is updated using migrations. If you are working database first, all changes must be made in the database, and then the classes are re-scaffolded. With some effort and planning, you can switch from database first to code first (and vice versa), but you should not be making manual changes to the code and the database at the same time.

The EF Core Global Tool CLI Commands

The dotnet-ef global CLI tool EF Core tooling contains the commands needed to scaffold existing databases into code, to create/remove database migrations, and to operate on a database (update, drop, etc.). Before you can use the dotnet-ef global tooling, it must be installed with the following command:

```
dotnet tool install --global dotnet-ef --version 6.0.0
```

■ **Note** If you have an earlier version of the EF Core command-line tooling installed, you will need to uninstall the older version before installing the latest version. To uninstall the global tool, use `dotnet tool uninstall --global dotnet-ef`.

To test the install, open a command prompt and enter the following command:

```
dotnet ef
```

If the tooling is successfully installed, you will get the EF Core Unicorn (the team's mascot) and the list of available commands, like this (the unicorn looks better on the screen):

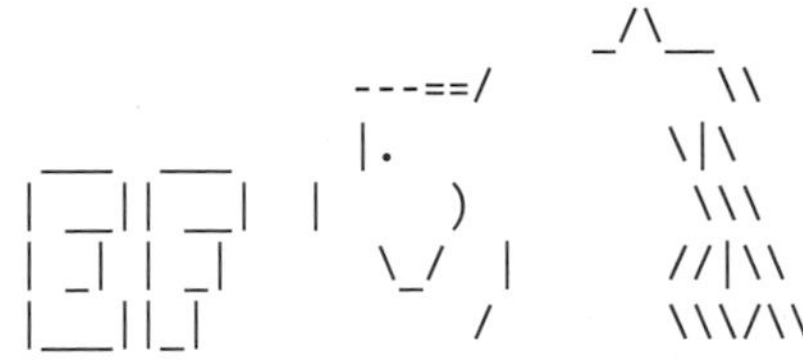

```
Entity Framework Core .NET Command-line Tools 6.0.0

Usage: dotnet ef [options] [command]

Options:
  --version        Show version information
  -h|--help        Show help information
  -v|--verbose     Show verbose output.
  --no-color       Don't colorize output.
  --prefix-output  Prefix output with level.
```

```
Commands:
  database    Commands to manage the database.
  dbcontext   Commands to manage DbContext types.
  migrations  Commands to manage migrations.

Use "dotnet ef [command] --help" for more information about a command.
```

Table 21-9 describes the three main commands in the EF Core global tool. Each main command has additional subcommands. As with all the .NET commands, each command has a rich help system that can be accessed by entering -h along with the command.

Table 21-9. *EF Core Tooling Commands*

Command	Meaning in Life
Database	Commands to manage the database. Subcommands include drop and update.
DbContext	Commands to manage the DbContext types. Subcommands include scaffold, list, and info.
Migrations	Commands to manage migrations. Subcommands include add, list, remove, and script.

The EF Core commands execute on .NET project files. The target project needs to reference the EF Core tooling NuGet package Microsoft.EntityFrameworkCore.Design. The commands operate on the project file located in the same directory where the commands are run, or a project file in another directory if referenced through the command-line options.

For the EF Core CLI commands that need an instance of a derived DbContext class (Database and Migrations), if there is only one in the project, that one will be used. If there are more than one, then the DbContext needs to be specified in the command-line options. The derived DbContext class will be instantiated using an instance of a class implementing the IDesignTimeDbContextFactory<TContext> interface if one can be located. If the tooling cannot find one, the derived DbContext will be instantiated using the parameterless constructor. If neither exists, the command will fail. Note that the using the parameterless constructor (and not the constructor that takes in the DbContextOptions<T>) requires the existence of the OnConfiguring override, which is not considered a good practice to have. The best (and really only) option is to always create an IDesignTimeDbContextFactory<TContext> for each derived DbContext that you have in your application.

There are common options available for the EF Core commands, shown in Table 21-10. Many of the commands have additional options or arguments.

Table 21-10. *EF Core Command Options*

Option (Shorthand || Longhand)	Meaning in Life
--c || --context <DBCONTEXT>	The fully qualified derived DbContext class to use. If more than one derived DbContext exists in the project, this is a required option.
-p || --project <PROJECT>	The project to use (where to place the files). Defaults to the current working directory.
-s || --startup-project <PROJECT>	The startup project to use (contains the derived DbContext). Defaults to the current working directory.
-h || --help	Displays the help and all of the options.
-v || --verbose	Shows verbose output.

To list all the arguments and options for a command, enter `dotnet ef <command> -h` in a command window, like this:

```
dotnet ef migrations add -h
```

■ **Note** It is important to note that the CLI commands are not C# commands, so the rules of escaping slashes and quotes do not apply.

The Migrations Commands

The `migrations` commands are used to add, remove, list, and script migrations. As migrations are applied to a base, a record is created in the `__EFMigrationsHistory` table. Table 21-11 describes the commands. The following sections explain the commands in detail.

Table 21-11. *EF Core Migrations Commands*

Command	Meaning in Life
`Add`	Creates a new migration based on the changes from the previous migration
`Remove`	Checks if the last migration in the project has been applied to the database and, if not, deletes the migration file (and its designer) and then rolls back the snapshot class to the previous migration
`List`	Lists all of the migrations for a derived `DbContext` and their status (applied or pending)
`Bundle`	Creates an executable to update the database.
`Script`	Creates a SQL script for all, one, or a range of migrations

The Add Command

The `add` command creates a new database migration based on the current object model. The process examines every entity with a `DbSet<T>` property on the derived `DbContext` (and every entity that can be reached from those entities using navigation properties) and determines whether there are any changes that need to be applied to the database. If there are changes, the proper code is generated to update the database. You'll learn more about that shortly.

The `Add` command requires a `name` argument, which is used to name the create class and files for the migration. In addition to the common options, the option `-o <PATH>` or `-output-dir <PATH>` indicates where the migration files should go. The default directory is named `Migrations` relative to the current path.

Each migration added creates two files that are partials of the same class. Both files start their name with a timestamp and the migration name used as the argument to the `add` command. The first file is named `<YYYYMMDDHHMMSS>_<MigrationName>.cs`, and the second is named `<YYYYMMDDHHMMSS>_<MigrationName>.Designer.cs`. The timestamp is based on when the file was created and will match exactly for both files. The first file represents the code generated for the database changes in *this* migration, and the designer file represents the code to create and update the database based on all migrations up to and including this one.

The main file contains two methods, Up() and Down(). The Up() method contains the code to update the database with this migration's changes, and the Down() method contains the code to roll back this migration's changes. A partial listing of the initial migration from earlier in this chapter is listed here (all of the migrations used in the previous examples are in the AutoLot.Samples project in the companion code):

```
public partial class Radio : Migration
{
  protected override void Up(MigrationBuilder migrationBuilder)
  {
    migrationBuilder.CreateTable(
      name: "Make",
      columns: table => new
        {
          Id = table.Column<int>(type: "int", nullable: false)
            .Annotation("SqlServer:Identity", "1, 1"),
          Name = table.Column<string>(type: "nvarchar(max)", nullable: true),
          TimeStamp = table.Column<byte[]>(type: "varbinary(max)", nullable: true)
        },
        constraints: table =>
        {
          table.PrimaryKey("PK_Make", x => x.Id);
        });
...
    migrationBuilder.CreateIndex(
      name: "IX_Cars_MakeId",
      table: "Cars",
      column: "MakeId");
  }

  protected override void Down(MigrationBuilder migrationBuilder)
  {
    migrationBuilder.DropTable(name: "Cars");
    migrationBuilder.DropTable(name: "Make");
  }
}
```

As you can see, the Up() method is creating tables, columns, indexes, etc. The Down() method is dropping the items created. The migrations engine will issue alter, add, and drop statements as necessary to ensure the database matches your model.

The designer file contains two attributes that tie these partials to the filename and the derived DbContext. The attributes are shown here with a partial list of the design class:

```
[DbContext(typeof(ApplicationDbContext))]
[Migration("20210613000105_Radio")]
partial class Radio
{
  protected override void BuildTargetModel(ModelBuilder modelBuilder)
  {
    //omitted for brevity
  }
}
```

The first migration creates an additional file in the target directory named for the derived DbContext in the format of <DerivedDbContextName>ModelSnapshot.cs. The format of this file is the same as the designer partial and contains the code that is the sum of all migrations. When migrations are added or removed, this file is automatically updated to match the changes.

■ **Note** It is extremely important that you don't delete migration files manually. This will result in the <DerivedDbContext>ModelSnapshot.cs becoming out of sync with your migrations, essentially breaking them. If you are going to manually delete them, delete them all and start over. To remove a migration, use the remove command, covered shortly.

The Remove Command

The remove command is used to remove migrations from the project and always operates on the last migration (based on the timestamps of the migrations). When removing a migration, EF Core will make sure it hasn't been applied by checking the __EFMigrationsHistory table in the database. If the migration has been applied, the process fails. If the migration hasn't yet been applied or has been rolled back, the migration is removed, and the model snapshot file is updated.

The remove command doesn't take any arguments (since it always works on the last migration) and uses the same options as the add command. There is one additional option, the force option (-f || --force). This will roll back the last migration and then remove it in one step.

The List Command

The list command is used to show all the migrations for a derived DbContext. By default, it will list all migrations and query the database to determine whether they have been applied. If they have not been applied, they will be listed as pending. There is an option to pass in a specific connection string and another option to not connect to the database at all and instead just list the migrations. Table 21-12 shows those options.

Table 21-12. *Additional Options for EF Core Migrations List Command*

Option (Shorthand || Longhand)	Meaning in Life
--connection <CONNECTION>	Connection string to the database. Defaults to the one specified in the instance of IDesignTimeDbContextFactory or the DbContext's OnConfiguring method.
--no-connect	Instructs the command to skip the database check.

The Bundle Command

The bundle command creates an executable to update the database. The generated executable, built for a target runtime (e.g., Windows, Linux), will apply all contained migrations to the database. Table 21-13 describes the most commonly used arguments with the bundle command.

Table 21-13. Common Arguments for the EF Core Migrations Bundle Command

Argument	Meaning in Life
-o | --output <file>	The path to the executable file to create.
-f | --force	Overwrite existing files.
--self-contained	Also bundle the .NET runtime with the executable.
-r | --target-runtime <RUNTIME ID>	Target runtime to bundle for. If no runtime is specified, the file will use the runtime of the current machine's operating system.

The executable will use the connection string from the IDesignTimeDbContextFactory; however, another connection string can be passed into the executable using the --connection flag. If the migrations have already been applied to the target database, they will not be reapplied.

When applying the --self-contained flag, the size of the executable will grow significantly. On my machine with the sample project from this chapter, the regular bundle file is 11MB in size, while the self-contained file is 74MB.

The Script Command

The script command creates a SQL script based on one or more migrations. The command takes two optional arguments representing the migration to start with and the migration to end with. If neither is entered, all migrations are scripted. Table 21-14 describes the arguments.

Table 21-14. Arguments for the EF Core Migrations Script Command

Argument	Meaning in Life
<FROM>	The starting migration. Defaults to 0 (zero), the starting migration.
<TO>	The target migration. Defaults to the last migration.

If no migrations are named, the script created will be the cumulative total of all the migrations. If named migrations are provided, the script will contain the changes between the two migrations (inclusive). Each migration is wrapped in a transaction. If the __EFMigrationsHistory table does not exist in the database where the script is executed, it will be created. The table will also be updated to match the migrations that were executed. Some examples are shown here:

```
//Script all of the migrations
dotnet ef migrations script
//script from the beginning to the Many2Many migrations
dotnet ef migrations script 0 Many2Many
```

There are some additional options available, as shown in Table 21-15. The -o option allows you to specify a file for the script (the directory is relative to where the command is executed), and -i creates an idempotent script. This means it contains checks to see whether a migration has already been applied and skips that migration if it has. The -no-transaction option disables the normal transactions that are added to the script.

Table 21-15. Additional Options for the EF Core Migrations Script Command

Option (Shorthand || Longhand)	Meaning in Life
`-o || -output <FILE>`	The file to write the resulting script to
`-i || --idempotent`	Generates a script that checks if a migration has already been applied before applying it
`--no-transactions`	Does not wrap each migration in a transaction

The Database Commands

There are two database commands, `drop` and `update`. The `drop` command deletes the database if it exists. The `update` command updates the database using migrations.

The Drop Command

The `drop` command drops the database specified by the connection string in the context factory of the `OnConfiguring` method of `DbContext`. Using the `force` option does not ask for confirmation and force closes all connections. See Table 21-16.

Table 21-16. EF Core Database Drop Options

Option (Shorthand || Longhand)	Meaning in Life
`-f || --force`	Don't confirm the drop. Force close all connections.
`--dry-run`	Show which database will be dropped but don't drop it.

The Database Update Command

The `update` command takes one argument (the migration name) and the usual options. The command has one additional option, `--connection <CONNECTION>`. This allows for using a connection string that isn't configured in the design-time factory or `DbContext`.

If the command is executed without a migration name, the command updates the database to the most recent migration, creating the database if necessary. If a migration is named, the database will be updated to that migration. All previous migrations that have not yet been applied will be applied as well. As migrations are applied, their names are stored in the `__EFMigrationsHistory` table.

If the named migration has a timestamp that is earlier than other applied migrations, all later migrations are rolled back. If a 0 (zero) is passed in as the named migration, all migrations are reverted, leaving an empty database (except for the `__EFMigrationsHistory` table).

The DbContext Commands

There are four DbContext commands. Three of them (list, info, script) operate on derived DbContext classes in your project. The scaffold command creates a derived DbContext and entities from an existing database. Table 21-17 shows the available commands.

***Table 21-17.** The DbContext Commands*

Command	Meaning in Life
Info	Gets information about a DbContext type
List	Lists available DbContext types
Optimize	Generates a compiled version of the model used by the DbContext
Scaffold	Scaffolds a DbContext and entity types for a database
Script	Generates SQL script from the DbContext based on the object model, bypassing any migrations

The list and info commands have the usual options available. The list command lists the derived DbContext classes in the target project. The info command provides details about the specified derived DbContext class, including the connection string, provider name, database name, and data source. The script command creates a SQL script that creates your database based on the object model, ignoring any migrations that might be present. The scaffold command is used to reverse engineer an existing database and is covered in the next section.

The DbContext Scaffold Command

The scaffold command creates the C# classes (derived DbContext and entities) complete with data annotations (if requested) and Fluent API commands from an existing database. There are two required arguments, the database connection string, and the fully qualified provider (e.g., Microsoft.EntityFrameworkCore.SqlServer). Table 21-18 describes the arguments.

***Table 21-18.** The DbContext Scaffold Arguments*

Argument	Meaning in Life
Connection	The connection string to the database
Provider	The EF Core database provider to use (e.g., Microsoft.EntityFrameworkCore.SqlServer)

The options available include selecting specific schemas and tables, the created context class name and namespace, the output directory and namespace of the generated entity classes, and many more. The standard options are also available. The extended options are listed in Table 21-19, with discussion to follow.

Table 21-19. The DbContext Scaffold Options

Option (Shorthand || Longhand)	Meaning in Life
`-d || --data-annotations`	Use attributes to configure the model (where possible). If omitted, only the Fluent API is used.
`-c || --context <NAME>`	The name of the derived `DbContext` to create.
`--context-dir <PATH>`	The directory to place the derived `DbContext`, relative to the project directory. Defaults to database name.
`-f || --force`	Replaces any existing files in the target directory.
`-o || --output-dir <PATH>`	The directory to put the generated entity classes into. Relative to the project directory.
`--schema <SCHEMA_NAME>...`	The schemas of the tables to generate entity types for.
`-t || --table <TABLE_NAME>...`	The tables to generate entity types for.
`--use-database-names`	Use the table and column names directly from the database.
`-n	--namespaces <NAMESPACE>`	The namespace for the generated entity classes. Matches the directory by default.
`--context-namespace <NAMESPACE>`	The namespace for the generated derived `DbContext` class. Matches the directory by default.
`--no-onconfiguring`	Does not generate `OnConfiguring` method.
`--no-pluralize`	Does not use the pluralizer.

The `scaffold` command has become much more robust with EF Core 6.0. As you can see, there are plenty of options to choose from. If the data annotations (`-d`) option is selected, EF Core will use data annotations where it can and fill in the differences with the Fluent API. If that option is not selected, the entire configuration (where different than the conventions) is coded in the Fluent API. You can specify the namespace, schema, and location for the generated entities and derived `DbContext` files. If you do not want to scaffold the entire database, you can select certain schemas and tables. The `--no-onconfiguring` option eliminates the `OnConfiguring()` method from the scaffolded class, and the `-no-pluralize` option turns off the pluralizer, which turns singular entities (`Car`) into plural tables (`Cars`) when creating migrations and turns plural tables into single entities when scaffolding.

New in EF Core 6, database comments on SQL tables and columns are also scaffolded into the entity classes and their properties.

The DbContext Optimize Command

The `optimize` command optimizes the derived `DbContext`, performing many of the steps that would normally happen when the derived `DbContext` is first used. The options available include specifying the directory to place the compiled results as well as what namespace to use. The standard options are also available. The extended options are listed in Table 21-20, with discussion to follow.

Table 21-20. *The DbContext Optimize Options*

<table>
<tr><th>Option (Shorthand || Longhand)</th><th>Meaning in Life</th></tr>
<tr><td>-o || --output-dir</td><td>The directory to put the files in. Paths are relative to the project directory.</td></tr>
<tr><td>-n | --namespace <NAMESPACE></td><td>The namespace to use. Matches the directory by default.</td></tr>
</table>

When the derived DbContext is compiled, the results include a class for each entity in your model, the compiled derived DbContext, and the compiled derived DbContext ModelBuilder. For example, you can compile AutoLot.Samples.ApplicationDbContext using the following command:

```
dotnet ef dbcontext optimize --output-dir CompiledModels
```

The compiled files are placed in a directory named CompiledModels. The files are listed here:

```
ApplicationDbContextModel.cs
ApplicationDbContextModelBuilder.cs
CarDriverEntityType.cs
CarEntityType.cs
CarMakeViewModelEntityType.cs
DriverEntityType.cs
MakeEntityType.cs
PersonEntityType.cs
RadioEntityType.cs
```

To use the compiled model, call the UseModel() method in the DbContextOptions, like this:

```
var optionsBuilder = new DbContextOptionsBuilder<ApplicationDbContext>();
var connectionString = @"server=.,5433;Database=AutoLotSamples;User Id=sa;Password=P
@ssw0rd;Encrypt=False;";
optionsBuilder.UseSqlServer(connectionString).UseModel(ApplicationDbContextModel.Instance);
var context = new ApplicationDbContext(optionsBuilder.Options);
```

Compiling the derived DbContext can significantly improve performance in certain situations, but there are some restrictions:

- Global query filters are not supported.
- Lazy loading proxies are not supported.
- Change tracking proxies are not supported.
- The model must be recompiled any time the model changes.

If these restrictions aren't an issue for your situation, making use of the DbContext optimization can significantly improve your applications performance.

Summary

This chapter started the journey into Entity Framework Core. This chapter examined EF Core fundamentals, how queries execute, and change tracking. You learned about shaping your model with conventions, data annotations, and the Fluent API. The final section covered the power of the EF Core command-line interface and global tools.

CHAPTER 22

Exploring Entity Framework Core

The previous chapter covered the components of EF Core. This chapter will dive into the capabilities of EF Core, starting with create, read, update, and delete (CRUD) operations. After covering the CRUD operations, specific EF Core features are explored, including global query filters, mixing SQL queries with LINQ, projections, and more.

Note This chapter's code picks up where the previous chapter left off, so you can continue to use the code from Chapter 21 if you have been coding along with the text. If you are starting with this chapter and want to code along with the text, start with the previous chapter's code from the repo.

To get started, clear out the `Program.cs` file and add the following `Console.WriteLine()`:

```
Console.WriteLine("***** More Fun with Entity Framework Core *****");
```

Creating Records

Records are added to the database by creating them in code, adding them to their `DbSet<T>`, and calling `SaveChanges()/SaveChangesAsync()` on the context. When `SaveChanges()` is executed, the `ChangeTracker` reports all the added entities, and EF Core (along with the database provider) creates the appropriate SQL statement(s) to insert the record(s). You saw examples of this earlier in this chapter when the sample records were added into the database.

As a reminder from Chapter 21, `SaveChanges()` executes in an implicit transaction, unless an explicit transaction is used. If the save was successful, the server-generated values are then queried to set the values on the entities. The handling of server-generated values is covered in depth later in this chapter.

All of the SQL statements shown in this section were collected using SQL Server Profiler.

Note Records can also be added using the derived `DbContext`. These examples will all use the `DbSet<T>` collection properties to add the records. Both `DbSet<T>` and `DbContext` have async versions of `Add()/AddRange()`. Only the synchronous versions are shown.

A. Troelsen and P. Japikse, *Pro C# 10 with .NET 6*, https://doi.org/10.1007/978-1-4842-7869-7_22

Entity State

When an entity is created through code but not yet added to a DbSet<T>, the EntityState is Detached. Once a new entity is added to a DbSet<T>, the EntityState is set to Added. After SaveChanges() executes successfully, the EntityState is set to Unchanged.

The following code shows a newly created Make record and its EntityState:

```
static void AddRecords()
{
  //The factory is not meant to be used like this, but it's demo code :-)
  var context = new ApplicationDbContextFactory().CreateDbContext(null);
  var newMake = new Make
  {
    Name = "BMW"
  };
  Console.WriteLine($"State of the {newMake.Name} is {context.Entry(newMake).State}");
}
```

After calling the AddRecords() method from the top-level statements, you should see the following output:

```
***** More Fun with Entity Framework Core *****
State of the BMW is Detached
```

Add a Single Record Using Add

To add a new Make record to the database, create a new entity instance and call the Add() method of the appropriate DbSet<T>. To trigger the persistence of the data, SaveChanges() of the derived DbContext class must also be called. The following code adds the new Make record to the database:

```
static void AddRecords()
{
...
  context.Makes.Add(newMake);
  Console.WriteLine($"State of the {newMake.Name} is {context.Entry(newMake).State}");
  context.SaveChanges();
  Console.WriteLine($"State of the {newMake.Name} is {context.Entry(newMake).State}");
}
```

Running the program again, you will see the following output in the console window. After the entity was added into the Change Tracker (using the Add() method), the state was changed to Added. The message about saving changes comes from the SavingChanges event handler, and the message "Saved 1 entities" came from the SavedChanges event handler. After SaveChanges() is called on the context, the entity's state is changed to Unchanged:

```
***** More Fun with Entity Framework Core *****
State of the BMW is Detached
State of the BMW is Added
Saving changes for server=.,5433;Database=AutoLotSamples;User Id=sa;Password=P@ssw0rd;
Saved 1 entities
State of the BMW is Unchanged
```

The executed SQL statement for the insert is shown here. The format of the query is due to the batching process used by EF Core to improve the performance of database operations. Batching is covered later in this chapter. All of the values passed into the SQL statement are parameterized to help reduce the threat of scripting attacks. Also notice that the recently added entity is queried for the database-generated properties. EF Core's handling of server-managed values is also covered later in this chapter.

```
exec sp_executesql N'SET NOCOUNT ON;
INSERT INTO [Makes] ([Name]) VALUES (@p0);

SELECT [Id], [TimeStamp]
FROM [Makes]
WHERE @@ROWCOUNT = 1 AND [Id] = scope_identity();

',N'@p0 nvarchar(50)',@p0=N'BMW'
```

Add a Single Record Using Attach

When an entity's primary key is mapped to an identity column in SQL Server, EF Core will treat that entity instance as Added when added to the ChangeTracker if the primary key property's value is zero. The following code adds the new Car record using the Attach() method instead of the Add() method. Note that SaveChanges() must still be called for the data to be persisted.

```
static void AddRecords()
{
...
  var newCar = new Car()
  {
    Color = "Blue",
    DateBuilt = new DateTime(2016, 12, 01),
    IsDrivable = true,
    PetName = "Bluesmobile",
    MakeId = newMake.Id
  };
  Console.WriteLine($"State of the {newCar.PetName} is {context.Entry(newCar).State}");
  context.Cars.Attach(newCar);
  Console.WriteLine($"State of the {newCar.PetName} is {context.Entry(newCar).State}");
  context.SaveChanges();
  Console.WriteLine($"State of the {newCar.PetName} is {context.Entry(newCar).State}");
}
```

Running the program again, you will see the following same progression of states as you saw with the Make entity:

```
***** More Fun with Entity Framework Core *****
...
State of the Bluesmobile is Detached
State of the Bluesmobile is Added
Saving changes for server=.,5433;Database=AutoLotSamples;User Id=sa;Password=P@ssw0rd;
Saved 1 entities
State of the Bluesmobile is Unchanged
```

The executed SQL statement for the insert is shown here:

```
exec sp_executesql N'SET NOCOUNT ON;
INSERT INTO [dbo].[Inventory] ([Color], [DateBuilt], [IsDrivable], [MakeId], [PetName])
VALUES (@p0, @p1, @p2, @p3, @p4);

SELECT [Id], [Display], [TimeStamp]
FROM [dbo].[Inventory]
WHERE @@ROWCOUNT = 1 AND [Id] = scope_identity();

',N'@p0 nvarchar(50),@p1 datetime2(7),@p2 bit,@p3 int,@p4 nvarchar(50)',@p0=N'Blue',
@p1='2016-12-01 00:00:00',@p2=1,@p3=1,@p4=N'Bluesmobile'
```

Add Multiple Records at Once

To insert multiple records in a single transaction, use the AddRange() method of a DbSet<T> property, as shown in the following example:

```
static void AddRecords()
{
...
  var cars = new List<Car>
  {
    new() { Color = "Yellow", MakeId = newMake.Id, PetName = "Herbie" },
    new() { Color = "White", MakeId = newMake.Id, PetName = "Mach 5" },
    new() { Color = "Pink", MakeId = newMake.Id, PetName = "Avon" },
    new() { Color = "Blue", MakeId = newMake.Id, PetName = "Blueberry" },
  };
  context.Cars.AddRange(cars);
  context.SaveChanges();
}
```

Even though four records were added, EF Core generated only one SQL statement for the inserts. The SQL statement for the inserts is shown here:

```
exec sp_executesql N'SET NOCOUNT ON;
DECLARE @inserted0 TABLE ([Id] int, [_Position] [int]);
MERGE [dbo].[Inventory] USING (
VALUES (@p0, @p1, @p2, 0),
```

```
(@p3, @p4, @p5, 1),
(@p6, @p7, @p8, 2),
(@p9, @p10, @p11, 3)) AS i ([Color], [MakeId], [PetName], _Position) ON 1=0
WHEN NOT MATCHED THEN
INSERT ([Color], [MakeId], [PetName])
VALUES (i.[Color], i.[MakeId], i.[PetName])
OUTPUT INSERTED.[Id], i._Position
INTO @inserted0;

SELECT [t].[Id], [t].[DateBuilt], [t].[Display], [t].[IsDrivable], [t].[TimeStamp] FROM
[dbo].[Inventory] t
INNER JOIN @inserted0 i ON ([t].[Id] = [i].[Id])
ORDER BY [i].[_Position];

',N'@p0 nvarchar(50),@p1 int,@p2 nvarchar(50),@p3 nvarchar(50),@p4 int,@p5 nvarchar(50),
@p6 nvarchar(50),@p7 int,@p8 nvarchar(50),@p9 nvarchar(50),@p10 int,@p11 nvarchar(50)',
@p0=N'Yellow',@p1=1,@p2=N'Herbie',@p3=N'White',@p4=1,@p5=N'Mach 5',@p6=N'Pink',@p7=1,
@p8=N'Avon',@p9=N'Blue',@p10=1,@p11=N'Blueberry'
```

Identity Column Considerations When Adding Records

When an entity has a numeric property that is defined as the primary key, that property (by default) gets mapped to an Identity column in SQL Server. EF Core considers any entity with the default value (zero) for the key property to be new, and any entity with a nondefault value to already exist in the database. If you create a new entity and set the primary key property to a nonzero number and attempt to add it to the database, EF Core will fail to add the record because identity insert is not enabled.

For SQL Server, identity insert is enabled by issuing the `SET IDENTITY_INSERT` command within an explicit transaction. This command requires the database schema and table name, not the C# namespace and entity name. To get the database information for an entity, use the `FindEntityType()` method of the `Model` property for the derived `DbContext`. Once you have the `EntityType`, use the `GetSchema()` and `GetTableName()` methods:

```
static void AddRecords()
{
...
  IEntityType metadata = context.Model.FindEntityType(typeof(Car).FullName);
  var schema = metadata.GetSchema();
  var tableName = metadata.GetTableName();
}
```

Recall from the previous chapter that when using an `ExecutionStrategy`, explicit transactions must execute within the scope of that strategy. For reference, here is the following sample from the previous chapter:

```
var strategy = context.Database.CreateExecutionStrategy();
strategy.Execute(() =>
{
  using var trans = context.Database.BeginTransaction();
  try
  {
    //actionToExecute();
  trans.Commit();
```

```
  Console.WriteLine($"Insert succeeded");
  }
  catch (Exception ex)
  {
    trans.Rollback();
    Console.WriteLine($"Insert failed: {ex.Message}");
  }
});
```

When adding a record using identity insert, the `actionToExecute()` placeholder in the previous code block is replaced by code to turn identity insert on, add the record(s), and then save the changes. If that all succeeds, the transaction is committed. If any part of it fails, the transaction is rolled back. In the `finally` block, identity insert is turned back off.

EF Core provides two methods to execute commands directly against the database. The `ExecuteSqlRaw()` method executes the string exactly as it is written, while `ExecuteSqlInterpolated()` uses C# string interpolation to create a parameterized query. For this example, use the `ExecuteSqlRaw()` version. Here is the updated code, with the new lines in bold:

```
var strategy = context.Database.CreateExecutionStrategy();
strategy.Execute(() =>
{
  using var trans = context.Database.BeginTransaction();
  try
  {
    context.Database.ExecuteSqlRaw(
      $"SET IDENTITY_INSERT {schema}.{tableName} ON");
    var anotherNewCar = new Car()
    {
      Id = 27,
      Color = "Blue",
      DateBuilt = new DateTime(2016, 12, 01),
      IsDrivable = true,
      PetName = "Bluesmobile",
      MakeId = newMake.Id
    };
    context.Cars.Add(anotherNewCar);
    context.SaveChanges();
    trans.Commit();
    Console.WriteLine($"Insert succeeded");
  }
  catch (Exception ex)
  {
    trans.Rollback();
    Console.WriteLine($"Insert failed: {ex.Message}");
  }
  finally
  {
    context.Database.ExecuteSqlRaw(
      $"SET IDENTITY_INSERT {schema}.{tableName} OFF");
  }
});
```

■ **Note** When using known values, as in this example, the `ExecuteSqlRaw()` method is safe to use. However, if you are collecting inputs from users, you should use the `ExecuteSqlInterpolated()` version for added protection.

The previous code executed the following commands against the database:

```
SET IDENTITY_INSERT dbo.Inventory ON
SAVE TRANSACTION [__EFSavePoint];
exec sp_executesql N'SET NOCOUNT ON;
INSERT INTO [dbo].[Inventory] ([Id], [Color], [DateBuilt], [IsDrivable], [MakeId],
[PetName])
VALUES (@p0, @p1, @p2, @p3, @p4, @p5);
SELECT [Display], [TimeStamp]
FROM [dbo].[Inventory]
WHERE @@ROWCOUNT = 1 AND [Id] = @p0;

',N'@p0 int,@p1 nvarchar(50),@p2 datetime2(7),@p3 bit,@p4 int,@p5 nvarchar(50)',@p0=27,
@p1=N'Blue',@p2='2016-12-01 00:00:00',@p3=1,@p4=1,@p5=N'Bluesmobile'
SET IDENTITY_INSERT dbo.Inventory OFF
```

Adding an Object Graph

When adding an entity to the database, child records can be added in the same call without specifically adding them into their own DbSet<T>. This is accomplished by adding them into the collection navigation property for the parent record. For example, a new Make entity is created, and a child Car record is added to the Cars property on the Make. When the Make entity is added to the DbSet<Make> property, EF Core automatically starts tracking the child Car record as well, without having to add it into the DbSet<Car> property explicitly. Executing SaveChanges() saves the Make and Car together. The following test demonstrates this:

```
static void AddRecords()
{
...
  var anotherMake = new Make {Name = "Honda"};
  var car = new Car { Color = "Yellow", PetName = "Herbie" };
  //Cast the Cars property to List<Car> from IEnumerable<Car>
  ((List<Car>) anotherMake.Cars).Add(car);
  context.Makes.Add(make);
  context.SaveChanges();
}
```

The executed SQL statements are shown here:

```
exec sp_executesql N'SET NOCOUNT ON;
INSERT INTO [Makes] ([Name])
VALUES (@p0);
SELECT [Id], [TimeStamp]
FROM [Makes]
```

```
WHERE @@ROWCOUNT = 1 AND [Id] = scope_identity();

',N'@p0 nvarchar(50)',@p0=N'Honda'

exec sp_executesql N'SET NOCOUNT ON;
INSERT INTO [dbo].[Inventory] ([Color], [MakeId], [PetName])
VALUES (@p1, @p2, @p3);
SELECT [Id], [DateBuilt], [Display], [IsDrivable], [TimeStamp]
FROM [dbo].[Inventory]
WHERE @@ROWCOUNT = 1 AND [Id] = scope_identity();

',N'@p1 nvarchar(50),@p2 int,@p3 nvarchar(50)',@p1=N'Yellow',@p2=2,@p3=N'Herbie'
```

Notice how EF Core retrieved the Id for the new Make record and automatically included that in the insert statement for the Car record.

Add Many-to-Many Records

With the new EF Core support for many-to-many tables, records can be added directly from one entity to the other without going through the pivot table. Now you can write the following code to add Driver records directly to the Car records:

```
//M2M
var drivers = new List<Driver>
{
  new() { PersonInfo = new Person { FirstName = "Fred", LastName = "Flinstone" } },
  new() { PersonInfo = new Person { FirstName = "Wilma", LastName = "Flinstone" } },
  new() { PersonInfo = new Person { FirstName = "BamBam", LastName = "Flinstone" } },
  new() { PersonInfo = new Person { FirstName = "Barney", LastName = "Rubble" } },
  new() { PersonInfo = new Person { FirstName = "Betty", LastName = "Rubble" } },
  new() { PersonInfo = new Person { FirstName = "Pebbles", LastName = "Rubble" } },
};
var carsForM2M = context.Cars.Take(2).ToList();
//Cast the IEnumerable to a List to access the Add method
//Range support works with LINQ to Objects, but is not translatable to SQL calls
((List<Driver>)carsForM2M[0].Drivers).AddRange(drivers.Take(..3));
((List<Driver>)carsForM2M[1].Drivers).AddRange(drivers.Take(3..));
context.SaveChanges();
```

When the SaveChanges() method is executed, two insert statements are executed. The first inserts the six Driver records into the Drivers table, and then the second inserts the six records into the InventoryDriver table (the pivot table). Here is the insert statement for the pivot table:

```
exec sp_executesql N'SET NOCOUNT ON;
DECLARE @inserted0 TABLE ([InventoryId] int, [DriverId] int, [_Position] [int]);
MERGE [dbo].[InventoryToDrivers] USING (
VALUES (@p12, @p13, 0),
(@p14, @p15, 1),
(@p16, @p17, 2),
(@p18, @p19, 3),
(@p20, @p21, 4),
```

```
(@p22, @p23, 5)) AS i ([InventoryId], [DriverId], _Position) ON 1=0
WHEN NOT MATCHED THEN
INSERT ([InventoryId], [DriverId])
VALUES (i.[InventoryId], i.[DriverId])
OUTPUT INSERTED.[InventoryId], INSERTED.[DriverId], i._Position
INTO @inserted0;

SELECT [t].[Id], [t].[TimeStamp] FROM [dbo].[InventoryToDrivers] t
INNER JOIN @inserted0 i ON ([t].[InventoryId] = [i].[InventoryId]) AND ([t].[DriverId] =
[i].[DriverId])
ORDER BY [i].[_Position];

',N'@p12 int,@p13 int,@p14 int,@p15 int,@p16 int,@p17 int,@p18 int,@p19 int,@p20 int,@p21
int,@p22 int,@p23 int',@p12=1,@p13=1,@p14=1,@p15=2,@p16=1,@p17=3,@p18=2,@p19=4,@p20=2,
@p21=5,@p22=2,@p23=6
```

This is a much better experience than past versions of EF Core when using many-to-many relationships, where you had to manage the pivot table yourself.

Add Sample Records

The final step is to add a series of Make and Car records for the query examples covered in the next section. The method creates several Make and Car entities and adds them to the database.

Start by creating the Make entities and add them to the Makes DbSet<Make> property of the derived ApplicationDbContext, and then call the SaveChanges() method. Repeat this process for the Car records, using the Cars DbSet<Car> property:

```
static void LoadMakeAndCarData()
{
  //The factory is not meant to be used like this, but it's demo code :-)
  var context = new ApplicationDbContextFactory().CreateDbContext(null);
  List<Make> makes = new()
  {
    new() { Name = "VW" },
    new() { Name = "Ford" },
    new() { Name = "Saab" },
    new() { Name = "Yugo" },
    new() { Name = "BMW" },
    new() { Name = "Pinto" },
  };
  context.Makes.AddRange(makes);
  context.SaveChanges();
  List<Car> inventory = new()
  {
    new() { MakeId = 1, Color = "Black", PetName = "Zippy" },
    new() { MakeId = 2, Color = "Rust", PetName = "Rusty" },
    new() { MakeId = 3, Color = "Black", PetName = "Mel" },
    new() { MakeId = 4, Color = "Yellow", PetName = "Clunker" },
    new() { MakeId = 5, Color = "Black", PetName = "Bimmer" },
    new() { MakeId = 5, Color = "Green", PetName = "Hank" },
    new() { MakeId = 5, Color = "Pink", PetName = "Pinky" },
```

```
    new() { MakeId = 6, Color = "Black", PetName = "Pete" },
    new() { MakeId = 4, Color = "Brown", PetName = "Brownie" },
    new() { MakeId = 1, Color = "Rust", PetName = "Lemon", IsDrivable = false },
  };
  context.Cars.AddRange(inventory);
  context.SaveChanges();
}
```

Clear the Sample Data

Later in this chapter, deleting records will be covered in depth. For now, we will create a method that clears out the sample data so when the examples are run multiple times, the previous executions don't interfere with the examples.

Create a new method called ClearSampleData(). The method uses the FindEntityType() method on the Model property of the ApplicationDbContext to get the table and schema name and then deletes the records. After the records are deleted, the code uses the DBCC CHECKIDENT command to reset the identity for each table.

```
static void ClearSampleData()
{
  //The factory is not meant to be used like this, but it's demo code :-)
  var context = new ApplicationDbContextFactory().CreateDbContext(null);
  var entities = new[]
  {
    typeof(Driver).FullName,
    typeof(Car).FullName,
    typeof(Make).FullName,
  };
  foreach (var entityName in entities)
  {
    var entity = context.Model.FindEntityType(entityName);
    var tableName = entity.GetTableName();
    var schemaName = entity.GetSchema();
    context.Database.ExecuteSqlRaw($"DELETE FROM {schemaName}.{tableName}");
    context.Database.ExecuteSqlRaw($"DBCC CHECKIDENT (\"{schemaName}.{tableName}\",
    RESEED, 0);");
  }
}
```

Add a call to this method at the beginning of the top-level statements to reset the database each time the program is executed. Also add a call after the AddRecords() method to clean up the examples that add individual records:

```
Console.WriteLine("***** More Fun with Entity Framework Core *****");
ClearSampleData();
AddRecords();
ClearSampleData();
LoadMakeAndCarData();
```

Querying Data

Querying data using EF Core is typically accomplished using LINQ queries. As a reminder, when using LINQ to query the database for a list of entities, the query isn't executed until the query is iterated over, converted to a `List<T>` (or an array), or bound to a list control (like a data grid). For single-record queries, the statement is executed immediately when the single record call (`First()`, `Single()`, etc.) is used.

■ **Note** This book is not a complete LINQ reference but shows just a few examples. For more examples of LINQ queries, Microsoft has published 101 LINQ samples at `https://code.msdn.microsoft.com/101-LINQ-Samples-3fb9811b`.

New in EF Core 5, you can call the `ToQueryString()` method in most LINQ queries to examine the query that gets executed against the database. The main exception is any immediate execution queries, such as `First()`/`FirstOrDefault()`. For split queries, the `ToQueryString()` method returns only the first query that will be executed.

Get All Records

To get all the records for a table, simply use the `DbSet<T>` property directly without any LINQ statements. For immediate execution, add `ToList()` to the `DbSet<T>` property. Add the following method to the `Program.cs` file:

```
static void QueryData()
{
  //The factory is not meant to be used like this, but it's demo code :-)
  var context = new ApplicationDbContextFactory().CreateDbContext(null);
  //Return all of the cars
  IQueryable<Car> cars = context.Cars;
  foreach (Car c in cars)
  {
    Console.WriteLine($"{c.PetName} is {c.Color}");
  }
  //Clean up the context
  context.ChangeTracker.Clear();
  List<Car> cars2 = context.Cars.ToList();
  foreach (Car c in cars2)
  {
    Console.WriteLine($"{c.PetName} is {c.Color}");
  }
}
```

Notice that the type returned is an `IQueryable<Car>` when using the `DbSet<Car>`, and the return type is `List<Car>` when using the `ToList()` method.

Filter Records

The Where() method is used to filter records from the DbSet<T>. Multiple Where() methods can be fluently chained to dynamically build the query. Chained Where() methods are always combined as and clauses in the created query. In the following example, the generated query for cars2 and cars3 are identical. To create an or statement, you must use the same Where() clause.

```
static void FilterData()
{
    //The factory is not meant to be used like this, but it's demo code :-)
    var context = new ApplicationDbContextFactory().CreateDbContext(null);
    //Return all yellow cars
    IQueryable<Car> cars = context.Cars.Where(c=>c.Color == "Yellow");
    Console.WriteLine("Yellow cars");
    foreach (Car c in cars)
    {
        Console.WriteLine($"{c.PetName} is {c.Color}");
    }
    context.ChangeTracker.Clear();

    //Return all yellow cars with a petname of Clunker
    IQueryable<Car> cars2 = context.Cars.Where(c => c.Color == "Yellow" && c.PetName ==
    "Clunker");
    Console.WriteLine("Yellow cars and Clunkers");
    foreach (Car c in cars2)
    {
        Console.WriteLine($"{c.PetName} is {c.Color}");
    }
    context.ChangeTracker.Clear();

    //Return all yellow cars with a petname of Clunker
    IQueryable<Car> cars3 = context.Cars.Where(c=>c.Color == "Yellow").Where(c=>c.PetName ==
    "Clunker");
    Console.WriteLine("Yellow cars and Clunkers");
    foreach (Car c in cars3)
    {
        Console.WriteLine($"{c.PetName} is {c.Color}");
    }
    context.ChangeTracker.Clear();

    //Return all yellow cars or cars with PetName of Clunker
    IQueryable<Car> cars4 = context.Cars.Where(c=>c.Color == "Yellow" || c.PetName ==
    "Clunker");
    Console.WriteLine("Yellow cars or Clunkers");
    foreach (Car c in cars4)
    {
        Console.WriteLine($"{c.PetName} is {c.Color}");
    }
    context.ChangeTracker.Clear();
}
```

Notice that the type returned is also an IQueryable<Car> when using a Where clause.

One improvement in EF Core 6 is the handling of converting string.IsNullOrWhiteSpace() into SQL. Examine the added code to the end of the FilterData() method:

```
static void FilterData()
{
...
  IQueryable<Car> cars5 = context.Cars.Where(c => !string.IsNullOrWhiteSpace(c.Color));
  Console.WriteLine("Cars with colors");
  foreach (Car c in cars5)
  {
    Console.WriteLine($"{c.PetName} is {c.Color}");
  }
  context.ChangeTracker.Clear();
}
```

Prior to EF Core 6, the resulting query was a mix of LTRIM/RTRIM commands. With the improvements in EF Core 6, the executed query is much cleaner:

```
SELECT [i].[Id], [i].[Color], [i].[DateBuilt], [i].[Display], [i].[IsDrivable], [i].
[MakeId], [i].[PetName], [i].[TimeStamp]
FROM [dbo].[Inventory] AS [i]
WHERE [i].[Color] <> N''
```

Sort Records

The OrderBy() and OrderByDescending() methods set the sort(s) for the query in either ascending or descending order, respectively. If subsequent sorts are required, use the ThenBy() and/or the ThenByDescending() methods.

```
static void SortData()
{
  //The factory is not meant to be used like this, but it's demo code :-)
  var context = new ApplicationDbContextFactory().CreateDbContext(null);
  //Return all cars ordered by color
  IOrderedQueryable<Car> cars = context.Cars.OrderBy(c=>c.Color);
  Console.WriteLine("Cars ordered by Color");
  foreach (Car c in cars)
  {
    Console.WriteLine($"{c.PetName} is {c.Color}");
  }
  context.ChangeTracker.Clear();
  //Return all cars ordered by color then Petname
  IOrderedQueryable<Car> cars1 = context.Cars.OrderBy(c=>c.Color).ThenBy(c=>c.PetName);
  Console.WriteLine("Cars ordered by Color then PetName");
  foreach (Car c in cars1)
  {
    Console.WriteLine($"{c.PetName} is {c.Color}");
  }
  context.ChangeTracker.Clear();
  //Return all cars ordered by color Descending
  IOrderedQueryable<Car> cars2 = context.Cars.OrderByDescending(c=>c.Color);
```

```
  Console.WriteLine("Cars ordered by Color descending");
  foreach (Car c in cars2)
  {
    Console.WriteLine($"{c.PetName} is {c.Color}");
  }
  context.ChangeTracker.Clear();
}
```

Notice that the datatype returned from a LINQ query with an `OrderBy()`/`OrderByDescending()` is `IOrderedQueryable<Car>`.

Ordering by ascending and descending can be intermixed, as is shown here:

```
static void SortData()
{
...
  //Return all cars ordered by Color then by PetName descending
  IOrderedQueryable<Car> cars3 = context.Cars.OrderBy(c=>c.Color).ThenByDescending(c=>
  c.PetName);
  Console.WriteLine("Cars ordered by Color then by PetName descending");
  foreach (Car c in cars3)
  {
    Console.WriteLine($"{c.PetName} is {c.Color}");
  }
  context.ChangeTracker.Clear();
}
```

Reverse Sort Records

The `Reverse()` method reverses the entire sort order, as shown here:

```
static void SortData()
{
...
  //Return all cars ordered by Color then Petname in reverse
  IQueryable<Car> cars1 = context.Cars.OrderBy(c=>c.Color).ThenBy(c=>c.PetName).Reverse();
  Console.WriteLine("Cars ordered by Color then PetName in reverse");
  foreach (Car c in cars1)
  {
    Console.WriteLine($"{c.PetName} is {c.Color}");
  }
  context.ChangeTracker.Clear();
}
```

Notice that the datatype returned from a LINQ query with a `Reverse()` clause is `IQueryable<Car>`, and not `IOrderedQueryable<Car>`.

The preceding LINQ query gets translated into the following:

```
SELECT [i].[Id], [i].[Color], [i].[DateBuilt], [i].[Display],
    [i].[IsDrivable], [i].[MakeId], [i].[PetName], [i].[TimeStamp]
FROM [dbo].[Inventory] AS [i]
ORDER BY [i].[Color] DESC, [i].[PetName] DESC
```

Paging

EF Core provides paging capabilities using Skip() and Take(). Skip() skips the specified number of records while Take() retrieves the specified number of records.

Using the Skip() method with SQL Server executes a query with an OFFSET command. The OFFSET command is the SQL Server version of skipping records that would normally be returned from the query. Add the following method to the Program.cs file:

```
static void Paging()
{
  //The factory is not meant to be used like this, but it's demo code :-)
  var context = new ApplicationDbContextFactory().CreateDbContext(null);
  Console.WriteLine("Paging");
  //Skip the first two records
  var cars = context.Cars.Skip(2).ToList();
}
```

■ **Note** The SQL Server OFFSET command has decreasing performance the more records are skipped. Most applications probably won't be using EF Core (or any ORM) with massive amounts of data, but make sure you performance test any calls that use Skip(). If there is a performance issue, it might be better to drop down to a FromSqlRaw()/FromSqlInterpolated() to optimize the query.

The example code skips the first two records and returns the rest. The slightly edited (for readability) query is shown here:

```
SELECT [i].[Id], [i].[Color], [i].[DateBuilt], [i].[Display],
    [i].[IsDrivable], [i].[MakeId], [i].[PetName], [i].[TimeStamp]
FROM [dbo].[Inventory] AS [i]
ORDER BY (SELECT 1)
OFFSET 2 ROWS
```

Notice that the generated query adds an ORDER BY clause, even though the LINQ statement did not have any ordering. This is because the SQL Server OFFSET command cannot be used without an ORDER BY clause.

The Take() method generates a SQL Server query that uses the TOP command. The following addition to the Paging() method uses the Clear() method on the ChangeTracker to reset the ApplicationDbContext and then uses the Take() method to return two records.

```
static void Paging()
{
...
  context.ChangeTracker.Clear();
  //Take the first two records
  cars = context.Cars.Take(2).ToList();
}
```

The executed query is shown here:

```
SELECT TOP(2) [i].[Id], [i].[Color], [i].[DateBuilt], [i].[Display],
    [i].[IsDrivable], [i].[MakeId], [i].[PetName], [i].[TimeStamp]
FROM [dbo].[Inventory] AS [i]
```

■ **Note** Recall from Chapter 13 that with .NET 6/C#10, the Take() method can take a range. This capability is not supported in EF Core.

Combing the Skip() and Take() method enables paging of the data. For example, if you have a page size of two (due to our small database size) and you need to get the second page, execute the following LINQ query:

```
static void Paging()
{
...
  //Skip the first two records and take the next two records
  cars = context.Cars.Skip(2).Take(2).ToList();
}
```

When combining Skip() and Take(), SQL Server doesn't use the TOP command, but another version of the OFFSET command, as shown here:

```
SELECT [i].[Id], [i].[Color], [i].[DateBuilt], [i].[Display], [i].[IsDrivable],
    [i].[MakeId], [i].[PetName], [i].[TimeStamp]
FROM [dbo].[Inventory] AS [i]
ORDER BY (SELECT 1)
OFFSET 2 ROWS FETCH NEXT 2 ROWS ONLY
```

Retrieve a Single Record

There are three main methods (with OrDefault variants) for returning a single record with a query: First()/FirstOrDefault(), Last()/LastOrDefault(), and Single()/SingleOrDefault(). While all three return a single record, their approaches all differ. The three methods and their variants are detailed here:

- First() returns the first record that matches the query condition and any ordering clauses. If no ordering is specified, then the record returned is based on database order. If no record is returned, an exception is thrown.
- The FirstOrDefault() behavior matches First() except that if no records match the query, the method returns the default value for the type (null).
- Single() returns the first record that matches the query condition and any ordering clauses. If no ordering is specified, then the record returned is based on database order. If no records or more than one record matches the query, then an exception is thrown.
- The SingleOrDefault() behavior matches Single() except that if no records match the query, the method returns the default value for the type (null).

- `Last()` returns the last record that matches the query condition and any ordering clauses. If no ordering is specified, an exception is thrown. If no record is returned, an exception is thrown.
- The `LastOrDefault()` behavior matches `Last()` except that if no records match the query, the method returns the default value for the type (null).

All the methods can also take an `Expression<Func<T, bool>>` to filter the result set. This means you can place the `Where()` expression inside the call for the `First()`/`Single()` methods as long as there is only a single `Where()` clause. The following statements are equivalent:

```
Context.Cars.Where(c=>c.Id < 5).First();
Context.Cars.First(c=>c.Id < 5);
```

Using First

When using the parameterless form of `First()` and `FirstOrDefault()`, the first record (based on database order or any preceding ordering clauses) will be returned. The following example gets the first record based on database order:

```
static void SingleRecordQueries()
{
  //The factory is not meant to be used like this, but it's demo code :-)
  var context = new ApplicationDbContextFactory().CreateDbContext(null);
  Console.WriteLine("Single Record with database Sort");
  var firstCar = context.Cars.First();
  Console.WriteLine($"{firstCar.PetName} is {firstCar.Color}");
  context.ChangeTracker.Clear();
}
```

The preceding LINQ query gets translated into the following:

```
SELECT TOP(1) [i].[Id], [i].[Color], [i].[DateBuilt], [i].[Display],
    [i].[IsDrivable], [i].[MakeId], [i].[PetName], [i].[TimeStamp]
FROM [dbo].[Inventory] AS [i]
```

The following code gets the first record based on `Color` order:

```
static void SingleRecordQueries()
{
...
  Console.WriteLine("Single Record with OrderBy sort");
  var firstCarByColor = context.Cars.OrderBy(c => c.Color).First();
  Console.WriteLine($"{firstCarByColor.PetName} is {firstCarByColor.Color}");
  context.ChangeTracker.Clear();
}
```

The preceding LINQ query gets translated into the following:

```
SELECT TOP(1) [i].[Id], [i].[Color], [i].[DateBuilt], [i].[Display],
    [i].[IsDrivable], [i].[MakeId], [i].[PetName], [i].[TimeStamp]
```

```
FROM [dbo].[Inventory] AS [i]
ORDER BY [i].[Color]
```

The following code shows `First()` being used with a `Where()` clause and then using `First()` as the `Where()` clause:

```
static void SingleRecordQueries()
{
...
  Console.WriteLine("Single Record with Where clause");
  var firstCarIdThree = context.Cars.Where(c => c.Id == 3).First();
  Console.WriteLine($"{firstCarIdThree.PetName} is {firstCarIdThree.Color}");
  context.ChangeTracker.Clear();

  Console.WriteLine("Single Record Using First as Where clause");
  var firstCarIdThree1 = context.Cars.First(c => c.Id == 3);
  Console.WriteLine($"{firstCarIdThree1.PetName} is {firstCarIdThree1.Color}");
  context.ChangeTracker.Clear();
}
```

Both preceding statements get translated into the following SQL:

```
SELECT TOP(1) [i].[Id], [i].[Color], [i].[DateBuilt], [i].[Display],
    [i].[IsDrivable], [i].[MakeId], [i].[PetName], [i].[TimeStamp]
FROM [dbo].[Inventory] AS [i]
WHERE [i].[Id] = 3
```

The following example shows that an exception is thrown if there isn't a match when using `First()`:

```
static void SingleRecordQueries()
{
...
  Console.WriteLine("Exception when no record is found");
  try
  {
    var firstCarNotFound = context.Cars.First(c => c.Id == 27);
  }
  catch (InvalidOperationException ex)
  {
    Console.WriteLine(ex.Message);
  }
  context.ChangeTracker.Clear();
}
```

The preceding LINQ query gets translated into the following:

```
SELECT TOP(1) [i].[Id], [i].[Color], [i].[DateBuilt], [i].[Display],
    [i].[IsDrivable], [i].[MakeId], [i].[PetName], [i].[TimeStamp]
FROM [dbo].[Inventory] AS [i]
WHERE [i].[Id] = 27
```

When using FirstOrDefault(), instead of an exception, the result is a null when no data is returned.

```
static void SingleRecordQueries()
{
...
  Console.WriteLine("Return Default (null) when no record is found");
  var firstCarNotFound = context.Cars.FirstOrDefault(c => c.Id == 27);
  Console.WriteLine(firstCarNotFound == true);
  context.ChangeTracker.Clear();
}
```

The preceding LINQ query gets translated into the same SQL as the previous example.

■ **Note** Also recall from Chapter 13 that with .NET 6/C#10, the OrDefault() methods can specify a default value when nothing is returned from the query. Unfortunately, this capability is also not supported in EF Core.

Using Last

When using the parameterless form of Last() and LastOrDefault(), the last record (based on any preceding ordering clauses) will be returned. When using Last(), the LINQ query must have an OrderBy()/OrderByDescending() clause or an InvalidOperationException will be thrown:

```
static void SingleRecordQueries()
{
...
  Console.WriteLine("Exception with Last and no order by");
  try
  {
    context.Cars.Last();
  }
  catch (InvalidOperationException ex)
  {
    Console.WriteLine(ex.Message);
  }
}
```

The following test gets the last record based on Color order:

```
static void SingleRecordQueries()
{
...
  Console.WriteLine("Get last record sorted by Color");
  var lastCar = context.Cars.OrderBy(c=>c.Color).Last();
  Console.WriteLine(firstCarNotFoundDefault == null);
  context.ChangeTracker.Clear();
}
```

EF Core reverses the ORDER BY statements and then takes the top(1) to get the result. Here is the executed query:

```
SELECT TOP(1) [i].[Id], [i].[Color], [i].[DateBuilt], [i].[Display],
    [i].[IsDrivable], [i].[MakeId], [i].[PetName], [i].[TimeStamp]
FROM [dbo].[Inventory] AS [i]
ORDER BY [i].[Color] DESC
```

Using Single

Conceptually, Single()/SingleOrDefault() works the same as First()/FirstOrDefault(). The main difference is that Single()/SingleOrDefault() returns Top(2) instead of Top(1) and throws an exception if two records are returned from the database.

The following tests retrieves the single record where Id == 1:

```
static void SingleRecordQueries()
{
...
  Console.WriteLine("Get single record");
  var singleCar = context.Cars.Single(c=>c.Id == 3);
  context.ChangeTracker.Clear();
}
```

The preceding LINQ query gets translated into the following:

```
SELECT TOP(2) [i].[Id], [i].[Color], [i].[DateBuilt], [i].[Display],
    [i].[IsDrivable], [i].[MakeId], [i].[PetName], [i].[TimeStamp]
FROM [dbo].[Inventory] AS [i]
WHERE [i].[Id] = 3
```

Single() throws an exception if no records are returned or more than one record is returned:

```
static void SingleRecordQueries()
{
...
  Console.WriteLine("Exception when more than one record is found");
  try
  {
     context.Cars.Single(c => c.Id > 1);
  }
  catch (InvalidOperationException ex)
  {
    Console.WriteLine(ex.Message);
  }
  context.ChangeTracker.Clear();

  Console.WriteLine("Exception when no records are found");
  try
  {
  context.Cars.Single(c => c.Id == 27);
  }
```

```
  catch (InvalidOperationException ex)
  {
    Console.WriteLine(ex.Message);
  }
  context.ChangeTracker.Clear();}
}
```

When using SingleOrDefault(), an exception is also thrown if more than one record is returned:

```
static void SingleRecordQueries()
{
...
  Console.WriteLine("Exception when more than one record is found");
  try
  {
    context.Cars.SingleOrDefault(c => c.Id > 1);
  }
  catch (InvalidOperationException ex)
  {
    Console.WriteLine(ex.Message);
  }
  context.ChangeTracker.Clear();
}
```

When using SingleOrDefault(), instead of an exception, the result is null when no data is returned.

```
static void SingleRecordQueries()
{
...
  var defaultWhenSingleNotFoundCar = context.Cars.SingleOrDefault(c => c.Id == 27);
  context.ChangeTracker.Clear();
}
```

Using Find

The Find() method also returns a single record but behaves a little differently than the other single record methods. The Find() method's parameter(s) represent the primary key(s) of the entity. It then looks in the ChangeTracker for an instance of the entity with the matching primary key and returns it if it's found. If not, it will then make a call to the database to retrieve the record.

```
static void SingleRecordQueries()
{
...
  var foundCar = context.Cars.Find(27);
  context.ChangeTracker.Clear();
}
```

If the entity has a compound primary key, then pass in the values representing the compound key:

```
var item = context.MyClassWithCompoundKey.Find(27,3);
```

Aggregation Methods

EF Core also supports server-side aggregate methods (Max(), Min(), Count(), and Average()). All aggregate methods can be used in conjunction with Where() methods and return a single value. The aggregation queries execute on the server side. Global query filters affect aggregate methods as well and can be disabled with IgnoreQueryFilters(). Global query filters are covered later in this chapter.

Note that each of the aggregate methods is a terminating function. In other words, they end the LINQ statement when executed since each method returns a single numeric value. Query execution also happens immediately, like the single record methods discussed earlier.

All of the SQL statements shown in this section were collected using SQL Server Profiler as the ToQueryString() method doesn't work with aggregation.

This first example counts all the Car records in the database.

```
static void Aggregation()
{
  //The factory is not meant to be used like this, but it's demo code :-)
  var context = new ApplicationDbContextFactory().CreateDbContext(null);
  var count = context.Cars.Count();
}
```

The executed SQL is shown here:

```
SELECT COUNT(*)
FROM [dbo].[Inventory] AS [i]
```

The Count() method can contain the filter expression, just like First() and Single(). The following examples demonstrate the Count() method with a where condition. The first adds the expression directly into the Count() method, and the second adds the Count() method to the end of the LINQ statement after the Where() method.

```
static void Aggregation()
{
...
  var countByMake = context.Cars.Count(x=>x.MakeId == 1);
  Console.WriteLine($"Count: {countByMake}");
  var countByMake2 = context.Cars.Where(x=>x.MakeId == 1).Count();
  Console.WriteLine($"Count: {countByMake2}");
}
```

Both lines of code create the same SQL calls to the server, as shown here:

```
SELECT COUNT(*)
FROM [dbo].[Inventory] AS [i]
WHERE [i].[MakeId] = 1
```

The next examples show Min(), Max(), and Average(). Each method takes an expression to specify the property that is being operated on:

```
static void Aggregation()
{
...
  var max = context.Cars.Max(x => x.Id);
```

```
  var min = context.Cars.Min(x => x.Id);
  var avg = context.Cars.Average(x => x.Id);
  Console.WriteLine($"Max ID: {max} Min ID: {min} Ave ID: {avg}");}

--Generated SQL
SELECT MAX([i].[Id]) FROM [dbo].[Inventory] AS [i]
SELECT MIN([i].[Id]) FROM [dbo].[Inventory] AS [i]
SELECT AVG(CAST([i].[Id] AS float)) FROM [dbo].[Inventory] AS [i]
```

Any( ) and All( )

The Any() and All() methods check a set of records to see whether any records match the criteria (Any()) or whether all records match the criteria (All()). Just like the aggregation methods, the Any() method (but not the All() method) can be added to the end of a LINQ query with Where() methods, or the filter expression can be contained in the method itself. Any() and All() methods execute on the server side, and a Boolean is returned from the query. Both are terminating functions. Global query filters affect Any() and All() methods functions as well and can be disabled with IgnoreQueryFilters().

The ToQueryString() method doesn't work with the Any()/All() functions either, so all of the SQL statements shown in this section were collected using SQL Server Profiler.

This first sample checks if *any* car records have a MakeId of 1.

```
static void AnyAndAll()
{
  //The factory is not meant to be used like this, but it's demo code :-)
  var context = new ApplicationDbContextFactory().CreateDbContext(null);
  var resultAny = context.Cars.Any(x => x.MakeId == 1);
  //This executes the same query as the preceding line
    var resultAnyWithWhere = context.Cars.IgnoreQueryFilters().Where(x => x.MakeId ==
    1).Any();

    Console.WriteLine($"Exist? {resultAny}");
    Console.WriteLine($"Exist? {resultAnyWithWhere}");
}
```

The executed SQL for the first example is shown here:

```
SELECT CASE
  WHEN EXISTS (
      SELECT 1
      FROM [dbo].[Inventory] AS [i]
      WHERE [i].[MakeId] = 1) THEN CAST(1 AS bit)
  ELSE CAST(0 AS bit)
END
```

This second example checks if *all* car records have a specific MakeId.

```
static void AnyAndAll()
{
...
  var resultAll = context.Cars.All(x => x.MakeId == 1);
  Console.WriteLine($"All? {resultAll}");
}
```

The executed SQL for the first theory test is shown here:

```
SELECT CASE
  WHEN NOT EXISTS (
      SELECT 1
      FROM [dbo].[Inventory] AS [i]
      WHERE [i].[MakeId] <> 1) THEN CAST(1 AS bit)
  ELSE CAST(0 AS bit)
END
```

Getting Data from Stored Procedures

The final data retrieval pattern to examine is getting data from stored procedures. While there are some gaps in EF Core in relation to stored procedures (compared to EF 6), remember that EF Core is built on top of ADO.NET. We just need to drop down a layer and remember how we called stored procedures pre-ORM.

The first step is to create the stored procedure in our database:

```
CREATE PROCEDURE [dbo].[GetPetName]
    @carID int,
    @petName nvarchar(50) output
AS
SELECT @petName = PetName from dbo.Inventory where Id = @carID
```

The following method creates the required parameters (input and output), leverages the ApplicationDbContext Database property, and calls ExecuteSqlRaw():

```
static string GetPetName(ApplicationDbContext context, int id)
{
  var parameterId = new SqlParameter
  {
    ParameterName = "@carId",
    SqlDbType = System.Data.SqlDbType.Int,
    Value = id,
  };

  var parameterName = new SqlParameter
  {
    ParameterName = "@petName",
    SqlDbType = System.Data.SqlDbType.NVarChar,
    Size = 50,
    Direction = ParameterDirection.Output
  };

  var result = context.Database
      .ExecuteSqlRaw("EXEC [dbo].[GetPetName] @carId, @petName OUTPUT",parameterId,
      parameterName);
  return (string)parameterName.Value;
}
```

The next step is to get the Car records (to get the Id values for each of the Car records), loop though them, and use the stored procedure to get their PetName:

```
static void GetDataFromStoredProc()
{
  //The factory is not meant to be used like this, but it's demo code :-)
  var context = new ApplicationDbContextFactory().CreateDbContext(null);
  var cars = context.Cars.IgnoreQueryFilters().ToList();
  foreach (var c in cars)
  {
    Console.WriteLine($"PetName: {GetPetName(context,c.Id)}");
  }
}
```

■ **Note** This example is somewhat contrived, as getting all of the Car records also gets the PetName properties for the records. Getting all of the records is a convenient way to demonstrate calling the stored procedure multiple times.

When the code is run, EF Core executes the following SQL for each Car in the list (only one is shown here):

```
declare @p4 nvarchar(50)
set @p4=N'Hank'
exec sp_executesql N'EXEC [dbo].[GetPetName] @carId, @petName OUTPUT',
  N'@carId int,@petName nvarchar(50) output',@carId=1,@petName=@p4 output
select @p4
```

Querying Related Data

Entity navigation properties are used to load an entity's related data. The related data can be loaded eagerly (one LINQ statement, one SQL query), eagerly with split queries (one LINQ statement, multiple SQL queries), explicitly (multiple LINQ calls, multiple SQL queries), or lazily (one LINQ statement, multiple on-demand SQL queries).

In addition to the ability to load related data using the navigation properties, EF Core will automatically fix up entities as they are loaded into the Change Tracker. For example, assume all the Make records are loaded into the DbSet<Make> collection property. Next, all the Car records are loaded into DbSet<Car>. Even though the records were loaded separately, they will be accessible to each other through the navigation properties.

Eager Loading

Eager loading is the term for loading related records from multiple tables in one database call. This is analogous to creating a query in T-SQL linking two or more tables with joins. When entities have navigation properties and those properties are used in the LINQ queries, the translation engine uses joins to get data from the related tables and loads the corresponding entities. This is usually much more efficient than executing one query to get the data from one table and then running additional queries for each of the related tables. For those times when it is less efficient to use one query, EF Core 5 introduced query splitting, covered next.

The Include() and ThenInclude() (for subsequent navigation properties) methods are used to traverse the navigation properties in LINQ queries. If the relationship is required, the LINQ translation engine will create an inner join. If the relationship is optional, the translation engine will create a left join.

For example, to load all the Car records with their related Make information, execute the following LINQ query:

```
static void RelatedData()
{
    //The factory is not meant to be used like this, but it's demo code :-)
    var context = new ApplicationDbContextFactory().CreateDbContext(null);
    var carsWithMakes = context.Cars.Include(c => c.MakeNavigation).ToList();
    context.ChangeTracker.Clear();
}
```

The previous LINQ executes the following query against the database:

```
SELECT [i].[Id], [i].[Color], [i].[DateBuilt], [i].[Display], [i].[IsDrivable],
  [i].[MakeId], [i].[PetName], [i].[TimeStamp],
  [m].[Id], [m].[Name], [m].[TimeStamp]
FROM [Dbo].[Inventory] AS [i]
INNER JOIN [dbo].[Makes] AS [m] ON [i].[MakeId] = [m].[Id]
```

■ **Note** The SELECT statement is returning all the fields for the Inventory and Makes tables. EF Core then wires up the data correctly, returning the correct object graph.

The MakeNavigation property is a required relationship since the MakeId property of the Car entity is non-nullable. Because it's required, the Make table is joined to the Inventory table with an INNER JOIN. If the navigation property was optional (MakeId was defined with a nullable int), the join would be an OUTER JOIN. The next example demonstrates optional relationships in the queries generated.

Multiple Include() statements can be used in the same query to join more than one entity to the original. To work down the navigation property tree, use ThenInclude() after an Include(). For example, to get all the Make records with their related Car records and the Driver records for the Cars, use the following statement:

```
var makesWithCarsAndDrivers = context.Makes.Include(c=>c.Cars).ThenInclude(d=>d.Drivers).
ToList();
```

■ **Note** The call to Clear() on the ChangeTracker is added to make sure that previous code examples don't interfere with the results of the code being discussed.

The previous LINQ executes the following query against the database:

```
SELECT [m].[Id], [m].[Name], [m].[TimeStamp], [t0].[Id], [t0].[Color], [t0].[DateBuilt],
    [t0].[Display], [t0].[IsDrivable], [t0].[MakeId], [t0].[PetName], [t0].[TimeStamp],
    [t0].[CarId],
    [t0].[DriverId], [t0].[Id0], [t0].[FirstName], [t0].[LastName], [t0].[TimeStamp0]
    FROM [Makes] AS [m]
```

```
  LEFT JOIN (
      SELECT [i].[Id], [i].[Color], [i].[DateBuilt], [i].[Display], [i].[IsDrivable], [i].
      [MakeId],
           [i].[PetName], [i].[TimeStamp], [t].[CarId], [t].[DriverId], [t].[Id] AS [Id0],
           [t].[FirstName],
           [t].[LastName], [t].[TimeStamp] AS [TimeStamp0]
    FROM [dbo].[Inventory] AS [i]
    LEFT JOIN (
        SELECT [c].[CarId], [c].[DriverId], [d].[Id], [d].[FirstName], [d].[LastName], [d].
        [TimeStamp]
        FROM [CarDriver] AS [c]
        INNER JOIN [Drivers] AS [d] ON [c].[DriverId] = [d].[Id]
    ) AS [t] ON [i].[Id] = [t].[CarId]
) AS [t0] ON [m].[Id] = [t0].[MakeId]
ORDER BY [m].[Id], [t0].[Id], [t0].[CarId], [t0].[DriverId], [t0].[Id0]
```

One thing that might seem odd is the ORDER BY clause, since the LINQ query did not include any ordering. When using chained includes (with the Include()/ThenInclude() statements), the LINQ translation engine will add an ORDER BY clause based on the order of the tables included and their primary and foreign keys. This is in addition to any ordering you specified in the LINQ query.

Take the following updated example:

```
var orderedMakes = context.Makes.Include(c => c.Cars).ThenInclude(d => d.Drivers).
OrderBy(d=>d.Name).ToList();
```

The SQL produced will be sorted by any (and all) ordering clauses in the LINQ query, suffixed with the autogenerated ORDER BY clauses:

```
SELECT [m].[Id], [m].[Name], [m].[TimeStamp], [t0].[Id], [t0].[Color], [t0].[DateBuilt],
    [t0].[Display], [t0].[IsDrivable], [t0].[MakeId], [t0].[PetName], [t0].[TimeStamp],
    [t0].[CarId],
    [t0].[DriverId], [t0].[Id0], [t0].[FirstName], [t0].[LastName], [t0].[TimeStamp0]
FROM [Makes] AS [m]
  LEFT JOIN (
     SELECT [i].[Id], [i].[Color], [i].[DateBuilt], [i].[Display], [i].[IsDrivable], [i].
     [MakeId],
           [i].[PetName], [i].[TimeStamp], [t].[CarId], [t].[DriverId], [t].[Id] AS [Id0],
           [t].[FirstName],
           [t].[LastName], [t].[TimeStamp] AS [TimeStamp0]
    FROM [dbo].[Inventory] AS [i]
    LEFT JOIN (
        SELECT [c].[CarId], [c].[DriverId], [d].[Id], [d].[FirstName], [d].[LastName], [d].
        [TimeStamp]
        FROM [CarDriver] AS [c]
        INNER JOIN [Drivers] AS [d] ON [c].[DriverId] = [d].[Id]
    ) AS [t] ON [i].[Id] = [t].[CarId]
) AS [t0] ON [m].[Id] = [t0].[MakeId]
ORDER BY [m].[Name], [m].[Id], [t0].[Id], [t0].[CarId], [t0].[DriverId], [t0].[Id0]
```

Filtered Include

Introduced in EF Core 5, the included data can be filtered and sorted. The allowable operations on the collection navigation are Where(), OrderBy(), OrderByDescending(), ThenBy(), ThenByDescending(), Skip(), and Take(). For example, if you want to get all Make records, but only the related Car records where the color is yellow, you filter the navigation property in the lambda expression, like this:

```
//Add to keep the demos clean
context.ChangeTracker.Clear();
var makesWithYellowCars = context.Makes
    .Include(x => x.Cars.Where(x=>x.Color == "Yellow"))
    .ToList();
```

The query that is executed is as follows:

```
SELECT [m].[Id], [m].[Name], [m].[TimeStamp], [t].[Id], [t].[Color], [t].[DateBuilt],
              [t].[Display], [t].[IsDrivable], [t].[MakeId], [t].[PetName], [t].[TimeStamp]
FROM [Makes] AS [m]
LEFT JOIN (
    SELECT [i].[Id], [i].[Color], [i].[DateBuilt], [i].[Display], [i].[IsDrivable], [i].[MakeId],
                  [i].[PetName], [i].[TimeStamp]
    FROM [dbo].[Inventory] AS [i]
    WHERE [i].[Color] = N'Yellow'
) AS [t] ON [m].[Id] = [t].[MakeId]
ORDER BY [m].[Id], [t].[Id]
```

Eager Loading with Split Queries

When a LINQ query contains a lot of includes, there can be a negative performance impact. To resolve this situation, EF Core 5 introduced split queries. Instead of executing a single query, EF Core will split the LINQ query into multiple SQL queries and then wire up all the related data. For example, the previous query can be expected as multiple SQL queries by adding AsSplitQuery() into the LINQ query, like this:

```
//Add to keep the demos clean
context.ChangeTracker.Clear();
var splitMakes = context.Makes.AsSplitQuery()
  .Include(x => x.Cars.Where(x=>x.Color == "Yellow")).ToList();
```

The queries that are executed are shown here:

```
SELECT [m].[Id], [m].[Name], [m].[TimeStamp]
FROM [dbo].[Makes] AS [m]
ORDER BY [m].[Id]

SELECT [t].[Id], [t].[Color], [t].[DateBuilt], [t].[Display], [t].[IsDrivable],
              [t].[MakeId], [t].[PetName], [t].[TimeStamp], [m].[Id]
FROM [Makes] AS [m]
INNER JOIN (
    SELECT [i].[Id], [i].[Color], [i].[DateBuilt], [i].[Display], [i].[IsDrivable], [i].
    [MakeId],
```

```
                [i].[PetName], [i].[TimeStamp]
    FROM [dbo].[Inventory] AS [i]
    WHERE [i].[Color] = N'Yellow'
) AS [t] ON [m].[Id] = [t].[MakeId]
ORDER BY [m].[Id]
```

There is a downside to using split queries: if the data changes between executing the queries, then the data returned will be inconsistent.

Many-to-Many Queries

The new EF Core support for designing many-to-many tables carries over to querying data with LINQ. Prior to the many-to-many support, queries would have to go through the pivot table. Now you can write the following LINQ statement to get the Car and related Driver records:

```
var carsAndDrivers = context.Cars.Include(x => x.Drivers).Where(x=>x.Drivers.Any());
```

As you can see from the generated SQL select statement, EF Core takes care of working through the pivot table to get the Car and Driver records matched up correctly:

```
SELECT [i].[Id], [i].[Color], [i].[DateBuilt], [i].[Display], [i].[IsDeleted], [i].
[IsDrivable], [i].[MakeId], [i].[PetName], [i].[Price], [i].[TimeStamp], [i].[ValidFrom],
[i].[ValidTo], [t].[InventoryId], [t].[DriverId], [t].[Id], [t].[TimeStamp], [t].[Id0], [t].
[TimeStamp0], [t].[FirstName], [t].[LastName]
FROM [dbo].[Inventory] AS [i]
LEFT JOIN (
    SELECT [i1].[InventoryId], [i1].[DriverId], [i1].[Id], [i1].[TimeStamp], [d0].[Id] AS
    [Id0], [d0].[TimeStamp] AS [TimeStamp0], [d0].[FirstName], [d0].[LastName]
    FROM [dbo].[InventoryToDrivers] AS [i1]
    INNER JOIN [dbo].[Drivers] AS [d0] ON [i1].[DriverId] = [d0].[Id]
) AS [t] ON [i].[Id] = [t].[InventoryId]
WHERE ([i].[IsDrivable] = CAST(1 AS bit)) AND EXISTS (
    SELECT 1
    FROM [dbo].[InventoryToDrivers] AS [i0]
    INNER JOIN [dbo].[Drivers] AS [d] ON [i0].[DriverId] = [d].[Id]
    WHERE [i].[Id] = [i0].[InventoryId])
ORDER BY [i].[Id], [t].[InventoryId], [t].[DriverId]
```

Explicit Loading

Explicit loading is loading data along a navigation property after the core object is already loaded. This process involves executing an additional database call to get the related data. This can be useful if your application selectively needs to get the related records instead of always pulling them.

The process starts with an entity that is already loaded and uses the `Entry()` method on the derived `DbContext`. When querying against a reference navigation property (e.g., getting the `Make` information for a car), use the `Reference()` method. When querying against a collection navigation property, use the `Collection()` method. The query is deferred until `Load()`, `ToList()`, or an aggregate function (e.g., `Count()`, `Max()`) is executed.

The following examples show how to get the related Make data as well as any Drivers for a Car record:

```
//Get the Car record
var car = Context.Cars.First(x => x.Id == 1);
//Get the Make information
context.Entry(car).Reference(c => c.MakeNavigation).Load();
//Get any Drivers the Car is related to
context.Entry(car).Collection(c => c.Drivers).Query().Load();
```

The previous statements generate the following queries:

```
//Get the Car record
SELECT TOP(1) [i].[Id], [i].[Color], [i].[DateBuilt], [i].[Display], [i].[IsDrivable],
    [i].[MakeId], [i].[PetName], [i].[TimeStamp]
FROM [dbo].[Inventory] AS [i]
WHERE [i].[Id] = 1
//Get the Make information
SELECT [m].[Id], [m].[Name], [m].[TimeStamp]
FROM [Makes] AS [m]
WHERE [m].[Id] = 5
//Get any Drivers the Car is related to
SELECT [t].[Id], [t].[FirstName], [t].[LastName], [t].[TimeStamp], [i].[Id], [t].[CarId],
[t].[DriverId],
    [t0].[CarId], [t0].[DriverId], [t0].[Id], [t0].[Color], [t0].[DateBuilt], [t0].[Display],
    [t0].[IsDrivable], [t0].[MakeId], [t0].[PetName], [t0].[TimeStamp]
FROM [dbo].[Inventory] AS [i]
INNER JOIN (
    SELECT [d].[Id], [d].[FirstName], [d].[LastName], [d].[TimeStamp], [c].[CarId], [c].
    [DriverId]
    FROM [CarDriver] AS [c]
    INNER JOIN [Drivers] AS [d] ON [c].[DriverId] = [d].[Id]
) AS [t] ON [i].[Id] = [t].[CarId]
LEFT JOIN (
    SELECT [c0].[CarId], [c0].[DriverId], [t1].[Id], [t1].[Color], [t1].[DateBuilt], [t1].
    [Display],
              [t1].[IsDrivable], [t1].[MakeId], [t1].[PetName], [t1].[TimeStamp]
    FROM [CarDriver] AS [c0]
    INNER JOIN (
        SELECT [i0].[Id], [i0].[Color], [i0].[DateBuilt], [i0].[Display], [i0].[IsDrivable],
               [i0].[MakeId], [i0].[PetName], [i0].[TimeStamp]
        FROM [dbo].[Inventory] AS [i0]
        WHERE [i0].[IsDrivable] = CAST(1 AS bit)
    ) AS [t1] ON [c0].[CarId] = [t1].[Id]
    WHERE [t1].[Id] = 1
) AS [t0] ON [t].[Id] = [t0].[DriverId]
WHERE [i].[Id] = 1
ORDER BY [i].[Id], [t].[CarId], [t].[DriverId], [t].[Id], [t0].[CarId], [t0].[DriverId],
[t0].[Id]
```

As you can see, that third and final query is doing a lot of work to simply get the Driver records for the selected Car record. This shows us two important facts: 1) If you can write it all on one query using eager loading, it is usually better to do so, which negates the need to go back to the database to get the related records, and 2) EF Core doesn't always create the best queries. I've already shown you how to use eager loading in the previous section. Later in this chapter, I will show you how to use SQL statements with or without additional LINQ statements to retrieve data from the database. This is useful when EF Core creates suboptimal queries.

Lazy Loading

Lazy loading is loading a record on-demand when a navigation property is used to access a related record that is not yet loaded into memory. Lazy loading is a feature from EF 6 that was added back into EF Core with version 2.1. While it might sound like a good idea to turn this on, enabling lazy loading can cause performance problems in your application by making potentially unnecessary round-trips to your database. Lazy loading can be useful in smart client (WPF, WinForms) applications but is recommended to not be used in web or service applications. For this reason, lazy loading is off by default in EF Core (it was enabled by default in EF 6).

To use lazy loading, the navigation properties to be lazily loaded must be marked as virtual. This is because the navigation properties are wrapped with a proxy. This proxy will then have EF Core make a call to the database if the navigation property has not been loaded when it is referenced in your application.

To use lazy loading with proxies, the derived `DbContext` must be correctly configured. Start by adding the `Microsoft.EntityFrameworkCore.Proxies` package to your project. You must then opt in to using the lazy loading proxies in the derived `DbContext` options. While this would normally be set in your application code when configuring your derived `DbContext`, we are going to opt in to the proxies using the `ApplicationDbContextFactory` class that we built earlier. Remember that this class is meant for design-time use and shouldn't be used in your application code. However, for learning and exploring, it will work just fine.

Open the `ApplicationDbContextFactory.cs` file and navigate to the `CreateDbContext()` method. We will take advantage of the `args` parameter to indicate that we want the method to return a derived `DbContext` configured to use the lazy loading proxies. Update the `CreateDbContext()` method to the following:

```
public ApplicationDbContext CreateDbContext(string[] args)
{
  var optionsBuilder = new DbContextOptionsBuilder<ApplicationDbContext>();
  var connectionString = @"server=.,5433;Database=AutoLotSamples;User Id=sa;Password=P
  @ssw0rd;";
  if (args != null && args.Length == 1 && args[0].Equals("lazy", StringComparison.
  OrdinalIgnoreCase))
  {
    optionsBuilder = optionsBuilder.UseLazyLoadingProxies();
  }
  optionsBuilder = optionsBuilder.UseSqlServer(connectionString);
  Console.WriteLine(connectionString);
  return new ApplicationDbContext(optionsBuilder.Options);
}
```

Next, update the Car class to the following:

```
[Table("Inventory", Schema = "dbo")]
[Index(nameof(MakeId), Name = "IX_Inventory_MakeId")]
[EntityTypeConfiguration(typeof(CarConfiguration))]
public class Car : BaseEntity
{
  private string _color;
```

```
  [Required, StringLength(50)]
  public string Color
  {
    get => _color;
    set => _color = value;
  }
  private bool? _isDrivable;

  public bool IsDrivable
  {
    get => _isDrivable ?? true;
    set => _isDrivable = value;
  }
  [DatabaseGenerated(DatabaseGeneratedOption.Computed)]
  public string Display { get; set; }
  public DateTime? DateBuilt { get; set; }
  [Required, StringLength(50)]
  public string PetName { get; set; }
  public int MakeId { get; set; }
  [ForeignKey(nameof(MakeId))]
  public virtual Make MakeNavigation { get; set; }
  public virtual Radio RadioNavigation { get; set; }

  [InverseProperty(nameof(Driver.Cars))]
  public virtual IEnumerable<Driver> Drivers { get; set; } = new List<Driver>();

  [InverseProperty(nameof(CarDriver.CarNavigation))]
  public virtual IEnumerable<CarDriver> CarDrivers { get; set; } = new List<CarDriver>();
}
```

Now that the properties are marked `virtual`, they can be used with lazy loading. Add the following method to your `Program.cs` file (notice that we are not using the `args` parameter of the `CreateDbContext()` method yet) and call the method from your top-level statements:

```
static void LazyLoadCar()
{
    //The factory is not meant to be used like this, but it's demo code :-)
  var context = new ApplicationDbContextFactory().CreateDbContext(null);

  var query = context.Cars.AsQueryable();
  var cars = query.ToList();
  var make = cars[0].MakeNavigation;
  Console.WriteLine(make.Name);
}
```

When you run this sample, you will receive a null reference exception when trying to access the `Name` property of the `Make` instance. This is because the `Make` record wasn't loaded, and we are not using the proxy-enabled version of the derived `DbContext()`. Update the method to pass in the "lazy" argument to `CreateDbContext()`, which enables the lazy loading proxy support:

```
var context = new ApplicationDbContextFactory().CreateDbContext(new string[] {"lazy"});
```

When you run the code again, you may be surprised to receive an `InvalidOperationException`. When using lazy proxies, *all* navigation properties on the models must be marked as virtual, even ones not directly involved in the executing code block. So far, we have updated only the `Car` entity. Update the rest of the models to the following (updates in bold):

```
//CarDriver
[Table("InventoryToDrivers", Schema = "dbo")]
public class CarDriver : BaseEntity
{
  public int DriverId {get;set;}
  [ForeignKey(nameof(DriverId))]
  public virtual Driver DriverNavigation {get;set;}

  [Column("InventoryId")]
  public int CarId {get;set;}
  [ForeignKey(nameof(CarId))]
  public virtual Car CarNavigation {get;set;}
}

//Driver.cs
[Table("Drivers", Schema = "dbo")]
[EntityTypeConfiguration(typeof(DriverConfiguration))]
public class Driver : BaseEntity
{
  public Person PersonInfo { get; set; } = new Person();
  [InverseProperty(nameof(Car.Drivers))]
  public virtual IEnumerable<Car> Cars { get; set; } = new List<Car>();
  [InverseProperty(nameof(CarDriver.DriverNavigation))]
  public virtual IEnumerable<CarDriver> CarDrivers { get; set; } = new List<CarDriver>();
}
//Make.cs
[Table("Makes", Schema = "dbo")]
public class Make : BaseEntity
{
...
  [InverseProperty(nameof(Car.MakeNavigation))]
  public virtual IEnumerable<Car> Cars { get; set; } = new List<Car>();
}
//Radio.cs
[Table("Radios", Schema = "dbo")]
[EntityTypeConfiguration(typeof(RadioConfiguration))]
public class Radio : BaseEntity
{
...
  [ForeignKey(nameof(CarId))]
  public virtual Car CarNavigation { get; set; }
}
```

■ **Note** Even though the `Owned` `Person` class represents a relationship, it is not a navigation property, and properties that are an `Owned` type do not need to be marked `virtual`.

Now, when you run the program again, the Make of the car will be printed to the console. When watching the SQL Server activity in profiler, you can clearly see that there were two queries executed:

```
--Get initial Inventory/Car records
SELECT [i].[Id], [i].[Color], [i].[DateBuilt], [i].[Display], [i].[IsDrivable],
    [i].[MakeId], [i].[PetName], [i].[TimeStamp]
FROM [dbo].[Inventory] AS [i]
--Get the Make record for the first Inventory/Car record
--Parameters removed for readability
SELECT [m].[Id], [m].[Name], [m].[TimeStamp]
FROM [Makes] AS [m]
WHERE [m].[Id] = 5
```

If you want to learn more about lazy loading and how to use it with EF Core, consult the documentation here: https://docs.microsoft.com/en-us/ef/core/querying/related-data/lazy.

Updating Records

Records are updated by loading them into DbSet<T> as a tracked entity, changing them through code, and then calling SaveChanges() on the context. When SaveChanges() is executed, the ChangeTracker reports all of the modified entities, and EF Core (along with the database provider) creates the appropriate SQL statement(s) to update the record(s).

Entity State

When a tracked entity is edited, EntityState is set to Modified. After the changes are successfully saved, the state is returned to Unchanged.

Update Tracked Entities

Updating a single record is much like adding a single record, except that the initial record is retrieved from the database and not created through code. Load the record from the database into a tracked entity, make some changes, and call SaveChanges(). Note that you do not have to call the Update()/UpdateRange() methods on the DbSet<T>, since the entities are already tracked. The following code updates only one record, but the process is the same if multiple tracked entities are updated and saved.

```
static void UpdateRecords()
{
  //The factory is not meant to be used like this, but it's demo code :-)
  var context = new ApplicationDbContextFactory().CreateDbContext(null);
  var car = context.Cars.First();
  car.Color = "Green";
  context.SaveChanges();
}
```

The executed SQL statement is listed here:

```
exec sp_executesql N'SET NOCOUNT ON;
UPDATE [dbo].[Inventory] SET [Color] = @p0
WHERE [Id] = @p1 AND [TimeStamp] = @p2;
SELECT [Display], [TimeStamp]
FROM [dbo].[Inventory]
WHERE @@ROWCOUNT = 1 AND [Id] = @p1;

',N'@p1 int,@p0 nvarchar(50),@p2 varbinary(8)',@p1=2,@p0=N'Green',@p2=0x0000000000000867
```

■ **Note** The previous where clause checked not only the Id column but also the TimeStamp column. This is EF Core using concurrency checking, covered later in this chapter.

Update Nontracked Entities

Untracked entities can also be used to update database records. The process is similar to updating tracked entities except that the entity is created in code (and not queried), and EF Core must be notified that the entity should already exist in the database and needs to be updated. There are two ways to notify EF Core that this entity needs to be processed as an update. The first is to call the Update() method on the DbSet<T>, which sets the state to Modified, like this:

```
context.Cars.Update(updatedCar);
```

The second is to use the context instance and the Entry() method to set the state to Modified, like this:

```
context.Entry(updatedCar).State = EntityState.Modified;
```

Either way, SaveChanges() must still be called for the values to persist.

■ **Note** You might be wondering when you might update an entity that is not tracked. Think of an ASP.NET Core post call that sends the values for an entity over HTTP. The updated data needs to be persisted, and using this technique negates the need for another call to the database to get the entity into the ChangeTracker.

The following example reads a record in as nontracked (simulating a postback in ASP.NET Core) and changes one property (Color). Then it sets the state as Modified by calling the Update() method on DbSet<T>.

```
static void UpdateRecords()
{
...
  var carToUpdate = context.Cars.AsNoTracking().First(x => x.Id == 1);
  carToUpdate.Color = "Orange";
  context.Cars.Update(carToUpdate);
  context.SaveChanges();
}
```

Since the entity is not tracked, EF Core updates all property values in the generated SQL:

```
exec sp_executesql N'SET NOCOUNT ON;
UPDATE [dbo].[Inventory] SET [Color] = @p0, [DateBuilt] = @p1, [IsDrivable] = @p2,
    [MakeId] = @p3, [PetName] = @p4
WHERE [Id] = @p5 AND [TimeStamp] = @p6;
SELECT [Display], [TimeStamp]
FROM [dbo].[Inventory]
WHERE @@ROWCOUNT = 1 AND [Id] = @p5;

',N'@p5 int,@p0 nvarchar(50),@p1 datetime2(7),@p2 bit,@p3 int,@p4 nvarchar(50),
@p6 varbinary(8)',@p5=1,@p0=N'Orange',@p1='2021-06-21 01:12:46.5800000',@p2=1,@p3=5,
@p4=N'Hank',@p6=0x000000000000088F
```

The next example follows the same logic, but instead of calling the `Update()` method, the code manually changes the `EntityState` to `Modified` and then calls `SaveChanges()`. The `Clear()` method is called on the `ChangeTracker` to make sure there isn't any crossover from the different execution paths. The generated SQL is the same as the previous example.

```
static void UpdateRecords()
{
  context.ChangeTracker.Clear();
  var carToUpdate2 = context.Cars.AsNoTracking().First(x => x.Id == 1);
  carToUpdate2.Color = "Orange";
  context.Entry(carToUpdate2).State = EntityState.Modified;
  context.SaveChanges();
}
```

Deleting Records

One or more entities are marked for deletion by calling `Remove()` (for a single entity) or `RemoveRange()` (for a list of entities) on the appropriate `DbSet<T>` property or by setting the state for the entity/entities to `Deleted`. The removal process will cause cascade effects on navigation properties based on the rules configured in `OnModelCreating()` (or by EF Core conventions). If deletion is prevented due to cascade policy, an exception is thrown.

Entity State

When the `Remove()` method is called on an entity that is being tracked, its `EntityState` is set to `Deleted`. After the `SaveChanges()` method is successfully executed, the entity is removed from the `ChangeTracker`, and its state is changed to `Detached`. Note that the entity still exists in your application unless it has gone out of scope and been garbage collected.

Delete Tracked Records

The delete process mirrors the update process. Once an entity is tracked, call `Remove()` on that instance, and then call `SaveChanges()` to remove the record from the database.

```
static void DeleteRecords()
{
  //The factory is not meant to be used like this, but it's demo code :-)
  var context = new ApplicationDbContextFactory().CreateDbContext(null);
  ClearSampleData();
  LoadMakeAndCarData();
  var car = context.Cars.First(x=>x.Color != "Green");
  context.Cars.Remove(car);
  context.SaveChanges();
}
```

The executed SQL call for the delete is listed here:

```
exec sp_executesql N'SET NOCOUNT ON;
DELETE FROM [dbo].[Inventory]
WHERE [Id] = @p0 AND [TimeStamp] = @p1;
SELECT @@ROWCOUNT;

',N'@p0 int,@p1 varbinary(8)',@p0=2,@p1=0x00000000000008EB
```

As a point of emphasis, after SaveChanges() is called, the entity instance still exists but is no longer in the ChangeTracker. When checking the EntityState, the state will be Detached.

```
static void DeleteRecords()
{
...
  Console.WriteLine($"{car.PetName}'s state is {context.Entry(car).State}");
}
```

Delete Nontracked Entities

Untracked entities can delete records the same way untracked entities can update records. The difference is that the entity is tracked by calling Remove()/RemoveRange() or setting the state to Deleted and then calling SaveChanges().

The following example follows the same pattern for updating nontracked entities. It reads a record in as nontracked and then uses the Remove() method on DbSet<T> (the first example) or manually changes the EntityState to Deleted (the second example). In each case, the code calls SaveChanges() to persist the deletion. The Clear() call on the ChangeTracker makes sure there isn't any pollution between the first example and the second.

```
static void DeleteRecords()
{
...
    context.ChangeTracker.Clear();
    var carToDelete = context.Cars.AsNoTracking().First(x=>x.Color != "Green");
    context.Cars.Remove(carToDelete);
    context.SaveChanges();

    context.ChangeTracker.Clear();
    var carToDelete2 = context.Cars.AsNoTracking().First(x=>x.Color != "Green");
    context.Entry(carToDelete2).State = EntityState.Deleted;
    context.SaveChanges();
}
```

Catch Cascade Delete Failures

EF Core will throw a DbUpdateException when an attempt to delete a record fails due to the cascade rules. The following test shows this in action:

```
static void DeleteRecords()
{
...
  context.ChangeTracker.Clear();
  var make = context.Makes.First();
  context.Makes.Remove(make);
  try
  {
    context.SaveChanges();
  }
  catch (DbUpdateException ex)
  {
    Console.WriteLine(ex.Message);
  }
}
```

This completes the content on Create, Read, Update, and Delete (CRUD) operations using EF Core. The next section covers notable EF Core features that provide benefit to data access code and developer productivity.

Notable EF Core Features

Many features from EF 6 have been replicated in EF Core, with more being added in every release. Many of those features have been greatly improved in their EF Core implementation, both in functionality and performance. In addition to bringing forward features from EF 6, EF Core has added many new features. The following are some of the more notable features in EF Core (in no particular order).

Global Query Filters

Global query filters enable a where clause to be added into all LINQ queries for a particular entity. For example, a common database design pattern is to use soft deletes instead of hard deletes. A field is added to the table to indicate the deleted status of the record. If the record is "deleted," the value is set to true (or 1), but not removed from the database. This is called a *soft delete*. To filter out the soft-deleted records from normal operations, every where clause must check the value of this field. Remembering to include this filter in every query can be time-consuming, if not problematic.

EF Core enables adding a *global query filter* to an entity that is then applied to every query involving that entity. For the soft delete example described earlier, you set a filter on the entity class to exclude the soft-deleted records. No longer do you have to remember to include the where clause to filter out the soft-deleted records in every query you write.

Presume that all Car records that are not drivable should be filtered out of the normal queries. Open the CarConfiguration class and add the following line to the Configure() method:

```
public void Configure(EntityTypeBuilder<Car> builder)
{
...
  builder.HasQueryFilter(c=>c.IsDrivable == true);
...
}
```

With the global query filter in place, queries involving the Car entity will automatically filter out the nondrivable cars. Take the following LINQ query that retrieves all cars except those excluded by the query filter:

```
static void QueryFilters()
{
  //The factory is not meant to be used like this, but it's demo code :-)
  var context = new ApplicationDbContextFactory().CreateDbContext(null);
  var cars = context.Cars.ToList();
  Console.WriteLine($"Total number of drivable cars: {cars.Count}");
}
```

The generated SQL is as follows:

```
SELECT [i].[Id], [i].[Color], [i].[DateBuilt], [i].[Display], [i].[IsDrivable],
    [i].[MakeId], [i].[PetName], [i].[TimeStamp]
FROM [dbo].[Inventory] AS [i]
WHERE [i].[IsDrivable] = CAST(1 AS bit)
```

■ **Note** Query filters are not additive. The last one in wins. If you were to add another query filter for the Car entity, it would *replace* the existing query filter.

If you need to retrieve all records, including those filtered with the global query filter, add the IgnoreQueryFilters() method into the LINQ query:

```
static void QueryFilters()
{
...
  var allCars = context.Cars.IgnoreQueryFilters().ToList();
  Console.WriteLine($"Total number of cars: {allCars.Count}");
  var radios = context.Radios.ToList();
  var allRadios = context.Radios.IgnoreQueryFilters().ToList();
}
```

With the IgnoreQueryFilters() added to the LINQ query, the generated SQL statement no longer has the where clause excluding the soft-deleted records:

```
SELECT [i].[Id], [i].[Color], [i].[DateBuilt], [i].[Display], [i].[IsDrivable],
    [i].[MakeId], [i].[PetName], [i].[TimeStamp]
FROM [dbo].[Inventory] AS [i]
```

It is important to note that calling IgnoreQueryFilters() removes the query filter for *every* entity in the LINQ query, including any that are involved in Include() or ThenInclude() statements.

■ **Note** Global query filters are entirely an EF Core construct. No changes are made to the database. Even with the filter to exclude nondrivable cars in place, if you open up SSMS/Azure Data Studio and run a query to select all Inventory (remember the Car entity is mapped to the Inventory table) records, you would see all records, even the nondrivable records.

Global Query Filters on Navigation Properties

Global query filters can also be set on navigation properties. Suppose you want to filter out any radios that are in a Car that is not drivable. The query filter is created on the Radio entity's CarNavigation navigation property, like this (using the RadioConfiguration class):

```
public void Configure(EntityTypeBuilder<Radio> builder)
{
...
  builder.HasQueryFilter(e=>e.CarNavigation.IsDrivable);
...
}
```

When executing a standard LINQ query, any orders that contain a nondrivable car will be excluded from the result. Here is the LINQ statement and the generated SQL statement:

```
//C# Code
static void QueryFilters()
{
...
  var radios = context.Radios.ToList();
}

/* Generated SQL query */
SELECT [r].[Id], [r].[InventoryId], [r].[HasSubWoofers],
   [r].[HasTweeters], [r].[RadioId], [r].[TimeStamp]
FROM [Radios] AS [r]
INNER JOIN (
    SELECT [i].[Id], [i].[IsDrivable]
    FROM [dbo].[Inventory] AS [i]
    WHERE [i].[IsDrivable] = CAST(1 AS bit)
) AS [t] ON [r].[InventoryId] = [t].[Id]
WHERE [t].[IsDrivable] = CAST(1 AS bit)
```

To remove the query filter, use IgnoreQueryFilters(). The following is the updated LINQ statements and the subsequent generated SQL:

```
//C# Code
static void QueryFilters()
{
...
  var allRadios = context.Radios.IgnoreQueryFilters().ToList();
}

/* Generated SQL query */
SELECT [r].[Id], [r].[InventoryId], [r].[HasSubWoofers], [r].[HasTweeters],
  [r].[RadioId], [r].[TimeStamp]
FROM [Radios] AS [r]
```

A word of caution here: EF Core does not detect cyclic global query filters, so use care when adding query filters to navigation properties.

Explicit Loading with Global Query Filters

Global query filters are also in effect when loading related data explicitly. For example, if you wanted to load the Car records for a Make, the IsDrivable filter will prevent nondrivable cars from being loaded into memory. Take the following code snippet as an example:

```
static void RelatedDataWithQueryFilters()
{
    //The factory is not meant to be used like this, but it's demo code :-)
    var context = new ApplicationDbContextFactory().CreateDbContext(null);
    var make = context.Makes.First(x => x.Id == 1);
    //Get the Cars collection
    context.Entry(make).Collection(c => c.Cars).Load();
    context.ChangeTracker.Clear();
}
```

By now it should be no surprise that the generated SQL query includes the filter for nondrivable cars.

```
SELECT [i].[Id], [i].[Color], [i].[DateBuilt], [i].[Display],
    [i].[IsDrivable], [i].[MakeId], [i].[PetName], [i].[TimeStamp]
FROM [dbo].[Inventory] AS [i]
WHERE ([i].[IsDrivable] = CAST(1 AS bit)) AND ([i].[MakeId] = 1)
```

There is a slight catch to ignoring query filters when explicitly loading data. The type returned by the Collection() method is CollectionEntry<Make,Car> and does not explicitly implement the IQueryable<T> interface. To call IgnoreQueryFilters(), you must first call Query(), which returns an IQueryable<Car>.

```
static void RelatedDataWithQueryFilters()
{
...
    //Get the Cars collection
    context.Entry(make).Collection(c => c.Cars).Query().IgnoreQueryFilters().Load();
}
```

It should come as no surprise now that the SQL generated by EF Core does not include the filter for nondrivable cars:

```
SELECT [i].[Id], [i].[Color], [i].[DateBuilt], [i].[Display], [i].[IsDrivable],
    [i].[MakeId], [i].[PetName], [i].[TimeStamp]
FROM [dbo].[Inventory] AS [i]
WHERE [i].[MakeId] = 1
```

The same process applies when using the `Reference()` method to retrieve data from a reference navigation property. First call `Query()` and then call `IgnoreQueryFilters()`.

Raw SQL Queries with LINQ

Sometimes getting the correct LINQ statement for a complicated query can be harder than just writing the SQL directly. Or the generated SQL from your LINQ query is suboptimal. Fortunately, EF Core has a mechanism to allow raw SQL statements to be executed on a `DbSet<T>`. The `FromSqlRaw()` and `FromSqlRawInterpolated()` methods take in a string that replaces the LINQ query. This query is executed on the server side.

If the raw SQL statement is nonterminating (e.g., neither a stored procedure, user-defined function, a statement that uses a common table expression, nor ends with a semicolon), then additional LINQ statements can be added to the query. The additional LINQ statements, such as `Include()`, `OrderBy()`, or `Where()` clauses, will be combined with the original raw SQL call and any global query filters, and the entire query is executed on the server side.

When using one of the `FromSql` variants, the query must be written using the data store schema and table name, and not the entity names. `FromSqlRaw()` will send the string in just as it is written. `FromSqlInterpolated()` uses C# string interpolation, and each interpolated string is translated in the SQL parameter. You should use the interpolated version whenever you are using variables for the added protection inherent in parameterized queries.

To get the database schema and table name, use the `Model` property on the derived `DbContext`. The `Model` exposes a method called `FindEntityType()` that returns an `IEntityType`, which in turn has methods to get the schema and table name. This was used earlier in the chapter to set identity insert for SQL Server. The following code displays the schema and table name:

```
static void UsingFromSql()
{
    //The factory is not meant to be used like this, but it's demo code :-)
    var context = new ApplicationDbContextFactory().CreateDbContext(null);
    IEntityType metadata = context.Model.FindEntityType(typeof(Car).FullName);
    Console.WriteLine(metadata.GetSchema());
    Console.WriteLine(metadata.GetTableName());
}
```

Presuming the global query filter from the previous section is set on the `Car` entity, the following LINQ statement will get the first inventory record where the `Id` is one, include the related `Make` data, and filter out nondrivable cars:

```
int carId = 1;
var car = context.Cars
  .FromSqlInterpolated($"Select * from dbo.Inventory where Id = {carId}")
  .Include(x => x.MakeNavigation)
  .First();
```

■ **Note** Unfortunately, the table and schema name cannot be added to the query using C# string interpolation, as SQL Server doesn't support the parameterization of those items.

The LINQ to SQL translation engine combines the raw SQL statement with the rest of the LINQ statements and executes the following query:

```
SELECT TOP(1) [c].[Id], [c].[Color], [c].[DateBuilt], [c].[Display],
    [c].[IsDrivable], [c].[MakeId], [c].[PetName], [c].[TimeStamp],
    [m].[Id], [m].[Name], [m].[TimeStamp]
FROM (
    Select * from dbo.Inventory where Id = @p0
) AS [c]
INNER JOIN [Makes] AS [m] ON [c].[MakeId] = [m].[Id]
WHERE [c].[IsDrivable] = CAST(1 AS bit)',N'@p0 int',@p0=1
```

Know that there are a few rules that must be observed when using raw SQL with LINQ.

- The SQL query must return data for all properties of the entity type.
- The column names must match the properties they are mapped to (an improvement over EF 6 where mappings were ignored).
- The SQL query can't contain related data.

Projections

In addition to using raw SQL queries with LINQ, view models can be populated with projections. A projection is where another object type is composed at the end of a LINQ query, *projecting* the data into another datatype. A projection can be a subset of the original data (e.g., getting all the Id values of Car entities that match a where clause) or a custom type, like the CarMakeViewModel.

To get the list of all the primary keys of the Car records, add the following method to your top-level statements:

```
static void Projections()
{
  //The factory is not meant to be used like this, but it's demo code :-)
  var context = new ApplicationDbContextFactory().CreateDbContext(null);
  List<int> ids = context.Cars.Select(x => x.Id).ToList();
}
```

The SQL generated for this statement is shown here. Notice the global query filter is honored in the projection:

```
SELECT [i].[Id]
FROM [dbo].[Inventory] AS [i]
WHERE [i].[IsDrivable] = CAST(1 AS bit)
```

To populate a custom type, use the new keyword in the Select() method. The values of the new type are populated using object initialization, and the LINQ to SQL translation engine takes care of ensuring the navigation properties used for the new type are retrieved from the database. This is done using eager loading, which is covered in detail later in this chapter. Update the Projections() method with the following code to create a list of CarMakeViewModel entities (note the additional using statement that must be added to the top of your file):

```
static void Projections()
{
...
  var vms = context.Cars.Select(x => new CarMakeViewModel
  {
    CarId = x.Id,
    Color = x.Color,
    DateBuilt = x.DateBuilt.GetValueOrDefault(new DateTime(2020, 01, 01)),
    Display = x.Display,
    IsDrivable = x.IsDrivable,
    Make = x.MakeNavigation.Name,
    MakeId = x.MakeId,
    PetName = x.PetName
  });
  foreach (CarMakeViewModel c in vms)
  {
    Console.WriteLine($"{c.PetName} is a {c.Make}");
  }
}
```

The SQL generated for this statement is shown next. Notice the inner join to retrieve the Make Name property and that the global query filter is once again honored:

```
SELECT [i].[Id], [i].[Color], [i].[DateBuilt], [i].[Display],
    [i].[IsDrivable], [m].[Name], [i].[MakeId], [i].[PetName]
FROM [dbo].[Inventory] AS [i]
INNER JOIN [Makes] AS [m] ON [i].[MakeId] = [m].[Id]
WHERE [i].[IsDrivable] = CAST(1 AS bit)
```

Handling Database-Generated Values

In addition to change tracking and the generation of SQL queries from LINQ, a significant advantage to using EF Core over raw ADO.NET is the seamless handling of database-generated values. After adding or updating an entity, EF Core queries for any database-generated data and automatically updates the entity with the correct values. In raw ADO.NET, you would need to do this yourself.

For example, the Inventory table has an integer primary key that is defined in SQL Server as an Identity column. Identity columns are populated by SQL Server with a unique number (from a sequence) when a record is added, and this primary key is not allowed to be updated during normal updates of the record (excluding the special case of having identity insert enabled). Additionally, the Inventory table has a Timestamp column used for concurrency checking. Concurrency checking is covered next, but for now just know that the Timestamp column is maintained by SQL Server and updated on any add or edit action. We also added two columns with default values to the table, DateBuilt and IsDrivable, and one computed column, Display.

The following code adds a new Car to the Inventory table, similar to the code used earlier in the chapter:

```
static void AddACar()
{
    //The factory is not meant to be used like this, but it's demo code :-)
```

```
    var context = new ApplicationDbContextFactory().CreateDbContext(null);
    var car = new Car
    {
        Color = "Yellow",
        MakeId = 1,
        PetName = "Herbie"
    };
    context.Cars.Add(car);
    context.SaveChanges();
}
```

When SaveChanges() is executed, there are two queries run against the database. The first, shown here, inserts the new record into the table:

```
--Process the insert
INSERT INTO [Dbo].[Inventory] ([Color], [MakeId], [PetName])
VALUES (N'Yellow', 1, N'Herbie');
```

The second returns the values for the primary key and all other server-generated data. In this case, the query is returning the Id, DateBuilt, Display, IsDrivable, and Timestamp values. EF Core then updates the entity with the server-generated values.

```
--Return the server maintained values to EF Core
SELECT [Id], [DateBuilt], [Display], [IsDrivable], [TimeStamp]
FROM [dbo].[Inventory]
WHERE @@ROWCOUNT = 1 AND [Id] = scope_identity();
```

■ **Note** EF Core actually executes parameterized queries, but I have simplified the SQL examples for readability.

When adding a record that assigns values to the properties with defaults, you will see that EF Core does not query for those properties, as the entity already has the correct values. Take the following example code:

```
static void AddACarWithDefaultsSet()
{
    //The factory is not meant to be used like this, but it's demo code :-)
    var context = new ApplicationDbContextFactory().CreateDbContext(null);
    var car = new Car
    {
        Color = "Yellow",
        MakeId = 1,
        PetName = "Herbie",
        IsDrivable = true,
        DateBuilt = new DateTime(2021,01,01)
    };
    context.Cars.Add(car);
    context.SaveChanges();
}
```

When SaveChanges() is executed, the following two SQL statements are run. Notice that only the Id (primary key), Display, and TimeStamp values are retrieved:

```
--Insert the values
INSERT INTO [dbo].[Inventory] ([Color], [DateBuilt], [IsDrivable], [MakeId], [PetName])
VALUES (N'Yellow','2021-01-01 00:00:00',1,1, N'Herbie');
--Get the database managed values
SELECT [Id], [Display], [TimeStamp]
FROM [dbo].[Inventory]
WHERE @@ROWCOUNT = 1 AND [Id] = scope_identity();
```

When updating records, the primary key values are already known, so only the nonprimary key fields that are database controlled are returned. Using the previous Car example, only the updated Timestamp value is queried and returned when the record is updated. The following code retrieves a Car record from the database, changes the color, and then saves the updated Car:

```
static void UpdateACar()
{
    //The factory is not meant to be used like this, but it's demo code :-)
    var context = new ApplicationDbContextFactory().CreateDbContext(null);
    var car = context.Cars.First(c => c.Id == 1);
    car.Color = "White";
    context.SaveChanges();
}
```

The SaveChanges() command executes the following SQL, which first saves the updates and then returns the new Display and TimeStamp values. Once again the SQL is simplified from the parameterized version. Don't worry about the TimeStamp value in the where clause; that will be explained in the next section.

```
//Update the Car Record
UPDATE [dbo].[Inventory] SET [Color] = N'White'
WHERE [Id] = 1 AND [TimeStamp] = 0x00000000000007E1;
//Return the updated Display and TimeStamp values to EF Core
SELECT [Display], [TimeStamp]
FROM [dbo].[Inventory]
WHERE @@ROWCOUNT = 1 AND [Id] = 1;
```

This process also works when adding and/or updating multiple items into the database. EF Core knows how to wire up the values retrieved from the database to the correct entities in your collection.

Concurrency Checking

Concurrency issues arise when two separate processes (users or systems) attempt to update the same record at roughly the same time. For example, User 1 and User 2 both get the data for Customer A. User 1 updates the address and saves the change. User 2 updates the credit rating and attempts to save the same record. If the save for User 2 works, the changes from User 1 will be reverted, since the address was changed after User 2 retrieved the record. Another option is to fail the save for User 2, in which case User 1's changes are persisted, but User 2's changes are not.

How this situation is handled depends on the requirements for the application. Solutions range from doing nothing (second update overwrites the first) to using optimistic concurrency (the second update fails) to more complicated solutions such as checking individual fields. Except for the choice of doing nothing (universally considered a bad programming idea), developers need to know when concurrency issues arise so they can be handled appropriately.

Fortunately, many modern databases have tooling to help the development team handle concurrency issues. SQL Server has a built-in data type called `timestamp`, a synonym for `rowversion`. If a column is defined with a data type of `timestamp`, when a record is added to the database, the value for the column is created by SQL Server, and when a record is updated, the value for the column is updated as well. The value is virtually guaranteed to be unique and is entirely controlled by SQL Server, so you don't have to do anything but "opt in."

EF Core can leverage the SQL Server `timestamp` data type by implementing a `Timestamp` property on an entity (represented as `byte[]` in C#). Entity properties defined with the `Timestamp` attribute or Fluent API designation are added to the `where` clause when updating or deleting records. Instead of just using the primary key value(s), the generated SQL adds the value of the timestamp property to the `where` clause, as you saw in the previous example. This limits the results to those records where the primary key and the timestamp values match. If another user (or the system) has updated the record, the timestamp values will not match, and the `update` or `delete` statement will not update the record. Here is the previous update example highlighting the query using the `Timestamp` column:

```
UPDATE [dbo].[Inventory] SET [Color] = N'White'
WHERE [Id] = 1 AND [TimeStamp] = 0x00000000000007E1;
```

Databases (such as SQL Server) report the number of records affected when adding, updating, or deleting records. If the database reports a number of records affected that is different than the number of records the `ChangeTracker` expected to be changed, EF Core throws a `DbUpdateConcurrencyException` and rolls the entire transaction back. The `DbUpdateConcurrencyException` contains information for all the records that did not persist, including the original values (when the entity was loaded from the database) and the current values (as the user/system updated them). There is also a method to get the current database values (this requires another call to the server). With this wealth of information, the developer can then handle the concurrency error as the application requires. The following code shows this in action:

```
static void ThrowConcurrencyException()
{
  //The factory is not meant to be used like this, but it's demo code :-)
  var context = new ApplicationDbContextFactory().CreateDbContext(null);
  try
  {
    //Get a car record (doesn't matter which one)
    var car = context.Cars.First();
    //Update the database outside of the context
    context.Database.ExecuteSqlInterpolated($"Update dbo.Inventory set Color='Pink' where Id
    = {car.Id}");
    //update the car record in the change tracker and then try and save changes
    car.Color = "Yellow";
    context.SaveChanges();
  }
  catch (DbUpdateConcurrencyException ex)
  {
    //Get the entity that failed to update
    var entry = ex.Entries[0];
```

```
    //Get the original values (when the entity was loaded)
    PropertyValues originalProps = entry.OriginalValues;
    //Get the current values (updated by this code path)
    PropertyValues currentProps = entry.CurrentValues;
    //get the current values from the data store -
    //Note: This needs another database call
    PropertyValues databaseProps = entry.GetDatabaseValues();
  }
}
```

Connection Resiliency

Transient errors are difficult to debug and more difficult to replicate. Fortunately, many database providers have a built-in retry mechanism for glitches in the database system (`tempdb` issues, user limits, etc.) that can be leveraged by EF Core. For SQL Server, `SqlServerRetryingExecutionStrategy` catches errors that are transient (as defined by the SQL Server team), and if enabled on the derived `DbContext` through `DbContextOptions`, EF Core automatically retries the operation until the maximum retry limit is reached.

For SQL Server, there is a shortcut method that can be used to enable `SqlServerRetryingExecutionStrategy` with all the defaults. The method used with `SqlServerOptions` is `EnableRetryOnFailure()` and is demonstrated here:

```
public ApplicationDbContext CreateDbContext(string[] args)
{
  var optionsBuilder = new DbContextOptionsBuilder<ApplicationDbContext>();
  var connectionString = @"server=.,5433;Database=AutoLot50;User Id=sa;Password=P@ssw0rd;";
  optionsBuilder.UseSqlServer(connectionString, options => options.EnableRetryOnFailure());
  return new ApplicationDbContext(optionsBuilder.Options);
}
```

The maximum number of retries and the time limit between retries can be configured per the application's requirements. If the retry limit is reached without the operation completing, EF Core will notify the application of the connection problems by throwing a `RetryLimitExceededException`. This exception, when handled by the developer, can relay the pertinent information to the user, providing a better experience.

```
try
{
  Context.SaveChanges();
}
catch (RetryLimitExceededException ex)
{
  //A retry limit error occurred
  //Should handle intelligently
  Console.WriteLine($"Retry limit exceeded! {ex.Message}");
}
```

When using an execution strategy, explicit transactions must be created within the context of the execution strategy:

```
static void TransactionWithExecutionStrategies()
```

```
{
  //The factory is not meant to be used like this, but it's demo code :-)
  var context = new ApplicationDbContextFactory().CreateDbContext(null);
  var strategy = context.Database.CreateExecutionStrategy();
  strategy.Execute(() =>
  {
    using var trans = context.Database.BeginTransaction();
    try
    {
      //actionToExecute();
      trans.Commit();
    }
    catch (Exception ex)
    {
      trans.Rollback();
    }
  });
}
```

For database providers that don't provide a built-in execution strategy, custom execution strategies can also be created. For more information, refer to the EF Core documentation: `https://docs.microsoft.com/en-us/ef/core/miscellaneous/connection-resiliency`.

Database Function Mapping

SQL Server functions can be mapped to C# methods and be included in LINQ statements. The C# method is merely a placeholder as the server function gets folded into the generated SQL for the query. Support for table-valued function mapping has been added in EF Core to the already existing support for scalar function mapping.

EF Core already supports many built-in SQL Server functions. The C# null coalescing operator (`??`) translates to the SQL Server `coalesce` function. `String.IsNullOrEmpty()` translates to a null check and uses the SQL Server `len` function to check for an empty string.

To see mapping a user-defined function in action, create a user-defined function that returns the number of `Car` records based on `MakeId`:

```
CREATE FUNCTION udf_CountOfMakes ( @makeid int )
RETURNS int
AS
BEGIN
    DECLARE @Result int
    SELECT @Result = COUNT(makeid) FROM dbo.Inventory WHERE makeid = @makeid
    RETURN @Result
END
GO
```

To use this in C#, create a new function in the derived `DbContext` class. The C# body of this function is never executed; it's merely a placeholder that is mapped to the SQL Server function. Note that this method can be placed anywhere, but it is usually placed in the derived `DbContext` class for discoverability:

```
[DbFunction("udf_CountOfMakes", Schema = "dbo")]
public static int InventoryCountFor(int makeId)
  => throw new NotSupportedException();
```

This function can now be used in LINQ queries and becomes part of the generated SQL. To see this in action, add the following code to your top-level statements:

```
static void UsingMappedFunctions()
{
  //The factory is not meant to be used like this, but it's demo code :-)
  var context = new ApplicationDbContextFactory().CreateDbContext(null);
  var makes = context.Makes
    .Where(x=>ApplicationDbContext.InventoryCountFor(x.Id)>1).ToList();
}
```

When this code is executed, the following SQL is executed:

```
SELECT [m].[Id], [m].[Name], [m].[TimeStamp]
FROM [Makes] AS [m]
WHERE [dbo].[udf_CountOfMakes]([m].[Id]) > 1
```

EF Core also supports mapping table-valued functions. Add the following function to your database:

```
CREATE FUNCTION udtf_GetCarsForMake ( @makeId int )
RETURNS TABLE
AS
RETURN
(
   -- Add the SELECT statement with parameter references here
   SELECT Id, IsDrivable, DateBuilt, Color, PetName, MakeId, TimeStamp, Display
   FROM Inventory WHERE MakeId = @makeId
)
GO
```

Add the following code to your ApplicationDbContext class:

```
[DbFunction("udtf_GetCarsForMake", Schema = "dbo")]
public IQueryable<Car> GetCarsFor(int makeId)
  => FromExpression(()=>GetCarsFor(makeId));
```

The FromExpression() call allows the function to be called directly on the derived DbContext instead of using a regular DbSet<T>. Add the following code to your top-level statements to exercise the table-valued function:

```
static void UsingMappedFunctions()
{
  //The factory is not meant to be used like this, but it's demo code :-)
  var context = new ApplicationDbContextFactory().CreateDbContext(null);
  var makes = context.Makes.Where(x=>ApplicationDbContext.InventoryCountFor(x.Id)>1).
ToList();
  var cars = context.GetCarsFor(1).ToList();
}
```

The following SQL gets executed (notice that the global query filter is honored when using the database function):

```
exec sp_executesql N'SELECT [u].[Id], [u].[Color], [u].[DateBuilt],
    [u].[Display], [u].[IsDrivable], [u].[MakeId],
    [u].[PetName], [u].[TimeStamp]
FROM [dbo].[udtf_GetCarsForMake](@__makeId_1) AS [u]
WHERE [u].[IsDrivable] = CAST(1 AS bit)',
N'@__makeId_1 int',@__makeId_1=1
```

For more information on database function mapping, consult the documentation: `https://docs.microsoft.com/en-us/ef/core/querying/user-defined-function-mapping`.

EF.Functions

The static EF class was created as a placeholder for CLR methods that get translated to database functions, using the same mechanism as database function mapping covered in the previous section. The main difference is that all the implementation details are handled by the database providers. Table 22-1 lists the functions available.

Table 22-1. *Functions Available Through EF.Functions*

Function	Meaning in Life
`Like()`	An implementation of the SQL `LIKE` operation. Case sensitivity and syntax are dependent on the database. For SQL Server, the comparison is not case sensitive, and the wildcard operator (%) must be provided.
`Random()`	Introduced in EF Core 6, this returns a pseudorandom number between 0 and 1, inclusive. Maps to SQL Server's RAND function.
`Collate<TProperty>()`	Specifies the collation to be used in a LINQ query.
`Contains()`	Maps to the SQL Server `CONTAINS` function. Table must be full-text indexed to use `Contains()`.
`FreeText()`	Maps to the server `FREETEXT` store function. Table must be full-text indexed to use `FreeText()`.
`DataLength()`	Returns number of bytes used to represent an expression.

(*continued*)

Table 22-1. (*continued*)

Function	Meaning in Life
DateDiffYear() DateDiffMonth() DateDiffWeek() DateDiffDay() DateDiffHour() DateDiffMinute() DateDiffSecond() DateDiffMillisecond() DateDiffMicrosecond() DateDiffNansecond()	Counts the number time interval of boundaries crossed between start date and end date. Maps to SQL Server's DATEDIFF function.
DateFromParts()	Initializes a new instance of the DateTime structure for specified year, month, day. Maps to SQL Server's DATEFROMPARTS function.
DateTime2FromParts()	Initializes a new instance of the DateTime structure for specified year, month, day, hour, minute, second, fractions, and precision. Maps to SQL Server's DATETIME2FROMPARTS function.
DateTimeFromParts()	Initializes a new instance of the DateTime structure for specified year, month, day, hour, minute, second, millisecond. Maps to SQL Server's DATETIMEFROMPARTS function.
DateTimeOffsetFromParts()	Initializes a new instance of the DateTimeOffset structure for specified year, month, day, hour, minute, second, fractions, hourOffset, minuteOffset, and precision. Maps to SQL Server's DATETIMEOFFSETFROMPARTS function.
SmallDateTimeFromParts()	Initializes a new instance of the DateTime structure to the specified year, month, day, hour, and minute. Corresponds to the SQL Server's SMALLDATETIMEFROMPARTS function.
TimeFromParts()	Initializes a new instance of the TimeSpan structure for the specified hour, minute, second, fractions, and precision. Maps to SQL Server's TIMEFROMPARTS function.
IsDate()	Validate if a given string is a date. Maps to SQL Server's ISDATE().

To demonstrate using the EF.Functions.Like method, add the following local function into your top-level statements:

```
static void UseEFFunctions()
{
  Console.WriteLine("Using Like");
  //The factory is not meant to be used like this, but it's demo code :-)
  var context = new ApplicationDbContextFactory().CreateDbContext(null);
```

```
  //Same as contains
  var cars = context.Cars.IgnoreQueryFilters().Where(x=>EF.Functions.Like(x.
  PetName,"%Clunk%")).ToList();
  foreach (var c in cars)
  {
    Console.WriteLine($"{c.PetName} was found");
  }
  //Same as Starts with
  cars = context.Cars.IgnoreQueryFilters().Where(x=>EF.Functions.Like(x.PetName,"Clun%")).
  ToList();
  foreach (var c in cars)
  {
    Console.WriteLine($"{c.PetName} was found");
  }
  //Same as Ends with
  cars = context.Cars.IgnoreQueryFilters().Where(x=>EF.Functions.Like(x.PetName,"%er")).
  ToList();
  foreach (var c in cars)
  {
    Console.WriteLine($"{c.PetName} was found");
  }
}
```

Notice that the SQL Server wildcard character (%) is used just like in a T-SQL query.

Batching of Statements

EF Core has significantly improved the performance when saving changes to the database by executing the statements in one or more batches. This decreases trips between the application and the database, increasing performance and potentially reducing cost (e.g., for cloud databases where customers are charged by the transaction).

EF Core batches the create, update, and delete statements using table-valued parameters. The number of statements that EF batches depends on the database provider. For example, for SQL Server, batching is inefficient below 4 statements and above 40, so EF Core will max out the number of statements at 42. Regardless of the number of batches, all statements still execute in a transaction. The batch size can also be configured through `DbContextOptions`, but the recommendation is to let EF Core calculate the batch size for most (if not all) situations.

If you were to insert four cars in one transaction like this:

```
static void Batching()
{
    //The factory is not meant to be used like this, but it's demo code :-)
    var context = new ApplicationDbContextFactory().CreateDbContext(null);
    var cars = new List<Car>
    {
    new Car { Color = "Yellow", MakeId = 1, PetName = "Herbie" },
    new Car { Color = "White", MakeId = 2, PetName = "Mach 5" },
    new Car { Color = "Pink", MakeId = 3, PetName = "Avon" },
    new Car { Color = "Blue", MakeId = 4, PetName = "Blueberry" },
    };
```

```
    context.Cars.AddRange(cars);
    context.SaveChanges();
}
```

EF Core would batch up the statements into a single call. The query generated is shown here:

```
exec sp_executesql N'SET NOCOUNT ON;
DECLARE @inserted0 TABLE ([Id] int, [_Position] [int]);
MERGE [dbo].[Inventory] USING (
VALUES (@p0, @p1, @p2, 0),
(@p3, @p4, @p5, 1),
(@p6, @p7, @p8, 2),
(@p9, @p10, @p11, 3)) AS i ([Color], [MakeId], [PetName], _Position) ON 1=0
WHEN NOT MATCHED THEN
INSERT ([Color], [MakeId], [PetName])
VALUES (i.[Color], i.[MakeId], i.[PetName])
OUTPUT INSERTED.[Id], i._Position
INTO @inserted0;

SELECT [t].[Id], [t].[DateBuilt], [t].[Display], [t].[IsDrivable], [t].[TimeStamp] FROM
[dbo].[Inventory] t
INNER JOIN @inserted0 i ON ([t].[Id] = [i].[Id])
ORDER BY [i].[_Position];

',N'@p0 nvarchar(50),@p1 int,@p2 nvarchar(50),@p3 nvarchar(50),@p4 int,@p5 nvarchar(50),
@p6 nvarchar(50),@p7 int,@p8 nvarchar(50),@p9 nvarchar(50),@p10 int,@p11 nvarchar(50)',
@p0=N'Yellow',@p1=1,@p2=N'Herbie',@p3=N'White',@p4=2,@p5=N'Mach 5',@p6=N'Pink',@p7=3,
@p8=N'Avon',@p9=N'Blue',@p10=4,@p11=N'Blueberry'
```

Value Converters

Value converters are used to automatically convert data when retrieved and saved to the database. EF Core ships with a long list of built-in value converters (you can see the complete list here: `https://docs.microsoft.com/en-us/dotnet/api/microsoft.entityframeworkcore.storage.valueconversion`). In addition to the built-in value converters, you can also create your own. For example, you can store the price of a `Car` in the database as a numeric value but display the price as a currency string.

Table 22-2 lists many of the built-in value converters available in EF Core. In addition to the converters that ship with EF Core, you can create your own.

Table 22-2. *Some of the EF Core Value Converters*

Value Converter	Meaning in Life
BoolToStringConverter	Converts Boolean values to and from two string values.
BytesToStringConverter	Converts arrays of bytes to and from strings.
CharToStringConverter	Converts a Char to and from a single-character String.
DateTimeOffsetToBinaryConverter	Converts DateTime to and from binary representation into a long. The DateTime is truncated beyond 0.1 millisecond precision.
DateTimeOffsetToBytesConverter	Converts DateTime to and from arrays of bytes.
DateTimeOffsetToStringConverter	Converts DateTimeOffset to and from strings.
DateTimeToBinaryConverter	Converts DateTime using ToBinary(). This will preserve the DateTimeKind.
DateTimeToStringConverter	Converts DateTime to and from strings.
DateTimeToTicksConverter	Converts DateTime to and from Ticks.
EnumToNumberConverter<TEnum,TNumber>	Converts enum values to and from their underlying numeric representation.
EnumToStringConverter<TEnum>	Converts enum values to and from their string representation.
GuidToStringConverter	Converts a Guid to and from a String using the standard "8-4-4-4-12" format.
NumberToStringConverter<TNumber>	Converts numeric values to and from their string representation.
StringToBoolConverter	Converts strings to and from Boolean values.
StringToBytesConverter	Converts strings to and from arrays of bytes.
StringToCharConverter	Converts strings to and from Char values.
StringToDateTimeConverter	Converts strings to and from DateTime values.
StringToDateTimeOffsetConverter	Converts strings to and from DateTimeOffset values.
StringToEnumConverter<TEnum>	Converts strings to and from enum values.
StringToGuidConverter	Converts strings to and from a Guid using the standard "8-4-4-4-12" format.
StringToNumberConverter<TNumber>	Converts strings to and from numeric values.
StringToTimeSpanConverter	Converts strings to and from TimeSpan values.
StringToUriConverter	Converts strings to and from Uri values.
TimeSpanToStringConverter	Converts TimeSpan to and from strings.
TimeSpanToTicksConverter	Converts TimeSpan to and from Ticks.
UriToStringConverter	Converts a Uri to and from a String.
ValueConverter	Defines conversions from an object of one type in a model to an object of the same or different type in the store.

Many of the built-in value converters don't require any configuration. For many situations, EF Core will automatically convert from a C# bool to a SQL Server bit data type without any intervention on your part.

■ **Note** Value converters are set on the model. While they allow mapping disparate data types between your model and the database, the converters will be used only when using EF Core to query the database. Querying the database directly will return the database type, and not the converted type.

For example, to return a string value from the database instead of a decimal, start by updating the Car class to have a string Price property:

```
public class Car : BaseEntity
{
...
  public string Price { get; set; }
...
}
```

If you are following along, make sure to update the database by creating and applying a migration:

```
dotnet ef migrations add Price -o Migrations -c AutoLot.Samples.ApplicationDbContext
dotnet ef database update Price  -c AutoLot.Samples.ApplicationDbContext
```

Add the following global using statements into the GlobalUsings.cs file:

```
global using Microsoft.EntityFrameworkCore.Storage.ValueConversion;
global using System.Globalization;
```

Next, add code into the CarConfiguration class's Configure() method to use the built-in StringToNumberConverter, like this:

```
public void Configure(EntityTypeBuilder<Car> builder)
{
...
  builder.Property(p=>p.Price).HasConversion(new StringToNumberConverter<decimal>());
...
}
```

If you want more control over the values, for example to format the price as currency, you can create a custom converter. Update the value conversion in the CarConfiguration class to the following:

```
public void Configure(EntityTypeBuilder<Car> builder)
{
...
  CultureInfo provider = new CultureInfo("en-us");
  NumberStyles style = NumberStyles.Number | NumberStyles.AllowCurrencySymbol;
  builder.Property(p => p.Price)
    .HasConversion(
      v => decimal.Parse(v, style, provider),
```

```
      v => v.ToString("C2"));
...
}
```

The first parameter is converting the values going *into* the database, and the second parameter is formatting the data coming *out* of the database.

Adding the Price column breaks the table-valued function from earlier in this chapter. To correct this, update the function to include the new column:

```
ALTER FUNCTION udtf_GetCarsForMake ( @makeId int )
  RETURNS TABLE
  AS
    RETURN
    (
      -- Add the SELECT statement with parameter references here
      SELECT Id, IsDrivable, DateBuilt, Color, PetName, MakeId, TimeStamp, Display, Price
      FROM Inventory WHERE MakeId = @makeId
    )
```

For more information on value conversion, please read the documentation at https://docs.microsoft.com/en-us/ef/core/modeling/value-conversions.

Shadow Properties

Shadow properties are properties that aren't explicitly defined on your model but exist due to EF Core. The value and state of these properties are maintained entirely by the Change Tracker. One example of the use of shadow properties is to represent foreign keys for navigation properties if the foreign key isn't defined as part of the entity. Another example is with temporal tables, discussed next.

Shadow properties that aren't added to an entity by EF Core can be defined only through the Fluent API using the Property() method. If the name of the property passed into the Property() method matches an existing property for the entity (either a previously defined shadow property or an explicit property), the Fluent API code configures the existing property. Otherwise, a shadow property is created for the entity. To add a shadow property of type bool? named IsDeleted to the Car entity with the default value of true, add the following code to the Configure() method of the CarConfiguration class:

```
public void Configure(EntityTypeBuilder<Car> builder)
{
  builder.Property<bool?>("IsDeleted").IsRequired(false).HasDefaultValue(true);
  //omitted for brevity
}
```

Shadow properties can be accessed only through the Change Tracker, so they must be loaded from the database as tracked entities. For example, the following code will not compile:

```
static void ShadowProperties()
{
  Console.WriteLine("Shadow Properties");
  //The factory is not meant to be used like this, but it's demo code :-)
  var context = new ApplicationDbContextFactory().CreateDbContext(null);
  var newCar = new Car
  {
```

```
    Color = "Blue",
    PetName = "TestRecord",
    MakeId = context.Makes.First().Id,
    //Can't do this (compile error):
    //IsDeleted = false
  };
}
```

Once the record is added to the Change Tracker, though, the IsDeleted property can be accessed:

```
static void ShadowProperties()
{
  Console.WriteLine("Shadow Properties");
  //omitted for brevity
  context.Cars.Add(newCar);
  context.Entry(newCar).Property("IsDeleted").CurrentValue = true;
}
```

Shadow properties can also be accessed in LINQ queries. The following code first loads all the Car records into the Change Tracker and then sets IsDeleted = false for every other record. After updating the database, the next LINQ query retrieves all of the deleted cars:

```
static void ShadowProperties()
{
  Console.WriteLine("Shadow Properties");
  //The factory is not meant to be used like this, but it's demo code :-)
  var context = new ApplicationDbContextFactory().CreateDbContext(null);
  //omitted for brevity

  var cars = context.Cars.ToList();
  foreach (var c in cars.Where(c=>c.Id % 2 == 0))
  {
    context.Entry(c).Property("IsDeleted").CurrentValue = false;
  }
  context.SaveChanges();
  var nonDeletedCars = context.Cars.Where(c=> !EF.Property<bool>(c,"IsDeleted")).ToList();
  foreach (Car c in nonDeletedCars)
  {
    Console.WriteLine($"{c.PetName} is deleted? {context.Entry(c).Property("IsDeleted").
    CurrentValue}");
  }
}
```

Adding the IsDeleted column also breaks the table-valued function from earlier in this chapter. Update the function to include the new column:

```
ALTER FUNCTION udtf_GetCarsForMake ( @makeId int )
  RETURNS TABLE
  AS
    RETURN
    (
```

```
    -- Add the SELECT statement with parameter references here
    SELECT Id, IsDrivable, DateBuilt, Color, PetName, MakeId, TimeStamp, Display, Price,
    IsDeleted
    FROM Inventory WHERE MakeId = @makeId
  )
```

SQL Server Temporal Table Support

SQL Server temporal tables automatically keep track of all data ever stored in the table. This is accomplished using a history table into which a timestamped copy of the data is stored whenever a change or deletion is made to the main table. Historical data is then available for querying, auditing, or restoring. EF Core 6 has added support for creating temporal tables, converting normal tables to temporal tables, querying historical data, and restoring data from a point in time.

Configure Temporal Tables

To add default temporal table support, use the `ToTable()` Fluent API method. This method can also be used to specify the table name and schema, but in our example, it's not needed due to the `Table` attribute on the `Car` entity. Update the `CarConfiguration` class's `Configure()` method to add a `ToTable()` call:

```
public void Configure(EntityTypeBuilder<Car> builder)
{
  //specify table name and schema - not needed because of the Table attribute
  //builder.ToTable("Inventory", "dbo", b=> b.IsTemporal());
  builder.ToTable(b=> b.IsTemporal());
  //omitted for brevity
}
```

■ **Note** Split tables are not supported for use as temporal tables. This includes any tables generated from entities using `Owned` entities.

After creating a new EF Core migration and updating the database, the `Inventory` table is converted to a system-versioned temporal table with two additional `datetime2` columns, `PeriodEnd` and `PeriodStart`. This also creates a history table named `<ClassName>History` (`CarHistory`, in this example) in the same schema as the main table (dbo, in this example). This history table is a clone of the updated `Inventory` table and stores the history of any changes to the `Inventory` table.

The names for the additional columns and the table (as well as the schema for the history table) can be controlled in the `IsTemporal()` method. The following example uses the names `ValidFrom` and `ValidTo` for `PeriodStart` and `PeriodEnd`, respectively; names the table `InventoryAudit`; and places the table in the `audits` schema:

```
builder.ToTable(b => b.IsTemporal(t =>
{
  t.HasPeriodEnd("ValidTo");
  t.HasPeriodStart("ValidFrom");
  t.UseHistoryTable("InventoryAudit", "audits");
}));
```

■ **Note** At the time of this writing, neither EF Core nor SQL Server will create the schema for the history table if the schema doesn't exist. Make sure you are using an existing schema or update the migration to ensure the schema exists by adding the following:`migrationBuilder.EnsureSchema("audits");`

After this change is migrated to the database, when you examine the tables using Azure Data Studio (or SSMS), you will see the `Inventory` table is labeled as System-Versioned, and when you expand the node, you will see the `audits.InventoryAudit` table. The `InventoryAudit` table is marked as History, as shown in Figure 22-1.

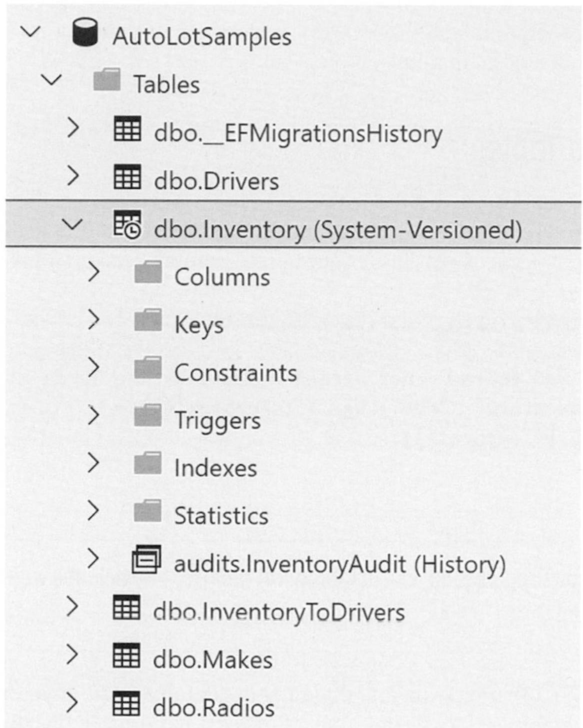

Figure 22-1. *The Inventory and InventoryAudit tables*

If you expand the Columns node, you will see the two new fields added to the table, and expanding the `InventoryAudit` table, you will see that the table is a clone of the `Inventory` table, as shown in Figure 22-2.

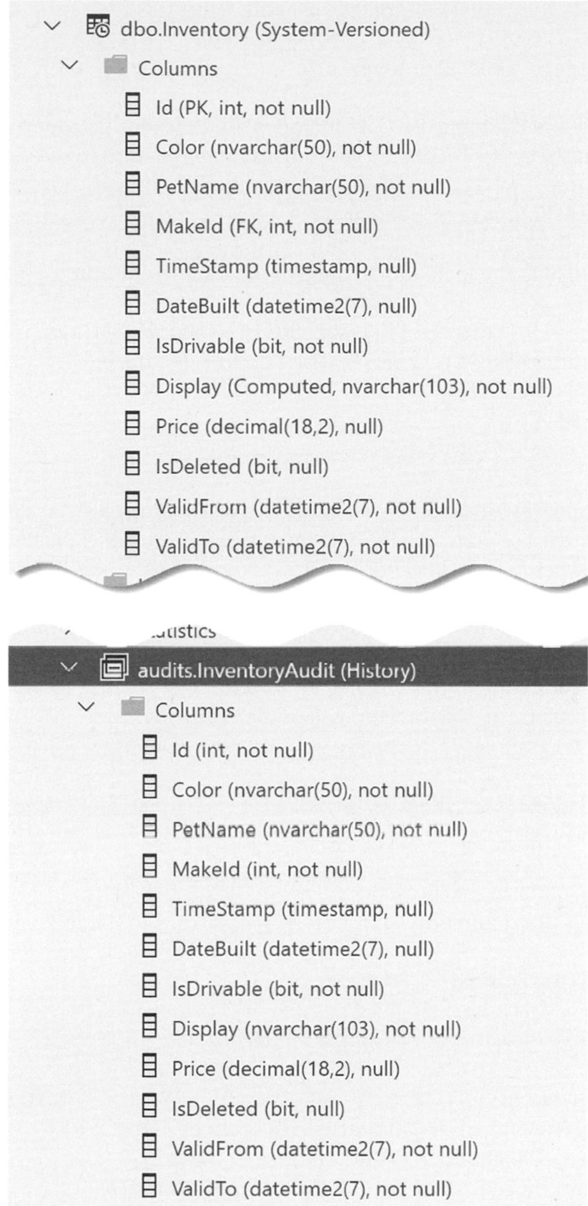

***Figure 22-2.** The Inventory and InventoryAudit columns*

An important note regarding temporal tables: regular queries will not return the timestamp fields as EF Core configures them as HIDDEN. If you execute the following query, you will see only the regular fields returned:

```
SELECT * FROM dbo.Inventory
```

To return the new fields, they must be explicitly specified, like this:

```
SELECT *,ValidFrom, ValidTo FROM dbo.Inventory
```

When using LINQ to query the table, EF Core includes the timestamp properties in the query. For example, the following query works as expected without any modification to the Car class:

```
var c = context.Cars.First();
```

Notice in the generated SQL the inclusion of the two timestamp columns:

```
SELECT TOP(1) [i].[Id], [i].[Color], [i].[DateBuilt], [i].[Display], [i].[IsDeleted],
    [i].[IsDrivable], [i].[MakeId], [i].[PetName], [i].[Price], [i].[TimeStamp],
    [i].[ValidFrom], [i].[ValidTo]
FROM [dbo].[Inventory] AS [i]
WHERE [i].[IsDrivable] = CAST(1 AS bit)
```

EF Core adds the additional columns onto your entity as shadow properties. As demonstrated in the previous section, shadow properties exist as columns in the database table, but are not explicitly defined on the entity.

The problem happens when you are instantiating classes using FromSqlRaw()/FromSqlInterpolated(), stored procedures, or user-defined functions. As you have learned when populating entities by any means other than LINQ, the query must return every property that is expected. Even though the ValidFrom and ValidTo properties are not defined on the Car entity, EF Core still expects them to be returned.

This breaks some previous code in this chapter. To fix it up, first go back to the UsingFromSql() local function and update the FromSqlInterpolated() call to the following:

```
var car = context.Cars
  .FromSqlInterpolated($"Select *,ValidFrom,ValidTo from dbo.Inventory where Id = {carId}")
  .Include(x => x.MakeNavigation)
  .First();
```

Next, update the table-valued function udtf_GetCarsForMake() to the following:

```
ALTER FUNCTION udtf_GetCarsForMake ( @makeId int )
RETURNS TABLE
AS
RETURN
(
   -- Add the SELECT statement with parameter references here
   SELECT Id, IsDrivable, DateBuilt, Color, PetName, MakeId,
      TimeStamp, Display, Price, IsDeleted, ValidFrom, ValidTo
   FROM Inventory WHERE MakeId = @makeId
)
```

Main Table and History Table Interactions

Because the PeriodStart and PeriodEnd column values are maintained by SQL Server, you can continue to use the Car entity as you did prior to adding in the temporal table support. Updates and deletions always target the main table, and queries that don't reference the shadow properties retrieve the current state of the table. While there doesn't appear to be any differences between a nontemporal and a temporal table when used with normal LINQ-based CRUD operations, behind the scenes there is constant interaction with the history table.

To see this in action, the following local function adds, updates, and then deletes a record from the Inventory table using normal EF Core interactions:

```
static void TemporalTables()
{
  Console.WriteLine("Temporal Tables");
  //The factory is not meant to be used like this, but it's demo code :-)
  var context = new ApplicationDbContextFactory().CreateDbContext(null);
  //ensure there is at least one Make record
  var make = new Make { Name = "Honda" };
  context.Makes.Add(make);
  context.SaveChanges();
  //create a Car record to work with
  var car = new Car
  {
    Color = "LightBlue",
    MakeId = context.Makes.First().Id,
    PetName = "Sky",
    IsDrivable = true,
    DateBuilt = new DateTime(2021, 01, 01)
  };
  context.Cars.Add(car);
  context.SaveChanges();
  car.Color = "Cloudy";
  context.Cars.Update(car);
  context.SaveChanges();
  context.Cars.Remove(car);
  context.SaveChanges();
}
```

Each insert, edit, or deletion is tracked in the history table. When a record is inserted into the table, the ValidFrom value is set to the time the insertion transaction started, and the ValidTo is set to the max date for a datetime2, which is 12/31/9999 23:59:59.9999999. Nothing exists in the history table.

■ **Note** All times are stored in UTC time and are recorded at the start of the transaction. Therefore, all rows in a transaction will have the same time recorded in their appropriate tracking fields.

If you step through the code and pause right after the SaveChanges() call that inserted the new Car entity, you can execute the following queries in Azure Data Studio (or SSMS) to verify that there is a record in the Inventory table and nothing in the InventoryAudit table, as well as examine the ValidFrom and ValidTo values:

```
SELECT *,ValidFrom,ValidTo FROM dbo.Inventory
SELECT * FROM audits.InventoryAudit
```

■ **Note** The history table does not hide the timestamp fields, so using the SELECT * syntax will retrieve all the columns. It's only the main table that hides the timestamp fields.

When the record is updated, a copy of the record to be updated is added into the history table (prior to the update statement), and the ValidTo value is set to the start of the transaction. In the main table, the ValidFrom value is set to the time of the update transaction started, and the ValidTo is set to the max date. If you query the tables after the SaveChanges() call that updates the Car record, you can see the two records, one in each table.

When a record is deleted, a copy of the record to be deleted is added into the history table (prior to the delete statement), and the ValidTo value is set to the start of the transaction. In the main table, the record is simply deleted. Now when you query the two tables, you will see there isn't any data in the Inventory table and two records in the InventoryAudit table.

Querying Temporal Tables

The previous example showed querying both the Inventory and InventoryAudit tables. While this showed the interactions between the two tables, there isn't any need to query the history table. SQL Server added the FOR SYSTEM_TIME clause that uses the main table and the history table to reconstruct the state of the data at the time(s) specified. There are five subclauses that can be used with the FOR SYSTEM_TIME clause, and they are listed in Table 22-3.

Table 22-3. *For System Time Subclauses When Querying Temporal Tables (T-SQL)*

Sub Clause	Qualifying Rows	Meaning in Life
AS OF <date_time>	PeriodFrom <= date_time and PeriodTo > date_time	Returns rows that were current at the specified point in time. Internally, a union between the main table and the history table to return the valid rows.
FROM <start_date_time> TO <end_date_time>	PeriodFrom < end_date_time and PeriodTo > start_date_time	Returns all row versions that were current within the specified time range. Note that the boundaries are exclusive.
BETWEEN <start_date_time> TO <end_date_time>	PeriodFrom <= end_date_time and PeriodTo > start_date_time	Returns all row versions that were current within the specified time range. Note that the PeriodFrom boundary is inclusive and the PeriodTo boundary is exclusive.
CONTAINED IN (<start_date_time>, <end_date_time>)	PeriodFrom >= start_date_time and PeriodTo >= end_date_time	Returns all rows that were active only within the specified time range. Note that the boundaries are inclusive.
ALL		Returns all records.

The FOR SYSTEM_TIME clause filters out records that have a period of validity that is zero (PeriodFrom = PeriodTo). To make our example a little more meaningful, add some Thread.Sleep() calls after each of the SaveChanges() calls:

```
static void TemporalTables()
{
..//omitted for brevity
  context.Cars.Add(car);
  context.SaveChanges();
  Thread.Sleep(5000);
  car.Color = "Cloudy";
  context.Cars.Update(car);
  context.SaveChanges();
  Thread.Sleep(5000);
  context.Cars.Remove(car);
  context.SaveChanges();
}
```

EF Core 6 has added query operators that are translated by the SQL Server provider into FOR SYSTEM_TIME and the subclauses listed in Table 22-3. Table 22-4 shows the new operators.

Table 22-4. *EF Core Support for the System Time Subclauses When Querying Temporal Tables*

Sub Clause	Translated To	Meaning in Life
TemporalAsOf()	AS OF <date_time>	Returns rows that were current at the specified point in time. Internally, a union between the main table and the history table to return the valid rows.
TemporalFromTo()	FROM <start_date_time> TO <end_date_time>	Returns all row versions that were current within the specified time range. Note that the boundaries are exclusive.
TemporalBetween()	BETWEEN <start_date_time> TO <end_date_time>	Returns all row versions that were current within the specified time range. Note that the PeriodFrom boundary is inclusive and the PeriodTo boundary is exclusive.
TemporalContainedIn()	CONTAINED IN (<start_date_time>, <end_date_time>)	Returns all rows that were active only within the specified time range. Note that the boundaries are inclusive.
TemporalAll()	ALL	Returns all records.

Remember that PeriodStart and PeriodEnd (ValidFrom and ValidTo in our example) are shadow properties, and not defined in the Car entity. Therefore, the following query won't work:

```
//This doesn't work with shadow properties
var cars = context.Cars.TemporalAll().OrderBy(e => e.ValidFrom);
```

Instead, you need to use the EF.Property<>() method to access the shadow properties:

```
var cars = context.Cars.TemporalAll().OrderBy(e => EF.Property<DateTime>(e, "ValidFrom"));
```

It is important to note that if you want the historical from and to dates, you must retrieve those explicitly in your query using the `EF.Property<>()` method. The following LINQ statement that returns all the current and historical data, using a projection to capture each row and its time values:

```
var cars = context.Cars
        .TemporalAll()
        .OrderBy(e => EF.Property<DateTime>(e, "ValidFrom"))
        .Select(
            e => new
            {
                Car = e,
                ValidFrom = EF.Property<DateTime>(e, "ValidFrom"),
                ValidTo = EF.Property<DateTime>(e, "ValidTo")
            });
foreach (var c in cars)
{
  Console.WriteLine(
    $"{c.Car.PetName} was painted {c.Car.Color} was active from {c.ValidFrom} to {c.ValidTo}");
}
```

When you examine the generated SQL, you can see that the call uses the `FOR SYSTEM_TIME` clause with the `ALL` subclause:

```
SELECT [i].[Id], [i].[Color], [i].[DateBuilt], [i].[Display], [i].[IsDeleted], [i].[IsDrivable],
    [i].[MakeId], [i].[PetName], [i].[Price], [i].[TimeStamp], [i].[ValidFrom], [i].[ValidTo]
FROM [dbo].[Inventory] FOR SYSTEM_TIME ALL AS [i]
WHERE [i].[IsDrivable] = CAST(1 AS bit)
ORDER BY [i].[ValidFrom]
```

As a final note on querying temporal tables, all queries using one of the temporal operators are nontracking queries. If you wanted to restore a record that was deleted, for example, you would use one of the temporal operators to get the historical record and call `Add()` on the `DbSet<T>` and then call `SaveChanges()`.

Clearing Temporal Tables

At this point, you might be wondering how you completely clear temporal tables. The short answer is that you can't, not without removing the versioning, clearing the historical data, and then adding the versioning back in. When versioning is turned off, the history table and the main table become disassociated. Then you can delete all records from the main table (which no longer records the history) and the history table; then you can turn versioning back on, and the tables will be re-associated. To do this in Azure Data Studio or SSMS, enter the following commands:

```
ALTER TABLE [dbo].[Inventory]
     SET (SYSTEM_VERSIONING = OFF)
DELETE FROM [dbo].[Inventory]
DELETE FROM [audits].[InventoryAudit]
ALTER TABLE [dbo].[Inventory]
     SET (SYSTEM_VERSIONING = ON (HISTORY_TABLE=audits.InventoryAudit))
```

If the history table has a custom name (like `audits.InventoryAudit`), it must be specified when turning versioning back on, or a new history table will be created.

To clear the history table using EF Core, the same statements are executed in an explicit transaction using the ExecuteSqlRaw() command on the context's database façade:

```
var strategy = context.Database.CreateExecutionStrategy();
strategy.Execute(() =>
{
  using var trans = context.Database.BeginTransaction();
  context.Database.ExecuteSqlRaw($"ALTER TABLE dbo.Inventory SET (SYSTEM_VERSIONING = OFF)");
  context.Database.ExecuteSqlRaw($"DELETE FROM audits.InventoryHistory");
  context.Database.ExecuteSqlRaw($"ALTER TABLE dbo.Inventory SET (SYSTEM_VERSIONING = ON
  (HISTORY_TABLE={historySchema}.{historyTable}))");
  trans.Commit();
});
```

Making this more generic is a bit more complicated. There is a method (IsTemporal()) on the entity that checks if a table is temporal, and two methods to get the history table name (GetHistoryTableName()) and schema (GetHistoryTableSchema()). While IsTemporal() works at runtime, the methods to get the table name and schema do not work against the runtime model. The runtime model contains just what is needed for EF Core (and your code) to execute, while the design-time model contains *everything*. To use these methods, you have to get an instance of the design-time model at runtime.

To enable access to the design time model at runtime, the project file must be updated. The Microsoft.EntityFrameworkCore.Design package is a DevelopmentDependency package. This means that the dependency won't flow into other projects, and you can't, by default, reference its types. To reference its types in your code, update the package metadata in the project file by removing the <IncludeAssets> tag:

```
<PackageReference Include="Microsoft.EntityFrameworkCore.Design" Version="6.0.0-rc.1.21452.10">
  <!--<IncludeAssets>runtime; build; native; contentfiles; analyzers; buildtransitive</
  IncludeAssets>-->
  <PrivateAssets>all</PrivateAssets>
</PackageReference>
```

To get the design-time model, create a new ServiceCollection and add the DbContextDesignTimeServices. After building the service provider, you can then get an instance of the design-time model:

```
var serviceCollection = new ServiceCollection();
serviceCollection.AddDbContextDesignTimeServices(context);
var serviceProvider = serviceCollection.BuildServiceProvider();
var designTimeModel = serviceProvider.GetService<IModel>();
```

■ **Note** If you are not familiar with the ServiceCollection, it is used by .NET Core for dependency injection. Dependency injection will be covered in depth in the ASP.NET Core chapters, later in this book.

With this in place, you can update the calls to clear the historical data as follows:

```
var strategy = context.Database.CreateExecutionStrategy();
strategy.Execute(() =>
{
  using var trans = context.Database.BeginTransaction();
  var designTimeEntity = designTimeModel.FindEntityType(entityName);
  var historySchema = designTimeEntity.GetHistoryTableSchema();
```

```
  var historyTable = designTimeEntity.GetHistoryTableName();
  context.Database.ExecuteSqlRaw(
    $"ALTER TABLE {schemaName}.{tableName} SET (SYSTEM_VERSIONING = OFF)");
  context.Database.ExecuteSqlRaw($"DELETE FROM {historySchema}.{historyTable}");
  context.Database.ExecuteSqlRaw(
  $"ALTER TABLE {schemaName}.{tableName} SET (SYSTEM_VERSIONING = ON (HISTORY_
  TABLE={historySchema}.{historyTable}))");
  trans.Commit();
});
```

Here is the updated ClearSampleData() method in its entirety:

```
static void ClearSampleData()
{
  //The factory is not meant to be used like this, but it's demo code :-)
  var context = new ApplicationDbContextFactory().CreateDbContext(null);
  var entities = new[]
  {
      typeof(Car).FullName,
      typeof(Make).FullName,
  };
  var serviceCollection = new ServiceCollection();
  serviceCollection.AddDbContextDesignTimeServices(context);
  var serviceProvider = serviceCollection.BuildServiceProvider();
  var designTimeModel = serviceProvider.GetService<IModel>();

  foreach (var entityName in entities)
  {
    var entity = context.Model.FindEntityType(entityName);
    var tableName = entity.GetTableName();
    var schemaName = entity.GetSchema();
    context.Database.ExecuteSqlRaw($"DELETE FROM {schemaName}.{tableName}");
    context.Database.ExecuteSqlRaw($"DBCC CHECKIDENT (\"{schemaName}.{tableName}\",
    RESEED, 0);");
    if (entity.IsTemporal())
    {
      var strategy = context.Database.CreateExecutionStrategy();
      strategy.Execute(() =>
      {
        using var trans = context.Database.BeginTransaction();
        var designTimeEntity = designTimeModel.FindEntityType(entityName);
        var historySchema = designTimeEntity.GetHistoryTableSchema();
        var historyTable = designTimeEntity.GetHistoryTableName();
        context.Database.ExecuteSqlRaw(
              $"ALTER TABLE {schemaName}.{tableName} SET (SYSTEM_VERSIONING = OFF)");
        context.Database.ExecuteSqlRaw($"DELETE FROM {historySchema}.{historyTable}");
```

```
          context.Database.ExecuteSqlRaw($"ALTER TABLE {schemaName}.{tableName} SET (SYSTEM_
          VERSIONING = ON (HISTORY_TABLE={historySchema}.{historyTable}))");
        trans.Commit();
      });
    }
  }
}
```

Summary

This chapter began with a long look at create, read, update, and delete (CRUD) operations using EF Core and then explored several EF Core features to help with developer productivity.

Now that you have a solid foundation for how EF Core works, the next chapter will build the `AutoLot` data access layer.

CHAPTER 23

Build a Data Access Layer with Entity Framework Core

The previous chapters covered the components and capabilities of EF Core. This chapter is focused on applying what you learned about EF Core to build the AutoLot data access layer. This chapter begins with creating one project for the entities and another for the data access library code. Separation of models from the data access code is a common design decision and will be taken advantage of in the ASP.NET Core chapters.

The next step is to scaffold the existing database from Chapter 20 into entities and a derived DbContext using the EF Core command-line interface (CLI). This demonstrates the *database first* process. Then the project is changed to *code first*, where the database design is driven by the C# entities.

The entities from Chapter 20 are updated to their final version, the new entities from Chapters 21 and 22 are added into the model, and the database is updated using EF Core migrations. Then the stored procedure, database view, and user-defined functions are integrated into the EF Core migration system, providing a singular mechanism for developers to get a complete copy of the database. The final EF Core migration completes the database.

The next step is to create repositories that provide encapsulated create, read, update, and delete (CRUD) access to the database. The final step in this chapter is to add data initialization code to provide sample data, a common practice used for testing the data access layer.

Create the AutoLot.Dal and AutoLot.Models Projects

The AutoLot data access layer consists of two projects, one to hold the EF Core–specific code (the derived DbContext, context factory, repositories, migrations, etc.) and another one to hold the entities and view models. Create a new solution named Chapter23_AllProjects, add a .NET Core class library named AutoLot.Models into the solution, and add the Microsoft.EntityFrameworkCore, Microsoft.EntityFrameworkCore.SqlServer, and System.Text.Json NuGet packages to the project.

The Microsoft.EntityFrameworkCore.Abstractions package provides access to many EF Core constructs (like data annotations), is lighter weight than the Microsoft.EntityFrameworkCore package, and would normally be used for model projects. However, support for the new IEntityTypeConfiguration<T> feature is not in the Abstractions package but the full EF Core package.

Add another .NET Core class library project named AutoLot.Dal to the solution. Add a reference to the AutoLot.Models project, and add the Microsoft.EntityFrameworkCore, Microsoft.EntityFrameworkCore.SqlServer, and Microsoft.EntityFrameworkCore.Design NuGet packages to the project.

As a refresher, the Microsoft.EntityFrameworkCore package provides the common functionality for EF Core. The Microsoft.EntityFrameworkCore.SqlServer package supplies the SQL Server data provider, and the Microsoft.EntityFrameworkCore.Design package is required for the EF Core command-line tools.

A. Troelsen and P. Japikse, *Pro C# 10 with .NET 6*, https://doi.org/10.1007/978-1-4842-7869-7_23

To complete all these steps using the command line, use the following (in the directory where you want the solution to be created):

```
dotnet new sln -n Chapter23_AllProjects

dotnet new classlib -lang c# -n AutoLot.Models -o .\AutoLot.Models -f net6.0
dotnet sln .\Chapter23_AllProjects.sln add .\AutoLot.Models
dotnet add AutoLot.Models package Microsoft.EntityFrameworkCore
dotnet add AutoLot.Models package Microsoft.EntityFrameworkCore.SqlServer
dotnet add AutoLot.Models package System.Text.Json

dotnet new classlib -lang c# -n AutoLot.Dal -o .\AutoLot.Dal -f net6.0
dotnet sln .\Chapter23_AllProjects.sln add .\AutoLot.Dal
dotnet add AutoLot.Dal package Microsoft.EntityFrameworkCore
dotnet add AutoLot.Dal package Microsoft.EntityFrameworkCore.Design
dotnet add AutoLot.Dal package Microsoft.EntityFrameworkCore.SqlServer

dotnet add AutoLot.Dal reference AutoLot.Models
```

■ **Note** If you are not using a Windows-based machine, adjust the directory separator character for your operating system in the previous commands. This adjustment will need to be done for all the CLI commands in this chapter.

The final step in creating the projects is to turn C#'s nullable reference types off. While EF Core supports this feature, we won't be using it in this solution. Update the project files for both projects to the following (change is in bold):

```
<PropertyGroup>
  <TargetFramework>net6.0</TargetFramework>
  <ImplicitUsings>enable</ImplicitUsings>
  <Nullable>disable</Nullable>
</PropertyGroup>
```

Finally, update AutoLot.Dal project file to enable access to the design-time model at runtime. Update the metadata for the `Microsoft.EntityFrameworkCore.Design` package to the following. This change is necessary for clearing out temporal tables, covered in the "Data Initialization" section:

```
<PackageReference Include="Microsoft.EntityFrameworkCore.Design" Version="6.0.0-
rc.1.21452.10">
  <!--<IncludeAssets>runtime; build; native; contentfiles; analyzers; buildtransitive</
IncludeAssets>-->
  <PrivateAssets>all</PrivateAssets>
</PackageReference>
```

Add the Database View

Before scaffolding the entities and derived `DbContext` from database, add a custom database view to the `AutoLot` database, which will be used later in this chapter. We are adding it now to demonstrate scaffolding support for views. Connect to the `AutoLot` database (using either SQL Server Management Studio or Azure Data Studio) and execute the following SQL statement:

```
CREATE VIEW [dbo].[CustomerOrderView]
AS
SELECT dbo.Customers.FirstName, dbo.Customers.LastName, dbo.Inventory.Color,
    dbo.Inventory.PetName, dbo.Makes.Name AS Make
FROM dbo.Orders
     INNER JOIN dbo.Customers ON dbo.Orders.CustomerId=dbo.Customers.Id
     INNER JOIN dbo.Inventory ON dbo.Orders.CarId=dbo.Inventory.Id
     INNER JOIN dbo.Makes ON dbo.Makes.Id=dbo.Inventory.MakeId;
```

■ **Note** In the repo's folder for Chapter 20 are database backups for Windows and Docker. If you need to restore the database, refer to the instructions in Chapter 20.

Scaffold the DbContext and Entities

The next step is to scaffold the AutoLot database using the EF Core CLI tools. Navigate to the AutoLot.Dal project directory in either a command prompt or Visual Studio's Package Manager Console. Use the EF Core CLI tools to scaffold the AutoLot database into the entities and the DbContext-derived class with the following command, updating the connection string as necessary (all on one line):

```
dotnet ef dbcontext scaffold "server=.,5433;Database=AutoLot;User Id=sa;Password=P@ssw0rd;"
Microsoft.EntityFrameworkCore.SqlServer --data-annotations --context ApplicationDb
Context --context-namespace AutoLot.Dal.EfStructures --context-dir EfStructures --no-
onconfiguring --namespace AutoLot.Models.Entities --output-dir ..\AutoLot.Models\
Entities --force
```

The previous command scaffolds the database located at the provided connection string (the example command uses the connection string for the Docker container used in Chapter 20) using the SQL Server database provider. The -data-annotations flag is to prioritize data annotations where possible (over the Fluent API). The --context names the context, --context-namespaces specifies the namespace for the context, --context-dir indicates the directory (relative to the current project) for the scaffolded context, --no-onconfiguring prevents the OnConfiguring method from being scaffolded, --output-dir is the output directory for the entities (relative to the project directory), and -n specifies the namespace for the entities. This command places all the entities in the AutoLot.Models project in the Entities folder and places the ApplicationDbContext.cs class in the EfStructures folder of the AutoLot.Dal project. The final option (--force) is used to force overwriting any existing files.

■ **Note** The EF Core CLI commands were covered in detail in Chapter 21.

Examine the Results

After running the command to scaffold the database into C# classes, you will see six entities in the AutoLot. Models project (in the Entities folder) and one derived DbContext in the AutoLot.Dal project (in the EfStructures folder). Each table is scaffolded into a C# entity class and added as a DbSet<T> property on the derived DbContext. Views are scaffolded into keyless entities, added as a DbSet<T>, and mapped to the proper database view using the Fluent API.

The scaffolding command that we used specified the --data-annotations flag to prefer annotations over the Fluent API. As you examine the scaffolded classes, you will notice there are a few misses with the annotations. For example, the TimeStamp properties do not have the [Timestamp] attribute but are instead configured as RowVersion ConcurrencyTokens in the Fluent API.

■ **Note** In my opinion, having the annotations in the class makes the code more readable than having all the configuration in the Fluent API. If you prefer to use the Fluent API, remove the -data-annotations option from the command.

Switch to Code First

Now that you have the database scaffolded into a derived DbContext and entities, it is time to switch from database first to code first. The process is not complicated, but also not something that should be done on a regular basis. It's better to decide on a paradigm and stick with it. Most agile teams prefer code first, as the emerging design of the application and its entities flows into the database. The process we are following here simulates starting a new project using EF Core targeting an existing database.

The steps involved in switching from database first to code first involves creating a DbContext factory (for the CLI tooling), creating an initial migration for the current state of the object graph, and then dropping the database and re-creating the database with either the migration or "fake" applied by tricking EF Core.

Create the DbContext Design-Time Factory

As you recall from the previous EF Core chapters, IDesignTimeDbContextFactory is used by the EF Core CLI tooling to create an instance of the derived DbContext class. Create a new class file named ApplicationDbContextFactory.cs in the AutoLot.Dal project in the EfStructures directory.

The details of the factory were covered in the previous chapter, so I'm just going to list the code here. Make sure to update your connection string to match your environment.

```
namespace AutoLot.Dal.EfStructures;

public class ApplicationDbContextFactory : IDesignTimeDbContextFactory<ApplicationDbContext>
{
  public ApplicationDbContext CreateDbContext(string[] args)
  {
    var optionsBuilder = new DbContextOptionsBuilder<ApplicationDbContext>();
    var connectionString = @"server=.,5433;Database=AutoLot;User Id=sa;Password=P@ssw0rd;";
    optionsBuilder.UseSqlServer(connectionString);
    Console.WriteLine(connectionString);
    return new ApplicationDbContext(optionsBuilder.Options);
  }
}
```

Create the Initial Migration

Recall that the first migration will create three files: the two files for the migration itself and the complete model snapshot. Enter the following in a command prompt (in the AutoLot.Dal directory) to create a new migration named Initial (using the ApplicationDbContext instance that was just scaffolded) and place the migration files in the EfStructures\Migrations folder of the AutoLot.Dal project:

```
dotnet ef migrations add Initial -o EfStructures\Migrations -c AutoLot.Dal.EfStructures.
ApplicationDbContext
```

■ **Note** It is important to make sure no changes are applied to the scaffolded files or the database until this first migration is created and applied. Changes on either side will cause the code and database to become out of sync. Once applied, all changes to the database need to be completed through EF Core migrations.

To confirm that the migration was created and is waiting to be applied, execute the list command.

```
dotnet ef migrations list -c AutoLot.Dal.EfStructures.ApplicationDbContext
```

The result will show the Initial migration pending (your timestamp will be different). The connection string is shown in the output due to Console.Writeline() in the CreateDbContext() method.

```
Build started...
Build succeeded.
server=.,5433;Database=AutoLot;User Id=sa;Password=P@ssw0rd;
20210703194100_Initial (Pending)
```

Applying the Migration

The easiest method of applying the migration to the database is to drop the database and re-create it. If that is an option, you can enter the following commands and move on to the next section:

```
dotnet ef database drop -f
dotnet ef database update Initial -c AutoLot.Dal.EfStructures.ApplicationDbContext
```

If dropping and re-creating the database is not an option (e.g., it is an Azure SQL database), then EF Core needs to *believe* that the migration has been applied. Fortunately, this is straightforward with EF Core doing most of the work. Start by creating a SQL script from the migration by using the following command:

```
dotnet ef migrations script --idempotent -o FirstMigration.sql
```

The relevant portions of this script are the parts that create the __EFMigrationsHistory table and then add the migration record into the table to indicate that it was applied. Copy those pieces to a new query in either Azure Data Studio or SQL Server Manager Studio. Here is the SQL code that you need (your timestamp will be different):

```
IF OBJECT_ID(N'[__EFMigrationsHistory]') IS NULL
BEGIN
    CREATE TABLE [__EFMigrationsHistory] (
        [MigrationId] nvarchar(150) NOT NULL,
        [ProductVersion] nvarchar(32) NOT NULL,
        CONSTRAINT [PK___EFMigrationsHistory] PRIMARY KEY ([MigrationId])
    );
```

```
END;
GO
...
IF NOT EXISTS(SELECT * FROM [__EFMigrationsHistory] WHERE [MigrationId] = N'20210703194100_
Initial')
BEGIN
    INSERT INTO [__EFMigrationsHistory] ([MigrationId], [ProductVersion])
    VALUES (N'20210703194100_Initial', N'6.0.0');
END;
GO
```

Now if you run the `list` command, it will no longer show the `Initial` migration as pending. With the initial migration applied, the project and database are in sync, and the development can continue code first. Before continuing with the database development, the project's custom exceptions need to be created.

Create the GlobalUsings Files

To tidy up the code in the projects, we are going to take advantage of the new C# 10 feature for global `using` statements. Rename the `Class1.cs` files in the AutoLot.Dal and AutoLot.Models projects to `GlobalUsings.cs`. Clear out all the code in each of the files and replace them as follows:

```
//AutoLot.Dal
//GlobalUsings.cs
global using AutoLot.Dal.EfStructures;
global using AutoLot.Dal.Exceptions;

global using AutoLot.Models.Entities;
global using AutoLot.Models.Entities.Configuration;
global using AutoLot.Models.Entities.Base;

global using System.Data;
global using System.Linq.Expressions;

global using Microsoft.Data.SqlClient;
global using Microsoft.EntityFrameworkCore;
global using Microsoft.EntityFrameworkCore.ChangeTracking;
global using Microsoft.EntityFrameworkCore.Design;
global using Microsoft.EntityFrameworkCore.Metadata;
global using Microsoft.EntityFrameworkCore.Migrations;
global using Microsoft.EntityFrameworkCore.Query;
global using Microsoft.EntityFrameworkCore.Storage;
global using Microsoft.Extensions.DependencyInjection;

//AutoLot.Models
//GlobalUsings.cs
global using AutoLot.Models.Entities.Base;
global using AutoLot.Models.Entities.Owned;
global using AutoLot.Models.Entities.Configuration;

global using Microsoft.EntityFrameworkCore;
global using Microsoft.EntityFrameworkCore.Metadata.Builders;
```

```
global using System.ComponentModel;
global using System.ComponentModel.DataAnnotations;
global using System.ComponentModel.DataAnnotations.Schema;
global using System.Globalization;
global using System.Xml.Linq;
```

■ **Note** Adding all the namespaces at once will prevent the code from compiling, as all of the namespaces listed here do not yet exist. Normally, you would add to this file as you develop your project. We are adding them most of them here in one shot to save space in an already long chapter.

Create Custom Exceptions

A common pattern in exception handling is to catch system exceptions (and/or EF Core exceptions, as in this example), log the exception, and then throw a custom exception. If a custom exception is caught in an upstream method, the developer knows the exception has already been logged and just needs to react to the exception appropriately in the current code block.

Create a new directory named `Exceptions` in the AutoLot.Dal project. In that directory, create four new class files: `CustomException.cs`, `CustomConcurrencyException.cs`, `CustomDbUpdateException.cs`, and `CustomRetryLimitExceededException.cs`. All four files are shown in the following listing:

```
//CustomException.cs
namespace AutoLot.Dal.Exceptions;

public class CustomException : Exception
{
  public CustomException() {}
  public CustomException(string message) : base(message) { }
  public CustomException(string message, Exception innerException)
      : base(message, innerException) { }
}

//CustomConcurrencyException.cs
namespace AutoLot.Dal.Exceptions;

public class CustomConcurrencyException : CustomException
{
  public CustomConcurrencyException() { }
  public CustomConcurrencyException(string message) : base(message) { }
  public CustomConcurrencyException(
    string message, DbUpdateConcurrencyException innerException)
      : base(message, innerException) { }
}

//CustomDbUpdateException.cs
namespace AutoLot.Dal.Exceptions;

public class CustomDbUpdateException : CustomException
```

```
{
  public CustomDbUpdateException() { }
  public CustomDbUpdateException(string message) : base(message) { }
  public CustomDbUpdateException(
    string message, DbUpdateException innerException)
      : base(message, innerException) { }
}

//CustomRetryLimitExceededException.cs
namespace AutoLot.Dal.Exceptions;

public class CustomRetryLimitExceededException : CustomException
{
  public CustomRetryLimitExceededException() { }
  public CustomRetryLimitExceededException(string message)
      : base(message) { }
  public CustomRetryLimitExceededException(
    string message, RetryLimitExceededException innerException)
      : base(message, innerException) { }
}
```

■ **Note** Custom exception handling was covered in detail in Chapter 7.

Finalize the Entities and ViewModel

This section updates scaffolded entities to their final version, adds the additional entities from the previous two chapters, and adds a logging entity.

■ **Note** Your projects will not compile until this section is complete.

The Entities

In the Entities directory of the AutoLot.Models project, you will find six files, one for each table in the database and one for the database view. Note that the names are singular and not plural (as they are in the database). This is a change starting with EF Core 5 where the pluralizer is on by default when scaffolding entities from the database. The pluralizer, as the name describes, maps singular entity names to plural table names, and vice versa.

The previous chapters covered the EF Core conventions, data annotations, and the Fluent API in depth, so most of this section will be code listings with brief descriptions.

The BaseEntity Class

The BaseEntity class will hold the Id and TimeStamp columns that are on every entity. Create a new directory named Base in the Entities directory of the AutoLot.Models project. In this directory, create a new file named BaseEntity.cs and update the code to match the following:

```
namespace AutoLot.Models.Entities.Base;

public abstract class BaseEntity
{
  [Key, DatabaseGenerated(DatabaseGeneratedOption.Identity)]
  public int Id { get; set; }
  [Timestamp]
  public byte[] TimeStamp { get; set; }
}
```

All of the entities (except for the logging entity) will be updated to use this base class throughout the next sections.

The Owned Person Entity

The Customer, CreditRisk, and Driver entities all have FirstName and LastName properties. Entities that have the same properties in each can benefit from owned classes. While moving these two properties to an owned class is a somewhat trivial example, owned entities help to reduce code duplication and increase consistency.

Create a new directory named Owned in the Entities directory of the AutoLot.Models project. In this new directory, create a new file named Person.cs. Update the code to match the following:

```
namespace AutoLot.Models.Entities.Owned;

[Owned]
public class Person
{
  [Required, StringLength(50)]
  public string FirstName { get; set; }

  [Required, StringLength(50)]
  public string LastName { get; set; }

  [DatabaseGenerated(DatabaseGeneratedOption.Computed)]
  public string FullName { get; set; }
}
```

Notice the additional computed column that combined the names into a FullName property. Owned classes are configured as part of the owning classes, so the configuration for the column name mapping and computed column takes place as part of the Customer, CreditRisk, and Driver configuration.

The Car (Inventory) Entity

The Inventory table was scaffolded to an entity class named Inventory. We are going to change the entity name to Car while leaving the table name alone. This is an example of mapping an entity to a table with a different name. This is easy to fix: change the name of the file to Car.cs and the name of the class to Car. The Table attribute is already applied correctly, so just add the dbo schema. Note that the schema parameter is optional because SQL Server defaults to dbo, but I include it for completeness. The namespaces can also be deleted, as they are covered with the global namespaces.

```
[Table("Inventory", Schema = "dbo")]
[Index(nameof(MakeId), Name = "IX_Inventory_MakeId")]
public partial class Car
{
...
}
```

Next, inherit from BaseEntity, and remove the Id (and its attribute) and TimeStamp properties as well as the constructor. This is the code for the class after these changes:

```
namespace AutoLot.Models.Entities;

[Table("Inventory", Schema = "dbo")]
[Index(nameof(MakeId), Name = "IX_Inventory_MakeId")]
public partial class Car  : BaseEntity
{
  public int MakeId { get; set; }
  [Required]
  [StringLength(50)]
  public string Color { get; set; }
  [Required]
  [StringLength(50)]
  public string PetName { get; set; }
  [ForeignKey(nameof(MakeId))]
  [InverseProperty("Inventories")]
  public virtual Make Make { get; set; }
  [InverseProperty(nameof(Order.Car))]
  public virtual ICollection<Order> Orders { get; set; }
}
```

Add the DisplayName attribute to the PetName property, add the Display property with the DatabaseGenerated attribute to hold the computed value from SQL Server, and add the Price and DateBuilt properties. Update the code to the following (changes in bold):

```
[Required]
[StringLength(50)]
[DisplayName("Pet Name")]
public string PetName { get; set; }

[DatabaseGenerated(DatabaseGeneratedOption.Computed)]
public string Display { get; set; }

public string Price { get; set; }
public DateTime? DateBuilt { get; set;}
```

■ **Note** The DisplayName attribute is used by ASP.NET Core and will be covered in that section.

The Make navigation property needs to be renamed to MakeNavigation, and the inverse property is using a magic string instead of the C# nameof() method. Here is the updated property:

```
[ForeignKey(nameof(MakeId))]
[InverseProperty(nameof(Make.Cars))]
public virtual Make MakeNavigation { get; set; }
```

■ **Note** This is a prime example of why naming the property the same as the class name becomes problematic. If the property name was left as Make, then the nameof function wouldn't work properly since Make (in this instance) is referring to the *property* and not the *type*.

The scaffolded code for the Orders navigation property does use the nameof() method in the inverse property but needs an update since all reference navigation properties will have the suffix Navigation added to their names. The final change for that navigation property is to have the type of the property typed as IEnumerable<Order> instead of ICollection<Order> and initialized with a new List<Order>. This is not a required change, as ICollection<Order> will also work. I prefer to use the lower-level IEnumerable<T> on collection navigation properties (since IQueryable<T> and ICollection<T> both derive from IEnumerable<T>). Update the code to match the following:

```
[InverseProperty(nameof(Order.CarNavigation))]
public virtual IEnumerable<Order> Orders { get; set; } = new List<Order>();
```

Add the collection navigation property for the Driver and CarDriver entities and the reference navigation property for the Radio entity:

```
[InverseProperty(nameof(Driver.Cars))]
public virtual IEnumerable<Driver> Drivers { get; set; } = new List<Driver>();

[InverseProperty(nameof(CarDriver.CarNavigation))]
public virtual IEnumerable<CarDriver> CarDrivers { get; set; } = new List<CarDriver>();

[InverseProperty(nameof(Radio.CarNavigation))]
public virtual Radio RadioNavigation { get; set; }
```

Next, add a NotMapped property that will display the Make value of the Car. If the related Make information was retrieved from the database with the Car record, the Make Name will be displayed. If the related data was not retrieved, the property displays "Unknown." As a reminder, NotMapped properties are not part of the database and exist only on the entity. Add the following:

```
[NotMapped]
public string MakeName => MakeNavigation?.Name ?? "Unknown";
```

Add an override for the ToString() method to display vehicle information.

```
public override string ToString()
{
  // Since the PetName column could be empty, supply
  // the default name of **No Name**.
  return $"{PetName ?? "**No Name**"} is a {Color} {MakeNavigation?.Name} with ID {Id}.";
}
```

Add the Required and DisplayName attributes to the MakeId. Even though the MakeId property is considered by EF Core to be required since it is non-nullable, I always add it for readability and UI framework support. Update the code to match the following:

```
[Required]
[DisplayName("Make")]
public int MakeId { get; set; }
```

The next change is to add the non-nullable bool IsDrivable property with a nullable backing field and a display name.

```
private bool? _isDrivable;

[DisplayName("Is Drivable")]
public bool IsDrivable
{
  get => _isDrivable ?? true;
  set => _isDrivable = value;
}
```

The final step for the Car class is to add the EntityTypeConfiguration attribute:

```
[Table("Inventory", Schema = "dbo")]
[Index(nameof(MakeId), Name = "IX_Inventory_MakeId")]
[EntityTypeConfiguration(typeof(CarConfiguration))]
public class Car : BaseEntity
{
...
}
```

That completes the updates to the Car entity class and is listed here in its entirety:

```
namespace AutoLot.Models.Entities;

[Table("Inventory", Schema = "dbo")]
[Index(nameof(MakeId), Name = "IX_Inventory_MakeId")]
[EntityTypeConfiguration(typeof(CarConfiguration))]
public partial class Car : BaseEntity
{
  [Required]
  [StringLength(50)]
  public string Color { get; set; }
  public string Price { get; set; }

  private bool? _isDrivable;
  [DisplayName("Is Drivable")]
  public bool IsDrivable
  {
    get => _isDrivable ?? true;
    set => _isDrivable = value;
  }
```

```
    public DateTime? DateBuilt { get; set; }

    [DatabaseGenerated(DatabaseGeneratedOption.Computed)]
    public string Display { get; set; }

    [Required]
    [StringLength(50)]
    [DisplayName("Pet Name")]
    public string PetName { get; set; }

    [Required]
    [DisplayName("Make")]
    public int MakeId { get; set; }
    [ForeignKey(nameof(MakeId))]
    [InverseProperty(nameof(Make.Cars))]
    public virtual Make MakeNavigation { get; set; }

    [InverseProperty(nameof(Radio.CarNavigation))]
    public virtual Radio RadioNavigation { get; set; }

    [InverseProperty(nameof(Driver.Cars))]
    public virtual IEnumerable<Driver> Drivers { get; set; } = new List<Driver>();

    [InverseProperty(nameof(CarDriver.CarNavigation))]
    public virtual IEnumerable<CarDriver> CarDrivers { get; set; } = new List<CarDriver>();

    [InverseProperty(nameof(Order.CarNavigation))]
    public virtual IEnumerable<Order> Orders { get; set; } = new List<Order>();

    [NotMapped]
    public string MakeName => MakeNavigation?.Name ?? "Unknown";
    public override string ToString()
    {
      // Since the PetName column could be empty, supply
      // the default name of **No Name**.
      return $"{PetName ?? "**No Name**"} is a {Color} {MakeNavigation?.Name} with ID {Id}.";
    }
}
```

Update the ApplicationDbContext Class

Since the Inventory class was renamed to Car, the ApplicationDbContext class must be updated. Locate the DbSet<Inventory> property and update the line to the following:

```
public virtual DbSet<Car> Cars { get; set; }
```

The CarConfiguration Class

Just as we did in Chapter 21, we will use `IEntityTypeConfiguration<T>` to hold the Fluent API code. This keeps the configuration for each entity in its own class, significantly decreasing the size of the `ApplicationDbContext OnModelCreating()` method. Start by creating a new directory named `Configuration` under the `Entities` directory. In this new directory, add a new file named `CarConfiguration.cs`, make it public, and implement the `IEntityTypeConfiguration<Car>` interface, like this:

```
namespace AutoLot.Models.Entities.Configuration;

public class CarConfiguration : IEntityTypeConfiguration<Car>
{
  public void Configure(EntityTypeBuilder<Car> builder)
  {
  }
}
```

Next, move the contents of the configuration for the `Car` entity (note that it will still be named `Inventory`) from the `OnModelCreating()` method in the `ApplicationDbContext` into the `Configure()` method of the `CarConfiguration` class. The scaffolded Fluent API code for each entity is wrapped in a construct similar to the following:

```
modelBuilder.Entity<Car>(entity =>
{
  //Fluent API code here
});
```

Each `IEntityTypeConfiguration<T>` is strongly typed to an entity, so the outer code for each entity is not needed, just the scaffolded inner code. Move the entire block, and then delete the entity specifier. Replace the `entity` variable in each of the inner code blocks with the `builder` variable, and then add the additional Fluent API code so the `Configure()` method looks like this:

```
public void Configure(EntityTypeBuilder<Car> builder)
{
  builder.HasQueryFilter(c => c.IsDrivable);

  builder.Property(p => p.IsDrivable)
    .HasField("_isDrivable")
    .HasDefaultValue(true);

  builder.Property(e => e.DateBuilt).HasDefaultValueSql("getdate()");

  builder.Property(e => e.Display)
  .HasComputedColumnSql("[PetName] + ' (' + [Color] + ')'", stored: true);

  CultureInfo provider = new CultureInfo("en-us");
  NumberStyles style = NumberStyles.Number | NumberStyles.AllowCurrencySymbol;
  builder.Property(p => p.Price)
    .HasConversion(
      v => decimal.Parse(v, style, provider),
      v => v.ToString("C2"));
```

```
  builder.HasOne(d => d.MakeNavigation)
    .WithMany(p => p.Cars)
    .HasForeignKey(d => d.MakeId)
    .OnDelete(DeleteBehavior.ClientSetNull)
    .HasConstraintName("FK_Inventory_Makes_MakeId");

  builder
    .HasMany(p => p.Drivers)
    .WithMany(p => p.Cars)
    .UsingEntity<CarDriver>(
      j => j
        .HasOne(cd => cd.DriverNavigation)
        .WithMany(d => d.CarDrivers)
        .HasForeignKey(nameof(CarDriver.DriverId))
        .HasConstraintName("FK_InventoryDriver_Drivers_DriverId")
        .OnDelete(DeleteBehavior.Cascade),
      j => j
        .HasOne(cd => cd.CarNavigation)
        .WithMany(c => c.CarDrivers)
        .HasForeignKey(nameof(CarDriver.CarId))
        .HasConstraintName("FK_InventoryDriver_Inventory_InventoryId")
        .OnDelete(DeleteBehavior.ClientCascade),
      j =>
        {
          j.HasKey(cd => new { cd.CarId, cd.DriverId });
        });
}
```

The Inventory table will be configured as a temporal table, so add the following to the Configure() method:

```
public void Configure(EntityTypeBuilder<Car> builder)
{
  //omitted for brevity
  builder.ToTable( b => b.IsTemporal(t =>
  {
    t.HasPeriodEnd("ValidTo");
    t.HasPeriodStart("ValidFrom");
    t.UseHistoryTable("InventoryAudit");
  }));
}
```

Make sure all the code in the OnModelBuilding() method (in the ApplicationDbContext.cs class) that configures the Inventory class is deleted, and add the following single line of code in its place:

```
protected override void OnModelCreating(ModelBuilder modelBuilder)
{
  new CarConfiguration().Configure(modelBuilder.Entity<Car>());
...
}
```

The Driver Entity

Chapter 21 added a new entity named Driver and set up a many-to-many relationship with the Car entity. Since this table wasn't in the Chapter 20 database, it is not in our scaffolded code. Add a new file named Driver.cs to the Entities folder and update the code in the file to match the following:

```
namespace AutoLot.Models.Entities;

[Table("Drivers", Schema = "dbo")]
[EntityTypeConfiguration(typeof(DriverConfiguration))]
public class Driver : BaseEntity
{
  public Person PersonInformation{ get; set; } = new Person();
  [InverseProperty(nameof(Car.Drivers))]
  public virtual IEnumerable<Car> Cars { get; set; } = new List<Car>();

  [InverseProperty(nameof(CarDriver.DriverNavigation))]
  public virtual IEnumerable<CarDriver> CarDrivers { get; set; } = new List<CarDriver>();
}
```

Update the ApplicationDbContext Class

Since this is a new table, a new DbSet<Driver> property must be added into the ApplicationDbContext class. Add the following to the DbSet<T> properties:

```
public virtual DbSet<Driver> Drivers { get; set; }
```

The DriverConfiguration Class

Add a new file named DriverConfiguration.cs into the Configuration folder, and update the code to the following:

```
namespace AutoLot.Models.Entities.Configuration;

public class DriverConfiguration : IEntityTypeConfiguration<Driver>
{
  public void Configure(EntityTypeBuilder<Driver> builder)
  {
    builder.OwnsOne(o => o. PersonInformation,
      pd =>
        {
          pd.Property<string>(nameof(Person.FirstName))
            .HasColumnName(nameof(Person.FirstName))
            .HasColumnType("nvarchar(50)");
          pd.Property<string>(nameof(Person.LastName))
            .HasColumnName(nameof(Person.LastName))
            .HasColumnType("nvarchar(50)");
          pd.Property(p => p.FullName)
            .HasColumnName(nameof(Person.FullName))
            .HasComputedColumnSql("[LastName] + ', ' + [FirstName]");
        });
```

```
    builder.Navigation(d => d.PersonInformation).IsRequired(true);
  }
}
```

The Driver entity uses the Person-owned property, so it cannot be configured as a temporal table.

Update the ApplicationDbContext OnModelCreating() method:

```
protected override void OnModelCreating(ModelBuilder modelBuilder)
{
  new CarConfiguration().Configure(modelBuilder.Entity<Car>());
  new DriverConfiguration().Configure(modelBuilder.Entity<Driver>());
}
```

The CarDriver Entity

Continuing with configuration the many-to-many relationship between Car and Driver, add a new class named CarDriver. Update the code to the following:

```
namespace AutoLot.Models.Entities;

[Table("InventoryToDrivers", Schema = "dbo")]
[EntityTypeConfiguration(typeof(CarDriverConfiguration))]
public class CarDriver : BaseEntity
{
  public int DriverId { get; set; }
  [ForeignKey(nameof(DriverId))]
  public virtual Driver DriverNavigation { get; set; }

  [Column("InventoryId")]
  public int CarId { get; set; }
  [ForeignKey(nameof(CarId))]
  public virtual Car CarNavigation { get; set; }
}
```

Update the ApplicationDbContext Class

Since this is a new table, a new DbSet<CarDriver> property must be added into the ApplicationDbContext class. Add the following to the DbSet<T> properties:

```
public virtual DbSet<CarDriver> CarsToDrivers { get; set; }
```

The CarDriverConfiguration Class

Because of the query filter for nondrivable cars on the Car class, the related tables (CarDriver and Order) need to have the same query filter applied to their navigation properties. Add a new file named CarDriverConfiguration.cs into the Configuration folder, and update the code to the following:

```
namespace AutoLot.Models.Entities.Configuration;
```

```
public class CarDriverConfiguration : IEntityTypeConfiguration<CarDriver>
{
  public void Configure(EntityTypeBuilder<CarDriver> builder)
  {
    builder.HasQueryFilter(cd=>cd.CarNavigation.IsDrivable);
  }
}
```

The InventoryToDrivers table will be configured as a temporal table, so add the following to the Configure() method:

```
public void Configure(EntityTypeBuilder<CarDriver> builder)
{
  //omitted for brevity
  builder.ToTable( b => b.IsTemporal(t =>
  {
    t.HasPeriodEnd("ValidTo");
    t.HasPeriodStart("ValidFrom");
    t.UseHistoryTable("InventoryToDriversAudit");
  }));
}
```

Update the ApplicationDbContext OnModelCreating() method:

```
protected override void OnModelCreating(ModelBuilder modelBuilder)
{
  new CarConfiguration().Configure(modelBuilder.Entity<Car>());
  new DriverConfiguration().Configure(modelBuilder.Entity<Driver>());
  new CarDriverConfiguration().Configure(modelBuilder.Entity<CarDriver>());
}
```

The Radio Entity

Chapter 21 also added a new entity named Radio and set up a one-to-one relationship with the Car entity. Add a new file named Radio.cs to the Entities folder and update the code in the file to match the following:

```
namespace AutoLot.Models.Entities;

[Table("Radios", Schema = "dbo")]
[EntityTypeConfiguration(typeof(RadioConfiguration))]
public class Radio : BaseEntity
{
  public bool HasTweeters { get; set; }
  public bool HasSubWoofers { get; set; }
  [Required, StringLength(50)]
  public string RadioId { get; set; }
  [Column("InventoryId")]
  public int CarId { get; set; }
  [ForeignKey(nameof(CarId))]
  public virtual Car CarNavigation { get; set; }
}
```

Update the ApplicationDbContext Class

Since this is a new table, a new DbSet<Radio> property must be added into the ApplicationDbContext class. Add the following to the DbSet<T> properties:

```
public virtual DbSet<Radio> Radios { get; set; }
```

The RadioConfiguration Class

Create a new class named RadioConfiguration, implement the IEntityTypeConfiguration<Radio> interface, and add the code from the ApplicationDbContext OnModelBuilding() method:

```
namespace AutoLot.Models.Entities.Configuration;

public class RadioConfiguration : IEntityTypeConfiguration<Radio>
{
  public void Configure(EntityTypeBuilder<Radio> builder)
  {
    builder.HasQueryFilter(r=>r.CarNavigation.IsDrivable);
    builder.HasIndex(e => e.CarId, "IX_Radios_CarId")
        .IsUnique();

    builder.HasOne(d => d.CarNavigation)
        .WithOne(p => p.RadioNavigation)
        .HasForeignKey<Radio>(d => d.CarId);
  }
}
```

The Radios table will be configured as a temporal table, so add the following to the Configure() method:

```
public void Configure(EntityTypeBuilder<Radio> builder)
{
  //omitted for brevity
  builder.ToTable( b => b.IsTemporal(t =>
  {
    t.HasPeriodEnd("ValidTo");
    t.HasPeriodStart("ValidFrom");
    t.UseHistoryTable("RadiosAudit");
  }));
}
```

Update the OnModelCreating() method in the ApplicationDbContext:

```
protected override void OnModelCreating(ModelBuilder modelBuilder)
{
  new CarConfiguration().Configure(modelBuilder.Entity<Car>());
  new DriverConfiguration().Configure(modelBuilder.Entity<Driver>());
  new CarDriverConfiguration().Configure(modelBuilder.Entity<CarDriver>());
  new RadioConfiguration().Configure(modelBuilder.Entity<Radio>());
}
```

The Customer Entity

The Customers table was scaffolded to an entity class named Customer. Inherit from BaseEntity and remove the Id and TimeStamp properties. Delete the constructor and add the Table attribute with schema. Remove the FirstName and LastName properties as they will be replaced by the Person-owned entity. This is where the class code stands at this time:

```
namespace AutoLot.Models.Entities;
[Table("Customers", Schema = "dbo")]
public partial class Customer : BaseEntity
{
  [InverseProperty(nameof(CreditRisk.Customer))]
  public virtual ICollection<CreditRisk> CreditRisks { get; set; }
  [InverseProperty(nameof(Order.Customer))]
  public virtual ICollection<Order> Orders { get; set; }
}
```

Like the Car entity, there are still some issues with this code that need to be fixed, and the owned entity must be added. The inverse property attributes need to be updated with the Navigation suffix and the types changed to an IEnumerable<T> and initialized. Update the code to match the following:

```
[InverseProperty(nameof(CreditRisk.CustomerNavigation))]
public virtual IEnumerable<CreditRisk> CreditRisks { get; set; } = new List<CreditRisk>();

[InverseProperty(nameof(Order.CustomerNavigation))]
public virtual IEnumerable<Order> Orders { get; set; } = new List<Order>();
```

The next step is to add the owned property. The relationship will be further configured in the Fluent API.

```
public Person PersonInformation { get; set; } = new Person();
```

The final step is to add the EntityTypeConfiguration attribute. Here is the complete class, with the final update in bold:

```
namespace AutoLot.Models.Entities;

[Table("Customers", Schema = "dbo")]
[EntityTypeConfiguration(typeof(CustomerConfiguration))]
public partial class Customer : BaseEntity
{
  public Person PersonInformation { get; set; } = new Person();
  [InverseProperty(nameof(CreditRisk.CustomerNavigation))]
  public virtual IEnumerable<CreditRisk> CreditRisks { get; set; } = new List<CreditRisk>();
  [InverseProperty(nameof(Order.CustomerNavigation))]
  public virtual IEnumerable<Order> Orders { get; set; } = new List<Order>();
}
```

The CustomerConfiguration Class

Add a new file named CustomerConfiguration.cs into the Configuration folder, and update the code to the following:

```
namespace AutoLot.Models.Entities.Configuration;

public class CustomerConfiguration : IEntityTypeConfiguration<Customer>
{
  public void Configure(EntityTypeBuilder<Customer> builder)
  {
    builder.OwnsOne(o => o. PersonInformation,
      pd =>
        {
          pd.Property<string>(nameof(Person.FirstName))
            .HasColumnName(nameof(Person.FirstName))
            .HasColumnType("nvarchar(50)");
          pd.Property<string>(nameof(Person.LastName))
            .HasColumnName(nameof(Person.LastName))
            .HasColumnType("nvarchar(50)");
          pd.Property(p => p.FullName)
            .HasColumnName(nameof(Person.FullName))
            .HasComputedColumnSql("[LastName] + ', ' + [FirstName]");
      });
    builder.Navigation(d => d. PersonInformation).IsRequired(true);
  }
}
```

The Customer entity uses the Person-owned property, so it cannot be configured as a temporal table.

Delete the Customer configuration code in the ApplicationDbContext OnModelCreating() method, and add the configuration line for the Customer:

```
protected override void OnModelCreating(ModelBuilder modelBuilder)
{
  new CarConfiguration().Configure(modelBuilder.Entity<Car>());
  new DriverConfiguration().Configure(modelBuilder.Entity<Driver>());
  new CarDriverConfiguration().Configure(modelBuilder.Entity<CarDriver>());
  new RadioConfiguration().Configure(modelBuilder.Entity<Radio>());
  new CustomerConfiguration().Configure(modelBuilder.Entity<Customer>());
}
```

The Make Entity

The Makes table was scaffolded to an entity class named Make. Inherit from BaseEntity and remove the Id and TimeStamp properties. Delete the constructor and add the Table attribute with schema. Here is the current state of the entity:

```
namespace AutoLot.Models.Entities;

[Table("Makes", Schema = "dbo")]
```

```
public partial class Make : BaseEntity
{
  [Required]
  [StringLength(50)]
  public string Name { get; set; }
  [InverseProperty(nameof(Inventory.Make))]
  public virtual ICollection<Inventory> Inventories { get; set; }
}
```

The following code shows the Cars navigation property corrected, renaming the Inventory/Inventories references to Car/Cars, the type changed to IEnumerable, and an initializer added:

```
[InverseProperty(nameof(Car.MakeNavigation))]
public virtual IEnumerable<Car> Cars { get; set; } = new List<Car>();
```

The MakeConfiguration Class

Create a new class named MakeConfiguration, implement the IEntityTypeConfiguration<Make> interface, and add the code from the ApplicationDbContext OnModelBuilding() method:

```
namespace AutoLot.Models.Entities.Configuration;

public class MakeConfiguration : IEntityTypeConfiguration<Make>
{
  public void Configure(EntityTypeBuilder<Radio> builder)
  {
  }
}
```

The Makes table will be configured as a temporal table, so add the following to the Configure() method:

```
public void Configure(EntityTypeBuilder<Make> builder)
{
  builder.ToTable( b => b.IsTemporal(t =>
  {
    t.HasPeriodEnd("ValidTo");
    t.HasPeriodStart("ValidFrom");
    t.UseHistoryTable("MakesAudit");
  }));
}
```

Delete the scaffolded configuration for the Make entity from the ApplicationDbContext Configure() method to complete the Make entity.

Update the OnModelCreating() method in the ApplicationDbContext:

```
protected override void OnModelCreating(ModelBuilder modelBuilder)
{
  new CarConfiguration().Configure(modelBuilder.Entity<Car>());
  new DriverConfiguration().Configure(modelBuilder.Entity<Driver>());
  new CarDriverConfiguration().Configure(modelBuilder.Entity<CarDriver>());
```

```
  new RadioConfiguration().Configure(modelBuilder.Entity<Radio>());
  new CustomerConfiguration().Configure(modelBuilder.Entity<Customer>());
  new MakeConfiguration().Configure(modelBuilder.Entity<Make>());
}
```

The CreditRisk Entity

The CreditRisks table was scaffolded to an entity class named CreditRisk. Inherit from BaseEntity and remove the Id and TimeStamp properties. Delete the constructor and add the Table attribute with schema. Remove the FirstName and LastName properties, as they will be replaced by the Person-owned entity. Here is the updated class code:

```
namespace AutoLot.Models.Entities;

[Table("CreditRisks", Schema = "dbo")]
[Index(nameof(CustomerId), Name = "IX_CreditRisks_CustomerId")]
[EntityTypeConfiguration(typeof(CreditRiskConfiguration))]
public partial class CreditRisk : BaseEntity
{
  public int CustomerId { get; set; }
  [ForeignKey(nameof(CustomerId))]
  [InverseProperty("CreditRisks")]
  public virtual Customer Customer { get; set; }
}
```

Fix the navigation property by using the nameof() method in the InverseProperty attribute and add the Navigation suffix to the property name.

```
[ForeignKey(nameof(CustomerId))]
[InverseProperty(nameof(Customer.CreditRisks))]
public virtual Customer CustomerNavigation { get; set; }
```

The final change is to add the owned property. The relationship will be further configured in the Fluent API.

```
public Person PersonInformation { get; set; } = new Person();
```

■ **Note** As discussed when the CreditRisk table was introduced, having the Person-owned class and a navigation property to the Customer table feels like an odd design, and in truth, it is. All of these tables were created to teach a different aspect of EF Core, and this is no different. Consider the extra FirstName/LastName as a place to put the uncreditworthy individual's alias.

That completes the CreditRisk entity.

The CreditRiskConfiguration Class

Add a new file named CreditRiskConfiguration.cs into the Configuration folder, and update the code to the following:

```
namespace AutoLot.Models.Entities.Configuration;

public class CreditRiskConfiguration : IEntityTypeConfiguration<CreditRisk>
{
  public void Configure(EntityTypeBuilder<CreditRisk> builder)
  {
    builder.HasOne(d => d.CustomerNavigation)
        .WithMany(p => p.CreditRisks)
        .HasForeignKey(d => d.CustomerId)
        .HasConstraintName("FK_CreditRisks_Customers");

    builder.OwnsOne(o => o.PersonInformation,
        pd =>
        {
          pd.Property<string>(nameof(Person.FirstName))
            .HasColumnName(nameof(Person.FirstName))
            .HasColumnType("nvarchar(50)");
          pd.Property<string>(nameof(Person.LastName))
            .HasColumnName(nameof(Person.LastName))
            .HasColumnType("nvarchar(50)");
          pd.Property(p => p.FullName)
            .HasColumnName(nameof(Person.FullName))
            .HasComputedColumnSql("[LastName] + ', ' + [FirstName]");
      });

    builder.Navigation(d => d.PersonInformation).IsRequired(true);
  }
}
```

The CreditRisk entity uses the Person-owned property, so it cannot be configured as a temporal table.

Update the ApplicationDbContext OnModelCreating() method by removing the CreditRisk configuration and adding the line for the CreditRiskConfiguration class:

```
protected override void OnModelCreating(ModelBuilder modelBuilder)
{
  new CarConfiguration().Configure(modelBuilder.Entity<Car>());
  new DriverConfiguration().Configure(modelBuilder.Entity<Driver>());
  new CarDriverConfiguration().Configure(modelBuilder.Entity<CarDriver>());
  new RadioConfiguration().Configure(modelBuilder.Entity<Radio>());
  new CustomerConfiguration().Configure(modelBuilder.Entity<Customer>());
  new MakeConfiguration().Configure(modelBuilder.Entity<Make>());
  new CreditRiskConfiguration().Configure(modelBuilder.Entity<CreditRisk>());
}
```

The Order Entity

The Orders table was scaffolded to an entity class named Order. Inherit from BaseEntity and remove the Id and TimeStamp properties. Delete the constructor and add the Table attribute with schema. Here is the current code:

```
namespace AutoLot.Models.Entities;

[Table("Orders", Schema = "dbo")]
[Index(nameof(CarId), Name = "IX_Orders_CarId")]
[Index(nameof(CustomerId), nameof(CarId), Name = "IX_Orders_CustomerId_CarId", IsUnique
= true)]
public partial class Order : BaseEntity
{
  public int CarId { get; set; }
  [ForeignKey(nameof(CarId))]
  [InverseProperty(nameof(Inventory.Orders))]
  public virtual Inventory Car { get; set; }

  public int CustomerId { get; set; }
  [ForeignKey(nameof(CustomerId))]
  [InverseProperty("Orders")]
  public virtual Customer { get; set; }
}
```

The Car and Customer navigation properties need the Navigation suffix added to their property names. The Car navigation property needs the type corrected to Car from Inventory. The inverse property needs the nameof() method to use Car.Orders instead of Inventory.Orders. The Customer navigation property needs to use the nameof() method for the InverseProperty.

```
[ForeignKey(nameof(CarId))]
[InverseProperty(nameof(Car.Orders))]
public virtual Car CarNavigation { get; set; }

[ForeignKey(nameof(CustomerId))]
[InverseProperty(nameof(Customer.Orders))]
public virtual Customer CustomerNavigation { get; set; }
```

The final step is to add the EntityTypeConfiguration attribute with the update in bold:

```
namespace AutoLot.Models.Entities;

[Table("Orders", Schema = "dbo")]
[Index(nameof(CarId), Name = "IX_Orders_CarId")]
[Index(nameof(CustomerId), nameof(CarId), Name = "IX_Orders_CustomerId_CarId", IsUnique
= true)]
[EntityTypeConfiguration(typeof(OrderConfiguration))]
public partial class Order : BaseEntity
{
...
}
```

That completes the Order entity.

The OrderConfiguration Class

Add a new file named OrderConfiguration.cs into the Configuration folder, and update the code to the following:

```
namespace AutoLot.Models.Entities.Configuration;

public class OrderConfiguration : IEntityTypeConfiguration<Order>
{
  public void Configure(EntityTypeBuilder<Order> builder)
  {
    builder.HasIndex(cr => new { cr.CustomerId, cr.CarId }).IsUnique(true);
    builder.HasQueryFilter(e => e.CarNavigation!.IsDrivable);
    builder.HasOne(d => d.CarNavigation)
        .WithMany(p => p.Orders)
        .HasForeignKey(d => d.CarId)
        .OnDelete(DeleteBehavior.ClientSetNull)
        .HasConstraintName("FK_Orders_Inventory");
    builder.HasOne(d => d.CustomerNavigation)
        .WithMany(p => p.Orders)
        .HasForeignKey(d => d.CustomerId)
        .HasConstraintName("FK_Orders_Customers");
  }
}
```

The Orders table will be configured as a temporal table, so add the following to the Configure() method:

```
public void Configure(EntityTypeBuilder<CarDriver> builder)
{
  //omitted for brevity
  builder.ToTable( b => b.IsTemporal(t =>
  {
    t.HasPeriodEnd("ValidTo");
    t.HasPeriodStart("ValidFrom");
    t.UseHistoryTable("OrdersAudit");
  }));
}
```

Update the ApplicationDbContext OnModelCreating() method by removing the Order configuration and adding the line for the OrderConfiguration class:

```
protected override void OnModelCreating(ModelBuilder modelBuilder)
{
  new CarConfiguration().Configure(modelBuilder.Entity<Car>());
  new DriverConfiguration().Configure(modelBuilder.Entity<Driver>());
  new CarDriverConfiguration().Configure(modelBuilder.Entity<CarDriver>());
  new RadioConfiguration().Configure(modelBuilder.Entity<Radio>());
  new CustomerConfiguration().Configure(modelBuilder.Entity<Customer>());
  new MakeConfiguration().Configure(modelBuilder.Entity<Make>());
  new CreditRiskConfiguration().Configure(modelBuilder.Entity<CreditRisk>());
  new OrderConfiguration().Configure(modelBuilder.Entity<Order>());
}
```

■ **Note** At this time, both the AutoLot.Models project and the AutoLot.Dal project should build properly.

The SeriLogEntry Entity

The database needs an additional table to hold log records. The ASP.NET Core projects later in this book use the SeriLog logging framework, and one of the options is to write log records to a SQL Server table. We are going to add the table now, knowing it will be used a few chapters from now.

The table does not relate to any other tables and does not use the `BaseEntity` class. Add a new class file named `SeriLogEntry.cs` in the `Entities` folder. The code is listed in its entirety here:

```
namespace AutoLot.Models.Entities;

[Table("SeriLogs", Schema = "Logging")]
[EntityTypeConfiguration(typeof(SeriLogEntryConfiguration))]
public class SeriLogEntry
{
  [Key, DatabaseGenerated(DatabaseGeneratedOption.Identity)]
  public int Id { get; set; }
  public string Message { get; set; }
  public string MessageTemplate { get; set; }
  [MaxLength(128)]
  public string Level { get; set; }
  [DataType(DataType.DateTime)]
  public DateTime TimeStamp { get; set; }
  public string Exception { get; set; }
  public string Properties { get; set; }
  public string LogEvent { get; set; }
  public string SourceContext { get; set; }
  public string RequestPath { get; set; }
  public string ActionName { get; set; }
  public string ApplicationName { get; set; }
  public string MachineName { get; set; }
  public string FilePath { get; set; }
  public string MemberName { get; set; }
  public int LineNumber { get; set; }
  [NotMapped]
  public XElement PropertiesXml => (Properties != null)? XElement.Parse(Properties):null;
}
```

■ **Note** The `TimeStamp` property in this entity is not the same as the `TimeStamp` property in the `BaseEntity` class. The names are the same, but in this table it holds the date and time of when the entry was logged and not the `rowversion` used in the other entities.

Update the ApplicationDbContext Class

Since this is a new table, a new DbSet<SeriLogEntry> property must be added into the ApplicationDbContext class. Add the following to the DbSet<T> properties:

```
public virtual DbSet<SeriLogEntry> SeriLogEntries { get; set; }
```

The SerilogEntryConfiguration Class

Add a new file named SeriLogEntryConfiguration.cs into the Configuration folder, and update the code to the following:

```
namespace AutoLot.Models.Entities.Configuration;

public class SeriLogEntryConfiguration : IEntityTypeConfiguration<SeriLogEntry>
{
  public void Configure(EntityTypeBuilder<SeriLogEntry> builder)
  {
    builder.Property(e => e.Properties).HasColumnType("Xml");
    builder.Property(e => e.TimeStamp).HasDefaultValueSql("GetDate()");
  }
}
```

Update the ApplicationDbContext OnModelCreating() method by adding the line for the SeriLogEntryConfiguration class:

```
protected override void OnModelCreating(ModelBuilder modelBuilder)
{
  new CarConfiguration().Configure(modelBuilder.Entity<Car>());
  new DriverConfiguration().Configure(modelBuilder.Entity<Driver>());
  new CarDriverConfiguration().Configure(modelBuilder.Entity<CarDriver>());
  new RadioConfiguration().Configure(modelBuilder.Entity<Radio>());
  new CustomerConfiguration().Configure(modelBuilder.Entity<Customer>());
  new CreditRiskConfiguration().Configure(modelBuilder.Entity<CreditRisk>());
  new OrderConfiguration().Configure(modelBuilder.Entity<Order>());
  new SeriLogEntryConfiguration().Configure(modelBuilder.Entity<SeriLogEntry>());
}
```

The View Models

The CustomerOrderView was scaffolded into a keyless entity along with the database tables. Another term used for keyless entities is view models, as they are designed to view data, usually from more than one table. This section will update the scaffolded entity into its final form as well as add a new view model to view temporal data. Start by adding a new folder named ViewModels in the AutoLot.Models project.

The CustomerOrderViewModel

Move the CustomerOrderView.cs class from the Entities folder into this folder and rename the file to CustomerOrderViewModel.cs and the class to CustomerOrderViewModel. Add an EntityTypeConfiguration attribute for the soon to be created configuration class. Also implement the INonPersisted interface (which will be created next):

```
namespace AutoLot.Models.ViewModels;

[Keyless]
[EntityTypeConfiguration(typeof(CustomerOrderViewModelConfiguration))]
public partial class CustomerOrderViewModel : INonPersisted
{
}
```

Add a new NotMapped property named FullDetail, as follows:

```
[NotMapped]
public string FullDetail => $"{FirstName} {LastName} ordered a {Color} {Make} named
{PetName}";
```

The FullDetail property is decorated with the NotMapped data annotation. Recall that this informs EF Core that this property is not to be included in the data coming from the database.

Next, add the four new properties for the Car entity to the view model:

```
public bool? IsDrivable { get; set; }
public string Display { get; set; }
public string Price {get;set; }
public DateTime? DateBuilt {get;set; }
```

Next add an override for the ToString() method. The ToString() override is also ignored by EF Core:

```
public override string ToString() => FullDetail;
```

That completes the changes to the view model. The complete file is shown here:

```
namespace AutoLot.Models.ViewModels;

[Keyless]
[EntityTypeConfiguration(typeof(CustomerOrderViewModelConfiguration))]
public partial class CustomerOrderViewModel : INonPersisted
{
  [Required]
  [StringLength(50)]
  public string FirstName { get; set; }
  [Required]
  [StringLength(50)]
  public string LastName { get; set; }
  [Required]
  [StringLength(50)]
  public string Color { get; set; }
  [Required]
  [StringLength(50)]
  public string PetName { get; set; }
  [Required]
```

```
  [StringLength(50)]
  public string Make { get; set; }
  public bool? IsDrivable { get; set; }
  public string Display { get;set; }
  [NotMapped]
  public string FullDetail => $"{FirstName} {LastName} ordered a {Color} {Make} named
{PetName}";
  public override string ToString() => FullDetail;
}
```

As a reminder, the KeyLess data annotation indicates this is an entity that works with data that does not have a primary key.

Add the INonPersisted Interface

Create a new folder named Interfaces in the ViewModels folder. In this folder, add a new interface named INonPersisted, and update the code to the following:

```
namespace AutoLot.Models.ViewModels.Interfaces;

public interface INonPersisted { }
```

Update the ApplicationDbContext Class

Since the CustomerOrderView class was renamed to CustomerOrderViewModel, the ApplicationDbContext class must be updated. Locate the DbSet< CustomerOrderView> property and update the line to the following:

```
public virtual DbSet< CustomerOrderViewModel> CustomerOrderViewModels { get; set; }
```

The CustomerOrderViewModelConfiguration Class

Create new folder named Configuration in the ViewModels folder. In this folder, add a new file named CustomerOrderViewModelConfiguration.cs into the Configuration folder, and update the code to the following:

```
namespace AutoLot.Models.ViewModels.Configuration;

public class CustomerOrderViewModelConfiguration : IEntityTypeConfiguration<CustomerOrder
ViewModel>
{
  public void Configure(EntityTypeBuilder<CustomerOrderViewModel> builder)
  {
    builder.ToView("CustomerOrderView");
  }
}
```

Update the ApplicationDbContext OnModelCreating() method by deleting the configuration for the CustomerOrderView class and adding the line for the CustomerOrderViewModelConfiguration class:

```
protected override void OnModelCreating(ModelBuilder modelBuilder)
{
  new CarConfiguration().Configure(modelBuilder.Entity<Car>());
  new DriverConfiguration().Configure(modelBuilder.Entity<Driver>());
  new RadioConfiguration().Configure(modelBuilder.Entity<Radio>());
  new CustomerConfiguration().Configure(modelBuilder.Entity<Customer>());
  new CreditRiskConfiguration().Configure(modelBuilder.Entity<CreditRisk>());
  new OrderConfiguration().Configure(modelBuilder.Entity<Order>());
  new SeriLogEntryConfiguration().Configure(modelBuilder.Entity<SeriLogEntry>());
  new CustomerOrderViewModelConfiguration()
    .Configure(modelBuilder.Entity<CustomerOrderViewModel>());
}
```

Update the GlobalUsings.cs Files

The new namespaces need to be added into the GlobalUsings.cs files in the AutoLot.Dal and AutoLot.Models projects. Add the following global using statements to each file:

```
//AutoLot.Models
global using AutoLot.Models.ViewModels.Configuration;
global using AutoLot.Models.ViewModels.Interfaces;

//AutoLot.Dal
global using AutoLot.Models.ViewModels;
global using AutoLot.Models.ViewModels.Configuration;
global using AutoLot.Models.ViewModels.Interfaces;
```

The TemporalViewModel

Recall from the previous chapter that when working with temporal data, it helps to have a class that stores the row along with the row's from and to dates. Create a new class named TemporalViewModel in the Entities folder. Update the code to the following:

```
namespace AutoLot.Models.ViewModels;

public class TemporalViewModel<T> where T: BaseEntity, new()
{
  public T Entity { get; set; }
  public DateTime ValidFrom { get; set; }
  public DateTime ValidTo { get; set; }
}
```

Since this class is only going to be used to store the results of queries on temporal tables, it does not need to be configured in ApplicationDbContext.

Update the ApplicationDbContext

It is time to update the ApplicationDbContext.cs file. Delete the default constructor, as we won't need it. It is only used in conjunction with an OnConfiguring() method, which, as discussed earlier, is considered not a good practice to use. The next constructor takes an instance of the DbContextOptions object and is fine for now. The event hooks for DbContext and ChangeTracker will be added later in this chapter.

Add the Mapped Database Functions

Recall that user-defined database functions can be mapped to C# functions for use in LINQ queries. Add the following functions to ApplicationDbContext for the two user-defined functions:

```
[DbFunction("udf_CountOfMakes", Schema = "dbo")]
public static int InventoryCountFor(int makeId)
  => throw new NotSupportedException();

[DbFunction("udtf_GetCarsForMake", Schema = "dbo")]
public IQueryable<Car> GetCarsFor(int makeId)
  => FromExpression(() => GetCarsFor(makeId));
```

Handling DbContext and ChangeTracker Events

Navigate to the constructor of ApplicationDbContext and add the three DbContext events discussed in the previous chapter.

```
public ApplicationDbContext(DbContextOptions<ApplicationDbContext> options)
  : base(options)
{
  SavingChanges += (sender, args) =>
  {
    string cs = ((ApplicationDbContext)sender).Database!.GetConnectionString();
    Console.WriteLine($"Saving changes for {cs}");
  };
  SavedChanges += (sender, args) =>
  {
    string cs = ((ApplicationDbContext)sender).Database!.GetConnectionString();
    Console.WriteLine($"Saved {args!.EntitiesSavedCount} changes for {cs}");
  };
  SaveChangesFailed += (sender, args) =>
  {
    Console.WriteLine($"An exception occurred! {args.Exception.Message} entities");
  };
}
```

Next, add handlers for the ChangeTracker, StateChanged, and Tracked events.

```
public ApplicationDbContext(DbContextOptions<ApplicationDbContext> options)
  : base(options)
{
...
  ChangeTracker.Tracked += ChangeTracker_Tracked;
  ChangeTracker.StateChanged += ChangeTracker_StateChanged;
}
```

As a refresher, EntityTrackedEventArgs holds a reference to the entity that triggered the event and whether it came from a query (loaded from the database) or was added programmatically. Add the following event handler in ApplicationDbContext:

```
private void ChangeTracker_Tracked(object sender, EntityTrackedEventArgs e)
{
  var source = (e.FromQuery) ? "Database" : "Code";
  if (e.Entry.Entity is Car c)
  {
    Console.WriteLine($"Car entry {c.PetName} was added from {source}");
  }
}
```

The StateChanged event is fired when a tracked entity's state changes. In the following event handler, if the entity's NewState is Unchanged, the OldState is examined to see whether the entity was added or modified. Add the following event handler into ApplicationDbContext:

```
private void ChangeTracker_StateChanged(object sender, EntityStateChangedEventArgs e)
{
  if (e.Entry.Entity is not Car c)
  {
    return;
  }
  var action = string.Empty;
  Console.WriteLine($"Car {c.PetName} was {e.OldState} before the state changed to
{e.NewState}");
  switch (e.NewState)
  {
    case EntityState.Unchanged:
      action = e.OldState switch
      {
        EntityState.Added => "Added",
        EntityState.Modified => "Edited",
        _ => action
      };
      Console.WriteLine($"The object was {action}");
      break;
  }
}
```

Override the Conventions

Add the override for ConfigureConventions. As a reminder, the following overrides will default strings to nvarchar(50) and will ignore entities that implement the INonPersisted interface. Any data annotations or Fluent API commands that contradict those two settings will override the configured conventions:

```
protected override void ConfigureConventions(ModelConfigurationBuilder configurationBuilder)
{
  configurationBuilder.Properties<string>().HaveMaxLength(50);
  configurationBuilder.IgnoreAny<INonPersisted>();
}
```

Override the SaveChanges Method

Recall that the SaveChanges() method on the base DbContext class persists the data updates, additions, and deletions to the database. Overriding that method in the derived DbContext enables exception handing to be encapsulated in one place. Add the following override to the SaveChanges() method:

```
public override int SaveChanges()
{
  try
  {
    return base.SaveChanges();
  }
  catch (DbUpdateConcurrencyException ex)
  {
    //A concurrency error occurred
    //Should log and handle intelligently
    throw new CustomConcurrencyException("A concurrency error happened.", ex);
  }
  catch (RetryLimitExceededException ex)
  {
    //DbResiliency retry limit exceeded
    //Should log and handle intelligently
    throw new CustomRetryLimitExceededException("There is a problem with SQL Server.", ex);
  }
  catch (DbUpdateException ex)
  {
    //Should log and handle intelligently
    throw new CustomDbUpdateException("An error occurred updating the database", ex);
  }
  catch (Exception ex)
  {
    //Should log and handle intelligently
    throw new CustomException("An error occurred updating the database", ex);
  }
}
```

Create the Next Migration and Update the Database

At this point in the chapter, we are ready to create another migration to update the database. Enter the following commands in the AutoLot.Dal project directory (each command must be entered on one line):

```
dotnet ef migrations add UpdatedEntities -o EfStructures\Migrations -c  AutoLot.Dal.
EfStructures.ApplicationDbContext

dotnet ef database update UpdatedEntities -c AutoLot.Dal.EfStructures.ApplicationDbContext
```

Use EF Migrations to Create/Update Database Objects

While the `CustomerOrderViewModel` was scaffolded from the `CustomerOrderView` in the database, the view itself is not represented in the C# code. If you were to drop the database and re-create it using the EF Core migrations, the view will not exist. For database objects, you have two options: maintain them separately and apply them using SSMS/Azure Data Studio or leverage the EF Core migrations to handle their creation.

Recall that each EF Core migration file has an `Up()` method (for applying the migration to the database) and a `Down()` method (for rolling the changes back). The `MigrationBuilder` also has a `Sql()` method that executes SQL statements directly against the database. By adding the `CREATE` and `DROP` statements into the `Up()` and `Down()` methods of a migration, the migration system will handle applying (and rolling back) database changes.

Add the MigrationHelpers Class

A helper class will hold all the SQL statements used by the custom migration. This separation prevents losing the code if the migration is removed from the system. Create a new `static` class named `MigrationHelpers.cs` in the `EfStructures` folder of the AutoLot.Dal project.

Add a new file named `MigrationHelpers.cs` in the `EfStructures` folder of the `AutoLot.Dal` project. Add a `using` statement for `Microsoft.EntityFrameworkCore.Migrations`, make the class `public` and `static`, and add the following methods, which use the `MigrationBuilder` to execute SQL statements against the database:

```
namespace AutoLot.Dal.EfStructures;

public static class MigrationHelpers
{
  public static void CreateCustomerOrderView(MigrationBuilder migrationBuilder)
  {
    migrationBuilder.Sql(@"exec (N'
        CREATE VIEW [dbo].[CustomerOrderView]
        AS
        SELECT c.FirstName, c.LastName, i.Color, i.PetName,
          i.DateBuilt, i.IsDrivable, i.Price, i.Display, m.Name AS Make
        FROM dbo.Orders o
        INNER JOIN dbo.Customers c ON c.Id = o.CustomerId
        INNER JOIN dbo.Inventory i ON i.Id = o.CarId
        INNER JOIN dbo.Makes m ON m.Id = i.MakeId')");
  }
  public static void DropCustomerOrderView(MigrationBuilder migrationBuilder)
  {
```

```
    migrationBuilder.Sql("EXEC (N' DROP VIEW [dbo].[CustomerOrderView] ')");
  }

  public static void CreateSproc(MigrationBuilder migrationBuilder)
  {
    migrationBuilder.Sql(@"exec (N'
        CREATE PROCEDURE [dbo].[GetPetName]
          @carID int,
          @petName nvarchar(50) output
        AS
          SELECT @petName = PetName from dbo.Inventory where Id = @carID')");
  }
  public static void DropSproc(MigrationBuilder migrationBuilder)
  {
    migrationBuilder.Sql("EXEC (N' DROP PROCEDURE [dbo].[GetPetName]')");
  }

  public static void CreateFunctions(MigrationBuilder migrationBuilder)
  {
    migrationBuilder.Sql(@"exec (N'
        CREATE FUNCTION [dbo].[udtf_GetCarsForMake] ( @makeId int )
        RETURNS TABLE
        AS
        RETURN
        (
          SELECT Id, IsDrivable, DateBuilt, Color, PetName, MakeId, TimeStamp,
          Display, Price
          FROM Inventory WHERE MakeId = @makeId
        )')");
    migrationBuilder.Sql(@"exec (N'
        CREATE FUNCTION [dbo].[udf_CountOfMakes] ( @makeid int )
        RETURNS int
        AS
        BEGIN
          DECLARE @Result int
          SELECT @Result = COUNT(makeid) FROM dbo.Inventory WHERE makeid = @makeid
          RETURN @Result
        END')");
  }
  public static void DropFunctions(MigrationBuilder migrationBuilder)
  {
    migrationBuilder.Sql("EXEC (N' DROP FUNCTION [dbo].[udtf_GetCarsForMake]')");
    migrationBuilder.Sql("EXEC (N' DROP FUNCTION [dbo].[udf_CountOfMakes]')");
  }
}
```

■ **Note** The CREATE statements are included in a SQL Server exec statement so they will successfully run when the migrations are scripted. Each migration process is wrapped in an IF block, and creation statements must be wrapped in exec statements when executed inside an IF.

Create and Update the Migration

Calling the dotnet migrations add command when there aren't any model changes will still create the properly timestamped migration files with empty Up() and Down() methods. Execute the following to create the empty migration (but do not apply the migration):

```
dotnet ef migrations add SQL -o EfStructures\Migrations -c AutoLot.Dal.EfStructures.
ApplicationDbContext
```

Open the newly created migration class and notice that the Up() and Down() methods are empty. That is the key to this technique. Using a blank migration that is updated using the MigrationHelpers methods prevents mixing custom code with EF Core–generated code. The static methods to create the database objects go into the migration's Up() method, and the methods to drop the database objects go into the migration's Down() method. When this migration is applied, the SQL Server objects are created, and when the migration is rolled back, the SQL Server objects are dropped. Here is the updated migration code listing:

```
namespace AutoLot.Dal.EfStructures.Migrations;

public partial class SQL : Migration
{
  protected override void Up(MigrationBuilder migrationBuilder)
  {
    MigrationHelpers.CreateCustomerOrderView(migrationBuilder);
    MigrationHelpers.CreateSproc(migrationBuilder);
    MigrationHelpers.CreateFunctions(migrationBuilder);
  }

  protected override void Down(MigrationBuilder migrationBuilder)
  {
    MigrationHelpers.DropCustomerOrderView(migrationBuilder);
    MigrationHelpers.DropSproc(migrationBuilder);
    MigrationHelpers.DropFunctions(migrationBuilder);
  }
}
```

Apply the Migration

If you dropped your database to run the initial migration, you can apply this migration and move on. Apply the migration by executing the following command:

```
dotnet ef database update -c AutoLot.Dal.EfStructures.ApplicationDbContext
```

If you did not drop your database for the first migration, the procedure and view already exist, and the create SQL statements for those database objects will fail, rolling the entire migration back. The simple fix is to drop the procedure and view using SSMS or Azure Data Studio, like this:

```
DROP VIEW [dbo].[CustomerOrderView]
GO
DROP PROCEDURE [dbo].[GetPetName]
GO
```

Now, apply the migration to add the SQL objects into the AutoLot database:

```
dotnet ef database update SQL -c AutoLot.Dal.EfStructures.ApplicationDbContext
```

■ **Note** You could also write code that will first check for an object's existence and drop it if it already exists, but I find that overkill for an issue happens only once when transitioning from database first to code first.

Add the Repositories

A common data access design pattern is the *repository pattern*. As described by Martin Fowler, the core of this pattern is to mediate between the domain and data mapping layers. Having a generic base repository that contains the common data access code helps to eliminate duplication of code. Having specific repositories and interfaces that derive from a base repository also works well with the dependency injection framework in ASP.NET Core.

■ **Note** This next section is not meant to be (nor does it pretend to be) a literal interpretation of Mr. Fowler's design pattern. If you are interested in the original pattern that motivated this version, you can find more information on the repository pattern at www.martinfowler.com/eaaCatalog/repository.html.

Each of the domain entities in the AutoLot data access layer will have a strongly typed repo to encapsulate all the data access work. To start, create a folder named Repos in the AutoLot.Dal project to hold all the classes.

Add the IBaseViewRepo Interface

The IBaseViewRepo interface exposes three methods for getting data from a view model. Make a new folder named Base in the Repos directory. Add a new interface into the Repos\Base folder named IBaseViewRepo. Update the code to match the following:

```
namespace AutoLot.Dal.Repos.Base;

public interface IBaseViewRepo<T>: IDisposable where T : class,new()
{
  ApplicationDbContext Context {get;}
  IEnumerable<T> ExecuteSqlString(string sql);
  IEnumerable<T> GetAll();
  IEnumerable<T> GetAllIgnoreQueryFilters();
}
```

Add the BaseViewRepo Implementation

Next, add a class named BaseViewRepo to the Repos\Base directory. This class will implement the IBaseViewRepo interface and provide the implementation for the interface. Make the class generic with type T and constrain the type to class and new(), which limits the types to classes that have a parameterless constructor. Implement the IBaseViewRepo<T> interface, as follows:

```
namespace AutoLot.Dal.Repos.Base;

public abstract class BaseViewRepo<T> : IBaseViewRepo<T> where T : class, new()
{
  //implementation goes here
}
```

The repo needs an instance of the ApplicationDbContext injected into a constructor. When used with the ASP.NET Core dependency injection (DI) container, the container will handle the lifetime of the context. A second constructor, used for integration testing, will accept an instance of DbContextOptions and use that to create an instance of the ApplicationDbContext. That context will need to be disposed since it isn't being managed by a DI container. Because this class is abstract, both constructors are protected. Add the following code for the public ApplicationDbContext, the two constructors, and the Dispose pattern:

```
private readonly bool _disposeContext;
public ApplicationDbContext Context { get; }

protected BaseViewRepo(ApplicationDbContext context)
{
  Context = context;
  _disposeContext = false;
}

protected BaseViewRepo(DbContextOptions<ApplicationDbContext> options) : this(new
ApplicationDbContext(options))
{
  _disposeContext = true;
}

public virtual void Dispose()
{
  Dispose(true);
  GC.SuppressFinalize(this);
}
private bool _isDisposed;
protected virtual void Dispose(bool disposing)
{
  if (_isDisposed)
  {
    return;
  }

  if (disposing)
  {
    if (_disposeContext)
    {
      Context.Dispose();
    }
  }
  _isDisposed = true;
}
```

```
~BaseViewRepo()
{
  Dispose(false);
}
```

The DbSet<T> properties of ApplicationDbContext can be referenced by using the DbContext.Set<T>() method. Create a public property named Table of type DbSet<T> and set the value in the initial constructor, like this:

```
public DbSet<T> Table { get; }
protected BaseViewRepo(ApplicationDbContext context)
{
  Context = context;
  Table = Context.Set<T>();
  _disposeContext = false;
}
```

Implement the Read Methods

The next series of methods returns records using LINQ statements or a SQL query. The GetAll() methods return all the records from the table. The first retrieves them in database order, and the second turns off all query filters.

```
public virtual IEnumerable <T> GetAll()
    => Table.AsQueryable();

public virtual IEnumerable<T> GetAllIgnoreQueryFilters()
    => Table.AsQueryable().IgnoreQueryFilters();
```

The ExecuteSqlString() method is there to execute FromSqlRaw() queries:

```
public IEnumerable<T> ExecuteSqlString(string sql) => Table.FromSqlRaw(sql);
```

Add the IBaseRepo Interface

The IBaseRepo interface exposes many of the common methods used in data access with the DbSet<T> properties where T is of type BaseEntity. Add a new interface into the Repos\Base folder named IBaseRepo. The full interface is listed here:

```
namespace AutoLot.Dal.Repos.Base;

public interface IBaseRepo<T> : IBaseViewRepo<T> where T : BaseEntity, new()
{
  T Find(int? id);
  T FindAsNoTracking(int id);
  T FindIgnoreQueryFilters(int id);
  void ExecuteParameterizedQuery(string sql, object[] sqlParametersObjects);
  int Add(T entity, bool persist = true);
  int AddRange(IEnumerable<T> entities, bool persist = true);
  int Update(T entity, bool persist = true);
```

```
    int UpdateRange(IEnumerable<T> entities, bool persist = true);
    int Delete(int id, byte[] timeStamp, bool persist = true);
    int Delete(T entity, bool persist = true);
    int DeleteRange(IEnumerable<T> entities, bool persist = true);
    int SaveChanges();
}
```

Add the BaseRepo Implementation

Next, add a class named BaseRepo to the Repos\Base directory. This class implements the IBaseRepo interface, inherits from the BaseViewRepo<T> abstract class, and provides the core functionality for the type-specific repos that will be built for each entity. Make the class generic with type T and constrain the type to BaseEntity and new(), which limits the types to classes that inherit from BaseEntity and have a parameterless constructor. Implement the IBaseRepo<T> interface, as follows:

```
namespace AutoLot.Dal.Repos.Base;

public abstract class BaseRepo<T> : BaseViewRepo<T>, IBaseRepo<T> where T :
BaseEntity, new()
{
  //implementation goes here
}
```

The repo leverages the BaseViewRepo<T> for the handling of the ApplicationDbContext instance as well as the Dispose() pattern implementation. Add the following code for the two constructors:

```
protected BaseRepo(ApplicationDbContext context) : base(context) {}
protected BaseRepo(DbContextOptions<ApplicationDbContext> options) : this(new
ApplicationDbContext(options))
{
}
```

Implement the SaveChanges Method

The BaseRepo has a SaveChanges() method that calls into the overridden SaveChanges() method on the ApplicationDbContext class. Add the following code to the BaseRepo class:

```
public int SaveChanges()
{
  try
  {
    return Context.SaveChanges();
  }
  catch (CustomException ex)
  {
    //Should handle intelligently - already logged
    throw;
  }
  catch (Exception ex)
  {
```

```
    //Should log and handle intelligently
    throw new CustomException("An error occurred updating the database", ex);
  }
}
```

Implement the Common Read Methods

The next series of methods returns records using LINQ statements. The `Find()` method takes the primary key value(s) and searches the `ChangeTracker` first. If the entity is already being tracked, the tracked instance is returned. If not, the record is retrieved from the database.

```
public virtual T Find(int? id) => Table.Find(id);
```

The two additional `Find()` methods augment the `Find()` base method. The next method demonstrates retrieving a record but not adding it to the `ChangeTracker` using `AsNoTrackingWithIdentityResolution()`. Add the following code to the class:

```
public virtual T FindAsNoTracking(int id) =>
  Table.AsNoTrackingWithIdentityResolution().FirstOrDefault(x => x.Id == id);
```

The next variation removes the query filters from the entity and then uses the shorthand version (skipping the `Where()` method) to get `FirstOrDefault()`. Add the following to the class:

```
public virtual T FindIgnoreQueryFilters(int id) =>
  Table.IgnoreQueryFilters().FirstOrDefault(x => x.Id == id);
```

The final method's next variation is used to execute a parameterized stored procedure. Add the final method to the class:

```
public virtual void ExecuteParameterizedQuery(string sql, object[] sqlParametersObjects)
  => Context.Database.ExecuteSqlRaw(sql, sqlParametersObjects);
```

The Add, Update, and Delete Methods

The next block of code to be added wraps the matching `Add()`/`AddRange()`, `Update()`/`UpdateRange()`, and `Remove()`/`RemoveRange()` methods on the specific `DbSet<T>` property. The `persist` parameter determines whether the repo executes `SaveChanges()` immediately when the repository methods are called. All the methods are marked `virtual` to allow for downstream overriding. Add the following code to your class:

```
public virtual int Add(T entity, bool persist = true)
{
  Table.Add(entity);
  return persist ? SaveChanges() : 0;
}
public virtual int AddRange(IEnumerable<T> entities, bool persist = true)
{
  Table.AddRange(entities);
  return persist ? SaveChanges() : 0;
}
public virtual int Update(T entity, bool persist = true)
```

```
{
  Table.Update(entity);
  return persist ? SaveChanges() : 0;
}
public virtual int UpdateRange(IEnumerable<T> entities, bool persist = true)
{
  Table.UpdateRange(entities);
  return persist ? SaveChanges() : 0;
}
public virtual int Delete(T entity, bool persist = true)
{
  Table.Remove(entity);
  return persist ? SaveChanges() : 0;
}
public virtual int DeleteRange(IEnumerable<T> entities, bool persist = true)
{
  Table.RemoveRange(entities);
  return persist ? SaveChanges() : 0;
}
```

There is one more `Delete()` method that doesn't follow the same pattern. This method uses `EntityState` to conduct the delete operation, which is used fairly often in ASP.NET Core operations to cut down on the network traffic. It is listed here:

```
public int Delete(int id, byte[] timeStamp, bool persist = true)
{
  var entity = new T {Id = id, TimeStamp = timeStamp};
  Context.Entry(entity).State = EntityState.Deleted;
  return persist ? SaveChanges() : 0;
}
```

This concludes the `BaseRepo` class, and now it's time to build the repo for temporal table support.

Add the ITemporalTableBaseRepo Interface

The `ITemporalTableBaseRepo` interface exposes the temporal capabilities of EF Core. Add a new interface into the `Repos\Base` folder named `ITemporalTableBaseRepo`. The full interface is listed here:

```
namespace AutoLot.Dal.Repos.Base;

public interface ITemporalTableBaseRepo<T> : IBaseRepo<T> where T : BaseEntity, new()
{
  IEnumerable<TemporalViewModel<T>> GetAllHistory();
  IEnumerable<TemporalViewModel<T>> GetHistoryAsOf(DateTime dateTime);
  IEnumerable<TemporalViewModel<T>> GetHistoryBetween(DateTime startDateTime, DateTime
endDateTime);
  IEnumerable<TemporalViewModel<T>> GetHistoryContainedIn(DateTime startDateTime, DateTime
endDateTime);
  IEnumerable<TemporalViewModel<T>> GetHistoryFromTo(DateTime startDateTime, DateTime
endDateTime);
}
```

Add the TemporalTableBaseRepo Implementation

Next, add a class named TemporalTableBaseRepo to the Repos\Base directory. This class implements the ITemporalTableBaseRepo interface, inherits from BaseRepo<T>, and provides the functionality for using temporal tables. Also make the class generic with type T and constrain the type to BaseEntity and new(). Implement the ITemporalTableBaseRepo<T> interface, as follows:

```
namespace AutoLot.Dal.Repos.Base;

public abstract class TemporalTableBaseRepo<T> : BaseRepo<T>, ITemporalTableBaseRepo<T>
    where T : BaseEntity, new()
{
  //implementation goes here
}
```

The repo leverages the BaseRepo<T> for the handling of the ApplicationDbContext instance as well as the Dispose() pattern implementation. Add the following code for the two constructors:

```
protected TemporalTableBaseRepo(ApplicationDbContext context) : base(context) {}
protected TemporalTableBaseRepo(DbContextOptions<ApplicationDbContext> options)
   : this(new ApplicationDbContext(options))
{
}
```

Implement the Helper Methods

There are two helper methods in this class. The first converts the current time (based on the TimeZoneInfo of the executing computer) to UTC time, and the second encapsulates the execution of the query and the projection to the TemporalViewModel. Add the following code to the class to convert the current time to UTC:

```
internal static DateTime ConvertToUtc(DateTime dateTime)
  => TimeZoneInfo.ConvertTimeToUtc(dateTime, TimeZoneInfo.Local);
```

The next method takes in an IQueryable<T>, adds the OrderBy clause for the ValidFrom field, and projects the results into a collection of TemporalViewModel instances:

```
internal static IEnumerable<TemporalViewModel<T>> ExecuteQuery(IQueryable<T> query)
  =>  query.OrderBy(e => EF.Property<DateTime>(e, "ValidFrom"))
                .Select(e => new TemporalViewModel<T>
                         {
                             Entity = e,
                             ValidFrom = EF.Property<DateTime>(e, "ValidFrom"),
                             ValidTo = EF.Property<DateTime>(e, "ValidTo")
                });
```

Implement the Temporal Methods

The final step is to implement the five temporal-based methods of the interface. They take in the required data parameters, call the relevant EF Core temporal method, and then pass execution to the ExecuteQuery() helper method:

```
public IEnumerable<TemporalViewModel<T>> GetAllHistory()
    => ExecuteQuery(Table.TemporalAll());

public IEnumerable<TemporalViewModel<T>> GetHistoryAsOf(DateTime dateTime)
    => ExecuteQuery(Table.TemporalAsOf(ConvertToUtc(dateTime)));

public IEnumerable<TemporalViewModel<T>> GetHistoryBetween(
    DateTime startDateTime, DateTime endDateTime)
    => ExecuteQuery(Table.TemporalBetween(ConvertToUtc(startDateTime),
ConvertToUtc(endDateTime)));
public IEnumerable<TemporalViewModel<T>> GetHistoryContainedIn(
    DateTime startDateTime, DateTime endDateTime)
    => ExecuteQuery(Table.TemporalContainedIn(ConvertToUtc(startDateTime),
ConvertToUtc(endDateTime)));
public IEnumerable<TemporalViewModel<T>> GetHistoryFromTo(
    DateTime startDateTime, DateTime endDateTime)
    => ExecuteQuery(Table.TemporalFromTo(ConvertToUtc(startDateTime), ConvertToUtc(endDa
teTime)));
```

Now that all the base repos are completed, it's time to build the entity-specific repos.

Entity-Specific Repo Interfaces

Each entity and view model will have a strongly typed repository derived from `BaseRepo<T>` and an interface that implements `IRepo<T>`. Add a new folder named `Interfaces` under the Repos directory in the AutoLot.Dal project. In this new directory, add the following interfaces:

- ICarDriverRepo
- ICarRepo.cs
- ICreditRiskRepo.cs
- ICustomerOrderViewModelRepo.cs
- ICustomerRepo.cs
- IDriverRepo
- IMakeRepo.cs
- IOrderRepo.cs
- IRadioRepo

The next sections complete the interfaces.

> ■ **Note** The interfaces in this section are simple and not indicative of a real-world application. When building production applications with this pattern, the entity specific interfaces will usually hold a significant number of additional methods. These examples are kept simple to show the pattern and how it is used.

The CarDriver Repository Interface

Open the ICarDriverRepo.cs interface. This interface doesn't add any functionality beyond what is provided in the TemporalTableBaseRepo. Update the code to the following:

```
namespace AutoLot.Dal.Repos.Interfaces;

public interface ICarDriverRepo : ITemporalTableBaseRepo<CarDriver>
{
}
```

The Car Repository Interface

Open the ICarRepo.cs interface. Change the interface to public and define the repo as follows:

```
namespace AutoLot.Dal.Repos.Interfaces;

public interface ICarRepo : ITemporalTableBaseRepo<Car>
{
  IEnumerable<Car> GetAllBy(int makeId);
  string GetPetName(int id);
}
```

The Credit Risk Interface

Open the ICreditRiskRepo.cs interface. This interface doesn't add any functionality beyond what is provided in the BaseRepo. Update the code to the following:

```
namespace AutoLot.Dal.Repos.Interfaces;

public interface ICreditRiskRepo : IBaseRepo<CreditRisk>
{
}
```

The CustomerOrderViewModel Repository Interface

Open the ICustomerOrderViewModelRepo.cs interface. This interface doesn't add any functionality beyond what is provided in the BaseViewRepo. Notice that it implements IBaseViewRepo<T> and not IBaseRepo<T>. Update the code to the following:

```
namespace AutoLot.Dal.Repos.Interfaces;

public interface ICustomerOrderViewModelRepo : IBaseViewRepo<CustomerOrderViewModel>
{
}
```

The Customer Repository Interface

Open the ICustomerRepo.cs interface. This interface doesn't add any functionality beyond what is provided in the BaseRepo. Update the code to the following:

```
namespace AutoLot.Dal.Repos.Interfaces;

public interface ICustomerRepo : IBaseRepo<Customer>
{
}
```

The Driver Repository Interface

Open the IDriverRepo.cs interface. This interface doesn't add any functionality beyond what is provided in the BaseRepo. Update the code to the following:

```
namespace AutoLot.Dal.Repos.Interfaces;

public interface IDriverRepo : IBaseRepo<Driver>
{
}
```

The Make Repository Interface

Open the IMakeRepo.cs interface. This interface doesn't add any functionality beyond what is provided in the TemporalTableBaseRepo. Update the code to the following:

```
namespace AutoLot.Dal.Repos.Interfaces;

public interface IMakeRepo : ITemporalTableBaseRepo<Make>
{
}
```

The Order Repository Interface

Open the IOrderRepo.cs interface. This interface doesn't add any functionality beyond what is provided in the TemporalTableBaseRepo. Update the code to the following:

```
namespace AutoLot.Dal.Repos.Interfaces;

public interface IOrderRepo : IBaseRepo<Order>
{
}
```

The Radio Repository Interface

Open the IRadioRepo.cs interface. Update the code to the following:

```
namespace AutoLot.Dal.Repos.Interfaces;

public interface IRadioRepo : ITemporalTableBaseRepo<Radio>
{
}
```

This completes the interfaces for the entity-specific repositories.

Implement the Entity-Specific Repositories

The implemented repositories gain most of their functionality from the base class. This section covers the functionality added to or overridden from the base repository. In the Repos directory of the AutoLot.Dal project, add the following repo classes:

- CarDriverRepo.cs
- CarRepo.cs
- CreditRiskRepo.cs
- CustomerOrderViewModelRepo.cs
- CustomerRepo.cs
- DriverRepo.cs
- MakeRepo.cs
- OrderRepo.cs

The next sections complete the repositories.

■ **Note** You will notice that none of the repository classes has error handling or logging code. This is intentional to keep the examples focused. You will want to make sure you are handling (and logging) errors in your production code.

The CarDriver Repository

Open the CarDriverRepo.cs file, change the class to public, inherit from TemporalTableBaseRepo<CarDriver>, and implement ICarDriverRepo.

```
namespace AutoLot.Dal.Repos;

public class CarDriverRepo : TemporalTableBaseRepo<CarDriver>, ICarDriverRepo
{
  //implementation code goes here
}
```

Each of the repositories must implement the two constructors from the BaseRepo. The first constructor will be used by ASP.NET Core and its built-in dependency injection process. The second will be used by the integration tests (covered in the next chapter) and in the Windows Presentation Foundation (WPF) chapters.

```
public CarDriverRepo(ApplicationDbContext context) : base(context)
{
}
internal CarDriverRepo(DbContextOptions<ApplicationDbContext> options) : base(options)
{
}
```

Next, create an `internal` method that includes the `CarNavigation` and `DriverNavigation` properties. Note that the return type is `IIncludableQueryable<CarDriver, Driver>`. When using multiple includes, the exposed type uses the base type (`CarDriver`) and the final Included type (`Driver`). This method will be used by the public methods of the repo.

```
internal IIncludableQueryable<CarDriver, Driver> BuildBaseQuery()
    => Table.Include(c => c.CarNavigation).Include(d=>d.DriverNavigation);
```

Override the `GetAll()`, `GetAllIgnoreQueryFilters()`, and `Find()` methods to utilize the internal method:

```
public override IEnumerable<CarDriver> GetAll()
    => BuildBaseQuery();

public override IEnumerable<CarDriver> GetAllIgnoreQueryFilters()
    => BuildBaseQuery().IgnoreQueryFilters();

public override CarDriver Find(int? id)
    => BuildBaseQuery().IgnoreQueryFilters().Where(x => x.Id == id).FirstOrDefault();
```

The Car Repository

Open the `CarRepo.cs` file and change the class to `public`, inherit from `TemporalTableBaseRepo<Car>`, and implement `ICarRepo` and the standard constructors:

```
namespace AutoLot.Dal.Repos;
public class CarRepo : TemporalTableBaseRepo<Car>, ICarRepo
{
  public CarRepo(ApplicationDbContext context) : base(context)
  {
  }
  internal CarRepo(DbContextOptions<ApplicationDbContext> options) : base(options)
  {
  }
    //remaining implementation code goes here
}
```

Next, create an `internal` method that includes the `MakeNavigation` and an `OrderBy()` for the `PetName` property. Note that the type returned is an `IOrderedQueryable<Car>`. This will be used by the public methods:

```
internal IOrderedQueryable<Car> BuildBaseQuery()
  => Table.Include(x => x.MakeNavigation).OrderBy(p=>p.PetName);
```

Add overrides for `GetAll()` and `GetAllIgnoreQueryFilters()`, using the base query, to include the `MakeNavigation` property and order by the `PetName` values.

```
public override IEnumerable<Car> GetAll()
    => BuildBaseQuery();
public override IEnumerable<Car> GetAllIgnoreQueryFilters()
    => BuildBaseQuery().IgnoreQueryFilters();
```

Implement the `GetAllBy()` method. This method gets all the `Inventory` records with the specified `MakeId`:

```
public IEnumerable<Car> GetAllBy(int makeId)
    => BuildBaseQuery().Where(x => x.MakeId == makeId);
```

Add an override for `Find()` to include the `MakeNavigation` property and ignore query filters.

```
public override Car Find(int? id)
  => Table
      .IgnoreQueryFilters()
      .Where(x => x.Id == id)
      .Include(m => m.MakeNavigation)
      .FirstOrDefault();
```

Finally, add the method to get a car's `PetName` value using the stored procedure. This uses the `ExecuteParameterizedQuery()` method of the base repo and returns the value of the `OUT` parameter.

```
public string GetPetName(int id)
{
  var parameterId = new SqlParameter
  {
    ParameterName = "@carId",
    SqlDbType = SqlDbType.Int,
    Value = id,
  };

  var parameterName = new SqlParameter
  {
    ParameterName = "@petName",
    SqlDbType = SqlDbType.NVarChar,
    Size = 50,
    Direction = ParameterDirection.Output
  };

  ExecuteParameterizedQuery("EXEC [dbo].[GetPetName] @carId, @petName OUTPUT",
          new[] {parameterId, parameterName});
  return (string)parameterName.Value;
}
```

The CreditRisk Repository

Open the `CreditRiskRepo.cs` file and change the class to `public`, inherit from `BaseRepo<CreditRisk>`, implement `ICreditRiskRepo`, and add the two required constructors.

```
namespace AutoLot.Dal.Repos;
public class CreditRiskRepo : BaseRepo<CreditRisk>, ICreditRiskRepo
{
  public CreditRiskRepo(ApplicationDbContext context) : base(context)
  {
  }
  internal CreditRiskRepo(DbContextOptions<ApplicationDbContext> options)
  : base(options)
  {
  }
}
```

The CustomerOrderViewModel Repository

Open the `CustomerOrderViewModelRepo.cs` file and change the class to `public`, inherit from `BaseViewRepo<CreditRisk>`, implement `ICreditRiskRepo`, and add the two required constructors.

```
namespace AutoLot.Dal.Repos;

public class CustomerOrderViewModelRepo
  : BaseViewRepo<CustomerOrderViewModel>, ICustomerOrderViewModelRepo
{
  public CustomerOrderViewModelRepo(ApplicationDbContext context) : base(context)
  {
  }
  internal CustomerOrderViewModelRepo(DbContextOptions<ApplicationDbContext> options)
  : base(options)
  {
  }
}
```

The Customer Repository

Open the `CustomerRepo.cs` file and change the class to `public`, inherit from `BaseRepo<Customer>`, implement `ICustomerRepo`, and add the two required constructors.

```
namespace AutoLot.Dal.Repos;

public class CustomerRepo : BaseRepo<Customer>, ICustomerRepo
{
  public CustomerRepo(ApplicationDbContext context)
    : base(context)
  {
  }
  internal CustomerRepo(DbContextOptions<ApplicationDbContext> options)
```

```
    : base(options)
  {
  }
}
```

The final step is to add the method that returns all Customer records with their orders sorted by LastName. Add the following method to the class:

```
public override IEnumerable<Customer> GetAll()
  => Table
      .Include(c => c.Orders)
      .OrderBy(o => o.PersonInformation.LastName);
```

The Driver Repository

Open the DriverRepo.cs file and change the class to public, inherit from BaseRepo<Driver>, implement IDriverRepo, and add the two constructors.

```
namespace AutoLot.Dal.Repos;

public class DriverRepo : BaseRepo<Driver>, IDriverRepo
{
  public  DriverRepo(ApplicationDbContext context) : base(context)
  {
  }
  internal DriverRepo(DbContextOptions<ApplicationDbContext> options) : base(options)
  {
  }
  //remaining implementation code goes here
}
```

Next, create an internal method that includes the order by the LastName and then FirstName properties of the PersonInformation-owned class. Note that the return type is IOrderedQueryable<Driver>. This will be used by the public functions:

```
internal IOrderedQueryable<Driver> BuildQuery()
  => Table
          .OrderBy(m => m.PersonInformation.LastName)
          .ThenBy(f => f.PersonInformation.FirstName);
```

Override the GetAll() and GetAllIgnoreQueryFilters() methods to utilize the internal method:

```
public override IEnumerable<Driver> GetAll() => BuildQuery();

public override IEnumerable<Driver> GetAllIgnoreQueryFilters()
    => BuildQuery().IgnoreQueryFilters();
```

The Make Repository

Open the MakeRepo.cs class and change the class to public, inherit from TemporalTableBaseRepo<Make>, implement IMakeRepo, and add the two required constructors.

```
namespace AutoLot.Dal.Repos;

public class MakeRepo : TemporalTableBaseRepo<Make>, IMakeRepo
{
  public MakeRepo(ApplicationDbContext context)
      : base(context)
  {
  }

  internal  MakeRepo(
    DbContextOptions<ApplicationDbContext> options)
      : base(options)
  {
  }
}
```

Next, create an internal method that includes the order by the Name property. Note that the return type is IOrderedQueryable<Make>:

```
internal IOrderedQueryable<Make> BuildQuery()
  => Table.OrderBy(m => m. Name);
```

The final methods to override are the GetAll() and GetAllIgnoreQueryFilters() methods, sorting the Make values by name.

```
public override IEnumerable<Make> GetAll() => BuildQuery();

public override IEnumerable<Make> GetAllIgnoreQueryFilters()
    => BuildQuery().IgnoreQueryFilters();
```

The Order Repository

Open the OrderRepo.cs class and change the class to public, inherit from TemporalTableBaseRepo<Order>, implement IOrderRepo, and add the two constructors:

```
namespace AutoLot.Dal.Repos;

public class OrderRepo : TemporalTableBaseRepo<Order>, IOrderRepo
{
  public OrderRepo(ApplicationDbContext context)
      : base(context)
  {
  }

  internal  OrderRepo(
    DbContextOptions<ApplicationDbContext> options)
```

```
      : base(options)
    {
    }
}
```

The Radio Repository

Open the RadioRepo.cs file and change the class to public, inherit from TemporalTableBaseRepo<CreditRisk>, implement ICreditRiskRepo, and add the two required constructors.

```
namespace AutoLot.Dal.Repos;

public class RadioRepo : TemporalTableBaseRepo<Radio>, IRadioRepo
{
  public RadioRepo(ApplicationDbContext context) : base(context)
  {
  }
  internal RadioRepo(DbContextOptions<ApplicationDbContext> options)
    : base(options)
  {
  }
}
```

That completes all the repositories. The next section will create the code to drop, create, seed, and clear the database.

Update the GlobalUsings.cs Files

The new repository namespaces need to be added into the GlobalUsings.cs file in the AutoLot.Dal project. Add the following global using statements to the file:

```
//AutoLot.Dal
global using AutoLot.Dal.Repos.Base;
global using AutoLot.Dal.Repos.Interfaces;
```

Programmatic Database and Migration Handling

The Database property of DbContext provides programmatic methods to drop and create the database as well as run all the migrations. Table 23-1 describes the methods related to these operations.

Table 23-1. Programmatically Working with the Database

Member of Database	Meaning in Life
`EnsureDeleted()`	Drops the database if it exists. Does nothing if it does not exist.
`EnsureCreated()`	Creates the database if it doesn't exist. Does nothing if it does. Creates the tables and columns based on the classes reachable from the `DbSet<T>` properties. Does not apply any migrations. **Note:** This should not be used in conjunction with migrations.
`Migrate()`	Creates the database if it doesn't exist. Applies all migrations to the database.

As mentioned in the table, the `EnsureCreated()` method will create the database if it doesn't exist and then creates the tables, columns, and indices based on the entity model. It does not apply any migrations. If you are using migrations (as we are), this will present errors when working with the database, and you will have to trick out EF Core (as we did earlier) to believe the migrations have been applied. You will also have to apply any custom SQL objects to the database manually. When you are working with migrations, always use the `Migrate()` method to programmatically create the database and not the `EnsureCreated()` method.

Drop, Create, and Clean the Database

During development, it can be beneficial to drop and re-create the development database and then seed it with sample data. This creates a stable and predictable database setup useful when testing (manual or automated). Create a new folder named `Initialization` in the AutoLot.Dal project. In this folder, create a new class named `SampleDataInitializer.cs`. Make the class `public` and `static` as shown here:

```
namespace AutoLot.Dal.Initialization;
public static class SampleDataInitializer
{
  //implementation goes here
}
```

Create a method named `DropAndCreateDatabase` that takes an instance of `ApplicationDbContext` as the single parameter. This method uses the `Database` property of `ApplicationDbContext` to first delete the database (using the `EnsureDeleted()` method) and then creates the database (using the `Migrate()` method).

```
internal static void DropAndCreateDatabase(ApplicationDbContext context)
{
  context.Database.EnsureDeleted();
  context.Database.Migrate();
}
```

■ **Note** This process works very well when you are using a local database (e.g., in a Docker container, on your local drive, etc.). This does not work when using SQL Azure, as the EF Core commands cannot create SQL Azure database instances. If you are using SQL Azure, use the `ClearData()` method instead, detailed next.

Create another method named `ClearData()` that deletes all the data in the database and resets the identity values for each table's primary key. The method loops through a list of domain entities and uses the `DbContext Model` property to get the schema and table name each entity is mapped to. Then it executes a `delete` statement and resets the identity for each table using the `ExecuteSqlRaw()` method on the `DbContext Database` property. If the table is temporal, it then clears out the history data.

```
internal static void ClearData(ApplicationDbContext context)
{
  var entities = new[]
  {
    typeof(Order).FullName,
    typeof(Customer).FullName,
    typeof(CarDriver).FullName,
    typeof(Driver).FullName,
    typeof(Radio).FullName,
    typeof(Car).FullName,
    typeof(Make).FullName,
    typeof(CreditRisk).FullName
  };
  var serviceCollection = new ServiceCollection();
  serviceCollection.AddDbContextDesignTimeServices(context);
  var serviceProvider = serviceCollection.BuildServiceProvider();
  var designTimeModel = serviceProvider.GetService<IModel>();
  foreach (var entityName in entities)
  {
    var entity = context.Model.FindEntityType(entityName);
    var tableName = entity.GetTableName();
    var schemaName = entity.GetSchema();
    context.Database.ExecuteSqlRaw($"DELETE FROM {schemaName}.{tableName}");
    context.Database.ExecuteSqlRaw($"DBCC CHECKIDENT (\"{schemaName}.{tableName}\",
    RESEED, 1);");
    if (entity.IsTemporal())
    {
      var strategy = context.Database.CreateExecutionStrategy();
      strategy.Execute(() =>
      {
        using var trans = context.Database.BeginTransaction();
        var designTimeEntity = designTimeModel.FindEntityType(entityName);
        var historySchema = designTimeEntity.GetHistoryTableSchema();
        var historyTable = designTimeEntity.GetHistoryTableName();
        context.Database.ExecuteSqlRaw(
            $"ALTER TABLE {schemaName}.{tableName} SET (SYSTEM_VERSIONING = OFF)");
        context.Database.ExecuteSqlRaw($"DELETE FROM {historySchema}.{historyTable}");
        context.Database.ExecuteSqlRaw($"ALTER TABLE {schemaName}.{tableName} SET (SYSTEM_
        VERSIONING = ON (HISTORY_TABLE={historySchema}.{historyTable}))");
        trans.Commit();
      });
    }
  }
}
```

■ **Note** The ExecuteSqlRaw() method of the database façade should be used carefully to prevent potential SQL injection attacks.

Now that you can drop and create the database and clear the data, it's time to create the methods that will add the sample data.

Data Initialization

We are going to build our own data seeding system that can be run on demand. The first step is to create the sample data and then add the methods into the SampleDataInitializer used to load the sample data into the database.

Create thc Sample Data

Add a new file named SampleData.cs to the Initialization folder. Make the class public and static:

```
namespace AutoLot.Dal.Initialization;

public static class SampleData
{
  //implementation goes here
}
```

The file consists of cight static methods that create the sample data.

```
public static List<Customer> Customers => new()
{
  new() { Id = 1, PersonInformation = new() { FirstName = "Dave", LastName = "Brenner" } },
  new() { Id = 2, PersonInformation = new() { FirstName = "Matt", LastName = "Walton" } },
  new() { Id = 3, PersonInformation = new() { FirstName = "Steve", LastName = "Hagen" } },
  new() { Id = 4, PersonInformation = new() { FirstName = "Pat", LastName = "Walton" } },
  new() { Id = 5, PersonInformation = new() { FirstName = "Bad", LastName = "Customer" } },
};

public static List<Make> Makes => new()
{
  new() { Id = 1, Name = "VW" },
  new() { Id = 2, Name = "Ford" },
  new() { Id = 3, Name = "Saab" },
  new() { Id = 4, Name = "Yugo" },
  new() { Id = 5, Name = "BMW" },
  new() { Id = 6, Name = "Pinto" },
};

public static List<Driver> Drivers => new()
{
  new() { Id = 1, PersonInformation = new() { FirstName = "Fred", LastName = "Flinstone" } },
  new() { Id = 2, PersonInformation = new() { FirstName = "Barney", LastName = "Rubble" } }
};
```

```
public static List<Car> Inventory => new()
{
  new() { Id = 1, MakeId = 1, Color = "Black", PetName = "Zippy" },
  new() { Id = 2, MakeId = 2, Color = "Rust", PetName = "Rusty" },
  new() { Id = 3, MakeId = 3, Color = "Black", PetName = "Mel" },
  new() { Id = 4, MakeId = 4, Color = "Yellow", PetName = "Clunker" },
  new() { Id = 5, MakeId = 5, Color = "Black", PetName = "Bimmer" },
  new() { Id = 6, MakeId = 5, Color = "Green", PetName = "Hank" },
  new() { Id = 7, MakeId = 5, Color = "Pink", PetName = "Pinky" },
  new() { Id = 8, MakeId = 6, Color = "Black", PetName = "Pete" },
  new() { Id = 9, MakeId = 4, Color = "Brown", PetName = "Brownie" },
  new() { Id = 10, MakeId = 1, Color = "Rust", PetName = "Lemon", IsDrivable = false },
};

public static List<Radio> Radios => new()
{
  new() { Id = 1, CarId = 1, HasSubWoofers = true, RadioId = "SuperRadio 1", HasTweeters = true },
  new() { Id = 2, CarId = 2, HasSubWoofers = true, RadioId = "SuperRadio 2", HasTweeters = true },
  new() { Id = 3, CarId = 3, HasSubWoofers = true, RadioId = "SuperRadio 3", HasTweeters = true },
  new() { Id = 4, CarId = 4, HasSubWoofers = true, RadioId = "SuperRadio 4", HasTweeters = true },
  new() { Id = 5, CarId = 5, HasSubWoofers = true, RadioId = "SuperRadio 5", HasTweeters = true },
  new() { Id = 6, CarId = 6, HasSubWoofers = true, RadioId = "SuperRadio 6", HasTweeters = true },
  new() { Id = 7, CarId = 7, HasSubWoofers = true, RadioId = "SuperRadio 7", HasTweeters = true },
  new() { Id = 8, CarId = 8, HasSubWoofers = true, RadioId = "SuperRadio 8", HasTweeters = true },
  new() { Id = 9, CarId = 9, HasSubWoofers = true, RadioId = "SuperRadio 9", HasTweeters = true },
  new() { Id = 10, CarId = 10, HasSubWoofers = true, RadioId = "SuperRadio 10", HasTweeters = true },
};

public static List<CarDriver> CarsAndDrivers => new()
{
  new() { Id = 1, CarId = 1, DriverId = 1 },
  new() { Id = 2, CarId = 2, DriverId = 2 }
};

public static List<Order> Orders => new()
{
  new() { Id = 1, CustomerId = 1, CarId = 5 },
  new() { Id = 2, CustomerId = 2, CarId = 1 },
  new() { Id = 3, CustomerId = 3, CarId = 4 },
  new() { Id = 4, CustomerId = 4, CarId = 7 },
  new() { Id = 5, CustomerId = 5, CarId = 10 },
};

public static List<CreditRisk> CreditRisks => new()
{
  new()
  {
    Id = 1,
    CustomerId = Customers[4].Id,
    PersonInformation = new()
```

```
    {
      FirstName = Customers[4].PersonInformation.FirstName,
      LastName = Customers[4].PersonInformation.LastName
    }
  }
};
```

Load the Sample Data

The internal SeedData() method in the SampleDataInitializer class adds the data from the SampleData methods into an instance of ApplicationDbContext and then persists the data to the database.

```
internal static void SeedData(ApplicationDbContext context)
{
  try
  {
    ProcessInsert(context, context.Customers, SampleData.Customers);
    ProcessInsert(context, context.Makes, SampleData.Makes);
    ProcessInsert(context, context.Drivers, SampleData.Drivers);
    ProcessInsert(context, context.Cars, SampleData.Inventory);
    ProcessInsert(context, context.Radios, SampleData.Radios);
    ProcessInsert(context, context.CarsToDrivers, SampleData.CarsAndDrivers);
    ProcessInsert(context, context.Orders, SampleData.Orders);
    ProcessInsert(context, context.CreditRisks, SampleData.CreditRisks);
  }
  catch (Exception ex)
  {
    Console.WriteLine(ex);
    //Set a break point here to determine what the issues is
    throw;
  }
  static void ProcessInsert<TEntity>(
    ApplicationDbContext context,
    DbSet<TEntity> table,
    List<TEntity> records) where TEntity : BaseEntity
  {
     if (table.Any())
     {
       return;
     }
    IExecutionStrategy strategy = context.Database.CreateExecutionStrategy();
    strategy.Execute(() =>
    {
      using var transaction = context.Database.BeginTransaction();
      try
      {
        var metaData = context.Model.FindEntityType(typeof(TEntity).FullName);
        context.Database.ExecuteSqlRaw(
            $"SET IDENTITY_INSERT {metaData.GetSchema()}.{metaData.GetTableName()} ON");
        table.AddRange(records);
        context.SaveChanges();
```

```
          context.Database.ExecuteSqlRaw(
              $"SET IDENTITY_INSERT {metaData.GetSchema()}.{metaData.GetTableName()} OFF");
          transaction.Commit();
        }
        catch (Exception)
        {
          transaction.Rollback();
        }
        });
  }
}
```

The SeedData() method uses a local function to process the data. It first checks to see whether the table has any records and, if not, proceeds to process the sample data. An ExecutionStrategy is created from the database façade, and this is used to create an explicit transaction, which is needed to turn identity insert on and off. The records are added, and if all is successful, the transaction is committed; otherwise, it's rolled back.

The next two methods are public and used to reset the database. InitializeData() drops and re-creates the database before seeding it, and the ClearDatabase() method just deletes all the records, resets the identity, and then seeds the data.

```
public static void InitializeData(ApplicationDbContext context)
{
  DropAndCreateDatabase(context);
  SeedData(context);
}

public static void ClearAndReseedDatabase(ApplicationDbContext context)
{
  ClearData(context);
  SeedData(context);
}
```

The initialization code will be exercised heavily in the next chapter.

Summary

This chapter used the knowledge gained in the previous chapter to complete the data access layer for the AutoLot database. You used the EF Core command-line tools to scaffold an existing database, updated the model to its final version, and then created migrations and applied them. Repositories were added for the encapsulation of the data access, and database initialization code with sample data can drop and create the database in a repeatable, reliable manner. The next chapter focuses on test-driving the data access layer.

CHAPTER 24

Test-Driving AutoLot

Now that you have the finished AutoLot data access layer, it's time to take it for a test-drive. Integration testing in an integral part of software development and is a great way to make sure your data access code behaves as expected. In this chapter, we will be using xUnit, a testing framework for .NET Core.

After creating the solution and test project, the AutoLot.Dal and AutoLot.Models projects are added to the solution. Next, xUnit will be explored to show how to run automated tests. Then the rest of the chapter is dedicated to creating and executing integration tests.

Setting Up the Test-Drives

Instead of creating a client application to test-drive the completed AutoLot data access layer, we are going to use automated integration tests. The tests will demonstrate create, read, update, and delete calls to the database. This allows us to examine the code without the overhead of creating another application. Each of the tests in this section will execute a query (either create, read, update, or delete) and then have one or more Assert statements to validate that the result is what was expected.

Create the Project

To get started, we are going to set up an integration test platform using xUnit, a .NET Core–compatible testing framework. Start by adding a new xUnit test project named AutoLot.Dal.Tests. In Visual Studio, this project type is named xUnit Test Project.

Note Unit tests are designed to test a single unit of code. What we will be doing throughout this chapter is technically creating *integration* tests, since we are testing the C# code *and* EF Core all the way to the database and back.

From the command-line interface, execute the following commands using the command-line interface (CLI):

```
dotnet new sln -n Chapter24_AllProjects
dotnet new xunit -lang c# -n AutoLot.Dal.Tests -o .\AutoLot.Dal.Tests -f net6.0
dotnet sln .\Chapter23_AllProjects.sln add AutoLot.Dal.Tests
```


A. Troelsen and P. Japikse, *Pro C# 10 with .NET 6*, https://doi.org/10.1007/978-1-4842-7869-7_24

Add the Microsoft.EntityFrameworkCore, Microsoft.EntityFrameworkCore.Design, Microsoft.EntityFrameworkCore.SqlServer, and Microsoft.Extensions.Configuration.Json NuGet packages to the AutoLot.Dal.Tests project. If using the CLI, use the following commands:

```
dotnet add AutoLot.Dal.Tests package Microsoft.EntityFrameworkCore
dotnet add AutoLot.Dal.Tests package Microsoft.EntityFrameworkCore.Design
dotnet add AutoLot.Dal.Tests package Microsoft.EntityFrameworkCore.SqlServer
dotnet add AutoLot.Dal.Tests package Microsoft.Extensions.Configuration.Json
```

The tests will use the data initializer code that clears the temporal data, so the same adjustment to the project file must be made regarding the Microsoft.EntityFrameworkCore.Design package. Update the package to remove (or comment out) the IncludeAssets tag:

```
<PackageReference Include="Microsoft.EntityFrameworkCore.Design" Version="6.0.
0-rc.1.21452.10">
  <!--<IncludeAssets>runtime; build; native; contentfiles; analyzers; buildtransitive
</IncludeAssets>-->
  <PrivateAssets>all</PrivateAssets>
</PackageReference>
```

The versions of the Microsoft.NET.Test.Sdk and coverlet.collector packages that ship with the xUnit project template typically lag behind the currently available versions. To update them, either use the NuGet Package Manager in Visual Studio to update all NuGet packages or use the CLI. To update them with the CLI, then add them again since adding packages from the command line will always retrieve the latest non-prerelease version. Here are the commands:

```
dotnet add AutoLot.Dal.Tests package Microsoft.NET.Test.Sdk
dotnet add AutoLot.Dal.Tests package coverlet.collector
```

Next, add project references to AutoLot.Models and AutoLot.Dal. To do this from the command line, execute the following (update the path and directory separator to your projects from Chapter 23):

```
dotnet add AutoLot.Dal.Tests reference ..\Chapter_23\AutoLot.Dal
dotnet add AutoLot.Dal.Tests reference ..\Chapter_23\AutoLot.Models
```

Finally, turn off nullable reference types and enable global implicit using statements in the project file:

```
<PropertyGroup>
  <TargetFramework>net6.0</TargetFramework>
  <IsPackable>false</IsPackable>
  <Nullable>disable</Nullable>
  <ImplicitUsings>enable</ImplicitUsings>
</PropertyGroup>
```

■ **Note** At the time of this writing, the xUnit project template does add the node for ImplicitUsings into the project file.

Make the AutoLot.Dal Internals Visible to AutoLot.Dal.Tests

To test (or use) the methods and classes in the AutoLot.Dal project that are marked internal, the internals need to be made visible to the AutoLot.Dal.Tests project. Open the AutoLot.Dal.csproj file and add the following:

```
<ItemGroup>
  <AssemblyAttribute Include="System.Runtime.CompilerServices.InternalsVisibleToAttribute">
    <_Parameter1>AutoLot.Dal.Tests</_Parameter1>
  </AssemblyAttribute>
</ItemGroup>
```

Add the GlobalUsings File

Create a new file named `GlobalUsings.cs` in the root of the AutoLot.Dal.Tests project. This will be the central location for all the `using` statements needed in this project. Update the code to match the following:

```
global using System.Data;
global using System.Linq.Expressions;

global using AutoLot.Dal.EfStructures;
global using AutoLot.Dal.Exceptions;
global using AutoLot.Dal.Initialization;
global using AutoLot.Dal.Repos;
global using AutoLot.Dal.Repos.Interfaces;

global using AutoLot.Dal.Tests.Base;

global using AutoLot.Models.Entities;
global using AutoLot.Models.Entities.Owned;

global using Microsoft.EntityFrameworkCore;
global using Microsoft.EntityFrameworkCore.ChangeTracking;
global using Microsoft.EntityFrameworkCore.Storage;
global using Microsoft.EntityFrameworkCore.Query;

global using Microsoft.Extensions.Configuration;

global using Xunit;
global using Xunit.Abstractions;
```

A First Look at xUnit

There are two types of tests that will be used in this chapter. Parameterless test methods are referred to as *facts* (and use the `Fact` attribute). Tests that take parameters are referred to as *theories* (and use the `Theory` attribute). Theory tests run multiple iterations of the test method passing in different values for each run. To demonstrate these test types, create a new class named `SampleTests.cs` in the `AutoLot.Dal.Tests` project and update the code to the following:

```
namespace AutoLot.Dal.Tests;

public class SampleTests
{
  //tests go here
}
```

Fact Test Methods

The first test to create is a Fact test. With Fact tests, all values are contained in the test method. The following (trivial) example tests 3+2=5:

```
[Fact]
public void SimpleFactTest()
{
  Assert.Equal(5,3+2);
}
```

There are a variety of Assert types available. In this example, the test is asserting the actual result (3+2) equals the expected result (5).

Theory Test Methods

When using Theory type tests, the values for the tests are passed into the test method. The previous test tested only one case, 3+2. Theories permit testing multiple use cases without having to repeat the test code multiple times. The values can come from the InlineData attribute, methods, or classes. For our purpose, we will only use the InlineData attribute. Create the following test that provided different addends and expected results to the test:

```
[Theory]
[InlineData(3,2,5)]
[InlineData(1,-1,0)]
public void SimpleTheoryTest(int addend1, int addend2, int expectedResult)
{
  Assert.Equal(expectedResult,addend1+addend2);
}
```

■ **Note** There will be many examples of Fact and Theory tests throughout this chapter, as well as additional capabilities for the xUnit testing framework. For more information in the xUnit test framework, consult the documentation located at https://xunit.net/.

Executing Tests

While the xUnit tests can be executed from the command line (using dotnet test), it is a better developer experience (in my opinion) to use Visual Studio to execute the tests. Launch the Test Explorer from the Test menu to have access to running and debugging all or selected tests.

Configure the Project and DbContext Instances

To retrieve the connection string at runtime, we are going to use the .NET Core configuration capabilities using a JSON file. Add a JSON file, named appsettings.testing.json, to the project and add your connection string information into the file in the following format (update your connection string from what is listed here as necessary):

```
{
  "ConnectionStrings": {
    "AutoLot": "server=.,5433;Database=AutoLot;User Id=sa;Password=P@ssw0rd;"
  }
}
```

Update the project file to have the settings file copied to the output folder on every build. Do that by adding the following ItemGroup to the AutoLot.Dal.Tests.csproj file:

```
<ItemGroup>
  <None Update="appsettings.testing.json">
    <CopyToOutputDirectory>Always</CopyToOutputDirectory>
  </None>
</ItemGroup>
```

Create the Integration Test Helper

The TestHelpers class will handle the application configuration as well as create new instances of ApplicationDbContext. Add a new public static class named TestHelpers.cs in the root of the project:

```
namespace AutoLot.Dal.Tests;

public static class TestHelpers
{
  //helper code goes here
}
```

Add a public static method to create an instance of the IConfiguration interface using the appsettings.testing.json file. Add the following code to the class:

```
public static IConfiguration GetConfiguration() =>
  new ConfigurationBuilder()
    .SetBasePath(Directory.GetCurrentDirectory())
    .AddJsonFile("appsettings.testing.json", true, true)
    .Build();
```

■ **Note** Configuration of assemblies is covered in Chapter 16.

Add another public static method to create instances of the ApplicationDbContext class using the IConfiguration instance. Add the following code to the class:

```
public static ApplicationDbContext GetContext(IConfiguration configuration)
{
  var optionsBuilder = new DbContextOptionsBuilder<ApplicationDbContext>();
  var connectionString = configuration.GetConnectionString("AutoLot");
  optionsBuilder.UseSqlServer(connectionString);
  return new ApplicationDbContext(optionsBuilder.Options);
}
```

Add another static method that will create a new instance of ApplicationDbContext. This demonstrates creating an instance of the ApplicationDbContext class from an existing instance to share the connection and transaction.public static ApplicationDbContext GetSecondContext(

```
  ApplicationDbContext oldContext,
  IDbContextTransaction trans)
{
  var optionsBuilder = new DbContextOptionsBuilder<ApplicationDbContext>();
  optionsBuilder.UseSqlServer(oldContext.Database.GetDbConnection());
  var context = new ApplicationDbContext(optionsBuilder.Options);
  context.Database.UseTransaction(trans.GetDbTransaction());
  return context;
}
```

Add the BaseTest Class

The BaseTest class handles the infrastructure for the tests in this chapter. Add a new folder named Base to the test project and add a new class file named BaseTest.cs to that folder. Make the class abstract and implement IDisposable. Add two protected readonly properties to hold the IConfiguration and ApplicationDbContext instances and dispose of the ApplicationDbContext instance in the virtual Dispose() method.

```
namespace AutoLot.Dal.Tests.Base;

public abstract class BaseTest : IDisposable
{
  protected readonly IConfiguration Configuration;
  protected readonly ApplicationDbContext Context;

  public virtual void Dispose()
  {
    Context.Dispose();
  }
}
```

The xUnit test framework provides a mechanism to run code before and after *each* test is executed. Test classes (called *fixtures*) that implement the IDisposable interface will execute the code in the class constructor in the inheritance chain before each test is run. This is commonly referred to as the *test setup*. After each test is executed, the code in the Dispose methods (through the inheritance chain) is executed. This is referred to as *test teardown*.

Add a protected constructor that creates an instance of IConfiguration and assigns it to the protected class variable. Use the configuration to create an instance of ApplicationDbContext using the TestHelper class and also assign it to the protected class variable.

```
protected BaseTest()
{
  Configuration = TestHelpers.GetConfiguration();
  Context = TestHelpers.GetContext(Configuration);
}
```

The ITestOutputHelper interface allows for content to be written to the test output window. When using the IDisposable pattern with xUnit test fixtures, the instance for this interface can be injected into the constructor. Add a protected readonly variable to hold the instance and update the constructor to the following:

```
protected readonly ITestOutputHelper OutputHelper;

protected BaseTest(ITestOutputHelper outputHelper)
{
  Configuration = TestHelpers.GetConfiguration();
  Context = TestHelpers.GetContext(Configuration);
  OutputHelper = outputHelper;
}
```

Add the Transacted Test Execution Helpers

The final two methods in the BaseTest class enable running test methods in a transaction. The methods will take an Action delegate as a single parameter, create an explicit transaction (or enlist an existing transaction), execute the Action delegate, and then roll back the transaction. We do this so any create/update/delete tests leave the database in the state it was in before the test was run. The transactions are executed inside an execution strategy in case the ApplicationDbContext is configured to enable retry on transient errors.

The ExecuteInATransaction() method executes the action delegate using a single instance of the ApplicationDbContext. Add the following code into your BaseTest class:

```
protected void ExecuteInATransaction(Action actionToExecute)
{
  var strategy = Context.Database.CreateExecutionStrategy();
  strategy.Execute(() =>
  {
    using var trans = Context.Database.BeginTransaction();
    actionToExecute();
    trans.Rollback();
  });
}
```

The ExecuteInASharedTransaction() method allows for multiple ApplicationDbContext instances to share a single transaction. Add the following code into your BaseTest class:

```
protected void ExecuteInASharedTransaction(Action<IDbContextTransaction> actionToExecute)
{
  var strategy = Context.Database.CreateExecutionStrategy();
  strategy.Execute(() =>
  {
    using IDbContextTransaction trans =
      Context.Database.BeginTransaction(IsolationLevel.ReadUncommitted);
    actionToExecute(trans);
    trans.Rollback();
  });
}
```

Add the EnsureAutoLotDatabase Test Fixture Class

The xUnit test framework provides a mechanism for running code before any of the tests are run (referred to as *fixture setup*) and after all the tests are run (referred to as *fixture teardown*). This practice is generally not recommended, but in our case, we want to ensure that the database is created and loaded with data before *any* tests are run instead of before *each* test is run. Test classes that implement IClassFixture<T> where T:

TestFixtureClass will have the constructor code of T (the TestFixtureClass) executed before any tests are run, and the Dispose() code will run after all tests are completed.

Add a new class named EnsureAutoLotDatabaseTestFixture.cs to the Base directory and implement IDisposable. Make the class public and sealed, and add the following using statements:

```
namespace AutoLot.Dal.Tests.Base;

public sealed class EnsureAutoLotDatabaseTestFixture : IDisposable
{
  //add implementation code here

  public void Dispose()
  {
  }
}
```

The constructor code uses the TestHelpers class to get the instance of IConfiguration and then gets an instance of the ApplicationDbContext. Next, it calls the ClearAndReseedDatabase() method from the SampleDataInitializer. The final line disposes of the context instance. In our examples, the Dispose() method doesn't have any code but needs to be implemented to satisfy the IDisposable interface. The following listing shows the updated constructor:

```
public EnsureAutoLotDatabaseTestFixture()
{
  var configuration =  TestHelpers.GetConfiguration();
  var context = TestHelpers.GetContext(configuration);
  SampleDataInitializer.ClearAndReseedDatabase(context);
  context.Dispose();
}
```

Add the Integration Test Classes

The next step is to add the classes that will hold the automated tests. These classes are referred to as *test fixtures*. Add a new folder named IntegrationTests in the AutoLot.Dal.Tests folder and add five files named CarTests.cs, CustomerOrderViewModelTests.cs, CustomerTests.cs, MakeTests.cs, and OrderTests.cs to this folder.

Depending on the capabilities of the test runner, xUnit tests are run in serial within a test fixture (class), but in parallel across test fixtures. This can be problematic when executing integration tests that interact with a database. Parallel database tests using a single database instance can cause blocks, produce erroneous results, and are generally problematic.

xUnit test execution can be changed to serial across test fixtures by adding them into the same test collection. Test collections are defined by name using the Collection attribute on the class. Add the following Collection attribute to the top of all four classes:

```
[Collection("Integration Tests")]
```

Next, inherit from BaseTest and implement the IClassFixture interface in both classes. Add a constructor to receive the ITestOutputHelper instance and pass it to the base class. Update each class to match the following:

```
//CarTests.cs
namespace AutoLot.Dal.Tests.IntegrationTests;

[Collection("Integation Tests")]
public class CarTests
  : BaseTest, IClassFixture<EnsureAutoLotDatabaseTestFixture>
{
  public CarTests(ITestOutputHelper outputHelper) : base(outputHelper)
  {
  }
}

//CustomerOrderViewModelTests.cs
namespace AutoLot.Dal.Tests.IntegrationTests;

[Collection("Integation Tests")]
public class CustomerOrderViewModelTests
  : BaseTest, IClassFixture<EnsureAutoLotDatabaseTestFixture>
{
  public CustomerOrderViewModelTests(ITestOutputHelper outputHelper)
    : base(outputHelper)
  {
  }
}

//CustomerTests.cs
namespace AutoLot.Dal.Tests.IntegrationTests;

[Collection("Integation Tests")]
public class CustomerTests
  : BaseTest, IClassFixture<EnsureAutoLotDatabaseTestFixture>
```

```
{
  public CustomerTests(ITestOutputHelper outputHelper) : base(outputHelper)
  {
  }
}

//MakeTests.cs
namespace AutoLot.Dal.Tests.IntegrationTests;

[Collection("Integation Tests")]
public class MakeTests
  : BaseTest, IClassFixture<EnsureAutoLotDatabaseTestFixture>
{
  public MakeTests(ITestOutputHelper outputHelper) : base(outputHelper)
  {
  }
}

//OrderTests.cs
namespace AutoLot.Dal.Tests.IntegrationTests;

[Collection("Integation Tests")]
public class OrderTests
  : BaseTest, IClassFixture<EnsureAutoLotDatabaseTestFixture>
{
  public OrderTests(ITestOutputHelper outputHelper):base(outputHelper)
  {
  }
}
```

For the CarTests class, update the constructor to create an instance of the CarRepo and assign the instance to a private readonly class-level variable. Override the Dispose() method, and in that method, dispose of the repo.

```
[Collection("Integration Tests")]
public class CarTests : BaseTest, IClassFixture<EnsureAutoLotDatabaseTestFixture>
{
  private readonly ICarRepo _carRepo;
  public CarTests(ITestOutputHelper outputHelper) : base(outputHelper)
  {
    _carRepo = new CarRepo(Context);
  }

  public override void Dispose()
  {
    _carRepo.Dispose();
    base.Dispose();
  }
}
```

Repeat the process for the CustomerOrderViewModelTests class, using the CustomerOrderViewModelRepo instead:

```
[Collection("Integration Tests")]
public class CustomerOrderViewModelTests : BaseTest, IClassFixture<EnsureAutoLotDatabase
TestFixture>
{
  private readonly ICustomerOrderViewModelRepo _repo;
  public CustomerOrderViewModelTests(ITestOutputHelper outputHelper) : base(outputHelper)
  {
    _repo = new CustomerOrderViewModelRepo(Context);
  }

  public override void Dispose()
  {
    _repo.Dispose();
    base.Dispose();
  }
}
```

The setup for the CustomerTests class is simpler, since it does not use the CustomerRepo:

```
[Collection("Integration Tests")]
public class CustomerTests : BaseTest, IClassFixture<EnsureAutoLotDatabaseTestFixture>
{
  public CustomerOrderViewModelTests(ITestOutputHelper outputHelper) : base(outputHelper)
  {
  }
}
```

The same process is needed for the MakeTests class, using MakeRepo:

```
[Collection("Integration Tests")]
public class MakeTests : BaseTest, IClassFixture<EnsureAutoLotDatabaseTestFixture>
{
  private readonly IMakeRepo _repo;
  public MakeTests(ITestOutputHelper outputHelper) : base(outputHelper)
  {
    _repo = new MakeRepo(Context);
  }

  public override void Dispose()
  {
    _repo.Dispose();
    base.Dispose();
  }
}
```

The final repository update is in the OrderTests class, using OrderRepo:

```
[Collection("Integration Tests")]
public class OrderTests : BaseTest, IClassFixture<EnsureAutoLotDatabaseTestFixture>
{
  private readonly IOrderRepo _repo;
  public OrderTests(ITestOutputHelper outputHelper) : base(outputHelper)
  {
    _repo = new OrderRepo(Context);
  }

  public override void Dispose()
  {
    _repo.Dispose();
    base.Dispose();
  }
}
```

Querying the Database

Recall that creating entity instances from a database data involves executing a LINQ statement or a SQL statement (using FromSqlRaw()/FromSqlInterpolated()) against the DbSet<T> properties. When using LINQ, the statements are converted to SQL by the database provider and the LINQ translation engine, and the appropriate data is read from the database. Data can also be loaded using the FromSqlRaw() or FromSqlInterpolated() method using raw SQL strings and, optionally, additional LINQ statements. Entities loaded into the DbSet<T> collections are added to the ChangeTracker by default but can be added without tracking. Data loaded in keyless DbSet<T> collections is never tracked.

If related entities are already loaded into the DbSet<T>, EF Core will wire up the new instances along the navigation properties. For example, if the Cars are loaded into the DbSet<Car> collection and then the related Orders are loaded into the DbSet<Order> of the same ApplicationDbContext instance, the Car.Orders navigation property will return the related Order entities without requerying the database.

Many of the methods demonstrated here have async versions available. The syntax of the LINQ queries are structurally the same, so I will only demonstrate the nonasync version.

LINQ Queries

The DbSet<T> collection type implements (among other interfaces) IQueryable<T>. This allows C# LINQ commands to be used to create queries to get data from the database. While all C# LINQ statements are available for use with the DbSet<T> collection type, some LINQ statements might not be supported by the database provider, and additional LINQ statements are added by EF Core. Unsupported LINQ statements that cannot be translated into the database provider's query language will throw a runtime exception. Some nontranslatable LINQ statements will execute on the client side if they are the last statement in the LINQ chain; however, others (like the update to the Take() method that works with ranges) will still throw an error unless the query is first executed using ToList() or a similar construct.

LINQ Execution

Where ToQueryString() is available, the tests in this next section set a variable (qs) to this value and are output to the test results using the ITestOutputHelper so you can examine the query while running the tests.

Get All Records

To get all the records for a table, simply use the DbSet<T> property directly without any LINQ statements. Add the following Fact to the CustomerTests.cs class:

```
[Fact]
public void ShouldGetAllOfTheCustomers()
{
  var qs = Context.Customers.ToQueryString();
  var customers = Context.Customers.ToList();
  Assert.Equal(5, customers.Count);
}
```

The statement gets translated into the following SQL:

```
SELECT [c].[Id], [c].[TimeStamp], [c].[FirstName], [c].[FullName], [c].[LastName]
FROM [Dbo].[Customers] AS [c]
```

The same process is used for Keyless entities, like the CustomerOrderViewModel, which is configured to get its data from the CustomerOrderView. Add the following test to the CustomerOrderViewModelTest.cs class to show getting data from the view:

```
[Fact]
public void ShouldGetAllViewModels()
{
  var qs = Context.CustomerOrderViewModels.ToQueryString();
  OutputHelper.WriteLine($"Query: {qs}");
  List<Models.ViewModels.CustomerOrderViewModel> list =
    Context.CustomerOrderViewModels.ToList();
  Assert.NotEmpty(list);
  Assert.Equal(5, list.Count);
}
```

The statement gets translated into the following SQL:

```
SELECT [c].[Color], [c].[DateBuilt], [c].[Display], [c].[FirstName],
    [c].[IsDrivable], [c].[LastName], [c].[Make], [c].[PetName], [c].[Price]
FROM [CustomerOrderView] AS [c]
```

Filter Records

The following test in the CustomerTests class shows querying for customers where the last name starts with a *W* (case insensitive):

```
[Fact]
public void ShouldGetCustomersWithLastNameW()
{
  IQueryable<Customer> query = Context.Customers
    .Where(x => x.PersonInformation.LastName.StartsWith("W"));
  var qs = query.ToQueryString();
  OutputHelper.WriteLine($"Query: {qs}");
```

```
  List<Customer> customers = query.ToList();
  Assert.Equal(2, customers.Count);
  foreach (var customer in customers)
  {
    var pi = customer.PersonInformation;
    Assert.StartsWith("W", pi.LastName, StringComparison.OrdinalIgnoreCase);
  }
}
```

The LINQ query gets translated into the following SQL:

```
SELECT [c].[Id], [c].[TimeStamp], [c].[FirstName], [c].[FullName], [c].[LastName]
FROM [dbo].[Customers] AS [c]
WHERE [c].[LastName] IS NOT NULL AND ([c].[LastName] LIKE N'W%')
```

The next test in the CustomerTests class demonstrates chaining Where() methods in a LINQ query to find the customers where the last name starts with a *W* and the first name starts with an *M*. Note that since SQL Server is case insensitive, these queries are also case insensitive:

```
[Fact]
public void ShouldGetCustomersWithLastNameWAndFirstNameM()
{
  IQueryable<Customer> query = Context.Customers
    .Where(x => x.PersonInformation.LastName.StartsWith("W"))
    .Where(x => x.PersonInformation.FirstName.StartsWith("M"));
  var qs = query.ToQueryString();
  OutputHelper.WriteLine($"Query: {qs}");
  List<Customer> customers = query.ToList();
  Assert.Single(customers);
  foreach (var customer in customers)
  {
    var pi = customer.PersonInformation;
    Assert.StartsWith("W", pi.LastName, StringComparison.OrdinalIgnoreCase);
    Assert.StartsWith("M", pi.FirstName, StringComparison.OrdinalIgnoreCase);
  }
}
```

This test in the CustomerTests class repeats the same filter using a single Where() method instead of two chained methods:

```
[Fact]
public void ShouldGetCustomersWithLastNameWAndFirstNameM()
{
  IQueryable<Customer> query = Context.Customers
    .Where(x => x.PersonInformation.LastName.StartsWith("W") &&
                     x.PersonInformation.FirstName.StartsWith("M"));
  var qs = query.ToQueryString();
  OutputHelper.WriteLine($"Query: {qs}");
  List<Customer> customers = query.ToList();
  Assert.Single(customers);
  foreach (var customer in customers)
```

```
  {
    var pi = customer.PersonInformation;
    Assert.StartsWith("W", pi.LastName, StringComparison.OrdinalIgnoreCase);
    Assert.StartsWith("M", pi.FirstName, StringComparison.OrdinalIgnoreCase);
  }
}
```

Both queries get translated into the following SQL:

```
SELECT [c].[Id], [c].[TimeStamp], [c].[FirstName], [c].[FullName], [c].[LastName]
FROM [dbo].[Customers] AS [c]
WHERE ([c].[LastName] IS NOT NULL AND ([c].[LastName] LIKE N'W%'))
  AND ([c].[FirstName] IS NOT NULL AND ([c].[FirstName] LIKE N'M%'))
```

The next test in the `CustomerTests` class demonstrates querying for customers where the last name starts with a *W* (case insensitive) *or* the last name starts with an *H* (case insensitive):

```
[Fact]
public void ShouldGetCustomersWithLastNameWOrH()
{
  IQueryable<Customer> query = Context.Customers
    .Where(x => x.PersonInformation.LastName.StartsWith("W") ||
                x.PersonInformation.LastName.StartsWith("H"));
  var qs = query.ToQueryString();
  OutputHelper.WriteLine($"Query: {qs}");
  List<Customer> customers = query.ToList();
  Assert.Equal(3, customers.Count);
  foreach (var customer in customers)
  {
    var pi = customer.PersonInformation;
    Assert.True(
      pi.LastName.StartsWith("W",StringComparison.OrdinalIgnoreCase) ||
      pi.LastName.StartsWith("H",StringComparison.OrdinalIgnoreCase));
  }
}
```

This gets translated into the following SQL:

```
SELECT [c].[Id], [c].[TimeStamp], [c].[FirstName], [c].[FullName], [c].[LastName]
FROM [dbo].[Customers] AS [c]
WHERE ([c].[LastName] IS NOT NULL AND ([c].[LastName] LIKE N'W%'))
    OR ([c].[LastName] IS NOT NULL AND ([c].[LastName] LIKE N'H%'))
```

The following in the `CustomerTests` class also queries for customers where the last name starts with a *W* (case insensitive) *or* the last name starts with an *H* (case insensitive). This test demonstrates using the `EF.Functions.Like()` method. Note that you must include the wildcard (%) yourself.

```
[Fact]
public void ShouldGetCustomersWithLastNameWOrH()
{
  IQueryable<Customer> query = Context.Customers
```

```
    .Where(x => EF.Functions.Like(x.PersonInformation.LastName, "W%") ||
                              EF.Functions.Like(x.PersonInformation.LastName, "H%"));
  var qs = query.ToQueryString();
  OutputHelper.WriteLine($"Query: {qs}");
  List<Customer> customers = query.ToList();
  Assert.Equal(3, customers.Count);
}
```

This gets translated into the following SQL (notice it does not check for null):

```
SELECT [c].[Id], [c].[TimeStamp], [c].[FirstName], [c].[FullName], [c].[LastName]
FROM [Dbo].[Customers] AS [c]
WHERE ([c].[LastName] LIKE N'W%') OR ([c].[LastName] LIKE N'H%')
```

The following test in the `CarTests.cs` class uses a `Theory` to query for the number of `Car` records (drivable or not) in the `Inventory` table based on a specified `MakeId`:

```
[Theory]
[InlineData(1, 2)]
[InlineData(2, 1)]
[InlineData(3, 1)]
[InlineData(4, 2)]
[InlineData(5, 3)]
[InlineData(6, 1)]
public void ShouldGetTheCarsByMake(int makeId, int expectedCount)
{
  IQueryable<Car> query =
    Context.Cars.IgnoreQueryFilters().Where(x => x.MakeId == makeId);
  var qs = query.ToQueryString();
  OutputHelper.WriteLine($"Query: {qs}");
  var cars = query.ToList();
  Assert.Equal(expectedCount, cars.Count);
}
```

Each `InlineData` row becomes a unique test in the test runner. For this example, six tests are processed, and six queries are executed against the database. Here is the SQL from one of the tests (the only difference in the queries from the other tests in the `Theory` is the value for `MakeId`):

```
DECLARE @__makeId_0 int = 1;

SELECT [i].[Id], [i].[Color], [i].[DateBuilt], [i].[Display], [i].[IsDrivable],
   [i].[MakeId], [i].[PetName], [i].[Price], [i].[TimeStamp]
FROM [dbo].[Inventory] AS [i]
WHERE [i].[MakeId] = @__makeId_0
```

The next test uses the `Car` repository to get the number of records for each `Make`. Since the `GetCarsBy()` method leaves the query filters in place, there is one less record when the `MakeId` is one.

```
[Theory]
[InlineData(1, 1)]
[InlineData(2, 1)]
[InlineData(3, 1)]
```

```
[InlineData(4, 2)]
[InlineData(5, 3)]
[InlineData(6, 1)]
public void ShouldGetTheCarsByMakeUsingTheRepo(int makeId, int expectedCount)
{
  var qs = _carRepo.GetAllBy(makeId).AsQueryable().ToQueryString();
  OutputHelper.WriteLine($"Query: {qs}");
  var cars = _carRepo.GetAllBy(makeId).ToList();
  Assert.Equal(expectedCount, cars.Count);
}
```

When examining the generated query, you can see the query filter that excluded records that aren't drivable:

```
DECLARE @__makeId_0 int = 1;

SELECT [i].[Id], [i].[Color], [i].[DateBuilt], [i].[Display], [i].[IsDrivable],
    [i].[MakeId], [i].[PetName], [i].[Price], [i].[TimeStamp], [m].[Id],
    [m].[Name], [m].[TimeStamp]
FROM [dbo].[Inventory] AS [i]
  INNER JOIN [dbo].[Makes] AS [m] ON [i].[MakeId] = [m].[Id]
WHERE ([i].[IsDrivable] = CAST(1 AS bit)) AND ([i].[MakeId] = @__makeId_0)
ORDER BY [i].[PetName]
```

Sort Records

Recall that sorting is achieved by using OrderBy()/OrderByDescending(). If more than one story level is required, add ThenBy()/ThenByDescending() for each subsequent property. Ascending and descending sorts for different properties can be used together, as shown in the following test in the CustomerTests.cs file:

```
[Fact]
public void ShouldSortByLastNameThenFirstName()
{
  //Sort by Last name then first name
  var query = Context.Customers
    .OrderBy(x => x.PersonInformation.LastName)
    .ThenByDescending(x => x.PersonInformation.FirstName);
  var qs = query.ToQueryString();
  OutputHelper.WriteLine($"Query: {qs}");
  var customers = query.ToList();
  for (int x = 0; x < customers.Count - 1; x++)
  {
    Compare(customers[x].PersonInformation, customers[x + 1].PersonInformation);
  }
  static void Compare(Person p1, Person p2)
  {
    var compareValue = string.Compare(p1.LastName, p2.LastName,
      StringComparison.CurrentCultureIgnoreCase);
    Assert.True(compareValue <=0);
    if (compareValue == 0)
```

```
    {
      //Descending first name sort
      Assert.True(string.Compare(p1.FirstName,p2.FirstName,
        StringComparison.CurrentCultureIgnoreCase) >= 0);
    }
  }
}
```

The preceding LINQ query gets translated into the following:

```
SELECT [c].[Id], [c].[TimeStamp], [c].[FirstName], [c].[FullName], [c].[LastName]
FROM [dbo].[Customers] AS [c]
ORDER BY [c].[LastName], [c].[FirstName] DESC
```

Reverse Sort Records

The Reverse() method reverses the entire sort order, as demonstrated in the next test:

```
[Fact]
public void ShouldSortByFirstNameThenLastNameUsingReverse()
{
  //Sort by Last name then first name descending then reverse the sort
  var query = Context.Customers
    .OrderBy(x => x.PersonInformation.LastName)
    .ThenByDescending(x => x.PersonInformation.FirstName)
    .Reverse();
  var qs = query.ToQueryString();
  var customers = query.ToList();
  //if only one customer, nothing to test
  if (customers.Count <= 1) { return; }

  for (int x = 0; x < customers.Count - 1; x++)
  {
    var pi1 = customers[x].PersonInformation;
    var pi2 = customers[x + 1].PersonInformation;
    var compareLastName = string.Compare(pi1.LastName,
    pi2.LastName, StringComparison.CurrentCultureIgnoreCase);
    Assert.True(compareLastName >= 0);
    if (compareLastName != 0) continue;
    var compareFirstName = string.Compare(pi1.FirstName,
    pi2.FirstName, StringComparison.CurrentCultureIgnoreCase);
    Assert.True(compareFirstName <= 0);
  }
}
```

The preceding LINQ query gets translated into the following, inverting the original OrderBy()/ThenByDescending() query:

```
SELECT [c].[Id], [c].[TimeStamp], [c].[FirstName], [c].[FullName], [c].[LastName]
FROM [dbo].[Customers] AS [c]
ORDER BY [c].[LastName] DESC, [c].[FirstName]
```

Single-Record Queries

Because of the immediate execution of the single-record LINQ statements, the ToQueryString() method isn't available. The listed query translations are provided by using SQL Server Profiler. All of the single-record tests are in the CustomerTests.cs file.

Using First

When using the parameterless form of First() and FirstOrDefault(), the first record (based on database order or any preceding ordering clauses) will be returned. The following test shows querying for the first record based on database order:

```
[Fact]
public void GetFirstMatchingRecordDatabaseOrder()
{
  //Gets the first record, database order
  var customer = Context.Customers.First();
  Assert.Equal(1, customer.Id);
}
```

The preceding LINQ query gets translated into the following:

```
SELECT TOP(1) [c].[Id], [c].[TimeStamp], [c].[FirstName], [c].[FullName], [c].[LastName]

FROM [Dbo].[Customers] AS [c]
```

The following test demonstrates getting the first record based on "last name, first name" order:

```
[Fact]
public void GetFirstMatchingRecordNameOrder()
{
  //Gets the first record, lastname, first name order
  var customer = Context.Customers
      .OrderBy(x => x.PersonInformation.LastName)
      .ThenBy(x => x.PersonInformation.FirstName)
      .First();
  Assert.Equal(1, customer.Id);
}
```

The preceding LINQ query gets translated into the following:

```
SELECT TOP(1) [c].[Id], [c].[TimeStamp], [c].[FirstName], [c].[FullName], [c].[LastName]
FROM [Dbo].[Customers] AS [c]
ORDER BY [c].[LastName], [c].[FirstName]
```

The following test asserts that an exception is thrown if there isn't a match when using First():

```
[Fact]
public void FirstShouldThrowExceptionIfNoneMatch()
{
```

```
  //Filters based on Id. Throws due to no match
  Assert.Throws<InvalidOperationException>(() => Context.Customers.First(x => x.Id == 10));
}
```

■ **Note** `Assert.Throws()` is a special type of assert statement. It is expecting an exception to the thrown by the code in the expression. If an exception *doesn't* get thrown, the assertion fails.

When using `FirstOrDefault()`, instead of an exception, the result is a null record when no data is returned. This test shows creating an expression variable:

```
[Fact]
public void FirstOrDefaultShouldReturnDefaultIfNoneMatch()
{
  //Expression<Func<Customer>> is a lambda expression
  Expression<Func<Customer, bool>> expression = x => x.Id == 10;
  //Returns null when nothing is found
  var customer = Context.Customers.FirstOrDefault(expression);
  Assert.Null(customer);
}
```

The preceding LINQ query gets translated into the same as the previous:

```
SELECT TOP(1) [c].[Id], [c].[TimeStamp], [c].[FirstName], [c].[FullName], [c].[LastName]
FROM [Dbo].[Customers] AS [c]
WHERE [c].[Id] = 10
```

Using Last

When using the parameterless form of `Last()` and `LastOrDefault()`, the last record (based on any preceding ordering clauses) will be returned. As a reminder, EF Core will throw an exception if no sort is specified. The following test gets the last record based on "last name, first name" order:

```
[Fact]
public void GetLastMatchingRecordNameOrder()
{
  //Gets the last record, lastname desc, first name desc order
  var customer = Context.Customers
      .OrderBy(x => x.PersonInformation.LastName)
      .ThenBy(x => x.PersonInformation.FirstName)
      .Last();
  Assert.Equal(4, customer.Id);
}
```

EF Core reverses the `order by` statements and then takes `top(1)` to get the result. Here is the executed query:

```
SELECT TOP(1) [c].[Id], [c].[TimeStamp], [c].[FirstName], [c].[FullName], [c].[LastName]
FROM [Dbo].[Customers] AS [c]
ORDER BY [c].[LastName] DESC, [c].[FirstName] DESC
```

This test confirms that EF Core throws an exception when `Last()` is used without an `OrderBy()/OrderByDescending()`:

```
[Fact]
public void LastShouldThrowIfNoSortSpecified()
{
  Assert.Throws<InvalidOperationException>(() => Context.Customers.Last());
}
```

Using Single

Conceptually, `Single()/SingleOrDefault()` works the same as `First()/FirstOrDefault()`. The main difference is that `Single()/SingleOrDefault()` returns `Top(2)` instead of `Top(1)` and throws an exception if two records are returned from the database. The following test retrieves the single record where `Id == 1`:

```
[Fact]
public void GetOneMatchingRecordWithSingle()
{
  //Gets the first record, database order
  var customer = Context.Customers.Single(x => x.Id == 1);
  Assert.Equal(1, customer.Id);
}
```

The preceding LINQ query gets translated into the following:

```
SELECT TOP(2) [c].[Id], [c].[TimeStamp], [c].[FirstName], [c].[FullName], [c].[LastName]
FROM [Dbo].[Customers] AS [c]
WHERE [c].[Id] = 1
```

```
Single() throws an exception if no records are returned.[Fact]
public void SingleShouldThrowExceptionIfNoneMatch()
{
  //Filters based on Id. Throws due to no match
  Assert.Throws<InvalidOperationException>(() => Context.Customers.Single(x => x.Id == 10));
}
```

When using `Single()` or `SingleOrDefault()` and more than one record is returned, an exception is thrown.

```
[Fact]
public void SingleShouldThrowExceptionIfMoreThenOneMatch()
{
  // Throws due to more than one match
  Assert.Throws<InvalidOperationException>(() => Context.Customers.Single());
}
[Fact]
public void SingleOrDefaultShouldThrowExceptionIfMoreThenOneMatch()
{
  // Throws due to more than one match
  Assert.Throws<InvalidOperationException>(() => Context.Customers.SingleOrDefault());
}
```

When using `SingleOrDefault()`, instead of an exception, the result is a null record when no data is returned.

```
[Fact]
public void SingleOrDefaultShouldReturnDefaultIfNoneMatch()
{
  //Expression<Func<Customer>> is a lambda expression
  Expression<Func<Customer, bool>> expression = x => x.Id == 10;
  //Returns null when nothing is found
  var customer = Context.Customers.SingleOrDefault(expression);
  Assert.Null(customer);
}
```

```
The preceding LINQ query gets translated into the following:
SELECT TOP(2) [c].[Id], [c].[TimeStamp], [c].[FirstName], [c].[FullName], [c].[LastName]
FROM [Dbo].[Customers] AS [c]
WHERE [c].[Id] = 10
```

Global Query Filters

Recall that there is a global query filter on the `Car` entity to filter out any cars where `IsDrivable` is false. Open the `CarTests.cs` class and add the following test that gets all the records that pass the query filter:

```
[Fact]
public void ShouldReturnDrivableCarsWithQueryFilterSet()
{
  IQueryable<Car> query = Context.Cars;
  var qs = query.ToQueryString();
  OutputHelper.WriteLine($"Query: {qs}");
  var cars = query.ToList();
  Assert.NotEmpty(cars);
  Assert.Equal(9, cars.Count);
}
```

Recall that we create 10 cars in the data initialization process, and one of them is set to be nondrivable. When the query is executed, the global query filter is applied, and the following SQL is executed:

```
SELECT [i].[Id], [i].[Color], [i].[DateBuilt], [i].[Display], [i].[IsDrivable],
    [i].[MakeId], [i].[PetName], [i].[Price], [i].[TimeStamp]
FROM [dbo].[Inventory] AS [i]
WHERE [i].[IsDrivable] = CAST(1 AS bit)
```

Disable the Query Filters

To disable global query filters for the entities in a query, add the `IgnoreQueryFilters()` method to the LINQ query. If there is more than one entity with a global query filter and some of the entities' filters are required, they must be added to the LINQ statement's `Where()` methods. Add the following test to the `CarTests.cs` class, which disables the query filter and returns all records:

```
[Fact]
public void ShouldGetAllOfTheCars()
{
  IQueryable<Car> query = Context.Cars.IgnoreQueryFilters();
  var qs = query.ToQueryString();
  OutputHelper.WriteLine($"Query: {qs}");
  var cars = query.ToList();
  Assert.Equal(10, cars.Count);
}
```

As one would expect, the where clause eliminating nondrivable cars is no longer on the generated SQL.

```
SELECT [i].[Id], [i].[Color], [i].[DateBuilt], [i].[Display], [i].[IsDrivable], [i].
[MakeId], [i].[PetName], [i].[Price], [i].[TimeStamp]
    FROM [dbo].[Inventory] AS [i]
```

Query Filters on Navigation Properties

In addition to the global query filter on the Car entity, we added a query filter to the CarNavigation property of the Order entity. To see this in action, add the following test to the OrderTests.cs class:

```
[Fact]
public void ShouldGetAllOrdersExceptFiltered()
{
  var query = Context.Orders.AsQueryable();
  var qs = query.ToQueryString();
  OutputHelper.WriteLine($"Query: {qs}");
  var orders = query.ToList();
  Assert.NotEmpty(orders);
  Assert.Equal(4,orders.Count);
}
```

```
The generated SQL is listed here:
SELECT [o].[Id], [o].[CarId], [o].[CustomerId], [o].[TimeStamp]
FROM [dbo].[Orders] AS [o]
INNER JOIN (
    SELECT [i].[Id], [i].[IsDrivable]
    FROM [dbo].[Inventory] AS [i]
    WHERE [i].[IsDrivable] = CAST(1 AS bit)
) AS [t] ON [o].[CarId] = [t].[Id]
WHERE [t].[IsDrivable] = CAST(1 AS bit)
```

Because the CarNavigation navigation property is a *required* navigation property, the query translation engine uses an INNER JOIN, eliminating the Order records where the Car is nondrivable.

```
To return all records, add IgnoreQueryFilters() to your LINQ query.[Fact]
public void ShouldGetAllOrders()
{
  var query = Context.Orders.IgnoreQueryFilters();
  var qs = query.ToQueryString();
  OutputHelper.WriteLine($"Query: {qs}");
```

```
  var orders = query.ToList();
  Assert.NotEmpty(orders);
  Assert.Equal(5, orders.Count);
}
```

You can see from the generated SQL that the where clause has been removed, and the query has been simplified:

```
SELECT [o].[Id], [o].[CarId], [o].[CustomerId], [o].[TimeStamp]
FROM [dbo].[Orders] AS [o]
```

Load Related Data Eagerly

Entities that are linked through navigation properties can be instantiated in one query using eager loading. The Include() method indicates a join to the related entity, and the ThenInclude() method is used for subsequent joins to other entities. Both of these methods will be demonstrated in these tests. When the Include()/ThenInclude() methods are translated into SQL, required relationships use an inner join, and optional relationships use a left join.

Add the following test to the CarTests.cs class to show a single Include():

```
[Fact]
public void ShouldGetAllOfTheCarsWithMakes()
{
  IIncludableQueryable<Car, Make> query =
  Context.Cars.Include(c => c.MakeNavigation);
  var qs = query.ToQueryString();
  OutputHelper.WriteLine($"Query: {qs}");
  var cars = query.ToList();
  Assert.Equal(9, cars.Count);
}
```

The query adds the MakeNavigation property to the results, performing an inner join with the following SQL being executed. The query returns all the columns from both tables, and then EF Core created Car and Make instances from the returned data. Notice the global query filter is in effect.

```
SELECT [i].[Id], [i].[Color], [i].[DateBuilt], [i].[Display], [i].[IsDrivable],
    [i].[MakeId], [i].[PetName], [i].[Price], [i].[TimeStamp], [m].[Id],
    [m].[Name], [m].[TimeStamp]
FROM [dbo].[Inventory] AS [i]
INNER JOIN [dbo].[Makes] AS [m] ON [i].[MakeId] = [m].[Id]
WHERE [i].[IsDrivable] = CAST(1 AS bit)
```

The next test demonstrates using two sets of related data. The first is getting the Make information (same as the previous test), while the second is getting the Orders and then the Customers attached to the Orders. The entire test is also filtering out the Car records that don't have any orders.

```
[Fact]
public void ShouldGetCarsOnOrderWithRelatedProperties()
{
```

```
  IIncludableQueryable<Car, Customer?> query = Context.Cars
    .Where(c => c.Orders.Any())
    .Include(c => c.MakeNavigation)
    .Include(c => c.Orders).ThenInclude(o => o.CustomerNavigation);
  var qs = query.ToQueryString();
  OutputHelper.WriteLine($"Query: {qs}");
  var cars = query.ToList();
  Assert.Equal(4, cars.Count);
  cars.ForEach(c =>
  {
    Assert.NotNull(c.MakeNavigation);
    Assert.NotNull(c.Orders.ToList()[0].CustomerNavigation);
  });
}
```

The generated query is rather lengthy. Here is the generated query:

```
SELECT [i].[Id], [i].[Color], [i].[DateBuilt], [i].[Display], [i].[IsDrivable],
    [i].[MakeId], [i].[PetName], [i].[Price], [i].[TimeStamp], [m].[Id],
    [m].[Name], [m].[TimeStamp], [t0].[Id], [t0].[CarId], [t0].[CustomerId],
    [t0].[TimeStamp], [t0].[Id0], [t0].[TimeStamp0], [t0].[FirstName],
    [t0].[FullName], [t0].[LastName], [t0].[Id1]
FROM [dbo].[Inventory] AS [i]
INNER JOIN [dbo].[Makes] AS [m] ON [i].[MakeId] = [m].[Id]
LEFT JOIN (
  SELECT [o0].[Id], [o0].[CarId], [o0].[CustomerId], [o0].[TimeStamp],
     [c].[Id] AS [Id0], [c].[TimeStamp] AS [TimeStamp0], [c].[FirstName],
     [c].[FullName], [c].[LastName], [t1].[Id] AS [Id1]
  FROM [dbo].[Orders] AS [o0]
  INNER JOIN (
    SELECT [i1].[Id], [i1].[IsDrivable]
    FROM [dbo].[Inventory] AS [i1]
    WHERE [i1].[IsDrivable] = CAST(1 AS bit)
  ) AS [t1] ON [o0].[CarId] = [t1].[Id]
  INNER JOIN [dbo].[Customers] AS [c] ON [o0].[CustomerId] = [c].[Id]
  WHERE [t1].[IsDrivable] = CAST(1 AS bit)
) AS [t0] ON [i].[Id] = [t0].[CarId]
WHERE ([i].[IsDrivable] = CAST(1 AS bit)) AND EXISTS (
  SELECT 1
  FROM [dbo].[Orders] AS [o]
  INNER JOIN (
    SELECT [i0].[Id], [i0].[Color], [i0].[DateBuilt], [i0].[Display],
       [i0].[IsDrivable], [i0].[MakeId], [i0].[PetName], [i0].[Price], [i0].[TimeStamp]
    FROM [dbo].[Inventory] AS [i0]
    WHERE [i0].[IsDrivable] = CAST(1 AS bit)
  ) AS [t] ON [o].[CarId] = [t].[Id]
WHERE ([t].[IsDrivable] = CAST(1 AS bit)) AND ([i].[Id] = [o].[CarId]))
ORDER BY [i].[Id], [m].[Id], [t0].[Id], [t0].[Id1], [t0].[Id0]
```

If you run the same query without the query filters, the query becomes much simpler. Here is the updated test that removes the query filters:

```
[Fact]
public void ShouldGetCarsOnOrderWithRelatedPropertiesIgnoreFilters()
{
  IIncludableQueryable<Car, Customer> query =
    Context.Cars.IgnoreQueryFilters().Where(c => c.Orders.Any())
            .Include(c => c.MakeNavigation)
            .Include(c => c.Orders).ThenInclude(o => o.CustomerNavigati
on)            ;
  var qs = query.ToQueryString();
  OutputHelper.WriteLine($"Query: {qs}");
  var cars = query.ToList();
  Assert.Equal(5, cars.Count);
  cars.ForEach(c =>
  {
    Assert.NotNull(c.MakeNavigation);
    Assert.NotNull(c.Orders.ToList()[0].CustomerNavigation);
  });
}
```

The generated query is rather lengthy. Here is the generated query:

```
SELECT [i].[Id], [i].[Color], [i].[DateBuilt], [i].[Display], [i].[IsDrivable], [i].
[MakeId], [i].[PetName], [i].[Price], [i].[TimeStamp], [m].[Id], [m].[Name], [m].
[TimeStamp], [t].[Id], [t].[CarId], [t].[CustomerId], [t].[TimeStamp], [t].[Id0], [t].
[TimeStamp0], [t].[FirstName], [t].[FullName], [t].[LastName]
    FROM [dbo].[Inventory] AS [i]
    INNER JOIN [dbo].[Makes] AS [m] ON [i].[MakeId] = [m].[Id]
    LEFT JOIN (
        SELECT [o0].[Id], [o0].[CarId], [o0].[CustomerId], [o0].[TimeStamp], [c].[Id] AS
[Id0], [c].[TimeStamp] AS [TimeStamp0], [c].[FirstName], [c].[FullName], [c].[LastName]
        FROM [dbo].[Orders] AS [o0]
        INNER JOIN [dbo].[Customers] AS [c] ON [o0].[CustomerId] = [c].[Id]
    ) AS [t] ON [i].[Id] = [t].[CarId]
    WHERE EXISTS (
        SELECT 1
        FROM [dbo].[Orders] AS [o]
        WHERE [i].[Id] = [o].[CarId])
    ORDER BY [i].[Id], [m].[Id], [t].[Id], [t].[Id0]
```

Splitting Queries on Related Data

The more joins added into a LINQ query, the more complex the resulting query becomes. As the previous examples demonstrated, query filters can make the queries even more complex. EF Core 5 introduced the ability to run complicated joins as split queries by adding the AsSplitQuery() method into the LINQ query. As discussed in the previous chapters, this can gain efficiency at the risk of data inconsistency. The following test demonstrates the same query just exercised, but as a split query:

```
[Fact]
public void ShouldGetCarsOnOrderWithRelatedPropertiesAsSplitQuery()
{
  IQueryable<Car> query = Context.Cars.Where(c => c.Orders.Any())
```

```
    .Include(c => c.MakeNavigation)
    .Include(c => c.Orders).ThenInclude(o => o.CustomerNavigation)
    .AsSplitQuery();
  var qs = query.ToQueryString();
  OutputHelper.WriteLine($"Query: {qs}");
  var cars = query.ToList();
  Assert.Equal(4, cars.Count);
  cars.ForEach(c =>
  {
    Assert.NotNull(c.MakeNavigation);
    Assert.NotNull(c.Orders.ToList()[0].CustomerNavigation);
  });
}
```

The ToQueryString() method returns only the first query, so the following queries were captured using SQL Server Profiler:

```
SELECT [i].[Id], [i].[Color], [i].[DateBuilt], [i].[Display], [i].[IsDrivable], [i].
[MakeId],
     [i].[PetName], [i].[Price], [i].[TimeStamp], [m].[Id], [m].[Name], [m].[TimeStamp]
FROM [dbo].[Inventory] AS [i]
INNER JOIN [dbo].[Makes] AS [m] ON [i].[MakeId] = [m].[Id]
WHERE ([i].[IsDrivable] = CAST(1 AS bit)) AND EXISTS (
  SELECT 1
  FROM [dbo].[Orders] AS [o]
  INNER JOIN (
    SELECT [i0].[Id], [i0].[Color], [i0].[DateBuilt], [i0].[Display], [i0].[IsDrivable],
            [i0].[MakeId], [i0].[PetName], [i0].[Price], [i0].[TimeStamp]
    FROM [dbo].[Inventory] AS [i0]
    WHERE [i0].[IsDrivable] = CAST(1 AS bit)
  ) AS [t] ON [o].[CarId] = [t].[Id]
  WHERE ([t].[IsDrivable] = CAST(1 AS bit)) AND ([i].[Id] = [o].[CarId]))
ORDER BY [i].[Id], [m].[Id]

SELECT [t0].[Id], [t0].[CarId], [t0].[CustomerId], [t0].[TimeStamp], [t0].[Id0],
    [t0].[TimeStamp0], [t0].[FirstName], [t0].[FullName], [t0].[LastName],
    [i].[Id], [m].[Id]
FROM [dbo].[Inventory] AS [i]
INNER JOIN [dbo].[Makes] AS [m] ON [i].[MakeId] = [m].[Id]
INNER JOIN (
  SELECT [o0].[Id], [o0].[CarId], [o0].[CustomerId], [o0].[TimeStamp],
      [c].[Id] AS [Id0], [c].[TimeStamp] AS [TimeStamp0], [c].[FirstName],
      [c].[FullName], [c].[LastName]
  FROM [dbo].[Orders] AS [o0]
  INNER JOIN (
    SELECT [i1].[Id], [i1].[IsDrivable]
    FROM [dbo].[Inventory] AS [i1]
    WHERE [i1].[IsDrivable] = CAST(1 AS bit)
  ) AS [t1] ON [o0].[CarId] = [t1].[Id]
  INNER JOIN [dbo].[Customers] AS [c] ON [o0].[CustomerId] = [c].[Id]
  WHERE [t1].[IsDrivable] = CAST(1 AS bit)
) AS [t0] ON [i].[Id] = [t0].[CarId]
```

```
WHERE ([i].[IsDrivable] = CAST(1 AS bit)) AND EXISTS (
  SELECT 1
  FROM [dbo].[Orders] AS [o]
  INNER JOIN (
    SELECT [i0].[Id], [i0].[Color], [i0].[DateBuilt], [i0].[Display], [i0].[IsDrivable],
      [i0].[MakeId], [i0].[PetName], [i0].[Price], [i0].[TimeStamp]
    FROM [dbo].[Inventory] AS [i0]
    WHERE [i0].[IsDrivable] = CAST(1 AS bit)
  ) AS [t] ON [o].[CarId] = [t].[Id]
  WHERE ([t].[IsDrivable] = CAST(1 AS bit)) AND ([i].[Id] = [o].[CarId]))
ORDER BY [i].[Id], [m].[Id]
```

Once again, removing the query filters greatly simplifies the queries generated. Here is the updated test:

```
[Fact]
public void ShouldGetCarsOnOrderWithRelatedPropertiesAsSplitQueryIgnoreQueryFilters()
{
  IQueryable<Car> query =
    Context.Cars.IgnoreQueryFilters()
                .Where(c => c.Orders.Any())
                .Include(c => c.MakeNavigation)
                .Include(c => c.Orders).ThenInclude(o => o.CustomerNavigation)
               .AsSplitQuery();
  var qs = query.ToQueryString();
  OutputHelper.WriteLine($"Query: {qs}");
  var cars = query.ToList();
  Assert.Equal(5, cars.Count);
  cars.ForEach(c =>
  {
    Assert.NotNull(c.MakeNavigation);
    Assert.NotNull(c.Orders.ToList()[0].CustomerNavigation);
  });
}
```

Here are the generated queries:

```
SELECT [i].[Id], [i].[Color], [i].[DateBuilt], [i].[Display], [i].[IsDrivable],
    [i].[MakeId], [i].[PetName], [i].[Price], [i].[TimeStamp], [m].[Id], [m].[Name], [m].
[TimeStamp]
FROM [dbo].[Inventory] AS [i]
INNER JOIN [dbo].[Makes] AS [m] ON [i].[MakeId] = [m].[Id]
WHERE EXISTS (
    SELECT 1
    FROM [dbo].[Orders] AS [o]
    WHERE [i].[Id] = [o].[CarId])
ORDER BY [i].[Id], [m].[Id]

SELECT [t].[Id], [t].[CarId], [t].[CustomerId], [t].[TimeStamp], [t].[Id0],
    [t].[TimeStamp0], [t].[FirstName], [t].[FullName], [t].[LastName], [i].[Id], [m].[Id]
FROM [dbo].[Inventory] AS [i]
INNER JOIN [dbo].[Makes] AS [m] ON [i].[MakeId] = [m].[Id]
```

```
INNER JOIN (
  SELECT [o0].[Id], [o0].[CarId], [o0].[CustomerId], [o0].[TimeStamp],
      [c].[Id] AS [Id0], [c].[TimeStamp] AS [TimeStamp0], [c].[FirstName], [c].[FullName],
[c].[LastName]
  FROM [dbo].[Orders] AS [o0]
  INNER JOIN [dbo].[Customers] AS [c] ON [o0].[CustomerId] = [c].[Id]
) AS [t] ON [i].[Id] = [t].[CarId]
WHERE EXISTS (
  SELECT 1
  FROM [dbo].[Orders] AS [o]
  WHERE [i].[Id] = [o].[CarId])
ORDER BY [i].[Id], [m].[Id]
```

Filtering Related Data

EF Core 5 introduces the ability to filter when including collection properties. Prior to EF Core 5, the only way to get a filtered list for a collection navigation property was to use explicit loading. Add the following test into the MakeTests.cs class, which demonstrates getting all the Make records and those cars that are yellow:

```
[Fact]
public void ShouldGetAllMakesAndCarsThatAreYellow()
{
  var query = Context.Makes.IgnoreQueryFilters()
      .Include(x => x.Cars.Where(x => x.Color == "Yellow"));
  var qs = query.ToQueryString();
  OutputHelper.WriteLine($"Query: {qs}");
  var makes = query.ToList();
  Assert.NotNull(makes);
  Assert.NotEmpty(makes);
  Assert.NotEmpty(makes.Where(x => x.Cars.Any()));
  Assert.Empty(makes.First(m => m.Id == 1).Cars);
  Assert.Empty(makes.First(m => m.Id == 2).Cars);
  Assert.Empty(makes.First(m => m.Id == 3).Cars);
  Assert.Single(makes.First(m => m.Id == 4).Cars);
  Assert.Empty(makes.First(m => m.Id == 5).Cars);
}
```

The generated SQL is as follows:

```
SELECT [m].[Id], [m].[Name], [m].[TimeStamp], [t].[Id], [t].[Color],
    [t].[DateBuilt], [t].[Display], [t].[IsDrivable], [t].[MakeId],
    [t].[PetName], [t].[Price], [t].[TimeStamp]
FROM [dbo].[Makes] AS [m]
LEFT JOIN (
  SELECT [i].[Id], [i].[Color], [i].[DateBuilt], [i].[Display], [i].[IsDrivable],
    [i].[MakeId], [i].[PetName], [i].[Price], [i].[TimeStamp]
  FROM [dbo].[Inventory] AS [i]
  WHERE [i].[Color] = N'Yellow'
) AS [t] ON [m].[Id] = [t].[MakeId]
ORDER BY [m].[Id], [t].[Id]
```

Changing the query to a split query yields this SQL (collection from SQL Server Profiler):

```
SELECT [m].[Id], [m].[Name], [m].[TimeStamp]
FROM [dbo].[Makes] AS [m]
ORDER BY [m].[Id]

SELECT [t].[Id], [t].[Color], [t].[DateBuilt], [t].[Display], [t].[IsDrivable],
    [t].[MakeId], [t].[PetName], [t].[Price], [t].[TimeStamp], [m].[Id]
FROM [dbo].[Makes] AS [m]
INNER JOIN (
  SELECT [i].[Id], [i].[Color], [i].[DateBuilt], [i].[Display], [i].[IsDrivable],
    [i].[MakeId], [i].[PetName], [i].[Price], [i].[TimeStamp]
  FROM [dbo].[Inventory] AS [i]
  WHERE [i].[Color] = N'Yellow'
) AS [t] ON [m].[Id] = [t].[MakeId]
ORDER BY [m].[Id]
```

Load Related Data Explicitly

If the related data needs to be loaded after the principal entity was queried into memory, the related entities can be retrieved from the database with subsequent database calls. This is triggered using the `Entry()` method on the derived `DbContext`. When loading entities on the many end of a one-to-many relationship, use the `Collection()` method on the `Entry` result. To load entities on the one end of a one-to-many (or in a one-to-one relationship), use the `Reference()` method. Calling `Query()` on the `Collection()` or `Reference()` method returns an `IQueryable<T>` that can be used to get the query string (as shown in the following tests) and to manage query filters (as shown in the next section). To execute the query and load the record(s), call the `Load()` method on the `Collection()`, `Reference()`, or `Query()` method. Query execution happens immediately when `Load()` is called.

The following test (back in the `CarTests.cs` class) shows how to load a reference navigation property on the `Car` entity:

```
[Fact]
public void ShouldGetReferenceRelatedInformationExplicitly()
{
  var car = Context.Cars.First(x => x.Id == 1);
  Assert.Null(car.MakeNavigation);
  var query = Context.Entry(car).Reference(c => c.MakeNavigation).Query();
  var qs = query.ToQueryString();
  OutputHelper.WriteLine($"Query: {qs}");
  query.Load();
  Assert.NotNull(car.MakeNavigation);
}
```

The generated SQL to get the `Make` information is as follows (the `Car` record was already queried):

```
DECLARE @__p_0 int = 1;

SELECT [m].[Id], [m].[Name], [m].[TimeStamp]
FROM [dbo].[Makes] AS [m]
WHERE [m].[Id] = @__p_0
```

This test shows how to load a collection navigation property on the Car entity:

```
[Fact]
public void ShouldGetCollectionRelatedInformationExplicitly()
{
  var car = Context.Cars.First(x => x.Id == 1);
  Assert.Empty(car.Orders);
  var query = Context.Entry(car).Collection(c => c.Orders).Query();
  var qs = query.ToQueryString();
  OutputHelper.WriteLine($"Query: {qs}");
  query.Load();
  Assert.Single(car.Orders);
}
```

The generated SQL is as follows:

```
DECLARE @__p_0 int = 1;

SELECT [o].[Id], [o].[CarId], [o].[CustomerId], [o].[TimeStamp]
FROM [dbo].[Orders] AS [o]
INNER JOIN (
  SELECT [i].[Id], [i].[IsDrivable]
  FROM [dbo].[Inventory] AS [i]
  WHERE [i].[IsDrivable] = CAST(1 AS bit)
) AS [t] ON [o].[CarId] = [t].[Id]
WHERE ([t].[IsDrivable] = CAST(1 AS bit)) AND ([o].[CarId] = @__p_0)
```

Load Related Data Explicitly with Query Filters

In addition to shaping queries generated when eagerly loading related data, global query filters are active when explicitly loading related data. Take the following test (in the MakeTests.cs class):

```
[Theory]
[InlineData(1,1)]
[InlineData(2,1)]
[InlineData(3,1)]
[InlineData(4,2)]
[InlineData(5,3)]
[InlineData(6,1)]
public void ShouldGetAllCarsForAMakeExplicitlyWithQueryFilters(int makeId, int carCount)
{
  var make = Context.Makes.First(x => x.Id == makeId);
  IQueryable<Car> query = Context.Entry(make).Collection(c => c.Cars).Query();
  var qs = query.ToQueryString();
  OutputHelper.WriteLine($"Query: {qs}");
  query.Load();
  Assert.Equal(carCount,make.Cars.Count());
}
```

This test is similar to ShouldGetTheCarsByMake() from the "Filter Records" section. However, instead of just getting the Car records that have a certain MakeId, the test first gets a Make record and then explicitly loads the Car records for the already retrieved Make record. The generated query is shown here:

```
DECLARE @__p_0 int = 1;

SELECT [i].[Id], [i].[Color], [i].[DateBuilt], [i].[Display], [i].[IsDrivable],
    [i].[MakeId], [i].[PetName], [i].[Price], [i].[TimeStamp]
FROM [dbo].[Inventory] AS [i]
WHERE ([i].[IsDrivable] = CAST(1 AS bit)) AND ([i].[MakeId] = @__p_0)
```

Notice that the query filter is still being used, even though the principal entity in the query is the Make record. To turn off query filters when explicitly loading records, call IgnoreQueryFilters() in conjunction with the Query() method. Here is the test that turns off query filters (again, in the MakeTests.cs class):

```
[Theory]
[InlineData(1, 2)]
[InlineData(2, 1)]
[InlineData(3, 1)]
[InlineData(4, 2)]
[InlineData(5, 3)]
[InlineData(6, 1)]
public void ShouldGetAllCarsForAMakeExplicitly(int makeId, int carCount)
{
  var make = Context.Makes.First(x => x.Id == makeId);
  IQueryable<Car> query =
    Context.Entry(make).Collection(c => c.Cars).Query().IgnoreQueryFilters();
  var qs = query.IgnoreQueryFilters().ToQueryString();
  OutputHelper.WriteLine($"Query: {qs}");
  query.Load();
  Assert.Equal(carCount, make.Cars.Count());
}
```

Temporal Queries

This section exercises EF Core's ability to retrieve historical data from temporal tables. As a reminder, the repos that derive from the TemporalTableBaseRepo contain the methods to query temporal tables using one of the five temporal query operators. To demonstrate this, open the MakeTests class, and add the following test at the bottom of the file:

```
[Fact]
public void ShouldGetAllHistoryRows()
{
  var make = new Make { Name = "TestMake" };
  _repo.Add(make);
  Thread.Sleep(2000);
  make.Name = "Updated Name";
  _repo.Update(make);
  Thread.Sleep(2000);
  _repo.Delete(make);
```

```
    var list = _repo.GetAllHistory().Where(x => x.Entity.Id == make.Id).ToList();
    Assert.Equal(2, list.Count);
    Assert.Equal("TestMake", list[0].Entity.Name);
    Assert.Equal("Updated Name", list[1].Entity.Name);
    Assert.Equal(list[0].ValidTo, list[1].ValidFrom);
}
```

The test creates a new Make record and adds it to the database. After pausing operation for two seconds, the Name is updated, and the change saved. After another two-second pause, the record is deleted. The test then uses the MakeRepo to get all the history for the Make record, confirms that there are two records in the history, makes sure the records are retrieved in ValidFrom order, and makes sure that the ValidTo of the first record exactly matches the ValidFrom of the second record.

SQL Queries with LINQ

This section exercises EF Core's ability to retrieve data using raw SQL queries using the DbSet<T>'s FromSqlRaw() or FromSqlInterpolated() methods. The first test (in the CarTests.cs class) uses a raw SQL query to get all the records from the Inventory table. Notice that the query must use the database names and not the entity names as well as add in the timestamp columns for the temporal functionality:

```
[Fact]
public void ShouldNotGetTheLemonsUsingFromSql()
{
  var entity = Context.Model.FindEntityType($"{typeof(Car).FullName}");
  var tableName = entity.GetTableName();
  var schemaName = entity.GetSchema();
  var query = Context.Cars
    .FromSqlRaw($"Select *,ValidFrom,ValidTo from {schemaName}.{tableName}");
  var qs = query.ToQueryString();
  OutputHelper.WriteLine($"Query: {qs}");
  var cars = query.ToList();
  Assert.Equal(9, cars.Count);
}
```

When using raw SQL queries, the query gets wrapped into a larger query by EF Core to support the query filter. If the statement was terminated with a semicolon, the query would not be executable on SQL Server.

```
SELECT [a].[Id], [a].[Color], [a].[DateBuilt], [a].[Display], [a].[IsDrivable], [a].
[MakeId], [a].[PetName], [a].[Price], [a].[TimeStamp], [a].[ValidFrom], [a].[ValidTo]
FROM (
    Select *,ValidFrom,ValidTo from dbo.Inventory
) AS [a]
WHERE [a].[IsDrivable] = CAST(1 AS bit)
```

When the query filter is removed, the generated SQL becomes the same SQL as the string passed into the FromSqlRaw() method:

```
Select *,ValidFrom,ValidTo from dbo.Inventory
```

The following test demonstrates using FromSqlInterpolated() with additional LINQ statements (including the MakeNavigation):

```
[Fact]
public void ShouldGetOneCarUsingInterpolation()
{
  var carId = 1;
  var query = Context.Cars
    .FromSqlInterpolated($"Select *,ValidFrom,ValidTo from dbo.Inventory where Id =
{carId}")
    .Include(x => x.MakeNavigation);
  var qs = query.ToQueryString();
  OutputHelper.WriteLine($"Query: {qs}");
  var car = query.First();
  Assert.Equal("Black", car.Color);
  Assert.Equal("VW", car.MakeNavigation.Name);
}
```

Here is the generated SQL:

```
DECLARE p0 int = 1;

SELECT [a].[Id], [a].[Color], [a].[DateBuilt], [a].[Display], [a].[IsDrivable], [a].[MakeId],
    [a].[PetName], [a].[Price], [a].[TimeStamp], [a].[ValidFrom], [a].[ValidTo],
    [m].[Id], [m].[Name], [m].[TimeStamp], [m].[ValidFrom], [m].[ValidTo]
FROM (
    Select *,ValidFrom,ValidTo from dbo.Inventory where Id = @p0
) AS [a]
INNER JOIN [dbo].[Makes] AS [m] ON [a].[MakeId] = [m].[Id]
WHERE [a].[IsDrivable] = CAST(1 AS bit)
```

Aggregate Methods

The next set of tests demonstrate the server-side aggregate methods (Max(), Min(), Count(), Average(), etc.). Aggregate methods can be added to the end of a LINQ query with Where() methods, or the filter expression can be contained in the aggregate method itself (just like First() and Single()). The aggregation executes on the server side, and the single value is returned from the query. Global query filters affect aggregate methods as well and can be disabled with IgnoreQueryFilters().

All the SQL statements shown in this section were collected using SQL Server Profiler.

This first test (in CarTests.cs) simply counts all the Car records in the database. Since the query filter is still active, the count returns nine cars.

```
[Fact]
public void ShouldGetTheCountOfCars()
{
  var count = Context.Cars.Count();
  Assert.Equal(9, count);
}
```

The executed SQL is shown here:

```
SELECT COUNT(*)
FROM [dbo].[Inventory] AS [i]
WHERE [i].[IsDrivable] = CAST(1 AS bit)
```

By adding `IgnoreQueryFilters()`, the `Count()` method returns 10, and the `where` clause is removed from the SQL query.

```
[Fact]
public void ShouldGetTheCountOfCarsIgnoreQueryFilters()
{
  var count = Context.Cars.IgnoreQueryFilters().Count();
  Assert.Equal(10, count);
}

--Generated SQL
SELECT COUNT(*) FROM [dbo].[Inventory] AS [i]
```

The following tests (also in `CarTests.cs`) demonstrate the `Count()` method with a `where` condition. The first test adds the expression directly into the `Count()` method, and the second adds the `Count()` method to the end of the LINQ statement.

```
[Theory]
[InlineData(1, 1)]
[InlineData(2, 1)]
[InlineData(3, 1)]
[InlineData(4, 2)]
[InlineData(5, 3)]
[InlineData(6, 1)]
public void ShouldGetTheCountOfCarsByMakeP1(int makeId, int expectedCount)
{
    var count = Context.Cars.Count(x=>x.MakeId == makeId);
    Assert.Equal(expectedCount, count);
}

[Theory]
[InlineData(1, 1)]
[InlineData(2, 1)]
[InlineData(3, 1)]
[InlineData(4, 2)]
[InlineData(5, 3)]
[InlineData(6, 1)]
public void ShouldGetTheCountOfCarsByMakeP2(int makeId, int expectedCount)
{
    var count = Context.Cars.Where(x => x.MakeId == makeId).Count();
    Assert.Equal(expectedCount, count);
}
```

Both tests create the same SQL calls to the server, as shown here (the MakeId changes with each test based on the InlineData):

```
exec sp_executesql N'SELECT COUNT(*)
FROM [dbo].[Inventory] AS [i]
WHERE ([i].[IsDrivable] = CAST(1 AS bit)) AND ([i].[MakeId] = @__makeId_0)'
,N'@__makeId_0 int',@__makeId_0=6
```

Any() and All()

The Any() and All() methods check a set of records to see whether any records match the criteria (Any()) or whether all records match the criteria (All()). Global query filters affect Any() and All() methods functions as well and can be disabled with IgnoreQueryFilters(). All the SQL statements shown in this section were collected using SQL Server Profiler.

This first test (in CarTests.cs) checks if *any* car records have a specific MakeId:

```
[Theory]
[InlineData(1, true)]
[InlineData(11, false)]
public void ShouldCheckForAnyCarsWithMake(int makeId, bool expectedResult)
{
  var result = Context.Cars.Any(x => x.MakeId == makeId);
  Assert.Equal(expectedResult, result);
}
```

The executed SQL for the first theory test is shown here:

```
exec sp_executesql N'SELECT CASE
    WHEN EXISTS (
        SELECT 1
        FROM [dbo].[Inventory] AS [i]
        WHERE ([i].[IsDrivable] = CAST(1 AS bit)) AND ([i].[MakeId] = @__makeId_0)) THEN
CAST(1 AS bit)
    ELSE CAST(0 AS bit)
END',N'@__makeId_0 int',@__makeId_0=1
```

This second test checks if *all* car records have a specific MakeId:

```
[Theory]
[InlineData(1, false)]
[InlineData(11, false)]
public void ShouldCheckForAllCarsWithMake(int makeId, bool expectedResult)
{
  var result = Context.Cars.All(x => x.MakeId == makeId);
  Assert.Equal(expectedResult, result);
}
```

The executed SQL for the first theory test is shown here:

```
exec sp_executesql N'SELECT CASE

    WHEN NOT EXISTS (
        SELECT 1
        FROM [dbo].[Inventory] AS [i]
        WHERE ([i].[IsDrivable] = CAST(1 AS bit)) AND ([i].[MakeId] <> @__makeId_0)) THEN
CAST(1 AS bit)
    ELSE CAST(0 AS bit)
END',N'@__makeId_0 int',@__makeId_0=1
```

Getting Data from Stored Procedures

The final test is to make sure that the CarRepo can get the PetName from the stored procedure. With this code in place, the test becomes trivial. Add the following test to the CarTests.cs class:

```
[Theory]
[InlineData(1, "Zippy")]
[InlineData(2, "Rusty")]
[InlineData(3, "Mel")]
[InlineData(4, "Clunker")]
[InlineData(5, "Bimmer")]
[InlineData(6, "Hank")]
[InlineData(7, "Pinky")]
[InlineData(8, "Pete")]
[InlineData(9, "Brownie")]
public void ShouldGetValueFromStoredProc(int id, string expectedName)
{
    Assert.Equal(expectedName, _carRepo.GetPetName(id));
}
```

Creating Records

Records are added to the database by creating them in code, adding them to their DbSet<T>, and calling S aveChanges()/SaveChangesAsync() on the context. When SaveChanges() is executed, the ChangeTracker reports all the added entities, and EF Core (along with the database provider) creates the appropriate SQL statement(s) to insert the record(s).

As a reminder, SaveChanges() executes in an implicit transaction, unless an explicit transaction is used. If the save was successful, the server-generated values are then queried to set the values on the entities. These tests will all use an explicit transaction so the changes can be rolled back, leaving the database in the same state as when the test execution began.

All the SQL statements shown in this section were collected using SQL Server Profiler.

■ **Note** Records can also be added using the derived DbContext as well. These examples will all use the DbSet<T> collection properties to add the records. Both DbSet<T> and DbContext have async versions of Add()/AddRange(). Only the synchronous versions are shown.

Add a Single Record

The following test demonstrates how to add a single record to the Inventory table:

```
[Fact]
public void ShouldAddACar()
{
  ExecuteInATransaction(RunTheTest);

  void RunTheTest()
  {
    var car = new Car
    {
      Color = "Yellow",
      MakeId = 1,
      PetName = "Herbie"
    };
    var carCount = Context.Cars.Count();
    Context.Cars.Add(car);
    Context.SaveChanges();
    var newCarCount = Context.Cars.Count();
    Assert.Equal(carCount+1,newCarCount);
  }
}
```

The executed SQL statement is shown here. Notice that the recently added entity is queried for the database-generated properties (Id and TimeStamp). When the results of the query come to EF Core, the entity is updated with the server-side values.

```
exec sp_executesql N'SET NOCOUNT ON;
INSERT INTO [dbo].[Inventory] ([Color], [MakeId], [PetName], [Price])
VALUES (@p0, @p1, @p2, @p3);
SELECT [Id], [DateBuilt], [Display], [IsDrivable], [TimeStamp]
FROM [dbo].[Inventory]
WHERE @@ROWCOUNT = 1 AND [Id] = scope_identity();
',
N'@p0 nvarchar(50),@p1 int,@p2 nvarchar(50),@p3 nvarchar(50)',@p0=N'Yellow',@p1=1,
@p2=N'Herbie',@p3=NULL
```

Add a Single Record Using Attach

The following test creates a new Car entity with the Id left at the default value of zero. When the entity is attached to the ChangeTracker, the state is set to Added, and calling SaveChanges() adds the entity to the database.

```
[Fact]
public void ShouldAddACarWithAttach()
{
  ExecuteInATransaction(RunTheTest);

  void RunTheTest()
  {
```

```
    var car = new Car
    {
      Color = "Yellow",
      MakeId = 1,
      PetName = "Herbie"
    };
    var carCount = Context.Cars.Count();
    Context.Cars.Attach(car);
    Assert.Equal(EntityState.Added, Context.Entry(car).State);
    Context.SaveChanges();
    var newCarCount = Context.Cars.Count();
    Assert.Equal(carCount + 1, newCarCount);
  }
}
```

Add Multiple Records at Once

To insert multiple records in a single transaction, use the AddRange() method of DbSet<T>, as shown in this test (note that with SQL Server, for batching to be used when persisting data, there must be at least four actions to execute):

```
[Fact]
public void ShouldAddMultipleCars()
{
  ExecuteInATransaction(RunTheTest);

  void RunTheTest()
  {
    //Have to add 4 to activate batching
    var cars = new List<Car>
    {
      new() { Color = "Yellow", MakeId = 1, PetName = "Herbie" },
      new() { Color = "White", MakeId = 2, PetName = "Mach 5" },
      new() { Color = "Pink", MakeId = 3, PetName = "Avon" },
      new() { Color = "Blue", MakeId = 4, PetName = "Blueberry" },
    };
    var carCount = Context.Cars.Count();
    Context.Cars.AddRange(cars);
    Context.SaveChanges();
    var newCarCount = Context.Cars.Count();
    Assert.Equal(carCount + 4, newCarCount);
  }
}
```

The add statements are batched into a single call to the database, and all the generated columns are queried. When the results of the query come to EF Core, the entities are updated with the server-side values. The executed SQL statement is shown here:

```
exec sp_executesql N'SET NOCOUNT ON;
DECLARE @inserted0 TABLE ([Id] int, [_Position] [int]);
MERGE [dbo].[Inventory] USING (
```

```
VALUES (@p0, @p1, @p2, @p3, 0),
(@p4, @p5, @p6, @p7, 1),
(@p8, @p9, @p10, @p11, 2),
(@p12, @p13, @p14, @p15, 3))
AS i ([Color], [MakeId], [PetName], [Price], _Position) ON 1=0
WHEN NOT MATCHED THEN
INSERT ([Color], [MakeId], [PetName], [Price])
VALUES (i.[Color], i.[MakeId], i.[PetName], i.[Price])
OUTPUT INSERTED.[Id], i._Position
INTO @inserted0;

SELECT [t].[Id], [t].[DateBuilt], [t].[Display], [t].[IsDrivable], [t].[TimeStamp]
FROM [dbo].[Inventory] t
INNER JOIN @inserted0 i ON ([t].[Id] = [i].[Id])
ORDER BY [i].[_Position];
',
N'@p0 nvarchar(50),@p1 int,@p2 nvarchar(50),@p3 nvarchar(50),
  @p4 nvarchar(50),@p5 int,@p6 nvarchar(50),@p7 nvarchar(50),
  @p8 nvarchar(50),@p9 int,@p10 nvarchar(50),@p11 nvarchar(50),
  @p12 nvarchar(50),@p13 int,@p14 nvarchar(50),@p15 nvarchar(50)',
  @p0=N'Yellow',@p1=1,@p2=N'Herbie',@p3=NULL,@p4=N'White',@p5=2,
  @p6=N'Mach 5',@p7=NULL,@p8=N'Pink',@p9=3,@p10=N'Avon',@p11=NULL,@p12=N'Blue',
  @p13=4,@p14=N'Blueberry',@p15=NULL
```

Adding an Object Graph

The following test demonstrates adding an object graph (related Make, Car, and Radio records):

```
[Fact]
public void ShouldAddAnObjectGraph()
{
  ExecuteInATransaction(RunTheTest);

  void RunTheTest()
  {
    var make = new Make {Name = "Honda"};
    var car = new Car
    {
      Color = "Yellow",
      MakeId = 1,
      PetName = "Herbie",
      RadioNavigation = new Radio
      {
        HasSubWoofers = true,
        HasTweeters = true,
        RadioId = "Bose 1234"
      }
    };
    //Cast the Cars property to List<Car> from IEnumerable<Car>
    ((List<Car>)make.Cars).Add(car);
    Context.Makes.Add(make);
```

```
        var carCount = Context.Cars.Count();
        var makeCount = Context.Makes.Count();
        Context.SaveChanges();
        var newCarCount = Context.Cars. Count();
        var newMakeCount = Context.Makes. Count();
        Assert.Equal(carCount+1,newCarCount);
        Assert.Equal(makeCount+1,newMakeCount);
    }
}
```

The executed SQL statements (one for each table) are shown here:

```
exec sp_executesql N'SET NOCOUNT ON;
INSERT INTO [dbo].[Makes] ([Name])
VALUES (@p0);
SELECT [Id], [TimeStamp]
FROM [dbo].[Makes]
WHERE @@ROWCOUNT = 1 AND [Id] = scope_identity();
',
N'@p0 nvarchar(50)',@p0=N'Honda'

exec sp_executesql N'SET NOCOUNT ON;
INSERT INTO [dbo].[Inventory] ([Color], [MakeId], [PetName], [Price])
VALUES (@p1, @p2, @p3, @p4);
SELECT [Id], [DateBuilt], [Display], [IsDrivable], [TimeStamp]
FROM [dbo].[Inventory]
WHERE @@ROWCOUNT = 1 AND [Id] = scope_identity();

',N'@p1 nvarchar(50),@p2 int,@p3 nvarchar(50),@p4 nvarchar(50)',@p1=N'Yellow',@p2=7,
@p3=N'Herbie',@p4=NULL

exec sp_executesql N'SET NOCOUNT ON;
INSERT INTO [dbo].[Radios] ([InventoryId], [HasSubWoofers],
  [HasTweeters], [RadioId])
VALUES (@p5, @p6, @p7, @p8);
SELECT [Id], [TimeStamp]
FROM [dbo].[Radios]
WHERE @@ROWCOUNT = 1 AND [Id] = scope_identity();
',
N'@p5 int,@p6 bit,@p7 bit,@p8 nvarchar(50)',@p5=11,
  @p6=1,@p7=1,@p8=N'Bose 1234'
```

Updating Records

Records are updated by loading them into DbSet<T> as a tracked entity, changing them through code, and then calling SaveChanges() on the context. When SaveChanges() is executed, the ChangeTracker reports all the modified entities, and EF Core (along with the database provider) creates the appropriate SQL statement(s) to update the record(s).

Update Tracked Entities

The following test updates a single record, but the process is the same if multiple tracked entities are updated and saved.

```
[Fact]
public void ShouldUpdateACar()
{
  ExecuteInASharedTransaction(RunTheTest);

  void RunTheTest(IDbContextTransaction trans)
  {
    var car = Context.Cars.First(c => c.Id == 1);
    Assert.Equal("Black",car.Color);
    car.Color = "White";
    //Calling update is not needed because the entity is tracked
    //Context.Cars.Update(car);
    Context.SaveChanges();
    Assert.Equal("White", car.Color);
    var context2 = TestHelpers.GetSecondContext(Context, trans);
    var car2 = context2.Cars.First(c => c.Id == 1);
    Assert.Equal("White", car2.Color);
  }
}
```

The prior code uses a shared transaction across two instances of ApplicationDbContext. This is to provide isolation between the context executing the test and the context checking the result of the test.

The executed SQL statement is listed here:

```
exec sp_executesql N'SET NOCOUNT ON;
UPDATE [dbo].[Inventory] SET [Color] = @p0
WHERE [Id] = @p1 AND [TimeStamp] = @p2;
SELECT [TimeStamp]
FROM [dbo].[Inventory]
WHERE @@ROWCOUNT = 1 AND [Id] = @p1;

',N'@p1 int,@p0 nvarchar(50),@p2 varbinary(8)',@p1=1,@p0=N'White',@p2=0x000000000000862D
```

Update Nontracked Entities

Untracked entities can also be used to update database records. The process is similar to updating tracked entities except that the entity is created in code (and not queried), and EF Core must be notified that the entity should already exist in the database and needs to be updated.

The following example reads a record in as nontracked, creates a new instance of the Car class from this record, and changes one property (Color). Then it either sets the state or uses the Update() method on DbSet<T>, depending on which line of code you uncomment. The Update() method also changes the state to Modified. The test then calls SaveChanges(). All of the extra contexts are there to ensure the test is accurate, and there isn't any crossover between contexts.

```
[Fact]
public void ShouldUpdateACarUsingState()
{
  ExecuteInASharedTransaction(RunTheTest);

  void RunTheTest(IDbContextTransaction trans)
  {
    var car = Context.Cars.AsNoTracking().First(c => c.Id == 1);
    Assert.Equal("Black", car.Color);
    var updatedCar = new Car
    {
      Color = "White", //Original is Black
      Id = car.Id,
      MakeId = car.MakeId,
      PetName = car.PetName,
      TimeStamp = car.TimeStamp,
      IsDrivable = car.IsDrivable
    };
    var context2 = TestHelpers.GetSecondContext(Context, trans);
    //Either call Update or modify the state
    context2.Entry(updatedCar).State = EntityState.Modified;
    //context2.Cars.Update(updatedCar);
    context2.SaveChanges();
    var context3 =
      TestHelpers.GetSecondContext(Context, trans);
    var car2 = context3.Cars.First(c => c.Id == 1);
    Assert.Equal("White", car2.Color);
  }
}
```

Concurrency Checking When Updating Records

The previous chapters covered concurrency checking in great detail. As a reminder, when an entity has a Timestamp property defined, the value of that property is used in the where clause when changes (updates or deletes) are being persisted to the database. Instead of just searching for the primary key, the TimeStamp value is added to the query, like this example:

```
UPDATE [dbo].[Inventory] SET [PetName] = @p0
WHERE [Id] = @p1 AND [TimeStamp] = @p2;
```

The following test shows an example of creating a concurrency exception, catching it, and using the Entries to get the original values, current values, and values that are currently stored in the database. Getting the current values requires another database call.

```
[Fact]
public void ShouldThrowConcurrencyException()
{
  ExecuteInATransaction(RunTheTest);

  void RunTheTest()
  {
```

```
    var car = Context.Cars.First();
    //Update the database outside of the context
    Context.Database.ExecuteSqlInterpolated(
      $"Update dbo.Inventory set Color='Pink' where Id = {car.Id}");
    car.Color = "Yellow";
    var ex = Assert.Throws<CustomConcurrencyException>(
      () => Context.SaveChanges());
    var entry = ((DbUpdateConcurrencyException) ex.InnerException)?.Entries[0];
    PropertyValues originalProps = entry.OriginalValues;
    PropertyValues currentProps = entry.CurrentValues;
    //This needs another database call
    PropertyValues databaseProps = entry.GetDatabaseValues();
  }
}
```

Deleting Records

A single entity is marked for deletion by calling Remove() on DbSet<T> or by setting its state to Deleted. A list of records are marked for deletion by calling RemoveRange() on the DbSet<T>. The removal process will cause cascade effects on navigation properties based on the rules configured in the Fluent API (or by EF Core conventions). If deletion is prevented due to cascade policy, an exception is thrown.

Delete Tracked Records

The delete process mirrors the update process. Once an entity is tracked, call Remove() on that instance, and then call SaveChanges() to remove the record from the database.

```
[Fact]
public void ShouldRemoveACar()
{
  ExecuteInATransaction(RunTheTest);

  void RunTheTest()
  {
    var carCount = Context.Cars. Count();
    var car = Context.Cars.First(c => c.Id == 9);
    Context.Cars.Remove(car);
    Context.SaveChanges();
    var newCarCount = Context.Cars.Count();
    Assert.Equal(carCount - 1, newCarCount);
    Assert.Equal(
      EntityState.Detached,
      Context.Entry(car).State);
  }
}
```

After SaveChanges() is called, the entity instance still exists, but is no longer in the ChangeTracker. When checking the EntityState, the state will be Detached.

The executed SQL call for the delete is listed here:

```
exec sp_executesql N'SET NOCOUNT ON;
DELETE FROM [dbo].[Inventory]
WHERE [Id] = @p0 AND [TimeStamp] = @p1;
SELECT @@ROWCOUNT;'
,N'@p0 int,@p1 varbinary(8)',@p0=2,@p1=0x0000000000008680
```

Delete Nontracked Entities

Untracked entities can delete records the same way untracked entities can update records. The difference is that the entity is tracked by calling Remove()/RemoveRange() or setting the state to Deleted and then calling SaveChanges().

The following example reads a record in as nontracked, creates a new instance of the Car class from this record, and changes one property (Color). Then it either sets the state or uses the Remove() method on DbSet<T> (depending on which line you uncomment). The test then calls SaveChanges(). All the extra contexts are there to ensure there isn't any crossover between contexts.

```
[Fact]
public void ShouldRemoveACarUsingState()
{
  ExecuteInASharedTransaction(RunTheTest);

  void RunTheTest(IDbContextTransaction trans)
  {
    var carCount = Context.Cars.Count();
    var car = Context.Cars.AsNoTracking().First(c => c.Id == 1);
    var context2 = TestHelpers.GetSecondContext(Context, trans);
    //Either call Remove or modify the state
    context2.Entry(car).State = EntityState.Deleted;
    //context2.Cars.Remove(car);
    context2.SaveChanges();
    var newCarCount = Context.Cars.Count();
    Assert.Equal(carCount - 1, newCarCount);
    Assert.Equal(
      EntityState.Detached,
      Context.Entry(car).State);
  }
}
```

Catch Cascade Delete Failures

EF Core will throw a DbUpdateException when an attempt to delete a record fails due to the cascade rules. The following test shows this in action:

```
[Fact]
public void ShouldFailToRemoveACar()
{
  ExecuteInATransaction(RunTheTest);
```

```
  void RunTheTest()
  {
    var car = Context.Cars.First(c => c.Id == 1);
    Context.Cars.Remove(car);
    Assert.Throws<CustomDbUpdateException>(
      ()=>Context.SaveChanges());
  }
}
```

Concurrency Checking When Deleting Records

Delete also uses concurrency checking if the entity has a `TimeStamp` property. See the section "Concurrency Checking" in the "Updating Records" section for more information.

Summary

This chapter used the knowledge gained in the previous chapter to complete the data access layer for the `AutoLot` database. You used the EF Core command-line tools to scaffold an existing database, updated the model to its final version, and then created migrations and applied them. Repositories were added for the encapsulation of the data access, and database initialization code with sample data can drop and create the database in a repeatable, reliable manner. The rest of the chapter focused on test-driving the data access layer. This completes our journey through data access and Entity Framework Core.

PART VIII

Windows Client Development

CHAPTER 25

Introducing Windows Presentation Foundation and XAML

When version 1.0 of the .NET platform was released, programmers who needed to build graphical desktop applications made use of two APIs named Windows Forms and GDI+, packaged up primarily in the `System.Windows.Forms.dll` and `System.Drawing.dll` assemblies. While Windows Forms and GDI+ are still viable APIs for building traditional desktop GUIs, Microsoft shipped an alternative GUI desktop API named Windows Presentation Foundation (WPF) beginning with the release of .NET 3.0. WPF and Windows Forms joined the .NET Core family with the release of .NET Core 3.0.

This initial WPF chapter begins by examining the motivation behind this new GUI framework, which will help you see the differences between the Windows Forms/GDI+ and WPF programming models. Next, you will come to know the role of several important classes, including `Application`, `Window`, `ContentControl`, `Control`, `UIElement`, and `FrameworkElement`.

This chapter will then introduce you to an XML-based grammar named *Extensible Application Markup Language* (XAML; pronounced "zammel"). Here, you will learn the syntax and semantics of XAML (including attached property syntax and the role of type converters and markup extensions).

This chapter wraps up by investigating the integrated WPF designers of Visual Studio by building your first WPF application. During this time, you will learn to intercept keyboard and mouse activities, define application-wide data, and perform other common WPF tasks.

The Motivation Behind WPF

Over the years, Microsoft has created numerous graphical user interface toolkits (raw C/C++/Windows API development, VB6, MFC, etc.) to build desktop executables. Each of these APIs provided a code base to represent the basic aspects of a GUI application, including main windows, dialog boxes, controls, menu systems, etc. With the initial release of the .NET platform, the Windows Forms API quickly became the preferred model for UI development, given its simple yet powerful object model.

While many full-featured desktop applications have been successfully created using Windows Forms, the fact of the matter is that this programming model is rather *asymmetrical*. Simply put, `System.Windows.Forms.dll` and `System.Drawing.dll` do not provide direct support for many additional technologies required to build a feature-rich desktop application. To illustrate this point, consider the ad hoc nature of GUI desktop development before the release of WPF (see Table 25-1).

A. Troelsen and P. Japikse, *Pro C# 10 with .NET 6*, https://doi.org/10.1007/978-1-4842-7869-7_25

Table 25-1. *Pre-WPF Solutions to Desired Functionalities*

Desired Functionality	Technology
Building windows with controls	Windows Forms
2D graphics support	GDI+ (`System.Drawing.dll`)
3D graphics support	DirectX APIs
Support for streaming video	Windows Media Player APIs
Support for flow-style documents	Programmatic manipulation of PDF files

As you can see, a Windows Forms developer must pull in types from several unrelated APIs and object models. While it is true that making use of these diverse APIs might look similar syntactically (it is just C# code, after all), you might also agree that each technology requires a radically different mindset. For example, the skills required to create a 3D rendered animation using DirectX are completely different from those used to bind data to a grid. To be sure, it is difficult for a Windows Forms programmer to master the diverse nature of each API.

Unifying Diverse APIs

WPF was purposely created to merge these previously unrelated programming tasks into a single unified object model. Thus, if you need to author a 3D animation, you have no need to manually program against the DirectX API (although you could) because 3D functionality is baked directly into WPF. To see how well things have cleaned up, consider Table 25-2, which illustrates the desktop development model ushered in as of .NET 3.0.

Table 25-2. *.NET 3.0+ Solutions to Desired Functionalities*

Desired Functionality	Technology
Building forms with controls	WPF
2D graphics support	WPF
3D graphics support	WPF
Support for streaming video	WPF
Support for flow-style documents	WPF

The obvious benefit here is that .NET programmers now have a single, *symmetrical* API for all common GUI desktop programming needs. After you become comfortable with the functionality of the key WPF assemblies and the grammar of XAML, you will be amazed how quickly you can create sophisticated UIs.

Providing a Separation of Concerns via XAML

Perhaps one of the most compelling benefits is that WPF provides a way to cleanly separate the look and feel of a GUI application from the programming logic that drives it. Using XAML, it is possible to define the UI of an application via XML *markup*. This markup (ideally generated using tools such as Microsoft Visual Studio or Blend for Visual Studio) can then be connected to a related C# code file to provide the guts of the program's functionality.

■ **Note** XAML is not limited to WPF applications. Any application can use XAML to describe a tree of .NET objects, even if they have nothing to do with a visible user interface.

As you dig into WPF, you might be surprised how much flexibility this "desktop markup" provides. XAML allows you to define not only simple UI elements (buttons, grids, list boxes, etc.) in markup but also interactive 2D and 3D graphics, animations, data-binding logic, and multimedia functionality (such as video playback).

XAML also makes it easy to customize how a control should render its visual appearance. For example, defining a circular button control that animates your company logo requires just a few lines of markup. As shown in Chapter 27, WPF controls can be modified through styles and templates, which allow you to change the overall look and feel of an application with minimum fuss and bother. Unlike Windows Forms development, the only compelling reason to build a custom WPF control from the ground up is if you need to change the *behaviors* of a control (e.g., add custom methods, properties, or events; subclass an existing control to override virtual members). If you simply need to change the *look and feel* of a control (again, such as a circular animated button), you can do so entirely through markup.

Providing an Optimized Rendering Model

GUI toolkits such as Windows Forms, MFC, or VB6 performed all graphical rendering requests (including the rendering of UI elements such as buttons and list boxes) using a low-level, C-based API (GDI), which has been part of the Windows OS for years. GDI provides adequate performance for typical business applications or simple graphical programs; however, if a UI application needed to tap into high-performance graphics, DirectX was required.

The WPF programming model is quite different, in that GDI is *not* used when rendering graphical data. All rendering operations (e.g., 2D graphics, 3D graphics, animations, control rendering, etc.) now make use of the DirectX API. The first obvious benefit is that your WPF applications will automatically take advantage of hardware and software optimizations. As well, WPF applications can tap into rich graphical services (blur effects, anti-aliasing, transparency, etc.) without the complexity of programming directly against the DirectX API.

■ **Note** Although WPF does push all rendering requests to the DirectX layer, I don't want to suggest that a WPF application will perform as fast as building an application using unmanaged C++ and DirectX directly. Although significant performance advances have been made in WPF with every release, if you are intending to build a desktop application that requires the fastest possible execution speed (such as a 3D video game), unmanaged C++ and DirectX are still the best approach.

Simplifying Complex UI Programming

To recap the story thus far, Windows Presentation Foundation (WPF) is an API for building desktop applications that integrates various desktop APIs into a single object model and provides a clean separation of concerns via XAML. In addition to these major points, WPF applications also benefit from a simple way to integrate services into your programs, which historically were quite complex to account for. The following is a quick rundown of the core WPF features:

- Multiple layout managers (far more than Windows Forms) to provide extremely flexible control over the placement and repositioning of content.
- Use of an enhanced data-binding engine to bind content to UI elements in a variety of ways.

- A built-in style engine, which allows you to define "themes" for a WPF application.
- Use of vector graphics, which allows content to be automatically resized to fit the size and resolution of the screen hosting the application.
- Support for 2D and 3D graphics, animations, and video and audio playback.
- A rich typography API, such as support for XML Paper Specification (XPS) documents, fixed documents (WYSIWYG), flow documents, and document annotations (e.g., a Sticky Notes API).
- Support for interoperating with legacy GUI models (e.g., Windows Forms, ActiveX, and Win32 HWNDs). For example, you can incorporate custom Windows Forms controls into a WPF application and vice versa.

Now that you have some idea of what WPF brings to the table, let's look at the various types of applications that can be created using this API. Many of these features will be explored in detail in the chapters to come.

Investigating the WPF Assemblies

WPF is ultimately little more than a collection of types bundled within .NET assemblies. Table 25-3 describes the key assemblies used to build WPF applications, each of which must be referenced when creating a new project. As you would hope, Visual Studio WPF projects reference these required assemblies automatically.

Table 25-3. *Core WPF Assemblies*

Assembly	Meaning in Life
`PresentationCore`	This assembly defines numerous namespaces that constitute the foundation of the WPF GUI layer. For example, this assembly contains support for the WPF Ink API, animation primitives, and numerous graphical rendering types.
`PresentationFramework`	This assembly contains a majority of the WPF controls, the `Application` and `Window` classes, support for interactive 2D graphics, and numerous types used in data binding.
`System.Xaml.dll`	This assembly provides namespaces that allow you to program against a XAML document at runtime. By and large, this library is useful only if you are authoring WPF support tools or need absolute control over XAML at runtime.
`WindowsBase.dll`	This assembly defines types that constitute the infrastructure of the WPF API, including those representing WPF threading types, security types, various type converters, and support for *dependency properties* and *routed events* (described in Chapter 27).

Collectively, these four assemblies define new namespaces and .NET classes, interfaces, structures, enumerations, and delegates. Table 25-4 describes the role of some (but certainly not all) of the important namespaces.

Table 25-4. *Core WPF Namespaces*

Namespace	Meaning in Life
System.Windows	This is the root namespace of WPF. Here, you will find core classes (such as Application and Window) that are required by any WPF desktop project.
System.Windows.Controls	This contains all the expected WPF widgets, including types to build menu systems, tooltips, and numerous layout managers.
System.Windows.Data	This contains types to work with the WPF data-binding engine, as well as support for data-binding templates.
System.Windows.Documents	This contains types to work with the documents API, which allows you to integrate PDF-style functionality into your WPF applications, via the XML Paper Specification (XPS) protocol.
System.Windows.Ink	This provides support for the Ink API, which allows you to capture input from a stylus or mouse, respond to input gestures, and so forth. This is useful for Tablet PC programming; however, any WPF can make use of this API.
System.Windows.Markup	This namespace defines several types that allow XAML markup (and the equivalent binary format, BAML) to be parsed and processed programmatically.
System.Windows.Media	This is the root namespace to several media-centric namespaces. Within these namespaces you will find types to work with animations, 3D rendering, text rendering, and other multimedia primitives.
System.Windows.Navigation	This namespace provides types to account for the navigation logic employed by XAML browser applications (XBAPs) as well as standard desktop applications that require a navigational page model.
System.Windows.Shapes	This defines classes that allow you to render interactive 2D graphics that automatically respond to mouse input.

To begin your journey into the WPF programming model, you will examine two members of the System.Windows namespace that are commonplace to any traditional desktop development effort: Application and Window.

■ **Note** If you have created desktop UIs using the Windows Forms API, be aware that the System.Windows.Forms.* and System.Drawing.* assemblies are not related to WPF. These libraries represent the original .NET GUI toolkit, Windows Forms/GDI+.

The Role of the Application Class

The System.Windows.Application class represents a global instance of a running WPF application. This class supplies a Run() method (to start the application), a series of events that you can handle in order to interact with the application's lifetime (such as Startup and Exit). Table 25-5 details some of the key properties.

Table 25-5. *Key Properties of the Application Type*

Property	Meaning in Life
Current	This static property allows you to gain access to the running Application object from anywhere in your code. This can be helpful when a window or dialog box needs to gain access to the Application object that created it, typically to access application-wide variables and functionality.
MainWindow	This property allows you to programmatically get or set the main window of the application.
Properties	This property allows you to establish and obtain data that is accessible throughout all aspects of a WPF application (windows, dialog boxes, etc.).
StartupUri	This property gets or sets a URI that specifies a window or page to open automatically when the application starts.
Windows	This property returns a WindowCollection type, which provides access to each window created from the thread that created the Application object. This can be helpful when you want to iterate over each open window of an application and alter its state (such as minimizing all windows).

Constructing an Application Class

Any WPF application will need to define a class that extends Application. Within this class, you will define your program's entry point (the Main() method), which creates an instance of this subclass and typically handles the Startup and Exit events (as necessary). Here is an example:

```
// Define the global application object
// for this WPF program.
class MyApp : Application
{
  [STAThread]
  static void Main(string[] args)
  {
    // Create the application object.
    MyApp app = new MyApp();

    // Register the Startup/Exit events.
    app.Startup += (s, e) => { /* Start up the app */ };
    app.Exit += (s, e) => { /* Exit the app */ };
  }
}
```

Within the Startup handler, you will most often process any incoming command-line arguments and launch the main window of the program. The Exit handler, as you would expect, is where you can author any necessary shutdown logic for the program (e.g., save user preferences, write to the Windows registry).

■ **Note** The Main() method of a WPF application must be attributed with the [STAThread] attribute, which ensures any legacy COM objects used by your application are thread-safe. If you do not annotate Main() in this way, you will encounter a runtime exception. Even with the introduction of top-level statements in C# 9.0, you will still want to use the more traditional Main() method in your WPF applications. In fact, the Main() method is autogenerated for you.

Enumerating the Windows Collection

Another interesting property exposed by Application is Windows, which provides access to a collection representing each window loaded into memory for the current WPF application. As you create new Window objects, they are automatically added into the Application.Windows collection. Here is an example method that will minimize each window of the application (perhaps in response to a given keyboard gesture or menu option triggered by the end user):

```
static void MinimizeAllWindows()
{
  foreach (Window wnd in Application.Current.Windows)
  {
    wnd.WindowState = WindowState.Minimized;
  }
}
```

You will build some WPF applications shortly, but until then, let's check out the core functionality of the Window type and learn about a number of important WPF base classes in the process.

The Role of the Window Class

The System.Windows.Window class (located in the PresentationFramework.dll assembly) represents a single window owned by the Application-derived class, including any dialog boxes displayed by the main window. Not surprisingly, Window has a series of parent classes, each of which brings more functionality to the table. Consider Figure 25-1, which shows the inheritance chain (and implemented interfaces) for System.Windows.Window as seen through the Visual Studio Object Browser.

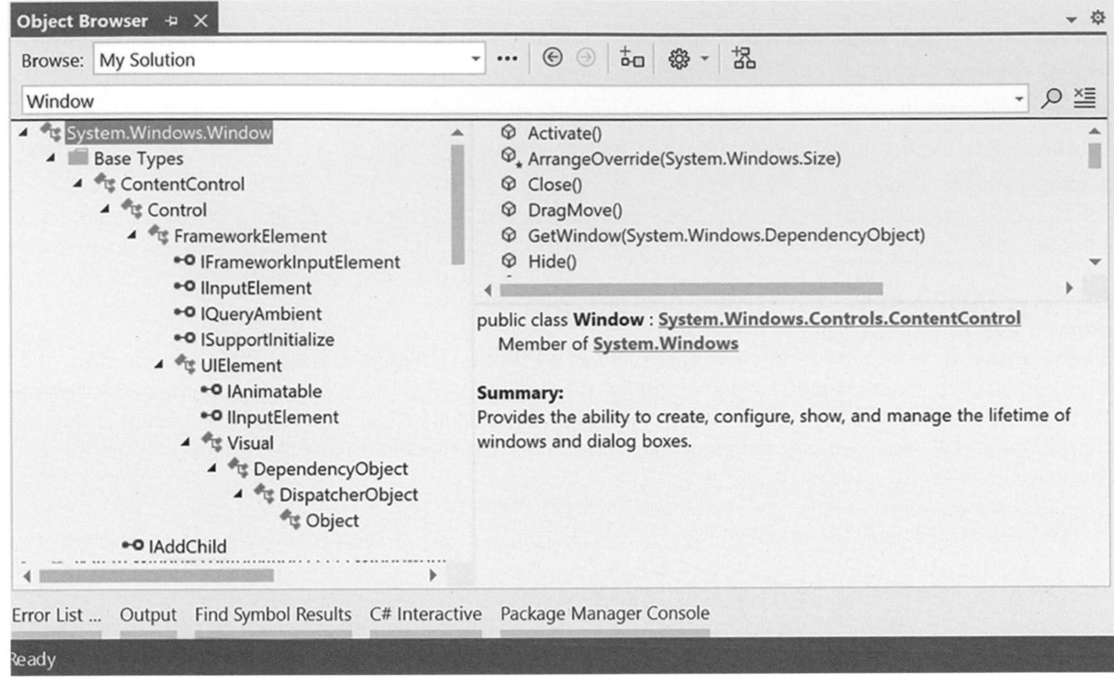

Figure 25-1. *The hierarchy of the Window class*

You will come to understand the functionality provided by many of these base classes as you progress through this chapter and the chapters to come. However, to whet your appetite, the following sections present a breakdown of the functionality provided by each base class (consult the .NET 6 documentation for full details).

The Role of System.Windows.Controls.ContentControl

The direct parent of `Window` is `ContentControl`, which is quite possibly the most enticing of all WPF classes. This base class provides derived types with the ability to host a single piece of *content*, which, simply put, refers to the visual data placed within the interior of the control's surface area via the `Content` property. The WPF content model makes it quite simple to customize the basic look and feel of a content control.

For example, when you think of a typical "button" control, you tend to assume that the content is a simple string literal (OK, Cancel, Abort, etc.). If you are using XAML to describe a WPF control and the value you want to assign to the `Content` property can be captured as a simple string, you may set the `Content` property within the element's opening definition as so (don't fret over the exact markup at this point):

```
<!-- Setting the Content value in the opening element -->
<Button Height="80" Width="100" Content="OK"/>
```

■ **Note** The `Content` property can also be set in C# code, which allows you to change the interior of a control at runtime.

However, content can be almost anything. For example, let's say you want to have a "button" that has something more interesting than a simple string, perhaps a custom graphic and a blurb of text. In other UI frameworks such as Windows Forms, you would be required to build a custom control, which could entail quite a bit of code and a whole new class to maintain. With the WPF content model, there is no need to do so.

When you want to assign the Content property to a value that cannot be captured as a simple array of characters, you cannot assign it using an attribute in the control's opening definition. Rather, you must define the content data *implicitly*, within the element's scope. For example, the following <Button> contains a <StackPanel> as content, which itself contains some unique data (an <Ellipse> and <Label>, to be exact):

```
<!-- Implicitly setting the Content property with complex data -->
<Button Height="80" Width="100">
  <StackPanel>
    <Ellipse Fill="Red" Width="25" Height="25"/>
    <Label Content ="OK!"/>
  </StackPanel>
</Button>
```

You can also make use of XAML's *property-element syntax* to set complex content. Consider the following functionally equivalent <Button> definition, which sets the Content property explicitly using property-element syntax (again, you will find more information on XAML later in this chapter, so don't sweat the details just yet):

```
<!-- Setting the Content property using property-element syntax -->
<Button Height="80" Width="100">
  <Button.Content>
    <StackPanel>
      <Ellipse Fill="Red" Width="25" Height="25"/>
      <Label Content ="OK!"/>
    </StackPanel>
  </Button.Content>
</Button>
```

Do be aware that not every WPF element derives from ContentControl and, therefore, not all controls support this unique content model (however, most do). As well, some WPF controls add a few refinements to the basic content model you have just examined. Chapter 26 will examine the role of WPF content in much more detail.

The Role of System.Windows.Controls.Control

Unlike ContentControl, all WPF controls share the Control base class as a common parent. This base class provides numerous core members that account for basic UI functionality. For example, Control defines properties to establish the control's size, opacity, tab order logic, the display cursor, background color, and so forth. Furthermore, this parent class provides support for *templating services*. As explained in Chapter 27, WPF controls can completely change the way they render their appearance using templates and styles. Table 25-6 documents some key members of the Control type, grouped by related functionality.

***Table 25-6.** Key Members of the Control Type*

Members	Meaning in Life
`Background`, `Foreground`, `BorderBrush`, `BorderThickness`, `Padding`, `HorizontalContentAlignment`, `VerticalContentAlignment`	These properties allow you to set basic settings regarding how the control will be rendered and positioned.
`FontFamily`, `FontSize`, `FontStretch`, `FontWeight`	These properties control various font-centric settings.
`IsTabStop`, `TabIndex`	These properties are used to establish tab order among controls on a window.
`MouseDoubleClick`, `PreviewMouseDoubleClick`	These events handle the act of double-clicking a widget.
`Template`	This property allows you to get and set the control's template, which can be used to change the rendering output of the widget.

The Role of System.Windows.FrameworkElement

This base class provides a number of members that are used throughout the WPF framework, such as support for storyboarding (used within animations) and support for data binding, as well as the ability to name a member (via the `Name` property), obtain any resources defined by the derived type, and establish the overall dimensions of the derived type. Table 25-7 hits the highlights.

***Table 25-7.** Key Members of the FrameworkElement Type*

Members	Meaning in Life
`ActualHeight`, `ActualWidth`, `MaxHeight`, `MaxWidth`, `MinHeight`, `MinWidth`, `Height`, `Width`	These properties control the size of the derived type.
`ContextMenu`	Gets or sets the pop-up menu associated with the derived type.
`Cursor`	Gets or sets the mouse cursor associated with the derived type.
`HorizontalAlignment`, `VerticalAlignment`	Gets or sets how the type is positioned within a container (such as a panel or list box).
`Name`	Allows to you assign a name to the type in order to access its functionality in a code file.
`Resources`	Provides access to any resources defined by the type (see Chapter 29 for an examination of the WPF resource system).
`ToolTip`	Gets or sets the tooltip associated with the derived type.

The Role of System.Windows.UIElement

Of all the types within a Window's inheritance chain, the UIElement base class provides the greatest amount of functionality. The key task of UIElement is to provide the derived type with numerous events to allow the derived type to receive focus and process input requests. For example, this class provides numerous events to account for drag-and-drop operations, mouse movement, keyboard input, stylus input, and touch.

Chapter 25 digs into the WPF event model in detail; however, many of the core events will look quite familiar (MouseMove, KeyUp, MouseDown, MouseEnter, MouseLeave, etc.). In addition to defining dozens of events, this parent class provides several properties to account for control focus, enabled state, visibility, and hit-testing logic, as shown in Table 25-8.

Table 25-8. *Key Members of the UIElement Type*

Members	Meaning in Life
Focusable, IsFocused	These properties allow you to set focus on a given derived type.
IsEnabled	This property allows you to control whether a given derived type is enabled or disabled.
IsMouseDirectlyOver, IsMouseOver	These properties provide a simple way to perform hit-testing logic.
IsVisible, Visibility	These properties allow you to work with the visibility setting of a derived type.
RenderTransform	This property allows you to establish a transformation that will be used to render the derived type.

The Role of System.Windows.Media.Visual

The Visual class type provides core rendering support in WPF, which includes hit-testing of graphical data, coordinate transformation, and bounding box calculations. In fact, the Visual class interacts with the underlying DirectX subsystem to draw data on the screen. As you will examine in Chapter 26, WPF provides three possible manners in which you can render graphical data, each of which differs in terms of functionality and performance. Use of the Visual type (and its children, such as DrawingVisual) provides the most lightweight way to render graphical data, but it also entails the greatest amount of manual code to account for all the required services. Again, more details to come in Chapter 28.

The Role of System.Windows.DependencyObject

WPF supports a particular flavor of .NET properties termed *dependency properties*. Simply put, this style of property provides extra code to allow the property to respond to several WPF technologies such as styles, data binding, animations, and so forth. For a type to support this new property scheme, it will need to derive from the DependencyObject base class. While dependency properties are a key aspect of WPF development, much of the time their details are hidden from view. Chapter 26 dives further into the details of dependency properties.

The Role of System.Windows.Threading.DispatcherObject

The final base class of the Window type (beyond System.Object, which I assume needs no further explanation at this point in the book) is DispatcherObject. This type provides one property of interest, Dispatcher, which returns the associated System.Windows.Threading.Dispatcher object. The Dispatcher class is the entry point to the event queue of the WPF application, and it provides the basic constructs for dealing with concurrency and threading. The Dispatcher class was explored in Chapter 15.

Understanding the Syntax of WPF XAML

Production-level WPF applications will typically make use of dedicated tools to generate the necessary XAML. As helpful as these tools are, it is a good idea to understand the overall structure of XAML markup. To help in your learning process, allow me to introduce a popular (and free) tool that allows you to easily experiment with XAML.

Introducing Kaxaml

When you are first learning the grammar of XAML, it can be helpful to use a free tool named *Kaxaml*. You can obtain this popular XAML editor/parser from https://github.com/punker76/kaxaml.

■ **Note** For many editions of this book, I've pointed users to www.kaxaml.com, but unfortunately, that site has been retired. Jan Karger (https://github.com/punker76) has forked the old code and has done some work on improving it. You can find his version of the tool on GitHub https://github.com/punker76/kaxaml/releases. Much respect and thanks to the original developers of Kaxaml and to Jan for keeping it alive; it is a great tool and has helped countless developers learn XAML.

Kaxaml is helpful, in that it has no clue about C# source code, event handlers, or implementation logic. It is a much more straightforward way to test XAML snippets than using a full-blown Visual Studio WPF project template. As well, Kaxaml has several integrated tools, such as a color chooser, a XAML snippet manager, and even an "XAML scrubber" option that will format your XAML based on your settings. When you first open Kaxaml, you will find simple markup for a <Page> control, as follows:

```
<Page
  xmlns="http://schemas.microsoft.com/winfx/2006/xaml/presentation"
  xmlns:x="http://schemas.microsoft.com/winfx/2006/xaml">
  <Grid>

  </Grid>
</Page>
```

Like a Window, a Page contains various layout managers and controls. However, unlike a Window, Page objects cannot run as stand-alone entities. Rather, they must be placed inside a suitable host such as a NavigationWindow or a Frame. The good news is that you can type identical markup within a <Page> or <Window> scope.

■ **Note** If you change the `<Page>` and `</Page>` elements in the Kaxaml markup window to `<Window>` and `</Window>`, you can press the F5 key to load a new window onto the screen.

As an initial test, enter the following markup into the XAML pane at the bottom of the tool:

```
<Page
  xmlns="http://schemas.microsoft.com/winfx/2006/xaml/presentation"
  xmlns:x="http://schemas.microsoft.com/winfx/2006/xaml">
  <Grid>
    <!-- A button with custom content -->
    <Button Height="100" Width="100">
      <Ellipse Fill="Green" Height="50" Width="50"/>
    </Button>
  </Grid>
</Page>
```

You should now see your page render at the upper part of the Kaxaml editor (see Figure 25-2).

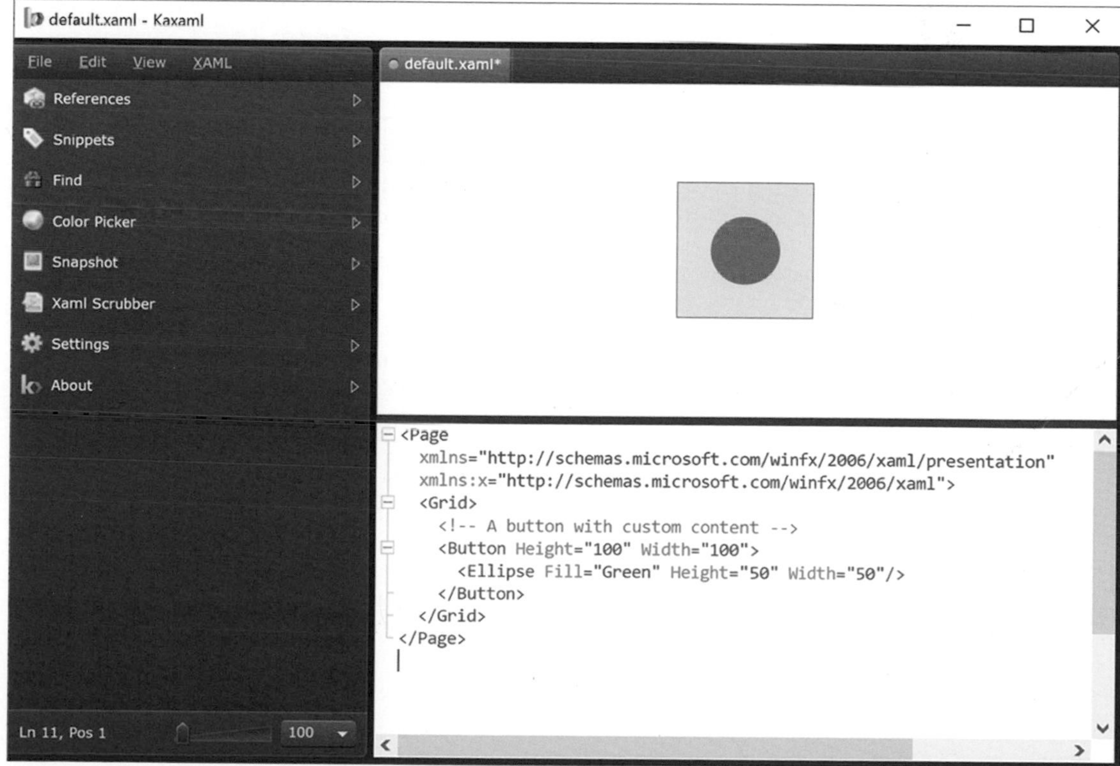

***Figure 25-2.** Kaxaml is a helpful (and free) tool used to learn the grammar of XAML*

As you work with Kaxaml, remember that this tool does not allow you to author any markup that entails code compilation (however, using x:Name is allowed). This includes defining an x:Class attribute (for specifying a code file), entering event handler names in markup, or using any XAML keywords that also entail code compilation (such as FieldModifier or ClassModifier). Any attempt to do so will result in a markup error.

XAML XML Namespaces and XAML "Keywords"

The root element of a WPF XAML document (such as a <Window>, <Page>, <UserControl>, or <Application> definition) will almost always reference the following two predefined XML namespaces:

```
<Page
  xmlns="http://schemas.microsoft.com/winfx/2006/xaml/presentation"
  xmlns:x="http://schemas.microsoft.com/winfx/2006/xaml">
  <Grid>

  </Grid>
</Page>
```

The first XML namespace, http://schemas.microsoft.com/winfx/2006/xaml/presentation, maps a slew of WPF .NET namespaces for use by the current *.xaml file (System.Windows, System.Windows.Controls, System.Windows.Data, System.Windows.Ink, System.Windows.Media, System.Windows.Navigation, etc.).

This one-to-many mapping is hard-coded within the WPF assemblies (WindowsBase.dll, PresentationCore.dll, and PresentationFramework.dll) using the assembly-level [XmlnsDefinition] attribute. For example, if you open the Visual Studio Object Browser and select the PresentationCore.dll assembly, you will see listings such as the following, which essentially imports System.Windows:

```
[assembly: XmlnsDefinition("http://schemas.microsoft.com/winfx/2006/xaml/presentation",
                           "System.Windows")]
```

The second XML namespace, http://schemas.microsoft.com/winfx/2006/xaml, is used to include XAML-specific "keywords" (for lack of a better term) as well as the inclusion of the System.Windows.Markup namespace, as follows:

```
[assembly: XmlnsDefinition("http://schemas.microsoft.com/winfx/2006/xaml",
                           "System.Windows.Markup")]
```

One rule of any well-formed XML document (remember, XAML is an XML-based grammar) is that the opening root element designates one XML namespace as the *primary namespace*, which is the namespace that contains the most common items. If a root element requires the inclusion of additional secondary namespaces (as seen here), they must be defined using a unique tag prefix (to resolve any possible name clashes). As a convention, the prefix is simply x; however, this can be any unique token you require, such as XamlSpecificStuff.

```
<Page
  xmlns="http://schemas.microsoft.com/winfx/2006/xaml/presentation"
  xmlns:XamlSpecificStuff="http://schemas.microsoft.com/winfx/2006/xaml">
  <Grid>
    <!-- A button with custom content -->
```

```
    <Button XamlSpecificStuff:Name="button1" Height="100" Width="100">
      <Ellipse Fill="Green" Height="50" Width="50"/>
    </Button>
  </Grid>
</Page>
```

The obvious downside of defining wordy XML namespace prefixes is you are required to type XamlSpecificStuff each time your XAML file needs to refer to one of the items defined within this XAML-centric XML namespace. Given that XamlSpecificStuff requires many additional keystrokes, just stick with x.

In any case, beyond the x:Name, x:Class, and x:Code keywords, the http://schemas.microsoft.com/winfx/2006/xaml XML namespace also provides access to additional XAML keywords, the most common of which are shown in Table 25-9.

Table 25-9. *XAML Keywords*

XAML Keyword	Meaning in Life
x:Array	Represents a .NET array type in XAML.
x:ClassModifier	Allows you to define the visibility of the C# class (internal or public) denoted by the Class keyword.
x:FieldModifier	Allows you to define the visibility of a type member (internal, public, private, or protected) for any named subelement of the root (e.g., a <Button> within a <Window> element). A *named element* is defined using the Name XAML keyword.
x:Key	Allows you to establish a key value for a XAML item that will be placed into a dictionary element.
x:Name	Allows you to specify the generated C# name of a given XAML element.
x:Null	Represents a null reference.
x:Static	Allows you to refer to a static member of a type.
x:Type	The XAML equivalent of the C# typeof operator (it will yield a System.Type based on the supplied name).
x:TypeArguments	Allows you to establish an element as a generic type with a specific type parameter (e.g., List<int> vs. List<bool>).

In addition to these two necessary XML namespace declarations, it is possible, and sometimes necessary, to define additional tag prefixes in the opening element of a XAML document. You will typically do so whenever you need to describe in XAML a .NET class defined in an external assembly.

For example, say you have built a few custom WPF controls and packaged them in a library named MyControls.dll. Now, if you want to create a new Window that uses these controls, you can establish a custom XML namespace that maps to your library using the clr-namespace and assembly tokens. Here is some example markup that creates a tag prefix named myCtrls, which can be used to access controls in your library:

```
<Window x:Class="WpfApplication1.MainWindow"
  xmlns="http://schemas.microsoft.com/winfx/2006/xaml/presentation"
  xmlns:x="http://schemas.microsoft.com/winfx/2006/xaml"
  xmlns:myCtrls="clr-namespace:MyControls;assembly=MyControls"
```

```
  Title="MainWindow" Height="350" Width="525">
  <Grid>
    <myCtrls:MyCustomControl />
  </Grid>
</Window>
```

The clr-namespace token is assigned to the name of the .NET namespace in the assembly, while the assembly token is set to the friendly name of the external *.dll assembly. You can use this syntax for any external .NET library you would like to manipulate in markup. While there is no need to do so at the current time, future chapters will require you to define custom XML namespace declarations to describe types in markup.

■ **Note** If you need to define a class in markup that is part of the current assembly but in a different .NET namespace, your xmlns tag prefix is defined without the assembly= attribute, like so: xmlns:myCtrls="clr-namespace:SomeNamespaceInMyApp".

Controlling Class and Member Variable Visibility

You will see many of these keywords in action where required in the chapters to come; however, by way of a simple example, consider the following XAML <Window> definition that makes use of the ClassModifier and FieldModifier keywords, as well as x:Name and x:Class (remember that kaxaml.exe will not allow you to make use of any XAML keyword that entails code compilation, such as x:Code, x:FieldModifier, or x:ClassModifier):

```
<!-- This class will now be declared internal in the *.g.cs file -->
<Window x:Class="MyWPFApp.MainWindow" x:ClassModifier ="internal"
  xmlns="http://schemas.microsoft.com/winfx/2006/xaml/presentation"
  xmlns:x="http://schemas.microsoft.com/winfx/2006/xaml">

  <!-- This button will be public in the *.g.cs file -->
  <Button x:Name ="myButton" x:FieldModifier ="public" Content = "OK"/>
</Window>
```

By default, all C#/XAML type definitions are public, while members default to internal. However, based on your XAML definition, the resulting autogenerated file contains an internal class type with a public Button variable.

```
internal partial class MainWindow :
System.Windows.Window,
  System.Windows.Markup.IComponentConnector
{
  public System.Windows.Controls.Button myButton;
...
}
```

XAML Elements, XAML Attributes, and Type Converters

After you have established your root element and any required XML namespaces, your next task is to populate the root with a *child element*. In a real-world WPF application, the child will be a layout manager (such as a Grid or StackPanel) that contains, in turn, any number of additional UI elements that describe the user interface. The next chapter examines these layout managers in detail, so for now just assume that your <Window> type will contain a single Button element.

As you have already seen over the course of this chapter, XAML *elements* map to a class or structure type within a given .NET namespace, while the *attributes* within the opening element tag map to properties or events of the type. To illustrate, enter the following <Button> definition into Kaxaml:

```
<Page
  xmlns="http://schemas.microsoft.com/winfx/2006/xaml/presentation"
  xmlns:x="http://schemas.microsoft.com/winfx/2006/xaml">
  <Grid>
    <!-- Configure the look and feel of a Button -->
    <Button Height="50" Width="100" Content="OK!"
            FontSize="20" Background="Green" Foreground="Yellow"/>
  </Grid>
</Page>
```

Notice that the values assigned to each property have been captured as a simple text value. This may seem like a complete mismatch of data types because if you were to make this Button in C# code, you would *not* assign string objects to these properties but would make use of specific data types. For example, here is the same button authored in code:

```
public void MakeAButton()
{
  Button myBtn = new Button();
  myBtn.Height = 50;
  myBtn.Width = 100;
  myBtn.FontSize = 20;
  myBtn.Content = "OK!";
  myBtn.Background = new SolidColorBrush(Colors.Green);
  myBtn.Foreground = new SolidColorBrush(Colors.Yellow);
}
```

As it turns out, WPF ships with several *type converter* classes, which will be used to transform simple text values into the correct underlying data type. This process happens transparently (and automatically).

While this is all well and good, there will be many times when you need to assign a much more complex value to a XAML attribute, which cannot be captured as a simple string. For example, let's say you want to build a custom brush to set the Background property of the Button. If you are building the brush in code, it is quite straightforward, as shown here:

```
public void MakeAButton()
{
...
  // A fancy brush for the background.
  LinearGradientBrush fancyBruch =
    new LinearGradientBrush(Colors.DarkGreen, Colors.LightGreen, 45);
  myBtn.Background = fancyBruch;
  myBtn.Foreground = new SolidColorBrush(Colors.Yellow);
}
```

How can you represent your complex brush as a string? Well, you cannot! Thankfully, XAML provides a special syntax that can be used whenever you need to assign a property value to a complex object, termed *property-element syntax*.

Understanding XAML Property-Element Syntax

Property-element syntax allows you to assign complex objects to a property. Here is a XAML description for a Button that makes use of a LinearGradientBrush to set its Background property:

```
<Button Height="50" Width="100" Content="OK!"
        FontSize="20" Foreground="Yellow">
  <Button.Background>
    <LinearGradientBrush>
      <GradientStop Color="DarkGreen" Offset="0"/>
      <GradientStop Color="LightGreen" Offset="1"/>
    </LinearGradientBrush>
  </Button.Background>
</Button>
```

Notice that within the scope of the <Button> and </Button> tags, you have defined a subscope named <Button.Background>. Within this scope, you have defined a custom <LinearGradientBrush>. (Do not worry about the exact code for the brush; you'll learn about WPF graphics in Chapter 28.)

Any property can be set using property-element syntax, which always breaks down to the following pattern:

```
<DefiningClass>
  <DefiningClass.PropertyOnDefiningClass>
    <!-- Value for Property here! -->
  </DefiningClass.PropertyOnDefiningClass>
</DefiningClass>
```

While any property *could* be set using this syntax, if you can capture a value as a simple string, you will save yourself typing time. For example, here is a much more verbose way to set the Width of your Button:

```
<Button Height="50" Content="OK!"
        FontSize="20" Foreground="Yellow">
...
  <Button.Width>
    100
  </Button.Width>
</Button>
```

Understanding XAML Attached Properties

In addition to property-element syntax, XAML defines a special syntax used to set a value to an *attached property*. Essentially, an attached property allows a child element to set the value for a property that is defined in a parent element. The general template to follow looks like this:

```
<ParentElement>
  <ChildElement ParentElement.PropertyOnParent = "Value">
</ParentElement>
```

The most common use of attached property syntax is to position UI elements within one of the WPF layout manager classes (Grid, DockPanel, etc.). The next chapter dives into these panels in some detail; for now, enter the following in Kaxaml:

```
<Page
  xmlns="http://schemas.microsoft.com/winfx/2006/xaml/presentation"
  xmlns:x="http://schemas.microsoft.com/winfx/2006/xaml">
  <Canvas Height="200" Width="200" Background="LightBlue">
    <Ellipse Canvas.Top="40" Canvas.Left="40" Height="20" Width="20" Fill="DarkBlue"/>
  </Canvas>
</Page>
```

Here, you have defined a Canvas layout manager that contains an Ellipse. Notice that the Ellipse can inform its parent (the Canvas) where to position its top-left position using attached property syntax.

There are a few items to be aware of regarding attached properties. First and foremost, this is not an all-purpose syntax that can be applied to *any* property of *any* parent. For example, the following XAML cannot be parsed without error:

```
<!-- Error! Set Background property on Canvas via attached property? -->
<Canvas Height="200" Width="200">
  <Ellipse Canvas.Background="LightBlue"
           Canvas.Top="40" Canvas.Left="90"
           Height="20" Width="20" Fill="DarkBlue"/>
</Canvas>
```

Attached properties are a specialized form of a WPF-specific concept termed a *dependency property*. Unless a property was implemented in a specific manner, you cannot set its value using attached property syntax. You will explore dependency properties in detail in Chapter 25.

■ **Note** Visual Studio has IntelliSense, which will show you valid attached properties that can be set by a given element.

Understanding XAML Markup Extensions

As explained, property values are most often represented using a simple string or via property-element syntax. There is, however, another way to specify the value of a XAML attribute, using *markup extensions*. Markup extensions allow a XAML parser to obtain the value for a property from a dedicated, external class. This can be beneficial given that some property values require several code statements to execute to figure out the value.

Markup extensions provide a way to cleanly extend the grammar of XAML with new functionality. A markup extension is represented internally as a class that derives from MarkupExtension. Note that the chances of you ever needing to build a custom markup extension will be slim to none. However, a subset of XAML keywords (such as x:Array, x:Null, x:Static, and x:Type) are markup extensions in disguise!

A markup extension is sandwiched between curly brackets, like so:

```
<Element PropertyToSet = "{MarkUpExtension}"/>
```

To see some markup extensions in action, author the following into Kaxaml:

```
<Page
  xmlns="http://schemas.microsoft.com/winfx/2006/xaml/presentation"
  xmlns:x="http://schemas.microsoft.com/winfx/2006/xaml"
  xmlns:CorLib="clr-namespace:System;assembly=mscorlib">

  <StackPanel>
    <!-- The Static markup extension lets us obtain a value
         from a static member of a class -->
    <Label Content ="{x:Static CorLib:Environment.OSVersion}"/>
    <Label Content ="{x:Static CorLib:Environment.ProcessorCount}"/>

    <!-- The Type markup extension is a XAML version of
         the C# typeof operator -->
    <Label Content ="{x:Type Button}" />
    <Label Content ="{x:Type CorLib:Boolean}" />

    <!-- Fill a ListBox with an array of strings! -->
    <ListBox Width="200" Height="50">
      <ListBox.ItemsSource>
        <x:Array Type="CorLib:String">
          <CorLib:String>Sun Kil Moon</CorLib:String>
          <CorLib:String>Red House Painters</CorLib:String>
          <CorLib:String>Besnard Lakes</CorLib:String>
        </x:Array>
      </ListBox.ItemsSource>
    </ListBox>
  </StackPanel>
</Page>
```

First, notice that the `<Page>` definition has a new XML namespace declaration, which allows you to gain access to the `System` namespace of `mscorlib.dll`. With this XML namespace established, you first make use of the `x:Static` markup extension and grab values from `OSVersion` and `ProcessorCount` of the `System.Environment` class.

The `x:Type` markup extension allows you to gain access to the metadata description of the specified item. Here, you are simply assigning the fully qualified names of the WPF `Button` and `System.Boolean` types.

The most interesting part of this markup is the `ListBox`. Here, you are setting the `ItemsSource` property to an array of strings declared entirely in markup! Notice here how the `x:Array` markup extension allows you to specify a set of subitems within its scope:

```
<x:Array Type="CorLib:String">
  <CorLib:String>Sun Kil Moon</CorLib:String>
  <CorLib:String>Red House Painters</CorLib:String>
  <CorLib:String>Besnard Lakes</CorLib:String>
</x:Array>
```

■ **Note** The previous XAML example is used only to illustrate a markup extension in action. As you will see in Chapter 26, there are much easier ways to populate `ListBox` controls!

Figure 25-3 shows the markup of this <Page> in Kaxaml.

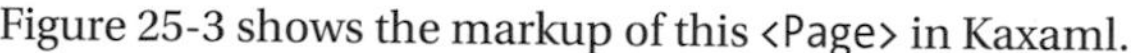

```
<StackPanel>
  <!-- The Static markup extension lets us obtain a value
       from a static member of a class -->
  <Label Content ="{x:Static CorLib:Environment.OSVersion}"/>
  <Label Content ="{x:Static CorLib:Environment.ProcessorCount}"/>

  <!-- The Type markup extension is a XAML version of
       the C# typeof operator -->
  <Label Content ="{x:Type Button}" />
  <Label Content ="{x:Type CorLib:Boolean}" />

  <!-- Fill a ListBox with an array of strings! -->
  <ListBox Width="200" Height="50">
    <ListBox.ItemsSource>
      <x:Array Type="CorLib:String">
        <CorLib:String>Sun Kil Moon</CorLib:String>
        <CorLib:String>Red House Painters</CorLib:String>
        <CorLib:String>Besnard Lakes</CorLib:String>
      </x:Array>
    </ListBox.ItemsSource>
  </ListBox>
</StackPanel>
</Page>
```

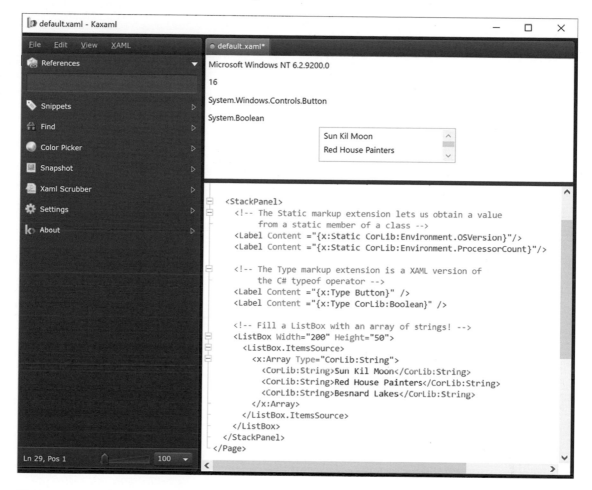

Figure 25-3. *Markup extensions allow you to set values via the functionality of a dedicated class*

You have now seen numerous examples that showcase each of the core aspects of the XAML syntax. As you might agree, XAML is interesting, in that it allows you to describe a tree of .NET objects in a declarative manner. While this is extremely helpful when configuring graphical user interfaces, do remember that XAML can describe *any* type from *any* assembly, provided it is a nonabstract type containing a default constructor.

Building WPF Applications Using Visual Studio

Let's examine how Visual Studio can simplify the construction of WPF programs. While you can build WPF applications using Visual Studio Code, Visual Studio Code does not have any designer support for building WPF applications. Visual Studio, with its rich XAML support, is a more productive IDE when building WPF applications.

■ **Note** Here, I will point out some key features of using Visual Studio to build WPF applications. Forthcoming chapters will illustrate additional aspects of the IDE where necessary.

The WPF Project Templates

The New Project dialog box of Visual Studio defines a set of WPF project templates, including WPF Application, WPF Class Library, WPF Custom Control Library, and WPF User Control Library. Create a new WPF Application project named WpfTesterApp.

■ **Note** When selecting WPF projects from the Visual Studio "Add a new project" screen, be sure to select the WPF project templates that do not have "(.NET Framework)" in the title. If you select a template with "(.NET Framework)" in the title, you will be building your app using .NET Framework 4.x.

Examining the project file, you can see that the SDK is set to `Microsoft.NET.Sdk`. The `TargetFramework` value is set to `net6.0-windows`, and the project will build an executable that uses WPF:

```
<Project Sdk="Microsoft.NET.Sdk">
  <PropertyGroup>
    <OutputType>WinExe</OutputType>
    <TargetFramework>net6.0-windows</TargetFramework>
    <UseWPF>true</UseWPF>
    <Nullable>disable</Nullable>
    <ImplicitUsings>enable</ImplicitUsings>
  </PropertyGroup>
</Project>
```

At the time of this writing, the WPF template doesn't set the flags for either implicit `using` statements or nullable reference types. Update the project file to enable implicit `using` statements and disables nullable reference types:

```
<Project Sdk="Microsoft.NET.Sdk">
  <PropertyGroup>
    <OutputType>WinExe</OutputType>
    <TargetFramework>net6.0-windows</TargetFramework>
    <UseWPF>true</UseWPF>
    <ImplicitUsings>enable</ImplicitUsings>
    <Nullable>disable</Nullable>
  </PropertyGroup>
</Project>
```

Beyond the project file, the template also provides an initial `Window`- and the `Application`-derived class, each represented using a XAML and C# code file.

The Toolbox and XAML Designer/Editor

Visual Studio provides a Toolbox (which you can open via the View menu) that contains numerous WPF controls. The top part of the panel holds the most common controls, and the bottom contains all controls (see Figure 25-4).

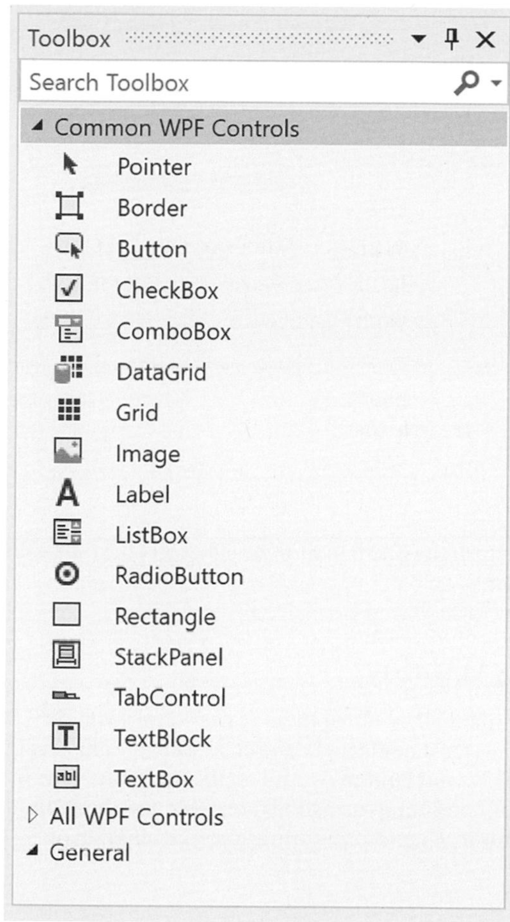

Figure 25-4. *The Toolbox contains the WPF controls that can be placed on the designer surface*

Using a standard drag-and-drop operation, you can place any of these controls onto the window's designer surface or drag the control into the XAML markup editor at the bottom of the designer. When you do, the initial XAML will be authored on your behalf. Use your mouse to drag a `Button` control and a `Calendar` control onto the designer surface. After you have done so, notice how you can relocate and resize your controls (and be sure to examine the resulting XAML generated based on your edits).

In addition to building the UI via the mouse and toolbox, you can manually enter your markup using the integrated XAML editor. As you can see in Figure 25-5, you do get IntelliSense support, which can help simplify the authoring of the markup. For example, try to add the `Margin` property to the `<Calendar>` element.

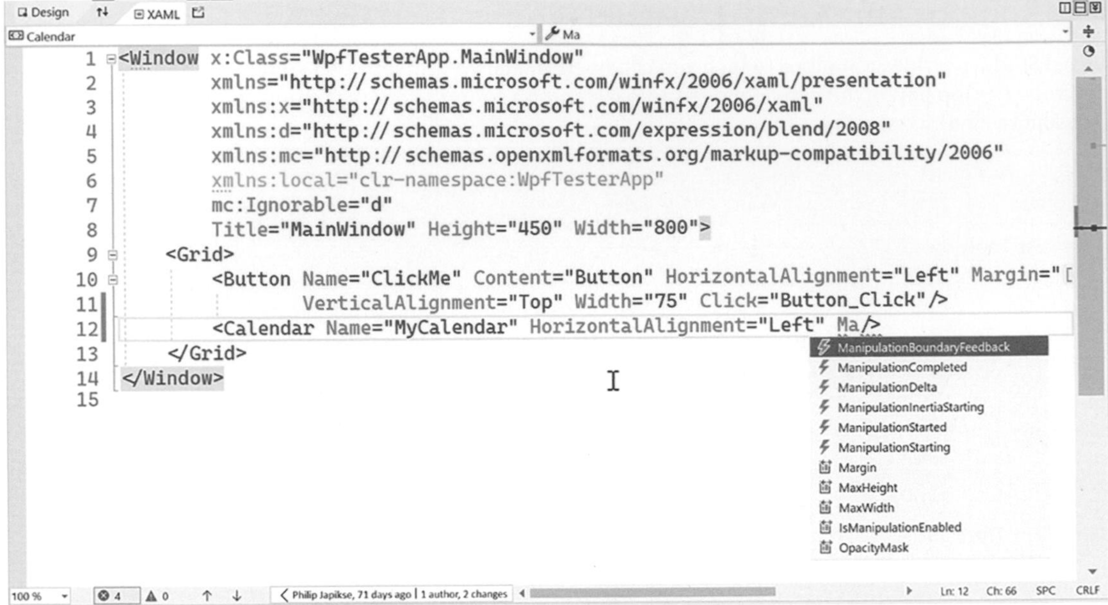

Figure 25-5. *The WPF Window designer*

Take a few moments to add some property values directly in the XAML editor. Be sure you take the time to become comfortable using this aspect of the WPF designer.

Setting Properties Using the Properties Window

After you have placed some controls onto your designer (or manually defined them in the editor), you can then make use of the Properties window to set property values for the selected control, as well as rig up event handlers for the selected control. By way of a simple test, select your `Button` control on the designer. Now, use the Properties window to change the `Background` color of the `Button` using the integrated Brushes editor (see Figure 25-6; you will learn more about the Brushes editor in Chapter 27, during your examination of WPF graphics).

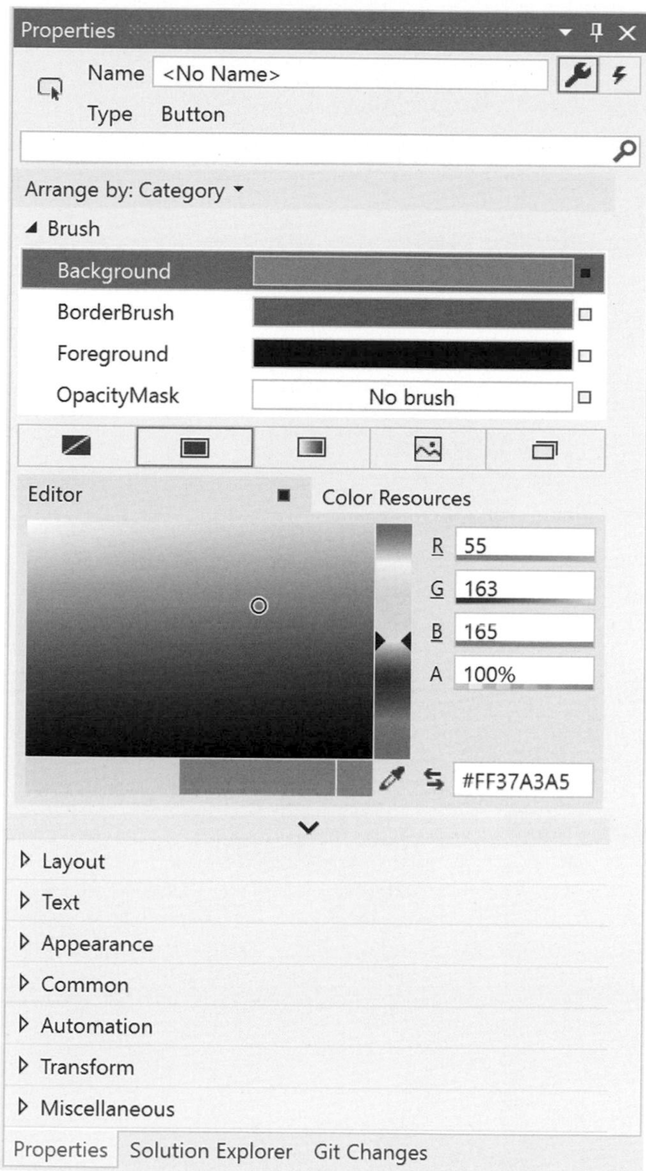

Figure 25-6. *The Properties window can be used to configure the UI of a WPF control*

■ **Note** The Properties window provides a search text area at the top. Type in the name of a property you would like to set to quickly find the item in question.

After you have finished tinkering with the Brushes editor, check out the generated markup. It might look something like this:

```
<Button Content="Button" HorizontalAlignment="Left" Margin="10,10,0,0"
VerticalAlignment="Top" Width="75">
  <Button.Background>
    <LinearGradientBrush EndPoint="0.5,1" StartPoint="0.5,0">
      <GradientStop Color="Black" Offset="0"/>
      <GradientStop Color="#FFE90E0E" Offset="1"/>
      <GradientStop Color="#FF1F4CE3"/>
    </LinearGradientBrush>
  </Button.Background>
</Button>
```

Handling Events Using the Properties Window

If you want to handle events for a given control, you can also make use of the Properties window, but this time you need to click the Events button at the upper right of the Properties window (look for the lightning bolt icon). Ensure that the button is selected on your designer and locate the `Click` event. Once you do, double-click directly on the `Click` event entry. This will cause Visual Studio to automatically build an event handler that takes the following general form:

NameOfControl_NameOfEvent

Since you did not rename your button, the Properties window shows that it generated an event handler named `Button_Click` (see Figure 25-7).

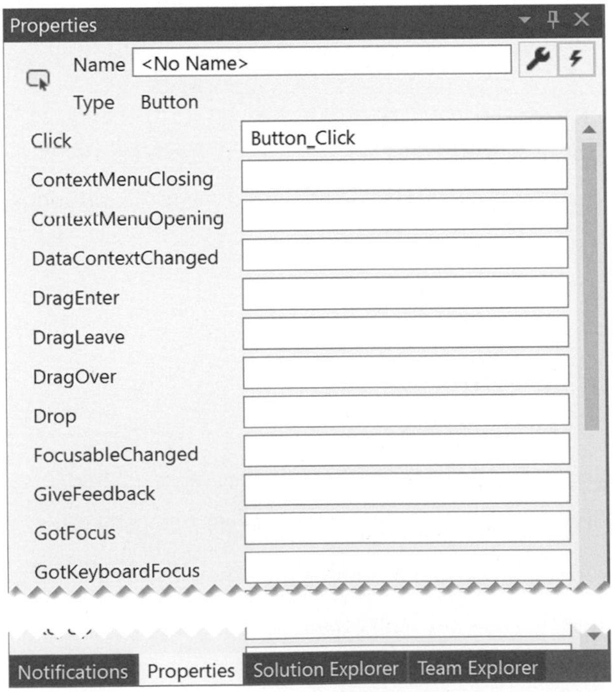

***Figure 25-7.** Handling events using the Properties window*

As well, Visual Studio generated the corresponding C# event handler in your window's code file. Here, you can add any sort of code that must execute when the button is clicked. For a quick test, just enter the following code statement:

```
private void Button_Click(object sender, RoutedEventArgs e)
{
  MessageBox.Show("You clicked the button!");
}
```

Handling Events in the XAML Editor

You can also handle events directly in the XAML editor. By way of an example, place your mouse within the `<Window>` element and type in the `MouseMove` event, followed by the equal sign. Once you do, you will see that Visual Studio displays any compatible handlers in your code file (if they exist), as well as the option to create a new event handler (see Figure 25-8).

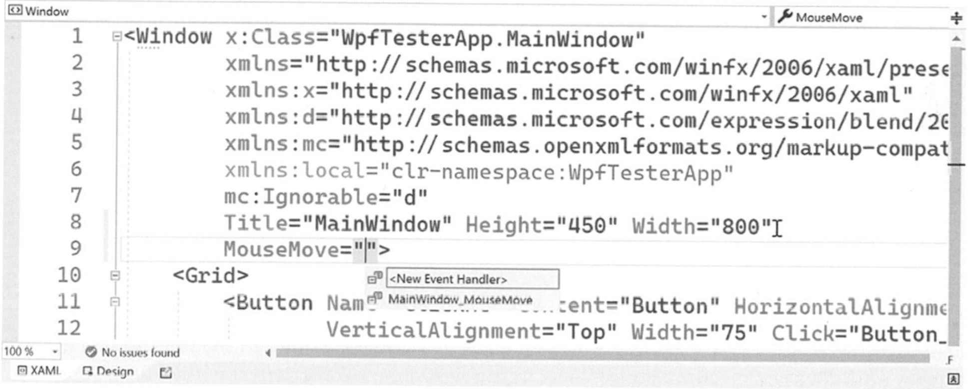

```
<Window x:Class="WpfTesterApp.MainWindow"
        xmlns="http://schemas.microsoft.com/winfx/2006/xaml/prese
        xmlns:x="http://schemas.microsoft.com/winfx/2006/xaml"
        xmlns:d="http://schemas.microsoft.com/expression/blend/20
        xmlns:mc="http://schemas.openxmlformats.org/markup-compat
        xmlns:local="clr-namespace:WpfTesterApp"
        mc:Ignorable="d"
        Title="MainWindow" Height="450" Width="800"
        MouseMove="">
    <Grid>
        <Button Nam  <New Event Handler>  ...tent="Button" HorizontalAlignme
                MainWindow_MouseMove
                VerticalAlignment="Top" Width="75" Click="Button_
```

Figure 25-8. Handling events using the XAML editor

Let the IDE create the `MouseMove` event handler, enter the following code, and then run the application to see the result:

```
private void MainWindow_MouseMove (object sender, MouseEventArgs e)
{
  this.Title = e.GetPosition(this).ToString();
}
```

■ **Note** Chapter 29 covers MVVM and the Command pattern, which is a much better way to handle click events in enterprise applications. But if you need only a simple app, handling click events with a straight event handler is perfectly acceptable.

The Document Outline Window

When you work with any XAML-based project, you will certainly make use of a healthy amount of markup to represent your UIs. When you begin to work with more complex XAML, it can be useful to visualize the markup to quickly select an item to edit on the Visual Studio designer.

Currently, your markup is quite tame because you have defined only a few controls within the initial `<Grid>`. Nevertheless, locate the Document Outline window in your IDE, mounted by default on the left side of Visual Studio (if you cannot locate it, simply activate it using the View ➤ Other Windows menu option). Now, make sure your XAML designer is the active window in the IDE (rather than the C# code file), and you will notice the Document Outline window displays the nested elements (see Figure 25-9).

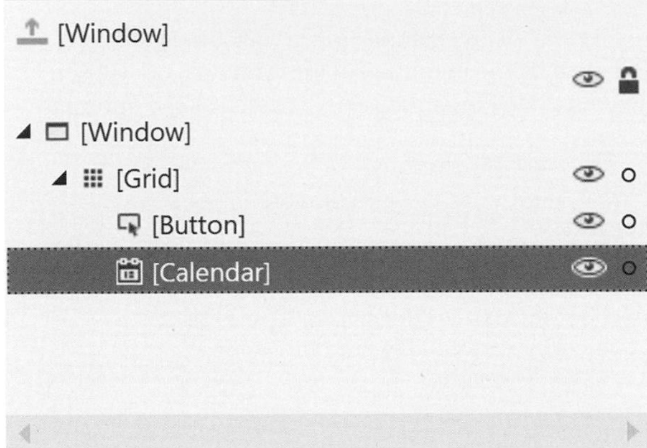

Figure 25-9. *Visualizing your XAML via the Document Outline window*

This tool also provides a way to temporarily hide a given item (or set of items) on the designer as well as lock items to prevent additional edits from taking place. In the next chapter, you will see how the Document Outline window also provides many other features to group selected items into new layout managers (among other features).

Enable or Disable the XAML Debugger

When you run the application, you will see the `MainWindow` on the screen. You will also see the interactive debugger, as shown in Figure 25-10 (minimized) and Figure 25-11 (expanded).

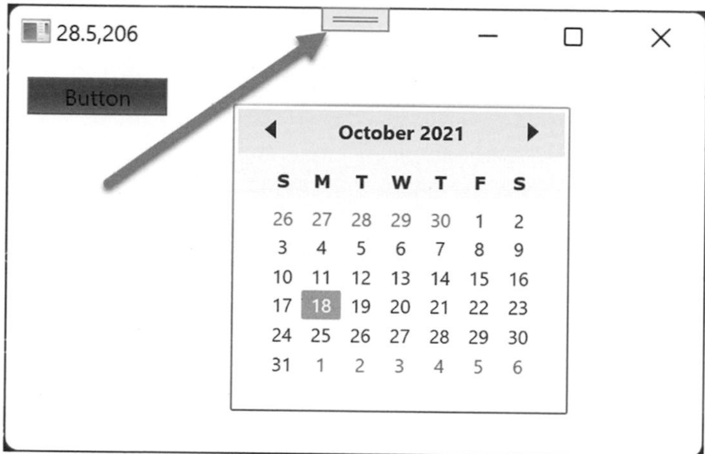

Figure 25-10. *XAML UI debugger (minimized)*

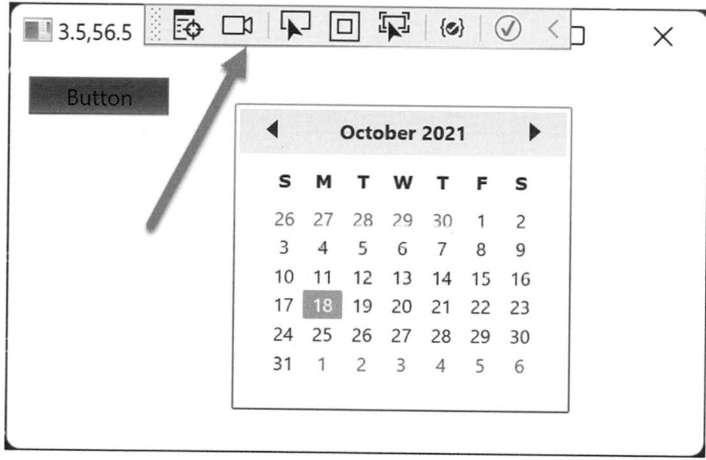

Figure 25-11. *XAML UI debugger*

If you want to turn this off, you will find the entries for XAML debugging under Tools ➤ Options ➤ Debugging ➤ XAML Hot Reload. Deselect the top box to prevent the debugger window from overlaying your windows. Figure 25-12 shows the entries.

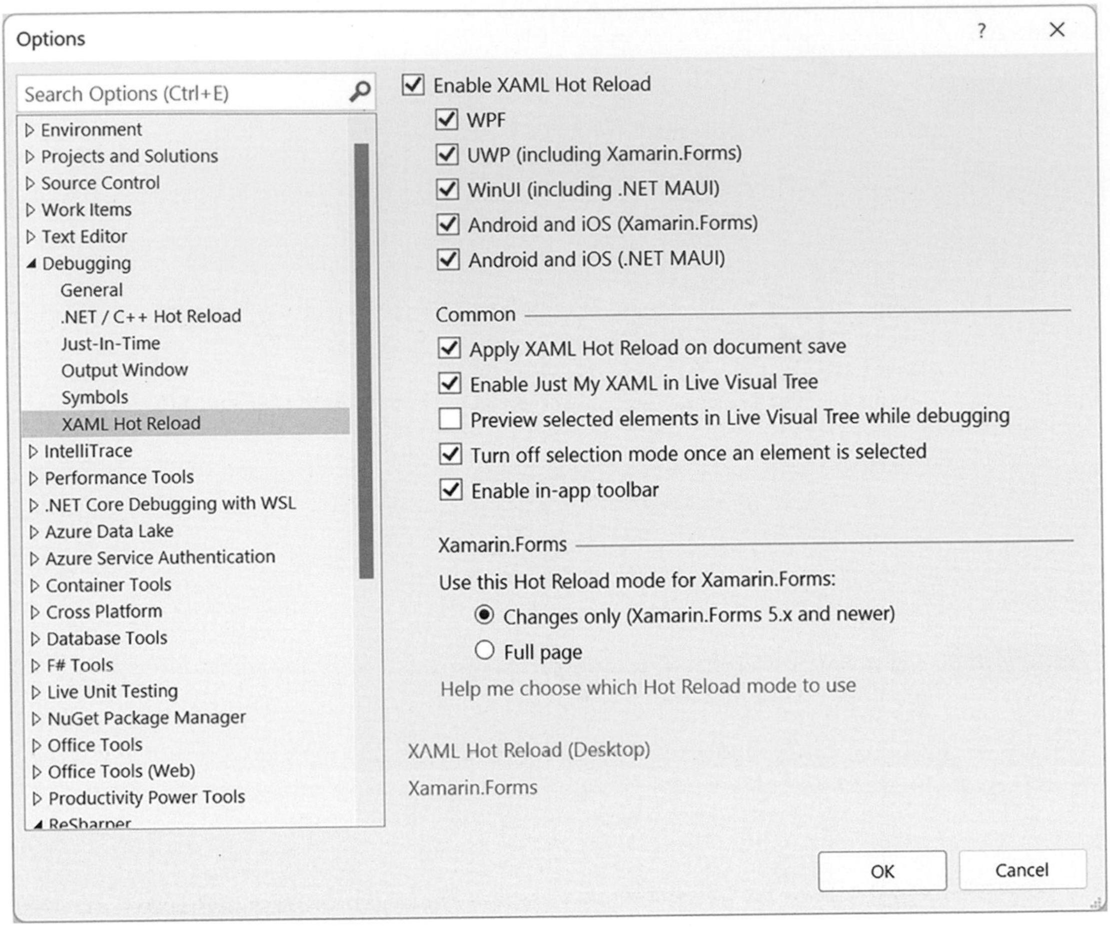

Figure 25-12. *Enabling/disabling XAML UI debugging*

Examining the App.xaml File

How did the project know what window to launch? Even more intriguing, if you examine the code files in your application, you will also see that there is not a `Main()` method anywhere to be found. You have learned throughout this book that applications must have an entry point, so how does .NET know how to launch your app? Fortunately, both plumbing items are handled for you through the Visual Studio templates and the WPF framework.

To solve the riddle of which window to launch, the `App.xaml` file defines an application class through markup. In addition to the namespace definitions, it defines application properties such as the `StartupUri`, application-wide resources (covered in Chapter 28), and specific handlers for application events such as `Startup` and `Exit`. The `StartupUri` indicates which window to load on startup. Open the `App.xaml` file and examine the markup, shown here:

```
<Application x:Class="WpfTesterApp.App"
             xmlns="http://schemas.microsoft.com/winfx/2006/xaml/presentation"
             xmlns:x="http://schemas.microsoft.com/winfx/2006/xaml"
```

```
             xmlns:local="clr-namespace:WpfTesterApp"
             StartupUri="MainWindow.xaml">
    <Application.Resources>
    </Application.Resources>
</Application>
```

Using the XAML designer and using Visual Studio code completion, add handlers for the Startup and Exit events. Your updated XAML should look like this (notice the change in bold):

```
<Application x:Class="WpfTesterApp.App"
             xmlns="http://schemas.microsoft.com/winfx/2006/xaml/presentation"
             xmlns:x="http://schemas.microsoft.com/winfx/2006/xaml"
             xmlns:local="clr-namespace:WpfTesterApp"
             StartupUri="MainWindow.xaml" Startup="App_OnStartup" Exit="App_OnExit">
    <Application.Resources>
    </Application.Resources>
</Application>
```

If you look at the App.xaml.cs file, it should look like this:

```
public partial class App : Application
{
  private void App_OnStartup(object sender, StartupEventArgs e)
  {
  }
  private void App_OnExit(object sender, ExitEventArgs e)
  {
  }
}
```

Note that the class is marked as partial. In fact, all the code-behind windows for XAML files are marked partial. That is key to solving the riddle of where the Main() method lives. But first, you need to examine what happens when msbuild.exe processes XAML files.

Mapping the Window XAML Markup to C# Code

When msbuild.exe processed your *.csproj file, it produced three files for each XAML file in your project with the form of *.g.cs (where g denotes auto*generated*), *.g.i.cs (where *i* denotes IntelliSense), and *.baml (for Binary Application Markup Language). These are saved into the \obj\Debug directory (and can be viewed in Solution Explorer by clicking the Show All Files button). You might have to hit the Refresh button in Solution Explorer to see them since they are not part of the actual project but build artifacts.

To make the most sense of the process, it is helpful to provide names for your controls. Go ahead and provide names for the Button and Calendar controls, as follows:

```
<Button Name="ClickMe" Content="Button" HorizontalAlignment="Left" Margin="10,10,0,0"
       VerticalAlignment="Top" Width="75" Click="Button_Click">
//omitted for brevity
</Button>
<Calendar Name="MyCalendar" HorizontalAlignment="Left" Margin="10,41,0,0"
VerticalAlignment="Top"/>
```

Now rebuild your solution (or project) and refresh the files in Solution Explorer. If you open the MainWindow.g.cs file into a text editor, you will find a class named MainWindow, which extends the Window base class. The name of this class is a direct result of the x:Class attribute in the <Window> start tag.

This class defines a private member variable of type bool (named _contentLoaded), which was not directly accounted for in the XAML markup. This data member is used to determine (and ensure) the content of the window is assigned only once. This class also contains a member variable of type System.Windows.Controls.Button, named ClickMe. The name of the control is based on the x:Name (or the shorthand form Name) attribute value within the opening <Button> declaration. What you do not see is a variable for the Calendar control. This is because msbuild.exe creates a variable for each *named* control in your XAML that has related code in the code-behind. If there is not any code, there isn't any need for a variable. To make matters more confusing, if you had not named the Button control, there wouldn't be a variable for it either. This is part of the magic of WPF and is tied into the IComponentConnector interface implementation.

The compiler-generated class also explicitly implements the WPF IComponentConnector interface defined in the System.Windows.Markup namespace. This interface defines a single method called Connect(), which has been implemented to prep each control defined in the markup and rig up the event logic as specified within the original MainWindow.xaml file. You can see the handler being set up for the ClickMe click event. Before the method completes, the _contentLoaded member variable is set to true. Here is the crux of the method:

```
void System.Windows.Markup.IComponentConnector.Connect(int connectionId, object target)
{
  switch (connectionId)
  {
    case 1:
    this.ClickMe = ((System.Windows.Controls.Button)(target));
    #line 11 "..\..\MainWindow.xaml"
    this.ClickMe.Click += new System.Windows.RoutedEventHandler(this.Button_Click);
    #line default
    #line hidden
    return;
  }
  this._contentLoaded = true;
}
```

To show the effects of unnamed controls with code, add an event handler for the SelectedDatesChanged event on the calendar. Rebuild the application, refresh the files, and reload the MainWindow.g.cs file. In the Connect() method, you now see the following code block:

```
#line 20 "..\..\MainWindow.xaml"
this.MyCalendar.SelectedDatesChanged += new
     System.EventHandler<System.Windows.Controls.SelectionChangedEventArgs>(
         this.MyCalendar_OnSelectedDatesChanged);
```

This tells the framework that the control on line 20 of the XAML file has the SelectedDatesChanged event handler assigned, as shown in the preceding code.

Finally, the MainWindow class defines and implements a method named InitializeComponent(). You might expect that this method contains code that sets up the look and feel of each control by setting various properties (Height, Width, Content, etc.). However, this is not the case! How then do the controls take on the correct UI? The logic with InitializeComponent() resolves the location of an embedded assembly resource that is named identical to the original *.xaml file, like so:

```
public void InitializeComponent() {
  if (_contentLoaded) {
    return;
    }
    _contentLoaded = true;
    System.Uri resourceLocater = new System.Uri("/WpfTesterApp;component/mainwindow.xaml",
        System.UriKind.Relative);
    #line 1 "..\..\MainWindow.xaml"
    System.Windows.Application.LoadComponent(this, resourceLocater);
    #line default
    #line hidden
}
```

At this point, the question becomes "what exactly is this embedded resource?"

The Role of BAML

As you might have guessed from the name, Binary Application Markup Language (BAML) is a compact, binary representation of the original XAML data. This `*.baml` file is embedded as a resource (via a generated `*.g.resources` file) into the compiled assembly. This BAML resource contains all the data needed to establish the look and feel of the UI widgets (again, such as the `Height` and `Width` properties).

The important takeaway here is to understand that a WPF application contains within itself a binary representation (the BAML) of the markup. At runtime, this BAML will be plucked out of the resource container and used to make sure all windows and controls are initialized to the correct look and feel.

Also, remember that the name of these binary resources are *identical* to the name of the stand-alone `*.xaml` files you authored. However, this does not imply in any way that you must distribute the loose `*.xaml` files with your compiled WPF program. Unless you build a WPF application that will dynamically load and parse `*.xaml` files at runtime, you will never need to ship the original markup.

Solving the Mystery of Main()

Now that you know how the MSBuild process works, open the `App.g.cs` file. Here you will find the autogenerated `Main()` method that initializes and runs your application object.

```
public static void Main() {
  WpfTesterApp.App app = new WpfTesterApp.App();
  app.InitializeComponent();
  app.Run();
}
```

The `InitializeComponent()` method configures the application properties, including the `StartupUri` and the event handlers for the `Startup` and `Exit` events.

```
public void InitializeComponent() {
    #line 5 "..\..\App.xaml"
    this.Startup += new System.Windows.StartupEventHandler(this.App_OnStartup);
    #line default
    #line hidden
    #line 5 "..\..\App.xaml"
    this.Exit += new System.Windows.ExitEventHandler(this.App_OnExit);
    #line default
```

```
    #line hidden
    #line 5 "..\..\App.xaml"
    this.StartupUri = new System.Uri("MainWindow.xaml", System.UriKind.Relative);
    #line default
    #line hidden
}
```

Interacting with Application-Level Data

Recall that the `Application` class defines a property named `Properties`, which allows you to define a collection of name-value pairs via a type indexer. Because this indexer has been defined to operate on type `System.Object`, you are able to store any sort of item within this collection (including your custom classes) to be retrieved at a later time using a friendly moniker. Using this approach, it is simple to share data across all windows in a WPF application.

To illustrate, you will update the current `Startup` event handler to check the incoming command-line arguments for a value named `/GODMODE` (a common cheat code for many PC video games). If you find this token, you will establish a `bool` value set to `true` within the properties collection of the same name (otherwise, you will set the value to `false`).

This sounds simple enough, but how are you going to pass the incoming command-line arguments (typically obtained from the `Main()` method) to your `Startup` event handler? One approach is to call the static `Environment.GetCommandLineArgs()` method. However, these same arguments are automatically added to the incoming `StartupEventArgs` parameter and can be accessed via the `Args` property. Here is the first update to the current code base:

```
private void App_OnStartup(object sender, StartupEventArgs e)
{
  Application.Current.Properties["GodMode"] = false;
  // Check the incoming command-line arguments and see if they
  // specified a flag for /GODMODE.
  foreach (string arg in e.Args)
  {
    if (arg.Equals("/godmode",StringComparison.OrdinalIgnoreCase))
    {
      Application.Current.Properties["GodMode"] = true;
      break;
    }
  }
}
```

Application-wide data can be accessed from anywhere within the WPF application. All you are required to do is obtain an access point to the global application object (via `Application.Current`) and investigate the collection. For example, you could update the `Click` event handler of the `Button` as so:

```
private void Button_Click(object sender, RoutedEventArgs e)
{
  // Did user enable /godmode?
  if ((bool)Application.Current.Properties["GodMode"])
  {
    MessageBox.Show("Cheater!");
  }
}
```

With this, if you enter the /godmode command-line argument into the Debug tab in the project properties and then run the program, you will be shamed, and the program will exit. You can also run the program from a command line by entering the following command (open a command prompt and navigate to the bin/debug directory):

```
WpfAppAllCode.exe /godmode
```

You will see the shameful message box displayed when terminating the application.

■ **Note** Recall that you can supply command-line arguments within Visual Studio. Simply double-click the Properties icon within Solution Explorer, click the Debug tab from the resulting editor, and enter /godmode within the "Command line arguments" editor.

Handling the Closing of a Window Object

End users can shut down a window by using numerous built-in system-level techniques (e.g., clicking the X close button on the window's frame) or by indirectly calling the Close() method in response to some user interaction element (e.g., File ➤ Exit). In either case, WPF provides two events that you can intercept to determine whether the user is *truly* ready to shut down the window and remove it from memory. The first event to fire is Closing, which works in conjunction with the CancelEventHandler delegate.

This delegate expects target methods to take System.ComponentModel.CancelEventArgs as the second parameter. CancelEventArgs provides the Cancel property, which when set to true will prevent the window from actually closing (this is handy when you have asked the user if he really wants to close the window or if perhaps he would like to save his work first).

If the user does indeed want to close the window, CancelEventArgs.Cancel can be set to false (which is the default setting). This will then cause the Closed event to fire (which works with the System.EventHandler delegate), making it the point at which the window is about to be closed for good.

Update the MainWindow class to handle these two events by adding these code statements to the current constructor, like so:

```
public MainWindow()
{
  InitializeComponent();
  this.Closed+=MainWindow_Closed;
  this.Closing += MainWindow_Closing;
}
```

Now, implement the corresponding event handlers as so:

```
private void MainWindow_Closing(object sender, System.ComponentModel.CancelEventArgs e)
{
  // See if the user really wants to shut down this window.
  string msg = "Do you want to close without saving?";
  MessageBoxResult result = MessageBox.Show(msg,
    "My App", MessageBoxButton.YesNo, MessageBoxImage.Warning);
```

```
  if (result == MessageBoxResult.No)
  {
    // If user doesn't want to close, cancel closure.
    e.Cancel = true;
  }
}

private void MainWindow_Closed(object sender, EventArgs e)
{
  MessageBox.Show("See ya!");
}
```

Now, run your program and attempt to close the window, either by clicking the X icon in the upper right of the window or by clicking the button control. You should see the confirmation dialog asking if you really want to leave. If you answer Yes, you will then see the farewell message. Clicking the No button will keep the window in memory.

Intercepting Mouse Events

The WPF API provides several events you can capture to interact with the mouse. Specifically, the UIElement base class defines mouse-centric events such as MouseMove, MouseUp, MouseDown, MouseEnter, MouseLeave, and so forth.

Consider, for example, the act of handling the MouseMove event. This event works in conjunction with the System.Windows.Input.MouseEventHandler delegate, which expects its target to take a System.Windows.Input.MouseEventArgs type as the second parameter. Using MouseEventArgs, you can extract the (x, y) position of the mouse and other relevant details. Consider the following partial definition:

```
public class MouseEventArgs : InputEventArgs
{
...
  public Point GetPosition(IInputElement relativeTo);
  public MouseButtonState LeftButton { get; }
  public MouseButtonState MiddleButton { get; }
  public MouseDevice MouseDevice { get; }
  public MouseButtonState RightButton { get; }
  public StylusDevice StylusDevice { get; }
  public MouseButtonState XButton1 { get; }
  public MouseButtonState XButton2 { get; }
}
```

■ **Note** The XButton1 and XButton2 properties allow you to interact with "extended mouse buttons" (such as the "next" and "previous" buttons found on some mouse controls). These are often used to interact with a browser's history list to navigate between visited pages.

The GetPosition() method allows you to get the (x, y) value relative to a UI element on the window. If you are interested in capturing the position relative to the activated window, simply pass in this. Handle the MouseMove event in the constructor of your MainWindow class, like so:

```
public MainWindow(string windowTitle, int height, int width)
{
...
  this.MouseMove += MainWindow_MouseMove;
}
```

Here is an event handler for MouseMove that will display the location of the mouse in the window's title area (notice you are translating the returned Point type into a text value via ToString()):

```
private void MainWindow_MouseMove(object sender,
  System.Windows.Input.MouseEventArgs e)
{
  // Set the title of the window to the current (x,y) of the mouse.
  this.Title = e.GetPosition(this).ToString();
}
```

Intercepting Keyboard Events

Processing keyboard input for the focused window is also straightforward. UIElement defines events that you can capture to intercept keypresses from the keyboard on the active element (e.g., KeyUp, KeyDown). The KeyUp and KeyDown events both work with the System.Windows.Input.KeyEventHandler delegate, which expects the target's second event handler to be of type KeyEventArgs, which defines several public properties of interest, shown here:

```
public class KeyEventArgs : KeyboardEventArgs
{
...
  public bool IsDown { get; }
  public bool IsRepeat { get; }
  public bool IsToggled { get; }
  public bool IsUp { get; }
  public Key Key { get; }
  public KeyStates KeyStates { get; }
  public Key SystemKey { get; }
}
```

To illustrate handling the KeyDown event in the constructor of MainWindow (just like you did for the previous events), implement the following event handler that changes the content of the button with the currently pressed key:

```
private void MainWindowOs_KeyDown(object sender, System.Windows.Input.KeyEventArgs e)
{
  // Display key press on the button.
  ClickMe.Content = e.Key.ToString();
}
```

At this point in the chapter, WPF might look like nothing more than yet another GUI framework that is providing (more or less) the same services as Windows Forms, MFC, or VB6. If this were in fact the case, you might question the need for yet another UI toolkit. To truly see what makes WPF so unique, you require an understanding of the XML-based grammar, XAML.

Summary

Windows Presentation Foundation (WPF) is a user interface toolkit introduced with the release of .NET 3.0. The major goal of WPF is to integrate and unify previously unrelated desktop technologies (2D graphics, 3D graphics, window and control development, etc.) into a single, unified programming model. Beyond this point, WPF programs typically make use of XAML, which allows you to declare the look and feel of your WPF elements via markup.

Recall that XAML allows you to describe trees of .NET objects using a declarative syntax. During this chapter's investigation of XAML, you were exposed to several new bits of syntax, including property-element syntax and attached properties, as well as the role of type converters and XAML markup extensions.

XAML is a key aspect for any production-level WPF application. The final example of this chapter gave you a chance to build a WPF application that showed many of the concepts discussed in this chapter. The next chapters will dive deeper into these concepts as well as introduce many more.

CHAPTER 26

WPF Controls, Layouts, Events, and Data Binding

Chapter 25 provided a foundation for the WPF programming model, including an examination of the Window and Application classes, the grammar of XAML, and the use of code files. Chapter 25 also introduced you to the process of building WPF applications using the designers of Visual Studio. In this chapter, you will dig into the construction of more sophisticated graphical user interfaces using several new controls and layout managers, learning about additional features of the WPF Visual Designer for XAML of Visual Studio along the way.

This chapter will also examine some important related WPF control topics such as the data-binding programming model and the use of control commands. You will also learn how to use the Ink and Documents APIs, which allow you to capture stylus (or mouse) input and build rich text documents using the XML Paper Specification, respectively.

A Survey of the Core WPF Controls

Unless you are new to the concept of building graphical user interfaces (which is fine), the general purpose of the major WPF controls should not raise too many issues. Regardless of which GUI toolkit you might have used in the past (e.g., VB6, MFC, Java AWT/Swing, Windows Forms, macOS, or GTK+/GTK# [among others]), the core WPF controls listed in Table 26-1 are likely to look familiar.

Table 26-1. *The Core WPF Controls*

WPF Control Category	Example Members	Meaning in Life
Core user input controls	Button, RadioButton, ComboBox, CheckBox, Calendar, DatePicker, Expander, DataGrid, ListBox, ListView, ToggleButton, TreeView, ContextMenu, ScrollBar, Slider, TabControl, TextBlock, TextBox, RepeatButton, RichTextBox, Label	WPF provides an entire family of controls you can use to build the crux of a user interface.
Window and control adornments	Menu, ToolBar, StatusBar, ToolTip, ProgressBar	You use these UI elements to decorate the frame of a Window object with input devices (such as the Menu) and user informational elements (e.g., StatusBar and ToolTip).

(continued)

A. Troelsen and P. Japikse, *Pro C# 10 with .NET 6*, https://doi.org/10.1007/978-1-4842-7869-7_26

Table 26-1. (*continued*)

WPF Control Category	Example Members	Meaning in Life
Media controls	`Image`, `MediaElement`, `SoundPlayerAction`	These controls provide support for audio/video playback and image display.
Layout controls	`Border`, `Canvas`, `DockPanel`, `Grid`, `GridView`, `GridSplitter`, `GroupBox`, `Panel`, `TabControl`, `StackPanel`, `Viewbox`, `WrapPanel`	WPF provides numerous controls that allow you to group and organize other controls for the purpose of layout management.

■ **Note** The intent of this chapter is *not* to walk through each and every member of each and every WPF control. Rather, you will receive an overview of the various controls with an emphasis on the underlying programming model and key services common to most WPF controls.

The WPF Ink Controls

In addition to the common WPF controls listed in Table 26-1, WPF defines additional controls for working with the digital Ink API. This aspect of WPF development is useful during tablet PC development because it lets you capture input from the stylus. However, this is not to say a standard desktop application cannot leverage the Ink API because the same controls can capture input using the mouse.

The `System.Windows.Ink` namespace of `PresentationCore.dll` contains various Ink API support types (e.g., `Stroke` and `StrokeCollection`); however, a majority of the Ink API controls (e.g., `InkCanvas` and `InkPresenter`) are packaged up with the common WPF controls under the `System.Windows.Controls` namespace in the `PresentationFramework.dll` assembly. You'll work with the Ink API later in this chapter.

The WPF Document Controls

WPF also provides controls for advanced document processing, allowing you to build applications that incorporate Adobe PDF-style functionality. Using the types within the `System.Windows.Documents` namespace (also in the `PresentationFramework.dll` assembly), you can create print-ready documents that support zooming, searching, user annotations (sticky notes), and other rich text services.

Under the covers, however, the document controls do not use Adobe PDF APIs; rather, they use the XML Paper Specification (XPS) API. To the end user, there will really appear to be no difference because PDF documents and XPS documents have an almost identical look and feel. In fact, you can find many free utilities that allow you to convert between the two file formats on the fly. Because of space limitation, these controls won't be covered in this edition.

WPF Common Dialog Boxes

WPF also provides you with a few common dialog boxes such as `OpenFileDialog` and `SaveFileDialog`. These dialog boxes are defined within the `Microsoft.Win32` namespace of the `PresentationFramework.dll` assembly. Working with either of these dialog boxes is a matter of creating an object and invoking the `ShowDialog()` method, like so:

```
using Microsoft.Win32;
//omitted for brevity
private void btnShowDlg_Click(object sender, RoutedEventArgs e)
{
  // Show a file save dialog.
  SaveFileDialog saveDlg = new SaveFileDialog();
  saveDlg.ShowDialog();
}
```

As you would hope, these classes support various members that allow you to establish file filters and directory paths and gain access to user-selected files. You will put these file dialogs to use in later examples; you will also learn how to build custom dialog boxes to gather user input.

A Brief Review of the Visual Studio WPF Designer

A majority of these standard WPF controls have been packaged up in the `System.Windows.Controls` namespace of the `PresentationFramework.dll` assembly. When you build a WPF application using Visual Studio, you will find most of these common controls contained in the toolbox, provided you have a WPF designer open as the active window.

Similar to other UI frameworks created with Visual Studio, you can drag these controls onto the WPF window designer and configure them using the Properties window (which you learned about in Chapter 25). While Visual Studio will generate a good amount of the XAML on your behalf, it is not uncommon to edit the markup yourself manually. Let's review the basics.

Working with WPF Controls Using Visual Studio

You might recall from Chapter 25 that when you place a WPF control onto the Visual Studio designer, you want to set the `x:Name` property through the Properties window (or through XAML directly) because this allows you to access the object in your related C# code file. You might also recall that you can use the Events tab of the Properties window to generate event handlers for a selected control. Thus, you could use Visual Studio to generate the following markup for a simple `Button` control:

```
<Button x:Name="btnMyButton" Content="Click Me!" Height="23" Width="140" Click="btnMyButton_
Click" />
```

Here, you set the `Content` property of the `Button` to a simple `string` with the value `"Click Me!"`. However, thanks to the WPF control content model, you could fashion a `Button` that contains the following complex content:

```
<Button x:Name="btnMyButton" Height="121" Width="156" Click="btnMyButton_Click">
  <Button.Content>
    <StackPanel Height="95" Width="128" Orientation="Vertical">
      <Ellipse Fill="Red" Width="52" Height="45" Margin="5"/>
      <Label Width="59" FontSize="20" Content="Click!" Height="36" />
    </StackPanel>
  </Button.Content>
</Button>
```

You might also recall that the immediate child element of a ContentControl-derived class is the implied content; therefore, you do not need to define a Button.Content scope explicitly when specifying complex content. You could simply author the following:

```
<Button x:Name="btnMyButton" Height="121" Width="156" Click="btnMyButton_Click">
  <StackPanel Height="95" Width="128" Orientation="Vertical">
    <Ellipse Fill="Red" Width="52" Height="45" Margin="5"/>
    <Label Width="59" FontSize="20" Content="Click!" Height="36" />
  </StackPanel>
</Button>
```

In either case, you set the button's Content property to a StackPanel of related items. You can also author this sort of complex content using the Visual Studio designer. After you define the layout manager for a content control, you can select it on the designer to serve as a drop target for the internal controls. At this point, you can edit each using the Properties window. If you were to use the Properties window to handle the Click event for the Button control (as shown in the previous XAML declarations), the IDE would generate an empty event handler, to which you could add your own custom code, like so:

```
private void btnMyButton_Click(object sender, RoutedEventArgs e)
{
  MessageBox.Show("You clicked the button!");
}
```

Working with the Document Outline Editor

You should recall from the previous chapter that the Document Outline window of Visual Studio (which you can open using the View ➤ Other Windows menu) is useful when designing a WPF control that has complex content. The logical tree of XAML is displayed for the Window you are building, and if you click any of these nodes, it is automatically selected in the visual designer and the XAML editor for editing.

With the current edition of Visual Studio, the Document Outline window has a few additional features that you might find useful. To the right of any node you will find an icon that looks similar to an eyeball. When you toggle this button, you can opt to hide or show an item on the designer, which can be helpful when you want to focus in on a particular segment to edit (note that this will *not* hide the item at runtime; this only hides items on the designer surface).

Right next to the "eyeball icon" is a second toggle that allows you to lock an item on the designer. As you might guess, this can be helpful when you want to make sure you (or your co-workers) do not accidentally change the XAML for a given item. In effect, locking an item makes it read-only at design time (however, you can change the object's state at runtime).

Controlling Content Layout Using Panels

A WPF application invariably contains a good number of UI elements (e.g., user input controls, graphical content, menu systems, and status bars) that need to be well organized within various windows. After you place the UI elements, you need to make sure they behave as intended when the end user resizes the window or possibly a portion of the window (as in the case of a splitter window). To ensure your WPF controls retain their position within the hosting window, you can take advantage of a good number of *panel types* (also known as *layout managers*).

By default, a new WPF Window created with Visual Studio will use a layout manager of type Grid (more details in just a bit). However, for now, assume a Window with no declared layout manager, like so:

```
<Window x:Class="MyWPFApp.MainWindow"
  xmlns="http://schemas.microsoft.com/winfx/2006/xaml/presentation"
  xmlns:x="http://schemas.microsoft.com/winfx/2006/xaml"
  Title="Fun with Panels!" Height="285" Width="325">

</Window>
```

When you declare a control directly inside a window that doesn't use panels, the control is positioned dead center in the container. Consider the following simple window declaration, which contains a single Button control. Regardless of how you resize the window, the UI widget is always equidistant from all four sides of the client area. The Button's size is determined by the assigned Height and Width properties of the Button.

```
<!- This button is in the center of the window at all times ->
<Window x:Class="MyWPFApp.MainWindow"
  xmlns="http://schemas.microsoft.com/winfx/2006/xaml/presentation"
  xmlns:x="http://schemas.microsoft.com/winfx/2006/xaml"
  Title="Fun with Panels!" Height="285" Width="325">

  <Button x:Name="btnOK" Height = "100" Width="80" Content="OK"/>
</Window>
```

You might also recall that if you attempt to place multiple elements directly within the scope of a Window, you will receive markup and compile-time errors. The reason for these errors is that a window (or any descendant of ContentControl for that matter) can assign only a single object to its Content property. Therefore, the following XAML yields markup and compile-time errors:

```
<!- Error! Content property is implicitly set more than once! ->
<Window x:Class="MyWPFApp.MainWindow"
  xmlns="http://schemas.microsoft.com/winfx/2006/xaml/presentation"
  xmlns:x="http://schemas.microsoft.com/winfx/2006/xaml"
  Title="Fun with Panels!" Height="285" Width="325">
  <!- Error! Two direct child elements of the <Window>! ->
  <Label x:Name="lblInstructions" Width="328" Height="27" FontSize="15" Content="Enter
Information"/>
  <Button x:Name="btnOK" Height = "100" Width="80" Content="OK"/>
</Window>
```

Obviously, a window that can contain only a single control is of little use. When a window needs to contain multiple elements, those elements must be arranged within any number of panels. The panel will contain all of the UI elements that represent the window, after which the panel itself is used as the single object assigned to the Content property.

The System.Windows.Controls namespace provides numerous panels, each of which controls how subelements are maintained. You can use panels to establish how the controls behave if the end user resizes the window, if the controls remain exactly where they were placed at design time, if the controls reflow horizontally from left to right or vertically from top to bottom, and so forth.

You can also intermix panel controls within other panels (e.g., a DockPanel that contains a StackPanel of other items) to provide a great deal of flexibility and control. Table 26-2 documents the role of some commonly used WPF panel controls.

Table 26-2. Core WPF Panel Controls

Panel Control	Meaning in Life
Canvas	Provides a classic mode of content placement. Items stay exactly where you put them at design time.
DockPanel	Locks content to a specified side of the panel (Top, Bottom, Left, or Right).
Grid	Arranges content within a series of cells, maintained within a tabular grid.
StackPanel	Stacks content in a vertical or horizontal manner, as dictated by the Orientation property.
WrapPanel	Positions content from left to right, breaking the content to the next line at the edge of the containing box. Subsequent ordering happens sequentially from top to bottom or from right to left, depending on the value of the Orientation property.

In the next few sections, you will learn how to use these commonly used panel types by copying some predefined XAML data into the kaxaml.exe application you installed in Chapter 25. You can find all these loose XAML files contained inside the PanelMarkup subfolder of your Chapter 26 code download folder. When working with Kaxaml, to simulate resizing a window, change the height or width of the Page element in the markup.

Positioning Content Within Canvas Panels

If you come from a WinForms background, you will probably feel most at home with the Canvas panel because it allows for absolute positioning of UI content. If the end user resizes the window to an area that is smaller than the layout maintained by the Canvas panel, the internal content will not be visible until the container is stretched to a size equal to or larger than the Canvas area.

To add content to a Canvas, you begin by defining the required controls within the scope of the opening and closing Canvas tags. Next, specify the upper-left corner for each control; this is where the rendering should begin using the Canvas.Top and Canvas.Left properties. You can specify the bottom-right area indirectly in each control by setting its Height and Width properties or directly by using the Canvas.Right and Canvas.Bottom properties.

To see Canvas in action, open the provided SimpleCanvas.xaml file using kaxaml.exe. You should see the following Canvas definition (if loading these examples into a WPF application, you will want to change the Page tag to a Window tag):

```
<Page
  xmlns="http://schemas.microsoft.com/winfx/2006/xaml/presentation"
  xmlns:x="http://schemas.microsoft.com/winfx/2006/xaml"
  Title="Fun with Panels!" Height="285" Width="325">
  <Canvas Background="LightSteelBlue">
    <Button x:Name="btnOK" Canvas.Left="212" Canvas.Top="203" Width="80" Content="OK"/>
    <Label x:Name="lblInstructions" Canvas.Left="17" Canvas.Top="14" Width="328" Height="27"
FontSize="15"
           Content="Enter Car Information"/>
    <Label x:Name="lblMake" Canvas.Left="17" Canvas.Top="60" Content="Make"/>
    <TextBox x:Name="txtMake" Canvas.Left="94" Canvas.Top="60" Width="193" Height="25"/>
    <Label x:Name="lblColor" Canvas.Left="17" Canvas.Top="109" Content="Color"/>
    <TextBox x:Name="txtColor" Canvas.Left="94" Canvas.Top="107" Width="193" Height="25"/>
```

```
    <Label x:Name="lblPetName" Canvas.Left="17" Canvas.Top="155" Content="Pet Name"/>
    <TextBox x:Name="txtPetName" Canvas.Left="94" Canvas.Top="153" Width="193" Height="25"/>
  </Canvas>
</Page>
```

You should see the window shown in Figure 26-1 in the top half of the screen.

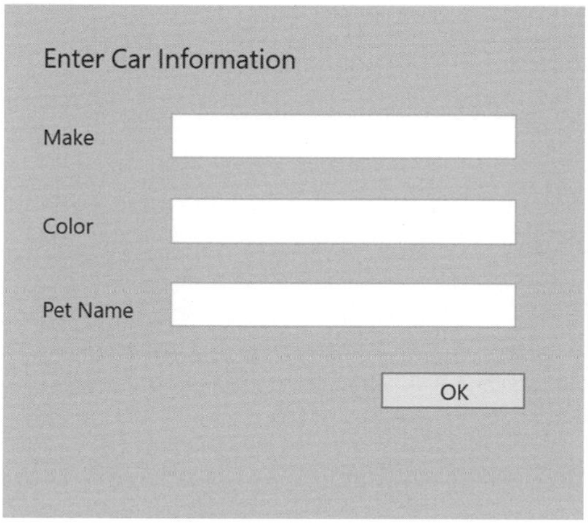

Figure 26-1. *The Canvas layout manager allows for absolute positioning of content*

Note that the order you declare content within a `Canvas` is not used to calculate placement; instead, placement is based on the control's size and the `Canvas.Top`, `Canvas.Bottom`, `Canvas.Left`, and `Canvas.Right` properties.

■ **Note** If subelements within a `Canvas` do not define a specific location using attached property syntax (e.g., `Canvas.Left` and `Canvas.Top`), they automatically attach to the extreme upper-left corner of `Canvas`.

Using the `Canvas` type might seem like the preferred way to arrange content (because it feels so familiar), but this approach does suffer from some limitations. First, items within a `Canvas` do not dynamically resize themselves when applying styles or templates (e.g., their font sizes are unaffected). Second, the `Canvas` will not attempt to keep elements visible when the end user resizes the window to a smaller surface.

Perhaps the best use of the `Canvas` type is for positioning *graphical content*. For example, if you were building a custom image using XAML, you certainly would want the lines, shapes, and text to remain in the same location, rather than see them dynamically repositioned as the user resizes the window! You'll revisit `Canvas` in Chapter 27 when you examine WPF's graphical rendering services.

Positioning Content Within WrapPanel Panels

A `WrapPanel` allows you to define content that will flow across the panel as the window is resized. When positioning elements in a `WrapPanel`, you do not specify top, bottom, left, and right docking values as you typically do with `Canvas`. However, each subelement is free to define a `Height` and `Width` value (among other property values) to control its overall size in the container.

Because content within a WrapPanel does not dock to a given side of the panel, the order in which you declare the elements is important (content is rendered from the first element to the last). If you were to load the XAML data found within the SimpleWrapPanel.xaml file, you would find it contains the following markup (enclosed within a Page definition):

```
<WrapPanel Background="LightSteelBlue">
  <Label x:Name="lblInstruction" Width="328" Height="27" FontSize="15" Content="Enter Car
  Information"/>
  <Label x:Name="lblMake" Content="Make"/>
  <TextBox x:Name="txtMake" Width="193" Height="25"/>
  <Label x:Name="lblColor" Content="Color"/>
  <TextBox x:Name="txtColor" Width="193" Height="25"/>
  <Label x:Name="lblPetName" Content="Pet Name"/>
  <TextBox x:Name="txtPetName" Width="193" Height="25"/>
  <Button x:Name="btnOK" Width="80" Content="OK"/>
</WrapPanel>
```

When you load this markup, the content looks out of sorts because it flows from left to right across the window (see Figure 26-2).

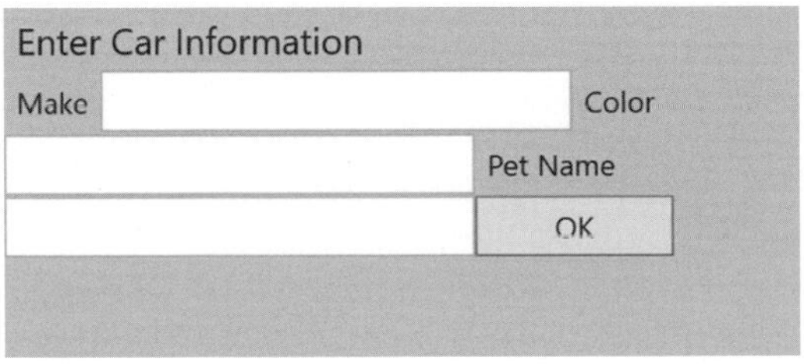

Figure 26-2. *Content in a WrapPanel behaves much like a traditional HTML page*

By default, content within a WrapPanel flows from left to right. However, if you change the value of the Orientation property to Vertical, you can have content wrap in a top-to-bottom manner.

```
<WrapPanel Background="LightSteelBlue" Orientation ="Vertical">
```

You can declare a WrapPanel (as well as some other panel types) by specifying ItemWidth and ItemHeight values, which control the default size of each item. If a subelement does provide its own Height and/or Width value, it will be positioned relative to the size established by the panel. Consider the following markup:

```
<Page
    xmlns="http://schemas.microsoft.com/winfx/2006/xaml/presentation"
    xmlns:x="http://schemas.microsoft.com/winfx/2006/xaml"
    Title="Fun with Panels!" Height="100" Width="650">
  <WrapPanel Background="LightSteelBlue" Orientation ="Horizontal" ItemWidth ="200"
  ItemHeight ="30">
  <Label x:Name="lblInstruction" FontSize="15" Content="Enter Car Information"/>
  <Label x:Name="lblMake" Content="Make"/>
  <TextBox x:Name="txtMake"/>
  <Label x:Name="lblColor" Content="Color"/>
```

```
  <TextBox x:Name="txtColor"/>
  <Label x:Name="lblPetName" Content="Pet Name"/>
  <TextBox x:Name="txtPetName"/>
  <Button x:Name="btnOK" Width ="80" Content="OK"/>
</WrapPanel>
</Page>
```

The rendered code looks like Figure 26-3 (notice the size and position of the `Button` control, which has a specified unique `Width` value).

Figure 26-3. *A WrapPanel can establish the width and height of a given item*

As you might agree after looking at Figure 26-3, a `WrapPanel` is not typically the best choice for arranging content directly in a window because its elements can become scrambled as the user resizes the window. In most cases, a `WrapPanel` will be a subelement to another panel type, allowing a small area of the window to wrap its content when resized (e.g., a `ToolBar` control).

Positioning Content Within StackPanel Panels

Like a `WrapPanel`, a `StackPanel` control arranges content into a single line that can be oriented horizontally or vertically (the default), based on the value assigned to the `Orientation` property. The difference, however, is that the `StackPanel` will *not* attempt to wrap the content as the user resizes the window. Rather, the items in the `StackPanel` will simply stretch (based on their orientation) to accommodate the size of the `StackPanel` itself. For example, the `SimpleStackPanel.xaml` file contains the following markup, which results in the output shown in Figure 26-4:

```
<Page
    xmlns="http://schemas.microsoft.com/winfx/2006/xaml/presentation"
    xmlns:x="http://schemas.microsoft.com/winfx/2006/xaml"
    Title="Fun with Panels!" Height="200" Width="400">
  <StackPanel Background="LightSteelBlue" Orientation ="Vertical">
    <Label Name="lblInstruction"
           FontSize="15" Content="Enter Car Information"/>
    <Label Name="lblMake" Content="Make"/>
    <TextBox Name="txtMake"/>
    <Label Name="lblColor" Content="Color"/>
    <TextBox Name="txtColor"/>
    <Label Name="lblPetName" Content="Pet Name"/>
    <TextBox Name="txtPetName"/>
    <Button Name="btnOK" Width ="80" Content="OK"/>
  </StackPanel>
</Page>
```

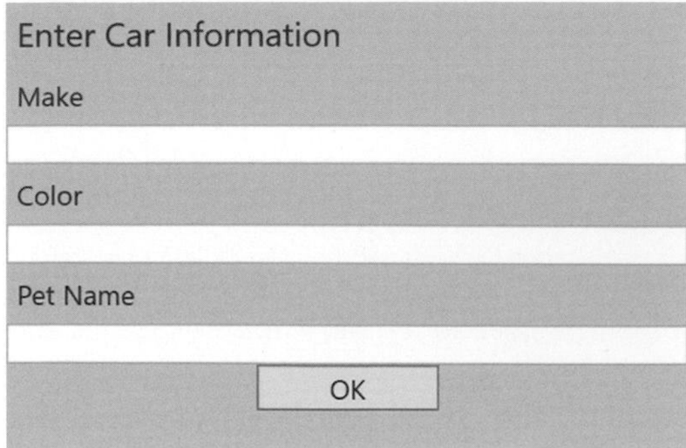

Figure 26-4. *Vertical stacking of content*

If you assign the Orientation property to Horizontal as follows, the rendered output will match that shown in Figure 26-5:

```
<StackPanel Background="LightSteelBlue" Orientation="Horizontal">
```

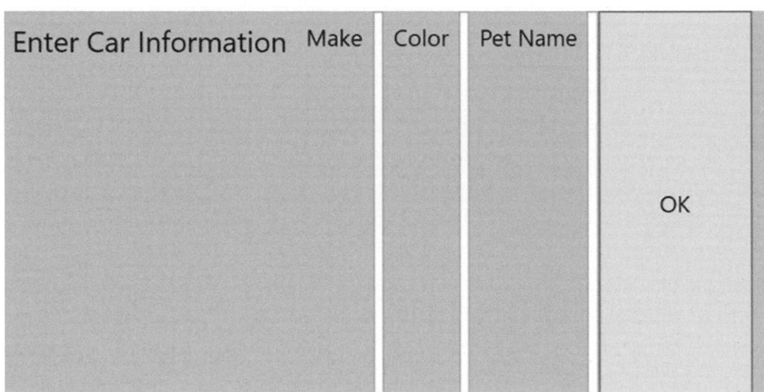

Figure 26-5. *Horizontal stacking of content*

Again, as is the case with the WrapPanel, you will seldom want to use a StackPanel to arrange content directly within a window. Instead, you should use StackPanel as a subpanel to a master panel.

Positioning Content Within Grid Panels

Of all the panels provided with the WPF APIs, Grid is far and away the most flexible. Like an HTML table, the Grid can be carved up into a set of cells, each one of which provides content. When defining a Grid, you perform these three steps:

1. Define and configure each column.
2. Define and configure each row.
3. Assign content to each cell of the grid using attached property syntax.

■ **Note** If you do not define any rows or columns, the `Grid` defaults to a single cell that fills the entire surface of the window. Furthermore, if you do not assign a cell value (column and row) for a subelement within a `Grid`, it automatically attaches to column 0, row 0.

You achieve the first two steps (defining the columns and rows) by using the `Grid.ColumnDefinitions` and `Grid.RowDefinitions` elements, which contain a collection of `ColumnDefinition` and `RowDefinition` elements, respectively. Each cell within a grid is indeed a true .NET object, so you can configure the look and feel and behavior of each cell as you see fit.

Here is a `Grid` definition (that you can find in the `SimpleGrid.xaml` file) that arranges your UI content, as shown in Figure 26-6:

```
<Grid ShowGridLines ="True" Background ="LightSteelBlue">
  <!-- Define the rows/columns -->
  <Grid.ColumnDefinitions>
    <ColumnDefinition/>
    <ColumnDefinition/>
  </Grid.ColumnDefinitions>
  <Grid.RowDefinitions>
    <RowDefinition/>
    <RowDefinition/>
  </Grid.RowDefinitions>

  <!-- Now add the elements to the grid's cells -->
  <Label x:Name="lblInstruction" Grid.Column ="0" Grid.Row ="0"
         FontSize="15" Content="Enter Car Information"/>
  <Button x:Name="btnOK" Height ="30" Grid.Column ="0"
          Grid.Row ="0" Content="OK"/>
  <Label x:Name="lblMake" Grid.Column ="1"
         Grid.Row ="0" Content="Make"/>
  <TextBox x:Name="txtMake" Grid.Column ="1"
           Grid.Row ="0" Width="193" Height="25"/>
  <Label x:Name="lblColor" Grid.Column ="0"
         Grid.Row ="1" Content="Color"/>
  <TextBox x:Name="txtColor" Width="193" Height="25"
           Grid.Column ="0" Grid.Row ="1" />

  <!-- Just to keep things interesting, add some color to the pet name cell -->
  <Rectangle Fill ="LightGreen" Grid.Column ="1" Grid.Row ="1" />
  <Label x:Name="lblPetName" Grid.Column ="1" Grid.Row ="1" Content="Pet Name"/>
  <TextBox x:Name="txtPetName" Grid.Column ="1" Grid.Row ="1"
           Width="193" Height="25"/>
</Grid>
```

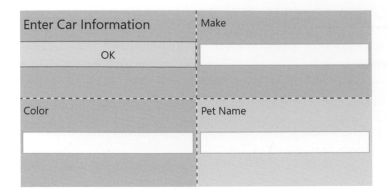

Figure 26-6. *The Grid panel in action*

Notice that each element (including a light green Rectangle element thrown in for good measure) connects itself to a cell in the grid using the Grid.Row and Grid.Column attached properties. By default, the ordering of cells in a grid begins at the upper left, which you specify using Grid.Column="0" Grid.Row="0". Given that your grid defines a total of four cells, you can identify the bottom-right cell using Grid.Column="1" Grid.Row="1".

Sizing Grid Columns and Rows

Columns and rows in a grid can be sized in one of three ways.

- Absolute sizing (e.g., 100)
- Autosizing
- Relative sizing (e.g., 3x)

Absolute sizing is exactly what you would expect; the column (or row) is sized to a specific number of device-independent units. Autosizing sizes each column or row based on the controls contained with the column or row. Relative sizing is pretty much equivalent to percentage sizing in CSS. The total count of the numbers in relatively sized columns or rows gets divided into the total amount of available space.

In the following example, the first row gets 25 percent of the space, and the second row gets 75 percent of the space:

```
<Grid.ColumnDefinitions>
  <ColumnDefinition Width="1*" />
  <ColumnDefinition Width="3*" />
</Grid.ColumnDefinitions>
```

Grids with GridSplitter Types

Grid objects can also support *splitters*. As you might know, splitters allow the end user to resize rows or columns of a grid type. As this is done, the content within each resizable cell will reshape itself based on how the items have been contained. Adding splitters to a Grid is easy to do; you simply define the GridSplitter control, using attached property syntax to establish which row or column it affects.

Be aware that you must assign a Width or Height value (depending on vertical or horizontal splitting) for the splitter to be visible on the screen. Consider the following simple Grid type with a splitter on the first column (Grid.Column = "0"). The contents of the provided GridWithSplitter.xaml file look like this:

```
<Grid Background ="LightSteelBlue">
  <!-- Define columns -->
  <Grid.ColumnDefinitions>
    <ColumnDefinition Width ="Auto"/>
    <ColumnDefinition/>
  </Grid.ColumnDefinitions>

  <!-- Add this label to cell 0 -->
  <Label x:Name="lblLeft" Background ="GreenYellow"
         Grid.Column="0" Content ="Left!"/>

  <!-- Define the splitter -->
  <GridSplitter Grid.Column ="0" Width ="5"/>

  <!-- Add this label to cell 1 -->
  <Label x:Name="lblRight" Grid.Column ="1" Content ="Right!"/>
</Grid>
```

First, notice that the column that will support the splitter has a Width property of Auto. Next, notice that the GridSplitter uses attached property syntax to establish which column it is working with. If you were to view this output, you would find a five-pixel splitter that allows you to resize each Label. Note that the content fills up the entire cell because you have not specified Height or Width properties for either Label (see Figure 26-7).

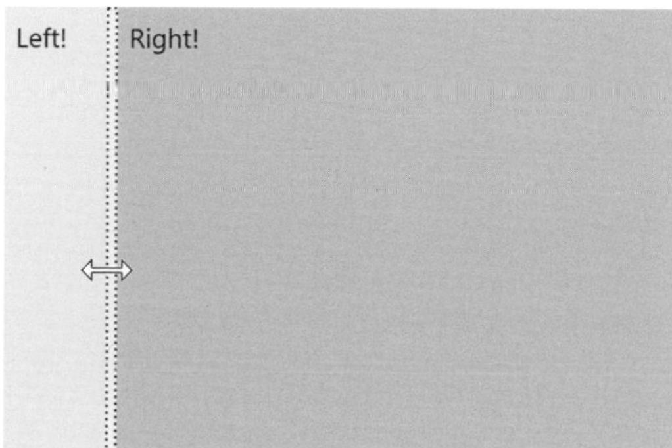

Figure 26-7. *Grid types containing splitters*

Positioning Content Within DockPanel Panels

DockPanel is typically used as a container that holds any number of additional panels for grouping related content. DockPanels use attached property syntax (as shown with the Canvas or Grid types) to control where each item docks itself within the DockPanel.

The SimpleDockPanel.xaml file defines the following simple DockPanel definition that results in the output shown in Figure 26-8:

```
<DockPanel LastChildFill ="True" Background="AliceBlue">
  <!-- Dock items to the panel -->
  <Label DockPanel.Dock ="Top" Name="lblInstruction" FontSize="15" Content="Enter Car
  Information"/>
  <Label DockPanel.Dock ="Left" Name="lblMake" Content="Make"/>
```

```
  <Label DockPanel.Dock ="Right" Name="lblColor" Content="Color"/>
  <Label DockPanel.Dock ="Bottom" Name="lblPetName" Content="Pet Name"/>
  <Button Name="btnOK" Content="OK"/>
</DockPanel>
```

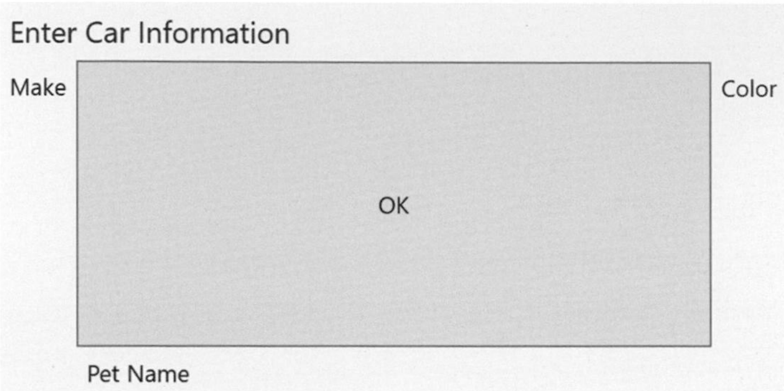

Figure 26-8. *A simple DockPanel*

■ **Note** If you add multiple elements to the same side of a DockPanel, they will stack along the specified edge in the order they are declared.

The benefit of using DockPanel types is that, as the user resizes the window, each element remains connected to the specified side of the panel (through DockPanel.Dock). Also notice that the opening DockPanel tag in this example sets the LastChildFill attribute to true. Given that the Button control is indeed the "last child" in the container, it will therefore be stretched within the remaining space.

Enabling Scrolling for Panel Types

It is worth pointing out that WPF supplies a ScrollViewer class, which provides automatic scrolling behaviors for data within panel objects. The SimpleScrollViewer.xaml file defines the following:

```
<ScrollViewer>
  <StackPanel>
    <Button Content ="First" Background = "Green" Height ="50"/>
    <Button Content ="Second" Background = "Red" Height ="50"/>
    <Button Content ="Third" Background = "Pink" Height ="50"/>
    <Button Content ="Fourth" Background = "Yellow" Height ="50"/>
    <Button Content ="Fifth" Background = "Blue" Height ="50"/>
  </StackPanel>
</ScrollViewer>
```

You can see the result of the previous XAML definition in Figure 26-9 (notice the scrollbar on the right since the window isn't sized to show all five buttons).

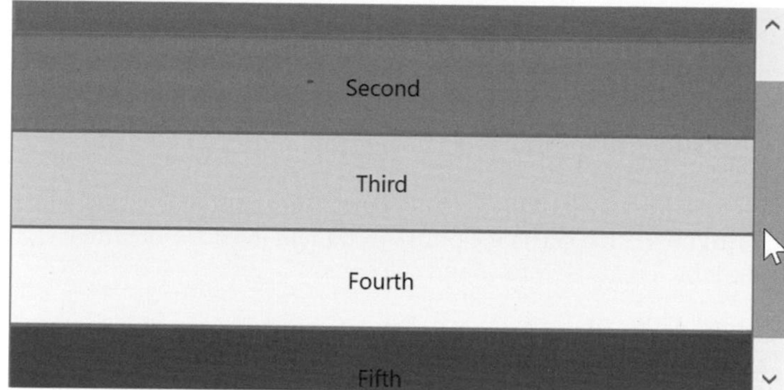

Figure 26-9. *Working with the ScrollViewer type*

As you would expect, each panel provides numerous members that allow you to fine-tune content placement. On a related note, many WPF controls support two properties of interest (`Padding` and `Margin`) that allow the control itself to inform the panel how it wants to be treated. Specifically, the `Padding` property controls how much extra space should surround the interior control, while `Margin` controls the extra space around the exterior of a control.

This wraps up this chapter's look at the major panel types of WPF, as well as the various ways they position their content. Next, you'll learn how to use the Visual Studio designers to create layouts.

Configuring Panels Using the Visual Studio Designers

Now that you have been given a walk-through of the XAML used to define some common layout managers, you will be happy to know that Visual Studio has very good design-time support for constructing your layouts. The key to doing so lies with the Document Outline window described earlier in this chapter. To illustrate some of the basics, create a new WPF application project named VisualLayoutTester.

Recall that the WFP Application project template doesn't set the options for implicit `using` statements or nullable reference types. For each of the projects in this chapter, I've enabled global implicit `using` statements and disabled nullable reference types at the project level.

```
<Project Sdk="Microsoft.NET.Sdk">
  <PropertyGroup>
    <OutputType>WinExe</OutputType>
    <TargetFramework>net6.0-windows</TargetFramework>
    <UseWPF>true</UseWPF>
    <Nullable>disable</Nullable>
    <ImplicitUsings>enable</ImplicitUsings>
  </PropertyGroup>
</Project>
```

Notice how your initial `Window` makes use of a `Grid` layout by default, as shown here:

```
<Window x:Class="VisualLayoutTester.MainWindow"
  xmlns="http://schemas.microsoft.com/winfx/2006/xaml/presentation"
  xmlns:x="http://schemas.microsoft.com/winfx/2006/xaml"
  xmlns:d="http://schemas.microsoft.com/expression/blend/2008"
  xmlns:local="clr-namespace:VisualLayoutTesterApp"
```

```
  mc:Ignorable="d"
    Title="MainWindow" Height="450" Width="800">
    <Grid>
    </Grid>
</Window>
```

If you are happy using the Grid layout system, notice in Figure 26-10 that you can easily carve out and resize the grid's cells using the visual layout. To do so, first select the Grid component in your Document Outline window and then click the grid's border to create new rows and columns.

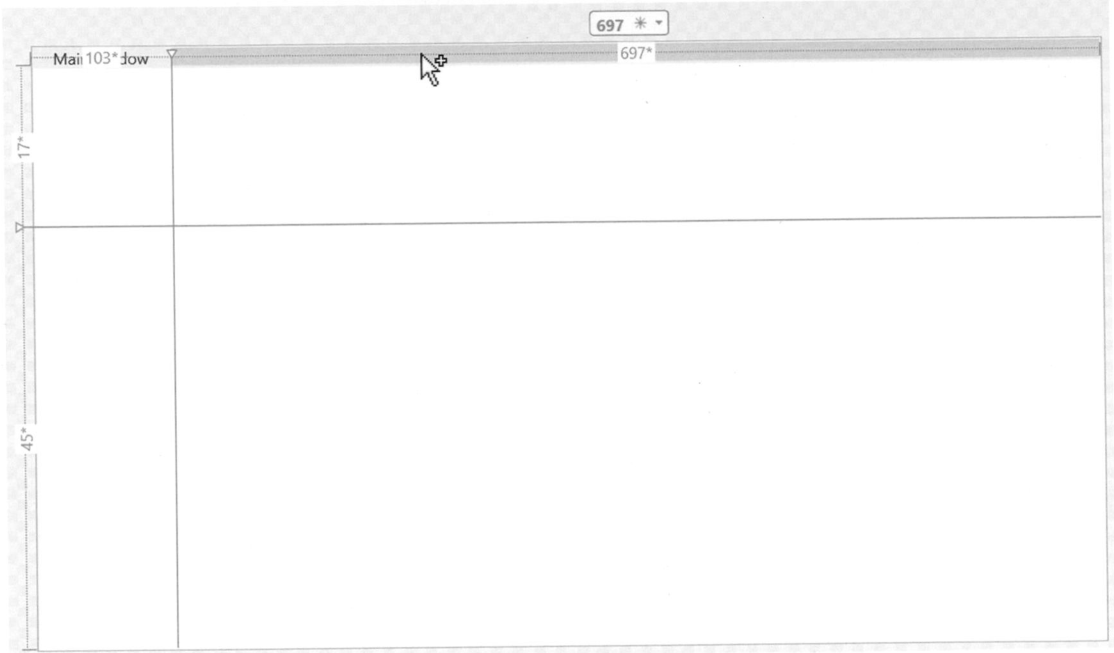

***Figure 26-10.** The Grid control can be visually cut into cells using the IDE's designer*

Now, let's say you have defined a grid with some number of cells. You can then drag and drop controls into a given cell of the layout system, and the IDE will automatically set the Grid.Row and Grid.Column properties of the control in question. Here is some possible markup generated by the IDE after dragging a Button into a predefined cell:

```
<Button x:Name="button" Content="Button" Grid.Column="0" HorizontalAlignment="Left"
Margin="21,21.4,0,0" Grid.Row="1" VerticalAlignment="Top" Width="75"/>
```

Now, let's say you would rather not use a Grid at all. If you right-click any layout node in the Document Outline window, you will find a menu option that allows you to change the current container into another (see Figure 26-11). Be aware that when you do so, you will (most likely) radically change the positioning of the controls because the controls will conform to the rules of the new panel type.

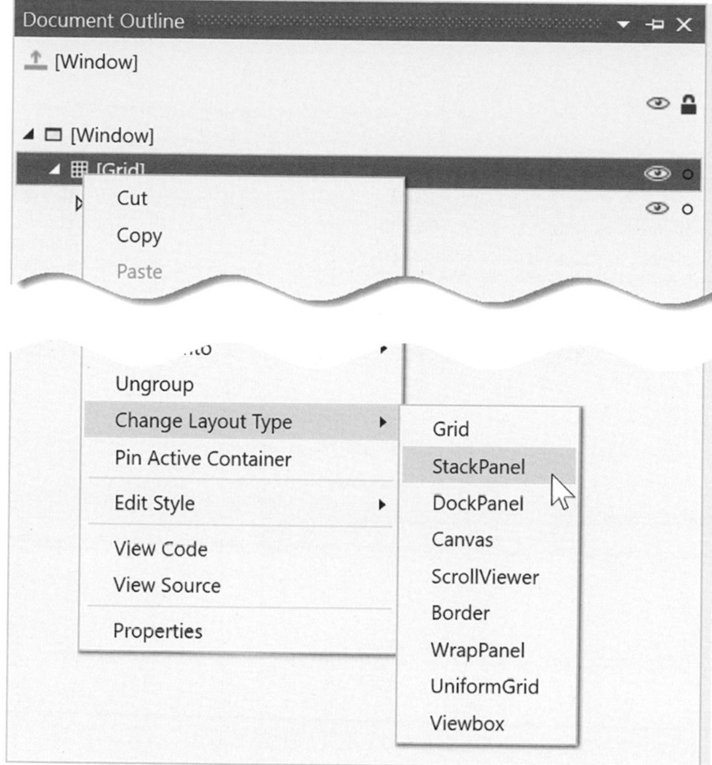

Figure 26-11. *The Document Outline window allows you to convert to new panel types*

Another handy trick is the ability to select a set of controls on the visual designer and group them into a new, nested layout manager. Assume you have a `Grid` that contains a set of random objects. Now, select a set of items on the designer by holding down the Ctrl key and clicking each item with the left mouse button. If you then right-click the selection, you can group the selected items into a new subpanel (see Figure 26-12).

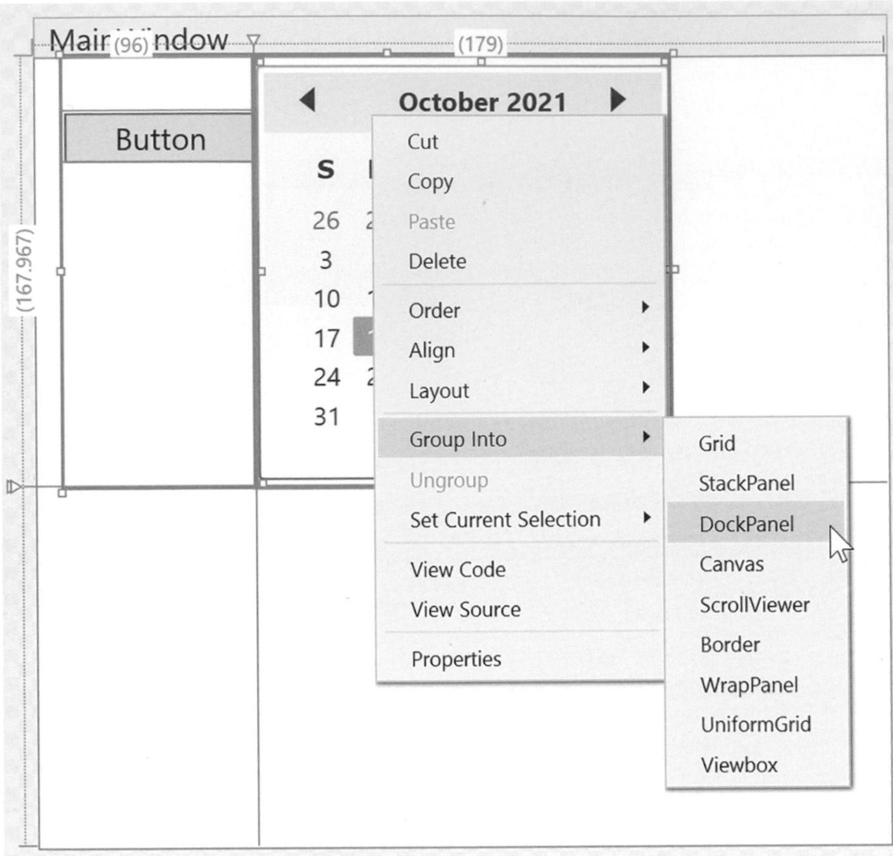

***Figure 26-12.** Grouping items into a new subpanel*

After you have done so, examine the Document Outline window once again to verify the nested layout system. As you build full-featured WPF windows, you will most likely always need to make use of a nested layout system, rather than simply picking a single panel for all of the UI display (in fact, the remaining WPF examples in the text will typically do so). On a final note, the nodes in the Document Outline window are all drag and droppable. For example, if you wanted to move a control currently in the DockPanel into the parent panel, you could do so as suggested in Figure 26-13.

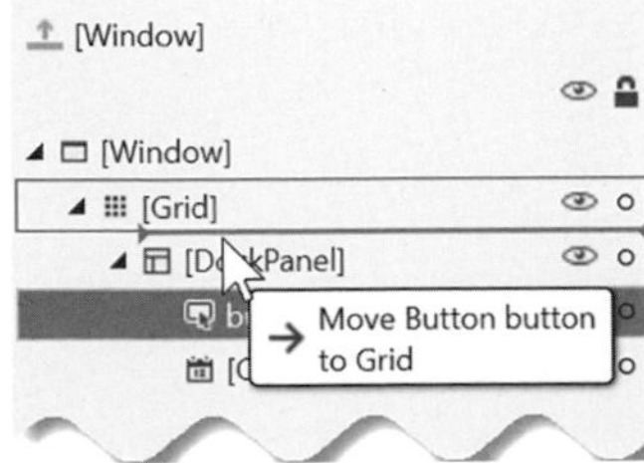

***Figure 26-13.** Relocating items via the Document Outline window*

As you work through the remaining WPF chapters, I'll point out additional layout shortcuts where possible. However, it's definitely worth your time to experiment and test various features yourself. To keep you moving in the right direction, the next example in the chapter will illustrate how to build a nested layout manager for a custom text processing application (with spell-checking!).

Building a Window's Frame Using Nested Panels

As mentioned, a typical WPF window will not use a single panel control but instead will nest panels within other panels to gain the desired layout system. Begin by creating a new WPF application named MyWordPad and enabling implicit `using` statements and disabling nullable reference types:

```
<Project Sdk="Microsoft.NET.Sdk">
  <PropertyGroup>
    <OutputType>WinExe</OutputType>
    <TargetFramework>net6.0-windows</TargetFramework>
    <UseWPF>true</UseWPF>
    <Nullable>disable</Nullable>
    <ImplicitUsings>enable</ImplicitUsings>
  </PropertyGroup>
</Project>
```

Your goal is to construct a layout where the main window has a topmost menu system, a toolbar under the menu system, and a status bar mounted on the bottom of the window. The status bar will contain a pane to hold text prompts that are displayed when the user selects a menu item (or toolbar button), while the menu system and toolbar will offer UI triggers to close the application and display spelling suggestions in an `Expander` widget. Figure 26-14 shows the initial layout you are shooting for; it also shows the spell-checking capabilities within WPF.

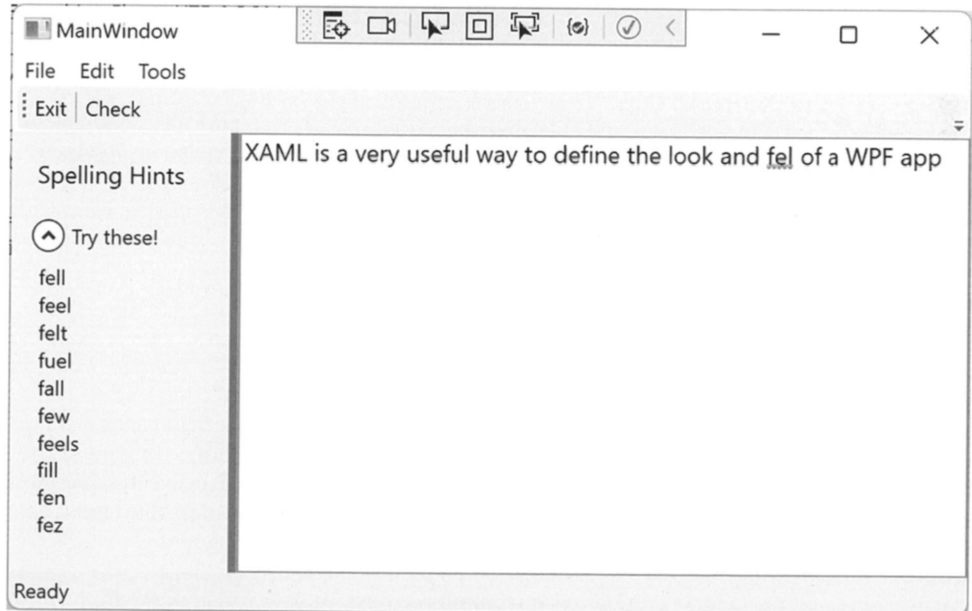

Figure 26-14. *Using nested panels to establish a window's UI*

To begin building this UI, update the initial XAML definition for your Window type so it uses a DockPanel child element, rather than the default Grid, as follows:

```
<Window x:Class="MyWordPad.MainWindow"
    xmlns="http://schemas.microsoft.com/winfx/2006/xaml/presentation"
    xmlns:x="http://schemas.microsoft.com/winfx/2006/xaml"
    xmlns:d="http://schemas.microsoft.com/expression/blend/2008"

    xmlns:local="clr-namespace:MyWordPad"
    mc:Ignorable="d"
    Title="My Spell Checker" Height="450" Width="800">
  <!-- This panel establishes the content for the window -->
  <DockPanel>
  </DockPanel>
</Window>
```

Building the Menu System

Menu systems in WPF are represented by the Menu class, which maintains a collection of MenuItem objects. When building a menu system in XAML, you can have each MenuItem handle various events. The most notable of these events is Click, which occurs when the end user selects a subitem. In this example, you begin by building the two topmost menu items (File and Tools; you will build the Edit menu later in this example), which expose Exit and Spelling Hints subitems, respectively.

In addition to handling the Click event for each subitem, you also need to handle the MouseEnter and MouseExit events, which you will use to set the status bar text in a later step. Add the following markup within your DockPanel scope:

```
<!-- Dock menu system on the top -->
<Menu DockPanel.Dock ="Top"
      HorizontalAlignment="Left" Background="White" BorderBrush ="Black">
  <MenuItem Header="_File">
    <Separator/>
    <MenuItem Header ="_Exit" MouseEnter ="MouseEnterExitArea"
              MouseLeave ="MouseLeaveArea" Click ="FileExit_Click"/>
    </MenuItem>
    <MenuItem Header="_Tools">
      <MenuItem Header ="_Spelling Hints"
          MouseEnter ="MouseEnterToolsHintsArea"
          MouseLeave ="MouseLeaveArea" Click ="ToolsSpellingHints_Click"/>
  </MenuItem>
</Menu>
```

Notice that you dock the menu system to the top of the DockPanel. Also, you use the Separator element to insert a thin horizontal line in the menu system, directly before the Exit option. Also notice that the Header values for each MenuItem contain an embedded underscore token (e.g., _Exit). You use this token to establish which letter will be underlined when the end user presses the Alt key (for keyboard shortcuts). This is a change from the & character used in Windows Forms since XAML is based on XML, and the & character has meaning in XML.

So far you've implemented the complete menu system definition; next, you need to implement the various event handlers. First, you have the File Exit handler, FileExit_Click(), which simply closes the window, which in turn terminates the application because this is your topmost window. The MouseEnter and MouseExit event handlers for each subitem will eventually update your status bar; however, for now, you will simply provide shells. Finally, the ToolsSpellingHints_Click() handler for the Tools Spelling Hints menu item will also remain a shell for the time being. Here are the current updates to your code-behind file (including the updated using statements):

```
using System.IO;
using System.Windows;
using System.Windows.Controls;
using System.Windows.Input;
using Microsoft.Win32;

namespace MyWordPad;

public partial class MainWindow : Window
{
  public MainWindow()
  {
    InitializeComponent();
  }

  protected void FileExit_Click(object sender, RoutedEventArgs args)
  {
    // Close this window.
    This.Close();
  }

  protected void ToolsSpellingHints_Click(object sender, RoutedEventArgs args)
  {
  }
  protected void MouseEnterExitArea(object sender, RoutedEventArgs args)
  {
  }
  protected void MouseEnterToolsHintsArea(object sender, RoutedEventArgs args)
  {
  }
  protected void MouseLeaveArea(object sender, RoutedEventArgs args)
  {
  }
}
```

Building Menus Visually

While it is always good to know how to manually define items in XAML, it can be a tad on the tedious side. Visual Studio supports visual design support for menu systems, toolbars, status bars, and many other UI controls. If you right-click the Menu control, you will notice an Add MenuItem option. As the name suggests, this adds a new menu item to the Menu control. After you have added a set of topmost items, you can then add submenu items and separators, expand or collapse the menu itself, and perform other menu-centric operations via a second right-click.

As you see for the remainder of the current MyWordPad example, I'll typically show you the final generated XAML; however, do take the time to experiment with the visual designers to simplify the task at hand.

Building the Toolbar

Toolbars (represented by the ToolBar class in WPF) typically provide an alternative manner for activating a menu option. Add the following markup directly after the closing scope of your Menu definition:

```
<!—Put Toolbar under the Menu -->
<ToolBar DockPanel.Dock ="Top" >
  <Button Content ="Exit" MouseEnter ="MouseEnterExitArea"
          MouseLeave ="MouseLeaveArea" Click ="FileExit_Click"/>
  <Separator/>
  <Button Content ="Check" MouseEnter ="MouseEnterToolsHintsArea"
          MouseLeave ="MouseLeaveArea" Click ="ToolsSpellingHints_Click"
          Cursor="Help" />
</ToolBar>
```

Your ToolBar control consists of two Button controls, which just so happen to handle the same events and are handled by the same methods in your code file. Using this technique, you can double up your handlers to serve both menu items and toolbar buttons. Although this toolbar uses the typical push buttons, you should appreciate that the ToolBar type "is-a" ContentControl; therefore, you are free to embed any types into its surface (e.g., drop-down lists, images, and graphics). The only other point of interest here is that the Check button supports a custom mouse cursor through the Cursor property.

■ **Note** You can optionally wrap the ToolBar element within a ToolBarTray element, which controls layout, docking, and drag-and-drop operations for a set of ToolBar objects.

Building the Status Bar

A StatusBar control will be docked to the lower portion of the DockPanel and contain a single TextBlock control, which you have not used prior to this point in the chapter. You can use a TextBlock to hold text that supports numerous textual annotations, such as bold text, underlined text, line breaks, and so forth. Add the following markup directly after the previous ToolBar definition:

```
<!-- Put a StatusBar at the bottom -->
<StatusBar DockPanel.Dock ="Bottom" Background="Beige" >
  <StatusBarItem>
    <TextBlock Name="statBarText" Text="Ready"/>
  </StatusBarItem>
</StatusBar>
```

Finalizing the UI Design

The final aspect of your UI design is to define a splittable Grid that defines two columns. On the left, place an Expander control that will display a list of spelling suggestions, wrapped within a StackPanel. On the right, place a TextBox control that supports multiple lines and scrollbars and includes enabled spell-checking. You mount the entire Grid to the left of the parent DockPanel. Add the following XAML markup directly under the StatusBar markup to complete the definition of your window's UI:

```
<Grid DockPanel.Dock ="Left" Background ="AliceBlue">
 --- Define the rows and columns -->
  <Grid.ColumnDefinitions>
    <ColumnDefinition />
    <ColumnDefinition />
  </Grid.ColumnDefinitions>

  <GridSplitter Grid.Column ="0" Width ="5" Background ="Gray" />
  <StackPanel Grid.Column="0" VerticalAlignment ="Stretch" >
    <Label Name="lblSpellingInstructions" FontSize="14" Margin="10,10,0,0">
     Spelling Hints
    </Label>

    <Expander Name="expanderSpelling" Header ="Try these!"
              Margin="10,10,10,10">
     --- This will be filled programmatically -->
      <Label Name ="lblSpellingHints" FontSize ="12"/>
    </Expander>
  </StackPanel>

 --- This will be the area to type within -->
  <TextBox  Grid.Column ="1"
            SpellCheck.IsEnabled ="True"
            AcceptsReturn ="True"
            Name ="txtData" FontSize ="14"
            BorderBrush ="Blue"
            VerticalScrollBarVisibility="Auto"
            HorizontalScrollBarVisibility="Auto">
  </TextBox>
</Grid>
```

Implementing the MouseEnter/MouseLeave Event Handlers

At this point, the UI of your window is complete. The only remaining tasks are to provide an implementation for the remaining event handlers. Begin by updating your C# code file so that each of the MouseEnter, MouseLeave, and MouseExit handlers sets the text pane of the status bar with a fitting message to help the end user, like so:

```
public partial class MainWindow : System.Windows.Window
{
...
  protected void MouseEnterExitArea(object sender, RoutedEventArgs args)
  {
    statBarText.Text = "Exit the Application";
  }
  protected void MouseEnterToolsHintsArea(object sender, RoutedEventArgs args)
  {
    statBarText.Text = "Show Spelling Suggestions";
  }
  protected void MouseLeaveArea(object sender, RoutedEventArgs args)
  {
```

```
    statBarText.Text = "Ready";
  }
}
```

At this point, you can run your application. You should see your status bar change its text based on which menu item/toolbar button you hover your mouse over.

Implementing the Spell-Checking Logic

The WPF API ships with built-in spell-checker support, which is independent of Microsoft Office products. This means you don't need to use the COM interop layer to use the spell-checker of Microsoft Word; instead, you can easily add the same type of support with only a few lines of code.

You might recall that when you defined the `TextBox` control, you set the `SpellCheck.IsEnabled` property to `true`. When you do this, misspelled words are underlined with a red squiggle, just as they are in Microsoft Office. Even better, the underlying programming model gives you access to the spell-checker engine, which allows you to get a list of suggestions for misspelled words. Add the following code to your `ToolsSpellingHints_Click()` method:

```
protected void ToolsSpellingHints_Click(object sender, RoutedEventArgs args)
{
  string spellingHints = string.Empty;

  // Try to get a spelling error at the current caret location.
  SpellingError error = txtData.GetSpellingError(txtData.CaretIndex);
  if (error != null)
  {
    // Build a string of spelling suggestions.
    foreach (string s in error.Suggestions)
    {
      spellingHints += $"{s}\n";
    }

    // Show suggestions and expand the expander.
    lblSpellingHints.Content = spellingHints;
    expanderSpelling.IsExpanded = true;
  }
}
```

The preceding code is quite simple. You simply figure out the current location of the caret in the text box by using the `CaretIndex` property to extract a `SpellingError` object. If there is an error at said location (meaning the value is not `null`), you loop over the list of suggestions using the aptly named `Suggestions` property. After you have all the suggestions for the misspelled word, you connect the data to the `Label` in the `Expander`.

So there you have it! With only a few lines of procedural code (and a healthy dose of XAML), you have the beginnings of a functioning word processor. An understanding of *control commands* can help you add a bit more pizzazz.

Understanding WPF Commands

WPF provides support for what might be considered *control-agnostic events* via the *command architecture*. A typical .NET Core event is defined within a specific base class and can be used only by that class or a derivative thereof. Therefore, normal .NET Core events are tightly coupled to the class in which they are defined.

In contrast, WPF commands are event-like entities that are independent from a specific control and, in many cases, can be successfully applied to numerous (and seemingly unrelated) control types. By way of a few examples, WPF supports copy, paste, and cut commands, which you can apply to a wide variety of UI elements (e.g., menu items, toolbar buttons, and custom buttons), as well as keyboard shortcuts (e.g., Ctrl+C and Ctrl+V).

While other UI toolkits (such as Windows Forms) provided standard events for such purposes, using them typically left you with redundant and hard-to-maintain code. Under the WPF model, you can use commands as an alternative. The end result typically yields a smaller and more flexible code base.

The Intrinsic Command Objects

WPF ships with numerous built-in control commands, all of which you can configure with associated keyboard shortcuts (or other input gestures). Programmatically speaking, a WPF command is any object that supports a property (often called `Command`) that returns an object implementing the `ICommand` interface, as shown here:

```
public interface ICommand
{
  // Occurs when changes occur that affect whether
  // or not the command should execute.
  event EventHandler CanExecuteChanged;

  // Defines the method that determines whether the command
  // can execute in its current state.
  bool CanExecute(object parameter);

  // Defines the method to be called when the command is invoked.
  void Execute(object parameter);
}
```

WPF provides various command classes, which expose close to 100 command objects, out of the box. These classes define numerous properties that expose specific command objects, each of which implements `ICommand`. Table 26-3 documents some of the standard command objects available.

Table 26-3. *The Intrinsic WPF Control Command Objects*

WPF Class	Command Objects	Meaning in Life
`ApplicationCommands`	`Close`, `Copy`, `Cut`, `Delete`, `Find`, `Open`, `Paste`, `Save`, `SaveAs`, `Redo`, `Undo`	Various application-level commands
`ComponentCommands`	`MoveDown`, `MoveFocusBack`, `MoveLeft`, `MoveRight`, `ScrollToEnd`, `ScrollToHome`	Various commands common to UI components
`MediaCommands`	`BoostBase`, `ChannelUp`, `ChannelDown`, `FastForward`, `NextTrack`, `Play`, `Rewind`, `Select`, `Stop`	Various media-centric commands
`NavigationCommands`	`BrowseBack`, `BrowseForward`, `Favorites`, `LastPage`, `NextPage`, `Zoom`	Various commands relating to the WPF navigation model
`EditingCommands`	`AlignCenter`, `CorrectSpellingError`, `DecreaseFontSize`, `EnterLineBreak`, `EnterParagraphBreak`, `MoveDownByLine`, `MoveRightByWord`	Various commands relating to the WPF Documents API

Connecting Commands to the Command Property

If you want to connect any of the WPF command properties to a UI element that supports the Command property (such as a Button or MenuItem), you have very little work to do. You can see how to do this by updating the current menu system so it supports a new topmost menu item named Edit and three subitems to account for copying, pasting, and cutting of textual data, like so:

```
<Menu DockPanel.Dock ="Top" HorizontalAlignment="Left" Background="White" BorderBrush
="Black">
  <MenuItem Header ="_File" >
    <MenuItem Header ="_Exit" MouseEnter ="MouseEnterExitArea" MouseLeave ="MouseLeaveArea"
        Click ="FileExit_Click"/>
  </MenuItem>

 <-- New menu item with commands! -->
  <MenuItem Header="_Edit">
    <MenuItem Command="ApplicationCommands.Copy" />
    <MenuItem Command="ApplicationCommands.Cut" />
    <MenuItem Command="ApplicationCommands.Paste" />
  </MenuItem>

  <MenuItem Header="_Tools">
    <MenuItem Header="_Spelling Hints"
        MouseEnter="MouseEnterToolsHintsArea"
        MouseLeave="MouseLeaveArea"
        Click="ToolsSpellingHints_Click" />
  </MenuItem>
```

Notice that each of the subitems on the Edit menu has a value assigned to the Command property. Doing this means that the menu items automatically receive the correct name and shortcut key (e.g., Ctrl+C for a cut operation) in the menu item UI; it also means that the application is now *copy, cut, and paste* aware with no procedural code!

If you run the application and select some of text, you can use your new menu items out of the box. As a bonus, your application is also equipped to respond to a standard right-click operation to present the user with the same options.

Connecting Commands to Arbitrary Actions

If you want to connect a command object to an arbitrary (application-specific) event, you will need to drop down to procedural code. Doing so is not complex, but it does involve a bit more logic than you see in XAML. For example, assume that you want to have the entire window respond to the F1 key so that when the end user presses this key, he will activate an associated help system. Also, assume your code file for the main window defines a new method named SetF1CommandBinding(), which you call within the constructor after the call to InitializeComponent().

```
public MainWindow()
{
  InitializeComponent();
  SetF1CommandBinding();
}
```

This new method will programmatically create a new CommandBinding object, which you can use whenever you need to bind a command object to a given event handler in your application. Here, you configure your CommandBinding object to operate with the ApplicationCommands.Help command, which is automatically F1 aware:

```
private void SetF1CommandBinding()
{
  CommandBinding helpBinding = new CommandBinding(ApplicationCommands.Help);
  helpBinding.CanExecute += CanHelpExecute;
  helpBinding.Executed += HelpExecuted;
  CommandBindings.Add(helpBinding);
}
```

Most CommandBinding objects will want to handle the CanExecute event (which allows you to specify whether the command occurs based on the operation of your program) and the Executed event (which is where you can author the content that should occur once the command occurs). Add the following event handlers to your Window-derived type (note the format of each method, as required by the associated delegates):

```
private void CanHelpExecute(object sender, CanExecuteRoutedEventArgs e)
{
  // Here, you can set CanExecute to false if you want to prevent the command from
  executing.
  e.CanExecute = true;
}

private void HelpExecuted(object sender, ExecutedRoutedEventArgs e)
{
  MessageBox.Sh“w("Look, it is not that difficult. Just type something!", "Help!");
}
```

In the preceding snippet, you implemented CanHelpExecute() so it always allows F1 help to launch; you do this by simply returning true. However, if you have certain situations where the help system should not display, you can account for this and return false when necessary. Your “help system” displayed within HelpExecuted() is little more than a message box. At this point, you can run your application. When you press the F1 key on your keyboard, you will see your message box appear.

Working with the Open and Save Commands

To complete the current example, you will add functionality to save your text data to an external file and open up *.txt files for editing. If you want to take the long road, you can manually add programming logic that enables or disables new menu items based on whether your TextBox has data inside it. Once again, however, you can use commands to decrease your burden.

Begin by updating the MenuItem element that represents your topmost File menu by adding the following two new submenus that use the Save and Open ApplicationCommands objects:

```
<MenuItem Head"r="_F"le">
  <MenuItem Comman" ="ApplicationCommands.O"en"/>
  <MenuItem Comman" ="ApplicationCommands.S"ve"/>
  <Separator/>
  <MenuItem Heade" ="_E"it"
```

```
            MouseEnte" ="MouseEnterExitA"ea"
            MouseLeav" ="MouseLeaveA"ea" Clic" ="FileExit_Cl"ck"/>
</MenuItem>
```

Again, remember that all command objects implement the ICommand interface, which defines two events (CanExecute and Executed). Now you need to enable the entire window so it can check whether it is currently okay to fire these commands; if so, you can define an event handler to execute the custom code.

You do this by populating the CommandBindings collection maintained by the window. Doing so in XAML requires that you use property-element syntax to define a Window.CommandBindings scope in which you place two CommandBinding definitions. Update your Window like this:

```
<Window x:Cla"s="MyWordPad.MainWin"ow"
  xml"s="http://schemas.microsoft.com/winfx/2006/xaml/presentat"on"
  xmlns"x="http://schemas.microsoft.com/winfx/2006/x"ml"
  Tit"e="MySpellChec"er" Heig"t=""31" Wid"h=""08"
  WindowStartupLocatio" ="CenterScr"en" >

 --- This will inform the Window which handlers to call,
      when testing for the Open and Save commands. -->
  <Window.CommandBindings>
    <CommandBinding Comma"d="ApplicationCommands.O"en"
                    Execut"d="OpenCmdExecu"ed"
                    CanExecu"e="OpenCmdCanExec"te"/>
    <CommandBinding Comma"d="ApplicationCommands.S"ve"
                    Execut"d="SaveCmdExecu"ed"
                    CanExecu"e="SaveCmdCanExec"te"/>
  </Window.CommandBindings>

 --- This panel establishes the content for the window -->
  <DockPanel>
  ...
  </DockPanel>
</Window>
```

Now right-click each of the Executed and CanExecute attributes in your XAML editor and pick the Navigate to Event Handler menu option. As you might recall from Chapter 25, this will automatically generate stub code for the event itself. At this point, you should have four empty handlers in the C# code file for the window.

The implementation of CanExecute event handlers will tell the window that it is okay to fire the corresponding Executed events at any time by setting the CanExecute property of the incoming CanExecuteRoutedEventArgs object.

```
private void OpenCmdCanExecute(object sender, CanExecuteRoutedEventArgs e)
{
  e.CanExecute = true;
}

private void SaveCmdCanExecute(object sender, CanExecuteRoutedEventArgs e)
{
  e.CanExecute = true;
}
```

The corresponding Executed handlers perform the actual work of displaying the open and save dialog boxes; they also send the data in your TextBox to a file. Begin by making sure that you import the System.IO and Microsoft.Win32 namespaces into your code file. The following completed code is straightforward:

```
private void OpenCmdExecuted(object sender, ExecutedRoutedEventArgs e)
{
  // Create an open file dialog box and only show XAML files.
  var openDlg = new OpenFileDialog { Filter"= "Text Files |*."xt"};

  // Did they click on the OK button?
  if (true == openDlg.ShowDialog())
  {
    // Load all text of selected file.
    string dataFromFile = File.ReadAllText(openDlg.FileName);

    // Show string in TextBox.
    txtData.Text = dataFromFile;
  }
}

private void SaveCmdExecuted(object sender, ExecutedRoutedEventArgs e)
{
  var saveDlg = new SaveFileDialog { Filter"= "Text Files |*."xt"};

  // Did they click on the OK button?
  if (true == saveDlg.ShowDialog())
  {
    // Save data in the TextBox to the named file.
    File.WriteAllText(saveDlg.FileName, txtData.Text);
  }
}
```

■ **Note** Chapter 29 will take a much deeper look into the WPF command system. In it, you will create custom commands based on the ICommand interface as well as create RelayCommands.

That wraps up this example and your initial look at working with WPF controls. Here, you learned how to work with basic commands, menu systems, status bars, toolbars, nested panels, and a few basic UI controls, such as TextBox and Expander. The next example will work with some more exotic controls while examining several important WPF services at the same time.

Understanding Routed Events

You might have noticed the RoutedEventArgs parameter instead of EventArgs in the previous code example. The routed events model is a refinement of the standard CLR event model designed to ensure that events can be processed in a manner that is fitting for XAML's description of a tree of objects. Assume you have a new WPF application project named WpfRoutedEvents. Now, update the XAML definition of the

MainWindow.xaml file by adding the following Button control, which has some complex content, inside the <Grid> (Window and Grid elements omitted for brevity):

```
<Button Name="btnClickMe" Height="75" Width = "250" Click ="btnClickMe_Clicked">
  <StackPanel Orientation ="Horizontal">
    <Label Height="50" FontSize ="20">Fancy Button!</Label>
    <Canvas Height ="50" Width ="100" >
      <Ellipse Name = "outerEllipse" Fill ="Green"
               Height ="25" Width ="50" Cursor="Hand"
               Canvas.Left="25" Canvas.Top="12"/>
      <Ellipse Name = "innerEllipse" Fill ="Yellow"
         Height = "15" Width ="36"
         Canvas.Top="17" Canvas.Left="32"/>
    </Canvas>
  </StackPanel>
</Button>
```

Notice in the Button's opening definition that you have handled the Click event by specifying the name of a method to be called when the event is raised. The Click event works with the RoutedEventHandler delegate, which expects an event handler that takes an object as the first parameter and a System.Windows.RoutedEventArgs as the second. Implement this handler as so:

```
public void btnClickMe_Clicked(object sender, RoutedEventArgs e)
{
  // Do something when button is clicked.
  MessageBox.Show("Clicked the button");
}
```

If you run your application, you will see this message box display, regardless of which part of the button's content you click (the green Ellipse, the yellow Ellipse, the Label, or the Button's surface). This is a good thing. Imagine how tedious WPF event handling would be if you were forced to handle a Click event for every one of these subelements. Not only would the creation of separate event handlers for each aspect of the Button be labor intensive, you would end up with some mighty nasty code to maintain down the road.

Thankfully, WPF *routed events* take care of ensuring that your single Click event handler will be called regardless of which part of the button is clicked automatically. Simply put, the routed events model automatically propagates an event up (or down) a tree of objects, looking for an appropriate handler.

Specifically speaking, a routed event can make use of three *routing strategies*. If an event is moving from the point of origin up to other defining scopes within the object tree, the event is said to be a *bubbling event*. Conversely, if an event is moving from the outermost element (e.g., a Window) down to the point of origin, the event is said to be a *tunneling event*. Finally, if an event is raised and handled only by the originating element (which is what could be described as a normal CLR event), it is said to be a *direct event*.

The Role of Routed Bubbling Events

In the current example, if the user clicks the inner yellow oval, the Click event bubbles out to the next level of scope (the Canvas), then to the StackPanel, and finally to the Button where the Click event handler is handled. In a similar way, if the user clicks the Label, the event is bubbled to the StackPanel and then finally to the Button element.

Given this bubbling routed event pattern, you have no need to worry about registering specific Click event handlers for all members of a composite control. However, if you want to perform custom clicking logic for multiple elements within the same object tree, you can do so.

By way of illustration, assume you need to handle the clicking of the outerEllipse control in a unique manner. First, handle the MouseDown event for this subelement (graphically rendered types such as the Ellipse do not support a Click event; however, they can monitor mouse button activity via MouseDown, MouseUp, etc.).

```
<Button Name="btnClickMe" Height="75" Width = "250"
        Click ="btnClickMe_Clicked">
  <StackPanel Orientation ="Horizontal">
    <Label Height="50" FontSize ="20">Fancy Button!</Label>
    <Canvas Height ="50" Width ="100" >
    <Ellipse Name = "outerEllipse" Fill ="Green"
             Height ="25" MouseDown ="outerEllipse_MouseDown"
             Width ="50" Cursor="Hand" Canvas.Left="25" Canvas.Top="12"/>
    <Ellipse Name = "innerEllipse" Fill ="Yellow" Height = "15" Width ="36"
             Canvas.Top="17" Canvas.Left="32"/>
    </Canvas>
  </StackPanel>
</Button>
```

Then implement an appropriate event handler, which for illustrative purposes will simply change the Title property of the main window, like so:

```
public void outerEllipse_MouseDown(object sender, MouseButtonEventArgs e)
{
  // Change title of window.
  this.Title = "You clicked the outer ellipse!";
}
```

With this, you can now take different courses of action depending on where the end user has clicked (which boils down to the outer ellipse and everywhere else within the button's scope).

■ **Note** Routed bubbling events always move from the point of origin to the *next defining scope*. Thus, in this example, if you click the innerEllipse object, the event will be bubbled to the Canvas, *not* to the outerEllipse because they are both Ellipse types within the scope of Canvas.

Continuing or Halting Bubbling

Currently, if the user clicks the outerEllipse object, it will trigger the registered MouseDown event handler for this Ellipse object, at which point the event bubbles to the button's Click event. If you want to inform WPF to stop bubbling up the tree of objects, you can set the Handled property of the EventArgs parameter to true, as follows:

```
public void outerEllipse_MouseDown(object sender, MouseButtonEventArgs e)
{
  // Change title of window.
  this.Title = "You clicked the outer ellipse!";
  // Stop bubbling!
  e.Handled = true;
}
```

In this case, you would find that the title of the window is changed, but you will not see the MessageBox displayed by the Click event handler of the Button. In a nutshell, routed bubbling events make it possible to allow a complex group of content to act either as a single logical element (e.g., a Button) or as discrete items (e.g., an Ellipse within the Button).

The Role of Routed Tunneling Events

Strictly speaking, routed events can be *bubbling* (as just described) or *tunneling* in nature. Tunneling events (which all begin with the Preview suffix; e.g., PreviewMouseDown) drill down from the topmost element into the inner scopes of the object tree. By and large, each bubbling event in the WPF base class libraries is paired with a related tunneling event that fires *before* the bubbling counterpart. For example, before the bubbling MouseDown event fires, the tunneling PreviewMouseDown event fires first.

Handling a tunneling event looks just like the processing of handling any other events; simply assign the event handler name in XAML (or, if needed, use the corresponding C# event-handling syntax in your code file) and implement the handler in the code file. Just to illustrate the interplay of tunneling and bubbling events, begin by handling the PreviewMouseDown event for the outerEllipse object, like so:

```
<Ellipse Name = "outerEllipse" Fill ="Green" Height ="25"
         MouseDown ="outerEllipse_MouseDown"
         PreviewMouseDown ="outerEllipse_PreviewMouseDown"
         Width ="50" Cursor="Hand" Canvas.Left="25" Canvas.Top="12"/>
```

Next, retrofit the current C# class definition by updating each event handler (for all objects) to append data about the current event into a string member variable named mouseActivity, using the incoming event args object. This will allow you to observe the flow of events firing in the background.

```
public partial class MainWindow : Window
{
  string _mouseActivity = string.Empty;
  public MainWindow()
  {
    InitializeComponent();
  }
  public void btnClickMe_Clicked(object sender, RoutedEventArgs e)
  {
    AddEventInfo(sender, e);
    MessageBox.Show(_mouseActivity, "Your Event Info");
    // Clear string for next round.
    _mouseActivity = "";
  }
  private void AddEventInfo(object sender, RoutedEventArgs e)
  {
    _mouseActivity += string.Format(
      "{0} sent a {1} event named {2}.\n", sender,
      e.RoutedEvent.RoutingStrategy,
      e.RoutedEvent.Name);
  }
  private void outerEllipse_MouseDown(object sender, MouseButtonEventArgs e)
  {
    AddEventInfo(sender, e);
  }
```

```
  private void outerEllipse_PreviewMouseDown(object sender, MouseButtonEventArgs e)
  {
    AddEventInfo(sender, e);
  }
}
```

Notice that you are not halting the bubbling of an event for any event handler. If you run this application, you will see a unique message box display based on where you click the button. Figure 26-15 shows the result of clicking the outer `Ellipse` object.

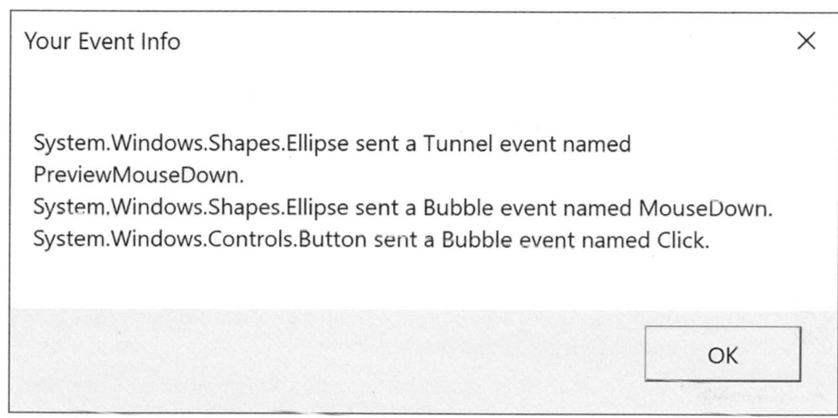

Figure 26-15. *Tunneling first, bubbling second*

So, why do WPF events typically tend to come in pairs (one tunneling and one bubbling)? The answer is that by previewing events, you have the power to perform any special logic (data validation, disable bubbling action, etc.) before the bubbling counterpart fires. By way of an example, assume you have a `TextBox` that should contain only numerical data. You could handle the `PreviewKeyDown` event, and if you see the user has entered non-numerical data, you could cancel the bubbling event by setting the `Handled` property to `true`.

As you would guess, when you are building a custom control that contains custom events, you could author the event in such a way that it can bubble (or tunnel) through a tree of XAML. For the purpose of this chapter, I will not be examining how to build custom routed events (however, the process is not that different from building a custom dependency property). If you are interested, check out the topic "Routed Events Overview" within the .NET Framework 4.7 SDK documentation. In it you will find a number of tutorials that will help you on your way.

A Deeper Look at WPF APIs and Controls

The remainder of this chapter will give you a chance to build a new WPF application using Visual Studio. The goal is to create a UI that consists of a `TabControl` widget containing a set of tabs. Each tab will illustrate some new WPF controls and interesting APIs you might want to make use of in your software projects. Along the way, you will also learn additional features of the Visual Studio WPF designers. To get started, create a new WPF application named WpfControlsAndAPIs.

Working with the TabControl

As mentioned, your initial window will contain a TabControl with three different tabs, each of which shows off a set of related controls and/or WPF APIs. Update the window's Width to 800 and Height to 350. Locate the TabControl control in the Visual Studio Toolbox, drop one onto your designer, and update the markup to the following:

```
<TabControl Name="MyTabControl" HorizontalAlignment="Stretch" VerticalAlignment="Stretch">
    <TabItem Header="TabItem">
        <Grid Background="#FFE5E5E5"/>
    </TabItem>
    <TabItem Header="TabItem">
        <Grid Background="#FFE5E5E5"/>
    </TabItem>
</TabControl>
```

You will notice that you are given two tab items automatically. To add additional tabs, you simply need to right-click the TabControl node in the Document Outline window and select the Add TabItem menu option (you can also right-click the TabControl on the designer to activate the same menu option) or just start typing in the XAML editor. Add one additional tab using either approach.

Now, update each TabItem control through the XAML editor and change the Header property for each tab, naming them Ink API, Data Binding, and DataGrid. At this point, your window designer should look like what you see in Figure 26-16.

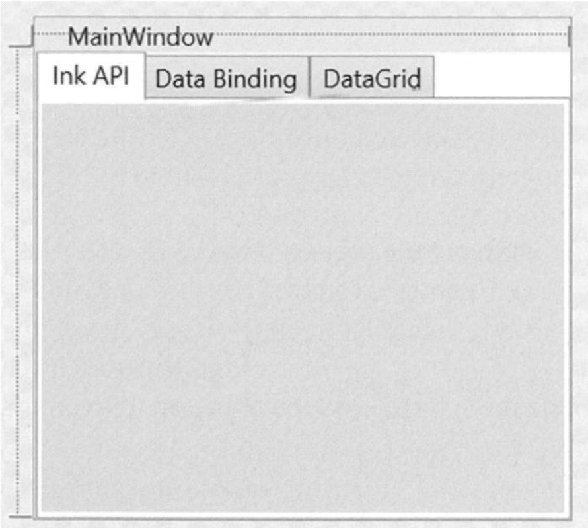

Figure 26-16. *The initial layout of the tab system*

Be aware that when you select a tab for editing, that tab becomes the active tab, and you can design that tab by dragging controls from the Toolbox window. Now that you have the core TabControl defined, you can work out the details tab by tab and learn more features of the WPF API along the way.

Building the Ink API Tab

The first tab will be used to show the overall role of WPF's digital Ink API, which allows you to incorporate painting functionality into a program easily. Of course, the application does not literally need to be a painting application; you can use this API for a wide variety of purposes, including capturing handwriting input.

■ **Note** For most of the rest of this chapter (and the next WPF chapters as well), I will be editing the XAML directly instead of using the various designer windows. While the dragging and dropping of controls works, more often than not the layout isn't what you want (Visual Studio adds margins and padding based on where you drop the control), and you spend a significant amount of time cleaning up the XAML anyway.

Begin by changing the `Grid` tag under the Ink API `TabItem` to a `StackPanel` and add a closing tag (make sure to remove "/" from the opening tag). Your markup should look like this:

```
<TabItem Header="Ink API">
  <StackPanel Background="#FFE5E5E5">
  </StackPanel>
</TabItem>
```

Designing the Toolbar

Add a new `ToolBar` control into the StackPanel (using the XAML editor) named `InkToolbar` with a height of 60.

```
<ToolBar Name="InkToolBar" Height="60">
</ToolBar>
```

Add three `RadioButton` controls inside a `WrapPanel`, inside a `Border` control, to the `ToolBar` as follows:

```
<Border Margin="0,2,0,2.4" Width="280" VerticalAlignment="Center">
  <WrapPanel>
    <RadioButton x:Name="inkRadio" Margin="5,10" Content="Ink Mode!" IsChecked="True" />
    <RadioButton x:Name="eraseRadio" Margin="5,10" Content="Erase Mode!" />
    <RadioButton x:Name="selectRadio" Margin="5,10" Content="Select Mode!" />
  </WrapPanel>
</Border>
```

When a `RadioButton` control is not placed inside of a parent panel control, it will take on a UI identical to a `Button` control! That's why I wrapped the `RadioButton` controls in the `WrapPanel`.

Next, add a `Separator` and then a ComboBox with a `Width` of 175 and a `Margin` of 10,0,0,0. Add three `ComboBoxItem` tags with content of Red, Green, and `Blue`, and follow the entire ComboBox with another `Separator` control, as follows:

```
<Separator/>
<ComboBox x:Name="comboColors" Width="175" Margin="10,0,0,0">
  <ComboBoxItem Content="Red"/>
  <ComboBoxItem Content="Green"/>
  <ComboBoxItem Content="Blue"/>
</ComboBox>
<Separator/>
```

The RadioButton Control

In this example, you want these three `RadioButton` controls to be mutually exclusive. In other GUI frameworks, ensuring that a group of related controls (such as radio buttons) were mutually exclusive required that you place them in the same group box. You don't need to do this under WPF. Instead, you can simply assign them all to the same *group name*. This is helpful because the related items do not need to be physically collected in the same area but can be anywhere in the window.

The RadioButton class includes an IsChecked property, which toggles between true and false when the end user clicks the UI element. Furthermore, RadioButton provides two events (Checked and Unchecked) that you can use to intercept this state change.

Add the Save, Load, and Delete Buttons

The final controls in the ToolBar control will be a Grid holding three Button controls. Add the following markup after the last Separator control:

```
<Grid>
  <Grid.ColumnDefinitions>
    <ColumnDefinition Width="Auto"/>
    <ColumnDefinition Width="Auto"/>
    <ColumnDefinition Width="Auto"/>
  </Grid.ColumnDefinitions>
  <Button Grid.Column="0" x:Name="btnSave" Margin="10,10" Width="70" Content="Save Data"/>
  <Button Grid.Column="1" x:Name="btnLoad" Margin="10,10" Width="70" Content="Load Data"/>
  <Button Grid.Column="2" x:Name="btnClear" Margin="10,10" Width="70" Content="Clear"/>
</Grid>
```

Add the InkCanvas Control

The final control for the TabControl is the InkCanvas control. Add the following markup after the closing ToolBar tag and before the closing StackPanel tag, as follows:

```
<InkCanvas x:Name="MyInkCanvas" Background="#FFB6F4F1" />
```

Preview the Window

At this point, you're ready to test the program, which you can do by pressing the F5 key. You should now see three mutually exclusive radio buttons, a combo box with three selections, and three buttons (see Figure 26-17).

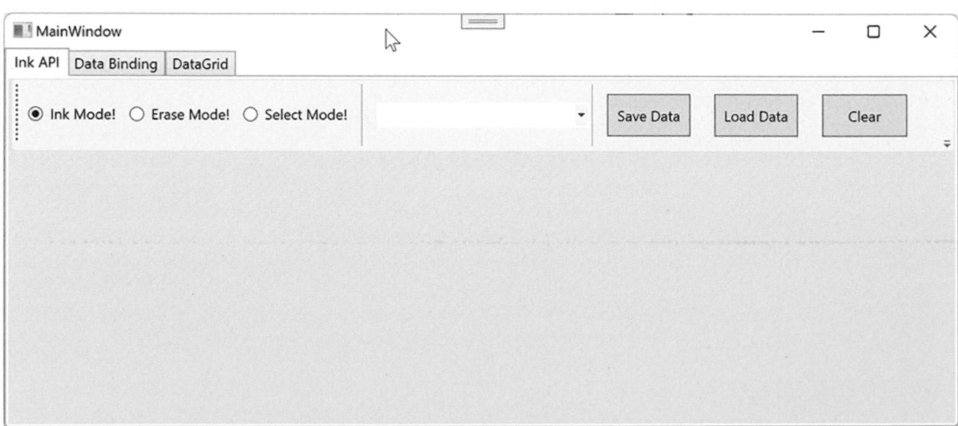

Figure 26-17. *The completed layout for the Ink API tab*

Handling Events for the Ink API Tab

The next step for the Ink API tab is to handle the Click event for each RadioButton control. As you have done in other WPF projects in this book, simply click the lightning bolt icon of the Visual Studio Properties editor to enter the names of event handlers. Using this approach, route the Click event for each button to the same handler, named RadioButtonClicked. After you handle all three Click events, handle the SelectionChanged event of the ComboBox using a handler named ColorChanged(). When you finish, you should have the following C# code:

```
public partial class MainWindow : Window
{
  public MainWindow()
  {
    this.InitializeComponent();

    // Insert code required on object creation below this point.
  }
  private void RadioButtonClicked(object sender,RoutedEventArgs e)
  {
    // TODO: Add event handler implementation here.
  }

  private void ColorChanged(object sender,SelectionChangedEventArgs e)
  {
    // TODO: Add event handler implementation here.
  }
}
```

You will implement these handlers in a later step, so leave them empty for the time being.

Add Controls to the Toolbox

You added an InkCanvas control by editing the XAML directly. If you wanted to use the UI to add it, the Visual Studio toolbox does *not* show you every possible WPF component by default. But you can update the items that are displayed in the Toolbox.

To do so, right-click anywhere in the Toolbox area and select the Choose Items menu option. After a moment or two, you will see a list of possible components to add to the Toolbox. For your purposes, you are interested in adding the InkCanvas control (see Figure 26-18).

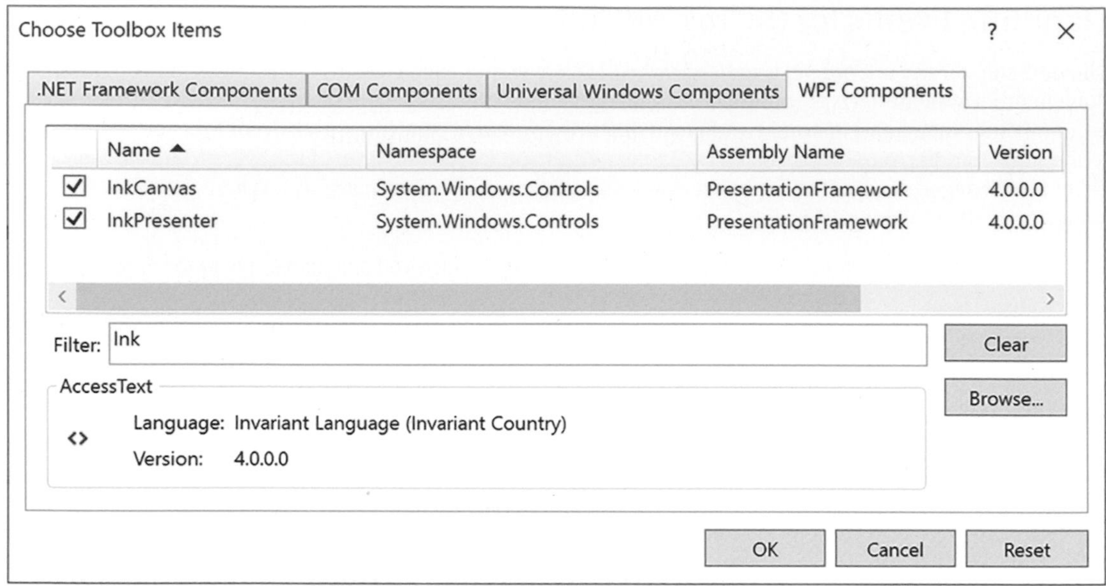

Figure 26-18. *Adding new components to the Visual Studio Toolbox*

■ **Note** The Ink controls are not compatible with the Visual Studio XAML designer in version 16.8.3 (the current version at the time of this writing) or Visual Studio 16.9 Preview 2. The controls can still be used, just not through the designer.

The InkCanvas Control

Just adding the InkCanvas enables drawing in your window. You can use your mouse or, if you have a touch-enabled device, your finger or a digitizer pen. Run the application and draw into the box (see Figure 26-19).

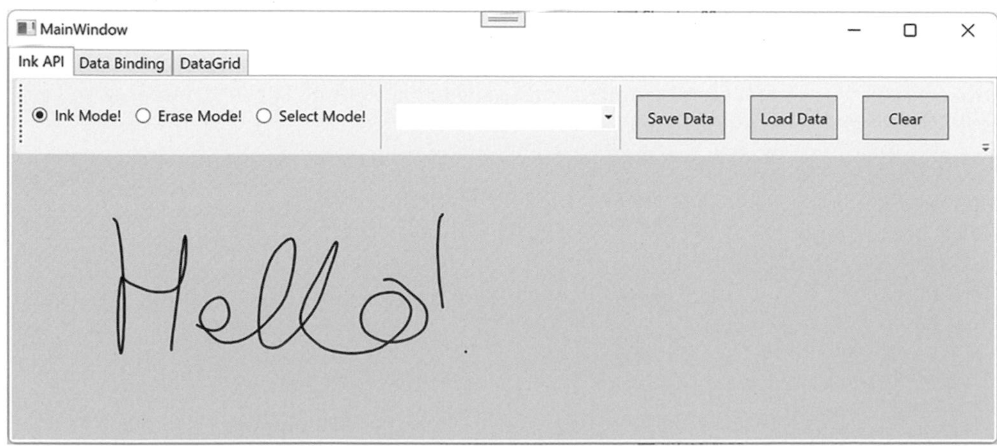

Figure 26-19. *The InkCanvas in action*

The InkCanvas does more than draw mouse (or stylus) strokes; it also supports a number of unique editing modes, controlled by the EditingMode property. You can assign this property any value from the related InkCanvasEditingMode enumeration. For this example, you are interested in Ink mode, which is the default option you just witnessed; Select mode, which allows the user to select a region with the mouse to move or resize; and EraseByStoke, which will delete the previous mouse stroke.

■ **Note** A *stroke* is the rendering that takes place during a single mouse down/mouse up operation. The InkCanvas stores all strokes in a StrokeCollection object, which you can access using the Strokes property.

Update your RadioButtonClicked() handler with the following logic, which places the InkCanvas in the correct mode, based on the selected RadioButton:

```
private void RadioButtonClicked(object sender,RoutedEventArgs e)
{
  // Based on which button sent the event, place the InkCanvas in a unique
  // mode of operation.
  this.MyInkCanvas.EditingMode = (sender as RadioButton)?.Content.ToString() switch
  {
    // These strings must be the same as the Content values for each
    // RadioButton.
    "Ink Mode!" => InkCanvasEditingMode.Ink,
    "Erase Mode!" => InkCanvasEditingMode.EraseByStroke,
    "Select Mode!" => InkCanvasEditingMode.Select,
    _ => this.MyInkCanvas.EditingMode
  };
}
```

Also, set the mode to Ink by default in the window's constructor. And while you are at it, set a default selection for the ComboBox (more details on this control in the next section), as follows:

```
public MainWindow()
{
  this.InitializeComponent();

  // Be in Ink mode by default.
  this.MyInkCanvas.EditingMode = InkCanvasEditingMode.Ink;
  this.inkRadio.IsChecked = true;
  this.comboColors.SelectedIndex = 0;
}
```

Now run your program again by pressing F5. Enter Ink mode and draw some data. Next, enter Erase mode and remove the previous mouse stroke you entered (you'll notice the mouse icon automatically looks like an eraser). Finally, enter Select mode and select some strokes by using the mouse as a lasso.

After you circle the item, you can move it around the canvas and resize its dimensions. Figure 26-20 shows your edit modes at work.

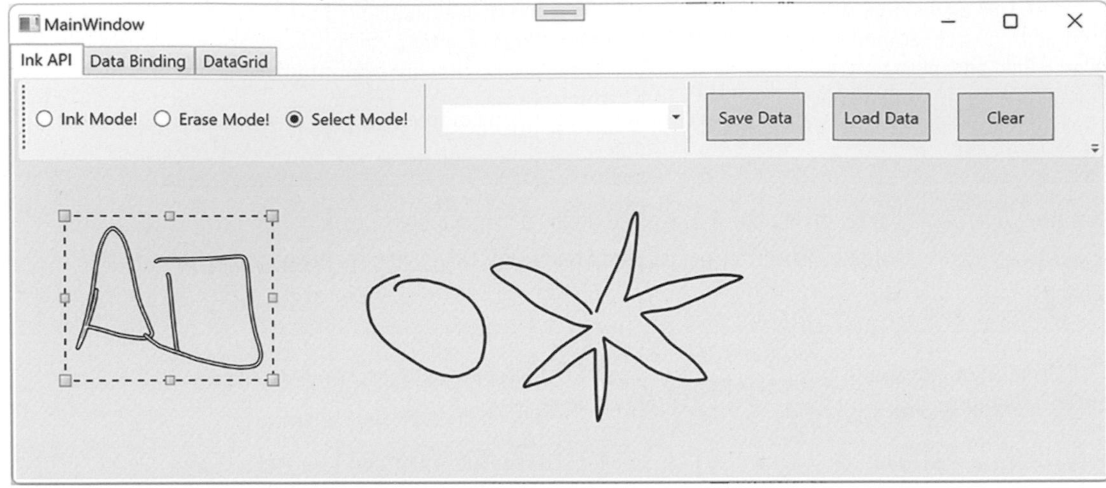

Figure 26-20. *The InkCanvas in action, with edit modes!*

The ComboBox Control

After you populate a ComboBox control (or a ListBox), you have three ways to determine the selected item. First, if you want to find the numerical index of the item selected, you can use the SelectedIndex property (which is zero based; a value of -1 represents no selection). Second, if you want to obtain the object within the list that has been selected, the SelectedItem property fits the bill. Third, the SelectedValue allows you to obtain the value of the selected object (typically obtained using a call to ToString()).

You need to add the last bit of code for this tab to change the color of the strokes entered on the InkCanvas. The DefaultDrawingAttributes property of InkCanvas returns a DrawingAttributes object that allows you to configure numerous aspects of the pen nib, including its size and color (among other settings). Update your C# code with this implementation of the ColorChanged() method:

```
private void ColorChanged(object sender, SelectionChangedEventArgs e)
{
  // Get the selected value in the combo box.
  string colorToUse =
    (this.comboColors.SelectedItem as ComboBoxItem)?.Content.ToString();

  // Change the color used to render the strokes.
  this.MyInkCanvas.DefaultDrawingAttributes.Color =
    (Color)ColorConverter.ConvertFromString(colorToUse);
}
```

Now recall that the ComboBox has a collection of ComboBoxItems. If you view the generated XAML, you'll see the following definition:

```
<ComboBox x:Name="comboColors" Width="100" SelectionChanged="ColorChanged">
  <ComboBoxItem Content="Red"/>
  <ComboBoxItem Content="Green"/>
  <ComboBoxItem Content="Blue"/>
</ComboBox>
```

When you call SelectedItem, you grab the selected ComboBoxItem, which is stored as a general Object. After you cast the Object as a ComboBoxItem, you pluck out the value of the Content, which will be the string Red, Green, or Blue. This string is then converted to a Color object using the handy ColorConverter utility class. Now run your program again. You should be able to change between colors as you render your image.

Note that the ComboBox and ListBox controls can contain complex content as well, rather than a list of text data. You can get a sense of some of the things that are possible by opening the XAML editor for your window and changing the definition of your ComboBox so it contains a set of StackPanel elements, each of which contains an Ellipse and a Label (notice that the Width of the ComboBox is 175).

```
<ComboBox x:Name="comboColors" Width="175" Margin="10,0,0,0" SelectionChanged="Colo
rChanged">
  <StackPanel Orientation ="Horizontal" Tag="Red">
    <Ellipse Fill ="Red" Height ="50" Width ="50"/>
    <Label FontSize ="20" HorizontalAlignment="Center"
           VerticalAlignment="Center" Content="Red"/>
  </StackPanel>

  <StackPanel Orientation ="Horizontal" Tag="Green">
    <Ellipse Fill ="Green" Height ="50" Width ="50"/>
    <Label FontSize ="20" HorizontalAlignment="Center"
           VerticalAlignment="Center" Content="Green"/>
  </StackPanel>

  <StackPanel Orientation ="Horizontal" Tag="Blue">
    <Ellipse Fill ="Blue" Height ="50" Width ="50"/>
    <Label FontSize ="20" HorizontalAlignment="Center"
           VerticalAlignment="Center" Content="Blue"/>
  </StackPanel>
</ComboBox>
```

Notice that each StackPanel assigns a value to its Tag property, which is a simple, fast, and convenient way to discover which stack of items has been selected by the user (there are better ways to do this, but this will do for now). With this adjustment, you need to change the implementation of your ColorChanged() method, like this:

```
private void ColorChanged(object sender, SelectionChangedEventArgs e)
{
  // Get the Tag of the selected StackPanel.
  string colorToUse = (this.comboColors.SelectedItem
      as StackPanel).Tag.ToString();
  ...
}
```

Now run your program again and take note of your unique ComboBox (see Figure 26-21).

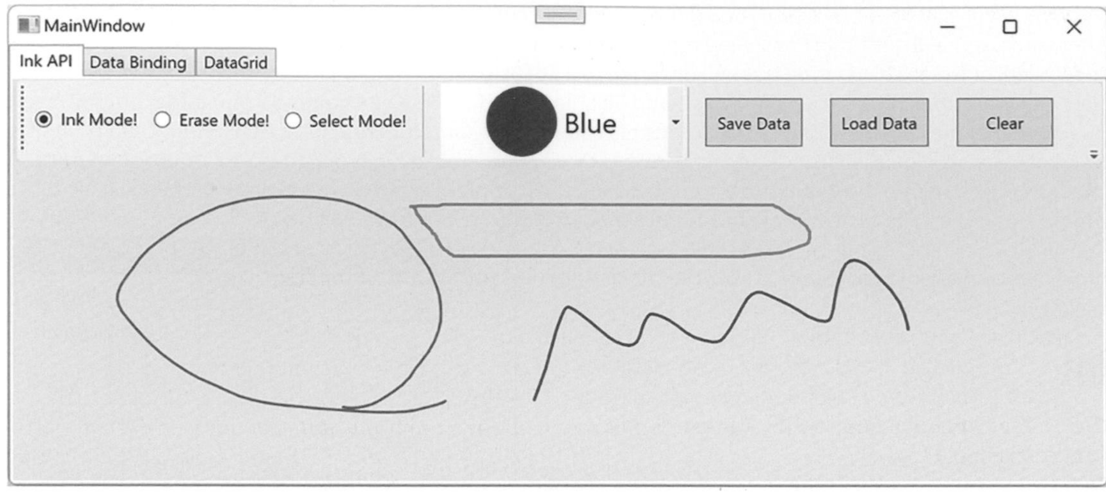

Figure 26-21. *A custom ComboBox, thanks to the WPF content model*

Saving, Loading, and Clearing InkCanvas Data

The last part of this tab will enable you to save and load your canvas data, as well as clear it of all content by adding event handlers for the buttons in the toolbar. Update the XAML for the buttons by adding markup for the click events, as follows:

```
<Button Grid.Column="0" x:Name="btnSave" Margin="10,10" Width="70" Content="Save Data"
Click="SaveData"/>
<Button Grid.Column="1" x:Name="btnLoad" Margin="10,10" Width="70" Content="Load Data"
Click="LoadData"/>
<Button Grid.Column="2" x:Name="btnClear" Margin="10,10" Width="70" Content="Clear"
Click="Clear"/>
```

Next, import the `System.IO` and `System.Windows.Ink` namespaces to your code file. Implement the handlers, like this:

```
private void SaveData(object sender, RoutedEventArgs e)
{
  // Save all data on the InkCanvas to a local file.
  using (FileStream fs = new FileStream("StrokeData.bin", FileMode.Create))
  this.MyInkCanvas.Strokes.Save(fs);
  fs.Close();
  MessageBox.Show("Image Saved","Saved");
}

private void LoadData(object sender, RoutedEventArgs e)
{
  // Fill StrokeCollection from file.
  using(FileStream fs = new FileStream("StrokeData.bin", FileMode.Open, FileAccess.Read))
  StrokeCollection strokes = new StrokeCollection(fs);
  this.MyInkCanvas.Strokes = strokes;
}
```

```
private void Clear(object sender, RoutedEventArgs e)
{
  // Clear all strokes.
  this.MyInkCanvas.Strokes.Clear();
}
```

You should now be able to save your data to a file, load it from the file, and clear the InkCanvas of all data. That wraps up the first tab of the TabControl, as well as your examination of the WPF digital Ink API. To be sure, there is more to say about this technology; however, you should be in a good position to dig into the topic further if that interests you. Next, you will learn how to use WPF data binding.

Introducing the WPF Data-Binding Model

Controls are often the target of various data-binding operations. Simply put, *data binding* is the act of connecting control properties to data values that might change over the course of your application's lifetime. Doing so lets a user interface element display the state of a variable in your code. For example, you might use data binding to accomplish the following:

- Check a CheckBox control based on a Boolean property of a given object.
- Display data in DataGrid objects from a relational database table.
- Connect a Label to an integer that represents the number of files in a folder.

When you use the intrinsic WPF data-binding engine, you must be aware of the distinction between the *source* and the *destination* of the binding operation. As you might expect, the source of a data-binding operation is the data itself (e.g., a Boolean property or relational data), while the destination (target) is the UI control property that uses the data content (e.g., a property on a CheckBox or TextBox control).

In addition to binding to traditional data, WPF enables element binding, as stated in the previous examples. This means you can bind (for example) the visibility of a property based on the checked property of a check box. You could certainly do this in WinForms, but it had to be done through code. The WPF framework provides a rich data-binding ecosystem that can be almost entirely handled in markup. This also enables you to ensure that the source and destination stay in sync if either of their values changes.

Building the Data Binding Tab

Using the Document Outline editor, change the Grid of your second tab to a StackPanel. Now, use the Toolbox and Properties editor of Visual Studio to build the following initial layout:

```
<TabItem x:Name="tabDataBinding" Header="Data Binding">
  <StackPanel Width="250">
    <Label Content="Move the scroll bar to see the current value"/>

    <!-- The scrollbar's value is the source of this data bind. -->
    <ScrollBar x:Name="mySB" Orientation="Horizontal" Height="30"
           Minimum = "1" Maximum = "100" LargeChange="1" SmallChange="1"/>

    <!-- The label's content will be bound to the scroll bar! -->
    <Label x:Name="labelSBThumb" Height="30" BorderBrush="Blue"
           BorderThickness="2" Content = "0"/>
  </StackPanel>
</TabItem>
```

Notice that the ScrollBar object (named mySB here) has been configured with a range between 1 and 100. The goal is to ensure that, as you reposition the thumb of the scrollbar (or click the left or right arrow), the Label will automatically update with the current value. Currently, the Content property of the Label control is set to the value "0"; however, you will change this via a data-binding operation.

Establishing Data Bindings

The glue that makes it possible to define a binding in XAML is the {Binding} markup extension. While you can define bindings through Visual Studio, it's just as easy to do it directly in the markup. Edit the Content property for the Label named labelSBThumb to the following:

```
<Label x:Name="labelSBThumb" Height="30" BorderBrush="Blue" BorderThickness="2"
       Content = "{Binding Path=Value, ElementName=mySB}"/>
```

Note the value assigned to the Label's Content property. The {Binding} statement denotes a data-binding operation. The ElementName value represents the source of the data-binding operation (the ScrollBar object), while the Path indicates the property being bound to, in this case the Value of the scrollbar.

If you run your program again, you will find that the content of the label updates based on the scrollbar value as you move the thumb!

The DataContext Property

You can define a data-binding operation in XAML using an alternative format, where it is possible to break out the values specified by the {Binding} markup extension by explicitly setting the DataContext property to the source of the binding operation, as follows:

```
<!-- Breaking object/value apart via DataContext -->
<Label x:Name="labelSBThumb" Height="30" BorderBrush="Blue" BorderThickness="2"
       DataContext = "{Binding ElementName=mySB}" Content = "{Binding Path=Value}" />
```

In the current example, the output would be identical if you were to modify the markup in this way. Given this, you might wonder when you would want to set the DataContext property explicitly. Doing so can be helpful because subelements can inherit its value in a tree of markup.

In this way, you can easily set the same data source to a family of controls, rather than having to repeat a bunch of redundant "{Binding ElementName=X, Path=Y}" XAML values to multiple controls. For example, assume you have added the following new Button to the StackPanel of this tab (you'll see why it is so large in just a moment):

```
<Button Content="Click" Height="200"/>
```

You could use Visual Studio to generate data bindings for multiple controls, but instead try entering the modified markup manually using the XAML editor, like so:

```
<!-- Note the StackPanel sets the DataContext property. -->
<StackPanel Background="#FFE5E5E5" DataContext = "{Binding ElementName=mySB}">
...
  <!-- Now both UI elements use the scrollbar's value in unique ways. -->
  <Label x:Name="labelSBThumb" Height="30" BorderBrush="Blue" BorderThickness="2"
```

```
        Content = "{Binding Path=Value}"/>

    <Button Content="Click" Height="200" FontSize = "{Binding Path=Value}"/>
</StackPanel>
```

Here, you set the DataContext property on the StackPanel directly. Therefore, as you move the thumb, you see not only the current value on the Label but also the font size of the Button grow and shrink accordingly, based on the same value (Figure 26-22 shows one possible output).

Figure 26-22. Binding the ScrollBar value to a Label and a Button

Formatting the Bound Data

The ScrollBar type uses a double to represent the value of the thumb, rather than an expected whole number (e.g., an integer). Therefore, as you drag the thumb, you will find various floating-point numbers displayed within the Label (e.g., 61.0576923076923). The end user would find this rather unintuitive because he is most likely expecting to see whole numbers (e.g., 61, 62, and 63).

If you want to format the data, you can add a ContentStringFormat property, passing in a custom string and a .NET Core format specifier, as follows:

```
<Label x:Name="labelSBThumb" Height="30" BorderBrush="Blue"
  BorderThickness="2" Content = "{Binding Path=Value}" ContentStringFormat="The value is:
  {0:F0}"/>
```

If you don't have any text in the format specification, then you need to lead with an empty set of braces, which is the escape sequence for XAML. This lets the processor know that the next characters are literals and not a binding statement, for example. Here is the updated XAML:

```
<Label x:Name="labelSBThumb" Height="30" BorderBrush="Blue"
  BorderThickness="2" Content = "{Binding Path=Value}" ContentStringFormat="{}{0:F0}"/>
```

■ **Note** If you are binding a `Text` property of a control, you can add a `StringFormat` name-value pair right in the binding statement. It only needs to be separate for `Content` properties.

Data Conversion Using IValueConverter

If you need to do more than just format the data, you can create a custom class that implements the `IValueConverter` interface of the `System.Windows.Data` namespace. This interface defines two members that allow you to perform the conversion to and from the target and destination (in the case of a two-way data binding). After you define this class, you can use it to qualify further the processing of your data-binding operation.

Instead of using the format property, you can use a value converter to display whole numbers within the `Label` control. To do this, add a new class (named `MyDoubleConverter`) to the project class. Next, add the following:

```
using System.Windows.Data;
namespace WpfControlsAndAPIs;

public class MyDoubleConverter : IValueConverter
{
  public object Convert(object value, Type targetType, object parameter,  System.
  Globalization.CultureInfo culture)
  {
    // Convert the double to an int.
    double v - (double)value;
    return (int)v;
  }

  public object ConvertBack(object value, Type targetType, object parameter,
    System.Globalization.CultureInfo culture)
  {
    // You won't worry about "two-way" bindings here, so just return the value.
    return value;
  }
}
```

The `Convert()` method is called when the value is transferred from the source (the `ScrollBar`) to the destination (the `Text` property of the `TextBox`). You will receive many incoming arguments, but you only need to manipulate the incoming `object` for this conversion, which is the value of the current `double`. You can use this type to cast the type into an integer and return the new number.

The `ConvertBack()` method will be called when the value is passed from the destination to the source (if you have enabled a two-way binding mode). Here, you simply return the value straightaway. Doing so lets you type a floating-point value into the `TextBox` (e.g., `99.9`) and have it automatically convert to a whole-number value (e.g., `99`) when the user tabs off the control. This "free" conversion happens because the `Convert()` method is called again, after a call to `ConvertBack()`. If you were simply to return `null` from `ConvertBack()`, your binding would appear to be out of sync because the text box would still be displaying a floating-point number.

To use this converter in markup, you first have to create a local resource representing the custom class you just built. Don't worry about the mechanics of adding resources; the next few chapters will dive deeper into this subject. Add the following just after the opening `Window` tag:

```
<Window.Resources>
  <local:MyDoubleConverter x:Key="DoubleConverter"/>
</Window.Resources>
```

Next, update the binding statement for the Label control to the following:

```
<Label x:Name="labelSBThumb" Height="30" BorderBrush="Blue"
    BorderThickness="2" Content = "{Binding Path=Value,Converter={StaticResource
    DoubleConverter}}" />
```

Now when you run the app, you see only whole numbers.

Establishing Data Bindings in Code

You can also register your data conversion class in code. Begin by cleaning up the current definition of the Label control in your data binding tab so that it no longer uses the {Binding} markup extension.

```
<Label x:Name="labelSBThumb" Height="30" BorderBrush="Blue" BorderThickness="2" />
```

Make sure there is a using for System.Windows.Data; then in your window's constructor, call a new private helper function called SetBindings(). In this method, add the following code (and make sure to call it from the constructor):

```
using System.Windows.Data;
...
namespace WpfControlsAndAPIs;

public partial class MainWindow : Window
{
  public MainWindow()
  {
    InitializeComponent();
    //ommitted for brevity
    SetBindings();
  }
//ommited for brevity
  private void SetBindings()
  {
    // Create a Binding object.
    Binding b = new Binding
    {
      // Register the converter, source, and path.
      Converter = new MyDoubleConverter(),
      Source = this.mySB,
      Path = new PropertyPath("Value")
      // Call the SetBinding method on the Label.
      this.labelSBThumb.SetBinding(Label.ContentProperty, b);
    }
  }
}
```

The only part of this function that probably looks a bit off is the call to `SetBinding()`. Notice that the first parameter calls a static, read-only field of the `Label` class named `ContentProperty`. As you will learn later in this chapter, you are specifying what is known as a *dependency property*. For the time being, just know that when you set bindings in code, the first argument will nearly always require you to specify the name of the class that wants the binding (the `Label`, in this case), followed by a call to the underlying property with the `Property` suffix. In any case, running the application illustrates that the `Label` prints out only whole numbers.

Building the DataGrid Tab

The previous data-binding example illustrated how to configure two (or more) controls to participate in a data-binding operation. While this is helpful, it is also possible to bind data from XML files, database data, and in-memory objects. To complete this example, you will design the final tab of your tab control so it displays data obtained from the `Inventory` table of the `AutoLot` database.

As with the other tabs, you begin by changing the current `Grid` to a `StackPanel`. Do this by directly updating the XAML using Visual Studio. Now define a `DataGrid` control in your new `StackPanel` named `gridInventory`, like so:

```
<TabItem x:Name="tabDataGrid" Header="DataGrid">
  <StackPanel>
    <DataGrid x:Name="gridInventory" Height="288"/>
  </StackPanel>
</TabItem>
```

Use the NuGet package manager to add the following packages to your project:

- `Microsoft.EntityFrameworkCore`
- `Microsoft.EntityFrameworkCore.SqlServer`
- `Microsoft.Extensions.Configuration`
- `Microsoft.Extensions.Configuration.Json`

If you prefer to use the .NET Core command-line interface (CLI) to add the packages, enter the following commands (from the solution directory):

```
dotnet add WpfControlsAndAPIs package Microsoft.EntityFrameworkCore
dotnet add WpfControlsAndAPIs package Microsoft.EntityFrameworkCore.SqlServer
dotnet add WpfControlsAndAPIs package Microsoft.Extensions.Configuration
dotnet add WpfControlsAndAPIs package Microsoft.Extensions.Configuration.Json
```

Next, right-click the solution, select Add ➤ Existing Project, and add the AutoLot.Dal and AutoLot.Dal.Models projects from Chapter 23 and project references to those projects. You can also use the CLI to add the references with the following command (you need to adjust your path for your projects' locations and computer's operation system):

```
dotnet sln .\Chapter26_AllProjects.sln add ..\Chapter_23\AutoLot.Models
dotnet sln .\Chapter26_AllProjects.sln add ..\Chapter_23\AutoLot.Dal
dotnet add WpfControlsAndAPIs reference ..\Chapter_23\AutoLot.Models
dotnet add WpfControlsAndAPIs reference ..\Chapter_23\AutoLot.Dal
```

Confirm that the project reference from AutoLot.Dal to AutoLot.Dal.Models is still in place. Add the following namespaces to MainWindow.xaml.cs:

```
using System.Linq;
using AutoLot.Dal.EfStructures;
using AutoLot.Dal.Repos;
using Microsoft.EntityFrameworkCore;
using Microsoft.Extensions.Configuration;
```

Add two module-level properties in MainWindow.cs to hold the instances of IConfiguration and ApplicationDbContext.

```
private IConfiguration _configuration;
private ApplicationDbContext _context;
```

Add a new method named GetConfigurationAndContext() to create those instances and call it from the constructor. The entire method is listed here:

```
private void GetConfigurationAndDbContext()
{
  _configuration = new ConfigurationBuilder()
    .SetBasePath(Directory.GetCurrentDirectory())
    .AddJsonFile("appsettings.json", true, true)
    .Build();
  var optionsBuilder =
    new DbContextOptionsBuilder<ApplicationDbContext>();
  var connectionString =
    _configuration.GetConnectionString("AutoLot");
  optionsBuilder.UseSqlServer(connectionString,
    sqlOptions => sqlOptions.EnableRetryOnFailure());
  _context = new ApplicationDbContext(optionsBuilder.Options);
}
```

Add a new JSON file named appsettings.json to the project and set its build status to copy always. This can be done by right-clicking the file in Solution Explorer, selecting Properties, and then entering **Copy always** for the Copy To Output Directory setting . You can also add this to the project file to accomplish the same thing:

```
<ItemGroup>
  <None Update="appsettings.json">
    <CopyToOutputDirectory>Always</CopyToOutputDirectory>
  </None>
</ItemGroup>
```

Update the JSON file to the following (updating your connection string to match your environment):

```
{
  "ConnectionStrings": {
    "AutoLotFinal": "server=.,5433;Database=AutoLot;User Id=sa;Password=P@ssw0rd;"
  }
}
```

Open MainWindow.xaml.cs, add a final helper function called ConfigureGrid(), and call it from your constructor after you have configured ApplicationDbContext. All you need to do is add a few lines of code, like so:

```
private void ConfigureGrid()
{
  using var repo = new CarRepo(_context);
  gridInventory.ItemsSource = repo.GetAllIgnoreQueryFilters().ToList()
    .Select(x=> new { x.Id, Make=x.MakeName, x.Color, x.PetName });
}
```

Now when you run the project, you see the data populating the grid. If you want to make the grid somewhat fancier, you can use the Visual Studio Properties window to edit the grid to make it more appealing.

That wraps up the current example. You'll see some other controls in action during later chapters; at this point, however, you should feel comfortable with the process of building UIs in Visual Studio and manually using XAML and C# code.

Understanding the Role of Dependency Properties

Like any .NET Core API, WPF makes use of each member of the .NET Core type system (classes, structures, interfaces, delegates, enumerations) and each type member (properties, methods, events, constant data, read-only fields, etc.) within its implementation. However, WPF also supports a unique programming concept termed a *dependency property*.

Like a "normal" .NET Core property (often termed a *CLR property* in the WPF literature), dependency properties can be set declaratively using XAML or programmatically within a code file. Furthermore, dependency properties (like CLR properties) ultimately exist to encapsulate data fields of a class and can be configured as read-only, write-only, or read-write.

To make matters more interesting, in almost every case you will be blissfully unaware that you have actually set (or accessed) a dependency property as opposed to a CLR property! For example, the Height and Width properties that WPF controls inherit from FrameworkElement, as well as the Content member inherited from ControlContent, are all, in fact, dependency properties.

```
<!-- Set three dependency properties! -->
<Button x:Name = "btnMyButton" Height = "50" Width = "100" Content = "OK"/>
```

Given all these similarities, why does WPF define a new term for such a familiar concept? The answer lies in how a dependency property is implemented within the class. You'll see a coding example in just a little bit; however, from a high level, all dependency properties are created in the following manner:

- First, the class that defined a dependency property must have DependencyObject in its inheritance chain.
- A single dependency property is represented as a public, static, read-only field in the class of type DependencyProperty. By convention, this field is named by suffixing the word Property to the name of the CLR wrapper (see the final bullet point).
- The DependencyProperty variable is registered via a static call to DependencyProperty.Register(), which typically occurs in a static constructor or inline when the variable is declared.
- Finally, the class will define a XAML-friendly CLR property, which makes calls to methods provided by DependencyObject to get and set the value.

Once implemented, dependency properties provide a number of powerful features that are used by various WPF technologies including data binding, animation services, styles, templates, and so forth. In a nutshell, the motivation of dependency properties is to provide a way to compute the value of a property based on the value of other inputs. Here is a list of some of these key benefits, which go well beyond those of the simple data encapsulation found with a CLR property:

- Dependency properties can inherit their values from a parent element's XAML definition. For example, if you defined a value for the `FontSize` attribute in the opening tag of a `Window`, all controls in that `Window` would have the same font size by default.
- Dependency properties support the ability to have values set by elements contained within their XAML scope, such as a `Button` setting the `Dock` property of a `DockPanel` parent. (Recall that *attached properties* do this very thing because attached properties are a form of dependency properties.)
- Dependency properties allow WPF to compute a value based on multiple external values, which can be important for animation and data-binding services.
- Dependency properties provide infrastructure support for WPF triggers (also used quite often when working with animation and data binding).

Now remember, in many cases you will interact with an existing dependency property in a manner identical to a normal CLR property (thanks to the XAML wrapper). In the previous section, which covered data binding, you saw that if you need to establish a data binding in code, you must call the `SetBinding()` method on the object that is the destination of the operation and specify the *dependency property* it will operate on, like so:

```
private void SetBindings()
{
  Binding b = new Binding
  {
    // Register the converter, source, and path.
    Converter = new MyDoubleConverter(),
    Source = this.mySB,
    Path = new PropertyPath("Value")
  };
  // Specify the dependency property!
  this.labelSBThumb.SetBinding(Label.ContentProperty, b);
}
```

You will see similar code when you examine how to start an animation in code in Chapter 28.

```
// Specify the dependency property!
rt.BeginAnimation(RotateTransform.AngleProperty, dblAnim);
```

The only time you need to build your own custom dependency property is when you are authoring a custom WPF control. For example, if you are building a `UserControl` that defines four custom properties and you want these properties to integrate well within the WPF API, you should author them using dependency property logic.

Specifically, if your properties need to be the target of a data-binding or animation operation, if the property must broadcast when it has changed, if it must be able to work as a `Setter` in a WPF style, or if it must be able to receive their values from a parent element, a normal CLR property will *not* be enough. If you were to use a normal CLR property, other programmers may indeed be able to get and set a value; however, if they attempt to use your properties within the context of a WPF service, things will not work as expected. Because you can never know how others might want to interact with the properties of your custom UserControl classes, you should get in the habit of *always* defining dependency properties when building custom controls.

Examining an Existing Dependency Property

Before you learn how to build a custom dependency property, let's take a look at how the Height property of the FrameworkElement class has been implemented internally. The relevant code is shown here (with my included comments):

```
// FrameworkElement is-a DependencyObject.
public class FrameworkElement : UIElement, IFrameworkInputElement,
  IInputElement, ISupportInitialize, IHaveResources, IQueryAmbient
{
...
  // A static read-only field of type DependencyProperty.
  public static readonly DependencyProperty HeightProperty;

  // The DependencyProperty field is often registered
  // in the static constructor of the class.
  static FrameworkElement()
  {
    ...
    HeightProperty = DependencyProperty.Register(
      "Height",
      typeof(double),
      typeof(FrameworkElement),
      new FrameworkPropertyMetadata((double) 1.0 / (double) 0.0,
        FrameworkPropertyMetadataOptions.AffectsMeasure,
        new PropertyChangedCallback(FrameworkElement.OnTransformDirty)),
      new ValidateValueCallback(FrameworkElement.IsWidthHeightValid));
    }

    // The CLR wrapper, which is implemented using
    // the inherited GetValue()/SetValue() methods.
    public double Height
    {
      get { return (double) base.GetValue(HeightProperty); }
      set { base.SetValue(HeightProperty, value); }
    }
}
```

As you can see, dependency properties require quite a bit of additional code from a normal CLR property! And in reality, a dependency can be even more complex than what you see here (thankfully, many implementations are simpler than Height).

First, remember that if a class wants to define a dependency property, it must have DependencyObject in the inheritance chain because this is the class that defines the GetValue() and SetValue() methods used in the CLR wrapper. Because FrameworkElement *is-a* DependencyObject, this requirement is satisfied.

Next, recall that the entity that will hold the actual value of the property (a double in the case of Height) is represented as a public, static, read-only field of type DependencyProperty. The name of this field should, by convention, always be named by suffixing the word Property to the name of the related CLR wrapper, like so:

```
public static readonly DependencyProperty HeightProperty;
```

Given that dependency properties are declared as static fields, they are typically created (and registered) within the static constructor of the class. The DependencyProperty object is created via a call to the static DependencyProperty.Register() method. This method has been overloaded many times; however, in the case of Height, DependencyProperty.Register() is invoked as follows:

```
HeightProperty = DependencyProperty.Register(
  "Height",
  typeof(double),
  typeof(FrameworkElement),
  new FrameworkPropertyMetadata((double)0.0,
    FrameworkPropertyMetadataOptions.AffectsMeasure,
    new PropertyChangedCallback(FrameworkElement.OnTransformDirty)),
  new ValidateValueCallback(FrameworkElement.IsWidthHeightValid));
```

The first argument to DependencyProperty.Register() is the name of the normal CLR property on the class (Height, in this case), while the second argument is the type information of the underlying data type it is encapsulating (a double). The third argument specifies the type information of the class that this property belongs to (FrameworkElement, in this case). While this might seem redundant (after all, the HeightProperty field is already defined within the FrameworkElement class), this is a clever aspect of WPF, in that it allows one class to register properties on another (even if the class definition has been sealed!).

The fourth argument passed to DependencyProperty.Register() in this example is what really gives dependency properties their own unique flavor. Here, a FrameworkPropertyMetadata object is passed that describes various details regarding how WPF should handle this property with respect to callback notifications (if the property needs to notify others when the value changes) and various options (represented by the FrameworkPropertyMetadataOptions enum) that control what is affected by the property in question. (Does it work with data binding? Can it be inherited?) In this case, the constructor arguments of FrameworkPropertyMetadata break down as so:

```
new FrameworkPropertyMetadata(
  // Default value of property.
  (double)0.0,

  // Metadata options.
  FrameworkPropertyMetadataOptions.AffectsMeasure,

  // Delegate pointing to method called when property changes.
  new PropertyChangedCallback(FrameworkElement.OnTransformDirty)
)
```

Because the final argument to the FrameworkPropertyMetadata constructor is a delegate, note that its constructor parameter is pointing to a static method on the FrameworkElement class named OnTransformDirty(). I won't bother to show the code behind this method, but be aware that any time you are building a custom dependency property, you can specify a PropertyChangedCallback delegate to point to a method that will be called when your property value has been changed.

This brings me to the final parameter passed to the DependencyProperty.Register() method, a second delegate of type ValidateValueCallback, which points to a method on the FrameworkElement class that is called to ensure the value assigned to the property is valid.

```
new ValidateValueCallback(FrameworkElement.IsWidthHeightValid)
```

This method contains logic you might normally expect to find in the set block of a property (more information on this point in the next section).

```
private static bool IsWidthHeightValid(object value)
{
  double num = (double) value;
  return ((!DoubleUtil.IsNaN(num) && (num >= 0.0))
    && !double.IsPositiveInfinity(num));
}
```

After the DependencyProperty object has been registered, the final task is to wrap the field within a normal CLR property (Height, in this case). Notice, however, that the get and set scopes do not simply return or set a class-level double-member variable but do so indirectly using the GetValue() and SetValue() methods from the System.Windows.DependencyObject base class, as follows:

```
public double Height
{
  get { return (double) base.GetValue(HeightProperty); }
  set { base.SetValue(HeightProperty, value); }
}
```

Important Notes Regarding CLR Property Wrappers

So, just to recap the story thus far, dependency properties look like normal everyday properties when you get or set their values in XAML or code, but behind the scenes they are implemented with much more elaborate coding techniques. Remember, the whole reason to go through this process is to build a custom control that has custom properties that need to integrate with WPF services that demand communication with a dependency property (e.g., animation, data binding, and styles).

Even though part of the implementation of a dependency property includes defining a CLR wrapper, you should never put validation logic in the set block. For that matter, the CLR wrapper of a dependency property should never do anything other than call GetValue() or SetValue().

The reason is that the WPF runtime has been constructed in such a way that when you write XAML that seems to set a property, such as

```
<Button x:Name="myButton" Height="100" .../>
```

the runtime will completely bypass the set block of the Height property and *directly* call SetValue()! The reason for this odd behavior has to do with a simple optimization technique. If the WPF runtime were to call the set block of the Height property, it would have to perform runtime reflection to figure out where the DependencyProperty field (specified by the first argument to SetValue()) is located, reference it in memory, and so forth. The same story holds true if you were to write XAML that retrieves the value of the Height property—GetValue() would be called directly.

Since this is the case, why do you need to build this CLR wrapper at all? Well, WPF XAML does not allow you to call functions in markup, so the following markup would be an error:

```
<!-- Nope! Can't call methods in WPF XAML! -->
<Button x:Name="myButton" this.SetValue("100") .../>
```

In effect, when you set or get a value in markup using the CLR wrapper, think of it as a way to tell the WPF runtime "Hey! Go call GetValue()/SetValue() for me since I can't directly do it in markup!" Now, what if you call the CLR wrapper in code like so:

```
Button b = new Button();
b.Height = 10;
```

In this case, if the set block of the Height property contained code other than a call to SetValue(), it *would* execute because the WPF XAML parser optimization is not involved.

The basic rule to remember is that when registering a dependency property, use a ValidateValueCallback delegate to point to a method that performs the data validation. This ensures that the correct behavior will occur, regardless of whether you use XAML or code to get/set a dependency property.

Building a Custom Dependency Property

If you have a slight headache at this point in the chapter, this is a perfectly normal response. Building dependency properties can take some time to get used to. However, for better or worse, it is part of the process of building many custom WPF controls, so let's take a look at how to build a dependency property.

Begin by creating a new WPF application named CustomDependencyProperty. Now, using the Project menu, activate the Add User Control (WPF) menu option, and create a control named ShowNumberControl.xaml.

■ **Note** You will learn more details about the WPF UserControl in Chapter 28, so just follow along as shown for now.

Just like a window, WPF UserControl types have a XAML file and a related code file. Update the XAML of your user control to define a single Label control in the Grid, like so:

```
<UserControl x:Class="CustomDepProp.ShowNumberControl"
    xmlns="http://schemas.microsoft.com/winfx/2006/xaml/presentation"
    xmlns:x="http://schemas.microsoft.com/winfx/2006/xaml"
    xmlns:d="http://schemas.microsoft.com/expression/blend/2008"
    xmlns:local="clr-namespace: CustomDependencyProperty"
    mc:Ignorable="d"
    d:DesignHeight="300" d:DesignWidth="300">
  <Grid>
    <Label x:Name="numberDisplay" Height="50" Width="200" Background="LightBlue"/>
  </Grid>
</UserControl>
```

In the code file of this custom control, create a normal, everyday .NET Core property that wraps an int and sets the Content property of the Label with the new value, as follows:

```
public partial class ShowNumberControl : UserControl
{
  public ShowNumberControl()
  {
    InitializeComponent();
  }
```

```
  // A normal, everyday .NET property.
  private int _currNumber = 0;
  public int CurrentNumber
  {
    get => _currNumber;
    set
    {
      _currNumber = value;
      numberDisplay.Content = CurrentNumber.ToString();
    }
  }
}
```

Now, update the XAML definition in `MainWindow.xml` to declare an instance of your custom control within a `StackPanel` layout manger. Because your custom control is not part of the core WPF assembly stack, you will need to define a custom XML namespace that maps to your control. Here is the required markup:

```
<Window x:Class="CustomDepPropApp.MainWindow"
    xmlns="http://schemas.microsoft.com/winfx/2006/xaml/presentation"
    xmlns:x="http://schemas.microsoft.com/winfx/2006/xaml"
    xmlns:d="http://schemas.microsoft.com/expression/blend/2008"
    xmlns:myCtrls="clr-namespace: CustomDependencyProperty"
    xmlns:local="clr-namespace: CustomDependencyProperty"
    mc:Ignorable="d"
    Title="Simple Dependency Property App" Height="450" Width="450"
    WindowStartupLocation="CenterScreen">
  <StackPanel>
    <myCtrls:ShowNumberControl HorizontalAlignment="Left" x:Name="myShowNumberCtrl"
    CurrentNumber="100"/>
  </StackPanel>
</Window>
```

As you can see, the Visual Studio designer appears to correctly display the value that you set in the `CurrentNumber` property (see Figure 26-23).

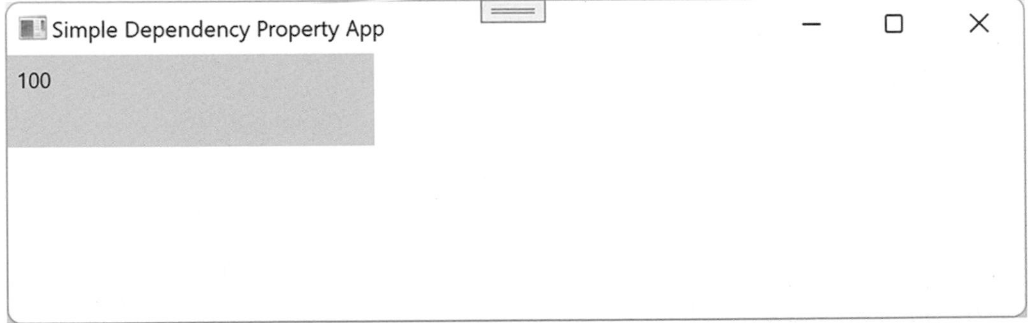

Figure 26-23. *It appears your property works as expected*

However, what if you want to apply an animation object to the CurrentNumber property so that the value changes from 100 to 200 over a period of 10 seconds? If you wanted to do so in markup, you might update your myCtrls:ShowNumberControl scope as so:

```
<myCtrls:ShowNumberControl x:Name="myShowNumberCtrl" CurrentNumber="100">
  <myCtrls:ShowNumberControl.Triggers>
    <EventTrigger RoutedEvent = "myCtrls:ShowNumberControl.Loaded">
      <EventTrigger.Actions>
        <BeginStoryboard>
          <Storyboard TargetProperty = "CurrentNumber">
            <Int32Animation From = "100" To = "200" Duration = "0:0:10"/>
          </Storyboard>
        </BeginStoryboard>
      </EventTrigger.Actions>
    </EventTrigger>
  </myCtrls:ShowNumberControl.Triggers>
</myCtrls:ShowNumberControl>
```

If you run your application, the animation object cannot find a proper target, and an exception is thrown. The reason is that the CurrentNumber property has not been registered as a dependency property! To fix matters, return to the code file of your custom control, and completely comment out the current property logic (including the private backing field).

Now, add the following code to create CurrentNumber as a dependency property:

```
public int CurrentNumber
{
  get => (int)GetValue(CurrentNumberProperty);
  set => SetValue(CurrentNumberProperty, value);
}
public static readonly DependencyProperty CurrentNumberProperty =
  DependencyProperty.Register("CurrentNumber",
  typeof(int),
  typeof(ShowNumberControl),
  new UIPropertyMetadata(0));
```

This is similar to what you saw in the implementation of the Height property; however, the code snippet registers the property inline rather than within a static constructor (which is fine). Also notice that a UIPropertyMetadata object is used to define the default value of the integer (0) rather than the more complex FrameworkPropertyMetadata object. This is the simplest version of CurrentNumber as a dependency property.

Adding a Data Validation Routine

Although you now have a dependency property named CurrentNumber (and the exception is no longer being thrown), you still won't see your animation take hold. The next adjustment you might want to make is to specify a function to call to perform some data validation logic. For this example, assume that you need to ensure that the value of CurrentNumber is between 0 and 500.

To do so, add a final argument to the DependencyProperty.Register() method of type ValidateValueCallback, which points to a method named ValidateCurrentNumber.

ValidateValueCallback is a delegate that can only point to methods returning bool and take an object as the only argument. This object represents the new value that is being assigned. Implement ValidateCurrentNumber to return true or false, if the incoming value is within the expected range.

```
public static readonly DependencyProperty CurrentNumberProperty =
  DependencyProperty.Register("CurrentNumber",
    typeof(int),
    typeof(ShowNumberControl),
    new UIPropertyMetadata(100),
    new ValidateValueCallback(ValidateCurrentNumber));

// Just a simple rule. Value must be between 0 and 500.
public static bool ValidateCurrentNumber(object value) =>
  Convert.ToInt32(value) >= 0 && Convert.ToInt32(value) <= 500;
```

Responding to the Property Change

So, now you have a valid number but still no animation. The final change you need to make is to specify a second argument to the constructor of UIPropertyMetadata, which is a PropertyChangedCallback object. This delegate can point to any method that takes a DependencyObject as the first parameter and a DependencyPropertyChangedEventArgs as the second. First, update your code as so:

```
// Note the second param of UIPropertyMetadata constructor.
public static readonly DependencyProperty CurrentNumberProperty =
  DependencyProperty.Register("CurrentNumber", typeof(int), typeof(ShowNumberControl),
  new UIPropertyMetadata(100, new PropertyChangedCallback(CurrentNumberChanged)),
  new ValidateValueCallback(ValidateCurrentNumber));
```

Within the CurrentNumberChanged() method, your ultimate goal is to change the Content of the Label to the new value assigned by the CurrentNumber property. You have one big problem, however: the CurrentNumberChanged() method is static, as it must be to work with the static DependencyProperty object. So, how are you supposed to gain access to the Label for the current instance of ShowNumberControl? That reference is contained in the first DependencyObject parameter. You can find the new value using the incoming event arguments. Here is the necessary code that will change the Content property of the Label:

```
private static void CurrentNumberChanged(DependencyObject
depObj,    DependencyPropertyChangedEventArgs args)
{
  // Cast the DependencyObject into ShowNumberControl.
  ShowNumberControl c = (ShowNumberControl)depObj;
  // Get the Label control in the ShowNumberControl.
  Label theLabel = c.numberDisplay;
  // Set the Label with the new value.
  theLabel.Content = args.NewValue.ToString();
}
```

Whew! That was a long way to go just to change the output of a label. The benefit is that your CurrentNumber dependency property can now be the target of a WPF style, an animation object, the target of a data-binding operation, and so forth. If you run your application once again, you should now see the value change during execution.

That wraps up your look at WPF dependency properties. While I hope you have a much better idea about what these constructs allow you to do and have a better idea of how to make your own, please be aware that there are many details I have not covered here.

If you find yourself in a position where you are building a number of custom controls that support custom properties, please look up the topic "Properties" under the "WPF Fundamentals" node of the .NET Framework 4.7 SDK documentation. In it you will find many more examples of building dependency properties, attached properties, various ways to configure property metadata, and a slew of other details.

Summary

This chapter examined several aspects of WPF controls, beginning with an overview of the control toolkit and the role of layout managers (panels). The first example gave you a chance to build a simple word processor application that illustrated the integrated spell-checking functionality of WPF, as well as how to build a main window with menu systems, status bars, and toolbars.

More importantly, you examined how to use WPF commands. Recall that you can attach these control-agnostic events to a UI element or an input gesture to inherit out-of-the-box services automatically (e.g., clipboard operations).

You also learned quite a bit about building complex UIs in XAML, and you learned about the WPF Ink API at the same time. You also received an introduction to WPF data-binding operations, including how to use the WPF `DataGrid` class to display data from your custom `AutoLot` database.

Finally, you investigated how WPF places a unique spin on traditional .NET Core programming primitives, specifically properties and events. As you have seen, a *dependency property* allows you to build a property that can integrate within the WPF set of services (animations, data bindings, styles, etc.). On a related note, *routed events* provide a way for an event to flow up or down a tree of markup.

CHAPTER 27

WPF Graphics Rendering Services

In this chapter, you'll examine the graphical rendering capabilities of WPF. As you'll see, WPF provides three separate ways to render graphical data: shapes, drawings, and visuals. After you understand the pros and cons of each approach, you will start learning about the world of interactive 2D graphics using the classes within `System.Windows.Shapes`. After this, you'll see how drawings and geometries allow you to render 2D data in a more lightweight manner. Finally, you'll learn how the visual layer gives you the greatest level of power and performance.

Along the way, you will explore several related topics, such as how to create custom brushes and pens, how to apply graphical transformations to your renderings, and how to perform hit-test operations. You'll see how the integrated tools of Visual Studio and an additional tool named Inkscape can simplify your graphical coding endeavors.

Note Graphics are a key aspect of WPF development. Even if you are not building a graphics-heavy application (such as a video game or multimedia application), the topics in this chapter are critical when you work with services such as control templates, animations, and data-binding customization.

Understanding WPF's Graphical Rendering Services

WPF uses a particular flavor of graphical rendering that goes by the term *retained-mode graphics*. Simply put, this means that since you are using XAML or procedural code to generate graphical renderings, it is the responsibility of WPF to persist these visual items and ensure that they are correctly redrawn and refreshed in an optimal manner. Thus, when you render graphical data, it is always present, even when the end user hides the image by resizing or minimizing the window, by covering the window with another, and so forth.

In stark contrast, previous Microsoft graphical rendering APIs (including Windows Forms' GDI+) were *immediate-mode* graphical systems. In this model, it was up to the programmer to ensure that rendered visuals were correctly "remembered" and updated during the life of the application. For example, in a Windows Forms application, rendering a shape such as a rectangle involved handling the `Paint` event (or overriding the virtual `OnPaint()` method), obtaining a `Graphics` object to draw the rectangle, and, most important, adding the infrastructure to ensure that the image was persisted when the user resized the window (e.g., creating member variables to represent the position of the rectangle and calling `Invalidate()` throughout your program).

The shift from immediate-mode to retained-mode graphics is indeed a good thing, as programmers have far less grungy graphics code to author and maintain. However, I'm not suggesting that the WPF graphics API is *completely* different from earlier rendering toolkits. For example, like GDI+, WPF supports various brush types and pen objects, techniques for hit-testing, clipping regions, graphical transformations,

A. Troelsen and P. Japikse, *Pro C# 10 with .NET 6*, https://doi.org/10.1007/978-1-4842-7869-7_27

and so on. So, if you currently have a background in GDI+ (or C/C++-based GDI), you already know a good deal about how to perform basic renderings under WPF.

WPF Graphical Rendering Options

As with other aspects of WPF development, you have a number of choices regarding how to perform your graphical rendering, beyond the decision to do so via XAML or procedural C# code (or perhaps a combination of both). Specifically, WPF provides the following three distinct ways to render graphical data:

- *Shapes*: WPF provides the `System.Windows.Shapes` namespace, which defines a small number of classes for rendering 2D geometric objects (rectangles, ellipses, polygons, etc.). While these types are simple to use and powerful, they do come with a fair amount of memory overhead if used with reckless abandon.
- *Drawings and geometries*: The WPF API provides a second way to render graphical data, using descendants from the `System.Windows.Media.Drawing` abstract class. Using classes such as `GeometryDrawing` or `ImageDrawing` (in addition to various *geometry objects*), you can render graphical data in a more lightweight (but less feature-rich) manner.
- *Visuals*: The fastest and most lightweight way to render graphical data under WPF is using the visual layer, which is accessible only through C# code. Using descendants of `System.Windows.Media.Visual`, you can speak directly to the WPF graphical subsystem.

The reason for offering different ways to do the same thing (i.e., render graphical data) has to do with memory use and, ultimately, application performance. Because WPF is such a graphically intensive system, it is not unreasonable for an application to render hundreds or even thousands of different images on a window's surface, and the choice of implementation (shapes, drawings, or visuals) could have a huge impact.

Do understand that when you build a WPF application, chances are good you'll use all three options. As a rule of thumb, if you need a modest amount of *interactive* graphical data that can be manipulated by the user (receive mouse input, display tooltips, etc.), you'll want to use members in the `System.Windows.Shapes` namespace.

In contrast, drawings and geometries are more appropriate when you need to model complex, generally noninteractive, vector-based graphical data using XAML or C#. While drawings and geometries can still respond to mouse events, hit-testing, and drag-and-drop operations, you will typically need to author more code to do so.

Last but not least, if you require the fastest possible way to render massive amounts of graphical data, the visual layer is the way to go. For example, let's say you are using WPF to build a scientific application that can plot out thousands of points of data. Using the visual layer, you can render the plot points in the most optimal way possible. As you will see later in this chapter, the visual layer is accessible only via C# code and is not XAML-friendly.

No matter which approach you take (shapes, drawings and geometries, or visuals), you will make use of common graphical primitives such as brushes (which fill interiors), pens (which draw exteriors), and transformation objects (which, well, transform the data). To begin the journey, you will start working with the classes of `System.Windows.Shapes`.

■ **Note** WPF also ships with a full-blown API that can be used to render and manipulate 3D graphics, which is not addressed in this text.

Rendering Graphical Data Using Shapes

Members of the System.Windows.Shapes namespace provide the most straightforward, most interactive, yet most memory-intensive way to render a two-dimensional image. This namespace (defined in the PresentationFramework.dll assembly) is quite small and consists of only six sealed classes that extend the abstract Shape base class: Ellipse, Rectangle, Line, Polygon, Polyline, and Path.

The abstract Shape class inherits from FrameworkElement, which inherits from UIElement. These classes define members to deal with sizing, tooltips, mouse cursors, and whatnot. Given this inheritance chain, when you render graphical data using Shape-derived classes, the objects are just about as functional (as far as user interactivity is concerned) as a WPF control!

For example, determining whether the user has clicked your rendered image is no more complicated than handling the MouseDown event. By way of a simple example, if you authored this XAML of a Rectangle object in the Grid of your initial Window:

```
<Rectangle x:Name="myRect" Height="30" Width="30" Fill="Green" MouseDown="myRect_MouseDown"/>
```

you could implement a C# event handler for the MouseDown event that changes the rectangle's background color when clicked, like so:

```
private void myRect_MouseDown(object sender, MouseButtonEventArgs e)
{
  // Change color of Rectangle when clicked.
  myRect.Fill = Brushes.Pink;
}
```

Unlike with other graphical toolkits you may have used, you do *not* need to author a ton of infrastructure code that manually maps mouse coordinates to the geometry, manually calculates hit-testing, renders to an off-screen buffer, and so forth. The members of System.Windows.Shapes simply respond to the events you register with, just like a typical WPF control (e.g., Button, etc.).

The downside of all this out-of-the-box functionality is that the shapes do take up a fair amount of memory. If you're building a scientific application that plots thousands of points on the screen, using shapes would be a poor choice (essentially, it would be about as memory intensive as rendering thousands of Button objects!). However, when you need to generate an interactive 2D vector image, shapes are a wonderful choice.

Beyond the functionality inherited from the UIElement and FrameworkElement parent classes, Shape defines a number of members for each of the children; Table 27-1 shows some of the more useful ones.

Table 27-1. *Key Properties of the Shape Base Class*

Properties	Meaning in Life
DefiningGeometry	Returns a Geometry object that represents the overall dimensions of the current shape. This object contains *only* the plot points that are used to render the data and has no trace of the functionality from UIElement or FrameworkElement.
Fill	Allows you to specify a brush object to fill the interior portion of a shape.
GeometryTransform	Allows you to apply transformations to a shape *before* it is rendered on the screen. The inherited RenderTransform property (from UIElement) applies the transformation *after* it has been rendered on the screen.

(*continued*)

Table 27-1. (*continued*)

Properties	Meaning in Life
Stretch	Describes how to fill a shape within its allocated space, such as its position within a layout manager. This is controlled using the corresponding System.Windows.Media.Stretch enumeration.
Stroke	Defines a brush object or, in some cases, a pen object (which is really a brush in disguise) that is used to paint the border of a shape.
StrokeDashArray, StrokeEndLineCap, StrokeStartLineCap, StrokeThickness	These (and other) stroke-related properties control how lines are configured when drawing the border of a shape. In a majority of cases, these properties will configure the brush used to draw a border or line.

■ **Note** If you forget to set the Fill and Stroke properties, WPF will give you "invisible" brushes, and, therefore, the shape will not be visible on the screen!

Adding Rectangles, Ellipses, and Lines to a Canvas

You will build a WPF application that can render shapes using XAML and C# and, while doing so, learn a bit about the process of hit-testing. Create a new WPF application named RenderingWithShapes and change the title of MainWindow.xaml to "Fun with Shapes!" Then update the initial XAML of the <Window>, replacing the Grid with a <DockPanel> containing a (now empty) <ToolBar> and a <Canvas>. Note that each contained item has a fitting name via the Name property.

```
<DockPanel LastChildFill="True">
  <ToolBar DockPanel.Dock="Top" Name="mainToolBar" Height="50">
  </ToolBar>
  <Canvas Background="LightBlue" Name="canvasDrawingArea"/>
</DockPanel>
```

Now, populate the <ToolBar> with a set of <RadioButton> objects, each of which contains a specific Shape-derived class as content. Notice that each <RadioButton> is assigned to the same GroupName (to ensure mutual exclusivity) and is also given a fitting name.

```
<ToolBar DockPanel.Dock="Top" Name="mainToolBar" Height="50">
  <RadioButton Name="circleOption" GroupName="shapeSelection" Click="CircleOption_Click">
    <Ellipse Fill="Green" Height="35" Width="35" />
  </RadioButton>
  <RadioButton Name="rectOption" GroupName="shapeSelection" Click="RectOption_Click">
    <Rectangle Fill="Red" Height="35" Width="35" RadiusY="10" RadiusX="10" />
  </RadioButton>
  <RadioButton Name="lineOption" GroupName="shapeSelection" Click="LineOption_Click">
    <Line Height="35" Width="35" StrokeThickness="10" Stroke="Blue"
          X1="10" Y1="10" Y2="25" X2="25"
          StrokeStartLineCap="Triangle" StrokeEndLineCap="Round" />
  </RadioButton>
</ToolBar>
```

As you can see, declaring Rectangle, Ellipse, and Line objects in XAML is quite straightforward and requires little comment. Recall that the Fill property is used to specify a *brush* to paint the interior of a shape. When you require a solid-colored brush, just specify a hard-coded string of known values, and the underlying type converter will generate the correct object. One interesting feature of the Rectangle type is that it defines RadiusX and RadiusY properties to allow you to render curved corners.

Line represents its starting and ending points using the X1, X2, Y1, and Y2 properties (given that *height* and *width* make little sense when describing a line). Here you are setting up a few additional properties that control how to render the starting and ending points of the Line, as well as how to configure the stroke settings. Figure 27-1 shows the rendered toolbar, as seen through the Visual Studio WPF designer.

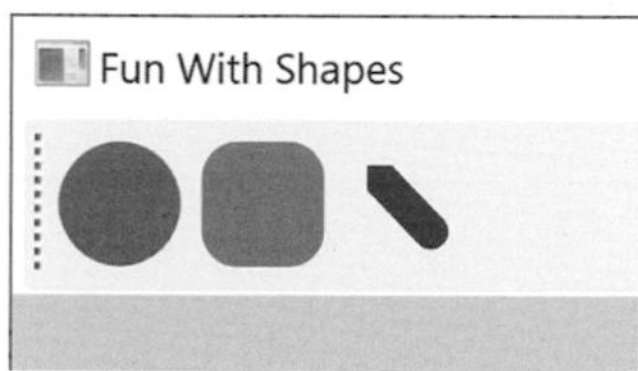

***Figure 27-1.** Using Shapes as content for a set of RadioButtons*

Now, using the Properties window of Visual Studio, handle the MouseLeftButtonDown event for the Canvas, and handle the Click event for each RadioButton. In your C# file, your goal is to render the selected shape (a circle, square, or line) when the user clicks within the Canvas. First, define the following nested enum (and corresponding member variable) within your Window-derived class:

```
public partial class MainWindow : Window
{
  private enum SelectedShape
  { Circle, Rectangle, Line }
  private SelectedShape _currentShape;
}
```

Within each Click event handler, set the currentShape member variable to the correct SelectedShape value, as follows:

```
private void CircleOption_Click(object sender, RoutedEventArgs e)
{
  _currentShape = SelectedShape.Circle;
}

private void RectOption_Click(object sender, RoutedEventArgs e)
{
  _currentShape = SelectedShape.Rectangle;
}

private void LineOption_Click(object sender, RoutedEventArgs e)
{
  _currentShape = SelectedShape.Line;
}
```

With the MouseLeftButtonDown event handler of the Canvas, you will render out the correct shape (of a predefined size), using the X,Y position of the mouse cursor as a starting point. Here is the complete implementation, with analysis to follow:

```
private void CanvasDrawingArea_MouseLeftButtonDown(object sender, MouseButtonEventArgs e)
{
  Shape shapeToRender = null;
  // Configure the correct shape to draw.
  switch (_currentShape)
  {
    case SelectedShape.Circle:
      shapeToRender = new Ellipse() { Fill = Brushes.Green, Height = 35, Width = 35 };
      break;
    case SelectedShape.Rectangle:
      shapeToRender = new Rectangle()
        { Fill = Brushes.Red, Height = 35, Width = 35, RadiusX = 10, RadiusY = 10 };
      break;
    case SelectedShape.Line:
      shapeToRender = new Line()
      {
        Stroke = Brushes.Blue,
        StrokeThickness = 10,
        X1 = 0, X2 = 50, Y1 = 0, Y2 = 50,
        StrokeStartLineCap= PenLineCap.Triangle,
        StrokeEndLineCap = PenLineCap.Round
      };
      break;
    default:
      return;
  }
  // Set top/left position to draw in the canvas.
  Canvas.SetLeft(shapeToRender, e.GetPosition(canvasDrawingArea).X);
  Canvas.SetTop(shapeToRender, e.GetPosition(canvasDrawingArea).Y);
  // Draw shape!
  canvasDrawingArea.Children.Add(shapeToRender);
}
```

■ **Note** You might notice that the Ellipse, Rectangle, and Line objects being created in this method have the same property settings as the corresponding XAML definitions! As you might hope, you can streamline this code, but that requires an understanding of the WPF object resources, which you will examine in Chapter 28.

As you can see, you are testing the currentShape member variable to create the correct Shape-derived object. After this point, you set the top-left value within the Canvas using the incoming MouseButtonEventArgs. Last but not least, you add the new Shape-derived type to the collection of UIElement objects maintained by the Canvas. If you run your program now, you should be able to click anywhere in the canvas and see the selected shape rendered at the location of the left mouse-click.

Removing Rectangles, Ellipses, and Lines from a Canvas

With the Canvas maintaining a collection of objects, you might wonder how you can dynamically remove an item, perhaps in response to the user right-clicking a shape. You can certainly do this using a class in the System.Windows.Media namespace called the VisualTreeHelper. Chapter 28 will explain the roles of "visual trees" and "logical trees" in some detail. Until then, you can handle the MouseRightButtonDown event on your Canvas object and implement the corresponding event handler like so:

```
private void CanvasDrawingArea_MouseRightButtonDown(object sender, MouseButtonEventArgs e)
{
  // First, get the X,Y location of where the user clicked.
  Point pt = e.GetPosition((Canvas)sender);
  // Use the HitTest() method of VisualTreeHelper to see if the user clicked
  // on an item in the canvas.
  HitTestResult result = VisualTreeHelper.HitTest(canvasDrawingArea, pt);
  // If the result is not null, they DID click on a shape!
  if (result != null)
  {
      // Get the underlying shape clicked on, and remove it from
      // the canvas.
      canvasDrawingArea.Children.Remove(result.VisualHit as Shape);
  }
}
```

This method begins by obtaining the exact X,Y location the user clicked in the Canvas and performs a hit-test operation via the static VisualTreeHelper.HitTest() method. The return value, a HitTestResult object, will be set to null if the user does not click a UIElement within the Canvas. If HitTestResult is *not* null, you can obtain the underlying UIElement that was clicked via the VisualHit property, which you are casting into a Shape-derived object (remember, a Canvas can hold any UIElement, not just shapes!). Again, you'll get more details on exactly what a "visual tree" is in the next chapter.

■ **Note** By default, VisualTreeHelper.HitTest() returns the topmost UIElement clicked and does not provide information on other objects below that item (e.g., objects overlapping by Z-order).

With this modification, you should be able to add a shape to the canvas with a left mouse-click and delete an item from the canvas with a right mouse-click!

So far, so good. At this point, you have used Shape-derived objects to render content on RadioButtons using XAML and populated a Canvas using C#. You will add a bit more functionality to this example when you examine the role of brushes and graphical transformations. On a related note, a different example in this chapter will illustrate drag-and-drop techniques on UIElement objects. Until then, let's examine the remaining members of System.Windows.Shapes.

Working with Polylines and Polygons

The current example used only three of the Shape-derived classes. The remaining child classes (Polyline, Polygon, and Path) are extremely tedious to render correctly without tool support (such as Microsoft Blend, the companion tool for Visual Studio designed for WPF developers, or other tools that can create vector graphics) simply because they require a large number of plot points to represent their output. Here is an overview of the remaining Shapes types.

The Polyline type lets you define a collection of (x, y) coordinates (via the Points property) to draw a series of line segments that do not require connecting ends. The Polygon type is similar; however, it is programmed so that it will always close the starting and ending points and fill the interior with the specified brush. Assume you have authored the following <StackPanel> in the Kaxaml editor:

```
<!-- Polylines do not automatically connect the ends. -->
<Polyline Stroke ="Red" StrokeThickness ="20" StrokeLineJoin ="Round" Points ="10,10 40,40
10,90 300,50"/>
<!-- A Polygon always closes the end points. -->
<Polygon Fill ="AliceBlue" StrokeThickness ="5" Stroke ="Green" Points ="40,10 70,80
10,50" />
```

Figure 27-2 shows the rendered output in Kaxaml.

Figure 27-2. *Polygons and polylines*

Working with Paths

Using the Rectangle, Ellipse, Polygon, Polyline, and Line types alone to draw a detailed 2D vector image would be extremely complex, as these primitives do not allow you to easily capture graphical data such as curves, unions of overlapping data, and so forth. The final Shape-derived class, Path, provides the ability to define complex 2D graphical data represented as a collection of independent *geometries*. After you have defined a collection of such geometries, you can assign them to the Data property of the Path class, where this information will be used to render your complex 2D image.

The Data property takes a System.Windows.Media.Geometry-derived class, which contains the key members described in Table 27-2.

Table 27-2. *Select Members of the System.Windows.Media.Geometry Type*

Member	Meaning in Life
Bounds	Establishes the current bounding rectangle containing the geometry.
FillContains()	Determines whether a given Point (or other Geometry object) is within the bounds of a particular Geometry-derived class. This is useful for hit-testing calculations.
GetArea()	Returns the entire area that a Geometry-derived type occupies.
GetRenderBounds()	Returns a Rect that contains the smallest possible rectangle that could be used to render the Geometry-derived class.
Transform	Assigns a Transform object to the geometry to alter the rendering.

The classes that extend Geometry (see Table 27-3) look very much like their Shape-derived counterparts. For example, EllipseGeometry has similar members to Ellipse. The big distinction is that Geometry-derived classes *do not know* how to render themselves directly because they are not UIElements. Rather, Geometry-derived classes represent little more than a collection of plot-point data, which say in effect "If a Path uses my data, this is how I would render myself."

Table 27-3. *Geometry-Derived Classes*

Geometry Class	Meaning in Life
LineGeometry	Represents a straight line
RectangleGeometry	Represents a rectangle
EllipseGeometry	Represents an ellipse
GeometryGroup	Allows you to group several Geometry objects
CombinedGeometry	Allows you to merge two different Geometry objects into a single shape
PathGeometry	Represents a figure composed of lines and curves

■ **Note** Path is not the only class in WPF that can use a collection of geometries. For example, DoubleAnimationUsingPath, DrawingGroup, GeometryDrawing, and even UIElement can all use geometries for rendering, using the PathGeometry, ClipGeometry, Geometry, and Clip properties, respectively.

The following is a Path that makes use of a few Geometry-derived types. Notice that you are setting the Data property of Path to a GeometryGroup object that contains other Geometry-derived objects such as EllipseGeometry, RectangleGeometry, and LineGeometry. Figure 27-3 shows the output.

```
<!-- A Path contains a set of geometry objects, set with the Data property. -->
<Path Fill = "Orange" Stroke = "Blue" StrokeThickness = "3">
  <Path.Data>
    <GeometryGroup>
      <EllipseGeometry Center = "75,70" RadiusX = "30" RadiusY = "30" />
    <RectangleGeometry Rect = "25,55 100 30" />
    <LineGeometry StartPoint="0,0" EndPoint="70,30" />
    <LineGeometry StartPoint="70,30" EndPoint="0,30" />
  </GeometryGroup>
  </Path.Data>
</Path>
```

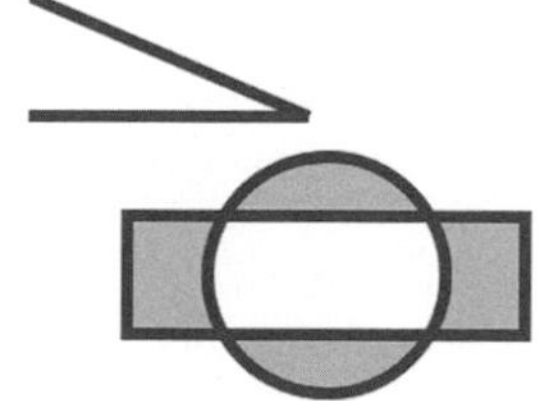

Figure 27-3. *A Path containing various Geometry objects*

The image in Figure 27-3 could have been rendered using the Line, Ellipse, and Rectangle classes shown earlier. However, this would have put various UIElement objects in memory. When you use geometries to model the plot points of what to draw and then place the geometry collection into a container that can render the data (Path, in this case), you reduce the memory overhead.

Now recall that Path has the same inheritance chain as any other member of System.Windows.Shapes and therefore can send the same event notifications as other UIElement objects. Thus, if you were to define this same <Path> element in a Visual Studio project, you could determine whether the user clicked anywhere in the sweeping line simply by handling a mouse event (remember, Kaxaml does not allow you to handle events for the markup you have authored).

The Path Modeling "Mini-Language"

Of all the classes listed in Table 27-3, PathGeometry is the most complex to configure in terms of XAML or code. This has to do with the fact that each *segment* of the PathGeometry is composed of objects that contain various segments and figures (e.g., ArcSegment, BezierSegment, LineSegment, PolyBezierSegment, PolyLineSegment, PolyQuadraticBezierSegment, etc.). Here is an example of a Path object whose Data property has been set to a <PathGeometry> composed of various figures and segments:

```
<Path Stroke="Black" StrokeThickness="1" >
  <Path.Data>
    <PathGeometry>
      <PathGeometry.Figures>
        <PathFigure StartPoint="10,50">
          <PathFigure.Segments>
           <BezierSegment
             Point1="100,0"
             Point2="200,200"
             Point3="300,100"/>
           <LineSegment Point="400,100" />
           <ArcSegment
             Size="50,50" RotationAngle="45"
             IsLargeArc="True" SweepDirection="Clockwise"
             Point="200,100"/>
           </PathFigure.Segments>
        </PathFigure>
      </PathGeometry.Figures>
    </PathGeometry>
  </Path.Data>
</Path>
```

Now, to be perfectly honest, few programmers will ever need to manually build complex 2D images by directly describing Geometry- or PathSegment-derived classes. Later in this chapter, you will learn how to convert vector graphics into path statements that can be used in XAML.

Even with the assistance of these tools, the amount of XAML required to define a complex Path object would be ghastly, as the data consists of full descriptions of various Geometry- or PathSegment-derived classes. To produce more concise and compact markup, the Path class has been designed to understand a specialized "mini-language."

For example, rather than setting the Data property of Path to a collection of Geometry- and PathSegment-derived types, you can set the Data property to a single string literal containing a number of known symbols and various values that define the shape to be rendered. Here is a simple example, and the resulting output is shown in Figure 27-4:

```
<Path Stroke="Black" StrokeThickness="3" Data="M 10,75 C 70,15 250,270 300,175 H 240" />
```

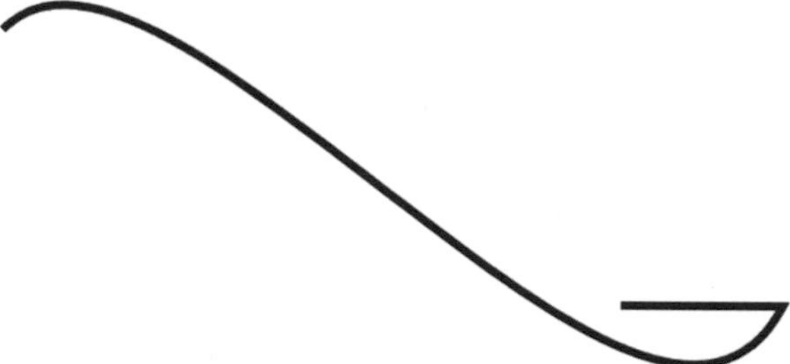

Figure 27-4. *The Path mini-language allows you to compactly describe a Geometry/PathSegment object model*

The `M` command (short for *move*) takes an X,Y position that represents the starting point of the drawing. The `C` command takes a series of plot points to render a *curve* (a cubic Bézier curve to be exact), while `H` draws a *horizontal* line.

Now, to be perfectly honest, the chances that you will ever need to manually build or parse a string literal containing Path mini-language instructions are slim to none. However, at the least, you will no longer be surprised when you view XAML-generated dedicated tools.

WPF Brushes and Pens

Each of the WPF graphical rendering options (shape, drawing and geometries, and visuals) makes extensive use of *brushes*, which allow you to control how the interior of a 2D surface is filled. WPF provides six different brush types, all of which extend `System.Windows.Media.Brush`. While `Brush` is abstract, the descendants described in Table 27-4 can be used to fill a region with just about any conceivable option.

Table 27-4. *WPF Brush-Derived Types*

Brush Type	Meaning in Life
`DrawingBrush`	Paints an area with a `Drawing`-derived object (`GeometryDrawing`, `ImageDrawing`, or `VideoDrawing`)
`ImageBrush`	Paints an area with an image (represented by an `ImageSource` object)
`LinearGradientBrush`	Paints an area with a linear gradient
`RadialGradientBrush`	Paints an area with a radial gradient
`SolidColorBrush`	Paints a single color, set with the `Color` property
`VisualBrush`	Paints an area with a `Visual`-derived object (`DrawingVisual`, `Viewport3DVisual`, and `ContainerVisual`)

The `DrawingBrush` and `VisualBrush` classes allow you to build a brush based on an existing `Drawing`- or `Visual`-derived class. These brush classes are used when you are working with the other two graphical options of WPF (drawings or visuals) and will be examined later in this chapter.

`ImageBrush`, as the name suggests, lets you build a brush that displays image data from an external file or embedded application resource, by setting the `ImageSource` property. The remaining brush types (`LinearGradientBrush` and `RadialGradientBrush`) are quite straightforward to use, though typing in the required XAML can be a tad verbose. Thankfully, Visual Studio supports integrated brush editors that make it simple to generate stylized brushes.

Configuring Brushes Using Visual Studio

Let's update your WPF drawing program, RenderingWithShapes, to use some more interesting brushes. The three shapes you have employed so far to render data on your toolbar use simple, solid colors, so you can capture their values using simple string literals. To spice things up a tad, you will now use the integrated brush editor. Ensure that the XAML editor of your initial window is the open window within the IDE and select the `Ellipse` element. Now, in the Properties window, locate the Brush category and then click `Fill` property listed on the top (see Figure 27-5).

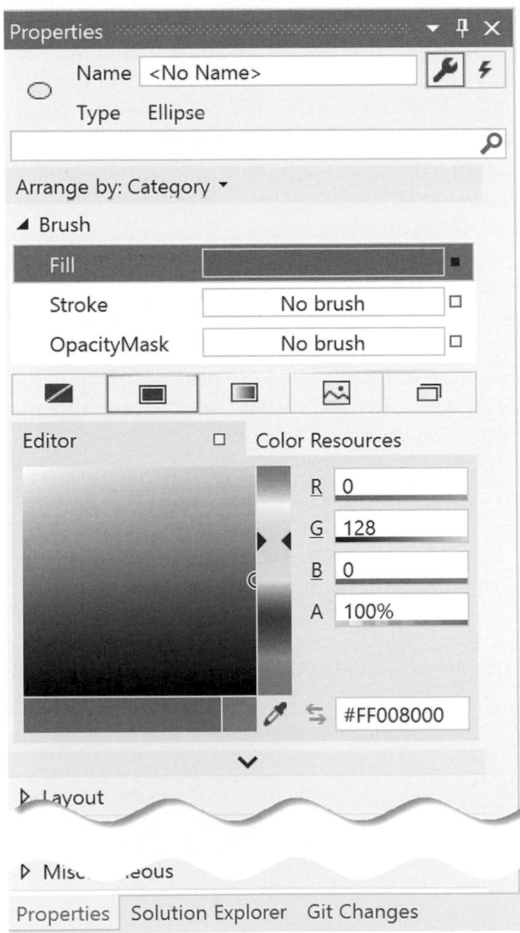

***Figure 27-5.** Any property that requires a brush can be configured with the integrated brush editor*

At the top of the Brushes editor, you will see a set of properties that are all "brush compatible" for the selected item (i.e., Fill, Stroke, and OpacityMask). Below this, you will see a series of tabs that allow you to configure different types of brushes, including the current solid color brush. You can use the color selector tool, as well as the ARGB (alpha, red, green, and blue, where "alpha" controls transparency) editors to control the color of the current brush. Using these sliders and the related color selection area, you can create any sort of solid color. Use these tools to change the Fill color of your Ellipse and view the resulting XAML. You will notice the color is stored as a hexadecimal value, as follows:

```
<Ellipse Fill="#FF47CE47" Height="35" Width="35" />
```

More interestingly, this same editor allows you to configure gradient brushes, which are used to define a series of colors and transition points. Recall that this Brushes editor provides you with a set of tabs, the first of which lets you set a *null brush* for no rendered output. The other four allow you to set up a solid color brush (what you just examined), gradient brush, tile brush, or image brush.

Click the gradient brush button, and the editor will display a few new options (see Figure 27-6). The three buttons on the lower left allow you to pick a linear gradient, pick a radial gradient, or reverse the gradient stops. The bottommost strip will show you the current color of each gradient stop, each of which is marked by a "thumb" on the strip. As you drag these thumbs around the gradient strip, you can control the gradient offset. Furthermore, when you click a given thumb, you can change the color for that particular gradient stop via the color selector. Finally, if you click directly on the gradient strip, you can add gradient stops.

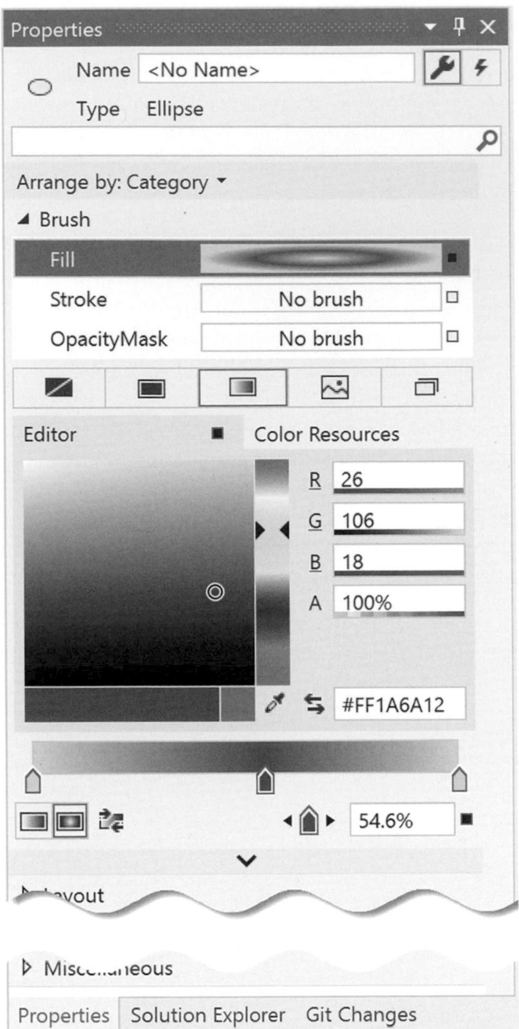

Figure 27-6. *The Visual Studio brush editor allows you to build basic gradient brushes*

Take a few minutes to play around with this editor to build a radial gradient brush containing three gradient stops, set to your colors of choice. Figure 27-6 shows the brush you just constructed, using three different shades of green.

When you are done, the IDE will update your XAML with a custom brush, set to a brush-compatible property (the `Fill` property of the `Ellipse` in this example) using property-element syntax, as follows:

```
<Ellipse Height="35" Width="35">
  <Ellipse.Fill>
    <RadialGradientBrush>
      <GradientStop Color="#FF17F800"/>
      <GradientStop Color="#FF24F610" Offset="1"/>
      <GradientStop Color="#FF1A6A12" Offset="0.546"/>
```

```
    </RadialGradientBrush>
  </Ellipse.Fill>
</Ellipse>
```

Configuring Brushes in Code

Now that you have built a custom brush for the XAML definition of your Ellipse, the corresponding C# code is out-of-date, in that it will still render a solid green circle. To sync things back up, update the correct case statement to use the same brush you just created. The following is the necessary update, which looks more complex than you might expect, just because you are converting the hexadecimal value to a proper Color object via the System.Windows.Media.ColorConverter class (see Figure 27-7 for the modified output):

```
case SelectedShape.Circle:
  shapeToRender = new Ellipse() { Height = 35, Width = 35 };
  // Make a RadialGradientBrush in code!
  RadialGradientBrush brush = new RadialGradientBrush();
  brush.GradientStops.Add(new GradientStop(
    (Color)ColorConverter.ConvertFromString("#FF77F177"), 0));
  brush.GradientStops.Add(new GradientStop(
    (Color)ColorConverter.ConvertFromString("#FF11E611"), 1));
  brush.GradientStops.Add(new GradientStop(
    (Color)ColorConverter.ConvertFromString("#FF5A8E5A"), 0.545));
  shapeToRender.Fill = brush;
  break;
```

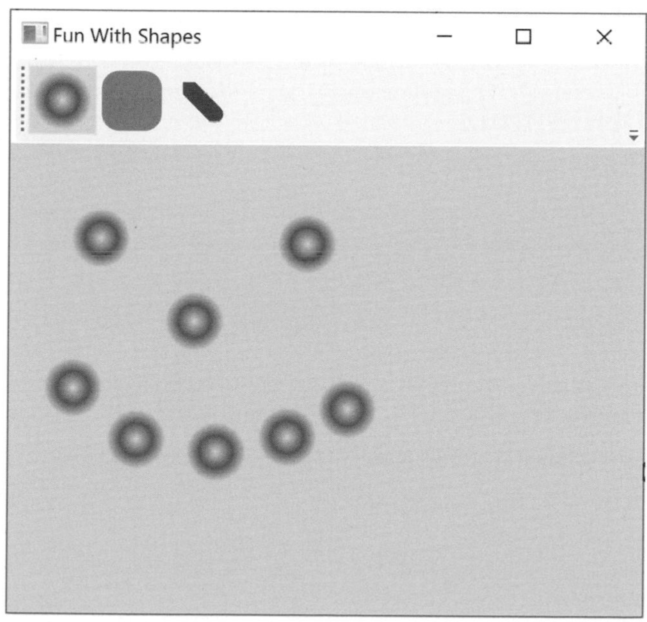

***Figure 27-7.** Drawing circles with a bit more pizzazz*

By the way, you can build GradientStop objects by specifying a simple color as the first constructor parameter using the Colors enumeration, which returns a configured Color object.

```
GradientStop g = new GradientStop(Colors.Aquamarine, 1);
```

Or, if you require even finer control, you can pass in a configured Color object, like so:

```
Color myColor = new Color() { R = 200, G = 100, B = 20, A = 40 };
GradientStop g = new GradientStop(myColor, 34);
```

Of course, the Colors enum and Color class are not limited to gradient brushes. You can use them anytime you need to represent a color value in code.

Configuring Pens

In comparison with brushes, a *pen* is an object for drawing borders of geometries or, in the case of the Line or PolyLine class, the line geometry itself. Specifically, the Pen class allows you to draw a specified thickness, represented by a double value. In addition, a Pen can be configured with the same sort of properties seen in the Shape class, such as starting and stopping pen caps, dot-dash patterns, and so forth. For example, you can add the following markup to a shape to define the pen attributes:

```
<Pen Thickness="10" LineJoin="Round" EndLineCap="Triangle" StartLineCap="Round" />
```

In many cases, you won't need to directly create a Pen object because this will be done indirectly when you assign a value to properties, such as StrokeThickness to a Shape-derived type (as well as other UIElements). However, building a custom Pen object is handy when working with Drawing-derived types (described later in the chapter). Visual Studio does not have a pen editor *per se*, but it does allow you to configure all the stroke-centric properties of a selected item using the Properties window.

Applying Graphical Transformations

To wrap up the discussion of using shapes, let's address the topic of *transformations*. WPF ships with numerous classes that extend the System.Windows.Media.Transform abstract base class. Table 27-5 documents many of the key out-of-the-box Transform-derived classes.

Table 27-5. *Key Descendants of the System.Windows.Media.Transform Type*

Type	Meaning in Life
MatrixTransform	Creates an arbitrary matrix transformation that is used to manipulate objects or coordinate systems in a 2D plane
RotateTransform	Rotates an object clockwise about a specified point in a 2D (x, y) coordinate system
ScaleTransform	Scales an object in the 2D (x, y) coordinate system
SkewTransform	Skews an object in the 2D (x, y) coordinate system
TranslateTransform	Translates (moves) an object in the 2D (x, y) coordinate system
TransformGroup	Represents a composite Transform composed of other Transform objects

Transformations can be applied to any UIElement (e.g., descendants of Shape as well as controls such as Button controls, TextBox controls, and the like). Using these transformation classes, you can render graphical data at a given angle, skew the image across a surface, and expand, shrink, or flip the target item in a variety of ways.

■ **Note** While transformation objects can be used anywhere, you will find them most useful when working with WPF animations and custom control templates. As you will see later in the chapter, you can use WPF animations to incorporate visual cues to the end user for a custom control.

Transformations (or a whole set of them) can be assigned to a target object (e.g., Button, Path, etc.) using two common properties, LayoutTransform and RenderTransform.

The LayoutTransform property is helpful, in that the transformation occurs *before* elements are rendered into a layout manager, and therefore the transformation will not affect Z-ordering operations (in other words, the transformed image data will not overlap).

The RenderTransform property, on the other hand, occurs after the items are in their container, and therefore it is quite possible that elements can be transformed in such a way that they could overlap each other, based on how they were arranged in the container.

A First Look at Transformations

You will add some transformational logic to your RenderingWithShapes project in just a moment. However, to see transformation objects in action, open Kaxaml and define a simple StackPanel in the root Page or Window and set the Orientation property to Horizontal. Now, add the following Rectangle, which will be drawn at a 45-degree angle using a RotateTransform object:

```
<!-- A Rectangle with a rotate transformation. -->
<Rectangle Height ="100" Width ="40" Fill ="Red">
  <Rectangle.LayoutTransform>
    <RotateTransform Angle ="45"/>
  </Rectangle.LayoutTransform>
</Rectangle>
```

Here is a <Button> that is skewed across the surface by 20 degrees, using a <SkewTransform>:

```
<!-- A Button with a skew transformation. -->
<Button Content ="Click Me!" Width="95" Height="40">
  <Button.LayoutTransform>
   <SkewTransform AngleX ="20" AngleY ="20"/>
  </Button.LayoutTransform>
</Button>
```

And for good measure, here is an Ellipse that is scaled by 20 degrees with a ScaleTransform (note the values set to the initial Height and Width), as well as a TextBox that has a group of transformation objects applied to it:

```
<!-- An Ellipse that has been scaled by 20%. -->
<Ellipse Fill ="Blue" Width="5" Height="5">
  <Ellipse.LayoutTransform>
```

```
    <ScaleTransform ScaleX ="20" ScaleY ="20"/>
  </Ellipse.LayoutTransform>
</Ellipse>
<!-- A TextBox that has been rotated and skewed. -->
<TextBox Text ="Me Too!" Width="50" Height="40">
  <TextBox.LayoutTransform>
    <TransformGroup>
      <RotateTransform Angle ="45"/>
      <SkewTransform AngleX ="5" AngleY ="20"/>
    </TransformGroup>
  </TextBox.LayoutTransform>
</TextBox>
```

Note that when a transformation is applied, you are not required to perform any manual calculations to correctly respond to hit-testing, input focus, or whatnot. The WPF graphics engine handles such tasks on your behalf. For example, in Figure 27-8, you can see that the TextBox is still responsive to keyboard input.

Figure 27-8. *The results of graphical transformation objects*

Transforming Your Canvas Data

Now, let's incorporate some transformational logic into your RenderingWithShapes example. In addition to applying a transformation object to a single item (e.g., Rectangle, TextBox, etc.), you can also apply transformation objects to a layout manager to transform all of the internal data. You could, for example, render the entire DockPanel of the main window at an angle.

```
<DockPanel LastChildFill="True">
  <DockPanel.LayoutTransform>
    <RotateTransform Angle="45"/>
  </DockPanel.LayoutTransform>
...
</DockPanel>
```

This is a bit extreme for this example, so let's add a final (less aggressive) feature that allows the user to flip the entire Canvas and all contained graphics. Begin by adding a final ToggleButton to your ToolBar, defined as follows:

```
<ToggleButton Name="flipCanvas" Click="FlipCanvas_Click" Content="Flip Canvas!"/>
```

Within the Click event handler, create a RotateTransform object and connect it to the Canvas object via the LayoutTransform property if this new ToggleButton is clicked. If the ToggleButton is not clicked, remove the transformation by setting the same property to null.

```
private void FlipCanvas_Click(object sender, RoutedEventArgs e)
{
  if (flipCanvas.IsChecked == true)
  {
    RotateTransform rotate = new RotateTransform(-180);
    canvasDrawingArea.LayoutTransform = rotate;
  }
  else
  {
    canvasDrawingArea.LayoutTransform = null;
  }
}
```

Run your application and add a bunch of graphics throughout the canvas area, making sure to go edge to edge with them. If you click your new button, you will find that the shape data flows outside of the boundaries of the canvas! This is because you have not defined a clipping region (see Figure 27-9).

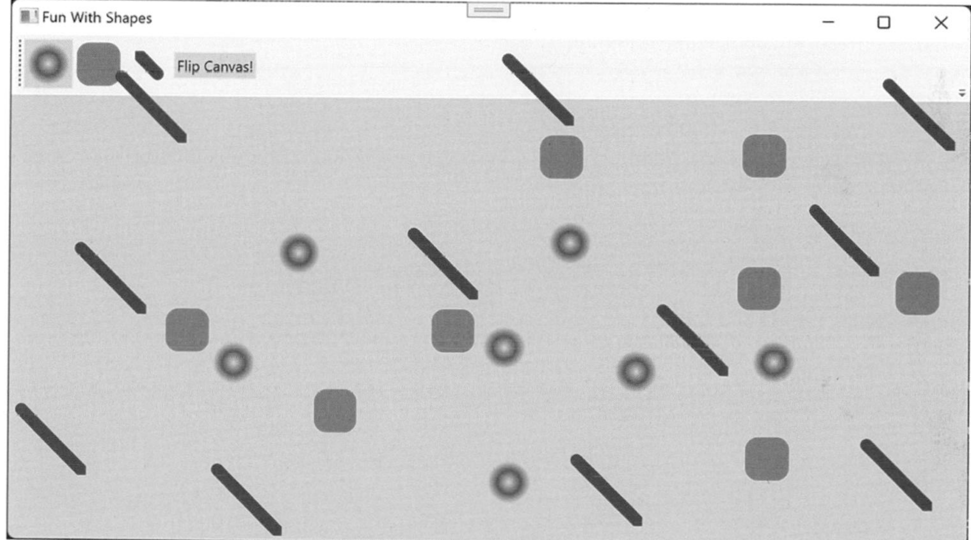

***Figure 27-9.** Oops! Your data is flowing outside of the canvas after the transformation!*

Fixing this is trivial. Rather than manually authoring complex clipping-logic code, simply set the `ClipToBounds` property of the `Canvas` to `true`, which prevents child elements from being rendered outside the parent's boundaries. If you run your program again, you'll find the data will not bleed off the canvas boundary.

```
<Canvas ClipToBounds = "True" ... >
```

The last tiny modification to make has to do with the fact that when you flip the canvas by pressing your toggle button and then click the canvas to draw a new shape, the point at which you click is *not* the point where the graphical data is applied. Rather, the data is rendered above the mouse cursor.

To resolve this issue, apply the same transformation object to the shape being drawn before the rendering occurs (via RenderTransform). Here is the crux of the code:

```
private void CanvasDrawingArea_MouseLeftButtonDown(object sender, MouseButtonEventArgs e)
{
  //omitted for brevity
  if (flipCanvas.IsChecked == true)
  {
    RotateTransform rotate = new RotateTransform(-180);
    shapeToRender.RenderTransform = rotate;
  }
  // Set top/left to draw in the canvas.
  Canvas.SetLeft(shapeToRender,
    e.GetPosition(canvasDrawingArea).X);
  Canvas.SetTop(shapeToRender,
    e.GetPosition(canvasDrawingArea).Y);

  // Draw shape!
  canvasDrawingArea.Children.Add(shapeToRender);
}
```

This wraps up your examination of System.Windows.Shapes, brushes, and transformations. Before looking at the role of rendering graphics using drawings and geometries, let's see how Visual Studio can be used to simplify how you work with primitive graphics.

Working with the Visual Studio Transform Editor

In the previous example, you applied various transformations by manually entering markup and authoring some C# code. While this is certainly useful, you will be happy to know that the latest version of Visual Studio ships with an integrated transformation editor. Recall that any UI element can be the recipient of transformational services, including a layout system containing various UI elements. To illustrate the use of Visual Studio's transform editor, create a new WPF application named FunWithTransforms.

Building the Initial Layout

First, split your initial Grid into two columns using the integrated grid editor (the exact size does not matter). Now, locate the StackPanel control within your Toolbox and add it to take up the entire space of the first column of the Grid; then add three Button controls to the StackPanel, like so:

```
<Grid>
  <Grid.ColumnDefinitions>
    <ColumnDefinition Width="*"/>
    <ColumnDefinition Width="*"/>
  </Grid.ColumnDefinitions>
  <StackPanel Grid.Row="0" Grid.Column="0">
    <Button Name="btnSkew" Content="Skew" Click="Skew"/>
    <Button Name="btnRotate" Content="Rotate" Click="Rotate"/>
    <Button Name="btnFlip" Content="Flip" Click="Flip"/>
  </StackPanel>
</Grid>
```

Add the handlers for the buttons to the code page, like this:

```
private void Skew(object sender, RoutedEventArgs e)
{
}
private void Rotate(object sender, RoutedEventArgs e)
{
}
private void Flip(object sender, RoutedEventArgs e)
{
}
```

To finalize the UI, create a graphic of your choosing (using any of the techniques discussed in this chapter) defined in the second column of the `Grid`. The markup used in the sample is listed here:

```
<Canvas x:Name="myCanvas" Grid.Column="1" Grid.Row="0">
  <Ellipse HorizontalAlignment="Left" VerticalAlignment="Top"
       Height="186"  Width="92" Stroke="Black"
       Canvas.Left="20" Canvas.Top="31">
    <Ellipse.Fill>
      <RadialGradientBrush>
        <GradientStop Color="#FF951ED8" Offset="0.215"/>
        <GradientStop Color="#FF2FECB0" Offset="1"/>
      </RadialGradientBrush>
    </Ellipse.Fill>
  </Ellipse>
  <Ellipse HorizontalAlignment="Left" VerticalAlignment="Top"
       Height="101" Width="110" Stroke="Black"
       Canvas.Left="122" Canvas.Top="126">
    <Ellipse.Fill>
      <LinearGradientBrush EndPoint="0.5,1" StartPoint="0.5,0">
        <GradientStop Color="#FFB91DDC" Offset="0.355"/>
        <GradientStop Color="#FFB0381D" Offset="1"/>
      </LinearGradientBrush>
    </Ellipse.Fill>
  </Ellipse>
</Canvas>
```

Figure 27-10 shows the final layout for the example.

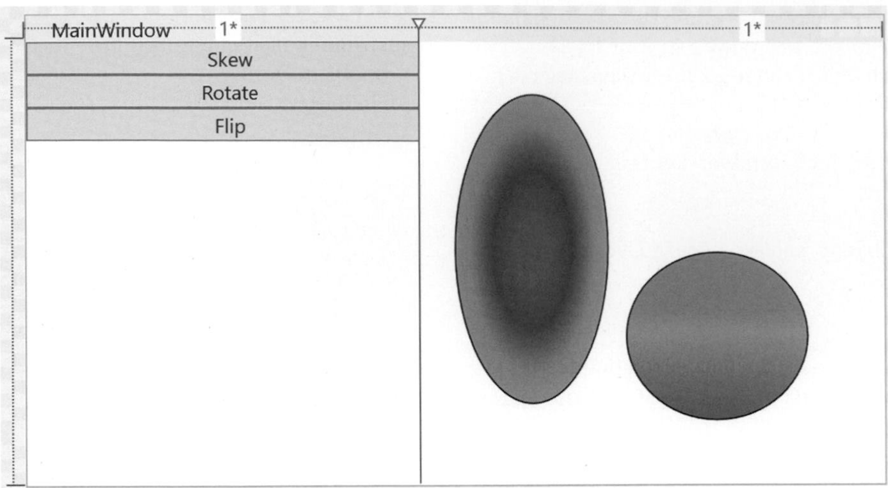

Figure 27-10. *The layout of your transformation example*

Applying Transformations at Design Time

As mentioned, Visual Studio provides an integrated Transform editor, which can be found in the Properties panel. Locate this area, and make sure you expand the Transform section to view the RenderTransform and LayoutTransform sections of the editor (see Figure 27-11).

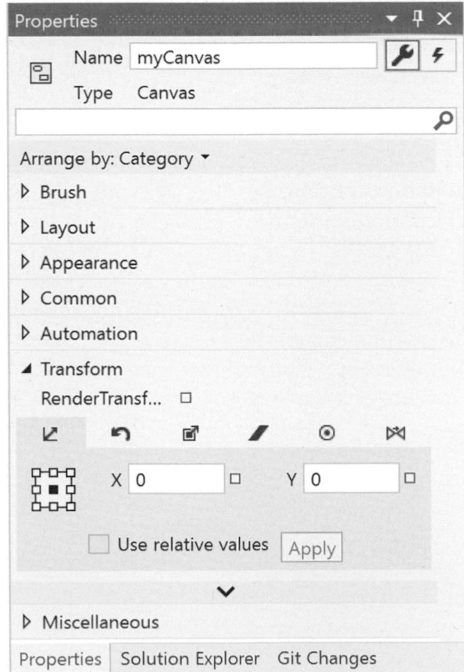

Figure 27-11. *The Transform editor*

Similar to the Brushes section, the Transform section provides a number of tabs to configure various types of graphical transformation to the currently selected item. Table 27-6 describes each transformation option, listed in the order of evaluating each tab from left to right.

Table 27-6. *Blend Transformation Options*

Transformation Option	Meaning in Life
Translate	Allows you to offset the location of an item on an X, Y position.
Rotate	Allows you to rotate an item on a 360-degree angle.
Scale	Allows you to grow or shrink an item by a factor in the X and Y directions.
Skew	Allows you to skew the bounding box containing the selected item by a factor in the X and Y directions.
Center Point	When you rotate or flip an object, the item moves relative to a fixed point, called the object's *center point*. By default, an object's center point is located at the object's center; however, this transformation allows you to change an object's center point to rotate or flip the object around a different point.
Flip	Flips a selected item based on an X or Y center point.

I suggest you test each of these transformations using your custom shape as a target (just press Ctrl+Z to undo the previous operation). Like many other aspects of the Transform Properties panel, each transformation section has a unique set of configuration options, which should become fairly understandable as you tinker. For example, the Skew transform editor allows you to set the X and Y skew values, the Flip transform editor allows you to flip on the x- or y-axis, and so forth.

Transforming the Canvas in Code

The implementation of each `Click` event handler will be more or less the same. You will configure a transformation object and assign it to the `myCanvas` object. Then, when you run the application, you can click a button to see the result of the applied transformation. Here is the complete code for each event handler (notice that you are setting the `LayoutTransform` property, so the shape data remains positioned relative to the parent container):

```
private void Flip(object sender, System.Windows.RoutedEventArgs e)
{
  myCanvas.LayoutTransform = new ScaleTransform(-1, 1);
}

private void Rotate(object sender, System.Windows.RoutedEventArgs e)
{
  myCanvas.LayoutTransform = new RotateTransform(180);
}

private void Skew(object sender, System.Windows.RoutedEventArgs e)
{
  myCanvas.LayoutTransform = new SkewTransform(40, -20);
}
```

Rendering Graphical Data Using Drawings and Geometries

While the Shape types allow you to generate any sort of interactive two-dimensional surface, they entail quite a bit of memory overhead due to their rich inheritance chain. And though the Path class can help remove some of this overhead using contained geometries (rather than a large collection of other shapes), WPF provides a sophisticated drawing and geometry programming interface that renders even more lightweight 2D vector images.

The entry point into this API is the abstract System.Windows.Media.Drawing class (in PresentationCore.dll), which on its own does little more than define a bounding rectangle to hold the rendering. The Drawing class is significantly more lightweight than Shape, given that neither UIElement nor FrameworkElement is in the inheritance chain.

WPF provides various classes that extend Drawing, each of which represents a particular way of drawing the content, as described in Table 27-7.

Table 27-7. *WPF Drawing-Derived Types*

Type	Meaning in Life
DrawingGroup	Used to combine a collection of separate Drawing-derived objects into a single composite rendering.
GeometryDrawing	Used to render 2D shapes in a very lightweight manner.
GlyphRunDrawing	Used to render textual data using WPF graphical rendering services.
ImageDrawing	Used to render an image file, or geometry set, into a bounding rectangle.
VideoDrawing	Used to play an audio file or video file. This type can only be fully exploited using procedural code. If you would like to play videos via XAML, the MediaPlayer type is a better choice.

Because they are more lightweight, Drawing-derived types do not have intrinsic support for handling input events, as they are not UIElements or FrameworkElements (although it is possible to programmatically perform hit-testing logic).

Another key difference between Drawing-derived types and Shape-derived types is that Drawing-derived types have no ability to render themselves, as they do not derive from UIElement! Rather, derived types must be placed within a hosting object (specifically, DrawingImage, DrawingBrush, or DrawingVisual) to display their content.

DrawingImage allows you to place drawing and geometries inside a WPF Image control, which typically is used to display data from an external file. DrawingBrush allows you to build a brush based on a drawing and its geometries to set a property that requires a brush. Finally, DrawingVisual is used only in the "visual" layer of graphical rendering, which is driven completely via C# code.

Although using drawings is a bit more complex than using simple shapes, this decoupling of graphical composition from graphical rendering makes the Drawing-derived types much more lightweight than the Shape-derived types while still retaining key services.

Building a DrawingBrush Using Geometries

Earlier in this chapter, you filled a Path with a group of geometries, like so:

```
<Path Fill = "Orange" Stroke = "Blue" StrokeThickness = "3">
  <Path.Data>
    <GeometryGroup>
```

```
      <EllipseGeometry Center = "75,70" RadiusX = "30" RadiusY = "30" />
    <RectangleGeometry Rect = "25,55 100 30" />
    <LineGeometry StartPoint="0,0" EndPoint="70,30" />
    <LineGeometry StartPoint="70,30" EndPoint="0,30" />
  </GeometryGroup>
  </Path.Data>
</Path>
```

By doing this, you gain interactivity from Path but are still fairly lightweight given your geometries. However, if you want to render the same output and have no need for any (out-of-the-box) interactivity, you can place the same <GeometryGroup> inside a DrawingBrush, like this:

```
<DrawingBrush>
  <DrawingBrush.Drawing>
    <GeometryDrawing>
      <GeometryDrawing.Geometry>
        <GeometryGroup>
            <EllipseGeometry Center = "75,70" RadiusX = "30" RadiusY = "30" />
            <RectangleGeometry Rect = "25,55 100 30" />
            <LineGeometry StartPoint="0,0" EndPoint="70,30" />
            <LineGeometry StartPoint="70,30" EndPoint="0,30" />
          </GeometryGroup>
        </GeometryDrawing.Geometry>
        <!-- A custom pen to draw the borders. -->
        <GeometryDrawing.Pen>
           <Pen Brush="Blue" Thickness="3"/>
        </GeometryDrawing.Pen>
        <!-- A custom brush to fill the interior. -->
        <GeometryDrawing.Brush>
          <SolidColorBrush Color="Orange"/>
        </GeometryDrawing.Brush>
      </GeometryDrawing>
    </DrawingBrush.Drawing>
</DrawingBrush>
```

When you place a group of geometries into a DrawingBrush, you also need to establish the Pen object used to draw the boundaries because you no longer inherit a Stroke property from the Shape base class. Here, you created a <Pen> with the same settings used in the Stroke and StrokeThickness values of the previous Path example.

Furthermore, since you no longer inherit a Fill property from Shape, you also need to use property-element syntax to define a brush object to use for the <DrawingGeometry>, which here is a solid-colored orange brush, just like the previous Path settings.

Painting with the DrawingBrush

Now that you have a DrawingBrush, you can use it to set the value of any property requiring a brush object. For example, if you are authoring this markup in Kaxaml, you could use property-element syntax to paint your drawing over the entire surface of a Page, like so:

```
<Page
  xmlns="http://schemas.microsoft.com/winfx/2006/xaml/presentation"
```

```
  xmlns:x="http://schemas.microsoft.com/winfx/2006/xaml">
  <Page.Background>
    <DrawingBrush>
    <!-- Same DrawingBrush as seen above. -->
    </DrawingBrush>
  </Page.Background>
</Page>
```

Or you can use this <DrawingBrush> to set a different brush-compatible property, such as the Background property of a Button.

```
<Page
  xmlns="http://schemas.microsoft.com/winfx/2006/xaml/presentation"
  xmlns:x="http://schemas.microsoft.com/winfx/2006/xaml">
  <Button Height="100" Width="100">
  <Button.Background>
    <DrawingBrush>
    <!-- Same DrawingBrush as seen above. -->
    </DrawingBrush>
  </Button.Background>
  </Button>
</Page>
```

No matter which brush-compatible property you set with your custom <DrawingBrush>, the bottom line is you are rendering a 2D vector image with much less overhead than the same 2D image rendered with shapes.

Containing Drawing Types in a DrawingImage

The DrawingImage type allows you to plug your drawing geometry into a WPF <Image> control. Consider the following:

```
<Image>
  <Image.Source>
    <DrawingImage>
      <DrawingImage.Drawing>
        <!--Same GeometryDrawing from above -->
      </DrawingImage.Drawing>
    </DrawingImage>
  </Image.Source>
</Image>
```

In this case, your <GeometryDrawing> has been placed into a <DrawingImage>, rather than a <DrawingBrush>. Using this <DrawingImage>, you can set the Source property of the Image control.

Working with Vector Images

As you might agree, it would be quite challenging for a graphic artist to create a complex vector-based image using the tools and techniques provided by Visual Studio. Graphic artists have their own set of tools that can produce amazing vector graphics. Neither Visual Studio nor its companion Expression Blend for Visual

Studio has that type of design power. Before you can import vector images into WPF application, they must be converted into Path expressions. At that point, you can program against the generated object model using Visual Studio.

■ **Note** You can find the image being used (LaserSign.svg) as well as the exported path (LaserSign.xaml) data in the Chapter 27 folder of the download files. The image is originally from Wikipedia, located at https://en.wikipedia.org/wiki/Hazard_symbol.

Converting a Sample Vector Graphic File into XAML

Before you can import complex graphical data (such as vector graphics) into a WPF application, you need to convert the graphics into path data. As an example of how to do this, start with a sample .svg image file, such as the laser sign referenced in the preceding note. Then download and install an open source tool called Inkscape (located at www.inkscape.org). Using Inkscape, open the LaserSign.svg file from the chapter download. You might be prompted to upgrade the format. Fill in the selections as shown in Figure 27-12.

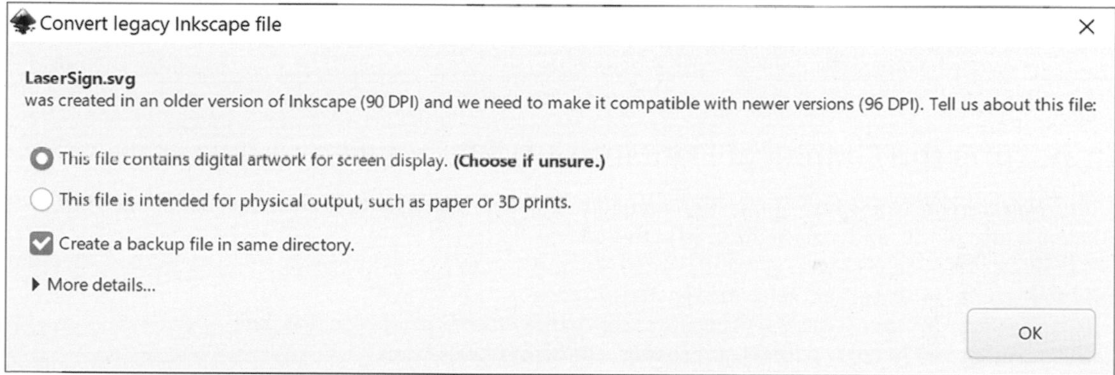

Figure 27-12. *Upgrading the SVG file to the latest format in Inkscape*

The next steps will seem a bit odd at first, but once you get over the oddity, it is a simple way to convert vector images to the correct XAML. When you have the image the way you want it, select the File ➤ Print menu option. Next, select the Microsoft XPS Document Writer as the printer target and then click Print. On the next screen, enter a filename and select where the file should be saved; then click Save. Now you have a complete *.xps (or *.oxps) file.

■ **Note** Depending on a number of variables with your system configuration, the generated file will have either the .xps or .oxps extension. Either way, the process works the same.

The *.xps and *.oxps formats are actually .zip files. Rename the extension of the file to .zip, and you can open the file in File Explorer (or 7-Zip, or your favorite archive tool). You will see that it contains the hierarchy shown in Figure 27-13.

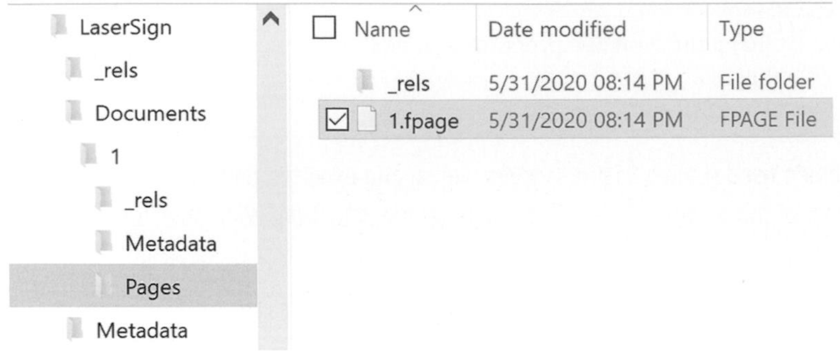

Figure 27-13. *The folder hierarchy of the printed XPS file*

The file that you need is in the Pages directory (Documents/1/Pages) and is named 1.fpage. Open the file with a text editor and copy everything except the <FixedPage> open and closing tags. The path data can then be copied into the Kaxaml and placed inside a Canvas in the main Window. Your image will show in the XAML window.

■ **Note** The latest version of Inkscape has an option to save the file as Microsoft XAML. Unfortunately, at the time of this writing, it is not compatible with WPF.

Importing the Graphical Data into a WPF Project

At this point, create a new WPF application named InteractiveLaserSign. Resize the Window to a Height of 600 and Width of 650, and replace the Grid with a Canvas.

```
<Window x:Class="InteractiveLaserSign.MainWindow"
        xmlns="http://schemas.microsoft.com/winfx/2006/xaml/presentation"
        xmlns:x="http://schemas.microsoft.com/winfx/2006/xaml"
        xmlns:d="http://schemas.microsoft.com/expression/blend/2008"

        xmlns:local="clr-namespace:InteractiveLaserSign"
        mc:Ignorable="d"
        Title="MainWindow" Height="600" Width="650">
    <Canvas>
    </Canvas>
</Window>
```

Copy the entire XAML from the 1.fpage file (excluding the outer FixedPage tag) and paste it into the Canvas control. View the Window in design mode, and you will see the sign reproduced in your application.

If you view the Document Outline, you will see that each part of the image is represented as a XAML Path element. If you resize your Window, the image quality stays the same, regardless of how big you make the window. This is because images represented by Path elements are rendered using the drawing engine and math instead of flipping pixels.

Interacting with the Sign

Recall that routed event tunnel and bubble, so any Path clicked inside the Canvas can be handled by a click event handler on the canvas. Update the Canvas markup to the following:

```
<Canvas MouseLeftButtonDown="Canvas_MouseLeftButtonDown">
```

Add the event handler with the following code:

```
private void Canvas_MouseLeftButtonDown(object sender, MouseButtonEventArgs e)
{
  if (e.OriginalSource is Path p)
  {
    p.Fill = new SolidColorBrush(Colors.Red);
  }
}
```

Now, run your application. Click the lines to see the effects.

You now understand the process of generating Path data for complex graphics and how to interact with the graphical data in code. As you might agree, the ability for professional graphic artists to generate complex graphical data and export the data as XAML is extremely powerful. Once the graphical data has been generated, developers can import the markup and program against the object model.

Rendering Graphical Data Using the Visual Layer

The final option for rendering graphical data with WPF is termed the *visual layer*. As mentioned, you can gain access to this layer only through code (it is not XAML-friendly). While a vast majority of your WPF applications will work just fine using shapes, drawings, and geometries, the visual layer does provide the fastest possible way to render huge amounts of graphical data. This low-level graphical layer can also be useful when you need to render a single image over a large area. For example, if you need to fill the background of a window with a plain, static image, the visual layer is the fastest way to do so. It can also be useful if you need to change between window backgrounds quickly, based on user input or whatnot.

I won't spend too much time delving into the details of this aspect of WPF programming, but let's build a small sample program to illustrate the basics.

The Visual Base Class and Derived Child Classes

The abstract System.Windows.Media.Visual class type supplies a minimal set of services (rendering, hit-testing, transformations) to render graphics, but it does not provide support for additional nonvisual services, which can lead to code bloat (input events, layout services, styles, and data binding). The Visual class is an abstract base class. You need to use one of the derived types to perform actual rendering operations. WPF provides a handful of subclasses, including DrawingVisual, Viewport3DVisual, and ContainerVisual.

In this example, you will focus only on DrawingVisual, a lightweight drawing class that is used to render shapes, images, or text.

A First Look at Using the DrawingVisual Class

To render data onto a surface using `DrawingVisual`, you need to take the following basic steps:

1. Obtain a `DrawingContext` object from the `DrawingVisual` class.
2. Use the `DrawingContext` to render the graphical data.

These two steps represent the bare minimum necessary for rendering some data to a surface. However, if you want the graphical data you've rendered to be responsive to hit-testing calculations (which would be important for adding user interactivity), you will also need to perform these additional steps:

1. Update the logical and visual trees maintained by the container upon which you are rendering.
2. Override two virtual methods from the `FrameworkElement` class, allowing the container to obtain the visual data you have created.

You will examine these final two steps in a bit. First, to illustrate how you can use the `DrawingVisual` class to render 2D data, create a new WPF application named RenderingWithVisuals. Your first goal is to use a `DrawingVisual` to dynamically assign data to a WPF `Image` control. Begin by updating the XAML of your window to handle the `Loaded` event, like so:

```
<Window x:Class="RenderingWithVisuals.MainWindow"
      <!--omitted for brevity -->
      Title="Fun With Visual Layer" Height="450" Width="800"
      Loaded="MainWindow_Loaded">
```

Next, replace the `Grid` with a `StackPanel` and add an `Image` in the `StackPanel`, like this:

```
<StackPanel Background="AliceBlue" Name="myStackPanel">
  <Image Name="myImage" Height="80"/>
</StackPanel>
```

Your `<Image>` control does not yet have a `Source` value because that will happen at runtime. The `Loaded` event will do the work of building the in-memory graphical data, using a `DrawingBrush` object. Make sure the following namespaces are at the top of `MainWindow.cs`:

```
using System;
using System.Windows;
using System.Windows.Media;
using System.Windows.Media.Imaging;
```

Here is the implementation of the `Loaded` event handler:

```
private void MainWindow_Loaded(
  object sender, RoutedEventArgs e)
{
  const int TextFontSize = 30;
  // Make a System.Windows.Media.FormattedText object.
  FormattedText text = new FormattedText(
    "Hello Visual Layer!",
    new System.Globalization.CultureInfo("en-us"),
    FlowDirection.LeftToRight,
```

```
    new Typeface(this.FontFamily, FontStyles.Italic,
      FontWeights.DemiBold, FontStretches.UltraExpanded),
    TextFontSize,
    Brushes.Green,
    null,
    VisualTreeHelper.GetDpi(this).PixelsPerDip);
  // Create a DrawingVisual, and obtain the DrawingContext.
  DrawingVisual drawingVisual = new DrawingVisual();
  using(DrawingContext drawingContext =
    drawingVisual.RenderOpen())
  {
    // Now, call any of the methods of DrawingContext to render data.
    drawingContext.DrawRoundedRectangle(
      Brushes.Yellow, new Pen(Brushes.Black, 5),
      new Rect(5, 5, 450, 100), 20, 20);
    drawingContext.DrawText(text, new Point(20, 20));
  }
  // Dynamically make a bitmap, using the data in the DrawingVisual.
  RenderTargetBitmap bmp = new RenderTargetBitmap(
    500, 100, 100, 90, PixelFormats.Pbgra32);
  bmp.Render(drawingVisual);
  // Set the source of the Image control!
  myImage.Source = bmp;
}
```

This code introduces a number of new WPF classes, which I will briefly comment on here. The method begins by creating a new `FormattedText` object that represents the textual portion of the in-memory image you are constructing. As you can see, the constructor allows you to specify numerous attributes such as font size, font family, foreground color, and the text itself.

Next, you obtain the necessary `DrawingContext` object via a call to `RenderOpen()` on the `DrawingVisual` instance. Here, you are rendering a colored, rounded rectangle into the `DrawingVisual`, followed by your formatted text. In both cases, you are placing the graphical data into the `DrawingVisual` using hard-coded values, which is not necessarily a great idea for production but is fine for this simple test.

The last few statements map the `DrawingVisual` into a `RenderTargetBitmap` object, which is a member of the `System.Windows.Media.Imaging` namespace. This class will take a visual object and transform it into an in-memory bitmap image. After this point, you set the `Source` property of the `Image` control, and sure enough, you will see the output in Figure 27-14.

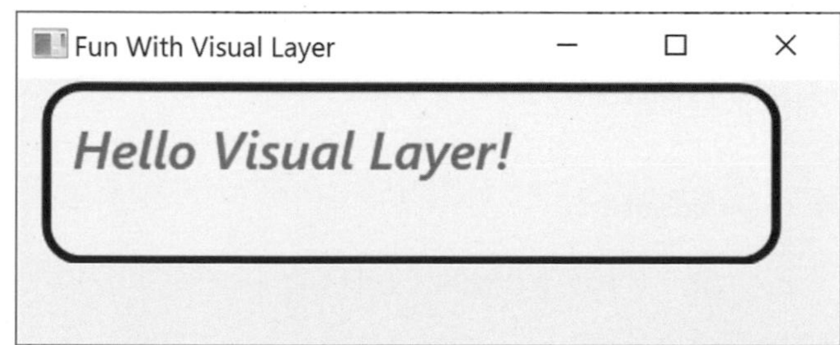

***Figure 27-14.** Using the visual layer to render an in-memory bitmap*

■ **Note** The System.Windows.Media.Imaging namespace contains a number of additional encoding classes that let you save the in-memory RenderTargetBitmap object to a physical file in a variety of formats. Check out the JpegBitmapEncoder class (and friends) for more information.

Rendering Visual Data to a Custom Layout Manager

While it is interesting to use DrawingVisual to paint onto the background of a WPF control, it is perhaps more common to build a custom layout manager (Grid, StackPanel, Canvas, etc.) that uses the visual layer internally to render its content. After you have created such a custom layout manager, you can plug it into a normal Window (or Page or UserControl) and have a part of the UI using a highly optimized rendering agent while the noncritical aspects of the hosting Window are using shapes and drawings for the remainder of the graphical data.

If you don't require the extra functionality provided by a dedicated layout manager, you could opt to simply extend FrameworkElement, which does have the necessary infrastructure to also contain visual items. To illustrate how this could be done, insert a new class to your project named CustomVisualFrameworkElement. Extend this class from FrameworkElement and import the System, System.Windows, System.Windows.Input, System.Windows.Media, and System.Windows.Media.Imaging namespaces.

This class will maintain a member variable of type VisualCollection, which contains two fixed DrawingVisual objects (of course, you could add new members to this collection via a mouse operation, but this example will keep it simple). Update your class with the following new functionality:

```
public class CustomVisualFrameworkElement : FrameworkElement
{
  // A collection of all the visuals we are building.
  VisualCollection theVisuals;
  public CustomVisualFrameworkElement()
  {
    // Fill the VisualCollection with a few DrawingVisual objects.
    // The ctor arg represents the owner of the visuals.
    theVisuals = new VisualCollection(this)
      {AddRect(),AddCircle()};
  }
  private Visual AddCircle()
  {
    DrawingVisual drawingVisual = new DrawingVisual();
    // Retrieve the DrawingContext in order to create new drawing content.
    using DrawingContext drawingContext =
      drawingVisual.RenderOpen()
    // Create a circle and draw it in the DrawingContext.
    drawingContext.DrawEllipse(Brushes.DarkBlue, null,
      new Point(70, 90), 40, 50);
    return drawingVisual;
  }
  private Visual AddRect()
  {
    DrawingVisual drawingVisual = new DrawingVisual();
```

```
    using DrawingContext drawingContext =
      drawingVisual.RenderOpen()
    Rect rect =
      new Rect(new Point(160, 100), new Size(320, 80));
    drawingContext.DrawRectangle(Brushes.Tomato, null, rect);
    return drawingVisual;
  }
}
```

Now, before you can use this custom FrameworkElement in your Window, you must override two key virtual methods mentioned previously, both of which are called internally by WPF during the rendering process. The GetVisualChild() method returns a child at the specified index from the collection of child elements. The read-only VisualChildrenCount property returns the number of visual child elements within this visual collection. Both methods are easy to implement because you can delegate the real work to the VisualCollection member variable.

```
protected override int VisualChildrenCount
  => theVisuals.Count;

protected override Visual GetVisualChild(int index)
{
  // Value must be greater than zero, so do a sanity check.
  if (index < 0 || index >= theVisuals.Count)
  {
    throw new ArgumentOutOfRangeException();
  }
  return theVisuals[index];
}
```

You now have just enough functionality to test your custom class. Update the XAML description of the Window to add one of your CustomVisualFrameworkElement objects to the existing StackPanel. Doing so will require you to add a custom XML namespace that maps to your .NET namespace.

```
<Window x:Class="RenderingWithVisuals.MainWindow"
  xmlns="http://schemas.microsoft.com/winfx/2006/xaml/presentation"
  xmlns:x="http://schemas.microsoft.com/winfx/2006/xaml"
  xmlns:local="clr-namespace:RenderingWithVisuals"
  Title="Fun with the Visual Layer" Height="350" Width="525"
  Loaded="Window_Loaded" WindowStartupLocation="CenterScreen">
    <StackPanel Background="AliceBlue" Name="myStackPanel">
          <Image Name="myImage" Height="80"/>
          <local:CustomVisualFrameworkElement/>
    </StackPanel>
</Window>
```

When you run the program, you will see the result shown in Figure 27-15.

Figure 27-15. *Using the visual layer to render data to a custom FrameworkElement*

Responding to Hit-Test Operations

Because `DrawingVisual` does not have any of the infrastructures of `UIElement` or `FrameworkElement`, you will need to programmatically add the ability to calculate hit-test operations. Thankfully, this is fairly easy to do in the visual layer because of the concept of *logical* and *visual* trees. As it turns out, when you author a blob of XAML, you are essentially building a logical tree of elements. However, behind every logical tree is a much richer description known as the *visual tree*, which contains lower-level rendering instructions.

Chapter 28 will delve into these trees in more detail, but for now, just understand that until you register your custom visuals with these data structures, you will not be able to perform hit-testing operations. Luckily, the `VisualCollection` container does this on your behalf (which explains why you needed to pass in a reference to the custom `FrameworkElement` as a constructor argument).

First, update the `CustomVisualFrameworkElement` class to handle the `MouseDown` event in the class constructor using standard C# syntax, like so:

```
this.MouseDown += CustomVisualFrameworkElement_MouseDown;
```

The implementation of this handler will call the `VisualTreeHelper.HitTest()` method to see whether the mouse is within the boundaries of one of the rendered visuals. To do this, you specify as a parameter to `HitTest()` a `HitTestResultCallback` delegate that will perform the calculations. If you click a visual, you will toggle between a skewed rendering of the visual and the original rendering. Add the following methods to your `CustomVisualFrameworkElement` class:

```
void CustomVisualFrameworkElement_MouseDown(object sender, MouseButtonEventArgs e)
{
  // Figure out where the user clicked.
  Point pt = e.GetPosition((UIElement)sender);
  // Call helper function via delegate to see if we clicked on a visual.
  VisualTreeHelper.HitTest(this, null,
  new HitTestResultCallback(myCallback), new PointHitTestParameters(pt));
}
```

```
public HitTestResultBehavior myCallback(HitTestResult result)
{
    // Toggle between a skewed rendering and normal rendering,
    // if a visual was clicked.
    if (result.VisualHit.GetType() == typeof(DrawingVisual))
    {
      if (((DrawingVisual)result.VisualHit).Transform == null)
      {
        ((DrawingVisual)result.VisualHit).Transform = new SkewTransform(7, 7);
      }
      else
      {
        ((DrawingVisual)result.VisualHit).Transform = null;
    }
  }
  // Tell HitTest() to stop drilling into the visual tree.
  return HitTestResultBehavior.Stop;
}
```

Now, run your program once again. You should now be able to click either rendered visual and see the transformation in action! While this is just a simple example of working with the visual layer of WPF, remember that you make use of the same brushes, transformations, pens, and layout managers as you would when working with XAML. As a result, you already know quite a bit about working with this `Visual`-derived classes.

That wraps up your investigation of the graphical rendering services of Windows Presentation Foundation. While you learned a number of interesting topics, the reality is that you have only scratched the surface of WPF's graphical capabilities. I will leave it in your hands to dig deeper into the topics of shapes, drawings, brushes, transformations, and visuals (and, to be sure, you will see some additional details of these topics in the remaining WPF chapters).

Summary

Because Windows Presentation Foundation is such a graphically intensive GUI API, it comes as no surprise that we are given a number of ways to render graphical output. This chapter began by examining each of three ways a WPF application can do so (shapes, drawings, and visuals) and discussed various rendering primitives such as brushes, pens, and transformations.

Remember that when you need to build interactive 2D renderings, shapes make the process very simple. However, static, noninteractive renderings can be rendered in a more optimal manner by using drawings and geometries, while the visual layer (accessible only in code) gives you maximum control and performance.

CHAPTER 28

WPF Resources, Animations, Styles, and Templates

This chapter introduces you to three important (and interrelated) topics that will deepen your understanding of the Windows Presentation Foundation (WPF) API. The first order of business is to learn the role of *logical resources*. As you will see, the logical resource (also known as an *object resource*) system is a way to name and refer to commonly used objects within a WPF application. While logical resources are often authored in XAML, they can also be defined in procedural code.

Next, you will learn how to define, execute, and control an animation sequence. Despite what you might think, WPF animations are not limited to video game or multimedia applications. Under the WPF API, animations can be as subtle as making a button appear to glow when it receives focus or expanding the size of a selected row in a `DataGrid`. Understanding animations is a key aspect of building custom control templates (as you will see later in this chapter).

You will then explore the role of WPF styles and templates. Much like a web page that uses CSS or the ASP.NET theme engine, a WPF application can define a common look and feel for a set of controls. You can define these styles in markup and store them as object resources for later use, and you can also apply them dynamically at runtime. The final example will teach you how to build custom control templates.

Understanding the WPF Resource System

Your first task is to examine the topic of embedding and accessing application resources. WPF supports two flavors of resources. The first is a *binary resource*, and this category typically includes items most programmers consider to be resources in the traditional sense (embedded image files or sound clips, icons used by the application, etc.).

The second flavor, termed *object resources* or *logical resources*, represents a named .NET object that can be packaged and reused throughout the application. While any .NET object can be packaged as an object resource, logical resources are particularly helpful when working with graphical data of any sort, given that you can define commonly used graphic primitives (brushes, pens, animations, etc.) and refer to them when required.

A. Troelsen and P. Japikse, *Pro C# 10 with .NET 6*, https://doi.org/10.1007/978-1-4842-7869-7_28

Working with Binary Resources

Before getting to the topic of object resources, let's quickly examine how to package up *binary resources* such as icons or image files (e.g., company logos or images for an animation) into your applications. If you would like to follow along, create a new WPF application named BinaryResourcesApp. Update the markup for your initial window to handle the Window Loaded event and to use a DockPanel as the layout root, like so:

```
<Window x:Class="BinaryResourcesApp.MainWindow"
  <!-- Omitted for brevity -->
    Title="Fun with Binary Resources" Height="500" Width="649" Loaded="MainWindow_OnLoaded">
  <DockPanel LastChildFill="True">
  </DockPanel>
</Window>
```

Now, let's say your application needs to display one of three image files inside part of the window, based on user input. The WPF Image control can be used to display not only a typical image file (*.bmp, *.gif, *.ico, *.jpg, *.png, *.wdp, or *.tiff) but also data in a DrawingImage (as you saw in Chapter 27). You might build a UI for your window that supports a DockPanel containing a simple toolbar with Next and Previous buttons. Below this toolbar you can place an Image control, which currently does not have a value set to the Source property, like so:

```
  <DockPanel LastChildFill="True">
    <ToolBar Height="60" Name="picturePickerToolbar" DockPanel.Dock="Top">
      <Button x:Name="btnPreviousImage" Height="40" Width="100" BorderBrush="Black"
              Margin="5" Content="Previous" Click="btnPreviousImage_Click"/>
      <Button x:Name="btnNextImage" Height="40" Width="100" BorderBrush="Black"
              Margin="5" Content="Next" Click="btnNextImage_Click"/>
    </ToolBar>
    <!-- We will fill this Image in code. -->
    <Border BorderThickness="2" BorderBrush="Green">
      <Image x:Name="imageHolder" Stretch="Fill" />
    </Border>
  </DockPanel>
```

Next, add the following empty event handlers:

```
private void MainWindow_OnLoaded(
  object sender, RoutedEventArgs e)
{
}
private void btnPreviousImage_Click(
  object sender, RoutedEventArgs e)
{
}
private void btnNextImage_Click(
  object sender, RoutedEventArgs e)
{
}
```

When the window loads, images will be added to a collection that the Next and Previous buttons will cycle through. Now that the application framework is in place, let's examine the different options for implementing this.

Including Loose Resource Files in a Project

One option is to ship your image files as a set of loose files in a subdirectory of the application install path. Start by adding a new folder (named Images) to your project. Into this folder add some images by right-clicking and selecting Add ➤ Existing Item. Make sure to change the file filter in the Add Existing Item dialog to *.* so the image files show. You can add your own image files or use the three image files named Deer.jpg, Dogs.jpg, and Welcome.jpg from the downloadable code.

Configuring the Loose Resources

To copy the content of your \Images folder to the \bin\Debug folder when the project builds, begin by selecting all the images in Solution Explorer. Now, with these images still selected, right-click and select Properties to open the Properties window. Set the Build Action property to Content, and set the Copy to Output Directory property to "Copy always" (see Figure 28-1).

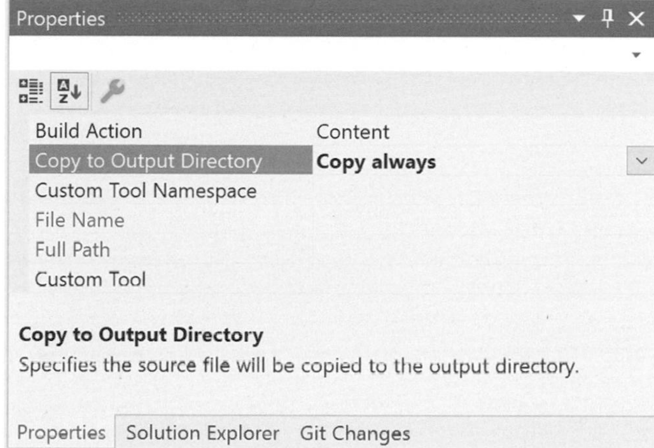

Figure 28-1. *Configuring the image data to be copied to your output directory*

■ **Note** You could also select Copy if Newer, which will save you time if you're building large projects with a lot of content. For this example, "Copy always" works.

If you build your project, you can now click the Show All Files button of Solution Explorer and view the copied Image folder under your \bin\Debug directory (you might need to click the Refresh button).

Programmatically Loading an Image

WPF provides a class named BitmapImage, which is part of the System.Windows.Media.Imaging namespace. This class allows you to load data from an image file whose location is represented by a System.Uri object. Add a List<BitmapImage> to hold the images, as well as an int to store the index of the currently displayed image.

```
// A List of BitmapImage files.
List<BitmapImage> _images=new List<BitmapImage>();
// Current position in the list.
private int _currImage=0;
```

In the Loaded event of your window, fill the list of images and then set the Image control source to the first image in the list.

```
private void MainWindow_OnLoaded(
  object sender, RoutedEventArgs e)
{
  try
  {
    string path=Environment.CurrentDirectory;
    // Load these images from disk when the window loads.
    _images.Add(new BitmapImage(new Uri($@"{path}\Images\Deer.jpg")));
    _images.Add(new BitmapImage(new Uri($@"{path}\Images\Dogs.jpg")));
    _images.Add(new BitmapImage(new Uri($@"{path}\Images\Welcome.jpg")));
    // Show first image in the List.
    imageHolder.Source=_images[_currImage];
  }
  catch (Exception ex)
  {
    MessageBox.Show(ex.Message);
  }
}
```

Next, implement the previous and next handlers to loop through the images. If the user gets to the end of the list, start them back at the beginning and vice versa.

```
private void btnPreviousImage_Click(
  object sender, RoutedEventArgs e)
{
  if (--_currImage < 0)
  {
    _currImage=_images.Count - 1;
  }
  imageHolder.Source=_images[_currImage];
}
private void btnNextImage_Click(
  object sender, RoutedEventArgs e)
{
  if (++_currImage >=_images.Count)
  {
    _currImage=0;
  }
  imageHolder.Source=_images[_currImage];
}
```

At this point, you can run your program and flip through each picture.

Embedding Application Resources

If you would rather configure your image files to be compiled directly into your .NET assembly as binary resources, select the image files in Solution Explorer (in the \Images folder, not in the \bin\Debug\Images folder). Change the Build Action property to Resource and set the Copy to Output Directory property to "Do not copy" (see Figure 28-2).

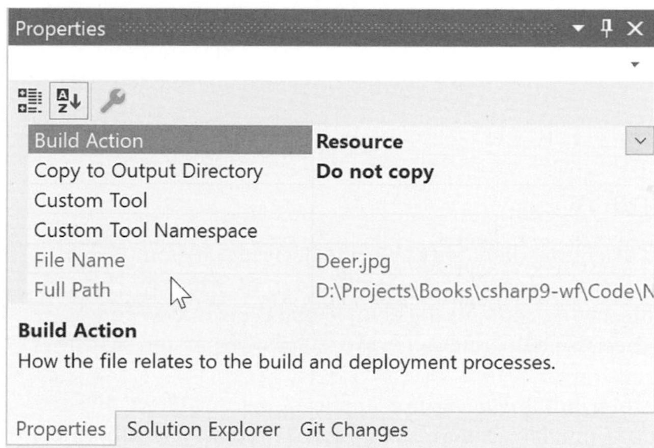

Figure 28-2. *Configuring the images to be embedded resources*

Now, using Visual Studio's Build menu, select the Clean Solution option to wipe out the current contents of \bin\Debug\Images and then rebuild your project. Refresh Solution Explorer and observe the absence of data in your \bin\Debug\Images directory. With the current build options, your graphical data is no longer copied to the output folder and is now embedded within the assembly itself. This ensures that the resources exist but also increases the size of your compiled assembly.

You need to modify your code to load these images into your list by extracting them from the compiled assembly.

```
// Extract from the assembly and then load images
_images.Add(new BitmapImage(new Uri(@"/Images/Deer.jpg", UriKind.Relative)));
_images.Add(new BitmapImage(new Uri(@"/Images/Dogs.jpg", UriKind.Relative)));
_images.Add(new BitmapImage(new Uri(@"/Images/Welcome.jpg", UriKind.Relative)));
```

In this case, you no longer need to determine the installation path and can simply list the resources by name, which considers the name of the original subdirectory. Also notice, when you create your Uri objects, you specify a UriKind value of Relative. At this point, your executable is a stand-alone entity that can be run from any location on the machine because all the compiled data is within the binary.

Working with Object (Logical) Resources

When you are building a WPF application, it is common to define a blurb of XAML to use in multiple locations within a window or perhaps across multiple windows or projects. For example, say you have created the *perfect* linear gradient brush, which consists of ten lines of markup. Now, you want to use that brush as the background color for every Button control in the project (which consists of eight windows) for a total of 16 Button controls.

The worst thing you could do is to copy and paste the XAML to every control. Clearly, this would be a nightmare to maintain, as you would need to make numerous changes any time you wanted to tweak the look and feel of the brush.

Thankfully, *object resources* allow you to define a blob of XAML, give it a name, and store it in a fitting dictionary for later use. Like a binary resource, object resources are often compiled into the assembly that requires them. However, you do not need to tinker with the `Build Action` property to do so. If you place your XAML into the correct location, the compiler will take care of the rest.

Working with object resources is a big part of WPF development. As you will see, object resources can be far more complex than a custom brush. You can define a XAML-based animation, a 3D rendering, a custom control style, a data template, a control template, and more, and package each one as a reusable resource.

The Role of the Resources Property

As mentioned, object resources must be placed in a fitting dictionary object to be used across an application. As it stands, every descendant of `FrameworkElement` supports a `Resources` property. This property encapsulates a `ResourceDictionary` object that contains the defined object resources. The `ResourceDictionary` can hold any type of item because it operates on `System.Object` types and may be manipulated via XAML or procedural code.

In WPF, all controls, `Windows`, `Pages` (used when building navigation applications), and `UserControls` extend `FrameworkElement`, so just about all widgets provide access to a `ResourceDictionary`. Furthermore, the `Application` class, while not extending `FrameworkElement`, supports an identically named `Resources` property for the same purpose.

Defining Window-wide Resources

To begin exploring the role of object resources, create a new WPF application named ObjectResourcesApp and change the initial `Grid` to a horizontally aligned `StackPanel` layout manager. Into this `StackPanel`, define two `Button` controls like so (you really do not need much to illustrate the role of object resources, so this will do):

```
<StackPanel Orientation="Horizontal">
  <Button Margin="25" Height="200" Width="200" Content="OK" FontSize="20"/>
  <Button Margin="25" Height="200" Width="200" Content="Cancel" FontSize="20"/>
</StackPanel>
```

Now, click the OK button and set the `Background` color property to a custom brush type using the integrated Brushes editor (discussed in Chapter 27). After you have done so, notice how the brush is embedded within the scope of the `<Button>` and `</Button>` tags, as shown here:

```
<Button Margin="25" Height="200" Width="200" Content="OK" FontSize="20">
  <Button.Background>
    <RadialGradientBrush>
      <GradientStop Color="#FFC44EC4" Offset="0" />
      <GradientStop Color="#FF829CEB" Offset="1" />
      <GradientStop Color="#FF793879" Offset="0.669" />
    </RadialGradientBrush>
  </Button.Background>
</Button>
```

To allow the Cancel button to use this brush as well, you should promote the scope of your `<RadialGradientBrush>` to a parent element's resource dictionary. For example, if you move it to the `<StackPanel>`, both buttons can use the same brush because they are child elements of the layout manager. Even better, you could package the brush into the resource dictionary of the `Window` itself so the window's content can use it.

When you need to define a resource, you use the property-element syntax to set the `Resources` property of the owner. You also give the resource item an `x:Key` value, which will be used by other parts of the window when they want to refer to the object resource. Be aware that `x:Key` and `x:Name` are not the same! The `x:Name` attribute allows you to gain access to the object as a member variable in your code file, while the `x:Key` attribute allows you to refer to an item in a resource dictionary.

Visual Studio allows you to promote a resource to a higher scope using its respective Properties window. To do so, first identify the property that has the complex object you want to package as a resource (the `Background` property, in this example). To the right of the property is a small square that, when clicked, will open a pop-up menu. From it, select the Convert to New Resource option (see Figure 28-3).

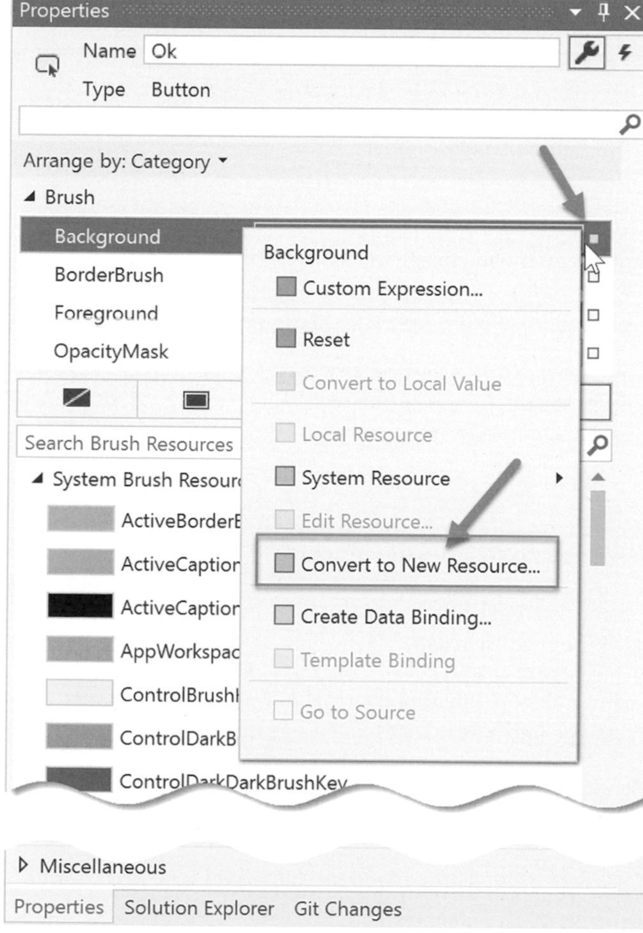

Figure 28-3. *Moving a complex object into a resource container*

You are asked to name your resource (myBrush) and specify where to place it. For this example, leave the default selection of the current document (see Figure 28-4).

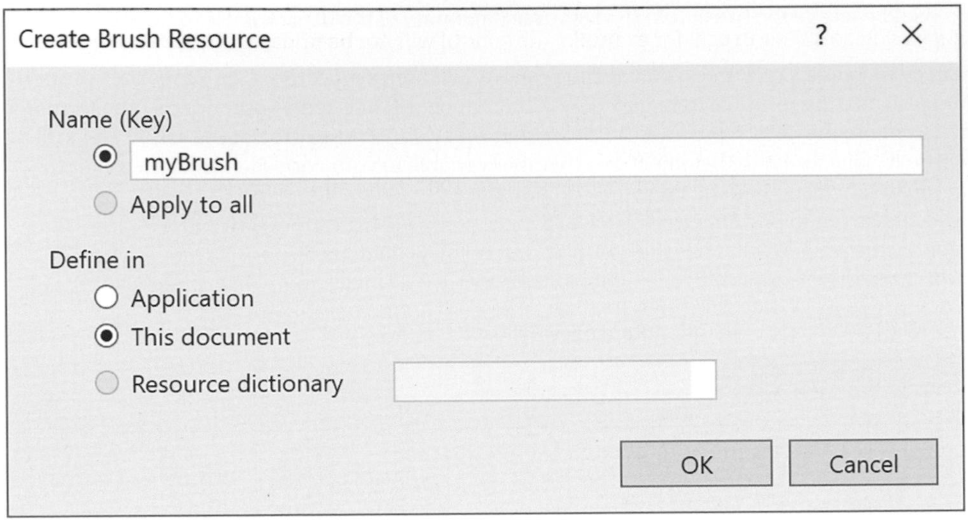

Create Brush Resource ? ×

Name (Key)

myBrush

Apply to all

Define in

Application

This document

Resource dictionary

OK Cancel

Figure 28-4. *Naming the object resource*

When you are done, you will see the brush has been moved inside the Window.Resources tag.

```
<Window.Resources>
  <RadialGradientBrush x:Key="myBrush">
    <GradientStop Color="#FFC44EC4" Offset="0" />
    <GradientStop Color="#FF829CEB" Offset="1" />
    <GradientStop Color="#FF793879" Offset="0.669" />
  </RadialGradientBrush>
</Window.Resources>
```

And the Button control's Background has been updated to use a new resource.

```
<Button Margin="25" Height="200" Width="200" Content="OK"
       FontSize="20" Background="{DynamicResource myBrush}"/>
```

The Create Resource Wizard creates the new resource as a DynamicResource. You will learn about DynamicResources later in the text, but for now, change it to a StaticResource, like this:

```
<Button Margin="25" Height="200" Width="200" Content="OK"
    FontSize="20" Background="{StaticResource myBrush}"/>
```

To see the benefit, update the Cancel Button's Background property to the same StaticResource, and you can see the reuse in action.

```
<Button Margin="25" Height="200" Width="200" Content="Cancel"
    FontSize="20" Background="{StaticResource myBrush}"/>
```

The {StaticResource} Markup Extension

The {StaticResource} markup extension applies the resource only once (on initialization) and stays "connected" to the original object during the life of the application. Some properties (such as gradient stops) will update, but if you create a new Brush, for example, the control will not be updated. To see this in action, add a Name and Click event handler to each Button control, as follows:

```
<Button Name="Ok" Margin="25" Height="200" Width="200" Content="OK"
    FontSize="20" Background="{StaticResource myBrush}" Click="Ok_OnClick"/>
<Button Name="Cancel" Margin="25" Height="200" Width="200" Content="Cancel"
    FontSize="20" Background="{StaticResource myBrush}" Click="Cancel_OnClick"/>
```

Next, add the following code to the Ok_OnClick() event handler:

```
private void Ok_OnClick(object sender, RoutedEventArgs e)
{
  // Get the brush and make a change.
  var b=(RadialGradientBrush)Resources["myBrush"];
  b.GradientStops[1]=new GradientStop(Colors.Black, 0.0);
}
```

■ **Note** You are using the Resources indexer to locate a resource by name here. Be aware, however, that this will throw a runtime exception if the resource cannot be found. You could also use the TryFindResource() method, which will not throw a runtime error; it will simply return null if the specified resource cannot be located.

When you run the program and click the OK Button, you see the gradients change appropriately. Now add the following code to the Cancel_OnClick() event handler:

```
private void Cancel_OnClick(object sender, RoutedEventArgs e)
{
  // Put a totally new brush into the myBrush slot.
  Resources["myBrush"]=new SolidColorBrush(Colors.Red);
}
```

Run the program again, click the Cancel Button, and nothing happens!

The {DynamicResource} Markup Extension

It is also possible for a property to use the DynamicResource markup extension. To see the difference, change the markup for the Cancel Button to the following:

```
<Button Name="Cancel" Margin="25" Height="200" Width="200" Content="Cancel"
               FontSize="20" Background="{DynamicResource myBrush}" Click="Cancel_OnClick"/>
```

This time, when you click the Cancel Button, the background for the Cancel Button changes, but the background for the OK Button remains the same. This is because the {DynamicResource} markup extension can detect whether the underlying keyed object has been replaced with a new object. As you might guess, this requires some extra runtime infrastructure, so you should typically stick to using {StaticResource} unless you know you have an object resource that will be swapped with a different object at runtime and you want all items using that resource to be informed.

Application-Level Resources

When you have object resources in a window's resource dictionary, all items in the window are free to make use of it, but other windows in the application cannot. The solution to share resources across your application is to define the object resource at the application level, rather than at the window level. There is no way to automate this within Visual Studio, so simply cut the current brush object out of the <Windows.Resources> scope and place it in the <Application.Resources> scope in your App.xaml file.

Now any additional window or control in your application is free to use this same brush. If you want to set the Background property for a control, the application-level resources are available for selection, as shown in Figure 28-5.

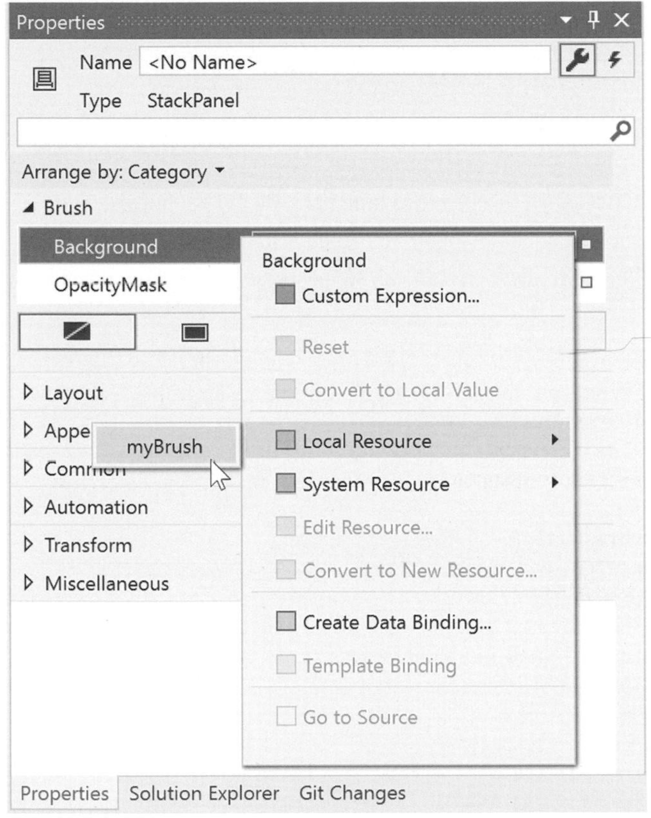

Figure 28-5. *Applying application-level resources*

■ **Note** Placing the resources at the application level and assigning it to a control's property will freeze the resource, preventing changing values at runtime. The resource can be cloned, and the clone can be updated.

Defining Merged Resource Dictionaries

Application-level resources are a quite often good enough, but they do not help reuse across projects. In this case, you want to define what is known as a *merged resource dictionary*. Think of it as a class library for WPF resources; it is nothing more than a XAML file that contains a collection of resources. A single project can have as many of these files as required (one for brushes, one for animations, etc.), each of which can be inserted using the Add New Item dialog box activated via the Project menu (see Figure 28-6).

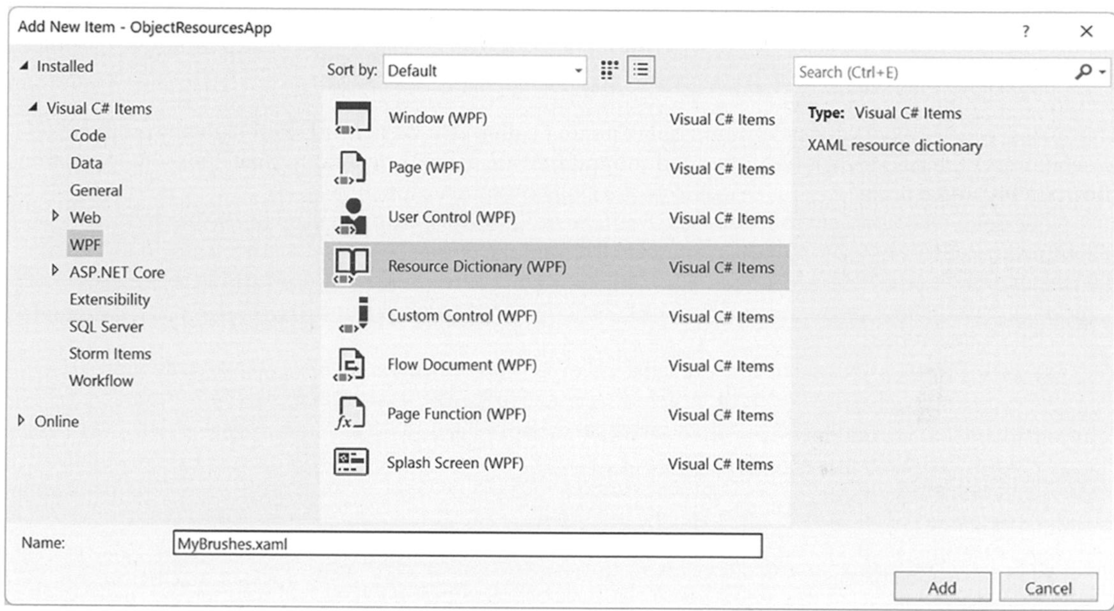

Figure 28-6. *Inserting a new merged resource dictionary*

In the new `MyBrushes.xaml` file, cut the current resources in the `Application.Resources` scope and move them into your dictionary, like so:

```
<ResourceDictionary xmlns=http://schemas.microsoft.com/winfx/2006/xaml/presentation
  xmlns:local="clr-namespace:ObjectResourcesApp"
  xmlns:x="http://schemas.microsoft.com/winfx/2006/xaml">
  <RadialGradientBrush x:Key="myBrush">
    <GradientStop Color="#FFC44EC4" Offset="0" />
    <GradientStop Color="#FF829CEB" Offset="1" />
    <GradientStop Color="#FF793879" Offset="0.669" />
  </RadialGradientBrush>
</ResourceDictionary>
```

Even though this resource dictionary is part of your project, all resource dictionaries must be merged (typically at the application level) into an existing resource dictionary to be used. To do this, use the following format in the `App.xaml` file (note that multiple resource dictionaries can be merged by adding multiple `<ResourceDictionary>` elements within the `<ResourceDictionary.MergedDictionaries>` scope):

```
<Application.Resources>
  <ResourceDictionary>
    <ResourceDictionary.MergedDictionaries>
```

```
        <ResourceDictionary Source="MyBrushes.xaml"/>
      </ResourceDictionary.MergedDictionaries>
    </ResourceDictionary>
  </Application.Resources>
```

The problem with this approach is that each resource file must be added to each project that needs the resources. A better approach for sharing resources is to define a .NET class library to share between projects, which you will do next.

Defining a Resource-Only Assembly

The easiest way to build a resource-only assembly is to begin with a WPF User Control Library project. Add such a project (named MyBrushesLibrary) to your current solution via the Add ➤ New Project menu option of Visual and add a project reference to it from the ObjectResourcesApp project.

Now, delete the `UserControl1.xaml` file from the project. Next, drag and drop the `MyBrushes.xaml` file into your `MyBrushesLibrary` project and delete it from the `ObjectResourcesApp` project. Finally, open `MyBrushes.xaml` in the `MyBrushesLibrary` project and change the `x:local` namespace in the file to `clr-namespace:MyBrushesLibrary`. Your `MyBrushes.xaml` file should look like this:

```
<ResourceDictionary xmlns="http://schemas.microsoft.com/winfx/2006/xaml/presentation"
                    xmlns:x="http://schemas.microsoft.com/winfx/2006/xaml"
                    xmlns:local="clr-namespace:MyBrushesLibrary">
    <RadialGradientBrush x:Key="myBrush">
        <GradientStop Color="#FFC44EC4" Offset="0" />
        <GradientStop Color="#FF829CEB" Offset="1" />
        <GradientStop Color="#FF793879" Offset="0.669" />
    </RadialGradientBrush>
</ResourceDictionary>
```

Compile your User Control Library project. Now, merge these binary resources into the application-level resource dictionary of the `ObjectResourcesApp` project. Doing so, however, requires some rather funky syntax, shown here:

```
<Application.Resources>
  <ResourceDictionary>
    <ResourceDictionary.MergedDictionaries>
      <!-- The syntax is /NameOfAssembly;Component/NameOfXamlFileInAssembly.xaml -->
      <ResourceDictionary Source="/MyBrushesLibrary;Component/MyBrushes.xaml"/>
    </ResourceDictionary.MergedDictionaries>
  </ResourceDictionary>
</Application.Resources>
```

First, be aware that this string is space sensitive. If you have extra whitespace around your semicolon or forward slashes, you will generate errors. The first part of the string is the friendly name of the external library (no file extension). After the semicolon, type in the word `Component` followed by the name of the compiled binary resource, which will be identical to the original XAML resource dictionary.

That wraps up the examination of WPF's resource management system. You will make good use of these techniques for most (if not all) of your applications. Next up, let's investigate the integrated animation API of Windows Presentation Foundation.

Understanding WPF's Animation Services

In addition to the graphical rendering services you examined in Chapter 27, WPF supplies a programming interface to support animation services. The term *animation* may bring to mind visions of spinning company logos, a sequence of rotating image resources (to provide the illusion of movement), text bouncing across the screen, or specific types of programs such as video games or multimedia applications.

While WPF's animation APIs could certainly be used for such purposes, animation can be used any time you want to give an application additional flair. For example, you could build an animation for a button on a screen that magnifies slightly when the mouse cursor hovers within its boundaries (and shrinks back once the mouse cursor moves beyond the boundaries). Or you could animate a window so that it closes using a particular visual appearance, such as slowly fading into transparency. A more business application-centric use is to fade in error messages on an application screen to improve the user experience. In fact, WPF's animation support can be used within any sort of application (a business application, multimedia programs, video games, etc.) whenever you want to provide a more engaging user experience.

As with many other aspects of WPF, the notion of building animations is nothing new. What is new is that, unlike other APIs you might have used in the past (including Windows Forms), developers are not required to author the necessary infrastructure by hand. Under WPF, there is no need to create the background threads or timers used to advance the animation sequence, define custom types to represent the animation, erase and redraw images, or bother with tedious mathematical calculations. Like other aspects of WPF, you can build an animation entirely using XAML, entirely using C# code, or using a combination of the two.

■ **Note** Visual Studio has no support for authoring animations using GUI animation tools. If you author an animation with Visual Studio, you will do so by typing in the XAML directly. However, Blend for Visual Studio (the companion product that ships with Visual Studio 2019) does indeed have a built-in animation editor that can simplify your life a good deal.

The Role of the Animation Class Types

To understand WPF's animation support, you must begin by examining the animation classes within the `System.Windows.Media.Animation` namespace of `PresentationCore.dll`. Here, you will find more than 100 different class types that are named using the `Animation` token.

These classes can be placed into one of three broad categories. First, any class that follows the name convention *DataType*`Animation` (`ByteAnimation`, `ColorAnimation`, `DoubleAnimation`, `Int32Animation`, etc.) allows you to work with linear interpolation animations. This enables you to change a value smoothly over time from a start value to a final value.

Next, the classes that follow the naming convention *DataType*`AnimationUsingKeyFrames` (`StringAnimationUsingKeyFrames`, `DoubleAnimationUsingKeyFrames`, `PointAnimationUsingKeyFrames`, etc.) represent "key frame animations," which allow you to cycle through a set of defined values over a period of time. For example, you could use key frames to change the caption of a button by cycling through a series of individual characters.

Finally, classes that follow the *DataType*`AnimationUsingPath` naming convention (`DoubleAnimationUsingPath`, `PointAnimationUsingPath`, among others) are path-based animations that allow you to animate objects to move along a path you define. By way of an example, if you were building a GPS application, you could use a path-based animation to move an item along the quickest travel route to the user's destination.

Now, obviously, these classes are *not* used to somehow provide an animation sequence directly to a variable of a particular data type (after all, how exactly could you animate the value "9" using an Int32Animation?).

For example, consider the Label type's Height and Width properties, both of which are dependency properties wrapping a double. If you wanted to define an animation that would increase the height of a label over a time span, you could connect a DoubleAnimation object to the Height property and allow WPF to take care of the details of performing the actual animation itself. By way of another example, if you wanted to transition the color of a brush type from green to yellow over a period of five seconds, you could do so using the ColorAnimation type.

To be clear, these Animation classes can be connected to any *dependency property* of a given object that matches the underlying types. As explained in Chapter 26, dependency properties are a specialized form of property required by many WPF services including animation, data binding, and styles.

By convention, a dependency property is defined as a static, read-only field of the class and is named by suffixing the word Property to the normal property name. For example, the dependency property for the Height property of a Button would be accessed in code using Button.HeightProperty.

The To, From, and By Properties

All Animation classes define the following handful of key properties that control the starting and ending values used to perform the animation:

- To: This property represents the animation's ending value.
- From: This property represents the animation's starting value.
- By: This property represents the total amount by which the animation changes its starting value.

Despite that all Animation classes support the To, From, and By properties, they do not receive them via virtual members of a base class. The reason for this is that the underlying types wrapped by these properties vary greatly (integers, colors, Thickness objects, etc.), and representing all possibilities using a single base class would result in complex coding constructs.

On a related note, you might also wonder why .NET generics were not used to define a single generic animation class with a single type parameter (e.g., Animate<T>). Again, given that there are so many underlying data types (colors, vectors, ints, strings, etc.) used to animated dependency properties, it would not be as clean a solution as you might expect (not to mention XAML has only limited support for generic types).

The Role of the Timeline Base Class

Although a single base class was not used to define virtual To, From, and By properties, the Animation classes do share a common base class: System.Windows.Media.Animation.Timeline. This type provides several additional properties that control the pacing of the animation, as described in Table 28-1.

Table 28-1. Key Members of the Timeline Base Class

Properties	Meaning in Life
AccelerationRatio, DecelerationRatio, SpeedRatio	These properties can be used to control the overall pacing of the animation sequence.
AutoReverse	This property gets or sets a value that indicates whether the timeline plays in reverse after it completes a forward iteration (the default value is false).
BeginTime	This property gets or sets the time at which this timeline should begin. The default value is 0, which begins the animation immediately.
Duration	This property allows you to set a duration of time to play the timeline.
FillBehavior, RepeatBehavior	These properties are used to control what should happen once the timeline has completed (repeat the animation, do nothing, etc.).

Authoring an Animation in C# Code

Specifically, you will build a Window that contains a Button, which has the odd behavior of spinning in a circle (based on the upper-left corner) whenever the mouse enters its surface area. Begin by creating a new WPF application named SpinningButtonAnimationApp. Update the initial markup to the following (note you are handling the button's MouseEnter event):

```
<Button x:Name="btnSpinner" Height="50" Width="100" Content="I Spin!"
      MouseEnter="btnSpinner_MouseEnter" Click="btnSpinner_OnClick"/>
```

In the code-behind file, import the System.Windows.Media.Animation namespace and add the following code in the window's C# code file:

```
private bool _isSpinning=false;

private void btnSpinner_MouseEnter(
  object sender, MouseEventArgs e)
{
  if (!_isSpinning)
  {
    _isSpinning=true;
    // Make a double animation object, and register
    // with the Completed event.
    var dblAnim=new DoubleAnimation();
    dblAnim.Completed +=(o, s)=> { _isSpinning=false; };
    // Set the start value and end value.
    dblAnim.From=0;
    dblAnim.To=360;
    // Now, create a RotateTransform object, and set
    // it to the RenderTransform property of our
    // button.
    var rt=new RotateTransform();
    btnSpinner.RenderTransform=rt;
```

```
    // Now, animation the RotateTransform object.
    rt.BeginAnimation(RotateTransform.AngleProperty, dblAnim);
  }
}
private void btnSpinner_OnClick(
  object sender, RoutedEventArgs e)
{

}
```

The first major task of this method is to configure a DoubleAnimation object, which will start at the value 0 and end at the value 360. Notice that you are handling the Completed event on this object as well, to toggle a class-level bool variable that is used to ensure that if an animation is currently being performed, you don't "reset" it to start again.

Next, you create a RotateTransform object that is connected to the RenderTransform property of your Button control (btnSpinner). Finally, you inform the RenderTransform object to begin animating its Angle property using your DoubleAnimation object. When you are authoring animations in code, you typically do so by calling BeginAnimation() and then pass in the underlying *dependency property* you would like to animate (remember, by convention, this is a static field on the class), followed by a related animation object.

Let's add another animation to the program, which will cause the button to fade into invisibility when clicked. First, add the following code in the Click event handler:

```
private void btnSpinner_OnClick(
  object sender, RoutedEventArgs e)
{
  var dblAnim=new DoubleAnimation
  {
    From=1.0,
    To=0.0
  };
  btnSpinner.BeginAnimation(Button.OpacityProperty, dblAnim);
}
```

Here, you are changing the Opacity property value to fade the button out of view. Currently, however, this is hard to do, as the button is spinning very fast! How, then, can you control the pace of an animation? Glad you asked.

Controlling the Pace of an Animation

By default, an animation will take approximately one second to transition between the values assigned to the From and To properties. Therefore, your button has one second to spin around a full 360-degree angle, while the button will fade away to invisibility (when clicked) over the course of one second.

If you want to define a custom amount of time for an animation's transition, you may do so via the animation object's Duration property, which can be set to an instance of a Duration object. Typically, the time span is established by passing a TimeSpan object to the Duration's constructor. Consider the following update that will give the button a full four seconds to rotate:

```
private void btnSpinner_MouseEnter(
  object sender, MouseEventArgs e)
{
  if (!_isSpinning)
  {
    _isSpinning=true;

    // Make a double animation object, and register
    // with the Completed event.
    var dblAnim=new DoubleAnimation();
    dblAnim.Completed +=(o, s)=> { _isSpinning=false; };

    // Button has four seconds to finish the spin!
    dblAnim.Duration=new Duration(TimeSpan.FromSeconds(4));

...
  }
}
```

With this adjustment, you should have a fighting chance of clicking the button while it is spinning, at which point it will fade away.

■ **Note** The BeginTime property of an Animation class also takes a TimeSpan object. Recall that this property can be set to establish a wait time before starting an animation sequence.

Reversing and Looping an Animation

You can also tell Animation objects to play an animation in reverse at the completion of the animation sequence by setting the AutoReverse property to true. For example, if you want to have the button come back into view after it has faded away, you could author the following:

```
private void btnSpinner_OnClick(object sender, RoutedEventArgs e)
{
  DoubleAnimation dblAnim=new DoubleAnimation
  {
    From=1.0,
    To=0.0
  };
  // Reverse when done.
  dblAnim.AutoReverse=true;
  btnSpinner.BeginAnimation(Button.OpacityProperty, dblAnim);
}
```

If you would like to have an animation repeat some number of times (or to never stop once activated), you can do so using the RepeatBehavior property, which is common to all Animation classes. If you pass in a simple numerical value to the constructor, you can specify a hard-coded number of times to repeat.

On the other hand, if you pass in a TimeSpan object to the constructor, you can establish an amount of time the animation should repeat. Finally, if you want an animation to loop *ad infinitum*, you can simply specify RepeatBehavior.Forever. Consider the following ways you could change the repeat behaviors of either of the DoubleAnimation objects used in this example:

```
// Loop forever.
dblAnim.RepeatBehavior=RepeatBehavior.Forever;

// Loop three times.
dblAnim.RepeatBehavior=new RepeatBehavior(3);

// Loop for 30 seconds.
dblAnim.RepeatBehavior=new RepeatBehavior(TimeSpan.FromSeconds(30));
```

That wraps up your investigation about how to animate aspects of an object using C# code and the WPF animation API. Next, you will learn how to do the same using XAML.

Authoring Animations in XAML

Authoring animations in markup is like authoring them in code, at least for simple, straightforward animation sequences. When you need to capture more complex animations, which may involve changing the values of numerous properties at once, the amount of markup can grow considerably. Even if you use a tool to generate XAML-based animations, it is important to know the basics of how an animation is represented in XAML because this will make it easier for you to modify and tweak tool-generated content.

■ **Note** You will find a number of XAML files in the XamlAnimations folder of the downloadable source code. As you go through the next several pages, copy these markup files into your custom XAML editor or into the Kaxaml editor to see the results.

For the most part, creating an animation is like what you saw already. You still configure an Animation object and associate it to an object's property. One big difference, however, is that WPF is not function call friendly. As a result, instead of calling BeginAnimation(), you use a *storyboard* as a layer of indirection.

Let's walk through a complete example of an animation defined in terms of XAML, followed by a detailed breakdown. The following XAML definition will display a window that contains a single label. As soon as the Label object loads into memory, it begins an animation sequence in which the font size increases from 12 points to 100 over a period of four seconds. The animation will repeat for as long as the Window object is loaded in memory. You can find this markup in the GrowLabelFont.xaml file, so copy it into Kaxaml (make sure to press F5 to show the window) and observe the behavior.

```
<Window
  xmlns="http://schemas.microsoft.com/winfx/2006/xaml/presentation"
  xmlns:x="http://schemas.microsoft.com/winfx/2006/xaml"
  Height="200" Width="600" WindowStartupLocation="CenterScreen" Title="Growing Label Font!">
  <StackPanel>
    <Label Content="Interesting...">
      <Label.Triggers>
        <EventTrigger RoutedEvent="Label.Loaded">
          <EventTrigger.Actions>
```

```
            <BeginStoryboard>
              <Storyboard TargetProperty="FontSize">
                <DoubleAnimation From="12" To="100" Duration="0:0:4"
                  RepeatBehavior="Forever"/>
              </Storyboard>
            </BeginStoryboard>
          </EventTrigger.Actions>
        </EventTrigger>
      </Label.Triggers>
    </Label>
  </StackPanel>
</Window>
```

Now, let's break this example down, bit by bit.

The Role of Storyboards

Working from the innermost element outward, you first encounter the <DoubleAnimation> element, which makes use of the same properties you set in procedural code (From, To, Duration, and RepeatBehavior).

```
<DoubleAnimation From="12" To="100" Duration="0:0:4"
                 RepeatBehavior="Forever"/>
```

As mentioned, Animation elements are placed within a <Storyboard> element, which is used to map the animation object to a given property on the parent type via the TargetProperty property, which in this case is FontSize. A <Storyboard> is always wrapped in a parent element named <BeginStoryboard>.

```
<BeginStoryboard>
  <Storyboard TargetProperty="FontSize">
    <DoubleAnimation From="12" To="100" Duration="0:0:4"
                     RepeatBehavior="Forever"/>
  </Storyboard>
</BeginStoryboard>
```

The Role of Event Triggers

After the <BeginStoryboard> element has been defined, you need to specify some sort of action that will cause the animation to begin executing. WPF has a few different ways to respond to runtime conditions in markup, one of which is termed a *trigger*. From a high level, you can consider a trigger a way of responding to an event condition in XAML, without the need for procedural code.

Typically, when you respond to an event in C#, you author custom code that will execute when the event occurs. A trigger, however, is just a way to be notified that some event condition has happened ("I'm loaded into memory!" or "The mouse is over me!" or "I have focus!").

Once you have been notified that an event condition has occurred, you can start the storyboard. In this example, you are responding to the Label being loaded into memory. Because it is the Label's Loaded event you are interested in, the <EventTrigger> is placed in the Label's trigger collection.

```
<Label Content="Interesting...">
  <Label.Triggers>
    <EventTrigger RoutedEvent="Label.Loaded">
      <EventTrigger.Actions>
```

```
        <BeginStoryboard>
          <Storyboard TargetProperty="FontSize">
            <DoubleAnimation From="12" To="100" Duration="0:0:4"
                             RepeatBehavior="Forever"/>
          </Storyboard>
        </BeginStoryboard>
      </EventTrigger.Actions>
    </EventTrigger>
  </Label.Triggers>
</Label>
```

Let's see another example of defining an animation in XAML, this time using a *key frame* animation.

Animation Using Discrete Key Frames

Unlike the linear interpolation animation objects, which can only move between a starting point and an ending point, the *key frame* counterparts allow you to create a collection of specific values for an animation that should take place at specific times.

To illustrate the use of a discrete key frame type, assume you want to build a `Button` control that animates its content so that over the course of three seconds the value "OK!" appears, one character at a time. You will find the following markup in the `AnimateString.xaml` file. Copy this markup into your `MyXamlPad.exe` program (or Kaxaml) and view the results:

```
<Window xmlns="http://schemas.microsoft.com/winfx/2006/xaml/presentation"
   xmlns:x="http://schemas.microsoft.com/winfx/2006/xaml"
   Height="100" Width="300"
   WindowStartupLocation="CenterScreen" Title="Animate String Data!">
   <StackPanel>
     <Button Name="myButton" Height="40"
             FontSize="16pt" FontFamily="Verdana" Width="100">
      <Button.Triggers>
        <EventTrigger RoutedEvent="Button.Loaded">
          <BeginStoryboard>
            <Storyboard>
              <StringAnimationUsingKeyFrames RepeatBehavior="Forever"
                Storyboard.TargetProperty="Content"
                Duration="0:0:3">
                <DiscreteStringKeyFrame Value="" KeyTime="0:0:0" />
                <DiscreteStringKeyFrame Value="O" KeyTime="0:0:1" />
                <DiscreteStringKeyFrame Value="OK" KeyTime="0:0:1.5" />
                <DiscreteStringKeyFrame Value="OK!" KeyTime="0:0:2" />
              </StringAnimationUsingKeyFrames>
            </Storyboard>
          </BeginStoryboard>
        </EventTrigger>
      </Button.Triggers>
    </Button>
  </StackPanel>
</Window>
```

First, notice that you have defined an event trigger for your button to ensure that your storyboard executes when the button has loaded into memory. The StringAnimationUsingKeyFrames class oversees changing the content of the button, via the Storyboard.TargetProperty value.

Within the scope of the <StringAnimationUsingKeyFrames> element, you define four DiscreteStringKeyFrame elements, which change the button's Content property over the course of two seconds (note that the duration established by StringAnimationUsingKeyFrames is a total of three seconds, so you will see a slight pause between the final ! and looping O).

Now that you have a better feel for how to build animations in C# code and XAML, let's look at the role of WPF styles, which make heavy use of graphics, object resources, and animations.

Understanding the Role of WPF Styles

When you are building the UI of a WPF application, it is not uncommon for a family of controls to require a shared look and feel. For example, you might want all button types to have the same height, width, background color, and font size for their string content. Although you could handle this by setting each button's individual properties to identical values, such an approach makes it difficult to implement changes down the road because you would need to reset the same set of properties on multiple objects for every change.

Thankfully, WPF offers a simple way to constrain the look and feel of related controls using *styles*. Simply put, a WPF style is an object that maintains a collection of property-value pairs. Programmatically speaking, an individual style is represented using the System.Windows.Style class. This class has a property named Setters, which exposes a strongly typed collection of Setter objects. It is the Setter object that allows you to define the property-value pairs.

In addition to the Setters collection, the Style class also defines a few other important members that allow you to incorporate triggers, restrict where a style can be applied, and even create a new style based on an existing style (think of it as "style inheritance"). Be aware of the following members of the Style class:

- Triggers: Exposes a collection of trigger objects, which allow you to capture various event conditions within a style
- BasedOn: Allows you to build a new style based on an existing style
- TargetType: Allows you to constrain where a style can be applied

Defining and Applying a Style

In almost every case, a Style object will be packaged as an object resource. Like any object resource, you can package it at the window or application level, as well as within a dedicated resource dictionary (this is great because it makes the Style object easily accessible throughout your application). Now recall that the goal is to define a Style object that fills (at minimum) the Setters collection with a set of property-value pairs.

Let's build a style that captures the basic font characteristics of a control in your application. Start by creating a new WPF application named WpfStyles. Open your App.xaml file and define the following named style:

```
<Application.Resources>
  <Style x:Key="BasicControlStyle">
    <Setter Property="Control.FontSize" Value="14"/>
    <Setter Property="Control.Height" Value="40"/>
    <Setter Property="Control.Cursor" Value="Hand"/>
  </Style>
</Application.Resources>
```

Notice that your BasicControlStyle adds three Setter objects to the internal collection. Now, let's apply this style to a few controls in your main window. Because this style is an object resource, the controls that want to use it still need to use the {StaticResource} or {DynamicResource} markup extension to locate the style. When they find the style, they will set the resource item to the identically named Style property. Replace the default Grid control with the following markup:

```
<StackPanel>
  <Label x:Name="lblInfo" Content="This style is boring..."
         Style="{StaticResource BasicControlStyle}" Width="150"/>
  <Button x:Name="btnTestButton" Content="Yes, but we are reusing settings!"
         Style="{StaticResource BasicControlStyle}" Width="250"/>
</StackPanel>
```

If you view the Window in the Visual Studio designer (or run the application), you will find that both controls support the same cursor, height, and font size.

Overriding Style Settings

While both of your controls have opted into the style, if a control wants to apply a style and then change some of the defined settings, that is fine. For example, the Button will now use the Help cursor (rather than the Hand cursor defined in the style).

```
<Button x:Name="btnTestButton" Content="Yes, but we are reusing settings!"
        Cursor="Help" Style="{StaticResource BasicControlStyle}" Width="250" />
```

Styles are processed before the individual property settings of the control using the style; therefore, controls can "override" settings on a case-by-case basis.

The Effect of TargetType on Styles

Currently, your style is defined in such a way that any control can adopt it (and must do so explicitly by setting the control's Style property), given that each property is qualified by the Control class. For a program that defines dozens of settings, this would entail a good amount of repeated code. One way to clean this style up a bit is to use the TargetType attribute. When you add this attribute to a Style's opening element, you can mark exactly once where it can be applied (in this example, in App.XAML).

```
<Style x:Key="BasicControlStyle" TargetType="Control">
  <Setter Property="FontSize" Value="14"/>
  <Setter Property="Height" Value="40"/>
  <Setter Property="Cursor" Value="Hand"/>
</Style>
```

■ **Note** When you build a style that uses a base class type, you needn't be concerned if you assign a value to a dependency property not supported by derived types. If the derived type does not support a given dependency property, it is ignored.

This is somewhat helpful, but you still have a style that can apply to any control. The TargetType attribute is more useful when you want to define a style that can be applied to only a particular type of control. Add the following new style to the application's resource dictionary:

```
<Style x:Key="BigGreenButton" TargetType="Button">
  <Setter Property="FontSize" Value="20"/>
  <Setter Property="Height" Value="100"/>
  <Setter Property="Width" Value="100"/>
  <Setter Property="Background" Value="DarkGreen"/>
  <Setter Property="Foreground" Value="Yellow"/>
</Style>
```

This style will work only on Button controls (or a subclass of Button). If you apply it to an incompatible element, you will get markup and compiler errors. Add a new Button that uses this new style, as follows:

```
<Button x:Name="btnAnotherButton" Content="OK!" Margin="0,10,0,0"
    Style="{StaticResource BigGreenButton}" Width="250" Cursor="Help"/>
```

You will see output like that shown in Figure 28-7.

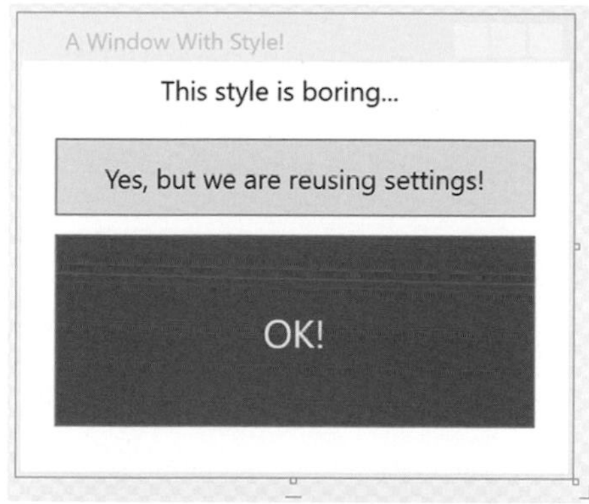

Figure 28-7. *Controls with different styles*

Another effect of TargetType is that the style will get applied to all elements of that type within the scope of the style definition if the x:Key property *does not* exist.

Here is another application-level style that will apply automatically to all TextBox controls in the current application:

```
<!-- The default style for all text boxes. -->
<Style TargetType="TextBox">
  <Setter Property="FontSize" Value="14"/>
  <Setter Property="Width" Value="100"/>
  <Setter Property="Height" Value="30"/>
  <Setter Property="BorderThickness" Value="5"/>
  <Setter Property="BorderBrush" Value="Red"/>
  <Setter Property="FontStyle" Value="Italic"/>
</Style>
```

You can now define any number of TextBox controls, and they will automatically get the defined look. If a given TextBox does not want this default look and feel, it can opt out by setting the Style property to {x:Null}. For example, txtTest will get the default unnamed style, while txtTest2 is doing things its own way.

```
<TextBox x:Name="txtTest"/>
<TextBox x:Name="txtTest2" Style="{x:Null}" BorderBrush="Black"
      BorderThickness="5" Height="60" Width="100" Text="Ha!"/>
```

Subclassing Existing Styles

You can also build new styles using an existing style, via the BasedOn property. The style you are extending must have been given a proper x:Key in the dictionary, as the derived style will reference it by name using the {StaticResource} or {DynamicResource} markup extension. Here is a new style based on BigGreenButton, which rotates the button element by 20 degrees:

```
<!-- This style is based on BigGreenButton. -->
<Style x:Key="TiltButton" TargetType="Button" BasedOn="{StaticResource BigGreenButton}">
  <Setter Property="Foreground" Value="White"/>
  <Setter Property="RenderTransform">
    <Setter.Value>
      <RotateTransform Angle="20"/>
    </Setter.Value>
  </Setter>
</Style>
```

To use this new style, update the markup for the button to this:

```
<Button x:Name="btnAnotherButton" Content="OK!" Margin="0,10,0,0"
    Style="{StaticResource TiltButton}" Width="250" Cursor="Help"/>
```

This changes the appearance to the image shown in Figure 28-8.

Figure 28-8. *Using a derived style*

Defining Styles with Triggers

WPF styles can also contain triggers by packaging up Trigger objects within the Triggers collection of the Style object. Using triggers in a style allows you to define certain <Setter> elements in such a way that they will be applied only if a given trigger condition is true. For example, perhaps you want to increase the size of a font when the mouse is over a button. Or maybe you want to make sure that the text box with the current focus is highlighted with a given color. Triggers are useful for these sorts of situations, in that they allow you to take specific actions when a property changes, without the need to author explicit C# code in a code-behind file.

Here is an update to the TextBox style that ensures that when a TextBox has the input focus, it will receive a yellow background:

```
<!-- The default style for all text boxes. -->
<Style TargetType="TextBox">
  <Setter Property="FontSize" Value="14"/>
  <Setter Property="Width" Value="100"/>
  <Setter Property="Height" Value="30"/>
  <Setter Property="BorderThickness" Value="5"/>
  <Setter Property="BorderBrush" Value="Red"/>
  <Setter Property="FontStyle" Value="Italic"/>
  <!-- The following setter will be applied only when the text box is in focus. -->
  <Style.Triggers>
    <Trigger Property="IsFocused" Value="True">
      <Setter Property="Background" Value="Yellow"/>
    </Trigger>
  </Style.Triggers>
</Style>
```

If you test this style, you'll find that as you tab between various TextBox objects, the currently selected TextBox has a bright yellow background (provided it has not opted out by assigning {x:Null} to the Style property).

Property triggers are also very smart, in that when the trigger's condition is *not true*, the property automatically receives the default assigned value. Therefore, as soon as a TextBox loses focus, it also automatically becomes the default color without any work on your part. In contrast, event triggers (examined when you looked at WPF animations) do not automatically revert to a previous condition.

Defining Styles with Multiple Triggers

Triggers can also be designed in such a way that the defined <Setter> elements will be applied when *multiple conditions* are true. Let's say you want to set the background of a TextBox to Yellow only if it has the active focus and the mouse is hovering within its boundaries. To do so, you can make use of the <MultiTrigger> element to define each condition, like so:

```
<!-- The default style for all text boxes. -->
<Style TargetType="TextBox">
  <Setter Property="FontSize" Value="14"/>
  <Setter Property="Width" Value="100"/>
  <Setter Property="Height" Value="30"/>
  <Setter Property="BorderThickness" Value="5"/>
  <Setter Property="BorderBrush" Value="Red"/>
  <Setter Property="FontStyle" Value="Italic"/>
  <!-- The following setter will be applied only when the text box is
  in focus AND the mouse is over the text box. -->
  <Style.Triggers>
    <MultiTrigger>
      <MultiTrigger.Conditions>
            <Condition Property="IsFocused" Value="True"/>
```

```
          <Condition Property="IsMouseOver" Value="True"/>
        </MultiTrigger.Conditions>
      <Setter Property="Background" Value="Yellow"/>
    </MultiTrigger>
  </Style.Triggers>
</Style>
```

Animated Styles

Styles can also incorporate triggers that kick off an animation sequence. Here is one final style that, when applied to Button controls, will cause the controls to grow and shrink in size when the mouse is inside the button's surface area:

```
<!-- The growing button style! -->
<Style x:Key="GrowingButtonStyle" TargetType="Button">
  <Setter Property="Height" Value="40"/>
  <Setter Property="Width" Value="100"/>
  <Style.Triggers>
    <Trigger Property="IsMouseOver" Value="True">
      <Trigger.EnterActions>
        <BeginStoryboard>
          <Storyboard TargetProperty="Height">
            <DoubleAnimation From="40" To="200"
                             Duration="0:0:2" AutoReverse="True"/>
          </Storyboard>
        </BeginStoryboard>
      </Trigger.EnterActions>
    </Trigger>
  </Style.Triggers>
</Style>
```

Here, the Triggers collection is on the lookout for the IsMouseOver property to return true. When this occurs, you define a <Trigger.EnterActions> element to execute a simple storyboard that forces the button to grow to a Height value of 200 (and then return to a Height of 40) over two seconds. If you want to perform other property changes, you could also define a <Trigger.ExitActions> scope to define any custom actions to take when IsMouseOver changes to false.

Assigning Styles Programmatically

Recall that a style can be applied at runtime as well. This can be helpful if you want to let end users choose how their UI looks and feels or if you need to enforce a look and feel based on security settings (e.g., the DisableAllButton style) or what have you.

During this project, you have defined several styles, many of which can apply to Button controls. So, let's retool the UI of your main window to allow the user to pick from some of these styles by selecting names in a ListBox. Based on the user's selection, you will apply the appropriate style. Here is the new (and final) markup for the <Window> element:

```
<DockPanel >
  <StackPanel Orientation="Horizontal" DockPanel.Dock="Top" Margin="0,0,0,50">
    <Label Content="Please Pick a Style for this Button" Height="50"/>
```

```
    <ListBox x:Name="lstStyles" Height="80" Width="150" Background="LightBlue"
             SelectionChanged="comboStyles_Changed" />
  </StackPanel>
  <Button x:Name="btnStyle" Height="40" Width="100" Content="OK!"/>
</DockPanel>
```

The ListBox control (named lstStyles) will be filled dynamically within the window's constructor, like so:

```
public MainWindow()
{
  InitializeComponent();
  // Fill the list box with all the Button styles.
  lstStyles.Items.Add("GrowingButtonStyle");
  lstStyles.Items.Add("TiltButton");
  lstStyles.Items.Add("BigGreenButton");
  lstStyles.Items.Add("BasicControlStyle");}
}
```

The final task is to handle the SelectionChanged event in the related code file. Notice in the following code how you can extract the current resource by name, using the inherited TryFindResource() method:

```
private void comboStyles_Changed(object sender, SelectionChangedEventArgs e)
{
  // Get the selected style name from the list box.
  var currStyle=(Style)TryFindResource(lstStyles.SelectedValue);
  if (currStyle==null) return;
  // Set the style of the button type.
  this.btnStyle.Style=currStyle;
}
```

When you run this application, you can pick from one of these four button styles on the fly. Figure 28-9 shows your completed application.

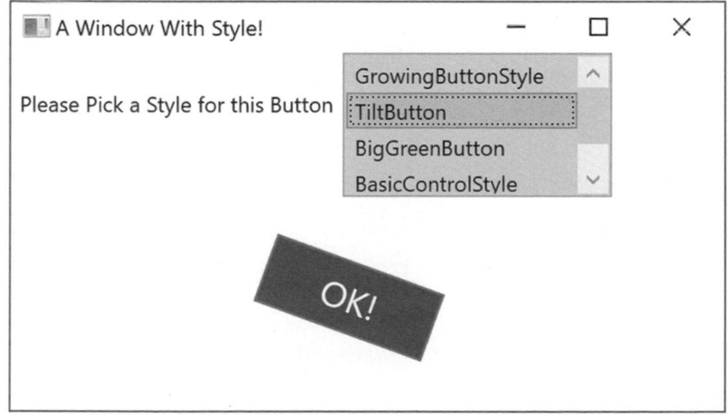

Figure 28-9. *Controls with different styles*

Logical Trees, Visual Trees, and Default Templates

Now that you understand styles and resources, there are a few more preparatory topics to investigate before you begin learning how to build custom controls. Specifically, you need to learn the distinction between a logical tree, a visual tree, and a default template. When you are typing XAML into Visual Studio or a tool such as kaxaml.exe, your markup is the *logical view* of the XAML document. As well, if you author C# code that adds new items to a layout control, you are inserting new items into the logical tree. Essentially, a logical view represents how your content will be positioned within the various layout managers for a main Window (or another root element, such as Page or NavigationWindow).

However, behind every logical tree is a much more verbose representation termed a *visual tree*, which is used internally by WPF to correctly render elements onto the screen. Within any visual tree, there will be full details of the templates and styles used to render each object, including any necessary drawings, shapes, visuals, and animations.

It is useful to understand the distinction between logical and visual trees because when you are building a custom control template, you are essentially replacing all or part of the default visual tree of a control and inserting your own. Therefore, if you want a Button control to be rendered as a star shape, you could define a new star template and plug it into the Button's visual tree. Logically, the Button is still of type Button, and it supports the properties, methods, and events as expected. But visually, it has taken on a whole new appearance. This fact alone makes WPF an extremely useful API, given that other toolkits would require you to build a new class to make a star-shaped button. With WPF, you simply need to define new markup.

■ **Note** WPF controls are often described as *lookless*. This refers to the fact that the look and feel of a WPF control is completely independent (and customizable) from its behavior.

Programmatically Inspecting a Logical Tree

While analyzing a window's logical tree at runtime is not a tremendously common WPF programming activity, it is worth mentioning that the System.Windows namespace defines a class named LogicalTreeHelper, which allows you to inspect the structure of a logical tree at runtime. To illustrate the connection between logical trees, visual trees, and control templates, create a new WPF application named TreesAndTemplatesApp.

Replace the Grid with the following markup that contains two Button controls and a large read-only TextBox with scrollbars enabled. Make sure you use the IDE to handle the Click event of each button. The following XAML will do nicely:

```
<DockPanel LastChildFill="True">
  <Border Height="50" DockPanel.Dock="Top" BorderBrush="Blue">
    <StackPanel Orientation="Horizontal">
      <Button x:Name="btnShowLogicalTree" Content="Logical Tree of Window"
            Margin="4" BorderBrush="Blue" Height="40" Click="btnShowLogicalTree_Click"/>
      <Button x:Name="btnShowVisualTree" Content="Visual Tree of Window"
            BorderBrush="Blue" Height="40" Click="btnShowVisualTree_Click"/>
    </StackPanel>
  </Border>
```

```
  <TextBox x:Name="txtDisplayArea" Margin="10" Background="AliceBlue" IsReadOnly="True"
         BorderBrush="Red" VerticalScrollBarVisibility="Auto" HorizontalScrollBarVisibility
         ="Auto" />
</DockPanel>
```

Within your C# code file, define a string member variable named _dataToShow. Now, within the Click handler for the btnShowLogicalTree object, call a helper function that calls itself recursively to populate the string variable with the logical tree of the Window. To do so, you will call the static GetChildren() method of LogicalTreeHelper. Here is the code:

```
private string _dataToShow=string.Empty;

private void btnShowLogicalTree_Click(object sender, RoutedEventArgs e)
{
  _dataToShow="";
  BuildLogicalTree(0, this);
  txtDisplayArea.Text=_dataToShow;
}

void BuildLogicalTree(int depth, object obj)
{
  // Add the type name to the dataToShow member variable.
  _dataToShow +=new string(' ', depth) + obj.GetType().Name + "\n";
  // If an item is not a DependencyObject, skip it.
  if (!(obj is DependencyObject))
    return;
  // Make a recursive call for each logical child.
  foreach (var child in LogicalTreeHelper.GetChildren((DependencyObject)obj))
  {
      BuildLogicalTree(depth + 5, child);
  }
}
private void btnShowVisualTree_Click(
  object sender, RoutedEventArgs e)
{
}
```

If you run your application and click this first button, you will see a tree print in the text area, which is just about an exact replica of the original XAML (see Figure 28-10).

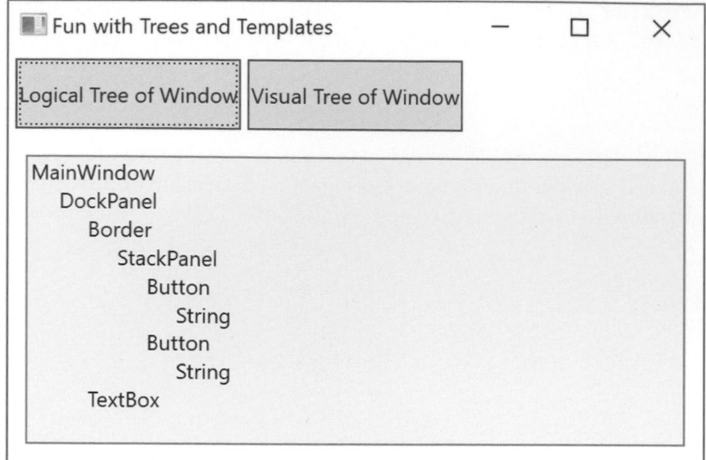

Figure 28-10. *Viewing a logical tree at runtime*

Programmatically Inspecting a Visual Tree

A Window's visual tree can also be inspected at runtime using the VisualTreeHelper class of System.Windows.Media. Here is a Click implementation of the second Button control (btnShowVisualTree), which performs similar recursive logic to build a textual representation of the visual tree:

```
using System.Windows.Media;

private void btnShowVisualTree_Click(object sender, RoutedEventArgs e)
{
  _dataToShow="";
  BuildVisualTree(0, this);
  txtDisplayArea.Text=_dataToShow;
}
void BuildVisualTree(int depth, DependencyObject obj)
{
  // Add the type name to the dataToShow member variable.
  _dataToShow +=new string(' ', depth) + obj.GetType().Name + "\n";
  // Make a recursive call for each visual child.
  for (int i=0; i < VisualTreeHelper.GetChildrenCount(obj); i++)
  {
    BuildVisualTree(depth + 1, VisualTreeHelper.GetChild(obj, i));
  }
}
```

As you can see in Figure 28-11, the visual tree exposes several lower-level rendering agents such as ContentPresenter, AdornerDecorator, TextBoxLineDrawingVisual, and so forth.

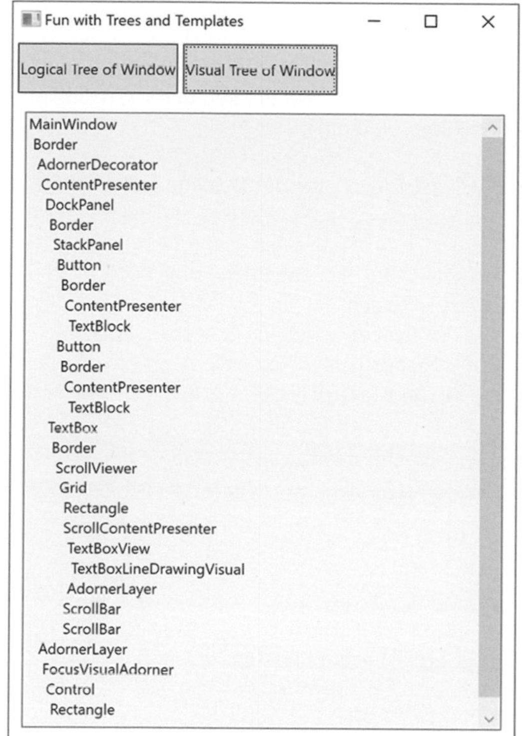

Figure 28-11. *Viewing a visual tree at runtime*

Programmatically Inspecting a Control's Default Template

Recall that a visual tree is used by WPF to understand how to render a `Window` and all contained elements. Every WPF control stores its own set of rendering commands within its default template. Programmatically speaking, any template can be represented as an instance of the `ControlTemplate` class. As well, you can obtain a control's default template by using the aptly named `Template` property, like so:

```
// Get the default template of the Button.
Button myBtn=new Button();
ControlTemplate template=myBtn.Template;
```

Likewise, you could create a new `ControlTemplate` object in code and plug it into a control's `Template` property as follows:

```
// Plug in a new template for the button to use.
Button myBtn=new Button();
ControlTemplate customTemplate=new ControlTemplate();

// Assume this method adds all the code for a star template.
MakeStarTemplate(customTemplate);
myBtn.Template=customTemplate;
```

While you could build a new template in code, it is far more common to do so in XAML. However, before you start building your own templates, let's finish the current example and add the ability to view the default template of a WPF control at runtime. This can be a useful way to look at the overall composition of a template. Update the markup of your window with a new StackPanel of controls docked to the left side of the master DockPanel, defined as so (placed just before the <TextBox> element):

```
<Border DockPanel.Dock="Left" Margin="10" BorderBrush="DarkGreen" BorderThickness="4"
Width="358">
  <StackPanel>
    <Label Content="Enter Full Name of WPF Control" Width="340" FontWeight="DemiBold" />
    <TextBox x:Name="txtFullName" Width="340" BorderBrush="Green"
             Background="BlanchedAlmond" Height="22" Text="System.Windows.Controls.Button" />
    <Button x:Name="btnTemplate" Content="See Template" BorderBrush="Green"
            Height="40" Width="100" Margin="5" Click="btnTemplate_Click"
            HorizontalAlignment="Left" />
    <Border BorderBrush="DarkGreen" BorderThickness="2" Height="260"
            Width="301" Margin="10" Background="LightGreen" >
      <StackPanel x:Name="stackTemplatePanel" />
    </Border>
  </StackPanel>
</Border>
```

Add an empty event handler function for the btnTemplate_Click() event like this:

```
private void btnTemplate_Click(
  object sender, RoutedEventArgs e)
{
}
```

The upper-left text area allows you to enter in the fully qualified name of a WPF control located in the PresentationFramework.dll assembly. Once the library is loaded, you will dynamically create an instance of the object and display it in the large square in the bottom left. Finally, the control's default template will be displayed in the right-hand text area. First, add a new member variable to your C# class of type Control, like so:

```
private Control _ctrlToExamine=null;
```

Here is the remaining code, which will require you to import the System.Reflection, System.Xml, and System.Windows.Markup namespaces:

```
private void btnTemplate_Click(
  object sender, RoutedEventArgs e)
{
  _dataToShow="";
  ShowTemplate();
  txtDisplayArea.Text=_dataToShow;
}
```

```
private void ShowTemplate()
{
  // Remove the control that is currently in the preview area.
  if (_ctrlToExamine !=null)
    stackTemplatePanel.Children.Remove(_ctrlToExamine);
  try
  {
    // Load PresentationFramework, and create an instance of the
    // specified control. Give it a size for display purposes, then add to the
    // empty StackPanel.
    Assembly asm=Assembly.Load("PresentationFramework, Version=4.0.0.0," +
      "Culture=neutral, PublicKeyToken=31bf3856ad364e35");
    _ctrlToExamine=(Control)asm.CreateInstance(txtFullName.Text);
    _ctrlToExamine.Height=200;
    _ctrlToExamine.Width=200;
    _ctrlToExamine.Margin=new Thickness(5);
    stackTemplatePanel.Children.Add(_ctrlToExamine);
    // Define some XML settings to preserve indentation.
    var xmlSettings=new XmlWriterSettings{Indent=true};
    // Create a StringBuilder to hold the XAML.
    var strBuilder=new StringBuilder();
    // Create an XmlWriter based on our settings.
    var xWriter=XmlWriter.Create(strBuilder, xmlSettings);
    // Now save the XAML into the XmlWriter object based on the ControlTemplate.
    XamlWriter.Save(_ctrlToExamine.Template, xWriter);
    // Display XAML in the text box.
    _dataToShow=strBuilder.ToString();
  }
  catch (Exception ex)
  {
    _dataToShow=ex.Message;
  }
}
```

The bulk of the work is just tinkering with the compiled BAML resource to map it into a XAML string. Figure 28-12 shows your final application in action, displaying the default template of the System.Windows.Controls.DatePicker control. The image shows the Calendar, which is accessed by clicking the button on the right side of the control.

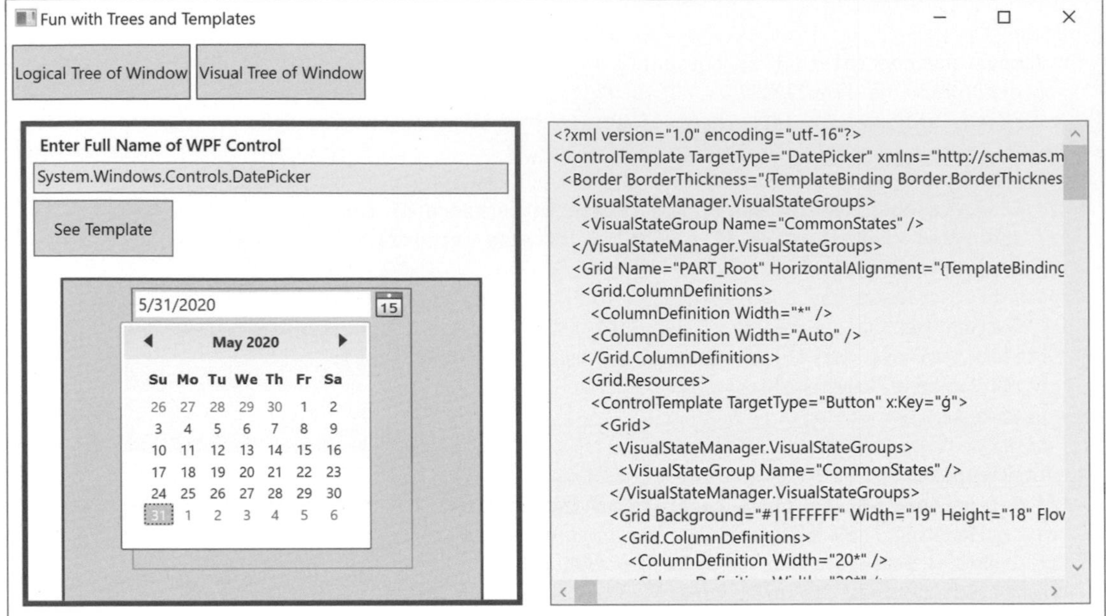

Figure 28-12. *Investigating a ControlTemplate at runtime*

Great! You should have a better idea about how logical trees, visual trees, and control default templates work together. Now you can spend the remainder of this chapter learning how to build custom templates and user controls.

Building a Control Template with the Trigger Framework

When you build a custom template for a control, you could do so with nothing but C# code. Using this approach, you would add data to a `ControlTemplate` object and then assign it to a control's `Template` property. Most of the time, however, you will define the look and feel of a `ControlTemplate` using XAML and add bits of code (or possibly quite a bit of code) to drive the runtime behavior.

In the remainder of this chapter, you will examine how to build custom templates using Visual Studio. Along the way, you will learn about the WPF trigger framework and the Visual State Manager (VSM), and you will see how to use animations to incorporate visual cues for the end user. Using Visual Studio alone to build complex templates can entail a fair amount of typing and a bit of heavy lifting. To be sure, production-level templates will benefit from the use of Blend for Visual Studio, the (now) free companion application installed with Visual Studio. However, given that this edition of the text does not include coverage of Blend, it is time to roll up your sleeves and pound out some markup.

To begin, create a new WPF application named ButtonTemplate. For this project, you are more interested in the mechanics of creating and using templates, so replace the `Grid` with the following markup:

```
<StackPanel Orientation="Horizontal">
  <Button x:Name="myButton" Width="100" Height="100" Click="myButton_Click"/>
</StackPanel>
```

In the Click event handler, simply display a message box (via MessageBox.Show()) to show a message confirming the clicking of the control. Remember, when you build custom templates, the *behavior* of the control is constant, but the *look* may vary.

Currently, this Button is rendered using the default template, which, as the previous example illustrated, is a BAML resource within a given WPF assembly. When you want to define your own template, you essentially replace this default visual tree with your own creation. To begin, update the definition of the <Button> element to specify a new template using the property-element syntax. This template will give the control a round appearance.

```
<Button x:Name="myButton" Width="100" Height="100" Click="myButton_Click">
  <Button.Template>
    <ControlTemplate>
      <Grid x:Name="controlLayout">
        <Ellipse x:Name="buttonSurface" Fill="LightBlue"/>
        <Label x:Name="buttonCaption"
        VerticalAlignment="Center"
        HorizontalAlignment="Center"
        FontWeight="Bold" FontSize="20" Content="OK!"/>
      </Grid>
    </ControlTemplate>
  </Button.Template>
</Button>
```

Here, you have defined a template that consists of a named Grid control containing a named Ellipse and a Label. Because your Grid has no defined rows or columns, each child stacks on top of the previous control, which centers the content. If you run your application now, you will notice that the Click event will fire *only* when the mouse cursor is within the bounds of the Ellipse! This is a great feature of the WPF template architecture: you do not need to recalculate hit-testing, bounds checking, or any other low-level detail. So, if your template used a Polygon object to render some oddball geometry, you can rest assured that the mouse hit-testing details are relative to the shape of the control, not the larger bounding rectangle.

Templates as Resources

Currently, your template is embedded to a specific Button control, which limits reuse. Ideally, you would place your template into a resource dictionary so you can reuse your round button template between projects or, at minimum, move it into the application resource container for reuse within this project. Let's move the local Button resource to the application level by cutting the template definition from the Button and pasting it into the Application.Resources tag in the App.xaml file. Add in a Key and a TargetType, as follows:

```
<Application.Resources>
  <ControlTemplate x:Key="RoundButtonTemplate" TargetType="{x:Type Button}">
    <Grid x:Name="controlLayout">
      <Ellipse x:Name="buttonSurface" Fill="LightBlue"/>
      <Label x:Name="buttonCaption" VerticalAlignment="Center" HorizontalAlignment="Center"
             FontWeight="Bold" FontSize="20" Content="OK!"/>
    </Grid>
  </ControlTemplate>
</Application.Resources>
```

Update the Button markup to the following:

```
<Button x:Name="myButton" Width="100" Height="100"
  Click="myButton_Click"
  Template="{StaticResource RoundButtonTemplate}">
</Button>
```

Now, because this resource is available for the entire application, you can define any number of round buttons just by simply applying the template. Create two additional Button controls that use this template for testing purposes (no need to handle the Click event for these new items).

```
<StackPanel>
  <Button x:Name="myButton" Width="100" Height="100"
    Click="myButton_Click"
    Template="{StaticResource RoundButtonTemplate}"></Button>
  <Button x:Name="myButton2" Width="100" Height="100"
    Template="{StaticResource RoundButtonTemplate}"></Button>
  <Button x:Name="myButton3" Width="100" Height="100"
    Template="{StaticResource RoundButtonTemplate}"></Button>
</StackPanel>
```

Incorporating Visual Cues Using Triggers

When you define a custom template, the visual cues of the default template are removed as well. For example, the default button template contains markup that informs the control how to look when certain UI events occur, such as when it receives focus, when it is clicked with the mouse, when it is enabled (or disabled), and so on. Users are quite accustomed to these sorts of visual cues because it gives the control somewhat of a tactile response. However, your RoundButtonTemplate does not define any such markup, so the look of the control is identical regardless of the mouse activity. Ideally, your control should look slightly different when clicked (maybe via a color change or drop shadow) to let the user know the visual state has changed.

This can be done using triggers, as you have already learned. For simple operations, triggers work perfectly well. There are additional ways to do this that are beyond the scope of this book, but there is more information available at https://docs.microsoft.com/en-us/dotnet/desktop-wpf/themes/how-to-create-apply-template.

By way of example, update your RoundButtonTemplate with the following markup, which adds two triggers. The first will change the color of the control to blue and the foreground color to yellow when the mouse is over the surface. The second shrinks the size of the Grid (and, therefore, all child elements) when the control is pressed via the mouse.

```
<ControlTemplate x:Key="RoundButtonTemplate" TargetType="Button" >
  <Grid x:Name="controlLayout">
    <Ellipse x:Name="buttonSurface" Fill="LightBlue" />
    <Label x:Name="buttonCaption" Content="OK!"
      FontSize="20" FontWeight="Bold"
      HorizontalAlignment="Center"
      VerticalAlignment="Center" />
  </Grid>
    <ControlTemplate.Triggers>
      <Trigger Property="IsMouseOver" Value="True">
```

```
        <Setter TargetName="buttonSurface" Property="Fill"
          Value="Blue"/>
        <Setter TargetName="buttonCaption"
          Property="Foreground" Value="Yellow"/>
      </Trigger>
      <Trigger Property="IsPressed" Value="True">
        <Setter TargetName="controlLayout"
           Property="RenderTransformOrigin" Value="0.5,0.5"/>
        <Setter TargetName="controlLayout"
          Property="RenderTransform">
          <Setter.Value>
            <ScaleTransform ScaleX="0.8" ScaleY="0.8"/>
          </Setter.Value>
        </Setter>
      </Trigger>
  </ControlTemplate.Triggers>
</ControlTemplate>
```

The Role of the {TemplateBinding} Markup Extension

The problem with the control template is that each of the buttons looks and says the same thing. Updating the markup to the following has no effect:

```
<Button x:Name="myButton" Width="100" Height="100"
  Background="Red" Content="Howdy!" Click="myButton_Click"
  Template="{StaticResource RoundButtonTemplate}" />
<Button x:Name="myButton2" Width="100" Height="100"
  Background="LightGreen" Content="Cancel!" Template="{StaticResource
  RoundButtonTemplate}" />
<Button x:Name="myButton3" Width="100" Height="100"
  Background="Yellow" Content="Format" Template="{StaticResource RoundButtonTemplate}" />
```

This is because the control's default properties (such as BackGround and Content) are overridden in the template. To enable them, they must be mapped to the related properties in the template. You can solve these issues by using the {TemplateBinding} markup extension when you build your template. This allows you to capture property settings defined by the control using your template and use them to set values in the template itself.

Here is a reworked version of RoundButtonTemplate, which now uses this markup extension to map the Background property of the Button to the Fill property of the Ellipse; it also makes sure the Content of the Button is indeed passed to the Content property of the Label:

```
<Ellipse x:Name="buttonSurface" Fill="{TemplateBinding Background}"/>
<Label x:Name="buttonCaption" Content="{TemplateBinding Content}"
  FontSize="20" FontWeight="Bold" HorizontalAlignment="Center"
  VerticalAlignment="Center" />
```

With this update, you can now create buttons of various colors and textual values. Figure 28-13 shows the result of the updated XAML.

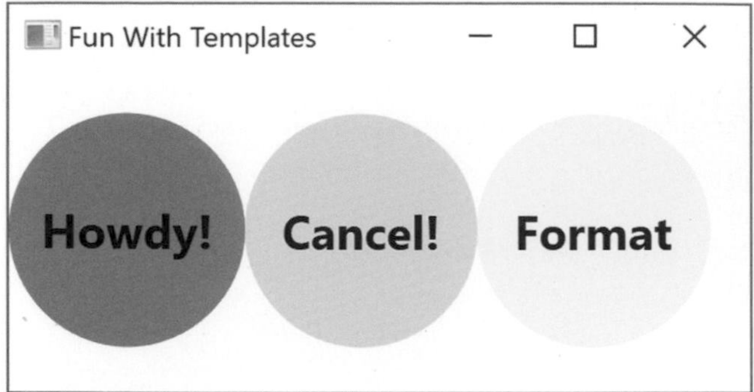

Figure 28-13. *Template bindings allow values to pass through to the internal controls.*

The Role of ContentPresenter

When you designed your template, you used a `Label` to display the textual value of the control. Like the `Button`, the `Label` supports a `Content` property. Therefore, given your use of `{TemplateBinding}`, you could define a `Button` that contains complex content beyond that of a simple string.

However, what if you need to pass in complex content to a template member that does *not* have a `Content` property? When you want to define a generalized *content display area* in a template, you can use the `ContentPresenter` class as opposed to a specific type of control (`Label` or `TextBlock`). There is no need to do so for this example; however, here is some simple markup that illustrates how you could build a custom template that uses `ContentPresenter` to show the value of the `Content` property of the control using the template:

```
<!-- This button template will display whatever is set to the Content of the hosting
button. -->
<ControlTemplate x:Key="NewRoundButtonTemplate" TargetType="Button">
  <Grid>
    <Ellipse Fill="{TemplateBinding Background}"/>
    <ContentPresenter HorizontalAlignment="Center" VerticalAlignment="Center"/>
  </Grid>
</ControlTemplate>
```

Incorporating Templates into Styles

Currently, your template simply defines a basic look and feel of the `Button` control. However, the process of establishing the basic properties of the control (content, font size, font weight, etc.) is the responsibility of the `Button` itself.

```
<!-- Currently the Button must set basic property values, not the template. -->
<Button x:Name="myButton" Foreground="Black" FontSize="20"
  FontWeight="Bold"
  Template="{StaticResource RoundButtonTemplate}"
  Click="myButton_Click"/>
```

If you want, you could establish these values *in the template*. By doing so, you can effectively create a default look and feel. As you might have already realized, this is a job for WPF styles. When you build a style (to account for basic property settings), you can define a template *within the style*! Here is your updated application resource in the application resources in App.xaml, which has been rekeyed as RoundButtonStyle:

```
<!-- A style containing a template. -->
<Style x:Key="RoundButtonStyle" TargetType="Button">
  <Setter Property="Foreground" Value="Black"/>
  <Setter Property="FontSize" Value="14"/>
  <Setter Property="FontWeight" Value="Bold"/>
  <Setter Property="Width" Value="100"/>
  <Setter Property="Height" Value="100"/>
  <!-- Here is the template! -->
  <Setter Property="Template">
    <Setter.Value>
      <ControlTemplate TargetType="Button">
          <!-- Control template from above example -->
      </ControlTemplate>
    </Setter.Value>
  </Setter>
</Style>
```

With this update, you can now create button controls by setting the Style property as so:

```
<Button x:Name="myButton" Background="Red" Content="Howdy!"
        Click="myButton_Click" Style="{StaticResource RoundButtonStyle}"/>
```

While the rendering and behavior of the button are identical, the benefit of nesting templates within styles is that you can provide a canned set of values for common properties. That wraps up your look at how to use Visual Studio and the trigger framework to build custom templates for a control. While there is still much more about the Windows Presentation Foundation API than has been examined here, you should be in a solid position for further study.

Summary

The first part of this chapter examined the resource management system of WPF. You began by looking at how to work with binary resources, and then you examined the role of object resources. As you learned, object resources are named blobs of XAML that can be stored at various locations to reuse content.

Next, you learned about WPF's animation framework. Here you had a chance to create some animations using C# code, as well as with XAML. You learned that if you define an animation in markup, you use <Storyboard> elements and triggers to control execution. You then looked at the WPF-style mechanism, which makes heavy use of graphics, object resources, and animations.

You examined the relationship between a *logical tree* and a *visual tree*. The logical tree is basically a one-to-one correspondence of the markup you author to describe a WPF root element. Behind this logical tree is a much deeper visual tree that contains detailed rendering instructions.

The role of a *default template* was then examined. Remember, when you are building custom templates, you are essentially ripping out all (or part) of a control's visual tree and replacing it with your own custom implementation.

CHAPTER 29

WPF Notifications, Validations, Commands, and MVVM

This chapter will conclude your investigation of the WPF programming model by covering the capabilities that support the Model-View-ViewModel (MVVM) pattern. The first section covers the Model-View-ViewModel pattern. Next, you learn about the WPF notification system and its implementation of the Observable pattern through observable models and observable collections. Having the data in the UI accurately portray the current state of the data automatically improves the user experience significantly and reduces the manual coding required in older technologies (such as WinForms) to achieve the same result.

Building on the Observable pattern, you will examine the mechanisms to add validation into your application. Validation is a vital part of any application—not only letting the user know that something is wrong but also letting them know *what* is wrong. To inform the user what the error is, you will also learn how to incorporate validation into the view markup.

Next, you will take a deeper dive into the WPF command system and create custom commands to encapsulate program logic, much as you did in Chapter 25 with the built-in commands. There are several advantages to creating custom commands, including (but not limited to) enabling code reuse, logic encapsulation, and separation of concerns.

Finally, you will bring all of this together in a sample MVVM application.

Introducing Model-View-ViewModel

Before you dive into notifications, validations, and commands in WPF, it would be good to understand the end goal of this chapter, which is the Model-View-ViewModel pattern (MVVM). Derived from Martin Fowler's Presentation Model pattern, MVVM leverages XAML-specific capabilities, discussed in this chapter, to make your WPF development faster and cleaner. The name itself describes the main components of the pattern: model, view, view model.

The Model

The *model* is the object representation of your data. In MVVM, models are conceptually the same as the models from your data access layer (DAL). Sometimes they are the same physical class, but there is no requirement for this. As you read this chapter, you will learn how to decide whether you can use your DAL models or whether you need to create new ones.

Models typically take advantage of the built-in (or custom) validations through data annotations and the `INotifyDataErrorInfo` interface and are configured as observable to tie into the WPF notification system. You will see all of this later in this chapter.

A. Troelsen and P. Japikse, *Pro C# 10 with .NET 6*, https://doi.org/10.1007/978-1-4842-7869-7_29

The View

The *view* is the UI of the application, and it is designed to be very lightweight. Think of the menu board at a drive-thru restaurant. The board displays menu items and prices, and it has a mechanism so the user can communicate with the back-end systems. However, there isn't any intelligence built into the board, unless it is specifically user interface logic, such as turning on the lights if it gets dark.

MVVM views should be developed with the same goals in mind. Any intelligence should be built into the application elsewhere. The only code in the code-behind file (e.g., `MainWindow.xaml.cs`) should be directly related to manipulating the UI. It should not be based on business rules or anything that needs to be persisted for future use. While not a main goal of MVVM, well-developed MVVM applications typically have very little code in the code-behind.

The View Model

In WPF and other XAML technologies, the *view model* serves two purposes.

- The view model provides a single stop for all the data needed by the view. This doesn't mean the view model is responsible for getting the actual data; instead, it is merely a transport mechanism to move the data from the data store to the view. Usually, there is a one-to-one correlation between views and view models, but architectural differences exist, and your mileage may vary.
- The second job is to act as the controller for the view. Just like the menu board, the view model takes direction from the user and relays that call to the relevant code to make sure the proper actions are taken. Quite often this code is in the form of custom commands.

Anemic Models or Anemic View Models

In the early days of WPF, when developers were still working out how best to implement the MVVM pattern, there were significant (and sometimes heated) discussions about *where* to implement items like validation and the Observable pattern. One camp (the anemic model camp) argued that it all should be in the view model since adding those capabilities to the model broke separation of concerns. The other camp (the anemic view model camp) argued it should all be in the models since that reduced duplication of code.

The real answer is, of course, it depends. When `INotifyPropertyChanged`, `IDataErrorInfo`, and `INotifyDataErrorInfo` are implemented on the model classes, this ensures that the relevant code is close to the target of the code (as you will see in this chapter) and is implemented only once for each model. That being said, there are times when your view model classes will need to be developed as observables themselves. At the end of the day, you need to determine what makes the most sense for your application, without over-complicating your code or sacrificing the benefits of MVVM.

■ **Note** There are multiple MVVM frameworks available for WPF, such as MVVMLite, Caliburn.Micro, and Prism (although Prism is much more than just an MVVM framework). This chapter discusses the MVVM pattern and the features in WPF that support implementing the pattern. I leave it to you, the reader, to examine the different frameworks and select the one that best matches your app's needs.

The WPF Binding Notification System

A significant shortcoming in the binding system for WinForms is a lack of notifications. If the data represented in the view is updated programmatically, the UI must also be refreshed programmatically to keep them in sync. This leads to a lot of calls to `Refresh()` on controls, typically more than are absolutely necessary in order to be safe. While usually not a significant performance issue to include too many calls to `Refresh()`, if you don't include enough, the experience for the user could be affected negatively.

The binding system built into XAML-based applications corrects this problem by enabling you to hook your data objects and collections into a notification system by developing them as observables. Whenever a property's value changes on an observable model or the collection changes (e.g., items are added, removed, or reordered) on an observable collection, an event is raised (either `NotifyPropertyChanged` or `NotifyCollectionChanged`). The binding framework automatically listens for those events to occur and updates the bound controls when they fire. Even better, as a developer, you have control over which properties raise the notifications. Sounds perfect, right? Well, it's not *quite* perfect. There can be a fair amount of code involved in setting this up for observable models if you are doing it all by hand. Fortunately, there is an open source framework that makes it much simpler, as you shall soon see.

Observable Models and Collections

In this section, you will create an application that uses observable models and collections. To get started, create a new WPF application named WpfNotifications. The application will be a master-detail form, allowing the user to select a specific car using a `ComboBox`, and then the details for that car will be displayed in the following `TextBox` controls. Update `MainWindow.xaml` by replacing the default Grid with the following markup:

```
<Grid IsSharedSizeScope="True" Margin="5,0,5,5">
  <Grid.RowDefinitions>
    <RowDefinition Height="Auto"/>
    <RowDefinition Height="Auto"/>
  </Grid.RowDefinitions>
  <Grid Grid.Row="0">
    <Grid.ColumnDefinitions>
      <ColumnDefinition Width="Auto"
        SharedSizeGroup="CarLabels"/>
      <ColumnDefinition Width="*"/>
    </Grid.ColumnDefinitions>
    <Label Grid.Column="0" Content="Vehicle"/>
    <ComboBox Name="cboCars"  Grid.Column="1"
      DisplayMemberPath="PetName" />
</Grid>
<Grid Grid.Row="1" Name="DetailsGrid">
  <Grid.ColumnDefinitions>
    <ColumnDefinition Width="Auto"
      SharedSizeGroup="CarLabels"/>
    <ColumnDefinition Width="*"/>
  </Grid.ColumnDefinitions>
  <Grid.RowDefinitions>
    <RowDefinition Height="Auto"/>
    <RowDefinition Height="Auto"/>
    <RowDefinition Height="Auto"/>
```

```
    <RowDefinition Height="Auto"/>
    <RowDefinition Height="Auto"/>
  </Grid.RowDefinitions>
  <Label Grid.Column="0" Grid.Row="0" Content="Id"/>
  <TextBox Grid.Column="1" Grid.Row="0" />
  <Label Grid.Column="0" Grid.Row="1" Content="Make"/>
  <TextBox Grid.Column="1" Grid.Row="1" />
  <Label Grid.Column="0" Grid.Row="2" Content="Color"/>
  <TextBox Grid.Column="1" Grid.Row="2" />
  <Label Grid.Column="0" Grid.Row="3" Content="Pet Name"/>
  <TextBox Grid.Column="1" Grid.Row="3" />
  <StackPanel Grid.Column="0" Grid.ColumnSpan="2" Grid.Row="4"
      HorizontalAlignment="Right" Orientation="Horizontal" Margin="0,5,0,5">
    <Button x:Name="btnAddCar" Content="Add Car" Margin="5,0,5,0" Padding="4, 2" />
    <Button x:Name="btnChangeColor" Content="Change Color" Margin="5,0,5,0"
      Padding="4, 2"/>
  </StackPanel>
  </Grid>
</Grid>
```

Your window will resemble Figure 29-1.

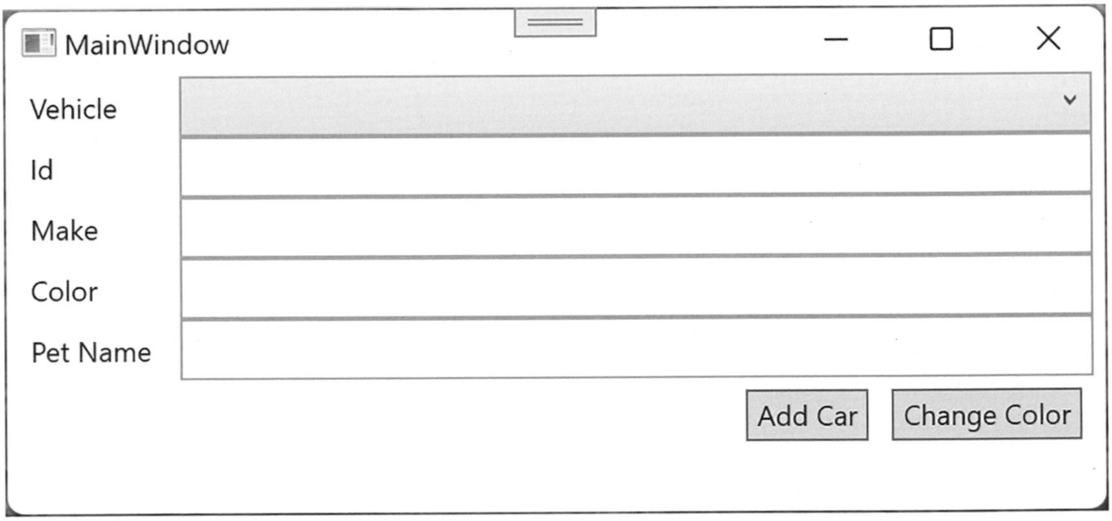

Figure 29-1. Master-detail window displaying Car details

The IsSharedSizeScope tag on the Grid control sets up child grids to share dimensions. The ColumnDefinitions marked SharedSizeGroup will automatically be sized to the same width without any programming needed. In this example, if the Pet Name label was changed to something much longer, the Vehicle column (which is in a different Grid control) would be sized to match it, keeping the window's appearance nice and tidy.

Next, right-click the project name in Solution Explorer, select Add ➤ New Folder, and name the folder Models. In this new folder, create a class named Car. The initial class is listed here:

```
public class Car
{
  public int Id { get; set; }
  public string Make { get; set; }
  public string Color { get; set; }
  public string PetName { get; set; }
}
```

Adding Bindings and Data

The next step is to add the binding statements for the controls. Remember that data-binding statements revolve around a data context, and this can be set on the control itself or on a parent control. Here, you are going to set the context on the DetailsGrid, so each control contained will inherit that data context. Set the DataContext to the SelectedItem property of the ComboBox. Update the Grid that holds the detail controls to the following:

```
<Grid Grid.Row="1" Name="DetailsGrid"
  DataContext="{Binding ElementName=cboCars, Path=SelectedItem}">
```

The text boxes in the DetailsGrid will show the individual properties of the select car. Add the appropriate text attributes and related bindings to the TextBox controls, like so:

```
<TextBox Grid.Column="1" Grid.Row="0" Text="{Binding Path=Id}" />
<TextBox Grid.Column="1" Grid.Row="1" Text="{Binding Path=Make}" />
<TextBox Grid.Column="1" Grid.Row="2" Text="{Binding Path=Color}" />
<TextBox Grid.Column="1" Grid.Row="3" Text="{Binding Path=PetName}" />
```

Finally, add data to the ComboBox. In MainWindow.xaml.cs, create a new list of Car records, and set the ItemsSource for the ComboBox to the list. Also, add the using statement for the Notifications.Models namespace.

```
using WpfNotifications.Models;
//omitted for brevity
public partial class MainWindow : Window
{
  readonly IList<Car> _cars = new List<Car>();
  public MainWindow()
  {
    InitializeComponent();
    _cars.Add(new Car {Id = 1, Color = "Blue", Make = "Chevy", PetName = "Kit"});
    _cars.Add(new Car {Id = 2, Color = "Red", Make = "Ford", PetName = "Red Rider"});
    cboCars.ItemsSource = _cars;
    }
}
```

Run the app. You'll see that the vehicle selector has two cars to choose from. Choose one of them, and the text boxes will be automatically populated with the vehicle detail. Change the color of one of the vehicles, select the other vehicle, and then go back to the vehicle you edited. You will see the new color is indeed still attached to the vehicle. This isn't anything remarkable; you've seen the power of XAML data binding in previous examples.

Programmatically Changing the Vehicle Data

While the previous example works as expected, if the data is changed programmatically, the UI will *not* reflect the changes unless you program the app to refresh the data. To demonstrate this, add an event handler for the btnChangeColor Button, like so:

```
<Button x:Name="btnChangeColor" Content="Change Color" Margin="5,0,5,0"
    Padding="4, 2" Click="BtnChangeColor_OnClick"/>
```

In the BtnChangeColor_Click() event handler, use the SelectedItem property of the ComboBox to locate the selected record from the cars list, and change the color to Pink. The code is listed here:

```
private void BtnChangeColor_OnClick(object sender, RoutedEventArgs e)
{
  _cars.First(x => x.Id == ((Car)cboCars.SelectedItem)?.Id).Color = "Pink";
}
```

Run the app, select a vehicle, and click the Change Color button. Nothing changes visibly. Select the other vehicle and go back to your originally selected vehicle. Now you will see the updated value. This is not a good experience for the user!

Now add an event handler to the btnAddCar button, like this:

```
<Button x:Name="btnAddCar" Content="Add Car" Margin="5,0,5,0" Padding="4, 2"
  Click="BtnAddCar_OnClick" />
```

In the BtnAddCar_Click event handler, add a new record to the Car list.

```
private void BtnAddCar_Click(object sender, RoutedEventArgs e)
{
  var maxCount = _cars?.Max(x => x.Id) ?? 0;
  _cars?.Add(new Car { Id=++maxCount,Color="Yellow",Make="VW",PetName="Birdie"});
}
```

Run the app, click the Add Car button, and examine the contents of the ComboBox. Even though you know there are three cars in the list, only two are displayed! To correct both of these problems, you will convert the Car class to an observable model and use an observable collection to hold all the Car instances.

Observable Models

The problem of data changing on a property of your model and not being displayed in the UI is resolved by implementing the INotifyPropertyChanged interface on your Car model class. The INotifyPropertyChanged interface contains a single event: PropertyChangedEvent. The XAML binding engine listens for this event for each bound property on classes that implement the INotifyPropertyChanged interface. The interface is shown here:

```
public interface INotifyPropertyChanged
{
  event PropertyChangedEventHandler PropertyChanged;
}
```

Add the following using statements to the Car.cs class:

```
using System.ComponentModel;
using System.Runtime.CompilerServices;
```

Next, implement the INotifyPropertyChanged interface on the class, as follows:

```
public class Car : INotifyPropertyChanged
{
  //Omitted for brevity
  public event PropertyChangedEventHandler PropertyChanged;
}
```

The PropertyChanged event takes an object reference and a new instance of the PropertyChangedEventArgs class, like in this example:

```
PropertyChanged?.Invoke(this,
  new PropertyChangedEventArgs("Model"));
```

The first parameter is the object instance that is raising the event. The PropertyChangedEventArgs constructor takes a string that indicates the property that was changed and needs to be updated. When the event is raised, the binding engine looks for any controls bound to the named property on that instance. If you pass String.Empty into the PropertyChangedEventArgs, all of the bound properties of the instance are updated.

You control which properties are enlisted in the automatic updates. Only those properties that raise the PropertyChanged event in the setter will be automatically updated. This is usually all the properties on your model classes, but you have the option of omitting certain properties based on your application's requirements. Instead of raising the event directly in the setter for each of the enlisted properties, a common pattern is to create a helper method (typically named OnPropertyChanged()) that raises the event on behalf of the properties, usually in a base class for your models. Add the following method and code into the Car.cs class:

```
protected void OnPropertyChanged([CallerMemberName] string propertyName = "")
{
  PropertyChanged?.Invoke(this,
    new PropertyChangedEventArgs(propertyName));
}
```

Next, update each of the automatic properties in the Car class to have a full getter and setter with a backing field. When the value is changed, call the OnPropertyChanged() helper method. Here is the Id property updated:

```
private int _id;
public int Id
{
  get => _id;
  set
  {
    if (value == _id) return;
    _id = value;
    OnPropertyChanged();
  }
}
```

Make sure you do the same for all the properties in the class and then run the app again. Select a vehicle and click the Change Color button. You will immediately see the change show up in the UI. First problem solved!

Using nameof

A feature added in C# 6 is the nameof operator, which provides the string name of the item passed into the nameof method. You can use this in the calls to OnPropertyChanged() in your setters, like this:

```
public string Color
{
  get { return _color; }
  set
  {
    if (value == _color) return;
    _color = value;
    OnPropertyChanged(nameof(Color));
  }
}
```

Note that you don't have to remove the CallerMemberName attribute from OnPropertyChanged() when you use the nameof method (although it becomes unnecessary). In the end, whether you use the nameof method or the CallerMemberName attribute comes down to a matter of personal choice.

Observable Collections

The next problem to resolve is updating the UI when the contents of a collection changes. This is done by implementing the INotifyCollectionChanged interface. Like the INotifyPropertyChanged interface, this interface exposes one event, the CollectionChanged event. Unlike the INotifyPropertyChanged event, implementing this interface by hand is more than just calling a method in the setter. You need to create a full List implementation and raise the CollectionChanged event any time your list changes.

Using the ObservableCollections Class

Fortunately, there is a much easier way than creating your own collection class. The ObservableCollection<T> class implements INotifyCollectionChanged, INotifyPropertyChanged, and Collection<T>, and it is part of the .NET Core Framework. No extra work! To see this, add a using statement for System.Collections.ObjectModel and then update the private field for _cars to the following:

```
private readonly IList<Car> _cars =
  new ObservableCollection<Car>();
```

Run the app again and click the Add Car button. You will see the new records appear appropriately.

Implementing a Dirty Flag

Another advantage of observable models is the ability to track state changes. Dirty tracking (tracking when one or more of an object's values have changed) with WPF is fairly trivial. Add a bool property named IsChanged to the Car class. Make sure to call OnPropertyChanged() just like the other properties in the Car class.

```
private bool _isChanged;
public bool IsChanged {
  get => _isChanged;
  set
  {
    if (value == _isChanged) return;
    _isChanged = value;
    OnPropertyChanged();
  }
}
```

You need to set the IsChanged property to true in the OnPropertyChanged() method. You also need to make sure you aren't setting IsChanged to true when IsChanged is updated, or you will hit a stack overflow exception! Update the OnPropertyChanged() method to the following (which uses the nameof method discussed earlier):

```
protected virtual void OnPropertyChanged(
  [CallerMemberName] string propertyName = "")
{
  if (propertyName != nameof(IsChanged))
  {
    IsChanged = true;
  }
  PropertyChanged?.Invoke(this,
    new PropertyChangedEventArgs(propertyName));
}
```

Open MainWindow.xaml and add an additional RowDefinition to the DetailsGrid. Add the following to the end of the Grid, which contains a Label and a CheckBox, bound to the IsChanged property, as follows:

```
<Label Grid.Column="0" Grid.Row="5" Content="Is Changed"/>
<CheckBox Grid.Column="1" Grid.Row="5" VerticalAlignment="Center"
    Margin="10,0,0,0" IsEnabled="False" IsChecked="{Binding Path=IsChanged}" />
```

If you were to run the app now, you would see that every single record shows up as changed, even though you haven't changed anything! This is because object creation sets property values, and setting any values calls OnPropertyChanged(). This sets the object's IsChanged property. To correct this, set the IsChanged property to false as the last property in the object initialization code. Open MainWindow.xaml.cs and change the code that creates the list to the following:

```
_cars.Add(
    new Car {Id = 1, Color = "Blue", Make = "Chevy", PetName = "Kit", IsChanged = false});
_cars.Add(
    new Car {Id = 2, Color = "Red", Make = "Ford", PetName = "Red Rider", IsChanged =
    false});
```

Run the app again, select a vehicle, and click the Change Color button. You will see the check box get selected along with the updated color.

Updating the Source Through UI Interaction

You might notice that if you type text into the UI, the Is Changed check box doesn't actually get selected until you tab out of the control being edited. This is because of the `UpdateSourceTrigger` property on the `TextBox` bindings. The `UpdateSourceTrigger` determines what event (such as changing the value, tabbing out, etc.) causes the UI to update the underlying data. There are four options, as shown in Table 29-1.

Table 29-1. *UpdateSourceTrigger Values*

Member	Meaning in Life
`Default`	Sets to the default for the control (e.g., `LostFocus` for `TextBox` controls).
`Explicit`	Updates the source object only when the `UpdateSource` method is called.
`LostFocus`	Updates when the control loses focus. This is the default for `TextBox` controls.
`PropertyChanged`	Updates as soon as the property changes. This is the default for `CheckBox` controls.

The default source trigger for a `TextBox` is the `LostFocus` event. Change this to `PropertyChanged` by updating the binding for the Color `TextBox` to the following XAML:

```
<TextBox Grid.Column="1" Grid.Row="2" Text="{Binding Path=Color, UpdateSourceTrigger=Proper
tyChanged}" />
```

Now, when you run the app and start typing into the Color text box, the check box is immediately selected. You might ask why the default is set to `LostFocus` for `TextBox` controls. Any validation (covered in a moment) for a model fires in conjunction with the `UpdateSourceTrigger`. For a `TextBox`, this would then potentially cause errors continually flashing until the user entered the correct values. For example, if the validation rules don't allow less than five characters in a `TextBox`, the error would show on each keystroke until the user got five or more entered. In those cases, it's best to wait for the user to tab out of the `TextBox` (after completing the change to the text) to update the source.

Wrapping Up Notifications and Observables

Using `INotifyPropertyChanged` on your models and `ObservableCollections` classes for your lists improves the user experience by keeping the data and the UI in sync. While neither interface is complicated, they do require updates to your code. Fortunately, Microsoft has included the `ObservableCollection` class to handle all of the plumbing to create observable collections. Just as fortunate is the update to the Fody project to add `INotifyPropertyChanged` functionality automatically. With these two tools in hand, there isn't any reason to not implement observables in your WPF applications.

WPF Validations

Now that you've implemented `INotifyPropertyChanged` and are using an `ObservableCollection`, it's time to add validations to your application. Applications need to validate user input and provide feedback to the user when the data entered is incorrect. This section covers the most common validation mechanisms for modern WPF applications, but these are still just a portion of the capabilities built into WPF.

Validation occurs when a data binding attempts to update the data source. In addition to built-in validations, such as exceptions in a property's setter, you can create custom validation rules. If *any* validation rule (built-in or custom) fails, the `Validation` class, discussed shortly, comes into play.

■ **Note** For each of the sections in this chapter, you can continue working in the same project from the previous section, or you can create a copy of the project for each new section. In the repo for this chapter, each section is a different project.

Updating the Sample for the Validation Examples

In the repo for this chapter, the new project (copied from the previous example) is called WpfValidations. If you are using the same project from the previous section, you just need to make note of the namespace changes when copying code into your project from the examples listed in this section.

The Validation Class

Before adding validations to your project, it's important to understand the `Validation` class. This class is part of the validation framework, and it provides methods and attached properties that can be used to display validation results. There are three main properties of the `Validation` class commonly used when handling validation errors (shown in Table 29-2). You will use each of these through the rest of this section.

Table 29-2. *Key Members of the Validation Class*

Member	Meaning in Life
`HasError`	Attached property indicating that a validation rule failed somewhere in the process
`Errors`	Collection of all active `ValidationError` objects
`ErrorTemplate`	Control template that becomes visible and adorns the bound element when `HasError` is set to `true`

Validation Options

As mentioned, XAML technologies have several mechanisms for incorporating validation logic into your application. You will examine three of the most commonly used validation choices in the next sections.

Notify on Exceptions

While exceptions should not be used to enforce business logic, exceptions can and do happen, and they should be handled appropriately. In case they aren't handled in code, the user should receive visual feedback of the problem. An important change from WinForms is that WPF binding exceptions are not, by default, propagated to the user as exceptions. They are, however, visually indicated, using an adorner (visual layer that resides on top of your controls).

To test this, run the app, select a record from the ComboBox, and clear out the Id value. Since the Id property is defined as an int (not a nullable int), a numeric value is required. When you tab out of the Id field, an empty string is sent to the Id property by the binding framework, and since an empty string can't be converted to an int, an exception is thrown in the setter. Normally, an unhandled exception would generate a message box to the user, but in this case, nothing like that happened. If you look in the Debug portion of the Output window, you will see the following:

```
System.Windows.Data Error: 7 : ConvertBack cannot convert value '' (type 'String').
BindingExpression:Path=Id; DataItem='Car' (HashCode=52579650); target element is
'TextBox' (Name=''); target property is 'Text' (type 'String') FormatException:'System.
FormatException: Input string was not in a correct format.
```

Visual display of the exception is a thin red box around the control, as shown in Figure 29-2.

Figure 29-2. *The default error template*

The red box is the ErrorTemplate property of the Validation object and acts as an adorner for the bound control. While the default error adorner shows that there is indeed an error, there isn't any indication as to *what* is wrong. The good news is that the ErrorTemplate is completely customizable, as you will see later in this chapter.

IDataErrorInfo

The IDataErrorInfo interface provides a mechanism for you to add custom validations to your model classes. This interface is added directly to your model (or view model) classes, and the validation code is placed inside your model classes (preferably in partial classes). This centralizes validation code in your project, in direct contrast to WinForms projects, where validation was typically done in the UI itself.

The IDataErrorInfo interface, shown here, contains two properties: an indexer and a string property named Error. Note that the WPF binding engine doesn't use the Error property.

```
public interface IDataErrorInfo
{
  string this[string columnName] { get; }
  string Error { get; }
}
```

You will be adding the Car partial class shortly, but first you need to update the Car.cs class and mark it as partial. Next, add another file to the Models directory named CarPartial.cs. Rename this class Car, make sure the class is marked as partial, and add the IDataErrorInfo interface. Finally, implement the API for the interface. The initial code is listed here:

```
public partial class Car : IDataErrorInfo
{
  public string this[string columnName] => string.Empty;
  public string Error { get;}
}
```

For a bound control to opt in to the IDataErrorInfo interface, it must add ValidatesOnDataErrors to the binding expression. Update the binding expression for the Make text box to the following (and update the rest of the binding statements in the same way):

```
<TextBox Grid.Column="1" Grid.Row="1" Text="{Binding Path=Make,
ValidatesOnDataErrors=True}" />
```

Once this update is made to the binding statements, the indexer on the model gets called each time the PropertyChanged event is raised. The property name from the event is used as the columnName parameter in the indexer. If the indexer returns string.Empty, the framework assumes that all validations passed, and no error condition exists. If the indexer returns anything but string.Empty, an error is presumed to exist on the property for that object instance, and each control that is bound to the property being validated on this specific instance of the class is considered to have an error, the HasError property of the Validation object is set to true, and the ErrorTemplate adorner is activated for the controls effected.

Next, you will add some simple validation logic to the indexer in CarPartial.cs. The validation rules are simple.

- If Make equals ModelT, set the error equal to "Too Old".
- If Make equals Chevy and Color equals Pink, set the error equal to $"{Make}'s don't come in {Color}".

Start by adding a switch statement for each of the properties. To avoid using magic strings in the case statements, you will again use the nameof method. If the code falls through the switch statement, return string.Empty. Next, add the validation rules. In the proper case statements, add a check of the property value based on the rules listed earlier. In the case statement for the Make property, first check to make sure the value isn't ModelT. If it is, return the error. If that passes, the next line will call into a helper method that returns an error if the second rule is violated, or it will return string.Empty if it is not. In the case statement for the Color property, also call the helper method. The code is as follows:

```
public string this[string columnName]
{
  get
  {
    switch (columnName)
    {
      case nameof(Id):
        break;
      case nameof(Make):
        return Make == "ModelT"
          ? "Too Old"
          : CheckMakeAndColor();
      case nameof(Color):
        return CheckMakeAndColor();
      case nameof(PetName):
        break;
    }
    return string.Empty;
  }
}

internal string CheckMakeAndColor()
{
  if (Make == "Chevy" && Color == "Pink")
  {
    return $"{Make}'s don't come in {Color}";
  }
  return string.Empty;
}
```

Run the app, select the Red Rider vehicle (the Ford), and change the Make to ModelT. Once you tab out of the field, the red error decorator appears. Now select Kit (which is a Chevy) from the drop-down and click the Change Color button to change the color to Pink. Immediately the red error adorner appears on the Color field but doesn't appear on the Make text box. Now, change Make to Ford, tab out of the text box, and note that the red adorner does *not* disappear!

This is because the indexer runs only when the PropertyChanged event is fired for a property. As discussed in earlier, the PropertyChanged event fires when the source object's property changes, and this happens either through code (such as clicking the Change Color button) or through user interaction (the timing of this is controlled through the UpdateSourceTrigger). When you changed the color, the Make property did not change, so the event did not fire for the Make property. Since the event didn't fire, the indexer did not get called, so the validation for the Make property didn't run.

There are two ways to fix this. The first is to change PropertyChangedEventArgs to update every bound property by passing in string.Empty instead of a field name. As discussed, this causes the binding engine to update *every* property on that instance. Update the OnPropertyChanged() method in the Car.cs class like this:

```
protected virtual void OnPropertyChanged([CallerMemberName] string propertyName = "")
{
  if (propertyName != nameof(IsChanged))
  {
    IsChanged = true;
  }
```

```
    //PropertyChanged?.Invoke(this, new PropertyChangedEventArgs(propertyName));
    PropertyChanged?.Invoke(this,
      new PropertyChangedEventArgs(string.Empty));
  }
```

Now, when you run the same test, you see that both the Make and Color text boxes are adorned with the error template when one of them is updated. So, why not always raise the event in this manner? It's largely a matter of performance. It's *possible* that refreshing every property on an object could hamper performance. Of course, there's no way to know without testing, and your mileage may (and probably will) vary.

The other solution is to raise the PropertyChanged event for the other dependent field(s) when one changes. The downside to using this mechanism is that you (or other developers who support your app) must know that the Make and Color properties are related through the validation code.

INotifyDataErrorInfo

The INotifyDataErrorInfo interface introduced in .NET 4.5 builds on the IDataErrorInfo interface and adds additional capabilities for validation. Of course, with additional power comes additional work! In a drastic shift from prior validation techniques that you had to specifically opt into, the ValidatesOnNotifyDataErrors binding property defaults to true, so adding the property to your binding statements is optional.

The INotifyDataErrorInfo interface is extremely small but does take a fair amount of plumbing code to make it effective, as you will see shortly. The interface is shown here:

```
public interface INotifyDataErrorInfo
{
  bool HasErrors { get; }
  event EventHandler<DataErrorsChangedEventArgs>
    ErrorsChanged;
  IEnumerable GetErrors(string propertyName);
}
```

The HasErrors property is used by the binding engine to determine whether there are *any* errors on any of the instance's properties. If the GetErrors() method is called with a null or empty string for the propertyName parameter, it returns all errors that exist in the instance. If a propertyName is passed into the method, only the errors for that particular property are returned. The ErrorsChanged event (like the PropertyChanged and CollectionChanged events) notifies the binding engine to update the UI for the current list of errors.

Implement the Supporting Code

When implementing INotifyDataErrorInfo, most of the code is usually pushed into a base model class, so it needs be written only once. Start by replacing IDataErrorInfo with INotifyDataErrorInfo in the CarPartial.cs class and add the interface members (you can leave the code from IDataErrorInfo in the class; you will be updating this later).

```
public partial class Car: INotifyDataErrorInfo, IDataErrorInfo
{
...
public IEnumerable GetErrors(string propertyName)
{
  throw new NotImplementedException();
}
```

```
public bool HasErrors { get; }
public event
  EventHandler<DataErrorsChangedEventArgs> ErrorsChanged;
}
```

Next, add a `Dictionary<string,List<string>>` that will hold any errors grouped by property name, as shown here:

```
private readonly Dictionary<string,List<string>> _errors
  = new Dictionary<string, List<string>>();
```

The `HasErrors` property should return `true` if there are *any* errors in the dictionary. This is easily accomplished like this:

```
public bool HasErrors => _errors.Any();
```

Next, create a helper method to raise the `ErrorsChanged` event (just like raising the `PropertyChanged` event) like this:

```
private void OnErrorsChanged(string propertyName)
{
  ErrorsChanged?.Invoke(this,
    new DataErrorsChangedEventArgs(propertyName));
}
```

As mentioned earlier, the `GetErrors()` method should return any and all errors in the dictionary if the parameter is empty or null. If a `propertyName` value is passed in, it will return any errors found for that property. If the parameter doesn't match (or there aren't any errors for a property), then the method will return null.

```
public IEnumerable GetErrors(string propertyName)
{
  if (string.IsNullOrEmpty(propertyName))
  {
    return _errors.Values;
  }
  return _errors.ContainsKey(propertyName)
    ? _errors[propertyName]
    : null;
}
```

The final set of helpers will add one or more errors for a property or clear all of the errors for a property (or all properties). Any time the dictionary changes, remember to call the `OnErrorsChanged()` helper method.

```
private void AddError(string propertyName, string error)
{
  AddErrors(propertyName, new List<string> { error });
}
private void AddErrors(
  string propertyName, IList<string> errors)
```

```
{
  if (errors == null || !errors.Any())
  {
    return;
  }
  var changed = false;
  if (!_errors.ContainsKey(propertyName))
  {
    _errors.Add(propertyName, new List<string>());
    changed = true;
  }
  foreach (var err in errors)
  {
    if (_errors[propertyName].Contains(err)) continue;
    _errors[propertyName].Add(err);
    changed = true;
  }
  if (changed)
  {
    OnErrorsChanged(propertyName);
  }
}
protected void ClearErrors(string propertyName = "")
{
  if (string.IsNullOrEmpty(propertyName))
  {
    _errors.Clear();
  }
  else
  {
    _errors.Remove(propertyName);
  }
  OnErrorsChanged(propertyName);
}
```

Now the question is "how is this code activated?" The binding engine listens for the ErrorsChanged event and will update the UI if there is a change in the errors collection for a binding statement. But the validation code still needs a trigger to execute. There are two mechanisms for this, and they will be discussed next.

Use INotifyDataErrorInfo for Validations

One place to check for errors is in the property setters, like the following example, simplified to just check for the ModelT validation:

```
public string Make
{
  get { return _make; }
  set
  {
    if (value == _make) return;
```

```
      _make = value;
      if (Make == "ModelT")
      {
        AddError(nameof(Make), "Too Old");
      }
      else
      {
        ClearErrors(nameof(Make));
      }
      OnPropertyChanged(nameof(Make));
      OnPropertyChanged(nameof(Color));
    }
  }
```

The main issue with this approach is you have to combine validation logic with property setters, making the code harder to read and support.

Combine IDataErrorInfo with INotifyDataErrorInfo for Validations

You saw in the previous section that `IDataErrorInfo` can be added to a partial class, which means you don't have to update your setters. You also saw that the indexer automatically gets called when `PropertyChanged` is raised on a property. Combining `IDataErrorInfo` and `INotifyDataErrorInfo` provides you with the additional features for validations from `INotifyDataErrorInfo` and with the separation from the setters provided by `IDataErrorInfo`.

The purpose of using `IDataErrorInfo` is not to run validations but to make sure your validation code that leverages `INotifyDataErrorInfo` gets called every time `PropertyChanged` is raised on your object. Since you aren't using `IDataErrorInfo` for validation, always return `string.Empty` from the indexer. Update the indexer and the `CheckMakeAndColor()` helper method to the following code:

```
public string this[string columnName]
{
  get
  {
    ClearErrors(columnName);
    switch (columnName)
    {
      case nameof(Id):
        break;
      case nameof(Make):
        CheckMakeAndColor();
        if (Make == "ModelT")
        {
          AddError(nameof(Make), "Too Old");
          hasError = true;
        }
        break;
      case nameof(Color):
        CheckMakeAndColor();
        break;
      case nameof(PetName):
```

```
        break;
    }
    return string.Empty;
  }
}
internal bool CheckMakeAndColor()
{
  if (Make == "Chevy" && Color == "Pink")
  {
    AddError(nameof(Make), $"{Make}'s don't come in {Color}");
    AddError(nameof(Color),
      $"{Make}'s don't come in {Color}");
    return true;
  }
  return false;
}
```

Run the app, select Chevy, and change the color to Pink. In addition to the red adorners around the Make and Model text boxes, you will also see a red box adorner around the entire grid that holds the Car details fields (shown in Figure 29-3).

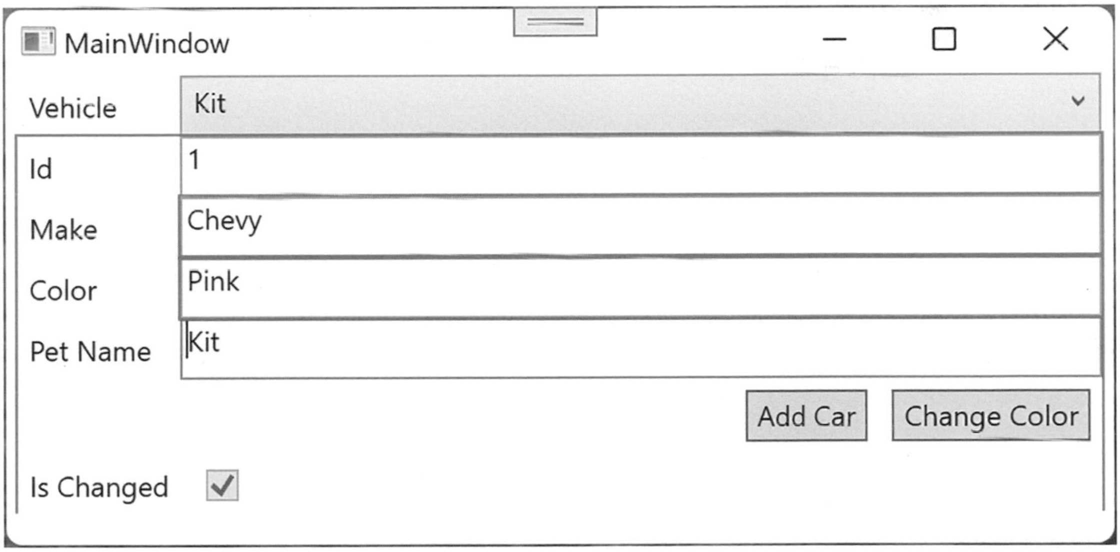

Figure 29-3. *The updated error adorner*

This is another advantage of using INotifyDataErrorInfo. In addition to the controls in error, the control defining the data context also gets adorned with the error template.

Show All Errors

The Errors property on the Validation class returns all the validation errors on a particular object in the form of ValidationError objects. Each ValidationError object has an ErrorContent property that contains the list of error messages for the property. This means the error messages you want to display are in this list within a list. To display them properly, you need to create a ListBox that holds a ListBox to display the data. It sounds a bit recursive, but it will make sense once you see it.

Start by adding another row to the DetailsGrid and make sure the Height of the Window is at least 300. Add a ListBox in the last row, and bind the ItemsSource to the DetailsGrid, using Validation.Errors for the path, as follows:

```
<ListBox Grid.Row="6" Grid.Column="0" Grid.ColumnSpan="2"
    ItemsSource="{Binding ElementName=DetailsGrid, Path=(Validation.Errors)}">
</ListBox>
```

Add a DataTemplate to the ListBox, and in the DataTemplate, add a ListBox that is bound to the ErrorContent property. The data context for each ListBoxItem in this case is a ValidationError object, so you don't need to set the data context, just the path. Set the binding path to ErrorContent, like this:

```
<ListBox.ItemTemplate>
  <DataTemplate>
    <ListBox ItemsSource="{Binding Path=ErrorContent}"/>
  </DataTemplate>
</ListBox.ItemTemplate>
```

Run the app, select Chevy, and set the color to Pink. You will see the errors displayed in Figure 29-4.

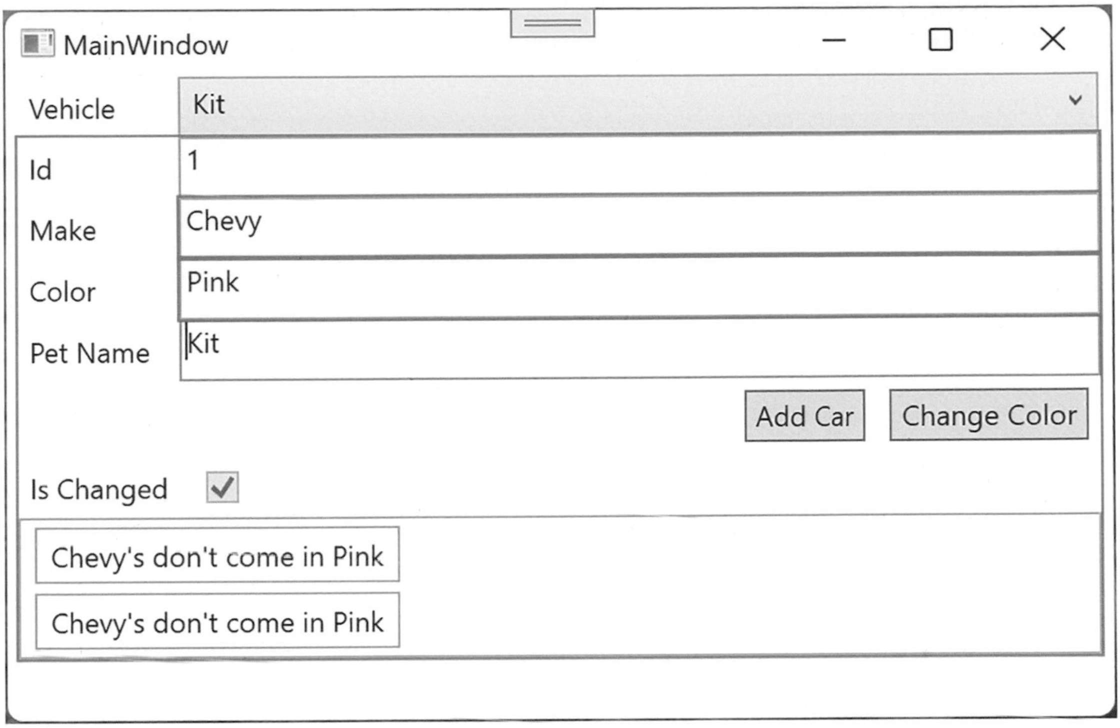

Figure 29-4. Showing the errors collection

This just scratches the surface of what you can do with validations and with displaying the errors generated, but it should have you well on your way to developing informative UIs that improve the user experience.

Move the Support Code to a Base Class

As you probably noticed, there is a lot of code now in the `CarPartial.cs` class. Since this example has only one model class, this isn't terrible. But, as you add models to a real application, you don't want to have to add all of that plumbing into each partial class for your models. The best thing to do is to push all of that supporting code down to a base class. You will do that now.

Add a new class file to the `Models` folder named `BaseEntity.cs`. Add `using` statements for `System.Collections` and `System.ComponentModel`. Make the class public, and add the `INotifyDataErrorInfo` interface, like this:

```
using System;
using System.Collections;
using System.Collections.Generic;
using System.ComponentModel;
using System.Linq;

namespace Validations.Models
{
  public class BaseEntity : INotifyDataErrorInfo
}
```

Move all of the code from CarPartial.cs that relates to INofityDataErrorInfo into the new base class. Any private methods and variables need to be made protected. Next, remove the INotifyDataErrorInfo interface from the CarPartial.cs class, and add BaseEntity as a base class, as follows:

```
public partial class Car : BaseEntity, IDataErrorInfo
{
 //removed for brevity
}
```

Now, any additional model classes you create will inherit all of the INotifyDataErrorInfo plumbing code.

Leverage Data Annotations with WPF

WPF can leverage data annotations as well for UI validation. Let's add some data annotations to the Car model.

Add Data Annotations to the Model

Open Car.cs and add a using statement for System.ComponentModel.DataAnnotations. Add the [Required] and [StringLength(50)] attributes to Make, Color, and PetName. The Required attribute adds a validation rule that the property must not be null (admittedly, this is redundant for the Id property since it is not a nullable int). The StringLength(50) attribute adds a validation rule that the value of the property cannot be longer than 50 characters.

Check for Data Annotation–Based Validation Errors

In WPF you have to programmatically check for data annotation-based validation errors. Two key classes for annotation-based validations are the ValidationContext and Validator classes. The ValidationContext class provides a context for checking a class for validation errors. The Validator class allows you to check an object for attribute-based errors within a ValidationContext.

Open BaseEntity.cs, and add the following using statements:

```
using System.ComponentModel;
using System.ComponentModel.DataAnnotations;
```

Next, create a new method named GetErrorsFromAnnotations(). This method is generic, takes a string property name and a value of type T as the parameters, and returns a string array. Make sure the method is marked as protected. The signature is listed here:

```
protected string[] GetErrorsFromAnnotations<T>(
  string propertyName, T value)
{}
```

In the method, create a List<ValidationResult> variable that will hold the results of validation checks and create a ValidationContext scoped to the property name passed into the method. When you have those two items in place, call Validate.TryValidateProperty, which returns a bool. If everything passes (in regard to data annotation validations), it returns true. If not, it returns false and populates the List<ValidationResult> with the errors. The complete code is shown here:

```
protected string[] GetErrorsFromAnnotations<T>(
```

```
  string propertyName, T value)
{
  var results = new List<ValidationResult>();
  var vc = new ValidationContext(this, null, null)
    { MemberName = propertyName };
  var isValid = Validator.TryValidateProperty(
    value, vc, results);
  return (isValid)
    ? null
    : Array.ConvertAll(
        results.ToArray(), o => o.ErrorMessage);
}
```

Now you can update the indexer method in CarPartial.cs to check for any errors based on data annotations. If any errors are found, add them to the errors collection supporting INotifyDataErrorInfo. This enables us to clean up the error handling. In the start of the indexer method, clear the errors for the column. Then process the validations and finally the custom logic for the entity. The updated indexer code is shown here:

```
public string this[string columnName]
{
  get
  {
    ClearErrors(columnName);
    var errorsFromAnnotations =
      GetErrorsFromAnnotations(columnName,
        typeof(Car)
        .GetProperty(columnName)?.GetValue(this,null));
    if (errorsFromAnnotations != null)
    {
      AddErrors(columnName, errorsFromAnnotations);
    }
    switch (columnName)
    {
      case nameof(Id):
        break;
      case nameof(Make):
        CheckMakeAndColor();
        if (Make == "ModelT")
        {
          AddError(nameof(Make), "Too Old");
        }
        break;
      case nameof(Color):
        CheckMakeAndColor();
        break;
      case nameof(PetName):
        break;
    }
    return string.Empty;
  }
}
```

Run the app, select one of the vehicles, and add text for the color that is longer than 50 characters. When you cross the 50-character threshold, the StringLength data annotation creates a validation error, and it is reported to the user, as shown in Figure 29-5.

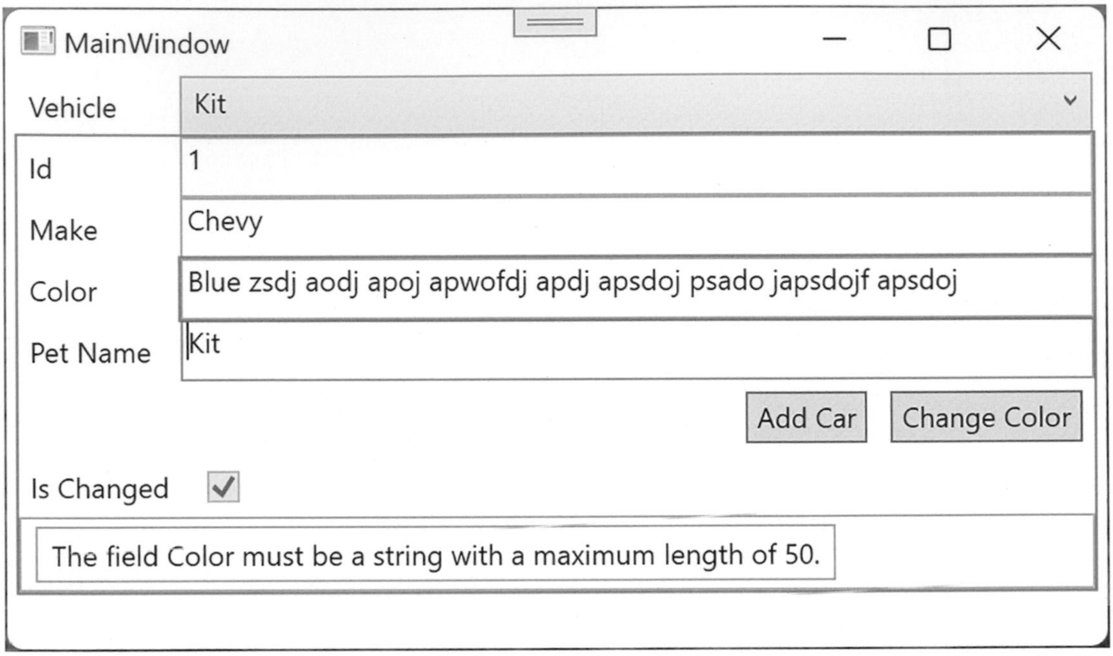

Figure 29-5. Validating the required data annotation

Customizing the ErrorTemplate

The final topic is to create a style that will be applied when a control is in error and also update the ErrorTemplate to display more meaningful error information. As you learned in Chapter 27, controls are customizable through styles and control templates.

Start by adding a new style in the Windows.Resources section of MainWindow.xaml with a target type of TextBox. Next, add a trigger on the style that sets properties when the Validation.HasError property is set to true. The properties and the values to set are Background (Pink), Foreground (Black), and Tooltip to the ErrorContent. The Background and Foreground setters are nothing new, but the syntax for setting the ToolTip needs some explanation. The binding points back to the control that this style is applied to, in this case, the TextBox. The path is the first ErrorContent value of the Validation.Errors collection. The markup is as follows:

```
<Window.Resources>
  <Style TargetType="{x:Type TextBox}">
    <Style.Triggers>
      <Trigger Property="Validation.HasError" Value="true">
        <Setter Property="Background" Value="Pink" />
        <Setter Property="Foreground" Value="Black" />
        <Setter Property="ToolTip"
```

```
            Value="{Binding RelativeSource={RelativeSource Self},
            Path=(Validation.Errors)[0].ErrorContent}"/>
      </Trigger>
    </Style.Triggers>
  </Style>
</Window.Resources>
```

Run the app and create an error condition. The result will be similar to Figure 29-6, complete with a tooltip showing the error message.

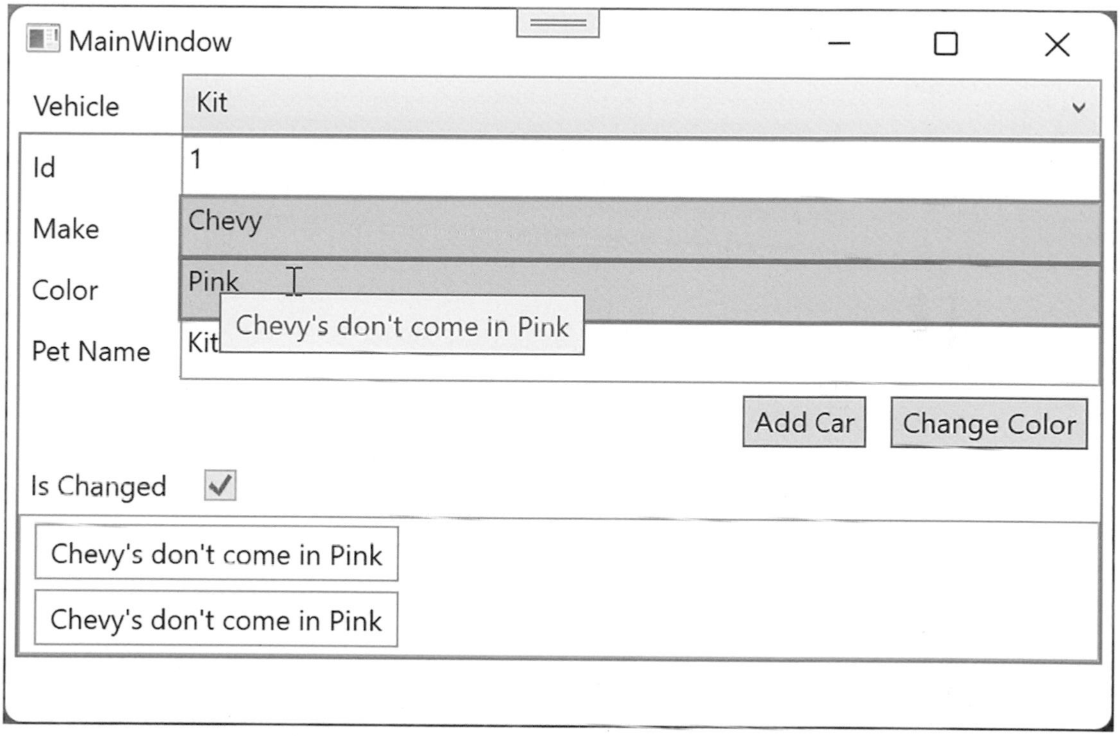

Figure 29-6. *Showing a custom ErrorTemplate*

The previous style changed the appearance of any `TextBox` that has an error condition. Next, you will create a custom control template to update the `ErrorTemplate` of the `Validation` class to show a red exclamation mark and set the tooltips for the exclamation mark. The `ErrorTemplate` is an *adorner*, which sits on top of the control. While the style just created updates the control itself, the `ErrorTemplate` will sit on top of the control.

Place a setter immediately after the `Style.Triggers` closing tag within the style you just created. You will be creating a control template that consists of a `TextBlock` (to show the exclamation mark) and a `BorderBrush` to surround the `TextBox` that contains the error(s). There is a special tag in XAML for the control that is being adorned with the `ErrorTemplate` named `AdornedElementPlaceholder`. By adding a name to this control, you can access the errors that are associated with the control. In this example, you want to access the `Validation.Errors` property so you can get the `ErrorContent` (just like you did in the `Style.Trigger`). Here is the full markup for the setter:

```
<Setter Property="Validation.ErrorTemplate">
  <Setter.Value>
    <ControlTemplate>
      <DockPanel LastChildFill="True">
        <TextBlock Foreground="Red" FontSize="20" Text="!"
          ToolTip="{Binding ElementName=controlWithError,
          Path=AdornedElement.(Validation.Errors)[0].ErrorContent}"/>
        <Border BorderBrush="Red" BorderThickness="1">
          <AdornedElementPlaceholder Name="controlWithError" />
        </Border>
      </DockPanel>
    </ControlTemplate>
  </Setter.Value>
</Setter>
```

Run the app and create an error condition. The result will be similar to Figure 29-7.

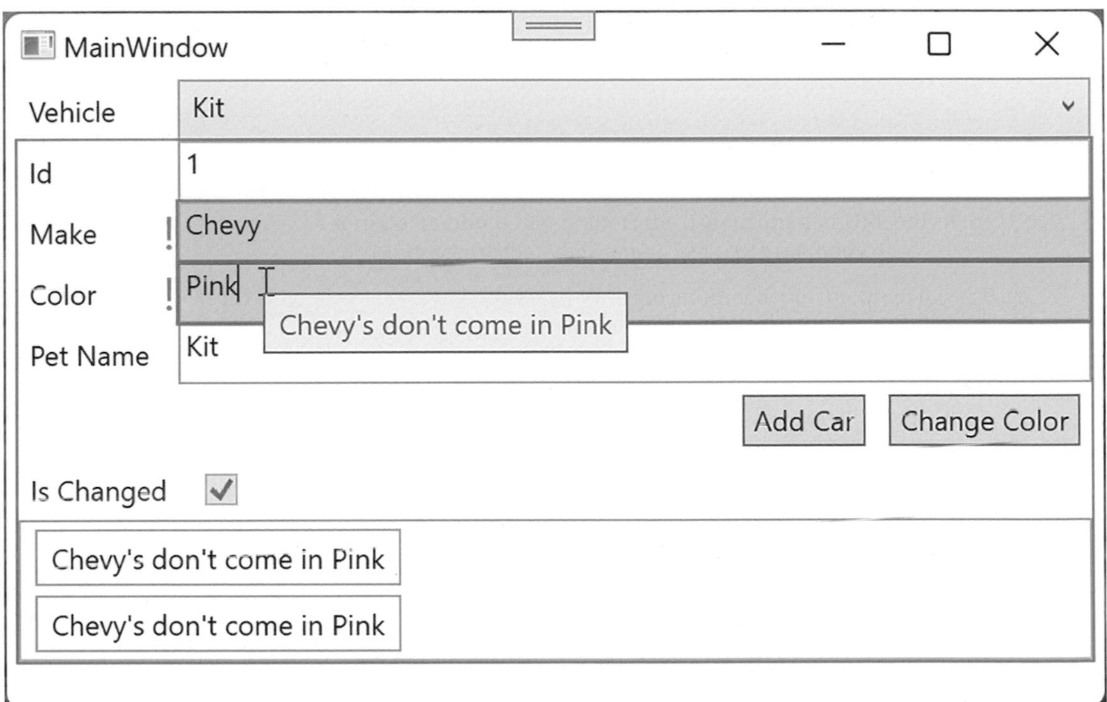

Figure 29-7. *Showing a custom ErrorTemplate*

Wrapping Up Validations

This completes your look at validation methods within WPF. Of course, there is much more that you can do. For more information, consult the WPF documentation.

Creating Custom Commands

As with the validations sections, you can continue working in the same project or create a new one and copy all of the code to it. I will create a new project named WpfCommands. If you are using the same project, be sure to pay attention to the namespaces in the code samples in this section and adjust them as needed.

As you learned in Chapter 25, commands are an integral part of WPF. Commands can be hooked up to WPF controls (such as `Button` and `MenuItem` controls) to handle user events, such as the `Click()` event. Instead of creating an event handler directly and adding the code directly into the code-behind file, the `Execute()` method of the command is executed when the click event fires. The `CanExecute()` method is used to enable or disable the control based on custom code. In addition to the built-in commands you used in Chapter 25, you can create your own custom commands by implementing the `ICommand` interface. By using commands instead of event handlers, you gain the benefit of encapsulating application code, as well as automatically enabling and disabling controls based on business logic.

Implementing the ICommand Interface

As a quick review from Chapter 25, the `ICommand` interface is listed here:

```
public interface ICommand
{
  event EventHandler CanExecuteChanged;
  bool CanExecute(object parameter);
  void Execute(object parameter);
}
```

Adding the ChangeColorCommand

The event handlers for your `Button` controls will be replaced with commands, starting with the Change Color button. Start by adding a new folder (named `Cmds`) in your project. Add a new class named `ChangeColorCommand.cs`. Make the class public, and implement the `ICommand` interface. Add the following `using` statements (the first one might vary depending on whether you created a new project for this sample):

```
using WpfCommands.Models;
using System.Windows.Input;
```

Your class should look like this:

```
public class ChangeColorCommand : ICommand
{
  public bool CanExecute(object parameter)
  {
    throw new NotImplementedException();
  }
  public void Execute(object parameter)
  {
    throw new NotImplementedException();
  }
  public event EventHandler CanExecuteChanged;
}
```

If the CanExecute() method returns true, any bound controls will be enabled, and if it returns false, they will be disabled. If a control is enabled (because CanExecute() returns true) and clicked, the Execute() method will fire. The parameter passed into both of these methods comes from the UI based on the CommandParameter property set on binding statements. The CanExecuteChanged event ties into the binding and notification system to inform the UI that the result of the CanExecute() method has changed (much like the PropertyChanged event).

In this example, the Change Color button should work only if the parameter is not null and of type Car. Update the CanExecute() method to the following:

```
public bool CanExecute(object parameter)
  => (parameter as Car) != null;
```

The value for the Execute() method parameter is the same as for the CanExecute() method. Since the Execute() method can execute only if the object is of type Car, the argument must be cast to an Car type and have the color updated, as follows:

```
public void Execute(object parameter)
{
  ((Car)parameter).Color="Pink";
}
```

Attaching the Command to the CommandManager

The final update for the command class is to type the command into the command manager. The CanExecute() method fires when the Window first loads and then when the command manager instructs it to reexecute. Each command class has to opt in to the command manager. This is done by updating the code regarding the CanExecuteChanged event, as follows:

```
public event EventHandler CanExecuteChanged
{
  add => CommandManager.RequerySuggested += value;
  remove => CommandManager.RequerySuggested -= value;
}
```

Updating MainWindow.xaml.cs

The next change is to create an instance of this class that the Button can access. For now, you will place this in the code-behind file for the MainWindow (later in this chapter, you will move this into a view model). Open MainWindow.xaml.cs and delete the Click event handler for the Change Color button. Add the following using statements to the top of the file (again, the namespace may vary based on whether you are still using the same project or you started a new one):

```
using WpfCommands.Cmds;
using System.Windows.Input;
```

Next, add a public property named ChangeColorCmd of type ICommand with a backing field. In the expression body for the property, return the backing property (make sure to instantiate a new instance of the ChangeColorCommand if the backing field is null).

```
private ICommand _changeColorCommand = null;
public ICommand ChangeColorCmd
  => _changeColorCommand ??= new ChangeColorCommand());
```

Updating MainWindow.xaml

As you saw in Chapter 25, clickable controls in WPF (like `Button` controls) have a `Command` property that allows you to assign a command object to the control. Start by connecting your command instantiated in the code-behind to the `btnChangeColor` button. Since the property for the command is on the `MainWindow` class, you use the `RelativeSourceMode` binding syntax to get to the `Window` that contains the `Button`, as follows:

```
Command="{Binding Path=ChangeColorCmd,
  RelativeSource={RelativeSource Mode=FindAncestor, AncestorType={x:Type Window}}}"
```

The `Button` still needs to send in a `Car` object as the parameter for the `CanExecute()` and `Execute()` methods. This is assigned through the `CommandParameter` property. You set this to the `SelectedItem` of the `cboCars` `ComboBox`, as follows:

```
CommandParameter="{Binding ElementName=cboCars, Path=SelectedItem}"
```

The complete markup for the button is shown here:

```
<Button x:Name="btnChangeColor" Content="Change Color" Margin="5,0,5,0"
    Padding="4, 2" Command="{Binding Path=ChangeColorCmd,
        RelativeSource={RelativeSource Mode=FindAncestor, AncestorType={x:Type Window}}}"
    CommandParameter="{Binding ElementName=cboCars, Path=SelectedItem}"/>
```

Testing the Application

Run the application. You will see that the Change Color command is *not* enabled, as shown in Figure 29-8, since there isn't a vehicle selected.

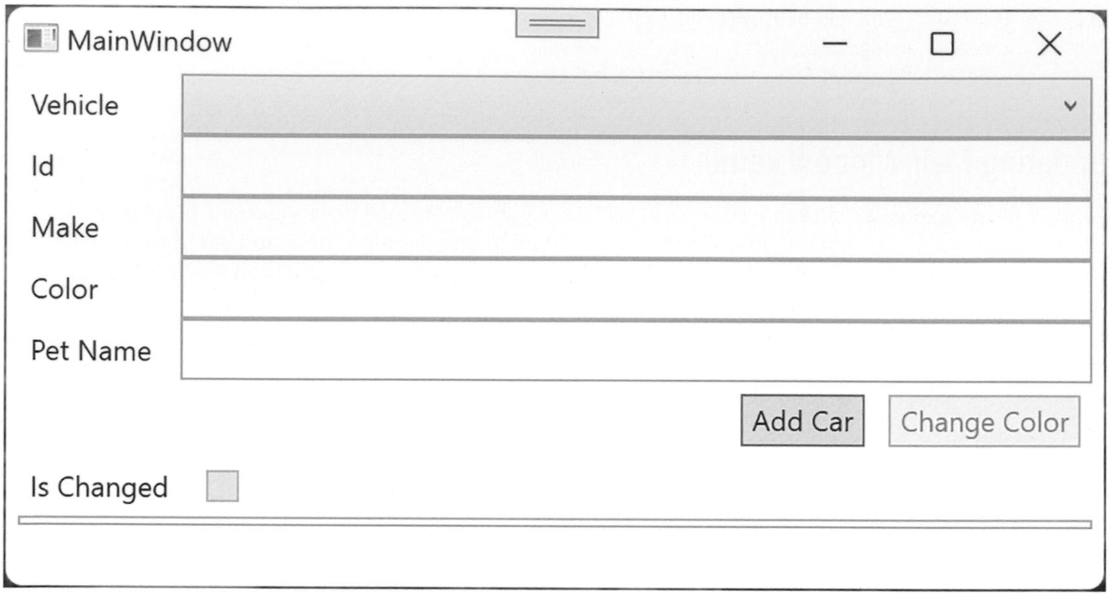

Figure 29-8. *A window with nothing selected*

Now, select a vehicle; the button will become enabled, and clicking it will change the color, as expected!

Creating the CommandBase Class

If you continued with this pattern for `AddCarCommand.cs`, there would be code that would be repeated between the classes. This is a good sign that a base class can help. Create a new class in the `Cmds` folder named `CommandBase.cs` and add a `using` for the `System.Windows.Input` namespace. Set the class to public and implement the `ICommand` interface. Change the class and the `Execute()` and `CanExecute()` methods to abstract. Finally, add in the updated `CanExecuteChanged` event from the `ChangeColorCommand` class. The full implementation is listed here:

```
using System;
using System.Windows.Input;

namespace WpfCommands.Cmds
{
  public abstract class CommandBase : ICommand
  {
    public abstract bool CanExecute(object parameter);
    public abstract void Execute(object parameter);
    public event EventHandler CanExecuteChanged
    {
      add => CommandManager.RequerySuggested += value;
      remove => CommandManager.RequerySuggested -= value;
    }
  }
}
```

Adding the AddCarCommand Class

Add a new class named AddCarCommand.cs to the Cmds folder. Make the class public and add CommandBase as the base class. Add the following using statements to the top of the file:

```
using System.Collections.ObjectModel;
using System.Linq;
using WpfCommands.Models;
```

The parameter is expected to be an ObservableCollection<Car>, so check to make sure of this in the CanExecute() method. If it is, then the Execute() method should add an additional car, just like the Click event handler.

```
public class AddCarCommand :CommandBase
{
  public override bool CanExecute(object parameter)
    => parameter is ObservableCollection<Car>;
  public override void Execute(object parameter)
  {
    if (parameter is not ObservableCollection<Car> cars)
    {
      return;
    }
    var maxCount = cars.Max(x => x.Id);
    cars.Add(new Car
    {
      Id = ++maxCount,
      Color = "Yellow",
      Make = "VW",
      PetName = "Birdie"
    });
  }
}
```

Updating MainWindow.xaml.cs

Add a public property named AddCarCmd of type ICommand with a backing field. In the expression body for the property, return the backing property (make sure to instantiate a new instance of the AddCarCommand if the backing field is null).

```
private ICommand _addCarCommand = null;
public ICommand AddCarCmd
  => _addCarCommand ??= new AddCarCommand());
```

Updating MainWindow.xaml

Update the XAML to remove the Click attribute and add the Command and CommandParameter attributes. The AddCarCommand will receive the list of cars from the cboCars combo box. The entire button's XAML is as follows:

```
<Button x:Name="btnAddCar" Content="Add Car" Margin="5,0,5,0" Padding="4, 2"
  Command="{Binding Path=AddCarCmd,
      RelativeSource={RelativeSource Mode=FindAncestor, AncestorType={x:Type Window}}}"
   CommandParameter="{Binding ElementName=cboCars, Path=ItemsSource}"/>
```

With this in place, you can now add cars and update the color of cars using reusable code contained in stand-alone classes.

Updating ChangeColorCommand

The final step is to update the ChangeColorCommand to inherit from CommandBase. Change ICommand to CommandBase, add the override keyword to both methods, and delete the CanExecuteChanged code. It's really that simple! The new code is listed here:

```
public class ChangeColorCommand : CommandBase
{
  public override bool CanExecute(object parameter)
    => parameter is Car;
  public override void Execute(object parameter)
  {
    ((Car)parameter).Color = "Pink";
  }
}
```

RelayCommands

Another implementation of the command pattern in WPF is the RelayCommand. Instead of creating a new class for each command, this pattern uses delegates to implement the ICommand interface. It is a lightweight implementation, in that each command doesn't have its own class. RelayCommands are usually used when there isn't any reuse needed for the implementation of the command.

Creating the Base RelayCommand

RelayCommands are typically implemented in two classes. The base RelayCommand class is used when there aren't any parameters needed for the CanExecute() and Execute() methods, and RelayCommand<T> is used when a parameter is required. You will start with the base RelayCommand class, which leverages the CommandBase class. Add a new class named RelayCommand.cs to the Cmds folder. Make the class public and add CommandBase as the base class. Add two class-level variables to hold the Execute() and CanExecute() delegates.

```
private readonly Action _execute;
private readonly Func<bool> _canExecute;
```

Create three constructors. The first is the default constructor (needed by the RelayCommand<T>-derived class), the second is a constructor that takes an Action parameter, and the third is a constructor that takes an Action parameter and a Func parameter, as follows:

```
public RelayCommand(){}
public RelayCommand(Action execute) : this(execute, null) { }
public RelayCommand(Action execute, Func<bool> canExecute)
{
  _execute = execute
    ?? throw new ArgumentNullException(nameof(execute));
  _canExecute = canExecute;
}
```

Finally, implement the CanExecute() and Execute() overrides. CanExecute() returns true if the Func is null; or if it is not null, it executes and returns true. Execute() executes the Action parameter.

```
public override bool CanExecute(object parameter)
  => _canExecute == null || _canExecute();
public override void Execute(object parameter) { _execute(); }
```

Creating RelayCommand<T>

Add a new class named RelayCommandT.cs to the Cmds folder. This class is almost a carbon copy of the base class, except that the delegates all take a parameter. Make the class public and generic, and add RelayCommand as the base class, as follows:

```
public class RelayCommand<T> : RelayCommand
```

Add two class-level variables to hold the Execute() and CanExecute() delegates:

```
private readonly Action<T> _execute;
private readonly Func<T, bool> _canExecute;
```

Create two constructors. The first takes an Action<T> parameter, and the second takes an Action<T> parameter and a Func<T,bool> parameter, as follows:

```
public RelayCommand(Action<T> execute):this(execute, null) {}
public RelayCommand(
  Action<T> execute, Func<T, bool> canExecute)
{
  _execute = execute
    ?? throw new ArgumentNullException(nameof(execute));
  _canExecute = canExecute;
}
```

Finally, implement the CanExecute() and Execute() overrides. CanExecute() returns true if the Func is null; or, if it is not null, it executes and returns true. Execute() executes the Action parameter.

```
public override bool CanExecute(object parameter)
  => _canExecute == null || _canExecute((T)parameter);
public override void Execute(object parameter)
  { _execute((T)parameter); }
```

Updating MainWindow.xaml.cs

When you use RelayCommands, all of the methods for the delegates need to be specified when a new command is constructed. This doesn't mean that the code needs to live in the code-behind (as is shown here); it just has to be accessible from the code-behind. It could live in another class (or even another assembly), providing the code encapsulation benefits of creating a custom command class.

Add a new private variable of type RelayCommand<Car> and a public property named DeleteCarCmd, as shown here:

```
private RelayCommand<Car> _deleteCarCommand = null;
public RelayCommand<Car> DeleteCarCmd
  => _deleteCarCommand ??=
     new RelayCommand<Car>(DeleteCar,CanDeleteCar));
```

The DeleteCar() and CanDeleteCar() methods must be created as well, as follows:

```
private bool CanDeleteCar(Car car) => car != null;
private void DeleteCar(Car car)
{
  _cars.Remove(car);
}
```

Notice the strong typing in the methods—this is one of the benefits of using RelayCommand<T>.

Adding and Implementing the Delete Car Button

The final step to tie it all together is to add the button and assign the Command and CommandParameter bindings. Add the following markup:

```
<Button x:Name="btnDeleteCar" Content="Delete Car" Margin="5,0,5,0" Padding="4, 2"
  Command="{Binding Path=DeleteCarCmd,
      RelativeSource={RelativeSource Mode=FindAncestor, AncestorType={x:Type Window}}}"
  CommandParameter="{Binding ElementName=cboCars, Path=SelectedItem}"/>
```

Now when you run the application, you can test that the Delete Car button is enabled only if a car is selected in the drop-down and that clicking the button does indeed delete the car from the Car list.

Wrapping Up Commands

This concludes your brief journey into WPF commands. By moving the event handling out of the code-behind file and into individual command classes, you gain the benefit of code encapsulating, reuse, and improved maintainability. If you don't need that much separation of concerns, you can use the lighter-weight RelayCommand implementation. The goal is to improve maintainability and code quality, so choose the method that works best for you.

Migrate Code and Data to a View Model

As in the "WPF Validations" section, you can continue working in the same project, or you can create a new one and copy all of the code over. I will create a new project named WpfViewModel. If you are using the same project, be sure to pay attention to the namespaces in the code samples in this section and adjust as needed.

Create a new folder named `ViewModels` in your project, and add a new class named `MainWindowViewModel.cs` into that folder. Add the following namespaces and make the class public:

```
using System.Collections.Generic;
using System.Collections.ObjectModel;
using System.Windows.Input;
using WpfViewModel.Cmds;
using WpfViewModel.Models;
```

■ **Note** A popular convention is to name the view models after the window they support. I typically follow that convention and will do so in this chapter. However, like any pattern or convention, this isn't a rule, and you will find a wide range of opinions on this.

Moving the MainWindow.xaml.cs Code

Almost all the code from the code-behind file will be moved to the view model. At the end, there will only be a few lines, including the call to `InitializeComponent()` and the code for setting the data context for the window to the view model.

Create a public property of type `IList<Car>` named `Cars`, like this:

```
public IList<Car> Cars { get; } =
  new ObservableCollection<Car>();
```

Create a default constructor and move all the `Car` creation code from the `MainWindow.xaml.cs` file, updating the list variable name. You can also delete the `_cars` variable from `MainWindow.xaml.cs`. Here is the view model constructor:

```
public MainWindowViewModel()
{
  Cars.Add(
    new Car { Id = 1, Color = "Blue", Make = "Chevy", PetName = "Kit", IsChanged = false });
    Cars.Add(
    new Car { Id = 2, Color = "Red", Make = "Ford", PetName = "Red Rider", IsChanged = false });
}
```

Next, move all the command-related code from the window code-behind file to the view model, updating the _cars variable reference to Cars. Here is just the changed code:

```
//rest omitted for brevity
private void DeleteCar(Car car)
{
  Cars.Remove(car);
}
```

Updating the MainWindow Code and Markup

Most of the code has been removed from the MainWindow.xaml.cs file. Remove the line that assigns the ItemsSource for the combo box, leaving only the call to InitializeComponent. It should now look like this:

```
public MainWindow()
{
    InitializeComponent();
}
```

Add the following using statement to the top of the file:

```
using WpfViewModel.ViewModels;
```

Next, create a strongly typed property to hold the instance of the view model.

```
public MainWindowViewModel ViewModel { get; set; }
  = new MainWindowViewModel();
```

Finally, add a DataContext property to the window's declaration in XAML.

```
DataContext="{Binding ViewModel, RelativeSource={RelativeSource Self}}"
```

Updating the Control Markup

Now that the DataContext for the Window is set to the view model, the XAML bindings for the controls need to be updated. Starting with the combo box, update the markup by adding an ItemsSource.

```
<ComboBox Name="cboCars" Grid.Column="1" DisplayMemberPath="PetName" ItemsSource="{Binding
Cars}" />
```

This works because the data context for the Window is the MainWindowViewModel, and Cars is a public property on the view model. Recall that binding calls walk up the element tree until a data context is located. Next, you need to update the bindings for the Button controls. This is straightforward; since the bindings are already set to the window level, you just need to update the binding statement to start with the DataContext property, as follows:

```
<Button x:Name="btnAddCar" Content="Add Car" Margin="5,0,5,0" Padding="4, 2"
    Command="{Binding Path=DataContext.AddCarCmd,
        RelativeSource={RelativeSource Mode=FindAncestor, AncestorType={x:Type Window}}}"
```

```
    CommandParameter="{Binding ElementName=cboCars, Path=ItemsSource}"/>
<Button x:Name="btnDeleteCar" Content="Delete Car" Margin="5,0,5,0" Padding="4, 2"
    Command="{Binding Path=DataContext.DeleteCarCmd,
        RelativeSource={RelativeSource Mode=FindAncestor, AncestorType={x:Type Window}}}"
    CommandParameter="{Binding ElementName=cboCars, Path=SelectedItem}" />
<Button x:Name="btnChangeColor" Content="Change Color" Margin="5,0,5,0" Padding="4, 2"
    Command="{Binding Path=DataContext.ChangeColorCmd,
        RelativeSource={RelativeSource Mode=FindAncestor, AncestorType={x:Type Window}}}"
    CommandParameter="{Binding ElementName=cboCars, Path=SelectedItem}"/>
```

Wrapping Up View Models

Believe it or not, you have just completed your first MVVM WPF application. You might be thinking, "This isn't a real application. What about data? The data in this example is hard-coded." And you would be correct. It's not a real app; it's demoware. However, that is the beauty of the MVVM pattern. The view doesn't know anything about where the data is coming from; it's just binding to a property on the view model. You can swap out view model implementations, perhaps using a version with hard-coded data for testing and one that hits the database for production.

There are a lot of additional points that could be discussed, including various open source frameworks, the View Model Locator pattern, and a host of differing opinions on how to best implement the pattern. That's the beauty of software design patterns—there are usually many correct ways to implement it, and then you just need to find the best manner based on your business and technical requirements.

Updating AutoLot.Dal for MVVM

If you want to update `AutoLot.Dal` for MVVM, you will have to apply the changes that we did for the `Car` class to all of the entities in the AutoLot.Dal.Models project, including the `BaseEntity`.

Summary

This chapter examined the WPF topics that support the Model-View-ViewModel pattern. You started off learning how to tie model classes and collections into the notification system in the binding manager. You implemented `INotifyPropertyChanged` and used `ObservableCollections` classes to keep the UI in sync with the bound data.

Next, you added validation code to the model using `IDataErrorInfo` and `INotifyDataErrorInfo` and checked for data annotation errors. You then displayed any validation errors in the UI so the user would know what the problem is and how to fix it, and you created a style and custom control template to render errors in a meaningful way.

Finally, you put it all together by adding a view model, and you cleaned up the UI markup and code-behind file to increase separation of concerns.

PART IX

ASP.NET Core

CHAPTER 30

Introducing ASP.NET Core

The final section of this book covers ASP.NET Core, C# and the .NET web development framework. The chapter begins with an introduction of ASP.NET MVC and the basics of the MVC pattern as implemented in ASP.NET Core. Next, you will create the solution and the three ASP.NET Core projects that will be developed over the course of the rest of the book. The first application, AutoLot.Api is an ASP.NET Core RESTful service, the second is an ASP.NET Core web application using the Model-View-Controller pattern and the final application is an ASP.NET Core web application using Razor pages. The RESTFul services serves as an optional back end to the MVC and Razor Page applications, and the AutoLot.Dal and AutoLot.Models projects that you built earlier in this book will serve as the data access layer for all of the applications.

After building the projects and solution, the next section demonstrates the many ways to run and debug ASP.NET Core projects using Visual Studio or Visual Studio Code. The rest of this chapter explores the many features from ASP.NET that were carried forward into ASP.NET Core. This includes controllers and actions, routing, model binding and validation, and finally filters.

A Quick Look Back at ASP.NET MVC

The ASP.NET MVC framework is based on the Model-View-Controller pattern and provided an answer to developers who were frustrated by WebForms, which was essentially a leaky abstraction over HTTP. WebForms was created to help client-server developers move to the Web, and it was pretty successful in that respect. However, as developers became more accustomed to web development, many wanted more control over the rendered output, elimination of view state, and adherence to a proven web application design pattern. With those goals in mind, ASP.NET MVC was created.

Introducing the MVC Pattern

The Model-View-Controller (MVC) pattern has been around since the 1970s, originally created as a pattern for use in Smalltalk. The pattern has made a resurgence recently, with implementations in many different and varied languages, including Java (Spring Framework), Ruby (Ruby on Rails), and .NET(ASP.NET MVC).

The Model

The *model* is the data of your application. The data is typically represented by plain old CLR objects (POCOs). View models are composed of one or more models and shaped specifically for the consumer of the data. One way to think about models and view models is to relate them to database tables and database views.

Academically, models should be extremely clean and not contain validation or any other business rules. Pragmatically, whether or not models contain validation logic or other business rules depends

A. Troelsen and P. Japikse, *Pro C# 10 with .NET 6*, https://doi.org/10.1007/978-1-4842-7869-7_30

entirely on the language and frameworks used, as well as specific application needs. For example, EF Core contains many data annotations that double as a mechanism for shaping the database tables and a means for validation in ASP.NET Core web applications. In this book (and in my professional work), the examples focus on reducing duplication of code, which places data annotations and validations where they make the most sense.

The View

The *view* is the user interface of the application. Views accept commands and render the results of those commands to the user. The view should be as lightweight as possible and not actually process any of the work, but hand off all work to the controller. Views are typically strongly typed to a model, although that is not required.

The Controller

The *controller* is the brains of the application. Controllers take commands/requests from the user (via the view) or client (through API calls) through action methods, and handle them appropriately. The results of the operation are then returned to the user or client. Controllers should be lightweight and leverage other components or services to handle the details of the requests. This promotes separation of concerns and increases testability and maintainability.

ASP.NET Core and the MVC Pattern

ASP.NET Core is capable of creating many types of web applications and services. Two of the options are web applications using the MVC pattern and RESTful services. If you have worked with ASP.NET "classic," these are analogous to ASP.NET MVC and ASP.NET Web API, respectively. The MVC web application and API application types share the "model" and the "controller" portion of the pattern, while MVC web applications also implement the "view" to complete the MVC pattern.

ASP.NET Core and .NET Core

Just as Entity Framework Core is a complete rewrite of Entity Framework 6, ASP.NET Core is a rewrite of the popular ASP.NET Framework. Rewriting ASP.NET was no small task, but it was necessary in order to remove the dependency on `System.Web`. Removing this dependency enabled ASP.NET applications to run on operating systems other than Windows and other web servers besides Internet Information Services (IIS), including self-hosted. This opened the door for ASP.NET Core applications to use a cross-platform, lightweight, fast, and open source web server called Kestrel. Kestrel presents a uniform development experience across all platforms.

■ **Note** Kestrel was originally based on LibUV, but since ASP.NET Core 2.1, it is now based on managed sockets.

Like EF Core, ASP.NET Core is being developed on GitHub as a completely open source project (`https://github.com/aspnet`). It is also designed as a modular system of NuGet packages. Developers only install the features that are needed for a particular application, minimizing the application footprint, reducing the overhead, and decreasing security risks. Additional improvements include a simplified startup, built-in dependency injection, a cleaner configuration system, and pluggable middleware.

One Framework, Many Uses

There are lots of changes and improvements in ASP.NET Core, as you will see throughout the rest of the chapters in this section. Besides the cross-platform capabilities, another significant change is the unification of the web application frameworks. ASP.NET Core encompasses ASP.NET MVC, ASP.NET Web API, and Razor Pages into a single development framework. Developing web applications and services with the ASP.NET (not ASP.NET Core) Framework presented several choices, including WebForms, MVC, Web API, Windows Communication Foundation (WCF), and WebMatrix. They all had their positives and negatives; some were closely related, and others were quite different. All of the choices available meant developers had to know each of them in order to select the proper one for the task at hand or just select one and hope for the best.

With ASP.NET Core, you can build applications that use Razor Pages, the Model-View-Controller pattern, RESTful services, and SPA applications using Blazor WebAssembly or JavaScript frameworks like Angular and React. While the UI rendering varies with choices between MVC, Razor Pages, and the JavaScript frameworks, the underlying server side development framework is the same across all choices. Blazor WebAssembly is a client side development framework, and doesn't have a server side component like the other ASP.NET Core application types. Two prior choices that have not been carried forward into ASP.NET Core are WebForms and WCF.

■ **Note** With all of the separate frameworks brought under the same roof, the former names of ASP.NET MVC and ASP.NET Web API have been officially retired. In this book, I still refer to ASP.NET Core web applications using the Model-View-Controller pattern as MVC or MVC based applications and refer to ASP.NET RESTful services as API or RESTful services for simplicity.

Create and Configure the Solution and Projects

Before diving into the some of the major concepts in ASP.NET Core, let's build the solution and projects that will be used through the rest of the chapters. The ASP.NET Core projects can be created using either Visual Studio or the command line. Both options will be covered in the next two sections.

Using Visual Studio 2022

Visual Studio has the advantage of a GUI to step you through the process of creating a solution and projects, adding NuGet packages, and creating references between projects.

Create the Solution and Projects

Start by creating a new project in Visual Studio. Select the C# template ASP.NET Core Web API from the "Create a new project" dialog. In the "Configure your new project" dialog, enter **AutoLot.Api** for the project name and **AutoLot** for the solution name, as shown in Figure 30-1.

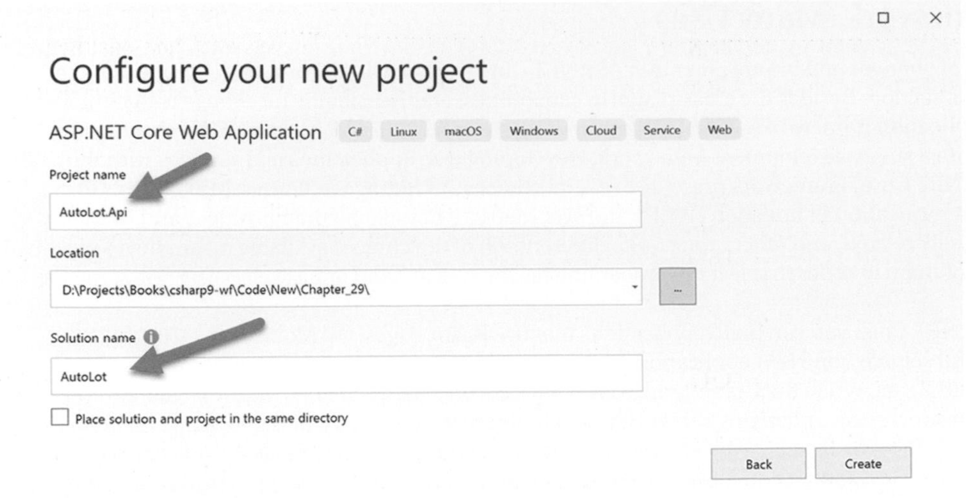

Figure 30-1. *Creating the AutoLot.Api project and AutoLot solution*

On the Additional information screen, select .NET 6.0 (Long-term support) for the Framework and leave the "Configure for HTTPS" and "Enable OpenAPI" check boxes checked, as shown in Figure 30-2. Then click Create.

■ **Note** Minimal APIs are a new feature in .NET 6 for creation without the traditional Controllers and action methods. These will not be covered in this text.

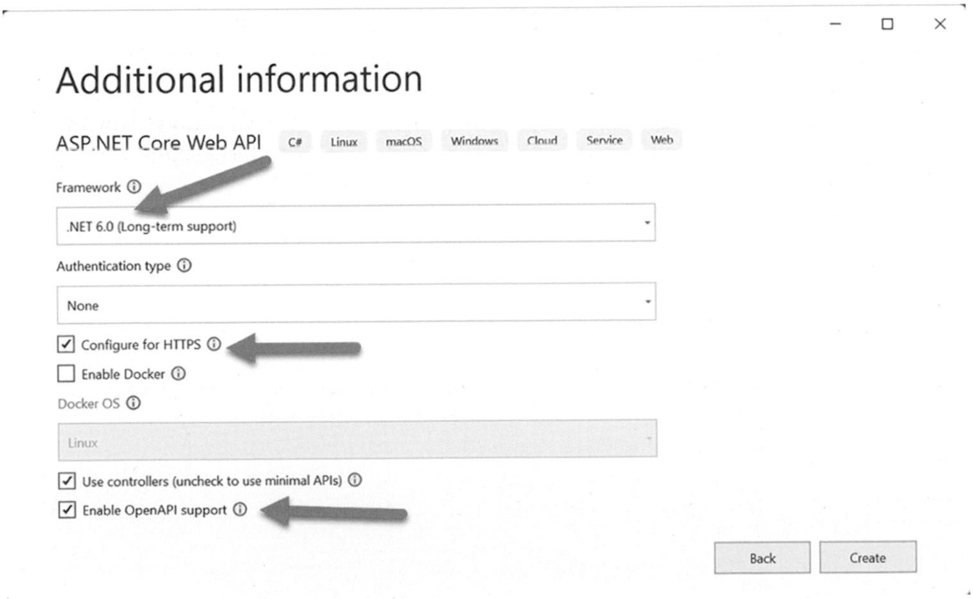

Figure 30-2. *Selecting the ASP.NET Core Web API template*

■ **Note** Hot reload is a new feature in .NET 6 that reloads your app while it is running when non-destructive changes are made, reducing the need to restart your application while developing to see changes. This has replaced Razor runtime compilation, which was used in .NET 5 to accomplish the same goal.

Now add another ASP.NET Core web application to the solution. Select the "ASP.NET Core Web App (Model-View-Controller)" template. Name the project **AutoLot.Mvc**, then make sure that .NET Core 6.0 is selected, and the "Configure for HTTPS" option is checked as shown in Figure 30-3.

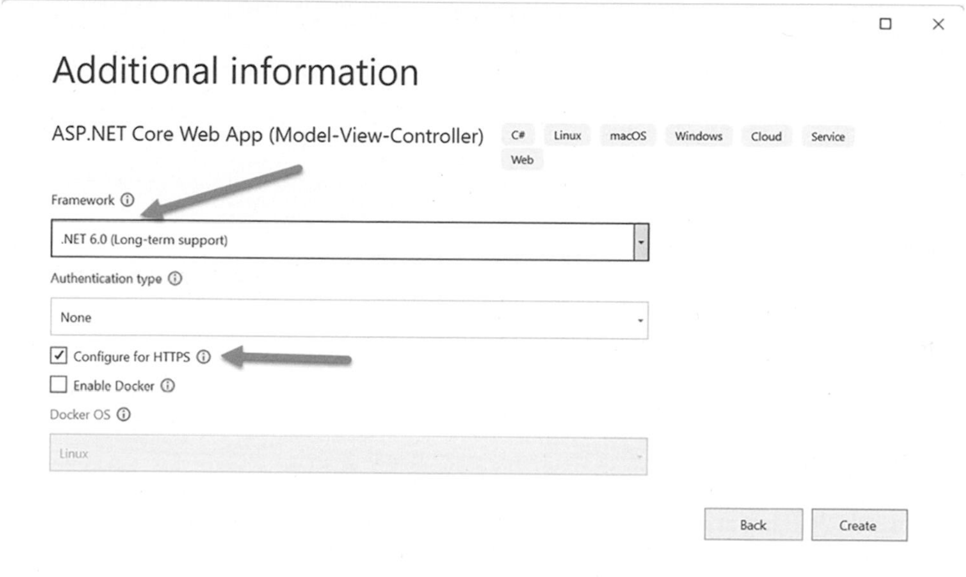

Additional information

ASP.NET Core Web App (Model-View-Controller) C# Linux macOS Windows Cloud Service Web

Framework

.NET 6.0 (Long-term support)

Authentication type

None

☑ Configure for HTTPS

☐ Enable Docker

Docker OS

Linux

Back Create

Figure 30-3. *Configuring the ASP.NET Core MVC based Web Application template*

Next, add the last ASP.NET Core web application to the solution. Select the "ASP.NET Core Web App" template. Name the project **AutoLot.Web**, then make sure that .NET Core 6.0 (Long-term support) is selected, and the "Configure for HTTPS" option is checked as shown in Figure 30-4.

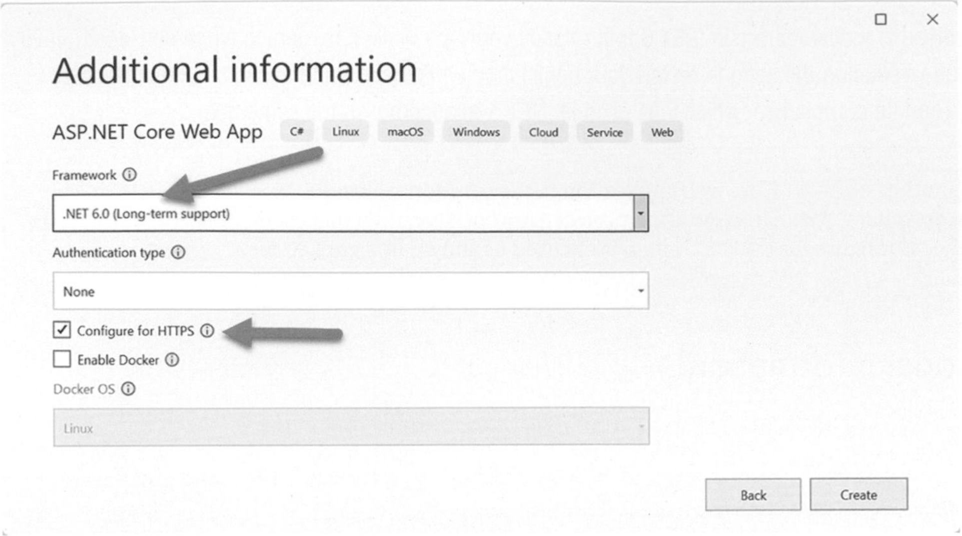

***Figure 30-4.** Configuring the ASP.NET Core Razor page MVC Web Application template*

Finally, add a C# Class Library to the project and name it **AutoLot.Services**.

Add in AutoLot.Models and AutoLot.Dal

The solution requires the completed data access layer which was completed in Chapter 23. You can also use the versions from Chapter 24, but that chapter was all about testing the finished data access layer and didn't make any changes to the data access layer projects. You can either copy the files into the current solution directory or leave them in the place where you built them. Either way, you need to right-click your solution name in Solution Explorer, select Add ➤ Existing Project, and navigate to the `AutoLot.Models.csproj` file and select it. Repeat for the AutoLot.Dal project by selecting the `AutoLot.Dal.csproj` file.

Add the Project References

Add the following project references by right-clicking the project name in Solution Explorer and selecting Add ➤ Project Reference for each project.

AutoLot.Api, AutoLot.Web, and AutoLot.Mvc reference the following:

- AutoLot.Models
- AutoLot.Dal
- AutoLot.Services

AutoLot.Services references the following:

- AutoLot.Models
- AutoLot.Dal

Add the NuGet Packages

Additional NuGet packages are needed to complete the applications.

To the AutoLot.Api project, add the following packages:

- `AutoMapper`
- `Microsoft.AspNetCore.Mvc.Versioning`
- `Microsoft.AspNetCore.Mvc.Versioning.ApiExplorer`
- `Microsoft.EntityFrameworkCore.Design`
- `Microsoft.EntityFrameworkCore.SqlServer`
- `Microsoft.VisualStudio.Web.CodeGeneration.Design`
- `Microsoft.VisualStudio.Threading.Analyzers`
- `System.Text.Json`
- `Swashbuckle.AspNetCore`
- `Swashbuckle.AspNetCore.Annotations`
- `Swashbuckle.AspNetCore.Swagger`
- `Swashbuckle.AspNetCore.SwaggerGen`
- `Swashbuckle.AspNetCore.SwaggerUI`

■ **Note** With the ASP.NET Core 6.0 API templates, `Swashbuckle.AspNetCore` is already referenced. The additional `Swashbuckle` packages add capabilities beyond the basic implementation.

To the AutoLot.Mvc project, add the following packages:

- `AutoMapper`
- `System.Text.Json`
- `LigerShark.WebOptimizer.Core`
- `Microsoft.Web.LibraryManager.Build`
- `Microsoft.VisualStudio.Web.CodeGeneration.Design`
- `Microsoft.EntityFrameworkCore.Design`
- `Microsoft.EntityFrameworkCore.SqlServer`
- `Microsoft.VisualStudio.Threading.Analyzers`

To the AutoLot.Web project, add the following packages:

- `AutoMapper`
- `System.Text.Json`
- `LigerShark.WebOptimizer.Core`
- `Microsoft.Web.LibraryManager.Build`

- `Microsoft.VisualStudio.Web.CodeGeneration.Design`
- `Microsoft.EntityFrameworkCore.Design`
- `Microsoft.EntityFrameworkCore.SqlServer`
- `Microsoft.VisualStudio.Threading.Analyzers`

To the AutoLot.Services project, add the following packages:

- `Microsoft.Extensions.Hosting.Abstractions`
- `Microsoft.Extensions.Options`
- `Serilog.AspNetCore`
- `Serilog.Enrichers.Environment`
- `Serilog.Settings.Configuration`
- `Serlog.Sinks.Console`
- `Serilog.Sinks.File`
- `Serilog.Sinks.MSSqlServer`
- `System.Text.Json`
- `Microsoft.VisualStudio.Threading.Analyzers`

Using the Command Line

As shown earlier in this book, .NET Core projects and solutions can be created using the command line. Open a prompt and navigate to the directory where you want the solution located.

■ **Note** The commands listed use the Windows directory separator. If you are using a non-Windows operating system, adjust the separator characters as needed. They also use a specific directory path when adding the AutoLot.Dal and AutoLot.Models projects to the solution, which will need to be updated based on the location of your projects.

The following commands create the AutoLot solution and add the existing AutoLot.Models and AutoLot.Dal projects into the solution using the same options that were shown when using Visual Studio 2022:

```
rem create the solution
dotnet new sln -n AutoLot
rem add autolot dal to solution update the path references as needed
dotnet sln AutoLot.sln add ..\Chapter_23\AutoLot.Models
dotnet sln AutoLot.sln add ..\Chapter_23\AutoLot.Dal
```

Create the AutoLot.Service project, add it to the solution, add the NuGet packages and the project references.

```
rem create the class library for the application services and add it to the solution
dotnet new classlib -lang c# -n AutoLot.Services -o .\AutoLot.Services -f net6.0
dotnet sln AutoLot.sln add AutoLot.Services
```

```
dotnet add AutoLot.Services package Microsoft.Extensions.Hosting.Abstractions
dotnet add AutoLot.Services package Microsoft.Extensions.Options
dotnet add AutoLot.Services package Serilog.AspNetCore
dotnet add AutoLot.Services package Serilog.Enrichers.Environment
dotnet add AutoLot.Services package Serilog.Settings.Configuration
dotnet add AutoLot.Services package Serilog.Sinks.Console
dotnet add AutoLot.Services package Serilog.Sinks.File
dotnet add AutoLot.Services package Serilog.Sinks.MSSqlServer
dotnet add AutoLot.Services package System.Text.Json
dotnet add AutoLot.Services  package Microsoft.VisualStudio.Threading.Analyzers

rem update the path references as needed
dotnet add AutoLot.Services reference ..\Chapter_23\AutoLot.Models
dotnet add AutoLot.Services reference ..\Chapter_23\AutoLot.Dal
```

Create the AutoLot.Api project, add it to the solution, add the NuGet packages and the project references.

```
dotnet new webapi -lang c# -n AutoLot.Api -au none -o .\AutoLot.Api -f net6.0
dotnet sln AutoLot.sln add AutoLot.Api

dotnet add AutoLot.Api package AutoMapper
dotnet add AutoLot.Api package Swashbuckle.AspNetCore
dotnet add AutoLot.Api package Swashbuckle.AspNetCore.Annotations
dotnet add AutoLot.Api package Swashbuckle.AspNetCore.Swagger
dotnet add AutoLot.Api package Swashbuckle.AspNetCore.SwaggerGen
dotnet add AutoLot.Api package Swashbuckle.AspNetCore.SwaggerUI
dotnet add AutoLot.Api package Microsoft.VisualStudio.Web.CodeGeneration.Design
dotnet add AutoLot.Api package Microsoft.EntityFrameworkCore.Design
dotnet add AutoLot.Api package Microsoft.EntityFrameworkCore.SqlServer
dotnet add AutoLot.Api package Microsoft.VisualStudio.Threading.Analyzers
dotnet add AutoLot.Api package System.Text.Json
dotnet add AutoLot.Api package Microsoft.AspNetCore.Mvc.Versioning
dotnet add AutoLot.Api package Microsoft.AspNetCore.Mvc.Versioning.ApiExplorer

rem add project references
rem update the path references as needed
dotnet add AutoLot.Api reference ..\Chapter_23\AutoLot.Dal
dotnet add AutoLot.Api reference ..\Chapter_23\AutoLot.Models
dotnet add AutoLot.Api reference AutoLot.Services
```

Create the AutoLot.Mvc project, add it to the solution, add the NuGet packages and the project references.

```
dotnet new mvc -lang c# -n AutoLot.Mvc -au none -o .\AutoLot.Mvc -f net6.0
dotnet sln AutoLot.sln add AutoLot.Mvc

rem add packages
dotnet add AutoLot.Mvc package AutoMapper
dotnet add AutoLot.Mvc package System.Text.Json
dotnet add AutoLot.Mvc package LigerShark.WebOptimizer.Core
dotnet add AutoLot.Mvc package Microsoft.Web.LibraryManager.Build
dotnet add AutoLot.Mvc package Microsoft.EntityFrameworkCore.Design
```

```
dotnet add AutoLot.Mvc package Microsoft.EntityFrameworkCore.SqlServer
dotnet add AutoLot.Mvc package Microsoft.VisualStudio.Threading.Analyzers
dotnet add AutoLot.Mvc package Microsoft.VisualStudio.Web.CodeGeneration.Design

rem add project references
rem update the path references as needed
dotnet add AutoLot.Mvc reference ..\Chapter_23\AutoLot.Models
dotnet add AutoLot.Mvc reference ..\Chapter_23\AutoLot.Dal
dotnet add AutoLot.Mvc reference AutoLot.Services
```

Finally, create the AutoLot.Web project, add it to the solution, add the NuGet packages, and add the project references.

```
dotnet new webapp -lang c# -n AutoLot.Web -au none -o .\AutoLot.Web -f net6.0
dotnet sln AutoLot.sln add AutoLot.Web

rem add packages
dotnet add AutoLot.Web package AutoMapper
dotnet add AutoLot.Web package System.Text.Json
dotnet add AutoLot.Web package LigerShark.WebOptimizer.Core
dotnet add AutoLot.Web package Microsoft.Web.LibraryManager.Build
dotnet add AutoLot.Web package Microsoft.EntityFrameworkCore.SqlServer
dotnet add AutoLot.Web package Microsoft.EntityFrameworkCore.SqlServer.Design
dotnet add AutoLot.Web package Microsoft.VisualStudio.Web.CodeGeneration.Design
dotnet add AutoLot.Web package Microsoft.VisualStudio.Threading.Analyzers

rem add project references
rem update the path references as needed
dotnet add AutoLot.Web reference ..\Chapter_23\AutoLot.Models
dotnet add AutoLot.Web reference ..\Chapter_23\AutoLot.Dal
dotnet add AutoLot.Web reference AutoLot.Services
```

That completes the setup using the command line. As you can probably see, it is much more efficient provided you don't need the Visual Studio GUI to help you.

■ **Note** At the time of this writing, Visual Studio created projects with files that use nested namespaces, while the CLI tooling creates files that use file scoped namespaces.

Update the Entity Framework Core Package Reference

Recall from the EF Core chapters that to clear out temporal tables, the `Microsoft.EntityFrameworkCore.Design` package reference must be modified. Update the reference in the project files for the AutoLot.Api, AutoLot.Mvc, and AutoLot.Web projects to the following:

```
<PackageReference Include="Microsoft.EntityFrameworkCore.Design" Version="6.0.0>
  <PrivateAssets>all</PrivateAssets>
  <!--<IncludeAssets>runtime; build; native; contentfiles; analyzers; buildtransitive</
IncludeAssets>-->
</PackageReference>
```

Disable Nullable Reference Types For All Projects

At this time, disable nullable reference types by updating each of the project files' PropertyGroup to the following:

```
<PropertyGroup>
  <TargetFramework>net6.0</TargetFramework>
  <Nullable>disable</Nullable>
  <ImplicitUsings>enable</ImplicitUsings>
</PropertyGroup>
```

Create a GlobalUsing.cs Class in Each Project

The final setup step is to add a file named GlobalUsings.cs to the root folder of each project and clear out any scaffolded code. These will be used to hold the using statements for each project.

Running ASP.NET Core Applications

Previous versions of ASP.NET web applications always ran using IIS (or IIS Express). With ASP.NET Core, applications typically run using the Kestrel web server with an option to use IIS, Apache, Nginx, etc., by way of a reverse proxy between Kestrel and the other web server. This shift from requiring IIS to allowing other web servers not only changes the deployment model, but also changes the development possibilities. During development, you can now run your applications in these ways:

- From Visual Studio, using Kestrel or IIS Express
- From a command prompt with the .NET CLI, using Kestrel
- From Visual Studio Code, using Kestrel, from the Run menu
- From Visual Studio Code's Terminal window using the .NET CLI and Kestrel

When using any of these options, the application's ports and environment are configured with a file named launchsettings.json located under the Properties folder. The launchsettings.json file for the AutoLot.Mvc project is listed here for reference (your ports for both the IIS Express and AutoLot.Mvc profiles will be different):

```
{
  "iisSettings": {
    "windowsAuthentication": false,
    "anonymousAuthentication": true,
    "iisExpress": {
      "applicationUrl": "http://localhost:42788",
      "sslPort": 44375
    }
  },
  "profiles": {
    "AutoLot.Mvc": {
      "commandName": "Project",
      "dotnetRunMessages": true,
      "launchBrowser": true,
      "applicationUrl": "https://localhost:5001;http://localhost:5000",
      "environmentVariables": {
        "ASPNETCORE_ENVIRONMENT": "Development",
```

```
      }
    },
    "IIS Express": {
      "commandName": "IISExpress",
      "launchBrowser": true,
      "environmentVariables": {
        "ASPNETCORE_ENVIRONMENT": "Development",
      }
    }
  }
}
```

Using Visual Studio

The first profile defines the settings when using Kestrel as the web server. The Kestrel profile is always named after the project (e.g., `AutoLot.Mvc`) when it is created, but can be changed to any other name. The `iisSettings` section and the `IIS Express` profile together define the settings when running the application using IIS Express as the web server. The most important settings to note are the `applicationUrl`, which also defines the port, and the `environmentVariables` block, which defines the environment variables to use when debugging. Any environment variables defined in this section supersede any user or machine environment settings with the same name.

The Run command in Visual Studio allows for choosing either the Kestrel or IIS Express profile, as shown in Figure 30-5. Once a profile is selected, you can run the project by pressing F5 (debug mode), pressing Ctrl+F5 (the same as "Start Without Debugging" in the Debug menu), or clicking the green run arrow (the same as "Start Debugging" in the Debug menu). New in .NET 6 and Visual Studio 2022, the Kestrel profile is set as the default.

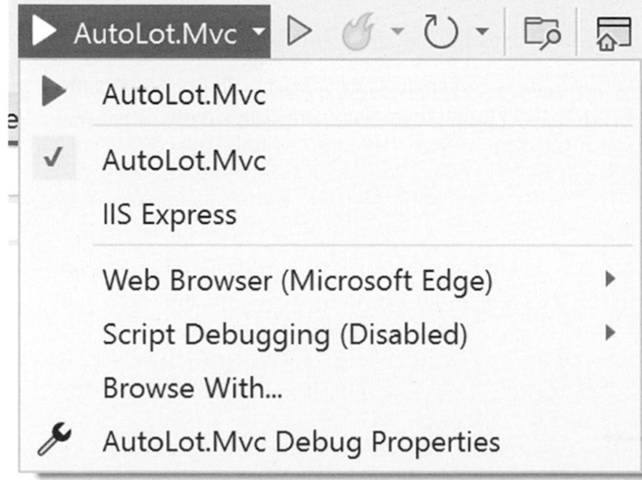

Figure 30-5. *The available Visual Studio debugging profiles*

■ **Note** There is also an option to create additional profiles, such as running using the WSL (Windows Subsystem for Linux). This feature isn't covered in this book, but if you are curious to learn more, there is a book on the topic titled *Pro Windows Subsystem for Linux* (`https://link.springer.com/book/10.1007/978-1-4842-6873-5z`)

Using Visual Studio Code

To run the projects from Visual Studio Code, open the folder where the solution is located. When you press F5 (or click Run), VS Code will prompt you to select the runtime to use (select .NET 6+ and .NET Core) and which project to run (AutoLot.Api, AutoLot.Web, or AutoLot.Mvc). It will then create a run configuration and place it in a file named `launch.json`. The launch settings only have to be configured the first time. Once the files exists, you can freely run/debug your application without having to make the selections again. Visual Studio Code uses the Kestrel profile when running your application.

Using the Command Line or Terminal Window

Running from the command line for ASP.NET Core apps is the same as any other .NET application that you have seen in this book. Simply navigate to the directory where the `csproj` file for your application is located and enter the following command:

```
dotnet run
```

This starts your application using the Kestrel profile. To end the process, press Ctrl+C.

Changing Code While Debugging

When running from the command line using `dotnet run`, the code in your application's projects can be changed, but the changes won't be reflected in the running app. To have the changes reflected in the running app, enter the following command:

```
dotnet watch
```

This command runs with Hot Reload enabled. Hot Reload is a new feature in .NET 6 that attempts to reload your app in real time when changes are made. This is a vast improvement over the .NET 5 `dotnet watch run` command, which restarted your entire app when a file watcher noticed changes.

Not all changes can be reloaded in real time, as some do require a restart of your app. If this is needed, you will be prompted to restart your application. If the prompt doesn't appear, you can force a reload by using Ctrl+R in the terminal window. To cancel the application, hit Ctrl+C.

Hot Reload is also available when debugging with Visual Studio 2022 or Visual Studio Code.

Debugging ASP.NET Core Applications

When running your application from Visual Studio or Visual Studio Code, debugging works as expected. When running from the command line, you have to attach to the running process before you can debug your application.

Attaching with Visual Studio

After launching your app (with `dotnet run` or `dotnet watch run`), select Debug ➤ Attach to Process in Visual Studio. When the Attach to Process dialog appears, filter the process by your application name, as shown in Figure 30-6.

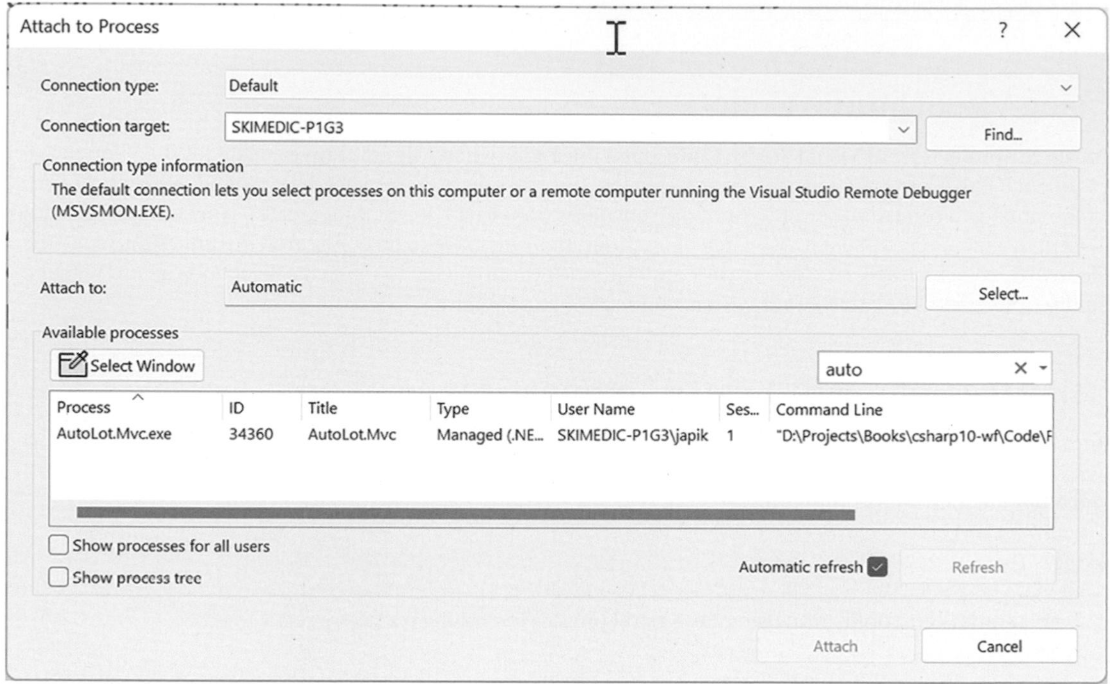

Figure 30-6. *Attaching to the running applications for debugging in Visual Studio*

Once attached to the running process, you can set breakpoints in Visual Studio, and debugging works as expected. Hot reload is enabled when you attach to the running process, so the edit and continue experience is getting better, although not yet to the level it was in prior versions of the .NET framework.

Attaching with Visual Studio Code

After launching your app (with `dotnet run` or `dotnet watch run`), select .NET Core Attach instead of .NET Core Launch (web) by clicking the green run arrow in VS Code, as shown in Figure 30-7.

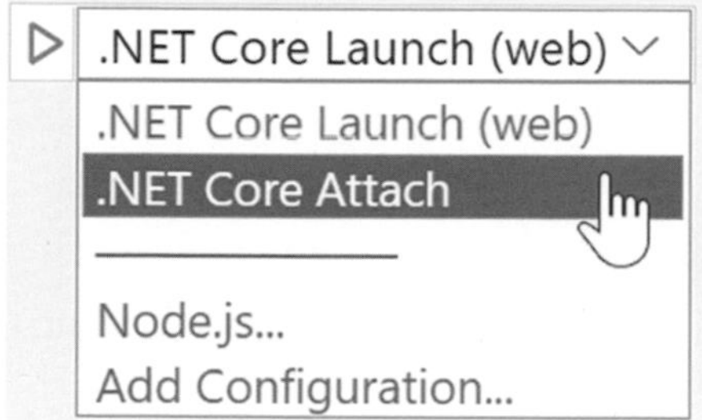

Figure 30-7. Attaching to the running applications for debugging in Visual Studio Code

When you click the Run button, you will be prompted to select which process to attach. Select your application. You can now set breakpoints as expected.

Update the AutoLot.Api and AutoLot.Web Kestrel Ports

You might have noticed that AutoLot.Api, AutoLot.Web, and AutoLot.Mvc have different ports specified for the IIS Express and Kestrel profiles. Instead of remembering each of the randomly assigned ports, update all of the projects settings as follows:

```
//AutoLot.Mvc launchSettins.json
"AutoLot.Mvc": {
  "commandName": "Project",
  "launchBrowser": true,
  "environmentVariables": {
  "ASPNETCORE_ENVIRONMENT": "Development"
  },
  "applicationUrl": "https://localhost:5001;http://localhost:5000",
  "dotnetRunMessages": true
},

//AutoLot.Api launchSettins.json
"AutoLot.API": {
  "commandName": "Project",
  "dotnetRunMessages": true,
  "launchBrowser": true,
  "launchUrl": "swagger",
  "applicationUrl": "https://localhost:5011;http://localhost:5010",
  "environmentVariables": {
    "ASPNETCORE_ENVIRONMENT": "Development"
  }
},

//AutoLot.Web launchSettins.json
"AutoLot.Web": {
  "commandName": "Project",
  "dotnetRunMessages": true,
  "launchBrowser": true,
  "applicationUrl": "https://localhost:5021;http://localhost:5020",
  "environmentVariables": {
```

```
    "ASPNETCORE_ENVIRONMENT": "Development"
  }
},
```

ASP.NET Core Concepts from MVC/Web API

Many of the design goals and features that brought developers to use ASP.NET MVC and ASP.NET Web API are still supported (and improved) in ASP.NET Core. Some of these (but not all) are listed here:

- Convention over configuration
- Controllers and actions
- Cleaner directory structure
- Model binding
- Model validation
- Routing
- Filters
- Layouts and Razor Views

These items are all covered in the next sections, except for layouts and Razor views, which are covered in a later chapter.

■ **Note** Razor page based applications are new in ASP.NET Core, however many of the concepts covered in this section also apply to this new application type. Razor page based applications will be formally introduced in the next chapter.

Convention over Configuration

ASP.NET MVC and ASP.NET Web API reduced the amount of configuration necessary by introducing certain conventions. When followed, these conventions reduce the amount of manual (or templated) configuration, but also require the developers to know the conventions in order to take advantage of them. Two of the main conventions include naming conventions and directory structure.

Naming Conventions

There are multiple naming conventions in ASP.NET Core, for MVC style and RESTful service applications as well as Razor page based applications. For example, controllers are typically named with the `Controller` suffix (e.g., `HomeController`) in addition to deriving from `Controller` (or `ControllerBase`). When accessed through routing, the `Controller` suffix is dropped. When routing to async action methods named with the suffix `Async`, the `Async` suffix is dropped. Razor pages' code behind files are named with the `Model` suffix (`ErrorModel`), which is dropped just like the `Controller` and `Async` suffixes. This convention of dropping the suffix is repeated throughout ASP.NET Core.

Another naming convention is used in locating the views for a controller's action methods. When looking for a controller's views, the controller name minus the suffix is the starting search location. By default, an action method will render the view of the same name as the method.

There will be many examples of ASP.NET Core conventions covered in the following chapters.

Controllers and Actions (MVC Based Web Apps and RESTful Services)

Just like ASP.NET MVC and ASP.NET Web API, controllers and action methods are the workhorses of an ASP.NET Core MVC style web application or RESTful service application.

■ **Note** Razor pages derive from the PageModel class, which will be covered in the next chapter.

The Controller Class

As mentioned already, ASP.NET Core unified ASP.NET MVC5 and ASP.NET Web API. This unification also combines the Controller, ApiController, and AsyncController base classes from MVC5 and Web API 2.2 into one new class, Controller, which has a base class of its own named ControllerBase. ASP.NET Core web application controllers inherit from the Controller class, while ASP.NET Core service controllers inherit from the ControllerBase class (covered next).

The Controller class provides a host of helper methods for MVC style web applications. Table 30-1 lists the most commonly used methods.

Table 30-1. *Some of the Helper Methods Provided by the Controller Class*

Helper Method	Meaning in Life
ViewDataTempDataViewBag	Provide data to the view through the ViewDataDictionary, TempDataDictionary, and dynamic ViewBag transport.
View	Returns a ViewResult (derived from ActionResult) as the HTTP response. Defaults to a view of the same name as the action method, with the option of specifying a specific view. All options allow specifying a view model that is strongly typed and sent to the View.
PartialView	Returns a PartialViewResult to the response pipeline.
ViewComponent	Returns a ViewComponentResult to the response pipeline.
Json	Returns a JsonResult containing an object serialized as JSON as the response.
OnActionExecuting	Executes before an action method executes.
OnActionExecutionAsync	Async version of OnActionExecuting.
OnActionExecuted	Executes after an action method executes.

The ControllerBase Class

The ControllerBase class provides the core functionality for both ASP.NET Core MVC style web applications and RESTful services, in addition to helper methods for returning HTTP status codes. Table 30-2 lists some of the core functionality in ControllerBase.

Table 30-2. Some of the Helper Methods Provided by the ControllerBase Class

Helper Method	Meaning in Life
`HttpContext`	Returns the `HttpContext` for the currently executing action.
`Request`	Returns the `HttpRequest` for the currently executing action.
`Response`	Returns the `HttpResponse` for the currently executing action.
`RouteData`	Returns the `RouteData` for the currently executing action (routing is covered later in this chapter).
`ModelState`	Returns the state of the model in regard to model binding and validation (both covered later in this chapter).
`Url`	Returns an instance of the `IUrlHelper`, providing access to building URLs for ASP.NET Core MVC applications and services.
`User`	Returns the `ClaimsPrincipal` user.
`Content`	Returns a `ContentResult` to the response. Overloads allow for adding a content type and encoding definition.
`File`	Returns a `FileContentResult` to the response.
`Redirect`	A series of methods that redirect the user to another URL by returning a `RedirectResult`.
`LocalRedirect`	A series of methods that redirect the user to another URL only if the URL is local. More secure than the generic `Redirect` methods.
`RedirectToActionRedirect ToPageRedirectToRoute`	A series of methods that redirect to another action method, Razor Page, or named route. Routing is covered later in this chapter.
`TryUpdateModelAsync`	Used for explicit model binding (covered later in this chapter).
`TryValidateModel`	Used for explicit model validation (covered later in this chapter).

And Table 30-3 covers some of the helper methods for returning HTTP status codes.

Table 30-3. Some of the HTTP Status Code Helper Methods Provided by the ControllerBase Class

Helper Method	HTTP Status Code Action Result	Status Code
`NoContent`	`NoContentResult`	204
`Ok`	`OkResult`	200
`NotFound`	`NotFoundResult`	404
`BadRequest`	`BadRequestResult`	400
`CreatedCreatedAt ActionCreatedAtRoute`	`CreatedResultCreatedAtAction ResultCreateAtRouteResult`	201
`AcceptedAcceptedAt ActionAcceptedAtRoute`	`AcceptedResultAccepted AtActionResultAcceptedAtRouteResult`	202

Actions

Actions are methods on a controller that return an IActionResult (or Task<IActionResult> for async operations) or a class that implements IActionResult, such as ActionResult or ViewResult.

This example returns a ViewResult in an MVC based application:

```
public async Task<IActionResult> Index()
    => View(await _serviceWrapper.GetCarsAsync());
```

This example returns an HTTP status code of 200 with a list of Car records as JSON:

```
[Produces("application/json")]
public ActionResult<IEnumerable<Car>> GetCarsByMake(int? id)
{
  return Ok(MainRepo.GetAll());
}
```

Actions and their return values will be covered more in the following chapters.

Antiforgery Tokens

ASP.NET Core uses antiforgery middleware to help combat against cross-site request forgery attacks. ASP.NET Core uses the Synchronizer Token Pattern (STP) which creates a server side token that is unique and unpredictable. That token is sent to the browser with the response. Any request that comes back to the server must include the correct token, or the request is refused.

Opting In (MVC Style Web Apps)

Receiving the token and validating it is handled in the action methods for MVC style web applications(MVC). To validate the token, simply add the ValidateAntiForgeryToken attribute to every HTTP Post method in your application, like this:

```
[HttpPost]
[ValidateAntiForgeryToken]
public async Task<IActionResult> Create (Car entity)
{
  //do important stuff
}
```

To opt out of the check, simply leave the ValidateAntiForgeryToken attribute off of the method.

■ **Note** Adding the antiforgery token to the response will be covered along with tag helpers and views.

Opting Out (Razor Page Web Apps)

Razor page base applications automatically participate in the antiforgery pattern. To opt out of participating, add the IgnoreAntiforgeryToken to the PageModel class:

```
[IgnoreAntiforgeryToken]
public class ErrorModel : PageModel
{
  //Omitted for brevity
}
```

Directory Structure Conventions

There are several folder conventions that you must understand to successfully build ASP.NET Core web applications and services. Many of the directories from Web API/MVC are the same (Controllers, Views, Areas) while there are some new ones (e.g., Pages, wwwroot). You will find the directory structure improved from MVC/WebAPI.

The Controllers Folder

By convention, the Controllers folder is where the ASP.NET Core MVC and API implementations (and the routing engine) expect that the controllers for your application are placed.

The Views Folder

The Views folder is where the views for an MVC style application are stored. Each controller gets its own folder under the main Views folder named after the controller name (minus the Controller suffix). The action methods will render views in their controller's folder by default. For example, the Views/Home folder holds all the views for the HomeController controller class.

The Shared Folder

A special folder under Views is named Shared. This folder is accessible to all controllers and their action methods. After searching the folder named for the controller, if the view can't be found, then the Shared folder is searched for the view.

The Pages Folder

The Pages folder is where the pages for the application are stored when building web applications using Razor pages. The directory structure under the Pages folder sets the base route for each page (more on routing later).

The Shared Folder

A special folder under Pages is named Shared. This folder is accessible to all pages in a Razor page based web application.

The Areas Folder

Areas are a feature that is used to organize related functionality into a group as a separate namespace for routing and folder structure for views and Razor pages. Each area gets its own set of controllers (API applications), controllers and views (MVC style applications), and pages (Razor page based applications). An application can have zero to many areas, and each area goes under the parent `Areas` folder.

The wwwroot Folder

An improvement in ASP.NET Core web applications over the previous framework versions is the creation of a special folder named `wwwroot`. In ASP.NET MVC, the JavaScript files, images, CSS, and other client-side content were intermingled with all the other folders. In ASP.NET Core, the client side files are all contained under the `wwwroot` folder. This separation of compiled files from client-side files significantly cleans up the project structure when working with ASP.NET Core.

There is an exception to this conventions that relates to view and page specific CSS files. Those are stored alongside the views/pages they target. They will be covered in later chapters.

Routing

Routing is how ASP.NET Core matches HTTP requests to the proper code (the executable *endpoints*) to handle those requests as well as create URLs from the executable end points. This is accomplished with routing middleware registered in the `Startup` class (pre-C# 10) or the top level statements in the `Program.cs` file (C# 10 and later).

A route in an MVC based web application consists of an (optional) area, a controller, an action method, an HTTP verb (POST or GET), and (optional) additional values (called *route values*). Routes in ASP.NET Core RESTful services consists of an (optional) area, a controller, an (optional) action method, an HTTP Verb (POST, PUT, GET, DELETE, etc.), and (optional) additional route values. When defining routes for ASP.NET RESTful services, an action method is not usually specified. Instead, once the controller is located, the action method to execute is based on the HTTP verb of the request. In MVC style web applications and RESTful services, routes can be configured along in the middleware or through route attributes on controllers and action methods.

A route in a Razor page based application is the directory structure of the application, an HTTP Verb, the page itself, and (optional) additional route values. In addition to the default constructs, all ASP.NET style applications can create a route that ignores the standard templates. In Razor page based applications, routes are based on the directory structure of the application, with additional tokens available as part of the `@page` directive. All of this is covered in more detail shortly.

URL Patterns and Route Tokens

Route definitions are composed of URL patterns that contain variable placeholders (called *tokens*) and (optional) literals placed into an ordered collection known as the *route table*. Each entry in the route table must define a different URL pattern to match. Table 30-4 lists the reserved token names and their definitions.

Table 30-4. Reserved Route Tokens for MVC Styled and RESTful Service Applications

Token	Meaning in Life
`Area`	Defines the area for the route
`Controller`	Defines the controller (minus the controller suffix)
`Action`	Defines the action method name
`* or **`	Catch-all parameter. When used as a prefix to a route parameter, it binds the rest of the URI. For example, `car/{**slug}` matches any URI that starts with `/car` and has any value following it. The following value is assigned to the `slug` route value. Using a double ** in the path preserves path separator characters while a single * does not.

Handling Duplicate C# Method Signatures

The `action` token by default matches the C# method name on a controller. The `ActionName` attribute can be used to change in relation to routing. For example, the following code specifies the HTTP Get and HTTP Post action methods with the name and same signature. C# doesn't allow two methods with the same signature with the same name, so a compiler error occurs:

```
[HttpGet]
public async Task<IActionResult> Create()
{
  //do something
}

[HttpPost]
[ValidateAntiForgeryToken]
//Compiler error
public async Task<IActionResult> Create()
{
  //Do something else
}
```

The solution is to rename one of the methods and add the `ActionName` attribute to change the name used by the routing engine:

```
[HttpPost]
[ActionName("Create")]
[ValidateAntiForgeryToken]
public async Task<IActionResult> CreateCar()
{
  //Do something else
}
```

Custom Route Tokens

In addition to the reserved tokens, routes can contain custom tokens that are mapped (model bound) to a controller action method's or Razor page handler method's parameters. When defining routes using tokens, there must be a literal value separating the tokens. While `{controller}/{action}/{id?}` is valid, `{controller}{action}{id?}` is not.

Route Token Constraints

Route tokens can also be constrained to disambiguate similar routes. Table 30-5 shows the available route token constraints. Note that the constraints are not meant to be used for validation. If a route value is invalid based on a constraint (e.g., too big for the int constraint), the routing engine will not find a match and returns a 404 (Not Found). However, business logic would probably require that a 400 (Bad Request) be returned instead.

Table 30-5. *Route Tokens Constraints for MVC Styled and RESTful Service Applications*

Constraint	Example	Meaning in Life
Int	{id:int}	Matches any integer.
Bool	{active:bool}	Matches true or false. Case insensitive.
datetime	{dob:datetime}	Matches a valid DateTime value in the invariant culture.
decimal	{price:decimal}	Matches a valid decimal value in the invariant culture.
double	{weight:double}	Matches a valid double value in the invariant culture.
Float	{weight:float}	Matches a valid float value in the invariant culture.
Guid	{id:guid}	Matches a valid GUID value.
Long	{ticks:long}	Matches a valid long value in the invariant culture.
minlength(value)	{name:minlength(4)}	String must be at least value characters long.
maxlength(value)	{name:maxlength(12)}	String must be at most value characters long.
length(value)	{name:length(12)}	String must be exactly value characters long.
min(value)	{age:min(18)}	Integer must be at least value
max(value)	{age:max(65)}	Integer must be at most value
range(min,max)	{age:range(12,65)}	Integer must be between min and max
alpha	{name:alpha}	String must only contain letters a-z, case insensitive.
regex(expression)	{ssn:regex(^\\d{{3}}-\\d{{2}}-\\d{{4}}$)}	String must match regular expression.
required	{name:required}	Value is required.

Conventional Routing (MVC Style Web Apps)

Conventional routing builds the route table in the Startup class (pre-.NET6) or in the Program.cs file's top level statements (.NET6+). The MapControllerRoute() method adds an endpoint into the route table. The method specifies a name, URL pattern, and any default values for the variables in the URL pattern. In the following code sample, the predefined {controller} and {action} placeholders refer to a controller (minus the Controller suffix) and an action method contained in that controller. The placeholder {id} is custom and is translated into a parameter (named id) for the action method. Adding a question mark to a route token indicates that it is an optional route value and is represented in the action method as a nullable parameter.

```
app.UseRouting();
app.MapControllerRoute(
    name: "default",
    pattern: "{controller=Home}/{action=Index}/{id?}"
);
```

When a URL is requested, it is checked against the route table. If there is a match, the HTTP Verb (Post, Get, etc.) of the request is also checked to make sure the code located at that application endpoint accepts the request's verb. For example, an HTTP Post with the URL (minus the scheme and domain) `Car/Delete/5` comes into the application. From the following two actions, the second delete action method would be targeted (since it is marked with the `[HttpPost]` attribute), passing in 5 as the value for the `id` parameter:

```
public class CarController : ControllerBase
{
  [HttpGet]
  public async Task<IActionResult> Delete(int? id)
  {
    //return a view
  }

  [HttpPost]
  [ValidateAntiForgeryToken]
  public async Task<IActionResult> Delete(int id, Car car)
  {
    //delete the record
  }
}
```

The defaults specify how to fill in the blanks for URLs that don't contain all of the defined components. In the previous code, if no additional route values were specified in the URL (such as `http://localhost:5001`), then the routing engine would call the `Index()` action method of the `HomeController` class, without an `id` parameter. The defaults are progressive, meaning that they can be excluded from right to left. However, route parts can't be skipped. Entering a URL like `http://localhost:5001/Delete/5` will fail the `{controller}/{action}/{id}` pattern.

Conventional routing is order dependent. The routing engine starts at the top of the route table and will attempt to find the first matching route based on the (optional) area, controller, action, custom tokens, and HTTP verb. If the routing engine finds more than one end point that matches the route plus HTTP Verb it will throw an `AmbiguousMatchException`. If the routing engine can't find a matching route, it will return a 404.

Notice that the route template doesn't contain a protocol or hostname. The routing engine automatically prepends the correct information when creating routes and uses the HTTP verb, path, and parameters to determine the correct application endpoint. For example, if your site is running on `https://www.skimedic.com`, the protocol (HTTPS) and hostname (`www.skimedic.com`) is automatically prepended to the route when created (e.g., `https://www.skimedic.com/Car/Delete/5`). For an incoming request, the routing engine uses the `Car/Delete/5` portion of the URL.

Area Routes

If your application contains an area, there is an additional route pattern that needs to be mapped. Instead of using `MapControllerRoute()`, call `MapAreaControllerRoute()`, like this:

```
app.UseRouting();
app.MapAreaControllerRoute(
    name:"areaRoute",
    areaName:"Admin",
    pattern:"Admin/{controller}/{action}/{id?}");
```

Since area routes are more specific than the non-area routes, they are typically added to the route table first, like this:

```
app.UseRouting();
app.MapAreaControllerRoute(
    name:"areaRoute",
    areaName:"Admin",
    pattern:"Admin/{controller}/{action}/{id?}");
app.MapControllerRoute(
    name: "default",
    pattern: "{controller=Home}/{action=Index}/{id?}");
```

Named Routes

Route names can be used as a shorthand to generate URLs from within the application. In the preceding conventional route, the endpoint is assigned the name `default`.

Attribute Routing (MVC Style Web Apps and RESTful Services)

Attribute routing works the same way as conventional routing when matching routes with application endpoints and HTTP verbs. The difference is how the routes are configured. In attribute routing, routes are defined using C# attributes on controllers and their action methods. This can lead to more precise routing, but can also increase the amount of configuration, since every controller and action needs to have routing information specified. Before we look at examples of attribute routing, it must be enabled in the `Startup` class (pre .NET 6) or the `Program.cs` file's top level statements (.NET6+) by calling `MapControllers()`:

```
app.MapControllers();
```

For an example of attribute routing, take the following code snippet. The four `Route` attributes on the `Index()` action method equate to the same default route defined earlier. The `Index()` action method is the application endpoint for

- `mysite.com ([Route("/")])`,
- `mysite.com/Home ([Route("/Home")])`,
- `mysite.com/Home/Index ([Route("/Home/Index")])`, or
- `mysite.com/Home/Index/5 ([Route("/Home/Index/{id?}")])`.

```
public class HomeController : Controller
{
  [Route("/")]
  [Route("/Home")]
  [Route("/Home/Index")]
  [Route("/Home/Index/{id?}")]
  public IActionResult Index(int? id)
  {
    ...
  }
}
```

In the previous example, the only route token used was for the optional id parameter. The same set of routes can be created using the controller and action route tokens, like this:

```
public class HomeController : Controller
{
  [Route("/")]
  [Route("/[controller]")]
  [Route("/[controller]/[action]")]
  [Route("/[controller]/[action]/{id?}")]
  public IActionResult Index(int? id)
  {
    ...
  }
}
```

The major difference between conventional routing and attribute routing is that conventional routing covers the application, while attribute routing covers just the controller and its action methods with the Route attribute. If conventional routing is not used, every controller will need to have their route defined with attribute routing or they will not be able to be accessed. For example, if there wasn't a default route defined in the route table (using conventional routing), the following code is not discoverable since the controller doesn't have any routing configured:

```
public class CarController : Controller
{
  public IActionResult Delete(int id)
  {
    ...
  }
}
```

■ **Note** Conventional and attribute routing can be used together. If the default controller route was set as in the conventional routing example, the preceding controller would be located by the route table.

When routes are added at the controller level, the action methods derive from that base route. For example, the following controller route covers the Delete() (and any other) action method:

```
[Route("[controller]/[action]/{id?}")]
public class CarController : Controller
{
  public IActionResult Delete(int id)
  {
    ...
  }
}
```

■ **Note** The built-in tokens are distinguished with square brackets ([ ]) in attribute routing instead of the curly braces ({ }) used in conventional routing. Custom tokens still use curly braces.

If an action method needs to restart the route pattern, prefix the route with a forward slash (/). For example, if the delete method should follow the URL pattern mysite.com/Delete/Car/5, configure the action as follows:

```
[Route("[controller]/[action]/{id?}")]
public class CarController : Controller
{
  [Route("/[action]/[controller]/{id}")]
  public IActionResult Delete(int id)
  {
    ...
  }
}
```

As shown with the default attribute route example, route definitions can use literal route values instead of using token replacement. The following code will produce the same result for the Delete() action method as the previous code sample:

```
[Route("[controller]/[action]/{id?}")]
public class CarController : Controller
{
  [Route("/Delete/Car/{id}")]
  public IActionResult Delete(int id)
  {
    ...
  }
}
```

Razor Page Routing

As mentioned already, Razor page routing is based on the folder structure of the application. To enable routing, call MapRazorPages() in the Startup class (pre .NET 6) or the Program.cs file's top level statements (.NET6+):

```
app.UseRouting();
app.MapRazorPages();
```

For Razor page based web applications, the Index page is the default page for a directory. This means that if an Index.cshtml page is located at Pages/Cars/Index.cshtml, then both the routes that map to that page include /Cars and /Cars/Index.

Additional route tokens can be added after the @page directive to refine the route. Suppose you have a Car folder under the Pages folder, and in the Cars folder, there is a page named Delete.cshtml. The default route for this page is /Cars/Delete. To add an optional id token to accept a URI like /Cars/Delete/5, update the @page directive to the following:

```
@page "{id?}"
```

Just like routing for MVC style applications, the route can be reset using a forward slash (/). Once reset, you can add literals and tokens to completely change the route. For example, the route for the Delete.cshtml page can be updated to /Delete/Vehicle/5 by using the following:

```
@page "/Delete/Vehicle/{id?}
```

Routing and HTTP Verbs

As we have already discussed, none of the route templates define an HTTP verb. In MVC based applications and RESTful services, the action methods are decorated with attributes to indicate which HTTP verb it should handle. For Razor page based applications, the different HTTP verbs are handled with specific page handler methods.

HTTP Verbs in MVC Styled Web Application Attribute Routing

As discussed earlier, a common pattern in web applications using the MVC pattern, there will be two application endpoints that match a particular route template. The discriminator in these instances is the HTTP verb, as we saw with the CarController's two Delete() action methods.

Routes can also be modified using the HTTP verb attributes. For example, the following shows the optional id route token added to the route template for both Delete() methods:

```
[Route("[controller]/[action]")]
public class CarController : Controller
{
  [HttpGet("{id?}")]
  public IActionResult Delete(int? id)
  {
    ...
  }
  [HttpPost("{id}")]
  [ValidateAntiForgeryToken]
  public IActionResult Delete(int id, Car recordToDelete)
  {
    ...
  }
}
```

■ **Note** Browsers only support `get` and `post` requests, so while you can decorate your MVC web application's methods with additional HTTP Verb attributes (like `HttpPut` and `HttpDelete`), browsers will not be able to make the appropriate requests to leverage those endpoints.

Routes can also be restarted using the HTTP verbs; just preface the route templated with a forward slash (/), as the following example demonstrates:

```
[HttpGet("/[controller]/[action]/{makeId}/{makeName}")]
public IActionResult ByMake(int makeId, string makeName)
{
  ViewBag.MakeName = makeName;
  return View(_repo.GetAllBy(makeId));
}
```

If an action method isn't decorated with an HTTP verb attribute, it defaults to accepting HTTP get requests. However, in MVC styled web applications, unmarked action methods can also respond to HTTP post requests, which might cause unexpected results. For this reason, it's considered a best practice to mark all action methods explicitly with the correct verb attribute.

HTTP Verbs in RESTful Service Routing

Route definitions used for RESTful services typically do not specify action methods. When action methods are not part of the route template, the action methods are selected based on the HTTP verb of the request (and optionally the content type). The following code shows an API controller with four methods that all match the same route template. Notice that the HTTP verb attributes are different for each of the action methods:

```
[Route("api/[controller]")]
[ApiController]
public class CarController : ControllerBase
{
  [HttpGet("{id}")]
  public IActionResult GetCarsById(int id)
  {
    ...
  }
  [HttpPost("{id}")]
  public IActionResult CreateANewCar(int id, Car entity)
  {
    ...
  }
  [HttpPut("{id}")]
  public IActionResult UpdateAnExistingCar(int id, Car entity)
  {
    ...
  }
```

```
  [HttpDelete("{id}")]
  public IActionResult DeleteACar(int id, Car entity)
  {
    ...
  }
}
```

If an action method doesn't have an HTTP verb attribute, it is treated as the application endpoint for HTTP get requests. Just as with MVC style applications, if the route requested is matched but there isn't an action method with the correct verb attribute, the server will return a 404 (not found).

■ **Note** ASP.NET Web API allowed you to omit the HTTP verb for a method if the name started with *Get*, *Put*, *Delete*, or *Post*. This convention has been removed in ASP.NET Core. If an action method does not have an HTTP verb specified, it will be called using an HTTP Get.

The final endpoint selector for API controllers is the optional Consumes attribute, which specifies the content type that is accepted by the endpoint. The request must use the matching content-type header, or a 415 Unsupported Media Type error will be returned. The following two example endpoints, both in the same controller, differentiate between JSON and XML:

```
[HttpPost]
[Consumes("application/json")]
public IActionResult PostJson(IEnumerable<int> values)
  => Ok(new { Consumes = "application/json", Values = values });

[HttpPost]
[Consumes("application/x-www-form-urlencoded")]
public IActionResult PostForm([FromForm] IEnumerable<int> values)
  => Ok(new { Consumes = "application/x-www-form-urlencoded", Values = values });
```

■ **Note** There is one additional (and optional) route selector for API controllers, and that involves versioning. Versioning API applications is covered in Chapter 32.

HTTP Verbs in Razor Page Routing

Once a Razor page is discovered as the endpoint for a route, the HTTP verb is used to determine the correct page handler method to execute. The following code sample for the Delete.cshtml page will execute the OnGet() method on get requests and the OnPost() method on post requests.

```
public class DeleteModel : PageModel
{
  public IActionResult OnGet(int? id)
  {
    //handle the get request here
  }
```

```
    public IActionResult OnPost(int? id)
    {
      //handle the post request here
    }
  }
```

This will be covered in more depth in the next chapter.

Redirecting Using Routing

Another advantage of routing is that you no longer have to hard-code URLs for other pages in your site. The routing entries are used to match incoming requests as well as build URLs. When building URLs, the scheme, host, and port are added based on the values of the current request.

When redirecting in server side code (e.g., in a controller's action method or in a Razor page), there are several redirect methods that can be used to redirect the execution path to another end point. Table 30-6 shows three of the redirect methods and their most commonly used overloads.

Table 30-6. *Methods for Server-Side Redirecting of Requests*

Method	Meaning in Life
`RedirectToAction()`	Redirects to an action. Overloaded parameter options include: actionName, controllerName, routeValues If any of the parameters are not supplied, the values will be supplied by the current HTTP request.
`RedirectToRoute()`	Redirects to a named route. Optional route values can be supplied.
`RedirectToPage()`	Redirects to a Razor Page. Optional route values can be supplied.

For an example, the following code redirects the request from the Delete method to the Index method in the same controller (since a controller name wasn't provided):

```
[HttpPost("{id}")]
public async Task<IActionResult> Delete(int id, Car car)
{
  //interesting code here
  return RedirectToAction(nameof(Index));
}
```

Model Binding

Model binding is the process where ASP.NET Core uses the name-value pairs submitted in an HTTP Post call to assign values to models. The values are submitted using form fields, request body (for API style controllers), route data, query string parameters, or uploaded files. To bind to a reference type, the name-value pairs come from the form values or the request body, the reference types must have a public default constructor, and the properties to be bound must be public and writable.

When assigning values, implicit type conversions (such as setting a `string` property value using an `int`) are used where applicable. If type conversion doesn't succeed, that property is flagged in error. Before discussing binding in greater detail, it's important to understand the `ModelState` dictionary and its role in the binding (and validation) process.

The ModelState Dictionary

The ModelState dictionary contains an entry for every property being bound and an entry for the model itself. If an error occurs during model binding, the binding engine adds the errors to the dictionary entry for the property and sets ModelState.IsValid = false. If all matched properties are successfully assigned, the binding engine sets ModelState.IsValid = true.

■ **Note** Model validation, which also sets the ModelState dictionary entries, happens after model binding. Both implicit and explicit model binding automatically call validation for the model. Validation is covered shortly.

How you handle the binding and/or validation errors varies based on the needs of your application. The following code sample from an API endpoint shows how to get all of the errors from the ModelState, create an anonymous object, and then return a BadRequestObject (HTTP status code 400) with the resulting object sent back in the body of the response as JSON:

```
[HttpPost]
[ValidateAntiForgeryToken]
public async Task<IActionResult> Update(Car entity)
{
  if (!ModelState.IsValid)
  {
    IEnumerable<string> errorList = ModelState.Values.SelectMany(v => v.Errors).Select(e=>e.
    ErrorMessage);
    var responseContent =
      new { Message = "One or more field validation errors occurred", Errors = errorList };
    apiLogEntry.ResponseContentBody = JsonSerializer.Serialize(responseContent);
    return new BadRequestObjectResult(responseContent);
  }
  //binding and validation was successful, execute the rest of the method
}
```

Adding Custom Errors to the ModelState Dictionary

In addition to the properties and errors added by the binding and validation engines, custom errors can be added to the ModelState dictionary. Errors can be added at the property level or for the entire model.

To add a specific error for a property (e.g., the PetName property of the Car entity), use the following:

```
ModelState.AddModelError("PetName","Name is required");
```

To add an error for the entire model, use string.Empty for the property name, like this:

```
ModelState.AddModelError(string.Empty, $"Unable to create record: {ex.Message}");
```

Clearing the ModelState Dictionary

There are times where you might need to clear the ModelState of all values and errors. To reset the ModelState, simply call the Clear() method, like this:

```
ModelState.Clear();
```

This is commonly used with explicit validation or when required properties are intentionally left out because of over posting concerns.

Implicit Model Binding

Implicit model binding occurs when the model to be bound is a parameter for an action method (MVC/API applications) or a handler method (Razor page applications). It uses reflection (and recursion for complex types) to match the model's writable property names with the names contained in the name-value pairs posted to the action method. If there is a name match, the binder uses the value from the name-value pair to attempt to set the property value. If multiple names from the name-value pairs match, the first matching name's value is used. If a property isn't found in the name-value pairs, the property is set to its default value. The order the name-value pairs are searched is as follows:

- Form values from an HTTP Post method (including JavaScript AJAX posts)
- Request body (for API controllers)
- Route values provided through ASP.NET Core routing (for simple types)
- Query string values (for simple types)
- Uploaded files (for `IFormFile` types)

For example, the following method will attempt to set all of the properties on the `Car` type implicitly. If the binding process completes without error, the `ModelState.IsValid` property returns `true`.

```
[HttpPost]
[ValidateAntiForgeryToken]
public ActionResult Create(Car entity)
{
  if (ModelState.IsValid)
  {
    //Save the data;
  }
}
```

Here an example `OnPostAsync()` method in a Razor page `PageModel` class that takes in an optional integer (from the route or query string) and an implicitly bound `Car` entity:

```
public async Task<ActionResult> OnPostAsync(int? id, Car entity)
{
  if (ModelState.IsValid)
  {
    //Save the data;
  }
}
```

Explicit Model Binding

Explicit model binding is executed with a call to `TryUpdateModelAsync()`, passing in an instance of the type being bound and the list of properties to bind. The method then uses reflection to find matches between the property names and the names in the name-value pairs in the request. If the model binding fails, the method returns `false` and sets the `ModelState` errors in the same manner as implicit model binding.

When using explicit model binding, the type being bound isn't a parameter of the action method (MVC/API) or handler method (Razor pages). For example, you could write the previous `Create()` method this way and use explicit model binding:

```
[HttpPost]
[ValidateAntiForgeryToken]
public async Task<IActionResult> Create()
{
  var newCar = new Car();
  if (await TryUpdateModelAsync(newCar ,"", c=>c.Color,c=>c.PetName,c=>c.MakeId))
  {
    //do something important
  }
}
```

Explicit model binding also works in Razor page handler methods:

```
public async Task<IActionResult> OnPostAsync()
{
  var newCar = new Car();
  if (await TryUpdateModelAsync(newCar ,"", c=>c.Color,c=>c.PetName,c=>c.MakeId))
  {
    //do something important
  }
}
```

■ **Note** The second parameter (set to an empty string in these examples) will be covered shortly in the Handling Property Name Prefixes section.

With implicit model binding, an instance is getting created for you. However, with explicit model binding, you must first create the instance then call `TryUpdateModelAsync()`, which attempts to update the values of that instance from the name value pairs sent in the request. Like explicit model binding, the binding engine ignores any properties without a matching name in the name-value pairs in the request.

Since you have to create the instance first with explicit model binding, you can set properties on your instance before calling `TryUpdateModelAsync()`, like this:

```
var newCar = new Car
{
  Color = "Purple",
  MakeId = 1,
  PetName = "Prince"
};
if (await TryUpdateModelAsync(newCar,"", c=>c.Color,c=>c.PetName,c=>c.MakeId))
{
    //do something important
}
```

In the previous example, any of the values set with the initial object initialization will retain their values if the property does not have a matching name in the name-value pairs in the request.

Property Model Binding

A property on a MVC style controller or a Razor page PageModel can be marked as the binding target for HTTP Post requests. This is accomplished by adding the public property to the class and marking it with the BindProperty attribute. When using property binding, the controller's action methods or PageModel handler methods do not take the property as a parameter. Here are two examples that uses property binding on a Car property for an MVC style application and a Razor page PageModel:

```
//CarsController - MVC
public class CarsController : Controller
{
  [BindProperty] public Car Entity { get; set; }

  [HttpPost("{id}")]
  [ValidateAntiForgeryToken]
  [ActionName("Edit")]
  public async Task<IActionResult> Edit(int id)
  {
    //Handle the post request
  }  //omitted for brevity
}

//EditPage -- Razor
public class EditModel : PageModel
{
  [BindProperty] public Car Entity { get; set; }

  public async Task<IActionResult> OnGet(int? id)
  {
    //Handle the HTTP Get request
  }
  public async Task<IActionResult> OnPost(int id)
  {
    //Handle the HTTP Get request
  }
}
```

By default, property binding only works with HTTP Post requests. If you need HTTP Get requests to also bind to the property, update the BindProperty attribute as follows:

```
[BindProperty(Name="car",SupportsGet = true)] public Car Entity { get; set; }
```

Handling Property Name Prefixes

Sometimes the data will come into your action method from a table, a parent-child construct, or a complex object that adds a prefix to the names in the name-value pairs. Recall that both implicit and explicit model binding uses reflection to match property names with names in the name-value pairs of the request, and prefixes to the names will prevent the matches from being made.

With implicit model binding, the Bind attribute is used to specify a prefix for the property names. The following example sets a prefix for the names:

```
[HttpPost]
[ValidateAntiForgeryToken]
public ActionResult Create([Bind(Prefix="CarList")]Car car)
{
  if (ModelState.IsValid)
  {
    //Save the data;
  }
  //handle the binding errors
}
```

With explicit model binding, the prefix is set in the TryUpdateModelAsync() method using the second parameter (which was just an empty string in the previous examples):

```
[HttpPost]
[ValidateAntiForgeryToken]
public async Task<IActionResult> Create()
{
  var newCar = new Car();
  if (await TryUpdateModelAsync(newCar,"CarList", c=>c.Color,c=>c.PetName,c=>c.MakeId))
  {
    //Save the data
  }
  //handle the binding errors
}
```

Preventing Over Posting

Over posting is when the request submits more values than you are expecting (or wanting). This can be accidental (the developer left too many fields in the form), or malicious (someone used browser dev tools to modify the form before submitting it). For example, presume you want the application to allow changing colors, names, or makes, but not the prices on Car records.

The Bind attribute in HTTP Post methods allows you to limit the properties that participate in implicit model binding. If a Bind attribute is placed on a reference parameter, the fields listed in the Include list are the only fields that will be assigned through model binding. If the Bind attribute is not used, all fields are bindable.

The following example uses the Bind attribute to only allow updating the PetName and Color fields in the Update() method:

```
[HttpPost]
[ValidateAntiForgeryToken]
public ActionResult Update([Bind(nameof(Car.PetName),nameof(Car.Color))]Car car)
{
  //body omitted for brevity
}
```

Here is the same example in a Razor page:

```
public async Task<ActionResult> OnPostAsync(int? id, [Bind(nameof(Car.PetName),nameof(Car.
Color))]Car car)
{
  //body omitted for brevity
}
```

To prevent over posting when using explicit model binding, you remove the properties in the body of the `TryUpdateModel()` method's body that shouldn't be accepted. The following example only allows updating the `PetName` and `Color` fields in the `Update()` method:

```
[HttpPost]
[ValidateAntiForgeryToken]
public async Task<IActionResult> Update()
{
  var newCar = new Car();
  if (await TryUpdateModelAsync(newCar,"", c=>c.Color,c=>c.PetName))
  {
    //save the data
  }
  //Handle the binding errors
}
```

When using this method of implicit method of model binding, the Bind attribute can be used to prevent over posting:

```
public async Task<ActionResult> OnPostAsync(int? id, [Bind(nameof(Car.PetName),nameof(Car.
Color))]Car car)
{
  //body omitted for brevity
}
```

You can also specify the binding source in Razor pages. The following instructs the binding engine to get the data from the request's `Form` data:

```
public async Task<ActionResult> OnPostAsync(int? id, [FromForm]Car car)
{
  //body omitted for brevity
}
```

Controlling Model Binding Sources in ASP.NET Core

Binding sources can be controlled through a set of attributes on the action parameters. Custom model binders can also be created; however, that is beyond the scope of this book. Table 30-7 lists the attributes that can be used to control model binding.

Table 30-7. *Controlling Model Binding Sources*

Attribute	Meaning in Life
`BindingRequired`	A model state error will be added if binding cannot occur instead of just setting the property to its default value.
`BindNever`	Tells the model binder to never bind to this parameter.
`FromHeaderFromQuery` `FromRouteFromForm`	Used to specify the exact binding source to apply (header, query string, route parameters, or form values).
`FromServices`	Binds the type using dependency injection (covered later in this chapter).
`FromBody`	Binds data from the request body. The formatter is selected based on the content of the request (e.g., JSON, XML, etc.). There can be at most one parameter decorated with the `FromBody` attribute.
`ModelBinder`	Used to override the default model binder (for custom model binding).

Here are two examples that show using the `FromForm` attribute. The first is in a RESTful service controller, and the second is from a Razor page handler method:

```
//API ActionMethod
[HttpPost]
public ActionResult<T> Create([FromForm] Car entity)
{
  //body omitted for brevity
}

//Razor page
public async Task<ActionResult> OnPostAsync(int? id, [FromForm]Car car)
{
  //body omitted for brevity
}
```

Model Validation

Model validation occurs immediately after model binding (both explicit and implicit). While model binding adds errors to the `ModelState` data dictionary due to conversion issues, validation failures add errors to the `ModelState` data dictionary due to broken validation rules. Examples of validation rules include required fields, strings that have a maximum allowed length, properly formatted phone numbers, or dates being within a certain allowed range.

Validation rules are set through validation attributes, either built-in or custom. Table 30-8 lists some of the built-in validation attributes. Note that several also double as data annotations for shaping the EF Core entities.

Table 30-8. *Some of the Built-in Validation Attributes*

Attribute	Meaning in Life
CreditCard	Performs a Luhn-10 check on the credit card number
Compare	Validates the two properties in a model match
EmailAddress	Validates the property has a valid email format
Phone	Validates the property has a valid phone number format
Range	Validates the property falls within a specified range
RegularExpression	Validates the property matches a specified regular expression
Required	Validates the property has a value
StringLength	Validates the property doesn't exceed a maximum length
Url	Validates the property has a valid URL format
Remote	Validates input on the client by calling an action method on the server

Custom validation attributes can also be developed and are covered later in this book.

Explicit Model Validation

Explicit model validation is executed with a call to `TryValidateModel()`, passing in an instance of the type being validated. The result of this call is a populated `ModelState` instance with any invalid properties. Valid properties do not get written to the `ModelState` object like they do with the binding/validation combination.

Take the following code as an example. This method uses explicit binding, leaving out the `Color` property. Since the color property is required, the `ModelState` reports as invalid. The `Color` is updated, explicit validation is called, and the `ModelState` is still invalid:

```
[HttpPost]
[ValidateAntiForgeryToken]
public async Task<IActionResult> CreateCar()
{
  var newCar = new Car();
  if (await TryUpdateModelAsync(newCar, "",c => c.PetName, c => c.MakeId))
  {
    //car is bound and valid - save it
  }

  var isValid = ModelState.IsValid; //false
  newCar.Color = "Purple";
  TryValidateModel(newCar);
  isValid = ModelState.IsValid; //still false
  //rest of the method
  }
}
```

In order for an object that has been through a validation pass to be revalidated, the `ModelState` must be cleared, as in the following update to the method:

```
[HttpPost]
[ValidateAntiForgeryToken]
public async Task<IActionResult> CreateCar()
{
  var newCar = new Car();
  if (await TryUpdateModelAsync(newCar, "",c => c.PetName, c => c.MakeId))
  {
    //car is bound and valid - save it
  }

  var isValid = ModelState.IsValid; //false
  newCar.Color = "Purple";
  TryValidateModel(newCar);
  isValid = ModelState.IsValid; //still false
  ModelState.Clear();
  TryValidateModel(newCar);
  isValid = ModelState.IsValid; //true
  //rest of the method
  }
}
```

Do know that calling `Clear()` clears out all ModelState data, including the binding information.

Filters

Filters in ASP.NET Core run code before or after specific stages of the request processing pipeline. There are built-in filters for authorization and caching, as well as options for assigning customer filters. Table 30-9 lists the types of filters that can be added into the pipeline, listed in their order of execution.

Table 30-9. *Filters Available in ASP.NET Core*

Filter	Meaning in Life
Authorization filters	Run first and determine if the user is authorized for the current request.
Resource filters	Run immediately after the authorization filter and can run after the rest of the pipeline has completed. Run before model binding.
Action filters	Run immediately before an action is executed and/or immediately after an action is executed. Can alter values passed into an action and the result returned from an action. Applies to MVC style web applications and RESTful services.
Page Filters	Can be built to run code after a handler method has been selected but before model binding, after the handler method executes after model binding is complete or immediately after the handler executed. Similar to Action filters but apply to Razor Pages.
Exception filters	Used to apply global policies to unhandled exceptions that occur before writing to the response body.
Result filters	Run code immediately after the successful execution of action results. Useful for logic that surrounds view or formatter execution.

Authorization Filters

Authorization filters work with the ASP.NET Core Identity system to prevent access to controllers or actions that the user doesn't have permission to use. It's not recommended to build custom authorization filters since the built-in `AuthorizeAttribute` and `AllowAnonymousAttribute` usually provide enough coverage when using ASP.NET Core Identity.

Resource Filters

Resource filters have two methods. The `OnResourceExecuting()` method executes after authorization filters and prior to any other filters, and the `OnResourceExecuted()` method executes after all other filters. This enables resource filters to short-circuit the entire response pipeline. A common use for resource filters is for caching. If the response is in the cache, the filter can skip the rest of the pipeline.

Action Filters

The `OnActionExecuting()` method executes immediately before the execution of the action method, and the `OnActionExecuted()` method executes immediately after the execution of the action method. Action filters can short-circuit the action method and any filters that are wrapped by the action filter (order of execution and wrapping are covered shortly).

Page Filters

The `OnHandlerSelected()` method executes after a handler method has been selected but before model binding occurs. The `OnPageHandlerExecuting()` method executes after model binding is complete and the `OnPageHandlerExecuted()` method executes after the handler method executes.

Exception Filters

Exception filters enable implementation of consistent error handling in an application. The `OnException()` method executes when unhandled exceptions are thrown in controller creation, model binding, action filters, or action methods, page filters, or page handler methods.

Result Filters

Result filters wrap the execution of the `IActionResult` for an action method. A common scenario is to add header information into the HTTP response message using a result filter. The `OnResultExecuting()` method executes before the response and `OnResultExecuted()` executes after the response has started.

Summary

This chapter introduced ASP.NET Core and is the first of a set of chapters covering ASP.NET Core. This chapter began with a brief look back at the history of ASP.NET and then looked at the features from classic ASP.NET MVC and ASP.NET Web API that also exist in ASP.NET Core.

The next section created the solution and the projects, updated the ports, and examined running and debugging ASP.NET Core web applications and services.

In the next chapter, you will dive into many of the new features added in ASP.NET Core.

CHAPTER 31

Diving Into ASP.NET Core

This chapter takes a deep look into the new features in ASP.NET Core. As you learn about the features, you will add them to the projects created in the previous chapter, Introducing ASP.NET Core.

What's New in ASP.NET Core

In addition to supporting the base functionality of ASP.NET MVC and ASP.NET Web API, Microsoft has added a host of new features and improvements over the previous frameworks. In addition to the unification of frameworks and controllers, a new style of web applications is now supported using Razor pages. Listed here are some additional improvements and innovations:

- Razor Page based web applications
- Environment awareness
- Minimal templates with top level statements
- Cloud-ready, environment-based configuration system
- Built-in dependency injection
- The Options pattern
- The HTTP Client Factory
- Flexible development and deployment models
- Lightweight, high-performance, and modular HTTP request pipeline
- Tag helpers (covered in a later chapter)
- View components (covered in a later chapter)
- Vast improvements in performance
- Integrated logging

Razor Pages

Another option for creating web applications with ASP.NET Core is using Razor pages. Instead of using the MVC pattern, Razor page applications are (as the name suggests) *page*-centric. Each Razor page consists of two files, the page file (e.g. `Index.cshtml`) is the view, and the `PageModel` C# class (e.g. `Index.cshtml.cs`), which serves as the code behind file for the page file.

A. Troelsen and P. Japikse, *Pro C# 10 with .NET 6*, https://doi.org/10.1007/978-1-4842-7869-7_31

■ **Note** Razor page based web applications also support partial and layout views, which will be covered in detail in later chapters.

The Razor Page File

Just like MVC based web applications, the Razor page file is responsible for rendering the content of the page, and receiving input from the user. It should be lightweight, and hand off work to the `PageModel` class. Razor page files will be explored in depth in Chapter 34.

The PageModel Class

Like the `Controller` class for MVC style applications, the `PageModel` class provides helper methods for Razor page based web applications. Razor pages derive from the `PageModel` class, and are typically named with the Model suffix, like `CreateModel`. The Model suffix is dropped when routing to a page. Table 31-1 lists the most commonly used methods and Table 31-2 lists the HTTP Status Code Helpers.

Table 31-1. *Some of the Helper Methods Provided by the Controller Class*

Helper Method	Meaning in Life
`HttpContext`	Returns the `HttpContext` for the currently executing action.
`Request`	Returns the `HttpRequest` for the currently executing action.
`Response`	Returns the `HttpResponse` for the currently executing action.
`RouteData`	Returns the `RouteData` for the currently executing action (routing is covered later in this chapter).
`ModelState`	Returns the state of the model in regard to model binding and validation (both covered later in this chapter).
`Url`	Returns an instance of the `IUrlHelper`, providing access to building URLs for ASP.NET Core MVC applications and services.
`ViewData` `TempData`	Provide data to the view through the `ViewDataDictionary` and `TempDataDictionary`
`Page`	Returns a `PageResult` (derived from `ActionResult`) as the HTTP response.
`PartialView`	Returns a `PartialViewResult` to the response pipeline.
`ViewComponent`	Returns a `ViewComponentResult` to the response pipeline.
`OnPageHandlerSelected`	Executes when a page handler method is selected but before model binding.
`OnPageHandlerExecuting`	Executes before a page handler method executes.
`OnPageHandlerExecutionAsync`	Async version of `OnPageHandlerExecuting`.
`OnPageHandlerExecuted`	Executes after a page handler method executes.

(*continued*)

Table 31-1. (*continued*)

Helper Method	Meaning in Life
OnPageHandlerSelectionAsync	Async version of OnPageHandlerSelected.
User	Returns the ClaimsPrincipal user.
Content	Returns a ContentResult to the response. Overloads allow for adding a content type and encoding definition.
File	Returns a FileContentResult to the response.
Redirect	A series of methods that redirect the user to another URL by returning a RedirectResult.
LocalRedirect	A series of methods that redirect the user to another URL only if the URL is local. More secure than the generic Redirect methods.
RedirectToAction RedirectToPage RedirectToRoute	A series of methods that redirect to another action method, Razor Page, or named route. Routing is covered later in this chapter.
TryUpdateModelAsync	Used for explicit model binding.
TryValidateModel	Used for explicit model validation.

Table 31-2. Some of the HTTP Status Code Helper Methods Provided by the PageModelClass

Helper Method	HTTP Status Code Action Result	Status Code
NotFound	NotFoundResult	404
Forbid	ForbidResult	403
BadRequest	BadRequestResult	400
StatusCode(int)StatusCode(int, object)	StatusCodeResultObjectResult	Defined by the int parameter.

You might be surprised to see some familiar methods from the Controller class. Razor page based applications share many of the features of MVC style applications as you have seen and will continue to see throughout these chapters.

Page Handler Methods

As discussed in the routing section, Razor pages define handler methods to handle HTTP Get and Post requests. The PageModel class supports both synchronous and asynchronous handler methods. The verb handled is based on the name of the method, with OnPost()/OnPostAsync() handling HTTP post requests, and OnGet()/OnGetAsync() handling HTTP get requests. The async versions are listed here:

```
public class DeleteModel : PageModel
{
  public async Task<IActionResult> OnGetAsync(int? id)
  {
    //handle the get request here
  }
```

```
  public async Task<IActionResult> OnPostAsync(int? id)
  {
    //handle the post request here
  }
}
```

The names of the handler methods can be changed, and multiple handler methods for each HTTP verb can exist, however overloaded versions with the same name are not permitted. This will be covered in Chapter 34.

Environmental Awareness

ASP.NET Core applications' awareness of their execution environment includes host environment variables and file locations through an instance of `IWebHostEnvironment`, which implement the `IHostEnvironment` interface. Table 31-3 shows the properties available through these interfaces.

Table 31-3. *The IWebHostEnvironment Properties*

Property	Functionality Provided
`ApplicationName`	Gets or sets the name of the application. Defaults to the name of the entry assembly.
`ContentRootPath`	Gets or sets the absolute path to the directory that contains the application content files.
`ContentRootFileProvider`	Gets or sets an `IFileProvider` pointing to the `ContentRootPath`.
`EnvironmentName`	Gets or sets the name of the environment. Sets to the value of the `ASPNETCORE_ENVIRONMENT` environment variable.
`WebRootFileProvider`	Gets or sets an `IFileProvider` pointing at the `WebRootPath`.
`WebRootPath`	Gets or sets the absolute path to the directory that contains the web-servable application content files.

In addition to accessing the relevant file paths, `IWebHostEnvironment` is used to determine the runtime environment.

Determining the Runtime Environment

ASP.NET Core automatically reads the value of the environment variable named `ASPNETCORE_ENVIRONMENT` to set the runtime environment. If the `ASPNETCORE_ENVIRONMENT` variable is not set, ASP.NET Core sets the value to `Production`. The value set is accessible through the `EnvironmentName` property on the `IWebHostEnvironment`.

While developing ASP.NET Core applications, this variable is typically set using the `launchSettings.json` file or the command line. Downstream environments (staging, production, etc.) typically use standard operating system environment variables.

You are free to use any name for the environment or the three that are supplied by the `Environments` static class.

```
public static class Environments
{
  public static readonly string Development = "Development";
  public static readonly string Staging = "Staging";
  public static readonly string Production = "Production";
}
```

The `HostEnvironmentEnvExtensions` class provides extensions methods on the `IHostEnvironment` for working with the environment name property. Table 31-4 lists the convenience methods available.

Table 31-4. *The HostEnvironmentEnvExtensions Methods*

Method	Functionality Provided
`IsProduction`	Returns true if the environment variable is set to `Production` (case insensitive)
`IsStaging`	Returns true if the environment variable is set to `Staging` (case insensitive)
`IsDevelopment`	Returns true if the environment variable is set to `Development` (case insensitive)
`IsEnvironment`	Returns true if the environment variable matches the string passed into the method (case insensitive)

These are some examples of using the environment setting:

- Determining which configuration files to load
- Setting debugging, error, and logging options
- Loading environment-specific JavaScript and CSS files

Examine the `Program.cs` file in the AutoLot.Mvc project. Near the end of the file, the environment is checked to determine if the standard exception handler and HSTS (HTTP Strict Transport Security Protocol) should be used:

```
if (!app.Environment.IsDevelopment())
{
    app.UseExceptionHandler("/Home/Error");
    app.UseHsts();
}
```

Update this block to flip it around:

```
if (app.Environment.IsDevelopment())
{
}
else
{
  app.UseExceptionHandler("/Home/Error");
  app.UseHsts();
}
```

Next, add the developer exception page into the pipeline when the app is running development. This provides debugging details like the stack trace, detailed exception information, etc. The standard exception handler renders a simple error page.

```
if (app.Environment.IsDevelopment())
{
  app.UseDeveloperExceptionPage();
}
else
{
  app.UseExceptionHandler("/Home/Error");
  app.UseHsts();
}
```

Update the AutoLot.Web project block to the following (notice the different route for the error handle in the Razor page based application):

```
if (app.Environment.IsDevelopment())
{
  app.UseDeveloperExceptionPage();
}
else
{
  app.UseExceptionHandler("/Error");
  app.UseHsts();
}
```

The AutoLot.Api project is a little different. It is checking for the development environment, and if it is running in development, Swagger and SwaggerUI are added into the pipeline. For this app, we are going to move the Swagger code out of the `if` block so it will always be available (leave the `if` block there, as it will be used later in this chapter):

```
if (app.Environment.IsDevelopment())
{
  //more code to be placed here later
}
app.UseSwagger();
app.UseSwaggerUI();
```

Since there isn't a UI associated with RESTful services, there isn't any need for the developer exception page. Swagger will be covered in depth in the next chapter.

■ **Note** Whether the Swagger pages are available outside of the development environment is a business decision. We are moving the Swagger code to run in all environments so that the Swagger page is always available as you work through this book. Swagger will be covered in depth in the next chapter.

You will see many more uses for environment awareness as you build the ASP.NET Core applications in this book.

The WebAppBuilder and WebApp

Unlike classic ASP.NET MVC or ASP.NET Web API applications, ASP.NET Core applications are .NET console applications that create and configure a `WebApplication`, which is an instance of `IHost`. The creation of configuration of the `IHost` is what sets the application up to listen and respond to HTTP requests.

The default templates for ASP.NET Core 6 MVC, Razor, and Service application are minimal. These files will be added to as you progress through the ASP.NET Core chapters.

■ **Note** Prior to .NET 6 and C# 10, a `WebHost` was created in the `Main()` method of the `Program.cs` file and configured for your application in the `Startup.cs` file. With the release of .NET 6 and C# 10, the ASP.NET Core template uses top level statements in the `Program.cs` file for creation and configuration and doesn't have a `Startup.cs` file.

The Program.cs File with RESTful Services

Open the `Program.cs` class in the AutoLot.Api application, and examine the contents, shown here for reference:

```
var builder = WebApplication.CreateBuilder(args);

// Add services to the container.

builder.Services.AddControllers();
// Learn more about configuring Swagger/OpenAPI at https://aka.ms/aspnetcore/swashbuckle
builder.Services.AddEndpointsApiExplorer();
builder.Services.AddSwaggerGen();

var app = builder.Build();

// Configure the HTTP request pipeline.
if (app.Environment.IsDevelopment())
{
  //more code to be placed here later
}
app.UseSwagger();
app.UseSwaggerUI();

app.UseHttpsRedirection();
app.UseAuthorization();
app.MapControllers();

app.Run();
```

If you are coming from a previous version of ASP.NET Core, the preceding code was split between the `Program.cs` file and the `Startup.cs` file. With ASP.NET Core 6, those file are combined into top level statements in the `Program.cs` file. The code before the call to `builder.Build()` was contained in the `Program.cs` file and the `ConfigureServices()` method in the `Startup.cs` file and is responsible for creating the WebApplicationBuilder and registering services in the dependency injection container. The code including the builder.Build() call and the rest of the code in the file was contained in the Configure() method and is responsible for the configuration of the HTTP pipeline.

The CreateBuilder() method compacts the most typical application setup into one method call. It configures the app (using environment variables and appsettings JSON files), it configures the default logging provider, and it sets up the dependency injection container. The returned WebApplicationBuilder is used to register services, add additional configuration information, logging support, etc.

The next set of methods adds the necessary base services into the dependency injection container for building RESTful services. The AddControllers() method adds in support for using controllers and action methods, the AddEndpointsApiExplorer() method provides information about the API (and is used by Swagger), and AddSwaggerGen() creates the basic OpenAPI support.

■ **Note** When adding services into the Dependency Injection container, make sure to add them into the top level statements using the comment //Add services to the container.They must be added before the builder.Build() method is called.

The builder.Build() method generates the WebApplication and sets up the next group of method calls to configure the HTTP pipeline. The Environment section was discussed previously. The next set of calls ensures all requests use HTTPS, enables the authorization middleware, and maps the controllers to their endpoints. Finally, the Run() method starts the application and gets everything ready to receive web requests and respond to them.

The Program.cs File with MVC Style Applications

Open the Program.cs class in the AutoLot.Mvc application, and examine the contents, shown here for reference (with differences from the AutoLot.Api application's file in bold):

```
var builder = WebApplication.CreateBuilder(args);

// Add services to the container.

builder.Services.AddControllersWithViews();

var app = builder.Build();

// Configure the HTTP request pipeline.
if (app.Environment.IsDevelopment())
{
  app.UseDeveloperExceptionPage();
}
else
{
  app.UseExceptionHandler("/Home/Error");
  app.UseHsts();
}

app.UseHttpsRedirection();
app.UseStaticFiles();
```

```
app.UseRouting();

app.UseAuthorization();

app.MapControllerRoute(
    name: "default",
    pattern: "{controller=Home}/{action=Index}/{id?}");

app.Run();
```

The first difference is the call to `AddControllersWithViews()`. ASP.NET Core RESTful services use the same controller/action method pattern as MVC style applications, just without views. This adds support for views into the application. The calls for Swagger and the API Explorer are omitted, as they are used by API service.

The next difference is the call to `UserExceptionHandler()` when the application is not running in a development environment. This is a user friendly exception handler that displays simple information (and no technical debugging data). That is followed by the `UseHsts()` method, which turns on HTTP Strict Transport Security, preventing users to switch back to HTTP once they have connected. It also prevents them from clicking through warnings regarding invalid certificates.

The call to `UseStaticFiles()` enables static content (images, JavaScript files, CSS files, etc.) to be rendered through the application. This call is not in the API style applications, as they don't typically have a need to render static content. The final changes add end point routing support and the default route to the application.

The Program.cs File with Razor Page Based Applications

Open the `Program.cs` class in the AutoLot.Web application, and examine the contents, shown here for reference (with the differences from the AutoLot.Mvc application shown in bold):

```
var builder = WebApplication.CreateBuilder(args);
// Add services to the container.

builder.Services.AddRazorPages();
var app = builder.Build();

// Configure the HTTP request pipeline.
if (app.Environment.IsDevelopment())
{
  app.UseDeveloperExceptionPage();
}
else
{
  app.UseExceptionHandler("/Error");
  app.UseHsts();
}
app.UseHttpsRedirection();
app.UseStaticFiles();
app.UseRouting();
app.UseAuthorization();
app.MapRazorPages();
app.Run();
```

There are only three differences between this file and the initial file for the AutoLot.Mvc application. Instead of adding support for controllers with views, there is a call to `AddRazorPages()` to add support for Razor pages, add routing for razor pages with the call to the `MapRazorPages()` method, and there isn't a default route configured.

Application Configuration

Previous versions of ASP.NET used the `web.config` file to configure services and applications, and developers accessed the configuration settings through the `System.Configuration` class. Of course, *all* configuration settings for the site, not just application-specific settings, were dumped into the `web.config` file making it a (potentially) complicated mess.

ASP.NET Core leverages the new .NET JSON-based configuration system first introduced in Chapter 16. As a reminder, it's based on simple JSON files that hold configuration settings. The default file for configuration is the `appsettings.json` file. The initial version of `appsettings.json` file (created by the ASP. NET Core web application and API service templates) simply contains configuration information for the logging, as well as allowing all hosts (e.g. https://localhost:xxxx) to bind to the app:

```
{
  "Logging": {
    "LogLevel": {
      "Default": "Information",
      "Microsoft.AspNetCore": "Warning",
    }
  },
  "AllowedHosts": "*"
}
```

The template also creates an `appsettings.Development.json` file. The configuration system works in conjunction with the runtime environment awareness to load additional configuration files based on the runtime environment. This is accomplished by instructing the configuration system to load a file named `appsettings.{environmentname}.json` after the `appSettings.json` file. When running under Development, the `appsettings.Development.json` file is loaded after the initial settings file. If the environment is Staging, the `appsettings.Staging.json` file is loaded, etc. It is important to note that when more than one file is loaded, any settings that appear in both files are overwritten by the last file loaded; they are not additive.

For each of the web application projects, add the following connection string information (updating the actual connection string to match your environment from Chapter 23 into the `appsettings.Development.json` files:

```
  "ConnectionStrings": {
    "AutoLot": "Server=.,5433;Database=AutoLot;User ID=sa;Password=P@ssw0rd;"
  }
```

■ **Note** Each item in the JSON must be comma delimited. When you add in the `ConnectionStrings` item, make sure to add a comma after the curly brace that proceeds the item you are adding.

Next, copy each of the appsettings.Development.json files to a new file named appsettings.Production.json into each of the web application projects. Update the connection string entries to the following:

```
"ConnectionStrings": {
  "AutoLot": "It's a secret"
},
```

This shows part of the power of the new configuration system. The developers don't have access to the secret production information (like connection strings), just the non-secret information, yet everything can still be checked into source control.

■ **Note** In production scenarios using this pattern, the secrets are typically tokenized. The build and release process replaces the tokens with the production information.

All configuration values are accessible through an instance of IConfiguration, which is available through the ASP.NET Core dependency injection system. In the top level statements prior to the web application being built, the configuration is available from the WebApplicationBuilder like this:

```
var config = builder.Configuration;
```

After the web application is built, the IConfiguration instance is available from the WebApplication instance:

```
var config = app.Configuration;
```

Settings can be accessed using the traditional methods covered in Chapter 16. There is also a shortcut for getting application connection strings.

```
config.GetConnectionString("AutoLot")
```

Additional configuration features, including the Options pattern, will be discussed later in this chapter.

Built-in Dependency Injection

Dependency injection (DI) is a mechanism to support loose coupling between objects. Instead of directly creating dependent objects or passing specific implementations into classes and/or methods, parameters are defined as interfaces. That way, any implementation of the interface can be passed into the classes or methods and classes, dramatically increasing the flexibility of the application.

DI support is one of the main tenets in the rewrite ASP.NET Core. Not only do the top level statements in the Program.cs file (covered later in this chapter) accept all the configuration and middleware services through dependency injection, your custom classes can (and should) also be added to the service container to be injected into other parts of the application. When an item is configured into the ASP.NET Core DI container, there are three lifetime options, as shown in Table 31-5.

Table 31-5. *Lifetime Options for Services*

Lifetime Option	Functionality Provided
`Transient`	Created *each* time they are needed.
`Scoped`	Created once for each request. Recommended for Entity Framework `DbContext` objects.
`Singleton`	Created once on first request and then reused for the lifetime of the object. This is the recommended approach versus implementing your class as a Singleton.

■ **Note** If you want to use a different dependency injection container, ASP.NET Core was designed with that flexibility in mind. Consult the docs to learn how to plug in a different container: `https://docs.microsoft.com/en-us/aspnet/core/fundamentals/dependency-injection`.

Services are added into the DI container by adding them to the `IServiceCollection` for the application. When using the top level statements template in .NET 6 web applications, the `IServiceCollection` is instantiated by the `WebApplicationBuilder`, and this instance is used to add services into the container.

When adding services to the DI container, make sure to add them before the line that builds the `WebApplication` object:

```
var app = builder.Build();
```

■ **Note** In pre-.NET 6 web applications, the startup process involved both a `Program.cs` class and another class named `Startup.cs` (by convention). In .NET 6, all of the configuration is done in top level statements in the `Program.cs` file. This will be covered in the section Configuring the Web Application.

Adding Web App Support To The Dependency Injection Container

When creating MVC based web applications, the `AddControllersWithView()` method adds in the necessary services to support the MVC pattern in ASP.NET Core. The following code (in the `Program.cs` file of the AutoLot.Mvc project) accesses the `IServiceCollection` of the `WebApplicationBuilder` and adds the required DI support for controllers and views:

```
var builder = WebApplication.CreateBuilder(args);
// Add services to the container.
builder.Services.AddControllersWithViews();
```

RESTful service web applications don't use views but do need controller support, so they use the `AddControllers()` method. The API template for ASP.NET Core also adds in support for Swagger (a .NET implementation of OpenAPI) and the ASP.NET Core end point explorer:

```
var builder = WebApplication.CreateBuilder(args);
// Add services to the container.
builder.Services.AddControllers();
builder.Services.AddEndpointsApiExplorer();
builder.Services.AddSwaggerGen();
```

■ **Note** Swagger and OpenAPI will be covered in the next chapter.

Finally, Razor page based applications must enable Razor page support with the AddRazorPages() method:

```
var builder = WebApplication.CreateBuilder(args);
// Add services to the container.
builder.Services.AddRazorPages();
```

Adding Derived DbContext Classes into the DI Container

Registering a derived DbContext class in an ASP.NET Core application allows the DI container to handle the initialization and lifetime of the context. The AddDbContext<>()/AddDbContextPool() methods add a properly configured context class into the DI container. The AddDbContextPool() version creates a pool of instances that are cleaned between requests, ensuring that there isn't any data contamination between requests. This can improve performance in your application, as it eliminates the startup cost for creating a context once it is added to the pool.

Start by adding the following global using statements into the GlobalUsings.cs for the AutoLot.Api, AutoLot.Mvc, AutoLot.Web projects:

```
global using AutoLot.Dal.EfStructures;
global using AutoLot.Dal.Initialization;
global using Microsoft.EntityFrameworkCore;
```

The following code (which must be added into each of the Program.cs files in the web projects) gets the connection string from the JSON configuration file and adds the ApplicationDbContext as a pooled resource into the services collection:

```
var connectionString = builder.Configuration.GetConnectionString("AutoLot");
builder.Services.AddDbContextPool<ApplicationDbContext>(
    options => options.UseSqlServer(connectionString,
        sqlOptions => sqlOptions.EnableRetryOnFailure().CommandTimeout(60)));
```

Now, whenever an instance of the ApplicationDbContext is needed, the dependency injection (DI) system will take care of the creation (or getting it from the pool) and recycling of the instance (or returning it to the pool).

EF Core 6 introduced a set of minimal APIs for adding derived DbContext classes into the services collection. Instead of the previous code, you can use the following short cut:

```
builder.Services.AddSqlServer<ApplicationDbContext>(connectionString, options =>
{
  options.EnableRetryOnFailure().CommandTimeout(60);
});
```

Note that the minimal API doesn't have the same level of capabilities. Several features, like DbContext pooling are not supported. For more information on the minimal APIs, refer to the documentation located here: https://docs.microsoft.com/en-us/ef/core/what-is-new/ef-core-6.0/whatsnew#miscellaneous-improvements.

Adding Custom Services To The Dependency Injection Container

Application services (like the repositories in the AutoLot.Dal project) can be added into the DI container using one of the lifetime options from Table 31-5. For example, to add the CarRepo as a service into the DI container, you would use the following

```
services.AddScoped<ICarRepo, CarRepo>();
```

The previous example added a scoped service (AddScoped<>()) into the DI container specifying the service type (ICarRepo) and the concrete implementation (CarRepo) to inject. You could add all of the repos into all of the web applications in the Program.cs file directly, or you can create an extension method to encapsulate the calls. This process keeps the Program.cs file cleaner.

Before creating the extension method, update the GlobalUsings.cs file in the AutoLot.Services project to the following:

```
global using AutoLot.Dal.Repos;
global using AutoLot.Dal.Repos.Base;
global using AutoLot.Dal.Repos.Interfaces;

global using AutoLot.Models.Entities;
global using AutoLot.Models.Entities.Base;

global using Microsoft.AspNetCore.Builder;

global using Microsoft.Extensions.DependencyInjection;
global using Microsoft.Extensions.Configuration;
global using Microsoft.Extensions.Hosting;
global using Microsoft.Extensions.Logging;

global using Serilog;
global using Serilog.Context;
global using Serilog.Core.Enrichers;
global using Serilog.Events;
global using Serilog.Sinks.MSSqlServer;

global using System.Data;
global using System.Runtime.CompilerServices;
```

Next, create a new folder named DataServices in the AutoLot.Services project. In this folder, create a new public static class named DataServiceConfiguration. Update this class to the following:

```
namespace AutoLot.Services.DataServices;

public static class DataServiceConfiguration
{
  public static IServiceCollection AddRepositories(this IServiceCollection services)
  {
    services.AddScoped<ICarDriverRepo, CarDriverRepo>();
    services.AddScoped<ICarRepo, CarRepo>();
    services.AddScoped<ICreditRiskRepo, CreditRiskRepo>();
    services.AddScoped<ICustomerOrderViewModelRepo, CustomerOrderViewModelRepo>();
```

```
    services.AddScoped<ICustomerRepo, CustomerRepo>();
    services.AddScoped<IDriverRepo, DriverRepo>();
    services.AddScoped<IMakeRepo, MakeRepo>();
    services.AddScoped<IOrderRepo, OrderRepo>();
    services.AddScoped<IRadioRepo, RadioRepo>();
    return services;
  }
}
```

Next, add the following to the GlobalUsings.cs file in each web application (AutoLot.Api, AutoLot.Mvc, AutoLot.Web):

```
global using AutoLot.Services.DataServices;
```

Finally, add the following code to the top level statements in each of the web applications, making sure to add them above the line that builds the WebApplication:

```
builder.Services.AddRepositories();
```

Dependency Hierarchies

When there is a chain of dependencies, all dependencies must be added into the DI container, or a run-time error will occur when the DI container tries to instantiate the concrete class. If you recall from our repositories, they each had a public constructor that took an instance of the ApplicationDbContext, which was added into the DI container before adding in the repositories. If ApplicationDbContext was not in the DI container, then the repositories that depend on it can't be constructed.

Injecting Dependencies

Services in the DI container can be injected into class constructors and methods, into Razor views, and Razor pages and PageModel classes. When injecting into the constructor of a controller or PageModel class, add the type to be injected into the constructor, like this:

```
//Controller
public class CarsController : Controller
{
  private readonly ICarRep _repo;
  public CarsController(ICarRepo repo)
  {
    _repo = repo;
  }
  //omitted for brevity
}

//PageModel
public class CreateModel : PageModel
{
  private readonly ICarRepo _repo;
```

```
  public CreateModel(ICarRepo repo)
  {
    _repo = repo;
  }
  //omitted for brevity
}
```

Method injection is supported for action methods and page handler methods. To distinguish between a binding target and a service from the DI container, the FromServices attribute must be used:

```
//Controller
public class CarsController : Controller
{
  [HttpPost]
  [ValidateAntiForgeryToken]
  public async Task<IActionResult> CreateAsync([FromServices]ICarRepo repo)
  {
    //do something
  }
  //omitted for brevity
}

//PageModel
public class CreateModel : PageModel
{
  public async Task<IActionResult> OnPostAsync([FromServices]ICarRepo repo)
  {
    //do somethng
  }
  //omitted for brevity
}
```

■ **Note** You might be wondering when you should use constructor injection vs method injection, and the answer, of course, is "it depends". I prefer to use constructor injection for services used throughout the class and method injection for more focused scenarios.

To inject into an MVC view or a Razor page view, use the @inject command:

```
@inject ICarRepo Repo
```

Getting Dependencies in Program.cs

You might be wondering how to get dependencies out of the DI container when you are in the top level statements in the Program.cs file. For example, if you want to initialize the database, you need an instance of the ApplicationDbContext. There isn't a constructor, action method, page handler method, or view to inject the instance into.

In addition to the traditional DI techniques, services can also be retrieved directly from the application's ServiceProvider. The WebApplication exposes the configured ServiceProvider through the Services property. To get a service, first create an instance of the IServiceScope. This provides a lifetime container to hold the service. Then get the ServiceProvider from the IServiceScope, which will then provide the services within the current scope.

Suppose you want to selectively clear and reseed the database when running in the development environment. To set this up, first add the following line to the appsettings.Development.json files in each of the web projects:

```
"RebuildDatabase": true,
```

Next, add the following line to each of the appsettings.Production.json files in each of the web projects:

```
"RebuildDatabase": false,
```

In the development block of the if statement in Program.cs, if the configured value for RebuildDatabase is true, then create a new IServiceScope to the an instance of the ApplicationDbContext and use that to call the ClearAndReseedDatabase() method (example shown from the AutoLot.Mvc project):

```
if (env.IsDevelopment())
{
  app.UseDeveloperExceptionPage();
  //Initialize the database
  if (app.Configuration.GetValue<bool>("RebuildDatabase"))
  {
    using var scope = app.Services.CreateScope();
    var dbContext = scope.ServiceProvider.GetRequiredService<ApplicationDbContext>();
    SampleDataInitializer.ClearAndReseedDatabase(dbContext);
  }
}
```

Make the exact same changes to the Program.cs file in the AutoLot.Web project. The Program.cs file update in the AutoLot.Api project is shown here:

```
if (app.Environment.IsDevelopment())
{
  //Initialize the database
  if (app.Configuration.GetValue<bool>("RebuildDatabase"))
  {
    using var scope = app.Services.CreateScope();
    var dbContext = scope.ServiceProvider.GetRequiredService<ApplicationDbContext>();
    SampleDataInitializer.ClearAndReseedDatabase(dbContext);
  }
}
```

Build the Shared Data Services

To wrap up the discussion on dependency injection, we are going to build a set of data services that will be used by both the AutoLot.Mvc and AutoLot.Web projects. The goal of the services is to present a single set of interfaces for all data access. There will be two concrete implementations of the interfaces, one that will call into the AutoLot.Api project and another one that will call into the AutoLot.Dal code directly. The concrete implementations that are added into the DI container will be determined by a project configuration setting.

The Interfaces

Start by creating a new directory named Interfaces in the DataServices directory of the AutoLot.Services project. Next, add the following IDataServiceBase<T> interface into the Interfaces directory:

```
namespace AutoLot.Services.DataServices.Interfaces;

public interface IDataServiceBase<TEntity> where TEntity : BaseEntity, new()
{
  Task<IEnumerable<TEntity>> GetAllAsync();
  Task<TEntity> FindAsync(int id);
  Task<TEntity> UpdateAsync(TEntity entity, bool persist = true);
  Task DeleteAsync(TEntity entity, bool persist = true);
  Task<TEntity> AddAsync(TEntity entity, bool persist = true);
  //implemented ghost method since it won't be used by the API data service
  void ResetChangeTracker() {}
}
```

The IMakeDataService interface simply implements the IDataServiceBase<Make> interface:

```
namespace AutoLot.Services.DataServices.Interfaces;

public interface IMakeDataService : IDataServiceBase<Make>
{
}
```

The ICarDataService interface implements the IDataServiceBase<Car> interface and adds a method to get Car records by Make Id:

```
namespace AutoLot.Services.DataServices.Interfaces;

public interface ICarDataService : IDataServiceBase<Car>
{
  Task<IEnumerable<Car>> GetAllByMakeIdAsync(int? makeId);
}
```

Add the following global using statement into the GlobalUsing.cs file:

```
global using AutoLot.Services.DataServices.Interfaces;
```

The AutoLot.Dal Direct Implementation

Start by creating a new directory named Dal in the DataServices directory, and add a new directory named Base in the Dal directory. Add a new class named DalServiceBase, make it public abstract and implement the IDataServiceBase<T> interface:

```
namespace AutoLot.Services.DataServices.Dal.Base;

public abstract class DalDataServiceBase<TEntity> : IDataServiceBase<TEntity>
  where TEntity : BaseEntity, new()
{
  //implementation goes here
}
```

Add a constructor that takes in an instance of the IBaseRepo<T> and assign it to a class level variable:

```
protected readonly IBaseRepo<TEntity> MainRepo;
protected DalDataServiceBase(IBaseRepo<TEntity> mainRepo)
{
  MainRepo = mainRepo;
}
```

Recall that all of the create, read, update, and delete (CRUD) methods on the base interface were defined as Task or Task<T>. They are defined this way because calls to a RESTful service are asynchronous calls. Also recall that the repo methods that were built with the AutoLot.Dal are not async. The reason for that was mostly for teaching purposes, and not to introduce additional friction into learning EF Core. As the rest of the data services implementation is complete, you can either leave the repo methods synchronous (as they will be shown here) or refactor the repos to add in async versions of the methods.

The base methods call the related methods in the MainRepo:

```
public async Task<IEnumerable<TEntity>> GetAllAsync()
  => MainRepo.GetAllIgnoreQueryFilters();
public async Task<TEntity> FindAsync(int id) => MainRepo.Find(id);
public async Task<TEntity> UpdateAsync(TEntity entity, bool persist = true)
{
  MainRepo.Update(entity, persist);
  return entity;
}
public async Task DeleteAsync(TEntity entity, bool persist = true)
  => MainRepo.Delete(entity, persist);
public async Task<TEntity> AddAsync(TEntity entity, bool persist = true)
{
  MainRepo.Add(entity, persist);
  return entity;
}
```

The final method resets the ChangeTracker on the context, clearing it out for reuse:

```
public void ResetChangeTracker()
{
  MainRepo.Context.ChangeTracker.Clear();
}
```

Add the following global using statements into the GlobalUsings.cs file:

```
global using AutoLot.Services.DataServices.Dal;
global using AutoLot.Services.DataServices.Dal.Base;
```

Add a new class named MakeDalDataService.cs in the Dal directory and update it to match the following:

```
namespace AutoLot.Services.DataServices.Dal;

public class MakeDalDataService : DalDataServiceBase<Make>,IMakeDataService
{
  public MakeDalDataService(IMakeRepo repo):base(repo) { }
}
```

Finally, add a class named CarDalDataService.cs and update it to match the following, which implements the one extra method from the interface:

```
namespace AutoLot.Services.DataServices.Dal;

public class CarDalDataService : DalDataServiceBase<Car>,ICarDataService
{
  private readonly ICarRepo _repo;
  public CarDalDataService(ICarRepo repo) : base(repo)
  {
    _repo = repo;
  }
  public async Task<IEnumerable<Car>> GetAllByMakeIdAsync(int? makeId) =>
    makeId.HasValue
      ? _repo.GetAllBy(makeId.Value)
      : MainRepo.GetAllIgnoreQueryFilters();
}
```

The API Initial Implementation

Most of the implementation for the API version of the data services will be completed after you create the HTTP client factory in the next section. This section will just create the classes to illustrate toggling implementations for interfaces. Start by creating a new directory named Api in the DataServices directory, and add a new directory named Base in the Api directory. Add a new class named ApiServiceBase, make it public abstract and implement the IDataServiceBase<T> interface:

```
namespace AutoLot.Services.DataServices.Api.Base;

public abstract class ApiDataServiceBase<TEntity> : IDataServiceBase<TEntity>
    where TEntity : BaseEntity, new()
{
  protected ApiDataServiceBase()
  {
  }

  public async Task<IEnumerable<TEntity>> GetAllAsync()
    => throw new NotImplementedException();
  public async Task<TEntity> FindAsync(int id) => throw new NotImplementedException();
  public async Task<TEntity> UpdateAsync(TEntity entity, bool persist = true)
  {
    throw new NotImplementedException();
  }
```

```
  public async Task DeleteAsync(TEntity entity, bool persist = true)
    => throw new NotImplementedException();
  public async Task<TEntity> AddAsync(TEntity entity, bool persist = true)
  {
    throw new NotImplementedException();
  }
}
```

Add the following global using statement into the GlobalUsings.cs file:

```
global using AutoLot.Services.DataServices.Api;
global using AutoLot.Services.DataServices.Api.Base;
```

Add a new class named MakeDalDataService.cs in the Dal directory and update it to match the following:

```
namespace AutoLot.Services.DataServices.Api;

public class MakeApiDataService : ApiDataServiceBase<Make>, IMakeDataService
{
  public MakeApiDataService():base()
  {
  }
}
```

Finally, add a class named CarDalDataService.cs and update it to match the following, which implements the one extra method from the interface:

```
namespace AutoLot.Services.DataServices.Api;

public class CarApiDataService : ApiDataServiceBase<Car>, ICarDataService
{
  public CarApiDataService() :base()
  {
  }

  public async Task<IEnumerable<Car>> GetAllByMakeIdAsync(int? makeId) =>
    throw new NotImplementedException();
}
```

Adding the Data Services to the DI Container

The final step is to add the ICarDataService and IMakeDataService into the services collection. Start by adding the following line into the appsettings.Development.json and appsettings.Production.json files in the AutoLot.Mvc and AutoLot.Web project:

```
  "RebuildDatabase": false,
  "UseApi": false,
```

Add the following global using statements to the GlobalUsings.cs file in both the AutoLot.Mvc and AutoLot.Web projects:

```
global using AutoLot.Services.DataServices.Api;
global using AutoLot.Services.DataServices.Dal;
```

Finally, add a new public static method named AddDataServices() to the DataServiceConfiguration class. In this method, check the value of the UseApi configuration flag, and if it is set to true, add the API versions of the data services classes into the services collection. Otherwise use the data access layer versions:

```
public static IServiceCollection AddDataServices(
    this IServiceCollection services,
    ConfigurationManager config)
{
  if (config.GetValue<bool>("UseApi"))
  {
    services.AddScoped<ICarDataService, CarApiDataService>();
    services.AddScoped<IMakeDataService, MakeApiDataService>();
  }
  else
  {
    services.AddScoped<ICarDataService, CarDalDataService>();
    services.AddScoped<IMakeDataService, MakeDalDataService>();
  }
  return services;
}
```

Call the new extension method in the top level statements in Program.cs in the AutoLot.Mvc and AutoLot.Web projects:

```
builder.Services.AddRepositories();
builder.Services.AddDataServices(builder.Configuration);
```

The Options Pattern in ASP.NET Core

The options pattern provides a mechanism to instantiate classes from configured settings and inject the configured classes into other classes through dependency injection. The classes are injected into another class using one of the versions of IOptions<T>. There are several versions of this interface, as shown in Table 31-6.

Table 31-6. *Some of the IOptions Interfaces*

Interface	Description
IOptionsMonitor<T>	Retrieves options and supports the following: notification of changes (with OnChange), configuration reloading, named options (with Get and CurrentValue), and selective options invalidation.
IOptionsMonitorCache<T>	Caches instances of T with support for full/partial invalidation/reload.
IOptionsSnaphot<T>	Recomputes options on every request.
IOptionsFactory<T>	Creates new instances of T.
IOptions<T>	Root interface. Doesn't support IOptionsMonitor<T>. Left in for backward compatibility.

Using the Options Pattern

A simple example is to retrieve car dealer information from the configuration, configure a class with that data, and inject it into a controller's action method for display. By placing the information into the settings file, the data is customizable without having to redeploy the site.

Start by adding the dealer information into the appsettings.json files for the AutoLot.Mvc and AutoLot.Web projects:

```
{
  "Logging": {
    "LogLevel": {
      "Default": "Information",
      "Microsoft.AspNetCore": "Warning"
    }
  },
  "AllowedHosts": "*",
  "DealerInfo": {
    "DealerName": "Skimedic's Used Cars",
    "City": "West Chester",
    "State": "Ohio"
  }
}
```

Next, we need to create a view model to hold dealer information. Create a new folder named ViewModels in the AutoLot.Services project. In that folder, add a new class named DealerInfo.cs. Update the class to the following:

```
namespace AutoLot.Services.ViewModels;
public class DealerInfo
{
    public string DealerName { get; set; }
    public string City { get; set; }
    public string State { get; set; }
}
```

■ **Note** The class to be configured must have a public parameterless constructor and be non-abstract. Properties are bound but fields are not. Default values can be set on the class properties.

Next, add the following global using statements to the AutoLot.Mvc and AutoLot.Web `GlobalUsings.cs` files:

```
global using AutoLot.Services.ViewModels;
global using Microsoft.Extensions.Options;
```

The `Configure<>()` method of the `IServiceCollection` maps a section of the configuration files to a specific type. That type can then be injected into classes and views using the options pattern. In the Program.cs files for the AutoLot.Mvc and AutoLot.Web `Program.cs` files, add the following after the line used to configure the repositories:

```
builder.Services.Configure<DealerInfo>(builder.Configuration.GetSection(nameof(Deal
erInfo)));
```

Now that the `DealerInfo` is configured, instances are retrieved by injection one of the `IOptions` interfaces into the class constructor, controller action method, or Razor page handler method. Notice that what is injected in is not an instance of the `DealerInfo` class, but an instance of the `IOptions<T>` interface. To get the configured instance, the `CurrentValue` (`IOptionsMonitor<T>`) or `Value` (`IOptionsSnapshot<T>`) must be used. The following example uses method injection to pass an instance if `IOptionsMonitor<DealerInfo>` into the `HomeController`'s `Index` method in the AutoLot.Mvc project, then gets the `CurrentValue` and passes the configured instance of the `DealerInfo` class to the view (although the view doesn't do anything with it yet).

```
public IActionResult Index([FromServices] IOptionsMonitor<DealerInfo> dealerMonitor)
{
  var vm = dealerMonitor.CurrentValue;
  return View(vm);
}
```

The following example replicates the process for the `Index` Razor page in the `Pages` folder in the AutoLot.Web project. Instead of passing the instance to the view, it is assigned to a property on the page. Update the `Index.cshtml.cs` by adding the same injection into the `OnGet()` method:

```
public DealerInfo DealerInfoInstance { get; set; }
public void OnGet([FromServices]IOptionsMonitor<DealerInfo> dealerOptions)
{
  DealerInfoInstance = dealerOptions.CurrentValue;
}
```

■ **Note** For more information on the options pattern in ASP.NET Core, consult the documentation: `https://docs.microsoft.com/en-us/aspnet/core/fundamentals/configuration/options?view=aspnetcore-6.0`.

The HTTP Client Factory

ASP.NET Core 2.1 introduced the IHTTPClientFactory, which can be used to create and configure HttPClient instances. The factory manages the pooling and lifetime of the underlying HttpClientMessageHandler instance, abstracting that away from the developer. It provides four mechanisms of use:

- Basic usage
- Named clients,
- Typed clients, and
- Generated clients.

After exploring the basic, named client, and typed client usages, we will build the API service wrappers that will be utilized by the data services built earlier in this chapter.

■ **Note** For information on generating clients, consult the documentation: https://docs.microsoft.com/en-us/aspnet/core/fundamentals/http-requests?view=aspnetcore-6.0.

Basic Usage

The basic usage registers the IHttpClientFactory with the services collection, and then uses the injected factory instance to create HttPClient instances. This method is a convenient way to refactor an existing application that is creating HttPClient instances. To implement this basic usage, add the following line into the top level statements in Program.cs (no need to actually do this, as the projects will use Typed clients):

```
builder.Services.AddHttpClient();
```

Then in the class that needs an HttpClient, inject the IHttpClientFactory into the constructor, and then call CreateClient():

```
namespace AutoLot.Services.DataServices.Api.Examples;

public class BasicUsageWithIHttpClientFactory
{
  private readonly IHttpClientFactory _clientFactory;
  public BasicUsageWithIHttpClientFactory(IHttpClientFactory clientFactory)
  {
    _clientFactory = clientFactory;
  }
  public async Task DoSomethingAsync()
  {
    var client = _clientFactory.CreateClient();
    //do something interesting with the client
  }
}
```

Named Clients

Named clients are useful when your application uses distinct HttpClient instances, especially when they are configured differently. When registering the IHttpClientFactory, a name is provided along with any specific configuration for that HttpClient usage. To create a client named AutoLotApi, add the following into the top level statements in Program.cs (no need to actually do this, as the projects will use Typed clients):

```
using AutoLot.Services.DataServices.Api.Examples;
builder.Services.AddHttpClient(NamedUsageWithIHttpClientFactory.API_NAME, client =>
{
    //add any configuration here
});
```

Then in the class that needs an HttpClient, inject the IHttpClientFactory into the constructor, and then call CreateClient() passing in the name of the client to be created. The configuration from the AddHttpClient() call is used to create the new instance:

```
namespace AutoLot.Services.DataServices.Api.Examples;

public class NamedUsageWithIHttpClientFactory
{
  public const string API_NAME = "AutoLotApi";
  private readonly IHttpClientFactory _clientFactory;
  public NamedUsageWithIHttpClientFactory(IHttpClientFactory clientFactory)
  {
    _clientFactory = clientFactory;
  }
  public async Task DoSomethingAsync()
  {
    var client = _clientFactory.CreateClient(API_NAME);
    //do something interesting with the client
  }
}
```

Typed Clients

Typed clients are classes that accept an HttpClient instance through injection into its constructor. Since the typed client is a class, it can be added into the service collection and injected into other classes, fully encapsulating the calls using an HttpClient. As an example, suppose you have a class named ApiServiceWrapper that takes in an HttpClient and implements IApiServiceWrapper as follows:

```
namespace AutoLot.Services.DataServices.Api.Examples;

public interface IApiServiceWrapperExample
{
  //interesting methods places here
}
```

```
public class ApiServiceWrapperExample : IApiServiceWrapperExample
{
  protected readonly HttpClient Client;
  public ApiServiceWrapperExample(HttpClient client)
  {
    Client = client;
  //common client configuration goes here
  }
  //interesting methods implemented here
}
```

With the interface and the class in place, they can be added to the service collection as follows:

```
builder.Services.AddHttpClient<IApiServiceWrapperExample,ApiServiceWrapperExample>();
```

Inject the IApiServiceWrapper interface into the class that needs to make calls to the API and use the methods on the class instance to call to the API. This pattern completely abstracts the HttpClient away from the calling code:

```
namespace AutoLot.Services.DataServices.Api.Examples;

public class TypedUsageWithIHttpClientFactory
{
  private readonly IApiServiceWrapperExample _serviceWrapper;

  public TypedUsageWithIHttpClientFactory(IApiServiceWrapperExample serviceWrapper)
  {
    _serviceWrapper = serviceWrapper;
  }
  public async Task DoSomethingAsync()
  {
    //do something interesting with the service wrapper
  }
}
```

In addition to the configuration options in the constructor of the class, the call to AddHttpClient() can also configure the client:

```
builder.Services.AddHttpClient<IApiServiceWrapperExample,ApiServiceWrapperExample>(client=>
{
  //configuration goes here
});
```

The AutoLot API Service Wrapper

The AutoLot API service wrapper uses a typed base client and entity specific typed clients to encapsulate all of the calls to the AutoLot.Api project. Both the AutoLot.Mvc and AutoLot.Web projects will use the service wrapper through the data services classes stubbed out earlier in this chapter and completed at the end of this section. The AutoLot.Api project will be finished in the next chapter.

Update the Application Configuration

The AutoLot.Api application endpoints will vary based on the environment. For example, when developing on your workstation, the base URI is `https://localhost:5011`. In your integration environment, the URI might be `https://mytestserver.com`. The environmental awareness, in conjunction with the updated configuration system, will be used to add these different values.

The `appsettings.Development.json` file will add the service information for the local machine. As code moves through different environments, the settings would be updated in each environment's specific file to match the base URI and endpoints for that environment. In this example, you only update the settings for the development environment. In the `appsettings.Development.json` files in the AutoLot.Mvc and AutoLot.Web projects, add the following after the `ConnectionStrings` entry (changes in bold):

```
"ConnectionStrings": {
  "AutoLot": "Server=.,5433;Database=AutoLot;User ID=sa;Password=P@ssw0rd;"
},
"ApiServiceSettings": {
  "Uri": "https://localhost:5011/",
  "UserName": "AutoLotUser",
  "Password": "SecretPassword",
  "CarBaseUri": "api/v1/Cars",
  "MakeBaseUri": "api/v1/Makes",
  "MajorVersion": 1,
  "MinorVersion": 0,
  "Status": ""
}
```

■ **Note** Make sure the port number matches your configuration for AutoLot.Api.

Create the ApiServiceSettings Class

The service settings will be populated from the settings the same way the dealer information was populated. In the AutoLot.Service project, create a new folder named `ApiWrapper` and in that folder, create a new folder named `Models`. In this folder, add a class named `ApiServiceSettings.cs`. The property names of the class need to match the property names in the JSON `ApiServiceSettings` section. The class is listed here:

```
namespace AutoLot.Services.ApiWrapper.Models;

public class ApiServiceSettings
{
  public ApiServiceSettings() { }
  public string UserName { get; set; }
  public string Password { get; set; }
  public string Uri { get; set; }
  public string CarBaseUri { get; set; }
  public string MakeBaseUri { get; set; }
  public int MajorVersion { get; set; }
  public int MinorVersion { get; set; }
  public string Status { get; set; }
```

```
  public string ApiVersion
    => $"{MajorVersion}.{MinorVersion}" + (!string.IsNullOrEmpty(Status)?$"-
{Status}":string.Empty);
}
```

■ **Note** API Versioning will be covered in depth in Chapter 32.

Add the following global using statement to the `GlobalUsings.cs` file in the AutoLot.Service project:

```
global using AutoLot.Services.ApiWrapper.Models;
```

Register the ApiServiceSettings Class

We are once again going to use an extension method to register everything needed for the API service wrapper, including configuring the `ApiServiceSettings.cs` using the Options pattern. Create a new folder named `Configuration` under the `ApiWrapper` folder, and in that folder create a new `public static` class named `ServiceConfiguration`, as shown here:

```
namespace AutoLot.Services.ApiWrapper.Configuration;

public static class ServiceConfiguration
{
  public static IServiceCollection ConfigureApiServiceWrapper(this IServiceCollection
services, IConfiguration config)
  {
    services.Configure<ApiServiceSettings>(config.GetSection(nameof(ApiServiceSettings)));
    return services;
  }
}
```

Add the following global using statement to the `GlobalUsings.cs` file for both the AutoLot.Mvc and AutoLot.Web projects:

```
global using AutoLot.Services.ApiWrapper.Configuration;
```

Add the following to the top level statements in `Program.cs` (in both AutoLot.Mvc and AutoLot.Web) before the call to `builder.Build()`:

```
builder.Services.ConfigureApiServiceWrapper(builder.Configuration);
```

The API Service Wrapper Base Class and Interface

The `ApiServiceWrapperBase` class is a generic base class that performs create, read, update, and delete (CRUD) operations against the AutoLot.Api RESTful service. This centralizes communication with the service, configuration of the HTTP client, error handling, and so on. Entity specific classes will inherit from this base class, and those will be added into the services collection.

The IApiServiceWrapperBase Interface

The AutoLot service wrapper interface contains the common methods to call into the AutoLot.Api service. Create a directory named `Interfaces` in the `ApiWrapper` directory. Add a new interface named `IApiServiceWrapper.cs` and update the interface to the code shown here:

```
namespace AutoLot.Services.ApiWrapper.Interfaces;

public interface IApiServiceWrapperBase<TEntity> where TEntity : BaseEntity, new()
{
  Task<IList<TEntity>> GetAllEntitiesAsync();
  Task<TEntity> GetEntityAsync(int id);
  Task<TEntity> AddEntityAsync(TEntity entity);
  Task<TEntity> UpdateEntityAsync(TEntity entity);
  Task DeleteEntityAsync(TEntity entity);
}
```

Add the following global using statement to the `GlobalUsings.cs` file for the AutoLot.Services project:

```
global using AutoLot.Services.ApiWrapper.Interfaces;
```

The ApiServiceWrapperBase Class

Before building the base class, add the following global using statements to the `GlobalUsings.cs` file:

```
global using AutoLot.Services.ApiWrapper.Base;
global using Microsoft.Extensions.Options;
global using System.Net.Http.Headers;
global using System.Net.Http.Json;
global using System.Text;
global using System.Text.Json;
```

Create a new folder named `Base` in the `ApiWrapper` directory of the AutoLot.Services project and add a class named `ApiServiceWrapperBase`. Make the class `public` and `abstract` and implement the `IApiServiceWrapperBase` interface. Add a `protected` constructor that takes an instance of `HttpClient` and `IOptionsMonitor<ApiServiceSettings>` and a `string` for the entity specific endpoint. Add a protected `readonly` string to hold the `ApiVersion` from the settings and initialize them all from the constructor like this:

```
namespace AutoLot.Services.ApiWrapper.Base;

public abstract class ApiServiceWrapperBase<TEntity>
  : IApiServiceWrapperBase<TEntity> where TEntity : BaseEntity, new()
{
  protected readonly HttpClient Client;
  private readonly string _endPoint;
  protected readonly ApiServiceSettings ApiSettings;
  protected readonly string ApiVersion;
```

```
  protected ApiServiceWrapperBase(
    HttpClient client, IOptionsMonitor<ApiServiceSettings> apiSettingsMonitor, string
    endPoint)
  {
    Client = client;
    _endPoint = endPoint;
    ApiSettings = apiSettingsMonitor.CurrentValue;
    ApiVersion = ApiSettings.ApiVersion;
  }
}
```

Configuring the HttpClient in the Constructor

The constructor adds the standard configuration to the HttpClient that will be used by all methods, including an AuthorizationHeader that uses basic authentication. Basic authentication will be covered in depth in the next chapter, Restful Services with ASP.NET Core, so for now just understand that basic authentication takes a username and password, concatenates them together (separated by a colon) and Base64 encodes them. The rest of the code sets the BaseAddress for the HttpClient and specifies that the client is expecting JSON.

```
public ApiServiceWrapperBase(
    HttpClient client, IOptionsMonitor<ApiServiceSettings> apiSettingsMonitor, string
    endPoint)
{
  Client = client;
  _endPoint = endPoint;
  ApiSettings = apiSettingsMonitor.CurrentValue;
  ApiVersion = ApiSettings.ApiVersion;
  Client.BaseAddress = new Uri(ApiSettings.Uri);
  client.DefaultRequestHeaders.Accept.Add(new MediaTypeWithQualityHeaderValue("application/
  json"));
  var authToken = Convert.ToBase64String(Encoding.UTF8.GetBytes($"{apiSettingsMonitor.
  CurrentValue.UserName}:{apiSettingsMonitor.CurrentValue.Password}"));
  client.DefaultRequestHeaders.Authorization = new AuthenticationHeaderValue("basic",
  authToken);
}
```

The Internal Support Methods

The class contains four support methods that are used by the public methods.

The Post and Put Helper Methods

These methods wrap the related HttpClient methods.

```
internal async Task<HttpResponseMessage> PostAsJsonAsync(string uri, string json)
{
  return await Client.PostAsync(uri, new StringContent(json, Encoding.UTF8, "application/
  json"));
}
```

```
internal async Task<HttpResponseMessage> PutAsJsonAsync(string uri, string json)
{
  return await Client.PutAsync(uri, new StringContent(json, Encoding.UTF8, "application/
  json"));
}
```

The HTTP Delete Helper Method Call

The final helper method is used for executing an HTTP delete. The HTTP 1.1 specification (and later) allows for passing a body in a delete statement, but there isn't yet an extension method of the `HttpClient` for doing this. The `HttpRequestMessage` must be built up from scratch.

The first step is to then create a request message using object initialization to set `Content`, `Method`, and `RequestUri`. Once this is complete, the message is sent, and the response is returned to the calling code. The method is shown here:

```
internal async Task<HttpResponseMessage> DeleteAsJsonAsync(string uri, string json)
{
  HttpRequestMessage request = new HttpRequestMessage
  {
    Content = new StringContent(json, Encoding.UTF8, "application/json"),
    Method = HttpMethod.Delete,
    RequestUri = new Uri(uri)
  };
  return await Client.SendAsync(request);
}
```

The HTTP Get Calls

There are two Get calls: one to get all records and one to get a single record. They both follow the same pattern. The `GetAsync()` method is called to return an `HttpResponseMessage`. The success or failure of the call is checked with the `EnsureSuccessStatusCode()` method, which throws an exception if the call did not return a successful status code. Then the body of the response is serialized back into the property type (either as an entity or a list of entities) and returned to the calling code. The endpoint is constructed from the settings, and the `ApiVersion` is appended as a query string value. Each of these methods is shown here:

```
public async Task<IList<TEntity>> GetAllEntitiesAsync()
{
  var response = await Client.GetAsync($"{ApiSettings.Uri}{_endPoint}?v={ApiVersion}");
  response.EnsureSuccessStatusCode();
  var result = await response.Content.ReadFromJsonAsync<IList<TEntity>>();
  return result;
}

public async Task<TEntity> GetEntityAsync(int id)
{
  var response = await Client.GetAsync($"{ApiSettings.Uri}{_endPoint}/{id}?v={ApiVersion}");
  response.EnsureSuccessStatusCode();
  var result = await response.Content.ReadFromJsonAsync<TEntity>();
  return result;
}
```

Notice the improvement in serializing the response body into an item (or list of items). Prior versions of ASP.NET Core would have to use the following code instead of the shorter ReadFromJsonAsync() method:

```
var result = await JsonSerializer.DeserializeAsync<IList<TEntity>>(await response.Content.
ReadAsStreamAsync());
```

The HTTP Post Call

The method to add a record uses an HTTP Post request. It uses the helper method to post the entity as JSON and then returns the record from the response body. The method is listed here:

```
public async Task<TEntity> AddEntityAsync(TEntity entity)
{
  var response = await PostAsJsonAsync($"{ApiSettings.Uri}{_endPoint}?v={ApiVersion}",
    JsonSerializer.Serialize(entity));
  if (response == null)
  {
    throw new Exception("Unable to communicate with the service");
  }

  var location = response.Headers?.Location?.OriginalString;
  return await response.Content.ReadFromJsonAsync<TEntity>() ?? await
  GetEntityAsync(entity.Id);
}
```

There are two lines of note. The first is the line getting the location. Typically, when an HTTP Post call is successful, the service returns an HTTP 201 (Created at) status code. The service will also add the URI of the newly created resource in the Location header. The preceding code demonstrates getting the Location header but isn't using the location in the code process.

The second line of note is reading the response content and creating an instance of the updated record. The service wrapper method needs to get the updated instance from the service to guarantee server generated values (like Id and TimeStamp) and are updated in the client app. Returning the updated entity in the response from HTTP post calls is not a guaranteed function of a service. If the service doesn't return the entity, then the method uses the GetEntityAsync() method. It could also use the URI from the location if necessary, but since the GetEntityAsync() supplies everything needed, getting the location value is merely for demo purposes.

The HTTP Put Call

The method to update a record uses an HTTP Put request by way of the PutAsJsonAsync() helper method. This method also assumes that the updated entity is in the body of the response, and if it isn't, calls the GetEntityAsync() to refresh the server generated values.

```
public async Task<TEntity> UpdateEntityAsync(TEntity entity)
{
  var response = await PutAsJsonAsync($"{ApiSettings.Uri}{_endPoint}/{entity.
  Id}?v={ApiVersion}",
      JsonSerializer.Serialize(entity));
  response.EnsureSuccessStatusCode();
  return await response.Content.ReadFromJsonAsync<TEntity>() ?? await GetEntityAsync(entity.Id);
}
```

The HTTP Delete Call

The final method to add, is for executing an HTTP Delete. The pattern follows the rest of the methods: use the helper method and check the response for success. There isn't anything to return to the calling code since the entity was deleted. The method is shown here:

```
public async Task DeleteEntityAsync(TEntity entity)
{
  var response = await DeleteAsJsonAsync($"{ApiSettings.Uri}{_endPoint}/{entity.
Id}?v={ApiVersion}",
      JsonSerializer.Serialize(entity));
  response.EnsureSuccessStatusCode();
}
```

The Entity Specific Interfaces

In the Interfaces directory, create two new interfaces named ICarApiServiceWrapper.cs and IMakeApiServiceWrapper.cs. Update the interfaces to the following:

```
//ICarApiServiceWrapper.cs
namespace AutoLot.Services.ApiWrapper.Interfaces;

public interface ICarApiServiceWrapper : IApiServiceWrapperBase<Car>
{
  Task<IList<Car>> GetCarsByMakeAsync(int id);
}

//IMakeApiServiceWrapper.cs
namespace AutoLot.Services.ApiWrapper.Interfaces;

public interface IMakeApiServiceWrapper : IApiServiceWrapperBase<Make>
{
}
```

The Entity Specific Classes

In the ApiWrapper directory, create two new classes named CarApiServiceWrapper.cs and MakeApiServiceWrapper.cs. The constructor for each class takes an instance of HttpClient and IOptions<ApiServiceSettings> and passes them into the base class along with the entity specific end point:

```
//CarApiServiceWrapper.cs
namespace AutoLot.Services.ApiWrapper;

public class CarApiServiceWrapper : ApiServiceWrapperBase<Car>, ICarApiServiceWrapper
{
  public CarApiServiceWrapper(HttpClient client, IOptionsMonitor<ApiServiceSettings>
  apiSettingsMonitor)
    : base(client, apiSettingsMonitor, apiSettingsMonitor.CurrentValue.CarBaseUri) { }
}
```

```
//MakeApiServiceWrapper.cs
namespace AutoLot.Services.ApiWrapper;

public class MakeApiServiceWrapper : ApiServiceWrapperBase<Make>, IMakeApiServiceWrapper
{
  public MakeApiServiceWrapper(HttpClient client, IOptionsMonitor<ApiServiceSettings>
  apiSettingsMonitor)
    : base(client, apiSettingsMonitor, apiSettingsMonitor.CurrentValue.MakeBaseUri) { }
}
```

The MakeApiServiceWrapper only needs the methods exposed in the ApiServiceWrapperBase to do its job. The CarApiServiceWrapper class has one additional method to get the list of Car records by Make. The method follows the same pattern as the base class's HTTP Get methods but uses a unique end point:

```
public async Task<IList<Car>> GetCarsByMakeAsync(int id)
{
  var response = await Client.GetAsync($"{ApiSettings.Uri}{ApiSettings.CarBaseUri}/bymake/
  {id}?v={ApiVersion}");
  response.EnsureSuccessStatusCode();
  var result = await response.Content.ReadFromJsonAsync<IList<Car>>();
  return result;
}
```

As a last step, register the two typed clients by updating the ConfigureApiServiceWrapper method in the ServiceConfiguration class to the following:

```
public static IServiceCollection ConfigureApiServiceWrapper(this IServiceCollection
services, IConfiguration config)
{
  services.Configure<ApiServiceSettings>(config.GetSection(nameof(ApiServiceSettings)));
  services.AddHttpClient<ICarApiServiceWrapper, CarApiServiceWrapper>();
  services.AddHttpClient<IMakeApiServiceWrapper, MakeApiServiceWrapper>();
  return services;
}
```

Complete the API Data Services

Now that the API service wrappers are complete, it's time to revisit the API data services and complete the class implementations.

Complete the ApiDataServiceBase Class

The first step to complete the base class is to update the constructor to receive an instance of the IApiServiceWrapperBase<TEntity> interface and assign it to a protected field:

```
protected readonly IApiServiceWrapperBase<TEntity> ServiceWrapper;
protected ApiDataServiceBase(IApiServiceWrapperBase<TEntity> serviceWrapperBase)
{
  ServiceWrapper = serviceWrapperBase;
}
```

The implementation for each of the CRUD methods calls the related method on the ServiceWrapper:

```
public async Task<IEnumerable<TEntity>> GetAllAsync()
  => await ServiceWrapper.GetAllEntitiesAsync();
public async Task<TEntity> FindAsync(int id)
  => await ServiceWrapper.GetEntityAsync(id);
  public async Task<TEntity> UpdateAsync(TEntity entity, bool persist = true)
{
  await ServiceWrapper.UpdateEntityAsync(entity);
  return entity;
}

public async Task DeleteAsync(TEntity entity, bool persist = true)
  => await ServiceWrapper.DeleteEntityAsync(entity);

public async Task<TEntity> AddAsync(TEntity entity, bool persist = true)
{
  await ServiceWrapper.AddEntityAsync(entity);
  return entity;
}
```

Complete the Entity Specific Classes

The CarApiDataService and MakeApiDataService classes need their constructors updated to receive their entity specific derived instance of the IApiServiceWrapperBase<TEntity> interface and pass it to the base class:

```
public class CarApiDataService : ApiDataServiceBase<Car>, ICarDataService
{
  public CarApiDataService(ICarApiServiceWrapper serviceWrapper) : base(serviceWrapper) { }
}

public class MakeApiDataService : ApiDataServiceBase<Make>, IMakeDataService
{
  public MakeApiDataService(IMakeApiServiceWrapper serviceWrapper):base(serviceWrapper) { }
}
```

The GetAllByMakeIdIdAsync() method determines if a value was passed in for the makeId parameter. If there is a value, the relevant method on the ICarApiServiceWrapper is called. Otherwise, the base GetAllAsync() is called:

```
public async Task<IEnumerable<Car>> GetAllByMakeIdAsync(int? makeId)
  => makeId.HasValue
           ? await ((ICarApiServiceWrapper)ServiceWrapper).
           GetCarsByMakeAsync(makeId.Value)
           : await GetAllAsync();
```

Deploying ASP.NET Core Applications

Prior versions of ASP.NET applications could only be deployed to Windows servers using IIS as the web server. ASP.NET Core can be deployed to multiple operating systems in multiple ways, using a variety of web servers. ASP.NET Core applications can also be deployed outside of a web server. The high-level options are as follows:

- On a Windows server (including Azure) using IIS
- On a Windows server (including Azure app services) outside of IIS
- On a Linux server using Apache or NGINX
- On Windows or Linux in a container

This flexibility allows organizations to decide the deployment platform that makes the most sense for them, including popular container-based deployment models (such as using Docker), as opposed to being locked into Windows servers.

Lightweight and Modular HTTP Request Pipeline

Following along with the principles of .NET, you must opt in for everything in ASP.NET Core. By default, nothing is loaded into an application. This enables applications to be as lightweight as possible, improving performance, and minimizing the surface area and potential risk.

Logging

Logging in ASP.NET Core is based on an `ILoggerFactory`. This enables different logging providers to hook into the logging system to send log messages to different locations, such as the Console. The `ILoggerFactory` is used to create an instance of `ILogger<T>`, which provides the following methods for logging by way of the `LoggerExtensions` class:

```
public static class LoggerExtensions
{
  public static void LogDebug(this ILogger logger, EventId eventId,
    Exception exception, string message, params object[] args)
  public static void LogDebug(this ILogger logger, EventId eventId, string message, params
  object[] args)
  public static void LogDebug(this ILogger logger, Exception exception, string message,
  params object[] args)
  public static void LogDebug(this ILogger logger, string message, params object[] args)

  public static void LogTrace(this ILogger logger, EventId eventId,
    Exception exception, string message, params object[] args)
  public static void LogTrace(this ILogger logger, EventId eventId, string message, params
  object[] args)
  public static void LogTrace(this ILogger logger, Exception exception, string message,
  params object[] args)
  public static void LogTrace(this ILogger logger, string message, params object[] args)
```

```
    public static void LogInformation(this ILogger logger, EventId eventId,
      Exception exception, string message, params object[] args)
    public static void LogInformation(this ILogger logger, EventId eventId, string message,
    params object[] args)
    public static void LogInformation(this ILogger logger, Exception exception, string
    message, params object[] args)
    public static void LogInformation(this ILogger logger, string message, params
    object[] args)

    public static void LogWarning(this ILogger logger, EventId eventId,
      Exception exception, string message, params object[] args)
    public static void LogWarning(this ILogger logger, EventId eventId, string message, params
    object[] args)
    public static void LogWarning(this ILogger logger, Exception exception, string message,
    params object[] args)
    public static void LogWarning(this ILogger logger, string message, params object[] args)

    public static void LogError(this ILogger logger, EventId eventId,
      Exception exception, string message, params object[] args)
    public static void LogError(this ILogger logger, EventId eventId, string message, params
    object[] args)
    public static void LogError(this ILogger logger, Exception exception, string message,
    params object[] args)
    public static void LogError(this ILogger logger, string message, params object[] args)

    public static void LogCritical(this ILogger logger, EventId eventId,
      Exception exception, string message, params object[] args)
    public static void LogCritical(this ILogger logger, EventId eventId, string message,
    params object[] args)
    public static void LogCritical(this ILogger logger, Exception exception, string message,
    params object[] args)
    public static void LogCritical(this ILogger logger, string message, params object[] args)

    public static void Log(this ILogger logger, LogLevel logLevel, string message, params
    object[] args)
    public static void Log(this ILogger logger, LogLevel logLevel, EventId eventId, string
    message, params object[] args)
    public static void Log(this ILogger logger, LogLevel logLevel,
      Exception exception, string message, params object[] args)
    public static void Log(this ILogger logger, LogLevel logLevel, EventId eventId,
      Exception exception, string message, params object[] args)
}
```

Add Logging with Serilog

Any provider that supplies an ILoggerFactory extension can be used for logging in ASP.NET Core, and Serilog is one such logging framework. The next sections cover creating a logging infrastructure based on Serilog and configuring the ASP.NET Core applications to use the new logging code.

The Logging Settings

To configure Serilog, we are going to use the application configuration files in conjunction with a C# class. Start by adding a new folder named Logging to the AutoLot.Service project. Create a new folder named Settings in the Logging folder, and in that new folder, add a class named AppLoggingSettings. Update the code to the following:

```
namespace AutoLot.Services.Logging.Settings;

public class AppLoggingSettings
{
  public GeneralSettings General { get; set; }
  public FileSettings File { get; set; }
  public SqlServerSettings MSSqlServer { get; set; }

  public class GeneralSettings
  {
    public string RestrictedToMinimumLevel { get; set; }
  }
  public class SqlServerSettings
  {
    public string TableName { get; set; }
    public string Schema { get; set; }
    public string ConnectionStringName { get; set; }
  }

  public class FileSettings
  {
    public string Drive { get; set; }
    public string FilePath { get; set; }
    public string FileName { get; set; }
    public string FullLogPathAndFileName =>

   $"{Drive}{Path.VolumeSeparatorChar}{Path.DirectorySeparatorChar}{FilePath}{Path.
   DirectorySeparatorChar}{FileName}";
  }
}
```

Add the following global using statement to the GlobalUsings.cs file in the AutoLot.Service project.

```
global using AutoLot.Services.Logging.Settings;
```

Next, use the following JSON to replace the scaffolded Logging details in the appsettings.Development.json files for the AutoLot.Api, AutoLot.Mvc, and AutoLot.Web projects:

```
"AppLoggingSettings": {
  "MSSqlServer": {
    "TableName": "SeriLogs",
    "Schema": "Logging",
    "ConnectionStringName": "AutoLot"
  },
```

```
  "File": {
    "Drive": "c",
    "FilePath": "temp",
    "FileName": "log_AutoLot.txt"
  },
  "General": {
    "RestrictedToMinimumLevel": "Information"
  }
},
```

Next, add the following AppName node to each of the files, customized for each app:

```
//AutoLot.Api
"AppName":"AutoLot.Api - Dev"

//AutoLot.Mvc
"AppName":"AutoLot.Mvc - Dev"

//AutoLot.Web
"AppName":"AutoLot.Web - Dev"
```

For reference, here is the complete listing for each project (notice the extra line at the beginning of the AutoLot.Web file – that will be covered in chapter 34):

```
//AutoLot.Api
{
  "AppLoggingSettings": {
    "MSSqlServer": {
      "TableName": "SeriLogs",
      "Schema": "Logging",
      "ConnectionStringName": "AutoLot"
    },
    "File": {
      "Drive": "c",
      "FilePath": "temp",
      "FileName": "log_AutoLot.txt"
    },
    "General": {
      "RestrictedToMinimumLevel": "Information"
    }
  },
  "ConnectionStrings": {
    "AutoLot": "Server=.,5433;Database=AutoLot;User ID=sa;Password=P@ssw0rd;"
  },
  "RebuildDatabase": true,
  "AppName": "AutoLot.Api - Dev"
}

//AutoLot.Mvc
{
  "AppLoggingSettings": {
    "MSSqlServer": {
```

```
      "TableName": "SeriLogs",
      "Schema": "Logging",
      "ConnectionStringName": "AutoLot"
    },
    "File": {
      "Drive": "c",
      "FilePath": "temp",
      "FileName": "log_AutoLot.txt"
    },
    "General": {
      "RestrictedToMinimumLevel": "Information"
    }
  },
  "ConnectionStrings": {
    "AutoLot": "Server=.,5433;Database=AutoLot;User ID=sa;Password=P@ssw0rd;"
  },
  "RebuildDatabase": true,
  "UseApi": false,
  "ApiServiceSettings": {
    "Uri": "https://localhost:5011/",
    "UserName": "AutoLotUser",
    "Password": "SecretPassword",
    "CarBaseUri": "api/v1/Cars",
    "MakeBaseUri": "api/v1/Makes"
  },
  "AppName": "AutoLot.Mvc - Dev"
}

//AutoLot.Web
{
  "DetailedErrors": true,
  "AppLoggingSettings": {
    "MSSqlServer": {
      "TableName": "SeriLogs",
      "Schema": "Logging",
      "ConnectionStringName": "AutoLot"
    },
    "File": {
      "Drive": "c",
      "FilePath": "temp",
      "FileName": "log_AutoLot.txt"
    },
    "General": {
      "RestrictedToMinimumLevel": "Information"
    }
  },
  "ConnectionStrings": {
    "AutoLot": "Server=.,5433;Database=AutoLot;User ID=sa;Password=P@ssw0rd;"
  },
  "RebuildDatabase": true,
  "UseApi": false,
```

```
  "ApiServiceSettings": {
    "Uri": "https://localhost:5011/",
    "UserName": "AutoLotUser",
    "Password": "SecretPassword",
    "CarBaseUri": "api/v1/Cars",
    "MakeBaseUri": "api/v1/Makes"
  },
  "AppName": "AutoLot.Web - Dev"
}
```

The final step is to clear out the Logging section of each of the appsettings.json files, leaving just the `AllowedHosts` entry in the `AutoLot.Api` project, and the `AllowedHosts` and the `DealerInfo` in the `AutoLot.Mvc` and `AutoLot.Web` projects:

```
//AutoLot.Api
{
  "AllowedHosts": "*"
}

//AutoLot.Mvc
{
  "AllowedHosts": "*",
  "DealerInfo": {
    "DealerName": "Skimedic's Used Cars",
    "City": "West Chester",
    "State": "Ohio"
  }
}

//AutoLot.Web
{
  "AllowedHosts": "*",
  "DealerInfo": {
    "DealerName": "Skimedic's Used Cars",
    "City": "West Chester",
    "State": "Ohio"
  }
}
```

The Logging Configuration

The next step is to configure Serilog. Get started by adding a new folder named Configuration in the Logging folder of the AutoLot.Service project. In this folder add a new class named `LoggingConfiguration`. Make the class `public` and `static`, as shown here:

```
namespace AutoLot.Services.Logging.Configuration;

public static class LoggingConfiguration
{
}
```

Serilog uses sinks to write to different logging targets. With this mechanism, a single call to SeriLog will write to many places. The targets we will use for logging in the ASP.NET Core apps are a text file, the database, and the console. The text file and database sinks require configuration, an output template for the text file sink, and a list of fields for the database sink.

To set up the file template, create the following static readonly string:

```
internal static readonly string OutputTemplate =
  @"[{Timestamp:yy-MM-dd HH:mm:ss} {Level}]{ApplicationName}:{SourceContext}{NewLine}
  Message:{Message}{NewLine}in method {MemberName} at {FilePath}:{LineNumber}{NewLine}
  {Exception}{NewLine}";
```

The SQL Server sink needs a list of columns identified using the SqlColumn type. Add the following code to configure the database columns:

```
internal static readonly ColumnOptions ColumnOptions = new ColumnOptions
{
  AdditionalColumns = new List<SqlColumn>
  {
    new SqlColumn {DataType = SqlDbType.VarChar, ColumnName = "ApplicationName"},
    new SqlColumn {DataType = SqlDbType.VarChar, ColumnName = "MachineName"},
    new SqlColumn {DataType = SqlDbType.VarChar, ColumnName = "MemberName"},
    new SqlColumn {DataType = SqlDbType.VarChar, ColumnName = "FilePath"},
    new SqlColumn {DataType = SqlDbType.Int, ColumnName = "LineNumber"},
    new SqlColumn {DataType = SqlDbType.VarChar, ColumnName = "SourceContext"},
    new SqlColumn {DataType = SqlDbType.VarChar, ColumnName = "RequestPath"},
    new SqlColumn {DataType = SqlDbType.VarChar, ColumnName = "ActionName"},
  }
};
```

Swapping the default logger with Serilog is a three-step process. The first is to clear the existing provider, the second is to add Serilog into the WebApplicationBuilder, and the third is to finish configuring Serilog. Add a new method named ConfigureSerilog(), which is an extension method for the WebApplicationBuilder. The first line clears out the default loggers, and the last line adds the fully configured Serilog framework into the WebApplicationBuilder's logging framework.

```
public static void ConfigureSerilog(this WebApplicationBuilder builder)
{
  builder.Logging.ClearProviders();
  var config = builder.Configuration;
  var settings = config.GetSection(nameof(AppLoggingSettings)).Get<AppLoggingSettings>();
  var connectionStringName = settings.MSSqlServer.ConnectionStringName;
  var connectionString = config.GetConnectionString(connectionStringName);
  var tableName = settings.MSSqlServer.TableName;
  var schema = settings.MSSqlServer.Schema;
  string restrictedToMinimumLevel = settings.General.RestrictedToMinimumLevel;
  if (!Enum.TryParse<LogEventLevel>(restrictedToMinimumLevel, out var logLevel))
  {
    logLevel = LogEventLevel.Debug;
  }
  var sqlOptions = new MSSqlServerSinkOptions
  {
    AutoCreateSqlTable = false,
```

```
    SchemaName = schema,
    TableName = tableName,
  };
  if (builder.Environment.IsDevelopment())
  {
    sqlOptions.BatchPeriod = new TimeSpan(0, 0, 0, 1);
    sqlOptions.BatchPostingLimit = 1;
  }

  var log = new LoggerConfiguration()
    .MinimumLevel.Is(logLevel)
    .Enrich.FromLogContext()
    .Enrich.With(new PropertyEnricher("ApplicationName", config.GetValue<string>("Applicati
    onName")))
    .Enrich.WithMachineName()
    .WriteTo.File(
       path: builder.Environment.IsDevelopment()? settings.File.FileName : settings.File.
       FullLogPathAndFileName,
       rollingInterval: RollingInterval.Day,
       restrictedToMinimumLevel: logLevel,
       outputTemplate: OutputTemplate)
    .WriteTo.Console(restrictedToMinimumLevel: logLevel)
    .WriteTo.MSSqlServer(
      connectionString: connectionString,
      sqlOptions,
      restrictedToMinimumLevel: logLevel,
      columnOptions: ColumnOptions);
  builder.Logging.AddSerilog(log.CreateLogger(),false);
}
```

With everything in place, it's time to create the logging framework that will use Serilog.

The AutoLot Logging Framework

The AutoLot logging framework leverages the built-in logging capabilities of ASP.NET Core to simplify using Serilog. It starts with the IAppLogging interface.

The IAppLogging Interface

The IApplogging<T> interface holds the logging methods for the custom logging system. Add new directory named Interfaces in the Logging directory in the AutoLot.Service project. In this directory, add a new interface named IAppLogging<T>. Update the code in this interface to match the following:

```
namespace AutoLot.Services.Logging.Interfaces;

public interface IAppLogging<T>
{
  void LogAppError(Exception exception, string message,
    [CallerMemberName] string memberName = "",
    [CallerFilePath] string sourceFilePath = "",
    [CallerLineNumber] int sourceLineNumber = 0);
```

```
    void LogAppError(string message,
      [CallerMemberName] string memberName = "",
      [CallerFilePath] string sourceFilePath = "",
      [CallerLineNumber] int sourceLineNumber = 0);

    void LogAppCritical(Exception exception, string message,
      [CallerMemberName] string memberName = "",
      [CallerFilePath] string sourceFilePath = "",
      [CallerLineNumber] int sourceLineNumber = 0);

    void LogAppCritical(string message,
      [CallerMemberName] string memberName = "",
      [CallerFilePath] string sourceFilePath = "",
      [CallerLineNumber] int sourceLineNumber = 0);

    void LogAppDebug(string message,
      [CallerMemberName] string memberName = "",
      [CallerFilePath] string sourceFilePath = "",
      [CallerLineNumber] int sourceLineNumber = 0);

    void LogAppTrace(string message,
      [CallerMemberName] string memberName = "",
      [CallerFilePath] string sourceFilePath = "",
      [CallerLineNumber] int sourceLineNumber = 0);

    void LogAppInformation(string message,
      [CallerMemberName] string memberName = "",
      [CallerFilePath] string sourceFilePath = "",
      [CallerLineNumber] int sourceLineNumber = 0);

    void LogAppWarning(string message,
      [CallerMemberName] string memberName = "",
      [CallerFilePath] string sourceFilePath = "",
      [CallerLineNumber] int sourceLineNumber = 0);
}
```

The attributes CallerMemberName, CallerFilePath, and CallerLineNumber inspect the call stack to get the values they are named for from the calling code. For example, if the line that calls LogAppWarning() is in the DoWork() function, in a file named MyClassFile.cs, and resides on line number 36, then the call:

```
_appLogger.LogAppError(ex, "ERROR!");
```

is converted into the equivalent of this:

```
_appLogger.LogAppError(ex,"ERROR","DoWork ","c:/myfilepath/MyClassFile.cs",36);
```

If values *are* passed into the method call for any of the attributed parameters, the values passed in are used instead of the values from the attributes.

Add the following global using statement to the GlobalUsings.cs file in the AutoLot.Services project:

```
global using AutoLot.Services.Logging.Interfaces;
```

The AppLogging Class

The AppLogging class implements the IAppLogging interface. Add a new class named AppLogging to the Logging directory. Make the class public and implement IAppLogging<T> and add a constructor that takes an instance of ILogger<T> and stores it in a class level variable.

```
namespace AutoLot.Services.Logging;

public class AppLogging<T> : IAppLogging<T>
{
  private readonly ILogger<T> _logger;

  public AppLogging(ILogger<T> logger)
  {
    _logger = logger;
  }
}
```

Serilog enables adding additional properties into the standard logging process by pushing them onto the LogContext. Add an internal method to log an event with an exception and push the MemberName, FilePath, and LineNumber properties. The PushProperty() method returns an IDisposable, so the method disposes everything before leaving the method.

```
internal static void LogWithException(string memberName,
  string sourceFilePath, int sourceLineNumber, Exception ex, string message,
  Action<Exception, string, object[]> logAction)
{
  var list = new List<IDisposable>
    {
      LogContext.PushProperty("MemberName", memberName),
      LogContext.PushProperty("FilePath", sourceFilePath),
      LogContext.PushProperty("LineNumber", sourceLineNumber),
    };
  logAction(ex,message,null);
  foreach (var item in list)
  {
    item.Dispose();
  }
}
```

Repeat the process for log events that don't include an exception:

```
internal static void LogWithoutException(string memberName,
  string sourceFilePath, int sourceLineNumber, string message,
  Action<string, object[]> logAction)
{
  var list = new List<IDisposable>
    {
      LogContext.PushProperty("MemberName", memberName),
      LogContext.PushProperty("FilePath", sourceFilePath),
      LogContext.PushProperty("LineNumber", sourceLineNumber),
    };
```

```
  logAction(message, null);
  foreach (var item in list)
  {
    item.Dispose();
  }
}
```

For each type of logging event, call the appropriate help method to write to the logs:

```
public void LogAppError(Exception exception, string message,
  [CallerMemberName] string memberName = "",
  [CallerFilePath] string sourceFilePath = "",
  [CallerLineNumber] int sourceLineNumber = 0)
{
  LogWithException(memberName, sourceFilePath, sourceLineNumber, exception, message, _
  logger.LogError);
}

public void LogAppError(string message,
  [CallerMemberName] string memberName = "",
  [CallerFilePath] string sourceFilePath = "",
  [CallerLineNumber] int sourceLineNumber = 0)
{
  LogWithoutException(memberName, sourceFilePath, sourceLineNumber, message, _logger.
  LogError);
}

public void LogAppCritical(Exception exception, string message,
  [CallerMemberName] string memberName = "",
  [CallerFilePath] string sourceFilePath = "",
  [CallerLineNumber] int sourceLineNumber = 0)
{
  LogWithException(memberName, sourceFilePath, sourceLineNumber, exception, message, _
  logger.LogCritical);
}

public void LogAppCritical(string message,
  [CallerMemberName] string memberName = "",
  [CallerFilePath] string sourceFilePath = "",
  [CallerLineNumber] int sourceLineNumber = 0)
{
  LogWithoutException(memberName, sourceFilePath, sourceLineNumber, message, _logger.
  LogCritical);
}

public void LogAppDebug(string message,
  [CallerMemberName] string memberName = "",
  [CallerFilePath] string sourceFilePath = "",
  [CallerLineNumber] int sourceLineNumber = 0)
{
  LogWithoutException(memberName, sourceFilePath, sourceLineNumber, message, _logger.LogDebug);
}
```

```
public void LogAppTrace(string message,
  [CallerMemberName] string memberName = "",
  [CallerFilePath] string sourceFilePath = "",
  [CallerLineNumber] int sourceLineNumber = 0)
{
  LogWithoutException(memberName, sourceFilePath, sourceLineNumber, message, _logger.
  LogTrace);
}

public void LogAppInformation(string message,
  [CallerMemberName] string memberName = "",
  [CallerFilePath] string sourceFilePath = "",
  [CallerLineNumber] int sourceLineNumber = 0)
{
  LogWithoutException(memberName, sourceFilePath, sourceLineNumber, message, _logger.
  LogInformation);
}

public void LogAppWarning(string message,
  [CallerMemberName] string memberName = "",
  [CallerFilePath] string sourceFilePath = "",
  [CallerLineNumber] int sourceLineNumber = 0)
{
  LogWithoutException(memberName, sourceFilePath, sourceLineNumber, message, _logger.
  LogWarning);
}
```

Final Configuration

The final configuration is to add the `IAppLogging<>` interface into the DI container and call the extension method to add SeriLog into the `WebApplicationBuilder`. Start by creating a new extension method in the `LoggingConfiguration` class:

```
public static IServiceCollection RegisterLoggingInterfaces(this IServiceCollection services)
{
  services.AddScoped(typeof(IAppLogging<>), typeof(AppLogging<>));
  return services;
}
```

Next, add the following global using statement to the `GlobalUsings.cs` file in each web project:

```
global using AutoLot.Services.Logging.Configuration;
global using AutoLot.Services.Logging.Interfaces;
```

Next, add both of the extension methods to the top level statements in the Program.cs file. Note that the `ConfigureSerilog()` method extends off of the `WebAppBuilder` (the builder variable) and the `RegisterLoggingInterfaces()` method extends off of the `IServiceCollection`:

```
//Configure logging
builder.ConfigureSerilog();
builder.Services.RegisterLoggingInterfaces();
```

Add Logging to the Data Services

With Serilog and the AutoLot logging system in place, it's time to update the data services to add logging capabilities.

Update the Base Classes

Starting with the ApiDataServiceBase and DalDataServiceBase classes, update the generic definition to also accept a class that implements IDataServiceBase<TEntity>. This is to allow for strongly typing the IAppLogging<TDataService> interface to each of the derived class. Here are the updated classes definitions:

```
//ApiDataServiceBase.cs
public abstract class ApiDataServiceBase<TEntity, TDataService> : IDataServiceBase<TEntity>
    where TEntity : BaseEntity, new()
    where TDataService : IDataServiceBase<TEntity>
{
  //omitted for brevity
}

//DalDataServiceBase.cs
public abstract class DalDataServiceBase<TEntity, TDataService> : IDataServiceBase<TEntity>
    where TEntity : BaseEntity, new()
    where TDataService : IDataServiceBase<TEntity>
{
  //omitted for brevity
}
```

Next, update each of the constructors to take an instance of IAppLogging<TDataService> and assign it to a protected class field:

```
//CarApiDataService.cs
protected readonly IApiServiceWrapperBase<TEntity> ServiceWrapper;
protected readonly IAppLogging<TDataService> AppLoggingInstance;

protected ApiDataServiceBase(IAppLogging<TDataService> appLogging,
    IApiServiceWrapperBase<TEntity> serviceWrapperBase)
{
  ServiceWrapper = serviceWrapperBase;
  AppLoggingInstance = appLogging;
}

//MakeApiDataService.cs
protected readonly IBaseRepo<TEntity> MainRepo;
protected readonly IAppLogging<TDataService> AppLoggingInstance;

protected DalDataServiceBase(IAppLogging<TDataService> appLogging, IBaseRepo<TEntity>
mainRepo)
{
  MainRepo = mainRepo;
  AppLoggingInstance = appLogging;
}
```

Update the Entity Specific Data Services Classes

Each of the entity specific classes need to change their inheritance signature to use the new generic parameter and also take an instance of IAppLogging in the constructor and pass it to the base class. Here is the code for the updated classes:

```
//CarApiDataService.cs
public class CarApiDataService : ApiDataServiceBase<Car,CarApiDataService>, ICarDataService
{
  public CarApiDataService(
      IAppLogging<CarApiDataService> appLogging,
      ICarApiServiceWrapper serviceWrapper)
    : base(appLogging, serviceWrapper) { }
  //omitted for brevity
}

//MakeApiDataService.cs
public class MakeApiDataService
  : ApiDataServiceBase<Make,MakeApiDataService>, IMakeDataService
{
  public MakeApiDataService(
        IAppLogging<MakeApiDataService> appLogging,
        IMakeApiServiceWrapper serviceWrapper)
    : base(appLogging,serviceWrapper) {  }
}

//CarDalDataService.cs
public class CarDalDataService : DalDataServiceBase<Car,CarDalDataService>,ICarDataService
{
  private readonly ICarRepo _repo;
  public CarDalDataService(IAppLogging<CarDalDataService> appLogging, ICarRepo repo) :
base(appLogging, repo)
  {
    _repo = repo;
  }
  //omitted for brevity
}

//MakeApiDataService.cs
public class MakeDalDataService : DalDataServiceBase<Make,MakeDalDataService>,IMakeD
ataService
{
  public MakeDalDataService(IAppLogging<MakeDalDataService> appLogging,IMakeRepo repo)
    : base(appLogging, repo) { }
}
```

Next, update the constructors to take the instance of IAppLogging<TDataService> and assign it to a protected class field:

Test-Drive the Logging Framework

To close out the chapter, let's test the logging framework. The first step is to update the HomeController in the AutoLot.Mvc project to use the new logging framework. Replace the ILogger<HomeController> parameter with IAppLogging<HomeController> and update the type of the field, like this:

```
public class HomeController : Controller
{
  private readonly IAppLogging<HomeController> _logger;
  public HomeController(IAppLogging<HomeController> logger)
  {
    _logger = logger;
  }
//omitted for brevity
}
```

With this in place, log a test error in the Index() method:

```
public IActionResult Index([FromServices]IOptionsMonitor<DealerInfo> dealerMoitor)
{
  _logger.LogAppError("Test error");
  var vm = dealerMonitor.CurrentValue;
  return View(vm);
}
```

Run the AutoLot.Mvc project. When the app starts, a record will be logged in the SeriLogs table as well as written to a file named log_AutoLotYYYYMMDD.txt.

When you open the log file, you might be surprised to see that there are a lot of additional entries that didn't come from the one call to the logger. That is because EF Core and ASP.NET Core emit very verbose logging when the log level is set to Information. To eliminate the noise, update the appsettings.Development.json files in the AutoLot.Api, AutoLot,Mvc, and AutoLot.Web projects so that the log level is Warning, like this:

```
"RestrictedToMinimumLevel": "Warning"
```

String Utilities

Recall that one of the conventions in ASP.NET Core removes the Controller suffix from controllers and the Async suffix from action methods when routing controllers and actions. When manually building up routes, it's common to have to remove the suffix through code. While the code is simple to write, it can be repetitive. To cut down on repeating the string manipulation code, the next step will create two string extension methods.

Add a new directory named Utilities in the AutoLot.Services project, and in that directory, create a new public static class named StringExtensions. In that class, add the following two extension methods:

```
namespace AutoLot.Services.Utilities

public static class StringExtensions
{
  public static string RemoveControllerSuffix(this string original)
      => original.Replace("Controller", "", StringComparison.OrdinalIgnoreCase);
```

```
  public static string RemoveAsyncSuffix(this string original)
      => original.Replace("Async", "", StringComparison.OrdinalIgnoreCase);
    public static string RemovePageModelSuffix(this string original)
        => original.Replace("PageModel", "", StringComparison.OrdinalIgnoreCase);
}
```

Next, add the following global using statement to the GlobalUsings.cs file in the AutoLot.Services project and all three web applications:

```
global using AutoLot.Services.Utilities;
```

Summary

This chapter dove into the new features introduced in ASP.NET Core and began the process of updating the three ASP.NET Core applications. In the next chapter, you will finish the AutoLot.Api application.

CHAPTER 32

RESTful Services with ASP.NET Core

The previous chapter introduced ASP.NET Core. After that introduction to the new features and implementing some cross cutting concerns, in this chapter, we will complete the AutoLot.Api RESTful service.

> **Note** The sample code for this chapter is in the `Chapter 32` directory of this book's repo. Feel free to continue working on the solution you started in Chapter 31.

Introducing ASP.NET Core RESTful Services

The ASP.NET MVC framework started gaining traction almost immediately upon release, and Microsoft released ASP.NET Web API with ASP.NET MVC 4 and Visual Studio 2012. ASP.NET Web API 2 was released with Visual Studio 2013 and then was updated to version 2.2 with Visual Studio 2013 Update 1.

From the beginning, ASP.NET Web API was designed to be a service-based framework for building **RE**presentational **S**tate **T**ransfer (RESTful) services. It is based on the MVC framework minus the *V* (view), with optimizations for creating headless services. These services can be called by any technology, not just those under the Microsoft umbrella. Calls to a Web API service are based on the core HTTP verbs (Get, Put, Post, Delete) through a uniform resource identifier (URI) such as the following:

```
http://www.skimedic.com:5001/api/cars
```

If this looks like a uniform resource locator (URL), that's because it is! A URL is simply a URI that points to a physical resource on a network.

Calls to Web API use the **H**yper**t**ext **T**ransfer **P**rotocol (HTTP) scheme on a particular host (in this example, `www.skimedic.com`) on a specific port (5001 in the preceding example), followed by the path (`api/cars`) and an optional query and fragment (not shown in this example). Web API calls can also include text in the body of the message, as you will see throughout this chapter. As discussed in the previous chapter, ASP.NET Core unified Web API and MVC into one framework.

A. Troelsen and P. Japikse, *Pro C# 10 with .NET 6*, https://doi.org/10.1007/978-1-4842-7869-7_32

Controller Actions with RESTful Services

Recall that actions return an `IActionResult` (or `Task<IActionResult>` for async operations). In addition to the helper methods in `ControllerBase` that return specific HTTP status codes, action methods can return content as formatted JavaScript Object Notation (JSON) responses.

■ **Note** Strictly speaking, action methods can return a wide range of formats. JSON is covered in this book because it is the most common.

Formatted JSON Response Results

Most RESTful APIs receive data from, and send data back to, clients using JSON (pronounced "jay-sawn"). A simple JSON example, consisting of two values, is shown here:

```
[
  "value1",
  "value2"
]
```

■ **Note** Chapter 19 covers JSON serialization in depth using `System.Text.Json`.

APIs also use HTTP status codes to communicate success or failure. Some of the HTTP status helper methods available in the `ControllerBase` class were listed in the Chapter 30 in Table 30-3. Successful requests return status codes in the 200 range, with 200 (OK) being the most common success code. In fact, it is so common that you don't have to explicitly return an OK. If there isn't an exception thrown and the code does not specify a status code, a 200 will be returned to the client along with any data.

To set up the following examples (and the rest of this chapter), add the following to the `GlobalUsing.cs` file:

```
global using Microsoft.AspNetCore.Mvc;
```

Next, add a new controller named `ValuesController.cs` in the `Controllers` directory of the AutoLot.Api project and update the code to match the following:

```
[Route("api/[controller]")]
[ApiController]
public class ValuesController : ControllerBase
{
}
```

■ **Note** If using Visual Studio, there is a scaffolder for controllers. To access this, right-click the `Controllers` folder in the AutoLot.Api project and select Add ➤ Controller. Select Common ➤ API in the left rail and then API Controller – Empty.

This code sets the route for the controller using a literal (api) and a token ([controller]). This route template will match URLs like www.skimedic.com/**api/values**. The next attribute (ApiController) opts in to several API-specific features in ASP.NET Core (covered in the next section). Finally, the controller inherits from ControllerBase. As discussed previously, ASP.NET Core rolled all of the different controller types available in classic ASP.NET into one, named Controller, with a base class ControllerBase. The Controller class provides view-specific functionality (the *V* in MVC), while ControllerBase supplies all the rest of the core functionality for MVC-style applications.

There are several ways to return content as JSON from an action method. The following examples all return the same JSON along with a 200 status code. The differences are largely stylistic. Add the following code to your ValuesController class:

```
[HttpGet]
public IActionResult Get()
{
  return Ok(new string[] { "value1", "value2" });
}
[HttpGet("one")]
public IEnumerable<string> Get1()
{
  return new string[] { "value1", "value2" };
}
[HttpGet("two")]
public ActionResult<IEnumerable<string>> Get2()
{
  return new string[] { "value1", "value2" };
}
[HttpGet("three")]
public string[] Get3()
{
  return new string[] { "value1", "value2" };
}
[HttpGet("four")]
public IActionResult Get4()
{
    return new JsonResult(new string[] { "value1", "value2" });
}
```

To test this, run the AutoLot.Api application, and you will see all the methods from ValuesController listed in the Swagger UI, as shown in Figure 32-1. Recall that when determining routes, the Controller suffix is dropped from the name, so the endpoints on the ValuesController are mapped as Values, not ValuesController.

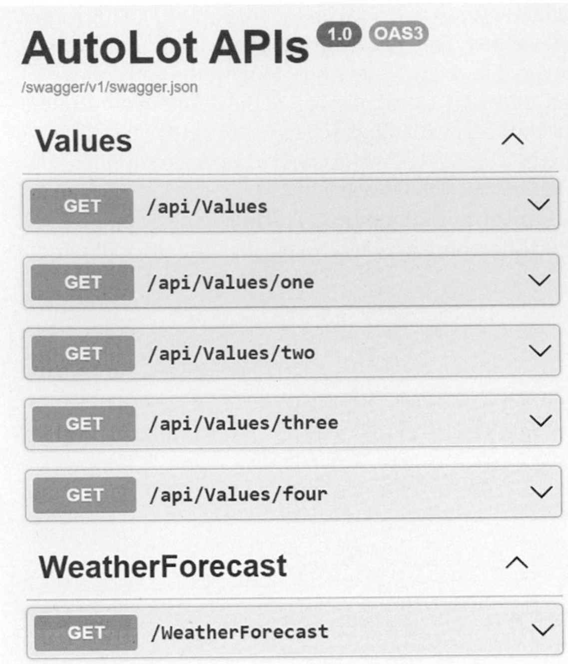

Figure 32-1. *The Swagger documentation page*

To execute one of the methods, click the **Get** button, the **Try it out** button, and then the **Execute** button. Once the method has executed, the UI is updated to show the results, with just the relevant portion of the Swagger UI shown in Figure 32-2.

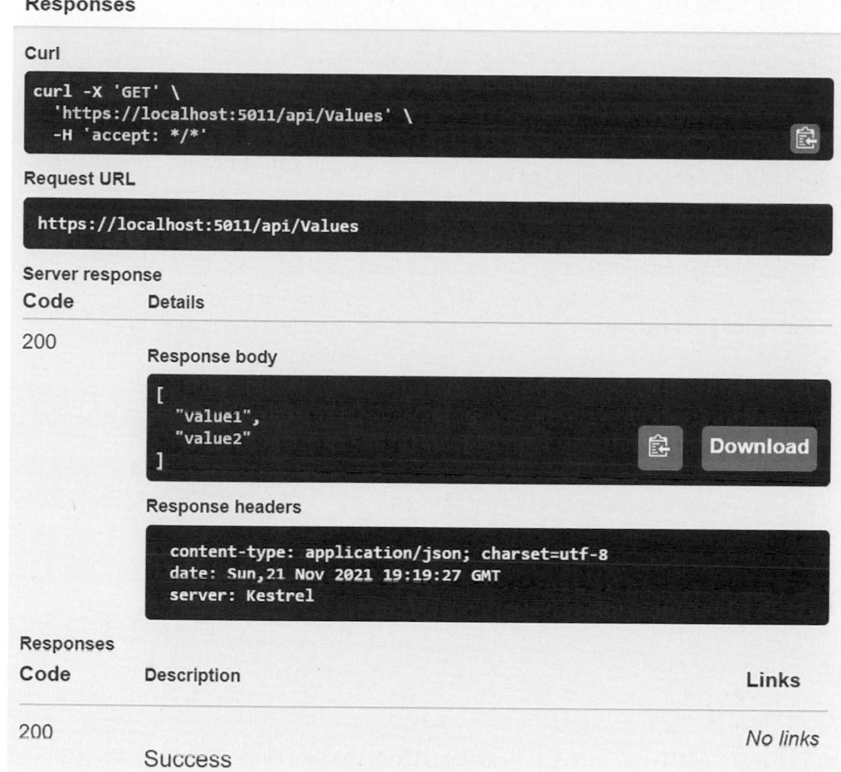

Figure 32-2. *The Swagger server response information*

You will see that executing each method produces the same JSON results.

Configuring JSON Handling

The `AddControllers()` method can be extended to customize JSON handling. The default for ASP.NET Core is to camel case JSON (first letter small, each subsequent word character capitalized like "**c**ar**R**epo"). This matches most of the non-Microsoft frameworks used for web development. However, prior versions of ASP.NET used Pascal casing (first letter small, each subsequent word character capitalized like "**C**ar**R**epo"). The change to camel casing was a breaking change for many applications that were expecting Pascal casing.

There are two serialization properties that can be set that help with this issue. The first is to make the JSON Serializer use Pascal casing by setting its `PropertyNamingPolicy` to null instead of `JsonNamingPolicy.CamelCase`. The second change is to use case insensitive property names. When this option is enabled, JSON coming into the app can be Pascal or camel cased. To make these changes, call `AddJsonOptions()` on the `AddControllers()` method:

```
builder.Services.AddControllers()
    .AddJsonOptions(options =>
    {
      options.JsonSerializerOptions.PropertyNamingPolicy = null;
      options.JsonSerializerOptions.PropertyNameCaseInsensitive = true;
    });
```

The next change is to make sure the JSON is more readable by writing it indented:

```
.AddJsonOptions(options =>
{
  options.JsonSerializerOptions.PropertyNamingPolicy = null;
  options.JsonSerializerOptions.PropertyNameCaseInsensitive = true;
  options.JsonSerializerOptions.WriteIndented = true;
});
```

Before making the final change, add the following global using to the `GlobalUsings.cs` file:

```
global using System.Text.Json.Serialization;
```

The final change (new to .NET 6) is to have the JSON serializer ignore reference cycles:

```
.AddJsonOptions(options =>
{
  options.JsonSerializerOptions.PropertyNamingPolicy = null;
  options.JsonSerializerOptions.PropertyNameCaseInsensitive = true;
  options.JsonSerializerOptions.WriteIndented = true;
  options.JsonSerializerOptions.ReferenceHandler = ReferenceHandler.IgnoreCycles;
});
```

The ApiController Attribute

The `ApiController` attribute, added in ASP.NET Core 2.1, provides REST-specific rules, conventions, and behaviors when combined with the `ControllerBase` class. These conventions and behaviors are outlined in the following sections. It's important to note that this works in base class scenarios as well. For example, if you have a custom base class decorated with the `ApiController` attribute, any derived controllers will behave as if the attribute is applied directly to them.

```
[ApiController]
public abstract class BaseCrudController : ControllerBase
{
}

//ApiController attribute is implicitly implied on this controller as well
public class CarsController : BaseCrudController
{
}
```

Lastly, the attribute can be applied at the assembly level, which then applies the attribute to every controller in the project. To apply the attribute to every controller in the project, add the following attribute to the top of the `Program.cs` file:

```
[assembly: ApiController]
```

Attribute Routing Requirement

When using the ApiController attribute, the controller must use attribute routing. This is just enforcing what many consider to be a best practice.

Automatic 400 Responses

If there is an issue with model binding, the action will automatically return an HTTP 400 (Bad Request) response code. This behavior is equivalent to the following code:

```
if (!ModelState.IsValid)
{
  return BadRequest(ModelState);
}
```

ASP.NET Core uses the ModelStateInvalidFilter action filter to do the preceding check. When there is a binding or a validation error, the HTTP 400 response in the body includes details for the errors, which is a serialized instance of the ValidationProblemDetails class, which complies with the RFC 7807 specification (https://datatracker.ietf.org/doc/html/rfc7807). This class derives from HttpProblemDetails, which derives from ProblemDetails. The entire hierarchy chain for the classes is shown here:

```
public class ProblemDetails
{
  public string? Type { get; set; }
  public string? Title { get; set; }
  public int? Status { get; set; }
  public string? Detail { get; set; }
  public string? Instance { get; set; }
  public IDictionary<string, object?> Extensions { get; } = new Dictionary<string,
  object?>(StringComparer.Ordinal);
}

public class HttpValidationProblemDetails : ProblemDetails
{
  public IDictionary<string, string[]> Errors { get; } = new Dictionary<string,
string[]>(StringComparer.Ordinal);
}

public class ValidationProblemDetails : HttpValidationProblemDetails
{
  public new IDictionary<string, string[]> Errors => base.Errors;
}
```

To see the automatic 400 error handling in action, update the ValuesController.cs file with the following HTTP Post action:

```
[HttpPost]
public IActionResult BadBindingExample(WeatherForecast forecast)
{
  return Ok(forecast);
}
```

Run the app, and on the Swagger page, click the POST version of the /api/Values end point, click Try it out, but before clicking Execute, clear out the autogenerated request body. This will cause a binding failure, and return the following error details:

```
{
  "type": "https://tools.ietf.org/html/rfc7231#section-6.5.1",
  "title": "One or more validation errors occurred.",
  "status": 400,
  "traceId": "00-2c35757698267491ad0a8554ac51ccd1-dbdfe43357cd6d3f-00",
  "errors": {
    "": [
      "A non-empty request body is required.”
    ]
  }
}
```

This behavior can be disabled through configuration in the ConfigureServices() method of the Startup.cs class.

```
Services.AddControllers()
  .AddJsonOptions( /* omitted for brevity */)
  .ConfigureApiBehaviorOptions(options =>
  {
    //suppress automatic model state binding errors
    options.SuppressModelStateInvalidFilter = true;
  });
```

When disabled, you can still send error information as an instance of ValidationProblemDetails. Update the top level statements to disable the automatic 400 response, and then update the BadBindingExample() action method to the following:

```
[HttpPost]
public IActionResult BadBindingExample(WeatherForecast forecast)
{
  return ModelState.IsValid ? Ok(forecast) : ValidationProblem(ModelState);
}
```

When you run the app and execute the BadBindingExample() code, you will see that the response contains the same JSON as the automatically handled error.

Binding Source Parameter Inference

The model binding engine will infer where the values are retrieved based on the conventions listed in Table 32-1.

Table 32-1. *Binding Source Inference Conventions*

Source	Parameters Bound
FromBody	Inferred for complex type parameters except for built-in types with special meaning, such as IFormCollection or CancellationToken. Only one FromBody parameter can exist, or an exception will be thrown. If binding is required on a simple type (e.g., string or int), then the FromBody attribute is still required.
FromForm	Inferred for action parameters of types IFormFile and IFormFileCollection. When a parameter is marked with FromForm, the multipart/form-data content type is inferred.
FromRoute	Inferred for any parameter name that matches a route token name.
FromQuery	Inferred for any other action parameters.

This behavior can bc disabled through configuration in the ConfigureServices() method of the Startup.cs class.

```
Services.AddControllers().ConfigureApiBehaviorOptions(options =>
{
  //suppress all binding inference
  options.SuppressInferBindingSourcesForParameters= true;
  //suppress multipart/form-data content type inference
  options. SuppressConsumesConstraintForFormFileParameters = true;
});
```

Problem Details for Error Status Codes

ASP.NET Core transforms an error result (status of 400 or higher) into a result of the same ProblemDetails shown earlier. To test this behavior, add another method to the ValuesController as follows:

```
[HttpGet("error")]
public IActionResult Error()
{
  return NotFound();
}
```

Run the app and use the Swagger UI to execute the new Error endpoint. The result is still a 404 (NotFound) status code, but additional information is returned in the body of the response. The following shows an example response (your traceId will be different):

```
{
  "type": "https://tools.ietf.org/html/rfc7231#section-6.5.4",
  "title": "Not Found",
  "status": 404,
  "traceId": "00-42432337d88a53a2f38bc0ab0e473f89-63d4e7b153a30b2d-00"
}
```

This behavior can be disabled through configuration in the ConfigureServices() method of the Startup.cs class.

```
services.AddControllers()
  .ConfigureApiBehaviorOptions(options =>
  {
    //omitted for brevity
    /'Don't create a problem details error object if set to true
    options.SuppressMapClientErrors = true;
  });
```

When the behavior is disabled, the call to the Error endpoint returns a 404 without any additional information.

When there is a client error (and the mapping of client errors is not suppressed), the Link and the Title text can be set to custom values that are more user friendly. For example, 404 errors can change the ProblemDetails Link to https://httpstatuses.com/404 and the Title to "Invalid Location" with the following code:

```
services.AddControllers()
  .ConfigureApiBehaviorOptions(options =>
  {
    /'Don't create a problem details error object if set to true
    options.SuppressMapClientErrors = false;
    options.ClientErrorMapping[StatusCodes.Status404NotFound].Link =
       "https://httpstatuses.com/404";
    options.ClientErrorMapping[StatusCodes.Status404NotFound].Title =
       "Invalid location";
  });
```

This updates the return values to the following:

```
{
  "type": "https://httpstatuses.com/404",
  "title": "Invalid location",
  "status": 404,
  "traceId": "00-e4cf79ad92807354bcc1f1bbe0faf92a-6b6a9d0578c15a77-00"
}
```

Reset the Settings

After you have completed testing the different options, update the code to the settings used in the rest of this chapter (and book), listed here:

```
builder.Services.AddControllers()
  .AddJsonOptions(/*omitted for brevity*/)
  .ConfigureApiBehaviorOptions(options =>
  {
    //suppress automatic model state binding errors
    options.SuppressModelStateInvalidFilter = true;
    //suppress all binding inference
    //options.SuppressInferBindingSourcesForParameters= true;
    //suppress multipart/form-data content type inference
    //options. SuppressConsumesConstraintForFormFileParameters = true;
    options.SuppressMapClientErrors = false;
```

```
    options.ClientErrorMapping[StatusCodes.Status404NotFound].Link =
    "https://httpstatuses.com/404";
    options.ClientErrorMapping[StatusCodes.Status404NotFound].Title = "Invalid location";
});
```

API Versioning

When building APIs, it's important to remember that humans don't interact with your end points, programs do. If an application UI changes, people can usually figure out the changes and keep on using your application. If an API changes, the client program just breaks. If your API is public facing, has more than one client, or you plan on making a change, you should add versioning support.

Microsoft's REST API Guidelines

Microsoft has published guidelines for REST APIs (located at `https://github.com/Microsoft/api-guidelines/blob/vNext/Guidelines.md`) and that guidance contains a section on versioning. In order to be compliant with the guidelines, APIs must support explicit versioning.

API versions are comprised of a major version and a minor version and are reported/requested as Major.Minor, such as `1.0`, `1.5`, etc. If the minor version is zero, it can be left off. In other words, `1` is the same as `1.0`. In addition to the major and minor version, a status can be added to the end of the version to indicate a version not yet production quality, such as `1.0-Beta` or `1.0.Beta`. Note that the status can be separated either by a period or a dash. When a version has a minor version of zero and a status, then the version can be specified as Major.Minor-Status (`1.0-Beta`) or Major-Status (`1-Beta`), using either dash or a period as the status separator).

In addition to `Major.Minor-Status` versions, there is also a group format that is an optional feature that is supported through non URL segment versioning. The group version format is defined as `YYYY-MM-DD`. The group format should not replace `Major.Minor-Status` versioning.

There are two options to specify the version in an API call, embedded in the URL (at the end of the service root), or as a query string parameter at the end of the URL. The following examples show calls to the version `1.0` API for the AutoLot.Api (presuming the host is `skimedic.com`):

```
www.skimedic.com/api/v1.0/cars
www.skimedic.com/api/cars?api-version=1.0
```

The following two examples call the same endpoint without specifying the minor version (since the minor version is zero):

```
www.skimedic.com/api/v1/cars
www.skimedic.com/api/cars?api-version=1
```

While APIs can use either URL embedding or query string parameters, the guidelines require that APIs be consistent. In other words, don't have some end points that use query strings and others that use URL embedding. It is permissible for all of the endpoints to support both methods.

■ **Note** The guidelines are definitely worth reading as you build .NET Core RESTful services. Again, the guideline can be read at `https://github.com/Microsoft/api-guidelines/blob/vNext/Guidelines.md`

Add Versioning NuGet Packages

To add full support for ASP.NET Core versioning, there are two NuGet packages that need to be added into your API projects. The first is the `Microsoft.AspNetCore.Mvc.Versioning` package which provides the version attributes, the `AddApiVersioning()` method, and the `ApiVersion` class. The second is the `Microsoft.AspNetCore.Mvc.Versioning.Explorer` NuGet package, which makes the `AddVersionedApiExplorer()` method available. Both of these packages were added to AutoLot.Api when the projects and solution were created.

For the rest of this section, add the following global using statements into the `GlobalUsings.cs`

```
global using Microsoft.AspNetCore.Mvc.ApiExplorer;
global using Microsoft.AspNetCore.Mvc.Versioning;
```

The ApiVersion Class

The `ApiVersion` class is the heart of API versioning support. It provides the container to hold the major and minor version and optional group and status information. It also provides methods to parse strings into `ApiVersion` instances and output properly formatted version string and overloads for equality and comparison operations. The class is listed here for reference.

```
public class ApiVersion
{
  //Constructors allowing for all combinations of group and versions
  public ApiVersion( DateTime groupVersion )
  public ApiVersion( DateTime groupVersion, string status )
  public ApiVersion( int majorVersion, int minorVersion )
  public ApiVersion( int majorVersion, int minorVersion, String? status )
  public ApiVersion( DateTime groupVersion, int majorVersion, int minorVersion )
  public ApiVersion( DateTime groupVersion, int majorVersion, int minorVersion, String? status)
//static method to return the same as ApiVersion(1,0)
  public static ApiVersion Default { get; }
//static method to return ApiVersion(null,null,null,null)
  public static ApiVersion Neutral { get; }
//Properties for the version information
  public DateTime? GroupVersion { get; }
  public int? MajorVersion { get; }
  public int? MinorVersion { get; } //(defaults to zero if null)
  public string? Status { get; }
//checks the status for valid format (all alpha-numeric, no special characters or spaces)
  public static bool IsValidStatus( String? status )
//Parsing strings into ApiVersion instances
  public static ApiVersion Parse( string text )
  public static bool TryParse( string text, [NotNullWhen( true )] out ApiVersion? version )
//Output properly formatted version string
  public virtual string ToString( string format ) => ToString( format, InvariantCulture );
  public override string ToString() => ToString( null, InvariantCulture );
//Equality overrides to quickly compare two versions
  public override bool Equals( Object? obj ) => Equals( obj as ApiVersion );
  public static bool operator ==( ApiVersion? version1, ApiVersion? version2 ) =>
  public static bool operator !=( ApiVersion? version1, ApiVersion? version2 ) =>
  public static bool operator <( ApiVersion? version1, ApiVersion? version2 ) =>
```

```
  public static bool operator <=( ApiVersion? version1, ApiVersion? version2 ) =>
  public static bool operator >( ApiVersion? version1, ApiVersion? version2 ) =>
  public static bool operator >=( ApiVersion? version1, ApiVersion? version2 ) =>
  public virtual bool Equals( ApiVersion? other ) => other != null && GetHashCode
  public virtual int CompareTo( ApiVersion? other )
}
```

Add API Version Support

The root of version support is added with the AddApiVersioning() method. This is a mega method that adds in a host of services into the DI container. To add standard API versioning support into the AutoLot.Api project, call this method on the IServiceCollection, like this (no need to add this to the Program.cs file at this time, as it will be done with an extension method shortly):

```
builder.Services.AddApiVersioning();
```

For more robust version support, the version support can be configured with the ApiBehaviorOptions class. Before using this, let's add an extension method to hold all of the version configuration code. Start by creating a new folder named ApiVersionSupport into the project. In this folder, add a new public static class named ApiVersionConfiguration.

```
Namespace AutoLot.Api.ApiVersionSupport;

public static class ApiVersionConfiguration
{
  //implementation goes here
}
```

Add the new namespace to the GlobalUsings.cs file:

```
global using AutoLot.Api.ApiVersionSupport;
```

Add an extension method for the IServiceCollection that also takes in an ApiVersion object that will be used to set the default version. If a default version isn't specified, create a new instance of the ApiVersion object with the version set to 1.0:

```
public static IServiceCollection AddAutoLotApiVersionConfiguration(
    this IServiceCollection services, ApiVersion defaultVersion = null)
{
  defaultVersion ??= ApiVersion.Default;
  //remaining implementation goes here
  return services;
}
```

Next, add in the call to AddApiVersioning() after the if statement for the default version:

```
if (defaultVersion == null)
{
  defaultVersion = ApiVersion.Default;
}
services.AddApiVersioning();
```

This method takes an optional `Action<ApiVersionOptions>` that can be used to configure all of the version options. Before adding the options, let's examine what's available. Table 32-2 lists the available options for versioning:

Table 32-2. *The APIVersioningOptions properties*

Option	Meaning in Life
`RouteConstraintName`	The route token when using URL versioning. Defaults to `apiVersion`.
`ReportApiVersions`	Indicates if system version information is sent in HTTP responses. When true, the HTTP headers `api-supported-versions` and `api-deprecated-versions` are added for all valid service routes. Defaults to `false`.
`AssumeDefaultVersionWhenUnspecified`	If set to `true`, uses the default API version when version information is not specified in the request. Version is based on the result of the call `IApiVersionSelector.SelectVersion()`. Defaults to `false`.
`DefaultApiVersion`	Sets the default API version to use when version information is not specified in the request and `AssumeDefaultVersionWhenUnspecified` is set to `true`. The default is `ApiVersion.Default` (1.0).
`ApiVersionReader`	Gets or sets the `ApiVersionReader` to use. Can use `QueryStringApiVersionReader`, `HeaderApiVersionReader`, `MediaTypeApiVersionReader`, `UrlSegmentApIVersionReader`. The default is `QueryStringApiVersionReader`.
`ApiVersionSelector`	Gets or sets the `ApiVersionSelector`. Defaults to `DefaultApiVersionSelector`.
`UseApiBehavior`	When true, API versioning policies only apply to controllers that have the `ApiController` attribute. Defaults to `true`.

Now that you understand the available options you can update the call to `AddApiVersioning()`. The following code first sets the default version from the parameter (or uses the default `1.0` version if the parameter is null). Then it sets the flag to use the default version if the client didn't specify a version. Next it filters out controllers without the `ApiController` attribute, reports the supported API versions in response headers. The final block enables all methods available for clients to specify the version in requests (make sure to comment out the original call to add versioning):

```
public static IServiceCollection AddAutoLotApiVersionConfiguration(
    this IServiceCollection services, ApiVersion defaultVersion = null)
{
  if (defaultVersion == null)
  {
    defaultVersion = ApiVersion.Default;
  }
  //services.AddApiVersioning();
  services.AddApiVersioning(
```

```
    options =>
    {
      //Set Default version
      options.DefaultApiVersion = defaultVersion;
      options.AssumeDefaultVersionWhenUnspecified = true;
      options.UseApiBehavior = true;
      // reporting api versions will return the headers "api-supported-versions"
      // and "api-deprecated-versions"
      options.ReportApiVersions = true;
      //This combines all of the avalialbe option as well as
      // allows for using "v" or "api-version" as options for
      // query string, header, or media type versioning
      options.ApiVersionReader = ApiVersionReader.Combine(
        new UrlSegmentApiVersionReader(),
        new QueryStringApiVersionReader(), //defaults to "api-version"
        new QueryStringApiVersionReader("v"),
        new HeaderApiVersionReader("api-version"),
        new HeaderApiVersionReader("v"),
        new MediaTypeApiVersionReader(), //defaults to "v"
        new MediaTypeApiVersionReader("api-version")
    );
  });
  //remaining implementation goes here
  return services;
}
```

The previous code sample enables all of the available ApiVersionReader options. As you can see, each of the non-URL segment options are specified twice. The first call for each pair enables the reader that uses api-version as the key. The second call takes a parameter into the constructor that instructs the reader to look for a custom key, in these examples, the simple key of v is accepted. When building real world applications, you probably wouldn't want to enable all of these options, they are shown here as an example of different reader configurations.

Update the Top Level Statements

The next step is to add the extension method to the top level statements in the Program.cs file. Add the call to the extension method into file right after the AddEndpointApiExplorer() (which adds in the ApiDescriptionProvider for end points):

```
builder.Services.AddEndpointsApiExplorer();
builder.Services.AddAutoLotApiVersionConfiguration(new ApiVersion(1, 0));
```

API Versions and Naming Convention Updates

When API versioning is enabled, controllers can be named with their version included, and it will be stripped off just like the Controller suffix. This means that you can have ValuesController and Values2Controller in your project, and the route for both is mysite.com/api/Values. It's important to understand that the number in the name has no relation on the actual version served by the controller, it's merely an update to the convention so you can separate controller classes by version and still have the same route.

The API Version Attributes

Now that versioning support is enabled, you can start decorating your controllers and action methods with version attributes. Table 32-3 lists the available attributes.

Table 32-3. *API Versioning Attributes*

Attribute	Meaning in Life
`ApiVersion`	Controller or Action level attribute that sets the API version that the controller/action method will accept. Can be used multiple times to indicate more than one version is accepted. Versions in `ApiVersion` attributes are discoverable.
`ApiVersionNeutral`	Controller level attribute that opts out of versioning. Query string version requests are ignored. Any well-formed URL when using URL versioning will be accepted, even if the placeholder represents an invalid version.
`MapToApiVersion`	Action level attribute that maps the action to a specific version when multiple versions are specified at the controller level. Versions in `MapToApiVersion` attributes aren't discoverable.
`AdvertiseApiVersions`	Advertises additional versions beyond what is contained in the app instance. Used when API versions are split across deployments and API information can't be aggregated through the API Version Explorer.

It's important to understand that once versioning is enabled, it's enabled for all API controllers. If a controller doesn't have a version specified, it will use the default version (`1.0` in the current configuration). To test this, run the application and run the following CURL commands, all of which produce the same result (recall that omitting the minor version is the same as specifying zero):

```
curl -G  https://localhost:5011/WeatherForecast
curl -G  https://localhost:5011/WeatherForecast?api-version=1
curl -G  https://localhost:5011/WeatherForecast?api-version=1.0
```

Now, update the call to this:

```
curl -G  https://localhost:5011/WeatherForecast?api-version=2.0
```

When asking for version `2.0`, the return value shows that it's an unsupported version:

```
{"error":{"code":"UnsupportedApiVersion","message":"The HTTP resource that matches the
request URI 'https://localhost:5011/WeatherForecast' does not support the API version
'2.0'.","innerError":null}}
```

To change the weather forecast endpoint to be available regardless of requested version, update the controller with the `[ApiVersionNeutral]` attribute:

```
[ApiVersionNeutral]
[ApiController]
[Route("[controller]")]
public class WeatherForecastController : ControllerBase
```

```
{
  //omitted for brevity
}
```

Now, regardless of the version requested (or no version requested), the forecast is returned.

Version Interleaving

A controller and/or action method can support more than one version, which is referred to as version interleaving. Let's start by updating the `ValuesController` to specifically support version `1.0`:

```
[ApiVersion("1.0")]
[ApiController]
[Route("api/[controller]")]
public class ValuesController : ControllerBase
{
  //omitted for brevity
}
```

If you want the `ValuesController` to also support version `2.0`, you can simply stack another `ApiVersion` attribute. The following change updates the controller and all of its methods to support version `1.0` and version `2.0`:

```
[ApiVersion("1.0")]
[ApiVersion("2.0")]
[ApiController]
[Route("api/[controller]")]
public class ValuesController : ControllerBase
{
  //omitted for brevity
}
```

Now, suppose you want to add a method to this controller that wasn't in version `1.0`. There are two way to do this. The first is to add the method into the controller and use the `ApiVersion` attribute:

```
[HttpGet("{id}")]
[ApiVersion("2.0")]
public IActionResult Get(int id)
{
  return Ok(new[] { "value1", "value2" });
}
```

The other option is to use the `MapToApiVersion` attribute, like this:

```
[HttpGet("{id}")]
[MapToApiVersion("2.0")]
```

```
public IActionResult Get(int id)
{
  return Ok(new[] { "value1", "value2" });
}
```

The difference between the two is very subtle, but important. In both instances, the /api/Values/1?api-version=2.0 route will hit the end point. However, versions in MapToApiVersion attributes aren't reported if they don't already exist in an ApiVersion attribute. To demonstrate, comment out the [ApiVersion("2.0")] attribute, then hit the endpoint with the following CURL:

```
curl -G  https://localhost:5011/api/Values/1?api-version=2.0 -i
```

The -i adds the response headers to the output. As you can see from the following output, even though the call was successful, only version 1.0 is reported:

```
HTTP/1.1 200 OK
Content-Type: application/json; charset=utf-8; v=2.0
Date: Thu, 11 Nov 2021 05:29:10 GMT
Server: Kestrel
Transfer-Encoding: chunked
api-supported-versions: 1.0
["values1","value2"]
```

Replace the [MapToApiVersion("2.0")] attribute on the Get(int id) method with the [ApiVersion("2.0")] attribute and run the same command. You will now see that both version 1.0 and 2.0 are reported in the headers as supported versions.

Controller Splitting

While version interleaving is fully supported by the tooling, it can lead to very messy controllers that become difficult to support over time. A more common approach is to use controller splitting. Leave all of the version 1.0 action methods in the ValuesController, but create a Values2Controller to hold all of the version 2.0 methods, like this:

```
[ApiVersion("2.0")]
[ApiController]
[Route("api/[controller]")]
public class Values2Controller : ControllerBase
{
    [HttpGet("{id}")]
    public IActionResult Get(int id)
    {
        return Ok(new[] { "value1", "value2" });
    }
}

[ApiVersion("1.0")]
```

```
[ApiController]
[Route("api/[controller]")]
public class ValuesController : ControllerBase
{
  //omitted for brevity
}
```

As discussed with the updated naming conventions, both controllers base routes are defined as /api/Values. The separation doesn't affect the exposed API, just provides a mechanism to clean up the code base.

Query String Version Requests and Routing

API versions (except with URL segment routing) come into play when a route is ambiguous. If a route is serviceable from two endpoints, the selection process will look for an explicit API version that matches the requested version. If an explicit match is not found, an implicit match is searched. If no match is found, then the route will fail.

As an example, the following two Get() methods are serviced by the same route of /api/Values:

```
[ApiVersion("2.0")]
[ApiController]
[Route("api/[controller]")]
public class Values2Controller : ControllerBase
{
  [HttpGet]
  public IActionResult Get()
  {
    return Ok(new[] { "Version2:value1", "Version2:value2" });
  }
}

[ApiVersion("1.0")]
[ApiController]
[Route("api/[controller]")]
public class ValuesController : ControllerBase
{
  [HttpGet]
  public IActionResult Get()
  {
    return Ok(new[] { "value1", "value2" });
  }
}
```

If you run the app and execute the following two CURL commands, they behave as expected:

```
curl -G  https://localhost:5011/api/Values?api-version=1.0 -i
curl -G  https://localhost:5011/api/Values?api-version=2.0 -i
```

If you take the version information out of either request, it will execute the ValuesController version since version 1.0 is the default. However, if you update the Values2Controller's attributes by adding the [ApiVersion("1.0")] attribute, the request fails with the following error:

```
//Updated attributes for Values2Controller
[ApiVersion("1.0")]
[ApiVersion("2.0")]
[ApiController]
[Route("api/[controller]")]
public class Values2Controller : ControllerBase

//Error returned from CURL request (just the relevant part of the message)
Microsoft.AspNetCore.Routing.Matching.AmbiguousMatchException: The request matched multiple
endpoints. Matches:

AutoLot.Api.Controllers.Values2Controller.Get (AutoLot.Api)
AutoLot.Api.Controllers.ValuesController.Get (AutoLot.Api)
```

Attribute Precedence

As previously stated, the ApiVersion attribute can be used at the controller or action level. The previous routing example, with duplicate [ApiVersion("1.0")] attributes at the controller level, failed due to an ambiguous match. Update the Values2Controller to move the [ApiVersion("1.0")] attribute to the Get() method like this:

```
[ApiVersion("2.0")]
[ApiController]
[Route("api/[controller]")]
public class Values2Controller : ControllerBase
{
  //omitted for brevity
  [ApiVersion("1.0")]
  [HttpGet]
  public IActionResult Get()
  {
    return Ok(new[] { "Version2:value1", "Version2:value2" });
  }
}
```

With this change, executing the CURL that is requesting the version 1.0 Get() method succeeds and returns the values from the Values2Controller. This is due to the order of precedence for the ApiVersion attribute. When applied at the controller level, the version specified is *implicitly* applied to all of the action methods in the controller. When the attribute is applied at the action level, the version is *explicitly* applied to the method. As discussed previously, explicit versions take precedence over implicit versions. As a final step, remove the [ApiVersion("1.0")] from the Values2Controller's Get action method.

Getting the API Version in Requests

When using version interleaving, it might be important to know the requested version. Fortunately, this is a simple endeavor. There are two methods to get the requested version. The first is calling the GetRequestedApiVersion() method on the HttpContext, and the second (introduced in ASP.NET Core 3.0) is to use model binding. Both are shown here in the updated Get() method in the Values2Controller:

```
[HttpGet("{id}")]
public IActionResult Get(int id, ApiVersion versionFromModelBinding)
{
  var versionFromContext = HttpContext.GetRequestedApiVersion();
  return Ok(new[] { versionFromModelBinding.ToString(), versionFromContext.ToString() });
}
```

When executed, the output is the formatted version `2.0` strings:

```
[ "2.0", "2.0" ]
```

Route Updates for URL Segment Versioning

Each of the previous examples used query string versioning. In order to use URL segment versioning, the Route attribute needs to be updated so the versioning engine knows what route parameter represents the version. This is accomplished by adding a route that uses the `{version:apiVersion}` route token, as follows:

```
[ApiVersion("2.0")]
[ApiController]
[Route("api/[controller]")]
[Route("api/v{version:apiVersion}/[controller]")]
public class Values2Controller : ControllerBase
{
  //omitted for brevity
}
```

Notice that the previous example has two routes defined. This is necessary to support URL segment versioning and non-URL segment routing. If the app will only support URL segment versioning, the `[Route("api/[controller]")]` attribute can be removed.

URL Segment Versioning and Version Status Values

Recall that a version can be defined with a text status, like `Beta`. This format is also supported with URL segment versioning by simply including the status in the URL. For example, update the `Values2Controller` to add a version `2.0-Beta`:

```
[ApiVersion("2.0")]
[ApiVersion("2.0-Beta")]
[ApiController]
[Route("api/[controller]")]
[Route("api/v{version:apiVersion}/[controller]")]
public class Values2Controller : ControllerBase
{
  //omitted for brevity
}
```

To request the `2.0-Beta` version of the API Calling into the API, you can use either a period or a dash as the separator. Both of these calls will successfully call into the 2.0-Beta version of the API:

```
rem separated by a dash
```

```
curl -G  https://localhost:5011/api/v2.0-Beta/Values/1 -i
rem separated by a period
curl -G  https://localhost:5011/api/v2.0.Beta/Values/1 -i
```

Deprecating Versions

As versions are added, it is a good practice to remove older, unused versions. However, you don't want to surprise anyone by suddenly deleting versions. The best way to handle older versions is to deprecate them. This informs the clients that this version will go away at some point in the future, and it's best to move to a different (presumably newer) version.

To mark a version as deprecated, simply add `Deprecated = true` to the `ApiVersion` attribute. Adding the following to the `ValuesController` marks version `0.5` as deprecated:

```
[ApiVersion("0.5", Deprecated = true)]
[ApiVersion("1.0")]
[ApiController]
[Route("api/[controller]")]
[Route("api/v{version:apiVersion}/[controller]")]
public class ValuesController : ControllerBase
{
  //omitted for brevity
}
```

The deprecated versions are reported as such in the headers, letting clients know that the version will be retired in the future:

```
HTTP/1.1 200 OK
Content-Type: application/json; charset=utf-8; v=2.0-beta
Date: Thu, 11 Nov 2021 19:04:02 GMT
Server: Kestrel
Transfer-Encoding: chunked
api-supported-versions: 1.0, 2.0-Beta, 2.0
api-deprecated-versions: 0.5
```

Unsupported Version Requests

As a reminder, if a client calls into the API with a valid, unambiguous route, but an unsupported version, the application will respond with an HTTP 400 (Bad Request) with the message shown after the CURL command:

curl -G https://localhost:5011/api/v2.0.RC/Values/1 -i

```
{"error":{"code":"UnsupportedApiVersion","message":"The HTTP resource that matches the
request URI 'https://localhost:5011/api/v2.0.RC/Values/1' does not support the API version
'2.0.RC'.","innerError":null}}
```

Add the API Version Explorer

If you don't plan on adding version support to your Swagger documentation, you can consider your versioning configuration complete at this point. However, to document the different versions available, an instance of the `IApiVersionDescriptionProvider` must be added into the DI container using the `AddVersionedApiExplorer()` extension method. This method takes an `Action<ApiExlorerOptions>` that is used to set options for the explorer. Table 32-4 lists the `ApiExplorerOptions`' properties:

Table 32-4. *Some of the APIExplorerOptions properties*

Option	Meaning in Life
`GroupNameFormat`	Gets or sets the format used to create group names from API versions. Default value is `null`.
`SubstitutionFormat`	Gets or sets the format used to format the API version substituted in route templates. Default value is "VVV", which formats major version and optional minor version.
`SubstitueApiVersionInUrl`	Gets or sets value indicating whether the API version parameter should be substituted in route templates. Defaults to `false`.
`DefaultApiVersionParameterDescription`	Gets or sets the default description used for API version parameters. Defaults to "The requested API version".
`AddApiVersionParametersWhenVersionNeutral`	Gets or sets a value indicating whether API version parameters are added when an API is version-neutral. Defaults to `false`.
`DefaultApiVersion`	Gets or sets the default version when request does not specify version information. Defaults to `ApiVersion.Default` (1.0).
`AssumeDefaultVersionWhenUnspecified`	Gets or sets a value indicating whether a default version is assumed when a client does not provide a service API version. Default derives from the property of the same name on the `ApiVersioningOptions`.
`ApiVersionParameterSource`	Gets or sets the source for defining API version parameters.

Add the call to the `AddVersionedApiExplorer ()` method into the `AddAutoLotApiVersionConfiguration()` method in the `ApiVersionConfiguration` class. The following code sets the default version, uses the default version if the client doesn't provide one, sets the reported version format to "v'Major.Minor-Status", and enables version substitution in URLs:

```
public static IServiceCollection AddAutoLotApiVersionConfiguration(
    this IServiceCollection services, ApiVersion defaultVersion = null)
{
  //omitted for brevity
  // add the versioned api explorer, which also adds IApiVersionDescriptionProvider service
  services.AddVersionedApiExplorer(
      options =>
```

```
        {
          options.DefaultApiVersion = defaultVersion;
          options.AssumeDefaultVersionWhenUnspecified = true;
          // note: the specified format code will format the version as "'v'major[.minor]
          [-status]"
          options.GroupNameFormat = "'v'VVV";
          // note: this option is only necessary when versioning by url segment. the
          SubstitutionFormat
          // can also be used to control the format of the API version in route templates
          options.SubstituteApiVersionInUrl = true;
        });
}
```

Update the Swagger/OpenAPI Settings

Swagger (also known as OpenAPI) is an open standard for documenting RESTful APIs. Two of the main open source libraries for adding Swagger into the ASP.NET Core APIs are Swashbuckle and NSwag. Since ASP.NET Core version 5,Swashbuckle has been included as part of the new project template (albeit a very basic implementation). Swashbuckle generates a `swagger.json` document for your application that contains information for the site, each endpoint, and any objects involved in the endpoints.

Swashbuckle also provides an interactive UI called Swagger UI that presents the contents of the `swagger.json` file, as you have already used in previous examples. This experience can be enhanced by adding additional application documentation into the generated `swagger.json` file.

To get started, add the following global using statements to the `GlobalUsings.cs` file:

```
global using Microsoft.Extensions.Options;
global using Microsoft.OpenApi.Any;
global using Microsoft.OpenApi.Models;
global using Swashbuckle.AspNetCore.Annotations;
global using Swashbuckle.AspNetCore.SwaggerGen;
global using System.Reflection;
global using System.Text.Json;
```

Add the XML Documentation File

.NET can generate an XML documentation file from your project by examining the method signatures as well as developer written documentation for methods contained in triple-slash (///) comments. You must opt-in to the generation of this file.

To enable the creation of the XML documentation file using Visual Studio, right-click the AutoLot.Api project and open the Properties window. Select Build/Output in the left rail, check the XML documentation file check box, and enter `AutoLot.Api.xml` for the filename, as shown in Figure 32-3.

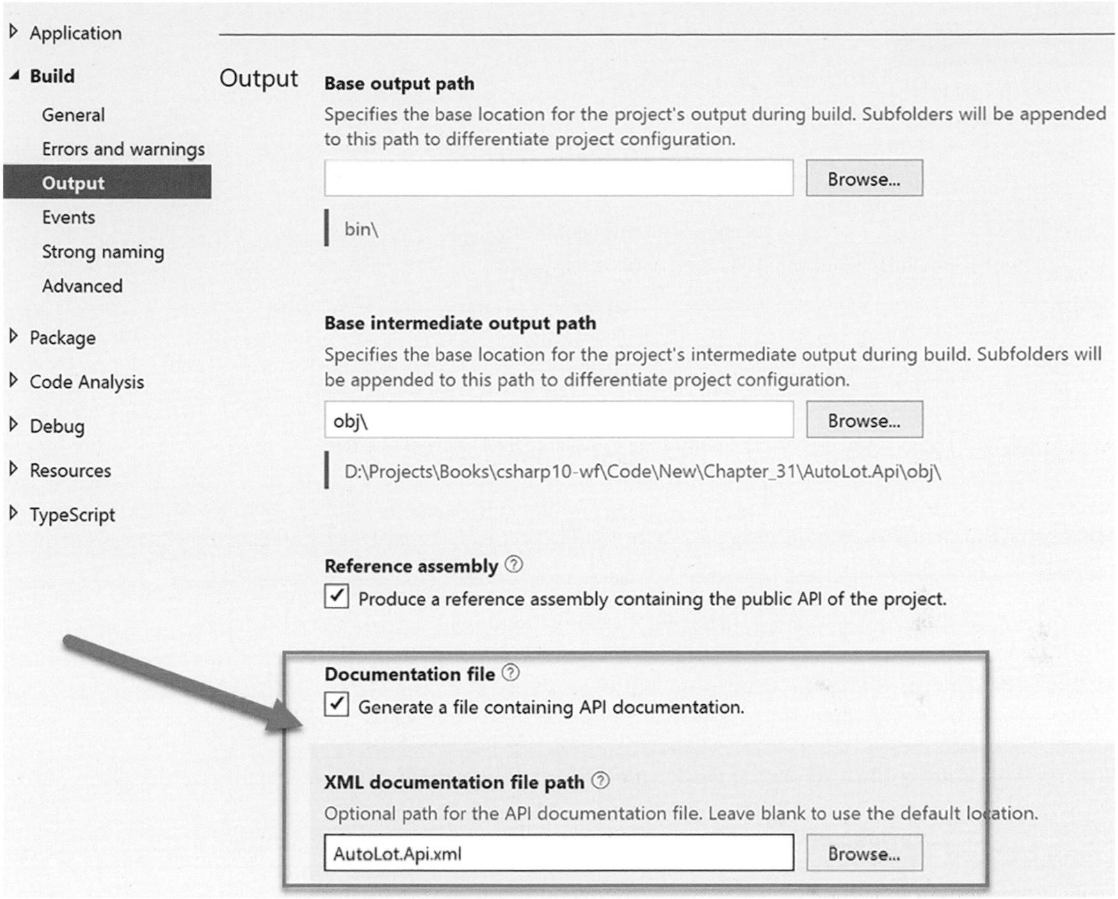

Figure 32-3. Adding the XML documentation file and suppressing 1591

Also, enter **1591** in the “Suppress warnings” text box, as shown in Figure 32-4. This setting turns off compiler warnings for methods that don’t have triple slash XML comments.

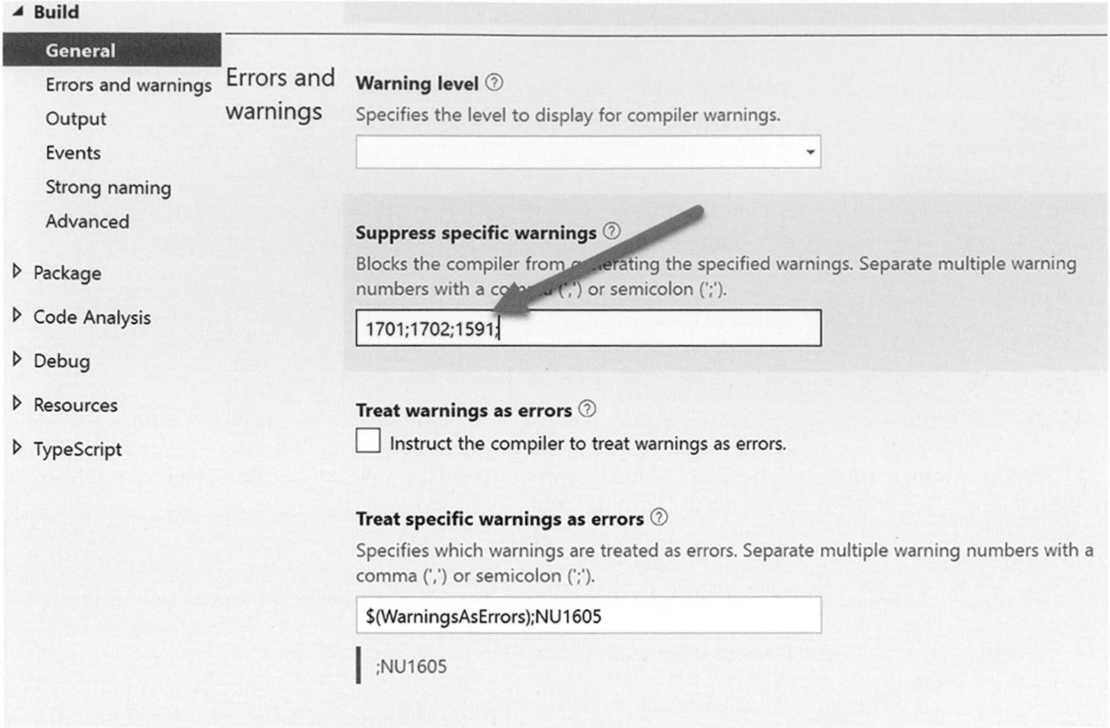

Figure 32-4. Adding the XML documenation file and suppressing 1591

■ **Note** The 1701 and 1702 warnings are carryovers from the early days of classic .NET that are exposed by the .NET Core compilers.

Updating the settings makes the following changes to the project file (shown in bold):

```
<PropertyGroup>
  <TargetFramework>net6.0</TargetFramework>
  <Nullable>disable</Nullable>
  <ImplicitUsings>enable</ImplicitUsings>
  <GenerateDocumentationFile>True</GenerateDocumentationFile>
  <DocumentationFile>AutoLot.Api.xml</DocumentationFile>
</PropertyGroup><PropertyGroup Condition="'$(Configuration)|$(Platform)'=='Debug|AnyCPU'">
  <NoWarn>1701;1702;1591</NoWarn>
</PropertyGroup>
<PropertyGroup Condition="'$(Configuration)|$(Platform)'=='Release|AnyCPU'">
  <NoWarn>1701;1702;1591</NoWarn>
</PropertyGroup>
```

The same process can be done directly in the project file with a more concise format:

```
<PropertyGroup>
  <DocumentationFile>AutoLot.Api.xml</DocumentationFile>
  <NoWarn>1701;1702;1591;1573</NoWarn>
</PropertyGroup>
```

Once the project is built, the generated file will be created in the root directory of the project. Lastly, set the generated XML file to always get copied to the output directory.

```
<ItemGroup>
  <None Update="AutoLot.Api.xml">
    <CopyToOutputDirectory>Always</CopyToOutputDirectory>
  </None>
</ItemGroup>
```

To add custom comments that will be added to the documentation file, add triple-slash (///) comments to the `Get()` method of the `ValuesController` to this:

```
/// <summary>
/// This is an example Get method returning JSON
/// </summary>
/// <remarks>This is one of several examples for returning JSON:
/// <pre>
/// [
///   "value1",
///   "value2"
/// ]
/// </pre>
/// </remarks>
/// <returns>List of strings</returns>
[HttpGet]
public IActionResult Get()
{
  return Ok(new string[“ { "value"", "value2" });
}
```

When you build the project, a new file named `AutoLot.Api.xml` is created in the root of the project. Open the file to see the comments you just added.

```
<?xml vers"on="1.0"?>
<doc>
  <assembly>
    <name>AutoLot.Api</name>
  </assembly>
  <members>
    <member name="M:AutoLot.Api.Controllers.ValuesController.Get">
      <summary>
        This is an example Get method returning JSON
      </summary>
      <remarks>This is one of several examples for returning JSON:
```

```
        <pre>
        [
         "value1",
         "value2"
        ]
        </pre>
      </remarks>
      <returns>List of strings</returns>
    </member>
  </members>
</doc>
```

■ **Note** When using Visual Studio, if you enter three backslashes before a class or method definition, Visual Studio will stub out the initial XML comments for you.

The XML comments will be merged into the generated swagger.json file shortly.

The Application's Swagger Settings

There are several customizable settings for the Swagger page, such as the title, description, and contact information. Instead of hard-coding these in the app, they will be made configurable using the Options pattern.

Start by creating a new folder named Swagger in the root of the AutoLot.Api project. In this folder, create another folder named Models. In the Models folder, create a new class named SwaggerVersionDescription.cs and update the class to the following:

```
namespace AutoLot.Api.Swagger.Models;

public class SwaggerVersionDescription
{
  public int MajorVersion { get; set; }
  public int MinorVersion { get; set; }
  public string Status {get;set;}
  public string Description { get; set; }
}
```

Next, create another class named SwaggerApplicationSettings.cs and update the class to the following:

```
namespace AutoLot.Api.Swagger.Models;

public class SwaggerApplicationSettings
{
    public string Title { get; set; }
    public List<SwaggerVersionDescription> Descriptions { get; set; } = new List<Swagger
VersionDescription>();
    public string ContactName { get; set; }
    public string ContactEmail {get; set; }
}
```

The settings are added to the appsettings.json file since they won't alter between environments:

```
{
  "AllowedHosts": "*",
  "SwaggerApplicationSettings": {
    "Title": "AutoLot APIs",
    "Descriptions": [
      {
        "MajorVersion": 0,
        "MinorVersion": 0,
        "Status": "",
        "Description": "Unable to obtain version description."
      },
      {
        "MajorVersion": 0,
        "MinorVersion": 5,
        "Status": "",
        "Description": "Deprecated Version 0.5"
      },
      {
        "MajorVersion": 1,
        "MinorVersion": 0,
        "Status": "",
        "Description": "Version 1.0"
      },
      {
        "MajorVersion": 2,
        "MinorVersion": 0,
        "Status": "",
        "Description": "Version 2.0"
      },
      {
        "MajorVersion": 2,
        "MinorVersion": 0,
        "Status": "Beta",
        "Description": "Version 2.0-Beta"
      }
    ],
    "ContactName": "Phil Japikse",
    "ContactEmail": "blog@skimedic.com"
  }
}
```

Update the GlobalUsings.cs file to include the new namespaces:

```
global using AutoLot.Api.Swagger;
global using AutoLot.Api.Swagger.Models;
```

Following the pattern of using extension methods to register services, create a new public static class named SwaggerConfiguration in the Swagger folder. Next, add a new public static extension method named AddAndConfigureSwagger() that extends the IServiceCollection, takes the IConfiguration instance, the path and name for the generated AutoLot.Api.xml file, and a bool to enable/disable the security features in Swagger UI:

```
namespace AutoLot.Api.Swagger;

public static class SwaggerConfiguration
{
  public static void AddAndConfigureSwagger(
        this IServiceCollection services,
        IConfiguration config,
        string xmlPathAndFile,
        bool addBasicSecurity)
  {
    //implementation goes here
  }
}
```

Now that the extension method is set up, register the settings using the Options pattern:

```
  public static void AddAndConfigureSwagger(
        this IServiceCollection services,
        IConfiguration config,
        string xmlPathAndFile,
        bool addBasicSecurity)
  {
    services.Configure<SwaggerApplicationSettings>(
      config.GetSection(nameof(SwaggerApplicationSettings)));
  }
```

Finally, call the extension method in the `Program.cs` file just before the call to `AddSwaggerGen()`:

```
builder.Services.AddAndConfigureSwagger(
    builder.Configuration,
    Path.Combine(AppContext.BaseDirectory, $"{Assembly.GetExecutingAssembly().GetName().
    Name}.xml"),
    true);
builder.Services.AddSwaggerGen();
```

The SwaggerDefaultValues Operation Filter

When APIs are versioned (as this one is), the Swagger code that came with the default ASP.NET Core RESTful service template isn't set up to handle the versions. Fortunately, the solution is provided by the good folks at Microsoft on the DotNet GitHub site (see the note for the link).

■ **Note** The original version of the `SwaggerDefaultValues.cs` and `ConfigureSwaggerOptions.cs` classes are from the DotNet GitHub site in the versioning sample, which is located here `https://github.com/dotnet/aspnet-api-versioning/blob/master/samples/aspnetcore/SwaggerSample/SwaggerDefaultValues.cs`

In the Swagger folder create a new class named SwaggerDefaultValues.cs and update the class to the following (which is direct from the sample with some minor cleanup):

```
namespace AutoLot.Api.Swagger;

public class SwaggerDefaultValues : IOperationFilter
{
  public void Apply(OpenApiOperation operation, OperationFilterContext context)
  {
    var apiDescription = context.ApiDescription;
    //operation.Deprecated = (operation.Deprecated | apiDescription.IsDeprecated())
    operation.Deprecated |= apiDescription.IsDeprecated();
    foreach (var responseType in context.ApiDescription.SupportedResponseTypes)
    {
      var responseKey = responseType.IsDefaultResponse ? "default" : responseType.
      StatusCode.ToString();
      var response = operation.Responses[responseKey];
      foreach (var contentType in response.Content.Keys)
      {
        if (responseType.ApiResponseFormats.All(x => x.MediaType != contentType))
        {
          response.Content.Remove(contentType);
        }
      }
    }
    if (operation.Parameters == null)
    {
      return;
    }

    foreach (var parameter in operation.Parameters)
    {
      var description = apiDescription.ParameterDescriptions.First(p => p.Name ==
      parameter.Name);
      parameter.Description ??= description.ModelMetadata?.Description;
      if (parameter.Schema.Default == null && description.DefaultValue != null)
      {
        var json = JsonSerializer.Serialize(description.DefaultValue, description.
        ModelMetadata.ModelType);
        parameter.Schema.Default = OpenApiAnyFactory.CreateFromJson(json);
      }
      parameter.Required |= description.IsRequired;
    }
  }
}
```

The ConfigureSwaggerOptions Class

The next class to add is also provided from the ASP.NET Core samples, but modified here to use the SwaggerApplicationSettings. Create a public class named ConfigureSwaggerOptions in the Swagger folder and make it implement IConfigureOptions<SwaggerGenOptions>, like this:

```
namespace AutoLot.Api.Swagger;

public class ConfigureSwaggerOptions : IConfigureOptions<SwaggerGenOptions>
{
  public void Configure(SwaggerGenOptions options)
  {
    throw new NotImplementedException();
  }
}
```

In the constructor, take an instance of the `IApiVersionDescriptionProvider` and the `OptionsMonitor` for the `SwaggerApplicationSettings`, and assign each to a class level variable (the code in bold is updated from the sample):

```
readonly IApiVersionDescriptionProvider _provider;
private readonly SwaggerApplicationSettings _settings;

public ConfigureSwaggerOptions(
  IApiVersionDescriptionProvider provider,
  IOptionsMonitor<SwaggerApplicationSettings> settingsMonitor)
{
  _provider = provider;
  _settings = settingsMonitor.CurrentValue;
}
```

The `Configure()` method loops through the API's versions, generating a Swagger document for each version. Add the following method (once again, the code in bold is added to the provided sample):

```
public void Configure(SwaggerGenOptions options)
{
  foreach (var description in _provider.ApiVersionDescriptions)
  {
    options.SwaggerDoc(description.GroupName, CreateInfoForApiVersion(description,
    _settings));
  }
}
internal static OpenApiInfo CreateInfoForApiVersion(
  ApiVersionDescription description,
  SwaggerApplicationSettings settings)
{
  throw new NotImplementedException();
}
```

The `CreateInfoForApiVersion()` method creates an instance of the `OpenApiInfo` object for each version. The `OpenApiInfo` holes the descriptive information for the application, such as the title, version information, description, etc. The code in bold is either custom information hardcoded for this app or leverages the `SwaggerApplicationSettings` to set the configured values:

```
internal static OpenApiInfo CreateInfoForApiVersion(
  ApiVersionDescription description,
  SwaggerApplicationSettings settings)
```

```
{
  var versionDesc = settings.Descriptions.FirstOrDefault(x =>
       x.MajorVersion == (description.ApiVersion.MajorVersion??0)
       && x.MinorVersion == (description.ApiVersion.MinorVersion ?? 0)
       && (string.IsNullOrEmpty(description.ApiVersion.Status) || x.Status==description.
       ApiVersion.Status));
var info = new OpenApiInfo()
  {
    Title = settings.Title,
    Version = description.ApiVersion.ToString(),
    Description = $"{versionDesc?.Description}",
    Contact = new OpenApiContact() { Name = settings.ContactName, Email = settings.
    ContactEmail },
    TermsOfService = new System.Uri("https://www.linktotermsofservice.com"),
    License = new OpenApiLicense() { Name = "MIT", Url = new System.Uri("https://opensource.
    org/licenses/MIT") }
  };
  if (description.IsDeprecated)
  {
    info.Description += "<p><font color='red'>This API version has been deprecated.
    </font></p>";
  }

  return info;
}
```

With these classes in place, add the following line to the AddAndConfigureSwagger() method so the SwaggerGenOptions are into the DI container:

```
public static void AddAndConfigureSwagger(
        this IServiceCollection services,
        IConfiguration config,
        string xmlPathAndFile,
        bool addBasicSecurity)
{
  services.Configure<SwaggerApplicationSettings>(config.GetSection(nameof(SwaggerApplication
  Settings)));
  services.AddTransient<IConfigureOptions<SwaggerGenOptions>, ConfigureSwaggerOptions>();
}
```

Update the SwaggerGen() Call

The default template simply called AddSwaggerGen(), in the Program.cs file top level statements, which adds very basic support. Remove that line from the top level statements and add it to the AddAndConfigureSwagger() method. In the following code, annotations are enabled, the OperationFilter is set, and XML comments are included. If security is not enabled, the method ends there. If security is requested, the rest of the method adds support for basic authentication into the Swagger UI. The call is listed here:

```
services.AddSwaggerGen(c =>
{
  c.EnableAnnotations();
  c.OperationFilter<SwaggerDefaultValues>();
  c.IncludeXmlComments(xmlPathAndFile);
  if (!addBasicSecurity)
  {
    return;
  }
  c.AddSecurityDefinition("basic", new OpenApiSecurityScheme
  {
    Name = "Authorization",
    Type = SecuritySchemeType.Http,
    Scheme = "basic",
    In = ParameterLocation.Header,
    Description = "Basic Authorization header using the Bearer scheme."
  });
  c.AddSecurityRequirement(new OpenApiSecurityRequirement
    {
      {
        new OpenApiSecurityScheme
        {
          Reference = new OpenApiReference
          {
            Type = ReferenceType.SecurityScheme,
            Id = "basic"
          }
        },
        new List<string> {}
      }
  });
});
```

Update the UseSwaggerUI() Call

The final step is to replace the `UseSwaggerUI()` call in the `Program.cs` file with a version that leverages all of the framework we just built. In the call, the instance of the `IApiVersionDescriptionProvider` is retrieved from the DI container and is used to loop through the API versions supported by the application, creating a new Swagger UI endpoint for each version.

Update the call to `UseSwaggerUI()` with the following code:

```
app.UseSwaggerUI(
    options =>
    {
        using var scope = app.Services.CreateScope();
        var versionProvider = scope.ServiceProvider.GetRequiredService<IApiVersionDescription
        Provider>();
        // build a swagger endpoint for each discovered API version
        foreach (var description in versionProvider.ApiVersionDescriptions)
```

```
    {
        options.SwaggerEndpoint($"/swagger/{description.GroupName}/swagger.json",
            description.GroupName.ToUpperInvariant());
    }
});
```

View the Results in the Swagger UI

Now that everything is in place, run the application and examine the Swagger UI. The first thing you will notice is that the version displayed in the UI is 0.5 (the deprecated version). This is because the UI displays the lowest version reported as the default. You can see the red message that the version has been deprecated, the description and contact information from the SwaggerApplicationSettings, a button to Authorize (for basic authentication), and all of the deprecated end points are grayed out and displayed with the font struck through. It's important to note that even though the endpoints look disabled, the page is still fully functional. All of the updates are merely cosmetic. Examine Figure 32-5 to see all of the updates to the UI:

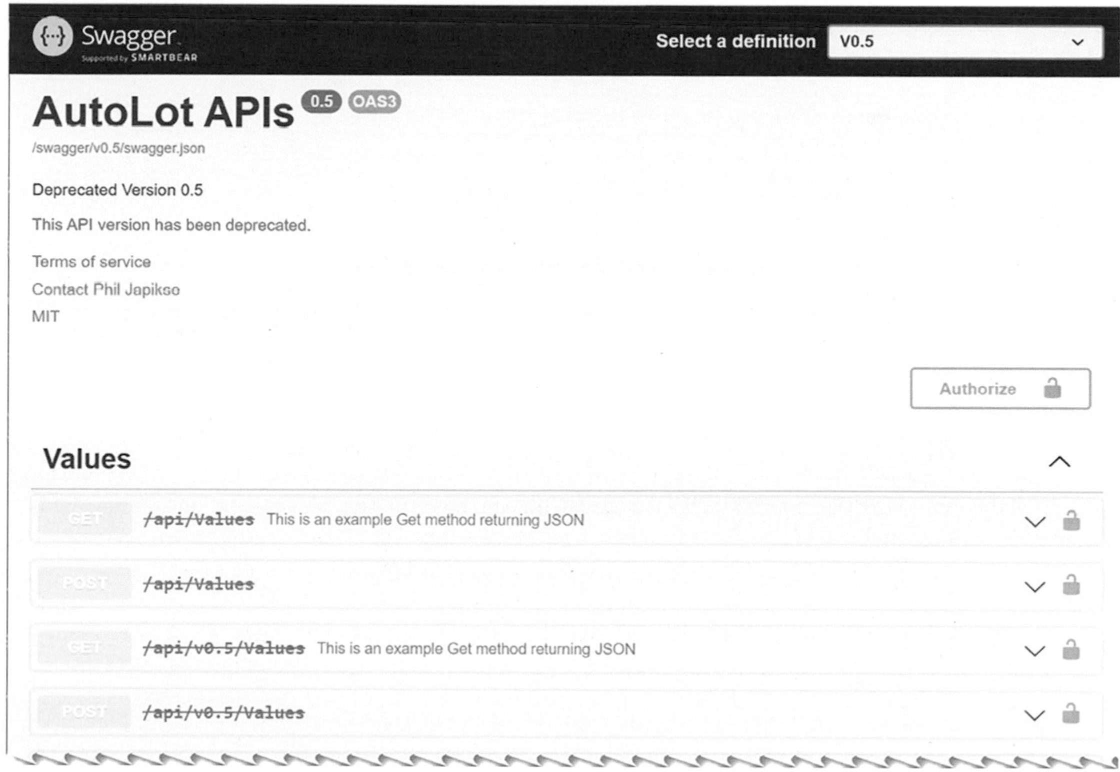

Figure 32-5. Updates to the Swagger UI page

Now, select version 1.0 with the version selector (Figure 32-6), and you will see all of the endpoints return to normal font and coloration and the red deprecated warning is gone.

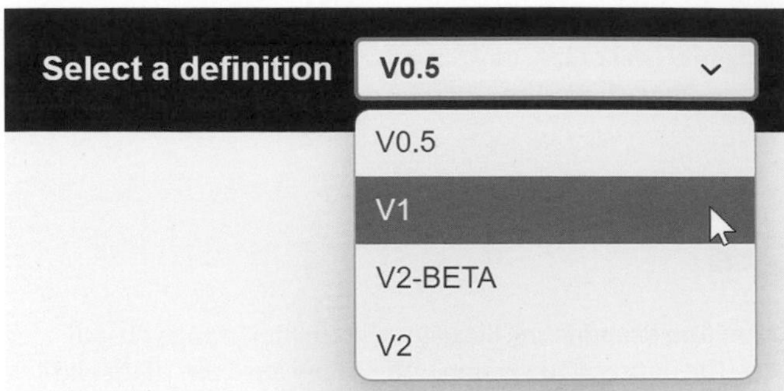

Figure 32-6. *The version selector on the Swagger UI page*

If you examine the HTTP Get /api/Values endpoint, you can see the XML comments have been incorporated into the UI, as show in Figure 32-7.

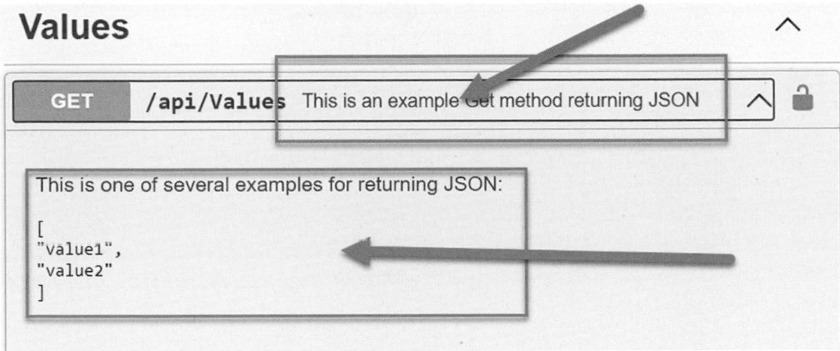

Figure 32-7. *XML documentation integrated into Swagger UI*

Another change is in the list of endpoints. With version 1.0 selected, you can see that there are two lines for each of the endpoints (Figure 32-8). This is because the app has URL segment versioning and non-URL segment versioning enabled.

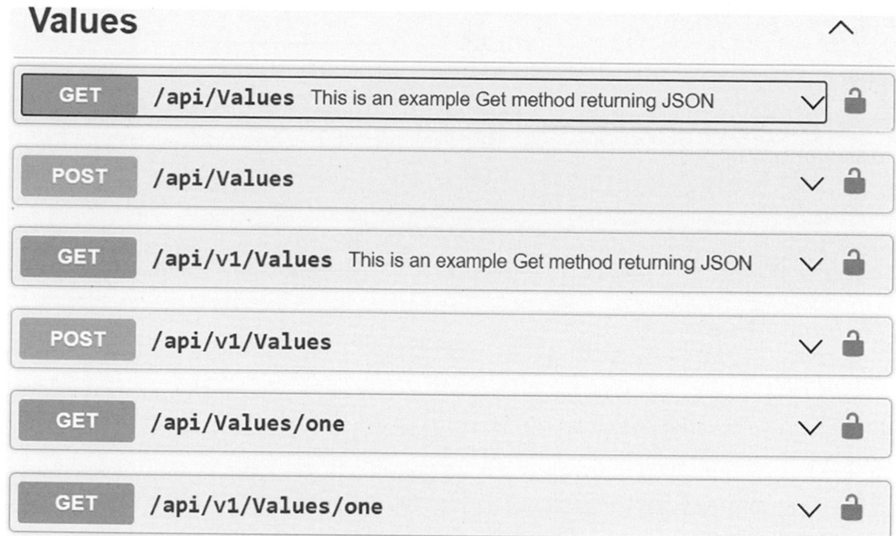

Figure 32-8. *Two entries for each end point*

The final change to examine has to do with executing the end points. When expanding one of the endpoints that use URL segment versioning (like `/api/v1/Values`), you see the normal Try it out button, and if you click that, you will see the option to enter any URL parameters (like `id`). However, with one of the non-URL segment routing end points (like `/api/Values`), when you expand the method, you see all of the version options available for input (Figure 32-9) in addition to any URL parameters. When you click Try it out, you have the option to enter an API version using one of the four methods.

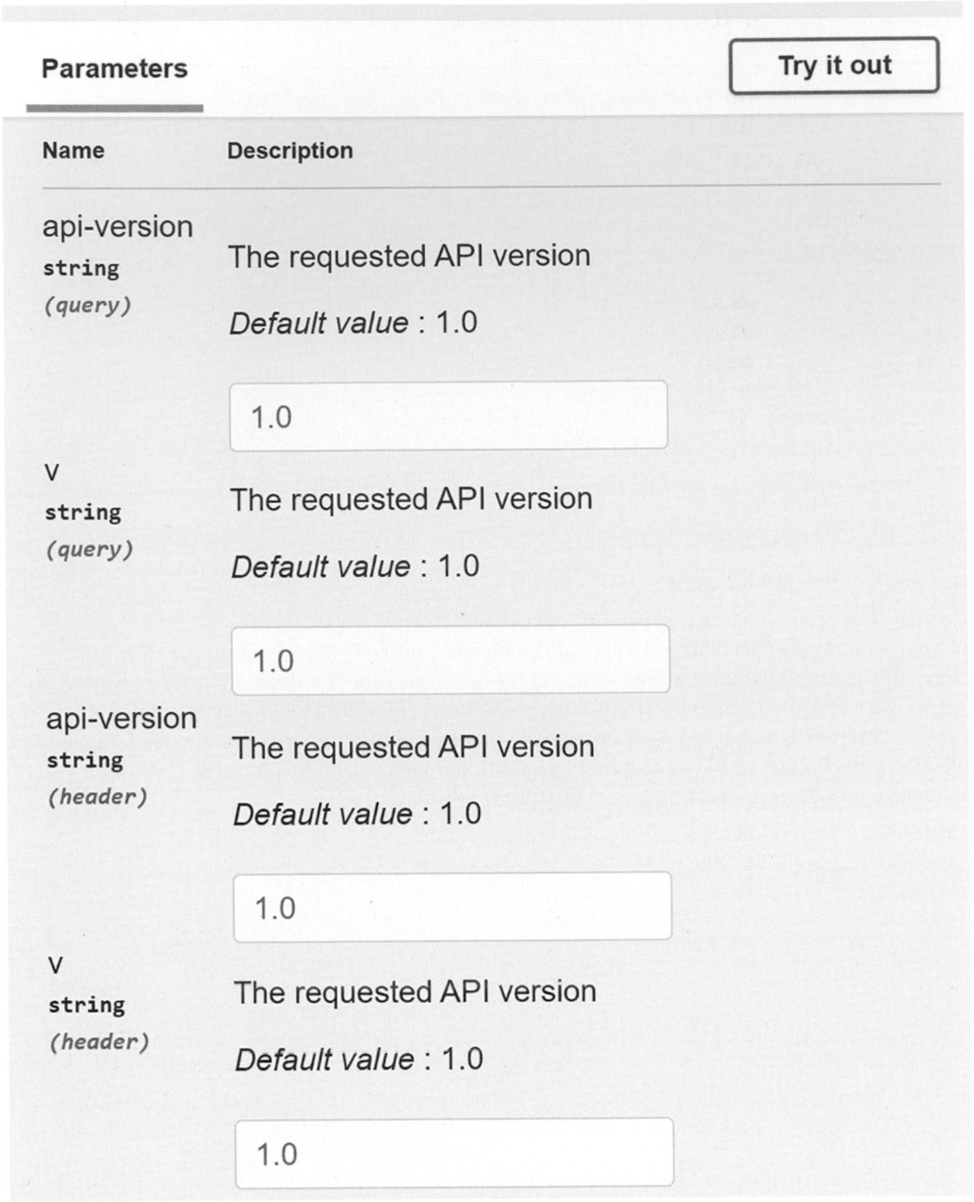

Parameters

Try it out

Name	Description
api-version string *(query)*	The requested API version *Default value* : 1.0 1.0
v string *(query)*	The requested API version *Default value* : 1.0 1.0
api-version string *(header)*	The requested API version *Default value* : 1.0 1.0
v string *(header)*	The requested API version *Default value* : 1.0 1.0

Figure 32-9. *Two entries for each end point*

The authorize button will be covered later in this chapter.

Additional Documentation Options for API Endpoints

There are additional attributes that augment the Swagger documentation. The Produces attribute indicates the content-type for the endpoint. The ProducesResponseType attribute uses the StatusCodes enumeration to indicate a possible return code for an endpoint. Update the Get() method of the ValuesController to specify application/json as the return type and that the action result will return either a 200 OK, a 400 Bad Request, or a 401 Unauthorized.

```
[HttpGet]
[Produces("application/json")]
[ProducesResponseType(StatusCodes.Status200OK)]
[ProducesResponseType(StatusCodes.Status400BadRequest)]
[ProducesResponseType(StatusCodes. Status401Unauthorized)]
public ActionResult<IEnumerable<string>> Get()
{
  return new string[] {"value1", "value2"};
}
```

While the ProducesResponseType attribute adds the response codes to the documentation, the information can't be customized. Fortunately, Swashbuckle adds the SwaggerResponse attribute for just this purpose. Update the Get() method to the following:

```
[HttpGet]
[Produces("application/json")]
[ProducesResponseType(StatusCodes.Status200OK)]
[ProducesResponseType(StatusCodes.Status400BadRequest)]
[ProducesResponseType(StatusCodes. Status401Unauthorized)]
[SwaggerResponse(200, "The execution was successful")]
[SwaggerResponse(400, "The request was invalid")]
[SwaggerResponse(401, "Unauthorized access attempted")]
public ActionResult<IEnumerable<string>> Get()
{
  return new string[] {"value1", "value2"};
}
```

Before the Swagger annotations will be picked up and added to the generated documentation, they must be enabled. They were already enabled in the AddAndConfigureSwagger() method. Now, when you view the responses section of the Swagger UI, you will see the customized messaging, as shown in Figure 32-10.

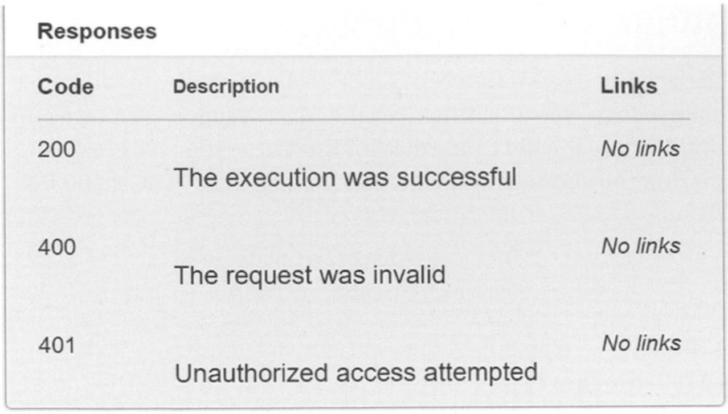

Responses

Code	Description	Links
200	The execution was successful	No links
400	The request was invalid	No links
401	Unauthorized access attempted	No links

Figure 32-10. *Updated responses in Swagger UI*

■ **Note** There is a lot of additional customization that Swashbuckle supports. Consult the docs at `https://github.com/domaindrivendev/Swashbuckle.AspNetCore` for more information.

Building The BaseCrudController

The majority of the functionality of the AutoLot.Api application can be categorized as one of the following methods:

- `GetOne()`
- `GetAll()`
- `UpdateOne()`
- `AddOne()`
- `DeleteOne()`

The main API methods will be implemented in a generic base API controller. Update the `GlobalUsings.cs` file by adding the following:

```
global using AutoLot.Dal.Exceptions;
global using AutoLot.Dal.Repos;
global using AutoLot.Dal.Repos.Base;
global using AutoLot.Dal.Repos.Interfaces;
global using AutoLot.Models.Entities;
global using AutoLot.Models.Entities.Base;
```

Next, create a new folder named Base in the `Controllers` directory. In this folder, add a new class named `BaseCrudController.cs` and update the class definition to the following:

```
namespace AutoLot.Api.Controllers.Base

[ApiController]
```

```
[Route("api/[controller]")]
[Route("api/v{version:apiVersion}/[controller]")]
public abstract class BaseCrudController<TEntity, TController> : ControllerBase
    where TEntity : BaseEntity, new()
    where TController : class
{
  //implementation goes here
}
```

Add the following global using statement into the `GlobalUsings.cs` file:

```
global using AutoLot.Api.Controllers.Base;
```

The class is `public` and `abstract` and inherits `ControllerBase`. The class accepts two generic parameters. The first type is constrained to derive from `BaseEntity` and have a default constructor, and the second must be a class (for the logging framework). As discussed earlier, when the `ApiController` attribute is added to a base class, derived controllers get the functionality provided by the attribute.

The Constructor

The next step is to add two protected class-level variables: one to hold an instance of `IRepo<TEntity>` and the other to hold an instance of `IAppLogging<TController>`. Both of these should be set using a constructor.

```
protected readonly IBaseRepo<TEntity> MainRepo;
protected readonly IAppLogging<TController> Logger;
protected BaseCrudController(IAppLogging<TController> logger, IBaseRepo<TEntity> repo)
{
  MainRepo = repo;
  Logger = logger;
}
```

The entity type for the repo matches the entity type for the derived controller. For example, the `CarsController` will be using the `CarRepo`. This allows for type specific work to be done in the derived controllers, but encapsulating simple CRUD operations in the base controller.

The Get Methods

There are four HTTP Get methods, `GetOnBad()`, `GetOneFuture()`, `GetOne()` and `GetAll()`. In this app, assume that the `GetOneBad()` method is deprecated as part of the `0.5` version. The `GetOneFuture()` is part of the next beta release (2.0-Beta), while the `GetOne()` and `GetAll()` methods are part of the version `1.0` production API.

Add the `GetAllBad()` method like this:

```
/// <summary>
/// DON'T USE THIS ONE. BAD THINGS WILL HAPPEN
/// </summary>
/// <returns>All records</returns>
[Produces("application/json")]
[ProducesResponseType(StatusCodes.Status200OK)]
[ProducesResponseType(StatusCodes.Status400BadRequest)]
```

```
[ProducesResponseType(StatusCodes.Status401Unauthorized)]
[SwaggerResponse(200, "The execution was successful")]
[SwaggerResponse(400, "The request was invalid")]
[SwaggerResponse(401, "Unauthorized access attempted")]
[ApiVersion("0.5", Deprecated = true)]
[HttpGet]
public ActionResult<IEnumerable<TEntity>> GetAllBad()
{
  throw new Exception("I said not to use this one");
}
```

■ **Note** When a version is deprecated, you must add the `Deprecated` flag to all of the `ApiVersion` attributes in your application to guarantee that Swagger will report the versions correctly.

Next, add in the future implementation of `GetAllFuture()` like this:

```
/// <summary>
/// Gets all records really fast (when it's written)
/// </summary>
/// <returns>All records</returns>
[Produces("application/json")]
[ProducesResponseType(StatusCodes.Status200OK)]
[ProducesResponseType(StatusCodes.Status400BadRequest)]
[ProducesResponseType(StatusCodes.Status401Unauthorized)]
[SwaggerResponse(200, "The execution was successful")]
[SwaggerResponse(400, "The request was invalid")]
[SwaggerResponse(401, "Unauthorized access attempted access attempted")]
[ApiVersion("2.0-Beta")]
[HttpGet]
public ActionResult<IEnumerable<TEntity>> GetAllFuture()
{
  throw new NotImplementedException("I'm working on it");
}
```

Now it's time to build the real get methods. First, add the `GetAll()` method. This method serves as the endpoint for the derived controller's get all route (e.g., `/Cars`).

```
/// <summary>
/// Gets all records
/// </summary>
/// <returns>All records</returns>
[Produces("application/json")]
[ProducesResponseType(StatusCodes.Status200OK)]
[ProducesResponseType(StatusCodes.Status400BadRequest)]
[ProducesResponseType(StatusCodes.Status401Unauthorized)]
[SwaggerResponse(200, "The execution was successful")]
[SwaggerResponse(400, "The request was invalid")]
[SwaggerResponse(401, "Unauthorized access attempted")]
```

```
[ApiVersion("1.0")]
[HttpGet]
public ActionResult<IEnumerable<TEntity>> GetAll()
{
  return Ok(MainRepo.GetAllIgnoreQueryFilters());
}
```

The next method gets a single record, based on the id, which is passed in as a required route parameter (e.g. /Cars/5).

```
/// <summary>
/// Gets a single record
/// </summary>
/// <param name="id">Primary key of the record</param>
/// <returns>Single record</returns>
[Produces("application/json")]
[ProducesResponseType(StatusCodes.Status200OK)]
[ProducesResponseType(StatusCodes.Status204NoContent)]
[ProducesResponseType(StatusCodes.Status400BadRequest)]
[ProducesResponseType(StatusCodes.Status401Unauthorized)]
[SwaggerResponse(200, "The execution was successful")]
[SwaggerResponse(204, "No content")]
[SwaggerResponse(400, "The request was invalid")]
[SwaggerResponse(401, "Unauthorized access attempted")]
[ApiVersion("1.0")]
[HttpGet("{id}")]
public ActionResult<TEntity> GetOne(int id)
{
  var entity = MainRepo.Find(id);
  if (entity == null)
  {
    return NoContent();
  }
  return Ok(entity);
}
```

The route value is automatically assigned to the id parameter (implicit [FromRoute]).

The UpdateOne Method

The HTTP Put verb represents an update to a record. The method is listed here, with explanation to follow:

```
/// <summary>
/// Updates a single record
/// </summary>
/// <remarks>
/// Sample body:
/// <pre>
/// {
///   "Id": 1,
///   "TimeStamp": "AAAAAAAAB+E="
```

```
///   "MakeId": 1,
///   "Color": "Black",
///   "PetName": "Zippy",
///   "MakeColor": "VW (Black)",
/// }
/// </pre>
/// </remarks>
/// <param name="id">Primary key of the record to update</param>
/// <param name="entity">Entity to update</param>
/// <returns>Single record</returns>
[Produces("application/json")]
[ProducesResponseType(StatusCodes.Status200OK)]
[ProducesResponseType(StatusCodes.Status400BadRequest)]
[ProducesResponseType(StatusCodes.Status401Unauthorized)]
[SwaggerResponse(200, "The execution was successful")]
[SwaggerResponse(400, "The request was invalid")]
[SwaggerResponse(401, "Unauthorized access attempted")]
[HttpPut("{id}")]
[ApiVersion("1.0")]
public IActionResult UpdateOne(int id, TEntity entity)
{
  if (id != entity.Id)
  {
    return BadRequest();
  }
  if (!ModelState.IsValid)
  {
    return ValidationProblem(ModelState);
  }
  try
  {
    MainRepo.Update(entity);
  }
  catch (CustomException ex)
  {
    //This shows an example with the custom exception
    //Should handle more gracefully
    return BadRequest(ex);
  }
  catch (Exception ex)
  {
    //Should handle more gracefully
    return BadRequest(ex);
  }
  return Ok(entity);
}
```

The method starts by setting the route as an `HttpPut` request based on the derived controller's route with the required `Id` route parameter. The route value is assigned to the `id` parameter (`implicit [FromRoute]`), and the entity is assigned from the body of the request (`implicit [FromBody]`).

The method checks to make sure the route value (id) matches the id in the body. If it doesn't, a BadRequest is returned. If it does, the explicit check for ModelState validity is used. If the ModelState isn't valid, a 400 (BadRequest) will be returned to the client. Remember that the explicit check for ModelState validity isn't needed if the implicit check is enabled with the ApiController attribute.

If all is successful to this point, the repo is used to update the record. If the update fails with an exception, a 400 is returned to the client. If all succeeds, a 200 (OK) is returned to the client with the updated record passed in as the body of the response.

■ **Note** The exception handling in this example (and the rest of the examples as well) is woefully inadequate. Production applications should leverage all you have learned up to this point in the book as well as exception filters (introduced later in this chapter) to gracefully handle problems as the requirements dictate.

The AddOne Method

The HTTP Post verb represents an insert to a record. The method is listed here, with an explanation to follow:

```
/// <summary>
/// <summary>
/// Adds a single record
/// </summary>
/// <remarks>
/// Sample body:
/// <pre>
/// {
///   "Id": 1,
///   "TimeStamp": "AAAAAAAAB+E="
///   "MakeId": 1,
///   "Color": "Black",
///   "PetName": "Zippy",
///   "MakeColor": "VW (Black)",
/// }
/// </pre>
/// </remarks>
/// <returns>Added record</returns>
[Produces("application/json")]
[ProducesResponseType(StatusCodes.Status201Created)]
[ProducesResponseType(StatusCodes.Status400BadRequest)]
[ProducesResponseType(StatusCodes.Status401Unauthorized)]
[SwaggerResponse(201, "The execution was successful")]
[SwaggerResponse(400, "The request was invalid")]
[SwaggerResponse(401, "Unauthorized access attempted")]
[HttpPost]
[ApiVersion("1.0")]
public ActionResult<TEntity> AddOne(TEntity entity)
{
    if (!ModelState.IsValid)
```

```
    {
        return ValidationProblem(ModelState);
    }
    try
    {
        MainRepo.Add(entity);
    }
    catch (Exception ex)
    {
        return BadRequest(ex);
    }

    return CreatedAtAction(nameof(GetOne), new { id = entity.Id }, entity);
}
```

This method starts off by defining the route as an HTTP Post. There isn't a route parameter since it's a new record. If `ModelState` is valid and the repo successfully adds the record, the response is `CreatedAtAction()`. This returns an HTTP 201 to the client, with the URL for the newly created entity as the `Location` header value. The body of the response is the newly added entity as JSON.

The DeleteOne Method

The HTTP Delete verb represents a removal of a record. Once you have the instance created from the body content, use the repo to process the delete. The entire method is listed here:

```
/// <summary>
/// Deletes a single record
/// </summary>
/// <remarks>
/// Sample body:
/// <pre>
/// {
///   "Id": 1,
///   "TimeStamp": "AAAAAAAAB+E="
/// }
/// </pre>
/// </remarks>
/// <returns>Nothing</returns>
[Produces("application/json")]
[ProducesResponseType(StatusCodes.Status200OK)]
[ProducesResponseType(StatusCodes.Status400BadRequest)]
[ProducesResponseType(StatusCodes.Status401Unauthorized)]
[SwaggerResponse(200, "The execution was successful")]
[SwaggerResponse(400, "The request was invalid")]
[SwaggerResponse(401, "Unauthorized access attempted")]
[HttpDelete("{id}")]
[ApiVersion("1.0")]
public ActionResult<TEntity> DeleteOne(int id, TEntity entity)
{
```

```
    if (id != entity.Id)
    {
      return BadRequest();
    }
    try
    {
      MainRepo.Delete(entity);
    }
    catch (Exception ex)
    {
      //Should handle more gracefully
      return new BadRequestObjectResult(ex.GetBaseException()?.Message);
    }
    return Ok();
  }
```

This method starts off by defining the route as an HTTP Delete with the id as a required route parameter. The id in the route is compared to the id sent with the rest of the entity in the body, and if they don't match, a BadRequest is returned. If the repo successfully deletes the record, the response is an OK; if there is an error, the response is a BadRequest.

If you recall from the EF Core chapters, an entity can be deleted with just its primary key and time stamp value. This allows deleting without the entire entity being sent in the request. If clients are using this abbreviated version of just sending the Id and TimeStamp, this method will fail if implicit ModelState checking is enabled and there are validation checks on the remaining properties.

As the final step, update the global using statements in the GlobalUsings.cs file to include the following:

```
global using AutoLot.Api.Controllers.Base;
```

The CarsController

The AutoLot.Api app needs an additional HTTP Get method to get the Car records based on a Make value. This will go into a new class called CarsController. Create a new empty API controller named CarsController in the Controllers folder. The CarsController derives from the BaseCrudController and the constructor takes in the entity-specific repo and an instance of the logger. Here is the initial controller layout:

```
namespace AutoLot.Api.Controllers

public class CarsController : BaseCrudController<Car, CarsController>
{
  public CarsController(IAppLogging<CarsController> logger, ICarRepo repo) :
base(logger,repo)
  {
  }
}
```

The CarsController extends the base class with another action method that gets all of the cars for a particular make. Add the following code, and the explanation will follow:

```
/// <summary>
/// Gets all cars by make
/// </summary>
/// <returns>All cars for a make</returns>
/// <param name="id">Primary key of the make</param>
[Produces("application/json")]
[ProducesResponseType(StatusCodes.Status200OK)]
[ProducesResponseType(StatusCodes.Status400BadRequest)]
[ProducesResponseType(StatusCodes.Status401Unauthorized)]
[SwaggerResponse(200, "The execution was successful")]
[SwaggerResponse(400, "The request was invalid")]
[SwaggerResponse(401, "Unauthorized access attempted")]
[HttpGet("bymake/{id?}")]
[ApiVersion("1.0")]
public ActionResult<IEnumerable<Car>> GetCarsByMake(int? id)
{
  if (id.HasValue && id.Value > 0)
  {
    return Ok(((ICarRepo)MainRepo).GetAllBy(id.Value));
  }
  return Ok(MainRepo.GetAllIgnoreQueryFilters());
}
```

The HTTP Get attribute extends the route with the bymake constant and then the optional id of the make to filter on, for example:

```
https://localhost:5021/api/cars/bymake/5
```

Next, it checks if a value was passed in for the id. If not, it gets all vehicles. If a value was passed in, it uses the GetAllBy() method of the CarRepo to get the cars by make. Since the MainRepo protected property of the base class is defined as IRepo<TEntity>, it must be cast back to the ICarRepo interface.

The Remaining Controllers

The remaining entity-specific controllers all derive from the BaseCrudController but don't add any additional functionality. Add seven more empty API controllers named CarDriversController, CreditRisksController, CustomersController, DriversController, MakesController, OrdersController, and RadiosController to the Controllers folder. The remaining controllers are all shown here:

```
//CarDriversController
namespace AutoLot.Api.Controllers;
public class CarDriversController : BaseCrudController<CarDriver, CarDriversController>
{
  public CarDriversController(IAppLogging<CarDriversController> logger,
ICarDriverRepo repo )
    : base(logger, repo)
```

```
  {
  }
}
//CreditRisksController.cs
namespace AutoLot.Api.Controllers;
public class CreditRisksController : BaseCrudController<CreditRisk, CreditRisksController>
{
  public CreditRisksController(IAppLogging<CreditRisksController> logger,
ICreditRiskRepo repo )
    : base(logger, repo)
  {
  }
}

//CustomersController.cs
namespace AutoLot.Api.Controllers;
public class CustomersController : BaseCrudController<Customer, CustomersController>
{
  public CustomersController(IAppLogging<CustomersController> logger, ICustomerRepo repo)
    : base(logger, repo)
  {
  }
}

//DriversController.cs
namespace AutoLot.Api.Controllers;
public class DriversController : BaseCrudController<Driver, DriversController>
{
  public DriversController(IAppLogging<DriversController> logger, IDriverRepo repo)
    : base(logger, repo)
  {
  }
}

//MakesController.cs
namespace AutoLot.Api.Controllers;
public class MakesController : BaseCrudController<Make, MakesController>
{
  public MakesController(IAppLogging<MakesController> logger, IMakeRepo repo)
    : base(logger, repo)
  {
  }
}

//OrdersController.cs
namespace AutoLot.Api.Controllers;
public class OrdersController : BaseCrudController<Order, OrdersController>
{
  public OrdersController(IAppLogging<OrdersController> logger,IOrderRepo repo)
```

```
    : base(logger, repo)
  {
  }
}

//RadiosController.cs
namespace AutoLot.Api.Controllers;
public class RadiosController : BaseCrudController<Radio, RadiosController>
{
  public RadiosController(IAppLogging<RadiosController> logger,IRadioRepo repo)
    : base(logger, repo)
  {
  }
}
```

This completes all of the controllers, and you can use the Swagger UI to test all of the functionality. If you are going to add/update/delete records, update the RebuildDataBase value to true in the appsettings.development.json file.

```
{
...
  "RebuildDataBase": true,
...
}
```

Exception Filters

When an exception occurs in a Web API application, there isn't an error page that gets displayed since the client is typically another application and not a human. Any information must be sent as JSON along with the HTTP status code. As discussed in Chapter 30 allows the creation of filters that run in the event of an unhandled exception. Filters can be applied globally, at the controller level, or at the action level. For this application, you are going to build an exception filter to send formatted JSON back (along with the HTTP 500) and include a stack trace if the site is running in debug mode.

■ **Note** Filters are an extremely powerful feature of .NET Core. In this chapter, we are only examining exception filters, but there are many more that can be created that can save significant time when building ASP.NET Core applications. For the full information on filters, refer to the documentation at https://docs.microsoft.com/en-us/aspnet/core/mvc/controllers/filters.

Create the CustomExceptionFilter

Before creating the filter, add the following global using statement to the GlobalUsings.cs file:

```
global using Microsoft.AspNetCore.Mvc.Filters;
```

Create a new directory named Filters, and in that directory add a new class named CustomExceptionFilterAttribute.cs. Change the class to public and inherit from ExceptionFilterAttribute. Override the OnException() method, as shown here:

```
namespace AutoLot.Api.Filters

public class CustomExceptionFilterAttribute : ExceptionFilterAttribute
{
  public override void OnException(ExceptionContext context)
  {
    //implementation goes here
  }
}
```

Unlike most filters in ASP.NET Core that have a before and after event handler, exception filters have only one handler: OnException() (or OnExceptionAsync()). This handler has one parameter, ExceptionContext. This parameter provides access to the ActionContext as well as the exception that was thrown.

Filters also participate in dependency injection, allowing for any item in the container to be accessed in the code. In this example, we need an instance of IWebHostEnvironment injected into the filter. This will be used to determine the runtime environment. If the environment is Development, the response should also include the stack trace. Add a class-level variable to hold the instance of IWebHostEnvironment and add the constructor, as shown here:

```
private readonly IWebHostEnvironment _hostEnvironment;
public CustomExceptionFilterAttribute(IWebHostEnvironment hostEnvironment)
{
  _hostEnvironment = hostEnvironment;
}
```

The code in the OnException() event handler checks the type of exception thrown and builds an appropriate response. If the environment is Development, the stack trace is included in the response message. A dynamic object that contains the values to be sent to the calling request is built and returned in an IActionResult. The updated method is shown here:

```
public override void OnException(ExceptionContext context)
{
  var ex = context.Exception;
  string stackTrace = _hostEnvironment.IsDevelopment() ? context.Exception.StackTrace :
string.Empty;
  string message = ex.Message;
  string error;
  IActionResult actionResult;
  switch (ex)
  {
    case DbUpdateConcurrencyException ce:
      //Returns a 400
      error = "Concurrency Issue.";
      actionResult = new BadRequestObjectResult(
        new {Error = error, Message = message, StackTrace = stackTrace});
      break;
```

```
    default:
      error = "General Error.";
      actionResult = new ObjectResult(
        new {Error = error, Message = message, StackTrace = stackTrace})
      {
        StatusCode = 500
      };
      break;
  }
  //context.ExceptionHandled = true; //If this is uncommented, the exception is swallowed
  context.Result = actionResult;
}
```

If you want the exception filter to swallow the exception and set the response to a 200 (e.g., to log the error but not return it to the client), add the following line before setting the `Result` (commented out in the preceding example):

```
context.ExceptionHandled = true;
```

Finally, add the following global using statement to the `GlobalUsings.cs` file:

```
global using AutoLot.Api.Filters;
```

Apply the Filter

As a reminder, filters can be applied to action methods, controllers, or globally to the application. The *before* code of filters executes from the outside in (global, controller, action method), while the *after* code of filters executes from the inside out (action method, controller, global). For the exception filter, the `OnException()` fires after an action method is executed.

Adding filters at the application level is accomplished in the `AddControllers()` method in the top line statements of the `Program.cs` file. Open the file and update the `AddControllers()` method to the following:

```
builder.Services.AddControllers(config =>
    {
            config.Filters.Add(new CustomExceptionFilterAttribute(builder.Environment));
    })
    .AddJsonOptions(options =>
    {
      //omitted for brevity
    })
    .ConfigureApiBehaviorOptions(options =>
    {
      //omitted for brevity
    });
```

Test the Exception Filter

To test the exception filter, run the application and exercise one of the deprecated `Get()` methods (like `/api/CarDrivers`) using Swagger. The response body in the Swagger UI should match the following output (the stack trace has been omitted in the listing):

```
{
  "Error": "General Error.",
  "Message": "I said not to use this one",
  "StackTrace": "<omitted>"
}
```

Add Cross-Origin Requests Support

APIs should have policies in place that allow or prevent clients that originate from another server to communicate with the API. These types of requests are called *cross-origin requests* (CORS). While this isn't needed when you are running locally on your machine in an all ASP.NET Core world, it is needed by JavaScript frameworks that want to communicate with your API, even when all are running locally.

■ **Note** For more information on CORS support, refer to the document article at `https://docs.microsoft.com/en-us/aspnet/core/security/cors`.

Create a CORS Policy

ASP.NET Core has rich support for configuring cores, including methods to allow/disallow headers, methods, origins, credentials, and more. In this example, we are going to leave everything as wide open as possible. Note that this is definitely not what you want to do with your real applications. Configuration starts by creating a CORS policy and adding the policy into the services collection. The policy is created with a name followed by the rules.

The following example creates a policy named `AllowAll` and then does just that. Add the following code to the top level statements in the `Program.cs` file before the call to `var app = builder.Build()`:

```
builder.Services.AddCors(options =>
{
  options.AddPolicy("AllowAll", builder =>
  {
    builder
        .AllowAnyHeader()
        .AllowAnyMethod()
        .AllowAnyOrigin();
  });
});
```

Add the CORS Policy to the HTTP Pipeline Handling

The final step is to add the CORS policy into the HTTP pipeline handling. Add the following line into the top level statements of the `Program.cs.cs` file, making sure it is after the `app.UseHttpsRedirection ()` method call:

```
app.UseHttpsRedirection();
//Add CORS Policy
app.UseCors("AllowAll");
```

Basic Authentication

Basic authentication is a method for securing HTTPs call using a username and a password. The username and password are concatenated together separated by a colon (`username:password`) and then Base64 encoded. This combination is placed in the Authorization header of the request in the format `Authorization Basic <CominedAndEncodedCredentials>`. It's important to note that the username and password are not encrypted, so calls using basic authentication should always use HTTPs as well as additional security mechanisms like IP address filtering.

There are two main attributes that are in the ASP.NET Core application that this example will use in relation to security. The first is `[Authorize]`, which requires a user to be authenticated in order to access the protected resource. The attribute can be applied at the controller or action level. If applied at the controller level, it is applied to all action methods in the controller.

The next attribute is `[AllowAnonymous]`, which turns off protection for the decorated resource. The attribute can also be applied at the controller or action level. It's important to note that the `AllowAnonymous` attribute always overrides the `Authorize` attribute, even if the `AllowAnonymous` attribute is applied at the controller level and the `Authorize` attribute is applied on an action of that controller.

■ **Note** This section is not meant to provide production ready authorization, but to demonstrate how to add custom authorization into an ASP.NET Core RESTful service. For more information on security, refer to the documentation starting at `https://docs.microsoft.com/en-us/aspnet/core/security/?view=aspnetcore-6.0`.

Add and Configure the Security Information

For this demonstration, we are going to do the least secure thing possible and store the username and password in the `appsettings.Development.json` file. Again, the goal is to show how to add security into the API and not serve as a primer on securing your application. Begin by adding the following section to the settings file:

```
"SecuritySettings": {
  "UserName": "AutoLotUser",
  "Password": "SecretPassword"
}
```

Next, provide a model to use with the Options pattern to get the security information. This model will live in the AutoLot.Services project so it can be shared with the ASP.NET Core web applications. Add a new class named `SecuritySettings`, into the `ViewModels` folder and update the code to match the following:

```
namespace AutoLot.Services.ViewModels;
public class SecuritySettings
{
```

```
  public string UserName { get; set; }
  public string Password { get; set; }
}
```

Add the new namespace to the GlobalUsings.cs file in the AutoLot.Api project:

```
global using AutoLot.Services.ViewModels;
```

Add the following to the top level statements in the Program.cs file in the AutoLot.Api project before the call to builder.Build():

```
builder.Services.Configure<SecuritySettings>(builder.Configuration.GetSection(nameof(Security
Settings)));
```

Before building the basic authentication handler, add the following global using statements to the GlobalUsings.cs file:

```
global using Microsoft.AspNetCore.Authentication;
global using Microsoft.AspNetCore.Authorization;
global using System.Net.Http.Headers;
global using System.Security.Claims;
global using System.Text;
global using System.Text.Encodings.Web;
```

The rest of the work in this chapter takes place in the AutoLot.Api project.

Build the Basic Authentication Handler

To build the basic authentication handler, begin by creating a new folder named Security. In that folder, create a new public class named BasicAuthenticationHandler.cs that inherits from AuthenticationHandl er<AuthenticationSchemeOptions>, like this:

```
namespace AutoLot.Api.Security;
public class BasicAuthenticationHandler : AuthenticationHandler<AuthenticationSchemeOptions>
{
  public BasicAuthenticationHandler(
    IOptionsMonitor<AuthenticationSchemeOptions> options,
    ILoggerFactory logger,
    UrlEncoder encoder,
    ISystemClock clock) : base(options, logger, encoder, clock)
 {
 }

  protected override async Task<AuthenticateResult> HandleAuthenticateAsync()
  {
    //implementation goes here
    throw new NotImplementedException();
  }
}
```

Next, update the required constructor to take the IOptionsMonitor for the application's SecuritySettings. Assign the SecuritySettings value to a class level variable:

```
private readonly SecuritySettings _securitySettings;

public BasicAuthenticationHandler(
        IOptionsMonitor<AuthenticationSchemeOptions> options,
        ILoggerFactory logger,
        UrlEncoder encoder,
        ISystemClock clock,
        IOptionsMonitor<SecuritySettings> securitySettingsMonitor)
        : base(options, logger, encoder, clock)
{
  _securitySettings = securitySettingsMonitor.CurrentValue;
}
```

There is one method that needs to be overridden, HandleAuthenticateAsync(). The first step is to check for the AllowAnonymous attribute, and if located, return an AuthenticateResult.NoResult(), which effectively allows access.

```
protected override async Task<AuthenticateResult> HandleAuthenticateAsync()
{
  // skip authentication if endpoint has [AllowAnonymous] attribute
  var endpoint = Context.GetEndpoint();
  if (endpoint?.Metadata?.GetMetadata<IAllowAnonymous>() != null)
  {
    return AuthenticateResult.NoResult();
  }
}
```

Next, check for the Authorization header key, and if not found, fail the authentication:

```
protected override async Task<AuthenticateResult> HandleAuthenticateAsync()
{
  // omitted for brevity

  if (!Request.Headers.ContainsKey("Authorization"))
  {
    return AuthenticateResult.Fail("Missing Authorization Header");
  }
}
```

The remainder of the method is listed here, with explanation to follow

```
try
{
  AuthenticationHeaderValue authHeader = AuthenticationHeaderValue.Parse(Request.
Headers["Authorization"]);
  byte[] credentialBytes = Convert.FromBase64String(authHeader.Parameter);
  string[] credentials = Encoding.UTF8.GetString(credentialBytes).Split(new[] { ':' }, 2);
  string userName = credentials[0];
```

```
    string password = credentials[1];
    if (userName.Equals(_securitySettings.UserName, StringComparison.OrdinalIgnoreCase) &&
       password.Equals(_securitySettings.Password, StringComparison.OrdinalIgnoreCase))
    {
      var claims = new[] {
          new Claim(ClaimTypes.NameIdentifier, userName),
          new Claim(ClaimTypes.Name, userName),
      };
      var identity = new ClaimsIdentity(claims, Scheme.Name);
      var principal = new ClaimsPrincipal(identity);
      var ticket = new AuthenticationTicket(principal, Scheme.Name);
      return AuthenticateResult.Success(ticket);
    }
    return AuthenticateResult.Fail("Invalid Authorization Header");
  }
  catch
  {
    return AuthenticateResult.Fail("Invalid Authorization Header");
  }
```

The first step is to parse the header for the `Authorization` attribute. If this succeeds, the parameter is changed back into plain text from the Base64 encoding, which, if the value is properly formatted, will yield a string in the format of `username:password`.

Next, the username and password are compared to the values in the settings file, and if they match, a new `ClaimsPrincipal` is created. The authorization process reports success, effectively logging in the new user.

If the username and password don't match, or if an exception occurs anywhere along the way, authentication fails.

The final step is to add the new namespace to the global using statements in `GlobalUsings.cs`:

```
global using AutoLot.Api.Security;
```

Register the Basic Authentication Handler and Secure the Controllers

The final steps are to register the handler, opt-in to authentication, and secure the controllers. Begin by adding the following to the `IServiceCollection` in the top level statements in Program.cs:

```
builder.Services.AddAuthentication("BasicAuthentication")
    .AddScheme<AuthenticationSchemeOptions, BasicAuthenticationHandler>("BasicAuthentication",
null);
```

Next, opt-in to authentication for the application:

```
//enable authorization checks
app.UseAuthentication();
app.UseAuthorization();
```

The final step is to add the Authorize to the BaseCrudController, which will secure all of the derived controllers as well:

```
[ApiController]
[Route("api/[controller]")]
[Route("api/v{version:apiVersion}/[controller]")]
[Authorize]
public abstract class BaseCrudController<TEntity, TController> : ControllerBase
    where TEntity : BaseEntity, new()
    where TController : class
{
}
```

As an alternative, you can set every controller to require authorization unless they are decorated with the [AllowAnonymous] attribute. There are a few ways to do this. The easiest way is to add the RequireAuthorization() method to the MapControllers() method:

```
app.MapControllers().RequireAuthorization();
```

If you need more control, you can create a policy, and add it as an Authorization policy. The following example creates an authorization policy that requires all calls to be authorized (unless the [AllowAnonymous] attribute is present):

```
builder.Services.AddControllers(config =>
    {
      config.Filters.Add(new CustomExceptionFilterAttribute(builder.Environment));
      var policy = new AuthorizationPolicyBuilder()
         .RequireAuthenticatedUser()
         .Build();
      config.Filters.Add(new AuthorizeFilter(policy));
    })
    .AddJsonOptions(options =>
    {
      //omitted for brevity
    })
    .ConfigureApiBehaviorOptions(options =>
    {
      //omitted for brevity
    });
```

Add the following global using statement to the GlobalUsings.cs file:

```
using Microsoft.AspNetCore.Mvc.Authorization;
```

In order to allow anonymous access to the WeatherController and the two ValuesControllers, you must add the [AllowAnonymous] attribute to those controllers:

```
//WeatherForecastController.cs
[ApiVersionNeutral]
[ApiController]
[Route("[controller]")]
```

```
[AllowAnonymous]
public class WeatherForecastController : ControllerBase
{
  //omitted for brevity
}

//ValuesController.cs
[ApiVersion("0.5", Deprecated = true)]
[ApiVersion("1.0")]
[ApiController]
[Route("api/[controller]")]
[Route("api/v{version:apiVersion}/[controller]")]
[AllowAnonymous]
public class ValuesController : ControllerBase
{
  //omitted for brevity
}

//Values2Controller.cs
[ApiVersion("2.0")]
[ApiVersion("2.0-Beta")]
[ApiController]
[Route("api/[controller]")]
[Route("api/v{version:apiVersion}/[controller]")]
[AllowAnonymous]
public class Values2Controller : ControllerBase
{
  //omitted for brevity
}
```

In order to test the new security, run the application, and click on the Authorize button, and enter the credentials (AutoLotUser, SecretPassword) as shown in Figure 32-11. Click Close, and then try one of the secured endpoints.

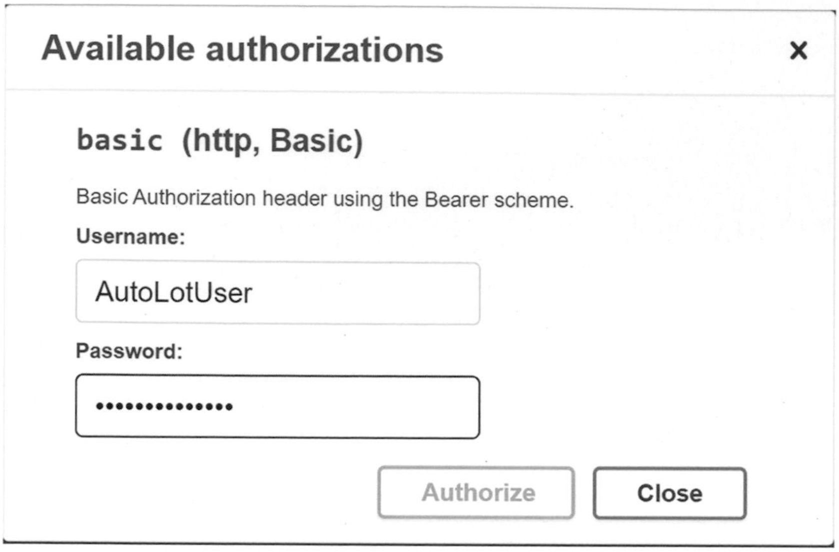

Figure 32-11. *The Swagger Authorize dialog*

Summary

This chapter continued our study of ASP.NET Core. We first learned about returning JSON from action methods and configuration of the JSON format. We then we looked at the `ApiController` attribute and the effect it has on API controllers. Next, versioning was added to the application, and the general Swashbuckle implementation was updated to include the application's XML documentation, additional information from action method attributes, and the support API Versions.

Next, the base controller was built, which holds most of the functionality of the application. After that, the derived, entity-specific controllers were added into the project. With the controllers in place, the application-wide exception filter was created and added to the filter collection, support for cross-origin requests was enabled, and finally, basic authentication was added into the application.

In the next chapter, Web Applications using MVC, you will go back to the ASP.NET Core web application using the MVC pattern that was started in Chapter 30.

CHAPTER 33

Web Applications with MVC

Chapter 30 introduced ASP.NET Core and many of the features common across all ASP.NET Core applications. This chapter covers areas, the user interface capabilities of ASP.NET Core, view components, managing client side libraries, and completes the AutoLot.Mvc web application. The chapter starts by putting the *V* back into MVC.

Note The sample code for this chapter is in the `Chapter 33` directory of this book's repo. Feel free to continue working with the solution you started in the previous ASP.NET Core chapters.

Introducing the "V" in ASP.NET Core

When building ASP.NET Core services, only the *M* (models) and the *C* (controllers) of the MVC pattern are used. The user interface is created using the *V*, or the views of the MVC pattern. Views are built using HTML, JavaScript, CSS, and Razor code. They optionally have a base layout view and are rendered from a controller action method or a view component. If you have worked in classic ASP.NET MVC, this should sound familiar.

ViewResults and Action Methods

As mentioned briefly in Chapter 30, `ViewResults` and `PartialView` results are `ActionResults` that are returned from an action method using the `Controller` helper methods. A `PartialViewResult` is designed to be rendered inside another view and doesn't use a layout view, while a `ViewResult` is typically rendered in conjunction with a layout view.

The convention in ASP.NET Core (as it was in ASP.NET MVC) is for the `View` or `PartialView` to render a `*.cshtml` file of the same name as the method. The view is expected to be located either in a folder named for the controller (less the controller suffix) or in the `Shared` folder (both located under the parent `Views` folder). For example, the following code will render the `SampleAction.cshtml` view located in the `Views\Sample` or `Views\Shared` folder:

```
[Route("[controller]/[action]")]
//Controller name is the main folder under the Views folder
public class SampleController: Controller
{
  //Action name is the default name for the view under the controller's folder
  public ActionResult SampleAction()
```


A. Troelsen and P. Japikse, *Pro C# 10 with .NET 6*, https://doi.org/10.1007/978-1-4842-7869-7_33

```
  {
    return View();
  }
}
```

■ **Note** This chapter uses Windows based directory separators (\). If you are using a non-Windows machine, use the appropriate directory separator for your operating system.

The view folder named after the controller is searched first. If the view cannot be found, the Shared folder is searched. If it still can't be found, an exception is thrown

To render a view with a name that is different than the action method name, pass in the name of the file (without the cshtml extension). The following code will render the CustomViewName.cshtml view:

```
public ActionResult SampleAction()
{
  return View("CustomViewName");
}
```

The final two overloads are for passing in a data object that becomes the model for the view. The first example uses the default view name, and the second example specifies a different view name.

```
public ActionResult SampleAction()
{
  var sampleModel = new SampleViewModel();
  return View(sampleModel);
}
public ActionResult SampleAction()
{
  var sampleModel = new SampleViewModel();
  return View("CustomViewName",sampleModel);
}
```

When a view isn't found for an action method, the behavior depends on the error handling configuration in the top level statements in the Program.cs file. When using the developer exception page, a lot of information is passed to the browser. To see this in action, open the HomeController and add a new action method as follows:

```
[HttpGet]
Public async Task<IActionResult> RazorSyntaxAsync()
{
  return View();
}
```

The action method is decorated with the [HTTPGet] attribute to set this method as the application endpoint for the /Home/RazorSyntax route (remember that the Async suffix is removed by the routing engine) as long as the request is an HTTP Get. The method returns a ViewResult using the View method. Since a view wasn't named, ASP.NET Core will look for a view named RazorSyntax.cshtml in the Views\Home directory or the Views\Shared directory. If the view it isn't found in either location, an exception will be returned to the client (browser).

Make sure the `UseApi` flag in the `appsettings.Development.json` file is set to `false`, then run the application and navigate to `https://localhost:5001/Home/RazorSyntax` URL to see the developer exception page as shown in Figure 33-1:

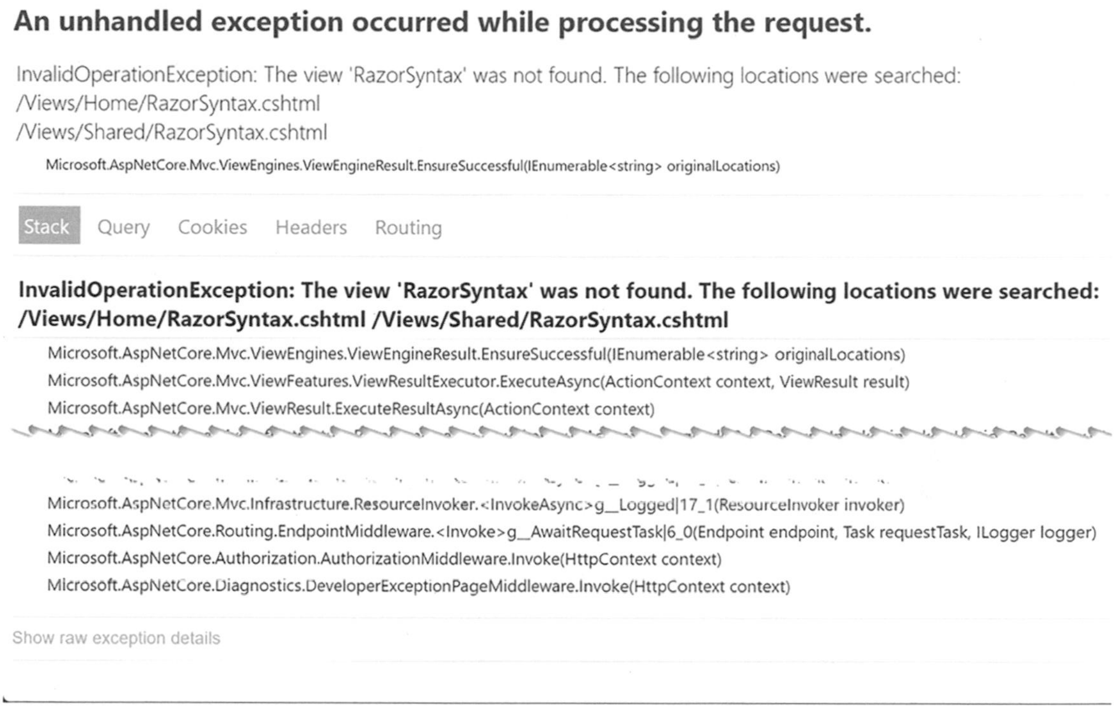

An unhandled exception occurred while processing the request.

InvalidOperationException: The view 'RazorSyntax' was not found. The following locations were searched:
/Views/Home/RazorSyntax.cshtml
/Views/Shared/RazorSyntax.cshtml

Microsoft.AspNetCore.Mvc.ViewEngines.ViewEngineResult.EnsureSuccessful(IEnumerable<string> originalLocations)

Stack Query Cookies Headers Routing

InvalidOperationException: The view 'RazorSyntax' was not found. The following locations were searched: /Views/Home/RazorSyntax.cshtml /Views/Shared/RazorSyntax.cshtml

Microsoft.AspNetCore.Mvc.ViewEngines.ViewEngineResult.EnsureSuccessful(IEnumerable<string> originalLocations)
Microsoft.AspNetCore.Mvc.ViewFeatures.ViewResultExecutor.ExecuteAsync(ActionContext context, ViewResult result)
Microsoft.AspNetCore.Mvc.ViewResult.ExecuteResultAsync(ActionContext context)

Microsoft.AspNetCore.Mvc.Infrastructure.ResourceInvoker.<InvokeAsync>g__Logged|17_1(ResourceInvoker invoker)
Microsoft.AspNetCore.Routing.EndpointMiddleware.<Invoke>g__AwaitRequestTask|6_0(Endpoint endpoint, Task requestTask, ILogger logger)
Microsoft.AspNetCore.Authorization.AuthorizationMiddleware.Invoke(HttpContext context)
Microsoft.AspNetCore.Diagnostics.DeveloperExceptionPageMiddleware.Invoke(HttpContext context)

Show raw exception details

Figure 33-1. *Error messaging from the developer exception page*

■ **Note** The sample URLs in this chapter all use Kestrel and port 5001. If you are using Visual Studio with IIS Express, use the URL from the `launchsettings.json` profile for IIS.

The developer exception page provides ample information to debug your application, including raw exception details complete with the stack trace. Now, comment out that line in the top level statements in the `Program.cs` file, replacing it with the "standard" error handler, like this:

```
if (app.Environment.IsDevelopment())
{
  //app.UseDeveloperExceptionPage();
  app.UseExceptionHandler("/Home/Error");
...
}
```

Run the app again and navigate to `http://localhost:5001/Home/RazorSyntax`, and you will see the standard error page, as shown in Figure 33-2.

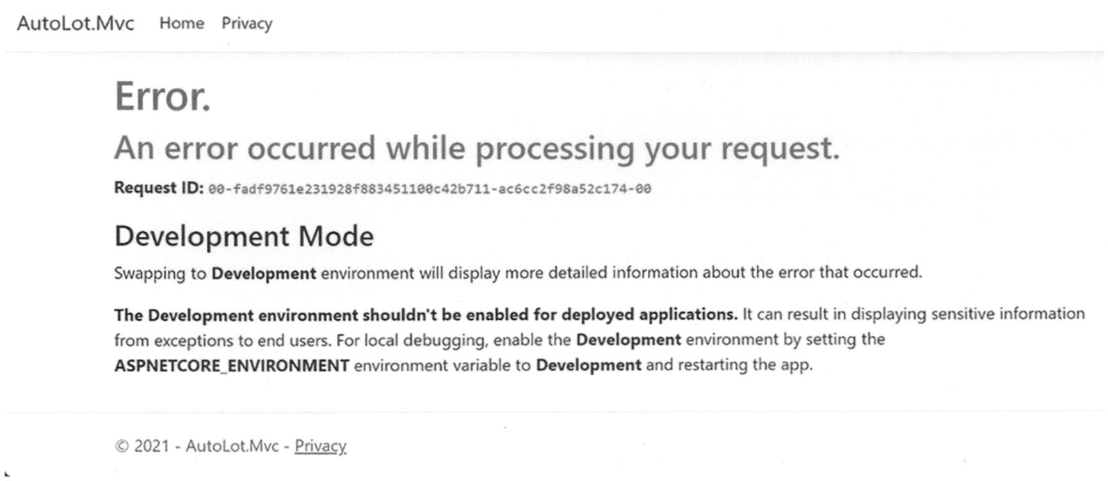

AutoLot.Mvc Home Privacy

Error.

An error occurred while processing your request.

Request ID: 00-fadf9761e231928f883451100c42b711-ac6cc2f98a52c174-00

Development Mode

Swapping to **Development** environment will display more detailed information about the error that occurred.

The Development environment shouldn't be enabled for deployed applications. It can result in displaying sensitive information from exceptions to end users. For local debugging, enable the **Development** environment by setting the **ASPNETCORE_ENVIRONMENT** environment variable to **Development** and restarting the app.

© 2021 - AutoLot.Mvc - Privacy

Figure 33-2. *Error messaging from the standard error page*

The standard error handler redirects errors to the HomeController's Error action method:

```
[ResponseCache(Duration = 0, Location = ResponseCacheLocation.None, NoStore = true)]
public IActionResult Error()
{
  return View(new ErrorViewModel { RequestId = Activity.Current?.Id ?? HttpContext.
TraceIdentifier });
}
```

If you examine the \Views\Home directory, you will see there isn't a view named Error.cshtml. This view is located in the \Views\Shared directory. If you want to customize the view, update the contents of the view.

Remember to return the Configure() method to use the developer exception page when finished experimenting with the error process:

```
if (app.Environment.IsDevelopment())
{
  app.UseDeveloperExceptionPage();
...
}
```

For more information on customizing error handling and additional options available, consult the documentation: https://docs.microsoft.com/en-us/aspnet/core/fundamentals/error-handling?view=aspnetcore-6.0.

The Razor View Engine and Razor Syntax

The Razor View Engine was designed as an improvement over the Web Forms View Engine and uses Razor as the core language. Razor is server-side code that is embedded into a view, is based on C#, and has corrected many annoyances with the Web Forms View Engine. The incorporation of Razor into HTML and CSS results in code that is much cleaner and easier to read than using the Web Forms View Engine syntax.

To get started, add a new view by right-clicking the Views\Home folder in the AutoLot.Mvc project and selecting Add ➤ View. Select Razor View – Empty from the Add New Scaffolded Item dialog and name the view RazorSyntax.cshtml.

Razor views are typically strongly typed by using the @model directive (note the lowercase *m*). Update the type of the new view to the Car entity by adding the following at the top of the view:

```
@model AutoLot.Models.Entities.Car
```

HTML, CSS, JavaScript, and Razor all work together in Razor view. Start by adding an <h1> tag to the top of the page to add a header:

```
<h1>Razor Syntax</h1>
```

Razor statement blocks open with an @ symbol and either are self-contained statements (like foreach) or are enclosed in braces, like the following examples:

```
@for (int i = 0; i < 15; i++)
{
    //do something
}

@{
    //Code Block
    var foo = "Foo";
    var bar = "Bar";
    var htmlString = "<ul><li>one</li><li>two</li></ul>";
}
```

To output the value of a variable to the view, just use the @ sign with the variable name. This is equivalent to Response.Write(). Notice that there isn't a closing semicolon after the statement when outputting directly to the browser.

```
@foo<br />
@htmlString<br />
@foo.@bar<br />
```

The previous example (@foo.@bar) combined two variables with a period (.) between them. This is not the usual C# "dot" notation of navigating a property chain. It's just two variables' output to the response stream with a physical period between them. If you need to "dot" your way down a variable, use the @ on the variable, and then write your code as normal.

```
@foo.ToUpper()<br/>
```

If you want to output raw HTML, you use what's referred to as an *HTML helper*. These are helpers built into the Razor View Engine. Here is the line to output the raw HTML:

```
@Html.Raw(htmlString)<br/>
<hr />
```

Code blocks can intermix markup and code. Lines that begin with markup are interpreted as HTML, while all other lines are interpreted as code. If a line starts with text that is *not* code, you must use the content indicator (@:) or the <text></text> content block indicator. Note that lines can transition back and forth. Here is an example:

```
@{
    @:Straight Text
    <div>Value:@Model.Id</div>
    <text>
        Lines without HTML tag
    </text>
    <br />
}
<hr/>
```

If you want to escape the @ sign, use a double @. Razor is also smart enough to handle email addresses, so they do not need to be escaped. If you need Razor to treat an @ sign like the Razor token, add parentheses.

```
Email Address Handling:<br/>
foo@foo.com<br />
@@foo<br />
test@foo<br/>
test@(foo)<br />
```

The preceding code outputs foo@foo.com, @foo, test@foo, and testFoo, respectively.

Razor comments are opened with @* and closed with *@.

```
@*
    Multiline Comments
    Hi.
*@
```

Razor supports inline functions as well. The following example function sorts a list of strings:

```
@functions {
    public static IList<string> SortList(IList<string> strings)  {
        var list = from s in strings orderby s select s;
        return list.ToList();
    }
}
```

The following code creates a list of strings, sorts them using the SortList() function, and then outputs the sorted list to the browser:

```
@{
    var myList = new List<string> {"C", "A", "Z", "F"};
    var sortedList = SortList(myList);
}
```

```
@foreach (string s in sortedList)
{
    @s@: 
}
<hr/>
```

Here is another example, which creates a delegate that can be used to set a string to bold:

```
@{
    Func<dynamic, object> b = @<strong>@item</strong>;
}
This will be bold: @b("Foo")
```

Razor also contains HTML helpers, which are methods supplied by ASP.NET Core. Two examples are `DisplayForModel()` and `EditorForModel()`. The former uses reflection on the view's model to display in the web page. The latter also uses reflection to create the HTML for an edit form (note that it does not supply the `Form` tags, just the markup for the model). HTML helpers will be examined in detail later in this chapter.

Finally, new in ASP.NET Core are tag helpers. Tag helpers combine markup and code and are covered later in this chapter.

Views

Views are special code files with a `cshtml` extension, written using a combination of HTML markup, CSS, JavaScript, and Razor syntax.

The Views Directory

The `Views` folder is where views are stored in ASP.NET Core projects using the MVC pattern. In the root of the `Views` folder, there are two files: `_ViewStart.cshtml` and `_ViewImports.cshtml`.

The `_ViewStart.cshtml` executes its code before any other view is rendered (excluding partial views and layouts). The file is generally used to set the default layout for views that don't specify one. Layouts are discussed in greater detail in the "Layouts" section. The `_ViewStart.cshtml` file is shown here:

```
@{
    Layout = "_Layout";
}
```

The `_ViewImports.cshtml` file is used for importing shared directives, like `@using` statements. The contents apply to all views in the same directory or subdirectory of the `_ViewImports` file. This file is the view equivalent of a `GlobalUsings.cs` file for C# code. Add a `@using` statement for the `AutoLot.Models.Entities`.

```
@using AutoLot.Mvc
@using AutoLot.Mvc.Models
@using AutoLot.Models.Entities
@addTagHelper *, Microsoft.AspNetCore.Mvc.TagHelpers
```

The `@addTagHelper` line will be covered along with tag helpers.

■ **Note** Why the leading underscore for `_ViewStart.html`, `_ViewImports.cshtml`, and `_Layout.cshtml`? The Razor View Engine was originally created for WebMatrix, which would not allow any file that starts with an underscore to be rendered directly. All core files (like layout and configuration files) had names that began with an underscore. This is not a convention that MVC cares about, since MVC doesn't have the same issue as WebMatrix, but the underscore legacy lives on anyway.

As mentioned, each controller gets its own directory under the `Views` folder where its specific views are stored. The names match the name of the controller (minus the word *Controller*). For example, the `Views\Cars` directory holds all the views for the `CarsController`. The views are typically named after the action methods that renders them, although the names can be changed, as shown earlier.

The Shared Directory

There is special directory under `Views` named `Shared`. This directory holds views that are available to all controllers and actions. As mentioned, if a requested view file can't be found in the controller-specific directory, the shared folder is searched.

The DisplayTemplates Folder

The `DisplayTemplates` folder holds custom templates that control how types are rendered and facilitate code reuse and display consistency. When the `DisplayFor()/DisplayForModel()` methods are called, the Razor View Engine looks for a template named the same as the type being rendered, for example, `Car.cshtml` for a `Car` class. If a custom template can't be located, the markup is rendered using reflection. The search path starts in the `Views\{CurrentControllerName}\DisplayTemplates` folder and, if it's not found, then it looks in the `Views\Shared\DisplayTemplates` folder. Display templates don't have to match the name of the class. If the template and class names aren't the same, the name of the templates must be passed into the `DisplayFor()/DisplayForModel()` methods.

■ **Note** The `DisplayFor()/DisplayForModel()` methods will be covered in depth later in this chapter. For now, know that the `DisplayFor()` method takes an expression to display a property on the model the view is bound typed to. The `DisplayForModel()` method displays the entire model.

The DateTime Display Template

Create a new folder named `DisplayTemplates` under the `Views\Shared` folder. Add a new view named `DateTime.cshtml` into that folder. Clear out all of the generated code and comments and replace them with the following:

```
@model DateTime?
@if (Model == null)
{
  @:Unknown
}
```

```
else
{
  if (ViewData.ModelMetadata.IsNullableValueType)
  {
    @:@(Model.Value.ToString("d"))
  }
  else
  {
    @:@(((DateTime)Model).ToString("d"))
  }
}
```

Note that the @model directive that strongly types the view uses a lowercase m. When referring to the assigned value of the model in Razor, an uppercase M is used. In this example, the model definition is nullable. If the value for the model passed into the view is null, the template displays the word Unknown. Otherwise, it displays the date in Short Date format, using the Value property of a nullable type or the actual model itself.

The Car Display Template

Create a new directory named Cars under the Views directory, and add a directory named DisplayTemplates under the Cars directory. Add a new view named Car.cshtml into that folder. Clear out all of the generated code and comments and replace them with the following code, which displays a Car entity:

```
@model AutoLot.Models.Entities.Car
<dl class="row">
  <dt class="col-sm-2">
    @Html.DisplayNameFor(model => model.MakeId)
  </dt>
  <dd class="col-sm-10">
    @Html.DisplayFor(model => model.MakeNavigation.Name)
  </dd>
  <dt class="col-sm-2">
    @Html.DisplayNameFor(model => model.Color)
  </dt>
  <dd class="col-sm-10">
    @Html.DisplayFor(model => model.Color)
  </dd>
  <dt class="col-sm-2">
    @Html.DisplayNameFor(model => model.PetName)
  </dt>
  <dd class="col-sm-10">
    @Html.DisplayFor(model => model.PetName)
  </dd>
  <dt class="col-sm-2">
    @Html.DisplayNameFor(model => model.Price)
  </dt>
  <dd class="col-sm-10">
    @Html.DisplayFor(model => model.Price)
  </dd>
```

```
  <dt class="col-sm-2">
    @Html.DisplayNameFor(model => model.DateBuilt)
  </dt>
  <dd class="col-sm-10">
    @Html.DisplayFor(model => model.DateBuilt)
  </dd>
  <dt class="col-sm-2">
    @Html.DisplayNameFor(model => model.IsDrivable)
  </dt>
  <dd class="col-sm-10">
    @Html.DisplayFor(model => model.IsDrivable)
  </dd>
</dl>
```

The DisplayNameFor() HTML helper displays the name of the property unless the property is decorated with either the Display(Name="") or DisplayName("") attribute, in which case the display value is used. The DisplayFor() method displays the value for the model's property specified in the expression. Notice that the navigation property for MakeNavigation is being used to get the make name.

The Car with Color Display Template

Copy the Car.cshtml view to another view named CarWithColors.cshtml in the Cars\DisplayTemplates directory. The difference is that this template changes the color of the *Color* text based on the model's Color property value. Update the new template's <dd> tag for Color to the following:

```
<dd class="col-sm-10" style="color:@Model.Color">
  @Html.DisplayFor(model => model.Color)
</dd>
```

To use this template instead of the Car.cshtml template, call DisplayForModel() with the name of the template (note the location rules still apply).

```
@Html.DisplayForModel("CarWithColors")
```

The EditorTemplates Folder

The EditorTemplates folder works the same as the DisplayTemplates folder, except the templates arc used for editing.

The Car Edit Template

Create a new directory named EditorTemplates under the Views\Cars directory. Add a new view named Car.cshtml into that folder. Clear out all of the generated code and comments and replace them with the following code, which represents the markup to edit a Car entity:

```
@model Car
<div asp-validation-summary="All" class="text-danger"></div>
<div>
    <label asp-for="MakeId" class="col-form-label"></label>
```

```
    <select asp-for="MakeId" class="form-control" asp-items="@ViewBag.
    LookupValues"></select>
    <span asp-validation-for="MakeId" class="text-danger"></span>
</div>
<div>
    <label asp-for="Color" class="col-form-label"></label>
    <input asp-for="Color" class="form-control"/>
    <span asp-validation-for="Color" class="text-danger"></span>
</div>
<div>
    <label asp-for="PetName" class="col-form-label"></label>
    <input asp-for="PetName" class="form-control" />
    <span asp-validation-for="PetName" class="text-danger"></span>
</div>
<div>
    <label asp-for="Price" class="col-form-label"></label>
    <input asp-for="Price" class="form-control"/>
    <span asp-validation-for="Price" class="text-danger"></span>
</div>
<div>
    <label asp-for="DateBuilt" class="col-form-label"></label>
    <input asp-for="DateBuilt" class="form-control"/>
    <span asp-validation-for="DateBuilt" class="text-danger"></span>
</div>
<div>
    <label asp-for="IsDrivable" class="col-form-label"></label>
    <input asp-for="IsDrivable" />
    <span asp-validation-for="IsDrivable" class="text-danger"></span>
</div>
```

The editor template uses several tag helpers (asp-for, asp-items, asp-validation-for, and asp-validation-summary). These will be covered later in this chapter.

Editor templates are invoked with the EditorFor()/EditorForModel() HTML helpers. Like the display templates, these methods will look for a view named after the type being displayed (e.g. Car.cshtml) or the view name passed into the method.

View CSS Isolation

CSS isolation is a new feature in ASP.NET Core 6 that enables view specific CSS files. As an example, the default template creates a _Layout.cshtml.css file along with the _Layout.cshtml file. The CSS contained in the _Layout.cshtml.css and any CSS in a view specific file (e.g. Index.cshtml.css) get combined into a file named {assembly_name}.styles.css. This is loaded into the rendered content that is sent to the browser. If you examine the site.css file in the wwwroot\css directory, you will notice it is very small. Most of the default CSS has been moved into the _Layout.cshtml.css file in the ASP.NET Core 6 templates.

Next, right click on the \Views\Home directory, and select Add ➤ New Item, navigate to ASP.NET Core/Web/Content in the left rail, and select Style Sheet and name it Index.cshtml.css. Update the content to the following:

```
h1 {
   background-color: blue;
}
```

When you run the application, you will see the background for the Welcome text on the home page has a blue background. Now navigate to the Privacy page by clicking on the link in the menu, and you will see that the heading does not have a blue background.

When you examine the sources in the developer tools, you will see the `site.css` file (in the `css` folder) and `AutoLot.Mvc.Styles.css`, which combines the CSS from the `_Layout.cshtml.css` and the `Index.cshtml.css` view, in the root. Open the combined file, and you will see that all of the CSS selectors are decorated with attribute selectors. Each file adds a generated attribute selector into the CSS it defines. For example, the CSS for the `Index.cshtml.css` file is listed here:

```
h1[b-7wgwza0zra] {
    background-color: blue;
}
```

These attributes are used to mark the elements contained within the scope of that CSS file. If you examine the elements, and navigate to the `<h1>` tag from the `Index` view, you will see the attribute on the generated HTML:

```
<h1 b-7wgwza0zra="" class="display-4">Welcome</h1>
```

This new feature allows very fine-grained control over the CSS in your site while still supporting general CSS in the `site.css` file.

One important caveat is that the `{assembly_name}.styles.css` file is only generated when running in Development or when the site is published. If you want to change the environment (e.g., through `launchSettings.json` file) when debugging, you must opt-in to using static web assets, like this (in the `Program.cs` file):

```
//Enable CSS isolation in a non-deployed session
if (!builder.Environment.IsDevelopment())
{
    builder.WebHost.UseWebRoot("wwwroot");
    builder.WebHost.UseStaticWebAssets();
}
```

Layouts

Similar to Web Forms master pages, MVC supports layouts that are shared among views to give the pages of the site a consistent look and feel. Navigate to the `Views\Shared` folder and open the `_Layout.cshtml` file. It is a full-fledged HTML file, complete with `<head>` and `<body>` tags. This file is the foundation that other views are rendered into. Layouts contain the navigation and any header and/or footer markup allowing views to be kept small, simple, and focused.

Scroll down in the file until you see the following line of Razor code:

```
@RenderBody()
```

That line instructs the layout page where to render the view. Now scroll down to the line just before the closing `</body>` tag. The following line creates a new section for the layout and makes it optional:

```
@await RenderSectionAsync("scripts", required: false)
```

Sections can also be marked as `required` by passing in `true` as the second parameter. They can also be rendered synchronously, like this:

```
@RenderSection("Header",true)
```

Any code and/or markup in a view file's `@section` block will not be rendered with the `@RenderBody()` call, but in the location of the layout's section definition. For example, presume you have a view with the following section implementation:

```
@section Scripts {
  <script src="~/lib/jquery-validation/dist/jquery.validate.js"></script>
}
```

The code from the view gets rendered to the layout in place of the section definition. If the layout has this definition:

```
<script src="~/lib/jquery/dist/jquery.min.js"></script>
<script src="~/lib/bootstrap/dist/js/bootstrap.bundle.min.js"></script>
<script src="~/js/site.js" asp-append-version="true"></script>
@await RenderSectionAsync("Scripts", required: false)
```

then the view's section gets added, resulting in this markup being sent to the browser:

```
<script src="~/lib/jquery/dist/jquery.min.js"></script>
<script src="~/lib/bootstrap/dist/js/bootstrap.bundle.min.js"></script>
<script src="~/js/site.js" asp-append-version="true"></script>
<script src="~/lib/jquery-validation/dist/jquery.validate.js"></script>
```

Two new options in ASP.NET Core are `@IgnoreBody()` and `@IgnoreSection()`. These methods, placed in a layout, will respectively not render the body of the view or a specific section. These enable turning features of a view on or off from the layout based on conditional logic, such as security levels.

The `asp-append-version` attribute is a tag helper, which will be covered later in this chapter.

Specifying the Layout for a View

To specify the layout for a view, add the following Razor block to the top of a view:

```
@{
    Layout = "_MyCustomLayout";
}
```

If a view doesn't have a layout specifically defined, the view will look for a `_ViewStart.cshtml` file in the same directory as the view. If one doesn't exist in the same directory, each directory above the current location is searched until one is found, using the first `_ViewStart.cshtml` file is located (whether or not a `Layout` is defined). If one isn't found, no layout is used, essentially rendering a partial view.

Partial Views

Partial views are conceptually similar to a user control in Web Forms. Partial views are useful for encapsulating UI, which helps to reduce repeated code and/or markup. A partial view does not use a layout and is injected into another view or is rendered with a view component (covered later in this chapter).

To render a view as a partial view from a controller's action method, use the `PartialView()` method instead of the `View()` method. For example, update the `HomeController Index()` action method to the following:

```
public IActionResult Index([FromServices] IOptionsMonitor<DealerInfo> dealerMonitor)
{
  //_logger.LogAppError("Test error");
  var vm = dealerMonitor.CurrentValue;
  return PartialView(vm);
}
```

When you run the app, you will see the content of the view, but none of the layout (menu, header, footer, etc.). Be sure to return the `Index()` method back to using the `View()` method.

Partial views can also be rendered from a view using the `<partial>` tag helper, which will be demonstrated in the next section.

Split the Layout into Partials

Sometimes layout files can become large and unwieldy. One technique to manage this is to split up the layout into a set of focused partials. You will also want to update the CSS and JavaScript referenced to current versions, as the client libraries that ship with the templates are typically a minor version or two behind. The next section will create the partials, the CSS and JavaScript libraries will be updated later in this chapter.

Create the Partials

Create a new folder named `Partials` under the `Shared` folder. Create three empty views named `_Head.cshtml`, `_JavaScriptFiles.cshtml`, and `_Menu.cshtml`.

The Head Partial

Cut the content in the layout that is between the `<head></head>` tags and paste it into the `_Head.cshtml` file.

```
<meta charset="utf-8" />
<meta name="viewport" content="width=device-width, initial-scale=1.0" />
<title>@ViewData["Title"] - AutoLot.Mvc</title>
<link rel="stylesheet" href="~/lib/bootstrap/dist/css/bootstrap.min.css" />
<link rel="stylesheet" href="~/css/site.css" />
<link rel="stylesheet" href="~/AutoLot.Mvc.styles.css" asp-append-version="true" />
```

In `_Layout.cshtml`, replace the deleted markup with the call to render the new partial:

```
<head>
  <partial name="Partials/_Head"/>
</head>
```

The <partial> tag is another example of a tag helper. The name attribute is the name of the partial with the path starting at the view's current directory (omitting the .cshtml extension), which in this case is Views\Shared.

The Menu Partial

For the menu partial, cut all the markup between the <header></header> tags (not the <head></head> tags) and paste it into the _Menu.cshtml file. Update the _Layout to render the Menu partial.

```
<header>
  <partial name="Partials/_Menu"/>
</header>
```

The JavaScript Files Partial

The final step at this time is to cut out the <script> tags for the JavaScript files and paste them into the JavaScriptFiles partial. Make sure to leave the RenderSection tag in place. Here is the JavaScriptFiles partial:

```
<script src="~/lib/jquery/dist/jquery.min.js"></script>
<script src="~/lib/bootstrap/dist/js/bootstrap.bundle.min.js"></script>
<script src="~/js/site.js" asp-append-version="true"></script>
```

Here is the current markup for the _Layout.cshtml file:

```
<!DOCTYPE html>
<html lang="en">
<head>
  <partial name="Partials/_Head" />
</head>
<body>
  <header>
    <partial name="Partials/_Menu" />
  </header>
  <div class="container">
    <main role="main" class="pb-3">
      @RenderBody()
    </main>
  </div>

  <footer class="border-top footer text-muted">
    <div class="container">
      &copy; 2021 - AutoLot.Mvc - <a asp-area="" asp-controller="Home" asp-
      action="Privacy">Privacy</a>
    </div>
  </footer>
  <partial name="Partials/_JavaScriptFiles" />
  @await RenderSectionAsync("Scripts", required: false)
</body>
</html>
```

The footer uses anchor tag helper attributes (asp-area/asp-controller/asp-action) which will be covered later in this chapter.

Sending Data to Views

There are multiple ways to send data into a view. When views are strongly typed, data can be sent when the views are rendered (either from an action method or through the <partial> tag helper).

Before continuing on, add the following global using statements to the GlobalUsings.cs file:

```
global using AutoLot.Mvc.Models;
global using AutoLot.Models.Entities;
global using AutoLot.Models.Entities.Base;

global using AutoLot.Mvc.Controllers;

global using AutoLot.Services.DataServices.Interfaces;

global using Microsoft.AspNetCore.Http.Features;
global using Microsoft.AspNetCore.Mvc;
global using Microsoft.AspNetCore.Mvc.Infrastructure;
global using Microsoft.AspNetCore.Mvc.Rendering;
global using Microsoft.AspNetCore.Mvc.Routing;
global using Microsoft.AspNetCore.Mvc.ViewComponents;
global using Microsoft.AspNetCore.Razor.TagHelpers;

global using Microsoft.Extensions.DependencyInjection.Extensions;

global using System.Diagnostics;
```

Strongly Typed Views and View Models

When a model or ViewModel is passed into the view method, the value gets assigned to the @model property of a strongly typed view, as shown here (note the lowercase *m*):

```
@model IEnumerable<Order>
```

The @model sets the type for the view and can then be accessed by using the @Model Razor command, like this (note the capital *M*):

```
@foreach (var item in Model)
{
  //Do something interesting here
}
```

If you recall, the RazorSyntax.cshtml view was strongly typed to the Car type, but nothing is being sent to the view. Update the action method to the following to use the ICarDataService to get a Car record (make sure the UseApi setting in the appsettings.Development.json file is set to false):

```
[HttpGet]
public async Task<IActionResult> RazorSyntaxAsync([FromServices]ICarDataService dataService)
```

```
{
  var car = await dataService.FindAsync(6);
  return View(car);
}
```

With the instance being passed to the view, add the following to the end of the view:

```
<hr/>
The Car named @Model.PetName is a <span style="color:@Model.Color">@Model.Color</span>
@Model.MakeNavigation.Name
```

When defining the type for a view, the `@model` directive uses a lower case `m`. When referring to the instance, use an upper case `M`. Notice that the Razor code is used in line with raw text, as a style value, and in a `<span>` tag, demonstrating some of the versatility of using Razor in HTML. The previous line outputs the following to the browser:

```
The Car named Hank is a Green BMW
```

A model value can also be passed into a partial view using the `<partial>` tag helper, as is demonstrated here:

```
<partial name="Partials/_CarListPartial" model="@Model"/>
```

As another example, recall that the `HomeController's Index()` action method is passing the configured `DealerInfo` to the view:

```
public IActionResult Index([FromServices] IOptionsMonitor<DealerInfo> dealerMonitor)
{
  var vm = dealerMonitor.CurrentValue;
  return View(vm);
}
```

To use that information, update the `Index.cshtml` file to the following:

```
@model AutoLot.Services.ViewModels.DealerInfo
@{
    ViewData["Title"] = "Home Page";
}

<div class="text-center">
    <h1 class="display-4">Welcome to @Model.DealerName</h1>
    <p class="lead">Located in @Model.City, @Model.State</p>
</div>
```

ViewBag, ViewData, and TempData

The `ViewBag`, `ViewData`, and `TempData` objects are mechanisms for sending small amounts of data into a view. Table 33-1 lists the three mechanisms to pass data from a controller to a view besides the passing a model into a view using the `View()/PartialView()` methods. These can also be used to pass data between views and controller action methods.

Table 33-1. Additional Ways to Send Data to a View

Data Transport Object	Description of Use
TempData	This is a short-lived object that works during the current request and next request only. Typically used when redirecting to another action method.
ViewData	A dictionary that allows storing values in name-value pairs (e.g., ViewData["Title"] = "My Page").
ViewBag	Dynamic wrapper for the ViewData dictionary (e.g., ViewBag.Title = "My Page").

Both ViewBag and ViewData point to the same object; they just provide different ways to access the data.

Let's take another look at the _HeadPartial.cshtml file you created earlier from the original _Layout.cshtml file (the important line is in bold):

```
<meta charset="utf-8" />
<meta name="viewport" content="width=device-width, initial-scale=1.0" />
<title>@ViewData["Title"] - AutoLot.Mvc</title>
<link rel="stylesheet" href="~/lib/bootstrap/dist/css/bootstrap.min.css" />
<link rel="stylesheet" href="~/css/site.css" />
```

You'll notice the <title> attribute uses ViewData to set the value. Since ViewData is a Razor construct, it's prefaced with the @ symbol. To see this in action, update the RazorSyntax.cshtml view with the following:

```
@model AutoLot.Models.Entities.Car
@{
    ViewData["Title"] = "RazorSyntax";
}
<h1>Razor Syntax</h1>
...
```

Now when you run the application and navigate to https://localhost:5001/Home/RazorSyntax, you will see the title "Razor Syntax – AutoLot.Mvc" in the browser tab.

Injecting Data

Anything that is in the IServiceCollection can be injected into a view. Add the following to the top of the _Layout.cshtml file, which injects the IWebHostEnvironment:

```
@inject IWebHostEnvironment _env
```

Next, update the footer to show the environment that the application is currently running in:

```
 &copy; 2021 - AutoLot.Mvc - @_env.EnvironmentName - <a asp-area="" asp-controller="Home"
asp-action="Privacy">Privacy</a>
```

Managing Client-Side Libraries

An important part of building the user interface for web application is managing the client side CSS and JavaScript libraries. The default template installed jQuery, jQuery Validation, and jQuery Validation Unobtrusive. However, those libraries are probably already out of data when you create a new project due the speed of updates for CSS and JavaScript libraries. To update them manually can be a tedious and time consuming task.

Fortunately, the LibraryManager project (originally built by Mads Kristensen) is now part of Visual Studio and also available as a .NET global tool. LibraryManager uses a simple JSON file to pull CSS and JavaScript tools from CDNJS.com, UNPKG.com, JSDeliver, or the file system. The referenced libraries can be set to pull on demand or with every build of the project.

Install Library Manager As a .NET Global Tool

Library Manager is now built into Visual Studio. To install it as a .NET global tool, enter the following command:

```
dotnet tool install --global Microsoft.Web.LibraryManager.Cli
```

Add Client-Side Libraries to AutoLot.Mvc

The default template loaded the CSS and JavaScript libraries into the `wwwroot\lib` directory. To switch to managing the libraries with LibraryManager, begin by deleting the entire `lib` directory and all of the directories and files it contains.

Add the libman.json File

The `libman.json` file controls what gets installed, from what sources, and the destination of the installed files.

Visual Studio

If you are using Visual Studio, right-click the AutoLot.Mvc project and select Manage Client-Side Libraries. This adds the `libman.json` file to the root of the project. There is also an option in Visual Studio to tie Library Manager into the MSBuild process. If you did not install the `Microsoft.Web.LibraryManager.Build` NuGet package prior to adding the `libmon.json` file (which we did when we built the projects in Chapter 30), right-click the `libman.json` file and select "Enable restore on build." This prompts you to allow the NuGet package to be added into the project. Allow the package to be installed if prompted. By installing the package first, the project is automatically set to restore on build.

The initial file specifies the default provider as `cdnjs`, which references api.cdnjs.com:

```
{
  "version": "1.0",
  "defaultProvider": "cdnjs",
  "libraries": []
}
```

Command Line

Create a new libman.json file with the following command (this sets the default provider to be cdnjs.com):

```
libman init --default-provider cdnjs
```

If you choose to not set a default provider with the command line, you will be prompted to select one, defaulting to cdnjs.

Update the libman.json File

When searching for libraries to install, CDNJS.com has a nice, human-readable API to use. List all of the available libraries with the following URL:

```
https://api.cdnjs.com/libraries?output=human
```

When you find the library you want to install, update the URL with the library name as it's listed to see all of the versions and files for each version. For example, to see everything available for jQuery, enter the following:

```
https://api.cdnjs.com/libraries/jquery?output=human
```

Once you settle on the version and files to install, add the library name (and version), the destination (typically wwwroot/lib/<library name>), and the files to load. For example, to load jQuery, enter the following in the library's JSON array:

```
{
  "library": "jquery@3.6.0",
  "destination": "wwwroot/lib/jquery",
  "files": [ "jquery.js"]
},
```

After adding all the files needed for this app, the entire libman.json file is shown here:

```
{
  //https://api.cdnjs.com/libraries?output=human
  //https://api.cdnjs.com/libraries/jquery?output=human
  "version": "1.0",
  "defaultProvider": "cdnjs",
  "defaultDestination": "wwwroot/lib",
  "libraries": [
    {
      "library": "jquery@3.6.0",
      "destination": "wwwroot/lib/jquery",
      "files": [ "jquery.js", "jquery.min.js", "jquery.min.map" ]
    },
    {
      "library": "jquery-validate@1.19.3",
      "destination": "wwwroot/lib/jquery-validation",
      "files": [ "jquery.validate.js", "jquery.validate.min.js", "additional-methods.js",
      "additional-methods.min.js" ]
```

```
},
{
  "library": "jquery-validation-unobtrusive@3.2.12",
  "destination": "wwwroot/lib/jquery-validation-unobtrusive",
  "files": [ "jquery.validate.unobtrusive.js", "jquery.validate.unobtrusive.min.js" ]
},
{
  "library": "bootstrap@5.1.3",
  "destination": "wwwroot/lib/bootstrap",
  "files": [
    "css/bootstrap.css",
    "css/bootstrap.css.map",
    "css/bootstrap.min.css",
    "css/bootstrap.min.css.map",
    "js/bootstrap.bundle.js",
    "js/bootstrap.bundle.js.map",
    "js/bootstrap.bundle.min.js",
    "js/bootstrap.bundle.min.js.map",
    "js/bootstrap.js",
    "js/bootstrap.js.map",
    "js/bootstrap.min.js",
    "js/bootstrap.min.js.map"
  ]
},
{
  "library": "font-awesome@5.15.4",
  "destination": "wwwroot/lib/font-awesome/",
  "files": [
    "js/all.js",
    "js/all.min.js",
    "css/all.css",
    "css/all.min.css",
    "sprites/brands.svg",
    "sprites/regular.svg",
    "sprites/solid.svg",
    "webfonts/fa-brands-400.eot",
    "webfonts/fa-brands-400.svg",
    "webfonts/fa-brands-400.ttf",
    "webfonts/fa-brands-400.woff",
    "webfonts/fa-brands-400.woff2",
    "webfonts/fa-regular-400.eot",
    "webfonts/fa-regular-400.svg",
    "webfonts/fa-regular-400.ttf",
    "webfonts/fa-regular-400.woff",
    "webfonts/fa-regular-400.woff2",
    "webfonts/fa-solid-900.eot",
    "webfonts/fa-solid-900.svg",
    "webfonts/fa-solid-900.ttf",
    "webfonts/fa-solid-900.woff",
```

```
        "webfonts/fa-solid-900.woff2"
      ]
    }
  ]
}
```

Once you save the file (in Visual Studio), the files will be loaded into the wwwroot\lib folder of the project. If running from the command line, enter the following command to reload all the files:

```
libman restore
```

Additional command-line options are available. Enter libman -h to explore all the options.

Update the JavaScript and CSS References

The location of many of the JavaScript and CSS files changed with the move to Library Manager. Bootstrap and jQuery were loaded from a \dist folder in the original scaffolded code. The update to using libman.json also added Font Awesome into the application.

The location for the Bootstrap files needs to be updated to ~/lib/bootstrap/css instead of ~/lib/boostrap/dist/css, and Font Awesome needs to be added. Update the _Head.cshtml file to the following:

```
<meta charset="utf-8" />
<meta name="viewport" content="width=device-width, initial-scale=1.0" />
<title>@ViewData["Title"] - AutoLot.Mvc</title>
<link rel="stylesheet" href="~/lib/bootstrap/css/bootstrap.min.css" />
<link rel="stylesheet" href="~/lib/font-awesome/css/all.css" />
<link rel="stylesheet" href="~/css/site.css" asp-append-version="true" />
<link rel="stylesheet" href="~/AutoLot.Mvc.styles.css" asp-append-version="true" />
```

Next, update _JavaScriptFiles.cshtml to take the \dist out of the jQuery and Bootstrap locations.

```
<script src="~/lib/jquery/jquery.min.js"></script>
<script src="~/lib/bootstrap/js/bootstrap.bundle.min.js"></script>
<script src="~/js/site.js" asp-append-version="true"></script>
```

The final change is to update the location of jquery.validation in the _ValidationScriptsPartial.cshtml partial view.

```
<script src="~/lib/jquery-validation/jquery.validate.min.js"></script>
<script src="~/lib/jquery-validation-unobtrusive/jquery.validate.unobtrusive.min.
js"></script>
```

Bundling and Minification

Library manager handles installing client side libraries into your project in an easy and efficient manner. Two additional considerations for building web applications with client-side libraries are bundling and minification for improved performance.

Bundling

Web browsers have a set limit of how many files they allow to be downloaded concurrently from the same endpoint. This can be problematic if you use SOLID development techniques with your JavaScript and CSS files, separating out related code and styles into smaller, more maintainable files. This provides a better development experience but can crush an application's performance while the files are waiting their turn to be downloaded. Bundling is simply concatenating files together to prevent them from being blocked while waiting for the browser download limit.

Minification

Also, for improved performance, the minification process changes CSS and JavaScript files to make them smaller. Unnecessary whitespace and line endings are removed, and non-keyword names are shortened. While this makes a file almost unreadable to a human, the functionality is not affected, and the size can be significantly reduced. This, in turn, speeds up the download process, thereby improving the performance of the application.

The WebOptimizer Solution

There are many development tools that can bundle and minify files as part of the build process. These are certainly effective but can be problematic if the processes become out of sync, since there really isn't a good comparer for the original files and the bundled and minified ones.

WebOptimizer is an open source package that uses middleware to bundle and minify files as part of the ASP.NET Core pipeline. This ensures that the bundled and minified files accurately represent the raw files. Not only are they accurate, but they are cached as part of the process, significantly cutting down on the number of disk reads for page requests.

WebOptimizer uses a cache-busting technique to make sure the files are always current. Every configured file link has the file's hash appended to the URL, like this:

```
https://localhost:5001/AutoLot.Mvc.styles.css?v=9Ozsx8PuquAgpHzcVo7FiIxEbbs
```

When the file changes, the hash changes, and the browser reloads the file since the URL has changed. This is the same way the `asp-append-version` tag helper functions. Tag helpers are covered later in this chapter.

You have already added the `Libershark.WebOptimizer.Core` NuGet package when the projects were created in Chapter 30. Now it is time to use it.

Add and Configure WebOptimizer

The first step is to add WebOptimizer into the pipeline. Open the `Program.cs` file in the AutoLot.Mvc project and add the following line (just before the `app.UseStaticFiles()` call):

```
app.UseWebOptimizer();
```

The next step is to configure what to minimize and bundle. Typically, when developing your application, you want to use the non-bundled/non-minified versions of the files and use the bundled/minified versions for staging and production. In the `Program.cs` file, add the following code block before `var app = builder.Build()`:

```
if (builder.Environment.IsDevelopment())
{
  builder.Services.AddWebOptimizer(false,false);
}
else
{
  builder.Services.AddWebOptimizer(options =>
  {
    //Configuration goes here
  });
}
```

In the preceding code block, if the environment is `Development`, all bundling and minification is disabled:

```
builder.Services.AddWebOptimizer(false,false);
```

WebOptimizer can be set to minify all CSS files and all JavaScript files found in the `wwwroot` directory:

```
options.MinifyCssFiles(); //Minifies all CSS files
options.MinifyJsFiles(); //Minifies all JS files
```

WebOptimizer can also be configured to minify a specific file or all files in a certain directory:

```
options.MinifyCssFiles("css/site.css"); //Minifies the site.css file
options.MinifyCssFiles("lib/**/*.css"); //Minifies all CSS files under the wwwroot/lib directory
options.MinifyJsFiles("js/site.js"); //Minifies the site.js file
options.MinifyJsFiles("lib/**/*.js"); //Minifies all JavaScript files under the wwwroot/
lib directory
```

The open source libraries already have the minified versions downloaded through Library Manager, so the only files that need to be minified are the project specific files, including the generated CSS file if you are using CSS isolation. Update the if block to the following:

```
if (builder.Environment.IsDevelopment())
{
    builder.Services.AddWebOptimizer(false,false);
    /*
    builder.Services.AddWebOptimizer(options =>
    {
        options.MinifyCssFiles("AutoLot.Mvc.styles.css");
        options.MinifyCssFiles("css/site.css");
        options.MinifyJsFiles("js/site.js");
    });
    */
}
else
{
    builder.Services.AddWebOptimizer(options =>
    {
```

```
            options.MinifyCssFiles("AutoLot.Mvc.styles.css");
            options.MinifyCssFiles("css/site.css");
            options.MinifyJsFiles("js/site.js");
        });
}
```

In the development scope, the code is setup for you to comment/uncomment the different options so you can replicate the production environment without switching to production.

WebOptimizer also supports bundling for CSS and JavaScript files. The first example creates a JavaScript bundle using file globbing, and the second creates a JavaScript bundle listing specific names.

```
options.AddJavaScriptBundle("js/validations/validationCode.js", "js/validations/**/*.js");
options.AddJavaScriptBundle("js/validations/validationCode.js", "js/validations/validators.js",
"js/validations/errorFormatting.js");
```

To bundle CSS files, use the `AddCssBundle()` method.

It's important to note that the minified and bundled files aren't actually on disk, but they are placed in cache. It's also important to note that the minified files keep the same name (`site.js`) and don't have the usual min in the name (`site.min.js`).

■ **Note** When updating your views to add the links for bundled files, Visual Studio will complain that the bundled file doesn't exist. Don't worry, it will still render from the cache.

Update _ViewImports.cshtml

The final step is to add the WebOptimizer tag helpers into the system. Add the following line to the end of the `_ViewImports.cshtml` file:

```
@addTagHelper *, WebOptimizer.Core
```

The Controllers

Before continuing the journey into the user interface aspects of MVC style applications, it's time to update the `HomeController` to use attribute routing and add the additional controllers for the main application. The AutoLot.Mvc has a base controller and two derived controllers.

The AutoLot.Mvc application will only use attribute routing, so the default route added by the MVC template can be removed. To make this change, comment out the `MapControllerRoute()` method in `Program.cs` and add the `MapControllers()` method:

```
app.MapControllers();
//app.MapControllerRoute(
//    name: "default",
//    pattern: "{controller=Home}/{action=Index}/{id?}");
```

The HomeController

When the default route was commented out, the routing engine can no longer locate the HomeController or it's action methods. This is corrected by adding in Route attributes on the controller and/or action methods. When a Route attribute is added at the controller level, all of the action methods inherit the same route template. Action methods can add to or reset the template. Update the controller declaration to add the controller's default route with the following Route attribute:

```
[Route("[controller]/[action]")]
public class HomeController : Controller
{
  //omitted for brevity
}
```

While the standard routing table allows the specification of default values for route tokens, attribute routing does not. This can cause routing issues if a fully qualified route isn't specified in the request. To create the equivalent of the default route, add the following three Route attributes to the Index() method like this:

```
[Route("/")]
[Route("/[controller]")]
[Route("/[controller]/[action]")]
public IActionResult Index([FromServices] IOptionsMonitor<DealerInfo> dealerMonitor)
```

Recall the route for an action method can be reset by starting the template with a forward slash (/). The first attribute ([Route("/")]) matches requests that don't specify any route parameters (e.g., www.skimedic.com). The second attribute ([Route("/[controller]")]) matches requests that only specify the controller portion of the route (www.skimedic.com/home), and the last one ([Route("/[controller]/[action]")]) matches routes with a controller and an action method (www.skimedic.com/home/index). These three route templates used together recreate the default route that was in the original application template.

■ **Note** Even though the controller route specifies the controller/action template, it must be repeated on the Index() method because the other Route attributes on the action method reset the controller route.

Finally, mark the Index() and the Privacy() methods the HttpGet attribute. The Error() method is not marked with the HttpGet attribute as it needs to execute any time there is an error, regardless of the HTTP verb of the request:

```
[HttpGet]
[Route("/")]
[Route("/[controller]")]
[Route("/[controller]/[action]")]
public IActionResult Index([FromServices] IOptionsMonitor<DealerInfo> dealerMonitor)

[HttpGet]
public IActionResult Privacy()
{
  Return View();
}
```

The BaseCrudController

The `BaseCrudController` contains the boilerplate create, read, update, and delete (CRUD) methods that will be used by derived controllers. Start building this base controller by adding a new directory named Base in the `Controllers` directory, right click the Base directory, select Add ➤ Controller, then select MVC Controller - Empty and name the controller `BaseCrudController`. Make it `public` and `abstract` and class generic, typed to the `BaseEntity` (for the CRUD methods) and any class (for logging). Assign the class the `[controller]/[action]` route:

```
namespace AutoLot.Mvc.Controllers.Base;

[Route("[controller]/[action]")]
public abstract class BaseCrudController<TEntity,TController>  : Controller
    where TEntity : BaseEntity, new()
    where TController: class
{
    public IActionResult Index()
    {
        return View();
    }
}
```

Add the following global using statement to the GlobalUsings.cs file:

```
global using AutoLot.Mvc.Controllers.Base;
```

Add a constructor that takes an instance of `IAppLogging<TController>` and `IDataService<TEntity>` and assign them to class level fields:

```
protected readonly IAppLogging<TController> AppLoggingInstance;
protected readonly IDataServiceBase<TEntity> MainDataService;

protected BaseCrudController(
    IAppLogging<TController> appLogging,
    IDataServiceBase<TEntity> mainDataService)
{
  AppLoggingInstance = appLogging;
  MainDataService = mainDataService;
}
```

Next, add a `protected` method to get a single entity using the injected data service:

```
protected async Task<TEntity> GetOneEntityAsync(int id)
  => await MainDataService.FindAsync(id);
```

Add a `protected abstract` method that will return a `SelectList` used to populate drop downs for lookup values like `Models` for the `Car` class:

```
protected abstract Task<SelectList> GetLookupValuesAsync();
```

The IndexAsync Method

The IndexAsync() method serves as the default method for the derived controllers, and as such needs to have the [controller] and [controller]/[action] routes defined just like the Index() method on the HomeController. Note that an application can only have one base route ([Route("/")]) defined, so make sure to just add the following two Route attributes along with the [HttpGet] attribute:

```
[HttpGet]
[Route("/[controller]")]
[Route("/[controller]/[action]")]
public IActionResult Index()
{
  return View();
}
```

All of the action methods on the base controller are marked virtual to allow derived controllers to override them and async to support the calls on the data service:

```
public virtual async Task<IActionResult> IndexAsync()
{
  return View();
}
```

Recall that when routing to an async action method with an Async suffix, the suffix is dropped. The route for the IndexAsync() method is /[controller]/Index, not /[controller]/IndexAsync.

The IndexAsync() method (and forthcoming view) is used to display a list of all of the entities. This list is retrieved using the GetAllAsync() method on the data service class and then passed to the view (note the change to use an expression body):

```
public virtual async Task<IActionResult> IndexAsync()
  => View(await MainDataService.GetAllAsync());
```

The DetailsAsync Method

The DetailsAsync() method is used to display a single record when called with an HTTP get request. The controller route is extended with an optional id value. Optional route tokens are indicated with a question mark in the token and represent nullable parameters on the action method. Add the following action method:

```
[HttpGet("{id?}")]
public virtual async Task<IActionResult> DetailsAsync(int? id)
{
}
```

The method body returns a BadRequest() if the parameter is null, otherwise calls the base class's GetOneEntityAsync() method. If an entity is not returned from the database/API, the method returns a NotFound() result. If the entity is found, it is returned to the view:

```
[HttpGet("{id?}")]
public virtual async Task<IActionResult> DetailsAsync(int? id)
{
  if (!id.HasValue)
```

```
  {
    return BadRequest();
  }
  var entity = await GetOneEntityAsync(id.Value);
  if (entity == null)
  {
    return NotFound();
  }
  return View(entity);
}
```

The BadRequest() and NotFound() methods are two of the ControllerBase helper methods discussed in Chapter 30. They are convenience methods for returning 400 and 404 HTTP status codes back to the client.

■ **Note** Simply returning 400 and 404 error codes to the browser might not receive the best reception from your users. For production applications, you will want to send a friendlier message. This will be demonstrated later in this chapter.

The CreateAsync Action Methods

The create process uses two action methods: one that is the endpoint for HTTP get requests and another that receives HTTP post requests.

The Get Method

The CreateAsync() get action method adds a SelectList of related records to the ViewData dictionary and returns the view.

```
[HttpGet]
public virtual async Task<IActionResult> CreateAsync()
{
  ViewData["LookupValues"] = await GetLookupValuesAsync();
  return View();
}
```

The Post Method

The CreateAsync() HTTP post action method uses implicit model binding to instantiate an entity of type TEntity from the form values. The code is listed here, with the explanation to follow:

```
[HttpPost]
[ValidateAntiForgeryToken]
public virtual async Task<IActionResult> CreateAsync(TEntity entity)
{
  if (ModelState.IsValid)
```

```
  {
    await MainDataService.AddAsync(entity);
    return RedirectToAction(nameof(DetailsAsync).RemoveAsyncSuffix(),new {id = entity.Id});
  }
  ViewData["LookupValues"] = await GetLookupValuesAsync();
  return View(entity);
}
```

The HttpPost attribute marks this as the application endpoint for the Controller/Create route when the request is a post. The ValidateAntiForgeryToken attribute requires and validates the hidden input value for the __RequestVerificationToken from the request. Adding the token to views will be covered later in this chapter.

The entity parameter is implicitly bound to the incoming request data. If the ModelState is valid, the entity is added to the database, and then the user is redirected to the IndexAsync() action method. This is the Post-Redirect-Get pattern. The user submitted a Post method (CreateAsync()) and is then redirected to a Get method (DetailsAsync()). This prevents the browser from resubmitting the post if the user refreshes the page. The nameof() method is used in the redirect command instead of simple strings to gain compiler checking. However, recall that routing removes the Async suffix from action methods, so to use the nameof() method the suffix must be removed. The RemoveAsyncSuffix() extension method is written to do just that.

As a final note for the redirect, the DetailsAsync() action requires the route parameter id. Route parameters are passed into the RedirectToAction() method using an anonymous object where the object's property names must match the route parameters names.

If the ModelState is not valid, the SelectList is added to the ViewData, and the entity that was submitted is sent back to the view to allow the user to correct the issues. ModelState is implicitly sent to the view as well so any errors can be displayed.

The EditAsync Action Methods

The edit process also uses two action methods: an HTTP get method to return the entity to be edited and an HTTP post method to submit the values of the updated record.

The Get Method

The EditAsync() HTTP get action method gets a single car by Id using the service wrapper and sends it to the view.

```
[HttpGet("{id?}")]
public virtual async Task<IActionResult> EditAsync(int? id)
{
  if (!id.HasValue)
  {
    ViewData["Error"] = "Bad Request";
    return View();
  }
  var entity = await GetOneEntityAsync(id.Value);
  if (entity == null)
  {
    ViewData["Error"] = "Not Found";
    return View();
  }
```

```
  ViewData["LookupValues"] = await GetLookupValuesAsync();
  return View(entity);
}
```

The route has an option id parameter that is then passed into the method using the id parameter. The method uses the GetOneEntityAsync() helper method to get the record. If the id is null or the record can't be located, the method adds an error message to ViewData and returns the view without any data. Otherwise, it creates a SelectList of the lookup values, adds it to the ViewData dictionary, and renders the view.

The Post Method

The EditAsync() HTTP post action method is similar to the CreateAsync() HTTP post method, except that it calls UpdateAsync() on the data services class:

```
[HttpPost("{id}")]
[ValidateAntiForgeryToken]
public virtual async Task<IActionResult> EditAsync(int id, TEntity entity)
{
  if (id != entity.Id)
  {
    ViewData["Error"] = "Bad Request";
    return View();
  }
  if (ModelState.IsValid)
  {
    await MainDataService.UpdateAsync(entity);
    return RedirectToAction(nameof(DetailsAsync).RemoveAsyncSuffix(),new {id});
  }
  ViewData["LookupValues"] = await GetLookupValuesAsync();
  return View(entity);
}
```

The EditAsync() HTTP post method takes a single required route parameter for the id. If this doesn't match the Id of the reconstituted entity, an error message and an empty view result is sent to the client. If the ModelState is valid, the entity is updated, and then the user is redirected to the DetailsAsync() action method, passing in the id parameter as the route value. Since the variable name matches the parameter name, the abbreviated method for creating the anonymous object (new {id})is used. This also used the Post-Redirect-Get pattern.

If the ModelState is not valid, the SelectList is added to ViewData, and the entity that was submitted is sent back to the view. ModelState is implicitly sent to the view as well so any errors can be displayed.

The DeleteAsync Action Methods

The Delete process also uses two action methods.

The Delete Get Method

The DeleteAsync() HTTP get action method functions the same as the EditAsync() get action method:

```
[HttpGet("{id?}")]
public virtual async Task<IActionResult> DeleteAsync(int? id)
{
  if (!id.HasValue)
  {
    ViewData["Error"] = "Bad Request";
    return View();
  }
  var entity = await GetOneEntityAsync(id.Value);
  if (entity == null)
  {
    ViewData["Error"] = "Not Found";
    return View();
  }
  return View(entity);
}
```

The Delete Post Method

The Delete() HTTP post action method creates a new entity only using the Id and TimeStamp, and then sends that instance to the data service:

```
[HttpPost("{id}")]
[ValidateAntiForgeryToken]
public virtual async Task<IActionResult> DeleteAsync(int id, TEntity entity)
{
  if (id != entity.Id)
  {
    ViewData["Error"] = "Bad Request";
    return View();
  }
  try
  {
    await MainDataService.DeleteAsync(entity);
    return RedirectToAction(nameof(IndexAsync).RemoveAsyncSuffix());
  }
  catch (Exception ex)
  {
    ModelState.Clear();
    ModelState.AddModelError(string.Empty,ex.Message);
    MainDataService.ResetChangeTracker();
    entity = await GetOneEntityAsync(id);
    return View(entity);
  }
}
```

The Delete() HTTP Post method is streamlined to only send the values needed by EF Core to delete a record. If the deletion succeeds, this isn't an issue since the user is redirected to the index page. However, if the deletion fails for some reason (such as a cascade issue), the remaining properties (and any necessary navigation properties) will all be null. This causes two problems. The first is that ModelState will likely be invalid. Secondly, the user won't be able to confirm that they are deleting the correct record since nothing will be displayed in the view.

To resolve this, the ModelState is cleared of any errors, then a model level error is added using the exception error message as the content. The next line calls into the data service to reset the ChangeTracker. This is only necessary when using the AutoLot.Dal code directly. The DbSet<TEntity>.Find() method (the back end method called when the GetOneEntityAsync() method is executed) will first check if an entity with the same primary key is already being tracked. If it is, that instance is returned. The problem in this workflow is that the instance currently being tracked only has the Id and TimeStamp properties populated. The call to ResetChangeTracker() forces the derived DbContext to stop tracking all entities (which in this case is only the entity to be deleted). After the ChangeTracker is cleared, the Find() method will go back to the database to get the full entity.

When using the AutoLot.Api as the back end, this isn't an issue since the API doesn't hold state between calls.

Using a BindProperty

Instead of receiving an entity parameter in each of the HTTP post methods, MVC controllers also support using a BindProperty. This is a public property on the controller that is marked with the BindProperty attribute, like this:

```
[BindProperty]
public TEntity Entity { get; set; }
```

With this in place, the post method signatures drop the entity parameter and use the controller level property. The model binding is still implicit, and ModelState works the same. If you want to try this, add in the Entity property to the controller and update the post signatures to the following (just showing the top line only):

```
namespace AutoLot.Mvc.Controllers.Base;

[Route("[controller]/[action]")]
public abstract class BaseCrudWithBindingPropertyController<TEntity, TController> :
Controller
    where TEntity : BaseEntity, new()
    where TController : class
{
  [BindProperty]
  public TEntity Entity { get; set; }

  [HttpPost]
  [ValidateAntiForgeryToken]
  [ActionName("Create")]
  public virtual async Task<IActionResult> CreatePostAsync()

  [HttpPost("{id}")]
  [ValidateAntiForgeryToken]
  [ActionName("Edit")]
  public virtual async Task<IActionResult> EditPostAsync(int id)
```

```
  [HttpPost("{id}")]
  [ValidateAntiForgeryToken]
  [ActionName("Delete")]
  public virtual async Task<IActionResult> DeletePostAsync(int id)
}
```

In addition to taking out the entity parameter, notice the changes to the action method names. This is due to the fact that when the CreateAsync() post method lost the parameter, it had the exact same name and signature as the CreateAsync() get method. While the routing engine is fine with this (since one is a post and one is a get), C# isn't. The solution is to change the name of the method then add the ActionName attribute. The ActionName attribute takes precedence over the method name, so the routing engine maps the CreatePostAsync() method back to the Create endpoint. The EditAsync() and DeleteAsync() post methods technically have different signatures than their get versions (which take a nullable int? instead of an int), I changed all of the names to be more consistent.

The last update to make to the controller is to rename entity to Entity in each of the methods, since the property is capitalized while the parameters were lower case.

You can find this controller in the sample code for this chapter.

The CarsController

The CarsController inherits from the BaseCrudController, gaining the base route and the standard CRUD operations. It is also strongly typed to the Car entity and the ICarDataService. Right click the Controllers directory, select Add ➤ Controller, then select MVC Controller - Empty and name the controller CarsController. Make it public and inherit from BaseCrudController, implement the abstract method, and add in the necessary constructor (make sure to add async to the override):

```
namespace AutoLot.Mvc.Controllers;

public class CarsController : BaseCrudController<Car,CarsController>
{
  public CarsController(IAppLogging<CarsController> appLogging, ICarDataService
mainDataService)
    : base(appLogging, mainDataService)
  {
  }

  protected override async Task<SelectList> GetLookupValuesAsync()
  {
    throw new NotImplementedException();
  }
}
```

The Car entities have related Make information, and when editing or adding Car records, the views will have drop down controls to allow the user to pick the Make by name. To build the Make SelectList, the controller needs an instance of the IMakeDataService. Update the constructor to take this in and assign it to a class level field:

```
private readonly IMakeDataService _lookupDataService;

public CarsController(IAppLogging<CarsController> appLogging, ICarDataService
mainDataService,
```

```
    IMakeDataService lookupDataService) : base(appLogging, mainDataService)
{
  _lookupDataService = lookupDataService;
}
```

With the data service in place, update the GetLookupValuesAsync() method to build the SelectList of the Make records:

```
protected override async Task<SelectList> GetLookupValuesAsync()
  => new SelectList(await _lookupDataService.GetAllAsync(), nameof(Make.Id),
  nameof(Make.Name));
```

There is one more action method needed, and that is used to get a list of cars that all have a certain Make. The route is extended with the [HttpGet] attribute to accept a makeId and makeName. The makeId is used to select the records, the makeName is added to the ViewBag for display in the view:

```
[HttpGet("{makeId}/{makeName}")]
public async Task<IActionResult> ByMakeAsync(int makeId, string makeName)
{
  ViewBag.MakeName = makeName;
  return View(await ((ICarDataService)MainDataService).GetAllByMakeIdAsync(makeId));
}
```

The following is the code from Chapter 30 that examined explicit model binding for your reference (it's also in the sample code for this chapter on GitHub):

```
[HttpPost]
[ActionName("Create")]
[ValidateAntiForgeryToken]
public override async Task<IActionResult> CreateAsync()
{
    var newCar = new Car();

    //var newCar = new Car
    //{
    //    Color = "Purple",
    //    MakeId = 1,
    //    PetName = "Prince"
    //};
    //if (await TryUpdateModelAsync(newCar, "",
    //        c => c.Color, c => c.PetName, c => c.MakeId))
    if (await TryUpdateModelAsync(newCar, "", c => c.PetName, c => c.MakeId))
    {
        await MainDataService.AddAsync(newCar);
        return RedirectToAction(nameof(IndexAsync).RemoveAsyncSuffix(), new { id =
        newCar.Id });
    }

    var isValid = ModelState.IsValid; //false
    newCar.Color = "Purple";
    TryValidateModel(newCar);
```

```
    isValid = ModelState.IsValid; //still false
    ModelState.Clear();
    TryValidateModel(newCar);
    isValid = ModelState.IsValid; //true
    ViewData["MakeId"] = await GetLookupValuesAsync();
    return View(newCar);
}
```

This completes the controllers for the main part of the application. Next we are going to examine Areas.

Areas

Areas are partitioned sections of an ASP.NET Core web application (either MVC or Razor page based) used to organize related functionality. They have their own namespace for routing as well as a distinct directory structure for views and Razor pages. When an Area is added to a project, the scaffolded files are created in the `Areas\[AreaName]` directory. There are four initial directories created under the `[AreaName]` directory:

- Controllers
- Models
- Data
- Views (MVC app) or Pages (Razor pages app)

Controllers for an Area must have the `[Area("[AreaName]")]` attribute (e.g., `[Area("Admin")]`) to identify them as an Area controller. While controllers for an area *typically* live in the `Areas\[AreaName]\Controllers` directory, they can technically live anywhere as long as they are properly attributed. The only restriction is for views and Razor pages. By default, views must live in one of the following directories (Razor pages and Areas are covered in detail in the next chapter):

```
/Areas/<Area-Name>/Views/<Controller-Name>/<Action-Name>.cshtml
/Areas/<Area-Name>/Views/Shared/<Action-Name>.cshtml
/Views/Shared/<Action-Name>.cshtml
```

Notice that the directory structure is the same as the main Views directory. A controller's views go into a folder named after the controller (minus the `Controller` suffix) or in the `Shared` directory in the Area's directory tree. If a view isn't found in one of those two places, the `Shared` folder in the main `Views` directory is searched. The main `Views\ControllerName` directory is never searched for an Area controller's views, even if the main app has a controller with the same name.

For the AutoLot.Mvc application, we are going to add an area to manage the `Make` records. To add an area, right click on the AutoLot.Mvc project, select Add ➤ New Scaffolded Item, then select MVC Area and name it `Admin`. Delete the `Models` and `Data` directories, as they are not needed.

Area Routing

When an Area is scaffolded, a `ScaffoldingReadMe.txt` file is added to the project with directions on adding the controller route for an Area. If you are using traditional routing, the suggested route is close to what you need to add (it hasn't been updated to ASP.NET Core 6 syntax as of the time of this writing). A better way to add an Area route is by using the `MapAreaControllerRoute()` method, like this (make sure to place Area routes before any non-Area routes):

```
app.MapAreaControllerRoute(
    name: "AdminArea",
    areaName:"Admin",
    pattern: "Admin/{controller=Home}/{action=Index}/{id?}"
);
```

Since AutoLot.Mvc is using attribute routing, the MapAreaControllerRoute() method is not needed.

The MakesController Area Controller

As mentioned previously, an Area's controllers must have the [Area] attribute applied. To demonstrate, add a new controller named MakesController in the Areas\Admin\Controllers directory. The initial code is exactly like the initial setup of the CarsController, except it is using the Make version of the data services and has the Area attribute applied:

```
namespace AutoLot.Mvc.Areas.Admin.Controllers;

[Area("Admin")]
[Route("Admin/[controller]/[action]")]
public class MakesController : BaseCrudController<Make, MakesController>
{
  public MakesController(IAppLogging<MakesController> logging,
        IMakeDataService mainDataService) : base(logging,mainDataService)
  {
  }
}
```

The GetLookupValuesAsync() isn't necessary, so set it to return Task.FromResult<SelectList>(null), which is the preferred way to return null from an async method:

```
protected override async Task<SelectList> GetLookupValuesAsync()
{
  return await Task.FromResult<SelectList>(null);
}
```

As a final change, override the IndexAsync() action method so the default route attributes can be applied, still using the base class's code:

```
[Route("/Admin")]
[Route("/Admin/[controller]")]
[Route("/Admin/[controller]/[action]")]
public override async Task<IActionResult> IndexAsync()
{
  return await base.IndexAsync();
}
```

To test that the routing works, add a simple view for the Index() action method. First add a new directory named Makes under the Areas\Admin\Views folder, and in that folder add a new empty Razor view named Index.cshtml. Next, run the app and navigate to https://localhost:5001/Admin, and a black screen should appear. You will find that it works with /Admin, /Admin/Makes, and Admin/Makes/Index.

To demonstrate that Area controllers can live outside of the Areas directory structure, move the MakesController to the main Controllers folder and test the routes again. You will find that they still work. However, if you move the Index.cshtml file to anywhere except Areas\Admin\Views\Makes, Areas\Admin\Views\Shared, or Views\Shared, you will find that the InvalidOperationException is thrown because of the missing view. Before continuing on with the chapter, make sure to return the controller and view back to their right places.

_ViewImports and _ViewStart

The _ViewImports.cshtml and _ViewStart.cshtml files apply to all views at the same directory level and below. The default location of these files is in the main \Views directory. With Areas, you can either copy the existing files (or create new ones) into the Areas\[ControllerName]\Views folder or move the existing files up to the project root so they cover all of the Area views as well. For this project, move the _ViewImports.cshtml and _ViewStart.cshtml files to the root on the project so they are applied to the entire project.

Tag Helpers

Tag helpers are a new feature introduced in ASP.NET Core. A *tag helper* is markup (a custom tag or an attribute on a standard tag) that represents server-side code. The server-side code then helps shape the HTML emitted. They greatly improve the development experience and readability of MVC views. If you are developing with Visual Studio, there is an added benefit of IntelliSense for the built-in tag helpers. Tag helpers largely replace Html helpers for individual tags.

■ **Note** If you are not familiar with Html helpers, they are Razor functions that emit HTML. The Html helpers that aren't replicated by tag helpers will be covered later in this chapter.

For example, the following HTML helper creates a label for the customer's FullName property:

```
@Html.Label("FullName","Full Name:",new {@class="customer"})
```

This generates the following HTML:

```
<label class="customer" for="FullName">Full Name:</label>
```

For the C# developer who has been working with ASP.NET MVC and Razor, the HTML helper syntax is probably well understood. But it's not intuitive, especially for someone who works in HTML/CSS/JavaScript and not C#.

The tag helper version looks like this:

```
<label class="customer" asp-for="FullName">Full Name:</label>
```

They produce the same output, but tag helpers, with their integration into the HTML tags, keep you "in the markup."

There are many built-in tag helpers, and they are designed to be used instead of their respective HTML helpers. However, not all HTML helpers have an associated tag helper. Table 33-2 lists the more commonly used tag helpers, their corresponding HTML helper, and the available attributes. They will be covered in detail throughout the rest of this chapter.

Table 33-2. *Commonly Used Built-in Tag Helpers in MVC Web Applications*

Tag Helper	HTML Helper	Available Attributes

`Form`	`Html.BeginForm`
	`Html.BeginRouteForm`
	`Html.AntiForgeryToken`
		`asp-route`—for named routes (can't be used with controller or action attributes).`asp-antiforgery`—if the antiforgery should be added (true by default).`asp-area`—the name of the area.`asp-controller`—the name of the controller.`asp-action`—the name of the action.`asp-route-<ParameterName>`—adds the parameter to the route, e.g., `asp-route-id="1"`.`asp-all-route-data`—dictionary for additional route values.

`Form Action (button or input type=image)`	`N/A`	`asp-route`—for named routes (can't be used with controller or action attributes).`asp-antiforgery`—if the antiforgery should be added (true by default).`asp-area`—the name of the area. `asp-controller`—the name of the controller.`asp-action`—the name of the action.`asp-route-<ParameterName>`—adds the parameter to the route, e.g., `asp-route-id="1"`.`asp-all-route-data`—dictionary for additional route values.
`Anchor`	`Html.ActionLink`	`asp-route`—for named routes (can't be used with controller or action attributes). `asp-area`—the name of the area. `asp-controller`—defines the controller. `asp-action`—defines the action. `asp-protocol`—HTTP or HTTPS.`asp-fragment`—URL fragment.`asp-host`—the host name.`asp-route-<ParameterName>`—adds the parameter to the route, e.g., `asp-route-id="1"`. `asp-all-route-data`—dictionary for additional route values.
`Input`	`Html.TextBox/TextBoxFor` `Html.Editor/EditorFor`	`asp-for`—a model property. Can navigate the model (`Customer.Address.AddressLine1`) and use expressions (`asp-for="@localVariable"`). The `id` and `name` attributes are autogenerated. Any HTML5 `data-val` attributes and `type` attributes are autogenerated.`asp-format` - the format string used to format the `asp-for` result
`TextArea`	`Html.TextAreaFor`	`asp-for`—a model property. Can navigate the model (`Customer.Address.Description`) and use expressions (`asp-for="@localVariable"`). The `id` and `name` attributes are autogenerated. Any HTML5 `data-val` attributes and `type` attributes are autogenerated.
`Label`	`Html.LabelFor`	`asp-for`—a model property. Can navigate the model (`Customer.Address.AddressLine1`) and use expressions (`asp-for="@localVariable"`). Displays the value of the `Display` attribute if it exists; otherwise uses property name.

(*continued*)

Table 33-2. (*continued*)

Tag Helper	HTML Helper	Available Attributes
Partial	Html.Partial(Async) Html.RenderPartial(Async)	name—the path and name of the partial view. for—model expression on current form to be the model in the partial.model—an object to be the model in the partial.view-data—ViewData for the partial.fallback-name— view to load if named view can't be locatedoptional—when optional, if the view can't be found the partial will no-op instead of throwing an error
Select	Html.DropDownListFor Html.ListBoxFor	asp-for—a model property. Can navigate the model (Customer.Address.AddressLine1) and use expressions (asp-for="@localVariable"). asp-items—specifies the options elements. Autogenerates the selected="selected" attribute. The id and name attributes are autogenerated. Any HTML5 data-val attributes are autogenerated.
Validation Message (span)	Html.ValidationMessageFor	asp-validation-for—a model property. Can navigate the model (Customer.Address.AddressLine1) and use expressions (asp-for="@localVariable"). Adds the data-valmsg-for attribute to the span.
Validation Summary (div)	Html.ValidationSummaryFor	asp-validation-summary—select one of All, ModelOnly, or None. Adds the data-valmsg-summary attribute to the div.
Link	N/A	asp-append-version—appends the file's hash as a version indicator to the filename (as query string) for cache-busting. href—address for the content delivery network version of the source. asp-fallback-href—fallback file to use if primary is not available; usually used with CDN sources. asp-fallback-href-include—globbed file list of files to include on fallback. asp-fallback-href-exclude—globbed file list of files to exclude on fallback. asp-fallback-test-*—properties to use on fallback test. Included are class, property, and value. asp-suppress-fallback-integrity - indicates if integrity check should be conducted on fallback file. Defaults to true.asp-href-include—globbed file pattern of files to include. asp-href-exclude—globbed file pattern of files to exclude.

(*continued*)

Table 33-2. *(continued)*

Tag Helper	HTML Helper	Available Attributes
Script	N/A	asp-append-version—appends the file's hash as a version indicator to the filename (as query string) for cache-busting. src—address for the content delivery network version of the source asp-fallback-src—fallback file to use if primary is not available; usually used with CDN sources. asp-fallback-src-include—globbed file list of files to include on fallback. asp-fallback-src-exclude—globbed file list of files to exclude on fallback. asp-fallback-test—the script method to use in fallback test. asp-suppress-fallback-integrity - indicates if integrity check should be conducted on fallback file. Defaults to true.asp-src-include—globbed file pattern of files to include. asp-src-exclude—globbed file pattern of files to exclude.
Image	N/A	asp-append-version—appends the file's hash as a version indicator to the filename (as query string) for cache-busting.
Environment	N/A	names—single host environment name or comma-separated list of names to trigger rendering of the content (ignores case).include—single host environment name or comma-separated list of names to trigger rendering of the content (ignores case).exclude—single host environment name or comma-separated list of names to exclude from rendering of the content (ignores case). Overrides and duplicates found in include or names

Enabling Tag Helpers

Tag helpers must be enabled in your project, as they are an opt-in feature. The _ViewImports.html file from the standard template already contains the following line to enable the tag helpers built into the ASP.NET Core framework:

```
@addTagHelper *, Microsoft.AspNetCore.Mvc.TagHelpers
```

This makes all tag helpers in the Microsoft.AspNetCore.Mvc.TagHelpers assembly (which contains all the built-in tag helpers) available to all the views at or below the directory level of the _ViewImports.cshtml file.

The Form Tag Helper

The <form> tag helper replaces the Html.BeginForm and Html.BeginRouteForm HTML helpers. For example, to create a form that submits to the HTTP Post version of the EditAsync action on the CarsController with one parameter (Id), use the following code and markup:

```
<form method="post" asp-controller="Cars" asp-action="Edit" asp-route-id="@Model.Id" >
<!-- Omitted for brevity -->
</form>
```

From a strictly HTML perspective, the `<form>` tag will work without the tag helper attributes. If none of the tag helper attributes are present, then it's just a plain old HTML form, and the antiforgery token must be added in manually. However, once one of the tag helpers is added, the antiforgery token is added into the form. The antiforgery token can be disabled by adding `asp-antiforgery="false"` into the form tag.

The Cars Create Form

The create form for the `Car` entity submits to the `Create` action method of the `CarsController`. Add a new empty Razor view named `Create.cshtml` in the `Views\Cars` directory. Update the view to the following:

```
@model Car

@{
  ViewData["Title"] = "Create";
}

<h1>Create a New Car</h1>
<hr/>
<div class="row">
  <div class="col-md-4">
    <form asp-controller="Cars" asp-action="Create">
    </form>
  </div>
</div>
```

This is not the complete view, but it's enough to show what we've covered so far plus the form tag helper. As a review, the first line strongly types the view to the `Car` entity class. The Razor block sets the view-specific title for the page. The HTML `<form>` tag has the `asp-controller` and `asp-action` attributes, which execute on the server side to shape the tag as well as add the antiforgery token.

Now run the application and navigate to `http://localhost:5001/Cars/Create`. Inspecting the source will reveal the form has the action attribute based on the `asp-controller` and `asp-action`, the method is set to `post`, and the `__RequestVerificationToken` was added as a hidden form input.

```
<form action="/Cars/Create" method="post">
  <input name="__RequestVerificationToken" type="hidden" value="CfDJ8EjcsTI5JRZFr8oJwqQ58P
  WHFcqWGyXdpU8sT-ELjcFZcI_6ks7lkomVuPQBOkOOtmlFSCxCk6JK6CZP4Q9Lvo2niGpfIXnHHPQXJGESFUOXS
  wr__XAuG9csJAoBrKDmEFr9KNERleQUD7T5obT3VM8">
</form>
```

Now update the `<form>` tag to disable the antiforgery token:

```
<form asp-controller="Cars" asp-action="Create" asp-antiforgery="false">
</form>
```

If you run the app and inspect the source of the page, the token is no longer there. If the user tried to post this form back, the request would fail because the `CreateAsync()` method has the `[ValidateAntiForgeryToken]` attribute. The request looks like a cross site request and is blocked.

To manually add the token back in, change the asp-antiforgery value to true, remove the attribute entirely (the default is true), or use the Html.AntiForgeryToken() helper to add a token:

```
<form asp-controller="Cars" asp-action="Create" asp-antiforgery="false">
@Html.AntiForgeryToken()
</form>
```

Once again looking at the generated HTML, you can see that the token is back in place. The recommended method for getting the token into your form is to use the default setting by omitting the asp-antiforgery attribute entirely.

The Form Action Button/Image Tag Helper

The form action tag helper is used on buttons and images to change the action for the form that contains them. For example, the following button added to the edit form will cause the post request to go to the Create endpoint of the current controller:

```
<button type="submit" asp-action="Create">Index</button>
```

The Anchor Tag Helper

The <anchor> tag helper replaces the Html.ActionLink HTML helper. It uses many of the same routing tags as the <form> tag helper. For example, to create a link for the RazorSyntax view, use the following code:

```
<a class="nav-link text-dark" asp-area="" asp-controller="Home" asp-action="RazorSyntax">
  Razor Syntax
</a>
```

To add a navigation menu item for the RazorSyntax page, update the _Menu.cshtml to the following, adding the new menu item between the Home and Privacy menu items (the <li> tags surrounding the <anchor> tags are needed when using the Bootstrap menu):

```
...
<li class="nav-item">
  <a class="nav-link text-dark" asp-area="" asp-controller="Home" asp-
  action="Index">Home</a>
</li>
<li class="nav-item">
  <a class="nav-link text-dark" asp-area="" asp-controller="Home" asp-
  action="RazorSyntax">Razor Syntax  <i class="fas fa-cut"></i></a>
</li>
<li class="nav-item">
  <a class="nav-link text-dark" asp-area="" asp-controller="Home" asp-
  action="Privacy">Privacy</a>
</li>
```

The markup after the "Razor Syntax" text is a FontAwesome icon to spruce up the menu.

The anchor tag helper can be combined with the view's model. For example, using the Car instance in the RazorSyntax view, the following anchor tag routes to the Details method passing in the Id as the route parameter:

```
<a asp-controller="Cars" asp-action="Details" asp-route-id="@Model.Id">@Model.PetName</a>
```

The Input Tag Helper

The <input> tag helper is one of the most versatile tag helpers. In addition to autogenerating the HTML id and name attributes, as well as any HTML5 data-val validation attributes, the tag helper builds the appropriate HTML markup based on the data type of the target property. Table 33-3 lists the HTML type that is created based on the .NET type of the property.

Table 33-3. *HTML Types Generated from .NET Types Using the Input Tag Helper*

.NET Type	Generated HTML Type
Bool	type="checkbox"
String	type="text"
DateTime	type="datetime"
Byte, Int, Single, Double	type="number"

Additionally, the <input> tag helper will add HTML5 type attributes based on data annotations. Table 33-4 lists some of the most common annotations and the generated HTML5 type attributes.

Table 33-4. *HTML5 Type Attributes Generated from .NET Data Annotations*

.NET Data Annotation	Generated HTML5 Type Attribute
EmailAddress	type="email"
Url	type="url"
HiddenInput	type="hidden"
Phone	type="tel"
DataType(DataType.Password)	type="password"
DataType(DataType.Date)	type="date"
DataType(DataType.Time)	type="time"

The Car.cshtml editor template contains <input> tags for the PetName and Color properties. As a reminder, just those tags are listed here:

```
<input asp-for="Petname" class="form-control" />
<input asp-for="Color" class="form-control" />
```

The <input> tag helper adds the name and id attributes to the rendered tag, the existing value for the property (if there is one), and HTML5 validation attributes. Both of the fields are required and have a string length limit of 50. Here is the rendered markup for those two properties:

```
<input class="form-control" type="text" data-val="true" data-val-length="The field Pet
Name must be a string with a maximum length of 50." data-val-length-max="50" data-val-
required="The Pet Name field is required." id="PetName" maxlength="50" name="PetName"
value="">

<input class="form-control" type="text" data-val="true" data-val-length="The field
Color must be a string with a maximum length of 50." data-val-length-max="50" data-val-
required="The Color field is required." id="Color" maxlength="50" name="Color" value="">
```

The TextArea Tag Helper

The <textarea> tag helper adds the id and name attributes automatically and any HTML5 validation tags defined for the property. For example, the following line creates a <textarea> tag for the Description property:

```
<textarea asp-for="Description"></textarea>
```

The Select Tag Helper

The <select> tag helper builds input <select> tags from a model property and a collection. As with the <input> tag helper, the id and name are added to the markup, as well as any HTML5 data-val attributes. If the model property value matches one of the select list item's values, that option gets the selected attribute added to the markup.

For example, take a model that has a property named Country and a SelectList named Countries, with the list defined as follows:

```
public List<SelectListItem> Countries { get; } = new List<SelectListItem>
{
  new SelectListItem { Value = "MX", Text = "Mexico" },
  new SelectListItem { Value = "CA", Text = "Canada" },
  new SelectListItem { Value = "US", Text = "USA"  },
};
```

The following markup will render the select tag with the appropriate options:

```
<select asp-for="Country" asp-items="Model.Countries"></select>
```

If the value of the Country property is set to CA, the following full markup will be output to the view:

```
<select id="Country" name="Country">
  <option value="MX">Mexico</option>
  <option selected="selected" value="CA">Canada</option>
  <option value="US">USA</option>
</select>
```

The Validation Tag Helpers

The validation message and validation summary tag helpers closely mirror the Html.ValidationMessageFor and Html.ValidationSummaryFor HTML helpers. The first is applied to an HTML span for a specific property on the model, and the latter is applied to a div tag and represents the entire model. The validation summary has the option of All errors, ModelOnly (excluding errors on model properties), or None.

Recall the validation tag helpers from the Car.cshtml file's EditorTemplate (shown here in bold):

```
<div asp-validation-summary="All" class="text-danger"></div>
<div>
    <label asp-for="PetName" class="form-label"></label>
    <input asp-for="PetName" class="form-control" />
    <span asp-validation-for="PetName" class="text-danger"></span>
</div>
<div>
    <label asp-for="MakeId" class="form-label"></label>
    <select asp-for="MakeId" class="form-control" asp-items="ViewBag.MakeId"></select>
    <span asp-validation-for="MakeId" class="text-danger"></span>
</div>
<div>
    <label asp-for="Color" class="form-label"></label>
    <input asp-for="Color" class="form-control"/>
    <span asp-validation-for="Color" class="text-danger"></span>
</div>
```

These helpers will display ModelState errors from binding and validation, as shown in Figure 33-3.

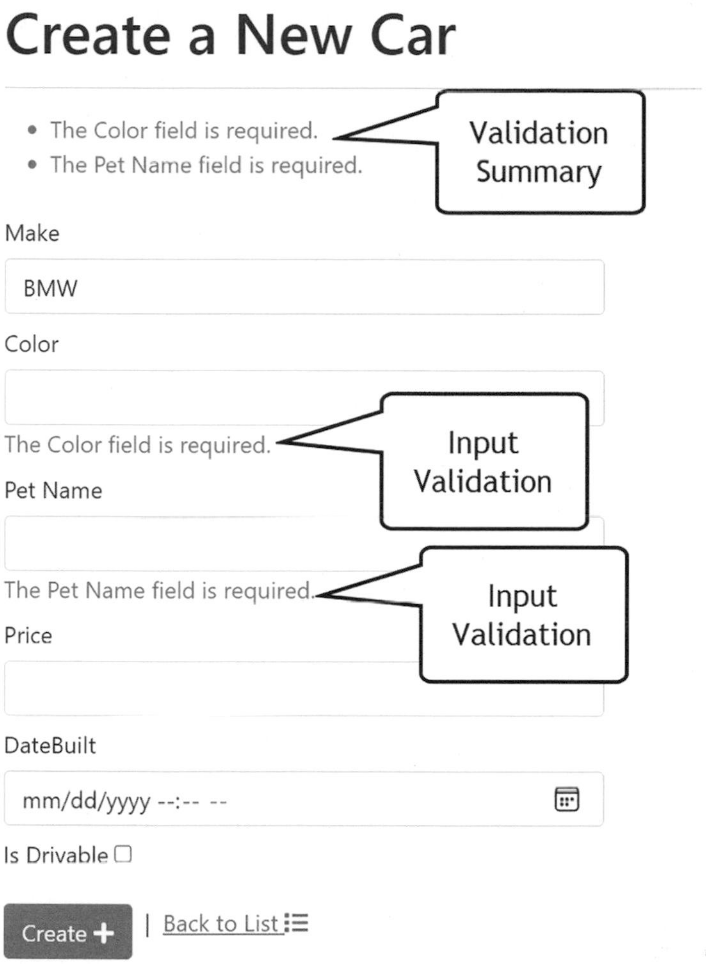

Create a New Car

- The Color field is required.
- The Pet Name field is required.

Validation Summary

Make

BMW

Color

The Color field is required.

Input Validation

Pet Name

The Pet Name field is required.

Input Validation

Price

DateBuilt

mm/dd/yyyy --:-- --

Is Drivable

Create | Back to List

Figure 33-3. The validaton tag helpers in action

The Environment Tag Helper

The <environment> tag helper is typically used to conditionally load JavaScript and CSS files (or any markup for that matter) based on the environment that the site is running under. Open the `_Head.cshtml` partial and update the markup to the following:

```
<meta charset="utf-8" />
<meta name="viewport" content="width=device-width, initial-scale=1.0" />
<title>@ViewData["Title"] - AutoLot.Mvc</title>
<environment include="Development">
    <link rel="stylesheet" href="~/lib/bootstrap/css/bootstrap.css" />
    <link rel="stylesheet" href="~/lib/font-awesome/css/all.css" />
</environment>
```

```
<environment exclude="Development">
    <link rel="stylesheet" href="~/lib/bootstrap/css/bootstrap.min.css" />
    <link rel="stylesheet" href="~/lib/font-awesome/css/all.min.css" />
</environment>
<link rel="stylesheet" href="~/css/site.css" asp-append-version="true" />
<link rel="stylesheet" href="~/AutoLot.Mvc.styles.css" asp-append-version="true" />
```

The first `<environment>` tag helper uses the `include="Development"` attribute to include the contained files when the environment is set to `Development`. In the preceding code, the non-minified versions of Bootstrap and Font Awesome are loaded. The second tag helper uses `exclude="Development"` to include the contained files when the environment is anything *but* `Development` and loads the minified versions. The last two files are minified by WebOptimizer, which is already configured for environment checking, so they are listed outside the `<environment>` tag helper.

Also, update the `_JavaScriptFiles.cshtml` partial to the following (notice the files in the `Development` section no longer have the `.min` extensions):

```
<environment include="Development">
    <script src="~/lib/jquery/jquery.js"></script>
    <script src="~/lib/bootstrap/js/bootstrap.bundle.js"></script>
</environment>
<environment exclude="Development">
    <script src="~/lib/jquery/jquery.min.js"></script>
    <script src="~/lib/bootstrap/js/bootstrap.bundle.min.js"></script>
</environment>
<script src="~/js/site.js" asp-append-version="true"></script>
```

The Link Tag Helper

The `<link>` tag helper has attributes used for both local and remote CSS files. The `asp-append-version` attribute, used with local files, adds the hash of the file as a query string parameter to the URL that is sent to the browser. When the file changes, the hash changes, updating the URL sent to the browser. Since the link changed, the browser purges the cache for that file and reloads it.

Update all of the link tags in the `_Head.cshtml` file to the following (notice that the `site.css` and `AutoLot.Mvc.styles.css` link tags already have the `asp-append-version` attribute):

```
<environment include="Development">
    <link rel="stylesheet" href="~/lib/bootstrap/css/bootstrap.css" asp-append-
    version="true" />
    <link rel="stylesheet" href="~/lib/font-awesome/css/all.css" asp-append-
    version="true" />
</environment>
<environment exclude="Development">
    <link rel="stylesheet" href="~/lib/bootstrap/css/bootstrap.min.css" asp-append-
    version="true" />
    <link rel="stylesheet" href="~/lib/font-awesome/css/all.min.css" asp-append-
    version="true" />
</environment>
<link rel="stylesheet" href="~/css/site.css" asp-append-version="true" />
<link rel="stylesheet" href="~/AutoLot.Mvc.styles.css" asp-append-version="true" />
```

The link sent to the browser for the `site.css` file now resembles the following (your hash will vary):

```
<link href="/css/site.css?v=v9cmzjNgxPHiyLIrNom5fw3tZj3TNT2QD7aOhBrSa4U" rel="stylesheet">
```

When loading CSS files from a content delivery network (CDN), the tag helpers provide a test mechanism to ensure the file was loaded properly. The test is looking for a specific value (`absolute`) for a property (`position`) on a specific CSS class, (`sr-only`) and if the property doesn't match, the tag helper will load the fallback file instead. Cross origin must be set to anonymous so no auth cookies are sent to the CDN, and the integrity check ensures the expected file is the one being downloaded. If the hash of the CDN file fails the integrity check, the tag helper will load the fallback file instead. Update the link tags enclosed by the `<environment exclude="Development">` tag helper to match the following:

```
<environment exclude="Development">
  <link rel="stylesheet" href="https://cdnjs.cloudflare.com/ajax/libs/bootstrap/5.1.3/css/
bootstrap.min.css"
          asp-fallback-href="~/lib/bootstrap/css/bootstrap.min.css"
          asp-append-version="true"
          asp-fallback-test-class="sr-only"
          asp-fallback-test-property="position"
          asp-fallback-test-value="absolute"
          crossorigin="anonymous"
          integrity="sha512-GQGUOfMMi238uA+a/bdWJfpUGKUkBdgfFdgBm72SUQ6BeyWjoY/tonOtEjH+OSH9
          iP4Dfh+7HMOI9f5eROL/4w=="/>
  <link rel="stylesheet" href="https://cdnjs.cloudflare.com/ajax/libs/font-awesome/5.15.4/
css/all.min.css"
          asp-fallback-href="~/lib/font-awesome/css/all.min.css"
          asp-append-version="true"
          asp-fallback-test-class="fab"
          asp-fallback-test-property="display"
          asp-fallback-test-value="inline-block"
          crossorigin="anonymous"
          integrity="sha512-1ycn6IcaQQ40/MKBW2W4Rhis/
          DbILU74C1vSrLJxCq57o941Ym01SwNsOMqvEBFlcgUa6xLiPY/NS5R+E6ztJQ=="/>
</environment>
```

An important note, especially if you are developing/deploying on Windows, is that the integrity check applies to both the CDN file and the local file. If your local file changes the line endings, then the hash of the local file won't match the hash in the integrity attribute and the resource will be blocked.

This be resolved by not conducting the integrity check on the fallback file by adding `asp-suppress-fallback-integrity="true"` to the link tag helpers:

```
<link rel="stylesheet" href="https://cdnjs.cloudflare.com/ajax/libs/bootstrap/5.1.3/css/
bootstrap.min.css"
  asp-fallback-href="~/lib/bootstrap/css/bootstrap.min.css"
  asp-append-version="true" asp-fallback-test-class="sr-only"
  asp-fallback-test-property="position" asp-fallback-test-value="absolute"
  asp-suppress-fallback-integrity="true"
  crossorigin="anonymous"
  integrity="sha512-GQGUOfMMi238uA+a/bdWJfpUGKUkBdgfFdgBm72SUQ6BeyWjoY/tonOtEjH+OSH9iP4Dfh+
  7HMOI9f5eROL/4w=="/>
```

```
<link rel="stylesheet" href="https://cdnjs.cloudflare.com/ajax/libs/font-awesome/5.15.4/
css/all.min.css"
        asp-fallback-href="~/lib/font-awesome/css/all.min.css"
        asp-append-version="true"
        asp-fallback-test-class="fab"
        asp-fallback-test-property="display"
        asp-fallback-test-value="inline-block"
        asp-suppress-fallback-integrity="true"
        crossorigin="anonymous"
        integrity="sha512-1ycn6IcaQQ40/MKBW2W4Rhis/
        DbILU74C1vSrLJxCq57o941Ym01SwNsOMqvEBFlcgUa6xLiPY/NS5R+E6ztJQ=="/>
```

■ **Note** If you decide to skip the integrity check for your local file, make sure that some other checks are in place to verify that the local file is indeed the correct file and hasn't been spoofed or hacked.

The Script Tag Helper

The `<script>` tag helper is similar to the `<link>` tag helper with cache busting and CDN fallback settings. The `asp-append-version` attribute works the same for scripts as it does for linked stylesheets. The `asp-fallback-*` attributes are also used with CDN file sources. The `asp-fallback-test` simply checks for JavaScript truthiness and, if it fails, loads the file from the fallback source.

Update the `_JavaScriptFiles.cshtml` partial to use the cache busting and the CDN fallback capabilities (notice that the `site.js` `script` tag already has the asp-append-version attribute):

```
<environment include="Development">
    <script src="~/lib/jquery/jquery.js" asp-append-version="true"></script>
    <script src="~/lib/bootstrap/js/bootstrap.bundle.js" asp-append-version="true"></script>
</environment>
<environment exclude="Development">
    <script src="https://cdnjs.cloudflare.com/ajax/libs/jquery/3.6.0/jquery.min.js"
            asp-append-version="true"
            asp-fallback-src="~/lib/jquery/jquery.min.js"
            asp-fallback-test="window.jQuery"
            asp-suppress-fallback-integrity="true"
            crossorigin="anonymous"
            integrity="sha512-894YE6QWD5I59HgZOGReFYm4dnWc1Qt5NtvYSaNcOP+u1T9qYdvdihzOPPSiiq
            n/+/3e7Jo4EaG7TubfWGUrMQ==">
    </script>
    <script src="https://cdn.jsdelivr.net/npm/bootstrap@5.1.3/dist/js/bootstrap.
    bundle.min.js"
            asp-append-version="true"
            asp-fallback-src="~/lib/bootstrap/js/bootstrap.bundle.min.js"
            asp-fallback-test="window.jQuery && window.jQuery.fn && window.jQuery.fn.modal"
            asp-suppress-fallback-integrity="true"
            crossorigin="anonymous"
           integrity="sha384-ka7Sk0Gln4gmtz2MlQnikT1wXgYsOg+OMhuP+IlRH9sENBO0LRn5q+8nbTov4+1p">
    </script>
```

```
</environment>
<script src="~/js/site.js" asp-append-version="true"></script>
```

The _ValidationScriptsPartial.cshtml needs to be updated with the <environment> and <script> tag helpers.

```
<environment include="Development">
  <script src="~/lib/jquery/dist/jquery.js" asp-append-version="true"></script>
  <script src="~/lib/jquery-validation-unobtrusive/jquery.validate.unobtrusive.js" asp-
  append-version="true"></script>
</environment>
<environment exclude="Development">
  <script src="https://cdnjs.cloudflare.com/ajax/libs/jquery-validate/1.19.3/jquery.
  validate.min.js"
          asp-fallback-src="~/lib/jquery-validation/jquery.validate.min.js"
          asp-fallback-test="window.jQuery && window.jQuery.validator"
          asp-append-version="true"
          crossorigin="anonymous"
          integrity="sha512-37T7leoNS06R80c8Ulq7cdCDU5MNQBwlYoy1TX/
          WUsLFC2eYNqtKlV0QjH7r8JpG/S0GUMZwebnVFLPd6SU5yg==">
  </script>
  <script src="https://cdnjs.cloudflare.com/ajax/libs/jquery-validation-unobtrusive/3.2.12/
  jquery.validate.unobtrusive.min.js"
          asp-fallback-src="~/lib/jquery-validation-unobtrusive/jquery.validate.
          unobtrusive.min.js"
          asp-fallback-test="window.jQuery && window.jQuery.validator && window.jQuery.
          validator.unobtrusive"
          asp-append-version="true"
          crossorigin="anonymous"
          integrity="sha512-o6XqxgrUsKmchwy9G5VRNWSSxTS4Urr4loO6/0hYdpWmFUfHqGzawGxeQGMDqY
          zxjY9sbktPbNlkIQJWagVZQg==">
  </script>
</environment>
```

The Image Tag Helper

The image tag helper provides the asp-append-version attribute, which works the same as described in the link and script tag helpers.

Custom Tag Helpers

Like the built-in tag helpers, custom tag helpers can be developed to help shape HTML tags or create custom tags. When building a CRUD based user interface, each of the screens typically has a set of links to navigate to other screens in the application. For example, the details page has links to edit, delete, and go back to the list. For AutoLot.Mvc, custom tag helpers will replace the HTML used to navigate around the Car CRUD screens reducing repetitive code and providing a consistent look and feel.

Set the Foundation

The custom tag helpers use a UrlHelperFactory and IActionContextAccessor to create the links based on routing.

Update Program.cs

To create an instance of the UrlFactory from a non-Controller-derived class, the IActionContextAccessor must be added to the services collection. Call the following line in Program.cs to add the IActionContextAccessor into the services collection:

```
builder.Services.TryAddSingleton<IActionContextAccessor, ActionContextAccessor>();
```

Create the Base Class

Create a new folder named TagHelpers in the root of the AutoLot.Mvc project. In this folder, create a new folder named Base, and in that folder, create a class named ItemLinkTagHelperBase.cs, make the class public and abstract, and inherit from TagHelper:

```
namespace AutoLot.Mvc.TagHelpers.Base;

public abstract class ItemLinkTagHelperBase : TagHelper
{
}
```

Add a constructor that takes instances of IActionContextAccessor and IUrlHelperFactory. Use the UrlHelperFactory with the ActionContextAccessor to create an instance of IUrlHelper, and store that in a class-level variable. The code is shown here:

```
protected readonly IUrlHelper UrlHelper;
protected ItemLinkTagHelperBase(IActionContextAccessor contextAccessor, IUrlHelperFactory
urlHelperFactory)
{
  UrlHelper = urlHelperFactory.GetUrlHelper(contextAccessor.ActionContext);
}
```

In the constructor, use the contextAccessor instance to get the current controller and assign it to a class level field:

```
protected readonly IUrlHelper UrlHelper;
private readonly string _controllerName;
protected ItemLinkTagHelperBase(IActionContextAccessor contextAccessor, IUrlHelperFactory
urlHelperFactory)
{
  UrlHelper = urlHelperFactory.GetUrlHelper(contextAccessor.ActionContext);
  _controllerName = contextAccessor.ActionContext.ActionDescriptor.
  RouteValues["controller"];
}
```

Add a protected property so the derived classes can indicate the action name for the route:

```
protected string ActionName { get; set; }
```

Add a single public property to hold the Id of the item, as follows:

```
public int? ItemId { get; set; }
```

Public properties on custom tag helpers are exposed as HTML attributes on the tag. The naming convention is that the property name is converted to lower-kabob-casing. This means every capital letter is lowercases and dashes (-) are inserted before each letter that is changed to lower case (except for the first one). This converts ItemId to item-id (like words on a shish-kabob).

When a tag helper is invoked, the Process() method is called. The Process() method takes two parameters: the TagHelperContext and the TagHelperOutput. The TagHelperContext is used to get any other attributes on the tag and a dictionary of objects used to communicate with other tag helpers targeting child elements. The TagHelperOutput is used to create the rendered output.

Since this is a base class, we will add a method called BuildContent() that the derived classes can call from the Process() method. Add the following method and code:

```
protected void BuildContent(
  TagHelperOutput output, string cssClassName, string displayText, string fontAwesomeName)
{
  output.TagName = "a"; // Replaces <item-> with <a> tag
  var target = (ItemId.HasValue)
    ? UrlHelper.Action(ActionName, _controllerName, new {id = ItemId})
    : UrlHelper.Action(ActionName, _controllerName);
  output.Attributes.SetAttribute("href", target);
  output.Attributes.Add("class",cssClassName);
  output.Content.AppendHtml($@"{displayText} <i class=""fas fa-{fontAwesomeName}""></i>");
}
```

The first line changes the tag from the tag used in the markup to the anchor tag. The next uses the UrlAction.Action() static method to generate the route, including the route parameter if one exists. The next two set the HREF of the anchor tag to the generated route and add the CSS class name. The final line adds the display text and a Font Awesome font as the text that is displayed to the user.

As the final step, add the following global using statement to the GlobalUsings.cs file:

```
global using AutoLot.Mvc.TagHelpers.Base;
```

The Item Details Tag Helper

Create a new class named ItemDetailsTagHelper.cs in the TagHelpers folder. Make the class public and inherit from ItemLinkTagHelperBase.

```
namespace AutoLot.Mvc.TagHelpers;

  public class ItemDetailsTagHelper : ItemLinkTagHelperBase
{
}
```

Add a constructor to take in the required object instances and pass them to the base class. The constructor also needs to assign the ActionName:

```
public ItemDetailsTagHelper(
    IActionContextAccessor contextAccessor,
    IUrlHelperFactory urlHelperFactory)
    : base(contextAccessor, urlHelperFactory)
  {
    ActionName = nameof(CarsController.DetailsAsync).RemoveAsyncSuffix();
  }
```

A note about the controller name used in the nameof() method: recall that the method returns the method name (DetailsAsync), and the controller name isn't output. For each of these custom tag helpers, the base class needs to know the action method name, and all of the basic CRUD actions are on the base controller. However, using nameof() with the generic BaseCrudController is a bit messy, so we are substituting an implementation of the BaseCrudController to use the nameof() method.

Override the Process() method, calling the BuildContent() method in the base class.

```
public override void Process(TagHelperContext context, TagHelperOutput output)
{
  BuildContent(output, "text-info", "Details", "info-circle");
}
```

This creates a Details link using the CSS class text-info, the text of Details with the Font Awesome info image:

```
<a asp-action="Details" asp-route-id="5" class="text-info">Details <i class="fas fa-info-circle"></i></a>
```

When invoking tag helpers, the TagHelper suffix is dropped, and the remaining name of class is lower-kebob-cased. In this case, the HTML tag is <item-details>. The asp-route-id value comes from the item-id attribute on the tag helper:

```
<item-details item-id="@item.Id"></item-details>
```

The Item Delete Tag Helper

Create a new class named ItemDeleteTagHelper.cs in the TagHelpers folder. Make the class public and inherit from ItemLinkTagHelperBase. Add the constructor to take in the required object instances and set the ActionName using the DeleteAsync() method name:

```
public ItemDeleteTagHelper(
    IActionContextAccessor contextAccessor,
    IUrlHelperFactory urlHelperFactory)
      : base(contextAccessor, urlHelperFactory)
{
  ActionName = nameof(CarsController.DeleteAsync).RemoveAsyncSuffix();
}
```

Override the Process() method, calling the BuildContent() method in the base class.

```
public override void Process(TagHelperContext context, TagHelperOutput output)
{
  BuildContent(output,"text-danger","Delete","trash");
}
```

This creates the Delete link with the Font Awesome garbage can image.

```
<a asp-action="Delete" asp-route-id="5" class="text-danger">Delete <i class="fas
fa-trash"></i></a>
```

The asp-route-id value comes from the item-id attribute on the tag helper:

```
<item-delete item-id="@item.Id"></item-delete>
```

The Item Edit Tag Helper

Create a new class named ItemEditTagHelper.cs in the TagHelpers folder. Make the class public, inherit from ItemLinkTagHelperBase and add the constructor that assign Edit as the ActionName:

```
namespace AutoLot.Mvc.TagHelpers;
public class ItemEditTagHelper : ItemLinkTagHelperBase
{
  public ItemEditTagHelper(
    IActionContextAccessor contextAccessor,
    IUrlHelperFactory urlHelperFactory)
      : base(contextAccessor, urlHelperFactory)
  {
    ActionName = nameof(CarsController.EditAsync).RemoveAsyncSuffix();
  }
}
```

Override the Process() method, calling the BuildContent() method in the base class.

```
public override void Process(TagHelperContext context, TagHelperOutput output)
{
  BuildContent(output,"text-warning","Edit","edit");
}
```

This creates the Edit link with the Font Awesome pencil image:

```
<a asp-action="Edit" asp-route-id="5" class="text-warning">Edit <i class="fas fa-
edit"></i></a>
```

The asp-route-id value comes from the item-id attribute on the tag helper:

```
<item-edit item-id="@item.Id"></item-edit>
```

The Item Create Tag Helper

Create a new class named ItemCreateTagHelper.cs in the TagHelpers folder. Make the class public, inherit from ItemLinkTagHelperBase and add the constructor that assigns "Create" as the ActionName:

```
namespace AutoLot.Mvc.TagHelpers;

public class ItemCreateTagHelper : ItemLinkTagHelperBase
{
  public ItemCreateTagHelper(
      IActionContextAccessor contextAccessor,
      IUrlHelperFactory urlHelperFactory)
        : base(contextAccessor, urlHelperFactory)
  {
    ActionName = nameof(CarsController.CreateAsync).RemoveAsyncSuffix();
  }

}
```

Override the Process() method, calling the BuildContent() method in the base class.

```
public override void Process(TagHelperContext context, TagHelperOutput output)
{
  BuildContent(output,"text-success","Create New","plus");
}
```

This creates the Create link with the Font Awesome plus image:

```
<a asp-action="Create" class="text-warning">Create New <I class="fas fa-plus"></i></a>
```

There isn't a route parameter with the Create action:

```
<item-create></item-create>
```

The Item List Tag Helper

Create a new class named ItemListTagHelper.cs in the TagHelpers folder. Make the class public, inherit from ItemLinkTagHelperBase and add the constructor that assigns "List" as the ActionName:

```
namespace AutoLot.Mvc.TagHelpers;

public class ItemListTagHelper : ItemLinkTagHelperBase
{
  public ItemListTagHelper(
    IActionContextAccessor contextAccessor,
    IUrlHelperFactory urlHelperFactory)
      : base(contextAccessor, urlHelperFactory)
  {
    ActionName = nameof(CarsController.IndexAsync).RemoveAsyncSuffix();
  }
}
```

Override the Process() method, calling the BuildContent() method in the base class.

```
public override void Process(TagHelperContext context, TagHelperOutput output)
{
  BuildContent(output,"text-default","Back to List","list");
}
```

This creates the Index link with the Font Awesome plus image:

```
<a asp-action="Index" class="text-default">Back to list <i class="fas fa-list"></i></a>
```

There isn't a route parameter with the Create action:

```
<item-list></item-list>
```

Making Custom Tag Helpers Visible

To make custom tag helpers visible, the @addTagHelper command must be executed for any views that use the tag helpers or are added to the _ViewImports.cshtml file. Open the _ViewImports.cshtml file in the root of the Views folder and add the following line:

```
@addTagHelper *, AutoLot.Mvc
```

HTML Helpers

While tag helpers have replaced many of the HTML helpers used in ASP.NET MVC, there are still several that don't have a tag helper equivalent. Table 33-5 lists some of the HTML helpers still commonly used (and used in this chapter).

Table 33-5. *Commonly Used HTML Helpers*

HTML Helper	Use
Html.DisplayFor()	Displays an object defined by the expression
Html.DisplayForModel()	Displays the model using the default template or a custom template
Html.DisplayNameFor()	Gets the Display name if it exists or the property name in the absence of a Display name
Html.EditorFor()	Displays an editor for an object defined by the expression
Html.EditorForModel()	Displays an editor for the model using the default template or a custom template

The DisplayFor HTML Helper

The DisplayFor() helper displays an object defined by an expression. If there is a display template for the type being displayed, then it will be used to create the HTML for the item. For example, on the RazorSyntax view, the Make information for the view's Car can be displayed using this:

```
@Html.DisplayFor(x=>x.MakeNavigation);
```

Since there isn't a custom template for Make class that is reachable (in the DisplayTemplates folder of the current controller's directory or the Shared directory), the view engine used reflection to emit the following HTML:

```
<div class="display-label">Name</div>
<div class="display-label">BMW</div>
<div class="display-label">Id</div>
<div class="display-label">5</div>
```

If a view named Make.cshtml exists and is reachable, then that view will be used to render the HTML (remember that the template name lookup is based on the type of an object, and not its property name). If there is a view named ShowMake.cshtml (for example), it can be used to render the object with the following call:

```
@Html.DisplayFor(x=>x.MakeNavigation, "ShowMake");
```

If a template isn't specified and there isn't a template for the class name, reflection is used to create the HTML for display.

The DisplayForModel HTML Helper

The DisplayForModel() helper displays the model for the view. If there is a display template for the type being displayed, then it will be used to create the HTML for the item. Add the following to the bottom of the RazorSyntax view:

```
@Html.DisplayForModel();
```

Just like the DisplayFor() helper, if a display template named for the type exists, it will be used. There is a Car.cshtml display template, but it is in the Cars directory structure, not the Home directory structure where the RazorSyntax view lives. To use a template from another directory structure, you have to not only specify the name of the view but the full path and file extension:

```
@Html.DisplayForModel("../Cars/DisplayTemplates/Car.cshtml")
```

Named templates can also be used. For example, to display the Car with the CarWithColors.html display template, use the following call (presuming the template is in the same directory structure or the Shared directory:

```
@Html.DisplayForModel("CarWithColors");
```

The EditorFor and EditorForModel HTML Helpers

The `EditorFor()` and `EditorForModel()` helpers function the same as their corresponding display helpers. The difference is that templates are searched in the `EditorTemplates` directory and HTML editors are displayed instead of a read-only representation of the object.

The Car Views

This section finishes the stubbed out views and adds the remaining views for the `CarsController`. If you set the `RebuildDatabase` flag in `appsettings.Development.json` to `true`, then any changes you make while testing these views will be reset the next time you start the application.

The Car List Partial View

There are two views available for the Index page. One shows the entire inventory of cars and one the list of cars by make. Since the UI is the same, the lists will be rendered using a partial view.

Create a new directory named `Partials` under the `Views\Cars` directory. In this directory, add a new view named `_CarListPartial.cshtml`, and clear out the existing code. Set `IEnumerable<Car>` as the type (it doesn't need to be fully qualified because we added the `AutoLot.Models.Entities` namespace to the `_ViewImports.cshtml` file).

```
@model IEnumerable< Car>
```

Next, add a Razor block with the set of a Boolean variables indicating whether the `Makes` should be displayed. When this partial is used by the entire inventory list, the `Makes` should be displayed. When it is showing only a single `Make`, the `Make` field should be hidden.

```
@{
    var showMake = true;
    if (bool.TryParse(ViewBag.ByMake?.ToString(), out bool byMake))
    {
        showMake = !byMake;
    }
}
```

The next markup uses the `ItemCreateTagHelper` to create a link to the `Create` HTTP Get method. As a reminder, when using custom tag helpers, the name is lower-kebab-cased. That means the `TagHelper` suffix is dropped, and then each Pascal-cased word is lowercased and separated with a hyphen:

```
<p>
  <item-create></item-create>
</p>
```

In the table headers, a Razor HTML helper is used to get the `DisplayName` for each of the properties. `DisplayName` will select the value of the `Display` or `DisplayName` attribute, and if neither are set, it will use the property name. This section uses a Razor block to show the `Make` information based on the view-level variable set earlier.

```
<table class="table">
  <thead>
  <tr>
    @if (showMake)
    {
      <th>@Html.DisplayNameFor(model => model.MakeId)</th>
    }
    <th>@Html.DisplayNameFor(model => model.Color)</th>
    <th>@Html.DisplayNameFor(model => model.PetName)</th>
    <th>@Html.DisplayNameFor(model => model.Price)</th>
    <th>@Html.DisplayNameFor(model => model.DateBuilt)</th>
    <th>@Html.DisplayNameFor(model => model.IsDrivable)</th>
    <th></th>
  </tr>
  </thead>
```

The final section loops through the records and displays the table records using the `DisplayFor` Razor HTML helper. This helper will look for a `DisplayTemplate` template name that matches the type of the property and, if not found, will create the markup in the default manner. For example, the `DateBuilt` property will use the `DateTime.cshtml` display template created earlier in the chapter.

This block also uses the `item-edit`, `item-details`, and `item-delete` custom tag helpers. As a reminder, when passing in values to public properties on a custom tag helper, the property name is lower-kebab-cased and added to the tag as an attribute.

```
<tbody>
  @foreach (var item in Model)
  {
    <tr>
      @if (showMake)
      {
        <td>@Html.DisplayFor(modelItem => item.MakeNavigation.Name)</td>
      }
      <td>@Html.DisplayFor(modelItem => item.Color) </td>
      <td>@Html.DisplayFor(modelItem => item.PetName)</td>
      <td>@Html.DisplayFor(modelItem => item.Price)</td>
      <td>@Html.DisplayFor(modelItem => item.DateBuilt)</td>
      <td>@Html.DisplayFor(modelItem => item.IsDrivable)</td>
      <td>
        <item-edit item-id="@item.Id"></item-edit> |
        <item-details item-id="@item.Id"></item-details> |
        <item-delete item-id="@item.Id"></item-delete>
      </td>
    </tr>
  }
  </tbody>
</table>
```

The Index View

With the `_CarListPartial` partial in place, the `Index` view is quite small, demonstrating the benefit of using partial views to cut down on repetitive markup. Create a new view named `Index.cshtml` in the `Views\Cars` directory. Clear out any generated code and add the following:

```
@model IEnumerable<Car>
@{
  ViewData["Title"] = "Index";
}
<h1>Vehicle Inventory</h1>
<partial name="Partials/_CarListPartial" model="@Model"/>
```

The partial `_CarListPartial` is invoked with the containing view's model value (`IEnumerable<Car>`) passed in with the `model` attribute. This sets the model of the partial view to the object passed into the `<partial>` tag helper. Recall that the `BaseCrudController's Index()` action method returns all records for the type.

To see this view in action, run the application and navigate to `https://localhost:5001/Cars/Index`, and you will see the list shown in Figure 33-4.

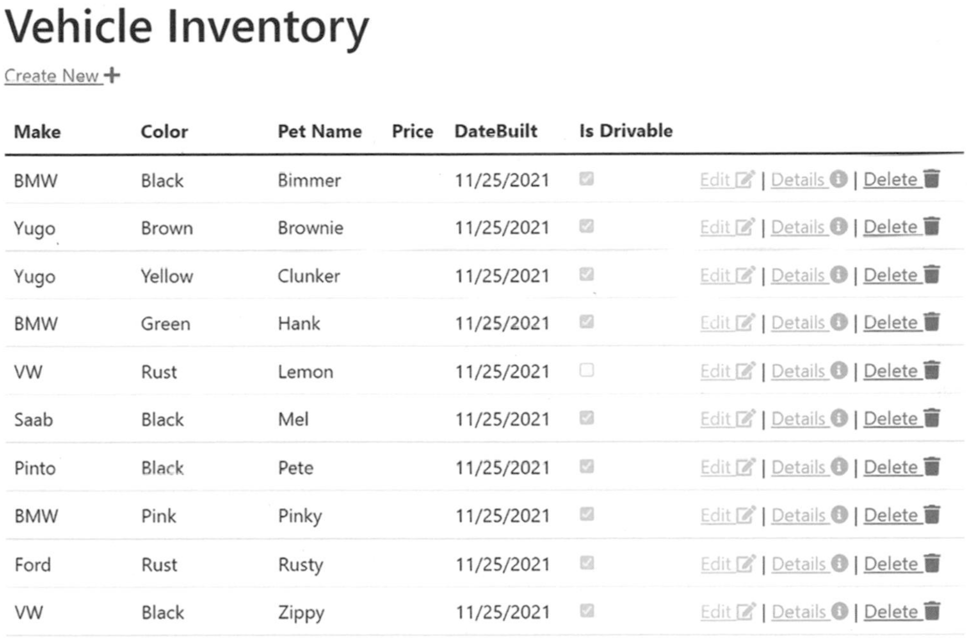

Vehicle Inventory

Create New +

Make	Color	Pet Name	Price	DateBuilt	Is Drivable	
BMW	Black	Bimmer		11/25/2021	☑	Edit | Details | Delete
Yugo	Brown	Brownie		11/25/2021	☑	Edit | Details | Delete
Yugo	Yellow	Clunker		11/25/2021	☑	Edit | Details | Delete
BMW	Green	Hank		11/25/2021	☑	Edit | Details | Delete
VW	Rust	Lemon		11/25/2021	☐	Edit | Details | Delete
Saab	Black	Mel		11/25/2021	☑	Edit | Details | Delete
Pinto	Black	Pete		11/25/2021	☑	Edit | Details | Delete
BMW	Pink	Pinky		11/25/2021	☑	Edit | Details | Delete
Ford	Rust	Rusty		11/25/2021	☑	Edit | Details | Delete
VW	Black	Zippy		11/25/2021	☑	Edit | Details | Delete

Figure 33-4. *The car inventory page*

The ByMake View

The `ByMake` view is similar to the `Index` but sets up the partial to not display `Make` information except in the title of the page. Create a new view named `ByMake.cshtml` in the `Views\Cars` directory. Clear out any generated code and add the following:

```
@model IEnumerable<Car>
@{
    ViewData["Title"] = "Index";
}
<h1>Vehicle Inventory for @ViewBag.MakeName</h1>
@{
    var mode = new ViewDataDictionary(ViewData) {{"ByMake", true}};
}
<partial name="Partials/_CarListPartial" model="Model" view-data="@mode"/>
```

There are two distinct differences. The first is it creates a new ViewDataDictionary containing the ByMake property from the ViewBag. This is then passed into the partial, along with the model, both of which are used by the _CarListPartial view.

Now that you have the Index view in place, run the application and navigate to https://localhost:5001/Cars/ByMake/5/BMW, and you will see the list shown in Figure 33-5.

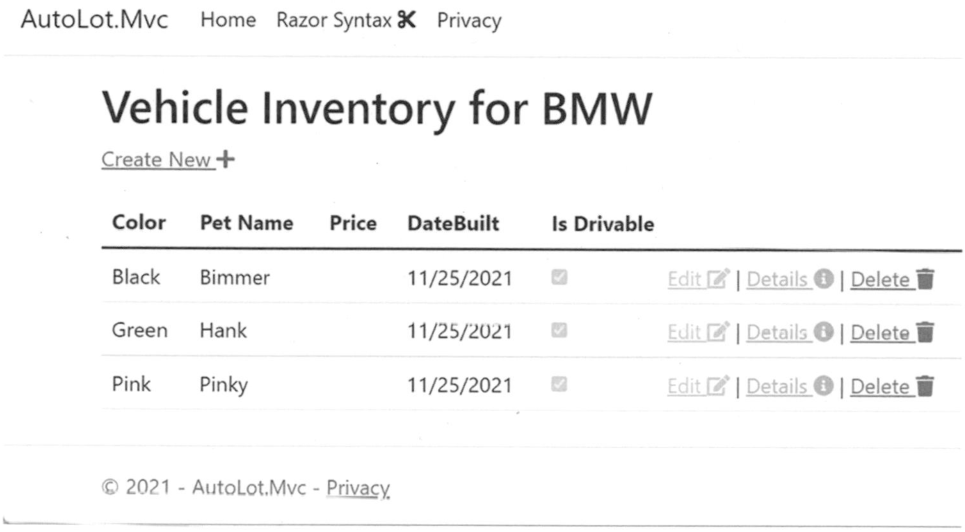

AutoLot.Mvc Home Razor Syntax Privacy

Vehicle Inventory for BMW

Create New

Color	Pet Name	Price	DateBuilt	Is Drivable	
Black	Bimmer		11/25/2021		Edit | Details | Delete
Green	Hank		11/25/2021		Edit | Details | Delete
Pink	Pinky		11/25/2021		Edit | Details | Delete

© 2021 - AutoLot.Mvc - Privacy

Figure 33-5. *The car inventory for a specific make*

The Details View

Create a new view named Details.cshtml in the Views\Cars directory. Clear out any generated code and add the following:

```
@model Car
@{
  ViewData["Title"] = "Details";
}
<h1>Details for @Model.PetName</h1>
@Html.DisplayForModel()
<div>
  <item-edit item-id="@Model.Id"></item-edit>
```

```
  <item-delete item-id="@Model.Id"></item-delete>
  <item-list></item-list>
</div>
```

The `@Html.DisplayForModel()` uses the display template (`Car.cshtml`) built earlier in this section to display the `Car` details. Run the application and navigate to `https://localhost:5001/Cars/Details/5`, and you will see the screen shown in Figure 33-6.

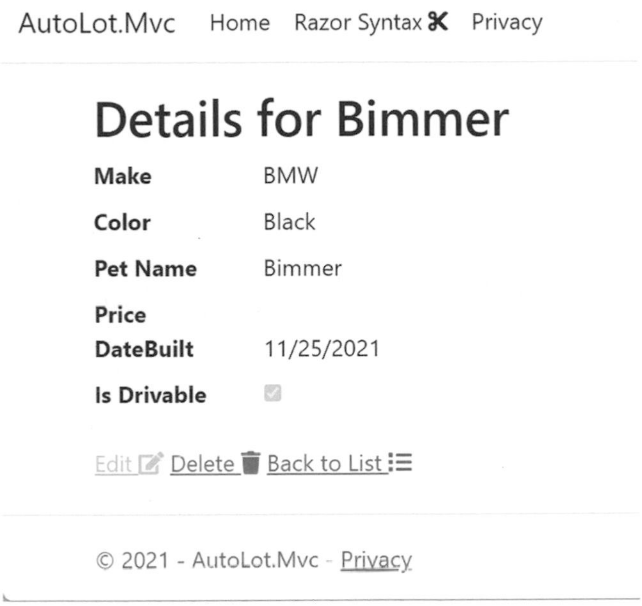

AutoLot.Mvc Home Razor Syntax Privacy

Details for Bimmer

Make BMW

Color Black

Pet Name Bimmer

Price

DateBuilt 11/25/2021

Is Drivable

Edit Delete Back to List

© 2021 - AutoLot.Mvc - Privacy

Figure 33-6. *The details for a specific car*

The `@Html.DisplayForModel()` line can be replaced with `@Html.DisplayForModel("CarWithColors")` to display the template that uses color in the display.

The Create View

The `Create` view was started earlier. Here is the full listing of the completed view:

```
@model Car

@{
    ViewData["Title"] = "Create";
}

<h1>Create a New Car</h1>
<hr/>
<form asp-controller="Cars" asp-action="Create">
  <div class="row">
    <div class="col-md-4">
      <div asp-validation-summary="ModelOnly" class="text-danger"></div>
```

```
        @Html.EditorForModel()
    </div>
  </div>
  <div class="d-flex flex-row mt-3">
    <button type="submit" class="btn btn-success">Create <i class="fas fa-plus"></
i></button>
        |  
    <item-list></item-list>
  </div>
</form>
@section Scripts {
    <partial name="_ValidationScriptsPartial" />
}
```

The `@Html.EditorForModel()` method uses the editor template (`Car.cshtml`) built earlier in this section to display the `Car` edit screen.

This view also brings in the `_ValidationScriptsPartial` in the `Scripts` section. Recall that in the layout this section occurs *after* loading jQuery. The sections pattern helps ensure that the proper dependencies are loaded before the contents of the section.

The create form can be viewed at `/Cars/Create` and is shown in Figure 33-7.

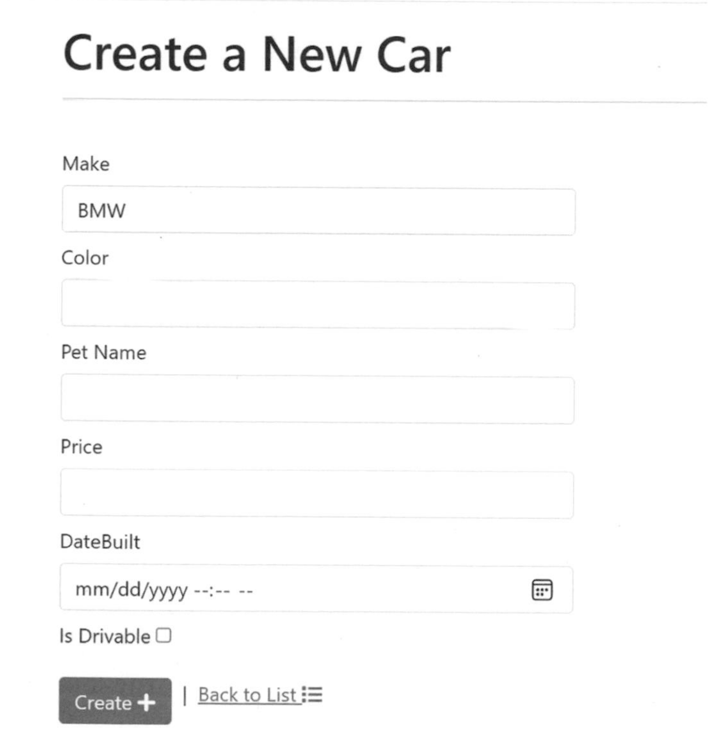

Create a New Car

Make

BMW

Color

Pet Name

Price

DateBuilt

mm/dd/yyyy --:-- --

Is Drivable

Create | Back to List

Figure 33-7. *The Create view*

The Edit View

Create a new view named Edit.cshtml in the Views\Cars directory. Clear out any generated code and add the following:

```
@model Car

@{
    ViewData["Title"] = "Edit";
}
@if (ViewData["Error"] != null)
{
    <div class="alert alert-danger" role="alert">
        @ViewData["Error"]
    </div>
}
else
{
  <h1>Edit @Model.PetName</h1>
  <hr />
  <form asp-area="" asp-controller="Cars" asp-action="Edit" asp-route-id="@Model.Id">
    <div class="row">
      <div class="col-md-4">
        @Html.EditorForModel()
      </div>
    </div>
    <div class="d-flex flex-row mt-3">
      <input type="hidden" asp-for="Id" />
      <input type="hidden" asp-for="TimeStamp" />
      <button type="submit" class="btn btn-primary">
         Save <i class="fas fa-save"></i></button>  |  
       <item-list></item-list>
    </div>
  </form>
}
@section Scripts {
    <partial name="_ValidationScriptsPartial" />
}
```

This view checks to see if there was an error passed from the controller, and if so, displays an alert and stops processing. Otherwise, it displays the edit form. This view also uses the @Html.EditorForModel() method and _ValidationScriptsPartial, but it also includes two hidden inputs for the Id and TimeStamp as well. These will be posted along with the rest of the form data but should not be edited by users. Without the Id and TimeStamp, the updates would not be able to be saved.

The edit form can be viewed at /Cars/Edit/1 and is shown in Figure 33-8.

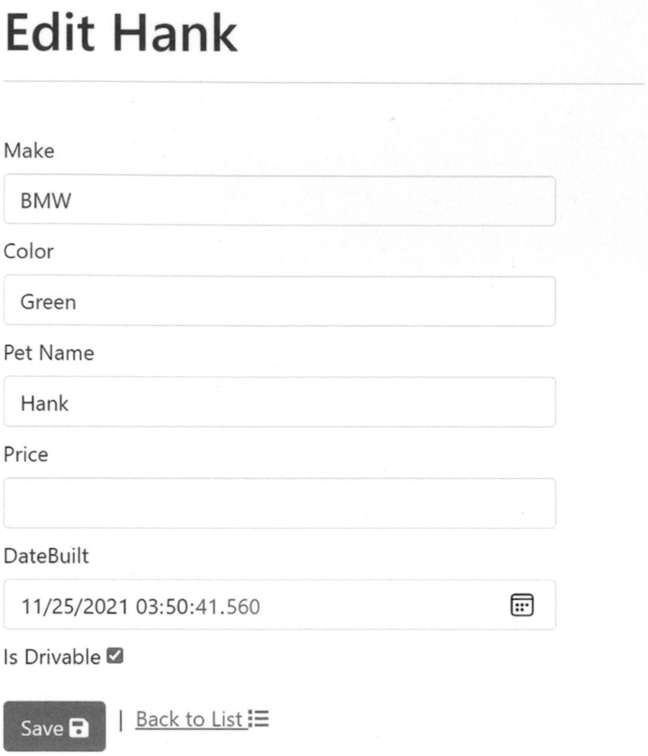

Figure 33-8. *The edit view*

The Delete View

Create a new view named `Delete.cshtml` in the `Views\Cars` directory. Clear out any generated code and add the following:

```
@model Car

@{
    ViewData["Title"] = "Delete";
}
@if (ViewData["Error"] != null)
{
    <div class="alert alert-danger" role="alert">
        @ViewData["Error"]
    </div>
}
else
{
  <h1>Delete @Model.PetName</h1>
  <h3>Are you sure you want to delete this car?</h3>
  <div>
```

```
    <div asp-validation-summary="All" class="text-danger"></div>
    @Html.DisplayForModel()
    <form asp-action="Delete">
      <input type="hidden" asp-for="Id"/>
      <input type="hidden" asp-for="TimeStamp"/>
      <button type="submit" class="btn btn-danger">Delete <i class="fas fa-trash"></i>
      </button>  |  
      <item-list></item-list>
    </form>
  </div>
}
```

This view also checks for an error and displays an alert if one is found. Otherwise it uses the `@Html.DisplayForModel()` method and the two hidden inputs for the `Id` and `TimeStamp`. These will be the only fields posted as the form data.

The delete form can be viewed at `/Cars/Delete/5` and is shown in Figure 33-9.

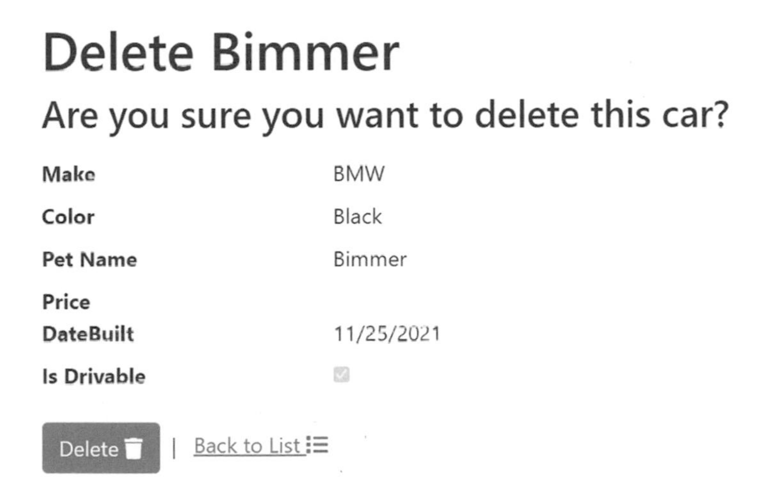

Delete Bimmer

Are you sure you want to delete this car?

Make	BMW
Color	Black
Pet Name	Bimmer
Price	
DateBuilt	11/25/2021
Is Drivable	☑

Delete | Back to List

Figure 33-9. *The delete view*

This completes the views and the controller for the `Car` entity.

View Components

View components are another new feature in ASP.NET Core. They combine the benefits of partial views with child actions to render parts of the UI. Like partial views, they are called from another view, but unlike partial views by themselves, view components also have a server-side component. This combination makes them a great fit for functions like creating dynamic menus (as shown shortly), login panels, sidebar content, or anything that needs to run server-side code but doesn't qualify to be a stand-alone view.

■ **Note** Child actions in classic ASP.NET MVC were action methods on a controller that could not serve as client-facing endpoints. They do not exist in ASP.NET Core.

For AutoLot, the view component will dynamically create the menu based on the makes that are in the database. The menu is visible on every page, so the logical place for it is in the _Layout.cshtml. But the _Layout.cshtml doesn't have a server-side component (unlike views), so every action in the app would have to supply the data to _Layout.cshtml. This can be done in the controller's OnActionExecuting event handler and the records placed in the ViewBag, but that can be messy to maintain. The blending of the server-side capabilities and the encapsulation of the UI make this scenario a perfect use case for view components.

The Server-Side Code

Create a new folder named ViewComponents in the root directory of the AutoLot.Mvc project. Add a new class file named MenuViewComponent.cs into this folder. The convention is to name the view component classes with the ViewComponent suffix, just like controllers. And just like controllers, the ViewComponent suffix is dropped when calling view components.

Change the class to public and inherit from ViewComponent. View components don't have to inherit from the ViewComponent base class, but like the Controller base class, inheriting from ViewComponent simplifies much of the work. Create a constructor that takes an instance of the IMakeDataService interface and assign that to a class-level field. The code at this point looks like this:

```
namespace AutoLot.Mvc.ViewComponents;

public class MenuViewComponent : ViewComponent
{
  private readonly IMakeDataService _dataService;
  public MenuViewComponent(IMakeDataService dataService)
  {
    _dataService = dataService;
  }
}
```

There are two methods that are available for view components, Invoke() and InvokeAsync(). One of them must be implemented, and since the IMakeDataService only makes async calls, add in the InvokeAsync() method, like this:

```
public async Task<IViewComponentResult> InvokeAsync()
{
}
```

When a view component is rendered from a view, the public method Invoke()/InvokeAsync() is called. This method returns an IViewComponentResult, which is conceptually similar to a PartialViewResult, but much more streamlined. In the Invoke() method, get the list of Makes from the data service and, if successful, return a ViewViewComponentResult (no, that's not a typo; it's actually the name of the type) using the list of makes as the view model. If the call to get the Make records fails, return a ContentViewComponentResult with an error message. Update the method to the following:

```
public async Task<IViewComponentResult> InvokeAsync()
{
  var makes = (await _dataService.GetAllAsync()).ToList();
  if (!makes.Any())
  {
```

```
    return new ContentViewComponentResult("Unable to get the makes");
  }
  return View("MenuView", makes);
}
```

The View helper method from the base ViewComponent class is similar to the Controller class helper method of the same name, with a couple of key differences. The first difference is that the default view file name is Default.cshtml instead of the name of the method. However, like the controller view helper method, the name of the view can be anything as long as the name is passed into the method call (without the .cshtml extension). The second difference is that the location of the view ***must*** be one of these three directories:

```
Views/< controller>/Components/<view_component_name>/<view_name>
Views/Shared/Components/<view_component_name>/<view_name>
Pages/Shared/Components/<view_component_name>/<view_name>
```

The C# class can live anywhere (even in another assembly), but <viewname>.cshtml must be in one of the directories listed earlier.

Build the Partial View

The partial view rendered by the MenuViewComponent will iterate through the Make records, adding each as a list item to be displayed in the Bootstrap menu. The All menu item is added first as a hard-coded value.

Create a new folder named Components under the Views\Shared folder. In this new folder, create another new folder named Menu. This folder name must match the name of the view component class created earlier, minus the ViewComponent suffix. In this folder, create a partial view named MenuView.cshtml.

Clear out the existing code and add the following markup:

```
@model IEnumerable<Make>
<div class="dropdown-menu">
<a class="dropdown-item text-dark" asp-area="" asp-controller="Cars" asp-
action="Index">All</a>

@foreach (var item in Model)
{
    <a class="dropdown-item text-dark" asp-controller="Cars" asp-action="ByMake" asp-route-
    makeId="@item.Id" asp-route-makeName="@item.Name">@item.Name</a>
}
</div>
```

Invoking View Components

View components are typically rendered from a view (although they can be rendered from a controller action method as well). The syntax is straightforward: Component.Invoke(<view component name>) or @await Component.InvokeAsync(<view component name>). Just like with controllers, the ViewComponent suffix must be removed when invoking a view component.

```
@await Component.InvokeAsync("Menu") //async version
@Component.Invoke("Menu") //non-async version
```

View components can be invoked using tag helper syntax. Instead of using Component.InvokeAsync()/Component.Invoke(), simply call the view component like this:

```
<vc:menu></vc:menu>
```

To use this method of calling view components, your application must opt in to using them. This is done by adding the @addTagHelper command with the name of the assembly that contains the view component. The following line must be added to the _ViewImports.cshtml file, which was already added for the custom tag helpers:

```
@addTagHelper *, AutoLot.Mvc
```

Updating the Menu

Open the _Menu.cshtml partial and navigate to just after the <li></li> block that maps to the Home/Index action method. Copy the following markup to the partial:

```
<li class="nav-item">
  <a class="nav-link text-dark" asp-area="" asp-controller="Home" asp-action="Index">Home
<i class="fa fa-home"></i></a>
</li>
<li class="nav-item dropdown">
  <a class="nav-link dropdown-toggle text-dark" data-bs-toggle="dropdown">Inventory
<i class="fa fa-car"></i></a>
  <vc:menu></vc:menu>
</li>
```

In the Home menu item, I added the Font Awesome home icon. The next line creates a Bootstrap drop down menu, and the MenuViewComponent is rendered inside the drop down menu.

Now when you run the application, you will see the Inventory menu with the makes listed as submenu items, as shown in Figure 33-10.

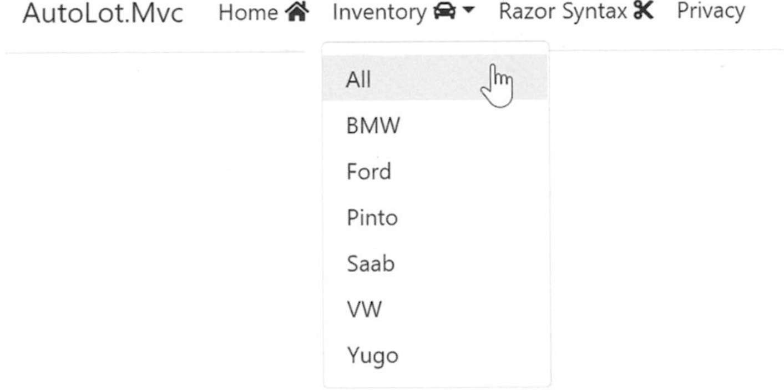

Figure 33-10. *The menu provided by MenuViewComponent*

Custom Validation Attributes

ASP.NET Core and EF Core contain a significant number of data annotations and validation attributes that you can apply to models (and view models). As you have seen, these attributes provide client-side and server-side validation. When client-side validation is enabled, the data is checked before a request is sent to the server, and in conjunction with the validation tag helpers, report the errors to the user. Server side validation occurs if JavaScript is enabled (or the jQuery Validation and jQuery Validation Unobtrusive libraries aren't loaded), server-side validation executes, and updates the `ModelState`. As you have already seen, if the `ModelState` isn't valid, the action methods return the data and the errors back to the view, resulting in the same effect as client side validation.

There are times where the built-in validations aren't sufficient, and custom validation is required to meet the business's needs. While you could write custom C# code (for server-side validation) and JavaScript (for client-side validation) each time it's needed, that could result in a lot of repeated code. It is better to encapsulate the validation code in a reusable component that can be added to the model in the form of a data annotation attribute.

For AutoLot, we need two custom validation attributes. The first one will require a value to be greater than zero, and the second one will require that a value on the model be less than or equal to another property on the model.

Set the Stage

Before building the validation attributes, we need to create the view, view model, and action method.

The ViewModel

It's a common practice to validate the quantity of items selected is greater than zero and less than or equal to the quantity available before the item can be added to their cart. With that is mind, create a new class named `AddToCartViewModel` in the `ViewModels` folder of the AutoLot.Services project:

```
namespace AutoLot.Services.ViewModels;

public class AddToCartViewModel
{
    public int Id { get; set; }
    public int StockQuantity { get; set; }
    public int ItemId { get; set; }
    public int Quantity { get; set; }
}
```

Add the following global using statements to the `GlobalUsings.cs` file in the AutoLot.Services project:

```
global using System.ComponentModel;
global using System.ComponentModel.DataAnnotations;
global using System.Reflection;
```

The View

Add a new blank Razor view named `Validation.cshtml` in the Views\Home folder of the AutoLot.Mvc project. Clear out the scaffolded comments and update the markup to the following:

```
@model AddToCartViewModel

@{
    ViewData["Title"] = "Validation";
}

<h1>Validation</h1>

<h4>Add To Cart</h4>
<hr />
<div class="row">
  <div class="col-md-4">
    <form asp-action="Validation">
      <div asp-validation-summary="ModelOnly" class="text-danger"></div>
      <div>
        <label asp-for="Id" class="col-form-label"></label>
        <input asp-for="Id" class="form-control" />
        <span asp-validation-for="Id" class="text-danger"></span>
      </div>
      <div>
        <label asp-for="StockQuantity" class="col-form-label"></label>
        <input asp-for="StockQuantity" class="form-control" />
        <span asp-validation-for="StockQuantity" class="text-danger"></span>
      </div>
      <div>
        <label asp-for="ItemId" class="col-form-label"></label>
        <input asp-for="ItemId" class="form-control" />
        <span asp-validation-for="ItemId" class="text-danger"></span>
      </div>
      <div>
        <label asp-for="Quantity" class="col-form-label"></label>
        <input asp-for="Quantity" class="form-control" />
        <span asp-validation-for="Quantity" class="text-danger"></span>
      </div>
        <div style="margin-top:5px">
          <input type="submit" value="Save" class="btn btn-primary" />
      </div>
    </form>
  </div>
</div>

@section Scripts {
    @{await Html.RenderPartialAsync("_ValidationScriptsPartial");}
}
```

The Validation Action Methods

The server side code for this sample is very simple: an HTTP get method to return a view with a new instance of the viewmodel, and an HTTP post to validate the data received from the user. Add the following action methods to the HomeController:

```
[HttpGet]
public IActionResult Validation()
{
  var vm = new AddToCartViewModel
  {
    Id = 1,
    ItemId = 1,
    StockQuantity = 2,
    Quantity = 0
  };
  return View(vm);
}

[HttpPost]
public IActionResult Validation(AddToCartViewModel viewModel)
{
  if (!ModelState.IsValid)
  {
    return View(viewModel);
  }
  return RedirectToAction(nameof(Validation));
}
```

The Validation Menu Item

The final setup before adding the validation attributes is to add a menu item to navigate to the Validation view. Add the following to the end of menu list (before the closing </ul> tag):

```
<li class="nav-item">
  <a class="nav-link text-dark" asp-area="" asp-controller="Home" asp-action="Validation"
title="Validation Example">Validation<i class="fas fa-check"></i></a>
</li>
```

Server-Side Validation

Although most modern web sites require JavaScript to be enabled, it's considered a best practice to add server-side validation to all of your custom validation attributes.

The MustBeGreaterThanZero Validation Attribute

Add a new directory named Validation to the AutoLot.Services project, and in that directory add a new class named MustBeGreaterThanZeroAttribute. Make the class public and inherit from ValidationAttribute and configure that attribute as property only:

```
namespace AutoLot.Services.Validation;

[AttributeUsage(AttributeTargets.Property)]
public class MustBeGreaterThanZeroAttribute : ValidationAttribute
{
  //implementation goes here
}
```

Validation attributes have a build in message, but also provide the ability to use a custom message. This same pattern is expected with custom validation attributes as well. Add to constructors, one that provides a default message, and another that allows for a custom message. The error message is then passed to the base constructor and is assigned to the protected ErrorMessageString property:

```
public MustBeGreaterThanZeroAttribute() : this("{0} must be greater than 0")
{
}

public MustBeGreaterThanZeroAttribute(string errorMessage) : base(errorMessage)
{
}
```

Notice the format string in the default message. This is used by the base FormatMessage() method, which needs to be overridden:

```
public override string FormatErrorMessage(string name)
{
  return string.Format(ErrorMessageString, name);
}
```

Server-side validation is conducted with the IsValid() virtual base method. If the method returns ValidationResult.Success, then the property is considered valid. If it returns a ValidationResult that contains a message, the message is added to ModelState and the property is marked Invalid. The check for this logic is quite simple, if the value of the property (passed in as an object) is null, not an int, or less than or equal to zero, fail the validation. Otherwise, return ValidationResult.Success. Notice that the ValidationContext instance provides the DisplayName property, which returns the DisplayName or Display(Name="") values if one is configured.

```
protected override ValidationResult IsValid(object value, ValidationContext
validationContext)
{
  if (!int.TryParse(value.ToString(), out int result))
  {
    return new ValidationResult(FormatErrorMessage(validationContext.DisplayName));
  }
```

```
    return result > 0
      ? ValidationResult.Success
      : new ValidationResult(FormatErrorMessage(validationContext.DisplayName));
}
```

Add the following using statement to the `GlobalUsings.cs` file:

```
global using AutoLot.Services.Validation;
```

Next, add the attribute to the view model (note that the `Attribute` suffix is dropped):

```
[MustBeGreaterThanZero]
public int Quantity { get; set; }
```

With this in place, run the application, navigate to the Validation page, and click Save (with the `Quantity` set to zero or a negative number) and you will see the validation message shown in Figure 33-11:

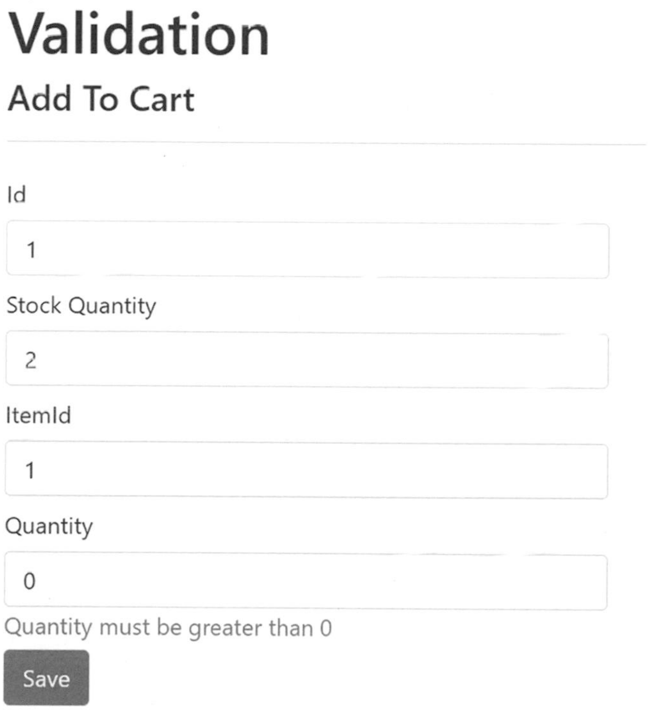

Validation

Add To Cart

Id

1

Stock Quantity

2

ItemId

1

Quantity

0

Quantity must be greater than 0

Save

Figure 33-11. *Custom validation message for zero quantity*

If you clear out any values from the `Quantity` fields and click Save, you will see a message stating that the value is required. This is because the property is defined as an `int`, and not a nullable `int?`.

The MustNotBeGreaterThan Validation Attribute

This custom attribute compares the property being validated with another property on the model. In the `Validation` directory add a new class named `MustNotBeGreaterThanAttribute`. Make the class `public` and inherit from `ValidationAttribute:`. This attribute could be added to the same property more than once, so it needs to be configured to allow multiple uses:

```
namespace AutoLot.Services.Validation;

[AttributeUsage(AttributeTargets.Property, AllowMultiple = true)]
public class MustNotBeGreaterThanAttribute : ValidationAttribute
{
  //implementation goes here
}
```

The attribute needs to know the other property for the comparison, and the validation message must refer to the other property to be meaningful to the user. Also, the other property might have a binding prefix. This will be necessary to capture for the client side validation. Create a constructor that provides a default message and prefix, and another that allows a custom message and optional prefix. Assign the other property name and prefix to class level fields:

```
readonly string _otherPropertyName;
readonly string _prefix;

public MustNotBeGreaterThanAttribute(string otherPropertyName, string prefix = "")
  : this(otherPropertyName, "{0} must not be greater than {1}", prefix)
{
}

public MustNotBeGreaterThanAttribute(string otherPropertyName, string errorMessage, string
prefix = "")
  : base(errorMessage)
{
  _otherPropertyName = otherPropertyName;
  _prefix = prefix;
}
```

The `MustBeGreaterThanZero` attribute showed getting the target property's display name from the `ValidationContext`. To get the other property's display name, you must use reflection. Create a method called `SetOtherPropertyName()` which retrieves the display name from either a `Display` or `DisplayName` attribute and assigns it to a class level field:

```
string _otherPropertyDisplayName;
internal void SetOtherPropertyName(PropertyInfo otherPropertyInfo)
{
  var displayAttribute =
    otherPropertyInfo.GetCustomAttributes<DisplayAttribute>().FirstOrDefault();
  if (displayAttribute != null)
  {
    _otherPropertyDisplayName = displayAttribute.Name;
    return;
  }
```

```
  var displayNameAttribute =
    otherPropertyInfo.GetCustomAttributes<DisplayNameAttribute>().FirstOrDefault();
  if (displayNameAttribute != null)
  {
    _otherPropertyDisplayName = displayNameAttribute.DisplayName;
    return;
  }
  _otherPropertyDisplayName = _otherPropertyName;
}
```

With the other property display name configured, override the FormatErrorMessage() method:

```
public override string FormatErrorMessage(string name)
{
  return string.Format(ErrorMessageString, name, _otherPropertyDisplayName);
}
```

The IsValid() override returns Success if the value is null since it can't be greater than any other value if it's null. It then checks that the value can be parsed into an int, and if not, fails validation. If it can, and the value is zero, validation succeeds. Next, it gets the other property's value using reflection, and if the other value is null or not numeric, validation fails. Finally, it compares that values, and if the target property is greater than the compare to property, validation fails:

```
protected override ValidationResult IsValid(object value, ValidationContext
validationContext)
{
  if (value is null)
  {
    return ValidationResult.Success;
  }
  if (!int.TryParse(value.ToString(), out int toValidate))
  {
    return new ValidationResult($"{validationContext.DisplayName} must be numeric.");
  }
  if (toValidate == 0)
  {
    return ValidationResult.Success;
  }
  var otherPropertyInfo = validationContext.ObjectType.GetProperty(_otherPropertyName);
  SetOtherPropertyName(otherPropertyInfo);
  var otherValue = otherPropertyInfo.GetValue(validationContext.ObjectInstance, null);
  if (otherValue is null)
  {
    return new ValidationResult($"{_otherPropertyDisplayName} must not be null.");
  }
  if (!int.TryParse(otherValue.ToString(),out int toCompare))
  {
    return new ValidationResult($"{_otherPropertyDisplayName} must be numeric.");
  }
```

```
  return toValidate > toCompare
    ? new ValidationResult(FormatErrorMessage(validationContext.DisplayName))
    : ValidationResult.Success;
}
```

Next, add the attribute to the view model:

```
[MustBeGreaterThanZero][MustNotBeGreaterThan(nameof(StockQuantity))]
public int Quantity { get; set; }
```

With this in place, run the application, navigate to the Validation page, and click Save with the `Quantity` set to a number higher than `Stock Quantity` and you will see the validation message shown in Figure 33-12:

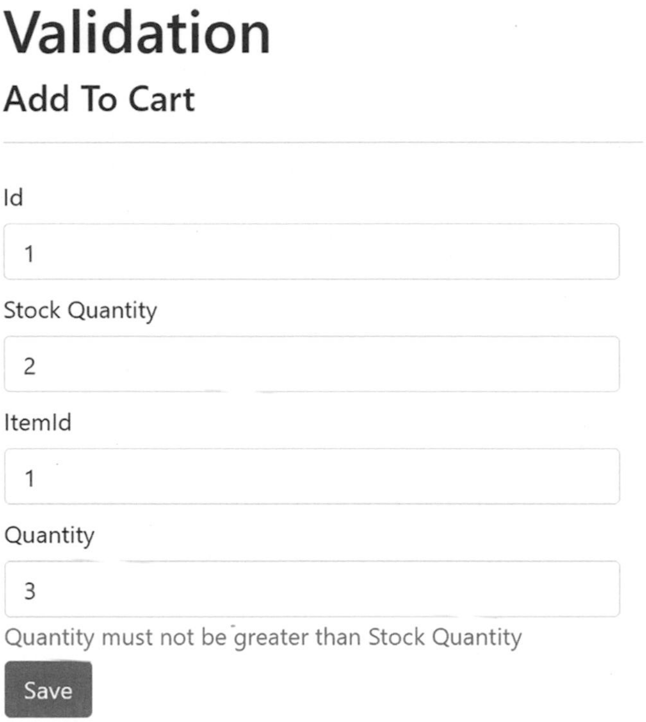

Figure 33-12. *Custom validation message for a quantity greater than stock quantity*

Client-Side Validation

Client-side validation support is added to custom attribute by implementing the `IClientValidator` interface and writing custom JavaScript that works with the jQuery validation libraries. Begin by adding the following global using statement to `GlobalUsings.cs` in AutoLot.Services:

```
global using Microsoft.AspNetCore.Mvc.ModelBinding.Validation;
```

Client-Side Error Formatting

Before completing the custom validation attributes, we are going to add some custom styling into the jQuery validation process. Add a new directory named `validations` under the `wwwroot\js` directory in the AutoLot.Mvc project. Add a new file named `errorFormatting.js` in the new directory and update the code to the following:

```
$.validator.setDefaults({
    highlight: function (element, errorClass, validClass) {
        if (element.type === "radio") {
            this.findByName(element.name).addClass(errorClass).removeClass(validClass);
        } else {
            $(element).addClass(errorClass).removeClass(validClass);
            $(element).closest('div').addClass('has-error');
        }
    },
    unhighlight: function (element, errorClass, validClass) {
        if (element.type === "radio") {
            this.findByName(element.name).removeClass(errorClass).addClass(validClass);
        } else {
            $(element).removeClass(errorClass).addClass(validClass);
            $(element).closest('div').removeClass('has-error');
        }
    }
});
```

The bulk of the method repeats what is already in jQuery-Validate. The two lines in bold add a custom style on the closest `<div>` tag to the element with the error. The final step is to add the custom style to the `site.css` file:

```
.has-error {
  border: 3px solid red;
  padding: 0px 5px;
  margin: 5px 0;}
```

This creates a red box around the label and the control with the error as shown in Figure 33-13:

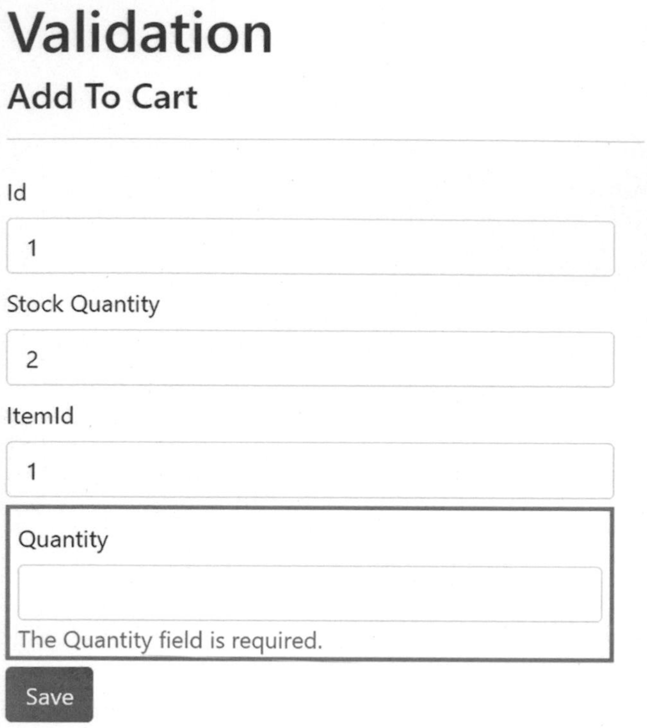

Validation

Add To Cart

Id

1

Stock Quantity

2

ItemId

1

Quantity

The Quantity field is required.

Save

Figure 33-13. *The updated error styling*

The MustBeGreaterThanZero Validation Attribute

Update the `MustBeGreaterThanZeroAttribute` class to implement the `IClientValidator` interface and the `AddValidation()` method:

```
[AttributeUsage(AttributeTargets.Property)]
public class MustBeGreaterThanZeroAttribute : ValidationAttribute, IClientModelValidator
{
  //omitted for brevity
  public void AddValidation(ClientModelValidationContext context)
  {
    //implementation goes here
  }
```

The `ClientModelValidationContext` is used to add HTML5 style `data-val` attributes to the markup. The format for the attribute is `data-val-[functiontoexecute]='error message'`. In this attribute, the message needs to be properly formatted with the target properties `DisplayName` (if assigned) or property name (if DisplayName isn't assigned), and the error message. Update the `AddValidation()` method to the following:

```
public void AddValidation(ClientModelValidationContext context)
{
  string propertyDisplayName =
    context.ModelMetadata.DisplayName ?? context.ModelMetadata.PropertyName;
  string errorMessage = FormatErrorMessage(propertyDisplayName);
  context.Attributes.Add("data-val-greaterthanzero", errorMessage);
}
```

With this in place, the rendered input changes to this:

```
<input class="form-control valid" type="number" data-val="true" data-val-
greaterthanzero="Quantity must be greater than 0" data-val-required="The Quantity field is
required." id="Quantity" name="Quantity" value="0" aria-describedby="Quantity-error" aria-
invalid="false">
```

Next up is to add the greaterthanzero() method into the jQuery validation system using the addMethod() function on the validator object. Create a new file named validators.js in the js\validations directory of the AutoLot.Mvc project. Update the code to the following:

```
$.validator.addMethod("greaterthanzero", function (value, element, params) {
  return value > 0;
});
```

Now, when the data-val attributes are parsed, the data-val-greaterthanzero attribute will cause the method to execute and will return true if the value is greater than zero. If not, false is returned, and the control is marked invalid.

The final step is to set the rules and message for the validation. This is a single control validation, so the rules property is simply set to true (to enable the validation), and the message is retrieved from the data-val-greaterthanzero attribute:

```
$.validator.unobtrusive.adapters.add("greaterthanzero", function (options) {
    options.rules["greaterthanzero"] = true;
    options.messages["greaterthanzero"] = options.message;
});
```

The MustNotBeGreaterThan Validation Attribute

Update the MustNotBeGreaterThanAttribute class to implement the IClientValidator interface and the AddValidation() method:

```
[AttributeUsage(AttributeTargets.Property, AllowMultiple = true)]
public class MustNotBeGreaterThanAttribute : ValidationAttribute, IClientModelValidator
{
  //omitted for brevity
  public void AddValidation(ClientModelValidationContext context)
  {
    //implementation goes here
  }
```

The JavaScript and setup for this attribute is a bit more complicated than the `MustBeGreaterThanZeroAttribute`, since it needs to access another property on the HTML form. The first step is to get the other property's display name and the formatted error message and assign that to the `data-val-notgreaterthan` attribute:

```
public void AddValidation(ClientModelValidationContext context)
{
  string propertyDisplayName = context.ModelMetadata.GetDisplayName();
  var propertyInfo = context.ModelMetadata.ContainerType.GetProperty(_otherPropertyName);
  SetOtherPropertyName(propertyInfo);
  string errorMessage = FormatErrorMessage(propertyDisplayName);
  context.Attributes.Add("data-val-notgreaterthan", errorMessage);
}
```

Additional data can be added to the validation process by extending the `data-val-` attribute. In this case, the other property name and prefix need to be added:

```
public void AddValidation(ClientModelValidationContext context)
{
  //omitted for brevity
  context.Attributes.Add("data-val-notgreaterthan-otherpropertyname", _otherPropertyName);
  context.Attributes.Add("data-val-notgreaterthan-prefix", _prefix);
}
```

With this in place, the rendered input changes to this:

```
<input class="form-control valid" type="number" data-val="true" data-val-
greaterthanzero="Quantity must be greater than 0" data-val-notgreaterthan="Quantity must not
be greater than Stock Quantity" data-val-notgreaterthan-otherpropertyname="StockQuantity"
data-val-notgreaterthan-prefix="" data-val-required="The Quantity field is required."
id="Quantity" name="Quantity" value="0" aria-describedby="Quantity-error" aria-
invalid="false">
```

The next step is to set the `rules` and `message` for the validation. The `rules` property is set to the fully qualified HTML id of the other property. The additional attribute values (`prefix`, `otherpropertyname`) are retrieved through the `options` parameter. The `message` is retrieved from the `data-val-greaterthanzero` attribute. Add the following to the `validators.js` file:

```
$.validator.unobtrusive.adapters.add("notgreaterthan", ["otherpropertyname","prefix"],
function(options) {
    options.rules["notgreaterthan"] = "#" + options.params.prefix + options.params.
otherpropertyname;
    options.messages["notgreaterthan"] = options.message;
});
```

Finally, add the `notgreaterthan()` method into the jQuery validation system. The other property's HTML id is available from the params parameter::

```
$.validator.addMethod("notgreaterthan", function (value, element, params) {
  return +value <= +$(params).val();
});
```

Update the Validation Scripts Partial

Before adding the new JavaScript files to the _ValidationScriptsPartial partial view, update the call to AddWebOptimizer() in the Program.cs top level statements to bundle the new files:

```
builder.Services.AddWebOptimizer(options =>
{
  //omitted for brevity
  options.AddJavaScriptBundle("/js/validationCode.js",
      "js/validations/validators.js", "js/validations/errorFormatting.js");
});
```

Next, update the _ValidationScriptsPartial partial to include the raw files in the development block and the bundled/minified files in the non-development block:

```
<environment include="Development">
    <script src="~/js/validations/errorFormatting.js" asp-append-version="true" ></script>
    <script src="~/js/validations/validators.js" asp-append-version="true" ></script>
</environment>
<environment exclude="Development">
    <script src="~/js/validationCode.js"></script>
</environment>
```

General Data Protection Regulation Support

The General Data Protection Regulation (GDPR) was enacted by the European Union to protect online users. There are several provisions to the regulation, including requiring the user to consent to any tracking cookies. Even though it's an EU rule, it applies to any website that can be accessed by an EU citizen, even if the website is not based in the EU.

■ **Note** The regulations are documented at https://ec.europa.eu/info/law/law-topic/data-protection/reform/what-does-general-data-protection-regulation-gdpr-govern_en. This book only covers ASP.NET Core support for the cookie provision and privacy policy page, it does not ensure compliance with the regulation. Please consult legal counsel for full compliance information.

ASP.NET Core added API support for the tracking cookie provisions in version 2.1 as well as a privacy policy page. The current template only includes the privacy page, and that is where your website's privacy and cookie policy needs to be placed.

Add Cookie Policy Support

Part of the policy is that users must agree to the use of cookies on your site, and if they don't, non-essential cookies can't be used. To enable the default cookie consent feature, start by adding the configured CookiePolicyOptions into the services collection. Add the following to the top level statements in the Program.cs file in the AutoLot.Mvc project:

```
builder.Services.Configure<CookiePolicyOptions>(options =>
{
    // This lambda determines whether user consent for non-essential cookies is
    // needed for a given request.
    options.CheckConsentNeeded = context => true;
    options.MinimumSameSitePolicy = SameSiteMode.None;
});
```

By default, session and TempData cookies are not considered essential. To change them as essential, add the following two lines of code just after configuring the CookiePolicyOptions:

```
// The TempData provider cookie is not essential. Make it essential
// so TempData is functional when tracking is disabled.
builder.Services.Configure<CookieTempDataProviderOptions>(options => { options.Cookie.
IsEssential = true; });
builder.Services.AddSession(options => { options.Cookie.IsEssential = true; });
```

The final change to the top level statements is to add cookie policy support to the HTTP pipeline:

```
app.UseStaticFiles();
app.UseCookiePolicy();
app.UseRouting();
```

The Cookie Support Partial View

The next step is to provide a user interface to allow users to consent to cookie use if they haven't already. Create a new empty view named _CookieConsentPartal.cshtml in the Views\Shared directory. If the user has consented, don't show the UI banner. At the top of the view, add a Razor block to check the ITrackingConsentFeature to see if the user has already consented, and if they have, don't show the banner. Finally, use the consent feature to create the cookie string:

```
@{
  var consentFeature = Context.Features.Get<ITrackingConsentFeature>();
  var showBanner = !consentFeature?.CanTrack ?? false;
  var cookieString = consentFeature?.CreateConsentCookie();
}
```

Next, if the user hasn't consented, show a banner that displays the cookie policy for the site and provides a button for the user to consent. If they do, a JavaScript function will add the cookie to the browser indicating that the user consented:

```
@if (showBanner)
{
  <div id="cookieConsent" class="alert alert-info alert-dismissible fade show" role="alert">
    Use this space to summarize your privacy and cookie use policy. <a asp-area="" asp-
controller="Home" asp-action="Privacy">Learn More</a>.
    <button type="button" class="accept-policy close" data-dismiss="alert" aria-
label="Close" data-cookie-string="@cookieString">
      <span aria-hidden="true">Accept</span>
    </button>
  </div>
```

```
  <script>
    (function () {
      var button = document.querySelector("#cookieConsent button[data-cookie-string]");
      button.addEventListener("click", function (event) {
        document.cookie = button.dataset.cookieString;
        window.location = '@Url.Action(nameof(HomeController.Index),nameof(HomeController).
RemoveControllerSuffix())';
      }, false);
    })();
  </script>
}
```

Finally, add the partial to the _Layout partial:

```
<div class="container">
    <partial name="_CookieConsentPartial"/>
    <main role="main" class="pb-3">
        @RenderBody()
    </main>
</div>
```

With this in place, when you run the application you will see the cookie consent banner, as shown in Figure 33-14:

Use this space to summarize your privacy and cookie use policy. Learn More. Accept

Figure 33-14. *The cookie consent banner*

If the user clicks Accept, the .AspNet.Content cookie is created. The next time the site loads, the banner will not be displayed.

Menu Support to Accept/Withdraw Cookie Policy Consent

The final change to the application is to add menu support to grant or withdraw consent. Add the following two action methods to the HomeController. Each method used the ITrackingConsentFeature to grant or withdraw consent, then redirect the user to the Index view:

```
[HttpGet]
public IActionResult GrantConsent()
{
  HttpContext.Features.Get<ITrackingConsentFeature>().GrantConsent();
  return RedirectToAction(nameof(Index), nameof(HomeController).RemoveControllerSuffix(),
    new { area = "" });
}

[HttpGet]
public IActionResult WithdrawConsent()
{
```

```
  HttpContext.Features.Get<ITrackingConsentFeature>().WithdrawConsent();
  return RedirectToAction(nameof(Index), nameof(HomeController).RemoveControllerSuffix(),
    new { area = "" });
}
```

Open the `_Menu.cshtml` partial, and add a Razor block to check if the user has granted consent:

```
@{
  var consentFeature = Context.Features.Get<ITrackingConsentFeature>();
  var showBanner = !consentFeature?.CanTrack ?? false;
}
```

If the banner is showing (the user hasn't granted consent), then display the menu link for the user to Accept the cookie policy. If they have granted consent, then show the menu link to withdraw consent. The following also updates the Privacy link to include a font awesome icon for secret:

```
<li class="nav-item">
  <a class="nav-link text-dark" asp-area="" asp-controller="Home" asp-action="Privacy">
    Privacy <i class="fa fa-user-secret"></i></a>
</li>
@if (showBanner)
{
  <li class="nav-item">
    <a class="nav-link text-dark" asp-controller="Home" asp-action="GrantConsent"
title="Accept Cookie Policy">Accept Cookie Policy <i class="fas fa-cookie-bite"></i></a>
  </li>
}
else
{
  <li class="nav-item">
    <a class="nav-link text-dark" asp-controller="Home" asp-action="WithdrawConsent"
title="Revoke Cookie Policy">Revoke Cookie Policy <i class="fas fa-cookie"></i></a>
  </li>
}
```

With this in place, you can see the two menu options, the first shown in Figure 33-15.

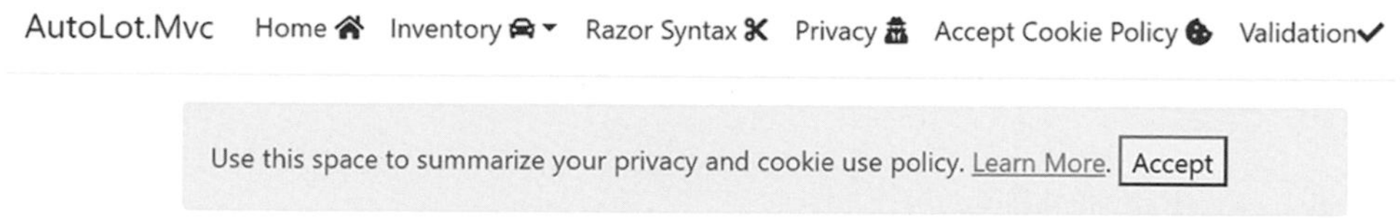

Figure 33-15. *Menu to grant cookie consent*

And the second shown in Figure 33-16.

Figure 33-16. *Menu to withdraw cookie consent*

Finish the Admin Area

The final step to complete the AutoLot.Mvc application is to add the remaining views for the Admin area. Add four empty Razor views, `Create.cshtml`, `Delete.cshtml`, `Details.cshtml`, and `Edit.cshtml` into the `Areas\Admin\Views\Make` directory. These views all follow the same pattern as the Cars views, so they are just listed here:

```
//Create.cshtml
@model Make
@{  ViewData["Title"] = "Create"; }
<h1>Create</h1>
<h4>Make</h4>
<hr/>
<form asp-action="Create">
  <div class="row">
    <div class="col-md-4">
      <div asp-validation-summary="ModelOnly" class="text-danger"></div>
        <label asp-for="Name" class="col-form-label"></label>
        <input asp-for="Name" class="form-control"/>
        <span asp-validation-for="Name" class="text-danger"></span>
      </div>
  </div>
  <div class="d-flex flex-row mt-3">
    <input type="submit" value="Create" class="btn btn-primary"/>  |  
    <item-list></item-list>
  </div>
</form>
@section Scripts {
    @{ await Html.RenderPartialAsync("_ValidationScriptsPartial"); }
}

//Delete.cshtml
@model Make
@{ ViewData["Title"] = "Delete"; }
<h1>Delete</h1>
<h3>Are you sure you want to delete this?</h3>
<div>
  <h4>Make</h4>
  <hr />
  <dl class="row">
    <dt class = "col-sm-2">@Html.DisplayNameFor(model => model.Name)</dt>
    <dd class = "col-sm-10">@Html.DisplayFor(model => model.Name)</dd>
  </dl>
  <form asp-action="Delete">
    <input type="hidden" asp-for="Id" />
    <input type="submit" value="Delete" class="btn btn-danger" /> |
    <item-list></item-list>
  </form>
</div>
```

```
//Details.cshtml
@model Make
@{ ViewData["Title"] = "Details"; }
<h1>Details</h1>
<div>
  <h4>Make</h4>
  <hr/>
  <dl class="row">
    <dt class="col-sm-2">@Html.DisplayNameFor(model => model.Name)</dt>
    <dd class="col-sm-10">@Html.DisplayFor(model => model.Name) </dd>
  </dl>
</div>
<div>
  <item-edit item-id="@Model.Id"></item-edit>
  <item-list></item-list>
</div>

//Edit.cshtml
@model Make
@{ ViewData["Title"] = "Edit"; }
<h1>Edit</h1>
<h4>Make</h4>
<hr/>
<form asp-action="Edit">
  <div class="row">
    <div class="col-md-4">
      <div asp-validation-summary="ModelOnly" class="text-danger"></div>
      <div>
        <label asp-for="Name" class="col-form-label"></label>
        <input asp-for="Name" class="form-control"/>
        <span asp-validation-for="Name" class="text-danger"></span>
      </div>
      <input type="hidden" asp-for="Id"/>
      <input type="hidden" asp-for="TimeStamp"/>
    </div>
  </div>
  <div class="d-flex flex-row mt-3">
    <input type="submit" value="Save" class="btn btn-primary"/>   |  
   <item-list></item-list>
  </div>
</form>
@section Scripts {
    @{ await Html.RenderPartialAsync("_ValidationScriptsPartial"); }
}

//Index.cshtml
@model IEnumerable<Make>

@{
    ViewData["Title"] = "Index";
}
```

```
<h1>Index</h1>
<p><a asp-action="Create">Create New</a></p>
<table class="table">
  <thead>
    <tr>
      <th>@Html.DisplayNameFor(model => model.Name) </th>
      <th></th>
    </tr>
  </thead>
  <tbody>
@foreach (var item in Model) {
    <tr>
      <td>@Html.DisplayFor(modelItem => item.Name)</td>
      <td>
        <item-edit item-id="@item.Id"></item-edit> |
        <item-details item-id="@item.Id"></item-details> |
        <item-delete item-id="@item.Id"></item-delete>
      </td>
    </tr>
}
  </tbody>
</table>
```

Next, update the _Menu.cshtml to add a menu link for the Admin area:

```
<li class="nav-item">
  <a class="nav-link text-dark" asp-area="Admin" asp-controller="Makes" asp-action="Index"
  title="Makes Admin">Makes Admin <i class="fas fa-cog"></i></a>
</li>
```

Run AutoLot.Mvc and AutoLot.Api Together

Up to this point, the demos have all been using the data access later of the data services. To switch to using the AutoLot.Api service as the back-end, change the UseApi flag in appsettings.Development.json to true. When running AutoLot.Mvc, AutoLot.Api must be running. This can be done with Visual Studio, the command line, or a combination of the two.

■ **Note** Remember that both AutoLot.Mvc and AutoLot.Api can be configured to rebuild the database every time they start. Make sure to turn at least one of them off or they will conflict. To speed up debugging, turn the flag off in both projects when you are testing functionality that doesn't change any data.

Using Visual Studio

You can configure Visual Studio to run multiple projects at the same time. This is accomplished by right-clicking the solution in Solution Explorer, selecting Select Startup Projects, and setting the actions for AutoLot.Api and AutoLot.Mvc to Start, as shown in Figure 33-17.

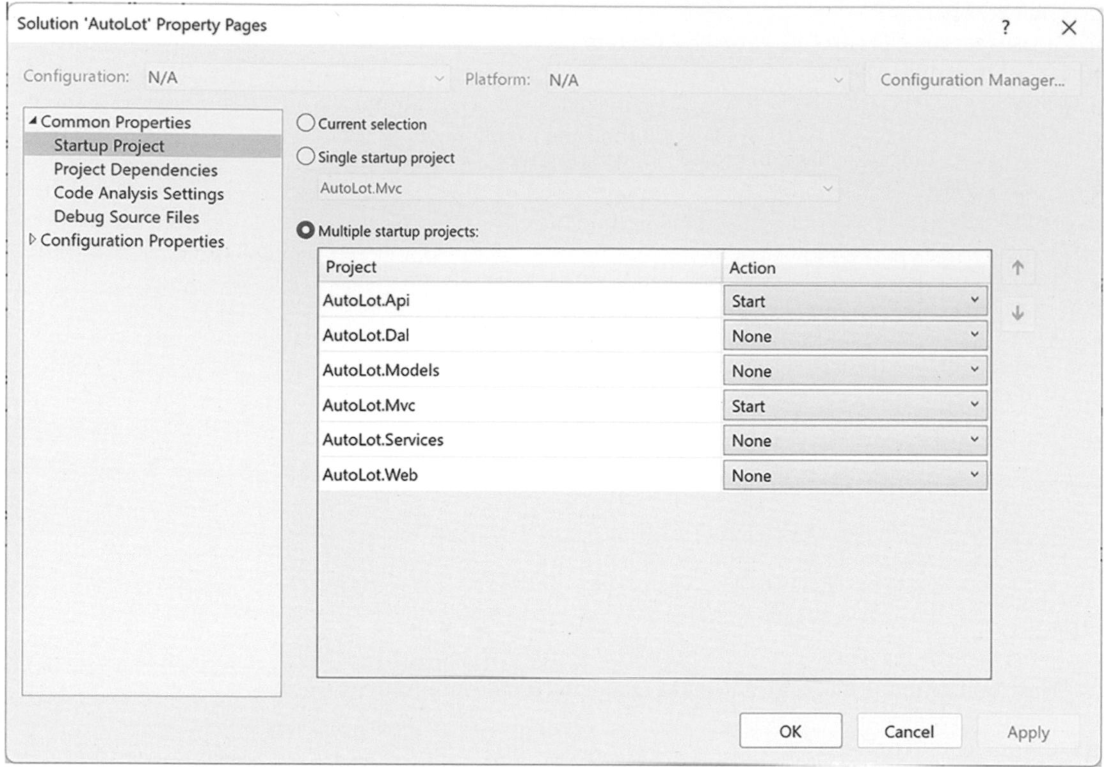

Figure 33-17. *Setting multiple startup projects in Visual Studio*

When you press F5 (or click the green run arrow), both projects will launch. There are some intricacies when you do this. The first is that Visual Studio remembers the last profile used to run an app. This means if you used IIS Express to run AutoLot.Api, running both together will run AutoLot.Api using IIS Express, and the port in the service settings will be incorrect. That's easy enough to fix. Either change the ports in the `appsettings.Development.json` file or run the app with Kestrel before configuring the multiple startup options.

The second comes down to timing. Both projects start at essentially the same time. If you have AutoLot.Api configured to re-create the database each time it runs, it will not be ready for AutoLot.Mvc when the `ViewComponent` executes to build the menu. A quick refresh of the AutoLot.Mvc browser (once you see the SwaggerUI in AutoLot.Api) will resolve this.

Using the Command Line

Open a command prompt in each of the project directories and enter `dotnet watch run`. This allows you to control the order and the timing and will also ensure that the apps are executed using Kestrel and not IIS. For information on debugging when running from the command line, please refer to Chapter 30.

Summary

This chapter completed the AutoLot.Mvc application. It began with a deep dive into views, partial views, and editor and display templates. The next set of topics covered client-side libraries, including management of what libraries are in the project as well as bundling and minification.

The `BaseCrudController` and the `CarsController` were developed, Areas were explored, and the `MakesController` was completed. Next was an examination of tag helpers and the creation of the projects custom tag helpers. The Cars views were created, and the `MenuViewComponent` was developed to make the menu dynamic. Next, two custom validation attributes were developed, GDPR support for cookie consent was added, and the Admin area was completed.

The next chapter will complete the AutoLot.Web application.

CHAPTER 34

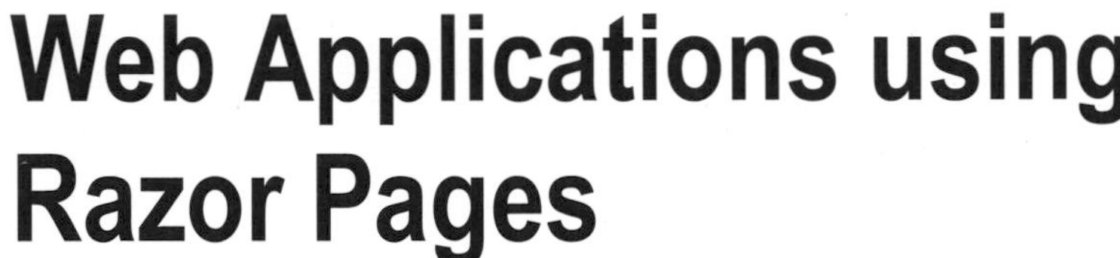

Web Applications using Razor Pages

This chapter builds on what you learned in the previous chapter and completes the AutoLot.Web Razor Page based application. The underlying architecture for Razor Page based applications is very similar to MVC style applications, with the main difference being that they are page based instead of controller based. This chapter will highlight the differences as the AutoLot.Web application is built, and assumes that you have read the previous chapters on ASP.NET Core.

Note The sample code for this chapter is in the `Chapter 34` directory of this book's repo. Feel free to continue working with the solution you started in the previous ASP.NET Core chapters.

Anatomy of a Razor Page

Unlike MVC style applications, views in Razor Page based applications are part of the page. To demonstrate, add a new empty Razor Page named `RazorSyntax` by right clicking the `Pages` directory in the AutoLot.Web project in Visual Studio, select Add ➤ Razor Page, and chose the Razor Page - Empty template. You will see two files created, `RazorSyntax.cshtml` and `RazorSyntax.cshtml.cs`. The `RazorSyntax.cshtml` file is the view for the page and the `RazorSyntax.cshtml.cs` file is the code behind file for the view.

Before proceeding, add the following global using statements to the `GlobalUsings.cs` file in the AutoLot.Web project:

```
global using AutoLot.Models.Entities;
global using Microsoft.AspNetCore.Mvc;
global using Microsoft.AspNetCore.Mvc.RazorPages;
global using AutoLot.Services.DataServices.Interfaces;
global using Microsoft.Build.Framework;
```

Razor Page PageModel Classes and Page Handler Methods

The code behind the file for a Razor Page derives from the `PageModel` base class and is named with the Model suffix, like `RazorSyntaxModel`. The `PageModel` base class, like the Controller base class in MVC style applications, provides many helper methods useful for building web applications. Unlike

A. Troelsen and P. Japikse, *Pro C# 10 with .NET 6*, https://doi.org/10.1007/978-1-4842-7869-7_34

the Controller class, Razor Pages are tied to a single view, have directory structure based routes, and have a single set of page handler methods to service the HTTP get (OnGet()/OnGetAsync()) and post (OnPost()/OnPostAsync()) requests.

Change the scaffolded RazorSyntaxModel class so the OnGet() page handler method is asynchronous and update the name to OnGetAsync(). Next, add an async OnPostAsync() page handler method for HTTP Post requests:

```
namespace AutoLot.Web.Pages;

public class RazorSyntaxModel : PageModel
{
  public async Task OnGetAsync()
  {
  }
  public async Task OnPostAsync()
  {
  }
}
```

■ **Note** The default names can be changed. This will be covered later in this chapter.

Notice how the page handler methods don't return a value like their action method counterparts. When the page handler method does return a value, the page implicitly returns the view that the page is associated with. Razor Page handler methods also support returning an IActionResult, which then requires explicitly returning an IActionResult. If the method is to return the class's view, the Page() method is returned. The method could also redirect to another page. Both scenarios are shown in this code sample:

```
public async Task<IActionResult> OnGetAsync()
{
  return Page();
}
public async Task OnPostAsync()
{
  return RedirectToPage("Index")
}
```

Derived PageModel classes support both method and constructor injection. When using method injection, the parameter must be marked with the [FromService] attribute, like this:

```
public async Task OnGetAsync([FromServices] ICarDataService carDataService)
{
  //Get a car instance
}
```

Since PageModel classes are focused on a single view, it is more common to use constructor injection instead of method injection. Update the RazorSyntaxModel class by adding a constructor that takes an instance of the ICarDataService and assigns it to a class level field:

```
private readonly ICarDataService _carDataService;

public RazorSyntaxModel(ICarDataService carDataService)
{
  _carDataService = carDataService;
}
```

If you inspect the Page() method, you will see that there isn't an overload that takes an object. While the related View() method in MVC is used to pass the model to the view, Razor Pages use properties on the PageModel class to send data to the view. Add a new public property named Entity of type Car to the RazorSyntaxModel class:

```
public Car Entity { get; set; }
```

Now, use the data service to get a Car record and assign it to the public property (if the UseApi flag in appsettings.Development.json is set to true, make sure AutoLot.Api is running):

```
public async Task<IActionResult> OnGetAsync()
{
  Entity = await _carDataService.FindAsync(6);
  return Page();
}
```

Razor Pages can use implicit binding to get data from a view, just like MVC action methods:

```
public async Task<IActionResult> OnPostAsync(Car entity)
{
  //do something interesting
  return RedirectToPage("Index");
}
```

Razor Pages also support explicit binding:

```
public async Task<IActionResult> OnPostAsync()
{
  var newCar = new Car();
  if (await TryUpdateModelAsync(newCar, "Entity",
      c => c.Id,
      c => c.TimeStamp,
      c => c.PetName,
      c => c.Color,
      c => c.IsDrivable,
      c => c.MakeId,
      c => c.Price
    ))
  {
    //do something interesting
  }
}
```

However, the common practice is to declare the property used by the HTTP get method as a BindProperty:

```
[BindProperty]
public Car Entity { get; set; }
```

This property will then be implicitly bound during HTTP post requests, and the OnPost()/OnPostAsync() methods use the bound property:

```
public async Task<IActionResult> OnPostAsync()
{
  await _carDataService.UpdateAsync(Entity);
  return RedirectToPage("Index");
}
```

Razor Page Views

Razor Pages views are specific for a Razor PageModel, begin with the @page directive and are typed to the code behind file, like this for the scaffolded RazorSyntax page:

```
@page
@model AutoLot.Web.Pages.RazorSyntaxModel
@{
}
```

Note that the view is not bound to the BindProperty (if one exists), but rather the PageModel derived class. The properties on the PageModel derived class (like the Entity property on the RazorSyntax page) are an extension of the @Model. To create the form necessary to test the different binding scenarios, add the following to the RazorSyntax.cshtml view, run the app, and navigate to https://localhost:5021/RazorSyntax:

```
<h1>Razor Syntax</h1>

<form asp-page="RazorSyntaxModel">
  <input type="hidden" asp-for="@Model.Entity.Id"/>
  <input type="hidden" asp-for="@Model.Entity.TimeStamp"/>
  <input asp-for="@Model.Entity.PetName"/>
  <input asp-for="@Model.Entity.Color"/>
  <input asp-for="@Model.Entity.IsDrivable"/>
  <input asp-for="@Model.Entity.MakeId"/>
  <input asp-for="@Model.Entity.Price"/>
  <input asp-for="@Model.Entity.DateBuilt"/>
  <button type="submit">Submit</button>
</form>
```

Note that the property doesn't need to be a BindProperty to access the values in the view. It only needs to be a BindProperty for the HTTP post method to implicitly bind the values.

Just like with MVC based applications, HTML, CSS, JavaScript, and Razor all work together in Razor Page views. All of the basic Razor syntax explored in the previous chapter is supported in Razor Page views, including tag helpers and HTML helpers. The only difference is in referring to the properties on the model, as previously demonstrated. To confirm this, update the view by adding the following from the Chapter 33 example, with the changes in bold (for the full discussion on the syntax, please refer to the previous chapter):

```
<h1>Razor Syntax</h1>
@for (int i = 0; i < 15; i++)
{
  //do something
}
@{
  //Code Block
  var foo = "Foo";
  var bar = "Bar";
  var htmlString = "<ul><li>one</li><li>two</li></ul>";
}
@foo<br />
@htmlString<br />
@foo.@bar<br />
@foo.ToUpper()<br/>
@Html.Raw(htmlString)<br/>
<hr />
@{
  @:Straight Text
  <div>Value:@Model.Entity.Id</div>
  <text>
      Lines without HTML tag
  </text>
  <br />
}

<hr/>
Email Address Handling:<br/>
foo@foo.com<br />
@@foo<br/>
test@foo<br/>
test@(foo)<br />
@*
    Multiline Comments
    Hi.
*@
@functions {
  public static IList<string> SortList(IList<string> strings)  {
    var list = from s in strings orderby s select s;
    return list.ToList();
  }
}
@{
  var myList = new List<string> {"C", "A", "Z", "F"};
  var sortedList = SortList(myList);
}
@foreach (string s in sortedList)
{
  @s@: 
}
<hr/>
```

```
@{
  Func<dynamic, object> b = @<strong>@item</strong>;
}
This will be bold: @b("Foo")
<hr/>
The Car named @Model.Entity.PetName is a <span style="color:@Model.Entity.Color">@Model.
Entity.Color</span>@Model.Entity.MakeNavigation.Name
<hr/>
Display For examples
Make:
@Html.DisplayFor(x=>x.Entity.MakeNavigation)
Car:
@Html.DisplayFor(c=>c.Entity)

@Html.EditorFor(c=>c.Entity)
```

Note the change in the last two lines. The _DisplayForModel()/EditorForModel() methods behave differently in Razor Pages since the view is bound to the PageModel, and not the entity/viewmodel like in MVC applications.

Razor Views

MVC style razor views (without a derived PageModel class as the code behind) and partial views are also supported in Razor Page applications. This includes the _ViewStart.cshtml, _ViewImports.cshtml (both in the \Pages directory) and the _Layout.cshtml files, located in the Pages\Shared directory. All three provide the same functionality as in MVC based applications. Layouts with Razor Pages will be covered shortly.

The _ViewStart and _ViewImports Views

The _ViewStart.cshtml executes its code before any other Razor Page view is rendered and is used to set the default layout. The _ViewStart.cshtml file is shown here:

```
@{
    Layout = "_Layout";
}
```

The _ViewImports.cshtml file is used for importing shared directives, like @using statements. The contents apply to all views in the same directory or subdirectory of the _ViewImports file. This file is the view equivalent of a GlobalUsings.cs file for C# code.

```
@using AutoLot.Web
@namespace AutoLot.Web.Pages
@addTagHelper *, Microsoft.AspNetCore.Mvc.TagHelpers
```

The @namespace declaration defines the default namespace where the application's pages are located.

The Shared Directory

The Shared directory under Pages holds partial views, display and editor templates, and layouts that are available to all Razor Pages.

The DisplayTemplates Folder

Display templates work the same in MVC and Razor Pages. They are placed in a directory named DisplayTemplates and control how types are rendered when the DisplayFor() method is called. The search path starts in the Pages\{CurrentPageRoute}\DisplayTemplates directory and, if it's not found, it then looks in the Pages\Shared\DisplayTemplates folder. Just like with MVC, the engine looks for a template with the same name as the type being rendered or looks to a template that matches the name passed into the method.

The DateTime Display Template

Create a new folder named DisplayTemplates under the Pages\Shared folder. Add a new view named DateTime.cshtml into that folder. Clear out all of the generated code and comments and replace them with the following:

```
@model DateTime?
@if (Model == null)
{
  @:Unknown
}
else
{
  if (ViewData.ModelMetadata.IsNullableValueType)
  {
    @:@(Model.Value.ToString("d"))
  }
  else
  {
    @:@(((DateTime)Model).ToString("d"))
  }
}
```

Note that the @model directive that strongly types the view uses a lowercase m. When referring to the assigned value of the model in Razor, an uppercase M is used. In this example, the model definition is nullable. If the value for the model passed into the view is null, the template displays the word Unknown. Otherwise, it displays the date in Short Date format, using the Value property of a nullable type or the actual model itself.

With this template in place, if you run the application and navigate to the RazorSyntax page, you can see that the BuiltDate value is formatted as a Short Date.

The Car Display Template

Create a new directory named Cars under the Pages directory, and add a directory named DisplayTemplates under the Cars directory. Add a new view named Car.cshtml into that folder. Clear out all of the generated code and comments and replace them with the following code, which displays a Car entity:

```
@model AutoLot.Models.Entities.Car
<dl class="row">
  <dt class="col-sm-2">
    @Html.DisplayNameFor(model => model.MakeId)
  </dt>
```

```
  <dd class="col-sm-10">
    @Html.DisplayFor(model => model.MakeNavigation.Name)
  </dd>
  <dt class="col-sm-2">
    @Html.DisplayNameFor(model => model.Color)
  </dt>
  <dd class="col-sm-10">
    @Html.DisplayFor(model => model.Color)
  </dd>
  <dt class="col-sm-2">
    @Html.DisplayNameFor(model => model.PetName)
  </dt>
  <dd class="col-sm-10">
    @Html.DisplayFor(model => model.PetName)
  </dd>
  <dt class="col-sm-2">
    @Html.DisplayNameFor(model => model.Price)
  </dt>
  <dd class="col-sm-10">
    @Html.DisplayFor(model => model.Price)
  </dd>
  <dt class="col-sm-2">
    @Html.DisplayNameFor(model => model.DateBuilt)
  </dt>
  <dd class="col-sm-10">
    @Html.DisplayFor(model => model.DateBuilt)
  </dd>
  <dt class="col-sm-2">
    @Html.DisplayNameFor(model => model.IsDrivable)
  </dt>
  <dd class="col-sm-10">
    @Html.DisplayFor(model => model.IsDrivable)
  </dd>
</dl>
```

The DisplayNameFor() HTML helper displays the name of the property unless the property is decorated with either the Display(Name="") or DisplayName("") attribute, in which case the display value is used. The DisplayFor() method displays the value for the model's property specified in the expression. Notice that the navigation property for MakeNavigation is being used to get the make name.

To use a template from another directory structure, you have to specify the name of the view as well as the full path and file extension. To use this template on the RazorSyntax view, update the DisplayFor() method to the following:

```
@Html.DisplayFor(c=>c.Entity,"Cars/DisplayTemplates/Car.cshtml")
```

Another option is to move the display templates to the Pages\Shared\DisplayTemplates directory

The Car with Color Display Template

Copy the `Car.cshtml` view to another view named `CarWithColors.cshtml` in the `Cars\DisplayTemplates` directory. The difference is that this template changes the color of the *Color* text based on the model's `Color` property value. Update the new template's `<dd>` tag for `Color` to the following:

```
<dd class="col-sm-10" style="color:@Model.Color">
  @Html.DisplayFor(model => model.Color)
</dd>
```

The EditorTemplates Folder

The `EditorTemplates` folder works the same as the `DisplayTemplates` folder, except the templates are used for editing.

The Car Edit Template

Create a new directory named `EditorTemplates` under the `Pages\Cars` directory. Add a new view named `Car.cshtml` into that folder. Clear out all of the generated code and comments and replace them with the following code, which represents the markup to edit a `Car` entity:

```
@model Car
<div asp-validation-summary="All" class="text-danger"></div>
<div>
    <label asp-for="MakeId" class="col-form-label"></label>
    <select asp-for="MakeId" class="form-control" asp-items="@ViewBag.
LookupValues"></select>
    <span asp-validation-for="MakeId" class="text-danger"></span>
</div>
<div>
    <label asp-for="Color" class="col-form-label"></label>
    <input asp-for="Color" class="form-control"/>
    <span asp-validation-for="Color" class="text-danger"></span>
</div>
<div>
    <label asp-for="PetName" class="col-form-label"></label>
    <input asp-for="PetName" class="form-control" />
    <span asp-validation-for="PetName" class="text-danger"></span>
</div>
<div>
    <label asp-for="Price" class="col-form-label"></label>
    <input asp-for="Price" class="form-control"/>
    <span asp-validation-for="Price" class="text-danger"></span>
</div>
<div>
    <label asp-for="DateBuilt" class="col-form-label"></label>
    <input asp-for="DateBuilt" class="form-control"/>
    <span asp-validation-for="DateBuilt" class="text-danger"></span>
</div>
```

```
<div>
    <label asp-for="IsDrivable" class="col-form-label"></label>
    <input asp-for="IsDrivable" />
    <span asp-validation-for="IsDrivable" class="text-danger"></span>
</div>
```

Editor templates are invoked with the `EditorFor()` HTML helper. To use this with the `RazorSyntax` page, update the call to `EditorFor()` to the following:

```
@Html.EditorFor(c=>c.Entity,"Cars/EditorTemplates/Car.cshtml")
```

View CSS Isolation

Razor Pages also support CSS isolation. Right click on the `\Pages` directory, and select Add ➤ New Item, navigate to ASP.NET Core/Web/Content in the left rail, and select Style Sheet and name it `Index.cshtml.css`. Update the content to the following:

```
h1 {
    background-color: blue;
}
```

This change makes the <h1> tag on the Index Razor Page blue but doesn't affect any other pages.

The same rules apply in Razor Pages as MVC with view CSS isolation: the CSS file is only generated when running in Development or when the site is published. To see the CSS in other environments, you have to opt-in:

```
//Enable CSS isolation in a non-deployed session
if (!builder.Environment.IsDevelopment())
{
    builder.WebHost.UseWebRoot("wwwroot");
    builder.WebHost.UseStaticWebAssets();
}
```

Layouts

Layouts in Razor Pages function the same as they do in MVC applications, except they are located in `Pages\Shared` and not `Views\Shared`. _ViewStart.cshtml is used to specify the default layout for a directory structure, and Razor Page views can explicitly define their layout using a Razor block:

```
@{
    Layout = "_MyCustomLayout";
}
```

Injecting Data

Add the following to the top of the `_Layout.cshtml` file, which injects the `IWebHostEnvironment`:

```
@inject IWebHostEnvironment _env
```

Next, update the footer to show the environment that the application is currently running in:

```
&copy; 2021 - AutoLot.Web - @_env.EnvironmentName - <a asp-area="" asp-page="/
Privacy">Privacy</a>
```

Partial Views

The main difference with partial views in Razor Pages is that a Razor Page view can't be rendered as a partial. In Razor Pages, they are used to encapsulate UI elements and are loaded from another view or a view component. Next, we are going to split the layout into partials to make the markup easier to maintain.

Create the Partials

Create a new directory named Partials under the Shared directory. Right click on the new directory and select Add ➤ New Item. Enter Razor View in the search box and select Razor View -Empty. Create three empty views named _Head.cshtml, _JavaScriptFiles.cshtml, and _Menu.cshtml.

Cut the content in the layout that is between the <head></head> tags and paste it into the _Head.cshtml file. In _Layout.cshtml, replace the deleted markup with the call to render the new partial:

```
<head>
  <partial name="Partials/_Head"/>
</head>
```

For the menu partial, cut all the markup between the <header></header> tags (not the <head></head> tags) and paste it into the _Menu.cshtml file. Update the _Layout to render the Menu partial.

```
<header>
  <partial name="Partials/_Menu"/>
</header>
```

The final step at this time is to cut out the <script> tags (after the closing </footer> tag) for the JavaScript files and paste them into the JavaScriptFiles partial. Make sure to leave the RenderSection tag in place.

```
  </footer>
  <partial name="Partials/_JavaScriptFiles" />
  @await RenderSectionAsync("Scripts", required: false)
```

Sending Data to Partials

A property on the derived PageModel can be passed into a partial view using the <partial> tag helper, as is demonstrated here:

```
<partial name="Partials/_CarListPartial" model="@Model.Entities"/>
```

ViewBag, ViewData, and TempData

Razor Pages also support the ViewBag, ViewData, and TempData objects. Recall that the <head> portion of the _Layout.cshtml view (now in _Head.cshtml) uses ViewData to set the title for a page:

```
<title>@ViewData["Title"] - AutoLot.Web</title>
```

With Razor Pages, you can reference ViewData in a Razor block in a view:

```
@page
@model AutoLot.Web.Pages.RazorSyntaxModel
@{
    ViewData["Title"] ="Razor Syntax";
}
```

You can also set ViewData properties by decorating PageModel properties with the [ViewData] attribute. The following code accomplishes the same result as the view Razor block shown in the previous code sample:

```
[ViewData]
public string Title => "Razor Syntax";
```

Now when you run the application and navigate to https://localhost:5001/Home/RazorSyntax, you will see the title "Razor Syntax - AutoLot.Web" in the browser tab.

This works the same for TempData.

Add Client-Side Libraries to AutoLot.Web

The default template loaded the CSS and JavaScript libraries into the wwwroot\lib directory. To switch to managing the libraries with LibraryManager, begin by deleting the entire lib directory and all of the directories and files it contains.

Add the libman.json File

The libman.json file controls what gets installed, from what sources, and the destination of the installed files.

Visual Studio

If you are using Visual Studio, right-click the AutoLot.Web project and select Manage Client-Side Libraries. This adds the libman.json file to the root of the project. There is also an option in Visual Studio to tie Library Manager into the MSBuild process. If you did not install the Microsoft.Web.LibraryManager.Build NuGet package prior to adding the libmon.json file (which we did when we built the projects in Chapter 30), right-click the libman.json file and select "Enable restore on build." This prompts you to allow the NuGet package to be added into the project. Allow the package to be installed if prompted. By installing the package first, the project is automatically set to restore on build.

Command Line

Create a new `libman.json` file with the following command (this sets the default provider to be `cdnjs.com`):

```
libman init --default-provider cdnjs
```

If you choose to not set a default provider with the command line, you will be prompted to select one, defaulting to `cdnjs`.

Update the libman.json File

After adding all the files needed for this app, the entire `libman.json` file is shown here:

```
{
  //https://api.cdnjs.com/libraries?output=human
  //https://api.cdnjs.com/libraries/jquery?output=human
  "version": "1.0",
  "defaultProvider": "cdnjs",
  "defaultDestination": "wwwroot/lib",
  "libraries": [
    {
      "library": "jquery@3.6.0",
      "destination": "wwwroot/lib/jquery",
      "files": [ "jquery.js", "jquery.min.js", "jquery.min.map" ]
    },
    {
      "library": "jquery-validate@1.19.3",
      "destination": "wwwroot/lib/jquery-validation",
      "files": [ "jquery.validate.js", "jquery.validate.min.js", "additional-methods.js",
"additional-methods.min.js" ]
    },
    {
      "library": "jquery-validation-unobtrusive@3.2.12",
      "destination": "wwwroot/lib/jquery-validation-unobtrusive",
      "files": [ "jquery.validate.unobtrusive.js", "jquery.validate.unobtrusive.min.js" ]
    },
    {
      "library": "bootstrap@5.1.3",
      "destination": "wwwroot/lib/bootstrap",
      "files": [
        "css/bootstrap.css",
        "css/bootstrap.css.map",
        "css/bootstrap.min.css",
        "css/bootstrap.min.css.map",
        "js/bootstrap.bundle.js",
        "js/bootstrap.bundle.js.map",
        "js/bootstrap.bundle.min.js",
        "js/bootstrap.bundle.min.js.map",
        "js/bootstrap.js",
        "js/bootstrap.js.map",
```

```
        "js/bootstrap.min.js",
        "js/bootstrap.min.js.map"
      ]
    },
    {
      "library": "font-awesome@5.15.4",
      "destination": "wwwroot/lib/font-awesome/",
      "files": [
        "js/all.js",
        "js/all.min.js",
        "css/all.css",
        "css/all.min.css",
        "sprites/brands.svg",
        "sprites/regular.svg",
        "sprites/solid.svg",
        "webfonts/fa-brands-400.eot",
        "webfonts/fa-brands-400.svg",
        "webfonts/fa-brands-400.ttf",
        "webfonts/fa-brands-400.woff",
        "webfonts/fa-brands-400.woff2",
        "webfonts/fa-regular-400.eot",
        "webfonts/fa-regular-400.svg",
        "webfonts/fa-regular-400.ttf",
        "webfonts/fa-regular-400.woff",
        "webfonts/fa-regular-400.woff2",
        "webfonts/fa-solid-900.eot",
        "webfonts/fa-solid-900.svg",
        "webfonts/fa-solid-900.ttf",
        "webfonts/fa-solid-900.woff",
        "webfonts/fa-solid-900.woff2"
      ]
    }
  ]
}
```

Once you save the file (in Visual Studio), the files will be loaded into the `wwwroot\lib` folder of the project. If running from the command line, enter the following command to reload all the files:

```
libman restore
```

Additional command-line options are available. Enter `libman -h` to explore all the options.

Update the JavaScript and CSS References

With the change of the location for the JavaScript and CSS libraries, the partials need to be updated. The `<environment>` and `<link>` tag helpers will also be added at this time. Start by updating the `_Head.cshtml` file to the following:

```
<meta charset="utf-8"/>
<meta name="viewport" content="width=device-width, initial-scale=1.0"/>
<title>@ViewData["Title"] - AutoLot.Web</title>
```

```
<environment include="Development">
  <link rel="stylesheet" href="~/lib/bootstrap/css/bootstrap.css" asp-append-version="true"/>
  <link rel="stylesheet" href="~/lib/font-awesome/css/all.css" asp-append-version="true"/>
</environment>
<environment exclude="Development">
  <link rel="stylesheet" href="https://cdnjs.cloudflare.com/ajax/libs/bootstrap/5.1.3/css/
bootstrap.min.css"
      asp-fallback-href="~/lib/bootstrap/css/bootstrap.min.css"
      asp-append-version="true"
      asp-fallback-test-class="sr-only"
      asp-fallback-test-property="position"
      asp-fallback-test-value="absolute"
      asp-suppress-fallback-integrity="true"
      crossorigin="anonymous"
      integrity="sha512-GQGU0fMMi238uA+a/bdWJfpUGKUkBdgfFdgBm72SUQ6BeyWjoY/ton0tEjH+0SH9iP4D
      fh+7HM0I9f5eR0L/4w=="/>
  <link rel="stylesheet" href="https://cdnjs.cloudflare.com/ajax/libs/font-awesome/5.15.4/
  css/all.min.css"
      asp-fallback-href="~/lib/font-awesome/css/all.min.css"
      asp-append-version="true"
      asp-fallback-test-class="fab"
      asp-fallback-test-property="display"
      asp-fallback-test-value="inline-block"
      asp-suppress-fallback-integrity="true"
      crossorigin="anonymous"
      integrity="sha512-1ycn6IcaQQ40/MKBW2W4Rhis/
DbILU74C1vSrLJxCq57o941Ym01SwNsOMqvEBFlcgUa6xLiPY/NS5R+E6ztJQ=="/>
</environment>
<link rel="stylesheet" href="~/css/site.css" asp-append-version="true"/>
<link rel="stylesheet" href="~/AutoLot.Web.styles.css" asp-append-version="true" />
```

Next, update _JavaScriptFiles.cshtml to change the location and add the <environment> and <script> tag helpers.

```
<environment include="Development">
  <script src="~/lib/jquery/jquery.js" asp-append-version="true"></script>
  <script src="~/lib/bootstrap/js/bootstrap.bundle.js" asp-append-version="true"></script>
</environment>
<environment exclude="Development">
  <script src="https://cdnjs.cloudflare.com/ajax/libs/jquery/3.6.0/jquery.min.js"
        asp-append-version="true"
        asp-fallback-src="~/lib/jquery/jquery.min.js"
        asp-fallback-test="window.jQuery"
        asp-suppress-fallback-integrity="true"
        crossorigin="anonymous"
        integrity="sha512-894YE6QWD5I59HgZOGReFYm4dnWc1Qt5NtvYSaNcOP+u1T9qYdvdihz0PPSiiqn/+
        /3e7Jo4EaG7TubfWGUrMQ==">
  </script>
  <script src="https://cdn.jsdelivr.net/npm/bootstrap@5.1.3/dist/js/bootstrap.bundle.min.js"
        asp-append-version="true"
        asp-fallback-src="~/lib/bootstrap/js/bootstrap.bundle.min.js"
        asp-fallback-test="window.jQuery && window.jQuery.fn && window.jQuery.fn.modal"
```

```
        asp-suppress-fallback-integrity="true"
        crossorigin="anonymous"
        integrity="sha384-ka7Sk0Gln4gmtz2MlQnikT1wXgYsOg+OMhuP+IlRH9sENBO0LRn5q+8nbTov4+1p">
  </script>
</environment>
<script src="~/js/site.js" asp-append-version="true"></script>
```

The final change is to update the location of `jquery.validation` and add the <environment> and <script> tag helpers in the `_ValidationScriptsPartial.cshtml` partial view.

```
<environment include="Development,Local">
  <script src="~/lib/jquery-validation/jquery.validate.js" asp-append-
             version="true"></script>
  <script src="~/lib/jquery-validation-unobtrusive/jquery.validate.unobtrusive.js" asp-
  append-version="true"></script>
</environment>
<environment exclude="Development,Local">
  <script src="https://cdnjs.cloudflare.com/ajax/libs/jquery-validate/1.19.3/jquery.
  validate.min.js"
        asp-fallback-src="~/lib/jquery-validation/jquery.validate.min.js"
        asp-fallback-test="window.jQuery && window.jQuery.validator"
        crossorigin="anonymous"
        integrity="sha512-37T7leoNS06R80c8Ulq7cdCDU5MNQBwlYoy1TX/WUsLFC2eYNqtKlVOQjH7r8JpG/
        SOGUMZwebnVFLPd6SU5yg==">
  </script>
  <script src="https://cdnjs.cloudflare.com/ajax/libs/jquery-validation-unobtrusive/3.2.12/
  jquery.validate.unobtrusive.min.js"
        asp-fallback-src="~/lib/jquery-validation-unobtrusive/jquery.validate.
        unobtrusive.min.js"
        asp-fallback-test="window.jQuery && window.jQuery.validator && window.jQuery.
        validator.unobtrusive"
        crossorigin="anonymous"
        integrity="sha512-o6XqxgrUsKmchwy9G5VRNWSSxTS4Urr4loO6/0hYdpWmFUfHqGzawGxeQGMDqYzxjY
        9sbktPbNlkIQJWagVZQg==">
  </script>
</environment>
```

Add and Configure WebOptimizer

Open the `Program.cs` file in the AutoLot.Web project and add the following line (just before the `app.UseStaticFiles()` call):

```
app.UseWebOptimizer();
```

The next step is to configure what to minimize and bundle. The open source libraries already have the minified versions downloaded through Library Manager, so the only files that need to be minified are the project specific files, including the generated CSS file if you are using CSS isolation. In the `Program.cs` file, add the following code block before `var app = builder.Build()`:

```
if (builder.Environment.IsDevelopment() || builder.Environment.IsEnvironment("Local"))
{
    builder.Services.AddWebOptimizer(false,false);
    /*
    builder.Services.AddWebOptimizer(options =>
    {
        options.MinifyCssFiles("AutoLot.Web.styles.css");
        options.MinifyCssFiles("css/site.css");
        options.MinifyJsFiles("js/site.js");
    });
    */
}
else
{
    builder.Services.AddWebOptimizer(options =>
    {
        options.MinifyCssFiles("AutoLot.Web.styles.css");
        options.MinifyCssFiles("css/site.css");
        options.MinifyJsFiles("js/site.js");
    });
}
```

In the development scope, the code is setup for you to comment/uncomment the different options so you can replicate the production environment without switching to production.

The final step is to add the WebOptimizer tag helpers into the system. Add the following line to the end of the _ViewImports.cshtml file:

```
@addTagHelper *, WebOptimizer.Core
```

Tag Helpers

Razor Pages views (and layout and partial views) also support Tag helpers. They function the same as in MVC applications, with only a few differences. Any tag helper that is involved in routing uses page-centric attributes instead of MVC centric attributes. Table 34-1 lists the tag helpers that use routing, their corresponding HTML helper, and the available Razor Page attributes. The differences will be covered in detail after the table.

Table 34-1. *Commonly Used Built-in Tag Helpers*

Tag Helper	HTML Helper	Available Attributes
Form	Html.BeginForm Html.BeginRouteForm Html.AntiForgeryToken	asp-route—for named routes (can't be used with controller, page, or action attributes).asp-antiforgery—if the antiforgery should be added (true by default).asp-area—the name of the area.asp-route-<ParameterName>—adds the parameter to the route, e.g., asp-route-id="1".asp-page—the name of the Razor Page.asp-page-handler—the name of the Razor Page handler.asp-all-route-data—dictionary for additional route values.
Form Action (button or input type=image)	N/A	Asp-route—for named routes (can't be used with controller, page, or action attributes).asp-antiforgery—if the antiforgery should be added (true by default).asp-area—the name of the area. asp-route-<ParameterName>—adds the parameter to the route, e.g., asp-route-id="1".asp-page—the name of the Razor Page.asp-page-handler—the name of the Razor Page handler.asp-all-route-data—dictionary for additional route values.
Anchor	Html.ActionLink	asp-route—for named routes (can't be used with controller, page, or action attributes). asp-area—the name of the area. asp-protocol—HTTP or HTTPS.asp-fragment—URL fragment.asp-host—the host name.asp-route-<ParameterName>—adds the parameter to the route, e.g., asp-route-id="1". asp-page—the name of the Razor Page. asp-page-handler—the name of the Razor Page handler.asp-all-route-data—dictionary for additional route values.

Enabling Tag Helpers

Tag helpers must be enabled in your project in the _ViewImports.html file by adding the following line (which was added by the default template):

```
@addTagHelper *, Microsoft.AspNetCore.Mvc.TagHelpers
```

The Form Tag Helper

With Razor Pages, the <form> tag helper uses asp-page instead of asp-controller and asp-action:

```
<form method="post" asp-page="Edit" asp-route-id="@Model.Entity.Id" >
<!-- Omitted for brevity -->
</form>
```

Another option available is to specify the name of the page handler method. When modifying the name, the format On<Verb><CustomName>() (OnPostCreateNewCar()) or On<Verb><CustomName>Async() (OnPostCreateNewCarAsync()) must be followed. With the HTTP post method renamed, the handler method is specified like this:

```
<form method="post" asp-page="Create" asp-page-handler="CreateNewCar">
<!-- Omitted for brevity -->
</form>
```

All Razor Page HTTP post handler methods automatically check for the antiforgery token, which is added whenever a `<from>` tag helper is used.

The Form Action Button/Image Tag Helper

The form action tag helper is used on buttons and images to change the action for the form that contains them and supports the `asp-page` and `asp-page-handler` attributes in the same manner as the `<form>` tag helper.

```
<button type="submit" asp-page="Create">Index</button>
```

The Anchor Tag Helper

The `<anchor>` tag helper replaces the `Html.ActionLink` HTML helper and uses many of the same routing tags as the `<form>` tag helper. For example, to create a link for the `RazorSyntax` view, use the following code:

```
<a class="nav-link text-dark" asp-area="" asp-page="/RazorSyntax">
  Razor Syntax
</a>
```

To add the navigation menu item for the `RazorSyntax` page, update the `_Menu.cshtml` to the following, adding the new menu item between the Home and Privacy menu items:

```
...
<li class="nav-item">
  <a class="nav-link text-dark" asp-area="" asp-page="/Index">Home</a>
</li>
<li class="nav-item">
  <a class="nav-link text-dark" asp-area="" asp-page="/RazorSyntax">Razor Syntax  <i
  class="fas fa-cut"></i></a>
</li>
<li class="nav-item">
  <a class="nav-link text-dark" asp-area="" asp-page="/Privacy">Privacy</a>
</li>
```

The anchor tag helper can be combined with the views model. For example, using the `Car` instance in the `RazorSyntax` page, the following anchor tag routes to the `Details` page passing in the Id as the route parameter:

```
<a asp-page="Cars/Details" asp-route-id="@Model.Entity.Id">@Model.Entity.PetName</a>
```

Custom Tag Helpers

Building custom tag helpers for Razor Pages is very similar to building them for MVC apps. They both inherit from `TagHelper` and must implement the `Process()` method. For AutoLot.Web, the difference from the MVC version is how the links are created since routing is different. Before starting, add the following global using statement to the `GlobalUsings.cs` file:

```
global using Microsoft.AspNetCore.Mvc.Infrastructure;
global using Microsoft.AspNetCore.Mvc.Routing;
global using Microsoft.AspNetCore.Razor.TagHelpers;
global using Microsoft.Extensions.DependencyInjection.Extensions;
```

Update Program.cs

Once again we need to use an UrlHelperFactory and IActionContextAccessor to create the links based on routing. To create an instance of the UrlFactory from a non-PageModel-derived class, the IActionContextAccessor must be added to the services collection. Call the following line in Program.cs to add the IActionContextAccessor into the services collection:

```
builder.Services.TryAddSingleton<IActionContextAccessor, ActionContextAccessor>();
```

Create the Base Class

Create a new folder named TagHelpers in the root of the AutoLot.Web project. In this folder, create a new folder named Base, and in that folder, create a class named ItemLinkTagHelperBase.cs, make the class public and abstract, and inherit from TagHelper:

```
namespace AutoLot.Web.TagHelpers.Base;

public abstract class ItemLinkTagHelperBase : TagHelper
{
}
```

Add a constructor that takes instances of IActionContextAccessor and IUrlHelperFactory. Use the UrlHelperFactory with the ActionContextAccessor to create an instance of IUrlHelper, and store that in a class-level variable. The code is shown here:

```
protected readonly IUrlHelper UrlHelper;
protected ItemLinkTagHelperBase(IActionContextAccessor contextAccessor, IUrlHelperFactory
urlHelperFactory)
{
  UrlHelper = urlHelperFactory.GetUrlHelper(contextAccessor.ActionContext);
}
```

In the constructor, use the contextAccessor instance to get the current Page and assign it to a class level field. The page route value is in the form of <directory>/<PageName>, like Cars/Index: The string is split to get only the directory name:

```
protected readonly IUrlHelper UrlHelper;
private readonly string _pageName;
protected ItemLinkTagHelperBase(IActionContextAccessor contextAccessor, IUrlHelperFactory
urlHelperFactory)
{
```

```
  UrlHelper = urlHelperFactory.GetUrlHelper(contextAccessor.ActionContext);
  _pageName = contextAccessor.ActionContext.ActionDescriptor.
      RouteValues["page"]?.Split("/",StringSplitOptions.RemoveEmptyEntries)[0];
}
```

Add a protected property so the derived classes can indicate the action name for the route:

```
protected string ActionName { get; set; }
```

Add a single public property to hold the Id of the item, as follows:

```
public int? ItemId { get; set; }
```

As a reminder, public properties on custom tag helpers are exposed as HTML attributes on the tag. The naming convention is that the property name is converted to lower-kabob-casing. This means every capital letter is lower cased and dashes (-) are inserted before each letter that is changed to lower case (except for the first one). This converts ItemId to item-id (like words on a shish-kabob).

The BuildContent() method is called by the derived classes to build the HTML that gets rendered instead of the tag helper:

```
protected void BuildContent(
  TagHelperOutput output, string cssClassName, string displayText, string fontAwesomeName)
{
  output.TagName = "a";
  var target = (ItemId.HasValue)
     ? UrlHelper.Page($"/{_pageName}/{ActionName}", new { id = ItemId })
     : UrlHelper.Page($"/{_pageName}/{ActionName}");
  output.Attributes.SetAttribute("href", target);
  output.Attributes.Add("class",cssClassName);
  output.Content.AppendHtml($@"{displayText} <i class=""fas fa-{fontAwesomeName}""></i>");
}
```

The first line changes the tag to the anchor tag. The next uses the UrlHelper.Page() static method to generate the route, including the route parameter if one exists. The next two set the HREF of the anchor tag to the generated route and add the CSS class name. The final line adds the display text and a Font Awesome font as the text that is displayed to the user.

As the final step, add the following global using statement to the GlobalUsings.cs file:

```
global using AutoLot.Web.TagHelpers.Base;
```

The Item Details Tag Helper

Create a new class named ItemDetailsTagHelper.cs in the TagHelpers folder. Make the class public and inherit from ItemLinkTagHelperBase.

```
namespace AutoLot.Web.TagHelpers;

  public class ItemDetailsTagHelper : ItemLinkTagHelperBase
{
}
```

Add a constructor to take in the required object instances and pass them to the base class. The constructor also needs to assign the ActionName:

```
public ItemDetailsTagHelper(
    IActionContextAccessor contextAccessor,
    IUrlHelperFactory urlHelperFactory)
    : base(contextAccessor, urlHelperFactory)
  {
    ActionName = "Details";
  }
```

Override the Process() method, calling the BuildContent() method in the base class.

```
public override void Process(TagHelperContext context, TagHelperOutput output)
{
  BuildContent(output, "text-info", "Details", "info-circle");
}
```

This creates a Details link using the CSS class text-info, the text of Details with the Font Awesome info image:

```
<a asp-page="Cars/Details" asp-route-id="5" class="text-info">Details <i class="fas fa-info-circle"></i></a>
```

When invoking tag helpers, the TagHelper suffix is dropped, and the remaining name of class is lower-kebob-cased. In this case, the HTML tag is <item-details>. The asp-route-id value comes from the item-id attribute on the tag helper:

```
<item-details item-id="@item.Id"></item-details>
```

The Item Delete Tag Helper

Create a new class named ItemDeleteTagHelper.cs in the TagHelpers folder. Make the class public and inherit from ItemLinkTagHelperBase. Add the constructor to take in the required object instances and set the ActionName using the DeleteAsync() method name:

```
public ItemDeleteTagHelper(
    IActionContextAccessor contextAccessor,
    IUrlHelperFactory urlHelperFactory)
      : base(contextAccessor, urlHelperFactory)
{
  ActionName = "Delete";
}
```

Override the Process() method, calling the BuildContent() method in the base class.

```
public override void Process(TagHelperContext context, TagHelperOutput output)
{
  BuildContent(output,"text-danger","Delete","trash");
}
```

This creates the Delete link with the Font Awesome garbage can image.

```
<a asp-page="Cars/Delete" asp-route-id="5" class="text-danger">Delete <i class="fas
fa-trash"></i></a>
```

The asp-route-id value comes from the item-id attribute on the tag helper:

```
<item-delete item-id="@item.Id"></item-delete>
```

The Item Edit Tag Helper

Create a new class named ItemEditTagHelper.cs in the TagHelpers folder. Make the class public, inherit from ItemLinkTagHelperBase and add the constructor that assigns Edit as the ActionName:

```
namespace AutoLot.Web.TagHelpers;

public class ItemEditTagHelper : ItemLinkTagHelperBase
{
  public ItemEditTagHelper(
    IActionContextAccessor contextAccessor,
    IUrlHelperFactory urlHelperFactory)
      : base(contextAccessor, urlHelperFactory)
  {
    ActionName = "Edit";
  }
}
```

Override the Process() method, calling the BuildContent() method in the base class.

```
public override void Process(TagHelperContext context, TagHelperOutput output)
{
  BuildContent(output,"text-warning","Edit","edit");
}
```

This creates the Edit link with the Font Awesome pencil image:

```
<a asp-page="Edit" asp-route-id="5" class="text-warning">Edit <i class="fas fa-
edit"></i></a>
```

The asp-route-id value comes from the item-id attribute on the tag helper:

```
<item-edit item-id="@item.Id"></item-edit>
```

The Item Create Tag Helper

Create a new class named ItemCreateTagHelper.cs in the TagHelpers folder. Make the class public, inherit from ItemLinkTagHelperBase and add the constructor that assigns Create as the ActionName:

```
namespace AutoLot.Web.TagHelpers;
```

```
public class ItemCreateTagHelper : ItemLinkTagHelperBase
{
  public ItemCreateTagHelper(
      IActionContextAccessor contextAccessor,
      IUrlHelperFactory urlHelperFactory)
        : base(contextAccessor, urlHelperFactory)
  {
    ActionName = "Create";
  }

}
```

Override the Process() method, calling the BuildContent() method in the base class.

```
public override void Process(TagHelperContext context, TagHelperOutput output)
{
  BuildContent(output,"text-success","Create New","plus");
}
```

This creates the Create link with the Font Awesome plus image:

```
<a asp-page="Cars/Create" class="text-warning">Create New <i class="fas fa-plus"></i></a>
```

There isn't a route parameter with the Create action:

```
<item-create></item-create>
```

The Item List Tag Helper

Create a new class named ItemListTagHelper.cs in the TagHelpers folder. Make the class public, inherit from ItemLinkTagHelperBase and add the constructor that assigns List as the ActionName:

```
namespace AutoLot.Web.TagHelpers;

public class ItemListTagHelper : ItemLinkTagHelperBase
{
  public ItemListTagHelper(
    IActionContextAccessor contextAccessor,
    IUrlHelperFactory urlHelperFactory)
      : base(contextAccessor, urlHelperFactory)
  {
    ActionName = "IndexAsync";
  }
}
```

Override the Process() method, calling the BuildContent() method in the base class.

```
public override void Process(TagHelperContext context, TagHelperOutput output)
{
  BuildContent(output,"text-default","Back to List","list");
}
```

This creates the Index link with the Font Awesome plus image:

```
<a asp-page="Cars/Index" class="text-default">Back to list <i class="fas fa-list"></i></a>
```

There isn't a route parameter with the Create action:

```
<item-list></item-list>
```

Making Custom Tag Helpers Visible

To make custom tag helpers visible, the `@addTagHelper` command must be executed for any views that use the tag helpers or are added to the `_ViewImports.cshtml` file. Open the `_ViewImports.cshtml` file in the root of the `Views` folder and add the following line:

```
@addTagHelper *, AutoLot.Web
```

The Cars Razor Pages

Next, we are going to create a base class that handles the common code across all pages. Before beginning, add the following global using statement to the `GlobalUsings.cs` file:

```
global using AutoLot.Models.Entities.Base;
```

The BasePageModel Class

Add a new directory named `Base` in the `Pages` directory. In that new directory, add a new class named `BasePageModel`. Make it abstract and generic (taking an entity type for data access and a class type for logging) and inherit from `PageModel`:

```
namespace AutoLot.Web.Pages.Base;

public abstract class BasePageModel<TEntity,TPageModel> : PageModel
  where TEntity : BaseEntity, new()
{
}
```

Next, add a protected constructor that takes an instance of `IAppLogging<TPageModel>`, an instance of the `IDataServiceBase<TEntity>`, and a string for the page's title. The interface instances get assigned to protected class fields, and the string gets assign to the `Title ViewData` property.

```
protected readonly IAppLogging<TPageModel> AppLoggingInstance;
protected readonly IDataServiceBase<TEntity> DataService;

[ViewData]
public string Title { get; init; }

protected BasePageModel(
    IAppLogging<TPageModel> appLogging,
```

```
    IDataServiceBase<TEntity> dataService,
    string pageTitle)
{
  AppLoggingInstance = appLogging;
  DataService = dataService;
  Title = pageTitle;
}
```

The base class has three public properties. An `TEntity` instance that is the `BindProperty`, a `SelectList` for lookup values, and an `Error` property to display a message in an error banner in the view:

```
[BindProperty]
public TEntity Entity { get; set; }
public SelectList LookupValues { get; set; }
public string Error { get; set; }
```

Next, add a method that takes in an instance of the `IDataServiceBase`, the `dataValue` and `dataText` property names, and builds the `SelectList`:

```
protected async Task GetLookupValuesAsync<TLookupEntity>(
  IDataServiceBase<TLookupEntity> lookupService, string lookupKey, string lookupDisplay)
  where TLookupEntity : BaseEntity, new()
{
  LookupValues = new(await lookupService.GetAllAsync(), lookupKey, lookupDisplay);
}
```

The `GetOneAsync()` method attempts to get a `TEntity` record by `Id`. If the `id` parameter is null or the record can't be located, the `Error` property is set. Otherwise, it assigns the record to the `Entity BindProperty`:

```
protected async Task GetOneAsync(int? id)
{
  if (!id.HasValue)
  {
    Error = "Invalid request";
    Entity = null;
    return;
  }
  Entity = await DataService.FindAsync(id.Value);
  if (Entity == null)
  {
    Error = "Not found";
    return;
  }
  Error = string.Empty;
}
```

The `SaveOneAsync()` method checks for `ModelState` validity, then attempts to save or update a record. If ModelState is invalid, the data is displayed in the view for the user to correct. If an error happens during the save/update call, the exception message is added to the `Error` property and `ModelState`, and then the view is returned to the user. The method takes in a `Func<TEntity, bool, Task<TEntity>>` so it can be called for both `AddAsync()` and `UpdateAsync()`:

```
protected virtual async Task<IActionResult> SaveOneAsync(Func<TEntity, bool, Task<TEntity>>
persistenceTask)
{
  if (!ModelState.IsValid)
  {
    return Page();
  }
  try
  {
    await persistenceTask(Entity, true);
  }
  catch (Exception ex)
  {
    Error = ex.Message;
    ModelState.AddModelError(string.Empty, ex.Message);
    AppLoggingInstance.LogAppError(ex, "An error occurred");
    return Page();
  }
  return RedirectToPage("./Details", new { id = Entity.Id });
}
```

The SaveWithLookupAsync() method does the same process as the SaveOneAsync(), but it also repopulates the SelectList when necessary. It takes in the data service to get the data for the lookup values, and the dataValue and dataText property names to build the SelectList:

```
protected virtual async Task<IActionResult> SaveWithLookupAsync<TLookupEntity>(
  Func<TEntity, bool, Task<TEntity>> persistenceTask,
  IDataServiceBase<TLookupEntity> lookupService, string lookupKey, string lookupDisplay)
  where TLookupEntity : BaseEntity, new()
{
  if (!ModelState.IsValid)
  {
    await GetLookupValuesAsync(lookupService, lookupKey, lookupDisplay);
    return Page();
  }
  try
  {
    await persistenceTask(Entity, true);
  }
  catch (Exception ex)
  {
    Error = ex.Message;
    ModelState.AddModelError(string.Empty, ex.Message);
    await GetLookupValuesAsync(lookupService, lookupKey, lookupDisplay);
    AppLoggingInstance.LogAppError(ex, "An error occurred");
    return Page();
  }
  return RedirectToPage("./Details", new { id = Entity.Id });
}
```

The DeleteOneAsync() method functions the same way as the Delete() HTTP Post method in the MVC version of AutoLot. The view is streamlined to only send the values needed by EF Core to delete a record, which is the Id and TimeStamp. If the deletion fails for some reason, ModelState is cleared, the ChangeTracker is reset, the entity is retrieved, and the Error property is set to the exception message:

```
public async Task<IActionResult> DeleteOneAsync(int? id)
{
  if (!id.HasValue || id.Value != Entity.Id)
  {
    Error = "Bad Request";
    return Page();
  }
  try
  {
    await DataService.DeleteAsync(Entity);
    return RedirectToPage("./Index");
  }
  catch (Exception ex)
  {
    ModelState.Clear();
    DataService.ResetChangeTracker();
    Entity = await DataService.FindAsync(id.Value);
    Error = ex.Message;
    AppLoggingInstance.LogAppError(ex, "An error occurred");
    return Page();
  }
}
```

Finally, add the following global using statement to the GlobalUsings.cs file:

```
global using AutoLot.Web.Pages.Base;
```

The Index Razor Page

The Index page will show a list of Car records and provide links to the other CRUD pages. The list will either be all of Car records in inventory, or just those with a certain Make value. Recall that in Razor Page routing, the Index Razor page is the default for a directory, reachable from both the /Cars and /Cars/Index URLs, so no additional routing is needed (unlike in the MVC version).

Start by adding an empty Razor Page named Index.cshtml to the Pages\Cars directory. The Index page doesn't need any of the functionality of the BasePageModel class, so leave it as inheriting from PageModel. Add a constructor that receives instances of IAppLogging<IndexModel> and the ICarDataService and assigns them to class level fields:

```
namespace AutoLot.Web.Pages.Cars;

public class IndexModel : PageModel
{
  private readonly IAppLogging<IndexModel> _appLogging;
  private readonly ICarDataService _carService;
  public IndexModel(IAppLogging<IndexModel> appLogging, ICarDataService carService)
  {
```

```
    _appLogging = appLogging;
    _carService = carService;
  }
}
```

Add three public properties on the class. Two hold the MakeName and MakeId properties used by the list of cars by Make, and the third holds the actual list of Car records. Note that it isn't a BindProperty since there won't be any HTTP post requests for the Index page.

```
public string MakeName { get; set; }
public int? MakeId { get; set; }
public IEnumerable<Car> CarRecords { get; set; }
```

The HTTP get method takes in optional parameters for makeId and makeName, then sets the public properties to those parameter values (even if they are null). The parameters are part of the route, which will be updated with the view. It then calls into the GetAllByMakeIdAsync() method of the data service, which will return all records if the makeId is null, otherwise it will return just the Car records to that Make:

```
public async Task OnGetAsync(int? makeId, string makeName)
{
  MakeId = makeId;
  MakeName = makeName;
  CarRecords = await _carService.GetAllByMakeIdAsync(makeId);
}
```

The Car List Partial View

There are two views available for the Index page. One shows the entire inventory of cars and one shows the list of cars by make. Since the UI is the same, the lists will be rendered using a partial view. This partial view is the same as for the MVC application, demonstrating the cross framework support for partial views.

Create a new directory named Partials under the Pages\Cars directory. In this directory, add a new view named _CarListPartial.cshtml, and clear out the existing code. Set IEnumerable<Car> as the type and add a Razor block to determine if the Makes should be displayed. When this partial is used by the entire inventory list, the Makes should be displayed. When it is showing only a single Make, the Make field should be hidden as it will be in the header of the page.

```
@model IEnumerable< Car>

@{
    var showMake = true;
    if (bool.TryParse(ViewBag.ByMake?.ToString(), out bool byMake))
    {
        showMake = !byMake;
    }
}
```

The next markup uses the ItemCreateTagHelper to create a link to the Create HTTP Get method (recall that tag helpers are lower-kebab-cased when used in Razor views). In the table headers, a Razor HTML helper is used to get the DisplayName for each of the properties. This section uses a Razor block to show the Make information based on the view-level variable set earlier.

```
<p>
  <item-create></item-create>
</p>

<table class="table">
  <thead>
  <tr>
    @if (showMake)
    {
      <th>@Html.DisplayNameFor(model => model.MakeId)</th>
    }
    <th>@Html.DisplayNameFor(model => model.Color)</th>
    <th>@Html.DisplayNameFor(model => model.PetName)</th>
    <th>@Html.DisplayNameFor(model => model.Price)</th>
    <th>@Html.DisplayNameFor(model => model.DateBuilt)</th>
    <th>@Html.DisplayNameFor(model => model.IsDrivable)</th>
    <th></th>
  </tr>
  </thead>
```

The final section loops through the records and displays the table records using the DisplayFor Razor HTML helper. This block also uses the item-edit, item-details, and item-delete custom tag helpers.

```
<tbody>
  @foreach (var item in Model)
  {
    <tr>
      @if (showMake)
      {
        <td>@Html.DisplayFor(modelItem => item.MakeNavigation.Name)</td>
      }
      <td>@Html.DisplayFor(modelItem => item.Color) </td>
      <td>@Html.DisplayFor(modelItem => item.PetName)</td>
      <td>@Html.DisplayFor(modelItem => item.Price)</td>
      <td>@Html.DisplayFor(modelItem => item.DateBuilt)</td>
      <td>@Html.DisplayFor(modelItem => item.IsDrivable)</td>
      <td>
        <item-edit item-id="@item.Id"></item-edit> |
        <item-details item-id="@item.Id"></item-details> |
        <item-delete item-id="@item.Id"></item-delete>
      </td>
    </tr>
  }
  </tbody>
</table>
```

The Index Razor Page View

With the `_CarListPartial` partial in place, the `Index` Razor Page view is quite small, demonstrating the benefit of using partial views to cut down on repetitive markup. The first step is to update the route information by adding two optional route tokens to the `@page` directive:

```
@page "{makeId?}/{makeName?}"
@model AutoLot.Web.Pages.Cars.IndexModel
```

The next step is to determine if the `PageModel`'s `MakeId` nullable in has a value. Recall that the `MakeId` and `MakeName` are update in the `OnGetAsync()` method based on the route parameters. If there is a value, display the `MakeName` in the header, and create a new `ViewDataDictionary` containing the `ByMake` property. This is then passed into the partial, along with the `CarRecords` model property, both of which are used by the `_CarListPartial` partial view. If `MakeId` doesn't have a value, invoke the `_CarListPartial` partial view with the `CarRecords` property but without the `ViewDataDictionary`:

```
@{
  if (Model.MakeId.HasValue)
  {
    <h1>Vehicle Inventory for @Model.MakeName</h1>
    var mode = new ViewDataDictionary(ViewData) { { "ByMake", true } };
    <partial name="Partials/_CarListPartial" model="@Model.CarRecords" view-data="@mode" />
  }
  else
  {
    <h1>Vehicle Inventory</h1>
    <partial name="Partials/_CarListPartial" model="@Model.CarRecords" />
  }
}
```

To see this view in action, run the application and navigate to `https://localhost:5001/Cars/Index` (or `https://localhost:5001/Cars`) to see the full list of vehicles. To see the list of BMW's, navigate to `https://localhost:5001/Cars/Index/5/BMW` (or `https://localhost:5001/Cars/5/BMW`).

The Details Razor Page

The `Details` page is used to display a single record when called with an HTTP get request. The route is extended with an optional id value. Update the code to the following, which takes advantage of the `BasePageModel` class:

```
namespace AutoLot.Web.Pages.Cars;

public class DetailsModel : BasePageModel<Car,DetailsModel>
{

  public DetailsModel(
    IAppLogging<DetailsModel> appLogging,
    ICarDataService carService) : base(appLogging, carService, "Details") { }

  public async Task OnGetAsync(int? id)
```

```
  {
    await GetOneAsync(id);
  }
}
```

The constructor takes instances of IAppLogging<T> and ICarDataService and passes them to the base class along with the page title. The OnGetAsync() page handler method takes in the optional route parameter then calls the base GetOneAsync() method. Since the method doesn't return an IActionResult, the view gets rendered when the method completes.

The Details Razor Page View

The first step is to update the route to include the optional id route token and add a header:

```
@page "{id?}"
@model AutoLot.Web.Pages.Cars.DetailsModel
<h1>Details for @Model.Entity.PetName</h1>
```

If there is a value in the Errors property, then the message needs to be displayed in a banner. If there isn't an error value, then use the Car display template to display the records information. Close out the view with the custom navigation tag helpers:

```
@if (!string.IsNullOrEmpty(Model.Error))
{
  <div class="alert alert-danger" role="alert">@Model.Error</div>
}
else
{
  @Html.DisplayFor(m => m.Entity)
  <div>
    <item-edit item-id="@Model.Entity.Id"></item-edit> |
    <item-delete item-id="@Model.Entity.Id"></item-delete> |
    <item-list></item-list>
  </div>
}
```

The @Html.DisplayFor() line can be replaced with @Html.DisplayFor(m=>m.Entity,"CarWithColors") to display the template that uses color in the display.

The Create Razor Page

The Create Razor Page inherits from BasePageModel. Clear out the scaffolded code and replace it with the following:

```
namespace AutoLot.Web.Pages.Cars;

public class CreateModel : BasePageModel<Car,CreateModel>
{
  //implementation goes here
}
```

In addition to the IAppLogging<T> and ICarDataService for the base class, the constructor takes an instance of the IMakeDataService and assigns it to a class level field:

```
private readonly IMakeDataService _makeService;
public CreateModel(
     IAppLogging<CreateModel> appLogging,
     ICarDataService carService,
     IMakeDataService makeService) : base(appLogging, carService, "Create")
{
  _makeService = makeService;
}
```

The HTTP get handler method populates the LookupValues property. Since there isn't a return value, the view is rendered when the method ends:

```
public async Task OnGetAsync()
{
  await GetLookupValuesAsync(_makeService, nameof(Make.Id), nameof(Make.Name));
}
```

The HTTP post handler method uses the base SaveWithLookupAsync() method and then returns the IActionResult from the base method. Note the non-standard name of the method. This will be addressed in the view form with the <form> tag helper:

```
public async Task<IActionResult> OnPostCreateNewCarAsync()
{
  return await SaveWithLookupAsync(
      DataService.AddAsync,
      _makeService,
      nameof(Make.Id),
      nameof(Make.Name));
}
```

The Create Razor Page View

The view uses the base route, so no changes are needed on the @page directive. Add the head and the error block:

```
@page
@model AutoLot.Web.Pages.Cars.CreateModel
<h1>Create a New Car</h1>
<hr/>
@if (!string.IsNullOrEmpty(Model.Error))
{
  <div class="alert alert-danger" role="alert">@Model.Error</div>
}
else
{
}
```

The <form> tag uses two tag helpers. The asp-page helper set the form's action to post back to the Create route (in the current directory, which is Cars). The asp-page-handler tag helper specifies the method name, less the OnPost prefix and Async suffix. Remember that if <form> tag helpers are used, the anti-forgery token is automatically added to the form data:

```
else
{
  <form asp-page="Create" asp-page-handler="CreateNewCar">
  </form>
}
```

The contents of the form is mostly layout. The two lines of note are the asp-validation-summary tag helper and the EditorFor() HTML helper. The EditorFor() method invokes the editor template for the Car class. The second parameter adds the SelectList into the ViewBag. The validation summary shows only model level errors since the editor template shows field level errors:

```
<form asp-page="Create" asp-page-handler="CreateNewCar">
  <div class="row">
    <div class="col-md-4">
      <div asp-validation-summary="ModelOnly" class="text-danger"></div>
      @Html.EditorFor(x => x.Entity, new { LookupValues = Model.LookupValues })
    </div>
  </div>
  <div class="d-flex flex-row mt-3">
    <button type="submit" class="btn btn-success">Create <i class="fas fa-plus"></i>
    </button>  |  
    <item-list></item-list>
  </div>
</form>
```

The final update is to add the _ValidationScriptsPartial partial in the Scripts section. Recall that in the layout this section occurs *after* loading jQuery. The sections pattern helps ensure that the proper dependencies are loaded before the contents of the section:

```
@section Scripts {
    <partial name="_ValidationScriptsPartial"/>
}
```

The create form can be viewed at /Cars/Create.

The Edit Razor Page

The Edit Razor Page follows the same pattern as the Create Razor Page. It inherits from BasePageModel. Clear out the scaffolded code and replace it with the following:

```
namespace AutoLot.Web.Pages.Cars;

public class EditModel : BasePageModel<Car,EditModel>
{
  //implementation goes here
}
```

In addition to the IAppLogging<T> and ICarDataService for the base class, the constructor takes an instance of the IMakeDataService and assigns it to a class level field:

```
private readonly IMakeDataService _makeService;
public EditModel(
     IAppLogging<EditModel> appLogging,
     ICarDataService carService,
     IMakeDataService makeService) : base(appLogging, carService, "Edit")
{
  _makeService = makeService;
}
```

The HTTP get handler method populates the LookupValues property and attempts to get the entity. Since there isn't a return value, the view is rendered when the method ends:

```
public async Task OnGetAsync(int? id)
{
  await GetLookupValuesAsync(_makeService, nameof(Make.Id), nameof(Make.Name));
  GetOneAsync(id);
}
```

The HTTP post handler method uses the base SaveWithLookupAsync() method and then returns the IActionResult from the base method:

```
public async Task<IActionResult> OnPostAsync()
{
  return await SaveWithLookupAsync(
      DataService.UpdateAsync,
      _makeService,
      nameof(Make.Id),
      nameof(Make.Name));
}
```

The Edit Razor Page View

The view takes in an optional id as a route token, which gets added to the @page directive. Update the directive and add the head and the error block:

```
@page "{id?}"
@model AutoLot.Web.Pages.Cars.EditModel
<h1>Edit @Model.Entity.PetName</h1>
<hr/>
@if (!string.IsNullOrEmpty(Model.Error))
{
    <div class="alert alert-danger" role="alert">
        @Model.Error
    </div>
}
else
{
}
```

The `<form>` tag uses two tag helpers. The `asp-page` helper set the form's `action` to post back to the `Edit` route (in the current directory, which is `Cars`). The `asp-route-id` tag helper specifies the value for the `id` route parameter:

```
else
{
  <form asp-page="Edit" asp-route-id="@Model.Entity.Id">
  </form>
}
```

The contents of the form is mostly layout. The four lines of note are the `asp-validation-summary` tag helper, the `EditorFor()` HTML helper, and the two hidden `input` tags. The `EditorFor()` method invokes the editor template for the `Car` class. The second parameter adds the `SelectList` into the `ViewBag`. The validation summary show only model level errors since the editor template shows field level errors. The two hidden input tags hold the values for the `Id` and `TimeStamp` properties, which are required for the update process, but have no meaning to the user:

```
<form asp-page="Edit" asp-route-id="@Model.Entity.Id">
  <div class="row">
    <div class="col-md-4">
      <div asp-validation-summary="ModelOnly"></div>
      @Html.EditorFor(x => x.Entity, new { LookupValues = Model.LookupValues })
      <input type="hidden" asp-for="Entity.Id"/>
      <input type="hidden" asp-for="Entity.TimeStamp"/>
    </div>
  </div>
  <div class="d-flex flex-row mt-3">
    <button type="submit" class="btn btn-primary">Save <i class="fas fa-save"></i></button>&
    nbsp; |  
    <item-list></item-list>
  </div>
</form>
```

The final update is to add the `_ValidationScriptsPartial` partial in the `Scripts` section. Recall that in the layout this section occurs *after* loading jQuery. The sections pattern helps ensure that the proper dependencies are loaded before the contents of the section:

```
@section Scripts {
    <partial name="_ValidationScriptsPartial"/>
}
```

The edit form can be viewed at `/Cars/Edit/1`.

The Delete Razor Page

The `Delete` razor page inherits from `BasePageModel` and has a constructor that takes the required two parameters:

```
namespace AutoLot.Web.Pages.Cars;
```

```
public class DeleteModel : BasePageModel<Car,DeleteModel>
{
  public DeleteModel(
   IAppLogging<DeleteModel> appLogging,
   ICarDataService carService) : base(appLogging, carService, "Delete")
  {
  }

  public async Task<IActionResult> OnPostAsync(int? id)
  {
    return await DeleteOneAsync(id);
  }
}
```

This view doesn't use the SelectList values, so the HTTP get handler method simply gets the entity. Since there isn't a return value for the method, the view is rendered when the method ends:

```
public async Task OnGetAsync(int? id)
{
  await GetOneAsync(id);
}
```

The HTTP post handler method uses the base DeleteOneAsync() method and then returns the IActionResult from the base method:

```
public async Task<IActionResult> OnPostAsync(int? id)
{
  return await DeleteOneAsync(id)
}
```

The Delete Razor Page View

The view takes in an optional id as a route token, which gets added to the @page directive. Update the directive and add the title, head, and the error block:

```
@page "{id?}"
@model AutoLot.Web.Pages.Cars.DeleteModel
<h1>Delete @Model.Entity.PetName</h1>
@if (!string.IsNullOrEmpty(Model.Error))
{
    <div class="alert alert-danger" role="alert">
        @Model.Error
    </div>
}
else
{
}
```

The <form> tag uses two tag helpers. The asp-page helper set the form's action to post back to the Delete route (in the current directory, which is Cars). The asp-route-id tag helper specifies the value for the id route parameter:

```
else
{
  <form asp-page="Delete" asp-route-id="@Model.Entity.Id">
  </form>
}
```

The view uses the Car display template outside of the form and hidden fields for the Id and TimeStamp properties inside the form. There isn't a validation summary since any errors in the delete process will show in the error banner:

```
<h3>Are you sure you want to delete this car?</h3>
<div>
  @Html.DisplayFor(c=>c.Entity)
  <form asp-page="Delete" asp-route-id="@Model.Entity.Id">
    <input type="hidden" asp-for="Entity.Id"/>
    <input type="hidden" asp-for="Entity.TimeStamp"/>
    <button type="submit" class="btn btn-danger">Delete <i class="fas fa-trash"></i>
    </button>  |  
    <item-list></item-list>
  </form>
</div>
```

The _ValidationScriptsPartial partial isn't needed, so that completed the Delete page view. The delete form can be viewed at /Cars/Delete/5.

View Components

View components in Razor Page based applications are built and function the same as in MVC styled applications. The main difference is where the partial views must be located. To get started in the AutoLot. Web project, add the following global using statement to the GlobalUsings.cs file:

```
global using Microsoft.AspNetCore.Mvc.ViewComponents;
```

Create a new folder named ViewComponents in the root directory. Add a new class file named MenuViewComponent.cs into this folder and update the code to the following (the same as was built in the previous chapter).

```
public class MenuViewComponent : ViewComponent
{
  private readonly IMakeDataService _dataService;

  public MenuViewComponent(IMakeDataService dataService)
  {
     _dataService = dataService;
  }
```

```
  public async Task<IViewComponentResult> InvokeAsync()
  {
    var makes = (await _dataService.GetAllAsync()).ToList();
    if (!makes.Any())
    {
      return new ContentViewComponentResult("Unable to get the makes");
    }
    return View("MenuView", makes);
  }
}
```

Build the Partial View

In Razor Pages, the menu items must use the asp-page anchor tag helper instead of the asp-controller and asp-action tag helpers. Create a new folder named Components under the Pages\Shared folder. In this new folder, create another new folder named Menu. In this folder, create a partial view named MenuView.cshtml. Clear out the existing code and add the following markup:

```
@model IEnumerable<Make>
<div class="dropdown-menu">
<a class="dropdown-item text-dark" asp-area="" asp-page="Cars/Index" >All</a>

@foreach (var item in Model)
{
    <a class="dropdown-item text-dark" asp-page="/Cars/Index" asp-route-makeId="@item.Id"
    asp-route-makeName="@item.Name">@item.Name</a>
}
</div>
```

To invoke the view component with the tag helper syntax, the following line must be added to the _ViewImports.cshtml file, which was already added for the custom tag helpers:

```
@addTagHelper *, AutoLot.Web
```

Finally, open the _Menu.cshtml partial and navigate to just after the <li></li> block that maps to the /Index page. Copy the following markup to the partial:

```
<li class="nav-item">
<a class="nav-link text-dark" asp-area="" asp-page="/Index">Home <i class="fa fa-
home"></i></a>
</li>
<li class="nav-item dropdown">
  <a class="nav-link dropdown-toggle text-dark" data-bs-toggle="dropdown">Inventory <i
class="fa fa-car"></i></a>
  <vc:menu></vc:menu>
</li>
```

Now when you run the application, you will see the Inventory menu with the Makes listed as submenu items.

Areas

Areas in Razor Pages are slightly different than in MVC based applications. Since Razor Pages are routed based on directory structure, there isn't any additional routing configuration to be handled. The only rule is that the pages must go in the `Areas\[AreaName]\Pages` directory. To add an area in AutoLot.Web, first add a directory named `Areas` in the root of the project. Next, add a directory named `Admin`, then add a new directory name `Pages`. Finally, add a new directory named `Makes`.

Area Routing with Razor Pages

When navigating to Razor Pages in an area, the Areas directory name is omitted. For example, the Index page in the `Areas\Admin\Makes\Pages` directory can be found at the `/Admin/Makes` (or `Admin/Makes/Index`) route.

_ViewImports and _ViewStart

In Razor Pages, the `_ViewImports.cshtml` and `_ViewStart.cshtml` files apply to all views at the same directory level and below. Move the `_ViewImports.cshtml` and `_ViewStart.cshtml` files to the root on the project so they are applied to the entire project.

The Makes Razor Pages

The pages to support the CRUD operations for the Make admin area follow the same pattern as the Cars pages. They will be listed here with minimal discussion.

The Make DisplayTemplate

Add a new directory named `DisplayTemplates` under the `Makes` directory in the `Admin` area. Add a new Razor View – Empty named `Make.cshtml` in the new directory. Update the content to the following:

```
@model Make
<hr/>
<dl class="row">
  <dt class="col-sm-2">@Html.DisplayNameFor(model => model.Name)</dt>
  <dd class="col-sm-10">@Html.DisplayFor(model => model.Name)</dd>
</dl>
```

The Make EditorTemplate

Add a new directory named `EditorTemplates` under the `Makes` directory in the `Admin` area. Add a new Razor View – Empty named `Make.cshtml` in the new directory. Update the content to the following:

```
@model Make
<div>
    <label asp-for="Name" class="col-form-label"></label>
    <input asp-for="Name" />
    <span asp-validation-for="Name" class="text-danger"></span>
</div>
```

The Index Razor Page

The Index page will show the list of Make records and provide links to the other CRUD pages. Add an empty Razor Page named Index.cshtml to the Pages\Makes directory and update the content to the following:

```
namespace AutoLot.Web.Areas.Admin.Pages.Makes;

public class IndexModel : PageModel
{
  private readonly IAppLogging<IndexModel> _appLogging;
  private readonly IMakeDataService _makeService;
  [ViewData]
  public string Title => "Makes";
  public IndexModel(IAppLogging<IndexModel> appLogging, IMakeDataService carService)
  {
    _appLogging = appLogging;
    _makeService = carService;
  }
  public IEnumerable<Make> MakeRecords { get; set; }
  public async Task OnGetAsync()
  {
    MakeRecords = await _makeService.GetAllAsync();
  }
}
```

The Index Razor Page View

Since the Make class is so small, a partial isn't used to show the list of records. Update the Index.cshtml file to the following:

```
@page
@model AutoLot.Web.Areas.Admin.Pages.Makes.IndexModel
<h1>Vehicle Makes</h1>
<p><item-create></item-create></p>
<table class="table">
  <thead>
  <tr>
    <th>@Html.DisplayNameFor(model => ((List<Make>)model.MakeRecords)[0].Name)</th>
    <th></th>
  </tr>
  </thead>
  <tbody>
  @foreach (var item in Model.MakeRecords) {
    <tr>
      <td>@Html.DisplayFor(modelItem => item.Name) </td>
    <td>
      <item-edit item-id="@item.Id"></item-edit> |
      <item-details item-id="@item.Id"></item-details> |
      <item-delete item-id="@item.Id"></item-delete>
    </td>
```

```
  </tr>
  }
  </tbody>
</table>
```

To see this view in action, run the application and navigate to `https://localhost:5001/Admin/Makes/Index` (or `https://localhost:5001/Admin/Makes`) to see the full list of records.

The Details Razor Page

The `Details` page is used to display a single record when called with an HTTP get request. Add an empty Razor Page named `Details.cshtml` to the `Pages\Makes` directory and update the content to the following:

```
namespace AutoLot.Web.Areas.Admin.Pages.Makes;
public class DetailsModel : BasePageModel<Make,DetailsModel>
{
  public DetailsModel(
    IAppLogging<DetailsModel> appLogging,
    IMakeDataService makeService)
    : base(appLogging, makeService,"Details") { }
  public async Task OnGetAsync(int? id)
  {
    await GetOneAsync(id);
  }
}
```

The Details Razor Page View

Update the `Details.cshtml` Razor Page view to the following:

```
@page "{id?}"
@model AutoLot.Web.Areas.Admin.Pages.Makes.DetailsModel

@{
    //ViewData["Title"] = "Details";
}

<h1>Details for @Model.Entity.Name</h1>
@if (!string.IsNullOrEmpty(Model.Error))
{
    <div class="alert alert-danger" role="alert">
        @Model.Error
    </div>
}
else
{
    @Html.DisplayFor(m => m.Entity)
    <div>
        <item-edit item-id="@Model.Entity.Id"></item-edit> |
```

```
        <item-delete item-id="@Model.Entity.Id"></item-delete> |
        <item-list></item-list>
    </div>
}
```

The Create Razor Page

Add an empty Razor Page named Create.cshtml to the Pages\Makes directory and update the content to the following:

```
namespace AutoLot.Web.Areas.Admin.Pages.Makes;
public class CreateModel : BasePageModel<Make,CreateModel>
{
  private readonly IMakeDataService _makeService;
  public CreateModel(
    IAppLogging<CreateModel> appLogging,
    IMakeDataService makeService)
    : base(appLogging, makeService, "Create") { }
  public void OnGet() { }
  public async Task<IActionResult> OnPostAsync()
  {
    return await SaveOneAsync(DataService.AddAsync);
  }
}
```

The Create Razor Page View

Update the Create.cshtml Razor Page view to the following:

```
@page
@model AutoLot.Web.Areas.Admin.Pages.Makes.CreateModel
<h1>Create a New Car</h1>
<hr/>
@if (!string.IsNullOrEmpty(Model.Error))
{
  <div class="alert alert-danger" role="alert">@Model.Error</div>
}
else
{
  <form asp-page="Create">
    <div class="row">
      <div class="col-md-4">
        <div asp-validation-summary="ModelOnly" class="text-danger"></div>
        @Html.EditorFor(x => x.Entity, new { LookupValues = Model.LookupValues })
      </div>
    </div>
    <div class="d-flex flex-row mt-3">
      <button type="submit" class="btn btn-success">Create <i class="fas fa-plus"></i
      button>  |  
```

```
      <item-list></item-list>
    </div>
  </form>
  @section Scripts {
    <partial name="_ValidationScriptsPartial"/>
  }
}
```

The Edit Razor Page

Add an empty Razor Page named Edit.cshtml to the Pages\Makes directory and update the content to the following:

```
namespace AutoLot.Web.Areas.Admin.Pages.Makes;
public class EditModel : BasePageModel<Make,EditModel>
{
  public EditModel(
    IAppLogging<EditModel> appLogging,
    IMakeDataService makeService)
    : base(appLogging, makeService, "Edit") { }
  public async Task OnGetAsync(int? id)
  {
    await GetOneAsync(id);
  }
  public async Task<IActionResult> OnPostAsync()
  {
    return await SaveOneAsync(DataService.UpdateAsync);
  }
}
```

The Edit Razor Page View

Update the Edit.cshtml Razor Page view to the following:

```
@page "{id?}"
@model AutoLot.Web.Areas.Admin.Pages.Makes.EditModel
<h1>Edit @Model.Entity.Name</h1>
<hr/>
@if (!string.IsNullOrEmpty(Model.Error))
{
  <div class="alert alert-danger" role="alert">@Model.Error</div>
}
else
{
  <form asp-page="Edit" asp-route-id="@Model.Entity.Id">
    <div class="row">
      <div class="col-md-4">
        <div asp-validation-summary="ModelOnly"></div>
        @Html.EditorFor(x => x.Entity)
        <input type="hidden" asp-for="Entity.Id"/>
```

```
        <input type="hidden" asp-for="Entity.TimeStamp"/>
      </div>
    </div>
    <div class="d-flex flex-row mt-3">
      <button type="submit" class="btn btn-primary">Save <i class="fas fa-save"></i>
      </button>  |  
      <item-list></item-list>
    </div>
  </form>
}
  @section Scripts {
    @{ await Html.RenderPartialAsync("_ValidationScriptsPartial");
  }
}
```

The Delete Razor Page

Add an empty Razor Page named Delete.cshtml to the Pages\Makes directory and update the content to the following:

```
namespace AutoLot.Web.Areas.Admin.Pages.Makes;
public class DeleteModel : BasePageModel<Make,DeleteModel>
{
  public DeleteModel(
    IAppLogging<DeleteModel> appLogging,
    IMakeDataService makeService)
    : base(appLogging, makeService, "Delete") { }
  public async Task OnGetAsync(int? id)
  {
    await GetOneAsync(id);
  }
  public async Task<IActionResult> OnPostAsync(int? id)
  {
    return await DeleteOneAsync(id);
  }
}
```

The Delete Razor Page View

Update the Delete.cshtml Razor Page view to the following:

```
@page "{id?}"
@model AutoLot.Web.Areas.Admin.Pages.Makes.DeleteModel
<h1>Delete @Model.Entity.Name</h1>
@if (!string.IsNullOrEmpty(Model.Error))
{
  <div class="alert alert-danger" role="alert">@Model.Error</div>
}
else
{
```

```
  <h3>Are you sure you want to delete this car?</h3>
  <div>
    @Html.DisplayFor(c=>c.Entity)
    <form asp-page="Delete" asp-route-id="@Model.Entity.Id">
       <input type="hidden" asp-for="Entity.Id"/>
       <input type="hidden" asp-for="Entity.TimeStamp"/>
       <button type="submit" class="btn btn-danger">Delete <i class="fas fa-trash"></i>
       </button>  |  
       <item-list></item-list>
    </form>
  </div>
}
```

Add the Area Menu Item

Update the _Menu.cshtml partial to add a menu item for the Admin area by adding the following:

```
<li class="nav-item">
    <a class="nav-link text-dark" asp-area="Admin" asp-page="Makes/Index"
    title="Makes Admin">Makes Admin <i class="fas fa-cog"></i></a>
</li>
```

When building a link to another area, the asp-area tag helper is required and the full path to the page must be placed in the asp-page tag helper.

Custom Validation Attributes

The custom validation attributes built in the previous chapter work with both MVC and Razor Page based applications. To demonstrate this, create a new empty Razor Page named Validation.cshtml in the main Pages directory. Update the ValidationModel code to the following:

```
namespace AutoLot.Web.Pages;
public class ValidationModel : PageModel
{
  [ViewData]
  public string Title => "Validation Example";
  [BindProperty]
  public AddToCartViewModel Entity { get; set; }
  public void OnGet()
  {
    Entity = new AddToCartViewModel
    {
      Id = 1,
      ItemId = 1,
      StockQuantity = 2,
      Quantity = 0
    };
  }
  public IActionResult OnPost()
  {
```

```
    if (!ModelState.IsValid)
    {
      return Page();
    }
    return RedirectToPage("Validation");
  }
}
```

The HTTP get handler method creates a new instance of the AddToCartViewModel and assigns it to the BindProperty. The page is automatically rendered when the method finishes.

The HTTP post handler method checks for ModelState errors, and if there is an error, returns the bad data to the view. If validation succeeds, it redirects to the HTTP get page handler following the post-redirect-get (PRG) pattern.

The Validation page view is shown here, which is the same code as the MVC version with the only difference is using the asp-page tag helper instead of the asp-action tag helper:

```
@page
@model AutoLot.Web.Pages.ValidationModel
@{
}
<h1>Validation</h1>

<h4>Add To Cart</h4>
<hr />
<div class="row">
  <div class="col-md-4">
    <form asp-page="/Validation">
      <div asp-validation-summary="ModelOnly" class="text-danger"></div>
      <div>
        <label asp-for="Entity.Id" class="col-form-label"></label>
        <input asp-for="Entity.Id" class="form-control" />
        <span asp-validation-for="Entity.Id" class="text-danger"></span>
      </div>
      <div>
        <label asp-for="Entity.StockQuantity" class="col-form-label"></label>
        <input asp-for="Entity.StockQuantity" class="form-control" />
        <span asp-validation-for="Entity.StockQuantity" class="text-danger"></span>
      </div>
      <div>
        <label asp-for="Entity.ItemId" class="col-form-label"></label>
        <input asp-for="Entity.ItemId" class="form-control" />
        <span asp-validation-for="Entity.ItemId" class="text-danger"></span>
      </div>
      <div>
        <label asp-for="Entity.Quantity" class="col-form-label"></label>
        <input asp-for="Entity.Quantity" class="form-control" />
        <span asp-validation-for="Entity.Quantity" class="text-danger"></span>
      </div>
      <div style="margin-top:5px">
        <input type="submit" value="Save" class="btn btn-primary" />
      </div>
```

```
    </form>
  </div>
</div>

@section Scripts {
    @{await Html.RenderPartialAsync("_ValidationScriptsPartial");}
}
```

Next, add the menu item to navigate to the Validation view. Add the following to the end of menu list (before the closing </ul> tag):

```
<li class="nav-item">
  <a class="nav-link text-dark" asp-area="" asp-page="Validation" title="Validation
Example">Validation<i class="fas fa-check"></i></a>
</li>
```

Server-side validation is built into the attributes, so you can play with the page and see the validation error returned to the page and displayed with the validation tag helpers.

Next, either copy the validation scripts from the previous chapter or you can create them from here. To create them, create a new directory name `validations` in the `wwwroot\js` directory. Create a new JavaScript file named `errorFormatting.js`, and update the content to the following:

```
$.validator.setDefaults({
    highlight: function (element, errorClass, validClass) {
        if (element.type === "radio") {
            this.findByName(element.name).addClass(errorClass).removeClass(validClass);
        } else {
            $(element).addClass(errorClass).removeClass(validClass);
            $(element).closest('div').addClass('has-error');
        }
    },
    unhighlight: function (element, errorClass, validClass) {
        if (element.type === "radio") {
            this.findByName(element.name).removeClass(errorClass).addClass(validClass);
        } else {
            $(element).removeClass(errorClass).addClass(validClass);
            $(element).closest('div').removeClass('has-error');
        }
    }
});
```

Next, add a JavaScript file named `validators.js` and update its content to this. Notice the Entity_ prefix update from the MVC version. This is due to the `BindProperty`'s name of `Entity`:

```
$.validator.addMethod("greaterthanzero", function (value, element, params) {
    return value > 0;
});
$.validator.unobtrusive.adapters.add("greaterthanzero", function (options) {
    options.rules["greaterthanzero"] = true;
    options.messages["greaterthanzero"] = options.message;
});
```

```
$.validator.addMethod("notgreaterthan", function (value, element, params) {
    return +value <= +$(params).val();
});
$.validator.unobtrusive.adapters.add("notgreaterthan", ["otherpropertyname","prefix"],
function(options) {
    options.rules["notgreaterthan"] = "#Entity_" + options.params.prefix + options.params.
    otherpropertyname;
    options.messages["notgreaterthan"] = options.message;
});
```

Update the call to AddWebOptimizer() in the Program.cs top level statements to bundle the new files when not in a Development environment:

```
builder.Services.AddWebOptimizer(options =>
{
  //omitted for brevity
  options.AddJavaScriptBundle("/js/validationCode.js",
      "js/validations/validators.js", "js/validations/errorFormatting.js");
});
```

```
Update site.css to include the error class:.has-error {
    border: 3px solid red;
    padding: 0px 5px;
    margin: 5px 0;
}
```

Finally, update the _ValidationScriptsPartial partial to include the raw files in the development block and the bundled/minified files in the non-development block:

```
<environment include="Development">
    <script src="~/js/validations/errorFormatting.js" asp-append-version="true" ></script>
    <script src="~/js/validations/validators.js" asp-append-version="true" ></script>
</environment>
<environment exclude="Development">
    <script src="~/js/validationCode.js"></script>
</environment>
```

General Data Protection Regulation Support

GDPR support in Razor Pages matches the support in MVC applications. Begin by adding CookiePolicyOptions and change the TempData and Session cookies to essential in the top level statements in Program.cs:

```
builder.Services.Configure<CookiePolicyOptions>(options =>
{
    // This lambda determines whether user consent for non-essential cookies is
    // needed for a given request.
    options.CheckConsentNeeded = context => true;
    options.MinimumSameSitePolicy = SameSiteMode.None;
});
```

```
// The TempData provider cookie is not essential. Make it essential
// so TempData is functional when tracking is disabled.
builder.Services.Configure<CookieTempDataProviderOptions>(options => { options.Cookie.
IsEssential = true; });
builder.Services.AddSession(options => { options.Cookie.IsEssential = true; });
```

The final change to the top level statements is to add cookie policy support to the HTTP pipeline:

```
app.UseStaticFiles();
app.UseCookiePolicy();
app.UseRouting();
```

Add the following global using statement to the `GlobalUsings.cs` file:

```
global using Microsoft.AspNetCore.Http.Features;
```

The Cookie Support Partial View

Add a new view named `_CookieConsentPartal.cshtml` in the `Pages\Shared` directory. This is the same view from the MVC application:

```
@{
  var consentFeature = Context.Features.Get<ITrackingConsentFeature>();
  var showBanner = !consentFeature?.CanTrack ?? false;
  var cookieString = consentFeature?.CreateConsentCookie();
}
@if (showBanner)
{
  <div id="cookieConsent" class="alert alert-info alert-dismissible fade show" role="alert">
    Use this space to summarize your privacy and cookie use policy. <a asp-area="" asp-
    page="Privacy">Learn More</a>.
    <button type="button" class="accept-policy close" data-dismiss="alert" aria-
    label="Close" data-cookie-string="@cookieString">
      <span aria-hidden="true">Accept</span>
    </button>
  </div>
  <script>
    (function () {
      var button = document.querySelector("#cookieConsent button[data-cookie-string]");
      button.addEventListener("click", function (event) {
        document.cookie = button.dataset.cookieString;
        window.location = '@Url.Page("/Index")';
      }, false);
    })();
  </script>
}
```

Finally, add the partial to the _Layout partial:

```
<div class="container">
    <partial name="_CookieConsentPartial"/>
```

```
    <main role="main" class="pb-3">
        @RenderBody()
    </main>
</div>
```

With this in place, when you run the application you will see the cookie consent banner. If the user clicks accept, the `.AspNet.Content` cookie is created. Next time the site loads, the banner will not show.

Menu Support to Accept/Withdraw Cookie Policy Consent

The final change to the application is to add menu support to grant or withdraw consent. Add a new empty Razor Page named `Consent.cshtml` to the main Pages directory. Update the `PageModel` to the following:

```
namespace AutoLot.Web.Pages;

public class ConsentModel : PageModel
{
  public IActionResult OnGetGrantConsent()
  {
    HttpContext.Features.Get<ITrackingConsentFeature>()?.GrantConsent();
    return RedirectToPage("./Index");
  }
  public IActionResult OnGetWithdrawConsent()
  {
    HttpContext.Features.Get<ITrackingConsentFeature>()?.WithdrawConsent();
    return RedirectToPage("./Index");
  }
}
```

The Razor page has two HTTP get page handlers. In order to call them, the link must use the `asp-page-handler` tag helper.

Open the `_Menu.cshtml` partial, and add a Razor block to check if the user has granted consent:

```
@{
  var consentFeature = Context.Features.Get<ITrackingConsentFeature>();
  var showBanner = !consentFeature?.CanTrack ?? false;
}
```

If the banner is showing (the user hasn't granted consent), then display the menu link for the user to Accept the cookie policy. If they have granted consent, then show the menu link to withdraw consent. The following also updates the Privacy link to include the Font Awesome secret icon. Notice the asp-page-handler tag helpers:

```
<li class="nav-item">
  <a class="nav-link text-dark" asp-area="" asp-page="/Privacy">
    Privacy <i class="fa fa-user-secret"></i></a>
</li>
@if (showBanner)
{
  <li class="nav-item">
```

```
    <a class="nav-link text-dark" asp-page="Consent" asp-page-handler="GrantConsent"
    title="Accept Cookie Policy">Accept Cookie Policy <i class="fas fa-cookie-bite"></i></a>
  </li>
}
else
{
  <li class="nav-item">
    <a class="nav-link text-dark" asp-page="Consent" asp-page-handler="WithdrawConsent"
    title="Revoke Cookie Policy">Revoke Cookie Policy <i class="fas fa-cookie"></i></a>
  </li>
}
```

Summary

This chapter completed the AutoLot.Web. It began with a deep dive into Razor Pages and page views, partial views, and editor and display templates. The next set of topics covered client-side libraries, including management of what libraries are in the project as well as bundling and minification.

Next was an examination of tag helpers and the creation of the project's custom tag helpers. The Cars Razor Pages were created along with a custom base class. A view component was added to make the menu dynamic, an admin area and its pages were added, and finally validation and GDPR support was covered.

Index

A

A. Troelsen and P. Japikse, *Pro C# 10 with .NET 6*, https://doi.org/10.1007/978-1-4842-7869-7

■ B

C

■ D

E

F

G

H

I

J

K

L

M

N

O

P

Q

R

S

T

U

V

W

X

Y, Z

Printed by Wilco bv, the Netherlands